4/1/00

*For Leslie and Bill,*
*with much*
*much love,*
*Nan*

SEEING
MARY
PLAIN

A Life of Mary McCarthy

# SEEING MARY PLAIN

Frances Kiernan

 W. W. NORTON & COMPANY

New York • London

CREDITS FOR PHOTOGRAPHS

Courtesy of Special Collections, Vassar College Libraries: photographs 1, 2, 3, 4, 5, 6, 7, 8, 9, 10, 11, 12, 13, 14, 16, 17, 18, 19, 20, 27, 29, 30, 31, 32, 33, 34, 36, 37, 38, 41
Courtesy of Alison West: 35
Courtesy of Edith Kurzweil: 24, 44, 45
Courtesy of Betty Rahv: 15
Courtesy of Nicholas Macdonald: 21
Courtesy of Lotte Kohler: 39
Courtesy of Thomas Mallon: 43

Since this page cannot legibly accommodate all the copyright notices, pages 811–14 constitute an extension of the copyright page.

In all cases where it has seemed appropriate, I have tried to reach the owner of the copyright for photographs and textual material included in this book. Any errors or omissions will be corrected in future printings.

For information about permission to reproduce selections from this book, write to Permissions, W. W. Norton & Company, Inc., 500 Fifth Avenue, New York, NY 10110

The text of this book is composed in Veljovic, with the display set in Serlio and Garton. Composition by Alice Bennett. Manufacturing by The Maple-Vail Book Manufacturing Group. Book design by Charlotte Staub.

Library of Congress Cataloging-in-Publication Data
Kiernan, Frances.
Seeing Mary plain: a life of Mary McCarthy / Frances Kiernan.
        p. cm.
Includes bibliographical references and index.
**ISBN 0-393-03801-7**
        1. McCarthy, Mary, 1912– 2. Authors, American—20th century—Biography.
I Title.
PS3525.A1435 Z69 2000
818'.5209—dc21
[B]    99-041098

W. W. Norton & Company, Inc., 500 Fifth Avenue, New York, N.Y. 10110
www.wwnorton.com

W. W. Norton & Company Ltd., 10 Coptic Street, London WC1A 1PU

1 2 3 4 5 6 7 8 9 0

To Howard

# Contents

*Photographs appear on pages
197–206 and 411–20*

# Preface

Ah, did you once see Shelley plain,
And did he stop and speak to you,
And did you speak to him again?
How strange it seems and new!

—ROBERT BROWNING from "Memorabilia," 1855

Most writers' lives are sadly lacking in drama. The dullest of people, it turns out, write witty and intelligent books. Once they push back their chairs and get up from their desks, they do little to warrant our attention. We would do best to grant them their privacy and turn our attention to the work itself. But if Mary Therese McCarthy had never written a single word, we would still want to know about her. Beautiful and never boring, reckless and endlessly maddening, this most analytical of writers shares with the great Romantic poets a gift for capturing the imagination by the simple, or not so simple, details of her life.

Only once did I see Mary McCarthy. She was smoking a cigarette in the twentieth-floor ladies room at *The New Yorker*. It must have been the midseventies, when she was working with William Shawn on an excerpt from Hannah Arendt's *The Life of the Mind*. You did not smoke in William Shawn's office, even if you were Mary McCarthy. Standing at an open window with her cigarette, she was not the glamorous dark lady of letters I remembered from photographs. Her hair, as I recall, fell just above her shoulders. It was not pulled back in a sleek black knot. There were enough gray strands to make her seem pale and washed out and even a bit dowdy. I had to look twice to make sure who she was.

A decade earlier I had read Mary McCarthy's big best-seller *The Group*. Recently I had read *Memories of a Catholic Girlhood*, the story of her orphaned upbringing. I was not a Catholic and I was not an orphan, but, like Mary McCarthy, I was part Jewish, and, like Mary McCarthy, I had been put in charge of my younger brothers and made to stay out in the cold for my health. Towering over my two brothers, I had stood in the snow on a freezing winter afternoon, waiting to be summoned home. Unlike Mary McCarthy, I had no wicked guardians to blame for this. And, unlike Mary McCarthy, I had made up no stories to help my brothers pass the time.

The woman I saw that day at *The New Yorker* was not as tall as I had expected. She was not as tall as I was. But, even so, she seemed formidable. To be sure, her reputation had preceded her. She was a great heroine to many young women my age. She was a heroine for her independence and her courage in speaking out in defense of lost causes and for her ability to combine great personal glamour with a ferocious intelligence. But just as she was celebrated for her green eyes and dark beauty, she was known for her refusal to suffer fools gladly. As a young editor in the magazine's fiction department, I had met enough famous writers to know that the writers you love are often better left on the page. I washed my hands at the sink and dried them. When I took my leave of the ladies room, she was still standing by that open window.

Mary McCarthy died in 1989. Although she was seventy-seven years old, her death seemed to me shockingly premature. Her sharp tongue and her inability to hold it may have had something to do with this. Certainly a refusal to accept injustice is a trait you expect to find in the very young. Then, too, there was a sense that between the two of us there was still some unfinished business. At the time of her death I was working at Houghton Mifflin, editing a writer she had gone out of her way to befriend before he had even begun his career. Thanks to him, I was beginning to see that there might be another Mary McCarthy—one altogether less daunting. His Mary McCarthy possessed the complexity and contradictions of a character in a novel. Along with the harshness, there was warmth and generosity and a crankiness that seemed at times to verge on the crackpot. Listening to him, I was sorry I had not had the courage to go up to her.

From the time I was a young girl I'd had a special fondness for older women. And from the time I was a girl I'd looked to novels the way others look to self-help books. For me they served as an introduction to the real world. By the time Mary McCarthy died, I had started to read biographies much the way I had once read fiction: to learn how to go about living my life. By the spring of 1990, when it was too late to tell Mary McCarthy how much *Memories of a Catholic Girlhood* had meant to me, I had concluded that she was one of those rare writers I wanted very much to get to know off the page. There was a literary portrait by Doris Grumbach, published in 1967, a biography by Carol Gelderman published in 1988, and now Carol Brightman was working on a book that had started out as an intellectual history, using Mary McCarthy as a window on her times. None of these books, for all their particular virtues, gave me what I was looking for. Although all three were conceived when their subject was still alive, they tended to treat her life as a fait accompli.

In the end, I chose to find my own way to Mary McCarthy. The book I have written is not a stately two-volume literary biography. Nor is it a pure oral history. It is intended for those who are intimate with the major events of Mary McCarthy's life as well as for those who know little more than her name. The cumulative effect is not unlike that of a novel, tracing the shape of this life, while conveying a sense of what it was like day to day.

The fact is, lives look very different when you look at them as they are being lived. Events that seem important at the time may prove to be of little or no consequence. A great career does not necessarily owe everything to planning and foresight. The lady of letters receiving you in her sitting room may have had very different plans for herself at the age of twenty.

From start to finish, Mary McCarthy wrote sentences that were clear and lucid and altogether beguiling, but if you look at the life mainly for the purpose of illuminating the work, you will discover very little you haven't already guessed. On the page, what you see is pretty much what you get. In this respect, the writer and woman would seem to be very much of a piece. For the most part, such lies as she told were lies of omission. No one was ever more determinedly direct and straightforward. No one was ever more hardworking. No one ever took greater pleasure in stirring up controversy. And no one ever elicited more wildly divergent responses from those who believed they understood her best.

In an effort to see Mary McCarthy "plain," I have sought her out everywhere from Seattle to Paris. Along the way I have tried to show her in good times and bad, falling in love and then out again, at her ease and doing battle, but always trying to put in at least three hours a day at her desk. To do this I have drawn on interviews with friends and family, the men and women she worked with, her fellow writers and casual acquaintances, many of whom have a reputation for being no less remarkable than she.

Of course recollections and anecdotes cannot tell us all we need to know about someone. Intentionally or not, there is a tendency in all of us to rewrite history—to bring to an incident in the past the greater wisdom of hindsight. Moreover, anecdotes, for all that they can be illuminating, are most vivid when they are most malicious. Even at their most amiable, they tend to cut their subjects down to size. Reviews and articles and letters and diaries can provide a necessary corrective; for all that they have a built-in bias, they have the advantage of telling us how things appeared at the time.

Unlike her second husband, Edmund Wilson, Mary McCarthy did not keep a diary. But having come of age too early for a long-distance phone call to become second nature, this most sociable of writers was an ardent, if erratic, correspondent. So were many of her closest friends. For much of her life she was at the center of a circle of men and women every bit as articulate as she was. In their letters she frequently figures large. In her own letters, on the other hand, we find not only the latest gossip and most intimate confidences but a face far less intimidating than the one she was accustomed to presenting to the world.

Always Mary McCarthy prided herself on being direct and forthright. But to see Mary McCarthy plain is not quite so simple as it sounds. Like most of us, she was more complicated than she liked to let on. Certainly she was more complicated than she believed herself to be.

The title *Seeing Mary Plain* conveys exactly what I hope to accomplish with this biography, but for me to call the woman I got a glimpse of two decades ago "Mary" can feel like a breach of decorum. For me she will always be "Mary McCarthy," the name she held on to as a published writer through four marriages and for close to sixty years. To be sure, on the jacket of her first book her publisher took care to point out that she was Mrs. Edmund Wilson. And in later years she made it a point to introduce herself to new acquaintances as Mary West. "Miss McCarthy," her last husband, James West, would sometimes call her. But for Jim West and all those who were close to her she was always "Mary." Only to her brother Kevin was she ever Mary Therese.

To the last, Mary Therese McCarthy prided herself on holding strong views on many subjects, and to the last she held strong views on the subject of biography. A writer's life was solely of interest, she believed, insofar as it illuminated the work. The rest was all gossip and "tittle-tattle." Here I beg to differ with her. After all, she is on record as saying that the novels she loved best were enlivened by the whisper of scandal that we get with good gossip.

However, when it comes to one important point I agree with her completely. In 1987, after reading the final draft of Carol Gelderman's *Mary McCarthy*, she wrote the author, "Balance is *not* what a biographer or historian should be after; rather, reality or truth, which rarely lies in the middle of a territory. The best history is partisan." Taking Mary McCarthy at her word, I have not tried for objectivity. It is my hope that in telling the story of her life I have come up with a portrait that might have made her crinkle her eyes and grin. From what I know of her, such a portrait would not have to be touched up or toned down to amuse her.

# SEEING
# MARY
# PLAIN

———————

# Chapter One

# MacDowell

On August 15, 1984, one month after a delicate operation to relieve the pressure of water on her brain, Mary McCarthy wrote her old friend Carmen Angleton. She had every reason to be pleased. Not only had her ataxia and headaches responded to surgery, but after four years of combating a punitive and highly publicized libel action mounted by the playwright Lillian Hellman, she was free to get on with her life. On June 30, Hellman had died, old, blind, and confined to a wheelchair. On August 10, at the behest of Hellman's executors, the $2.25 million suit had been dropped.

For speaking her mind McCarthy had suffered physically and financially. If at this point she had begun to temper her words, it would not have been surprising. "I went swimming the day before yesterday, and the incapacitating headaches have greatly diminished," she wrote from the lovely old house in Maine, where she and her husband, Jim West, now lived half the year, dividing their time between Castine and Paris. Then she moved on to her big news: "It looks as if we would surely be able to drive to Peterborough, New Hampshire, to get the MacDowell Colony award. I don't know whether I told you about that, but it's another medal for literary good behavior, unfortunately with no money attached. The honor, however, is supposed to be considerable; I'd be more sensitive to that if, back in the sixties, Hellman had not been given it."

Although Hellman's lawsuit had been dropped, Mary McCarthy was not about to forgive and forget. After watching the playwright, who had achieved fame decades earlier for such Broadway hits as *The Little Foxes*, attract legions of new admirers with three volumes of memoirs glossing over her years as a defender of Stalin and playing up her refusal to name names to the House Committee on Un-American Activities, McCarthy had finally erupted. In a taped interview with Dick Cavett first aired in January 1980, she had proclaimed, "[E]very word she [Hellman] writes is a lie, including 'and' and 'the.'" For four years, all the while McCarthy had been working on book reviews and essays and starting her own memoir, she had lived with the prospect of being stripped of every cent.

Lillian Hellman had, in fact, been given the MacDowell Medal for excellence in the seventies, not the sixties—1976, to be exact. McCarthy would be the tenth writer to receive the award, which was accompanied by no money but possessed an undeniable luster—in large part owing to the reputation of the colony, which had been founded in 1906 as a retreat for writers, artists, and musicians, freeing them to work without interruption for weeks at a time. In 1960 the first medal had been awarded to the playwright Thornton Wilder, who had written *Our Town* during a long stay at the colony. Since then, twenty-four painters, composers, sculptors, and writers—among them, Georgia O'Keeffe, Aaron Copland, Isamu Noguchi, and McCarthy's second husband, the critic Edmund Wilson— had made the journey to New Hampshire to receive the award.

For all her offhand manner, Mary McCarthy, at seventy-two, was hardly accustomed to such honors. Over five decades she had published more than twenty books of fiction, essays, and criticism. There had been respectful and admiring reviews from critics known to be fastidious. Her short story collection *The Company She Keeps* had broken ground for young women who came after her. *Memories of a Catholic Girlhood*, her account of her orphaned childhood, was regarded by many as a masterpiece. Her Vietnam reporting was regarded as articulate and uncompromising even by those who did not agree with it. *The Group*, her best-seller, had sold millions of copies. *The Stones of Florence* and *Venice Observed* remained perpetually in print. Nonetheless, there had been little recognition from the literary establishment. At an age when she might expect to be inducted into the American Academy of Arts and Letters, she remained in the larger and less august chamber of the National Institute. Although she had sat on—and influenced—a fair number of prize juries, for her own work there had been no National Book Award, no citation from the National Book Critics Circle, no Pulitzer.

By never hesitating to speak harsh truths, she had made enemies less litigious than Lillian Hellman but no more forgiving. Only recently had she received any serious institutional recognition. On May 3, at the New York Public Library she had been awarded the National Medal for Literature, a bronze medal accompanied by a check for $15,000, to honor a lifetime's achievement. Robert Silvers, her editor at *The New York Review of Books*, had been chairman of the nominating committee. While there had been friends of Hellman on the committee, the critic and novelist Elizabeth Hardwick, an old friend and Castine neighbor, had been there to plead her cause. Hardwick, as it happened, was also on the MacDowell Board.

Mary McCarthy was to be awarded her medal on Sunday, August 26. The drive from Castine to Peterborough could take as long as six hours. Saturday night, she and Elizabeth Hardwick, who had been chosen to present the award, had to attend a dinner for colony patrons and board members. Sunday, before an audience of several hundred listeners, each woman would have to stand up and deliver a prepared speech.

Beginning with a painful eruption of shingles in 1980, McCarthy had been suffering from one debilitating ailment after another. The shingles had subsided, to be followed by a new neurological disorder—an impairment of voluntary muscular control, which at one point was diagnosed as Parkinson's disease and then as possibly the effects of juvenile alcoholism. In July, at New York Hospital, a neurosurgeon had drilled a hole in her skull and inserted a plastic tube to serve as a drain, or shunt, to siphon fluid off to her leg. She had been home from the hospital barely three weeks. After everything she had been through, she could be forgiven a lack of enthusiasm. Indeed, she could be forgiven for not making the trip to Peterborough at all.

**SALLY AUSTIN**   Before Mary had the brain shunt, Jim told me that in Paris he would watch her walk across the street and find that she was absolutely stuck in the middle, paralyzed, with cars coming. That was one of the things that was happening to her. She couldn't make her legs move. The most awful things were happening, and Mary just simply never let you know. She just put it aside.

**JAMES WEST**   I had encouraged her to pay more attention to her health and of course she tried as hard as she could, but she was more interested in ideas than in her health.

**ELEANOR PERÉNYI**   Until Mary's health began to fail, I never knew anyone so tireless. It was only after she got shingles that I could keep up with her. Up at dawn when we traveled together, ready to explore every inch of whatever town we were in. And no naps. I think it was all part of being brave about life, facing everything head-on, good or bad. The Hellman lawsuit, for instance, that would have terrified me.

**JAMES WEST**   Mary hated anything that was lying. Mary would say that Lillian Hellman's political history had a lot to do with lying—her testimony that she had nothing to do with the Soviets, when she had plenty to do with them. Mary thought that most of Hellman's so-called mature work was a history of a deception, among other things. Lillian wanted her blood. She wanted Mary to say, "I'm sorry I said that." And Mary wouldn't.

**ELIZABETH HARDWICK**   Once that thing had started, to my horror Mary didn't say, "Oh, I didn't mean that," and let it drop. She wasn't about to. Which was what the rest of us would do. No, she had this idea of her own truthfulness. She would have bankrupted herself for that. It was terrible. I don't know what would have happened, had Lillian not died.

Only after Hellman's death did she feel free to check into the hospital and attend to the condition some doctors believed would end by confining *her* to a wheelchair. The operation performed at New York Hospital was regarded by her surgeons as delicate, though not especially difficult. She herself was famously difficult, but as a patient she proved to be remarkably undemanding—eating the hospital food without complaint and making no fuss when a floor nurse was late with her medication. She also proved to be remarkably resilient.

**SUSAN ANDERSON**  When I first met Mary McCarthy, she had just come back from surgery. I had been assigned as her special duty nurse. When I went into the room, she was lying flat, because that was the doctor's orders, and she had prism glasses on to try and read a book. Her head had been shaved for the surgery and was bandaged. There were about six or eight of her friends around the bed. They were sitting there and talking to her and joking with her, concerned about how she was. I had to climb over people to take her blood pressure. She made suffering look easy. Other people didn't have the sense of how much she suffered. She would be witty and entertaining for people. But she knew that *I* knew it was very hard.

**ELEANOR PERÉNYI**  One thing she couldn't tolerate was commiseration, being fussed over. I went down to New York to see her after the first brain operation. She lay there with her head bandaged, looking awful. But she hadn't a word to say about the operation. I had brought her a bucketful of lilies from my garden, and as I recall it, they were the sole topic of conversation.

### FROM MARY McCARTHY'S LETTER TO FRANI BLOUGH MUSER, AUGUST 15, 1984

> The operation worked, and I am now recuperating—more time to read than I've had since adolescence, for, like an adolescent, I lie flat on a bed or sofa most of the time. Unluckily half my hair was shaved off, and I would look like the Last of the Mohicans if I weren't wearing little Directoire-style caps that Maria has been knitting for me.

**JAMES WEST**  Her recovery surprised me. It was very steady and quicker than one would suppose. Of course one tends to think that tampering with the head or brain is terribly critical. Well, some of that work is and some of it ain't. Some of it is sculpture. With the installation of the shunt you have to know where you're going, but when you know, it's not too bad. Her ability to approach things really made me wonder. But there were times when she was a bit low that summer. After that suit's going on all that time, there was a little letdown when the suit got dropped.

She was to be honored at MacDowell and there was to be no begging off at the last minute. A long announcement had been printed in the colony's spring newsletter and mention had been made of the award in *The New York Times*.

Fortunately, the medal ceremony began to take on something of the aspect of a holiday outing, thanks to two summer visitors of Elizabeth Hardwick's—Esther and Peter Brooks, who had a sprawling summer cottage with spectacular views of Mt. Monadnock, in Dublin, New Hampshire, just down the road from Peterborough. An invitation was extended one night when Mary McCarthy and Jim West were over at Hardwick's for dinner. Esther Brooks proposed that everyone at the table come stay for Medal Day weekend. The Wests would spend their first night at the director's house at MacDowell, but Elizabeth Hardwick—as well as Sally Austin and Jon Jewett, two young Castine friends—would stay with the Brookses both nights.

The morning of Saturday, August 25, Jon Jewett picked up the Wests promptly at eight. Journeys by car were a great thing in the West marriage. But this was unlike any such journey they had made in the past.

**JAMES WEST**    Sometimes on one of the long car trips Mary and I used to take—in the Black Forest or on the way to Rome—when I was driving and I felt I was beginning to get a little tired, Mary would risk singing, and she'd hum a little bit. And it was very pleasant. Then she'd stop because she was bashful, I guess, about her singing. Hers was a very deep voice and it was hardly the tune involved, but nonetheless it was very pleasant. She sang old Irish ballads and occasional Scottish ballads. She knew what the tune was, but the voice control was not there. As with everything, she aimed at perfection, and she got so that finally she sang those ballads as they were written to be sung. Oh, she loved the words.

**JON JEWETT**    We had just typical light gossip in the car, but I was sort of tense, which I'm usually not. I was worried about getting Mary there. Jim didn't have a lot to say. It was terribly hot. Lizzie and Mary just chatted on the way they always did. It wasn't until we were well into New Hampshire that Mary just sort of groaned and started to collapse. We had hospital pillows and she curled up and rested her head on Lizzie. Lizzie claimed to know where the colony was, but in Peterborough we got lost.

Hillcrest, where Mary McCarthy and Jim West were staying, was the oldest building at the colony. At one time it had been the home of the colony's founders, the composer Edward MacDowell and his wife, Marian. Now it housed the resident director. Built as a plain eighteenth-century farmhouse, it was enlarged in 1896 and then embellished with gables, balustrades, porches, and a verandah. A beautiful music room was added on. In this music room, with its pine wainscotting, exposed beams, built-in window seats, and gold embossed Japanese wallpaper, sits Edward MacDowell's piano. Waiting for McCarthy at Hillcrest were Chris Barnes, the colony's resident director, Margaret Carson, the colony's publicist, and Samuel G. Freedman, a reporter from *The New York Times*.

**MARGARET CARSON**   When I learned that Mary McCarthy was to receive the MacDowell Colony Medal, I telephoned *The New York Times* and asked if they were interested in doing a story. They were, and they assigned one of their best reporters, Samuel G. Freedman, to interview Ms. McCarthy at the colony. I knew she had been ill, so I suggested we schedule the interview for late afternoon and that would give her a chance to rest before seeing Mr. Freedman. That seemed agreeable to her and arrangements were made. She was pleased about *The New York Times*. The next day, however, when I asked her to talk to the *Seattle Post-Intelligencer*, her hometown paper, she snapped, "How much will they pay me to do it?" I pointed out that she had not asked me to request payment from *The New York Times*. "That's different," she said. I told the *Seattle Post-Intelligencer* what she had said. The answer to me was "Forget it." I did not forget it, and I did not dismiss it. From then on, I did not arrange any more interviews with Mary McCarthy. There's nothing in the book that says you have to be an easy person to get along with. There's only something that says if you're going to be an artist, be a damn good one. When she came down that afternoon, she didn't seem frail—not a bit. I saw to it that she got together with Sam Freedman and then I left.

**SAMUEL G. FREEDMAN**   For my generation, the feud with Lillian Hellman was the only thing that brought Mary McCarthy into public consciousness— except for a handful of women I knew, who found Mary McCarthy through *Memories of a Catholic Girlhood*. I expected a literary lioness, and she was feisty and opinionated. She certainly hadn't been brought low by either illness or the formality of the occasion. Liking did not enter into our relations that much. I admired the zest and fierce intellect—especially from someone at that age.

Dinner was a sit-down buffet at the director's house. Some fifty guests were invited and tables were set up in the living room, the back hall, and the music room. Virtually all of the colony's board members were there, and at least two had met the guest of honor in the past—the writer Brendan Gill, who had reviewed two of her early novels for *The New Yorker*, and Lael Wertenbaker, who had enjoyed a distinguished career as a journalist and written one highly regarded memoir that told of her husband's harrowing death from cancer. After dinner some of the heartier dinner guests went on to join the colonists, who were holding a dance in the tent set up for the ceremony on the lawn behind Colony Hall.

**BRENDAN GILL**   At MacDowell dinner is an especially pretty occasion because Hillcrest is so nice and old-fashioned and everybody always feels good and excited about the affirmative nature of things. That night, everybody was startled by Mary's wearing a knit cap. There was a sense of not being sure what it meant. She and I just chatted a little bit. I think she was glad to see somebody she'd known for a long time. Then I introduced her to a couple of people. There are always people who are hovering about, hoping to meet the great person.

**LAEL WERTENBAKER**   At Hillcrest I felt like I was going to swim into those sweetly smiling jaws and be chewed up. I had known her before. I'd met her at least three times. I met her in Paris at one point. It was in the late forties and my husband and I were living in Paris and she was visiting. I dislike her writing intensely. She certainly was a good stylist, which I admire, but I disapprove of the way she uses real people in her fiction. She invades other people's privacy. I didn't go up to her. I sat across the room, terrified.

**JAMES WEST**   She seemed to me that first night a tiny bit weak and a tiny bit tired. Frail is not a word I would use for her. She got around—not quite as fast as usual—but she did talk with a number of people and did seem to enjoy it. And then she wore out a little faster than usual. The two of us went down to the tent after dinner. At MacDowell, after all her troubles with Hellman and with her health, she was out and in public and she was like herself. People. Fun. Music. Do you think she'd miss that? We had one little dance.

Sunday morning, while the heat was still bearable, a handful of workmen were busy tidying up the green-and-white tent, where the dance had been held the night before. Hundreds of folding chairs were set up in long rows. Wooden armchairs for all the speakers were placed at the rear of a raised platform, and a podium, equipped with a microphone, was set up at the front. The morning was glorious, but promised to be sultry. George Kendall, resident director of the colony from 1951 to 1970, was looking forward to watching the ceremony from the first row.

**GEORGE KENDALL**   When Edmund Wilson got the award he had just turned down a similar award from one of the New York organizations—I think it was the Century Club. But he accepted the MacDowell award because he felt it really represented something from the artists themselves, sweating away. I think there's a little bit of a fraternal link there. That's what makes it particularly moving for an artist to receive the medal.

**JAMES WEST**   It was Mary's day and like a good photographer I stayed out of the way. I made sure as much as I could that everything was okay for Mary. She was having a tiny bit of trouble walking after the operation. But it was not nearly as bad as it had been.

*The Colony Newsletter* would later report that it was the most beautiful day of the summer. In spite of the heat, more than seven hundred people crowded into the tent. Although most of McCarthy's friends were tied up with summer vacation plans, the poet James Merrill was able to make it to Peterborough, as did Arthur Schlesinger's first wife, Marian, who had a house in the area. Among the colonists there were no close friends. However, taking a special interest in the proceedings were the poet Jane Cooper, who had run into McCarthy over the years, and the novelist Meg Wolitzer, who had written her to say how much she loved *Memories of a Catholic Girlhood* and then received two notes back.

William Banks, the colony's vice chairman, opened the Medal Day ceremony by announcing a bequest from the daughter of Dubose Heyward, colyricist of the opera *Porgy and Bess*. The soprano Nora Bostaph sang two songs from *Porgy and Bess* and then Trevor Cushman, the colony's president, introduced Elizabeth Hardwick, who was to make the "presentation address." Hardwick had been Mary McCarthy's friend for over three decades. In that time she had been called to speak and write about her more than once. While her prepared talk drew on observations that had been made in the past, it was put together with considerable care.

In the limited time she was allotted, Elizabeth Hardwick did her best to cover all bases—to suggest the special nature of Mary McCarthy's achievements, while placing them in a larger historical context. She began with the writing. After doing justice to the "purity of the diction," the "classical sonority of [the] balanced clauses," and the "mastery of prose composition," Hardwick went on to say that the writing was never an end in itself but always "in the service of striking ideas."

In discussing the writing Hardwick tended to concentrate on the fiction. She made much of the fact that even though a major theme of McCarthy's fiction had been ideological follies now long forgotten, her stories and novels had not dated in the slightest. As Hardwick saw it, the reason for this was simple enough: "The conflict between abstract ideas and self-advancement, between probity and the wish to embrace the new and clamorously fashionable is an enduring historical theme."

Next Hardwick went on to speak of the woman herself. After making much of McCarthy's "dashing, slashing and puncturing wit," Hardwick spoke of her character. She spoke of her refusal to let pass anything she believed was wrong. And she spoke of the fundamental conservatism underlying her liberal politics. "The technological utopia is not to this author's taste," she announced.

But Hardwick did not leave it at that. She went so far as to assert that McCarthy's rejection of the fruits of modern technology was no crank prejudice. "There is the suggestion of the lost ideal America," Hardwick said, "the America of enlightened self-respect and self-reliance, of truthfulness, decent education and moral courage at home and in defense of the Bill of Rights." Finally, Hardwick declared that with both her life and her writing the author being honored that day belonged to a longstanding and honorable American tradition.

### FROM ELIZABETH HARDWICK'S PRESENTATION ADDRESS

[I]f Mary McCarthy is a scourge she is a very cheerful one, light-hearted and even optimistic. I do not see in any of her work a trace of despair or alienation but instead rather romantic expectation. She always expects better of persons and of the nation. She seems to believe in love and her heroines are ready to rush out to it again and again. To me this writer from Seattle, New York, Paris and Maine belongs in the line of cranky, idealistic American genius[. . . .] There is something of Henry James in her and more of William James; you can find Emerson and Margaret Fuller and even the deflating slyness of Mark Twain.

**JANE COOPER**   Elizabeth touched on so much and with such delicacy. And to do that for an old and dear friend is the hardest thing. It's much easier to do it for a stranger.

**JAMES MERRILL**   I always have an impression of Lizzie's presence. She's a very vivid presence. I remember the tone of voice and the kind of sweetness that came through at MacDowell. She seemed very pleased to be doing this. I think Lizzie was always rather insecure vis-à-vis Mary. She probably spent a lot of energy trying to cover it up.

Elizabeth Hardwick's presentation address was all that it should be. The decorum of the occasion demanded that she restrict herself to whole-hearted celebration. To smile at her friend's domestic conservatism was the most she could permit herself.

For Mary McCarthy, on the other hand, decorum was less compelling than a chance to express exactly how she felt. The speech she gave that morning was not like any she had ever delivered. But before she had even opened her mouth to speak, she had departed from MacDowell custom by delivering her written talk from a chair. (The *Times* the following day would ascribe this to the fact that she was recovering from surgery on her "scalp.")

Seated at a small wooden table with a microphone and a water pitcher, Mary McCarthy began by letting her listeners know that for her this was hardly an occasion for celebration. "Ladies and gentlemen," she announced, "in accepting this award I've been driven to review my career, a somewhat saddening business, for I, as person and writer, seem to have had little effect, in the sense of improving the world I came into or even of maintaining a previous standard." The only improvement she could see was in the proliferation of labor-saving devices, which she saw as no real progress at all.

"I like labor-intensive implements and practices," she informed her listeners and went on to explain why: "The amount of labor that goes into a human manufacture determines the success of the enterprise." As examples she gave "cranking by hand an ice cream freezer" or "pushing a fruit or vegetable through a sieve," and then went on to invoke Michelangelo, who had spoken "of leaving some mark of the tools on the marble rather than have a smooth, polished surface." "I think it has something to do with truth," she said.

She told of how she had fought off the electric typewriter, the Cuisinart, and credit cards, only to find the electric typewriter itself was fast becoming "obsolescent." She acknowledged that her objection to many of these technological advances was perhaps nothing more than "prejudice," but she made it clear that she objected to credit cards on "political" grounds. "I am against the forced registration of citizens," she explained.

Although the greater part of her talk was devoted to the sorry state of a world that was less and less to her liking, her failure to have any lasting effect on that world was never far from her mind. Toward the end of her talk, trying to leaven her words with such humor as she could muster, she returned to this theme.

### FROM MARY MCCARTHY'S ACCEPTANCE SPEECH

[W]hy should I care that I have lived my life as a person and writer in vain? We all live our lives more or less in vain. That is the normal common fate, and the fact of having a small *name* should not make us hope to be exceptions, to count for something or other. At best, we writers, artists in general, give pleasure to some, and the pleasure we have offered our readers comes to seem a sort of bribe that will persuade them to listen to us when no pleasure is involved[. . . . ] But I wonder, will anyone listen if I make a pitch, here, for Mondale?

**JAMES MERRILL**   Mary gave a very touching reply to Lizzie's presentation, stressing all the things that we loved and sometimes deplored about her. Her reluctance to join the modern world. Her boycotting of mechanical kitchen appliances and electric typewriters and credit cards. She came through as a very crusty survivor, full of charm.

**JANE COOPER**   I thought it took tremendous courage to appear as she appeared and to give this speech sitting down. And when she said, I feel sad because my work never changed the world, I thought, You're one of the few people who meant your work to change the world.

**MEG WOLITZER**   The main thing I remember is her railing against credit cards. I gave it a lot of thought because I was really broke. I was subletting my apartment so that I could go to MacDowell. I didn't have a credit card. It was the one thing about which I felt, Oh, good, she'd approve of me. But what does it mean, not wanting credit cards? It seemed that there was a conspiracy-theory quality to her speech.

**GEORGE KENDALL**   That day she seemed charged with intellectual and physical energy, although she wore a bonnet on her head that looked like a nightcap. I know she'd just had surgery. I don't know how old she was. I assumed she was in her sixties. She was very dynamic. She was courageous and sparkling. She came across as someone you would be delighted to sit next to at a dinner. You would hope to run across her again later.

**JAMES MERRILL**   This was the only medal ceremony I'd ever been to. It's not the sort of experience I really go in search of. It's sad, because in the nicest possible way the person being honored is being kicked upstairs.

**SAMUEL G. FREEDMAN**   People like her were becoming marginal, through no fault of their own. First, she was seeing the death of intellectual life in this country. The culture had moved away from ideas and words to images. Second, during the Reagan era anyone from the Left who was old or dying—whether he was a Stalinist, Trotskyite, Lovestoneite, social democrat, or anarchist—would have to feel that it was all a failure. If you had fought battles on the Left for social democracy and an enlightened kind of welfare state and racial equality and at the end of all your fighting what you were left with was Reagan, it would make you want to hit your head against the wall.

**JAMES WEST**   When Mary said her actions hadn't counted for much it was heartbreaking. She had been low that summer, but it hurt me when she said things like that. But the talk ended on a much brighter note. The audience really went for her Mondale pitch. She'd said her say and she must have been pleased that she could do that after all she'd been through.

As always on Medal Day, tables were set up outside the tent for the box lunches. Samuel Freedman did not stay on for the picnic, and Esther Brooks was in a hurry to get back to her house in Dublin and start dinner. Although Mary McCarthy was beginning to tire, she kept smiling and shaking hands and posing for photographs. She and Elizabeth Hardwick were walking down an alley of trees, on their way back to the car, when Nancy Crampton, the photographer there to cover the ceremony for the colony, snapped one last picture.

Although the guest of honor got to bed before midnight, it had been a long, demanding, and by no means carefree day. Monday morning, three of the travelers from Maine were up early, eager to get on the road. However, no one was surprised to see that the Wests were still in their room. At the Brookses', with Mt. Monadnock in the distance and no other house in sight, the real world can seem continents away.

**JON JEWETT**   Around eight thirty I went up to Mary and Jim's room and listened and I could hear someone was in the shower. I went downstairs, and Lizzie said, "Hurry up and get the trays." Esther and I fixed up two trays with a poached egg, an English muffin, and an old-fashioned coffee thermos for each. We didn't need Lizzie—we had two trays and two people—but Lizzie was like a schoolgirl going up the stairs ahead of us. Mary and Jim were propped up on their pillows waiting. Jim looked at his watch. In Castine, I guess Maria brought them their breakfast promptly at eight thirty.

**ESTHER BROOKS**   Elizabeth left with Sally around nine. Afterward the rest of us all had a great breakfast on the screened porch behind the dining room. It took about an hour to get that organized and Peter, Jon, and I had just started our breakfast, when Mary and Jim came downstairs fully dressed and sat down with us and ate all over again. They took a helping of everything. The phone rang, and I said, "Mary, it's a newspaperman on the phone, do you want to speak to him?" Jim said, "Perhaps I'd better take it, Mary." He was still trying to protect her. She went out and took the call and came back looking very pleased with herself. The reporter had wanted to know about how she felt now that the Hellman suit had been dropped. She'd told him she'd really been looking forward to the lawsuit, and Jim said, "You could have said something better than that, dear."

As it happened Mary McCarthy had already said "something better"— or if not better, then more elaborate—to Samuel G. Freedman whose piece ran that morning in the *Times.* To ensure that readers did not miss it, the piece was cited in a boxed index on the front page. In addition, the opening sentence to her MacDowell speech was quoted in the paper's "Quote of the Day."

### FROM "McCARTHY IS RECIPIENT OF MacDOWELL MEDAL," *THE NEW YORK TIMES,* AUGUST 27, 1984

Mary McCarthy, literary lioness, received the Edward MacDowell Medal here today for her career as an author. She proceeded to show that, at the age of 72, she still has her growl and her claws[. . . .] Miss McCarthy assailed J. D. Salinger when he was at his height and defended James Farrell when it was chic to dismiss him. She was a stout anti-Stalinist from the time of the Moscow purge trials, yet she remains far to the left in American politics and visited North Vietnam during the war.

And in the incident that brought her perhaps more fame than her books, Miss McCarthy was sued for libel by Lillian Hellman in 1980[. . . .] "I'm absolutely unregenerate," Miss McCarthy said[. . . .] "I didn't want her to die. I wanted her to lose in court. I wanted her around for that."

**JAMES WEST**    I regretted her public statement that she was sorry that Lillian died because she would have liked to have taken her to the mat and won the case. I thought that was a bit gross myself. A little too much. After all, that's almost cannibalistic.

**ESTHER BROOKS**    I just thought, This is going to be very bad publicity for Mary. I knew Lillian much better than I knew Mary. What Mary said about Lillian is true, but I don't think you can say those things. And what does it mean to say that the "ands" and the "buts" are a lie. In the end it wasn't pretty and it wasn't funny. It was appalling.

**SAMUEL G. FREEDMAN**    I thought in terms of historical context. I mean, here was somebody who has been fighting the same political battle—the Stalinist Left vs. the non-Stalinist Left—for fifty years. I think she probably felt the way Muhammad Ali felt when Joe Frazier retired. You've lost your best and longest antagonist. What's life going to be like if you have no one to hate?

**ESTHER BROOKS**    After they left, I came into the living room to find the plaster was falling down from one corner of the ceiling. There was an old claw-footed tub in the bathroom Mary and Jim were using. The tub has a shower curtain attachment, and you have to tuck the curtain inside the bathtub. That's fairly rudimentary. Well, Mary didn't. She flooded the bathroom floor and never told anybody. You know the way water goes through old houses. We had to have the ceiling redone.

Samuel Freedman's piece in the *Times* ended on a note of triumph, with her making her pitch for Mondale and receiving "raucous applause" from her listeners. Her head in a little knit cap, unable to stand at the podium, she was no longer an object of pity. The speech was a success. If all went well, she would soon be hard at work on her own memoirs. Yet the opening words of her speech, when highlighted in the *Times*'s "Quotation of the Day," sounded an undeniably plaintive note: "As a person and a writer, I seem to have had little effect on improving the world I came into." This air of sorrow, or regret, did not go unremarked on Monday morning by at least one *Times* reader, who sat at the desk of his Wall Street law office with a pen and a long yellow legal pad and wrote out a detailed memorandum:

Memo: From Louis Auchincloss
*Re*: Mary McCarthy's having lived her life in vain
*To*: Mary McCarthy

*Facts*: I have considered Mary McCarthy's effect on *my* life, and I discover the following:
1) As a reporter she convinced me, a Republican desperately seeking to believe in this party that:
   a) R. Nixon was the arch villain of Watergate.
   b) [The war in] Viet Nam was an unjustified moral and tactical disaster.
2) As a critic she introduced me to the delights of Compton-Burnett and Sarraute, two authors I had not previously known how to enjoy. And she reintroduced me to Dickens.
3) As a travel writer, she immensely intensified my love of Florence, revisited twice, her book in hand.
4) As a novelist she gave me reassurance that form, plot, character delineation and *intelligence* are still as vital to fiction as a "bleeding heart" and that fiction still has a great role to play in our society.
5) As a religious writer she opened my eyes as none other to the reality of Catholicism in America—what it is *really* like.
*Conclusion*: Multiply me by *thousands*, and it will appear that McC's life has been lived in vain only if *all* lives are lived in vain.

Louis Auchincloss was not a close friend. They had met over the years at dinners in New York and at literary gatherings, and in 1965 Auchincloss had included an admiring chapter on her fiction in *Pioneers and Caretakers: A Study of Nine American Women Novelists*. His memo was sent off in the morning mail with a scribbled note. Later, Mary confided to her friend Cleo Paturis that his words had meant a good deal to her, but seeing her response you might not necessarily know this. On September 5, she sent Louis Auchincloss a brief typed letter. She said that while his words had had a "cheering effect," she did not want him to think she was "fishing." To repay him for his "testimonial" and his "kindness" she recommended he read the second volume of Hilary Spurling's biography of Ivy Compton-Burnett, which had just come out. But to his memo's conclusion, she offered a mild demurral. Not quite ready to accept his tightly reasoned argument, she wrote, "Maybe I really feel, though, that *all* lives are lived somehow in vain."

# Chapter Two

# MINNEAPOLIS

For Mary McCarthy to suggest that perhaps *all* lives were lived in vain was hardly coy or disingenuous. At the age of six, with the death of her two young parents, she was made to feel the fragility of every bond and assumption most of us take for granted. But even before these two untimely losses there had been intimations of trouble. From the moment her parents had met and fallen in love at an Oregon resort in the summer of 1910, neither family had approved of the match. At twenty-one, Tess Preston was one of the most beautiful girls in Seattle. Roy McCarthy, eight years older and prematurely gray, was charming and good-looking but held no steady job. For most of his adult life he had been supported by his father.

When it came down to it, the objections raised to the marriage were not purely financial. If necessary, there was sufficient money to help the young couple get started. Harold Preston, Tess's father, was a highly regarded Seattle lawyer. J. H. (James Henry) McCarthy was renowned in Minneapolis for his shrewd management of the family's extensive grain-elevator holdings. In a quiet way he was rich.

Nor were the objections entirely religious. Roy's mother, Elizabeth Sheridan McCarthy, was a devout and belligerent Catholic and had little use for Protestants or Jews. Harold Preston was nominally Protestant and his wife, Augusta, was Jewish. Neither of them gave much thought to religion, but the McCarthys would have been happier if they had been Catholics. Still, McCarthy men had been known to marry outside the faith. What seemed to trouble both families was the uncertain health of the prospective bridegroom, who was not only eight years older than his beautiful young bride but suffering from a bad heart.

The wedding took place in April 1911. After a false start in Minneapolis, the couple returned to Seattle, and a first child, Mary Therese McCarthy, was born on June 21, 1912. That fall, Roy began law school at the University of Washington, and the McCarthys bought the little family a suitable house, not large by the standards of either family but comfortable. Three years later, having earned his degree, Roy McCarthy was forced to recognize that he did not have the physical stamina to practice law full-time—or to carry the expenses of his relatively modest but far from frugal household.

By 1917 Tess McCarthy had given birth to three boys: Kevin, Preston, and Sheridan. All Tess's children, except for the last, had the dark hair, fair skin, and green eyes fringed with black lashes characteristic of McCarthy men. In this rapidly expanding family, colds, coughs, and stomach upsets were passed from toddler to infant to parent and back again. Still, there was time for birthday celebrations, for fairy teas and an ermine muff for little Mary. There was time to attend mass and for the children to be taught their prayers. Sometimes there was a resident cook, and for a while there was a Japanese houseboy; occasionally a nurse had to be brought in, but it was hard to keep help of any competence. Before long, Roy was staying home because of his bad heart.

In 1918, the seventh year of the marriage, matters came to a head. The McCarthys were contributing eight or nine hundred dollars a month for the family's maintenance and the Prestons were putting in another hundred. Roy McCarthy's health was visibly deteriorating. With the four children getting older, expenses were getting out of hand. Nine hundred a month was no longer sufficient. If anyone was going to take charge, or turn things around, it was not the Prestons, who lived close by in Seattle. It would have to be the McCarthys, half a continent away, who at one point had sent their youngest son, Louis, to keep an eye on Roy and Tess while he was attending the University of Washington. The McCarthys, after all, were meeting the bills.

With Louis now training to be a pilot in Pensacola, Florida, and soon to go overseas to fight in the war in Europe, the McCarthys suddenly turned their attention to their oldest son's family in Seattle. Later, no one was quite sure exactly what prompted them to suddenly step in. Tess, an enthusiastic convert to Catholicism, had enrolled her only daughter as a day student at the Forest Ridge Convent of the Sacred Heart, when, with no warning, she and Roy were ordered to pack up at once and move the family east, to a modest yellow house that J. H. McCarthy had purchased just down the street from his own handsome residence on Blaisdell Avenue.

Why this great haste? According to one newspaper account, Roy wished to see his younger brother, Louis, before Louis shipped out for overseas. As explanations go, this was certainly preferable to any suggestion that J. H. McCarthy had let Roy know that he had finally had enough. Unfortunately, Roy's trouble maintaining his growing family was merely another episode in a long sorry history. Before he had met and married Tess Preston, Roy McCarthy had been a serious drunk. At a physical his first year at the University of Minnesota, it was discovered he had a badly damaged heart. Although Roy eventually finished college, upon hearing this news he virtually dropped out.

More than once Roy had been hospitalized for alcoholism, and when all else failed, he had been shipped out west to Portland. In the west, where no one, least of all the Prestons, knew of his drinking, Roy had pieced together a new life. During the first months of his marriage to Tess, this new life had threatened to unravel. When the newlyweds first moved back to Minneapolis in 1911, so Roy could work for his father, Roy had begun to drink again. The McCarthys had advised his new wife to leave him. Instead, she had returned with him to Seattle and when his daughter, Mary, was born, he had stopped drinking for good.

But the time had come to summon the prodigal home. To ensure that all went smoothly, a third brother, Harry, and his wife, Zula, were dispatched to Seattle to help with the packing. That September Tess had been hospitalized with the flu. Mary had been forced to miss the start of school because of chicken pox. Whether Harry and Zula were any help remains open to question. But one thing is certain: after the little house was stripped and the furniture placed in storage, there were loose ends to be tied up and farewells to be made. For several days the party of four adults and four children put up at a local hotel.

Unwelcome as the move was, it might have gone as planned if not for an outbreak of Spanish influenza. With no antibiotics or sulfa drugs to treat its side effects, the infection often developed into a pneumonia to which young adults were particularly susceptible. In the end the epidemic would claim more than 20 million victims, 675,000 of them in the United States. By the time the McCarthy party boarded their train in Seattle at least one member was noticeably feverish. In the course of the three-day journey all four children took sick. When, at last, the train arrived in Minneapolis, two of the four adults had to be lifted down to the station platform on stretchers and taken to the second floor of the J. H. McCarthy house on Blaisdell Avenue. A makeshift infirmary was set up for the stricken children in their grandmother's sewing room on the first floor.

On November 7, 1918, in one of the substantial but rarely used guest bedrooms of that dark, imposing, and rigorously dusted house at 2114 Blaisdell Avenue, Therese Preston McCarthy, twenty-nine years old, a Child of Mary and member of the sodality of the Ladies of the Sacred Heart, succumbed to influenza. Roy McCarthy had died the previous day, in a bedroom down the hall. Kept ignorant of their parents' fate, the four orphaned children continued to convalesce in the iron beds set up for

them downstairs in the sewing room. When they were deemed sufficiently recovered, the three boys were taken away to the modest yellow
house J. H. McCarthy had bought.

Mary, the eldest, was left behind to come to terms, in the company of
two grandparents she knew only from brief visits, with the fact of her
parents' deaths. At six, she was old enough to have vivid memories of her
parents, although soon these memories would be colored by stories she
heard from her grandparents, her aunts and uncles, and from family
friends. In time these memories would be further embroidered and
interwoven with her brother Kevin's recollections until she was not
always certain what was myth and what was hard fact.

Certain details, however, seemed incontrovertible: her mother had
been by anyone's standard beautiful. Her tall gray-haired father, reduced
to spending a good many of his days in bed with his books and calendar
diary and his not always disciplined offspring, had, quite simply, adored
her. To their entrancing but chaotic household Augusta Preston would
pay an occasional visit, driving her very own electric car and wearing a
linen duster, her hat swathed in veils.

The recommended course of action during an epidemic is the same
today as it was in 1918: stay put within the walls of your own house,
where you are least likely to run the risk of contagion. Of course not
everyone has this luxury. William Maxwell, later one of McCarthy's editors at *The New Yorker*, lost his young mother in that same epidemic of
Spanish influenza because in the last days of her pregnancy a doctor
rushed her to the local hospital for a difficult delivery. Still, that doctor
was only doing what was necessary to save his patient's life. He felt he
had no choice. The McCarthys, on the other hand, *did* have a choice.
They could have let Roy and his wife stay where they were—at least until
the war was over.

The deaths of Tess and Roy McCarthy were a family tragedy. But for
the children their deaths were a disaster. Almost immediately the four
children were packed up by Roy's mother, Elizabeth Sheridan (Lizzie)
McCarthy and thrust into a makeshift household governed by two totally
unqualified poor relations, her aging, recently married sister Margaret
and her husband Myers. The fact that this sister had no prior experience
with young children seems never to have troubled Lizzie McCarthy, a
woman of strong opinions and few misgivings. By paying Margaret and
Myers Shriver to take charge of the four homeless orphans she would be
keeping Roy's little family intact while securing an income for her sister's new husband. If the investment sometimes seemed costly, she could
always console herself with the thought that she was getting double value
for her money. Moreover, she was keeping the children safe from their
Protestant grandfather and his Jewish wife.

After church, scrubbed and dressed in their modest Sunday best, the four orphaned children were invited to pay an afternoon call on their McCarthy grandmother or join her for a rare family outing. With the elder McCarthys—particularly with their grandfather—there was a possibility of a cookie or piece of candy. Unhappily, the erratic traffic that existed between the two houses on Blaisdell Avenue went only one way. The elder McCarthys saw no need to set foot in the yellow stucco house. As the years passed, no one seemed to notice what a poor return they were getting for their money—or to take note of the level to which that grim little establishment had sunk. No one, that is, except the two oldest children.

In early middle age, Mary McCarthy wrote eight memoirs portraying her childhood and adolescence, most of which were published over the course of ten years in *The New Yorker*. The memoirs were then brought together in *Memories of a Catholic Girlhood*. In the book's first three chapters she tried to make sense of what happened in Minneapolis. By that time she had heard from her three brothers and her Uncle Harry—who called the shots as he saw them, without benefit of punctuation or capital letters—and had revised some of her facts and conclusions. To all but the last chapter she attached an afterword, making clear what was hitherto muddied and pointing out where she had fudged the truth or slipped into pure invention in the interests of telling a good story.

Her determined but not altogether satisfactory forays into the past led her to go on at some length about the unreliability of memory—the way it fused events and details and perpetuated misunderstandings until over time an incident that had never happened came to be accepted as incontrovertible fact. She wrote, "My own son, Reuel, for instance, used to be convinced that Mussolini had been thrown off a bus in North Truro, on Cape Cod, during the war. This memory goes back to one morning in 1943 when, as a young child, he was waiting with his father and me beside the road in Wellfleet to put a departing guest on the bus to Hyannis. The bus came through, and the bus driver leaned down to shout the latest piece of news: 'They've thrown Mussolini out.'"

Reuel had been fortunate enough to have two parents to set him right about what had taken place. As an orphan, with no adults available to verify important details, she was admittedly ill equipped to fix and interpret key events of her early life. But this did not stop her from trying. And it did not stop her from fixing blame where she felt it deserved to be laid.

### FROM "TO THE READER" IN *MEMORIES OF A CATHOLIC GIRLHOOD*

It is our parents, normally, who not only teach us our family history but who set us straight on our childhood recollections, telling us that *this* cannot have happened the way we think it did and that *that*, on the other hand, did occur, just as we remember it, in such and such a summer when So-and-So was our nurse.

## FROM MARY MCCARTHY'S REVIEW OF MONIQUE WITTIG'S OPOPONAX IN THE NEW STATESMAN, JULY 1966

Everybody's childhood is the same in its essentials. For a child, it is a story he is memorizing under his breath, beginning with his name.

**PRESTON MCCARTHY**  A few years ago, Kevin found a desk calendar our father had kept at home. Reading that, you see everybody was sick all the time. Almost every page was "Dr. So-and-So came to see So-and-So. And he had some of his prescriptions listed—the digitalis. One entry I remember was: "I got downstairs today to find Kevin having cut Pomps' hair." Kevin couldn't pronounce Preston. I still have that lock of hair.

## FROM HARRY MCCARTHY'S LETTER TO MARY MCCARTHY, MARCH 8, 1952

your lovely mother had vainly tried to install some sign of discipline in the seattle house but my brother would say in a mealy sort of voice "no tess, come mary in bed with daddy and he will read to you," the day we left seattle all sick, you filled your mother's perfume bottles with ink and kevin started a fire in the house

**CYNTHIA MCCARTHY SANDBERG**  When my father, Louis, was a very young boy, his two older brothers were kind of wild, and he and his mother would go out with the chauffeur to find them. Harry and Roy had early careers that were not dissimilar.

## FROM "TO THE READER"

My father, I used to maintain, was so tall that he could not get through a door without bending his head. This was an exaggeration. He was a tall man, but not remarkably so, as I can see from pictures, like all the McCarthy men, he had a torso that was heavy-boned and a little too long for his legs. He wore his gray hair in a pompadour and carried a stick when he walked. He read to me a great deal, chiefly Eugene Field and fairy tales, and I remember we heard a nightingale together, on the boulevard, near the Sacred Heart convent. But there are no nightingales in North America.

**PRESTON MCCARTHY**  The difference between Mary and the rest of us was that Mary knew our parents and we didn't. And then, too, she was the apple of her father's eye.

She had enjoyed a special position in that little paradise in Seattle and she would enjoy a position no less special once she got her bearings in Minneapolis. If there was blame to be placed for what had happened to her and her brothers, it was not going to be with the father she loved.

## FROM "YONDER PEASANT, WHO IS HE?" IN
## *MEMORIES OF A CATHOLIC GIRLHOOD*

Our father had put us beyond the pale by dying suddenly of influenza and taking our young mother with him, a defection that was remarked on with horror and grief commingled, as though our mother had been a pretty secretary with whom he had wantonly absconded into the irresponsible paradise of the hereafter. Our reputation was clouded by this misfortune. There was a prevailing sense, not only in the family but among storekeepers, servants, streetcar conductors, and other satellites of our circle, that my grandfather, a rich man, had behaved with extraordinary munificence in allotting a sum of money for our support and installing us with some disagreeable middle-aged relations in a dingy house two blocks distant from his own. What alternative he had was not mentioned; presumably he could have sent us to an orphan asylum and no one would have thought the worse of him. At any rate, it was felt, even by those who sympathized with us, that we led a privileged existence, privileged because we had no rights, and the very fact that at the yearly Halloween or Christmas party given at the home of an uncle we appeared so dismal, ill clad, and unhealthy, in contrast to our rosy, exquisite cousins, confirmed the judgment that had been made on us—clearly, it was a generous impulse that kept us in the family at all.

**KEVIN MCCARTHY**   Sometimes, not very often, we were taken down to Grandma's house (only two blocks away: a five-minute walk). That big white house with grand furnishings inside was called *Grandma's* house. (Obviously she was the more dominant figure, therein.) Grandpa was lame; he had broken his hip in a buggy accident years earlier and walked with a cane. He would lead Mary, my brother "Pomps," and me back to a great big kitchen and talk to us and offer us cookies. I remember Grandma McCarthy had a big chest—a big "front porch." She had a bulldog face and a jutting jaw. Later on, I heard her described by one of our McCarthy relatives as the one who wanted to save Catholicism from the Pope, who wasn't as fervent or fierce a Catholic as she and some of her Irish biddies felt he ought to be. An Italian is a questionable character, after all.

**PRESTON MCCARTHY**   Our grandmother McCarthy was a domineering woman, you could see that. She was a fanatic Catholic. She had a special chair where she did a lot of her handiwork—needlepoint and such, with scenes. When she sat there, her spine never touched the back of her chair. She was a tough one. I remember one time she and my grandfather gave us boys a whopping. I don't think my uncles got many hugs from her.

## FROM HARRY MCCARTHY'S LETTER OF MARCH 8, 1952

father advanced $41,700 during those years, each year he would write preston and inquire if he could not spare a bob or so for his grandchildren and preston sure did open up the purse strings, he sent two checks for one hundred each from 1918 to 1923. when I would inquire if any funds ever arrived from seattle, father would say, he is probably hard up, besides father was very fond of tess and roy and could afford it.

**CYNTHIA McCARTHY SANDBERG**  Mary's feeling that the Prestons were taking care of her made Dad kind of cross. He realized that her impression was that she'd been totally abandoned financially, and that wasn't the case. I presume that the figures that Harry gives Mary in his letter are my father's and I know they are accurate because my father kept good records of everything. I could, if I went through things, find the cost of a snowsuit I had when I was three. My father was a very kind man, and when Tess and Roy died he was only twenty-three and not married yet. He laughed when Mary's book came out, because he was treated rather gently. "That's because I'm alive," he said.

At the yellow stucco house on Blaisdell Avenue, with its cinder-block walls, its cemented front lawn, and its rooms furnished with castoffs and pieces from the Salvation Army, the four children were left to make the best of it. Their grandmother's sister Margaret, pinched and worn and rescued from an old maid's fate by a marriage in her fifties to a man several years her junior, was as different from their mother as night from day. Lord and master of this new domain was Myers Shriver, every bit as fat as his wife was thin. To help with all the work Margaret had enlisted a sweet-faced old lady called "Aunt Mary," said to be her eldest sister but relegated to a bare attic room, where, in the manner of pensioners from time immemorial, she spent her days at mending and needlework.

**KEVIN McCARTHY**  Suddenly we were presented to this couple and to a considerably older lady—"Aunt Mary," a vague shadowy figure, almost like a ghost to us little kids, who was living alone in the attic of the house where we were being installed. She was probably our grandmother's very elderly sister. So this inexperienced middle-aged pair, Myers Shriver and his wife, Margaret, became instant foster parents as they were handed these four orphan kids and told, "Here, take care of them." Can you imagine what a terrible burden this must have been on those benighted people who had no children of their own?

**PRESTON McCARTHY**  For those two old people—Shriver and Aunt Margaret—Mary must have been a handful. When I think of those old people being responsible for caring for us, it explains a lot.

**FROM "A TIN BUTTERFLY" IN *MEMORIES OF A CATHOLIC GIRLHOOD***
Myers was the perfect type of rootless municipalized man who finds his pleasures in the handouts or overflow of an industrial civilization. He enjoyed sitting on a curbstone, watching parades, the more nondescript the better[. . . .] He liked bandstands, band concerts, public parks devoid of grass[. . . .] He collected coupons and tinfoil, bundles of newspaper for the old rag-and-bone man [. . .] free tickets given out by a neighborhood movie house to the first installment of a serial—in all the years we lived with him, we never saw a full-length movie but

only those truncated beginnings[. . . .] In the winter, he spent the days at home in the den, or in the kitchen, making candy. He often had enormous tin trays of decorated fondants cooling in the cellar[. . . .] The bonbons, with their pecan or almond topping, that he laid out in such perfect rows were for his own use; we were permitted to watch him set them out, but never—and my brother Kevin confirms this—did we taste a single one.

**KEVIN McCARTHY**  When Uncle Myers made candy, which he did quite frequently, he didn't want any help; his little charges could stand back away from the stove and watch. But he did insist on having Pomps and me help him on days when he was ready to make peanut brittle. I remember having to go and sit in the basement and get the skins off raw peanuts that had been soaked in water. It's so painstaking to get the brown skin off a peanut that hasn't been roasted. I don't remember Mary being stuck with this black-hole assignment. I guess she was doing something of value: her homework.

**PRESTON McCARTHY**  I always remember one Christmas in that house. We were in the living room and a big "ho-ho-ho" was coming down the stairs, and then there was Shriver in a beard. We all knew it was Shriver. In that room there was a sort of divider and I got laughing so hard I fell off. He was, I would guess, a lost person with nothing to do all day. He never helped with the housework, but I can remember working with him out in the garage. It was some sort of carpentry he was doing—he was building something—and he teased me about how I kept my tongue out when I worked. He kept after me, saying, "Pomps, you're going to bite your tongue off."

**KEVIN McCARTHY**  I would think that to a certain extent Preston had it easier than Mary and I. Aren't people inclined to go easier on the younger ones? And of course he and Sheridan were a little further from the so-called accident of our parents' disappearance.

At St. Stephen's Church and at St. Stephen's School Mary did find a measure of solace. If the church itself offered immediate comfort, the school offered rewards that were to be long lasting. Both held little appeal for her youngest brothers or for Kevin. But at their shabby neighborhood parochial school, Mary led her class not only in all academic subjects but in athletics. In a statewide contest, she won a first prize of twenty-five dollars for her essay on "The Irish in American History." With her high scholastic average she was able to talk her parish priest into letting her take first communion a year early. In later years she would say, "I am not sorry to have *been* a Catholic, first of all for practical reasons. It gave me a certain knowledge of the Latin language and of the saints and their stories which not everyone is lucky enough to have. Latin, when I came to study it, was easy for me and attractive, too, like an old friend." But the church offered her more than that. She would go on to say that religion had made all the difference in Minneapolis. But it was by no means the religion of her McCarthy grandmother.

### FROM THE INTRODUCTION TO *MEMORIES OF A CATHOLIC GIRLHOOD*

Looking back, I see that it was religion that saved me. Our ugly church and parochial school provided me with my only aesthetic outlet, in the words of the Mass and the litanies and the old Latin hymns, in the Easter lilies around the altar, rosaries, ornamented prayer books, votive lamps, holy cards stamped in gold and decorated with flower wreaths and a saint's picture. This side of Catholicism, much of it cheapened and debased by mass production, was for me, nevertheless, the equivalent of Gothic cathedrals and illuminated manuscripts and mystery plays[. . . .]

There was the Catholicism I learned from my mother and from the simple parish priests and nuns in Minneapolis, which was, on the whole, a religion of beauty and goodness, however imperfectly realized. Then there was the Catholicism practiced in my grandmother McCarthy's parlor and in the home that was made for us down the street—a sour, baleful doctrine in which old hates and rancors had been stewing for generations, with ignorance proudly stirring the pot[. . . .]

From what I have seen, I am driven to the conclusion that religion is only good for good people[. . . .] For the others, it is too great a temptation—a temptation to the deadly sins of pride and anger, chiefly, but one might also add sloth.

Even though the Shriver establishment was two short blocks away, for Lizzie and J. H. McCarthy it might as well have been situated on another continent. At the Shrivers', when a child was caught doing something forbidden, punishment was swift. To Mary and her brothers the blows that descended upon them frequently seemed to come for no good reason. By the standards of the life they had led, they were doing nothing wrong. Much of what was said to be for their health, or their own good, felt like punishment. It was as if with their parents' death they had stepped through the looking glass and everything was the opposite of the way it had been before. Yet no one in the family seemed to remark on this or to question it—least of all their Minneapolis grandparents.

### FROM "A TIN BUTTERFLY"

[W]hen I was ten, I wrote an essay for a children's contest on "The Irish in American History," which won first the city and then the state prize[. . . .] At any rate, there was a school ceremony, at which I was presented the city prize (twenty-five dollars, I think, or perhaps that was the state prize); my aunt was in the audience in her best mallard-feathered hat, looking, for once, proud and happy. She spoke kindly to me as we walked home, but when we came to our ugly house, my uncle silently rose from his chair, led me into the dark downstairs lavatory, which always smelled of shaving cream, and furiously beat me with the razor strop—to teach me a lesson, he said, lest I become stuck-up[. . . .]

We were beaten all the time, as a matter of course, with the hair-brush across the bare legs for ordinary occasions, and with the razor strop across the bare bottom for special occasions, like the prize-win-ning. It was as though these ignorant people, at sea with four fright-ened children, had taken a Dickens novel—*Oliver Twist*, perhaps, or *Nicholas Nickleby*—for a navigation chart.

**KEVIN MCCARTHY**  Mary and I got punished for dumb things—things we weren't aware of having done. Suddenly, inexplicably, the razor strap or hairbrush is lashing away at your backside and you are being scolded during the assault for the fact, let's say, that the soap has been found in the bottom of the bathtub instead of in its dish. If the hairbrush was found on the floor you got spanked. You couldn't do right.

### FROM HARRY MCCARTHY'S LETTER OF MARCH 8, 1952

i readily admit that i did not see much of your home life, why should i? i lived a very full life had nice children of my own and many friends, the adults in your house bored me and you and kevin particularly were the worst spoiled brats i knew[. . . .] if I had heard that meyer's was lay-ing his heavy hand on your tender derriere, i would probably have smiled.

**CYNTHIA MCCARTHY SANDBERG**  I know one instance when Dad stepped in. It was an unpleasant situation with the old people, Myers and Margaret. I think Mary may have been a difficult child, but, my Lord, they had suffered such a horrible horrible thing! And I remember hearing the story once that Mary broke her glasses and she was just told she wouldn't have glasses any-more. Dad was furious and said that was the most absurd thing he'd ever heard and he immediately got her a new pair of glasses.

### FROM "A TIN BUTTERFLY"

A distinction must be made between my uncle's capricious brutality and my aunt's punishments and repressions, which seem to have been dictated to her by her conscience. My aunt was not a bad woman; she was only a believer in method. Since it was the family theory that we had been spoiled, she undertook energetically to remedy this by quasi-scientific means[. . . .] [O]ur day's menu consisted of parsnips, turnips, rutabagas, carrots, boiled potatoes, boiled cabbage, onions, Swiss chard, kale [. . . .] We must have had meat, but I have only the most indistinct recollection of pale lamb stews in which carrots outnumbered the pieces of white, fatty meat and bone and gristle.

**KEVIN MCCARTHY**  That awful meat with its pieces of fat. I well remem-ber trying to hide the sickening fat under my knife.

**PRESTON MCCARTHY**  Mary was right about the food. The parsnips.

**KEVIN MCCARTHY**  At some point in our occasional sessions of recollec-tion, when we were trying to figure out what happened to us—trying to sys-temize the mysterious odyssey of those years—I became aware that my sister seemed to be in a competition with me for the worst wounds. It was-n't *known* but as a child I had adenoids and had to breathe through my mouth. This annoyed Myers intensely and finally he got a big roll of heavy adhesive tape and every night, just before we'd go to bed he'd cut a big swatch off and put it completely over my mouth. He was going to make me breathe properly. In the morning, before breakfast, he'd bring out the spirits of ether and dab with the stuff right under my nose to help in pulling off the sticky tape and its gummy residue. On weekends, if Myers had seen too much of us, I might have adhesive on my mouth during the day. I sharply recall one very dramatic—wild—Sunday morning when Mary got the tape put on as punishment for sassing Uncle Myers; but I had it on every night for months. Then, by luck, it was discovered that I had adenoids and they were cut out. But that's not the way Mary remembered it. It troubles me that I never really challenged her for appropriating my hallmarks.

### FROM "A TIN BUTTERFLY"

[W]e were put to bed at night with our mouths sealed with adhesive tape to prevent mouth-breathing; ether, which made me sick, was used to help pull the tape off in the morning, but a grimy, gray, rubbery remainder was usually left on our upper lips and in the indentations of our pointed chins when we set off for school in our heavy outer clothes, long underwear, black stockings, and high shoes. Our pillows were taken away from us; we were given a sulphur-and-molasses spring tonic, and in the winter, on Saturdays and Sundays, we were made to stay out three hours in the morning and three in the afternoon, regardless of the temperature. We had come from a mild climate, in Seattle, and at fifteen, twenty, or twenty-four below zero we could not play, even if we had had something to play with, and used simply to stand in the snow, crying, and beating sometimes on the window with our frozen mittens, till my aunt's angry face would appear there and drive us away.

### FROM "YONDER PEASANT, WHO IS HE?"

Independently of each other, [Kevin] and I had evolved an identical project—to get ourselves placed in an orphan asylum. We had noticed the heightening of interest that mention of our parentless condition seemed always to produce in strangers, and this led us to interpret the word "asylum" in the old Greek sense and to look on a certain red brick building, seen once from a streetcar near the Mississippi River, as a haven of security. So, from time to time, when our lives became too painful, one of us would set forth.

**KEVIN MCCARTHY**     There was snow on the ground everywhere. I was miles and miles from Blaisdell Avenue, clear across town, near the river. It was cold—early December—and three or four hundred yards away, within sight, was the Shriner's Home for disabled and impoverished children. I had told Mary I was going to try to find an orphanage and ask them to let me live there and then Mary could come and live there, too. The Shriner's Home was yellow sandstone and it looked institutional, but it was called the Sheltering Arms! Darkness was falling fast, my shoes were wet and my feet were cold and I was in a little jacket and I had to go to the bathroom so bad. I was just getting ready to knock on the door when a tremendous voice yelled,

"Hey! Hey!" I ran. I ran until I came to this ordinary little street with bungalows and I saw a man coming toward me. I threw myself down in a great big bank of snow and began to sob. The man stopped and asked why I was crying. "I'm lost," cried I. It turned out this scene was played almost at his front door. The man and his wife were young and had no furniture in their house to speak of. "Do you want to go to the bathroom?" he asked. I said no. They made me soup and sat me at a little card table. I lied about where I lived and where I went to school. I thought if they couldn't find where I came from, maybe they'd let me stay with them and I could be their child. Upstairs, in a bare kind of attic room, they found me a sheet and a blanket and a pillow without a pillowcase. He helped me off with my wet pants and wet socks. "I thought you told me you didn't have to go to the bathroom," he said. There was a bedstead and mattress and I was so tired that the lightbulb shining over my head made me close my eyes. The next thing I knew there was my Uncle Louis's face looking at me. He had my grandmother's limousine outside with the chauffeur. He bundled me up and took me downstairs—thanked those people, I suppose—and put me in this great big Pierce Arrow with a fur lap robe. "Well, son," Lou said, "tell me what happened." I said, "I did something bad and I'm . . . I'm not going to get any Christmas presents." Lou must have been twenty-eight or twenty-nine. He put his arm around me. "Now, Kevie, don't you worry. You are going to get Christmas!"

After five long years the sorry domestic arrangement on Blaisdell Avenue was dismantled as abruptly, and inexplicably, as it had been cobbled together. In the early fall of 1923, Harold Preston paid a visit to Minneapolis and in the course of a leisurely walk saw fit to question his granddaughter, Mary, and her brother Kevin. By the time that walk was over, Harold Preston had heard all he needed to know. Within days, Kevin and Preston were back in their grandmother McCarthy's sewing room; Sheridan, having been permitted to stay on with the Shrivers, was awaiting their departure for Indiana; Mary alone of the three children was accompanying her grandfather on the train ride back to Seattle.

**CYNTHIA MCCARTHY SANDBERG**   I don't think the Prestons swept into town and saved those poor orphaned children. I think the decision had been made. And I wouldn't be surprised a bit if my father had had a hand in it. I know that Mary had been in a lot of trouble. As a matter of fact, at one point my grandmother apparently considered a place in St. Paul that was for wayward girls. Dad heard about that and the idea was dropped immediately.

**PRESTON MCCARTHY**   For a few months after the removal of Shriver, Kevin and I stayed with our grandparents. Kevin and I would get into Grandpa's study and sneak a little brandy. I remember talking a lot with the chauffeur. The garage was a converted barn and it had a turntable for the three cars and Kevin and I used to get on the turntable and make that thing *go.* When it came down to it, I would have preferred to be with Shriver and Aunt Margaret.

**CYNTHIA McCARTHY SANDBERG**   Pretty soon the boys came to live with Mother and Dad and their family. Mother and Dad, as a matter of fact, sold a house that they had built, and loved, because they didn't think that it would be adequate for more children.

**PRESTON McCARTHY**   If the family thought things had really been bad, I don't believe that they would have let Sheridan go with Shriver and Margaret. I remember Shriver came back for a visit one time and he was staying in a rooming house—a real fleabag. Kevin and I went to stay overnight with him—we were big boys by then—and there was this double bed, and Kevin was on one side of Shriver and I was on the other, and I remember being able to see Kevin over that big mound of Shriver's belly and thinking how strange it was. The way our grandmother behaved toward Shriver—not putting him up in her house or treating him like family—I wonder if that didn't have some effect on what went on with all of us. Mary and I never really talked about this. There was never a time to say, "Mary, I don't have the same ideas as you about some things."

**WILLIAM MAXWELL**   It was a great age for pretending not to know, when everybody knew perfectly well what was happening. Certainly choosing not to, when it was too inconvenient. She and I were both involved in the same catastrophe. I was surrounded by loving aunts and grandmothers and she was stranded with those dreadful, dreadful guardians. If they'd put her off the train in the middle of nowhere, it would have been kinder.

From a perspective made possible by Harold Preston's rescue, Mary McCarthy could see that the suffering and upheaval brought on by her parents' deaths had somehow been the making of her. In the introduction to *Memories of a Catholic Girlhood*, she wrote, "I sometimes wonder what I would have been like now if Uncle Harry and Aunt Zula had not come on, if the journey had never been undertaken. My father, of course, might have died anyway, and my mother would have brought us up. If they had both lived, we would have been a united Catholic family, rather middle class and wholesome. I would probably be a Child of Mary. I can see myself married to an Irish lawyer and playing golf and bridge, making occasional retreats and subscribing to a Catholic Book Club. I suspect I would be rather stout."

By setting out on their misbegotten mission to Seattle, Harry and Zula had snatched her from the comfortable suburban life of a plump Catholic matron she proclaimed to be her natural destiny. Precisely what kind of life she had earned through her suffering she didn't feel it appropriate to go into at length. That she had become a writer, unchastened, unbowed, and full of anger and high spirits, with a taste for paradox and irony, would argue for a miraculous escape from permanent damage in the face of shocking mistreatment. Not only had she survived to tell a grim tale with wit and ingenuity but she had gone on to marry, to make contact with the three brothers who shared that early nightmare existence, and to have a child of her own.

In her twenties, during her second marriage, Mary McCarthy spent four years in analysis and concluded she had little use for its theories, its terminologies, or its insights. By the time she began writing the stories in *Memories of a Catholic Girlhood*, she saw no need for psychoanalytic theory in trying to make sense of her past. In seeking how she might have come to be a writer she was inclined to look to heredity. Most congenial to her were her father's McCarthy ancestors who had been "wreckers," or pirates, luring passing ships too close to the Nova Scotia rocks and taking the salvaged cargoes as plunder. As she grew older, investigations by family members and her first biographer forced her to accept the fact that the McCarthys had come from Newfoundland, not Nova Scotia, and had been law-abiding farmers. But about Freudian theories of childhood trauma she was not about to revise her opinion.

In 1979, in an interview for *People* magazine, when her brother Kevin asked if she felt that in becoming a writer she had been "compensating . . . for some of those wounds," her answer was firm: "That sort of psychiatric stuff doesn't compel my belief. Its tendency is to take any mystery out of our experience, and to imply one has a kind of knowledge one doesn't have." All the same, she couldn't deny that she had been affected by the loss of her parents. "It's natural that we as orphan children—rather looked down on, different from other children—would try to distinguish ourselves favorably," she said. "I know that as a child I had this attention-getting business very strongly, and [*laughing*] alas, I still have."

# Chapter Three

# SEATTLE

Living with her grandparents in a tall shingle house overlooking Seattle's Lake Washington, Mary McCarthy was no longer a poor orphan but a young lady whose wardrobe and social life required careful supervision. Whether she was being driven to mass on Sundays by the Preston chauffeur or sent as a five-day boarder to the Forest Ridge Convent of the Sacred Heart, every effort was made to see to it that she picked up where her old life left off. In any self-respecting fairy tale, her return to Seattle would have been an unequivocally happy ending. The evil guardians had been banished. She was living with two well-intentioned people who loved her.

There were no onerous tasks to perform. No threats of corporal punishment. When she opened her mouth to voice an opinion, no one made fun of her. From the wallpaper on her bedroom walls to the linens on her bed, every item was costly and chosen with an eye to pleasing the senses. Her grandparents employed a cook, a maid, and a chauffeur. She had the run of the public rooms downstairs and of the extensive gardens. Her clothes were no longer threadbare. The dresses her grandmother's seamstress fitted on her were pretty, if not entirely to her taste. Never again would she be forced to eat a turnip or suck the white cord from the scrawny neck of some ancient boiled hen. The ample meals she was served were delicious, if unconscionably rich.

When she was home from school, she was free to join her grandmother for a lunch at the country club or for some shopping downtown. But Augusta Preston, beautifully clothed and taciturn, did not seek out her company. Instead, every morning, without fail, she was on the telephone with her sister Rosie Gottstein, her confidante and best friend. In the afternoon, her face rouged and powdered and her glossy black hair arranged to her satisfaction, Augusta Preston would drive downtown.

There she would make the rounds of her favorite saleswomen at Seattle's better department stores before picking up her husband from work. For shopping she had infinite patience. For her granddaughter she seemed to have none.

Although Augusta Preston set a fine table, she saw no need to invite anyone outside the family to sit down to it. Sunday, the cook's night off, her older son, Frank, and his wife, Isabel, would come over for a cold supper. Sometimes Eva Aronson, her widowed sister, was invited to join them. Twice a year she gave a tea party, where both of her sisters were asked to help pour. That was the extent of her entertaining.

In her first years in Seattle, Mary McCarthy had few friends she was tempted to bring home with her. At Forest Ridge, all the popular girls, with one exception, showed no interest in getting to know her. Only the misfits sought her out. Weekends and holidays she was left to amuse herself as best she was able. From the family chauffeur she learned to make fried potatoes. For the most part, though, the kitchen was off-limits. She made too much of a mess, her grandmother said.

When her other uncle, Harold Junior, brought friends from the University of Washington home, he marched them straight upstairs, to the private sitting room off his bedroom. Her grandparents tended to keep to themselves, shut away for long hours upstairs in *their* suite of rooms. Given free range by her grandfather of the matched sets on the oak shelves of his library and a subscription to any magazine he deemed suitable, she had many spare hours to sample the pleasures of Dickens and Tolstoy and to gaze longingly at the leather-bound volumes of Dumas, every one of which, save for *The Count of Monte Cristo*, was on the Catholic Church's index of forbidden books.

Twice she wrote about her years in Seattle—first in early middle age in the somewhat fictionalized memoirs collected and elaborated upon in *Memories of a Catholic Girlhood*, and then at the very end of her life in her intellectual autobiography, *How I Grew*. For confirmation of her Minneapolis memories, she'd had her brothers Kevin and Preston to fall back on. When she wrote about the years after her rescue, she had no one to turn to for help. Her grandparents were dead and her uncles had spent little time with her. Friends and relations were of limited assistance. Her only obligation was to the facts as she knew them. Her only imperatives were those common to all writers: to give shape to the tale she was telling and to make it as lively as possible.

In *Memories of a Catholic Girlhood*, she brought to her return to Seattle flashes of disappointment but no real anger. Following on the heels of her tribulations in Minneapolis, her West Coast years seemed, if only by contrast, sunny. While her Preston grandparents regarded her as something of a handful, her rebellions were those one might expect from any independent-minded adolescent girl kept on a tight rein. Such punishment as was dealt out to her was prompted by concern and love.

With the publication of *How I Grew* it was clear that the troubles in Seattle had not been as muted as she had once suggested. But even in her earlier book, she could not suppress an undercurrent of sadness. Although she had survived the torments of Minneapolis, it had been at some cost. By the time she was taken back to her Grandmother Preston's house, she was no longer the adorably precocious six-year-old who had boarded the train for Minneapolis with her brothers and beloved parents. On Blaisdell Avenue she had grown not only older but wiser in ways that the adults around her could not imagine and had no wish to explore.

If she had been altered with time, so had the world she had remembered in vivid detail. As small children, visiting their Seattle grandmother for Sunday lunch, she and her brothers had loved to play under the dining room table, pressing the button by their grandmother's foot and setting off a bell summoning the maid from the kitchen. At one point, before their departure for Minneapolis, the button had vanished. Safe at last in her grandmother's house, no longer a visitor but a member of the family, she found the button back where it had originally been but nothing else was quite the way she remembered it.

### FROM "ASK ME NO QUESTIONS" IN *MEMORIES OF A CATHOLIC GIRLHOOD*

The other thing [my brothers and I] liked to do was, after lunch, to roll down her terraces, which dropped in grassy tiers from her tall house right down, I remembered, to Lake Washington[. . . .] The grass was like velvet, and there were flower beds all around and a smell of roses; a sprinkler was going somewhere, and there were raspberries that we ate off bushes. Alas, when I came back, I found I had been dreaming. The grounds did not go down to the lake but only to the next block, below, and there was only one grass bank; the second one was wild, covered with blackberry prickers, and it had always been so, they said. I rolled a few times down the single green slope, but it was not the same; only five or six turns and I reached the bottom; I could not recapture the delicious dizzy sensation I remembered so well. And the raspberries, which I had been looking forward to eating, did not belong to us but to the people next door.

**KEVIN MCCARTHY** I keep wondering, Where did everything go? Where did all the things go? Where is our mother's ring? Mary got the silverware and various other things, and I realize that as far as I know I was never given anything that came down from my mother and father. Mary probably made a point of knowing about such things. Probably because she lived with somebody that paid attention—Grandma and Grandpa Preston.

## From the Afterword to "Names" In *Memories of a Catholic Girlhood*

Meanwhile, my brothers remained in Saint Benedict's Academy; my youngest brother, Sheridan, had joined the other two. They were kept there, with the nuns, during Christmas and Easter vacations; in the summer they were parceled out among relations or sent to camp[. . . .] I was a child of wealth, and they were little pensioners on the trust fund that was left by my grandfather McCarthy when he died[. . . .] When I review my [Preston] grandfather's character, I find this very puzzling[. . . .] Order, exactitude, fairness—these were the traits my grandfather was famous for and the traits I always found in him. How, especially knowing what he did of the treatment we received in Minneapolis, did he fail to concern himself with what happened later to my brothers? I cannot explain this[. . . .] Until I was grown up, the idea never crossed my mind that something might have been done by the Prestons for my brothers as well as for me. The only persons, evidently, to whom this idea occurred were the McCarthys.

## From Harry McCarthy's Letter to Mary McCarthy, March 8, 1952

from 1927 to 1938 my brother as executor mailed to mary mccarthy in care of her grandpapa preston, $11,200.00[. . . .] that my friend is what your mccarthy grandparents did for you and you have the nerve to try and look down your subversive schnabel at them.

The house on Thirty-fifth Avenue retained vestiges of a child's fairy land, but, like Sleeping Beauty's castle smothered in a tangle of vines and creepers, it seemed transfixed by some dark spell. In perpetual mourning for her lost daughter, Augusta Preston was a glamorous though restless presence presiding over its richly decorated rooms. Some days it seemed as if the sadness had always been there. Nothing Harold Preston did could offset the gloom. With everything in readiness to receive visitors, why did Augusta Preston invite no one outside the family? Why was she so reluctant to talk about her daughter? Why did she and her husband take in only one of Tess's children? To broach any of these subjects was to risk immediate rebuff. One thing was incontrovertible: in 1918 at the house on Thirty-fifth Avenue all possibility for real happiness had been cut short. To search for answers within the silent confines of this opulent domain was endlessly enticing. But if there were any answers to be had, they seemed to reside with Augusta Preston. Her granddaughter would be in her thirties before stumbling upon at least one.

## From "Ask Me No Questions"

This body of hers was the cult object around which our household revolved. As a young girl, I knew her shoe size and her hat size and her glove size, her height and weight, the things she ate and didn't eat, her

preferences in underwear and nightgowns and stockings, the contents
of her dressing table in the bathroom, down to the pumice stone which
she used for removing an occasional hair from under her arms; one of
her beauty attributes was that her white, shapely arms and legs were
almost totally hairless, so that she never had to depend on a depilatory
or a razor.

### FROM HARRY MCCARTHY'S LETTER OF MARCH 8, 1952

the first time i saw mrs morganstein [sic] preston, we gave a luncheon at the new washington, in came this excellently groomed and
corseted woman, the figure really exploded youth, then i got a look at
the kisser, it fascinated me, those big lumps at the bottom of the cheeks
were really startling, it puzzled me completely and i could not ask tess
what was the trouble and one day she said you probably are wondering about the disfigurement of my mother's face, in her attempt to look
young she had some quack fill her cheeks with parafine to remove the
wrinkles and the para melted.

### FROM "ASK ME NO QUESTIONS"

"Your grandmother's tragedy"—so I first heard the face lifting alluded
to, if I remember rightly, by one of my friends, who had heard of it
from her mother. And I will not query the appropriateness of the term
according to the Aristotelian canon; in this case, common usage seems
right. It was a tragedy, for her, for her husband and family, who,
deprived of her beauty through an act of folly, came to live in silence,
like a house accursed.

My grandmother's withdrawal from society must have dated, really,
from this period, and not from the time of my mother's death, which
came as the crowning blow. That was why we were so peculiar, so unso-
cial, so, I would add, slightly inhuman; we were all devoting ourselves,
literally, to the cult of a relic, which was my grandmother's body, laved
and freshened every day in the big bathroom, and then paraded before
the public in the downtown stores.

If the whole family was willing to devote itself to "the cult of a relic,"
its newest addition did so with reservations. There was much about her
grandmother that made young Mary McCarthy uneasy. Although she
herself was one quarter Jewish, she had been raised as a Catholic. That
had been her mother's heart's desire. By enrolling her at the Forest Ridge
Convent of the Sacred Heart her Grandfather Preston was doing his best
to honor his dead daughter's wishes as well as to carry on where the
McCarthys had left off. If it was the path of least resistance, it was also
the correct thing to do. At Forest Ridge she was with girls of fine family
and nuns of gentle spirit. But that was not the sort of Catholic upbringing had she been subjected to in Minneapolis. There she had been inoc-
ulated with prejudices and biases that would prove hard to shake off.

Twice in later years her impulse to keep a healthy distance from her grandmother's Jewish origins would result in an amusing orthographic confusion. Despite corrections from both Edmund Wilson and her biographer Carol Gelderman, she would persist in spelling her grandmother's maiden name "Morganstern" rather than "Morgenstern" until she wrote *How I Grew*. Even late in life, when she was writing her autobiography and correcting the misspelling, her frankness on this subject could sound a wrong note. As a grown woman she might deplore any illiberal sentiments that smacked of anti-Semitism, but she came by them naturally thanks to her early years with the McCarthys.

### FROM *HOW I GREW*

At this point I had not given much thought to Jews or what it meant to be one. There were several kinds evidently (corresponding, I now see, to the degree of assimilation): the kind represented by my grandmother and her sisters; another represented by their brother, Uncle Elkan Morgenstern, and his huge-breasted little wife, Aunt Hennie (in that family girls were fat and boys went through some rite at the age of confirmation called the bar mitzvah with presents and a party afterward, where you got sweetbreads and mushrooms in patty shells, cheese puffs, and Crab Louie); and still a stranger kind, in funny clothes, whom I used to look at from the Madrona streetcar, which went by their houses—the poor Orthodox Jews from the Pale[. . . .] And nearer home, our next-door neighbors, Mr. and Mrs. Gerber, afflicted with heavy accents, had two long-nosed sons, Len and Sid, who dressed "old" and kept apart from the neighborhood. Unlike my young uncle Harold and his friends, they were destined for "business," I heard, as though it were a vocation, like the priesthood.

### FROM HARRY McCARTHY'S LETTER OF MARCH 8, 1952

you definitely are a throw back to the maternal side of your breeding which explains your inability to resist this urge particularily as you apparently have a ready market, many jews have told me and it is recognized by all who stop to wonder, why all this race creed and color lament, it is because most of all owe their present position of advancement to the constant cry of persecution

**ISAIAH BERLIN**   One had no idea that Mary was part Jewish. It never showed in any way. The Irish Catholic yes.

**MARY GORDON**   Like her, I was part Jewish. But I grew up in an Irish neighborhood in which I *looked* Jewish. And although I don't think she looked Jewish, it makes for a sense of being an outsider, which I think she had.

On the train back to Seattle she had brought little with her save for her Catholic faith, but the Forest Ridge Convent of the Sacred Heart—with its ties to the Jesuits, its *Mesdames* and *Mère Supérieure* and pretty green, blue, and pink moire ribbons for good conduct, its *congés* and *goûters* and "curtsies dipped in the hall"—was very different from St. Stephen's modest parochial school. Different in ways that were at once seductive and chastening.

### FROM "THE BLACKGUARD" IN *MEMORIES OF A CATHOLIC GIRLHOOD*

[O]ur days were a tumult of emotion. In the first place, we ate, studied, and slept in that atmosphere of intrigue, rivalry, scandal, favoritism, tyranny, and revolt that is common to all girls' boarding schools and that makes "real" life afterward seem a long and improbable armistice, a cessation of the true anguish of activity. But above the tinkling of this girlish operetta, with its clink-clink of changing friendships, its plot of smuggled letters, notes passed from desk to desk, secrets, there sounded in the Sacred Heart convent heavier, more solemn strains, notes of a great religious drama, which was also all passion and caprice, in which salvation was the issue and God's rather sultanlike and elusive favor was besought, scorned, despaired of, connived for, importuned.

She had been liked and admired by her classmates at St. Stephen's School, but here at Forest Ridge her classmates seemed to see something in her they found absurd or ridiculous. They even gave her a nickname, C.Y.E., whose meaning, much to her mortification, she could not make out. At home, her grandfather encouraged her to persist in her studies, but much of what she was taught at school was as alien to him as a foreign language. At the convent, she might savor the drama of daily life and the romantic thread underlying her history lessons. She might relish a novel like *A Tale of Two Cities* that was read aloud by an older nun while she and the other girls sewed a fine seam. But her pleasure was the piquant sensation of coming upon a pretty curiosity. None of it seemed natural to her, and always she seemed to get things wrong.

Not long after she arrived at Forest Ridge, fired by a sermon preached by a particularly rigorous visiting Jesuit missionary, she began to fear for her Protestant grandfather's salvation—because he had been baptized, he had "sufficient knowledge" and would be damned to hell unless he saw the error of his ways.

She soon made the mistake of repeating to her grandfather a rebuke from the most severe and exacting of the nuns, who had said before an entire class, "You're just like Lord Byron, brilliant but unsound." This rebuke so filled her with delight she repeated it her very next weekend home. She was not beaten with a razor strop for getting above herself, but her grandfather was on the telephone at once with the Mother Superior. Monday she had to hear this nun announce to the class that Mary McCarthy "did not resemble Lord Byron in any particular" and was "neither brilliant, loose-living, nor unsound."

In Minneapolis, in an effort to get attention she had gotten into more trouble than she'd bargained for. In Seattle, if her attempts to shine led to misadventure, her punishment was of a different sort. In her second year as a full boarder at the convent, she announced that she had lost her faith. In making this startling bid for attention she believed she had little or nothing to lose.

## FROM "C'EST LE PREMIER PAS QUI COÛTE" IN
## MEMORIES OF A CATHOLIC GIRLHOOD

People are always asking me how I came to lose my faith, imagining a period of deep inward struggle. The truth is the whole momentous project simply jumped at me, ready-made[. . . .] Starting Monday morning, we were going to have a retreat, to be preached by a stirring Jesuit. If I lost my faith on, say, Sunday, I could regain it during the three days of retreat, in time for Wednesday confessions. Thus there would be only four days in which my soul would be in danger if I should happen to die suddenly[. . . .] It was a miracle that someone had not thought of it already, the idea seemed so obvious, like a store waiting to be robbed[. . . .]

I found that I had always been a little suspicious of the life after death. Perhaps it was really true that the dead just rotted and I would never rejoin my parents in Heaven?[. . .] At the last trump, all the bodies of men, from Adam onward, were supposed to leap from their graves and rejoin the souls that had left them; this was why the Church forbade cremation[. . . .] What about cannibals? If God divided the cannibal into the component bodies he had digested, what would become of the cannibal?[. . .] At that time, I did not know that this problem had been treated by Aquinas, and with a child's pertinacity, I mined away at the foundations of the Fortress Rock.

**NICCOLÒ TUCCI**  Mary was a pagan Christian. She didn't have a clear idea of what her faith was, because the Catholic school where she went, as most Catholic schools, was an extremely limited place mentally. The teaching was made mostly in view of keeping a flock of imbeciles within the church. From the Jewish grandmother I saw in Mary the vitality and also the mania for reasoning—that was very rabbinical.

**MAUREEN HOWARD**  Her Catholic girlhood, and the convent school Mary McCarthy was sent to, were out of the ordinary. She understood that about her life at home, but not about the school. Religion classes as I experienced them with the Sisters of Mercy, a less intellectual order than the Mesdames de Sacre Coeur, did not allow for theological discussion. In matters of faith, the sisters did not want girls to question or even to know too much. It is mind-boggling to me that the theological arguments in *Memories* were conducted at a prep school with a Jesuit chaplain. I think: 1) that she was an extraordinary kid; 2) that she must have thought through her arguments as a mature writer. Indeed, as most gifted autobiographers do, she re-envisions the scene: "My own questions are a mixture of memory and conjecture." There was an inspired amount of invention in the justification of her loss of faith.

**FATHER PATRICK SAMWAY**   I think she gives leaving the church greater substance than in fact it may have had. For a woman of twenty it might have been something meaningful. We're talking about a twelve-year-old girl who is living in an environment where a nun sits behind a curtain when she takes a bath. A lot of the appeal of the church for her seems to have been the drama. She talks about proofs and arguments. For the five proofs of God's existence she tells us in the afterword that she had to turn to the Catholic Encyclopedia. That's the giveaway. Belief for her seems to have been not a commitment to a loving God, but a little black box, or a set of keys, which one day she lost.

**EILEEN SIMPSON**    I remember that while we were in Paris a story came out in *The New Yorker* about a girl who was in a Convent of the Sacred Heart. The story was somehow critical, and Mary said, "The trouble with her is that she didn't stay long enough." She was very loyal—not to Catholicism but to that period of her education.

**MARY GORDON**   She was formed by a kind of romantic Catholicism, and so she had that kind of extremely high-colored way of looking at the world which comes from that brand of Catholicism. It was something that I understood. There was never anything that she didn't look at morally. It seemed to me that she combined purity of style with a rigorous moral honesty. A relentless moral perspective on the world.

### FROM HARRY McCARTHY'S LETTER OF MARCH 8, 1952

> . . . your mother told me her father was an agnostic so there is no trouble figuring where you received the hatred training for the catholic church, that is his doubtful privelege, there will always be agnostics i presume just like there will always be guys who wear white sox or bow ties.

### FROM THE AFTERWORD TO "C'EST LE PREMIER PAS QUI COÛTE"

> Contrary to what the McCarthys believed, my grandfather Preston made it his duty to see that I kept up my religion. It was a pact between us that I would continue to go to church on Sundays until I was a little older. But he never questioned my sincerity. When I told him I had lost my faith (and by then it was true), he did not treat it as a dodge for getting out of Mass.

**NICHOLAS KING**   She declares herself an atheist but I don't know. She had a lot of interest in the Church. Someone who's interested in history cannot help but be. At the end of her life she was doing this book about Gothic cathedrals. And she knew the Church very well. She knew Catholic doctrine.

### FROM "A BELIEVING ATHEIST," PUBLISHED POSTHUMOUSLY IN *VASSAR VIEWS,* NOVEMBER 1992

> In fact, had it not been for the accident of being sent by my grandparents to an Episcopal boarding-school, I might still be as thorough an atheist as the convent had made me. Instead, through the hymns, through the book of Common Prayer, through our mild Sacred Study course, I regained bit by bit the underlying Christian doctrine which I accept today as being part of me, whether I like it or not.

I do not believe in God or an afterlife or in the divinity of Christ. But I am aware that Jesus did. He thought he was God's messenger to mankind. I feel that was a tragic mistake, but tragedy is no joke. He found virtue in suffering and taught the *Via Crucis*. I agree with that, though I certainly do not aim to illustrate it by imitation. He had an amusing mind, much given to paradox as in the case of Magdalen, whom none of my [McCarthy] relatives would have had in the house.

Once she announced she had lost her faith, there was no going back. Her Grandfather Preston waited a decent interval and then removed her from the convent, sending her first to Garfield High School, a coeducational Seattle public school, where she came close to failing all her courses, and then to the Annie Wright Seminary, an Episcopal boarding school for girls in Tacoma, where she not only found some of the comfort she had once derived from the services at St. Stephen's but people and ideas that excited her imagination.

At Garfield High School she fell for the school's football captain and developed a series of mostly unrequited crushes which led her grandparents to believe she had become "boy crazy." But she also discovered the Seattle Public Library and found a best friend in "Ted" Rosenberg, a girl who dressed like a boy and whose passion for *Green Mansions* was not unlike her own passion for Garfield athletes. Most important, she met her first intellectuals.

In *How I Grew* her recollections of Garfield were fond but clearsighted. In *Memories of a Catholic Girlhood* her portrayal of the Annie Wright Seminary was so gentle as to be almost loving, as was her portrait of the principal, who every so often took an errant girl onto her slippery lap for a good cry before welcoming her back to the fold. At Annie Wright she first glimpsed the life she wanted for herself. Soon after her arrival she came under the spell of a good-looking young woman who taught sophomore English, a recent Vassar graduate, who encouraged her to try her hand at writing short stories—going so far as to send one story off for criticism to an editor in New York.

Owing to the allure of this young and good-looking teacher, she decided not to follow her Uncle Harold to the University of Washington but to go east to Vassar. For admission to the college she needed three years of Latin. Starting that summer, with her grandfather's encouragement, she set about cramming three years of Latin into two with the help of a plain, exacting Scotswoman from Canada (Ethel Mackay in real life and "Miss Gowrie" in this fictionalized memoir). In the process she learned to love Caesar, but only after a brief infatuation with Catiline, a sardonic rebel very much to her taste, whose part she took senior year in a Latin Club play.

Unfortunately, the attractive girls at Annie Wright were all older. Still, there were small pleasures to be had—sundaes in town, weekly horse-back rides at a nearby stable kept by a British major. One time she ran away with a fellow boarder with no real destination in mind and was saved from expulsion only by her high grades. Annie Wright couldn't afford to lose a girl going on to an eastern college.

Her misadventures seemed comic rather than sordid. One summer she had a chance to take the measure of two of her schoolmates when she went home with two sisters from Montana. Her grandfather would not permit her to go out with boys, but for three weeks, as the sisters' guest, she was free to join in their totally unfettered social life, even to date a married man and drink bootleg gin until she passed out. Junior year, sitting on the ledge of an open window, trying to keep from being discovered smoking in her room, she nearly toppled two stories to the ground.

Senior year, from sheer contrariness she decided to turn her severe and unbending Latin teacher into a class pet by strenuously promoting her as a chaperone for outings at which she was sure to be a wet blanket. Enjoying this newfound ability to sway public opinion, she then began lobbying to have a plain but easygoing girl chosen as May Queen. By the end of her last spring at school, she was sneaking off to meet a handsome local boy who had lost his leg in some feckless adventure. Then, almost on the eve of commencement, she was caught climbing in the window from a late date and nearly didn't graduate. Only after a last-minute concession and a teary interlude on the principal's lap was she permitted to give her commencement address as class valedictorian.

In *How I Grew*, written three decades later, her adolescent rebellions took on a darker cast. In densely packed chapters in which she eschewed the omissions and transpositions and sheer artifice that had made the raw facts of her personal history so satisfying to earlier readers, she revealed that the company she kept in Seattle had been seamy, even by today's fairly relaxed standards. Although she went on to make friends at Annie Wright Seminary, her best friend had continued to be Ted Rosenberg, who wore her hair short, dressed like a boy, and was an avid reader of any poetry or prose that reflected sensibility rather than sense.

Teya Rosenberg, whose given name was Ethel and whose father was a tailor, introduced her to fiction and poetry that would never find its way to the shelves of her grandfather's library—books by Walter Pater, Aubrey Beardsley, and Oscar Wilde. With Ted's large family she spent as much time as she could manage. It was Ted Rosenberg who introduced her to a louche artistic set, which led to her capturing the attention of a blond painter possessed of a mustache and a certain talent and a white-haired Russian "baron" who sold greeting cards, both of whom made no secret of what they wanted from her.

As it turned out, her early crushes and romances hadn't been nearly as innocent as she had once suggested. Nor had her setbacks been quite so painless. Owing to her resentment at not being permitted to go out with boys until she turned eighteen, her stay with her Seattle grandparents had not been nearly as placid as she had made out. Harold Preston had been in many ways exemplary—he had been the "just, laconic, severe, magnanimous, detached" figure she described earlier—but, while she might admire his moral integrity, he did not approve of many of the things she did. Augusta Preston, frankly, did not approve of *her*. And this feeling, from the start, was mutual. *She* might be happy to take refuge with the Rosenbergs, but the Jewishness of her grandmother and her grandmother's relatives—Aunt Rosie and Uncle Moses Gottstein, in particular—upset her more than she'd cared to admit in the earlier book.

Furthermore, the Annie Wright Seminary was decidedly second-rate. The teachers were better than adequate, but the same could not be said for most of the students. Despite every effort, the principal, Miss Adelaide Preston (no relation to her grandfather, but said to share a common ancestor), was constantly losing all her best students to boarding schools in the east. If it hadn't been for her earlier brush with real intellectuals at Garfield High School, Mary might have fared no better than the majority of her classmates, who passed through the seminary as one might a finishing school. Although she did make it to the rostrum to deliver the class valedictory, up until the last minute she was suffering from the aftereffects of a late-night "drinking picnic" and vomiting in the sink.

Of course both portraits of Annie Wright were highly colored and highly subjective. So it is not surprising that some of her classmates remembered her time inside the classroom and outside of it rather differently. By all accounts, when it came to her studies, she managed to steer a true course with little effort. But it would seem that owing to her need to astonish and impress, she was not always quite so adept.

**BETH GRIFFITH**   I was first aware of Mary when we were in Miss Dorothy Atkinson's English class. Mary had read some very strange novels that I had only read about. They were difficult and written with a good deal of symbolism. They were almost in a foreign language. We were very much impressed with the fact that she could talk about them with Miss Atkinson. But we didn't know what in the world they were talking about. The class would turn into a conversation between them. Looking back, I wonder why the teachers let a lot of things happen. They let Mary take the bit in her mouth and run with it. They let her say things in class that were indiscreet and really not very nice. And the bullying that she did! Mary would make fun of people in class who couldn't answer a question. In French class if somebody got up and was fumbling for the answer, she would say, "Teacher, she doesn't have the answer. Ask me, ask me." First of all, her hand spoke for her. She would have that hand really beating the air, trying to get the teacher to let her answer the question. She did that only once to me and I turned around and I had it out with her right in class.

**BARBARA DOLE LAWRENCE**   She didn't have a life that was quite as simple as most of ours. I think we were aware of that. We knew that she was an orphan. We knew all that. She was exceptional in her ambitions. She'd had less of what we'd had. She was hungrier. I never felt sorry for her. I thought she could handle anything.

**BETH GRIFFITH**   When she wasn't being nasty, she could be pretty, but beautiful never. I doubt completely that she had boyfriends. I think that is a fiction. I'll tell you why. When she came into our class sophomore year, there was a boyfriend I had who had a funny car—a classic car—and he was dropping me off at school or picking me up and she saw me with him. I couldn't stand him. I went into the study hall and Mary took me aside and questioned me. You can't believe the questions she asked me about this fellow. I think his mother had introduced him to my aunt in Seattle and she'd introduced us. He was older than we were. I had the most animated quiz from Mary and what came out of the quiz was that she was very, very young and very inexperienced in these realms. I think she'd had a very protected environment. Her questions were gauche. It was like a much younger girl who'd just heard about sex. She would have liked to ask me all about his petting technique. I don't think she understood dates. Not only that, she'd read so much that she wanted to go right from A to Z. She wanted things to develop fast. She'd read about being a mistress and having a lover and I think she wanted to jump into this area rather quickly.

### FROM *HOW I GREW*

In my first year at Annie Wright Seminary, I lost my virginity. I am not sure whether this was an "educational experience" or not. The act did not lead to anything and was not repeated for two years. But at least it dampened my curiosity about sex and so left my mind free to think about other things. Since in that way it was formative, I had better tell about it.

It took place in a Marmon roadster, in the front seat—roadsters had no back seats, though there was often a rumble, outside, in the rear, where the trunk is now. That day the car was parked off in a lonely Seattle boulevard. It was a dark winter afternoon, probably during Thanksgiving vacation, since I was home from school. In my memory it feels like a Saturday. "His" name was Forrest Crosby; he was a Phi Delt, I understood, and twenty-three years old, a year or so out of the University[. . . .]

I might say that what happened was my grandparents' own fault; *they* had forced me into clandestinity[. . . .] The tight rein they tried to keep on me while my contemporaries were allowed to run loose was a mistake and kept me from having any easy or natural relation with boys; I never even learned to dance with one of them properly. Moreover, the prohibitions I labored under led me into all kinds of deceptions. I lied to my grandparents about where I had been, with whom, how long, and so on. I lied to my partner in deception, in this case Forrest

Crosby, because I was sure he would despise me if I avowed my inexperience, and I lied to other girls to keep them from knowing of my trammels, in short from discovering all of the above. The lying became a necessity, imposed by my grandparents in the first instance, but then the habit was formed, as the wish to appear other than I was permitted to be dominated every social relation except those with my teachers.

**BARBARA DOLE LAWRENCE** We never took her too seriously when she told us about her adventures. We thought she was kidding.

**JEAN EAGLESON** Mary was pretty shocking. I'd pretend not to be shocked, but I was shocked out of my skin.

One thing is certain: in her first year at Annie Wright she showed a great interest in writing poems and stories. Much of her writing was done in study hall and consisted of recopying romantic poems of other poets' making. Her stories, works of her own creation, written out by hand and copied in a fine script, were not of the sort one might expect from a gently reared schoolgirl. One that she showed her English teacher sophomore year had a Jewish lothario called Mose Nordstrom who preyed on faded beauties. In all the stories she seemed to be punishing her heroines for their self-delusions and inadequacies.

## FROM AN UNTITLED STORY WRITTEN SOPHOMORE YEAR
Then, at exactly the psychological moment when Gracia was hanging coyly over the counter, opening her pale blue eyes with a baby stare, enter the Prince! He was a small, stout Jewish gentleman with a heavy jaw, and a flabby, dissipated face, with great pouches under hard bright eyes. He was really, however, an innocent looking little man to the unprejudiced observer, though several of the "old-timers" around the store smiled suggestively at each other on seeing him approach one of the counters, and ask for something unknown, all the while appraising the salesgirls one by one[. . . .]

Evidently Mr. Nordstrom was not one of those who seek to drink at the Fountain of Youth, for he instantly crossed to the cosmetics counter. Though enormously rich, he was not quite good-looking enough to succeed in seducing sixteen year-olds, much as they might crave to be initiated into an unknown world. Oh, yes, Mose Nordstrom was wise.

Summer vacation of junior year, through Ted Rosenberg's offices, she made a debut of sorts in Seattle society—albeit not the sort of society she had courted at Annie Wright. She was taken by Ted to the home of Czerna Wilson, a handsome lesbian married to the owner of a local bookstore, who presided over a literary and artistic salon. "I was attracted to Czerna aesthetically, as a superb foreign object, as a possibility of what one might become, with resolution," she would later write. She was attracted to

Czerna Wilson's long red braid, her beautifully tailored jackets, her air of sophistication, and, above all, her insouciance.

### From *How I Grew*

She made no advances to me, and I never went there without Ted till one day toward the end of the summer when she told me that she would like me to come to a party, by myself, as Ted could not make it[. . . .] I had just let my hair grow into a knot at the nape of my neck, and my prayers were being answered—I was finally getting pretty. Not as beautiful as my mother, "the most beautiful woman in Seattle," but not bad, let us say winsome, because of my Irish blood[. . . .] In Czerna's crowded living-room that night I sensed that I was "launched." To a certain extent this proved to be true: it was my coming-out party—the only one I would have.

She was launched, but she was not truly prepared for the sort of attentions a pretty girl is likely to receive in this particular society. Soon she was entangled in an affair with a local painter named Kenneth Callahan, which proved to be no less painful to contemplate than her defloration in the Marmon roadster.

### From *How I Grew*

On the whole, I was relieved late that fall when Kenneth, having sold almost no paintings, decided to go to sea to earn a living[. . . .] He bored me; he was weak; he lisped slightly, and his studio was squalid. The best thing about it was the companionway-like approach. And some of the things he did in bed made me cringe with shame to think of afterward.

It was these sexual practices of his that taught me while still a senior at Annie Wright how to deal with shame and guilt. When you have committed an action that you cannot bear to think about, that causes you to writhe in retrospect, do not seek to evade the memory: *make* yourself relive it, confront it repeatedly over and over, till finally, you will discover, through sheer repetition that it loses its power to pain you. It works, I guarantee you, this sure-fire guilt-eradicator, like a homeopathic medicine—like in small doses applied to like. It works, but I am not sure that it is a good thing.

Senior year at Annie Wright she was president of the French club and secretary of the Latin Club. She played Catiline in her Latin teacher's play and the heroine in Goldoni's *The Fan*. She was taking riding lessons on Saturdays. It was her hope to one day become an actress. But she was preparing for the college boards, with the hope of getting into Vassar. On her own she was reading poems by Ezra Pound, Edwin Arlington Robinson, and Edna St. Vincent Millay, perhaps Vassar's most celebrated graduate.

**FROM A LETTER SENT BY MISS ETHEL MACKAY [MISS GOWRIE],**
**INSTRUCTOR IN LATIN AT THE ANNIE WRIGHT SEMINARY,**
**TO THE ADMISSIONS DEPARTMENT OF VASSAR COLLEGE**

Mary McCarthy is a student of quite unusual intelligence. She has studied Latin with me for two years, and in my opinion has a remarkable aptitude for languages. I have always found her industrious and pleasant to deal with in the class-room.

Mary also has considerable dramatic ability, and played the leading part in the senior play this year[. . . .] She has a strong will and plenty of ambition, and a magnetic and charming personality.

**FROM *HOW I GREW***

In her worst nightmares that dear Latinist could not have pictured my frequentations [ . . .] the mountain of lies. Nonetheless, I wonder. Invincible in her ignorance, she may have known me better than I knew myself. That is, *I* was deceived by the will-less passive self I seemed to be living with, and Miss Mackay was not.


When she sat for her college boards in June 1929, Mary did not do as well in Latin as she and "Miss Gowrie" had anticipated, but she did well enough to be accepted as a freshman at Vassar. To get some good out of her summer she enrolled in classes in "eurhythmics" and phonetics at Seattle's Cornish School, which was determinedly avant-garde but not so firmly entrenched in the vanguard as to be alarming to the grandparents who were meeting her tuition. At the end-of-summer recital, with some reluctance she assumed the role of a drowned pirate, just another member of a wretched crew of brigands weaving before the footlights as if making their way across the ocean's floor.

This was not the sort of drama she had aspired to. Already she had her eye on a real actor she had spotted the summer before playing the part of a Red Cross Knight in a pageant commemorating the signing of the Magna Carta. Lean and tall, with a broken nose and receding hairline, he looked nothing like the men and boys she knew. His name, she had discovered, was Harold Johnsrud. She finally had a chance to meet him at a lunch at Ted Rosenberg's—a lunch she attended wearing a dress she had sewn herself, which had an unfortunate tendency to hike up over her knees and which may have had something to do with why he laughingly referred to her as "the child Mary."

By the end of summer, she was on her way to Vassar, her trunks packed with a wardrobe of more becoming and better tailored outfits. Traveling on her own by train, she stopped off in Minneapolis to visit her McCarthy grandmother. J. H. McCarthy was dead and her brothers were away at school, but she had the pleasure of turning down Lizzie McCarthy's gift of an electric donut maker and of hearing a priest, enlisted to lecture her on the sinfulness of Vassar, state that she would be receiving a first-rate education.

Unfortunately, her triumphant journey east came to a disappointing end when, on her first visit to New York, she was forced to share rooms with two chaperones, her grandmother Preston and her Uncle Frank's wife, Isabel, at the irreproachable but irredeemably stodgy Roosevelt Hotel. Isabel and Augusta Preston wanted only to see the hit Broadway shows, shop at the better stores, and dine at respectable restaurants. At the Metropolitan Museum of Art, she finally had enough. Refusing to join the two women for a tour of the American Wing, she ran off in tears, only to fall headlong down the flight of marble stairs leading to the museum's entrance.

Miraculously she survived the fall intact. Barely bruised but battered in spirit, she was walking back to her hotel when she ran into Harold Johnsrud on the street, one block from the Roosevelt. Thanks to Harold Johnsrud, she got to go to a gallery showing modern art and to a matinee in Greenwich Village of a play by Mike Gold, who wrote a column for *The Daily Worker*. If the two Preston women didn't quite approve of this twenty-six-year-old actor who sought out the company of their seventeen-year-old charge, they couldn't quite bring themselves to forbid her to see him. Particularly when the two principals were so soon to be separated.

By the time she boarded her train for Poughkeepsie she had Harold Johnsrud's phone number and address safely in hand. It didn't matter that she had Augusta and Isabel Preston trailing along behind her. Already she had it in mind to lose her virginity still again. Nothing was going to stop this bright and desperately ambitious young adventurer, who had turned her back on Seattle and set her sights on Vassar, where she was not about to settle for second best and where she was going to distinguish herself at all costs.

# Chapter Four

# VASSAR

"Like Athena, goddess of wisdom, Vassar College sprang in full battle dress from the head of a man," wrote Mary McCarthy in her controversial essay "The Vassar Girl," published more than two decades after her much anticipated arrival. "Incorporated at Poughkeepsie, New York, in 1861, the year of Lincoln's inauguration and the emancipation of the serfs in Russia, it was the first woman's college to be conceived as an idea, a manifesto, a declaration of rights, and a proclamation of equality."

After introducing her alma mater with a flourish sure to delight the hearts of the most self-satisfied fellow graduates, she went on to note that the man to whom the college owed its existence was "not a gentleman of parts or a social reformer, but a self-educated Poughkeepsie brewer, the keeper of an ale and oyster house." However, she did not leave it at that. She pointed out that, although Matthew Vassar might be an unlikely progenitor for this noble institution, he was a fitting one. "His maiden speech to the Board of Trustees at the initial meeting in February, 1861, had the resonance of a sovereign pronouncement[. . . .] The authoritative tone is characteristic; it is as though, speaking through the mouth of the elderly, didactic brewer, were the first, fresh Vassar girl."

Mary McCarthy entered Vassar in September 1929, one of 289 well-prepared, gently reared freshmen. She arrived at the tail end of the Jazz Age, but by the time she graduated there was a worldwide depression. Her second month at Vassar the New York stock market crashed. Inevitably, this economic crisis had a direct effect on her and on a good many, if not all, of her classmates. Whether the effect was lasting or beneficial was open to question. As to the quality of her Vassar education she never entertained a moment's doubt. Not only was Vassar the best of the Ivy League women's colleges but it was "the very best college in America."

What made the Vassar of 1929 unique, she believed, was neither the caliber of its students nor the beauty of its campus but the special nature of the classroom experience. Starting with the very first session of her class in English composition, an entering freshman was taught to mistrust the orthodoxies of her parents, to question cherished assumptions, and to learn to think on her own.

For most of the Vassar faculty—above all, for Anna Kitchel, her teacher for freshman composition, and Helen Sandison, who taught Shakespeare and presided over her seminar in the English Renaissance—McCarthy had only kind words. However, when it came to her Vassar classmates, she was hardly unstinting in her praise. Frani Blough was always held dear. Martha McGahan had a special place in her heart. Elizabeth Bishop, from the class of '34, was viewed with respect. Julia Denison was remembered with affection. But for the debutantes, the girls who had arrived at Vassar fresh from boarding school, with their pearls and Brooks Brothers sweaters, the "blue-eyed Republican girls," as she called them, she appeared, as the years passed, to have diminishing forbearance.

Three times—first in "The Vassar Girl," published in *Holiday* in 1951, then in *The Group* in 1963, and finally in *How I Grew*—she tried to convey her feelings about her old college. In her first effort, written when she was living quietly with her son, Reuel, and her third husband, Bowden Broadwater, in a farmhouse near Newport, Rhode Island, she credited the school with a history marked by a blend of the heroic and the commonplace, and then went on to suggest the special allure possessed by the campus of her day: "Bucolically set in rolling orchard country just outside the town of Poughkeepsie, with the prospect of long walks and rides along curving back roads and cold red apples to bite; framed by two mirror-like lakes, by a lively off-campus street full of dress shops, antique stores, inns, which were brimming now with parents, brothers, and fiancés, Vassar, still warm and summery, gave the impression of a cornucopia overflowing with promises [. . .] the vaulted library; the catalogue already marked and starred for courses like Psychology and Philosophy [. . .] the trolley tracks running past the spiked fence downtown to further shopping, adventure, the railroad station, New York [. . .] all this seemed to foretell four years of a Renaissance lavishness, in an academy that was a Forest of Arden and a Fifth Avenue department store combined."

If there was a touch of mockery to this portrait of a sybaritic Dutchess County idyll, that mockery was gentle. At the same time, she portrayed herself as being in no way appreciably different from the other carefully nurtured and splendidly outfitted members of the class of '33. At most, she might have been more wildly romantic: "I myself was an ardent literary little girl in an Episcopal boarding school on the West Coast, getting up at four in the morning to write a seventeen-page medieval romance before breakfast, smoking on the fire-escape and thinking of suicide, meeting a crippled boy in the woods by the cindery athletic field, composing a novelette in study hall about the life of a middle-aged prostitute."

In her reflections on her time at Vassar there was no hint of the neglect or privations of her orphaned childhood. Not a word about her precocious sex life. Only the barest intimation that her taste had never run to Yale boys. And no mention of Harold Johnsrud, the older actor who had teased her in Seattle and then picked her up on a New York City street. Without betraying her true feelings about these long-standing Vassar traditions, she touched briefly on the Daisy Chain of graduation attendants, with its white-clad sophomore beauties, and on the Saturday night "J" dances, where a girl could go stag and, after a brief introduction, cut in on any of the hapless males dragged there by their less than enchanted Vassar dates. Recalling the "bareheaded Yale boys" lounging outside Taylor Gate, with their roadsters and whiskey flasks, the department store charge accounts and trunk shows, the artichokes and mushrooms under glass shared with classmates in rustic inns and long vanished roadhouses, she suggested a life of ease and camaraderie and careless flirtation.

Writing in her late thirties, Mary McCarthy was painting a picture that might have satisfied the longings of the most romantic boarding school girl. She had come to this academic paradise overlooking an industrial river town in the fall of 1929 harboring dreams of becoming a famous actress or writer, of being accepted and embraced by her classmates, of being recognized as special. While she was recognized at once as an outstanding student, her other dreams were not realized quite so readily. As an actress, only once did she get beyond a supporting role in a Hall play, when her friend Frani Blough cast her as the Virgin in a nativity pageant. With the majority of her classmates she was not an immediate favorite. On the well-stocked shelves of Thompson Library she came closest to finding what she was seeking, working long hours for Miss Kitchel and Miss Sandison, teachers who had fired her imagination. Proud to call herself an "aesthete," and a "royalist," she professed to have no interest in politics, and when she chose a major it was English, with a specialty in the English Renaissance. It was as a writer that she made her mark at Vassar, and when early on Miss Kitchel suggested she had no talent for fiction, she was disappointed but undaunted and concentrated on writing criticism.

She had come east to Vassar knowing no other girls. By train, a round-trip journey to Seattle consumed a full week of school vacation, and, unless she was going home for the summer, it was hardly worth the trouble. Holidays she was left to her own devices or the mercy of her classmates. From the beginning, New York offered a refuge that was at once seductive and convenient. Any weekend Harold Johnsrud felt inclined to see her, she was quick to grab a train down to the city. For at least one Christmas holiday, she resorted to his Greenwich Village apartment, fully aware that if he had a job out of town, she would be left behind on her own.

Her first two years at Vassar, living alone in Davison, a redbrick dormitory on the quadrangle, she learned to detest the voices of the New York debutantes on her floor while spending time with Virginia Johnston and Elinor Coleman. Under the Vassar system of "grouping," students sorted themselves into small permanent communities within the various dormitories. Seniors all lived in Main.

In "The Vassar Girl," Mary McCarthy told of a visit she had paid to her old college in the fall of 1949, when she had found little to please her. After doing ample justice to the school's place in both the public's imagination and her own, she wrote, "To the returning alumna whose college years were both more snobbish and sectarian, on the one hand, and more Bohemian, rebellious, and lyrical, on the other, the administrative cast, so to speak, of the present Vassar mold is both disquieting and praiseworthy. A uniform, pliant, docile undergraduate seems to be resulting from the stress on the group and the community that prevails at Vassar today. The outcast and the rebel are almost equally known [sic]."

In locating the source of the problem she did not pull her punches. But while she deplored the sorry state of her alma mater, she was almost gentle in her portrayal of her own undergraduate experience. No doubt it served the purposes of her argument to suffuse the past with a pretty roseate glow. However, her own years at Vassar had been by no means untroubled. Vassar society had been highly stratified. If a rebel was tolerated, she was rarely embraced. Inevitably there had been friction. In later years, when she turned again to her time as an undergraduate, first in her best-selling novel *The Group* and then in a personal memoir, she would subject the college and her classmates to a scrutiny far less benign.

### FROM *THE GROUP*

"To the Class of Thirty-three," he toasted. The others drank to the Vassar girls. "Bottoms up!" cried the man's wife. From the silent best man came a cackling laugh. Tiddly as she was, Priss could tell that she and her friends, through no fault of their own, had awakened economic antagonism. Vassar girls, in general, were not liked by the world at large; they had come to be a sort of symbol of superiority.

In the class of '33 you could find daughters of diplomats and the niece of the vice president, along with a Wurlitzer, a Dole pineapple, and a Welch's grape juice. To hold your own in such a class was no easy matter. A new girl was likely to arrive having met at least one of her classmates—either at prep school or summer camp or vacationing on the coast of New England. More than likely, she was about to be presented to society at a dinner dance or small tea. If she was fond of riding, she might keep her favorite horse stabled close by. For Lucille Fletcher, a scholarship student from Brooklyn, the difficulty of making a place for herself was manifestly apparent. For an orphan from a second-rank boarding school in Tacoma, with no family close by and only the most tenuous of ties to an older actor in New York, the immediate prospect was no less bleak.

### FROM *HOW I GREW*

Having seen me installed in my room, which shocked my grandmother by its lack of amenities, she and Isabel left, with assurances from the house warden that a lamp, a rug, bedcover, and so on, could be bought downtown at a store called Luckey Platt. I was alone (no roommate!) in Davison Hall[. . . .] Soon I would have to eat in the dining-hall with perfect strangers. The outlook was as friendless as New York had been until I saw Johnsrud coming briskly toward me on East 46th Street. It would be better when classes started, but on that first night I did not know a soul at Vassar[. . . .] Johnsrud had given me his address: 50 Garden Place Brooklyn. Not to seem too eager, maybe I let a week elapse before writing.

**HELEN DOWNES LIGHT**  At the reception desk you went in and gave your name. We felt very protected. The guards were on at the Main Gate and you gave your credentials if you wanted in or out. They stopped every car and asked where it was going. And then we had a night watchman who prowled the corridors. There was a family feeling to the dormitory. We had waitresses and we had maids.

### FROM "CAN IT BE FIFTY YEARS?," DELIVERED BY
### LUCILLE FLETCHER WALLOP AT THE FIFTIETH REUNION
### OF THE CLASS OF '33, JUNE 1983

My group lived in "Main" where I roomed with Janet McLeod and [Beth] Osborne in a large drafty suite consisting of a living-room and two small bedrooms. The living-room had a fireplace and two enormous windows, and the bedrooms had windows fronting on a corridor. These accommodations were typical of "Main" at that time, relics of Matthew Vassar's day, when he had built his female college in the style of Versailles.

Like Versailles, there were no closets, only huge black armoires fastened to the wall. Matthew Vassar didn't believe in closets. He felt that all a female needed for her garments were two hooks, one for her nightgown and one for her Sunday dress.

**FRANI BLOUGH MUSER**  It wasn't like boarding school. It was like being in a hotel. After dinner, coffee was served in the drawing room of the house. You would go in and somebody would be pouring coffee, and you would sit around and chat before you went to your room to study or to the smoking room to play bridge.

In time, most members of the class of '33 came to recognize the serious nature of October's stock market crash.

### FROM "MEMOIRS OF LITERATAE AND SOCIALISTS 1929–33," BY EUNICE CLARK JESSUP

Those were the years when the Bonus Marchers, an army of 20,000 ragged people, marched on Washington and camped for three months demanding their World War I bonuses, only to be dispersed by the U.S. Army with tear gas; when the farmers of Iowa were pouring tanks of milk over rural roads, when stockbrokers were jumping out of windows; when there were calls for martial law; when Hitler came to power and the Japanese were chewing up Manchuria; when breadlines wove all through American cities; when there was no Social Security, no unemployment, no Federal Deposit Insurance.

**FRANI BLOUGH MUSER**   My friends and I didn't march, but we spent a lot of time talking about how to reorganize the economic structure of the country. There were all kinds of proposals to overturn the structure that had brought about the bank failures and all that. We were dominated by the classical style but we lived in the real world. We were all socialists. Norman Thomas was a parent at the school. He was very popular, and he was running for president. Of course he was the one we always voted for.

**ELINOR COLEMAN GUGGENHEIMER**   In October 1929 there were those incredible headlines which said that some billions had been lost in the market, but the figures seemed so outlandish to us, none of us understood what it was that was really happening. Some girls were called back because their parents had lost money. So it was a very strange period. On the other hand, I think what it did was shake us up, because we knew that everything wasn't always going to be the same.

That November, however, events on Wall Street were hardly foremost on everyone's mind.

### FROM MARY MCCARTHY'S LETTER TO TED ROSENBERG, NOVEMBER 1, 1929

Miss Mary McCarthy announces that she is about to flunk out of Vassar College on February 1st 1930. On being questioned Miss McCarthy stated that there was no reason for her action[. . . .]

About college—it's all right, better than the [University of Washington] anyway. But there is too much smart talk, too many labels for things, too much pseudo-cleverness. I suppose I'll get that way, too, though I'm doing my best to avoid it[. . . .]

There is one girl here I like very much—Virginia Johnston of Waterbury, Connecticut. She has nice, quiet blue-grey eyes, and a wonderful sense of humor. I'm going home with her for a week-end whence we are going to Yale[. . . .]

My English teacher is a joy. She's homely, raw-boned and middle-aged. She ought to be named Kate. But she's real, Ted, actually; she's sincere, and she has a good hearty sense of humor. I enjoy the class tremendously: it usually turns into long conversations between her and me.

Not only was Anna Kitchel a joy but she was quick to take an interest in this outspoken freshman from the west. Soon Miss Kitchel was her advisor as well as her teacher for English 105. On her "comment card" for the first term of English 105, Miss Kitchel wrote, "Delightfully eager and keen, with logic and imagination both working. Has read widely and thoroughly and contributes *greatly* to class discussion." There were a handful of required subjects for which she had little aptitude or patience, but when it came to writing and literature she had no equal. At Vassar the competition was keener than it had been at Annie Wright, but she saw no reason to modify her behavior in class. Here again, her protracted conversations with sympathetic teachers and her lack of tolerance for less gifted students did not escape the notice of the other girls in the class.

**FRANI BLOUGH MUSER**   The way I met Mary was we were neighbors in chemistry lab our first year. We were doing these childish experiments where there were supposed to be three kinds of odors—sweet, sour, sharp or salt or something like that. Finding the precise word for each odor became a great challenge. Mary and I worked away trying to find the *mot juste*. She was no better at chemistry than I was, but English was different. There she would speak right up.

**ELINOR COLEMAN GUGGENHEIMER**   One of the most discouraging things in the world was being in an English class freshman year with Mary McCarthy. Before Vassar, I was very much considered an incipient writer, but she was so much better, I think I was discouraged for life. She had a facility with words that was sensational. She had a command of language second to none. Second to no one in college, at least in my time. She wasn't kind about anyone else's writing either.

**LUCILLE FLETCHER WALLOP**   In freshman English we would turn in our papers to Miss Kitchel and she would put them in a folder, and we were supposed to read them all and discuss them. But Mary was the chief attraction in our class because she was far advanced. The writing in her papers was very good but it was mostly the content that interested me. That was the only class I took with her—I don't believe we ever exchanged more than a couple of sentences—but I found her remarkable and intimidating. And she absolutely destroyed one's own ego. Mary would not be rude to your face. It was just an air of superiority.

In class you were expected to speak up. That was the Vassar way—to discuss and to question long cherished beliefs and assumptions. Later on, Mary McCarthy credited Vassar with instilling the skepticism that she was famous for. But one could argue that by the time she arrived at

Vassar skepticism was already second nature to her. Given all she had lived through, she had little reason to take anything on faith.

Both in the classroom and outside of it she knew what she liked and what she didn't. From the start, she knew the kind of friends she wished to make. Early on, in one of her classes, she found herself seated next to a girl from Cleveland with black hair and dark brown eyes and a name that fell right after hers in the class roster. Martha McGahan was an Irish Catholic who had lost her mother at an early age. She had been raised by her two aunts and a bookish father and educated in parochial schools. Her decision to apply to Vassar was perhaps the most rebellious act of her life. Her godson would later say, "She was the secret Catholic girl in Mary." Although there was a mutual and lasting sympathy, the friendship flourished only after college. But, then, Mary McCarthy had not gone to Vassar to spend her days with the likes of Martha McGahan.

Frani Blough was a different story. With her fair curly hair and her long Parisian policeman's cape she had something of the aspect of a merry adolescent boy. She was a gifted musician and possessed of a dry sense of humor. Like Mary McCarthy, she had a great fondness for Renaissance literature. Her touch was lighter, but, then, as the only child of loving parents she'd had an easier time of it. Her father was an executive with a big Pittsburgh steel company. Having skipped two grades, she was younger than most of her classmates, but that didn't seem to hurt her any. Beloved by both the blue-eyed Republicans and those who had no use for them, she was a popular campus figure.

In no time Mary McCarthy and Frani Blough were seeing each other every day, even though they lived in dormitories a good distance apart. And in no time the two of them were taken up by Helen Sandison and Anna Kitchel, who lived in adjoining apartments in faculty housing and made it a point to invite the two girls, together and individually, for afternoon tea on the screened porch they shared.

The Vassar system of education suited Mary McCarthy particularly when it came to the study of English literature. She loved Helen Sandison and she loved Anna Kitchel. For only one teacher in the English department, Helen Lockwood, did she show anything but admiration and for that teacher her scorn was so open that years later it was the stuff of Vassar legend.

**FRANI BLOUGH MUSER** Miss Lockwood was not literary the way Miss Kitchel and Miss Sandison were, but she was an exceedingly good critic of writing. She was very specific and knew exactly what good writing was about. She was famous for the Press course. It was reading newspapers from all over the country and analyzing the styles of the writing and the presentation of the subject. I took it senior year, but as it turned out it wasn't really what I wanted. I wanted something I could go out with in my hand to get a job. But the course was very popular and highly respected. And there were people who kissed the ground Miss Lockwood walked on.

## FROM *HOW I GREW*

A young person who disliked certitudes of any kind was proof against the recruiting methods of the "charismatic" Miss Lockwood, who had a moustache and a deep "thrilling" voice. There was an instant antagonism between us, which did not come to a head, though, until junior year when the Blake-to-Keats course, which I had been taking with my own dear favorite, Miss Kitchel was turned over at mid-years to Miss Lockwood[. . . .]

Many years later, over an Old-Fashioned in a downtown Poughkeepsie restaurant Miss Kitchel told me the story, as she heard it, of a famous passage-at-arms between the dread Miss Lockwood and a very pert me. One morning, it seemed, Miss Lockwood, who was much given to leaning across the professorial desk, chin in hand and raking the class with her burning gaze, had fired an opening question at us in her profoundest bass: "GIRLS, what is poetry?" At which, from a back row, I put up a saucy hand and sweetly recited: "*Coleridge* says it's the best words in the best order." She could have slapped me, I imagine.

To Vassar Mary McCarthy had brought a passionate desire for attention. Once she began taking the train down to the city to see Harold Johnsrud, she was not slow to let her classmates know of her involvement with this older Broadway actor. Harold Johnsrud might be sarcastic and elusive, but—unlike her former beaux—he was no demon lover to keep under wraps. Well regarded in his profession and sought out by Broadway producers, he was a graduate of Carleton College and had attended the Yale Drama School.

When she had the chance freshman year, she drew on her burgeoning relations with Johnsrud to dazzle classmates less sexually sophisticated. If she'd had her wish, she would gladly have dazzled them with her beauty. "All my friends have got the bug for getting tanned," she wrote Ted Rosenberg her first May. "They lie out on the grass on blankets all day. I've been out plucking violets, but right at present I, too, am lying on the grass under a large black umbrella, for I am trying to retain my gorgeous ivory skin." At Czerna Wilson's her pale skin and black hair had elicited the kind of admiration she had spent so much of her adolescence longing for. Here, owing in part to the strong and identifiable cast of her handsome features, the response was decidedly mixed.

## FROM THE UNPUBLISHED MEMOIRS OF LUCILLE FLETCHER WALLOP

[S]he was lined up for a physical exam and wearing only an "angel robe" over her nakedness. I had never seen a face more strikingly beautiful—and avid. It stood out in the dim basement light like the illuminated portrait of some rebellious young queen or a vision from some Celtic poet's dream. Her hair was long and black, hanging low in a massive coil at the back of her neck, and her features were flushed and contemptuous . . . the lips curled, the nostrils arched, and the slanting green eyes with their heavy black eyebrows alive with intelligence and disdain. She looked like a Gaelic mermaid just risen from the sea—to do harm to a curragh of passing fishermen.

**ELINOR COLEMAN GUGGENHEIMER**   She had fascinating eyes. And a fascinating kind of crooked smile. She walked badly, but she was in a sense beautiful because her face was so alive. Even though she was impossible, I was more interested in her, and I wanted more for her to like me than anyone else I can remember at Vassar.

**KAY MCLEAN**   She had a wicked gleam in her eyes. Her hair was straight and limp and in those days she just pulled it back and then into a bun at the nape of her neck. Some of the pictures I've seen of her seem to be glamorized. She was awfully thin.

**JULIA DENISON RUMSEY**   Pretty is too soft a word for her. She had an unfortunate Cheshire cat kind of grin.

**FRANI BLOUGH MUSER**   She wasn't Daisy Chain material. She wasn't pretty in that way.

**HELEN DAWES WATERMULDER**   When Frani cast Mary as the Madonna in a Christmas pageant, people asked, "Why on earth are you doing that?" Mary at that time resembled Charles Addams's Morticia. But with the blue in Mary's costume and the way that she was posed she was perfectly beautiful.

**ELEANOR GRAY CHENEY**   If Mary had stood up straight and washed her face she might have been pretty. She had a beautiful complexion, as I remember. And a very Irish face. You hate to say that, but there is such a thing.

Her first fall at Vassar Harold Johnsrud, or "John" as she had taken to calling him, was cast in a play adapted by George S. Kaufman and Alexander Woollcott from a story by Guy de Maupassant. The play, which she later described in *How I Grew* as "witty" and "well staged and well acted," and "among the three best of the season," lasted for only sixty performances. She attributed its failure to attract a large following to the stock market crash. That winter, Johnsrud moved to a cheaper apartment in Greenwich Village, on Bank Street, where, she wrote, "I lost my virginity for the third time."

With friends and acquaintances she saw no reason to keep the sexual nature of her relationship with Johnsrud a secret. At the same time, she was eager to have them meet him when he came to visit her at Vassar on weekends. Wisely or not, she had fallen in love with this older actor. The tone he took toward her remained superior and mocking, but that did not keep her from making plans for their future. "John and I were engaged, I told my friends, not knowing for sure whether we were or what it meant."

**FRANI BLOUGH MUSER**   John was older and a professional and also a literary aspirant. He wanted to be a playwright and he was full of the affectations that went with the role that he was playing. He would come up and Mary would bring him over, and of course Miss Kitchel and Miss Sandison just fell for him like a ton of bricks. The two ladies were very interested in that romance. They were all for romance.

**MARGARET MILLER**   Johnsrud was most attractive—rangy and tall and he moved very well. He was bald and had a broken nose, but he had very beautiful eyes. I think the eyes that Mary attributes to Philip Rahv in her last memoir were John's.

**KAY MCLEAN**   Johnsrud was sort of fascinating. I think that fundamentally he was probably a pretty nice guy passing himself off as . . . he sent a wire to Mary one time I remember saying, "Meet you in Central Park in sheep's clothing."

**FROM THE UNPUBLISHED MEMOIRS OF LUCILLE FLETCHER WALLOP**
[A]s soon as I read her stories in our Freshman English folder which had been placed in the Vassar Library by our English teacher, Miss Kitchel, I was awed by her love life, the numerous affairs she had had. She wrote about losing her virginity at an early age and all about the older man, a Broadway actor and stage manager she was visiting every weekend in his Greenwich Village apartment. I learned from her short stories that devilled ham was fatal to a proper orgasm and that lettuce was a powerful aphrodisiac. I had never heard of orgasms or aphrodisiacs, but I lapped up her descriptions, as did the rest of the class, who often lined up in a long queue waiting for the folder.

**ROSILLA HORNBLOWER HAWES**   There were three or four of us from Chapin all in the same house freshman year, with Mary. We used to be staggered when we heard Mary talking in the community bathroom we all shared. At least I was. Mary would regale whoever was listening about her sex life and abortions—I don't know that they were *her* abortions, but it was an eye opener.

**ELINOR COLEMAN GUGGENHEIMER**   One of my outstanding memories is her lecture on douching. I remember it still today. It was one of the high points of freshman year. I didn't know what the hell she was talking about. Mary of course loved to shock us.

**FROM "MEMOIRS OF LITERATAE AND SOCIALISTS 1929–33,"**
**BY EUNICE CLARK JESSUP**
We considered Mary McCarthy to be on a level of sophistication we couldn't attain until after marriage, if then[. . . .] Not only was she going to marry an actor, a species that none of us had ever seen except across the footlights, but she bought her clothes at Saks instead of Peck & Peck. Another girl said to me once, "Mary McCarthy says there are perverts

who make love to dead bodies. Can that be true?" "Well," I answered weakly, "if Mary says so."

In Greenwich Village Mary was eating her lettuce and staying clear of deviled ham and at Vassar she was doing little to ensure the kind of general popularity that makes for a class officer or for the editor of a school newspaper or literary magazine. If you caught her at the wrong moment, she could be careless or abrupt. If she unearthed any hidden fault or defect, she was not above using it as a weapon, especially if it was a defect she shared. When she didn't care for something you said, she did not hesitate to let you know. With time, certain of her schoolmates learned to be on their guard around her. For some, one brush with her was sufficient.

**ELINOR COLEMAN GUGGENHEIMER**   We were friends sometimes, but Mary could be absolutely brutal. She would decide she didn't like you one day, and she would sneer at you. Her command of language made it extremely difficult to stand up to her.

**ELEANOR GRAY CHENEY**   Mary liked people to be honest. We got along in that sense. I knew her right through college. She was rather different from the rest of us in that she was somewhat loose, and very very bright. The only thing she ever got mad at me about was that I loved Kipling. It was the only time I ever knew her to be irrational.

**KAY MCLEAN**   Mary was very opinionated on all subjects. I resented it at the time. *Brave New World* came out and Mary thought it was the most disgusting book that she'd ever read, and I thought it was fascinating because I was also taking zoology and various things like that. I said I thought that from a scientific point of view it was very interesting. Mary's reply was: "Our minds are just at opposite poles."

She was prepared to be sarcastic and biting when she felt that the occasion called for it. But sometimes she caused hurt feelings without really meaning to.

**FROM *HOW I GREW***

At Vassar, my Davison friends, [Virginia Johnston] excepted, had rapidly lost interest for me. Even before Thanksgiving, I was tired of hearing about Alice Butler's boarding-school roommate, and Betty Brereton's father in the Navy. Yet something had happened that condemned us to stick together[. . . .] [W]e were still friends, all of us, when one afternoon in the dormitory someone—I no longer know who—came to tell us that Elinor Coleman was Jewish. We laughed. If charming golden snub-nosed sheltered Elly resembled anything, it was a girl straight out of a convent[. . . .] We were slow to catch on, the slowest being big fair Alice Butler from New Haven, who just could not contain her guffaws.

**ELINOR COLEMAN GUGGENHEIMER**  I was very very blond with greenish eyes and a small nose and I've never been recognized as Jewish. There was nothing that would have ever identified me, and the end result is that I guess it was an awful shock to Mary and those other girls in the dormitory to find this out. It was nothing I hid from them, but I would have loved to have. I wanted to be accepted. I didn't want to be rejected. I wanted to be liked. There was something so upsetting about the evening they confronted me. Their sense of shock, which I felt extremely destroyed by. I knew that this was something I would never forget—and that no one who had been in that room would forget, either.

After that evening, Mary would make remarks sometimes. At one moment she was ultraliberal and then she would do that. I had no idea she had a Jewish grandmother. I only found out years later. She never let on. Never. If anything, she was anti-Semitic. She made me feel awful being Jewish. She couldn't wait to distance herself from me, although she did continue at times—she was very erratic—to be friendly. One minute she was your best friend and the next minute she was your enemy. Depending.

## FROM *HOW I GREW*

[A]s Elly's house guest, I finally "made it" into New York society—coming-out parties with "name" bands and the young men in dinner jackets, a stag line[. . . .] I was in high society, no question. The only thing was that it was *Jewish* high society[. . . .]

It was garment money [. . .] and jewelry money rather than banking money that was clasping me to its shirt front in my long ice-green satin dress.

**ELINOR COLEMAN GUGGENHEIMER**  Mary came to stay with us one Thanksgiving weekend—I think it was after all that had happened. I remember there was a dance at the Plaza Hotel one night. But what I remember mostly is that one night she went out at eleven o'clock to a hotel to meet Harold Johnsrud, who was in a play. That was counter to anything that young women did in those days. My mother couldn't stand her. I think my mother was ready to take me out of Vassar. At the end of sophomore year, I left.

By the end of sophomore year Mary McCarthy's informal group in Davison had broken up—Virginia Johnston had gone off to get married, Elinor Coleman had quit school, and a third member had moved away. Junior year she moved over to Cushing, where she would be near Frani Blough, her best friend at school. Having Frani living close by did not make all that much difference: she continued to see Frani all the time, the way she had before. But through a modest alteration in her living arrangements, she began, in her view, to come into her own.

It was in her junior year that she first came up against a major campus figure, Eunice Clark, a great admirer of Helen Lockwood and soon to be the editor of the Vassar paper, the *Miscellany News*. She also got to know Elizabeth Bishop, a quirky, amusing, and highly literary girl from

Nova Scotia who had gone to boarding school with Frani and was one class behind theirs.

No less important, in Cushing's Tudor dining room, she met up with some handsome rich girls more to her liking than the debutantes at Davison. At dinner and then in the smoking room, she began to spend time with Julia Denison and Dottie Newton, Rosilla Hornblower and Helen Kellogg, and Kay McLean and Maddie Aldrich, a group of gently reared young women, whose most formidable member was Nathalie Swan. Statuesque and undeniably good-looking, Nathalie Swan came from a wealthy New York family (her mother was a cofounder of the Junior League). This rarefied circle of society girls would figure large in Mary's last two years at Vassar and then go on to provide inspiration for many characters in her most famous work of fiction.

While her social life at Vassar was more to her liking, her relations with Harold Johnsrud were no more tranquil than they had been at the start. Still, she persisted in relying on him to help her through the long school holidays. In letters to Frani Blough written during the school holidays, she would occasionally let hints of her unhappiness slip through. Her letters to Ted Rosenberg had stopped, but at Vassar she'd had the good luck to find in Frani a friend for life. It was through Frani that she became better acquainted with Elizabeth Bishop, who had also lost her parents when she was young and who had a talent for writing poetry that was precise and deft and on occasion pungent.

### AN UNTITLED POEM ATTRIBUTED TO ELIZABETH BISHOP
> Ladies and gents, ladies and gents,
> Flushing away your excrements,
> I sit and hear beyond the wall
> The sad continual waterfall
> That sanitary pipes can give
> To still our actions primitive.

**FRANI BLOUGH MUSER**    When we were friends at Vassar I could have envisioned the life for Mary that she had. Just as I was sure Elizabeth Bishop would be a great poet. Elizabeth Bishop stood out as a gifted person. Mary stood out, but not in the same way. She stood out for her brains and her accomplishments. Mary had tremendous . . . "dedication" isn't quite the word. She had a capacity for not being deflected from her purpose. She liked to work. She always got her papers in on time and they were good.

**MARGARET MILLER**    I didn't get to know Mary until junior year, when I met her through Elizabeth Bishop. We would see each other in a group of people. Never alone. She was fun to be with, but I learned to be on my guard with her. One time, I was in one of the Hall plays, and I'm not usually malicious, but I said something about a girl we knew who was working on the scenery. Anyway, Mary loved it. And several weeks later we were all at a table and the conversation came around to scenery and Mary quoted what I had said. So she was able to embarrass both the girl and me. I don't think she appreciated how embarrassing it was. I don't think she was capable of imagining. And I don't think she cared. She was reckless.

## FROM *HOW I GREW*

At Cushing we belonged to the so-called smoking-room set[. . . .] [O]n some nights the smoking-room would turn into a debating society as girls would drop in from Students or from their own dormitories and we would discuss questions such as "What makes Cézanne's apples beautiful?" I argued that it was purely the arrangement of the shapes and colors, while hoarse-voiced Eunice Clark, editor-to-be of the *Miscellany News*, kept earnestly repeating "But it's the *spirit* of the apples that counts," whereupon I led a round of derisive laughter.

## FROM *HOW I GREW*

[M]ost nights at the dinner-hour each table in the dining-hall was the preserve of a constituted group. If I did not see Frani from where I stood in the doorway (or there was no empty place beside her), I had nowhere, literally, to go[. . . .] And that was how, Reader—gradually, very gradually—I came to join the group.

At their table, near the door, there was quite often an empty place[. . . .]

At first I hardly knew any of these mostly rich and handsome girls to speak to, only the Sphinx of the smoking-room, the untalkative Nathalie Swan, and Julia Denison, who was in my Blake-to-Keats class[. . . .]

On nights when there was an empty place Julia would smile at me encouragingly as I surveyed the diners from the doorway. "Come on, sit with us," she pantomimed, and the full-breasted, inscrutable Nathalie Swan, who looked like an Edwardian beauty in a corset, would nod a greeting.

**JULIA DENISON RUMSEY**   I began to see Mary when I was in Cushing, my junior year. Oddly enough, she seemed rather lonesome. She seemed vulnerable underneath. Why exactly I can't say. Maybe it had to do with the way Harold Johnsrud treated her. He was a bit of a sadist I always felt, though I also liked him. And he was a tease. I don't think he would have approached her the way he did if he didn't know she was sensitive. Someone who wasn't sensitive wouldn't have put up with all of that.

## FROM MARY MCCARTHY'S LETTER TO FRANI BLOUGH, DECEMBER 25, 1931

I am writing to you to keep myself out of a psychopathic state. It's Christmas night, and I've enjoyed the charms of my own society exclusively since ten-thirty this morning. For, at eleven John left for Washington[. . . .] Haven't minded particularly all day, for I did nothing more than lie about reading books; but when I had to wander about the Village this evening, looking for an inexpensive restaurant in which to eat my Christmas dinner, and then ate it, and read a good book; well, on my return from that adventure, the situation got a bit too much for me; and I have been indulging in some good old self-pity.

In the summer of 1932, Mary McCarthy did not return to Seattle. When Nathalie Swan set off for Europe, to study for a year at the Bauhaus, Mary and Kay McLean both found work. She managed to get Kay a job as an apprentice with Harold Johnsrud, who was running a summer theater at Scarborough, in Westchester County. And she took a job as a secretary to a man named Mannie Rousuck, the owner and manager of a less than reputable New York art gallery. At the time, her job at the Carleton Galleries seemed no more than emblematic of a dismal summer. A decade later, it would provide the setting for a short story, with her employer's active sideline in animal portraiture transmogrified to dog portraits on crystal cuff links.

### FROM MARY MCCARTHY'S LETTER TO FRANI BLOUGH, JULY 22, 1932

You see me installed in my position as a member of the proletariat. What an absurd job it is! My boss is a nice, sweet, battered soul who spends his time skulking about, avoiding the sheriff. He now owes me eighteen dollars, and there is very little prospect of collecting it, unless I enlist my grandfather's services and join the ranks of the vultures who are hovering about the poor man, ready to pounce[. . . .]

You will get no literary letters from me this summer, my dear, or at least not yet awhile. It is much too hot for intellectual activity. I even find it difficult to plough through a detective story. I dip into Proust at night in bed when it's too hot and sticky to sleep normally. And I put aside my critical faculties when I go up to Scarborough to have a look at the Theatre, and merely commend and bow and scrape, a state of affairs which seems to suit John very well.

### FROM "ROGUE'S GALLERY," BY MARY MCCARTHY

Mr. Sheer was a dealer in objects of art, a tall, pale-eyed man with two suits and many worries. Downstairs in the building directory he was listed as The Savile Galleries, and the plural conveyed a sense of endless vistas of rooms gleaming with collector's items. Like Mr. Sheer himself, that plural was imaginative, winged with ambition, but untrustworthy[. . . .]

"Dogs," Mr. Sheer said. "Wear your dog on your sleeve." I stared at him. He went into the inner office and came back with a jeweler's box in which lay a pair of crystal cuff links. Buried in the crystals, one could see a tiny pair of scotties[. . . .]

He was fond of the fine arts, fond of long words, and fond of me, but was this simply because he felt that between us we could make a prosperous gentleman out of him? I am not sure. He could never use the long words correctly and he could hardly tell a Cellini from a Rembrandt; yet surely there was a kind of integrity in that very lack of taste.

When the season ended at Scarborough, Harold Johnsrud returned to New York and she quit her job at the Carleton Galleries and moved in with him. Kay McLean, who was dating Johnsrud's younger brother, had also come down to New York. It had been Kay's impression that Johnsrud had been living with his leading lady for most of the summer, and she may have intimated enough of this to ensure that Mary would recall the summer as a total disaster. But, then, Johnsrud himself did his part in seeing to that.

### FROM *HOW I GREW*

We had a month before college reopened, the worst month, I believe, of my life. I had not thought that anyone could suffer so much. I cried every day, usually more than once[. . . .] And almost the worst was my total mystification. What made him so hateful I never found out, and this left me with a sense of being hopelessly stupid, which I fear John liked[. . . .]

In the fall, John was hired as a writer by MGM at a salary of $200 a week. Out there he lived in a house in Laurel Canyon and did not come back till May of the following year. In time to see me play Leontes in *The Winter's Tale* and tell me I could never be an actress.

That fall, when Johnsrud went off to California, she returned to Vassar, to join the rich girls from Cushing's dining room in a living arrangement whereby she was made a provisional part of their "group." Out of self-interest as much as good fellowship they had invited her and another girl to share a suite of rooms with them.

**HELEN KELLOGG EDEY**   I don't remember meeting Mary, but suddenly senior year she was there with us in Main. There was this business of signing up for a "group." Sometimes it was three or four. But there was this tower in Main and you had to be eight. Everybody seemed to think it was a desirable place. The people in the "group" that I knew the best and did the most with and am still close to were my roommate Maddie Aldrich, Rosilla Hornblower, and Dottie Newton. The four of us were all from New York—Dottie was from Boston, but it was the same thing. And then of the four others, we saw more of Julia and Kay. But the two in the middle rooms, Clover Benson and Mary, just sort of appeared there. I mean, we'd known them the year before obviously, but we decided to include them in the group so that we could get this suite.

Ensconced in that coveted suite in the South Tower of Main, bent on making a place for herself in a circle of longtime friends, Mary was also laboring long hours in secret with Frani Blough, Elizabeth Bishop, Eunice Clark, and Margaret Miller to put out a rebel literary magazine. She had taken Miss Kitchel's criticism to heart and had ceased writing stories guaranteed to shock and titillate her classmates. On one of her trips west, stopping off in Minneapolis, she had been reunited with her brothers Preston and Kevin. Not long after this visit, she made an attempt at dramatizing the shocking mistreatment they had all suffered at the hands of the guardians the McCarthys had put in charge of them.

With the group in South Tower, proximity began to breed a measure of intimacy. In time the more tenderhearted members of the group granted her a tantalizing, never-to-be-forgotten introduction to a rarefied and confident world she had glimpsed in Augusta Preston's copies of *Vogue*—a world campus radicals like Eunice Clark had little use for.

### FROM *THE GROUP*

> "You people were aesthetes. We were the politicals," Norine continued. "We eyed each other across the barricades[. . . .] You were Sandison. We were Lockwood[. . . .] [Y]our crowd was sterile. Lockwood taught me that. But, God, I used to envy you![. . .] Poise. Social savvy. Looks. Success with men. Proms. Football games. Junior Assemblies. We called you the Ivory Tower Group. Aloof from the battle."

**KAY MCLEAN**   The group were all bright interesting people but they had a different type of social background than Mary did. My father had lost his money in the Depression, but I had been brought up in that way. I was going to debutante parties while Mary was meeting up with the wolf in sheep's clothing. When I was visiting those girls, I was simply seeing what I'd always seen, but for Mary it was a fascinating thing learning about how the other half lived. I don't think she really felt comfortable with them or that they felt comfortable with her. It seems to me I heard that at one of the houses she visited she was nasty to the butler, the way that people who haven't been brought up with servants in the house sometimes are. They're sort of scared and don't know what to do about them.

**HELEN KELLOGG EDEY**   Mary basically ran around with a somewhat different crowd. She was literary. And there was this group in the North Tower and in some other building whom she seemed to have more social life with. Here she was inhabiting the same living room and the same bathroom, but I didn't feel I knew her terribly well. She would talk to us about the adjustment—about her Catholic girlhood. She never talked about any parents. I knew she lived with her grandparents.

**MADDIE ALDRICH DE MOTT**   I was aware of the fact that she was an orphan. She talked about how awful her relatives were and how she was living with her grandparents. She seemed to like her brother Kevin very much.

**MARGARET MILLER**   Her last year, I remember Mary had just come from a conference—she had been studying playwriting and shown the teacher something she had written about her childhood—and she was ecstatic. I'd never seen her so moved by anything as she was by the teacher's response to her own life experience. It was both a source of boastful exuberance and a balm—something you'd apply to a burn. The idea that this might be something magnificent—something she could use—made her as exuberant as I'd ever seen her. But beneath the exuberance there was this feeling not so much of being understood as that there was something redemptive about it.

### FROM *HOW I GREW*

By senior year I was well aware of having a Jewish grandmother and aware of it —let me be blunt—as something to hide. I excused myself by saying to my conscience that I could not fight on all fronts at once.

**HELEN KELLOGG EDEY**    I had her down for weekends. We lived in a house, not an apartment. We had a butler. My parents were on the cool side. I was becoming pretty damned liberal politically and my parents were pretty conservative. So I would bring these strange people into the house, and my parents were very, very benevolent. They tolerated these people. And Mary looked at my parents and decided they must be awful because they happened to be snobbish and have money.

### FROM MARY MCCARTHY'S UNSENT LETTER TO THE
### *NEW YORK HERALD TRIBUNE*, FEBRUARY 6, 1964

I think they were practicing tolerance, since I was so different from them, though this difference was not a matter of proms, clothes, men (I loved clothes, proms, and men), but was mainly a matter of what they would call "breeding." I was not ill-bred, but untrained and "wild," which meant not just living-with-a-man-before-marriage and drinking (most of them liked to drink too) and breaking the rules, but being very outspoken and extreme in all my enthusiasms and dislikes. And, unlike them, I was not practicing tolerance.

**MADDIE ALDRICH DE MOTT**    One Christmas, I think it was senior year, I brought Mary home with me to Barrytown. I wasn't looking for volunteer work, but she was lonesome. She wasn't a close friend, but something had to be done about her.

**HELEN KELLOGG EDEY**    Mary would go home for vacations or go away someplace or go off to New York and come back to school and we always got the feeling that she was making a new adjustment to our life. I think we probably made it harder for her than if she'd been at North Tower or some other place because the four of us were already sort of an "in" and we were quite different from Mary. We had money, homes, family. My four had money. I don't think Julia had a nickel. I remember she couldn't afford to get the newspaper. Kay was better off than that. I'm sure there was envy on Mary's part of these secure rich New Yorkers. If she'd been in a different group it might have been fine. She would make remarks like "You don't know what you're talking about." I think she felt sort of superior and she didn't bother to hide it. We just didn't measure up to her intellectual ambitions and she didn't have much time for us.

Although it was not entirely to her new group's liking, she was spending much of her free time that year laboring over *Con Spirito*, the new magazine that was to be a dazzling alternative to the stodgy *Vassar Review*. As she later told it, she and Frani Blough and Elizabeth Bishop were its founding members. Eventually they were joined by Margaret Miller, Muriel Rukeyser, and Eunice Clark and her younger sister, Eleanor. Originally the name for the magazine had been *The Battleaxe*. The title they finally came up with played with the whole notion of conspiracy. Contributions were to be anonymous. The editorial board was to be kept secret. Inevitably the magazine caused a sensation. It also stirred up a fair share of ill will.

As Frani Blough remembered it, the idea had actually come from Eunice Clark, "who just loved to put out anything in print." According to Frani, Eunice got the idea from Selden Rodman, a Yale man she was dating, who was one of the founding editors of a Yale undergraduate publication sympathetic to avant-garde and left-wing writing. Eleanor and Eunice Clark both had their own memories of *Con Spirito*, which never quite jibed with Mary's or Frani's. Margaret Miller tended to see it more Mary's way. Since nothing was recorded and everything was secret, there is no way to set the record straight. All that is certain is that for a brief period *Con Spirito* was a great success and that Mary McCarthy wrote a review in an early issue attacking Aldous Huxley's *Brave New World*.

**ELEANOR CLARK**  Mary got *Con Spirito* all mixed up with another magazine called *The Housatonic*, which was got out by my sister, Eunice, and me, with the help of Muriel Rukeyser, from our mother's home in Connecticut, the summer of 1932. *Con Spirito* was the following fall. Muriel Rukeyser had left college by then, so she had nothing to do with it; and I had nothing to do with it because I had decided to leave Vassar and go to Barnard for that year.

**MARGARET MILLER**  We had the meetings in speakeasys. Forbidden territory. So that lent an air of suspense. Elizabeth Bishop and Mary were the two who seemed most in charge.

### FROM "MEMOIRS OF LITERATAE AND SOCIALISTS 1929–33," BY EUNICE CLARK JESSUP

The official literary magazine, *The Vassar Review*, looked to us like the Bastille. They didn't print our avant-garde contributions and they altered our sentences to sound more like Matthew Arnold.

So a group of us gathered in an Italian speakeasy in lower Poughkeepsie in the spring of 1933 [*sic*] to produce the counter-establishment blast[. . . .] I was in funds, $300, due to the bonus from editing the *Miscellany News*, which was enough to pay the printer.

The product was brilliant. I sent it to the *N. Y. Herald Tribune*, where Lewis Gannett commented on us in the Book Review. The literatae volunteered to peddle it around the college, and they all collected enough money except for Mary McCarthy, who was not cut out to be a peddler.

### FROM "TWO CRYSTAL-GAZING NOVELISTS", *CON SPIRITO*, FEBRUARY 1933

When the Huxley book was published a year ago the usual polite applause that Huxley as a stylist has always been given was succeeded by a general groan. One by one the literary demi-gods of the nineteen twenties were collapsing. Lawrence, with the sentimental mysticism of his later work, was probably the first to go. Joyce was gradually deflating into a comfortable unintelligibility. Virginia Woolf was masking her new lack of hard thinking which was later to appear undisguised in the simple "pretty" femininity of *The Second Common Reader*, in a pretense of acute feeling and "experimentation with a new form"[. . . .]

If one places *Brave New World* side by side with *Public Faces* [by Harold Nicolson], the easiness and superficiality of Huxley's recent thinking becomes glaringly apparent[. . . .] The intellectual attainment that it represents could be duplicated by any half-trained mathematician, who cared to take a few contemporary tendencies and raise them to the nth degree. Worst of all, it represents so definitely a distinct social point of view, the point of view of a social coterie which believes, for snobbish and academic reasons, that standardization is a hideous fate to which mass-production, the movies, and the subway system are relentlessly hastening us.

In later years she would share not a few of Aldous Huxley's "snobbish" views, but with this review of *Brave New World* an aspiring critic was finding her voice. As a model she had chosen Rebecca West, a British writer twenty years older, known for her wit, her striking looks, her socialist politics, and for her glamorous circle of male friends. Already it was evident that Mary herself had a gift. What was less evident was how to go about making use of it. In a paper for her seminar in Elizabethan literature, she wrote of the prolific poet and pamphleteer Robert Greene, who tried to live by his pen and died in abject poverty. In an essay awarded half the Furness Prize for Elizabeth Studies, she wrote with keen sympathy of the early promise and failed ambitions of Sir John Harington, translator of *Orlando Furioso*, favorite of Queen Elizabeth, and inventor of "the modern water closet."

**FRANI BLOUGH MUSER** I remember we would talk about what we would be when we were thirty, and Mary was hoping to have a kind of salon. Interesting people and all that. She'd imagined herself as a figure from literary history, you see. So she had put herself in a salon, like Madame de Staël. I think an awful lot of our aspirations came out of literary sources—especially theatrical or dramatic presentations. We were always imitating somebody or other. Margaret Marshall, that woman on *The Nation* who later encouraged Mary, was very well known and she would have been a model for Mary when Mary was thinking of writing criticism. And Rebecca West.

## MARY MCCARTHY AT CITY ARTS & LECTURES, SAN FRANCISCO, MAY 10, 1985

[Rebecca West] had a great influence on me when I was young, when I was at Vassar. The incisiveness of her mind made a great impression on me. I did not like her much as she grew older. It seemed to me that she developed all kinds of prejudices[. . . .] Every now and then she would come through, even very old, with some brilliant, incisive piece of work. She was a strange mixture of extreme common sense and a certain irrationality.

In November 1932, Franklin Delano Roosevelt was elected president on the promise that he would somehow get the country out of what was coming to be called the Great Depression. While Rebecca West exerted an influence on Mary McCarthy's writing, other, more immediate, influences were being brought to bear on her politics—politics, which, with her fondness for lost causes like that of the French pretender or Bonnie Prince Charlie, she delighted in calling "royalist."

### FROM *HOW I GREW*

[T]he course senior year that had the greatest visible influence on my future was Miss Peebles' Contemporary Prose Fiction, in which we studied the "river-novel" and something she called "multiplicity"[. . . .] [W]e read Dos Passos' *The 42nd Parallel* [. . .] and, one thing leading to another, I was prompted to go to the library basement and find Dos Passos' pamphlet on Sacco and Vanzetti, which turned me around politically from one day to the next (or so it seemed). There was no more talk from me of royalism; instead, I was pursuing the Tom Mooney case through the back numbers of *The New Republic*.

**FRANI BLOUGH MUSER**   Our last year at school was the worst year of the Crash—1933, when the banks folded and you couldn't get any of your money out. I remember writing my father, "I have eighty-five cents, so I'll be all right."

**MADDIE ALDRICH DE MOTT**   Although Mary always felt that my family was land poor—intelligent but not rich—we really had plenty of money. We just didn't throw it around. I didn't have any problems with money during the Depression. I've often wondered why not. I've never investigated. Rosilla never had any trouble and Helen was fine. We never even discussed it. We never even thought about it. The people that didn't have money we just automatically paid for without thinking about it.

**JULIA DENISON RUMSEY**   Because of the Depression my father had no money to pay for my tuition. I was going to quit the middle of senior year. Mary McCarthy and Dottie Newton thought that was crazy. They went to the dean and persuaded her that I should be given a special scholarship that was reserved for valuable seniors. Up until then I had a C average. But Mary had leverage with the dean because of her standing in the class and she persuaded the dean that I was worth financial assistance. Of course from then on, for the last term, I got straight A's. Dottie Newton was a close friend, so it was natural that she would have done that. But Mary was not a close friend.

Four years into the Depression, old assumptions and attitudes no longer offered reliable support, no matter how rich you were. As senior year drew to a close, virtually all of Mary McCarthy's classmates had some intention of putting to use their fine educations. The question was how to go about doing this. Most relied on family connections. Others had to venture out on their own. Helen Downes was offered a job placing unemployed executives by a woman she sat next to at a big dinner party. Kay McLean, who had planned to work in the theater, considered herself fortunate to be offered a job in a training program at Macy's. Helen Kellogg, who had planned to train as a doctor, was now making plans to get married. She had just fallen in love and she couldn't have it both ways.

Mary had aspirations that were at once more specific and more ambitious than those of her classmates. Then, too, she had no parents to fall back on. She began her job hunting in New York during Easter vacation. In a thank-you note to Frani Blough's mother, who had entertained her over the holiday weekend, she wrote of "tramping from part to outlying part of Manhattan," visiting various magazines, looking for editorial work. So far her efforts had come to nothing more than "raw material for an article for *Harper's*, entitled in typical *Harper's* fashion, 'The Girl Graduate in the Greater World.' " The one prospect that seemed in any way promising did not involve a paying job. "I had a little success with *The New Republic*," she wrote, "which promised to go so far as to send me a book to review, providing I send it back." Up until May, she had no idea what role Johnsrud intended to play in her future.

### FROM *HOW I GREW*

It was not clear to anyone whether John and I were going to be married or not. This was partly because John in his histrionic style could not accept the thought of being predictable. But [. . .] my own feelings had changed, mainly because of what John had put me through, overestimating my capacity for suffering[. . . .] What must have made it harder to "sort my feelings out" was that his return was a great triumph for me, to put in the eye of the egregious Kay McLean (whom I had come to positively hate) and all the other doubters and skeptics. Just to have him on campus was to show them.

Around that time I "made" Phi Beta Kappa[. . . .] John had been Phi Bete at Carleton and as soon as he heard, he offered to give me his key, so that by not sending for mine I could save the six dollars. This struck us as clever, I am afraid, like a high-brow equivalent of being "pinned" by your man's fraternity pin[. . . .] Clearly I still considered myself engaged to him[. . . .] As our class prepared for graduation, I was wearing his key on a chain.

**JULIA DENISON RUMSEY**   I always felt very strongly about Johnsrud—not personally so much as abstractly—because he came from a background that was pretty poor. He had helped a younger brother through college.

**FRANI BLOUGH MUSER**   John was around all the time and we all knew that Mary would marry him.

### FROM *HOW I GREW*

It was mid-June the morning we graduated, and I fainted in the chapel from the heat. Afterwards Frani's parents took several of us to lunch at the Silver Swan. My grandparents had not come on for the occasion, to hear me get my *cum laude* (no *magna*); they sent me the money the trip would have cost them. That was my graduation present[. . . .] Besides that, my grandfather sent me a check for what they might have given me for a trip to Europe, such as Frani was getting from her parents—*that* was a wedding present, he wrote. Yes, the decision had been made. We had even sublet an apartment, furnished, on East 52nd Street, from Miss Sandison's sister, Lois Howland, who taught Latin at Chapin.

Right after graduation Frani Blough went off to France, for the summer session at the American school of music at Fontainebleau. In the fall she would start at a Pittsburgh nursery school. Rosilla Hornblower, one of the South Tower debutante suitemates, immediately went to work at the National Consumer's League, where she would be helping push through child labor laws and legislation providing minimum wages for workers. Helen Dawes, the glamorous niece of Hoover's vice president and a class leader, got a job right away as a hostess at the World's Fair in Chicago, called the "Century of Progress." Although not everyone's future was so neatly resolved, almost everyone ended up with some kind of work.

**LUCILLE FLETCHER WALLOP**   I looked for a job in New York for about three months and the only thing I could get was typing at Columbia Broadcasting for fifteen dollars a week—that included Saturdays—or else working at Macy's in the toy department. When I went for that interview at Macy's, there were four hundred people sitting there waiting to get a chance to sell toys. So I took the job at CBS.

**MADDIE ALDRICH DE MOTT**   I didn't have a regular job, but I did start up this business in New York of exercising other people's dogs. It was called "the Dog Trot," which I thought was a wonderful name for it.

### FROM *THE GROUP*

[T]here was not one of them who did not propose to work this coming fall, at a volunteer job if need be. Libby MacAusland had a promise from a publisher; Helena Davison, whose parents, out in Cincinnati, no, Cleveland, lived on the income of their income, was going into teaching[. . . .] The worst fate, they utterly agreed, would be to become like Mother and Dad, stuffy and frightened. Not one of them, if she could help it, was going to marry a broker or a banker or a cold-fish corporation lawyer, like so many of Mother's generation.

Sixteen years after her graduation, when Mary McCarthy was pulling together facts and figures for "The Vassar Girl," she learned that, according to a survey taken not long after graduation, most of her fellow classmates had given up the careers they had struggled to establish as well as the jobs they had taken as a stopgap. By 1949 the average member of the class of '33 had produced "two-plus children and was married to a Republican lawyer." Her conclusion was not only depressing but sweeping: "[T]he statistical fate of the Vassar girl, thanks to Mother and Dad and the charge account, is already decreed. And the result is that the Vassar alumna, uniquely among American college women, is two persons—the housewife or matron, and the yearner and regretter."

By the time she wrote these words, it was clear that with two works of fiction to her credit and a considerable reputation as a critic, she was neither a regretter nor a matron. Miraculously she had escaped the fate of the majority of her classmates, but, then, unlike the majority of her classmates, she had no Mother and Dad to cosset or support her or deflect her from her chosen course. She was an orphan. And while she might be an orphan with an income from a family trust fund, compared to most of her classmates she was little better than a charity case.

Having been told by Harold Johnsrud that she had no future as an actress, she chose to go to New York and try to make a name for herself as a writer. At graduation, with the Depression showing no signs of abating, this plan must have seemed highly impractical. Unfortunately, there were few, if any, attractive alternatives. Such family as she could lay claim to appeared to have little time for her. When he stopped off at Seattle on his way back from California, Johnsrud had seen the Prestons, but she herself hadn't seen them for more than a year. Her grandparents had not felt it necessary to attend her graduation. It was left to Frani Blough's parents to take her to lunch afterward.

She was the first member of her class to marry. Her grandparents sent money in lieu of their blessings and did not trouble to come east to see her wed an actor they had been prepared to put up for the night but not necessarily greet with open arms. When Johnsrud, who had teased her for four years and dallied with her affections, proposed marriage, she had good reason to reject his offer, but in the end she accepted. Once the decision was made, she left no time for second thoughts. With Johnsrud, she would have a measure of company. In addition, she would have the blessings of Miss Kitchel and Miss Sandison. And with a husband to help meet the rent it wouldn't be quite so reckless to go off to New York and gamble, against all odds, on making a name for herself in the literary world.

From the day of her graduation Mary McCarthy believed that something irrevocable had taken place in Poughkeepsie. If she had stayed in Seattle and gotten her degree at the University of Washington she might have gone on to make a name for herself, but it would have been of a different order. Toward the end of her life, she was still insisting on the special nature of her college education. Over the years, she might turn her back on Vassar, the way she had turned away from the Catholic Church, but always she would carry its prejudices with her as well as its precepts, defined by them even as she was bent on denying them, through good times and bad, for better or worse.

# Chapter Five

## MRS. HAROLD JOHNSRUD

At Vassar Mary McCarthy had delighted in slipping off for an illicit weekend, openly boasting of her assignations with the older New York actor who sometimes took the train up to see her, but, upon graduation, she seemed to rush to embrace the very conventions she'd made it a point to flaunt. On June 21, 1933, in a ceremony at St. George's Episcopal Church, on Stuyvesant Square in Manhattan, with a scattering of classmates in attendance, she vowed to honor and obey Harold Johnsrud. If she'd had her wish, two things would have been different: the rector, not his curate, would have presided at the altar and Frani Blough, studying music at the Conservatoire Americain at Fontainebleau, would have been at her side.

After a wedding breakfast very much like the one Kay Strong throws for herself in the opening chapter of *The Group*, the new bride left with her new husband for a one-night stay at an inn, close to the city, in Briarcliff. She was proud to have been the first in her class to marry. Once she had been joined before man and God to the lover who for four years had teased and tormented her, she was bent on making the best of it. To her friends she admitted to no second thoughts.

In the apartment on East Fifty-second Street sublet for the summer from Miss Sandison's sister, Mary McCarthy Johnsrud prepared to receive old friends. With the sublet came a "colored" maid and some estimable if rather traditional pieces of furniture. Lois Howland's husband had lost his job in the Depression and to make ends meet the couple had been forced to retreat to a room at the National Arts Club. At the end of the summer, with the Howlands' approval, the furniture and maid accompanied the Johnsruds in their move to a one-room apartment on Beekman Place, closer to the East River. As a student Mary had appreciated the allure of living a bohemian life in the Village. But as a young matron she chose to live with her actor husband in a more conventional setting.

Although the rent was said to be reasonable for such a fashionable location, the Beekman Place apartment was by no means a bargain. An apartment in the Village or Brooklyn Heights would have made better sense. Johnsrud's father, a retired high school principal in St. Cloud, Minnesota, had neither the means nor the inclination to come to their assistance. The wedding and graduation checks from her grandfather in Seattle were the only dowry she was likely to receive from her family. The poor orphan now received an income from the McCarthy trust, but her income depended entirely on the current performance of her Capital Elevator stock.

In the first years of Roosevelt's presidency, it was becoming apparent, even to those who had initially tried to dismiss the stock market crash as a necessary corrective, that the United States had settled into a full-blown depression. Johnsrud was scrambling to make a living in the theater—not an easy matter in the best of times—directing, acting, working as an assistant stage manager for Jed Harris. At one point, he was playing a blind man in two Broadway plays, Maxwell Anderson's *Winterset* and Archibald MacLeish's *Panic*, racing between the two theaters by cab. Casting directors saw in his lined face, his bald head, and broken nose a villain or seer, or perhaps a saturnine *poète maudit*. At his ease in his British tweeds he had the look, if not the bearing, of a writer or intellectual. In a long stretch between jobs, he would sometimes turn his hand to playwriting.

More fortunate than most of her fellow graduates, Mary McCarthy had been quick to get a promise of review assignments, first from *The New Republic* and then from *The Nation*, periodicals that could lay claim to distinguished histories while embracing the latest political ideologies. At *The New Republic* she would come up against politics that were not merely liberal but unabashedly Communist and a book review editor who seemed to have little enthusiasm for her efforts. At *The Nation*, with Joseph Wood Krutch and Margaret Marshall, she would fare better. If her reviews tended to be on the harsh side, that seemed to suit them fine. Still, the checks received for these short pieces were not of a size to pay even the most modest of rents.

To make money she tried collaborating with her husband on writing a screenplay. When that came to nothing, she started a project of her own. Hoping to put to good use an appetite for murder mysteries she feared was growing into an addiction, she started to write one herself. Following the time-honored dictum of writing teachers world over, she chose for the crime a setting she knew firsthand: the Carleton Galleries, where she had sweated over letters for Mannie Rousuck the summer before her senior year.

Unlike the Howlands, she was not about to accommodate herself to the exigencies of an economic depression. She was out to have a good time. When she wasn't making her way among the Stalinists at *The New Republic* or striving to sound the right political note in a book review, she was scarcely affected by the political currents around her. With her smart wedding gifts, her dancing in Harlem, her endless games of bridge, her Sunday brunches that would not break up until late into the night, her falling off the wagon and climbing back on again, she might have been mistaken for one of the young flappers in a Dorothy Parker story.

No doubt the company she and Johnsrud kept was conducive to this careless existence. On occasion they saw Johnsrud's friends from the theater. But most of the people they saw were girls she knew from Vassar. And as she noted in 1951 in writing about her alma mater, a Vassar girl, when she chooses a husband, tends to look to boys of good family from schools like Harvard or Yale. Julia Denison and Rosilla Hornblower had married young men starting out in business, as had Maddie Aldrich (although her husband, Chris Rand, went on to become a writer). Margaret Miller and Elizabeth Bishop, with no young men laying claim to their time, were free to respond to a last-minute invitation or to turn a brunch into a moveable feast.

No landlord is eager to evict a tenant if there is little likelihood of finding a replacement. Even on Beekman Place, good tenants were few and far between. She and Johnsrud found their rent could remain unpaid for as long as a year, with no repercussions. Electricity came free with the apartment. When the phone company threatened to cut off service, she would go down to their offices to charm the man in charge of the account. When necessary, she was able to earn a few dollars by writing catalog copy and glowing letters describing the latest offerings of her old boss Mannie Rousuck, who had moved on from the Carleton Galleries to more savory quarters, trading dog portraits for eighteenth-century English hunting scenes. With her labors she was not only helping pay for groceries but culling additional details for her murder mystery.

Johnsrud was by nature inclined to view politics of every persuasion with ironic detachment, but as an actor he took work where he found it. He had parts in productions of *Black Pit*, *The Sailors of Cattaro*, and Gorky's *The Mother* mounted by the Theatre Union, a downtown group founded in 1933 by Charles and Adelaide Walker, which performed at the old Civic Repertory Theatre. Although he liked and respected Charles Walker (a translator of Aeschylus and Sophocles) and Walker's beautiful wife, Adelaide, he kept his distance from his fellow actors and from their radical politics. The Sunday night that Clifford Odets's *Waiting for Lefty* was first performed at a Theatre Union benefit, he brought Mary downtown to see it, but at his own dinner table he was heard to ask, "Odets, where is thy sting?"

A handful of Mary's Vassar schoolmates were settling down with unconventional husbands of their own, but for the most part these husbands were also from fine old families and Ivy League colleges. In 1934, Eunice Clark, the ardent disciple of Miss Lockwood, married Selden Rodman, not long out of Yale and one of the two founding editors of *Common Sense*. Left of center without being Marxist, *Common Sense* printed articles by noted writers and intellectuals, book reviews, and poetry but no fiction whatsoever. In 1935, Selden Rodman's sister, Nancy, one year ahead of Mary at Vassar, married Dwight Macdonald, a graduate of Exeter and Yale who had been writing since 1929 for Henry Luce's *Fortune*. The Macdonalds lived in a high-rise on East Fifty-second, not far from the Johnsruds. The Rodmans lived a few blocks south. They had rented a basement apartment in a town house that had a garden and they had painted the walls of the apartment black.

When the Johnsruds weren't spending their evenings at a bridge table with the Rodmans, they might join them for a trip to Harlem or a night on the town with a visiting politician who had won the approval of *Common Sense*. Or they might join them in their garden for a cocktail party to promote a new literary review, or to raise money for the latest worthy cause. While the speakers might be dull or the problems under discussion unamenable to solution, the evening need not necessarily be grim. As time passed and economic conditions seemed to worsen, gatherings of this sort threatened to become commonplace.

It was not unthinkable, given the climate of the times, to wholeheartedly embrace certain radical causes. To see your interests as closely allied with that of the workingman. Or to seriously consider joining the Communist Party. Rosilla Hornblower no longer seemed remarkable for taking a job fighting for legislation to provide a minimum wage and to keep children from being exploited by factory owners. Nancy and Dwight Macdonald were making their high-rise apartment available for parties to raise money for sharecroppers. Eunice Clark, mocked in the smoking room at Cushing for the radical causes she supported with such vehemence, now appeared to be firmly positioned in the vanguard of fashionable politics.

If times were hard and funds were tight, the Johnsruds put a brave face on it. They managed to amuse and entertain their friends and, more often than not, themselves as well. Gradually, the teasing and taunting of their long Vassar courtship stopped. However, the placid surface of their days did not necessarily indicate a change for the better. If to most observers the marriage appeared to be fairly solid, more than one close friend would later observe that there had been cause for concern.

As a writer Mary McCarthy never scrupled to mine her own life for material. In 1938, in her first short story "Cruel and Barbarous Treatment," she presented a modern comedy of manners, a witty variation on the theme of the breakup of a marriage not unlike her own. In 1963, in her novel *The Group*, she bestowed her first husband on her poor foolish heroine Kay Strong, and then gave Kay a set of friends bearing a striking resemblance to her own friends from Vassar. Finally, in the second volume of her autobiography, *Intellectual Memoirs*, she examined the marriage at length, trying to make sense of what had happened. By then the facts of the case had blended with the fabrications of her fiction, so that the line of demarcation was sometimes difficult to make out. All the same, like Pokey at Kay's wedding in the opening chapter of *The Group*, she was certain she could see precisely where things began to go wrong. But while Pokey spotted trouble in a failure of decorum, she believed it stemmed from a failure invisible to the average bystander.

### FROM *THE GROUP*

Pokey made use of her *lorgnon*, squinting up her pale-lashed eyes like an old woman; this was her first appraisal of Harald, for she had been away hunting for the weekend the one time he had come to college. "Not too bad," she pronounced. "Except for the shoes." The groom was a thin, tense young man with black straight hair and a very good, supple figure, like a fencer's; he was wearing a blue suit, white shirt, brown suède shoes, and dark-red tie. Her scrutiny veered to Kay, who was wearing a pale-brown thin silk dress with a big white *mousseline de soie* collar and a wide black taffeta hat wreathed with white daisies; around one tan wrist was a gold bracelet that had belonged to her grandmother; she carried a bouquet of field daisies mixed with lilies of the valley. With her glowing cheeks, vivid black curly hair, and tawny hazel eyes, she looked like a country lass on some old tinted post card; the seams of her stockings were crooked, and the backs of her black suède shoes had worn spots, where she had rubbed them against each other. Pokey scowled. "Doesn't she know," she lamented, "that black's bad luck for weddings?"

### FROM *HOW I GREW*

[I]t was exactly one week after Commencement and my twenty-first birthday when we "stood up" together in the chapel. I had a beige dress and a large black silk hat with a wreath of daisies. Most of the group were present; Frani had already sailed for Fontainebleau to study music, and Bishop, I think, was not there either. We had a one-night honeymoon at an inn in Briarcliff, and there all of a sudden I had an attack of panic. This may have had something to do with an applejack punch we served at the reception or with the disturbing proximity of

Scarborough, suffused with bad memories of the summer before. As we climbed into the big bed, I knew, too late, that I had *done the wrong thing.* To marry a man without loving him, which was what I had just done, not really perceiving it, was a wicked action, I saw.

Not content with giving Kay her own wedding, she went so far as to give her one of her own favorite gifts.

### FROM *THE GROUP*

Kay's first wedding present, which she had picked out herself, was a Russel Wright cocktail shaker in the shape of a skyscraper and made out of oak ply and aluminum with a tray and twelve little round cups to match—light as a feather and nontarnishable, of course.

In *Intellectual Memoirs* she wrote at some length of how she and John-srud used part of their wedding money to buy a Russel Wright cocktail shaker, along with a chromium hors d'oeuvre tray and "six silver Old-Fashioned spoons with a simulated cherry at one end and the bottom of the spoon flat, for crushing sugar and Angostura." Like a fondue pot of the sixties, the cocktail shaker was a fashion of the moment and an expression of the personal style of the young couple who purchased it. In retrospect, it came to seem a bit silly. A lapse in taste. An aesthetic misstep. But also a purchase called into question by the irony of its having been made four years too late. By 1933 13 million people were out of work.

### FROM "MY CONFESSION"

[I]n New York I used to see apple-sellers on the street corners, and, now and then, a bread line, but I had a very thin awareness of mass poverty[. . . .] I was conscious of the suicides of stockbrokers and businessmen, and of the fact that some of my friends had to go on scholarships and had their dress allowances curtailed, while their mothers gaily turned to doing their own cooking. To most of us at Vassar, I think, the depression was chiefly an upper-class phenomenon.

So long as she was busy setting up house it was easy to make light of what was going on all around her.

### FROM ELIZABETH HARDWICK'S FOREWORD TO
### *INTELLECTUAL MEMOIRS*, BY MARY MCCARTHY

What, perhaps, might be asked nowadays is why the gifted and beautiful young woman was so greatly attracted to marriage in the first place, why she married at twenty-one. She seemed swiftly to overlook the considerable difficulties of unmarried couples "living together" at the time: the subterfuge about staying overnight, facing the elevator man, hiding the impugning clothes when certain people appeared[. . . .]

There were many things Mary didn't believe in, but she certainly believed in marriage, or rather in being married.

## FROM MARY MCCARTHY'S LETTER TO FRANI BLOUGH, JULY 21, 1933

I was [. . .] intensely sorry that you were not among those heaving rice at my hapless form. I could almost say that it was no fun at all being married without you, but that would not be strictly true, so I won't say it. Bishop couldn't come either, chiefly from lack of funds[. . . .] But to get back to the wedding—it was all very exciting. Ten of us had breakfast at the Hotel Lafayette, with a swell punch with an applejack base, and there were a few more people at the church. My powerful bass voice (last heard in *The Winter's Tale*) changed to a faint, trembling soprano, which could not be heard, I learn, beyond the first pew. My knees shook so that I could hardly stand. Dottie and Phil stood up with us, and knelt at all the wrong places. Afterwards, in the vestry, we got your telegram, and our hearts were warmed[. . . .]

P.P.S. I forgot to mention it, but, in case you're interested, I am happily married. John's character has undergone a remarkable transformation, indeed, a metamorphosis. He is so goddamned nice that he puts me to shame. I am so glad we stopped being sensible and got married.

With no real home to return to, she might well be glad she had ceased to be "sensible." If nothing else a husband would help protect her from an economic crisis that showed no signs of abating. However, as it turned out, marriage suited her. She welcomed its rituals and prerogatives. With fresh paint on the walls, venetian blinds on the windows, and a few astute purchases from Macy's, the Howland furniture could be made to seem less conventional. As if to impart her blessing, Miss Sandison had given the newlyweds a beautiful cherry-wood card table with a blue suede top.

Before long, there were some striking modernist touches. With a little ingenuity and the advice of Nathalie Swan, back from studying at the Bauhaus, the Howlands' two single beds were turned into rather handsome brown couches. If a visitor didn't know better, he might mistake their single room on Beekman Place for the living room of a much larger establishment.

Most of the guests the Johnsruds invited for dinner, or for a game at their splendid new card table, were holdovers from Vassar—Maddie Aldrich, Julia Denison, Rosilla Hornblower, and Clover Benson from the South Tower group; Nathalie Swan, Eleanor Gray Cheney, and Eunice Clark; Margaret Miller and Elizabeth Bishop, still at school in Poughkeepsie; and of course Frani Blough whenever she came in from Pittsburgh, where she was living with her parents and teaching. Elizabeth Bishop had presented the couple with a colored print called *Geometry*, which she had bought for them in Paris. For many of these young women the neighborhood of the Johnsruds' establishment was both congenial and convenient. Moreover, it was regarded as suitable by their parents, who on occasion invited the Johnsruds for tea or lunch. At the beginning, before she learned to ridicule it, Mary delighted in her new role as a smart young East Side matron with a dashing actor for a husband and an ambitious social life. She was pleased to give a glimpse of this life, not only to her friends but to her brother, who was at school at Georgetown.

**KEVIN MCCARTHY**   One weekend for $3.45 I made my first trip ever to New York City via the Pennsylvania Railroad. It must have been the autumn of 1934, before I had to leave the Georgetown School of Foreign Service because of blowing the second-semester tuition money, which was in my care until it wasn't. That was long before Mary and I became close, but it was a good beginning. Preston and I had seen our sister only once in the ten years since Myers Shriver got the boot and we kids were all separated; Mary was on her way between Seattle and Vassar, and she did a brief stopover in Minneapolis—we said hello and maybe had a sandwich together, that was all, and she seemed to us very glamorous. But now it's 1934 and I'm about to meet a stranger, my married sister and her husband! My train was a nightime-coach affair and arrived in Manhattan that Saturday at the crack of dawn. Well, I got directions and walked all the way to the East River and Fiftieth—found Beekman Place, and must have been buzzing their door probably before 7:00 A.M., and I guess I finally woke them! Mary got the door open a crack and exclaimed, "Oh my god! Kevin! You'll have to go walk around for an hour or two. We can get together at eight." For lunch Mary took me to a place called the Richmond Grill, which was a speakeasy, and we had a cocktail. She took me to a matinee at the Henry Miller. It was called *Mrs. Wiggs of the Cabbage Patch.* That was our first time at the theater together and years before I had any idea that I was going to be an actor. It was after the play, I think, that I met Harold Johnsrud; I recall him as being somewhat reserved and sardonical. I didn't stay overnight.

**MARGARET MILLER**   I got to know Mary better when she was married. I would come for dinner and we'd talk. When I was in a room with her I sometimes watched her. She was amusing to watch. She had a tremor in her hand, and she developed a mannerism—a way of holding it to her side. She wore her hair pulled back in those days.

**NANCY MACDONALD**   I remember when she came to a cocktail party at our house—it must have been around 1935—and she had this sort of orange hat that went over her eyes and she was blinking her eyes and I kept thinking, What's coming out from there? You never knew what to expect. She was beautiful and I was terrified of her. Her intellectuality was a little bit too much for me. When I got to know her, I saw she had a soft side, too.

**KAY MCLEAN**   I really didn't continue to see Mary after she was married. I started working at Macy's the day after Labor Day and I was living at the Allerton House for Women on the corner of Fifty-seventh Street and Lexington. I can remember worrying whether I could afford the 75-cent dinner or whether I should stick to the 50-cent dinner. I was making $15 a week. My parents were subsidizing the rent, which was $8 a week. Mary had launched herself into intellectual circles and she was making her way in that world. As Mary said to me at Vassar, our minds were far apart. She didn't have any use for me. She could be ruthless. That was just the way she was.

Prohibition had made drinking glamorous and had given rise to a whole cornucopia of libations, a veritable soda parlor of mixed drinks. Perhaps owing to her eagerness to put her new cocktail shaker to use, a convivial evening at Two Beekman Place could end in crossed signals or a sudden argument. Sometimes it seemed as if misunderstandings of every sort attended her early social forays in New York.

**ROSILLA HORNBLOWER HAWES**   We had a friend who was young, just out of college, and rather innocent in her way. She came to me in a state of shock. She had gone to something in New York City and it was too late to go back to Bronxville, so she accepted an invitation to stay overnight at Mary's apartment. I think she was foolish to do that. It was a one-room apartment and it had two day beds—one along one wall, the second at a right angle along the other, and they were sofas during the day. Well, Mary and John made love in the very next bed to my friend. She was terribly upset.

Not even a game of bridge was without peril, particularly when at least one of the players felt herself to be at loose ends.

### FROM MARY MCCARTHY'S LETTER TO FRANI BLOUGH, DECEMBER 7, 1933

I find that I am becoming a prey to boredom, the boredom that sends young wives out to join bridge clubs, where they become still more bored. Not boredom with John, not at all, just a feeling of vacancy that must come with the end of a four years routine. Housework and a book review or two are not effective substitutes for sixteen hours of classes a week.

**ROSILLA HORNBLOWER HAWES**   Mary would come to play bridge with Julia and her husband and then she'd come, as I remember, to play bridge with me and my husband. We couldn't really understand why she wanted to see us because we were so conventional. We liked Johnsrud. Because he was in the theatrical business, they'd stay up very late and we couldn't do that. So we would let the liquor run out. But then they took to bringing their own liquor.

**JULIA DENISON RUMSEY**   One night they arrived around ten o'clock with cards and a bottle. We were in bed, and I jumped up and dressed, ready to play. My husband did, too, but then he said afterward, "Now that's the last time I'll play bridge." My husband didn't care for them. They were too bohemian.

From J. Donald Adams at *The New York Times Book Review* and Irita Van Doren at the *Herald Tribune*'s "Books" she received not a single review assignment. From Irita Van Doren she received one piece of advice: "We on this paper believe that there's somethin' good in evvra book that should be brought to the attention of evvra reader." With Malcolm Cowley, at *The New Republic*, she fared only marginally better. There, however, her difficulties seemed to owe more to the politics of the staff than to any wish to avoid negative criticism.

But if the book business sometimes seemed to be moribund, she was not about to give up. Her pieces in *The Nation* were attracting attention. She was writing for her sometime bridge partner Selden Rodman at *Common Sense*. With books, as with people, she knew what she liked and what she didn't. When the rest of the critics were singing his praises, she saw nothing whatsoever to like in John Steinbeck. But on the rare occasion that she admired a book, like Robert Graves's *I, Claudius*, she was able to make clear precisely what she saw in it.

### FROM MARY MCCARTHY'S REVIEW OF JOHN STEINBECK'S *IN DUBIOUS BATTLE* IN *THE NATION*, MARCH 11, 1936

For the most part, however, the author and his characters remind one of those tedious persons who in the theater indefatigably chat through the climaxes of the play, and whose vocal efforts have nothing to recommend them but their loudness.

### FROM MARY MCCARTHY'S REVIEW OF ROBERT GRAVES'S *I, CLAUDIUS* IN *THE NATION*, JUNE 13, 1934

[Mr. Graves] has put into the mouth of the unfortunate emperor an autobiography of such learning, spirit, and perspicacity that long-dead Claudius ought surely to live again[. . . .] In no respect is Mr. Graves guilty of writing history to suit his fancy, though, if presented with two tenable theories, he will, like any lively biographer, choose the more dramatic. His book is amazingly accurate and well informed, and at the same time full of color and imagination.

**SELDEN RODMAN**    I always had a high opinion of Mary's critical faculties, and I was glad to get her to review books for us. I don't think I would have dared cut or emend anything Mary wrote, because she already had a reputation for being touchy about such things. Not that I would have had to.

### FROM ELIZABETH HARDWICK'S FOREWORD TO *INTELLECTUAL MEMOIRS*

She was a prodigy from the first. I remember coming across an early review when I was doing some work in the New York Public Library. It was dazzling, a wonderfully accomplished composition, written soon after she left college.

She may have been a prodigy, but not everyone was prepared to recognize this. At the end of her life she wrote at length about her vexed relations with Malcolm Cowley, the books editor at *The New Republic*. Part of their trouble, she asserted, stemmed from his being a fellow traveler—not quite a Communist Party member but a subscriber to the Party's doctrine and also to its cant. Cowley had made it clear to her when she went for a job interview her last year at college that if she wasn't starving or a genius she had little claim on his attention. Early on he gave her a small review or two. After that the assignments stopped. All the same, every Wednesday she took the El down to West 21 Street and joined the cluster of hopeful reviewers waiting in the magazine's reception room, until finally one Wednesday she received what she believed might be her big break.

### FROM *INTELLECTUAL MEMOIRS*

[O]ne by one we mounted to Cowley's office, where shelves of books for review were ranged behind the desk, and there again we waited while he wriggled his eyebrows and silently puffed at his pipe as though trying to make up his mind[. . . .]

Cowley had [a cohort] by the name of Otis Ferguson, a real proletarian, who had been a sailor in the merchant marine. "Oat" was not in the book department; he wrote movie reviews. But he carried great weight with Cowley, though he may not have been a Marxist—he was more of a free-ranging literary bully without organizational ties. I had a queer time with him one evening when John and I went to look him up at his place on Cornelia Street, the deepest in the Village I had yet been. At our ring he came downstairs, but instead of asking us up to his place, he led us out to a bar for a drink, which seemed unfriendly, after he had given me his address and told me to drop by[. . . .] Anyway, whatever happened that evening and whatever caused it cannot have been the reason for my sudden fall from favor at *The New Republic*. No.

It was a book: *I Went to Pit College*, by Lauren Gilfillan, a Smith girl who had spent a year working in a coal mine[. . . .] The book was causing a stir, and Cowley, as he handed it over to me, benignly, let me understand that he was *giving me my chance*[. . . .] He was allowing me plenty of space, to do a serious review, not another three-hundred-word bit. And with my name, I dared hope, on the cover. I got the message: I was supposed to like the book. For the first time, and the last, I wrote to order[. . . .] With the result, of course, that I wrote a lifeless review, full of simulated praise. In short, a cowardly review.

### FROM MARY MCCARTHY'S REVIEW OF LAUREN GILFILLAN'S *I WENT TO PIT COLLEGE* IN *THE NEW REPUBLIC*, MAY 2, 1934

Marxian critics may not approve of Miss Gilfillan's book, since it is obstinately impartial and refuses to suggest remedies, but they and all its readers cannot help but feel the terrific reality it gives its subject.

### FROM *INTELLECTUAL MEMOIRS*

Cowley had second thoughts about the book. Whether the Party line had changed on it or whether for some other reason, he now decided that it was overrated[. . . .] [H]e printed my laudatory piece and followed it with *a correction*. The correction was signed only with initials: O.C.F. Oat of course[. . . .] I did not write for *The New Republic* again (nor was I asked to) till six years had passed; Cowley was gone, and [Edmund] Wilson had returned temporarily to his old post as book editor.

### FROM A CORRECTION SIGNED "OCF," *THE NEW REPUBLIC*, MAY 2, 1934

This book is of worth only in so far as the personal record of what happened to Miss Gilfillan rises above the artificiality of the whole business: it should never be taken for a gripping social document or even an unstudied and humanitarian gesture.

**ROB COWLEY**   There is nothing like an article gone wrong or sour to turn you forever against the person you deemed to be responsible. And with people like Mary McCarthy or Hemingway you have real haters. Boy, did those people hate. Whenever the subject of Mary McCarthy came up, there was always some crack or other from my father. I remember him saying she had a wonderful talent—for fouling her own nest. You have to remember that most of the time my father was an easy man to get along with.

*The New Republic* wasn't the only place where Mary McCarthy encountered class-war problems. She was aware that it was risky, if not foolhardy, to proclaim yourself a "royalist." But to call yourself a Roosevelt Democrat was hardly sufficient. Even old friends from Vassar were Norman Thomas socialists. It was the Communist Party that provided entrée at a significant number of publishing houses and magazines. Radical politics made good business sense—not only in publishing but in the theater. Like it or not, as time passed, politics and pleasure could not always be kept separate.

**SELDEN RODMAN**   We could see Roosevelt was not doing any of the things we'd hoped he'd be doing to cope. The New Deal had been put into effect in a halfhearted way, but none of the things he instituted were effective.

**ROSILLA HORNBLOWER HAWES**   Mary had never been political in school. Not at all. I used to lunch with her in New York in 1933 and 1934 when I was working for the Consumer's League down at Twentieth and Fifth Avenue, pushing labor legislation, and she seemed no more political then than she had at Vassar.

**SELDEN RODMAN**   She was less interested in politics than she was literary. She talked a lot about politics anyway, though I couldn't tell you what she said.

### FROM "MY CONFESSION"

[T]hrough our professional connections, [John and I] began to take part in a left-wing life, to which we felt superior, which we laughed at, but which nevertheless was influencing us without our being aware of it. If the composition of the body changes every seven years, the composition of our minds during the seven years changed, so that though our thoughts looked the same to us, inside we had been altered, like an old car which has had part after part replaced in it under the hood.

We wore our rue with a difference; we should never have considered joining the Communist Party. We were not even fellow-travelers; we did not sign petitions or join "front" groups. We were not fools, after all[. . . .] We argued with the comrades backstage in the dressing rooms and at literary cocktail parties; I was attacked by a writer in the *New Masses*. We knew about Lovestoneites and Trotskyites, even while we were ignorant of the labor theory of value, the law of uneven development, the theory of permanent revolution *vs.* socialism in one country, and so on. "Lovestone is a Lovestoneite!" John wrote in wax on his dressing-room mirror, and on his door in the old Civic Repertory he put up a sign: "Through these portals pass some of the most beautiful tractors in the Ukraine."

After a brief post-Prohibition debauch of gin slingers and manhattans, now, more often than not, you had to stand or sit on the floor and make do with straight gin in a paper cup or glass tumbler that was none too well washed. Despite its sleek chrome lines, that Russel Wright cocktail shaker was fast becoming an anachronism. As were bridge parties and quiet dinners at home. Now you went to dances at Webster Hall and parties in borrowed apartments to raise money for the sharecroppers and the Scottsboro boys or the latest worthy cause.

When there was a host and hostess things tended to be more civilized. You did not have to pay for your drink or sit on the floor and on occasion you met someone who would become a friend for life. But of course if you were looking for real excitement a cocktail party couldn't hold a candle to a strike or demonstration.

### FROM *INTELLECTUAL MEMOIRS*

At Dwight Macdonald's apartment near the river, on East 51st Street, I went to a cocktail party for the sharecroppers, wearing a big mustard-yellow sombrero-like felt hat[. . . .] Fred Dupee, a Yale classmate of Dwight's, was much taken with my hat; he was just back from a year in Mexico, and I was meeting him for the first time. I was struck by his very straight, almost black hair, like an Indian's, by his blue eyes, and by a certain jauntiness. This must have been about the time of his conversion to Communism[. . . .] It was possibly through Fred that Dwight, who was still on *Fortune*, was giving a party for sharecroppers and making an embarrassed speech before literally passing the hat[. . . .] The Macdonald drinks were free and in glasses, and to sit on they had dark-blue outsize furniture looking like a design edict and made by a firm called Modernage.

**SELDEN RODMAN**   In the late winter of 1934 I organized a walkout at the Waldorf in support of the waiters, who were out on strike. The hotel had hired scabs to take the place of the waiters who were outside the hotel marching on a picket line. I called up all the intellectuals I knew—and, from *Common Sense*, I knew them all—and asked them to join us. Dreiser was there at my invitation, as well as Robert Benchley and Dorothy Parker. We were all dressed up. At one point I jumped up on a table and said, "All of the waiters in this hotel are on strike for a decent wage, but they're not the only ones on strike. The guests are going to strike with them."

## FROM *INTELLECTUAL MEMOIRS*

> Johnsrud and I joined, also in evening dress—Eunice was wearing a tiara. At another table Dorothy Parker and Alexander Woollcott and Heywood Broun got up to walk out, too[. . . .] It was all in the papers the next day, though Johnsrud and I were too unknown to be in the story[. . . .] It was the only time I saw Dorothy Parker close up, and I was disappointed by her dumpy appearance. Today television talk shows would have prepared me.

The Waldorf strike might seem more than a bit like a collegiate prank, but the plight of the workingman, whether he was a waiter or a coal miner, was all too real. Times were hard. Still, for a graduate of Vassar or Yale there were almost always possibilities for employment. At Beekman Place review assignments continued to trickle in. The correction signed O.C.F. was no more than a temporary embarrassment. Johnsrud was working fairly steadily in the theater, although casting directors passed him over for starring roles.

## FROM "MY CONFESSION"

> There was something about [John] both baleful and quizzical; whenever he stepped on the stage he had the ironic air of a symbol. This curious appearance of his disqualified him for most Broadway roles; he was too young for character parts and too bald for juveniles. Yet just this disturbing ambiguity—a Communist painter friend did a drawing of him that brought out a resemblance to Lenin—suited the portentous and equivocal atmosphere of left-wing drama. He smiled dryly at Marxist terminology, but there was social anger in him[. . . .] I suppose there was something in him of both the victim and the leader, an undertone of totalitarianism; he was very much interested in the mythic qualities of leadership and talked briskly about a Farmer-Labor party in his stage English accent[. . . .] In personal life he was very winning, but that is beside the point here.

In April 1934, there was some welcome news. A Broadway producer, who held an option on a Clifford Odets play that would later become *Awake and Sing*, took a six-month option on a play Johnsrud had written. At last, it seemed as if all the promise his wife and her friends had seen in Harold Johnsrud would be fulfilled. Under the circumstances, a bit of celebration seemed in order.

### FROM MARY MCCARTHY'S LETTER TO FRANI BLOUGH, N.D. [C. APRIL 1934]

Today, after four sidecars apiece, we go on the wagon[. . . .] We played bridge with Eunice and Selden this evening, using them as a means of sobering up, like a Turkish bath or a brisk walk. (Eunice tends more to the Turkish bath school of revivification.) Last Saturday night we went up to Harlem to a pansy joint, and relived all the early works of Carl Van Vechten[. . . .] There were Lesbians in tailored suits, fairies with lipstick dating each other up, a foul ladies room, a lot of drunks, and an effeminate one who quietly vomited in the middle of the room. The ventilation was almost nonexistent. The evening was unsuccessful to a degree.

For months she and Johnsrud put off paying their rent, comfortable in the knowledge that they would make it good when Frank Merlin mounted a production of the play he had optioned. However, that fall, Merlin let his option lapse. Johnsrud scrambled to find another patron, with no success. All of this she touched on in her memoirs, without suggesting how crushing the blow had been at the time.

### FROM MARY MCCARTHY'S LETTER TO FRANI BLOUGH, SEPTEMBER 23, 1934

Did you hear about Merlin?[. . .] [T]he gist of it is that Merlin's backer faded out on him, and *Anti-Climax* is now back on the market[. . . .] The futility of all this scrabbling for money sometimes overwhelms me, and I sometimes wonder what would happen, if, when the money runs out as it soon will, we didn't frantically exert ourselves to borrow more for purposes of survival, but just stopped fighting and let ourselves go.

All her life, whenever Mary McCarthy was faced with a situation she found intolerable, her health broke. That October, she was rushed to New York Hospital with abdominal pain—acute appendicitis. From her hospital bed she had to place an emergency call to her grandfather Preston for help with her medical bills. But by Christmas she was back home and had regained her taste for gossip, even if she was going to have to do without champagne for a while.

In the summer of 1935, she was asked by *The Nation* to write a series on the lamentable state of book reviewing in America. She accepted at once. Either to lend weight to the series or to keep her pen in check, Margaret Marshall was brought in as co-author. The series, which started in November, ran in five installments, bringing both authors instant notoriety. In later years, when there was no one alive to dispute her claim,

Mary McCarthy would say that although she and Margaret Marshall shared the research for the series, the writing was mostly hers. Reading the pieces, one can only believe her. As each bailiwick of the book reviewing establishment is held up to scrutiny, a voice that is clear and unflinching and very like that of the mature Mary McCarthy never hesitates to pass judgment. Two critics she singled out for praise: John Chamberlain, the daily reviewer for the *Times*, and Edmund Wilson, who she noted was the only practicing American critic to make "any extended effort to relate what is valuable in modern literature to the body of literature of the past." Most of their fellow practitioners, who were so quick to praise as to form a veritable "publisher's claque," received short shrift.

### FROM "OUR CRITICS, RIGHT OR WRONG. II: THE ANTI-INTELLECTUALS"

Unequipped to deal with complicated artistic or intellectual problems, [the anti-intellectuals] instinctively resist them and affect to despise them. They write rave notices of second-rate, untaxing novels[. . . .] They plug their favorite writers, applaud one another's efforts, and bolster one another's opinions at literary teas.

### FROM "OUR CRITICS, RIGHT OR WRONG. IV: THE PROLETARIANS"

The Marxist critic, as he appears in the pages of the *New Masses*, is an extremely complicated animal. Though he has cut himself off from the bourgeois critics, a number of vestigial traces of the bourgeois intellectual life still cling to him[. . . .] Moreover, he has not abjured the literary back-scratching which goes on in high-powered capitalist literary circles

### FROM "BOOKS OF THE TIMES," BY JOHN CHAMBERLAIN, DECEMBER 12, 1935

The main topic of conversation in that unidentified section of the town known as "literary New York" is a series that has been running fortnightly in *The Nation* [. . .] the concoction of Mary McCarthy and Margaret Marshall, two bright girls who have not been conspicuously reverent even toward their own literary editor, Mr. Joseph Wood Krutch[. . . .] But the outcries of the wounded, which range in tone from the bitter to the jocose, are not particularly concerned with impartiality[. . . .] All I can say for myself is that I have been let off very lightly and have therefore no personal complaints to utter.

If her career was taking off, there was little financial gain to show for it. To supplement what she was earning, she had to take a job as a secretary to Margaret Marshall's former lover Ben Stolberg, a well-regarded labor writer. The social rewards, however, were almost immediate. Soon she was being invited to parties by the writer James T. Farrell. Years later, she would write that Farrell had looked her up because she had given a good review in *Common Sense* to *The Young Manhood of Studs Lonigan*, but as Farrell himself remembered it, the pieces in *The Nation* were what turned the trick.

#### FROM *INTELLECTUAL MEMOIRS*

All we had in common was being Irish, Middle Western, ex-Catholic, and liking baseball (and I was only half-Midwestern and half-Irish). But Farrell, gregarious and hospitable, took to me anyway.

**MADDIE ALDRICH DE MOTT**   Mary had been such a student at college and she'd had only John as a boyfriend, and I think that the fact that she was becoming quite successful with people in New York began to go to her head. She and I were talking about somebody who had gone off with another man and I said innocently, "But she'd only just been married." Mary, who was far more sophisticated, said, "Well, you just wait and see. That doesn't mean a thing."

By 1936, in smart New York circles, fascism was coming to be regarded as a greater threat to world peace than communism. Party members were urging socialists to join forces to present a popular front against Hitler and Mussolini, much as they had done with great success in France. To support Stalin was to support a strong, if occasionally intemperate, force for world order. It was still possible to overlook Stalin's attacks upon his former Bolshevik comrades. The first of the Moscow trials would not come until the summer. Trotsky was in exile, seeking asylum, but still very much alive. The Fascists in Spain, with help from Mussolini, were making significant strides in undermining the Loyalist government, but a full-blown civil war was yet to erupt.

At a dance at Webster Hall, Mary McCarthy was introduced to a tall young man by the name of John Porter. The introduction was made by Eunice Clark, who had put her marriage to Selden Rodman firmly behind her and was savoring the sudden intimacies fostered by radical politics. That spring, Harold Johnsrud was out of town, touring with Maxwell Anderson's *Winterset*. Upon Johnsrud's return, later in May, Mary asked for a divorce.

#### FROM *INTELLECTUAL MEMOIRS*

"FelLOW WORKers, join our RANKS!" It was 1936, and there I was, Mary Johnsrud, marching down lower Broadway in a May Day parade, chanting that slogan at the crowds watching on the sidewalk. "FelLOW WORKers!" Nobody, I think, joined us; they just watched. We were having fun. Beside me marched a tall fair young man, former correspondent of the Paris *Herald*.

### From Elizabeth Hardwick's Foreword to
### Intellectual Memoirs

So, we meet her here in 1936, marching in a Communist May Day parade, marching along with John Porter, a new man who looked like Fred MacMurray. The conjunction of romance and the events of the day is characteristic of Mary at all points in her life.

### From Intellectual Memoirs

John Porter was tall, weak, good-looking, a good dancer; his favorite writer was Rémy de Gourmont, and he had an allergy to eggs in any form. He went to Williams (I still have his Psi U pin) and was the only son of elderly parents. When I met him, he had been out of work for some time and lived by collecting rents on Brooklyn and Harlem real estate for his mother. The family, de-gentrifying, occupied the last "white" house in Harlem, on East 122nd Street, and owned the beautiful old silver Communion cup from Trinity Church in Brooklyn; it must have been given to an ancestor as the last vestryman[. . . .]

He was in love with me or thought he was; my energy must have made an appeal to him—he probably hoped it would be catching. Despite his unemployment, dour mother, rent-collecting, he was gay and full of charm. He was fond of making love and giving pleasure.

**Eleanor Perényi** I met John Porter in Taxco, Mexico, in the summer of 1936. I was eighteen and he was one of several boyfriends. He looked like Fred MacMurray, and was a good dancer. He had a dilapidated old jalopy that kept breaking down on expeditions. Frankly, when I discovered all those years later that he was the Young Man in the first chapter of *The Company She Keeps*, I was amazed. He was such a lightweight I would never have thought him eligible for somebody of Mary's caliber.

### From Intellectual Memoirs

I had "told" John, who was back from playing *Winterset* on the road. I said I was in love with John Porter and wanted to marry him. This was in Central Park while we watched some ducks swimming, as described in "Cruel and Barbarous Treatment." Except for that detail, there is not much resemblance between the reality and the story I wrote two years later—the first I ever published[. . . .] I was trying, I think, to give some form to what had happened between John, John Porter, and me—in other words, to explain it to myself.

Rather than continue sharing the one room on Beekman Place, she moved in with her Cushing friend Nathalie Swan, "the Sphinx of the smoking-room," who was living with her parents on the Upper East Side. Safe in the Swans' fine Georgian town house, she waited for her grandfather Preston to secure for her the best lawyer in Reno. But why smash apart a perfectly adequate marriage for no good reason and then rush off to a young man she had only just met? It was a question her closest

friends made some attempt to answer. It was a question she herself tried
to answer two years later, skimming over the whole tangled issue of sex,
in "Cruel and Barbarous Treatment"—a story as stylized as any comedy
of manners, which she liked to say she wrote under the pernicious influence of Henry James.

## FROM "CRUEL AND BARBAROUS TREATMENT"

She could not bear to hurt her husband. She impressed this on the
Young Man, on her confidantes, and finally on her husband himself.
The thought of Telling Him actually made her heart turn over in a sudden and sickening way, she said. This was true, and yet she knew that
being a potential divorcee was deeply pleasurable in somewhat the
same way that being an engaged girl had been[. . . .]

She told him at breakfast in a fashionable restaurant, because, she
said, he would be better able to control his feelings in public. When he
called at once for the check, she had a spasm of alarm lest in an access
of brutality or grief he leave her there alone, conspicuous, and, as it
were, unfulfilled. But they walked out of the restaurant together and
through the streets, hand in hand, tears streaming "unchecked," she
whispered to herself, down their faces. Later they were in the Park, by
an artificial lake, watching the ducks swim. The sun was very bright,
and she felt a kind of superb pathos in the careful and irrelevant attention they gave to the pastoral scene. This was, she knew, the most profound, the most subtle, the most idyllic experience of her life.

**MARGARET MILLER**   I felt Mary had outgrown John. What Frani told me
was that he was jealous of Mary's success, her going off and writing those
book reviews.

**SELDEN RODMAN**   I tolerated Johnsrud, but I can't say I was drawn to him.
He had a kind of snide sense of humor. I didn't see the charming side to him.
Maybe that was something he reserved for women.

## FROM INTELLECTUAL MEMOIRS

He took it hard, much harder than I had been prepared for. I felt bad
for him; in fact I was torn. The worst was that, when it came down to
it, I did not know why I was leaving him. I still had love of some sort
left for him, and seeing him suffer made me know it.

When it came time to board a train for Nevada, John Porter was at the
station to see her off. After Reno, she would spend some time with her
grandparents in Seattle before returning to this young lover, who was
already beginning to bore her. Not recognizing that her interest was waning, Porter had gotten a contract to write a travel book on Mexico. He had
every intention of combining business with pleasure and turning the
book project into a cheap honeymoon. On her way west, alone in the
club car, she was free to read and smoke, to work on a book review, to

fend off the advances of the occasional traveling salesman, and to figure
out how she was going to tell John Porter she did not want to go with him
to Mexico. When the right salesman came along, wearing a custom-
ordered shirt with a monogram on the sleeve, she, like Margaret Sargent
in her short story "The Man in the Brooks Brothers Shirt," was free to follow him back to his compartment. And afterward, she, like Margaret Sargent, did not draw back from that whole tangled issue of sex.

### FROM "THE MAN IN THE BROOKS BROTHERS SHIRT"

*She liked him.* Why, it was impossible to say. The attraction was not sexual, for, as the whisky went down in the bottle, his face took on a more
and more porcine look that became so distasteful to her that she could
hardly meet his gaze, but continued to talk to him with a large, remote
stare, as if he were an audience of several hundred people[. . . .]

The train woke her the next morning as it jerked into a Wyoming station. "Evanston?" she wondered. It was still dark. The Pullman shade
was drawn, and she imagined at first that she was in her own lower
berth. She knew that she had been drunk the night before, but reflected
with satisfaction that Nothing Had Happened. It would have been terrible if . . . She moved slightly and touched the man's body[. . . .]

Waves of shame began to run through her, like savage internal
blushes, as fragments of the night before presented themselves for
inspection[. . . .] She had fought him off for a long time, but at length
her will had softened. She had felt tired and kind, and thought, why
not? Then there had been something peculiar about the love-making
itself—but she could not recall what it was. She had tried to keep aloof
from it, to be present in body but not in spirit. Somehow that had not
worked out and she had been dragged in and humiliated.

In Reno, and then in Seattle, where she was staying with her grandparents for the first time since college, the former Mrs. Harold Johnsrud
received a barrage of phone calls from John Porter. Stuck with time on
her hands, she did not dwell on her faltering romance or failed marriage,
but turned her attention to writing a book review and then reporting a
political piece for *The Nation.* Although both efforts reflected a deepen-
ing interest in radical politics, the conclusions she arrived at owed little
to an understanding of Marxist theory or current developments in the
Soviet Union. What fascinated her about the politicians from her home
state of Washington was their flamboyant personalities. And what drew
her to the novel, along with the political message and the quality of the
writing, was the story of a love between two women—Sophia Willoughby,
"a country gentlewoman of birth, means, intelligence, force, and practicality," and Minna Lemuel, her estranged husband's mistress, a middle-
aged "Jewish *diseuse* and romantic revolutionary" with a beautiful voice
and charismatic personality.

## FROM "MY CONFESSION"

The first Moscow trial took place in August. I knew nothing of this event because I was in Reno and did not see the New York papers. Nor did I know that the Party line had veered to the right and that all the fellow-travelers would be voting, not for Browder as I was now prepared to do (if only I remembered to register), but for Roosevelt. Isolated from these developments in the mountain altitudes, I was blossoming like a lone winter rose overlooked by the frost into a revolutionary thinker of the pure, uncompromising strain. The detached particles of the past three years' experience suddenly "made sense," and I saw myself as a radical. "Book Bites Mary," wrote back a surprised literary editor when I sent him, from Reno, a radiant review of a novel about the Paris Commune [*sic*] that ended with the heroine sitting down to read the *Communist Manifesto*.

## FROM MARY MCCARTHY'S REVIEW OF SYLVIA TOWNSEND WARNER'S *SUMMER WILL SHOW* IN *THE NATION*, AUGUST 15, 1936

[Sophia] works, singing on street corners, distributing leaflets, scavenging scrap metal for bullets; works because she loves the Jewess, and because it is her nature to be efficient. Out of the defeat of the Paris Communists, Sophia salvages no shred of her personal life; she loses her husband, her money, her family connections; even the rebellious Jewess she forfeits on the barricades. The novel ends with the Englishwoman, physically beaten, shabby, sitting in the disordered apartment of her dead friend, opening, for the first time, the leaflets she has circulated, discovering the *Communist Manifesto*.

As the dénouement of *Summer Will Show*, where elegance burns into fervor, seems to me the most triumphal single moment in revolutionary fiction, so the whole elaborate, fine-spun novel seems the most skilful, the most surefooted, sensitive, witty piece of prose yet to have been colored by left-wing ideology.

As it turned out, Minna Lemuel would have a more lasting hold on Mary McCarthy's imagination than the *Communist Manifesto* or John Porter. Once Mary returned from Seattle she would have to somehow make this pleasure-loving young man understand that she had no wish to spend the rest of her life with him. Fortunately, it never came to that. In the belief that she would join him later, John Porter set off for Mexico without her. His first stop was Washington, D.C., where he made sure to telephone daily. She still had not told him when he finally set off in his car for the Mexican border. For a time she sent letters almost every day to the address he'd given her, general delivery in Laredo, but she never heard from him again.

In late fall, she received a strange package from someone whose name she didn't recognize. By then she was living in Greenwich Village and Johnsrud was living at a nearby hotel. "I am ashamed to say that I asked Johnsrud if he would come over and be with me while I opened it," she later wrote. "First we listened to be sure we could not hear any-thing ticking—but inside all we found was a quite hideous pony-skin throw lined with the cheapest sleaziest sky-blue rayon, totally unlike Porter." When she wired the sender, she got a telegram saying "PACKAGE COMES FROM JOHN PORTER MEXICO." More than a year later she learned that John Porter was dead. Ever after she blamed herself.

### FROM *INTELLECTUAL MEMOIRS*

If it had not been for me, he would never have *been* in Mexico. He would still be collecting rents for his parents. And, if I had gone along with him, instead of copping out, I would *never* have let him overstay his visa, which had caused him to land in prison, which caused him to contract diphtheria or typhus or whatever it was that killed him when, on his release, the woman he had been living with let him come back and stay in her stable.

**ELEANOR PERÉNYI**   The story Mary had of Johnny's death was so differ-ent from the one my mother had heard in Mexico, and I'm fairly sure ours was the correct one. Mary was told that he caught some tropical bug and died of neglect. What she didn't know until we told her was that he had been hav-ing an affair with the wife of an important Mexican politico, and down there it was believed that the politician had simply had someone slip poison into Johnny's drink. Obviously, this version was a less attractive explanation for his having so mysteriously vanished from her life, and she didn't really accept it. She wrote me shortly before she died asking me, not for the first time, what I thought had happened because she was going to put it in her autobiography. But when she did, she still told it wrong. She said, for instance, that he'd got into trouble over his visa—quite a new touch, and you didn't need a visa for Mexico, only a tourist card. Yet she was such a stickler for accuracy, it's strange.

No divorce in real life is as free of painful recriminations as the divorce in "Cruel and Barbaric Treatment." With the confessions and rev-elations attending the breakup of McCarthy's marriage, it had become clear that her liaison with John Porter was by no means the first infi-delity. Each partner had been unfaithful to the other: she with three men who were little better than strangers; Johnsrud at the theater and then closer to home, with two of the wives who came over with their hus-bands to play cards, most notably Eunice Clark.

That fall, she moved from temporary quarters at the Lafayette Hotel to a tiny studio apartment on Gay Street. For John Porter, whom she had so sadly disappointed, she had no immediate replacement. Her new apartment had few male visitors. When the real man in the Brooks Brothers shirt turned up—a married businessman from Pittsburgh who sold bathroom fixtures—she was happy enough to accompany him to the World Series, but not quite so pleased at the thought of being seen with him. To have sex in her new apartment with this man who had picked her up on the train was completely out of the question.

All the men who had flirted with her when she was safely married had vanished. For company she had to fall back on a few loyal friends and her former husband. When she wanted to go out to a bar for a drink, she would call him. After all, he was living close by. Having passed on the Howlands' furniture to someone who had some use for it, he had put a trunk of her possessions in storage and was staying at the Hotel Brevoort.

Why, if she had in fact loved him, had she walked out on Harold Johnsrud? At the end of her life, she would write, "No psychoanalyst ever offered a clue, except to tell me that I felt compelled to leave the man I loved because my parents had left *me*." With her low opinion of psychoanalysis, she was not inclined to bring forth such a theory unless it was to wreak havoc upon it. But at the end it was the best explanation she could come up with. For her, it may have promised the balm of a secular pardon. Seen in such a light, her smashing apart the household she had willed into being owed nothing to recklessness or caprice. It was simply an irresistible impulse she had inherited along with her Capital Elevator stock.

# Chapter Six

## PARTISAN REVIEW

In the fall of 1936, Mary McCarthy was suddenly free to embrace the unconventional life she had flirted with in college. Single again and living in a studio apartment in the Village, possessed of enviable good looks and a bit of a "name," she was well equipped to take advantage of her new freedom. If the men who had flocked to her side when she was Mrs. Harold Johnsrud saw fit to shun her company, she was not without options. From her walk-up she could make her way to men more inclined to appreciate her. Like Madame de Staël, she could gather about her a group of congenial intellectuals and writers. Or, like Czerna Wilson, she could partake of the pleasures of a bohemian salon.

Instead, she remained at home. For two months she struggled to piece together a life that was sensible and independent and not unduly extravagant. From her grandfather Preston, she was receiving $25 a week. Working half days for the gallery owner Mannie Rousuck she made another $15. Most nights she ate by herself at Shima's, a local place where the food was cheap and you did not stand out if you kept a book open by your plate. Sundays James Farrell's publisher would sometimes invite her to lunch with his family in Hartsdale.

Once in a while she would have an old friend over for a dinner cooked on a hot plate, but she could afford no lavish entertaining. If there was space at her table for only two guests, it didn't much matter. Martha McGahan, who was living and working in New York, *did* come to dinner, but Julia Denison had moved from the city, Maddie Aldrich was in California, and Frani Blough was busy getting her master's at Columbia.

Rather than stay home alone, she began to accept almost any invitation that came her way. Briefly she took up with Bob Misch, the secretary of the Wine and Food Society and continued to attend his dinners, making conversation and new connections with a table full of Stalinists and fellow travelers, long after she had tired of him.

One weekend, looking for help, she took the train up to Vassar to visit Miss Sandison. "Learn to live without love if you want to live *with* it," her old teacher told her. Always a gifted student, she was quick to grasp the import of Miss Sandison's advice. But to put this regimen into effect—to implement it within the confines of her small Village walk-up—seemed completely beyond her. "This thought greatly struck me, and still does," she wrote in her *Intellectual Memoirs*. "I am sure it is true but, unlike Miss Sandison, I am not up to it. I have seldom been capable of living without love, not for more than a month or so."

In 1952, in "My Confession," Mary McCarthy wrote of the powerful part played by chance in altering her personal and political history. She wrote of how, in November 1936, at a cocktail party to celebrate the publication of a book by Art Young, a *New Masses* cartoonist, "a novelist friend" came over and asked whether she thought Trotsky had a right to a hearing. Embarrassed by her ignorance, she had to ask him what he meant. A chance to answer Stalin's charges of treason, he explained. The "dimple-faced, shaggy-headed, earnest" friend was James Farrell. While she had been off at Reno, Zinovyev and Kamanev and sixteen other party officials had been convicted of treason and Trotsky had been convicted of plotting with the Nazis to overthrow Stalin. Once she was presented with the facts of the case, she said that of course Trotsky deserved a hearing. Farrell then moved on to the next group.

The way she saw it, if she had answered no, or had skipped the party, her life might have taken an altogether different direction. Within days she found her name listed on the letterhead of the Committee for the Defense of Leon Trotsky. Just as she was about to make an angry phone call to Farrell, demanding to have her name removed, she began receiving calls urging her—for her own good—to take her name off the letterhead. In the end she did not telephone Farrell and her name stayed on.

But having come to this decision out of inertia as much as sentiment, she now made it a point to get hold of the trial transcripts. Once she was satisfied that Zinovyev and his fellow defendants were indeed innocent, she began attending meetings of the Trotsky Defense Committee. Soon she was taking part in discussions and joining in the projects of a group of radicals who supported Trotsky but did not go along with his call for world revolution. For all that they were ready to rally to the defense of the "old man," they were not Trotskyists. They were anti-Stalinists, and that was as far as it went.

At those committee meetings she met a group of men who would inform her taste and color her opinions for more than two decades. But the immediate result of her staying on the committee's letterhead was to totally transform the tentative single life she had made for herself. No longer would she have to depend on her former husband or Bob Misch for an escort. She was having a flurry that not only rivaled but far surpassed that of her old friend and sometime rival Eunice Clark.

In "My Confession," written when she was just forty, Mary McCarthy portrayed her political conversion as the fortuitous culmination of an ebullient autumn spent dabbling in radical politics. She depicted it as the fitting conclusion to a liberation that had begun when she put her first marriage firmly behind her and set up on her own downtown. In *Intellectual Memoirs*, written when she was nearing the end of her life, she painted a less lighthearted picture of her first months on her own. Indeed she seemed to suggest that her decision to stay on the Trotsky Defense Committee may have been grounded in personal need as much as it had been in pure chance.

### FROM "MY CONFESSION"

This was in September and I was back in New York. The Spanish Civil War had begun. The pay-as-you-go parties were now all for the Loyalists, and young men were volunteering to go and fight in Spain. I read the paper every morning with tears of exaltation in my eyes, and my sympathies rained equally on Communists, Socialists, Anarchists, and the brave Catholic Basques. My heart was tense and swollen with popular-front solidarity. I applauded the Lincoln Battalion, protested nonintervention, hurried into Wanamaker's to look for cotton-lace stockings: I was boycotting silk on account of Japan in China. I was careful to smoke only union-made cigarettes; the white package with Sir Walter Raleigh's portrait came proudly out of my pocketbook to rebuke Chesterfields and Luckies.

### FROM *INTELLECTUAL MEMOIRS*

The one-room apartment I moved into on Gay Street had eleven sides. I counted one day when I was sick in bed. The normal quota, including floor and ceiling, would have been six. But my place had many jogs, many irregularities. There was a tiny kitchen and a bath suited to a bird[. . . .] All this was very different from our life on Beekman Place; it was as though the number of my friends had shrunk to fit the space I now lived in.

In early November, when James Farrell approached her at that cocktail party, he was setting in motion a chain of events that would cut her loose from her old life more completely than any divorce ever could. But, as she saw it, there were no " 'great' decisions" in life. History was riddled with the "whims of chance" and with "inadvertence." As it happened, she was not the only one to see things that way.

### FROM "MY CONFESSION"

Trotsky himself, looking at his life in retrospect, was struck, as most of us are on such occasions, by the role chance had played in it. He tells how one day, during Lenin's last illness, he went duck-shooting with an old hunter in a canoe on the River Dubna, walked through a bog in felt boots—only a hundred steps—and contracted influenza. This was the reason he was ordered to Sukhu for the cure, missed Lenin's funeral, and had to stay in bed during the struggle for primacy that raged that autumn and winter.

Once people began to telephone to urge her to drop off the committee's letterhead, she was no more able to take her name off than she had been able to give up on dour "Miss Gowrie" when Annie Wright classmates declared her to be the worst possible chaperone for their Saturday horseback rides. Decades later, she and Farrell would still be arguing about whether he had the right to bring her to such a pass. The debate continued even though she had every reason to believe he had done her a great favor.

### FROM JAMES FARRELL'S LETTER TO MARY McCARTHY, SEPTEMBER 15, 1967

A matter of memory and the past[. . . .] The party was not solemn and all Trotsky worship. I did not misrepresent in getting you to join the Committee for the Defense of Leon Trotsky. There was a very distinguished list of people on the Committee. You were not much known then. I was complimenting you, and making a small opportunity for you.

### FROM McCARTHY'S LETTER TO FARRELL, OCTOBER 25, 1967

I knew you were complimenting me when you asked my opinion (for I really had no title to one) but I didn't think I was being asked for a signature. But I've never held that against you; it changed my life—for the better.

At first, neither she nor her friends seemed to take her political conversion seriously. The only immediate effect was to push her into an entirely new social set, one which possessed a certain glamour, even though she did not find all of its members congenial.

### FROM INTELLECTUAL MEMOIRS

I remember a downtown meeting of some Trotskyist group where I first saw Diana Trilling; with her dark eyes and flaring nostrils, she looked like Katharine Cornell. Among Stalinist males, I heard, the Trotskyists were believed to have a monopoly on "all the beautiful" girls. That included Diana and Eunice's sister, Eleanor Clark, who would soon marry a secretary of Trotsky's to get him U.S. citizenship. It was said to have been a "white" marriage, like Auden's with Erika Mann. Pretentious, I thought. I didn't like Eleanor Clark, and we barely acknowledged each other, though we belonged politically to the same circle and had been a class apart at Vassar.

**ROSILLA HORNBLOWER HAWES**   I used to lunch with Mary. We were good friends. One day at lunch she announced that she had become an anti-Stalinist and there was a glint of mischief in her eye. I thought it was just Mary running against the tide. I didn't think that Mary had any political convictions at all, one way or another. The truth is all her friends at the time were Stalinists. She was taking the opposite side just to be contrary, to *épater les bourgeois*.

Because he had no power and no way to implement any plan or program, Leon Trotsky offered little for a political novice to criticize—particularly a political novice with a lifelong fondness for deposed princes in exile. For the time being, she was prepared to put aside her customary skepticism. If nothing else, by joining the Trotsky Defense Committee she was allying herself with radicals whose style was very much to her taste. Unfortunately, this style was not to the taste of her friend Bob Misch. In a story called "The Genial Host," she would later describe a gathering not unlike one of Misch's dinners held at the home of a man-about-town called Pflaumen—a gathering where her heroine, Meg Sargent, throws the entire table into an uproar by lashing out at a fellow guest who expresses his disgust at all the "petty political squabbles" between the various leftist factions in Spain.

## FROM "THE GENIAL HOST"

Suddenly you knew that you must cut yourself off from these people, must demonstrate conclusively that you did not belong here. You took a deep breath and leaned across the table toward John Peterson. "God damn you," you said in a very loud voice, such as you had once heard a priest use to denounce sinners from the pulpit, "God damn you, what about Andrés Nin?" You felt your body begin to shake with stage fright and the blood rush up into your face and you heard the gasp go around the table, and you were gloriously happy because you had been rude and politically unfashionable, and really carried beyond yourself, an angel with a flaming sword[. . . .]

You knew that you were not a violent Trotskyist[. . . .] It was just that you were temperamentally attracted to unpopular causes: when you were young, it had been the South, the Dauphin, Bonnie Prince Charlie; later it was Debs and now Trotsky that you loved. You admired this romantic trait in yourself and you would confess humorously: "All I have to do is be *for* somebody and he loses." Now it came to you that perhaps that was just another way of showing off, of setting yourself apart from the run of people. Your eyes began to fill with tears of shame; you felt like Peter in the Garden, but yours was, you knew, the greater blasphemy: social pressure had made Peter deny the Master; it had made you affirm him—it was the difference between plain and fancy cowardice.

Meg Sargent's moment of dispiriting self-knowledge no doubt owes something to a similar discovery made by her creator. But at the end of her life Mary McCarthy would dismiss the story out of hand. She would fault it not for anything it said about Meg Sargent but for what it did *not* say about her ties to Misch-Pflaumen.

### FROM *INTELLECTUAL MEMOIRS*

If I may give an opinion, it is the weakest thing in the book. No doubt that is because I was unwilling to face the full reality of the relationship. In real life I slept with him and in the story I don't. I suppose I was ashamed. Misch was eager to give me expensive presents (such as handbags) and to do services for me that I didn't want. Even after I stopped sleeping with him, which was soon, he kept on asking me to those dinners, and I kept on accepting, because of his insistence and because, as the chapter says, (though without mentioning the sex between us), I was not quite ready to break with him, being still "so poor, so loverless, so lonely."

The guests at those little dinners were mostly Stalinists, which was what smart, successful people in that New York world were. And they were mostly Jewish; as was often pointed out to me, with gentle amusement, I was the only non-Jewish person in the room.

Just as she had never been at ease with Elinor Coleman her first year at Vassar, she was never totally comfortable with Bob Misch or his particular kind of Jewishness. With his "short, stocky, dark, well-fed body" and his love of rich food and fine wine and expensive furniture, he was in fact more than a little reminiscent of the Seattle Morgensterns. It would be years before she would acknowledge her own Jewish blood.

By joining the Trotsky Defense Committee she had not only allied herself with radicals who were very much to her taste but she had also vastly improved her social life. Suddenly she had meetings and fund-raisers and cocktail parties to attend. She was running into men she had glimpsed as Mrs. Harold Johnsrud and meeting new ones with whom she found she now had a great deal in common. Soon the men in her life began to increase at a dizzying rate—men of every description, from truck drivers to Yale graduates. The men did not have to be handsome for her to find them attractive. Not all of them were anti-Stalinists. Some of them would go on to become lifelong friends.

### FROM *INTELLECTUAL MEMOIRS*

Once I got started, I saw all sorts of men that winter. Often one led to another. Most of them I slept with at least one time[. . . .] I did not go to bars alone, so someone must have taken me—probably John— and then left.

It was getting rather alarming. I realized one day that in twenty-four hours I had slept with three different men. And one morning I was in bed with somebody while over his head I talked on the telephone with somebody else. Though slightly scared by what things were coming to, I did not *feel* promiscuous. Maybe no one does. And maybe more girls sleep with more men than you would ever think to look at them.

**FROM JEAN STROUSE'S REVIEW OF *INTELLECTUAL MEMOIRS* IN *THE NEW YORK TIMES BOOK REVIEW*, MAY 24, 1992**

Maybe nobody *does* feel promiscuous—McCarthy simply did in the 1930's what other women have done before and since, she just wrote about it earlier and more frankly than most—but what did she feel in all this frenetic activity? What was she searching for in the eyes and sexual responses of men?

**SUSAN SONTAG**   I know very little about Mary's sexual life except for what she chose to tell—which was simply to give us the names and some suggestion of quantity. But I never have the feeling that she enjoyed sex from anything she ever wrote. There's no sensuality in her writing. I never feel that. It's just something you know how to do and that men like to do and because you're so pretty they want to do it with you. And then when they do it with you, you have something on them. You also have something to say for yourself which you are pleased with. And then you have some connection or power over them. And that seems to be all that it was about.

**FROM RICHARD EDER'S REVIEW OF *INTELLECTUAL MEMOIRS* IN THE *LOS ANGELES TIMES*, MAY 12, 1992**

It would be a mistake to think that any of this sex is set down sexily. *Catalogue* is the right word. One suspects that in their frequent-flier phase, the affairs were the study of an idea. They were the Vassar woman's passage through Bohemia; a course number might be assigned: Emancipation 202.

**DIANA TRILLING**   You've no doubt read the account from the second volume of her memoirs, all about her sexual life when she first lived in New York. Now, you're going to have to put this in a context which I supply of very great sexual tolerance. And within this context of my sexual tolerance, I think of that kind of promiscuity—sleeping with a different person every day, as she says she did, and sometimes different people twice or three times a day—as pathological. It has nothing to do with the fact that she is a woman. I would think that was pathological in a man. Never to have enough emotion generated out of the sexual encounter to want to reproduce that situation with that individual and not go on to experiment with another one immediately. I don't care if she wanted to sleep around, but not in this way. It gives me the creeps.

**FROM *INTELLECTUAL MEMOIRS***

I was able to compare the sexual equipment of the various men I made love with, and there were amazing differences, in both length and massiveness. One handsome married man, who used to arrive with two Danishes from a very good bakery, had a penis about the size and shape of a lead pencil; he shall remain nameless. In my experience, there was usually a relation to height, as Philip Rahv and Bill Mangold, both tall men, bore out. There may be dwarfish men with monstrously large organs, but I have never known one.

In her seventies, as Mary McCarthy went on to list the sizes and shapes of the male organs she encountered during her stay on Gay Street, she seemed intent on leaving nothing out. At moments she seemed almost elated. Her excitement did not seem to be sexual and one had the feeling it never was: it was the sheer scope of her adventures that seems to galvanize her. All the same, she recognized that the list was alarming. But this frisson was nothing to the alarm she must have felt fifty years earlier, that morning on Gay Street when her life seemed to be spinning out of control.

In the early winter of 1936, Mary was careful to make sure that her life *appeared* to be in order. On a good morning it may have seemed that way to her, too. Just before leaving for Reno, she had been introduced by Eunice Clark to the publisher Pat Covici, who had read her pieces in *The Nation*. At their first meeting she had let him know that she would be interested in an editorial position, and he had promised to keep her in mind. That fall, her precarious financial situation took a turn for the better when she was offered a part-time job as a reader at the publishing house of Covici-Friede. At the end of the year she was hired as a full-time editorial assistant at twenty-five dollars a week. The job was not glamorous and she had very little power. But by joining Covici-Friede, she was getting a chance to see the book business from the other side.

That winter, with the same thoroughness she brought to her reviewing for *The Nation* she proceeded to acquire the skills of a first-rate proofreader and copy editor. With little effort she mastered the arcane symbols, signs, marks, and abbreviations of her new craft—precise notations that she would avail herself of, whether it was called for or not, throughout her writing life. When she had the time, she tried to take advantage of the pleasant distractions afforded by her new job. There were book parties to attend, and long lunches and drinks with promising young authors. There was one memorable lunch, when Pat Covici asked her along to meet John Steinbeck, the house's most celebrated author. But if there was no love lost between the author of *In Dubious Battle* and his book's most acerbic critic, her employer did not seem to notice.

Any trouble she ran into at Covici-Friede seemed to stem from the politics of her co-workers, many of them fellow travelers or outright Stalinists. In her view, they were little better than the Stalinists who ran the books department of *New Masses*. Concerned with the political content and utility of a book rather than its quality, certain of their judgments, oblivious of aesthetics, they were the spiritual heirs of the Puritans and latter-day "Zeal-of-the-land-Busys." Chief among them was the woman who shared her office—a "long-nosed Stalinist" who disapproved of her long lunches and frequent phone calls and eventually reported her for "persistent lateness to work."

Much of the time it was not only her harried social life that was taking time from her paying job. She was continuing to do both book reviewing and longer pieces for *The Nation* and that winter she began preparing a follow-up to the attention-getting series she had done with Margaret Marshall. This time she was taking a look at a season's worth of theater criticism, and she was not going to have to share the credit. Unfortunately, she was not quite so confident of her opinions here. When she went to see one of the plays she would be discussing, she frequently called on her former husband for his company and expertise. With Johnsrud at her side, she did not shrink from casting a jaundiced eye upon the nation's most revered drama critics or from laying bare the limitations of two beloved icons of the American stage. In "Our Actors and the Critics," which ran in the spring of 1937, she announced that Katharine Cornell was regarded by members of her profession as "no actress at all, but an ambitious, unimaginative mediocre young woman whose fortune it is to own a face that is an exotic mask." She then went on to inform readers that "Lynn Fontanne's talents are completely worn out."

In the end, this two-part series for *The Nation* did not have the impact of its predecessor. Indeed, in later years McCarthy would choose to make no mention of it. But it was no small achievement. At the same time that she was holding her own at *The Nation* and holding down a publishing job, she was making her way among a group of tough-minded radicals. She was securing a place for herself, and, in addition, she was going to some lengths to make a place for Dwight Macdonald, who had quit his job at *Fortune* over censorship of a damning piece he had written on U.S. Steel and was living with his wife Nancy in a walk-up on East Tenth Street, scraping by on their savings and her trust fund and whatever he could earn with his writing.

## FROM DWIGHT MACDONALD'S INTRODUCTION OF MARY MCCARTHY AT THE 92ND STREET Y, NEW YORK CITY, NOVEMBER 10, 1963

The time was the winter of 1937. The place was the Old English Coffee Shoppe, which was paneled in fumed oak and located on Fortieth Street, near the Public Library. My companions at lunch were Margaret Marshall, who was then the literary editor of *The Nation*, and Mary McCarthy. Up to that time I'd been a mild fellow traveler, contributed to sharecroppers and so on. The *Time-Fortune* unit of the Newspaper Guild was actually founded in my apartment, and that the organizer of it was a perfectly avowed Communist didn't bother me at the time—didn't bother anybody at the time.

But now, on this day, these two women were taking it for granted

that the Moscow trials—the second of which had just been concluded—
were frame-ups. As usual, I was incredulous. I said it couldn't be and
why did they confess and so on. And also, as usual, to my credit, I was
somewhat shaken. Shaken enough to buy a few days later the transcript of the trial, which the comrades were foolish enough to sell at a
cheap price. And when I read the record of the second Moscow trial I
concluded that Mary had been right, that indeed it was a frame-up.

#### FROM "MY CONFESSION"

Most of us who became anti-Communists at the time of the trials were
drawn in, like me, by accident and almost unwillingly. Looking back,
as on a love affair, a man could say that if he had not had lunch in a
certain restaurant on a certain day, he might not have been led to ponder the facts of the Moscow trials. Or not then at any rate.

Her arguments may have been enough to persuade Dwight Macdonald and they may have been as well reasoned as those of the most committed anti-Stalinist, but, in the view of her friends from the thirties and
forties as well as those acquaintances who had little use for her, her politics were not to be taken seriously. Sometimes she herself seemed to
subscribe to this view. In "My Confession," written in the early fifties,
she presented herself as having been more ignorant of the Moscow trials than was plausible for anyone who had access to a radio and newspapers, and a close connection with *The Nation*. At the same time, she
was pleased to speak of a political conversion the way you would of an
everyday love affair.

When she was writing "My Confession," this may have been the wis-
est tone to take. Dwight Macdonald brought some of the same amused
skepticism to his political memoirs of the same period. But it seems
likely that her motives were not political. At heart she *had* been ignorant, although she may not have been totally uninformed. And told this
way, it made a better story.

**ISAIAH BERLIN**   You couldn't talk to Mary about socialism or Marxism or
conservatism. No good asking her, "What do you think about John Stuart
Mill's book *On Liberty*?" She was no good on abstract ideas. She was fine on
life in general. People. Society. People's reactions. Character. She responded
very sensitively and sharply. Mary was a good writer, but ideas were not her
thing at all. She was a great wit, but she was not a great thinker. Like many
creative people, she had no gift for academic thought.

**WILLIAM PHILLIPS**   My main criticism is that she substituted morality for
politics. She was always moralizing. She was always taking the high road. It
could be annoying.

**DIANA TRILLING**   I took my politics too seriously to be amused by
Mary. She was stupid politically. Irresponsible. She did harm. She presented herself to the world as the most responsible of people but she was

irresponsible really. And she was awfully smug about her liberal bona fides. They don't impress me very much; they were too easily come by. I like a little hard thinking instead.

The Trotsky Defense Committee met in Farrell's apartment, and it was soon apparent that not every committee member leavened his politics with a dash of irony or was capable of sharing her delight in the fact that no one else in the room happened to be aware that they were meeting on St. Valentine's Day. At least two took their politics *very* seriously: Philip Rahv had been a member of the Communist Party; William Phillips, while professing never to have been an actual member, had nonetheless had close Party ties. Since 1934 Rahv and Phillips had been editing *Partisan Review*, a magazine of densely written and closely reasoned political and literary analysis funded by the John Reed Clubs, the Party's literary arm. (At the urging of her Beekman Place stationers, she had bought more than one issue of this deliberately recondite publication and found it hard going.)

In 1936, just as *Partisan Review*'s two main editors were concluding that they could not follow international communism in its shift to the right, or accept Stalin's killing off all his old allies in Russia, the Party dissolved the John Reed Clubs and withdrew all financial support. That December, the last issue of *Partisan Review* came out. The magazine's demise was viewed as timely by both the Party and its disaffected editors, but Rahv and Phillips did not plan to leave the corpse decently buried. They were secretly hoping to resurrect the *Partisan Review* as an anti-Stalinist monthly. With Communist plots and atrocities coming to light in Russia and in Spain, they saw a pressing need for a publication that could offer a sharp response to the Stalinist line. What they envisioned was a literate and independent alternative to the *New Masses*. Having broken with the Party, the two editors were not about to hold their peace.

Compared to the Stalinists at Covici-Friede, Philip Rahv and William Phillips possessed the glamour of cossacks or pirates. Prepared at all times to go on the attack, they had a polemical stance that was not unlike McCarthy's own. When it came to judging the merits of a piece of writing, they had a relatively enlightened attitude. Both Philip Rahv and William Phillips were married, although Rahv and his wife were separated. Of the two men Phillips, slender, with fine features and blue eyes, was the more traditionally handsome. But it was Rahv, tall and bearlike, who caught her eye. Born in Russia in 1908, Rahv had lived for a time with his parents in Palestine, and then joined an older brother who had immigrated to Providence, Rhode Island. He had started life with the name Ilya Greenberg and spoke Russian and German. Always his spoken English retained a hint of a Russian accent.

From Providence, Rahv had drifted to Portland, Oregon, where he wrote advertising copy. He never attended college. When he lost his job in the Depression, he moved back east, to New York, where he slept on park benches if nothing better offered and spent as much time as possible at the New York Public Library on Forty-second Street. Through his reading he found his way not only to Dostoyevsky and Henry James but to Marxism and the John Reed Clubs. It was there that he met William Phillips.

Rahv had none of the polish of Harold Johnsrud, and he lacked the boyish appeal of John Porter. He was proud, but he was also pragmatic. Although he disapproved of Roosevelt's New Deal in principle, he was reconciled to accepting money to live on from the Writers' Project of the Works Progress Administration. He was quick tempered, passionate, and defiantly self-educated. "Manic-impressive," Delmore Schwartz would later call him. Or "Philip Slav."

**FROM *THE INTELLECTUAL FOLLIES*, BY LIONEL ABEL**
Philip was tall, powerfully built, and handsome, not in the way movie stars are, but rather as a prizefighter might be, with a square jaw and a nose flattened not of course by an opponent's blow but by whatever genetic forces have been Asianing noses in the Ukraine, where, as it happens, Philip was born. He was not highly imaginative, but he was very intelligent, in fact one of the most intelligent men I have had the luck to be acquainted with.

**ISAIAH BERLIN**   Rahv had a very powerful mind. He was a Marxist of course. More than the others. But his Marxism was extremely intelligent and interesting. Intellectually powerful. It was individual and thought out. He wasn't a particularly nice man.

**IRVING HOWE**   He was a very complex figure. He had a lot of malice in him but he was also very kind. He gave me a boost. He gave me a hand. What else do you want from an editor? But he could say things about people that were just terrible. I often was grateful that I wasn't around to hear what he said about me.

**EVE GASSLER STWERTKA**   When I was working for him and William Phillips in the late forties, he used to take me to lunch rather a lot. You know who he reminded me of? Mr. Rochester in *Jane Eyre*.

**DWIGHT MACDONALD IN A 1979 INTERVIEW WITH DIANA TRILLING, *PARTISAN REVIEW*, FALL 1984**
For some reason or other, women loved him. My wife thought he was adorable. He was quite a womanizer but also quite avuncular with women. But boy, with his equals and with men he could be pretty damn tough. And he had a power complex too. He thought power was a big thing. He was very paranoiac, very suspicious, as power people are.

By the time Rahv caught her eye, she was seeing a lot of one of the men who had made their way to her bed on Gay Street—Bill Mangold, a pipe-smoking Yale graduate who was working to raise money for medical aid for the Loyalists in Spain. Mangold, like Rahv, was separated from his wife, but his wife was not quite so far in the background as Rahv's was. In addition, *he* was undergoing analysis. Until his analysis was completed he was not allowed to make any significant life changes, whether it might be to get a divorce or to move in with a good-looking anti-Stalinist.

Having signed on with the Writers' Project of the WPA, Rahv had to check in every day and do some writing for them to earn his keep. In his free time he wrote book reviews for *The Daily Worker* and *The Nation*. As a critic he was not without experience. One of the things that had brought Rahv to her attention, she would recall shortly after his death, was not his looks or the impressive figure he cut in radical circles, but the unexpected inflection of an early book review he had written.

### FROM "PHILIP RAHV, 1908–1973," BY MARY MCCARTHY, *THE NEW YORK TIMES BOOK REVIEW*, FEBRUARY 17, 1974

I remember when I first knew him, back in the mid-thirties, at a time when he was an intransigent (I thought), pontificating young Marxist, and I read a short review he had done of *Tender Is the Night*—the tenderness of the review, despite its critical stance, startled me. I would not have suspected in Rahv that power of sympathetic insight into a writer glamorized by rich Americans on the Riviera. Fitzgerald, I must add, was "out" then and not only for the disagreeable crowd at the *New Masses*.

While she may have possibly stumbled upon a copy of Rahv's 1934 review in *The Daily Worker*, it is more likely that she read it later, when she was beginning to see him—in which case, "sympathetic insight" and "tenderness" owe something to the eye of the beholder. While Rahv gave Fitzgerald credit for being "the voice and character of the jazz age," he held him accountable for having "surrendered to the standards of the *Saturday Evening Post*."

At Covici-Friede, she had been encouraged to search the little magazines and quarterlies for promising new writers. In this capacity she sent a letter to a young writer named Eudora Welty, only to have nothing come of it. In addition, she was free to scout for books on the lists of foreign publishers and to assign likely books to readers sufficiently fluent in the language to determine whether they were worth publishing in translation. In this capacity she called on the multilingual Philip Rahv. Having dazzled James Farrell and his set with her silk stockings and pretty dresses, she was not unaware of the figure she cut among writers and intellectuals. It was the rare man among them who remained indifferent to her attractions.

**LIONEL ABEL**   Mary was beautiful. You have no idea. A real beauty. You don't expect that in someone so bright. That's what was so unusual about her.

**WILLIAM PHILLIPS**   She was very handsome. Her legs weren't good, but the upper part was. You couldn't take your eyes off her. One got fascinated with her. And she was bright in her conversation—sharp and bright—which added to her charms. She was less slashing in person than she was in her writing.

**ALFRED KAZIN**   I have to confess that despite a lifetime of girl chasing I was never attracted to her. I found her a little too clever and talkative. And then there was that Irish jaw. And a pronounced emphasis to everything she did—a hearty Irish laugh, a nervous laugh.

By late spring Philip Rahv was living with her on Gay Street. By early summer, they had moved into a furnished walk-up on Beekman Place, not far from her old apartment, lent to them by a couple she knew. The wife was a descendant of the founder of Sears, Roebuck and the apartment came with a maid. To earn extra money, she was working as a ghostwriter for the radio commentator H. V. Kaltenborn, patching together a book from old radio scripts. For the conservative Kaltenborn she wrote chapters providing an anti-Stalinist perspective on labor's recent triumphs in the automobile industry, on Léon Blum's newly elected Popular Front government in France, and on the Loyalist attempts to stave off the rebel forces in the early months of the Spanish Civil War—only to have all her efforts undone when Kaltenborn's Stalinist son came down from Harvard and took a look at the manuscript and made her sound like a bubbleheaded fellow traveler.

Meanwhile, Rahv was actively working with Phillips to resurrect *Partisan Review*. The plan was for the new magazine to follow an anti-Stalinist line that was independent of Trotsky. But for the magazine's editorial board he and Phillips chose no veterans of the radical movement with degrees from City College or the New York Public Library. They solicited no first- or second-generation Jews. Instead, they turned to newcomers to radical politics who seemed to arrive, like Jim Barnett in McCarthy's "Portrait of the Intellectual as a Yale Man," fresh from "the happy center of things."

Invited to join the editorial board were Rahv's handsome girlfriend from Vassar and her friend Dwight Macdonald. With him, Macdonald brought along two old friends from Yale—Fred Dupee, who had passable radical credentials, having worked as an organizer on the waterfront and as literary editor at the *New Masses*; and George L. K. Morris, a painter with a trust fund, who was breathtakingly ignorant about radical politics but happy to sign on as the magazine's first art critic and chief financial backer. Macdonald's wife, Nancy, took the job of business manager.

Once Morris joined the magazine it became possible to rent office space, pay contributors, pay a printer, and make concrete plans. The new *Partisan Review* was announced as "a literary monthly." Although it would be proudly and unabashedly anti-Stalinist, literary standards would not be compromised for the sake of ideology. For the first issue the editors agreed to seek out writers with established reputations and new writers just beginning to make names for themselves. While Macdonald was soliciting contributions from the respected critic Edmund Wilson and from Trotsky himself, McCarthy was trying to secure a piece of criticism from a young professor of comparative literature at Harvard.

**HARRY LEVIN**   I first heard from Mary when the *Partisan Review* was getting started. I had written, as she had, for *The New Republic* and *The Nation*. She wrote asking me if I'd be interested in contributing. That was when they ceased to be a young Communist publication. They were still all young New York leftists, but they wanted to be independent. And I was quite sympathetic to that because I was a Minnesota leftist. My state was the Farmer-Labor state at the time. That was my orientation. I always said I never needed Marx because I had Thorstein Veblen.

### FROM *A PARTISAN VIEW*, BY WILLIAM PHILLIPS

   Though we felt some continuity with the spirit of the twenties and early thirties when we started the new *Partisan Review*, we were actually representing—or creating—a new intellectual atmosphere[. . . .] Of the established figures who associated themselves with us, the one whom we respected most was Edmund Wilson, a strange, remote, impressive figure. A man of immense literary scholarship, he was making an effort to master Marxist theory and radical politics.

### FROM PHILIP RAHV'S LETTER TO DWIGHT MACDONALD, AUGUST 4, 1937

   Your letter made us all feel good. The contact you have made with [Edmund] Wilson is really important; once we get him to contribute regularly we have set the pace for others of his calibre. All of us feel that the article he proposes on Marxist criticism would make a swell beginning for the first number, and his poem by the way is not at all bad. Mary and Fred like it too.

That summer, Mary McCarthy may have had moments when she believed that she had managed to secure for herself the best of Gay Street and Beekman Place. She was helping bring about the birth of a new leftist magazine—soliciting contributions and translating a piece on the Soviet Union by André Gide—but at the same time she was seeing a lot of her rich Vassar friend Nathalie Swan. Her lover was on the dole, supported by the WPA, but she was once again living on Beekman Place amid furniture as sleek and modern as her Russel Wright cocktail shaker. With a little ingenuity and a willingness to compromise, it seemed that a strong political commitment did not preclude the pleasures of a fine home or a good dinner, or even rule out a weekend of skinny dipping with the Macdonalds at the house they had rented in Connecticut.

By the end of the summer she was shopping for furniture at Macy's with the approval of her lover and trying to find a suitable apartment on the Upper East Side. But if opposites attract, they do not necessarily enjoy a moment's peace in each other's company. In her last memoir she would recall how, in the privacy of their apartment, Rahv would balk at some expense he regarded as unnecessary or mock her for the bourgeois prejudices she could not seem to shed. He would accuse her of being unwilling to acknowledge her latent anti-Semitism. She in turn would mock his ignorance when it came to the New Testament. Or point out his inability to buy himself a well-cut suit. However, to the outside world none of this discord was evident. As a couple she and Rahv were striking and unlikely and a source of endless fascination. For Delmore Schwartz—who was obsessed with her and had little liking for Rahv—their relationship was the inspiration for a short story he never finished.

### FROM "THE COMPLETE ADVENTURESS," A FRAGMENT BY DELMORE SCHWARTZ

When Helena met Stanislaus, a big and powerful radical politician, she felt for the first time that she was with one who pleased her whole being[. . . .] She soon found that there was a roughness about Stanislaus and a rudeness and a habit of being too serious in conversation which she did not like in the least. She tried to correct his rudeness and roughness, his habit of getting into taxis before she did, and his brusqueness in conversing with persons he did not estimate highly[. . . .] Stanislaus was so pleased with Helena that he tried to improve himself, although lightness was foreign to his whole being.

**ALFRED KAZIN** The first time I saw Mary McCarthy was in 1936 or 1937, I believe. It was at one of those writers' congresses the Communists were always putting on in those days. There was Mary in the auditorium of the New School on West Twelfth Street. She and Rahv were sitting together and they were whispering and making fun of the proceedings, which I found utterly understandable. I was sitting behind her. Funny the things you remember.

### FROM THE TRUANTS, BY WILLIAM BARRETT

Rahv sat on the sofa beside Mary McCarthy. They were lovers, and they were living together. That was a daring thing at the time, or at least to the youthful minds of Delmore [Schwartz] and myself, and in our eyes it cast a certain aura about them. Not that Miss McCarthy had need of any additional aura beyond what nature had furnished her with[. . . .] She did not seem to worry about her clothes or appearance generally, and I noticed—an odd detail to remember now!—that her legs were unshaved. Probably it was no affectation, she had simply been too busy to attend to her toilette; but it reinforced the touch of gamine about her[. . . .] As she sat beside him, she listened intently to whatever Rahv said, and her hand rested on his knee affectionately now and then. Later, when we had left, Delmore grumbled to me, "Did you see Mary McCarthy giving Rahv a feel?"

**WILLIAM PHILLIPS**   She and Rahv didn't seem terribly happy together. I don't know why, but they weren't. It wasn't that there was so much bickering in front of other people. It was just that you didn't get the impression that they really liked each other that much. He was stricken with her. I would not say he adored her. She had a certain kind of charisma obviously. She was handsome and she was sophisticated and bright.

By the fall of 1937, she and Rahv were living with their new furniture not far from Gracie Mansion, a location she found congenial but not at all convenient for commuting downtown to a nine-to-five job. While she was rushing to Covici-Friede, Rahv was making his leisured way to the Writers' Project or the offices he had found for the new magazine just off Union Square.

Although the space at 22 East Seventeenth Street was no more than a long shoebox with a glass partition separating the front from the back, it was ample enough for the new magazine's current needs. From these offices it was easy to send out letters to potential contributors, vet submissions, edit manuscripts, and store growing stacks of correspondence. The offices made it official: meetings took on a less provisional aspect. Here, as they came together on the fringes of a neighborhood steeped in radicalism, the editors had occasion to take one another's measure. For one editor at least the distinctions were fairly clear-cut.

### FROM *MARY MCCARTHY'S THEATRE CHRONICLES*

The "boys" were still committed to Marxism, and so were the other young men who figured on the masthead as editors, except one—the backer. The backer, a young abstract painter from a good old New York family, was so "confused" politically that one day he went into the Workers' Bookshop (Stalinist) and asked for a copy of Trotsky's *The Revolution Betrayed*; he was wearing spats that day, too, and carrying a cane, and the thought of the figure he must have cut made the rest of us blanch. "Did anyone recognize you? Do you think they knew who you were?" we all immediately demanded.

My position was something like the backer's; that is, I was a source of uneasiness and potential embarrassment to the magazine, which had accepted me, unwillingly, as an editor because I had a minute "name" and was the girl friend of one of the "boys," who had issued a ukase on my behalf. I was not a Marxist; I should have liked, rather, to be one, but I did not know the language, which seemed really like a foreign tongue[. . . .] All my habits of mind were bourgeois, my fellow editors used to tell me. They were always afraid that I was going to do something, in real life or in print that would "disgrace *Partisan Review*"; this was a fear that worried me even more than it did them.

While Rahv and Phillips had no use for the Stalinists or for their popular front, they had not been above borrowing a recent Stalinist stratagem in recruiting for their editorial board attractive, personable Ivy League graduates. If they were hoping, however, to recruit a group of intellectual fellow travelers, delighted to rubber stamp their decisions, they were in for a rude awakening. From the beginning there would be no unanimity of opinion. Alliances would shift, individuals would come and go, but, as the political ground shifted and the magazine's position underwent modification, character as much as ideology would inform editorial debate.

**WILLIAM PHILLIPS**   When it came to decisions about what was to be published we all voted. It was always done by committee, with a lot of factionalism, a lot of jockeying—Dwight Macdonald was always able to influence George Morris, and Dwight and Mary constituted a kind of team that paraded under the banner of moral scrupulousness. Rahv and I tended more to side with each other on practical grounds. We considered ourselves politically more sophisticated than the others. Fred Dupee was kind of independent. Fred Dupee was a good editor. He had great sensitivity and sensibility. A very sharp literary sense. He was not a strong person. The most insistent person was Macdonald. There was a lot of bluster, a lot of aggression, a lot of argumentation. Rahv was a close second. Fred was not like that. So there were these shifting attitudes and relationships. We had violent meetings—yelling, screaming, arguing. Not on every piece but on many pieces. Everybody had an equal vote, although some people yelled louder. Macdonald and Rahv yelled the loudest. Mary was the firmest and most acidic.

### FROM *THE TRUANTS*, BY WILLIAM BARRETT
To my youthful eyes they belonged to the great world outside the walls of academy where I was still drudging for a degree. Theirs was the world of bohemia and the arts, of political movements and countermovements, bold and sweeping ideologies; and they were the intrepid spirits who bravely walked within that world. They were therefore beings invested in my eyes with a strange and mysterious glamour; and I felt tongue-tied and stupid in their presence.

**ISAIAH BERLIN**   Philip Rahv was by far and away the cleverest in that *Partisan Review* circle. He was formidable. Rather ugly, but of all those people far superior. Mary agreed when I said, "Philip is far superior to all the others." *"D'accord,"* she said.

**ALFRED KAZIN**   These people were extremists and kept a certain Bolshevik habit of mind. I really think—though I can't prove it—that the key to their character was their infatuation with the Russian Bolshevik style. They were so bitterly, unforgivingly anti-Stalinist and they felt that only nincompoops were still loyal Communists. There was definitely an elitist, snooty attitude about all this. People were dismissed as not being very clever—as being what William Phillips would call "your average Jewish dentist." They were the most terrible gossips and backbiters you've ever seen. They made a point of sitting around—people drank more than they do now—and just knocking everybody to pieces. William Phillips had a wife, Edna, and when she died not too many years ago William asked me to go to Frank E. Campbell's for her service, and I'm glad I did because every speaker eulogizing Edna made the same point—which was that she was the only person at these parties who never slandered anyone. She was a nice Brooklyn schoolteacher.

In the offices of *Partisan Review* it was Philip Rahv who ran the show. Years later, writing an introduction for a collection of her theater pieces for the magazine, Mary McCarthy would assert that it was only to please Rahv that the other editors agreed to let her do them at all. She was assigned the theater because she had once been married to an actor and because most of the editors believed that the theater didn't matter anyway.

### FROM *MARY MCCARTHY'S THEATRE CHRONICLES*

If I made mistakes, who cared? This argument won out. Being an editor, at least in name, I had to be allowed to do *something*, and the "Theatre Chronicle" (we spelled it "theater") was "made work," like the W.P.A. jobs of the period. I could not fail to see this or to be aware that nobody had much confidence in my powers as a critic. Nevertheless, I was determined to make good.

**WILLIAM PHILLIPS**   Mary's saying that we gave her the theater reviews because we didn't take them seriously is a typical effort by Mary to be witty at all costs. She got the "Theater Chronicle" because she indicated a strong critical sense and a kind of slashing temperament and style that we felt the theater needed at that time.

**IRVING HOWE**   I think it's probably true that the boys had Mary writing that criticism because they didn't care about the theater to begin with. Rahv was a very canny character, and he probably thought that this would be a place for Mary to practice. And it didn't make much difference what she said about theater. They weren't going to get any theater ads anyway. And none of the people who read *PR* went to the theater very much. They couldn't afford it or weren't interested.

**LIONEL ABEL**   I think it's probably true that they gave it to her because Rahv and Phillips didn't think it was important. About the theater she was almost always wrong.

The first issue of the new *Partisan Review* came out in December 1937, exactly one year after the old *Partisan Review* had shut down. Leading off with "In Dreams Begin Responsibilities," a first story by a handsome twenty-four-year-old newcomer named Delmore Schwartz, it went on to present writing by Lionel Trilling, James T. Farrell, Pablo Picasso, James Agee, Sidney Hook, and Edmund Wilson. There was a poem by Wallace Stevens. Harry Levin's book review, as it turned out, would not appear in the magazine until its second issue. Almost all the contributors had politics that were left of center, but in keeping with the spirit of *Partisan Review*'s avowed editorial policy, they were allied with a nice variety of sects, factions, and splinter groups.

### FROM THE EDITORIAL STATEMENT OF *PARTISAN REVIEW*, DECEMBER 1937

> *Partisan Review* is aware of its responsibility to the revolutionary movement in general, but we disclaim obligation to any of its organized political expressions. Indeed we think that the cause of revolutionary literature is best served by a policy of no commitments to any political party.

When staking out a position for itself, a new magazine may find it easier to say what it is *not* going to be than to predict exactly what it will in time become. The new *Partisan Review* was definitely not going to be like the old one. And it was not going to be like the *New Masses*. In the magazine's first issue, it was left to Dwight Macdonald to make it abundantly clear that there was also no chance of its becoming anything like *The New Yorker*.

### FROM "LAUGH AND LIE DOWN," BY DWIGHT MACDONALD

> The *New Yorker* is the last of the great family journals. Its inhibitions stretch from sex to the class struggle. It can be read aloud in mixed company without calling a blush to the cheek of the most virtuous banker[. . . .]
>
> In the class war the *New Yorker* is ostentatiously neutral. It makes fun of subway guards and of men-about-town, of dowagers and laundresses, of shop-girls and debutantes[. . . .] Its neutrality is itself a form of upper class display, since only the economically secure can afford such Jovian aloofness from the common struggle.

In the pages of *Partisan Review* there would be no inhibitions and no pretense of neutrality. There would be wit and, above all, there would be "ideas."

**IRVING HOWE**   When the first issue of the *Partisan Review* came out in 1937 the circulation was tiny. But it had more influence then, when it was selling maybe three thousand copies, than it ever did again, because it had a defined point of view. It stood for something. That's the trouble with *The New Yorker*. It finally doesn't stand for anything. The *Partisan Review* stood for two things, and they thought that it was possible to combine them. Later it became clear that it probably wasn't. But they thought it was possible to combine anti-Stalinist radicalism and avant-garde culture. For a time it seemed to work, because there we had André Gide contributing and George Orwell and T. S. Eliot and Stephen Spender. It really made a dent in the whole Stalinist intellectual world. It attracted younger readers.

**HARRY LEVIN**   I wrote a couple of long reviews for two of the early issues, but then I gave up on it because it seemed to me that it was quite as doctrinaire as the Communists—only a slightly different Trotskyist doctrine.

**IRVING HOWE**   The *Partisan Review* mattered tremendously in the late thirties because it became the focus for the anti-Stalinists. Now, some people have tried to minimize this and say there weren't that many Stalinists. It wasn't a question of numbers. Their influence on intellectual life was enormous.

**ALFRED KAZIN**   At its best *Partisan Review* was a very brilliant magazine— one that I loved reading and writing for. For many years, whenever I moved offices, like an idiot I kept all my old copies with me.

**ISAIAH BERLIN**   The *Partisan Review* was a remarkable publication. They were a coterie, and that's a very good thing. Coteries lead to very good writing, because they all write for each other. And they criticize each other. And they go by each other's views. And it sharpens their minds. When people write for each other they know what they're talking about, they understand each other's language. It liberates them and it sharpens them.

**WILLIAM PHILLIPS**   I think *Partisan Review* was the best magazine America has ever put out, frankly. I think I'm objective. Its strength was its sharpness, its courage, its polemicists, its willingness to be polemical. But of course it was the content of our polemics that was important. We were out to destroy Stalinism, stupid politics, stupid criticism, parochialism. But we were also perhaps even lucky—well, partly lucky—in the sense that a lot of talent appeared at that time. An awful lot of talent. And I say partly lucky because to some extent we corralled that talent, attracted it, encouraged it.

One of the magazine's most talented writers turned out to be the boss's girlfriend. When Mary McCarthy later wrote of how the "Theater Chronicle" began as glorified make-work, she chose not to mention that she had recently written about the current theater season for *The Nation*. She was hardly coming to the subject cold. With the first of her reviews, dissecting minor efforts by Ben Hecht and Maxwell Anderson, she set the tone for all her theater criticism to come: she was not impressed by popular success and she was not disposed to settle for the best Broadway could offer. To many readers her theater pieces seemed emblematic of much that *Partisan Review* stood for. At the same time, they set her apart as someone to watch.

**FROM "THEATER CHRONICLE," PARTISAN REVIEW, DECEMBER 1937**
Though Mr. Anderson has lately been hailed as America's first dramatist, it has long been obvious that he was essentially a popular playwright, distinguished from his fellows only by his ambition[. . . .] Mr. Anderson's mind is like a musty, Middle Western law office of thirty years ago, full of heterogeneous books, on the law, on American history, on philosophy, and the morocco-bound complete works of William Shakespeare.

**ALFRED KAZIN** The *Partisan Review* was Mary's magazine. William Phillips said Mary was the star of the magazine because she could dust off anyone.

**DIANA TRILLING** In those early days I thought Mary had such a shine on everything she wrote—there was a kind of brilliance in her writing that I very much admired and envied. I never thought that she was sound. I thought she was brilliant. For instance, she wrote of Margaret Sullavan, I believe, "She was the kind of woman who would go hatless in the rain at forty." There is nothing you can't do with a statement like that—turn it inside out, it has just as much meaning. Or lack of meaning. I never thought that was any way to write. It has great dazzle. Those reviews are fun to read. But I passed an intellectual judgment. I thought that she had been gifted with something I wished I had, but which wasn't very useful in the world. I could envy it, but I didn't think it was sufficient.

**IRVING HOWE** Mary was essentially a polemical writer. And *PR* was totally polemical. It was a fighting magazine, and that's what made it interesting. Mary didn't write essays for the ages. She wasn't like Thomas Mann positioning himself for posterity. It was always in response to something. That was the sense of the essay that we all did. And that's why none of us is likely to survive. That's the training we had. That's what makes for a good magazine. It doesn't necessarily make for a great career.

Polemical writing may not necessarily make for literary longevity. However, if you bring to it not only brilliance on the page but extraordinary physical beauty, then possibly you have the makings of a great career after all. Certainly, when her brothers Kevin and Preston and their friend Martin Swensen arrived early that winter, Mary McCarthy appeared to be assured a very bright future. Fresh from the University of Minnesota, the three young men were hoping to make their way in the big city— Kevin and Martin as actors and Preston as a photographer. From the vantage point of the one furnished room they shared in a brownstone on West Twenty-third Street, her progress seemed nothing short of splendid.

**PRESTON McCARTHY** What surprised me most was that she had become an author.

**KEVIN McCARTHY** She seemed like such a civilized and practical person; at the same time there was something glamorous about her. She took us out to dinner, to an exotic restaurant in Greenwich Village, and then one time we made dinner for her. I think we made salmon croquettes and canned peas and maybe potatoes. Whatever we did was on this little tiny stove. There was no bathroom in the apartment. You had to "go" down the hall.

**MARTIN SWENSEN**  Mary wanted to know what Kevin had put in the salmon croquettes and how he molded them and how he made them in the oven. She had this wonderful natural curiosity about things. And she ate her croquettes all up. She thought they were fine, and they were, too. It wasn't a dinner party. We were living on a shoestring. Here we were off the prairie and Mary looked ready for the magazines and all. She looked wonderful. She was pretty, you know. But she was not intimidating. Not in the least. She was just a lot of fun to be with.

Within months the three good-looking young men would be making plans to skip out on their landlord. Soon Preston's Ford and Leica camera would be sold and they would be living on the streets, sleeping in a church and shaving in a garage rest room. Kevin was able to find a job or two modeling. Martin Swensen briefly drove a produce wagon. For all that the economy was said to be improving, there was little pick-up work. By the fall, Preston was back in school in Minnesota, Martin Swensen was in Washington, and Kevin, with no remnants of his inheritance to finance further education, was returning from his daily round of agents' offices, auditions, and casting calls to a bed in a flophouse on Bleecker Street.

In four short years, thanks to a combination of good luck and hard work, Mary McCarthy had been able to make a very nice life for herself in New York. The night she joined her brothers for salmon croquettes she was living in a comfortable apartment in a good neighborhood with a man whom she would later profess to love deeply. In addition, she was close to achieving the two goals she had set for herself at Vassar. Not only was she rapidly acquiring a "name," but she had a place of honor at the center of a formidable group of writers and intellectuals whose rough-and-ready evenings were beginning to partake of the cachet if not the style associated with the rarefied gatherings presided over by Madame de Staël.

She had managed to cut a bold swathe in a world not inclined to embrace an ambitious newcomer, no matter how good-looking. Whether this had been at some cost to herself or to those around her was not a question she was inclined to raise. What she had done seemed to her only natural. Depending on your perspective, her success could seem natural or inevitable or totally inexplicable. But whatever you chose to make of her precipitous rise, her next move was astonishing. Just when she was getting a name for herself in the New York literary world, she in effect turned her back on that world and walked off.

Perhaps, as that psychiatrist said, she was doomed to leave the men in her life: it was simply her orphan's fate. Certainly, by leaving Philip Rahv before he had a chance to tire of her or to take her for granted, she saw to it that she would be the one who was missed. But for all that it was sudden, this departure was not undertaken lightly. Unlike her brothers, she was no innocent when it came to the practicalities of living. She had let her marriage to Johnsrud drag on for three years. She did not live with Rahv for even one. When she had walked out on Johnsrud, her departure had not smacked of self-interest. She had left him for a careless young man who could not even support himself. This time, matters were not quite so clear-cut.

# Chapter Seven

# EDMUND WILSON

When it came time to seek contributions and credibility for their new venture, the editors of *Partisan Review* turned at once to Edmund Wilson. In practical terms, their overture made excellent sense. He brought to this group of political rebels and literary outsiders an aura of respectability. A generation older, he was already quite famous. Then, as a disenchanted Marxist, he shared many of their political ideas. Finally, and no less important, he subscribed to their belief that a participation in radical politics was perfectly compatible with a commitment to serious literature.

Wilson was not about to limit himself to the library. Or to restrict himself to the scrutiny of a writer's work without reference to the circumstances of his life. He was best known for *Axel's Castle*, a collection of essays on the Symbolists, which celebrated the accomplishments of writers like Yeats, Valéry, and Proust while taking exception to the way they led their lives. Always he liked to think of himself as a literary journalist, a reporter who went out in the world, gathered facts, examined and made sense of them, and then gave a precise account of what he had learned. Whether he was writing about Proust or striking coal miners in Pennsylvania, he strove to make his points clearly and forcibly and to be intelligible to the widest possible audience. He never hesitated to say where his own sympathies lay.

Born in 1895, in Red Bank, New Jersey, Edmund Wilson, was related on his mother's side to Cotton Mather, but was named for his father, a respected trial lawyer who served under Woodrow Wilson (no relation), as Attorney General of New Jersey. The Wilsons were staunch Republicans and Presbyterians. His mother's family, the Kimballs, with their large landholdings in New Jersey and in upstate New York and their roots in the seventeenth century, could be said to belong to America's landed aristocracy. From both sides of the family he inherited a sense of entitlement and a susceptibility to nervous illness. A spate of hard work could precipitate a depression that kept his father locked in his room for months—or, worse, led to his being institutionalized. His mother's response to his father's first bout of melancholia had been immediate and dramatic. Overnight she had turned stone-deaf. Not surprisingly, Wilson's happiest memories were of the summers he had spent in a rural backwater in upstate New York, at the Kimballs' handsome old stone house in Talcottville.

In 1912, the year Mary McCarthy was born, Wilson started at Princeton, where he would go on to study European literature with Christian Gauss, forge close friendships with F. Scott Fitzgerald and John Peale Bishop, write for the *Lit*, and show no aptitude whatsoever for science or mathematics. He graduated in 1916, just as America was about to enter the war in Europe. He preferred to think of himself as a man of the twenties and, like many of his generation, he surrendered his fair share of illusions when he went overseas to tend the wounded in France. In 1919, upon being demobilized, he settled in New York City and in a year's time he was contributing to *Vanity Fair* and *The New Republic*, eventually serving briefly at each publication as managing editor. In his capacity as a critic he did much to bring to the attention of the reading public the novels of his friend Scott Fitzgerald—novels that both celebrated and defined the spirit of the decade. Sadly, there seemed to be no way he could manage to do the same for his own twenties novel, *I Thought of Daisy*, when it came out in 1929.

While Mary McCarthy had been sitting in study hall and writing about wronged shop girls, Wilson had been living out his own variation on *The Beautiful and Damned*. First, he had fallen in love with a beautiful red-haired Vassar graduate, the poet Edna St. Vincent Millay. Then he had fallen for the poet Léonie Adams. When it became evident that they had no wish to requite his passion, he tumbled into bed with a taxi dancer and a waitress from Childs and any attractive woman who would have him. In 1923, he married the actress Mary Blair and had one daughter, Rosalind, by her, but their life together was far from tranquil. Six years later, Wilson was hospitalized with a nervous breakdown and he and Mary Blair were divorced. In 1930, he tried marriage again, this time with Margaret Canby, an old friend and drinking companion, only to be devastated two years later, when she died after tumbling down a flight of stone steps one night on a hillside in Santa Barbara.

Wilson may have been a man of the twenties, but it was in the thirties that he made his reputation. In 1931, with the publication of *Axel's Castle*, his study of the modernist masters and their roots in the Symbolists, he began to receive the kind of widespread recognition that his first novel had failed to bring him. He was among the few critics praised by

Mary McCarthy and Margaret Marshall in their 1935 series in *The Nation*. Indeed he was singled out for being the only one to make "any extended effort to relate what is valuable in modern literature to the body of literature of the past." By then, however, he had turned much of his attention to writing a series of pieces on the Depression in America—reporting that would be brought together in *The American Jitters*.

Like many writers and intellectuals, Wilson went from being contemptuous of the plutocrats who were running the country to wanting to do away with them entirely. To his credit, he did not settle for supporting the striking waiters at the Waldorf but went out and confronted the economic depression in less luxurious quarters. For the first issue of Selden Rodman's *Common Sense* he reported on a milk strike in Pennsylvania. He delivered food to striking coal miners in Pennsylvania and wrote about the harsh life of the workers who were still employed on the assembly lines in Detroit or in the mills in New England. Such hope as he saw for the future seemed to reside in the Marxist dialectic. In 1933, Wilson began a series of essays for *The New Republic* tracing the development of Marxism from its roots in the French Revolution. The essays would become part of *To The Finland Station*. In 1935, he spent six months in Russia on a Guggenheim Fellowship.

By 1937, when Dwight Macdonald approached him as a potential contributor, Wilson had been living for almost two years at Trees, a house overlooking the Mianus River in Stamford, Connecticut, rented from Margaret de Silver, an heiress sympathetic to radical causes. He was the author of six books. In addition to his first novel and *Axel's Castle*, he was responsible for two volumes of reporting, *The American Jitters* and *Travels in Two Democracies*, an account of his recent Russian visit juxtaposed with his travels in his own country. Over the years he had developed a fondness for the works of Walt Disney and a passion for magic—having taken this passion so far as to pay a call on Harry Houdini. His enthusiasms were wide-ranging and on occasion surprising. While his two years in the country had been productive, he was beginning to tire of his solitary nights. In the city, he had enjoyed close friendships with the poet Louise Bogan and the novelist Dawn Powell, but neither woman was interested in him as a lover or a husband—or in coming up to live with him in a remote house in Connecticut.

At Trees, Wilson had been writing the essays that would become the final chapters of *To The Finland Station* and bringing to them a perspective very different from that of 1933. No longer could he blame political repression in the Soviet Union on centuries of czarist tyranny or see in Russia any vestige of democracy. He had ceased to look to Marxism as a secular alternative to religion—as a way for man to manage his own fate. As it happened, he had few spare moments to dwell on this loss of faith.

He was busy writing critical pieces on Shaw, James, Housman, and Flaubert for a book to be called *The Triple Thinkers*. As a successful man of letters in the tradition of Sainte-Beuve and Samuel Johnson, he had learned to be thrifty with his time, getting double value from his essays by sending them off to be published separately in a suitable periodical before bringing them together in a book.

Upon further consideration, Wilson chose not to write about Marxist criticism for the first issue of *Partisan Review*, but to save this for a later issue. Instead, he gave the editors an essay on Flaubert's politics—a piece he had completed the previous spring. All this was settled one warm Saturday in October when he stopped by the magazine's offices to meet the six editors for lunch. For this occasion Mary McCarthy wore her best black dress and carried a silver fox stole—a costume "more suited to a wedding reception," she would later recall. At lunch at a restaurant just around the corner, everyone but Wilson ordered a drink. In fact, he was nursing a hangover, but McCarthy had no way of knowing this. She had seen Wilson only once before, when he had come to lecture at Vassar and stammered his way through a prepared talk on Flaubert. This second encounter, while hardly an easy afternoon among equals, proved more satisfactory. A week later, Wilson called Margaret Marshall at *The Nation* to suggest she join him for dinner and bring along her former collaborator on "Our Critics, Right or Wrong."

Their first dinner got off to a bad start, Mary McCarthy would always say, because she had let Fred Dupee fortify her with a couple of stiff daiquiris for what she feared would be a long sober evening. As soon as she joined Wilson and Margaret Marshall at an Italian restaurant in the Village, she saw that Wilson was no teetotaler. With dinner they each had two double manhattans, followed by red wine and tumblers of B&B. By the end of the evening she had exhausted herself with a talking jag and had to be put to bed by her two companions, who had no idea where she lived.

Wilson behaved like the gentleman he gave every indication of being, and took a room for the two women at the Chelsea Hotel, where he was staying. The next morning, a shaken Mary had her roommate call an "angry" and worried Philip Rahv. But if she suffered pangs of remorse, these pangs seem to have subsided quickly, because on a Saturday night not long afterward she and Margaret Marshall were again having dinner with Wilson at the very same restaurant. This time they accompanied their host, who did not own a car and did not drive, on a long taxi ride up to his rented house in Stamford. And this time she did not pass out. While Margaret Marshall slept in the guest bedroom, she slipped down the hall and joined Wilson in his study, where she succumbed to his drunken advances on his couch.

Sunday morning, Mary called Philip Rahv to come collect her and, at Wilson's suggestion, invited him to join them for lunch. When Rahv accepted and took the train up to Stamford, he may have thought it a good idea to humor a valued contributor. Or a good idea to get to know that contributor better. Possibly he had nothing else to do with his day off. According to her, it did not occur to Rahv that in Wilson he had a potential rival. And, according to her, until she placed that phone call, Wilson did not know that she and Rahv were a couple. If her phone call was placed in all innocence, she soon had cause to think twice about its implications. Her lover was at a great disadvantage from the moment he availed himself of Wilson's hospitality, sipped his wine, and sat down to a lunch cooked by his "colored" maid Hatty.

At the end of the day, Rahv brought his girlfriend home on the train, still unaware of what had transpired in the study. Had he suspected, it might have made little difference. By entering into a conspiracy with Wilson, she had already begun to distance herself from the man she lived with. In no time she and Wilson were corresponding, with Wilson sending his letters to Covici-Friede, where their incriminating contents would be safe from discovery.

Twice Mary McCarthy would return in her writing to the couch in Wilson's study. The first time was some twenty years later in a novel called *A Charmed Life*, in which Martha Sinnott, her fine-boned blonde heroine, succumbs to an overbearing and physically repellent lay analyst and sometime playwright named Miles Murphy. The second time was in her last memoir, in which she warned readers that "though derived, like all books, from experience," her novel had not been autobiographical. In this memoir, to the best of her ability, she tried to make sense of a discomfiting and perplexing lapse that had altered the course of her life. When writing about her political conversion, she had always been perfectly willing to blame her decision to join the Trotsky Defense Committee on pure chance. But when it came to this particular romantic entanglement, she was not quite so ready to make light of her decision. She seemed intent on examining her conscience, on taking full responsibility for her actions. But to the very end she was still insisting that she had never really wanted things to turn out the way they had.

### FROM *A CHARMED LIFE*

She did not understand what had happened. She had only, she bemoaned, wanted to talk to him—a well-known playwright and editor, successful, positive, interested in her ideas and life-history. And yet he must be right; even her teachers would think so. She would never, surely, have yielded to his embraces, shrinking, as she did, from his swollen belly and big, crooked nose, if some deep urge in herself, which *he* seemed to understand, had not decreed it.

## FROM *INTELLECTUAL MEMOIRS*

One day, a bit afterward, when we were finally able to talk—I had come out to Trees on the train, and we did not drink—I tried to explain to [Wilson] my motives in returning to his study that night. But he would not listen to what I felt sure was the truth; only facts spoke to him, and the fact was that I had let him make love to me. Again, I gave up. You cannot argue against facts. And yet to this very day I am convinced that he had me wrong: I only wanted to talk to him.

Wilson was not the first unappetizing man she had tumbled into bed with. And this was not the first time that a night of hard drinking had ended in a sexual misadventure. For all that such misadventures could be embarrassing, their effect did not have to be lasting. Even the man in the Brooks Brothers shirt had listened to reason. It would seem that in both these accounts she had left something crucial out. It was something that she would suggest in a later scene in *A Charmed Life*, when Martha Sinnott, having divorced Miles Murphy, returns to the village of New Leeds and is raped by her former husband on the Empire sofa in her own parlor. It was something Wilson would not merely suggest but would go into at disconcerting length in an unpublished segment of his journal.

## FROM *A CHARMED LIFE*

The only thing that shamed her, looking back on the encounter, was the fact that her senses had awakened under Miles's touch. She would have liked to blot out that part, which was only a minute or two, from her memory. But honesty compelled her to remember, with a half-desirous shudder, that moment when his hand had first squeezed her expectant breast and languorous delight had possessed her, like a voluptuary.

## FROM THE JOURNALS OF EDMUND WILSON, JANUARY 1, 1943

With Mary at the Little Hotel: I invented, first, a trick of running my tongue around on the inside of her lips—then a smooth unbroken rotary motion that didn't have the element of jerkiness that brought you down to the ground—it was wonderful, almost like flying in a dream, and it carried her along, too. I began to intensify it by speeding up a little and pressing in—and she came before I did. Then I doubled up her knees and put her legs back over her body and drove in from above. I asked her if she enjoyed it, and she answered, "Couldn't you tell?" A wonderful transporting discovery. Afterwards, my penis did not lose its stiffness and still felt as if it had some kind of enchantment on it, as if it had been dipped in an invisible magic fluid that could prolong in the organ withdrawn the magic that was in her—only gradually fading off. I am happy tonight.

That sex meant a good deal to Wilson, there is no question. In bed, or out of it, whatever you thought of Edmund Wilson, he was not easily dismissed.

### FROM *INTELLECTUAL MEMOIRS*

He bustled into our office, short, stout, middle-aged, breathy [. . .] with popping reddish-brown eyes and fresh pink skin, which looked as though he had just bathed. Perhaps it was this suggestion of baths—the tepidarium—and his fine straight nose that gave him a Roman air. I think he was wearing a gray two-piece suit and a white shirt.

**CLEMENT GREENBERG**  From first glance I had enormous respect for Wilson. As a human being. Not just as a writer. But he wasn't my idea of fun. In the end respect counts for more than anything. I liked him, no matter what. He was short and he'd put on weight, but there was something attractive about him.

**HARRY LEVIN**  I'm on record with my literary appreciation, but he was rather an impossible person. He was curiously shy. He was an only child. I don't think growing up he'd ever had to get along with people. He was a great investigative reporter, and he was terribly good if you happened to be connected with something that he was interested in. He had all the questions lined up to fire at you. But he didn't have any small talk. Or social conversation.

**ALFRED KAZIN**  He was used to having his own way in everything. He was an only child who had never been refused anything. And then because of his extraordinary position in American literature—everyone thought of him as *the* great critic—he was naturally bossy. Despite his enormous gifts, he was quite a terrible man.

**SAUL BELLOW**  There was no Mister Magoo in those days, but as soon as I saw Mister Magoo I thought I recognized Edmund Wilson.

By the late thirties Wilson might, with some justification, be said to resemble a fat squinty-eyed cartoon character with a skull like a squashed melon. But as a young man he had been good-looking. Although he was never as handsome as his friend Fitzgerald, his profile was not in the least like *A Charmed Life*'s Miles Murphy's. Indeed it could be called noble. The passage of time has a way of smoothing out certain fine distinctions. In the photographs we see of Philip Rahv in his fifties, he looks to be obese and hypothyroid. In fact he looks no better than Edmund Wilson. But in 1937 Rahv was a virtually unknown young man of twenty-eight. Wilson, on the other hand, was a famous man of forty-two who looked older than his years. He was also the much-talked-of author of essays and books that were not only on their way to becoming classics but were free of cant and sentimentality and of a sort to make you fall in love with the man who had written them.

### FROM "THE OLD STONE HOUSE," BY EDMUND WILSON, WRITTEN IN 1933

Let people who have never known country life complain that the farmer has been spoiled by his radio and his Ford. Along with the memory of exaltation at the immensity and freedom of that country-side, I have memories of horror at its loneliness: houses burning down at night, sometimes with people in them, where there was no fire department to save them, and husbands or wives left alone by death—the dark nights and the prisoning winters. I do not grudge the sacrifice of the Sugar River falls for the building of the new state highway, and I do not resent the hot-dog stand.

### FROM "MIDTOWN AND THE VILLAGE," BY ALFRED KAZIN, *HARPER'S*, JANUARY 1971

From the time I first read *Axel's Castle*, I loved Wilson's writing passionately and knew that he was not only a remarkable critic because he put you directly in touch with any work he discussed, but also an original, an extraordinary literary artist who wove his essays out of the most intense involvement with his materials[. . . .] It was his intense personal experience of writers that had always fascinated me in Wilson, that had sent me back many times to the last paragraph of the essay on Proust in *Axel's Castle* in which he spoke of him as a "many-faceted fly," to the sections on Dickens's early struggles in *The Wound and the Bow*, to the portrait of [Jules] Michelet in *To the Finland Station*, for the felt reverberations of the life behind the book.

### FROM *A PARTISAN VIEW*, BY WILLIAM PHILLIPS

A man of immense literary scholarship, he was making an effort to master Marxist theory and radical politics. I recall long talks with him about Marx and Marxist aesthetics, when my awe of his reputation and knowledge was tempered by the realization that I knew more about radical theory and the movement of the left than he did. But I really felt legitimized only when he praised something I had written, for that meant recognition by someone noted for his critical sense and his prose.

**DANIEL AARON**  Edmund Wilson could be blunt and stern in his literary judgments, but usually there was little rancor in them. He took hostile comments pretty impersonally, wasn't resentful or feline.

**PHILIP HAMBURGER**  I would see Edmund Wilson in the office at *The New Yorker*, and then I got to know him during the war, when we were in Italy together. I was really crazy about him. First, I admired the great mind. Then, I found him very funny and wonderfully agreeable. He appreciated me, which always helps in a relationship. He laughed a lot. He would believe stories I told him, which is also pleasing. And I would believe his stories. But, then, I'm not a woman.

At the time Wilson met Mary McCarthy, his first wife, Mary Blair, was dying of tuberculosis. Their daughter, Rosalind, was fourteen years old and in need of a mother. You did not have to fall in love with Wilson's work, or think he was infallible, to sense the force of his personality. But what exactly did Edmund Wilson see in the young Mary McCarthy? And what did she come to see in him?

**FRANI BLOUGH MUSER**   Edmund was a very bright man—an extremely intellectual man—and that would have appealed to her. And very entertaining.

**DANIEL AARON**   I think he liked and admired talented literary women and remained friends with them long after the affair was over. He continued to read their work and to advise them and to bolster flagging egos.

**ISAIAH BERLIN**   He liked women, you see. When it came to women, he was a man of no great judgment. He was a very, so to speak, sexually obsessed man. And I think Mary admired him very much and was impressed by him. And I think she thought him very sexy, which he was.

**SUSAN SONTAG**   The one thing that follows from her being so pretty, which I've seen in my own knowledge of women and men, is that extremely beautiful people don't care about good looks in their partners. The great beauties often have homely mates. The Greta Garbos, as it were. They don't care. They've got enough beauty for two.

**ALISON LURIE**   There's one disadvantage very beautiful women have and that is they often become the prize of not the nicest man or the most intelligent or attractive man, but of the toughest man. Men will elbow each other out of their way for a woman who looks like Mary McCarthy. And I think that's why she began with these strong older men. Partly.

At the *Partisan Review* offices, Wilson had met a beautiful young woman who not only deferred to his literary judgment but took the trouble to get all dressed up for his benefit. At their second and third meetings, whether owing to alcohol or something deeper, she proved to be incapable of taking leave of him. Indeed, the fatal night in his study she left behind a book, which offered Wilson and his guest a perfect excuse to immediately get in touch. In the golden age of the postal service, when a letter dispatched in the morning might conceivably be delivered by late afternoon, two letters, both sent off on Monday, crossed in the mail. The difference in tone is palpable. Her letter telling Wilson he can throw out the book if he likes and warning him not to send it on to *Partisan Review*, was typed single spaced on Covici-Friede stationery and signed "Well, good-bye, and thank you. Yours, Mary McCarthy."

### FROM MARY MCCARTHY'S LETTER TO EDMUND WILSON, NOVEMBER 29, 1937

I don't know what you think, but I think I must have been guilty of an extraordinary and irresponsible presumptuousness. If this is so, and reason assures me it must be, I am sorry, really. . . . Yesterday I was so painfully self-conscious, trying to avoid the double entendres and meaningful looks that these situations so often inspire. Anyway, forgive me, please. I want you to, very much.

## FROM WILSON'S LETTER TO McCARTHY, NOVEMBER 29, 1937

You left your book again. I miss you. How about coming back here soon? Could you come out here for an evening? Just call me up and leap on the train.

Wilson's letter was signed "Love, Edmund W." Apparently that was all that was needed. McCarthy signed her letter of Tuesday afternoon, "Love to you, too." This time, she was promising to come up again and confessing to a recent fit of jealousy.

## FROM MARY McCARTHY'S LETTER TO EDMUND WILSON, NOVEMBER 30, 1937

Sunday was a bad day for me. [. . .] You tried me sorely, too. When you took Peggy [Margaret Marshall] on your lap, something happened to my face that I couldn't stop. Philip leaned over to me and said, "I know something about you," and I said, "I know you do," and he said, "You're jealous," and I said, "Yes." He attributed it, however, to an extreme coquettishness, and didn't look farther for explanations.

That week, she wrote Wilson from work every day but Thursday. The effort expended on the correspondence was decidedly one-sided. Wilson's letters were affectionate and direct but they were little more than a scribbled or poorly typed note. On November 30, she had mentioned a plan to do an essay on Lord Byron ("emphasis on political and satirical qualities"). "I've felt a sweet affinity with the wicked Lord, ever since I was eleven years old and had read *The Prisoner of Chillon*," she wrote. Thursday, Wilson dispensed with Byron's politics in one sentence: "Byron was always on the side of the rebel, but had no politics properly speaking—will give you a long lecture on the subject if you will submit and if I ever see you long enough to do so."

Friday, she was reporting at length on a dinner the previous evening with Delmore Schwartz. "He is the most intellectual creature I have ever seen, so intellectual that he is inhuman," she wrote and then went on to explain why. "He makes one feel that to admit in his cerebral presence any natural inclination or appetite—for food, company, love, gossip, comfort—would be to commit a most indecent solecism."

She herself was not above admitting to appetites. Sunday night, she joined Wilson in Stamford and later, taking the milk train back to the city, she "bummed a cigarette from the only person who was awake." Monday she wrote, "I want very much to see you. But no more milk trains!" In case Wilson took this ultimatum too much to heart, she added that she feared he was feeling "sensible and renunciatory." While she could understand why he felt this way, she would be "very sad" if he "carried it into stern practice."

Wilson *may* have been feeling renunciatory, but it did not last for long, and the following week she was back at Stamford, relying for her alibi for Rahv on the morning papers and the kindness of strangers.

### FROM MARY MCCARTHY'S LETTER TO EDMUND WILSON, N.D. [C. DECEMBER 14, 1937]

You remember my telling you in the taxi on the way out that I was supposed to be at the fight? Well, the taxi-driver, it seems, was a man of heart. As soon as I got in the cab at your house, he said without any preliminaries: "I suppose you'd like to hear about the fight." Then he went on to give me a round-by-round description of it. I thanked him at the station, got out (no tip), and didn't even buy a morning tabloid in the station to have a picturesque account of the fight at my fingertips.

Later that December, she was writing Wilson, "I think you're wonderful. I miss you." And she was telling him of a party where she had been introduced to his landlady. Upon learning that they had a mutual friend, Margaret de Silver had spoken of how she was going to have to ask Wilson to find another place to live. Although the prospect of Wilson's leaving Trees was dismaying, the conversation had afforded a certain pleasure: "You know the delight of speaking the name of someone with whom one is privately intimate to a third person to whom the name is just like any other one mentions? It's wonderful. Such conversations have a kind of pleasing dramatic irony."

The Christmas holidays put an end to all letters and all visits. When they resumed writing at the beginning of January, the tone of their letters changed rapidly. Wilson was recovering from a miserable holiday week at Red Bank and she was coming to terms with her grandfather Preston's death from a stroke. On the visit after her trip to Reno, she'd grown close to him again—he'd helped her out when she was setting up her life on Gay Street—and she was taking it hard. Wilson appreciated the seriousness of her loss, but he was soon having troubles of his own. ("writing a lot of inconsequential articles in order to pay my bills.") In their mutual misery they seem to have forged a deeper bond. "I don't think you do take care of yourself enough," Wilson wrote on January 18. He signed his letter, "Love, as ever" and added "with * * * (though you say they mean comparatively little to you)."

"You are wrong about kisses," she responded. "They mean a great deal to me, but I put them in the classification of hors d'oeuvres." In that same letter she let him know, "I think I must be a little bit in love." Indeed she had gone so far as to purchase a pair of reserved seats at Radio City Music Hall for a Saturday matinee of *Snow White*, a movie she would never have attended on her own, much less gone out of her way to see. Wilson's stature was such that he could indulge his appetite for Walt Disney and remain unsullied.

Wilson's final letter, written as the month drew to a close, told of a recent visit to Boston, where he had delivered a lecture at Harvard and been wined and dined by the faculty. With one of his hosts, Harry Levin, he had discussed the doctrinal rigidity of *Partisan Review*'s editors. But this particular discussion was not one he felt free yet to share with her. In any case, what he'd had to tell her was of greater urgency. He missed her and wanted her to be with him.

In later life, as Mary McCarthy read over her letters to Wilson, she was startled by "the intimacy and friendliness" and by "a note of tenderness and teasing." She was quick to add: "What I hear in the letters is not love, though—I never loved Wilson—but sympathy, affection, friendship." In addition to the tenderness and teasing, a more disinterested reader might glimpse an effort to beguile, but every now and then there is a hint of something deeper. A hint that could easily encourage a lover who is looking to find evidence that his passion is reciprocated.

We have no record of the letters Mary McCarthy wrote to the men she had been entangled with before Edmund Wilson, but it is reasonable to assume that with Wilson she was rising to the occasion. These were no ordinary letters, but, then, Wilson was no ordinary man. His written responses, if brief, were encouraging. It is only natural to find wonderful someone who finds you wonderful—particularly when you feel you are at the top of your form.

If she'd had her way, she might have let the affair with Edmund Wilson drag on indefinitely. But common sense dictated that they take some action—it was only a matter of time before they were caught by Rahv. Wilson was adamant: Mary had to make a choice. And if she chose him she was going to have to choose marriage and give up her job. He did not want her to come and live with him in Connecticut without benefit of clergy. His proposal was simple and direct. Her response was less so. She made a full confession to Rahv. To his credit, on learning that the woman he lived with had betrayed him, Rahv did not get angry. He did not throw her out. "What do you want to do, Mary?" he said. But he did nothing to persuade her to stay. The decision was left to her. Rahv urged her not to be hasty and sent her off to the country, to Nathalie Swan's mother's house, to give her time to come to her senses. Fortified by a week of luxury and motherly concern, she decided to go ahead and marry Wilson.

**NANCY MACDONALD**   Here she was living with Rahv, seemingly happy with him, and out of the blue suddenly she was off with Wilson. Why did she do it? Security, maybe. I don't think Rahv had much in the way of money. Wilson certainly was a big name. But she seemed very much in love with Rahv.

**DWIGHT MACDONALD, IN A 1979 INTERVIEW WITH DIANA TRILLING,** *PARTISAN REVIEW*, **FALL 1984**

It was a crushing blow to Rahv. I remember Rahv saying, my God, why did I ever introduce her to that guy. Of course Wilson was a very eminent guy, and so on. Also she might have had an instinct that she needed him as a kind of, you know, guide.

**LIONEL ABEL**   What Phil said was: "Mary has no imagination. When she married Edmund Wilson, it never entered her mind she'd have to sleep with him."

**WILLIAM PHILLIPS**   Rahv concealed his emotions. He worked at it, or maybe it came naturally to him. He'd sort of brush everything aside. And he sort of brushed personal feelings aside and personal relations aside in order to get to the real meat of life—to politics and literature and thinking. So that his real upset probably didn't come out. He was upset when she left him for Wilson, but he was able to squelch it more than some people could have. I couldn't have.

**HARRY LEVIN**   I can see Edmund being enchanted by Mary and taking her off from Philip Rahv. I didn't have a very high opinion of Rahv, for that matter, although he was in many ways a strong character and a lot of women seem to have liked him. The gossip—the rumor—was that Mary said, "Here is this man who is in such an eminent position, what could I do."

**SELDEN RODMAN**   I can't see why anyone would have married Edmund Wilson, who was the most repulsive person on Earth, other than for the prestige of being his wife. He looked like a pig.

**WILLIAM BARRETT**   I hashed it all over with Delmore. Ambition undoubtedly figured in her leaving Rahv for Wilson, but there were concrete reasons besides that. I tended to think that she really loved Rahv, but she would be off with the old and on with the new. Mary was hard-pressed financially. And Rahv offered no relief that way. With Wilson, for a short while when they were hitting it off, she lived like a queen.

Mary McCarthy married Edmund Wilson on February 10, 1938, in Red Bank, New Jersey, in a civil ceremony. This time there were no relations and no friends in attendance. Just the borough clerk and two witnesses. The marriage rocked the *Partisan Review* circle, sending aftershocks as far north as Cambridge. Ever afterward she would be at a loss to explain why she had left a man she loved to marry a man whom she did not love and whom she found physically repugnant. What had caused her to do such a thing?

## FROM *INTELLECTUAL MEMOIRS*

So finally I agreed to marry Wilson as my punishment for having gone to bed with him—this was certainly part of the truth. As a modern girl, I might not have called that a "sin"; I thought in logical rather than religious terms. The logic of having slept with Wilson compelled the sequence of marriage if that was what he wanted. Otherwise my action would have no consistency; in other words, no meaning. I could not accept the fact that I had slept with this fat, puffing man for no reason, simply because I was drunk. No, it had to make sense. Marrying him, though against my inclinations, *made* it make sense.

Besides this "logical" explanation there were others that she was prepared to offer. Her grandfather's death had left her shaken; Wilson came from the same kind of Anglo-Saxon Presbyterian background as Harold Preston; Wilson promised that they would read Juvenal together, that they would take long walks in the woods, pick wildflowers, go trout fishing, ride horses; and, most important, Wilson promised he would "do something" for her: No great fan of her "Theater Chronicles"—"You draw a crushing brief against a play," observed this former theater reviewer— he was going to help her develop what he saw as a considerable talent for "imaginative writing." But for all that Wilson's promise to further her career was tempting, McCarthy later asserted, it did not determine her decision. If anything, his appeal to her "self-interest" put her off.

Eventually, having riffled through some fairly unpalatable possible causes for her defection, she settled for "a single one." In keeping with the period, she chose a "Marxist explanation." Compared to Rahv, Wilson was upper-class. Her decision had nothing to do with money, she said; Rahv was doing fine on the WPA. But from Wilson she would receive no lectures on her hopelessly middle-class manners and mores. In addition, he had promised her they would have children. "That was all there was to it," she said. Not everyone was convinced.

## FROM ELIZABETH HARDWICK'S FOREWORD TO *INTELLECTUAL MEMOIRS*

The account of the moral struggles is a most curious and interesting one, an entangled conflict between inclination and obligation; the inclination to stay with Rahv and the obligation to herself, her principles, incurred when she got drunk and slept with Wilson and therefore had to marry him. The most engaging part of this struggle is not its credibility or inner consistency but the fact that Mary believed it to be the truth. There was a certain Jesuitical aspect to her moral life which for me was part of her originality and one of the outstanding charms of her presence.

**WILLIAM PHILLIPS** Reading the third chapter of the last memoir, it seemed to me that Mary was remembering things the way she wanted to. I don't think what she wrote corresponded to her behavior at the time. She was reconstructing the past, the way we all do to a lesser or greater extent. She did it to a greater extent.

**FROM JEAN STROUSE'S REVIEW OF *INTELLECTUAL MEMOIRS***
Again and again she puts her behavior on trial, judging herself harshly (and inviting readers to judge her) as if to forestall conviction in a higher court—yet somehow the confessions seem always slightly to miss the point, amounting to a sort of moral sidestep, as if none of this really has anything to do with *her*.

**GORE VIDAL**  Women like Mary marry for a purpose.

**PAULINE KAEL**  It's a peculiar piece because there's so much left out. Her account just doesn't tell us enough. Wilson wrote lucidly and beautifully but I've never been a great admirer of his work. Still, so many people were that it conferred an enormous position on him. When I met him (for the only time) in the early sixties he was heavy-lidded and unmoving—a petulant dragon. He was like an overgrown Truman Capote. He expected me to stand up a group of Canadian filmmakers who were waiting for me downtown and go to dinner with him. (He indicated that if I didn't spend this evening with him I wouldn't get another chance—which was fine with me.)

**ALISON LURIE**  Going with a stronger older man was then and still is now a way of getting ahead in the world. It is a way of instantly skipping ten or twenty years socially and professionally. There's a downside to this that comes later when you realize that you're only Mrs. So-and-So. It's a trade-off. But if you go into it with your eyes open, it does have its advantages. It can work out if you're fast on your feet, like Mary was.

If she could not quite explain why she had left Rahv for Wilson, she was sure of one thing: her leaving Rahv had been a mistake.

**FROM *INTELLECTUAL MEMOIRS***
If it had been left to Rahv, I never would have written a single "creative" word. And I do not hold it against him; on the contrary. His love, unlike Wilson's, was from the heart. He cared for what I was, not for what I might evolve into. Whatever I might be *made* to be, with skillful encouragement, did not interest him. To say this today may seem hard on Wilson, as well as ungrateful on my part for what he did, in the first months of our marriage, to push me into "creativity"[. . . .] I would not be the "Mary McCarthy" you are now reading. Yet, awful to say, I am not particularly grateful.

**ELIZABETH HARDWICK**  Mary's saying all those things about Edmund does not make any sense. In my experience he was adorable, though by no means easy to handle. But why all that anger on Mary's part? My feeling is that with all the other husbands Mary was always in control. And Mary couldn't bend to anybody. She just went through the other ones. With Edmund she couldn't do that.

From the first day they were married, Edmund Wilson determined how he and his young wife would spend their time, where they would live, and whom they would see. As soon as they were officially joined before the borough clerk and two witnesses at the Red Bank town hall, Wilson brought his new bride to lunch at his mother's house. Once they had eaten, he left her to make the best of it with his mother and her ear trumpet while he slipped upstairs for a nap. There was no honeymoon. That night, they took a room at the New Weston Hotel in New York, and in bed, after too many drinks with her brothers Kevin and Preston, Wilson accused her of tricking him into marrying her so that she could turn him over to her brothers, who were agents of the GPU (the KGB of that day). The next morning no mention was made of Wilson's wild accusation, but once again Mary spent her wedding night wide awake, nursing the sad realization that she had made a mistake.

## FROM *INTELLECTUAL MEMOIRS*

During that bad night I assessed my situation. I was alone, with no one to turn to. Philip and my job were gone. Grandpa was dead; my only friends were people like Eunice Clark who were not real friends[. . . .] My marriage was a mistake. I clearly saw that I never should have married that peculiar man, yet I did not have the courage to take my suitcase and go off somewhere by myself. That would have been Miss Sandison's counsel.

For all her formidable powers of observation, when it came time to marry, she seemed to suffer from an astonishing myopia. This time, though, her misgivings seemed to be no more than a bride's wedding night jitters. Certainly, in his journal and his letters, Wilson showed every evidence of being delighted with his new marriage and his young wife. At Trees, it was a beautiful February. Sometimes the afternoons were warm enough for a long walk. He was working late at night. In April he was inviting friends like Louise Bogan and the poet and critic Allen Tate to take the train up and see how well he had done for himself. *The Triple Thinkers*, his second book of literary criticism, had just come out and he wanted to know what they thought of it. He was hoping to have his book on Marxism finished by the fall. He was full of plans for the immediate future—he had found a place for them to stay in Bermuda after they left Trees. Already he had started work on a new book "to be hung on the *Philoctetes* myth of the man with the incurable wound and the invincible bow."

By May, Wilson's new wife was not only pregnant but had written a short story. With admirable dispatch Wilson had made good on both of his prenuptial promises. Much like the Monsieur Willy of Colette's legend, he had sat his young wife down at a desk in the small guest bedroom at Trees and closed the door. Although he did not go so far as to lock that door, the result was nonetheless impressive. She had typed "Cruel and Barbarous Treatment" straight out, confirming Wilson's belief in her talent for "imaginative" writing—a talent not even her fondest teachers at Vassar had been willing to grant her. In those December letters Wilson may have found grounds for holding such a belief. Certainly in more than one can be found the germ of this short story, which commences by contrasting the pleasures of an extramarital affair with those of a secret engagement.

### From "Cruel and Barbarous Treatment"

[W]ith the extramarital courtship, the deception was prolonged where it had been ephemeral, necessary where it had been frivolous, con-spiratorial where it had been lonely. It was, in short, serious where it had been dilettantish. That it was accompanied by feelings of guilt, by sharp and genuine revulsions, only complicated and deepened its delights, by abrading the sensibilities, and by imposing a sense of out-lawry and consequent mutual dependence upon the lovers.

Shut away in that small room in Connecticut, she had returned to the precipitate breakup of her first marriage and written of a young woman who leaves her husband for a Young Man not unlike John Porter. Edmund Wilson was no John Porter, but the heroine's wish to savor her delicious secret as long as possible was very fresh in her mind. To the telling of the story she brought irony and distance, not even troubling to name the young man or the philandering wife. She also brought a con-trol that could be seen as reflecting the order and stability of her new life in Connecticut and the immediate rewards of the recent bargain she had struck.

"Cruel and Barbarous Treatment" would come out one year later in the *Southern Review*. The Woman with a Secret, the Young Man, and the husband she had no wish to hurt—a triangle as old as storytelling itself but refurbished and made to seem quite modern—would immediately strike a responsive chord in readers. The response would be sufficiently gratifying for her to go on to write more stories that would have as their heroine a fiercely intelligent, courageous, foolhardy, and surprisingly vulnerable young woman who would in time acquire the name Meg Sar-gent and who would owe almost every detail of her being to her creator.

Unfortunately, as Mary McCarthy's first spring with her new husband drew to a close, her wedding night fears proved to be all too well founded. On June 7, Allen Tate and his wife, Caroline Gordon came to dinner. A highly regarded novelist, Caroline Gordon was not about to be impressed by one promising short story. The three old friends had much to say to one another and not all that much to say to Wilson's pregnant new wife. At some point during the bibulous evening Mary left her guests and went off to bed. She always claimed that what followed was a mystery to her, but one can see that there might have been some cause for what subsequently took place.

If the Tates' visit was much anticipated by Wilson it was not without attendant stress. For one thing, he was introducing them to a wife seventeen years his junior. For another, the time was fast approaching when he and his wife were going to have to leave Trees—not for a house in Bermuda, but for a summer with his mother in Red Bank. Furthermore, while he might profess to be eager to hear what Allen Tate had to say about *The Triple Thinkers*, he believed that Tate had completely misunderstood aspects of *Axel's Castle*. Indeed, he had told him as much.

By the end of that June dinner, Wilson had consumed more than his customary considerable allotment of alcohol. After seeing the Tates on their way, he went upstairs and joined his pregnant wife in bed. What happened next is open to conjecture. All that is certain is that it ended with Wilson's wife receiving a black eye and being rushed by taxi down to New York Hospital, where she was admitted as a psychiatric patient to the Payne Whitney Clinic. Seven years later Mary McCarthy would provide a vivid account of the entire incident when she applied for a legal separation from Edmund Wilson. One part of this sworn affidavit would turn up in the tabloids and go on to dog her to the very end of her life.

### FROM MARY MCCARTHY'S AFFIDAVIT OF MARCH 12, 1945

Late in the evening, after my husband had spent the evening drinking with some friends, he came into my room, woke me up, hit me, kicked me, and after a tirade of abuse finally slumped into bed and went to sleep. After receiving this shocking treatment, I stayed awake most of the night, and when my husband woke up in the morning I asked him what he meant by his treatment of the night before, and informed him that I would stand for it no longer. I had just about expressed myself, when he punched me in the face, held me down on the bed and began to hit me all over the face, breasts and stomach saying "Now will you shut up you goddam bitch?" I was terrified, and started to scream and then cry and finally went into the bathroom and threw up—and I could not stop either crying or vomiting. I was in the period of pregnancy which brings on morning sickness at the time, and this condition was aggravated by my husband's brutal conduct.

In this affidavit, McCarthy stated that as the day wore on, Wilson grew alarmed at her condition and called in a doctor, who suggested that she be taken to Harkness Pavilion. She suggested New York Hospital, where she'd had her appendectomy. By the time she and Wilson got to the hospital, it was late at night and she had a black eye. After what she called "some confusion," she was checked into the psychiatric wing. The staff on duty assumed her black eye was self-inflicted and sent her to the admissions ward, where she immediately "went to bed." The next morning, when she was feeling more like herself, she talked to the doctor who came to examine her. After "a complete check-up," she was moved to "the Convalescent or Outgoing Floor, and was diagnosed not as a psychotic but possibly in need of some private psychoanalytic treatment."

Later, in her 1963 novel *The Group*, she had something very like this befall her heroine Kay, whose husband Harald Petersen beats her violently, gives her a black eye, and then signs her into Payne Whitney. Harald Petersen dumps his wife at the admissions desk and then cannot be located until the following night. What makes the incident particularly horrifying—and in one key respect different from the incident described in the affidavit—is that Harald Petersen does not inform Kay that she is being admitted to a psychiatric clinic. When Kay's friend Polly Andrews comes to see her the next morning, Kay tells her that her committal is a misunderstanding—that both she and Harold believed she was simply going to New York Hospital for a rest. She tells how she chose New York Hospital over Harkness because of the "rough-weave yellow curtains and pure white walls" and how she was just starting to look for the gift shop in the lobby when a doctor came over and asked how she got her black eye. "I laughed and said I'd run into a door, but he didn't get the joke," she tells Polly. It is left to Polly to set Kay straight.

**FROM *THE GROUP***
> "Harald committed me?" cried Kay. "He must have," said Polly. "Unless you committed yourself. Did you?" "No." Kay was positive. "That must have been those forms he filled out in the office," she said. The two girls' eyes dilated. "But that means," Kay said slowly, "that he knew what kind of place this was when he left me."

In the years following publication of *The Group*, Mary McCarthy would tell three biographers that she, like Kay, had been misled by Wilson, who had checked her into Payne Whitney without telling her where she was going. To Carol Brightman, she mentioned the considerable appeal for her of the "yellow roughly woven curtains" at New York Hospital—curtains she had first seen at the time of her 1934 appendectomy. To both Brightman and Carol Gelderman, she said that Wilson had come up from his evening with the Tates to find her sleeping on new blue sheets that she'd had Hatty put on the bed. He had ripped the sheets, which were not to his liking, off the bed and thrown her onto the floor. He did not turn up until the afternoon following the committal, she said, a good deal the worse for drink.

In public Edmund Wilson always maintained a gentlemanly silence, but in the affidavit he had filed in February 1945, a month prior to

McCarthy's, he gave a very different version of the events of that day and night. For decades Wilson's affidavit remained in the court record, available for anyone to see. Then, at the end of his life, when he was readying his journals from the thirties for publication, Wilson wrote down his version of this incident—a version that would be edited out when the journals were published posthumously, in order to spare the still living McCarthy. According to Wilson, it was the doctor in Connecticut who sent her to Payne Whitney and there was no subterfuge about it. That was that. In time, the whole question would come up again when McCarthy was interviewed later by Wilson's biographer and the journals' last editor.

### FROM EDMUND WILSON'S AFFIDAVIT OF FEBRUARY 23, 1945

I discovered shortly after my marriage to plaintiff that she was a psychiatric case. In May of 1938 [sic], during her first pregnancy, she developed an acute hysterical condition and I took her to the Payne Whitney Clinic at the Medical Center. She was there confined to the ward for violent cases for a period of time. She remained at the Payne Whitney Pavilion for a number of weeks[. . . .]

At no time did I ever attack her. I have found it necessary to protect myself against violent assaults by her in the course of which she would kick me, bite me, scratch me and maul me in any way she could.

### FROM EDMUND WILSON'S RETROSPECTIVE NOTE

I made fewer entries in this journal during the years I was married to Mary, and those usually about other people. She was a hysteric of the classical kind who makes scenes[. . . .] Her pregnancy brought this on in an acute form. I did not know what to do about her, but Hatty, who was getting scared, having had the experience of her insane daughter, on her own initiative called a local doctor. He evidently knew nothing about such disorders; he assumed Mary was simply insane and sent her to the Payne-Whitney Clinic in New York. I took her up in a taxi in the middle of the night[. . . .]

Mary's fits of alienation at times made life very difficult—I was always having to cover them up. I could not bear to write about it. But she was also, in spite of the distortion of her view, an amusing and provocative companion, and I really till the very end never ceased to be extremely fond of her. Except in the use of her intellect, she had always remained a child. You were sorry for her and wanted to rescue her. Her tantrums would end in tears. She said that she had never cried before in her life, and [psychoanalyst Sándor] Rado told me that this was a favorable sign: she had before been so sealed-up and frozen that she could not express her emotion. In her spells of hysteria, she would be likely to identify me with the uncle by marriage whom she had hated and with whom she and Kevin had been sent to live after her parents' death. She was under the impression—which must have been exaggerated—that he had beaten her every day.

### FROM LEWIS DABNEY'S NOTE TO EDMUND WILSON'S *THE SIXTIES*

In June 1938, after a bitter quarrel with EW, McCarthy spent three weeks in this psychiatric hospital in New York City. She later claimed they had gone to a psychiatric hospital by accident rather than on their Stamford doctor's advice, though when I asked about this she laughed, admitting a certain doubt.

Life can imitate art, particularly in retrospect, when a story is told so frequently it begins to impose itself on the original version. Depositions for divorce tend to lead to exaggeration, particularly when the custody of a child is at issue. No one would argue against the fact that Wilson drank to excess. That he was capable of hitting a wife seems highly possible. That at some point he believed he was only subduing a hysterical wife is also possible. While there was no witness to what happened in the Wilson bedroom, there was one witness to what went on throughout the seven years of the marriage.

**ROSALIND WILSON**   I knew Mary McCarthy from 1937 to 1944. She married my father when I was fourteen, and she left him seven years later, when I was twenty-one. Reuel says that his mother changed very much in later life. I can only talk about the person I knew. Also, one thing to remember is that Mary was never a very sympathetic intellect to me. Had my father married Dawn Powell I would have found her sympathetic and someone I really wanted to be with. During those seven years I was naturally away at school and college. I spent a lot of the time at the home of my friend Jeannie Clymer. And I spent a lot of time with my grandmother. But I was with them quite a lot in the summer and one winter work period, when I was living in New York. I was with them enough certainly to be the person who saw that marriage from the inside and is in a position to talk about it.

Mary, at the time that she married my father and all through the marriage, would have these terrible . . . I can only call them "seizures." It wasn't like anything I've ever seen. The gestures were the same every time. It was like the mad wife of Mr. Rochester. Mary, in her letter to me about my book said, "Well, everyone knows that your father had drunken fights with his wives." This has nothing to do with drunken fights, which occasionally happened. This was something separate, unto itself. And Mary could have them at any time of the day or night. Mary would begin to scream and yell and attack him—it had nothing to do with drink, it had nothing to do with anything he was doing—and she was a big girl and it was frightening. It was terribly, terribly frightening.

Naturally, I didn't say anything to him the first times I heard it, which was at Stamford. But it was so frightening that my father then took me for a walk when we were at Red Bank and explained it to me. Because he *had* to explain it to me. It's a good thing he did. He explained that because of her childhood trauma, her parents dying and all that, that she'd been left ill. But she hadn't told him about it before her marriage to him. He'd talked to the doctors who said she was a classical hysterical case—the sort of stuff that witches were made from. And she did look like a witch when she got into one of those spells. He said that she had to go to the doctor and he explained about that. And he repeated again and again that she'd never told him about this before they were married.

Rosalind Wilson had little cause to love her stepmother, but her words cannot be ignored. One fact everyone agrees on: the doctors quickly determined that Wilson's bruised and battered wife could use "private psychoanalytic treatment." In a matter of days, Wilson was put in touch with Sándor Rado, a noted analyst and head of the Psychoanalytic Institute, who was about to spend his summer vacation in Stamford, at Shippan Point. Rado consented to look in on her at the hospital. Although he was reluctant to take on a patient on a temporary basis, he agreed to do so, and then to turn her over to another analyst in the fall. Wilson changed his plans for the summer. Instead of taking their things down to Red Bank, he rented a furnished house just down the street from Rado, so that it would be easy for his wife to see Rado for psychoanalysis three times a week.

According to McCarthy, Wilson confessed to her doctors on his first visit that he had been the one to give her the black eye. He reassured them it was not self-inflicted. Having done that, like Harald Petersen in *The Group*, he urged her to spare herself further stress by staying on at Payne Whitney while he took care of their move. With her hospital insurance from Covici-Friede, he argued, staying there for a few weeks would be cheaper than going to a hotel. He also urged his wife to get an abortion. To the stay at Payne Whitney, she agreed readily, but she had no wish to have the abortion. She did not subscribe to the theory voiced by her husband and the doctor who had briefly treated her in Stamford that a protracted pregnancy would be dangerous in light of her precarious mental state.

In her first letter from Payne Whitney, she attempted to persuade Wilson to let her carry their child to term. She assured him that there would be no repetition of the unpleasant incident that had landed her in the hospital. The letter is at once poignant and deeply troubling. It can be read two ways: either as verification of Wilson's assertion that it was an attack of hysteria that landed her in the hospital, or as the placating gesture of a typical battered wife.

**FROM MARY MCCARTHY'S LETTER TO EDMUND WILSON, JUNE 9, 1938**
  I had an extremely cheerful interview with Dr. Ripley last night[. . . .] As for the psychiatric aspect of the matter, he says that observation of My Case indicates that a continuance of the pregnancy will almost certainly not make me worse and possibly even better. He thinks from your point of view the Worst may be over, that you may not have

to witness anything like the last thing you did witness. He says there
are some types of cases that would grow much more violent during
pregnancy, but that I am not in that category. I told him that you told
me that the Stamford doctor had advised abortion, and he said that the
Stamford doctor's advice was based, in all probability, on the fact that
he had only seen me during what we will call for politeness sake a
seizure, and presumed that I was continuously in that condition[. . . .]

Tonight we are going to have a Community Sing. I bet you didn't
have that in *your* insane asylum. We played anagrams last night, a different sort from ours and much faster[. . . .] I am learning to play pool.
Once I've mastered it you won't be able to distinguish me from Studs
Lonigan at high noon.


The letter, which is single spaced, is at times reminiscent of her letters from the previous December. When she goes on to say that she has
been reading the advance copy of a historical novel Wilson brought her,
she lapses into the voice of her old *Nation* book notes. Like Kay in *The
Group*, she has turned out to be absolutely normal on her metabolic tests.
But, unlike Kay, she asks her husband for typing paper. Already among
her fellow patients she finds much to occupy her. ("It was just the same
at college. The Jewish girl on the corridor, however middling her family's income, always kept the larder for all the rest of us.") She is so
intent on sounding like her old self that in time she seems to forget that
she isn't.

Wilson, on the other hand, is intent on persuading her to have an
abortion. ("I can't come to any other conclusion but that you mustn't go
through with a child at this time.") It is a "disappointment," he acknowl-
edges, but the only practical course, given the fact that they have little
money to spare. Not only will her psychoanalysis be costly but with a
baby she will be "badly tied down." As he sees it, there is only one solution: "So get the thing over and then you can come to Stamford and you
can start a gay summer life between New York and the psychoanalyst
and your loving husband."

As his young wife prepared to leave the hospital, Wilson was careful
to reassure her that *he* didn't feel that with their marriage they had made
a "false start." Mary McCarthy was discharged from Payne Whitney on
June 29, 1938. She had been in the hospital three weeks. (In his affidavit
Wilson would say "several" and in hers she would say "two.") The diagnosis was "without psychosis; anxiety reaction." Mary had been allowed
to keep her child. Her analysis with Rado was to commence at once. By
entering analysis, she was agreeing to go along with its tenets, one of
which she had come up against when she was seeing an unhappily married Bill Mangold. Until her analysis was completed she was not to get a
divorce or in any way change her life.

After a visit to Provincetown in August, the Wilsons, for want of anything better, returned to finish out the year at the house in Shippan Point. Sándor Radó had referred his patient to a Dr. Richard Frank in New York. Although living in Stamford was cheaper than living in the city, it was hardly convenient. The Wilsons did not keep a car and neither of them drove. Mary had to take the train to see Dr. Frank at his office on Park Avenue. She had cut back on her "Theater Chronicles." For 1938 she did five "Chronicles," all told.

The cost of psychoanalysis was upsetting Wilson's precariously balanced budget. In October, he wrote his old teacher Christian Gauss, looking for a job. With a new baby coming he was going to need more money, he explained. He made no mention of the psychoanalysis. He went on to tell of a visit from a newly sober Scott Fitzgerald, who had made it all the way east from California. The visit seems to have touched a raw nerve. If Fitzgerald's new girl, Sheilah Graham, was "less interesting" than crazy Zelda, he observed, she had the virtue of keeping him in "better order." On their vacation Wilson had taken his pregnant wife to stay at the Provincetown house of John Dos Passos, whose writing had first brought to her attention the plight of Sacco and Vanzetti. That fall she was entertaining Scott Fitzgerald.

On the face of it, her life sounded every bit as glamorous as the one she had anticipated. She was not being asked to earn a living. She could devote as much time as she liked to working on short stories, to developing her gift for "imaginative writing." Encouraging her to do so was one of the world's leading literary critics. If Wilson sometimes had to resort to his mother to meet the phone bill, this wasn't reflected in the cabs they took, the books they bought, or the liquor they consumed. She might have liked to have worn jewels and beautiful dresses, but she was living in a nicely furnished house on a spit of land jutting out into Long Island Sound. If there was serious discord in the marriage, her friends and family continued for the moment to be unaware of it. If she seemed different, that was only to be expected. Indeed there was much about the marriage that could be viewed as attractive and appealing and altogether enviable.

**KEVIN McCARTHY**  When Preston and Marty Swensen gave up on New York and left town, I was damn near dead broke and coming down with a severe cold and I was worried I wouldn't be able to do my CBS radio audition. I called Mary up in Stamford and asked if I could come out and stay with her for a couple of days and recuperate. She said, "We'll meet the train." I remember being with Mary out there and seeing little Reuel, and Mary and I walking along the lovely Mianus River. She seemed to be living an agreeable life.

**FRANI BLOUGH MUSER**  When she married Edmund Wilson, I was abroad again. By the time I came back that summer—I'd decided to get married myself and was catching up with old friends—she was Mrs. Edmund Wilson and she was pregnant. Edmund was a very masterful person. And I think she was looking for a little of being pushed into shape. He said, "Mary, go up there and stay in your room every morning nine to noon and write." And she did. And that's really what got her going writing books. When I left she'd been living with Philip Rahv in the Village. It was an entirely different person that I met when I came back. She suddenly seemed to be kind of tempery, I must say. But that I ascribed to her pregnancy. She wasn't somebody who took those things easily.

**Margaret Miller**   I was in Europe for a year—I went in June of 'thirty-seven and came back in September of 'thirty-eight, after the Anschluss—and she was married to Edmund Wilson. He was an admirable man. He was older and he was apt to see more sides to a question. He could have tremendous charm. If you read his letters, he was constantly helping people. And he did that for Mary. I remember not long after I got back we had lunch one day and she announced that she was going to write fiction in an essayist's style. This was the beginning of her writing fiction. It was because she had been told she couldn't bring people to life on the page.

**Jason Epstein**   You can see why she married him and he married her, because you imagine that kind of thing will work, but of course it can't. It's not like Joan Didion and John Gregory Dunne, who manage to stay on pretty separate tracks. Wilson and Mary were going right head-to-head. And he was helping her—forcing her—to go head-to-head. Wilson encouraged Mary to write fiction, but, then, he would encourage *himself* to write fiction.

Wilson encouraged her to write fiction, but he did not encourage her to have much to do with her old friends at *Partisan Review*. Before the March issue came out, she had resigned from the magazine's editorial board. Living at Stamford made it difficult to keep in close touch with the magazine and its editors—to take the train into the city for a meeting was no laughing matter—but there seemed to be more to her departure from the editorial board than that.

In January, on his visit to Boston, Wilson had told Harry Levin he shared his misgivings about the *Partisan Review*'s Trotskyist rigidity. That same month, in a brief letter to the magazine, printed under the heading "Riposte," his words of praise for the first issue were offset by a schoolmaster's brisk rap on the wrist.

**"Riposte," Signed Edmund Wilson,**
**Partisan Review, January 1938**
I thought the first number of the *Review* was very good. The only thing wrong with it was the proof-reading, which you really ought to watch in the next issue.

### FROM *THE TRUANTS*, BY WILLIAM BARRETT

I told him I had joined the staff of *Partisan Review*; he merely laughed and remarked of Rahv and Phillips "Potash and Perlmutter." He was citing an early comedy of his own playgoing years. Potash and Perlmutter are the eternal pair of bumbling Jewish businessmen, yoked together and perpetually querulous about each other, but somehow managing a business that survives by the skin of its teeth.

**IRVING HOWE**   I think there was some kind of personal rivalry between Rahv and Wilson over Mary McCarthy because she had been Rahv's girlfriend before Wilson. And he was a little contemptuous of what he called the Partisansky Review.

**CLEMENT GREENBERG**   Wilson was anti-Semitic in a social way. Which is more aesthetic. There were remarks that Mary reported to me. Remarks like: "You mustn't have too many Jews at a party."

When it came to his wife's friends from Vassar, Wilson was more tolerant, though he could never be said to be at ease in their company. All the same, he agreed to escort his pregnant wife to Frani Blough's wedding on the day of Christmas Eve. The baby was expected late December or early January, which provided Mary with a perfect excuse to stay home. Then there was a false labor that sent her to the hospital the morning of the ceremony. But even if it meant coming down all the way from Connecticut in a taxi, she had no intention of missing the wedding breakfast.

**LUCILLE FLETCHER WALLOP**   At Frani's wedding she looked tired and frazzled. At college she had this wonderful color in her cheeks. With that fresh Irish color, her green eyes, and coal-black hair, she was so striking looking. But she had lost all that rosiness, that wonderful color.

**FRANI BLOUGH MUSER**   After the breakfast and some champagne she and Edmund decided to walk down to Brooks Brothers, which was a great help getting the thing going. And by the time they got there she was ready to go to the hospital again. Reuel was born the next day. He's the one person to whom I say, "I always know how old you are." He's always the age of our marriage.

At New York Hospital, she finally got to see those woven yellow curtains she had so admired during her appendectomy. In addition, there was a river view and another Vassar classmate on her floor. For the length of her stay she was pampered and coddled. If she did not look exactly the way she had at college, she briefly manifested a bit of her old desire to outrage and shock. Her classmate Rosilla Hornblower Hawes, who had her baby in an adjoining room, would later recall, "She had to walk up and down the hall for long periods to bring on labor and, Mary-like, she paraded up and down in a very transparent nightgown. Of course there were all the fathers and uncles and grandfathers around. Everybody was offended." But when it came time to choose a name for the baby she acceded to her husband's wishes. The baby was named Reuel, for Edmund's mother's favorite brother, the successful manager of the Kimball family fortune. And when it came time to leave the hospital, she returned with her baby and a makeshift layette to the rented house at Shippan Point.

Wilson's mother came to their rescue with a baby carriage. But whether he liked it or not, Wilson had to find himself a job. When Christian Gauss failed to come up with a teaching position at Princeton, Wilson managed to obtain a position for the summer at the University of Chicago. Two days a week he was to lecture on the novels of Charles Dickens. His academic duties, while by no means congenial, did not sound especially onerous. His salary might buy him time to work on his projected essays for *The Atlantic* and complete his much anticipated book on Marxism. In mid-June, Wilson set off by train for Chicago with his young family and a maid who helped care for the baby. They arrived just as the city was about to suffer the onslaught of another Midwest summer. He had sublet an apartment belonging to a faculty member who was teaching that summer in Austin, but it was immediately apparent that the apartment, with only one bedroom and a tiny maid's room, was going to be much too small.

**WALTER BLAIR**   We met them the day they came and the thing that impressed itself on us was, my God, Edmund was sweaty. He was larding the green earth. He was already fit to be tied by the time they got to the apartment with the luggage. He and Mary McCarthy were barking at each other. I don't think she particularly impressed us. They came, as I say, under the least enhancing circumstances. It was a terribly hot day.

**CLEANTH BROOKS**   I remember meeting the couple who had rented their apartment to the Wilsons. I was teaching there the following year. The wife couldn't get over how she had been helping Mary unpack and had come upon the most beautiful slippers. When she said how lovely they were, Mary told her that they had cost thirty-five dollars. You have to remember that that was an extraordinary amount of money for those days.

In the small apartment on Kimbark Avenue, with the help of the maid they had brought with them from Stamford, Mary tended the baby and got meals on the table. If her living conditions were a good deal more cramped than they had been, her social life had improved perceptibly. As a distinguished visitor, Wilson was expected to show up with his young wife for faculty cocktail parties and dinners. Before long, there were small dinners and a weekend picnic by Lake Michigan. At these occasions she was no mere appendage. She was not only a contributor to *Partisan Review* but the author of a short story that had just come out in a respected literary quarterly.

### FROM EDMUND WILSON'S JOURNAL, SUMMER OF 1939

*Picnic with Gerry Allard*[. . . .] The food and beer, of which there was a lot, on high trestle tables. The setting of Hyde Park: figures in bathing suits and shorts on the green grass. The parks in Chicago are not so well policed as in New York, so that people are more likely to get robbed or murdered, but on the other hand they have a much better time[. . . .] The baseball game—Gerry's wonderful faculty of making everybody feel at ease and mixing different kinds of people[. . . .] Mary playing ball with the others, in her pink flowered bathing suit (she had taken off the red skirt and blue top [?] of her beach dress), long legs, straight figure, olivish skin.

### FROM EDMUND WILSON'S LETTER TO JOHN DOS PASSOS, JULY 16, 1939

We've been having an awfully good time out here. The situation at the university is something fantastic—I can't do justice to it in a letter; but the faculty are much more lively and up-to-date and the students much more serious-minded than they've seemed to me in general in the East[. . . .] I have students in my courses of all races, religions, nationalities, and colors—including a German Catholic nun. Some of them are very bright[. . . .] Mary sends love. She has written about your book for *Partisan Review*, so that if you don't know how to write the next one, it won't be our fault.

Although he might wax enthusiastic about the faculty and student body, Wilson found teaching difficult. Preparing the papers to read to his classes was taking more time than he'd anticipated. The sessions were an hour and a half long. The extreme heat did nothing to make any of this easier. In no time it was clear that the apartment in Chicago was too small to quietly contain two adults who might be in perfect accord about the virtues of Edith Wharton or the failings of Archibald MacLeish but could rarely agree about something so simple as the appropriate time to sit down to eat. With the arrival of Rosalind matters weren't helped any.

**WALTER BLAIR**   One of my friends became quite well acquainted with Wilson and he wrote me at Austin, saying, "I hear that the apartment hasn't been greatly damaged, but they did call in the police last night." The two of them were fighting like cats and dogs. The police were called on several occasions. The maid got a black eye. She got between them, trying to save one of their lives.

### FROM *NEAR THE MAGICIAN*, BY ROSALIND WILSON

There were some happy social times, but on the whole it was a tense and tortuous household. For instance, they were two people who should never have eaten a meal together at home. Mary was a very good cook of the gourmet-perfectionist variety, not the girl to get the meal on the table for the threshers at harvest time. My father was always ready to criticize the food and really wouldn't have felt everything was normal if he didn't. He was compulsively late for meals, so the soufflé whatnot had fallen or the meringue had toughened up. The combination made for some ghastly meals preceded by dread on all sides. Mary longed for the constant assurance that everything was perfect, and my father was the last person to give it to her.

At the end of July, shortly after Rosalind joined them, Mary McCarthy left with Reuel to pay a long visit to her grandmother in Seattle. The maid stayed behind. Absence can make the heart grow fonder, even when you have good reason to know better. "I keep thinking of how cute [Reuel] looked on his hands and knees in the upper berth, looking out with his bright little eyes," Wilson wrote in his first letter. This time, it was Wilson who shouldered the weight of a correspondence full of anecdotes and plans for their future. In response to his letters, Mary sent off one cable to announce her safe arrival in Seattle with the "infant Hercules" and one long letter of her own. For the moment, it would seem that on Wilson's side all was forgiven, or simply forgotten—at least until she took it in her head to ask him to buy her a fur coat. The two of them had made the trip to Chicago without any firm plans for the future. Once again it was Wilson who determined their next step.

### FROM EDMUND WILSON'S LETTER TO MARY MCCARTHY, AUGUST 14, 1939

As I told you on the phone, I've now decided to go straight to Provincetown from here as soon as I've finished my courses week after next[. . . .] It's always possible to get a house there easily and cheaply—I'll take it just up to Christmas. It's delightful there in September and October—though you'll have to expect some pretty damp and dreary weather in November and December[. . . .]

I am missing you terribly. Last night I dreamed that you were back and that Reuel had learned to talk and was saying rather interesting things. I'm getting back into my old nocturnal habits, though making an effort to struggle against them—have been writing letters all night: it's now four in the morning[. . . .] As I hadn't had anything to drink for a week, the whisky I consumed with the guests last night laid me low all day today with one of my celebrated nervous headaches. Celibacy is beginning to tell on me.

## FROM WILSON'S LETTER TO MCCARTHY, AUGUST 19, 1939

I can't buy you a fur coat now, because I am completely cleaned out and will have to borrow money to get away. I still have Dr. Frank, the moving and storage bill and gas and electric bill at Stamford to pay. But if you can pick one out and get them to set it aside for you, I'll try to get it for you at Christmas.

It was her first visit to Seattle since her grandfather Preston's death, and the first since her divorce in Reno. If there were losses, there were also compensations. At the brown shingle house overlooking Lake Washington, she enjoyed the benefit of her grandmother's full attention. Augusta Preston, well along in her seventies, had lost neither her lustrous raven-black hair nor her passion for shopping. Having settled in with her infant son and hired a girl to take care of him, Mary surrendered to the blandishments of a household whose mistress saw no need to stint.

By the end of her stay, she was writing her husband that Reuel was not only sitting up but standing. He weighed $24\frac{1}{2}$ pounds. Her grandmother was "absolutely mad about him." The sole book she could find to read in the house was *War and Peace*. Although she expressed some sympathy at Wilson's financial plight, safe in her old bedroom at Thirty-fifth Avenue she didn't seem to take it very seriously. She had been keeping close to home, she informed Wilson—not seeking out her old friends, much as she might have liked to. Her grandmother was about to make a gift to her of the fur coat Wilson could not afford. She had been playing up to her grandmother and her efforts had been rewarded in more ways than one.

As a girl of eleven, new to this household from Minneapolis, she had been full of questions—trying to determine whether Augusta Preston's Jewish heritage had contributed to her bitterness or to her withdrawal from Seattle society. As a grown woman, her curiosity was once again piqued. These were not questions she was able to mention to Wilson or to broach with her grandmother. However, much of what she saw and heard that summer would have immediate consequences and lasting effects.

The Seattle visit ended with a day at the races. Accompanying her and her grandmother on this outing was Augusta Preston's favorite sister, Rose Gottstein, overweight, lacking in material possessions, happily unassimilated, and in almost every respect Augusta's opposite. At the track the two sisters placed their bets and held court. That night, with no warning, Rose died. If Mary had been hoping to discover the secret of her grandmother's affections, she was rewarded. But if she had cherished any hope of securing a place in her grandmother's heart, the futility of such a hope was brought home to her.

### FROM "ASK ME NO QUESTIONS"

My grandmother understood before I could tell her, before I had set down the telephone. A terrible scream—an unearthly scream—came from behind the closed door of her bedroom; I have never heard such a sound, neither animal nor human, and it did not stop [. . . .] I saw her, on her bed, the covers pushed back; her legs were sprawled out, and her yellow batiste nightgown, trimmed with white lace, was pulled up, revealing her thighs. She was writhing on the bed; the cook and I could barely get hold of her[. . . .] [A]ll at once she would remember Rosie and shriek out her name; no one could take Rosie's place, and we both knew it. I felt like an utter outsider. It seemed clear to me that night, as I sat stroking her hair, that she had never really cared for anyone but her sister; that was her secret.

For Mary McCarthy there was no refuge to be found in Seattle with Augusta Preston. No place for her to stay with her young son. She had no choice but to take the train east, knowing full well that the celebrated older man she had believed would somehow rescue her was in desperate need of rescue himself. To help with their son's layette he'd had to turn to his mother. He could barely afford the price of her train ticket. Worse, the life he led was anything but settled. He was not her grandfather Preston, calm, reasonable, and impartial in his judgments. Nor was he cool, rational, and enlightened. All of these qualities were reserved for his books.

By the time she set off to join Wilson on the Cape she had every reason to believe that he had misled her terribly. Six years later, one particular grievance would rankle. "Before we were married," she would inform the court, "he gave the appearance of a man of quiet habits with an interest in books, pictures and music. He was well known as a literary critic and I admired his work even before I met him. During his courtship he held out great promise of a quiet settled life and the rearing of a large family. Directly after our marriage I discovered that he was addicted to drink."

If her second husband resembled anyone, it was not Harold Preston but Myers Shriver, her tormentor from Blaisdell Avenue. Certainly his big belly and reddish blond hair recalled the well-fed tyrant who had beaten and starved her. They were in fact the same body type. But it was in their brutality that the true resemblance lay. According to McCarthy, there was nothing Wilson would stop at. "After I became pregnant he began beating me with his fists, he would kick me out of bed and again when I was on the floor. A short time before our son was born he knocked me down in the kitchen and kicked me in the stomach."

Whether Wilson had done any of this or not, she felt she had been brutally beaten. In a matter of months he had undone all the good of her years safe in Seattle, her time at Vassar, her first marriage and her independent life in the city. She had left behind her friends and her job to marry him. More important, she had left behind a man who said he loved her. She had no money to speak of. Her grandfather was dead, and her grandmother offered no refuge. Her brothers could barely take care of themselves. With an eight-month-old baby she couldn't very well hop off the train in New York and go look for a job. She couldn't take Reuel with her to live in the city and she couldn't possibly leave him to his father. She had little choice but to see the marriage through.

In Minneapolis she had found solace in the liturgy and sacraments of the Catholic Church. For recognition and approval she had relied on the nuns at St. Stephen's School. In Connecticut, having long since jettisoned her faith, she had found some comfort at the office of Dr. Richard Frank. On the Cape, she would have no doctor to turn to. She would have only Wilson, her mentor and oppressor. Wilson had promised they would find Portuguese help to come in and cook and clean, so that she could get on with her writing. She had a long autumn ahead of her. Three hours every morning she was expected to go into her room and write. If once again she had made a terrible error in judgment, reason dictated that she try to get some benefit out of it.

# Chapter Eight

# THE MINOTAUR

At the end of her life Mary McCarthy did not shrink from calling Edmund Wilson a "monster." In her very last memoir she confided that for years her name for him had been "the minotaur." Trying to make plain why she had married him, she wrote, "I may have felt a kind of friendship for the poor minotaur in his maze, so sadly dependent on the yearly sacrifice of maidens. But if, sensing that need, I warmed to Wilson, solitary among his trees, I did not guess that I would be one of the Athenian maidens with never a Theseus to rescue me."

By the time she met him, Wilson *did* bear a physical resemblance to the bellowing monster that Daedalus had quite sensibly shut away in a labyrinth. When he was drunk, the resemblance may have been marked. On his mother's side, as she noted, "he was even related to the Bull family." Still, by definition, a minotaur is a very special kind of monster. He is half bull and half man, and he, no less than the maiden, is confined within the maze. If he devours her, it is not out of malice but because it is his nature to do so. He has no choice. Still, his role is hardly ambiguous. He is the villain of the tale.

In Wilson's predicament there was undeniable pathos. But in Wilson at his best there was generosity and grandeur. His intelligence ensured that he was not a ridiculous figure. Indeed, he was not without his appeal. All the same, a few short years before he captured McCarthy, the poet Louise Bogan had deftly and persistently resisted all his offers to take her in hand and make her his own. To the great critic's strange intermingling of brilliance and brutality McCarthy seems to have been at first shockingly blind and then unusually susceptible. For seven years, one way or another, Wilson would manage to hold her in his thrall.

Readers not entirely sympathetic to her view of her second marriage have sometimes noted that by the time Mary McCarthy met up with

Edmund Wilson and went off with him to Connecticut she was no Attic maiden. In addition, she was not lacking in friends. Inevitably they go on to say that Wilson, who had encouraged her in her writing, sent her off to a psychiatrist, and hired her a housekeeper, hardly sounds like your typical monster.

But to be fair, her life with Wilson may well have seemed so solitary and encumbered as to be tantamount to captivity. Having married him and had a child by him, she was effectively cut off from her friends and from any new lover who might rescue her. Indeed, she was cut off from almost everything she had held dear. She was reduced to the company of a brilliant husband who was jealous and impossible to live with, and to such visitors as he chose to make welcome. When you are in your twenties a year can seem an eternity. If you are ambitious, it can seem as if the whole world has passed you by.

By October 1939 she and Wilson were hard at work and living on Cape Cod, in Truro Center, one of a cluster of small villages situated more than seventy-five miles out in the Atlantic on the narrowing spit of land that runs from Chatham to Provincetown. The house they were renting belonged to Wilson's old friend Polly Boyden and was on a bluff overlooking the bay. For Wilson it was ideal. Although Truro had no town center to speak of, it was a short taxi ride from John and Katy Dos Passos in Provincetown or Charles and Adelaide Walker in Wellfleet. Best of all, it was well beyond commuting distance from McCarthy's friends at *Partisan Review*. A visit to Truro was tantamount to a pilgrimage, calling for a long train ride to Providence and then a long bus ride to the tip of the Cape. Not only did it offer a perfect refuge from the clamor of debates he had no wish to take part in, but it would be a perfect refuge from the escalating conflict in Europe.

That summer, while Wilson had been finishing up in Chicago, the world had undergone a sea change. On August 23, with no warning, the Soviet Union had signed a nonaggression pact with Germany (and Stalin had secretly joined Hitler in carving up Poland). The implications of this turn of events had to be weighed and digested by leftists of every faction—even Trotsky in Mexico was forced to take a position. On the American Left, the Stalinists ceased to control the political agenda. Whether they liked it or not, the editors at *Partisan Review* were now part of the radical establishment, if only because events had proved them right.

On September 1, just as Wilson's young wife was preparing to leave Seattle, Hitler invaded Poland. She was on the streamliner headed east, on her way to join him on the Cape, when France declared war on Germany, and England immediately followed suit. Almost exactly a year after Neville Chamberlain had promised "peace in our time," the great

powers were preparing to go to war. In November, while winter was closing in on the Cape and all but the last diehards were returning to New
York, the Russians invaded Finland.

As Marxists, Mary McCarthy and Edmund Wilson were committed to
sitting back and letting the great capitalist nations destroy one another.
For Wilson this posed few problems. Having witnessed at first hand one
bloody war in Europe, he had no wish to see the United States become
embroiled in another. At heart Wilson was a creature of the twenties, literary and not deeply political. Faced with this wave of disappointments,
he was simply reverting to type. For his wife, Wilson's unwavering isolationist stance would eventually become untenable. For the moment,
though, she was prepared, at least here, to follow his lead.

By the time McCarthy joined Wilson on the Cape, she had good reason to know that he was not the man she had thought he was. While he
might sometimes promise to mend his ways, he was at heart a crusty old
bachelor with a bundle of long established habits. She was a young
woman with a mind of her own and a will that simply would not bend to
his. He was an alcoholic and he was violent. But little as she could bear
to stay with him, for five more years she could not seem to find a place
she liked better.

Although they would pick up and move many times, from the
moment they arrived in Truro she and Wilson regarded the Cape as their
true home. Here, as a couple they had some of their best periods. And at
least one of their worst. But in good times and bad, she had a chance to
savor the Cape's many pleasures. Wilson wrote of their time there in his
journals. She never had a chance to finish her own factual account of
their marriage. Nonetheless, she managed to examine those years with
some rigor in interviews and in her fiction. For her and for Martha Sinnott, the heroine of A Charmed Life, the Cape would possess an almost
fatal allure.

### FROM EDMUND WILSON'S NOTES FOR A NOVEL TO BE CALLED "THE THREE WISHES," FROM THE THIRTIES

If the weather was good enough, we went out for a walk with the
baby and pushed the carriage up and down the hills. We had a drink
every day at five, and some nights we kept on drinking in the evening.
At noon we went for the mail. We subscribed to a number of magazines
and read them all very carefully and sent for things that were adver-
tized in them. Whenever there promised to be anything a little better
than Charlie Chan, we went into Provincetown to the movies.

### FROM A CHARMED LIFE

Martha had forgotten how beautiful New Leeds was out of season, with
its steel-blue fresh-water ponds and pine forests and mushrooms and
white bluffs dropping to a strangely pebbled beach.

Once winter closed in, the population on the Cape was reduced to the natives who had lived there for generations and a handful of stragglers. Wilson had promised that they would remain only until Christmas, but they ended up staying on through spring. Whenever they were in need of company, they could turn to fellow diehards, like Anna and Norman Matson, who had a large house in the Wellfleet woods.

**ANNA MATSON HAMBURGER**   If the community had been larger, I don't think Edmund and my husband, Norman, would have seen each other. Back then there were very few people who read *The New York Times*, and the ones who read the *Times* hung out together. In the summer, of course, it was different. Despite the fact that I don't think Edmund and Norman had any real meeting of the minds, there was an intimacy that comes from living in an igloo. I remember once we were leaving a dinner party at Polly Boyden's house and it was raining—we had just gotten into our Pontiac—and Edmund followed us out to the car and rapped on our window. Norman rolled the window down, and Edmund said, "Norman, do you find that you fight with your wife more often in February?"

For all that their days and nights were quiet, they were never entirely free of discord. When it came to politics or ideas—to collaborating on a poem about events in Spain or composing a letter in response to *Partisan Review*'s rejection of Wilson's long essay on Lenin—husband and wife were in complete agreement. But when it came to something as simple as the sky above their heads they rarely saw eye to eye.

**A POEM CREDITED TO "E.W. AND M. McC."**
**IN *PARTISAN REVIEW*, FALL 1939**

> SOME AMERICANS STILL IN SPAIN TO SOME
> STALINISTS STILL IN AMERICA
>
> You sent us here, and here we rot:
> The fight we propped has gone to pot.
> The Pope and all his priests in Spain
> Are safe as in the Vatican;
> And you who sent us, safe at home,
> Are pliant to the Pope of Rome.
> —Now tell us plainly, teachers dear,
> Which folks our comrades most shall fear:
> Grandees who boast the Pope their boss
> Or Communists who kiss the Cross?

**FROM EDMUND WILSON'S LETTER TO FRED DUPEE, MAY 16, 1940**

> You people are getting as bad as *The New Republic*[. . . .] You are developing the occupational disease of editors—among them, thinking up idiotic ideas for articles that you want the writers to write instead

of printing what they want to write. (Mary wants me to ask you whether you think you're the *Saturday Evening Post*.) I've thought there was something wrong in your shop ever since you passed up that short story of Mary's, which seemed to me the best thing she had written. You people certainly owed her a chance to develop, since she was one of your original group.

### FROM *THE THIRTIES*, BY EDMUND WILSON

Full moon, on night of terrific wind, we looked at it through the panes on the upper story of Polly Boyden's house, and saw the inky clouds driven rapidly across it, showing their silver hems as they passed[. . . .] The moon remained fixed and supreme. Mary said she always thought it was moving—I always thought it was standing still.

If these months tucked away in Truro were productive, they were not without losses. On December 23, 1939, *The New York Times* reported that Harold Johnsrud, who had been acting in the play *Key Largo*, had been badly burned in a fire in his two-room suite at the Hotel Brevoort. After spreading the alarm to two fellow actors asleep in the adjoining apartment, he had returned to his rooms to retrieve "personal belongings." The following day, the *Times* reported Johnsrud's death in Misericordia Hospital. He was thirty-six years old. The personal belongings were believed to be the script of a play.

Johnsrud's death was the most severe blow Mary McCarthy experienced her first year on the Cape, but it was not the only one. That spring, Nathalie Swan, the stately Vassar classmate who had been a reliable refuge during romantic turmoil, took everyone by surprise by marrying Philip Rahv. "I guess I hadn't adjusted to her being one of the great serious brains in New York," said one classmate decades later. "I never thought she was very bright. I see Mary as being connected with that marriage. I think Nathalie Swan probably hung on to Mary in some way." At the time Mary McCarthy professed to be unfazed by the marriage, but it could scarcely have pleased her. For all that Rahv had found it difficult to accept her bourgeois prejudices and her sudden departure, he seemed to have had no trouble finding both a replacement and a taste for the ways of the truly rich.

On the Cape, it was proving impossible to hide not only from news on the domestic front but from news from overseas. With the coming of spring, the war in Western Europe had ceased to be largely a matter of bluster and saber rattling. On April 9, 1940, the "phony war" ended when the Germans invaded Norway. A month later, on May 10, Hitler marched into Holland and on into Belgium and France. By the end of the month, the British were evacuating Dunkirk.

In June, the Wilsons moved from Truro to a rental in the more substantial village of Wellfleet, with its full-leafed shade trees and fine old houses. In *A Charmed Life* Mary McCarthy sketched a comic picture of Wellfleet, which she called New Leeds. When readers accused her of enlarging on the truth or writing satire, she persisted in saying that she was simply trying to describe the village as she saw it.

### FROM *A CHARMED LIFE*

[T]he essence of New Leeds was a kind of exaggeration. Everything here multiplied, like the jellyfish in the harbor. There were *three* village idiots, grinning, in the post office; the average winter resident who settled here had had three wives; there were eight young bohemians, with beards, leaning from their pickup trucks; twenty-one town drunkards. In wife-beating, child neglect, divorce, automobile accidents, falls, suicide, the town was on a sort of statistical rampage, like the highways on a holiday week end.

The summer of 1940 was the first of five consecutive summers she spent on the Cape. It marked the beginning of a close friendship with Adelaide Walker, who with her husband Charles had managed the Theatre Union when Johnsrud was acting there.

**ROSALIND WILSON**   Mary and Adelaide Walker were very much the two beautiful women going to parties together and it was almost a sister act. I didn't realize until I read Mary's memoirs that Mary had known Adelaide before she married my father. Adelaide Walker would have made a wonderful actress.

**ADELAIDE WALKER**   My husband had been at Yale when Edmund was at Princeton. We'd lived in Wellfleet for a long time. They came to Wellfleet really more or less because of us. From the beginning Mary and I got along very well. Edmund had this thing with his wives. He didn't drive himself and he did everything possible to keep them from driving. I think it meant a kind of independence from him that he didn't like. So I took Mary out a great deal and on these trips I was the driver. Later on, she bought a car and learned to drive. It was one of her declarations of independence.

At Wellfleet, Mary learned to drive and to cook perfect meals using the very freshest of ingredients from her garden. Although driving was not something she ever much cared for, she developed a passion for domesticity, which would grow with time and never cease to characterize her.

**ANNA MATSON HAMBURGER**   Our things were from Woolworth's but Mary had lovely china and silver. She was an excellent cook. I remember her telling me that after you've been baking a cake you should always leave the door of the oven open. She read *Good Housekeeping*. I didn't go in for that. Or maybe I'd gone in for that earlier and I was over it. Mary and I were never close friends, but we had in common being the same age and being married to older men who were writers. In those days she was very girlish. We were in our late twenties. I wore blue jeans all the time. She wore skirts. When we had supper—we didn't have "dinners"—we put on Mexican shirts.

With the coming of warm weather, she began to partake of the myriad pleasures that attract summer visitors—chief among them, picnics at the freshwater ponds and on the long stretch of beach by the ocean.

### FROM *THE FORTIES*, BY EDMUND WILSON

Today we cleared a space under the low branches of the pines so that we could get a little shade, and the light openwork shadows rippled on Mary's white skin[. . . .] For lunch we had had from the brown picnic basket the classical boiled eggs, bean salad in glass jars, cucumber sandwiches, and sandwiches filled with some mixture of green chopped herbs and white cottage cheese (and there were bananas, tomatoes, and sliced sweetish green cucumber pickles which we didn't get around to eating).

**ANNA MATSON HAMBURGER**   The thing about the Cape then was that we swam on this great huge expanse of beach and in the old days in midsummer, at the public beach about a quarter mile away, there would be maybe fifty people, like little dots. Our bathing suits were wool and they never dried, so those of us who were swimming by ourselves or with our children never bothered to put bathing suits on when we went in the water. We all swam without bathing suits. If anybody started walking toward us, we had plenty of time to put our bathing suit on. It had nothing to do with exhibitionism. It had to do with being practical. I didn't swim in company without my bathing suit because I didn't think it was aesthetic. I'd already had children. Mary had a very nice figure, but nothing special in the way of bosom. She was skinny and bony. Her legs were a little too far apart and her backbone had bumps.

**ROSALIND WILSON**   My father and Mary never went in for the nude bathing scene. I don't remember it. Maybe they did it on the sly. I mean, we were always dressed when we went to the beach.

### FROM "MIDTOWN AND THE VILLAGE," BY ALFRED KAZIN, *HARPER'S*, JANUARY 1971

Many years later, when I teased [Wilson] at Wellfleet on Cape Cod about wearing a formal white shirt to the beach, he replied, "I have only one way of dressing."

In his dress and in his prejudices the great critic was very much a man of his generation, but he shared with ordinary mortals no pressing need to be consistent. While he was not without his own streak of anti-Semitism, he secretly applauded his wife's sticking it to guests of his old Princeton friend John Peale Bishop at a dinner party in Chatham.

### FROM *THE THIRTIES*, BY EDMUND WILSON

Old stuffed shirts from Chatham: none of us went except Mary and
Nina Chavchavadze. Mary and man she sat beside at dinner: anti-
Semitic, joke about many cats in the Bronx, also many Katzes—asked
her whether she didn't think that was funny; she said she couldn't find
it very funny, since her own maiden name was Katz. Everyone
became silent, people didn't talk to her after that.

Early in the summer of 1940, when the Wilsons were finally settled
in Wellfleet, France capitulated to the Germans. Later that summer,
Hitler began his bombing of Britain, and Trotsky was felled by an assas-
sin. In Wellfleet, Wilson, who suddenly found himself welcoming a succession of visitors, may have had occasion to reconsider his distaste for
the stuffed shirts in Chatham. Whether it suited him or not, the Cape was
fast becoming a northern outpost of Greenwich Village. There you could
find young writers starting out, like Alfred Kazin. Philip Rahv and his new
wife were renting a house in Provincetown for the season. In addition,
the Wilsons were putting up assorted houseguests, like David Grene, a
classics scholar who had befriended Edmund in Chicago and then kept
him company after Mary's departure. Grene came with his wife and
stayed for six weeks. Although Wilson rarely had the Wellfleet house to
himself, he could always go off in the morning to write in a studio he
rented next door to the local real estate agent. Wilson's wife had no such
option. She managed, however, not only to get meals on the table and
finish a draft of a short story but to make her presence felt.

**DAVID GRENE**    There was less gaiety than there had been in Chicago, but
Bunny Wilson was just a marvelous fellow. He could do magic tricks in a way
that would ravish any child's heart. He could produce rabbits out of hats; he
could make the most fantastic shadows on the wall with his hands. He was
wonderful with Reuel. But it wasn't all that cozy between Edmund and Mary.
Mary had rather a thing against drinking. She *did* drink, but not very much.
It was one of those things where she would rather snippily say, "Edmund, *of
course* you don't remember. How *would* you?" Jolly comments like that. Most
mornings we would all go off and write for three or four hours. It was a rambling sort of house and I had a place to myself. After lunch I walked with
Edmund on the beach.

### FROM *STARTING OUT IN THE THIRTIES*, BY ALFRED KAZIN

She had, I thought, a wholly destructive critical mind, shown in her
unerring ability to spot the hidden weakness or inconsistency in any
literary effort and every person. To this weakness she instinctively
leaped with cries of pleasure—surprised that her victim, as he lay torn
and bleeding, did not applaud her perspicacity. She seemed to regard
her intelligence as essentially impersonal; truth, in the person of this

sharply handsome twenty-eight year-old Vassar graduate, had come to pass judgment on the damned in Provincetown.

**CLEMENT GREENBERG**   In some ways Mary saw people surprisingly clearly. Sometimes. As if she were detachment itself, she had these insights and perceptions. When it came to who she respected, who she didn't, she was maybe accurate without being fair.

**ADELAIDE WALKER**   I was one of her few friends who never suffered her sharpness, and I think I owe that to the fact that she was fond of me. But being fond of somebody wouldn't have kept her from being sharp. She couldn't resist being witty at somebody's expense.

After the last summer guests had departed, the Wilsons did not settle in at Wellfleet for another solitary winter. In the fall of 1940, they returned to the house on Margaret de Silver's property in Connecticut where they had spent their first night and the first months of their marriage. That October, Scribner's brought out *To The Finland Station* and Wilson resumed his former duties as literary editor of *The New Republic*, filling in for his wife's old nemesis Malcolm Cowley, who had taken a job in Washington.

In November, Wilson wrote Scott Fitzgerald in Los Angeles to say that he was glad to know that he'd liked *To The Finland Station* and that he hoped that Fitzgerald's own new book was going to be about Hollywood. On December 21, Fitzgerald died of a heart attack. Wilson stayed on at *The New Republic* until March in order to put out a literary supplement that paid tribute to his old college friend. After that, he put together a workable manuscript of Fitzgerald's partially completed Hollywood novel, *The Last Tycoon*. He then assembled a volume of Fitzgerald's uncollected writing, which he called *The Crack-up*.

Fitzgerald's publishers paid Wilson for his work, but all royalties went to Fitzgerald's widow and daughter. While his labors were for a good cause, they took valuable hours from his own writing. They also exacted an emotional toll. Fitzgerald had been a year younger than Wilson and, for that reason alone, his death came as a shock. But it was only the last and most personal loss he had suffered in the course of that year. "Yeats, Freud, Trotsky, and Joyce have all gone in so short a time—it is almost like the death of one's father," he wrote John Peale Bishop, while soliciting a poem for him for the Fitzgerald memorial. "I'm sorry you're feeling exhausted—but come! Somebody's got to survive and write." A mere three years later John Peale Bishop, too, would be dead.

In the late winter of 1941, when he was feeling the full effect of Fitzgerald's death, Wilson did not give in to the depression that threatened to overwhelm. Instead, he went out and bought a piece of Cape property. By borrowing $1500 from his mother and then taking out a large mortgage, he was able to purchase a nineteenth-century frame house, just off Highway 6—a rambling old house said to have been built for a ship's captain, with wide floorboards, handsome metal latches, and lovely views from its downstairs windows. For this house he paid $4000. For another $1000 he had it painted and fixed up. It was his plan to live there year-round.

A tenant, when he is ready to leave, can simply lock the door and walk away. But an owner can never quite put behind nagging questions about the reliability of the furnace or the state of the roof. With an old house such questions seem to multiply geometrically. That March, in order to better oversee the work necessary to render his new purchase both attractive and habitable, Wilson decided to pack up his family and take over the Walkers' vacant house, which was virtually around the corner and one road back from the highway.

Living in Connecticut, it had been possible for Mary to resume commuting to the city for her analysis with Dr. Frank. From Wellfleet, continuing even a truncated analysis was out of the question. Once again, the decision had been Wilson's. But, then, Wilson wrote the checks and paid the bills. Having agreed early on in the marriage to put all her financial affairs completely in her husband's hands, she had come to see the error of her ways. As long as this policy continued she was completely at his mercy. Wilson was not a miser or a skinflint. He liked to live as well as the next man. The trouble was, he was not about to relinquish a single financial prerogative, even if it was the signature power on a bank account that contained so little money as to be of almost no value.

**ROSALIND WILSON**  When she was married to my father it's true there were bad times—my father would often give you a blank check which was totally bad—but the fact of the matter is that during all those years he and Mary always had a decent place to live, a nurse for Reuel, and usually a maid of sorts. And when they were in New York they always ordered everything from Gristede's. She didn't have to go out and walk around looking for the cheaper cuts of meat or anything like that.

**ANNA MATSON HAMBURGER**  It was another one of those cold rainy winter days on the Cape and there was only one joy and that was the ice cream parlor. Newcomb's made the most wonderful sodas, with heavy cream. Norman and I had taken the children down there to get some ice cream, when Mary walked in. She had bicycled from her house, which was not very far away, with Reuel on the back of the bicycle. She bought Reuel a cone for five cents, and then she turned to my husband and said, "Norman, will you treat me to a cone? Edmund wouldn't give me any more money, and I'm dying for some ice cream." Edmund was not poor at that time. They didn't have a lot of money but we always thought of him as rich. It was one of the ways he had of holding on to her.

**MARY MCCARTHY, IN AN INTERVIEW WITH CAROL BRIGHTMAN,**
**THE NATION, MAY 19, 1984**

> When I inherited a little bit of money from the McCarthy family—and
> I was earning a little bit of money from my writing—he made me put
> it into his bank account. And of course, I couldn't have signature
> power on his bank account. I had to ask him for a nickel to make a tele-
> phone call.

In the end, Mary McCarthy would take a stand and insist on her own
bank account. Whether this was at the suggestion of her analyst, she
would never be sure. The secrets of the analyst's couch must remain invi-
olate, and no work of fiction, no matter how close to real life, should be
mistaken for straight autobiography. All the same, in "Ghostly Father, I
Confess," we seem to be coming uncomfortably close to real life. As
McCarthy's heroine stretches out on the couch for a fifty-minute session
and begins to sift through her past and her dreams, the details of her story
begin to sound eerily familiar. Rid of her first husband and now married
to an older architect named Frederick, Meg Sargent is being treated by a
Dr. James for what sounds like a nervous breakdown. The doctor has
maple furniture in his waiting room and an etching of Chartres over his
desk and the best that can be said of him is that he is rather dull and colorless. Enduring what she sees as the modern equivalent of the priest's
confessional, Meg Sargent believes she has little choice. Trapped in a marriage she now views as a mistake, with a string of affairs and a failed first
marriage behind her, she sees in Dr. James her last hope.

"Let me suggest to you, Margaret, that this ordeal of your childhood
has been the controlling factor of your life," says Dr. James. But while
Meg Sargent's bleak, loveless childhood owes a good deal to McCarthy's
own, in almost every important respect it is less vicious. Having suffered
the loss of only one parent, Meg Sargent has been raised by a remote
lawyer father and a razor-strop-wielding aunt whom the father saw fit to
put in charge of the household. The aunt, it turns out, was Catholic and
rather vulgar; the father was Presbyterian and upper-middle-class. Only
after considerable damage had been done did the lawyer father step in
and take over the rearing of his dead wife's child.

"Ghostly Father, I Confess," was published in *Harper's Bazaar* in the
spring of 1942. Reading it, we feel as though we're catching glimpses of
McCarthy's disastrous childhood in a fun-house mirror while we're looking at her recent marital history head-on. Some details we have come
upon in the depositions for the Wilson separation. Some we have heard
from her in interviews. Very little about the marriage, aside from Frederick's profession, seems to have been made up out of whole cloth.

Pinned like some poor broken butterfly to Dr. James's couch, Meg Sargent views her predicament with an amusement so sardonic as to be

almost savage. But clever as she is, both she and her creator are on to every one of her tricks. They are also on to the fact that her doctor is not going to provide her with any satisfactory release from the trouble she finds herself in. As long as Dr. James brings to Meg Sargent's analysis the orthodox insights of his profession, she never for an instant relinquishes her skepticism. How, she asks, can she become the creature that Dr. James and Frederick want her to be and still keep that part of her that refuses to say what's politic or to deny the evidence before her very eyes. She never wavers until the end of the session, when Dr. James speaks of her "mind" and "beauty" and gives her an extra five minutes.

### FROM "GHOSTLY FATHER, I CONFESS"

On the street, she felt very happy. "He likes me," she thought, "he likes me the best." She walked dreamily down Madison Avenue, smiling, and the passers-by smiled back at her[. . . .] Suddenly, her heart turned over. She shuddered. It had all been a therapeutic lie. There was no use talking. *She knew*. The mind was powerless to save her. Only a man. . . She was under a terrible enchantment, like the beleaguered princesses in the fairy tales. The thorny hedge had grown up about her castle so that the turrets could hardly be seen, the road was thick with brambles[. . . .] But supposing he *should* fall in love with her, would she have the strength to remind herself that he was a fussy, methodical young man whom she would never ordinarily have looked at?[. . .]

"Oh, my God," she said, pausing to stare in at a drugstore window that was full of hot-water bottles, "do not let them take this away from me. If the flesh must be blind, let the spirit see."

Both as fiction and as document, the story makes painful reading. Finally, what are we to make of it? If Meg Sargent admits to having hysterical fits, does that mean that Mary McCarthy also had them? Possibly. But, then, she was writing this story knowing Edmund Wilson would be her first reader. In addition, she was writing it for public consumption when she and Wilson were still very much a couple.

Above all, Mary McCarthy, like any good writer, was writing for herself. As she went along, she was trying to discover just how she felt about all that was happening to her heroine. In the process it would be hard not to reflect on what was happening in her own life. Had she, like Margaret Sargent, been altered by her analysis? Had she been beaten down? Had she become some sort of invalid? Was she less inclined to speak her mind? Was she losing the qualities that most defined her?

**ROSALIND WILSON**  I was never comfortable with Mary. Never. In all the time I was with her. Only once did I ever stand up to her and it was so totally exhausting I never did it again. The very thought that something about her wasn't perfect was unacceptable.

**ARTHUR SCHLESINGER**   Harry Levin, who was a professor of comparative literature, and his wife, Elena, invited my then wife, me, and Mary and Edmund to dinner at their house in Cambridge. I was married in the summer of 1940, so this would have been later that year. I was twenty-three years old. I absolutely adored Mary. I was transfixed by her. She was so beautiful, so witty, so much fun to talk to. And I remember my feeling of outrage that this beautiful young woman should be married to what seemed to me to be an old man.

**MARIAN SCHLESINGER**   I wasn't struck by the disparity in age or Mary's beauty. She was full of ideas and conversation. There was a lot of gossip, which of course is fun. I was wary of her. She had a tongue like a viper.

**ELENA LEVIN**   All the men of course fell for Mary because she was beautiful. Very. When she entered a room with that smile, the whole room became alive. She had wonderful gray eyes—searching eyes.

At the very least, she had not lost her ability to create an indelible impression.

### FROM "MIDTOWN AND THE VILLAGE," BY ALFRED KAZIN, *HARPER'S*, JANUARY 1971

It was a strange, sulfurous afternoon. Wilson and his wife Mary McCarthy were staying in a borrowed apartment somewhere in the East Thirties near the Third Avenue El; he seemed at loose ends, uncomfortable with himself as well as with me[. . . .]

He had summoned me to hear his opinion of my book [*On Native Grounds*], and I heard it. He was brief and conclusive. He was not much interested in it. Then the afternoon took a strange turn. Wilson had been merely impatient with my book. Mary McCarthy was much more thorough. She went into my faults with great care. Since her brilliance in putting down friends, enemies, and various idols of the tribe was already known to me from her stories in *Partisan Review* and our previous meeting at Provincetown in 1940, I was fascinated by her zeal. She warmed to her topic with positive delight; she looked beautiful in the increasing crispness of her analysis.

While the secrets of the analyst's couch are no less sacred than those of the confessional, from a letter Mary McCarthy wrote to Fred Dupee we do know this much: in the winter of 1941 Dr. Richard Frank helped his patient with a story that she was working on—a story that later prompted Wilson to write in a letter to Christian Gauss, his old teacher, "I'm not sure she isn't the woman Stendhal." This was a discovery he had seen fit to share with the writer herself. As a husband Wilson might not be pleased with his wife's progress, but as a first reader and mentor he was not loath to sing her praises or to demand for her work the recognition he felt it deserved. Whether or not his letter to Fred Dupee had anything to do with it, *Partisan Review* had set their "shop" in order and made up their mind to give Wilson's wife a "chance to develop." They were taking her latest story.

### FROM MARY MCCARTHY'S LETTER TO FRED DUPEE, N.D. [C. 1941]

Your letter pleases me very much. Edmund was gratified, too, because he says it's just what he's been saying. His line is that I'm a female Stendhal. Think of that![. . .] I am anxious to hear what the other boys think of it. I am anxious also to get it back so that I can re-read the passages you admire. As is always the case, the part you like is the part I was most worried about. I had a terrible struggle with the scene in the berth. It kept getting too torrid for the rest of the story. Incidently, my psychoanalyst explained to me why I was having trouble with it, and after that it was all right.

The story was "The Man in the Brooks Brothers Shirt," and the scene in the berth was the making of Mary McCarthy. It became the cornerstone of a celebrity that was to far surpass any recognition she had received from the pieces with Margaret Marshall or her "Theater Chronicles." Meg Sargent's one-night stand with a fat middle-aged traveling salesman was shocking in its day, and it has not ceased to elicit strong responses even now. For *Partisan Review*, bringing it out showed an uncharacteristic generosity of spirit—or an astonishing lack of self-awareness.

### FROM "THE MAN IN THE BROOKS BROTHERS SHIRT"

And if she had felt safe with the different men who had been in love with her it was because—she saw it now—in one way or another they were all of them lame ducks. The handsome ones, like her fiancé, were good-for-nothings, the reliable ones, like her husband, were peculiar-looking, the well-to-do ones were short and wore lifts in their shoes or fat with glasses, the clever ones were alcoholic or slightly homosexual, the serious ones were foreigners or else wore beards or black shirts or were desperately poor and had no table manners. Somehow each of them was handicapped for American life and therefore humble in love. And was she too disqualified, did she really belong to this fraternity of cripples, or was she not a sound and normal woman who had been spending her life in self-imposed exile, a princess among the trolls?

**WILLIAM PHILLIPS** We knew the story was going to be shocking. That was part of my hesitation. To be that brazen in our editorial policy. In that time for publishing things like that you could get into trouble with the post office authorities. We then were tax exempt, if I remember correctly. You could lose your tax exemption. You could lose your second-class-mailing rights. It was a risk. It wasn't putting your life in danger, but it was a slight risk.

**LIONEL ABEL** I don't think that she ever wrote anything else that was as true a confession, that had as much meaning, that was as well written, that had that kind of import. It's really one of the best American short stories. It should be in any anthology.

**CLEMENT GREENBERG**  I was on the magazine when the story came in, and I thought, Well done, but it's middle-brow stuff. And then I reread it years later and I thought, Well done—better done than I'd realized.

To be sure, Meg Sargent comes off little better than the trolls she has surrounded herself with. Certainly she is not permitted to walk away from her one-night stand scot-free:

**FROM "THE MAN IN THE BROOKS BROTHERS SHIRT"**
Softly, she climbed out of the berth and began to look for her clothes. In the darkness, she discovered her slip and dress neatly hung by the wash basin—the man must have put them there, and it was fortunate, at least, that he was such a shipshape character, for the dress would not be rumpled. On the floor she collected her stockings and a pair of white crepe-de-chine pants, many times mended, with a button off and a little brass pin in its place. Feeling herself blush for the pin, she sat down on the floor and pulled her stockings on. One garter was missing.

For more than one generation of young women, Meg Sargent, with her bravado and underpants held together with a safety pin, would become a personal heroine. But the story had an immediate and striking effect on three young women who went on to become writers themselves.

**FROM "ODE TO A WOMAN WELL AT EASE," BY EILEEN SIMPSON, LEAR'S, APRIL 1990**
The scene was the college lunchroom, sometime in my junior year. A lively discussion was going on about a story by Mary McCarthy in a recent issue of *Partisan Review*[. . . .] If the author of "The Man in the Brooks Brothers Shirt" hoped to *épater* her readers, she certainly succeeded with us. It was one thing for a writer to dazzle her audience with astringent theater chronicles and uncompromising book reviews[. . . .] It was quite another to turn irony on herself, as she seemed to be doing in this story, which read like a hilarious confession of scandalous behavior[. . . .] "Wouldn't you think," one voice at the lunch table said, "that even if her conscience hadn't kept her from going *all the way*, having a safety pin in her underpants would have?"

**PAULINE KAEL**  Mary McCarthy really was the culture heroine of my generation. And I felt how different things were now when I watched that "Man in the Brooks Brothers Shirt" on television. It's very well done. Elizabeth McGovern is hip and smart in the central role. What's missing is the importance the story had when it first appeared. In the 1940s it was wonderfully giddy and daring. It was tonic. It was the story that bright people—women especially—talked about and identified with. This was a feminist heroine who was strong and foolish; it was before feminist writing got bogged down in victimization. She was asinine but she wasn't weak. I looked at the reviews of the television production and the people writing about it didn't seem to get it at all. It was just a story.

**ALISON LURIE**  It's hard now to realize how shocking it was at the time. The attitude toward men. That you could have a relationship with a man just for the fun of it and you didn't have to feel guilty or upset or anything like that.

For male readers the story tended to have an effect that was more astringent.

**SAUL BELLOW**  I remember reading the story and coming across those sentences that say in effect: She lay like a piece of white lamb on a sacrificial altar. "Bullshit," I said.

**ALFRED KAZIN**  There was a contempt for men in Mary's writing, which I thought was rather unpleasant. Describing her heroine's intercourse on the train, she says that she waited for the man to exhaust himself. It was as if she was not involved.

**GEORGE PLIMPTON**  I read it when I was sixteen, because all of the women I knew wanted me to read it. At that age what stunned me was that people could write about things like that. The candor. And also the fact that somebody had printed such a thing so explicitly. Everybody talked about it. I was at Exeter at the time and it made almost as much an impression as Pearl Harbor.

"The Man in the Brooks Brothers Shirt" came out in the summer of 1941, just as Mary McCarthy was getting settled in her new house, unpacking books and possessions long in storage and trying to bring some order to an ambitious garden that had gone wild with neglect. The war in Europe had been under way for more than a year when, on June 22, Hitler had suddenly invaded Russia, putting an end to an alliance that had placed many radicals in an ideological quandary. If you were a committed Stalinist, Hitler was now the enemy. If you were a committed anti-Stalinist matters were not so clear-cut. In the same issue of *Partisan Review* that ran "The Man in the Brooks Brothers Shirt," you could find a piece by Dwight Macdonald and Clement Greenberg called "10 Propositions on the War." Here Macdonald and Greenberg were at pains to present still again the traditional arguments of the Left for biding one's time and letting the great powers slug it out until they were weakened enough for the workers to rise up. But with the Germans occupying Paris and most of eastern Europe and well on their way to occupying Moscow, the ten propositions and the arguments buttressing them didn't carry the same kind of conviction they might have a year earlier.

By November Hitler's troops were in fact surrounding Moscow. In the November–December issue of *Partisan Review*, in a piece called "10 Propositions and 8 Errors," Philip Rahv responded to his fellow editors' arguments and concluded that to allow Hitler to go on unchecked would be to put an end to any possibility for social revolution in the future. The only way to stop Hitler, he argued, was to forge an alliance between "Anglo-American imperialism and Stalin's Red Army." Having spoken his mind, Rahv, like some nervous suitor, drew back at the last minute from making any binding commitment. "In a sense this war, even if it accomplishes the destruction of fascism, is not yet *our* war," he wrote. It was a hesitation that Greenberg and Macdonald, both staunch isolationists, would immediately fault him for. "In what sense? 'Not yet'—then when? *Whose* war, then?" they asked in a reply printed in the same issue. And it was a hesitation Mary McCarthy would forget entirely when telling her *Paris Review* interviewer of how Rahv helped change her view of the war.

### MARY MCCARTHY, IN AN INTERVIEW WITH ELISABETH NIEBUHR, *PARIS REVIEW*, WINTER–SPRING 1962

At the beginning of the war we were all isolationists, the whole group. Then I think the summer after the fall of France—certainly before Pearl Harbor—Philip Rahv wrote an article in which he said in a measured sentence, "In a certain sense, this is our war."

On December 7, 1941, the Japanese bombed Pearl Harbor and the United States entered the war, immediately rendering all such arguments moot. All the same, lines had been drawn. Rahv's heated exchange with Macdonald and Greenberg marked the beginning of a major fissure in *Partisan Review*'s editorial board. In 1943, after a two-year moratorium on all war editorials, Clement Greenberg was drafted into the army. Macdonald, who had never hesitated to voice his dissatisfaction with the way modernist literature was replacing radical politics in the magazine's pages, found himself suddenly without a strong ally. Rather than stay on without Greenberg, he quit, taking his wife Nancy, the magazine's business manager, with him. After the departure of Greenberg and the Macdonalds, *Partisan Review* came out in support of the war.

Mary McCarthy was in complete sympathy with the stand taken by her old friend Dwight Macdonald. But much as she might want to support his position, her husband had effectively removed her from *Partisan Review*'s editorial battles. At this point she was just a contributor, like any other. And not necessarily a frequent contributor at that. In 1941 and '42 she gave the magazine no "Theater Chronicles." In 1943, the year of the

big rupture, she wrote three. Geography had done much to make for distance. But in fact that first winter on the Cape had been the Wilsons' last.

Although Wilson had bought the house in Wellfleet as a permanent
residence, he and Mary never lived there year-round. Starting in 1941–42
the Wilsons spent the bulk of the winter months in New York. For much
of that first winter they made their home at the Little Hotel on West
Fifty-second Street. The winter of 1942–43 they took part of an apartment on Stuyvesant Square. The winter of 1943–44, they were living in
an apartment at the Gramercy Park Hotel.

But even if she was staying only a subway ride from her old friends
at *Partisan Review*, Mary could never again be part of the inner circle. For
one thing, the inner circle was not what it had been, with Greenberg and
Macdonald giving way to Delmore Schwartz and eventually William Barrett. For another, her husband's testy relations with its editors did not
get better with time. Wilson saw no need to mince words and, much as
she might have wished to, she could not altogether distance herself
from what he said. She might appear wonderfully brave and independent, but through most of her marriage she was firmly tied to Wilson,
who might occasionally give the magazine a backhanded compliment but
had little or no use for its editors. Indeed, in April 1942 he went so far as
to write Harold Ross at *The New Yorker* asking for advice about starting
up a magazine of his own. Inevitably, Wilson's faint praise was returned
in kind.

### FROM "THE WRITING OF EDMUND WILSON," BY DELMORE SCHWARTZ, *PARTISAN REVIEW*, 1942

[I]f we look for literary judgment in Wilson, we find a singular weakness and lack of critical pioneering[. . . .] Wilson speaks in the same
sentence of Proust and Dorothy Parker, and compares Max Eastman
favorably with Gide.

**ISAIAH BERLIN**  I first came into contact with *Partisan Review* in 1941.
They didn't like Edmund Wilson. They thought he was rather old-fashioned.
He was no good to them. They underestimated him. They liked Trotskyism
and a certain kind of Marxism. I remember they were very disparaging
about him. I used to defend him to them. Wilson was much more gifted than
they were, much more serious. He was a critic—they were reviewers.

In the end, though, it was not Wilson's troubled relations with his
wife's old friends so much as his encouragement of her "imaginative
writing" that finally broke their hold on her. The publication of "Cruel
and Barbarous Treatment" had established her as a dazzling new talent.
Maria Leiper, a young editor at Simon and Schuster, spotted the story in
the *Southern Review* and quickly signed its gifted author to a contract.

Her subsequent stories were not as short or as stylized as her first effort, but they all had the same tension between highly charged events and a cool, almost analytical, presentation. For all the decorum of their tone and syntax, the material could sometimes seem nakedly confessional. At some point she suggested to Maria Leiper that the stories could be joined together to form part of a novel to be called *The Company She Keeps*. In all she would write six self-contained stories, which had as their heroine or narrator a young woman whose politics were radical and whose companions of choice were a circle of New York intellectuals.

With irony and wit she was probing personal areas scarcely mined by women writing literary fiction. At Simon and Schuster, known mostly for its crossword puzzles, the staff believed they had now found a literary author who could reach a wide audience. The reception accorded "The Man in the Brooks Brothers Shirt" had done nothing to shake this belief. Nina Bourne, a young poet who worked as secretary to Dick Simon, the head of the house, shared this belief. It would seem that Simon, the man who ultimately controlled all advertising and support for the book, did, too.

**MARIA LEIPER**   I made a habit of reading little magazines and saying to the authors of stories I liked, "Do you have a short story collection or novel to show me?" Mary brought the manuscript in as a novel. That was her idea. I was wildly enthusiastic about her and her book. She was charming, delightful, and agreeable. She never had her back up. She never said, No, I won't have this comma changed. She wasn't prickly. Maybe one reason I got on with her was I was Vassar '28. We were five years apart.

**NINA BOURNE**   We were not the first port of call for literature. The book must have been other places. At Simon and Schuster everyone fell in love with the book. It sent out vibrations. They knew it was for them. Dick Simon deserves the credit for publishing it. He was totally smitten with "The Man in the Brooks Brothers Shirt." And I'm sure he must have been smitten with her, too, although he was very much married. When Mary McCarthy first came to the offices, she was beautiful in the way someone like Ingrid Bergman was beautiful. Physically she had that melting look but what came out was sharper. She was tall; he was a man on a large scale; and they matched.

**MARIA LEIPER**   When she came into my office, she did not look like the jacket photograph. But, then, she was only coming to see me at my office. She became beautiful with success. I don't remember Dick Simon's having anything to do with the book. I'm not sure he even read it. If he did, I doubt that he would have liked it. He was very puritanical.

In May 1942, with a bit of advertising and much fanfare, Simon and Schuster brought out *The Company She Keeps*. The book was touted as "a novel in six parts." Two of the parts, "Rogue's Gallery" and "Portrait of the

Intellectual as a Yale Man," were appearing for the first time. The book carried no dedication. Binding all six parts together was a foreword, which ran the risk of sounding pretentious and would be dropped from later editions. On the front and back flap of the dust jacket a reader could find a précis of each of the six parts. Gracing the back of the book was a photograph by Philippe Halsmann that made the author look like a movie star.

### FROM THE FOREWORD TO *THE COMPANY SHE KEEPS*

"When did you have it last?" the author adjures the distracted heroine, who is fumbling in her spiritual pocketbook for a missing object, for the ordinary, indispensable self that has somehow got mislaid. It is a case of lost identity. The author and the reader together accompany the heroine back over her life's itinerary, pausing occasionally to ask: "Was it here? Did you still have it at this point?"

The foreword, she would later claim, had been entirely the publisher's idea. But the publisher was not solely responsible for the "Note About the Author." This four-paragraph history, which follows the last chapter and also runs beneath her photograph on the dust jacket, states that the author's "favorite literary character is Byron" and her "favorite writer is Shakespeare" and that she lives in Wellfleet with her husband, Edmund Wilson, and their "small son." At Vassar, it goes on to say, the author "helped organize a rebel literary magazine together with Elizabeth Bishop, the poet, and others."

The Wilson connection did not escape the notice of reviewers. Special mention of it was made not only in *Book Review Digest* but in *The New York Times*, where in his opening sentences John Chamberlain, the daily reviewer, also made mention of Tess Slesinger, who eight years earlier had written a much praised novel about life among the New York intellectuals.

### FROM *BOOK REVIEW DIGEST 1942*

MCCARTHY, MARY (MRS. EDMUND WILSON), Company she keeps. 304p $2.50 Simon & Schuster

### FROM JOHN CHAMBERLAIN'S REVIEW IN *THE NEW YORK TIMES*, MAY 16, 1942

Several years ago Tess Slesinger wrote a memorable story of bohemian and radical New York. She called it *The Unpossessed*—meaning that its characters, unlike those of a Dostoievsky, acted out of an inner sterility[....] In spite of Miss Slesinger's judgment, however, bohemian and radical New York still persists. Now, in *The Company She Keeps*, Mary McCarthy, the sharp-eyed wife of Edmund Wilson, has done *The Unpossessed* from a different angle.

**NINA BOURNE**   It was not typical to refer to someone in a review as "Mrs. Edmund Wilson."

**MARIA LEIPER**   We never referred to her as Mrs. Edmund Wilson. I never realized she was married to Edmund Wilson until later. I would think she would have been upset by having it mentioned.

In every way that was decently possible the author and her publisher tried to control the book's reception. But with all this effort they succeeded primarily in getting some backs up—even the back of Robert Penn Warren, who had been happy enough to take two chapters for the *Southern Review* but now faulted her for what he saw as her "coy" introductory disclaimer with regard to her heroine's "selves." In the end, the critical response to the book was decidedly mixed.

### FROM WILLIAM ABRAHAMS'S REVIEW IN THE *BOSTON GLOBE*, MAY 13, 1942

Mary McCarthy looks like a glamour girl, and writes like a man who has been around for a long time. *The Company She Keeps* is her first novel, and it is, without any reservations, the book of the year.

### FROM MALCOLM COWLEY'S REVIEW IN *THE NEW REPUBLIC*, MAY 25, 1942

*The Company She Keeps* is not a likable book, nor is it very well put together, but it has the still unusual quality of having been lived.

### FROM CLIFTON FADIMAN'S REVIEW IN *THE NEW YORKER*, MAY 16, 1942

Miss McCarthy is no novelist (the book does not hold together in the least) but she has considerable talent for dissecting people and leaving a nasty mess on the table. One has the feeling that her characters are drawn from life and that all of them are really much pleasanter and decenter people than Miss McCarthy gives them credit for being. Her book, however, has the definite attraction of high-grade back-fence gossip.

### FROM ROBERT PENN WARREN'S REVIEW IN *PARTISAN REVIEW*, NOVEMBER–DECEMBER 1942

*The Company She Keeps* is a shrewd, witty, malicious, original, and often brilliantly written book, which is "a novel in six parts" but which might more accurately be called a heroine in six parts.

Robert Penn Warren went on to give the book full credit for "seriousness" and "values," while questioning the premise of its satire. Either he did not suspect, or was loath to mention, that for many of the novel's most striking characters there were recognizable real life models.

By 1942 both Harold Johnsrud and John Porter, the husband and young man of McCarthy's first story, were dead. The man in the Brooks Brothers shirt had dropped from sight. Bob Misch, the model for the genial Pflaumen, had lost contact with the writer and had no way of protecting himself. However, Mannie Rousuck, the model for Mr. Sheer in "Rogue's Gallery," was very much around and very much alive. One night, while he and Mary were dining alone at her hotel, Rousuck had somehow managed to get hold of the manuscript and, having literally taken matters into his own hands, refused to surrender any pages until she agreed to make changes in his fictional portrait.

John Chamberlain, the physical model for Jim Barnett, the clean-cut Stalinist poster boy in "Portrait of the Intellectual as a Yale Man," had the unenviable task of reviewing the book. Like Jim Barnett, John Chamberlain had a wife and child, a degree from Yale, and a well-known sympathy for left-wing causes. While other Yale men, like Dwight Macdonald and Bill Mangold, had contributed to Jim Barnett's makeup, only Chamberlain was recognizable as the intellectual who made you think of Huckleberry Finn and Boy Scouts. But McCarthy did not leave it at that. In recounting the story of Jim Barnett's brief flirtation with radical politics— a flirtation that ends in bitter self-knowledge—she had him go to bed with his Trotskyist co-worker Meg Sargent and then renounce her in a fashion no Boy Scout would be proud of.

### From "Portrait of the Intellectual as a Yale Man"

Why was it that she, only she, had the power to make him feel, feel honestly, unsentimentally, that his life was a failure, not a tragedy exactly, but a comedy with pathos? That single night and day when he had been almost in love with her had taught him everything. He had learned that he must keep down his spiritual expenses—or else go under[. . . .] He had never been free, but until he had tried to love the girl, he had not known he was bound.

In 1962, Mary McCarthy would tell her interviewer from the *Paris Review*, "What I really do is take real plums and put them in an imaginary cake." Unfortunately, if you were a plum, it could be a source of public embarrassment. John Chamberlain might deny any involvement with her, but there was so much that was real and convincing in his portrait that it was only natural for people to believe that the two of them had had an affair. After all, in their piece on mainstream reviewers, she and Margaret Marshall had let him off very lightly. Years later, when the harm was done, she would try to set the record straight. At the time, all Chamberlain could do was write a balanced review of the book, say "its satire is administered as gently and as murderously as a cat administers death to a mouse," and score a few points.

### FROM JOHN CHAMBERLAIN'S REVIEW IN *THE NEW YORK TIMES*, MAY 16, 1942

Two of the characters in *The Company She Keeps* are identifiable to me as compounds of living people. The first is Mr. Pflaumen of the episode called "The Genial Host." The second is Jim Barnett of "Portrait of the Intellectual as a Yale Man," which may be taken as the unconscious tribute which bohemianism pays to health. As a graduate of Yale I should not be asked to comment on a chapter which manhandles certain New York publications as well as my alma mater. Yet there is a rough justice in Miss McCarthy's portrait: Yale "intellectuals," so called, frequently do lack a final seriousness of purpose, the ability to muster the sustaining moral conviction to carry through enterprises of book length. Some of them, as a matter of fact, may be convicted of the heinous sin of preferring journalism, which is a nether world to the snob in Meg Sargent.

Wilson, who appeared only briefly as an offstage character in the novel's final chapter, saw no need for a balanced approach to his wife's fiction. For all six parts he had been an enthusiastic first reader, urging them on old friends like Robert Penn Warren and taking issue with any editor obtuse enough to turn them down. It did not escape the notice of new friends and even casual acquaintances that the way to Wilson's heart was praise of his talented young wife.

### FROM VLADIMIR NABOKOV'S LETTER TO EDMUND WILSON, MAY 6, 1942

Now about Mary's book. I have read it. It has been a habit of mine to be absolutely outspoken in such cases, i.e. especially when it concerns friends. So I hope you will take what I have to say in the right spirit. When I see you I shall discuss the book exhaustively but until then I want to tell you that it is a splendid thing, clever, poetic and new. In fact I am quite flabbergasted—if that's the right word.

### FROM RANDALL JARRELL'S LETTER TO EDMUND WILSON, AUGUST 5, 1941

My wife and I were charmed with your wife's story["The Man in the Brooks Brothers Shirt"] in *Partisan Review*; we were in Baton Rouge when we read it, and we got into long arguments with the *Southern Review* staff, saying that they should have printed it instead of their own stories.

Once you got past the entrenched critical establishment, enthusiasm for *The Company She Keeps* was immediate and enduring. For women the book had a special appeal. But you did not have to be a young woman to feel its power.

**ALISON LURIE** Mary McCarthy's heroine may have setbacks but she doesn't admit that men are in charge of the world and she doesn't admit that she has done anything wrong. I think all the women I knew read her with this in mind. She made us think it was possible to get away with it as a writer and possible to get away with it as a person.

**JOHN UPDIKE**   Like Hemingway, she began at the top of her form; her fiction never got better than *The Company She Keeps*. Maybe it was too hard to get better than that. She was a writer before she began to write fiction, so that there isn't this sense of stumbling or groping that you sometimes get in early stories; she was a thoroughly sharpened tool. Those stories are so exhilarating in their freedom and in their candor.

**NORMAN MAILER**   I was so much in awe of Mary McCarthy in those days. I read *The Company She Keeps* my sophomore year at Harvard. It was a consummate piece of work. It seemed so finished. And at the same time she was taking this risk. She was revealing herself in ways she never did again. She was letting herself be found out. That first book had a felicity to it. I hoped for more from her in her later work. I kept thinking she'd write a great novel. In those days I had no idea how difficult it is to write a great novel.

*The Company She Keeps* ends with Margaret Sargent's resolving to stay in her marriage and make the best of it, while she prays to a God she does not believe in to let her continue to see things as they really are. For almost three more years Mary McCarthy remained in her marriage to Edmund Wilson, winning small concessions like the signature power on his bank account, or a car of her own (an old Chevy a bit the worse for wear) and the right to drive it, but never fundamentally altering the terms of their relations. If she was tempted to leave, she had one compelling reason to stay. Unlike Margaret Sargent she had a young child.

**ADELAIDE WALKER**   Edmund said she was a terrible mother. I don't know why he said that. I could never figure it out. Edmund and I fought about this later. I thought she was a very good mother. Reuel was a big bone of contention between them. But Mary seemed to manage Reuel very well as a small boy. She was kind and firm and obviously loved him dearly. Reuel was a darling child. Very cunning. I don't remember Mary's playing games with Reuel so much. That wasn't her style. But she read to him a great deal—as did his father.

**ANNA MATSON HAMBURGER**   Mary was very good with Reuel. She was the way mothers are with children.

**EILEEN SIMPSON**   I saw Mary as a nervous mother. I met her on the street one day when Reuel was ill in bed with a cold. She was very upset. And indulgent. She was buying him a big sailboat. She was not a natural mother, but she wanted to do things right. They used to tell jokes on the Cape about how, when Reuel would reach for a plant or a flower, she would say, "Reuel, smell, don't touch." Careful to give the positive suggestion first.

**ROSALIND WILSON**   I must say something positive for her, and that is my brother, Reuel, is a wonderful human being and she must have had something to do with that.

By the time *The Company She Keeps* came out in 1942, Mary McCarthy was back on the Cape receiving visitors. To most visitors—whether they were old friends from college or a fond brother with a camera—her life there seemed to suit her. In 1941, Kevin had married Augusta Dabney, whom he had met while performing in his first New York play. By the next summer, he was serving in the army as an MP, responsible for escorting German prisoners by train to detention camps within the continental United States. Both Kevin and Augusta McCarthy were welcome guests at Wellfleet. Augusta, too, was doing a bit of traveling and that summer she had a job with a stock company in Chatham. At some point, Augusta and Kevin converged on the Wilsons for a family visit and an orgy of picture taking, which would document for posterity the tenor of the household and strike terror into the senior member's heart.

**AUGUSTA DABNEY**   Mary's attitude toward the camera was wonderful. She'd show her best side. Or she'd look straight into the camera. There was no "Oh I won't let him take my picture." There was none of that nonsense.

**FROM EDMUND WILSON'S LETTER TO MARY MCCARTHY, SEPTEMBER 22, 1942**
> I found those pictures that Kevin took. The one with you and Reuel is my favorite picture of you, and the one of Reuel alone is awfully cute. The pictures of me are downright disgusting and have given me quite a turn. I seem to be taking snuff in one of them.

If the camera's eye was unsparing, the eye of the photographer's wife, like that of the bulk of the Wilsons' visitors, passed lightly over anything out of the ordinary. Only one friend seemed to be privy to the sorry state of their domestic life.

**AUGUSTA DABNEY**   I remember Mary complained a bit, but you know you confuse what you've read with what actually happened or what you remember and what you've seen in photographs. Mary was always a candid person and yet a private person.

**ANNA MATSON HAMBURGER**   She never gave me the idea that life had become so intolerable that she was thinking of leaving. I don't think she had the ability to be that intimate with anyone. She may have told Adelaide. Actually, Mary *did* confide in me. She would tell me, one after another, that people were in love with her. Everybody was in love with her. I don't know whether they were or not. Maybe it was true. But in her mind it was. And it was important to her to be adored.

**ADELAIDE WALKER**   Mary confided in me. We talked all the time. We would take trips to Boston together with our children. That was one of the things that Edmund held against me. Edmund was an alcoholic and he would just take to the bottle and be impossible. He could be very abusive. When Edmund was drinking, you would just avoid him. But a wife couldn't. Mary always claimed Edmund beat her. He always claimed he didn't. I never saw him do it. She felt beaten anyway.

By the summer of 1942, not all her conquests were imaginary and not all Wilson's suspicions were without foundation. The way her step-daughter saw it, "She was Anna Karenina without the warmth, and if there was a Vronsky, he was not a handsome officer but a complicated Jewish intellectual." More than once, she got into the car with her suitcase. Sometimes she actually drove off.

**ROSALIND WILSON**   There must have been ten times I remember when one really wished she would leave and she just didn't. She came back. And the reason she came back was it's a relationship that everyone got in with my father—I certainly got in it—it's the ambivalence. He could be so darned interesting and it could be quite a lot of fun to be around him.

Before the end of the summer, she discovered she was pregnant. She barely had time to consider the implications of this turn of events when she suffered a miscarriage.

**ADELAIDE WALKER**   Mary's miscarriage was one of the sad things in our life. Edmund was away and we went to Provincetown and had a drink or two with that psychiatrist Edmund was always jealous of [Sándor Rado]. And then she was feeling bad and she spent the night with Katy Dos Passos while I came home, and that night she had a miscarriage. Edmund accused me of being Mary's accomplice in this and accused Mary of aborting the fetus. It was utterly untrue. It was a miscarriage. To accuse her like that was awful. And quite unjust.

### FROM *NEAR THE MAGICIAN*, BY ROSALIND WILSON

Dos and Katy thought she'd planned it and were not happy about it, discussing it cynically afterward. I went and brought her home in our old car. The brakes gave on the way home and it was frightening: part of the whole ambiance of our lives.

That September, Edmund Wilson was living in Wellfleet and his wife was living in New York, which had become a refuge not only from harsh winters but from bad times in the marriage. Whenever relations became intolerable, Wilson or his young wife would pack a bag and head south. Most often it was his wife. Because her departure was not official, it was rarely a source of public embarrassment. Wilson could then talk her into returning or prevail upon her to let him join her. Because the conflicts in the marriage were enduring, these reconciliations inevitably proved illusory. By Christmas, Mary McCarthy had been living in New York for four months. The ostensible reason for her stay in the city was that she had resumed psychotherapy, this time with a Dr. Abraham Kardiner (Dr. Frank had been drafted). She had been subletting a portion of an apartment on Stuyvesant Square belonging to Polly Boyden, commuting some weekends to Wellfleet, and even accompanying her husband to Smith College, where to earn extra money he was delivering a series of lectures on language. At Christmas, Wilson came down to New York with Reuel and his nurse, and they took over the entire apartment.

Fortunately, Mary's inability to disentangle herself from a union not to her liking did not necessarily spill over to other areas of her life. Having made quite a splash with her first novel, she soon discovered she had made no real money to speak of. To rub salt into this wound, Simon and Schuster had sold the film rights to her novel to RKO without consulting her and pocketed half the profits. Although it seems to have been a point of dispute at the time, she later professed to have no memory of the incident. Her troubles with Simon and Schuster, she contended, first stemmed from Dick Simon's pressing her to sign a multibook contract and then from his insisting she get an agent. At his recommendation she chose Bernice Baumgarten at Brandt and Brandt, who then concluded that Simon and Schuster was not the best house for a literary writer. Time has a way of altering memory, but it would seem that Dick Simon wasn't the only one urging her to get an agent and it wasn't only literary considerations that prompted her to pull away.

**MARIA LEIPER**   My distinct recollection is that the business department sold the title of her book to the movies and took 50 percent, which is an awful lot. They sold it without my knowledge. I was furious and she was furious at the time. Fifty percent was indeed too greedy. If she'd had an agent to protect her that would never have happened.

### FROM EDMUND WILSON'S LETTER TO MARY MCCARTHY, AUGUST 10, 1942

I came down on the train yesterday with [Arthur] Schlesinger, who asked how you can come out with Simon & Schuster, and told me very seriously that I oughtn't to let you "go around there unchaperoned." He said that they were so hard-boiled and unscrupulous that either I or an agent ought to handle your business with them.

By early October, five months after Simon and Schuster had brought out *The Company She Keeps*, she was writing Bernice Baumgarten to say that she wanted to sign up to do a book with Robert Linscott at Houghton

Mifflin. For a novel to be called *Better to Burn* she was to receive an advance of $2250, with $750 upon signing the contract. Baumgarten was a well-regarded agent with a long list of famous clients and this start on the road to financial independence appeared auspicious. But for the moment, much of her effort was directed toward earning a living with her free-lance writing.

That fall, William Maxwell, a young fiction editor at *The New Yorker*, wrote to ask if she had any stories to show him. Most of what she had was too long, she responded, but she agreed to meet him for lunch. By February, she had sold *The New Yorker* a story called "The Company Is Not Responsible," a first-person account of a grueling wartime bus ride, where the passengers not only rise to the occasion but form a brief but intense bond. The story was mild and even heartwarming and nothing like anything she had ever written. She was paid for the story and it was set in galleys, only to linger in the fiction bank for over a year.

She was rapidly discovering that she might be the talk of literary New York, but for magazine editors she was just another writer trying to sell them a story or article that did not necessarily suit them. By the spring of 1943, she was back in Wellfleet with Wilson, older and wiser and visibly annoyed.

### FROM MARY MCCARTHY'S LETTER TO BERNICE BAUMGARTEN, MAY 29, 1943

But what does Harry Bull [at *Town and Country*] mean it is not in the form of the New York letter I suggested?[. . .] Just what *are* his intentions? I certainly would not undertake to do a regular piece for seventy-five dollars. Since this is already written, I shall have to take what I can get for it. What about the possibility of *Harper's Bazaar*?[. . .] By the way, when you talk to Harry Bull, would you ask him to return the story of mine he has?

### FROM MCCARTHY'S LETTER TO BAUMGARTEN, JUNE 23, 1943

Your letter [. . .] arrived practically on the heels of a printed rejection slip which accompanied a story I had sent to [the *Atlantic*. . . .] Frankly, the *Atlantic* proposition does not seem too brilliant to me. It simply boils down, doesn't it, to doing an occasional article on spec for them? What I am looking for is a regular and predictable source of income, something which could be done once a month and simply consigned to the mail[. . . .] I cannot get worked up about the *Atlantic* as a market, because aside from the rejection slip matter, they turned down practically every story in my book.

By September 1943, she was asking Bernice Baumgarten to send a story already rejected by *The New Yorker*, *The Atlantic*, and *Town and Country* off to *Mademoiselle*. She had changed the story's title from "Cultural Phenomena" to "C.Y.E." Having touched on her childhood in a highly fictionalized and not altogether convincing fashion in "Ghostly Father, I Confess," she was now approaching it directly with a piece of old-fashioned reminiscence. (A sign the narrator sees on Union Square prompts her to remember the suffering she endured years before, when two older girls christened her with a nickname she now believes was an acronym for "Clever Young Egg"—a meaning that was evident to everyone in the school but her.)

In her packet to Baumgarten, along with this first serious attempt to write directly about her childhood, she included a story that in tone and format harkened back to *The Company She Keeps*. The story was titled "The Weeds," and told of a young woman trying to tear herself away from an overbearing architect husband and from a beloved garden, which her husband has come to view as his enemy. Eventually, the young woman finds the courage to run off, only to end up sitting alone in her hotel room. Five days later, when her husband comes to fetch her, the weeds have overtaken and destroyed her garden.

*Mademoiselle* quickly decided to take "C.Y.E.," but it would be months before "The Weeds" found a publisher. For the magazines she was now looking at, this new story was strong stuff. However, for the moment, her need for money was not quite so pressing. Wilson's letter to Harold Ross had not secured a backer for his proposed literary magazine but it resulted in the offer of a full-time job. In October 1943 Wilson joined *The New Yorker* as their regular book reviewer, replacing Clifton Fadiman, who, along with just about every other able-bodied male in publishing, had been drafted into the armed forces. "I've decided to take it for a year," he wrote a friend, "though I doubt whether anything good but money will come of it." For the first time in more than a decade Wilson was bringing home a respectable paycheck.

Because his work at *The New Yorker* required him to be in the city, Wilson took an apartment for his family at the Gramercy Park Hotel and enrolled Reuel in a nearby kindergarten. On New Year's Eve he and Mary had a handful of friends join them, including Dawn Powell, Clement Greenberg, Margaret Miller, and Philip Rahv. As midnight approached, Miller later recalled, Mary was sitting on the floor with her back against the wall and her legs straight out in front of her. She had her eyes closed and Philip Rahv's head in her lap.

What Wilson made of this scene there is no knowing. The marriage continued into the new year and he continued to support his wife's work. On April 22, 1944, "The Company Is Not Responsible" appeared in *The New Yorker*. To anyone aware of the writer's avowed isolationist stance, its tone may have been a bit puzzling. But by this time, as she explained to an interviewer in 1962, she was coming to have a very different view of the war. "I'd go to a movie—there was a marvelous documentary called *Desert Victory* about the British victory over Rommel's Africa Corps—and I'd find myself weeping madly when Montgomery's bagpipers went through to El Alamein."

Cause and effect can be difficult to sort out, particularly when it comes to solidifying a writer's position at a magazine. In later years Mary McCarthy also liked to tell interviewers that her connection to *The New Yorker* had been forged when William Maxwell spotted one of her early published stories and urged her to send more. In short, she had made it there on her own. But her first fiction did not make it into the magazine until Edmund Wilson took over the "Books" column, William Maxwell went off on leave, and Katharine White returned from a five-year hiatus in Maine. It was Katharine White who shepherded the story into print, while buying a second story and giving her a first-reading agreement.

Over the years Katharine White had edited Wilson's poetry, parts of *To The Finland Station*, and virtually everything but his book reviews. Not only had she listened to Wilson's repeated recommendations that she upgrade the literary quality of the magazine's fiction but she had heeded his pleas on behalf of his good friend Vladimir Nabokov. Indeed, it was at the apartment of Edmund Wilson and Mary McCarthy that White met Nabokov for the first time.

Given Wilson's willingness to intercede on behalf of writers he admired, and his tendency to do so on behalf of his wife, McCarthy's sudden success at the magazine may not be pure coincidence. On the other hand, there may be no connection whatsoever. What is interesting is that she was careful in later years to see to it that no one entertained such a suspicion. Nevertheless, it would seem that no one in the fiction department thought twice about asking Wilson to serve as his wife's messenger.

### FROM MARY MCCARTHY'S LETTER TO BERNICE BAUMGARTEN, MAY 27, 1944

Here is a check for $100, which represents 10% of the $1000 option check I got from the *New Yorker*. The check was handed to Edmund just before we left [for Wellfleet] and in the flurry of moving, etc., I've neglected to send you your commission. Forgive this disorderly way of handling the thing.

The check Wilson had taken home was for a story that bore no relation to her first *New Yorker* effort and that was totally unlike any story that had appeared in the magazine's pages. It was the story called "The Weeds." The magazine would not publish the story until the fall, but as had happened before in her marriage to Wilson, life proceeded to imitate art and then outdo it with a vengeance. At Wellfleet, in the early summer of 1944, the fraying fabric of the Wilson marriage began to rip past the

point of repair. Propelled by a violent episode that she would describe in
her initial affidavit asking for a legal separation and then make part of
Martha Sinnott's marital history in her novel *A Charmed Life*, Mary fled
into the night.

### FROM *A CHARMED LIFE*

Martha's story was famous, and not only from her own telling. She
had left her first husband's second house in the middle of the night, in
a nightgown, driving his Plymouth sedan, which ran out of gas and
stranded her on the road.

### FROM MARY MCCARTHY'S AFFIDAVIT OF FEBRUARY 23, 1945

On July 5, 1944 while drunk he hit me with a chair, put his arm
through a window pane and cut himself so badly that he almost bled
to death before preventive measures could be applied. Since that time
he has threatened me from time to time and by his actions has seemed
so menacing that I have fled from our home for safety.

In real life she had fled in a Chevrolet, not a Plymouth, and she had
taken Rosalind Wilson with her. Once again a quarrel had erupted when
Wilson had had too much to drink and the guests had gone home. And
once again she, like Martha Sinnott, had been unable to hold her tongue.

### FROM *A CHARMED LIFE*

Their penultimate quarrel, for example, had exploded in the middle of
the night, after a party, when she was carrying out two overflowing
pails of garbage and he refused, with a sardonic bow, to hold open the
screen door for her. There she was, manifestly, the injured party, but
instead of leaving it at that and taxing him with it the next day, when
he was weakened with a hangover, she immediately distributed the
guilt by setting down one pail of garbage and slapping him across his
grinning face. She never knew how to make him feel sorry for what he
had done.

Toward the end of her life she would recall how Wilson had returned
the slap and then chased her into Reuel's room, where much of the subsequent beating had taken place. Rosalind Wilson had then accompanied
her in her flight from the house. Their car had taken the two women only
as far as Gull Pond. Looking back on the incident, she had no idea how
she and Rosalind made it home. Rosalind Wilson remembered the incident somewhat differently.

**ROSALIND WILSON**   What happened was that my father and Mary were
upstairs, and I was in Reuel's room. He was drunk and they were having a
fight. I was always one who wanted to swim at any time of the day or night,
and I said to Mary, "Let's take a swim at Gull Pond." Which we did. That's all
there was to it. She and I went off and took a swim while he stayed behind.

1. Augusta Preston with Harold Junior, c. 1914

3. Tess and Augusta Preston

2. Harold Preston

4. Roy McCarthy before his marriage to Tess

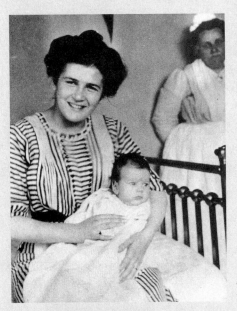

5. Tess McCarthy with infant Mary, 1912

6. Mary, Kevin, and Preston

7. Roy McCarthy, Kevin, J. H. McCarthy, Mary, Elizabeth Sheridan
McCarthy holding Sheridan, Tess McCarthy, and Preston, 1917

8. The McCarthy children in
Minneapolis: Mary and Kevin
stand, while Preston and
Sheridan pose astride an itinerant photographer's pony.

9. Mary before leaving Vassar

11. Elizabeth Bishop

10. Frani Blough

12. Miss Sandison

13. Miss Kitchel

14. Mary and Harold Johnsrud on their wedding day, June 21, 1933

15. Philip Rahv, 1940s

16. Mary McCarthy and Edmund Wilson, Wellfleet,
summer of 1943 (Sylvia Salmi)

17. Reuel Wilson,
Wellfleet, summer
of 1943 (Sylvia Salmi)

18. Jacket photo for *The Company She Keeps*, 1942 (Philippe Halsmann)

19. Bowden Broadwater (Kevin McCarthy)

20. Mary McCarthy and Bowden Broadwater, late 1940s

21. Dwight Macdonald, 1940s (Bertrand de Geofroy)

22. Alfred Kazin, 1946 (Henri Cartier-Bresson/Magnum)

23. Saul Bellow, 1950s
(Richard Meeker)

24. William Phillips, 1950s

And then he managed to put his hand through the glass panel of the front door when we came back. Now, I ask you, who got hurt there? My father was the one hurt.

One thing everyone is agreed on: Wilson put his hand through the glass of the front door. McCarthy later recalled how on their return they discovered a trail of blood that led upstairs to the master bedroom, where Wilson had passed out on the bed. The two women left him there until the morning, when the housekeeper arrived for work. A doctor was called and when Wilson turned the doctor away, McCarthy packed her bags and left for New York.

For the rest of the summer, Wilson did everything in his power to get his wife to return to Wellfleet "on a purely friendly basis." It would be a shame for her to miss the best months, he argued, and it would be especially hard on Reuel. Why not wait, he suggested, and separate in the fall when Reuel was at school.

Once again Wilson promised to turn over a new leaf. He gave his wife credit for trying hard to take good care of him and their son. He took the greater part of the blame for the sorry state of the marriage on himself. He then blamed their recent upset on the presence of Rosalind, who "upsets the balance of the family when she comes." He attributed their long-standing difficulties to the difference in their ages, which led to her wanting to do things he had ceased to enjoy and to her inability to appreciate the "miseries" of a man in his forties ("the death of old friends, bad habits and diseases of one's own, and a certain inevitable disillusion with the world"). At one point he went so far as to say, "it may be that you and I are psychologically impossible for one another anyway." Whether he intended this or not, his plea for her return had something of the retrospective tone of someone tallying up the score after the game has been lost.

#### FROM EDMUND WILSON'S LETTER TO MARY MCCARTHY, JULY 13, 1944
I have really loved you more than any other woman and have felt closer to you than to any other human being. I think, though, that it is true that, as lovers, you and I scare and antagonize each other in a way that has been getting disastrous lately (though sometimes I have been happier and more exalted with you than I have ever been with anybody). [. . . .] I'm entering on a period of sobriety and work (have even initiated a diet) which may be tiresome for you; but I will do my best to be considerate and not nag you. In the meantime, I want your company, which, aside from other considerations, I prefer to anybody else's.

"The Weeds" came out in *The New Yorker* on September 16, 1944. By the time the story was being read by their friends, Wilson had persuaded her to come back with him, at least temporarily, and they were living in a dark narrow house on Henderson Place, just off East End Avenue at Eighty-sixth Street. Frani Blough was in an apartment around the corner. They were only blocks away from St. Bernard's, where Reuel was enrolled in first grade. At *The New Yorker*, "The Weeds" was breaking new ground.

**BRENDAN GILL**   I remember to this day someone telling me about "The Weeds" and the number of inches in the galleys. It was seventy inches or something and people walked up and down the corridors talking about it. It was stunning. When Mary came along with "The Weeds," it was almost like a scandal, it was so exciting and unexpected. Mary represented to us at that time a major transition in the ambitiousness of the magazine. Irwin Shaw at about the same time also began writing longer stories. I think she and Irwin were terribly important. These people altered the nature of the magazine. They were breaking out of the small form and the more or less still quite plotless form into something new. The distinction of the magazine was in its welcoming them instead of rejecting them. These things, because they succeed, appear not ever to have been in a position to fail. But they were not inevitable.

For Wilson, too, this story marked a breakthrough. He had taken his wife's previous stories in stride, even the one that touched on their marriage and her analysis. As was her custom, she had asked him to take a look at this new story when she finished it. So the story was by no means new to him. Nonetheless, seeing it in *The New Yorker*'s pages was something else again.

**MARY MCCARTHY IN *CONTEMPORARY AUTHORS,
NEW REVISION SERIES*, VOLUME 16 (1984)**
> I remember I wrote a story in which he more or less figured as a character—this was when we were married—and it was not a very favorable picture. But it was not a portrait; it was somebody who was in the same position vis-a-vis the heroine as he was to me. I gave it to him to read, and he had no comment on that aspect of it. I can't remember what he said about the story in general—it was one called "The Weeds"[. . . .] I sent it to the *New Yorker*, and they took it, and it came out. And he was really quite mad. I said, "But I showed it to you before." And he said, "But you've improved it!"

Between the husband and wife in "The Weeds" there is no buffer of a psychiatrist, no pretense that the individual is in conflict with society. There is no more than a veneer of wit masking the anger. It was by now an open secret that her stories were frequently closer to fact than fantasy. If in the past she had been fairly circumspect about how bad things were in the marriage, the story put an end to her reticence once and for all.

Once everyone read "The Weeds" in the pages of *The New Yorker*, the end of her unhappy marriage was effectively assured. Like the young wife in "Cruel and Barbarous Treatment," she had taken the game to a level that she could not hope to sustain for any length of time. To do so would be to risk public ridicule—or boredom. Whether she had intended this or not, she had propelled herself to the front door. It was only a matter of waiting for the next violent incident. Only a matter of time before she would step out the door and shut it firmly behind her. Only a question of whether she could bring this exit off with style. When the time came, she trusted to a pencil, three small slips of paper, and a dash of rue to offset the anger.

### FROM MARY MCCARTHY'S FAREWELL NOTE TO EDMUND WILSON, N.D.

This is the note in the pincushion, I'm afraid. I don't see what else there is to do. Perhaps the fighting is mostly my fault, but that's not a reason for staying together. Reuel had the wits scared out of him last night, and whoever is responsible, he isn't. I will go 50-50 with you on him; you can have him in the summer, and in the winter or vice versa. If you want to make it legal it's all right with me[. . . .] I will try to get money, if only a loan, from Simon & Schuster—and maybe work for Mannie in the mornings[. . . .] Up to the last ten days, I thought if I didn't have drinks every day, it might make a difference—but no. I'm sorry, this could probably all be managed with less éclat, but the only way I can ever break off anything is to run away.

In effect she had written herself out of the marriage. By January she was living at the Stanhope Hotel, within walking distance of Reuel's school. Once again, as she said in her note to Wilson, she had walked out. Now it was a question of getting official custody of her son and the money needed to support the two of them. It was also necessary to ignore Wilson's efforts to forestall her making their separation final. Not only was he promising to turn over a new leaf, he was promising to leave the country. He had gotten *The New Yorker* to send him to Europe as a correspondent to cover the closing days of the war. With the extra money he would be earning, he could easily afford to support her and Reuel at Henderson Place. He was asking her to hold off on any action until he returned from overseas.

When faced with a husband who would not consent to release her, she, like the good lawyer's granddaughter that she was, resorted to the courts. On February 23, 1945, she sued for a separation. On March 12, she filed papers in response to Wilson's testimony—testimony in which he was claiming that she would "kick me, bite me, scratch me and maul me in any way she could." To start with, he made it clear that she was "a psychiatric case" and had been confined to "the ward for violent cases." He went on to say that she had broken down the door of his study and "pushed paper under the door to my study and set fire to it." In an attempt to reply to her husband's charges and discredit them, she turned to her stepdaughter, to her psychiatrists, to one stranger, and to two friends. That spring she was granted her separation. The divorce trial would not take place for another year and a half.

**ADELAIDE WALKER**   If I'd had to go to court and testify, I certainly wouldn't have said that he beat her because I had no evidence. I would have said that he was very irascible and very difficult. I would have said that he was pretty impossible as a husband, which he was.

**ROSALIND WILSON**   I refused to testify at the trial because I didn't want Reuel saying to me someday, If you hadn't testified I wouldn't have ended up with father or Mary or whatever. It seems to me that Adelaide might have taken the same stance. But God knows we all do stupid things.

**ADELAIDE WALKER**   I didn't actually testify for Mary in the divorce because it didn't come to that. But I went into court with Mary saying that I would. Then the judge called them up and scolded both of them. And they settled it without anybody testifying and airing all the accusations and counteraccusations. It was very fortunate. The judge saved them from themselves. And I think the lawyers must have helped too. But Mary and Edmund were prepared to take it down to the line.

To every fresh start, along with all their cherished belongings, Mary McCarthy and Edmund Wilson had persisted in bringing a growing load of sour grievances. As they prepared to go to court, every grievance came spilling out. All three of Mary's psychiatrists signed affidavits declaring her to be sane and to be suffering in large part from the effects of her troubled marriage. Once again her old friend Nathalie Swan came through in a time of marital crisis, swearing in an affidavit that she had seen Wilson abuse his wife verbally in front of their friends and their son and had seen him torture her with his unwarranted jealousy, making her pay for being more popular than he was. In her affidavit Adelaide Walker swore to returning with her from a trip to Boston to find Wilson drunk and raving about the men his wife was meeting there on the sly.

For two years Wilson would not speak to Adelaide Walker. She had betrayed him, he said. They were old friends and her first loyalty was therefore to him. For Adelaide Walker, much as she regretted the breach in the friendship, there had been no choice. "Mary was the underdog," she would explain. "She didn't have many people who were going to stand up for her. She had lots of friends, but they hadn't been through this marriage. They didn't have the real facts. Edmund was a much more powerful figure than she was and I didn't feel she had very good defenses. You see, she wasn't really famous then."

In the end Mary McCarthy managed to break free from the minotaur and his maze, even though she could find no hero to rescue her. To get out of the marriage she'd had to trust to her own efforts—to her writing and her intelligence and her refusal to mistake appearance for substance. When it came time to go to court, two women friends had stood by her— one married to her former lover and one married to her husband's best friend. For the moment, she seemed to have put aside any notion of trusting to a new romantic adventure to help her make her life over. Two things she had learned from her unhappy marriage. First, you do best to cherish, and keep close by you, the friends you love and rely on. Second, but no less important, when forging a reputation as a writer you cannot dismiss the value of discipline and sheer craft. That second lesson would be difficult to master. Both would prove invaluable. The next time she turned to a divorce court to rid herself of a husband she had no use for, not even the most tenderhearted observer would call her a poor underdog with no one to stand up for her.

# Chapter Nine

# THE SUMMER OF '45

Edmund Wilson, like Mary McCarthy, had a taste for Greek fables. By the time the two of them married, he had found in Sophocles' *Philoctetes* a way to make sense of the emotional chaos that at some point marks the life of virtually every writer. As summarized by Wilson, the fable is simple enough: On his way to Troy, Philoctetes acquires a magic bow that renders him invincible in battle, but soon afterward he receives a nasty snakebite on his ankle—an ugly suppurating wound so repellent that Odysseus and his fellow warriors leave him to rot on a desert island. Both the wound and the bow are bestowed on Philoctetes by the Gods. Ten years later, when the Greeks return for him, it is not because they believe they have wronged him but because they have been advised by a Trojan soothsayer that without his assistance they will never capture Troy. Once Philoctetes relents, and agrees to help them, his snakebite is cured.

In the title essay of *The Wound and the Bow*, published in 1941, Wilson wrote, "I should interpret the fable as follows. The victim of a malodorous disease which renders him abhorrent to society and periodically degrades him and makes him helpless is also the master of a superhuman art which everybody has to respect and which the normal man finds he needs." In short, if you want the artist you must take him wounds and all.

At this point in his life, Wilson had a grudging respect for Freud and his disciples, particularly when their insights conformed to his own ideas. With its ties to the Attic world, the story of Philoctetes was more to Wilson's taste than a bald statement of the standard psychoanalytic insight that sees the artist as marked by emotional damage incurred in childhood. But in fact it was virtually identical. If other readers might view Sophocles' drama somewhat differently, Wilson's interpretation was not a wild misreading of the text. And if there was a hint of self-justification to his interpretation, it was self-justification of the highest order.

Thanks to its lack of specificity, Wilson's fable could be made to apply to his wife no less than to himself. With *The Company She Keeps* Mary McCarthy had made an astonishing publishing debut. Her willingness to reveal the worst about her heroine (and, by implication, herself) contributed in no small part to the strong impression the book made. Because almost every section was written while she was undergoing psychoanalysis, one might argue that analysis had fostered this candor. However, one could argue that if it had not been for Edmund Wilson, she would not have been on that analyst's couch in the first place.

According to this second view, the misery of her marriage to Wilson— a marriage that had brought the childhood she believed she had put behind her crashing down on top of her—had pushed her past some barrier. Psychoanalysis, then, simply provided the support that made it possible for her to write. To this view, the author of *The Wound and the Bow* would have subscribed wholeheartedly, although he would have described his role somewhat differently. In February 1945, after his wife had left Henderson Place for good, he was writing his friend Helen Muchnic, a Russian scholar at Smith, "[D]on't take too seriously anything Mary may have said when you saw her. Her way of seeing herself in a drama doesn't always make connections with reality. Lately she has been acting out a novel when she ought to be writing one."

As Wilson saw it, the upheaval in their marriage was almost entirely of his wife's making. But if Wilson had indeed reopened his wife's childhood wounds and left them to suppurate, thereby stimulating her imaginative writing, what was going to happen to her now that she had finally broken with him? If one gave credence to Wilson's theory, the conclusion was obvious: Leave the marriage and you risk losing the bow.

In the early spring of 1945, finally free of the husband who had prodded and shaped and thoroughly tormented her, Mary McCarthy was left to make her own way as a writer of fiction. At the same time, she had to make a home for herself and her small son. According to the terms of the separation agreement Wilson was to give her sixty dollars a week from his *New Yorker* salary. While he was on assignment in Europe, the magazine would pay the allowance directly to her. Even with the help of Bernice Baumgarten, she had been unable to find a regular market for her free-lance writing. She had yet to write the novel she had promised Houghton Mifflin. To earn enough money to support herself she was going to have to find a job.

Exactly what kind of job was another question. She could not possibly go back to *Partisan Review*. The magazine as she had known it had ceased to exist, the majority of its founding editors having been scattered by the war, by their efforts to earn a living, and by what Rahv, never one to spare a colleague his sharp tongue, chose to call his own "analytic exuberance." Fred Dupee had left New York and was now teaching at Bard College, having severed his ties with the editorial board. Clement Greenberg, who had taken her place at the magazine, had left for the army in 1943. Dwight Macdonald had departed that same year. Delmore Schwartz, with whom her relations were always vexed, had then joined Rahv and Phillips in an uneasy triumvirate.

There was no possibility of a full time job with Dwight Macdonald, who soon after his departure had started up *politics*, a monthly journal of opinion, which relied on submissions from like-minded friends and his own prodigious gifts as a writer and editor. As Macdonald moved toward an anarchist view of the international situation, he had taken his magazine with him, all the while continuing to attract a small but enthusiastic readership. But by choice and by necessity, it was a family operation. His wife, Nancy, was serving as managing editor.

More urgent than finding an acceptable job to supplement her monthly payment from Wilson, however, was making a life on her own. In February she had taken Reuel from the house Wilson had rented on Henderson Place. For most of spring she made do with temporary quarters at Kevin and Augusta's apartment or at the Stanhope Hotel. All of her plans that spring were made with trepidation and all of them were provisional.

In 1936, when she left Harold Johnsrud, it had been for a handsome young man she believed she was going to marry. When the young man hadn't worked out, she had found herself possessed of a small name and some skill as a writer, adrift in a one-room Village apartment. In 1944, when she left Edmund Wilson, things were very different. She had a child to consider and no romantic refuge in the offing. "There was no other man in the picture when I left him," she told her brother Kevin in their 1979 interview for *People*. "It was desperation!"

Sadly, in this drama where Edmund was the villain and she was the victim there had been no leading man to play the hero. Still, there had been a reasonably viable supporting actor, one happy to observe the unfolding drama even though he was never asked to take an active part in it. Born in the Bronx and raised in Norfolk, Virginia, Clement Greenberg was three years older than she was. Although he harbored some ambition to be a painter, he had taken a degree in literature at Syracuse University. By 1945 he had established his reputation with two essays published in *Partisan Review*, "Avant-garde and Kitsch" and "Towards a Newer Laocoon," in which he argued that, contrary to what radicals wished to believe, avant-garde art required a wealthy capitalist class for its support. "Avant-garde and Kitsch" had begun as a letter to the magazine's editor, in response to an article by Dwight Macdonald on Soviet cinema. At that time Greenberg had been working as a clerk at the U.S. Customs House.

Mary McCarthy had first met Clement Greenberg at a *Partisan Review* party back in 1941, but not until his release from the army in 1944 did the two of them start an affair, which both would later dismiss as a fling. In Greenberg she had found a man who was forceful and perhaps brilliant but who was gaining a reputation for settling arguments with his fists. Like Philip Rahv before him, he was separated from a wife he saw no compelling reason to divorce. In addition, he had a school-age son. Never an easy relationship, their affair lurched on through the fall and winter of 1944, before finally coming to a dead halt once the separation from Wilson was complete. It left a considerable residue of bad feeling.

**CLEMENT GREENBERG**  Mary's reputation preceded her. I was intimidated by her, but I got to like her. She was fun to be with. If you had something to say, she'd toss the ball back. She'd toss the ball at you, too. I had good times with Mary. She was once telling me how Phil Rahv was sensual—the way he'd stroke a piece of cloth. And she said, "You're not sensual and I'm not either." I think it was less true of her than of me, maybe. Mary would correct your diction and pronunciation and all that. She was a bit of a prig at times. Prigs tend to go by the book.

### DWIGHT MACDONALD, IN A 1979 INTERVIEW WITH DIANA TRILLING, *PARTISAN REVIEW*, FALL 1984

I got Greenberg on the magazine. In fact, I invented Clem Greenberg[. . . .] I'm not so sure that he did know anything about art. But he had something that was very important: a moralistic approach to everything. He made people feel guilty if they didn't like Jackson Pollock, that's what it amounts to. And that's very powerful medicine with all this worried, jumped-up, wartime-educated public[. . . .] He used morality as a way to make people feel guilty.

**CLEMENT GREENBERG**  Once I was with Mary and something came up—I forget what—and I said, "I think you're more than a quarter Jewish." Her eyes blazed at me. She took me seriously. For one week I thought I wanted to marry Mary. When she was in between men. I didn't know enough to listen to my entrails. But I didn't pursue it. In any case Mary wouldn't have married me. She wasn't going to marry a Jew.

Whether she was prepared to marry a Jew is open to question. But Greenberg's religion would seem to have been the least of his drawbacks. To close friends her taste in men could be bewildering. But to a casual observer, meeting up with her when she was in the throes of divesting herself of Wilson, she was a striking and often appealing figure.

**SYBILLE BEDFORD**  My view, obviously limited, of Mary McCarthy in the New York of the early 1940s was that she conducted herself much as a prima donna—in public, that was, at the somewhat wild hard-drinking parties of the time. With cause: beauty, great attraction for men, dazzling literary reputation. Due homage was paid to her, by the *Partisan Review* crowd, the Peggy

Guggenheim circle, the French surrealist refugees. . . . I can still see her reclining on a chaise longue—had they actually carried her in like Cleopatra on a litter?—worshiped by a swarm of men, at Jean Connolly's East Sixties apartment.

Then, one damp Sunday afternoon in the country in upstate New York, complete reversal. A mutual friend, Esther Murphy Arthur, Gerald Murphy's sister and a chum of Bunny Wilson's since their Prohibition youth, suggested that we should go and see Mary, who was living somewhere in those parts. (That was soon after she had left Wilson.) We found a forlorn figure sitting at a kitchen table—no makeup, no flamboyance, just a rather solitary thin young woman, glad (or so it seemed to us) of some human company. She perked up a bit talking about her little boy, *so* clever, reading Henry James. Esther, a formidable personage in her own right, looked skeptical. The kitchen was cold. We left feeling baffled and sad.

**WILLIAM MAXWELL**   There was a Schrafft's on Madison Avenue and Eighty-eighth Street where I used to go for breakfast at the counter. Mary and Reuel would come in at about the same time I did. Over a period of weeks we used to sit having breakfast together in a very cozy fashion. Mary was staying at a nearby hotel. She was perfectly relaxed and friendly. Never terrifying or anything. She was very beautiful and she was lovely with Reuel.

For the role of the new man in her life there were at least three possibilities. By the time spring turned to summer she was entertaining hopes of capturing Hardwick Moseley, who had replaced her original editor at Houghton Mifflin. By late summer she was simultaneously encouraging and fending off advances from Theodore Spencer, a professor of English at Harvard. But by then there was Bowden Broadwater, a recent Harvard graduate working in *The New Yorker*'s checking department, whom she would later say she had met the very night she finally walked out on Edmund Wilson.

**NICCOLÒ TUCCI**   Mary met Bowden at my house. Bowden and his sister were friends of this group of Dutch boys and girls. Bowden published a magazine of poetry and he was an excellent editor. He had flair. He knew when a piece of writing was good or bad. She came for dinner one evening and he was so kind to her and he accompanied her home. When people said he was homosexual, Mary said, "No, he's just light on his feet."

At twenty-five Bowden Broadwater was eight years younger than she was. Although she persisted in looking remarkably girlish, the disparity in their ages did not go unnoticed. Nor did the fact that he was totally unlike any of the other men in her life. At *The New Yorker* he was known for his long scarf and yellow socks. "The office aesthete," E. B. White called him. At Harvard, as one Radcliffe graduate would later recall, he had gone from Bob Broadwater to Robert Broadwater to R. Bowden Broadwater before finally arriving at the name he would sign to the eight stories that appeared in *The Advocate*. While some people found him attractive, others felt he looked like a frog.

**WILLIAM ABRAHAMS**   I must have met Bowden about 1940. The proper word for Bowden at Harvard—everybody tries to be tactful, and I've thought about it a great deal—was "fey." He was a very fey young man. Alarmingly thin. Very affected. Strange. I mean, it did not fall into any slot except that he reminded me of what I'd read about Ronald Firbank. You would never have guessed where he came from—which seemed to be a rather dull and stodgy little family down in Maryland. His affectations were amazing. His way of talking. He would prolong the syllables. I'd never heard anyone who talked like this. But I found him charming. He was very strange looking. He had orangy red hair and he wore the thickest glasses I'd ever seen, so that his eyes looked as though they were headlights. He was amusing, but he also turned out to be very talented. He was a most precocious and interesting and eccentric writer. Thanks chiefly to me, if I may say so, he was taken onto the staff of *The Harvard Advocate*. I also militantly argued for his being admitted to the Signet Society. He did not meet the definition of what would now be called a gay man. That was not what he was. He was certainly "other." "Queer" was not yet in style. There was something about him that upset all these rather nice ordinary American upper-class boys.

**NORMAN MAILER**   I knew Bowden from *The Advocate*. We liked each other. I think we respected each other. In those days we were in hostile camps. To put it generally, I belonged to the group you might call the realists, who were the minority. We admired writers like Farrell and Dos Passos. The power in *The Advocate* belonged to the aesthetes. I think Bowden had the major influence on that group. Everyone was terrified of his wit. He had an absolutely savage and immaculate wit. It was almost as good then as it is now. The difference was we were all so young that it was truly impressive. Bowden and I never clashed openly because you'd get your head handed to you if you cut across Bowden's bow.

In the spring of 1945, Mary McCarthy had no serious plans for the future. Before his departure for Europe, Wilson had offered her the use of the house on Henderson Place and she had declined his offer, seeing it as no more than a trick to lure her back. She had also declined his offer of the house in Wellfleet. Rather than return to her books and pots and pans and her garden, she chose to take Reuel to Truro, to Polly Boyden's, where she and Wilson had passed their first winter on the Cape.

Always she would say that the summer of 1945 was the best summer of her life. By the fall she would have to somehow come up with a job. She would also have to come up with a place to live. But for the summer she was on holiday. Not only did she immediately issue invitations to old friends like Eunice Clark Jessup and old lovers like Clement Greenberg and Philip Rahv but she was quick to join in the activities of a congenial group of neighbors—a group that included Dwight and Nancy Macdonald as well as the composer Gardner Jencks and his wife, Ruth.

Unfortunately, she could not afford a holiday from writing. She continued to owe Houghton Mifflin a book. Making the rounds of the various magazines but meeting with no success was a story called "The Friend of the Family," an ironic inquiry into the case of one Francis Cleary, the nonentity every couple keeps in reserve who offends and pleases no one. In late June she wrote to her agent Bernice Baumgarten to say she had given up hope on this old story and that she was sitting down at her desk in the mornings and finishing a new one. This story, too, was nothing like the stories in *The Company She Keeps*. It was called "The Unspoiled Reaction" and was a pared-down, almost allegorical account of a children's puppet show that goes wildly out of control. She did not see any need to describe this new story to her agent, but she did let her know that with a young son on her hands, getting down to work at that desk wasn't always easy.

### From Mary McCarthy's Letter to Bernice Baumgarten, June 20, 1945

If you have any news for me (and my presentiments are all ominous), I am here for the summer. We are living next door to Phyllis Dugaune, and it is a question every morning which mother's work is going to be demolished for the day by the children. So far I have gotten the best of it, and today their interest was deflected from us: they discovered the pleasure of flitting Phyllis's mother with the flit gun.

By the time she arrived at Truro, she knew Bowden Broadwater well enough to start a lively correspondence and to invite him up for the weekend. Joining her in extending this invitation was her six-year-old son. Bowden Broadwater had an easy way with children and for a hard-pressed single mother he had much to recommend him.

### From Mary McCarthy's Letter to Bowden Broadwater, June 23, 1945

Surely you must come up here. We miss you, both mother and child[. . . .] There is a room in this house called The Delmore Schwartz Memorial Chamber. You may occupy it if you like.

Although she was always careful to make light of Reuel's illnesses, she could count on her new friend's taking an interest in them. And she could count on his appreciating the terror they elicited.

### FROM MARY McCARTHY'S LETTER TO BOWDEN BROADWATER, N.D. [JULY 1945]

Did I write you that Reuel had mumps? I regarded it as a test of character for all men who set foot in the house. Mr. Moseley passed it honorably (really nobly); Dos Passos got zero. Oddly enough, the men who shrank away from Reuel were the men whose lives wouldn't have been visibly changed by Reuel's most fearsome germs.

### FROM McCARTHY'S LETTER TO BROADWATER, AUGUST 3, 1945

Reuel has infected toe. Going to Provincetown to doctor in morning. Worried[. . . .] Pray for Reuel. The lives of all mothers of my age are haunted by the memory of the Coolidge boy who got an infected foot from a tennis shoe. But now, I suppose, there is sulfanilamide.

No less important, she could count on Bowden Broadwater's being entertained by her descriptions of life in Truro. On those occasions she felt an impulse to unburden herself further, she felt no need to hold back. Not long after meeting her, Bowden Broadwater had had a falling out with Niccolò Tucci, the dashing and volatile Italian *New Yorker* writer who had brought the two of them together. In no time he was serving up tales of Tucci's perfidity. But his loyalty to her seems never to have been in question. From the start it was understood that, for all that he dearly loved gossip, he was not going to betray her. Bowden Broadwater's world was not her world and here the difference in their ages worked to her advantage. When he joined her in the company of her friends, he might carry off these encounters with a bravado that verged on effrontery, but he depended on her for support. When he wrote her a letter, he went to great lengths to amuse her, much the way she had once sought to amuse Edmund Wilson. From the anecdotes he recounted, he appeared to share her fondness for portraits that verged on caricatures. Possibly he was tailoring his anecdotes to her taste. But even if she suspected him of playing up to her, at this point in her life such a bid for her approval could only be welcome.

On her arrival in Truro, Mary had discovered that without Edmund Wilson, she was not necessarily on every hostess's A-list. Old friends of Wilson, like Katy and John Dos Passos, had taken it upon themselves to snub her; even those who did not go so far as to actually shun her saw little reason to seek her out. When it came down to it, she could count on the Dwight Macdonalds, Polly Boyden, and Ruth and Gardner Jencks. For all that she might make light of her new role as social pariah, she could not quite manage to ignore it. Once the summer got under way and Wellfleet swelled with visitors, she would in all likelihood be fine. But while she was still smarting from these pointed rebuffs she was at least able to turn them into high comedy, confident that her correspondent would not presume to doubt her word.

**FROM MCCARTHY'S LETTER TO BOWDEN BROADWATER, JUNE 23, 1945**
The Robert Nathans (*Portrait of Jennie*) are entertaining the Charlie
Jacksons (*The Lost Weekend*) during the week of the 2nd to the 9th. Mr.
Jackson does not like to meet more than seven or eight people at a
time (he masochistically counts the drinks, I suppose, and higher mul-
tiplication or simple accumulation of envy unsettles him), so they are
having two parties for him. Mrs. Nathan, through lack of information,
invited me to the inferior, non-intellectual one, and now Mr. Nathan is
scrambling around desperately trying to repair the mistake and he's
finally floundered into asking me to both, but I shall accept Mrs.
Nathan's category.

Not only had she suffered at the hands of Wilson's old friends but she
had been battered by her own houseguest. Clement Greenberg had come
to stay and proceeded to wreak havoc on both her household and her self-
esteem. But by this time she had finished the short story she was writing, freeing her to put all her recent suffering to immediate fictional use.

**FROM MCCARTHY'S LETTER TO BOWDEN BROADWATER,
N.D. [JULY 1945]**
Clem was perfectly odious all the time he was here. He did nothing
but criticize me, *not* help with the dishes, sleep until one and want both
breakfast and lunch, fleck imaginary specks off my face and costume,
and flirt with my worst enemies[. . . .] It has become the subject of a
witty novelette, now reaching page thirty-five, by a lady writer, M.M.
The novelette is called "The Lost Week."

The novelette was set in Nottingham, a pretty village of failed artists,
which can be seen as a rough sketch for the community she would portray seven years later in *A Charmed Life*:

**FROM "THE LOST WEEK"**
Nottingham was a kind of asylum for the derelicts of the American
creative life, a rural Foreign Legion which incorporated a man into its
ranks and asked no questions about his past or indeed about his present. Most of these charming people, with their gardens, their domestic arts, their shelves full of pickles and jellies, their home-made bread,
their coffee mills, their chickens, their beautiful old houses which they
had modernized, often with their own hands, their water lily pools,
their aquariums, had something to forget, sometimes a sexual scandal,
sometimes a financial indiscretion, but most often a sadder secret—the
failure of talent.

But it was not the village of Nottingham that interested her as much
as its inhabitants. When she sat down at her desk every morning, she
was settling a score with a writer of popular novels who had thought so

little of her as to invite her to a B-list party. Of Jim Theobald, whom she had modeled on Bob Nathan, she wrote, "By adroit manipulation (that is, by never making any single book so good that the next could be put in the shade by it) he had evaded the cruel hazard that confronts every writer—loss of critical esteem."

No less important, she was getting back at a former lover who had flirted with her enemies. Of Martin Samuels, a writer and critic who owed much to Clement Greenberg, she wrote, "[H]e never entered a friend's apartment without making some criticism of the lighting, decor or ventilation; he rearranged books on people's bookshelves, turned out the gas under dishes the cook had left simmering on the stove, took the knitting out of old ladies' hands to criticize the stitch they were using, and once went so far in his usurpation of some one else's domesticity as to spank a lively child while he was waiting for its mother."

As she trotted out harsh truths in the guise of writing satire, she did not spare herself. Of Frani Farrar, the pretty young novelist who was both her stand-in and heroine, she wrote, "[S]he practiced self-criticism with such openness and assiduity that she had a monopoly in the field and left no avenue open for the assault of competitors."

Writing Bowden Broadwater, she'd had the pleasure of settling some scores while entertaining her reader. Writing Edmund Wilson, she sent off a very different kind of letter. Thanks to the efforts of Fred Dupee, she had been offered an appointment for the fall at Bard College, a small liberal arts college in Annandale-on-Hudson, just up the river from Vassar, where she would receive three thousand dollars a year. The job would start September 15 and looked as if it would pay her enough to live on. She used this good news as an occasion to let Wilson know of the quiet life she was leading, of Reuel's positively flourishing in his absence, and of her plans to go to Nova Scotia for a few weeks at the end of August.

## FROM MARY MCCARTHY'S LETTER TO EDMUND WILSON, JULY 18, 1945

Reuel is well and is having a good summer with Eben [Given], Charlie Jencks, and Mike Macdonald. I have a part-time college girl helping to look after him, but he and Eben spend most of their time together. He is learning to swim; yesterday at Boundbrook he swam five strokes twice. He has been to stay several times at the Jencks's where he is very popular[. . . .] There is virtually nothing to eat on this end of the Cape, which has had the effect of thinning him down[. . . .] We are alone here[. . . .] [T]he Jessups with their little boys are coming up to spend ten days with us. When you come back, Reuel will come over to stay with you. He is looking forward to it very much.

The life she was leading was not quite as quiet as she made it out to be when writing her estranged husband. The fact was, she was not lacking in diversion. The Macdonalds had rented a two-story house on a bluff overlooking the North Truro Fish Factory and Provincetown Bay, with room enough for guests and for six-year-old Mike and his baby brother. In later years the Macdonalds would take other houses, eventually buying one in the Wellfleet woods, not far from the ocean. Dwight Macdonald would start up a softball game, where every Saturday anyone who showed up could join a team and play. Sometimes there were as many as twenty on a side. He would also start up a beach picnic that would take place on Saturday nights. That summer the more formal conventions of the Macdonalds' informal Cape life were not yet in place but there were still many picnics and dinners.

**MIKE MACDONALD**   At the picnics I seem to recall that she would always have very elegant stuff. The hamburgers would somehow be better hamburgers than anybody else had. And she'd have a nice little salad. In the evening there would be fires. John Berryman would recite "The Monkey's Paw," that marvelous old horror story. He would do it in a very undramatic way, which made it very dramatic.

**DANIEL AARON**   On these Wellfleet nights with Dwight Macdonald and Nancy there would be these moonlight dips sans bathing suits. I have mental pictures of Mary coming out of the water and toweling herself in the firelight.

**PENELOPE JENCKS**   I remember her going to the beach with my parents. I remember going to the ponds and she and my father would sit down by the pond and they would brush their hands in the sand, so that they'd make these patterns in the sand—these round ridges that would come out from their feet, spraying out beside them—and they'd sit there for hours talking about "truth."

To occupy her attention Mary had concerns every bit as pressing as "truth" or the Robert Nathans. During her marriage to Wilson, taking any active interest in the war would have meant running up against his staunch isolationism. On her own at Truro, she was at liberty to come out in full support of the Allied effort. She was free to debate with friends the implications of a victory that would render the United States the richest and most powerful nation in the Western world. If she liked, she could reject all previously held convictions. She could do virtually anything she wished—even support the war effort by donating a pint of blood. At Truro she was not on every hostess's A-list, but she continued to be a much-sought-after guest.

**FROM "ODE TO A WOMAN WELL AT EASE," BY EILEEN SIMPSON, *LEAR'S*, APRIL 1990**
At a cocktail party my hostess pointed out Mary across the crowded room. She stood in what I later recognized as a characteristic stance,

right foot forward and balanced on a high heel. In one hand she held a cigarette, in the other a martini. Her hair was parted in the middle and drawn back in a bun (à la Virginia Woolf and Elizabeth Bowen), setting off her elegant profile. Surrounded by men, she was in animated, even disputatious, conversation with them. It was about politics, whether So-and-So was or was not an anti-Stalinist.

As far as the poet John Berryman's young wife, Eileen Simpson, was concerned, she was the cynosure of all eyes.

**EILEEN SIMPSON** People in Wellfleet talked about Mary McCarthy a bit. And she knew it. I don't think she minded. That is to say, she felt (perhaps), They've got it all wrong, but I'm not going to bother to correct it.

For all that she might be smarting from the snubs she had received earlier that summer, she was not above administering a snub or two of her own. When an eager hostess introduced Berryman's wife to her as a fellow orphan, Mary made it clear just how little their mutual background counted for with her.

**EILEEN SIMPSON** She wanted me to know that she did not like at all to hear references to her orphanhood. (Like me, she wanted to believe that it had not damaged her in any way.)

That summer there were other visitors to the Cape whom she was more than happy to welcome. Visitors in whom she was not likely to see mirrored her own inadequacies and sad history. By 1945, thanks to Hitler and Stalin, even on the farthest reaches of the Cape you could find foreign intellectuals of every persuasion. With them they seemed to bring an aura of glamour and a less parochial perspective. To their experienced eyes, America did not necessarily appear bankrupt of promise. Although the war was drawing to an end, the ranks of these refugees did not appear to be thinning in the slightest.

By expressing sympathy for "poor Hitler" at a *Partisan Review* gathering the previous year, she had run afoul of the German philosopher Hannah Arendt. Still, she did not lack for friends from abroad. In the autumn of 1940, with Edmund Wilson she had come to know the Russian writer Vladimir Nabokov. Later, through Dwight Macdonald she had met the Italian writer Niccolò Tucci and the artist Saul Steinberg. Then, in the summer of 1943, through Macdonald, she had been introduced to an Italian refugee by the name of Nicola Chiaromonte.

Upon his arrival on the Cape in the summer of 1945, Nicola Chiaromonte began to have an immediate and lasting effect not merely on her political views but on the way she saw the world. In the vehemence of her response to Chiaromonte she was by no means unique in her circle. If nothing else, his personal history was of a sort to appeal to writers and intellectuals. An anarchist who had been forced to leave Mussolini's Italy in the early thirties, he had taken part in the war in Spain and fought in André Malraux's squadron alongside the Loyalists. After Franco's victory, he sought refuge in Paris and met and married an Austrian artist who had come to live there with her parents. His wife's father had been the editor of an important newspaper in Vienna and was said to be a Communist. When the Germans marched into Paris, Chiaromonte's father-in-law killed himself. One step ahead of the Nazis, Chiaromonte had escaped with his wife to Toulouse, where, stranded and waiting for exit papers, she died of tuberculosis. Eventually Chiaromonte was able to get hold of forged papers and find temporary refuge in North Africa. There he met and befriended the writer Albert Camus. In 1941, he came to the United States.

At one time a man of action who took time off from battle to read Plato, Chiaromonte had become a pacifist. He had rejected all systems of thought, whether they were progressive or reactionary. A passionate admirer of Tolstoy, he shared with the great novelist a mistrust of both the State and of History with a capital "H." He had long since ceased to believe in the Enlightenment or in the inevitability of progress. All the same, he believed in the power of individuals to change the world for the better by working within small communities. At the end of the war, when all systems of thought seemed to have produced little but bloodshed and carnage, the message he was carrying was particularly welcome.

In the years he had been in the United States, Nicola Chiaromonte had made something of a name for himself with articles in *The New Republic*, *The Nation*, and *politics*. He was widely known to be a character in Malraux's *Man's Hope*. But back in 1941, when Chiaromonte had turned up at the door of a New York City high school teacher with an introduction from George Santayana, he had presented a far from prepossessing figure. The suit he was wearing did not fit him properly. He could read English and understand it perfectly, but he did not speak it very well. That first evening he had seemed uncomfortable and embarrassed and sad. With some misgivings, the high school teacher agreed to help him with his English. Chiaromonte's father-in-law, she learned, had left instructions before committing suicide that his clothing be sent on to Nicola. Chiaromonte and his tutor were married in 1942. Now they had taken a small cottage not far from the house McCarthy was renting—a cottage she and Reuel had to pass on their way to the beach. In the course of many beach picnics and evening visits, there was plenty of occasion to get to know one another better.

**MARY MCCARTHY, IN AN INTERVIEW WITH CAROL BRIGHTMAN, *THE NATION*, MAY 19, 1984**

We talked about Tolstoy and about Dostoyevsky, and the *change* from someone like Edmund and his world was absolutely stunning. Nicola did not like Dostoyevsky and he had an absolute passion for Tolstoy [. . . .] One might have said that of course T. was a much better stylist and D. wrote bad Russian and so on. But that was a completely empty literary point of view by comparison. And in some way a self-satisfied point of view: it really didn't involve thinking about what these writers were saying! Talking with Nicola Chiaromonte was an absolute awakening and I never got over it.

**FROM MARY MCCARTHY'S INTRODUCTION TO *THE WORM OF CONSCIOUSNESS AND OTHER ESSAYS*, BY NICOLA CHIAROMONTE**

I heard a characteristic story about him from the organizer of a group of American Unitarians who was in Toulouse helping anti-Fascist escapees to get away, trying to secure them visas from the consulate, providing them with bogus papers: on being stopped one day by a Vichy policeman ("Let's see your papers!"), Chiaromonte was obliging: "Do you want the false ones or the real ones?"

**SAUL STEINBERG**  I think he and Mary were alike in that they were passionate. She admired passion. What she liked about Chiaromonte was the teddy bear. He was a hedgehog, but he was at the same time a bear—more a bear than a badger. On the fattish side, but not an obese man. He was a man who was meant to be shaped that way. It was his style. A very good dancer, too.

For some time Chiaromonte had been a contributor to *politics*, where his ideas could be seen reflected in the magazine's editorials. In the process, he and Dwight Macdonald had become close friends. It was owing to the Macdonalds that Chiaromonte and his wife, Miriam, had taken the house in Truro. To the end of her days Mary cherished a memory of Nicola in a blue ruffled apron sweeping out the cottage that he shared with Miriam. For her he was a remarkable and endearing figure. But while many who met him were willing to grant him moral superiority, not everyone shared her reverence for his ideas.

**NICCOLÒ TUCCI**  He was like a Benedictine monk. Very much so. One of the very few Italians who use the language politely and precisely. He was a great man. He was both brilliant and truly good.

**LIONEL ABEL**  I admired Nick more morally than intellectually. I don't know anything he wrote that I would say is a great work of thought. But I've never had a better friend.

**SAUL BELLOW**  I had a more reserved view of Chiaromonte than the rest of them did—partially because he held such sway over the New York intellectuals. I thought there must be something wrong somewhere. Of course he was everything they admired. He had been in Spain with Malraux. He had had a tragic first marriage. He was a very romantic character. He talked classics and especially Plato to them. And they behaved as if they'd never heard of Plato. Anyhow, they sat at his feet, listening to him. I was never a great one for sitting at anyone's feet.

**WILLIAM PHILLIPS**   People thought he was a genius because he was silent. Because he didn't talk much. He felt a lot. I don't want to put him down. He had qualities. He wasn't a great man but he was all right. He was intelligent and he had abilities. They needed a moral force. And he was the moral force. He fit Mary's needs. If he hadn't existed, she might have created him.

When you are caught up in savoring and then testing the limits of your new freedom, you may have little real desire to spend your summer at a desk in a dark room. Particularly if you have a constant stream of houseguests. Matters aren't helped any if you are the mother of an active small boy—not even when you have a young college girl from Simmons to help you take care of him.

With her future assured for the moment, thanks to the teaching job at Bard, writing a novel to satisfy Houghton Mifflin had ceased to be a dire necessity. She could afford to shift some of her attention from her satire to a more pressing project—one that was of immediate interest to the friends she was seeing every day on the beach. She was soon devoting her afternoons to translating into English an essay on *The Iliad* by a young Frenchwoman named Simone Weil, who had died during the Occupation, refusing all food and sustenance, a virtual suicide. Dwight Macdonald was eager to run her translation in *politics* as soon as it was ready. The essay had been published in 1940, on the heels of the Nazi invasion, in *Cahiers du Sud*, but it had never been published in English. Niccolò Tucci had discovered it and then taken her to see it in the Reading Room of the New York Public Library.

### FROM MARY MCCARTHY'S INTRODUCTION TO *THE RAIN CAME LAST AND OTHER STORIES*, BY NICCOLÒ TUCCI

Hatred and grief were almost palpable in the text [he] had found— hatred of the victors and grief for the defeated. Homer's *Iliad* was offered as an allegory (description of one thing under the image of another) of 1940, yet the correspondences were not exact. "Greeks" did not translate into "Nazis" or "Trojans" into "anti-Nazis." In Simone Weil's thinking there was no place for equal signs. Her subject was force, might, power, always fearsome, always at fault, whoever wielded it, Hector or Achilles[. . . .] I was used to thinking in opposites, and I can date a radical change in my mental life from the meeting with Tucci in the reading-room, which led to my translating the essay for Dwight's magazine. That was on Cape Cod, in Truro[. . . .] I took my typewriter to the beach and got sand in it.

If her need for Chiaromonte, like her passionate admiration for Simone Weil, owed something to the world situation, her fondness for him did not derive exclusively from his ideas. On both sides the relationship was rooted in quotidian pleasures. But on one side at least there were some reservations at first. Still, when she made the effort, she was hard to resist.

**MIRIAM CHIAROMONTE**   The first time I really met Mary was on the Cape. She did something that I think was typical of her and which I think I'm particularly vulnerable to. She gave me a present. Mary was a marvelous present giver and she gave me some wonderful soap that she said reminded her of me. I know that she was considered formidable and I know that she was, but we always had a quite, I should say, tender relationship.

**NICCOLÒ TUCCI**   She was amused by everything and therefore a discussion with her was always interesting. Everybody felt inspired to give his best. It was like a competition—a natural competition, a friendly competition. She was happy to be in the world. She loved to drink, she loved to cook, she loved to make love, she loved to have friends, she loved to fight. You don't often find that.

**SAUL STEINBERG**   I like people who still look the way they looked when they were children. On her it was obvious. She had kept not only the physical resemblance but there was a certain eagerness—a desire for gifts that a child has. Curiosity and innocence.

**NICCOLÒ TUCCI**   My friend Chiaromonte didn't like Mary at the beginning, but then she conquered him.

**LIONEL ABEL**   One evening that summer, we all read *Henry IV* at Mary's suggestion. Her brother Kevin was Prince Hal. I was Falstaff. And she cast herself as Hotspur's wife and Nick as Hotspur. It was quite an evening. I think Miriam was very frightened of Mary. At that time Mary had left Wilson and she really liked Nick enormously, so Miriam had some reason to be afraid of her. She was a very attractive personality, Mary. Did they have an affair? I think not. Mary liked Nick because she thought he was a very pure person, and she knew he would not leave Miriam. I think that at the moment when it might have happened she met Bowden.

Toward the end of July Bowden Broadwater took Mary McCarthy up on her invitation and paid a visit to the Cape. While no one close to his hostess was quite prepared to envision Bowden Broadwater in the role of her new lover, it was apparent that the two of them had a special affinity. She made no secret of valuing his ideas and his opinions. Indeed, reading her letters, it is clear that from the start she valued him sufficiently to wish to make him exquisitely aware of her own worth. Thanks to her epistolary flirtation with Wilson, she was no novice when it came to a correspondence between an older writer and one who is just starting out. Already in June she was addressing him as "Dearest Bowden" and signing her letters with "much love." He, on the other hand, persisted in addressing her as "Dear McCarthy" or "Dear Mary" and signing with a "Love" or a "Yours." Although he was slow to follow her lead, his stay at Truro seems to have taken relations to a new level. In his letter of August 10, he addressed her as "Dearest, darling Mary."

With her separation from Edmund Wilson, she had not lost her fondness for gossip or for regaling those she cared about with tales of her romantic conquests. When she wrote Bowden Broadwater of a close call with an ardent suitor or a recent visit from a former lover, it may have been no more than force of habit. But a hint of concern on his part was bound to be gratifying.

### FROM MARY MCCARTHY'S LETTER TO BOWDEN BROADWATER, N.D. [JULY 1945]

[Clement Greenberg] told me that the trouble was that he couldn't forgive me for the fact that he hadn't fallen in love with me. I exercised more *caritas* than I or Jim Agee thought I had in me by refraining from saying that the facts lent themselves to another and even a contrary interpretation—I just nodded understandingly and went on cooking his scrambled eggs.

### FROM MCCARTHY'S LETTER TO BROADWATER, AUGUST 3, 1945

In Wellfleet met Gardner Jencks. Car ride to garage, followed by declaration of love. (*Secret.*) "What I feel about you I can only express in music." Answer: "But I can't hear it; I'm tone deaf." Practical application of feelings fortunately seen as hopeless. I terribly embarrassed. Oh dear, isn't life awful, never felt such a dead lump of matter.

### FROM MCCARTHY'S LETTER TO BROADWATER, N.D [EARLY AUGUST 1945]

Gardner Jencks (I adore putting the *c* in his name), having made his declaration, has slunk away to the moors of Bound Brook and I see him no more. Always the way[. . . .]

John Berryman kissed me on the road outside Joan Colebrook's house. This kiss, in which the element of surprise played the same part as at Pearl Harbor, was witnessed by R. and G. Jencks, P. Boyden, and, alas, N. Chiaromonte.

**MIRIAM CHIAROMONTE**   I like Bowden very much, but I did not like what happened with the two of them together. Mary and Bowden fed each other. All the talk was cruel, brilliant—not gossip, just destruction of people. It was malicious. And one became that way, too—when you're in a group like that, you all start. It's terrible. It's hard to resist. You don't like yourself for it, and you resent having been part of it.

**KEVIN MCCARTHY**   When Mary and Bowden used to be in a room together, she would say something and he would go, "Hmmmm," and you would become aware that Mary had picked up on Bowden's innuendo of a difference of opinion and she was not about to let it pass. "Yes?! What is it?" There was this electricity in the air from the positive and negative elements.

**WILLIAM BARRETT**   To some extent I thought Mary became the consort of the man she was with. Mary tended to support the man she was with 120 percent. She would become like him. And then more so.

Nicola Chiaromonte, who was careful never to openly voice disapproval of any aspect of his friend Mary's character, saw no reason for such tact when it came to discussing her young friend. She, for her part, saw no reason to refrain from passing along his less than flattering though delicately phrased comment.

### FROM MARY MCCARTHY'S LETTER TO BOWDEN BROADWATER, JULY 28, 1945

Slight discussion of Bowden. Bowden living in very late Henry James novel, posthumous, dating from master's 100th year. Bowden supersubtleizes, imagines the non-existent. I said: but I am in it too, imprisoned in late novel, can't get out.

In her letters to Bowden Broadwater, she did not scruple to refer to Chiaromonte behind his back as "The Master" or "Le Maître." But while she might dare to speak of her new Italian mentor with irony in a letter, she was nonetheless in Chiaromonte's thrall. She was not about to cross him, and she was not about to take sides against him. For all that she might profess her willingness to reside alongside Bowden Broadwater in this posthumous novel by Henry James, she showed every intention of keeping one foot planted firmly in the beach cottage down the road. Defending her young friend to Chiaromonte, she did not refute his nonetoo-veiled criticism but chose, rather, to disarm it with her wit. When defending him to a less prepossessing attacker, her response was swift and direct.

### FROM MARY MCCARTHY'S LETTER TO BOWDEN BROADWATER, JULY 28, 1945

Long visit from Barbara Lawrence[. . . .] Criticism of Bowden's character from psychoanalyzed point of view—negativistic, snobbish, unrelaxed, freezing natural gifts by fear-produced inhibition. Impassioned defence of Bowden. Point carried. Miss Lawrence looks at Bowden in new light.

Happily, when it came to psychoanalysis, her allegiance was undivided. Neither Bowden Broadwater nor Nicola Chiaromonte had any use for it. Nor did she. The three psychoanalysts who had treated her may have helped rid her of her attacks of hysteria, but they had also helped perpetuate her husband's hold on her. Even as she was filing for a separation, Wilson had been urging her to go back and talk to Dr. Kardiner. At moments of crisis, he had always been pushing her down onto some analyst's couch.

During prior summers on the Cape, she had shown no aversion to analysts or their insights. Indeed at one point she had sought out the company of her first doctor, Sándor Rado. But by the summer of 1945 she had little wish to see Rado or to have anything further to do with psychoanalysis. She felt she had no need of it. To justify her wholesale rejection of its precepts and methods, she would eventually argue that it fostered in patients a most unattractive self-pity. She would also argue that it had no claims to being a science. In 1979, when her brother Kevin suggested that there might be more to it than that, she wasn't hearing any of it. "I think the whole thing is an absurd series of myths," she said. "It's never in any way been empirically verified." A few years later, when her friend and former student Eve Stwertka confided that she sometimes suffered from terrible anxiety, she countered by saying, "I never ever feel that."

**EVE GASSLER STWERTKA**   I think it's one of the things that made her so strong. Because anxiety is very draining. It saps a lot of energy. It impairs your efficiency. Whatever Mary's personality was, she was not what used to be defined by the Freudians as neurotic. I think she rather looked down on neurosis. I think she thought neurosis was an illness of the bourgeoisie. The middle class. The aristocracy went mad.

The summer of her liberation from both Edmund Wilson and psychoanalysis closed on a somber note. On August 6, Truman ordered an atomic bomb to be dropped on Hiroshima. On August 9, a second bomb was dropped on Nagasaki. A debate over whether or not to give blood began to seem irrelevant, if not frivolous. At the same time, passages she had been translating on the beach, with the help of friends delighted to offer encouragement, began to sound alarmingly prescient.

**FROM "THE ILIAD OR, THE POEM OF FORCE," BY SIMONE WEIL**
[V]iolence obliterates anybody who feels its touch. It comes to seem just as external to its employer as to its victim. And from this springs the idea of a destiny before which executioner and victim stand equally innocent, before which conquered and conqueror are brothers in the same distress. The conquered brings misfortune to the conqueror, and vice versa.

One year later, she would attack the writer John Hersey for not suggesting the sheer horror of what had taken place.

### FROM MARY MCCARTHY'S LETTER TO THE EDITOR OF *POLITICS*, NOVEMBER 1946

May I add something to your comment on the Hiroshima *New Yorker*? The editors of that magazine imagined, and you yourself in your comment take for granted, that the Hersey piece was an indictment of atomic warfare. Its real effect, however, was quite the opposite. What it did was to minimize the atom bomb by treating it as though it belonged to the familiar order of catastrophes—fires, floods, earthquakes—which we have always had with us and which offer to the journalist, from Pliny down to Mr. Hersey, an unparalleled wealth of human-interest stories, examples of the marvelous, and true-life narratives of incredible escapes.

Fifteen years later, writing of how this event had cast into question the assumptions underlying realistic fiction, she would recall how it cast into question *all* underlying assumptions.

### FROM "THE FACT IN FICTION," *PARTISAN REVIEW*, SUMMER 1960

I remember reading the news of Hiroshima in a little general store on Cape Cod in Massachusetts and saying to myself as I moved up to the counter, "What am I doing buying a loaf of bread?"

**MIRIAM CHIAROMONTE**   We were all horrified. I remember the discussions. We spoke of nothing else after it happened.

**WILLIAM PHILLIPS**   I don't know. I would guess that she was putting on a bit. She was self-dramatizing. I don't say that about Hiroshima with any certainty. But the rest of us were not self-dramatizing in that way. She was always moralizing. And she found a moral principle here. She was always taking the high road. It was annoying.

At the time, however, her most immediate worry was Edmund Wilson's impending return from Europe. "Really in frightful state of anxiety as date for docking approaches," she wrote Bowden Broadwater. "Rosalind thinks Father will stay New York one week before coming up here." By late August it was impossible to regard Wilson's return with equanimity. Her plan was to take a plane from Boston to check on arrangements at Bard. Soon she was going to have to take her leave of Truro. To make her leave-taking easier, the Jenckses had invited Reuel to come stay with them. To give her a proper send-off, the Chiaromontes were throwing a farewell party on the beach. Well before Wilson set foot in Wellfleet, she was hoping to be miles away. Just where, she was not entirely sure.

In the end, Mary did indeed go off to Nova Scotia—to a business hotel in Yarmouth, where she holed up for one week with her typewriter and the manuscript of "The Lost Week." Just as she was preparing to depart she learned that Bernice Baumgarten had sold "The Unspoiled Reaction" to *The Atlantic.* On her way north she stopped off in Boston and stayed over at the apartment of Herbert Solow, who treated her to "a coarse leer" at breakfast while she was encouraging another putative suitor, Theodore Spencer. Keeping Bowden Broadwater abreast of her latest romantic escapades, while swearing him to secrecy, she informed him that she was tempted to get Theodore Spencer to propose to her even though he had committed the solecism of attempting to write an atom bomb sonnet and could lay claim to only $2500 a year.

Once she was safely in Nova Scotia, it was her intention to finish her novelette. Alone in her hotel room she would have no friends to distract her. For company she had a volume of Spinoza. Unfortunately, she had no letters from Bowden waiting to reward her at general delivery. Having asked twice if there were any, she let him know, she "felt utterly neglected." She believed she was suspected of being a spy. The surrounding countryside was "beautiful," but Yarmouth offered nothing to attract a real American tourist.

### FROM MCCARTHY'S LETTER TO BOWDEN BROADWATER, N.D. [LATE AUGUST 1945]

Everything looks like a frontier street in the movies and you expect people to come out shooting[. . . .] [N]o liquor sold except bottled in a government liquor store, permit required; no drinking of any kind allowed in public places; venereal warnings (VD it's called—I thought at first it was a new kind of victory) plastered over every public toilet. All this gives the impression that socialism has arrived in a kind of dreary and antique form. The food reminds me poignantly of the unpleasant part of my childhood: the taste and smell of soda permeates everything, bread, vegetables, even meat. Blanc-mange, rice pudding, plums, balls of mashed potatoes, turnips, squash—I feel as if my hair and teeth were going to fall out.

Regrettably, owing to a bad cold, she did not feel up to leaving her "large and vaguely unpleasant" hotel and traveling to some resort where she could get the benefit of some of that beautiful local scenery. And, regrettably, the anger that had fueled the novelette had abated considerably. The fact was, much had happened since the week of July Fourth. Once her social life had picked up, Robert Nathan's slights had lost much of their sting and Clement Greenberg's transgressions had come to seem like ancient history. Then, too, the bombings of Hiroshima and Nagasaki could not be ignored. If nothing else, they called into question, at least for the moment, the assumptions that underlie a comedy of manners. Still, she persisted with her project.

In the final pages of the manuscript of "The Lost Week," she had Martin Samuels, the Clement Greenberg character, take it upon himself to tell Frani Farrar that there is a direct link between her "observance of social formality" and her success with commercial magazines. As he sees it, commercial magazines are incapable of publishing "a serious piece of fiction by a serious writer" and Frani is "the half-emancipated slave of convention." Broadly drawn and thoroughly outrageous, Martin Samuels is the only character in the manuscript who has any claim to life.

But it is not revenge or social satire that occupies the author of "The Lost Week." The visit of Charles Jackson, the author of *The Lost Weekend*, has led her to contemplate the future of a writer she calls Herbert Harper, who has made his reputation by writing a confessional novel.

### FROM "THE LOST WEEK"

Herbert Harper could not duplicate his first success [. . .] for such early successes can never be duplicated. The mood of self-revelation comes but once to an author; it cannot be revived but only counterfeited. In fear and trembling, he lays his whole soul on the table, risking universal condemnation for the sake of some higher forgiveness—"Love me," he cries, "as I am." It is this sense of risk, this mixture of temerity and terror, that authenticates his story; but once he has won the gamble, been accepted, admired, forgiven, his confessions, if he persists in them, will become spurious, since he is sure in advance of absolution. Moreover, his private life is no longer private; it is a museum through which he himself has shown visitors, and if he continues to live in it, it is only as a custodian or janitor. Yet it was the very privacy of his private life that was the bond between him and his readers; in the sense of having something to hide, something unspoken, unadmitted, he was exactly like them—as a prominent author who has made a holy spectacle of himself in print, he will never again be on an equal footing with them. If he is to go on with his career, it must be on a different basis; he himself must disappear from his work or appear in it disjointed, as it were, one part of him being given to one character, one to another, one part to the style, so that the work of art is an assemblage of *disjuncta membra poetae*.

Early in the summer, Mary McCarthy had worried that her novelette would wind up sounding too much like John Marquand. In the end it faltered not because it was derivative but because it began to sound too much like a writer talking to herself. Writing of Herbert Harper and Frani Farrar, she stayed clear of any theory locating the source of artistic creation in psychic misery. She rejected all myths, be they religious or secular. She restricted herself to empirical observation. And what she saw gave her grounds for concern. At this point her future as a novelist seemed far from assured. She feared that with her first big success she had painted herself into a corner. If anything, her current labors seemed to confirm her worst fear.

After a week of solitary confinement, she had come nowhere near completing her projected one hundred pages. Judging from Wilson's brief unhappy stint at the University of Chicago, once she started teaching she would have little energy to spare for her own work. Her appointment to the Bard faculty was for the entire academic year. With her salary from Bard, augmented by her payments from Wilson, she would be able to afford the furnished house she had found for herself and Reuel. With the promise of a job had come a measure of security and a greater sense of liberty. She had bought herself peace of mind, but she had not bought herself time.

At Yarmouth, lonely and bored, she had sent off a brace of typewritten letters to Bowden Broadwater—letters which, for all that they spill over with depictions of provincial tedium, are themselves never dreary or boring. If Wilson had been at her elbow, he might have accused her of "acting out a novel when she ought to be writing one." But there was no Wilson at her elbow or anywhere in sight. At the end of her week's retreat, cured of her cold but still carrying on her well-documented flirtation with Theodore Spencer, she packed up her manuscript and typewriter. Putting her novelette away for good, she set off for the Cape, to face down the husband who had ceased to hold any sway over her and to pick up her young son.

# Chapter Ten

# BARD

One of the essays in Edmund Wilson's collection *The Wound and the Bow* was called "Justice to Edith Wharton." Here Wilson attempted to salvage the reputation of a writer whose writing had fallen off so precipitously toward the end of her life as to obscure her early triumphs. To restore some lustre to Wharton's sadly tarnished reputation Wilson had set about relieving her of the burden of standing forever in the shadow of her good friend Henry James. Instead of treating her as a lesser disciple of a writer whose interests were for the most part "esthetic," he chose to see her as a realist, a writer of tragedies in the vein of Aeschylus, and a "social prophet."

Written in December 1937, when Mary McCarthy was stealing away from Philip Rahv to visit Wilson in his lair at Stamford and when the author of *The House of Mirth* and *The Age of Innocence* was barely cold in her grave, "Justice to Edith Wharton" seems eerily prescient. Whether one agrees with Wilson's assessment of Wharton's career or not, one can see that it has some bearing on Mary McCarthy's case. According to Wilson, all Edith Wharton's important novels were written about an individual coming into conflict with the rules of society. And all were written during a twelve year period in which she was suffering through a terrible emotional crisis that brought back the sorrow and isolation of her privileged New York childhood. As he saw it, not only the novelist's great theme but the intensity of her treatment derived from the misery of her marriage. Once she moved permanently to France and rid herself of the insane husband who made her life miserable, her work fell apart.

For the young Mary McCarthy, Wilson's generous appraisal of Wharton's strengths may well have provided both validation and guidance. But eight years later, when she was finally breaking free of Wilson, his account of Wharton's subsequent career could easily be read as a cautionary tale. Or seal of doom. Wilson wrote, "It is sometimes true of women writers—less often I believe of men—that a manifestation of something like genius may be stimulated by some exceptional strain, but will disappear when the stimulus has passed. With a man, his professional, his artisan's life is likely to persist and evolve as a partially independent organism through the vicissitudes of his emotional experience. Henry James in a virtual vacuum continued to possess and develop his *métier* up to his very last years. But Mrs. Wharton had no *métier* in this sense." In 1937 Wilson could with perfect impunity take on the magisterial inflections of Wharton's friend and mentor as he set about proclaiming a literary double standard. As he saw it, women writing fiction lacked the discipline of a lifetime's commitment to their craft. Once they ceased to chafe under their psychic wounds, they not only risked losing the bow but were for all practical purposes assured of doing so.

Having finally escaped her unhappy marriage and been rewarded by a pleasant but unproductive summer in Truro, McCarthy had grounds to fear that by upsetting the status quo she had lost the sense of vocation that Wilson had instilled in her. Her experience at the hotel in Yarmouth had hardly boded well for her future. Moreover, what followed had done nothing to reassure her. She had returned to the Cape in early September to discover that Wilson had made off with their six-year-old son.

Waiting for her at Truro was a letter from Wilson accusing her of not letting him know that she had taken Reuel out of school at St. Bernard's. Her July 18 letter, sent to him in Italy had apparently failed to reach him. Putting her on notice, Wilson was simply repaying what he saw as her own high-handed behavior. "You can take Reuel this winter and I will give you money for him while he is with you," he wrote. "Later I will take him to Europe for a whole year. Otherwise, we will share him six months and six months[. . . .] I decide all matters of his education."

Her worst fears, it seemed, had been realized. Fortunately, Wilson was ill equipped to take on the care and management of an active six-year-old. Instead of making off with Reuel for good, he had immediately deposited the boy for safekeeping with his grandmother in Red Bank. Reuel was in fact free to go live with his mother at Bard. But in case she had harbored any lingering hope that relations with Wilson might some day be amicable, this incident let her know that she could look forward to neither a tranquil separation nor a quick, painless divorce.

On a flying visit to Bard in August, she had rented a substantial old Victorian house in the neighboring village of Upper Red Hook, New York. The house was not only furnished but appeared, at first glance, to have much to recommend it. With the money she was making teaching and her sixty dollars a week from Wilson, she would be able to live in some style. Once she moved in, her first task was to make a settled home for Reuel. Her next task was to pick up the dangling threads of her writing career. About to embark on her first year as a single working mother and her first year of teaching, she could only hope that with all the turmoil of the past months she had not permanently mislaid her *métier*.

Certainly if she was expecting to find at Bard something along the lines of her own undergraduate experience, she was destined for disappointment. In 1860, when the brewer Matthew Vassar had been proclaiming the establishment of a college to educate young women, John Bard had been quietly signing over part of his Hudson River estate to establish "an Episcopal men's college with a strong classical curriculum" to be called St. Stephen's. In 1928 the college had been taken over by Columbia University, which soon instituted an academic regimen relying on tutors and small seminars and owing not a little to Oxford. In 1934, the name of the college was changed to Bard. In 1944 Bard began admitting women, while severing its ties with Columbia and retaining only the loosest of ties with the Episcopal Church. From that moment, Bard began to acquire the freewheeling reputation of Bennington or Sarah Lawrence.

In the full splendor of her halcyon days at Truro, Mary McCarthy had contemplated half seriously a retreat from the world with a group of like-minded friends. By accepting an appointment at Bard she effectively removed herself from the world as she knew it. However, her retreat was not entirely by choice and her companions in exile were not necessarily ones she herself would have chosen. One exception of course was Fred Dupee, who had brought her to the campus. Eight years her senior and possessed of great charm, brilliant blue eyes, and a fondness for gossip, he was someone whose company she had invariably sought out. It was Fred Dupee who had fortified her with the two fatal daiquiris before her first date with Edmund Wilson. Of all the editors at *Partisan Review*, he had been the one Wilson found least objectionable. He had been her editor for "The Man in the Brooks Brothers Shirt." At one point Wilson had suspected him of being her lover as well.

While she was not to be permitted the privilege of choosing her companions in exile, there was every reason to believe that she would have little difficulty finding company to tide her over during the school year. Teachers at Bard tended to be young and iconoclastic. The chairman of the humanities division, Artine Artinian—born in Bulgaria but educated in America—was only five years older than she was. The most senior member of the division, the Dante scholar Irma Brandeis, was in her forties.

More typical of the Bard faculty were Vida Ginsberg, two years out of Radcliffe and an instructor in both drama and English literature, and Fritz Shafer, who had a young wife and new baby and did double duty as college chaplain and lecturer in religion. In a community of rebels and misfits one faculty member, Lincoln Reis, stood out. A widely published assistant professor of philosophy in the division of social sciences and a veteran of more than one institution of higher learning, Reis was not about to conform to standards and rules he viewed as foolish, even though he had a wife and two young daughters to support.

As a new and totally inexperienced teacher, Mary McCarthy had been fortunate to find employment at an institution that prided itself on being slow to pass judgment. She herself felt no such reluctance, but for the moment she announced no plans to make use of all she observed of her students and colleagues in any "imaginative writing." With two courses to teach each semester, she had little time to spare for such an ambitious project. Instead, she restricted her satiric portraits to her active correspondence with Bowden Broadwater.

Not until 1952 would she dredge up her Bard memories in *The Groves of Academe*, a novel in which an academic veteran and Joyce scholar by the name of Henry Mulcahy receives notice that his one-year teaching contract will not be renewed and immediately lets it be known that his wife is desperately ill, that he has been hired with the promise of tenure, and that the school's president, an avowed liberal and champion of political freedom, has fired him solely because he is a member of the Communist Party. By then, with a term at Sarah Lawrence behind her, she could speak with some authority about the absurdities and incongruities endemic to progressive education. For the school in her novel she chose the name Jocelyn. Publicly she claimed that its campus was inspired by a small girls' academy in Lititz, Pennsylvania, the home of the pretzel, and that its faculty was made up from whole cloth. When pressed by an interviewer from *Paris Review*, she later granted that "it was quite a bit like Bard."

If her fictional portrait was not of a sort to gladden the heart of anyone who held the college and its "experimental" traditions sacred, she tended in later years to recall her time at Annandale-on-Hudson in terms that bordered on the idyllic. With rare exceptions, her students had had nothing like the grounding in Latin and Greek or the familiarity with English literature that her generation had taken for granted, but they were eager to learn. Always she made it a point to say how much she had enjoyed teaching them. However, in the fall of 1945 it was not a love of teaching that brought her to academia. About to set off for Bard with a good Vassar education, an active six-year-old son, no place to stay for the night, and virtually no preparation whatsoever, she paused, at the last minute, to send off one desperate postcard.

### MARY McCARTHY TO FRED DUPEE, N.D. [SEPTEMBER 1945]

Dear Fred: Is Richards' *Practical Criticism* in a class with [Thomas Carlyle's] *Past and Present* as far as college courses go nowadays, or is it still possible to use it? Arriving Saturday evening by car with Reuel. Can you put us up or shall we register at Red Hook hotel. House not available till 16th. Reply Truro if possible. *Love*, Mary.

Although Fred Dupee was not disposed to offer her a bed or prepared to allay her fears about I. A. Richards and the New Critics, he had an investment in seeing that her stay at Bard got off to a smooth start. By vouching for her, he had in effect been responsible for her hiring. In some sense, whether he intended it or not, he was responsible for all that was to follow.

**ARTINE ARTINIAN** I hadn't read any of Mary's work and was at first going on Fred Dupee's say-so. I'd had Fred Dupee as a teacher in speech when I was a freshman at Bowdoin. That was in 1927. Then lo and behold in 1944, I was chairman of the division, and I was interviewing *him* for a job.

**VIDA GINSBERG DEMING** Fred, Irma Brandeis, and I all came when Bard became coed in 1944. Before Mary arrived at Bard I sketched—we all sketched—a novel that she would write after leaving. The people that she'd pick. The kind of names she'd give. And that was great fun. I pretty well guessed right. I didn't know the episode she would use, which came later.

When Mary McCarthy first set foot on the Bard campus, it was a pastoral backwater, just emerging from a state of all-male innocence and feeling the first effects of coeducation. At this point Russia was still a valued ally, there was no loyalty oath, no House Committee on Un-American Activities, and no ferreting out of Communists. Her first brush with academia was at once less dramatic and more complicated than anything she would later portray in her novel. True to her word, on Saturday, September 15, she arrived at Annandale-on-Hudson accompanied by her young son, an aura of glamour, a hint of scandal, and a reputation for a take-no-prisoners approach to everything from a book or theater review to a perfectly ordinary dinner party.

**MARGARET SHAFER** The first time I met Mary was at a party in a basement apartment at the college. I was wild to meet the person who had written *The Company She Keeps*. She was wearing this white lace dress, off the shoulder, and it was not what you expect to see people wearing in October. Of course she had everybody riveted. She was very glamorous. I was too much in awe to speak to her. She really liked my husband, Fritz, very much—I think she was intrigued to find an Episcopal chaplain to whom she could talk and whose mind she could respect. She almost immediately invited us over.

**ARTINE ARTINIAN** At a party she seemed self-assured and confident. But she was not as articulate as she was on the page. Frequently she was in slight disarray.

**VIDA GINSBERG DEMING** Her smile fractured her face. It was a very spontaneous smile, but suddenly the face was all in pieces, which was strange and unnerving. It was like a Picasso. I liked her when I first met her, but there were off-putting things. I remember getting very angry when she would speak of herself as a girl. I was considerably younger, and I didn't see her as this young thing. She was over thirty. Now I can understand it. Having older friends helps maintain girlishness. And she moved, in general, in older circles, where they thought of her as "our *enfant terrible.*"

For the fall term, McCarthy was responsible for overseeing four sophomores who were embarking on projects of their own and for teaching a class in the Russian novel. In 1962 she told the *Paris Review* interviewer, "I liked teaching because I loved this business of studying." In her love of studying, if nothing else, she bore a striking resemblance to the Russian bluestocking Domna Rejnev, the heroine of *The Groves of Academe*, whose students "were quick to discover that they could not please Miss Rejnev better than by discovering a wish to study an author she had not read, preferably an old author, in some forgotten cranny of culture."

**MARY MCCARTHY, IN AN INTERVIEW WITH ELISABETH NIEBUHR, *PARIS REVIEW*, WINTER–SPRING 1962**
Well, you had to call everything at Bard either modern or contemporary, or the students wouldn't register for it. Everyone thinks this is a joke, but it was true. I originally was going to teach a whole course on critical theory, from Aristotle to T. S. Eliot or something, and only three students registered for it, but if it had been called "Contemporary Criticism," then I think we would have had a regular class. So we called this course "The Modern Novel," and it began with Jane Austen, I think, and went up, well, certainly to Henry James.

With the faculty and with students like Barbara ("Andy") Anderson, who would go on to marry Fred Dupee, her reputation had preceded her.

**BARBARA DUPEE** Fred had been ecstatic that Mary was coming, because he was by then a very old friend. They must have known each other for ten years. When Mary lived in Stamford with Edmund Wilson, she would call Fred up and say she was coming to New York, and they'd go to the movies in the afternoon, have drinks, and gossip. I think Fred thought of her as the most marvelous creature that had ever been. I met Mary my first day of class. And she was so beautiful and disheveled. I knew she'd been writing for money since she was practically a child. She had no money and she was just an ordinary person. Later she went to designers and spent God knows how much on clothes. But she was really at her best with her hair not quite caught and everything flying about.

**EVE GASSLER STWERTKA** The first time I met Mary was at an office that had been assigned to her and I was waiting in the office to sign up for her tutorial. The office was empty. When you registered at Bard you didn't go stand on line in some gymnasium, you simply went up to each instructor. On her desk was a book, *The Little Red Hen*. I didn't know *The Little Red Hen*, so I picked it up and I was reading it, and then I heard this voice—Mary's voice was quite distinctive. She had Reuel with her. I don't think Reuel went to school at that time. When she came in, she was surrounded by an entourage. She was followed by three faculty members—all male. She really had a vibration all around her, an aura. Her hair was not long then and it was a little curled and parted on the side. She looked in, went out again, and I heard her say to somebody, "One of my students is reading *The Little Red Hen*."

As long as she met with her advisees, presided over her classes, read her students' papers, and turned in reasonably appropriate grades, no one was about to think the worst of her. Faced with a sea of blank faces, most teachers quickly learn to adjust their standards accordingly. However, for her class on the Russian novel, she cobbled together an ambitious reading list and then proceeded to stick with it. Following in the tradition of Miss Kitchel and Miss Sandison, she did not make allowances. Her students had to struggle to keep up, but she was soon struggling every bit as hard as they were.

**MARY McCARTHY, IN AN INTERVIEW WITH ELISABETH NIEBUHR, *PARIS REVIEW*, WINTER–SPRING 1962**
It was all quite mad, crazy. I had never taught before, and I was staying up till two in the morning every night trying to keep a little bit behind my class. Joke[. . . .]
I found it quite impossible to give a course unless I'd read the material the night before. I absolutely couldn't handle the material unless it was fresh in my mind. Unless you give canned lectures, it really has to be—though that leads, I think to all sorts of very whimsical, perhaps, and capricious interpretations; that is, you see the whole book, say *Anna Karenina*, in terms that are perhaps dictated by the moment. One wonders afterwards whether one's interpretation of *Anna Karenina* that one had rammed down the throats of those poor students was really as true as it seemed to one at the time.

**ARTINE ARTINIAN**   Now, you must remember that Bard at the time did not have a lecturing type of teaching. It was seminars. So that we would assign a book to be read by the class and we met once a week for a two hour session to discuss that particular assignment. Believe me, the teacher was under the gun constantly. You had twelve or fifteen bright students who had just read that book more carefully than you had time for. And they would come up with all sorts of questions.

**ELLEN ADLER OPPENHEIM**   In the Russian novel course, I remember we started with an assignment to read the first chapters of *Anna Karenina*. There were about fourteen of us and we sat around a table. It seems to me that Mary asked the girls for a show of hands as to which of us would fall in

love with Vronksy and which would fall in love with Levin. All but one raised
our hands for Vronsky. The poor soul who raised her hand for Levin hit
Mary's bad list and remained there all term. I think Mary took her for a middle-brow because it was quite obvious that if both Kitty and Anna were in
love with Vronsky, Tolstoy intended his reader to be too.

Supervising four sophomore projects each term, she tried her best to
be rigorous. With her advisees and her students she seemed incapable of
doing anything by rote or by halves.

**ARTINE ARTINIAN**   My office was next to her classroom and I could not
believe how almost inarticulate she was in class. She hesitated and hemmed
and hawed, seeking the perfect word that she wanted to use. When you were
with her in a social situation, she wasn't like that in conversation. And of
course in her writing she was brilliant. I couldn't hear what she was saying
in the next room, but I could hear the hesitations.

**ELLEN ADLER OPPENHEIM**   October came and Mary wanted to have the
Russian class outside. We sat outside and the autumn leaves were coming
down. It was a really sharp October day. Somebody lit a cigarette and some
boy said, "Let me near the fire." Mary looked up and said, "Are you cold?" I
mean, it was thirty degrees.

At Bard, unlike Vassar, contact with students outside the classroom was
not limited to quiet afternoon tea on a screened sunporch.

**JAMES MERRILL**   The point of Bard is that the students always have access
to you. And the students at Bard were demanding. I was teaching there the
year after Mary and I think Mary always had a good deal more sense of
responsibility toward her students than I ever did. I would cluster my classes
in the middle of the week and then drive down to New York for a four-day
weekend. So I escaped.

**EVE GASSLER STWERTKA**   When faculty had a party, they always invited
students. Eventually at Mary's parties I met all the *Partisan Review* people. I
met Dwight Macdonald. I also met Elizabeth Hardwick. She and Mary were
just starting to be friends.

Early on it became apparent to both students and faculty that this new
addition to the literature division was like no other faculty member. She
had rented a big old house with a view of the Hudson in Upper Red
Hook—a tiny village long on charm and short on practicality, with an
array of pretty Victorian gingerbread houses and no place to shop. The
house, which had been abandoned for some time, was not in good shape.
It was cold and it was damp, but it had a parlor and a living room and a
number of bedrooms upstairs. Best of all, there was a big kitchen in the
basement, with a stone floor and a huge old stove, and a large overgrown
garden in the back.

**MARGARET SHAFER**   As we walked into her house, the first thing that met my eye was a huge bouquet of flowers. Bard people just didn't have huge bowls of fresh flowers in November.

**VIDA GINSBERG DEMING**   The house may have had lots of problems, but it had wonderful old engravings on the wall, wonderful bound books, and wonderful old furniture.

At Bard, where faculty and students lived in each other's pockets, there were few secrets.

**EVE GASSLER STWERTKA**   I became Reuel's baby-sitter, and that's really how the friendship between Mary and myself grew. Mary loved for me to read to Reuel. She had a book of Russian fairy tales, which were quite unusual because Russian fairy tales never seem to have a moral. She had no money at all at that point, but she always believed in buying the best. Her clothes were almost nonexistent, but she had one really fancy dress from Bergdorf Goodman. And Reuel was wearing a little gray flannel Brooks Brothers suit with short pants.

Although Mary McCarthy had seen very little of Bowden Broadwater over the summer, she had seen enough to know she enjoyed his company. In her first letter from Bard, she was already issuing an invitation to come spend the weekend. If the house was not quite ready to receive guests, she knew from experience that this particular guest could be counted on to not merely beguile or entertain but pitch in and help. Reuel told Andy Anderson, "Bowden makes Mummy laugh," but the fact was he also made Reuel laugh. Indeed Reuel was reported to have asked, "Is Bowden only a jester?" Still, it would be fair to say that not all of the Bard community was amused by this frequent visitor. From the start no one was quite sure what to make of him. Even so, there were those who saw in him something that was appealing—or, failing that, believed they saw what his hostess saw in him.

**EVE GASSLER STWERTKA**   I thought Bowden was a little bit of an odd choice for Mary, but he was very charming. He was like a beautiful English boy. Like Christopher Robin grown to be twenty-eight. His coloring was so blond—sort of like the Duke of Windsor's. He had very English looks. A very elongated, slender figure. Very graceful. And of course he had his suits made for him at Brooks Brothers. The suits would fit like a glove. And always three pieces. A summer suit and a winter suit. And I used to think in my innocence that he had an income from his family.

**VIDA GINSBURG DEMING**   I thought Bowden was foolish. I remember he had a beautiful lavender sweater. I kept wondering if she'd marry him, and it seemed almost impossible. And then I thought, What is it that she finds in him? He seemed a caricature of a limp gay man. And not pretty at all. I mean, very homely. He had great aspirations of elegance. He and Mary had that in common. Mary had social aspirations and she wanted elegance. Which I guess she had been deprived of in many ways. I remember she gave a party once and Bowden hand-painted mints and suspended them from the trees in the garden. And they had a trio playing chamber music on the back porch, which was elevated, and the party was down on the lawn. At some point the laundry man turned up shouting, "Where's the laundry?"

Glamorous as her life might appear to a casual visitor, the cracks showed through, the way the laundry man popped up during the interlude of chamber music. The glamour was achieved at no small cost and against considerable odds. Her wonderful house was a white elephant. A house in Annandale-on-Hudson, within easy walking distance of the Bard campus, would have made better sense. Or a smaller house with a furnace that she could trust.

In fact, her early days at Bard were no more carefree than her first days at Truro. The problems she faced were simply of a different order. On the Cape, she had been living within her means and she had been living in a house she had lived in before, with the owner sometimes in residence and the college girl from Simmons there to help out. During the summer she could look forward to Reuel's spending the day with Mike Macdonald or Charlie Jencks; in emergencies she could count on his staying with the Jencks family. At Bard, she arrived with no one to help her manage the house and with no sitter for Reuel. Most of her colleagues were either single or had very young children. None had boys Reuel's age. Worst of all, the standards of the Red Hook public school were not the same as St. Bernard's. In her view, they were more rigorous. The bottom line was his teachers wanted to put Reuel back a year. Reuel, understandably, wanted very much to stay where he was.

As a single parent with a full-time job, her first concern was for her son. Ignoring the recommendation of his teachers, she went along with Reuel's wishes and secured him a tutor to help him with his reading. She had already found him a kitten and a canary he quickly named Limeade and Lemonade. She had imported a temporary sitter from New York and then enlisted the services of her favorite students as baby-sitters. She also got a local woman to stay with him when school let out.

Her second concern was to somehow mollify Edmund Wilson. In late September Wilson had written to say that because no one had informed St. Bernard's of Reuel's departure, the school had held a place for him and would be well within their rights to dun Wilson for a term's tuition. In November, having waited more than a month for Wilson to cool down, she finally told him about Reuel's setback at Red Hook, insisting that it was temporary and that if fault was to be found it resided with St.

Bernard's. Unfortunately, her letter caught Wilson when he was still blaming her for the St. Bernard's mix-up.

In almost every respect, the move to Bard had been more disruptive than she had anticipated. At home she was managing as best she was able, trying all the while to carry it off with some style. At Bard she was making every effort not to let her domestic responsibilities interfere with her teaching. But she could never manage to catch up. Trying her best to cope with one disappointment after another, she turned to Bowden Broadwater. During the dull stretches between tutorials, or late at night when she was the only member of the household awake, she wrote to her young friend at *The New Yorker*, sometimes two letters on the same day, filling them with the sort of intimate details that one expects to find in diaries. Occasionally she would include a brief letter dictated by Reuel. Even as she made an effort to put a comic face on her misadventures, she did not gloss over the difficulties she was facing. In her opening letter, she freely admitted that on closer inspection the house she had rented back in August looked to be a disaster. Indeed the whole move, from her current perspective, could be seen as a mistake.

### FROM MARY MCCARTHY'S LETTER TO BOWDEN BROADWATER, SEPTEMBER 19, 1945

Hate it here. Violently unhappy. Not used to being so—don't know how to deal with it[. . . .] Please don't commiserate—I am beyond commiseration. Think of me as one dead[. . . .] House is dirty almost beyond hope. No competent cleaning woman or child-watchers available; old man who was promised to fix furnace declines further traffic with it; "only did it for the family." Reuel hates school and little oafs in it, longs for St. Bernard's. Only joy is non-housebroken kitten, which adds to parent's sorrow. Nausea twice a day at hour of cat's function[. . . .] Only exotic specimen on faculty tall member of French department with black beard and broken neck which he wears in a brown leather corset. Asked president whether he had seen photograph of employee before hiring. President (very progressive) gave loud shocked laugh and said, "Why, Miss McCarthy, how conventional you are." Only moment of real satisfaction.

In her letters to Bowden Broadwater she might make light of her problems, but they were no laughing matter. Having almost never been subject to bouts of paralysis or depression, she found she was suffering from something remarkably like writer's block. But that was not the all of it.

### FROM MARY MCCARTHY'S LETTER TO BOWDEN BROADWATER, NOVEMBER 13, 1945

I can't write, haven't written, because I find myself in a state of utter desolation. I don't want to describe it. Everything has turned black.

Never felt worse, or at least cannot recall anything comparable—however, scientists say we cannot remember pain. Degradation, despair, strong ascetic impulse—would like to write long *boring* epic poem. I feel like the ice box yesterday morning, stripped of provisions, and the machine double-frosted with diseased-looking ice. Creation, dear Bowden, is, at such moments, the only replenishing force, but no time for that. I *did* teach all my courses yesterday, having decided that to add professional remorse to other griefs was to court insanity.

### FROM REUEL WILSON'S LETTER TO BOWDEN BROADWATER, DICTATED TO HIS MOTHER, NOVEMBER 3, 1945

Cat's been going to the bathroom in the fireplace because Mrs. Donerley has reported it; he is a nice cat so far. The cat and me had a yummy dinner last night; it was better than an advertisement in a magazine. Cat sleeps outdoors now; he does messes in the house so he sleeps outdoors all night. I have gotten poison sumach now. When are you coming over here again? Please answer. Please come soon.

Bowden Broadwater, writing from his desk at *The New Yorker* or just across the street at the Harvard Club, was always quick to reply in kind, whether he was writing a short note to Reuel or a long letter to Reuel's mother. When he wasn't filling her in on the latest news of Nancy Macdonald's Committee for War Relief, Bowden was delighted to fill her in on the most recent activities of her estranged husband. Having started by calling Wilson "Fatso," "Buster," or "Noodle," he was prompted by Wilson's long *New Yorker* piece on Crete to settle on "the Monster," "the Minotaur," or "*le Monstre.*"

Not everyone saw the humor of these nicknames. Still, no one was about to raise an objection. Bowden Broadwater enjoyed a privileged position. There was no reward to be gained by criticizing him—something that Fred Dupee had already discovered. Before Mary's arrival at Bard, Fred Dupee had been looking forward to being reunited with her, just as she had been counting on a tender reunion with him. If she had been hoping for more from their relationship, she gave no such indication. From her first letter she was urging Bowden Broadwater to come up and join her for the weekend. Possibly she was only lonely. Possibly she had come to realize how much she cared for him. Possibly something else was going on.

She had settled in at Upper Red Hook, not far from where Fred Dupee was living, only to find that he was in the final stages of psychoanalysis and showing every sign of being deeply conflicted about his feelings for her. Almost immediately she let him know that she had a mysterious man in her life—someone whose identity must remain secret. According to her, jealousy reared its ugly head as soon as she tried to secure the services of one of his students as a live-in sitter and furnace tender. Relations did not improve any during the next two weeks; in early October they reached a crisis, resulting in a late-night scene, which, in keeping with her policy at Truro, she did not hesitate to report to Bowden.

### FROM MARY MCCARTHY'S LETTER TO BOWDEN BROADWATER, OCTOBER 1, 1945

First a wild lunge, then You-know-*I*-have-always-loved-you, then an unflattering comparison (Don't find you nearly as attractive as little boys). Each element in this complex sounded equally spurious, bald, *voulu*. Found myself equally skeptical of passion for self and passion for little boys[. . . .] Next day a pretended loss of memory, a pretense gracefully acquiesced in by me.

**MARGARET SHAFER** Fred seemed sweet on Mary, but it was complicated all around. I mean, Mary and Bowden knew certain things about Fred that most of us didn't know at that point. Fred was an extraordinarily charming man. And sometimes Mary resented and resisted it.

**BARBARA DUPEE** Mary apparently was easily infatuated. Sort of the way a snake is fascinated by a snake charmer, she was fascinated and unquestioning about Bowden. Fred and Mary ended the year at Bard on quite bad terms because Bowden and Fred just really didn't get along.

The Thanksgiving holidays marked a watershed. For the long weekend, she and Bowden had put together a house party that included both the Chiaromontes and the Tuccis, with the guests spilling over into the Dupee household. For the duration of the holiday a temporary truce had been declared. On one level at least the weekend was a complete success. Afterward, none of the party felt any need to ponder further the nature of her relations with Bowden Broadwater. They could no longer deny the evidence before their eyes.

**MIRIAM CHIAROMONTE** Someone had said that something was going on between Mary and Bowden, but everyone said no, that's impossible. Tucci was there and he walked into the bedroom and found it *wasn't* impossible.

### FROM NICOLA CHIAROMONTE'S THANK-YOU NOTE TO MARY MCCARTHY, NOVEMBER 25, 1945

According to that most talked-about philosopher, Martin Heidegger, only foolish men (and women) would enjoy "freedom from care." But since neither Plato nor Tolstoi ever said such a thing, I feel perfectly free to tell you that that's what we did in Red Hook: we felt perfectly free from care. Yours (and Bowden's—it is only fair to add) unlimited devotion to friendship and hospitality were such[. . . .]

**MIRIAM CHIAROMONTE** At Bard the house was very pretty and the meals were wonderful, but at the meals all the talk was cruel, brilliant—not gossip, just destruction of people. Yet there was another part of their being together.

I think they helped each other with their work. I *know* he helped Mary with her writing. And he was very good with Reuel.

**CLEMENT GREENBERG**   Mary couldn't be alone at night—that's what she told me—she panicked when she was alone. She saw to it that she wasn't alone. When Reuel was there, Reuel's baby-sitter would stay on. She told me this. I didn't observe it. She was rather desperate then. She had a crush on Hardwick Moseley—he worked for her publisher, a nice guy who had been married and his marriage was breaking up—but he wasn't coming through with any declaration. And she was reduced to Bowden, as it were.

At Bard, despite her taste for a certain kind of propriety, she was gaining a reputation for ignoring the basic social conventions that make for common courtesy. When Stella Adler and Harold Clurman came to visit Adler's daughter, Ellen, Mary made it clear how little she liked their politics. Because many members of the Group Theatre were known to be Party members, she felt free to dismiss them both as Stalinists.

**ELLEN ADLER OPPENHEIM**   My mother and stepfather were friendly with Fred, and when they came to see me at Bard we went over to Fred's house. Fred then of course asked Mary, who was with Bowden. I remember the absolute contemptuousness of Mary for those professional theater people. I was very sensitive and these were my parents. She had absolutely no interest in them. She felt above it. She felt that they were left-wing Broadwayniks. Mary didn't have that glorious flaw of self-questioning. What she thought was what it was. The way she saw it was the way it was, in her eyes.

**BARBARA DUPEE**   I'm not sure how this whole reputation for unpleasantness began, but I think a lot of it must have had to do with jealousy. She was beautiful. And then there was the way she had of concentrating on one person, the way she did with one boy in the Russian novel class—always looking at him when we were having discussions in class. So many people I know have said, "She cut me dead, she didn't say a word to me." In other words, her social graces were not really the greatest. She was punctilious about doing the right thing about people who were her friends, but I think at parties probably when she was young and she saw someone she really liked or really wanted to talk to, she went right by someone else. I'm not sure that she meant to do this.

**EVE GASSLER STWERTKA**   Bowden was quite malicious and it's possible that his maliciousness turned Mary quite malicious, too. Because she did have that reputation. Naughtiness more than malice.

Credited with encouraging bad behavior in his hostess, Bowden Broadwater had undoubtedly made some enemies at Bard. But among the Bard faculty he acquired two unexpected supporters in Lincoln Reis and his wife, Mary. To be sure, Reis himself was in great need of support, having been told by Bard's president that his contract would not be renewed at the end of the school year. As he saw it, he had been fired without cause. By mid-December matters were slowly but surely coming to a head. Irma Brandeis was threatening to resign if Reis wasn't rehired. Having been promised Mary McCarthy's backing in his battle to stay on, Reis was understandably eager to please her.

## FROM MCCARTHY'S LETTER TO BOWDEN BROADWATER, DECEMBER 18, 1945

By the way, I forgot to tell you (didn't I?) that the Reises expressed great enthusiasm for you: "Sorry I didn't talk to Bowden more; he seems like a wonderful person (Mary)."

Lincoln Reis and his wife were good for a late-night hamburger, but they were by no means the Macdonalds. The Shafers, for all their many virtues, were busy with their baby. Among the faculty you could find a handful of refugees from Hitler, but they were a poor substitute for the Italian friend who had fought alongside Malraux in Spain, befriended Camus in North Africa, and taught her to love Tolstoy.

**MARGARET SHAFER** When we first came to Bard, there were a lot of European refugees. Highly intelligent, all of them, but I'm not sure how well Mary got along with all those people. Not too well, I think. Maybe she felt they were drab. They were poor. I don't think Mary liked that really. Even when she was poor, she was not drab. The wives were striding around in heavy shoes. There was no chic about them. They were not people to whom she was attracted at all. Perhaps they were too much like orphans.

**BARBARA DUPEE** I don't think Mary liked the poor, the downtrodden, or the stupid very much. I think she had very little patience with them. I think she was aware of this. We would talk about it, though just glancingly. I mean, I would not say, "Mary, the poor are always with us." She would feel very sorry for masses of people who were being destroyed by wars and other disasters, but as to their individual fates, I don't think that she much cared.

Exhausted by a week's teaching, Mary would frequently head down to the city, where the company was more exciting. If she was lucky, she would find a friend's apartment that was vacant for the weekend. Sometimes she was able to stay with Mannie Rousuck, who had moved his gallery to more luxurious quarters on Fifty-seventh Street and had taken an apartment on Park Avenue. When all else failed, she had Bowden find her a room at some hotel. On occasion she would drop Reuel off with his father. Sometimes she would bring a student to help look after him. One time she stopped off with him at Schrafft's and had breakfast at the counter, just like the old days.

When she could find the time she would do a bit of shopping, stopping at Kresge's to pick up some miniature toy trains for the Anna Karenina necklace she was planning to wear at a party for her Russian novel class or looking in at Bergdorf's to see if she could find another "good dress." After one such shopping expedition, Bowden Broadwater introduced her to a slender young woman with straight black hair, an old friend from his Harvard days who was not drab or downtrodden and whose family was about to return with her to Europe (and whose brother James would one day be second in command of the CIA).

**CARMEN ANGLETON**   I think we met at a friend's apartment behind the Museum of Modern Art. As I recall, Mary arrived in a kind of flurry of bandboxes—obviously she'd been shopping madly. She was very beautiful. We had tea, and I think that later we had drinks with Bowden at a nearby hotel. She was not intimidating. At this point I hadn't read anything by Mary, but naturally once I met her it was only correct to read her. We liked each other. I approved of her shopping. She was full of energy. She was both witty and sparkling. There was real gaiety to her—really like something out of Shakespeare, something out of *A Midsummer Night's Dream*.

Returning the favor, Mary introduced Bowden to a beautiful and fastidious friend from Vassar.

**MARGARET MILLER**   The last time I saw Mary was after her marriage to Edmund Wilson had ended. She called up from the desk and when I came down I saw she had a very young man with her. I took the two of them into the garden. We sat and he scooted down and was leaning against a seat with his legs up on another seat, the way a child would. In front of all the people in the garden Mary bent over and acted with him exactly the way I'd seen her with Reuel on the Cape. I couldn't stand it another minute, and I got up and left. That was Bowden Broadwater.

Once again she seemed to see life in New York as more promising and more appealing than life at school. This time, instead of running off to spend a weekend with a sardonic actor whose behavior verged on the demonic, she was setting off with the intention of mixing business with pleasure. She might be going down to see a new play and then on to dinner with the Macdonalds or Kevin and Augusta. Or she might be going down to put in an appearance at one of the many parties being thrown by the editors of *Partisan Review*.

At these gatherings she was always welcome. But, for all that she might still consider herself a girl, she was hardly a fresh face. During those years when she had been trying to break free from Edmund Wilson, a good-looking writer from Colorado named Jean Stafford had turned up in New York. In 1944, Stafford's first novel, *Boston Adventure*, had been published to glowing reviews. That same year, two stories by Stafford had appeared in *Partisan Review*'s pages along with a lead review giving her full credit for having written a Proustian epic. *Boston Adventure* was a genuine best-seller, earning Stafford sufficient money to buy, renovate, and then furnish a large early-nineteenth-century house in Maine and to throw her husband, the poet Robert Lowell, into a protracted tailspin.

Early in September, Bowden Broadwater wrote that he had just learned that Jean Stafford and Robert Lowell had tried to get teaching jobs at Bard and been turned down. In the letters exchanged that fall and winter, Stafford's name came up with no great frequency—but when it did, you could be sure not a kind word was said.

### FROM MARY McCARTHY'S LETTER TO BOWDEN BROADWATER, FEBRUARY 13, 1946

Must tell you my discovery—I must get Joe Campbell to *blazon* it in the *Saturday Review of Literature*—*Boston Adventure* is straight out of *Jude the Obscure.* That is, the only good thing in [it], the glittering dome of the State House across the water, the City of Light seen by the child of poor family et cetera, is pure, raw Hardy. How can it be intimated to Miss Stafford that we know?

She might make light of her writer's block or make fun of Miss Stafford, but both were no laughing matter. That fall she had watched the poet John Berryman have his first story, "The Imaginary Jew," come out in *Kenyon Review* while her own stories were languishing on various editors' desks. With her non-fiction she was faring little better. Having agreed to write an article on the theater for Charles Henri Ford's *View*, she had to apologize for the makeshift piece she turned in.

### FROM MARY McCARTHY'S LETTER TO CHARLES HENRI FORD, N.D. [FALL 1945]

The last disaster to the theatre piece was this college. I am inundated by it, and do nothing but read Plato, Aristotle, Tolstoi, Horace Walpole and James T. Farrell from quarter of seven until midnight. This regimen obviously cannot go on, but whether I or it will be abolished I don't yet know.

In August Bernice Baumgarten had placed "The Unspoiled Reaction" with *The Atlantic.* Then, finally, in November, Harry Bull at *Town and Country* made an offer for "The Friend of the Family." The purchase was contingent on her making major revisions along lines he suggested. The trouble was, she could never seem to find a spare moment to sit down and go over the manuscript. In late November she wrote Bernice Baumgarten, "There is no time here for a literary thought, let alone a composition, but we do have a six weeks vacation at Christmas time." It was her hope that during Christmas vacation—the "field period" cherished by

Bard students and faculty alike—she would be able to give the story her full attention.

That Christmas, she found herself a virtual shut-in. Fred Dupee was in Nassau. Bowden Broadwater was off in Maryland with his family. The students had dispersed to points unknown. Unfortunately, the quiet and isolation in Upper Red Hook were not of a sort to facilitate a serious revision of the story. Both she and Reuel were running fevers. According to the terms of the separation, Reuel was supposed to spend the vacation with his father, but, having kept Reuel long enough to celebrate his birthday on Christmas Day, she ended up having to keep her convalescing son for the entire holiday. Confined to bed with bronchitis, she was at the mercy of a failing car, a faulty furnace, and Lincoln Reis, who was carrying in supplies and ferrying her letters to the post office.

Later on, when she was finally divorced from Edmund Wilson, there would be times when relations between the two of them were not merely friendly but almost affectionate. At this point, however, their legal separation was marked by fury and vitriol, with both parties insisting on asserting every possible prerogative. After Christmas, Wilson suddenly found himself facing a bleak financial future, and relations deteriorated further. Because *The New Yorker* was not going to be taking all the reporting from his months in Europe, he was not going to have the kind of regular income envisioned when the separation agreement had been drawn up.

For her, any reduction in Wilson's weekly payments was unthinkable. The rent on the house in Upper Red Hook was within her budget, but the house cost a fortune to heat. Once Wilson began defaulting on his payments, she was in serious trouble—a fact she tried to make clear to him in a letter where she listed all her major expenses, only to realize she had forgotten to include the money that went for Reuel's clothing, their doctor, their telephone bills, and the woman who took care of Reuel after school. "I can't get through the rest of this winter without the $60 which you, after all, committed yourself to pay," she wrote. The figures bore her out. Her basic expenses came to $312. Meanwhile her after-tax salary came to $207 a month.

In February, when she was desperately short of money, Bowden Broadwater took it on himself to send her a check for $50. He let her know that she could always pay him back when things got better and that he wished he could have sent her more. Living with his sister in an old-law tenement on East Fifty-seventh Street and earning a pittance at *The New Yorker*, Bowden had little money to spare. Wilson may have been strapped for cash, but he *did* have a wealthy mother in Red Bank. Eventually Wilson sent her money for coal. Then, when she announced it might be better if he kept Reuel for only half of Easter vacation, he erupted.

## FROM EDMUND WILSON'S LETTER TO MARY MCCARTHY, MARCH 21, 1946

You will remember that you took him away from the house in the middle of February a year ago without even letting me know where he was: that after I got back from Europe, he was with me for only a few days before you took him away to Red Hook, where it was impossible for me to see him except during vacations[. . . .] I have seen almost nothing of him for more than a year[. . . .] I know how much satisfaction this kind of thing gives you, and that you are always able to find excellent reasons for the unpleasant things that you do, and I know that I must be prepared to settle down to a lifetime of unpleasantness with you wherever Reuel is concerned. But I want to remind you that I am also in a position to make things difficult and uncomfortable for you, and that it is not a good thing for Reuel to be made the object of continual hostilities between us.

By late April Wilson was sounding more reasonable. With the publication of *Memoirs of Hecate County*, a collection of sexually explicit stories he liked to describe as demonic, he was, for the first time in his long writing career, beginning to see the possibility of earning sizable royalties. Thanks to its notoriety, the book was selling briskly. Critics and friends might be disturbed or offended by the book, but they were finally taking his fiction seriously.

On April 30, Wilson sent her a check for $120, with a warning to hold off cashing it until the end of the week. With the end of the spring term in sight, he asked if she had plans to stay on at Bard, declaring himself perfectly willing to have her do so and keep Reuel in school at Red Hook another year. He had decided against taking the boy to Europe. Instead, he would be keeping his son for the summer at Wellfleet.

*Memoirs of Hecate County* may have made her relations with Wilson easier, but the collection's success was not of a kind to lift the spirits of a writer who has been unable to steal many hours for her own work. In February, pushed into action by a cable from her agent, she had finally sent off a revised version of "The Friend of the Family," which, she confessed, had been "lying around on my desk like a watch with its insides out." In March "The Unspoiled Reaction" had finally come out in *The Atlantic*. From her time at Bard she would eventually get the setting, the plot, and the characters for her novel *The Groves of Academe*. But that April she had little tangible to show for her strenuous efforts aside from the fact that Harold Gray, Bard's president, had asked her back for the coming year.

After making sure Reuel would be free to return to St. Bernard's, she chose to leave Bard at the end of the spring term. Almost every tie binding her and her son to Upper Red Hook had been severed. Lemonade, the canary, had died in late March and had been put to rest by Reuel with a proper "military funeral." Limeade, the cat, had died a natural death and been buried to "Taps." Although Mary had no fixed plans and no immediate prospects, she had no wish to commit herself to another year of teaching. As a writer, she simply could not afford it. Still, she could take pride in a job well done. No one could fault her efforts. And for some students she had made a difference.

**EVE GASSLER STWERTKA**   Living with Mary and knowing Mary was like being in a book. Life had a heightened quality. That was just her. Her perceptions had a heightened quality. And nothing was ever humdrum or dull or everyday. Ever. If she was sad, then the sadness had a special piquancy. Though she was very seldom sad. Almost never. Even when she was sick, she didn't dwell on it. She changed my life. There's no doubt about that.

**ELLEN ADLER OPPENHEIM**   It was a privilege to study with somebody very ethical and high-minded and serious, when you had other teachers who were very lackluster. She was a big woman and you knew it. And a big thinker. But if you were a student, you really couldn't like Mary unless you worshiped her. You couldn't just like her. And if you were going to be a friend, you had to have a crush on her.

**BARBARA DUPEE**   She was wonderful. Anybody would have missed something by not meeting her because she was really a whole world unto herself somehow. I can't even imagine anybody being as wonderful as Mary. Anything that I say about foibles of one sort or another is absolutely a footnote. Mary was never petty. She was like a goddess in our midst.

During the school year, to little apparent effect, she had been regaling Bowden Broadwater with tales of infatuated men leaping upon her and declaring their love. He, for his part, had remained helpful and attentive but uncommitted. At some point during that year the balance of power in their relations had shifted. Now he was leaving his job at *The New Yorker*, taking off for Europe for the summer, and meeting up with Carmen Angleton in Paris. Mary's plan for the fall was to return to New York and find an apartment convenient to both Bowden and St. Bernard's. But her immediate plan was to join Bowden in France.

In the end she was not able to accompany him when he left for Europe at the start of July. She had packing to tend to, Reuel to send off to his father, supplies to lay in, a court date to meet, and business affairs to settle—not least among them, turning over title to her moribund 1937 Chevrolet to Dwight Macdonald for one dollar. Fortunately, while she was abroad she would be making some money to offset her expenses.

Harry Bull at *Town and Country*, pleased with her revision of "The Friend of the Family," had commissioned her to do a letter from Europe. While she was abroad, she would also have a chance to get some of her own writing done—a possibility that had become particularly appealing, now that she was back writing stories.

At the end of June, *The New Yorker* had finally taken and paid for a piece of reminiscence that drew on her memories of her early months at Forest Ridge Academy. Called "The Blackguard," it told of her terror on hearing a visiting priest preach a sermon that seemed to her to make it clear that her Protestant grandfather had no hope of salvation. And it closed with an episode that she had recounted with no little pride during her courtship with Wilson. Once again, as in the days when her correspondence with Wilson had been a joy to them both, she told the story of the brief moment of glory when her favorite teacher at the convent had turned on her and said, "You're just like Lord Byron, brilliant but unsound."

The story was one she had pulled out and reworked several times in the past. The sale meant a lot to her, but, desperate as she was for the money, there had been a brief unhappy moment when she had been prepared to withdraw the story because of unacceptable changes she had discovered in the retyped manuscript. Explanations were offered, adjustments were made, and relations with Katharine White were once again on an even keel. But back in May, when the edited manuscript could have meant the end of her relationship with *The New Yorker*, she had chosen to take a droll view of this latest crisis when writing to Bowden.

### FROM MARY MCCARTHY'S LETTER TO BOWDEN BROADWATER, MAY 8, 1946

The only news is that your publication has mortally insulted me. Do not be alarmed if this letter should attract to itself some of the phrases from the running letter I am mentally composing to Mrs. White. Your editors have hired a typist to re-copy my manuscript and insert from her own vocabulary (phrase out of the proposed White letter) such clauses as "[my grandfather], whom I adored." This typist has also supplied a name for my convent: St. Catherine of the Woods, which evokes perhaps the kind of convent *she* attended, but not mine. She (and of course the typist is Mrs. White) has furthermore re-named the story, "A Very Fine Man, A Very Fine Woman." I am hesitating between the rupture letter which demands the instant return of my original manuscript, which they have probably taken the precaution of burning; and the *démarche* [sic] letter which will leave the door open for an apology.

Mary McCarthy had never been to Europe. The money her grandparents had sent to mark her graduation from Vassar had gone to setting up the apartment on Beekman Place. Eager to get to Paris, where she would meet up with Bowden Broadwater, before going on to Lausanne (where her beloved Lord Byron had written *The Prisoner of Chillon*), she had to cool her heels in New York. Her ship's departure date was delayed by bad weather. The load of flour it was taking to Europe couldn't be packed, she wrote Reuel, "for fear of getting it wet. (If it got wet, I suppose they would have a shipload of paste.)"

But the delay was the least of her problems. She was confined to bed, suffering from the aftereffects of a vaccination for typhoid and smallpox. When her fever turned to viral pneumonia, she was forced to let the boat leave without her. Fortunately, by July 8 she could write Bowden Broadwater that she had been able to secure a seat on a plane. Eventually, the plane, too, left without her as the pneumonia gave way to a streptococcus infection. Stranded in New York, with her lover an ocean away and her son with his father on the Cape, she was relying on the generosity of friends and acquaintances—shuttling back and forth between a vacant apartment on Central Park West and Mannie Rousuck's more sumptuous apartment on Park Avenue, sometimes attended by a practical nurse. She could not afford to stay at a hospital.

Shortly after Bastille Day, weighed down with two suitcases and a footlocker of goods and staples, Mary boarded a train for Montreal. From Montreal she went on to Halifax, where she met up with a small Cunard liner. In her *Town and Country* piece, she started off by making light of her illnesses, her cumbersome luggage, and the many precautions she had been urged to take by well-meaning friends.

### FROM "LAUSANNE," *TOWN AND COUNTRY*, NOVEMBER 1946

Warnings of the most definite and frightening kind mingled with the formulas and perhaps also the substance of envy: *You must live off Bovril and saltines in your hotel room (if you can find one), because there isn't a thing to eat in Paris; oh, how I wish I were going.* And of all the dangers that threatened, the most solid and terrible was, if you listened to the undertones of my friends' conversation, a purely social one: the danger of appearing ignorant[. . . .] One of my friends even hinted that I would be wise to wear (like a dotted veil) an expression of concern on my face (you mustn't seem *gay* in Europe); this suggestion at least had the merit of costing nothing and taking up no space in a suitcase.

Having taken her friends' advice about transporting quantities of goods to pave her way in war-torn Europe, she discovered upon landing at Liverpool that she could have saved herself the trouble. Her footlocker of staples had been lost between Montreal and Halifax. In Paris, she was met with another disappointment—one that did not find its way into the piece for *Town and Country*. If she'd had qualms about intruding on Bowden Broadwater's arrangements with Carmen Angleton when she first envisioned this trip abroad, she was hardly reassured when she finally arrived.

**BARBARA DUPEE**   She once told me about sort of chasing Bowden to Paris the year that she'd given the Russian novel course. She was madly in love with him. He had a friend, Carmen Angleton, and he apparently led Mary to believe that he had a romantic interest in her. Or had had. Mary rushed off to Paris, and she and Carmen one day went off and tried on bathing suits. And you know trying on bathing suits is a very *fraught* experience. But doing it with a girlfriend who is also your rival . . . Bowden was torturing her with Carmen and she was feeling worse and worse about herself.

**ANGÉLIQUE LEVI**   I saw the three of them together. Nicola Chiaromonte had sent them to us. My husband, Mario, was Nicola's friend. When I first met Mary we lived in a dilapidated but charming private house across from the Musée Rodin. I did not find Mary beautiful when I first met her because I was struck by the beauty of Carmen Angleton. It was much later that I noticed Mary's beautiful eyes.

When it came time to leave Paris for Italy, the three Americans were joined by the art collector and gallery owner Peggy Guggenheim, who was going on to Venice to see if she could find a *palazzo* to buy. The four boarded a train for Dijon with six suitcases, a typewriter, "a hatbox from a Royal hatter," and a picnic basket stuffed with provisions. At Dijon the journey by train turned into a journey on the "Hell Express." Although the trip took on different dimensions depending on your perspective, it is agreed that Mary McCarthy became seriously ill and Carmen Angleton's feet became so swollen her sandals had to be cut off.

**CARMEN ANGLETON**   Of course it was soon after the war and things were a little bit rough, but we had a very good time together. First we went on a kind of army train, and there was Peggy all dressed in red flirting with the soldiers onboard. Mary and I had brought a wonderful picnic, which we of course shared with everyone. I'm sure there was chicken and wine. We were traveling in third class. We were thrown off the train at Dijon because it didn't go where we wanted to go. We had to change trains and had to wait at the station for a train to Switzerland, and it was there that Mary began to fade.

**FROM "LAUSANNE"**
   Wedged into the train so tightly that the door could not be opened behind us, crouching on suitcases pressed up against the door of the filthy *lavabo*, we quickly became a slum—our food turned to garbage, the royal hatbox crumpled, and the pearl-gray hat bounded about, hand after strange hand retrieving it, with each jolt of the moving train. In the Swiss customs house five hours later my temperature was 102°. We removed from the Hell Express and took a local. But we had no Swiss visas.

**CARMEN ANGLETON**   She stayed at Lausanne with Bowden. She couldn't ignore her illness. Throughout her life she always had bronchial trouble—many pneumonias, many bronchitises. It was her weak physical point. I had an appointment with my father in Milan. I got a couple of calls from Mary in Milan, where she sounded a little bit lonely in spite of Bowden's being with her. But I think it was because she was sick. She wanted to talk. Sympathy she had. I'm sure she had a great deal of sympathy from Bowden.

**FROM "LAUSANNE"**

> [A] sinister Swiss doctor with a gray spade-shaped beard prescribed a mustard plaster, a fearful purgative, and *boissons alcooliques*. We called him Dr. Gargoyle, and he would not stop coming, even though we telephoned and told him to discontinue his services. My temperature went to 104°. The Alpine scenery, the somehow dubious hotel, the anxiety about the visas, the perpetual soft knock on the door, followed by Dr. Gargoyle and his murderous remedies, made us believe we were in a Hitchcock movie.

Convalescing at Lausanne, with a view of Lake Léman and a blue funicular that every fifteen minutes slid down to the lake, she managed to write her piece for *Town and Country* and send it off to her agent. Although she tried to sound lighthearted in the opening paragraphs, there was a darker undercurrent to both the piece and her accompanying letter to Bernice Baumgarten.

**FROM "LAUSANNE"**

> Poor Keats lies dead in Rome; Lord Byron, in 1816, wrote *The Prisoner of Chillon* in a room at the Hotel de l'Ancre, Ouchy; did he actually journey to Chillon, or did he too see it on a postcard as he lay confined to his bed with one of those illnesses that were always assaulting him on the Continent until the last, most ferocious fever successfully carried him off at Missolonghi? You remember those Henry James heroines, Daisy Miller and Milly Theale, who came to Europe only to die, and Isabel Archer who died the death of the soul there.

**FROM MCCARTHY'S LETTER TO BERNICE BAUMGARTEN,**
**AUGUST 28, 1946**

> Can you stuff this down *Town and Country*'s throat? Is there any prospect of getting more money from them?[. . .] I am destitute (as you might guess from the contents)[. . . .] I am better, though I still have the faint remains of the lung infection and am supposed to lead an invalid's life—which is impossible.

Recovering her spirits and the better part of her health, Mary McCarthy set off with Bowden Broadwater on a pilgrimage from Lausanne to Milan and then Florence and Venice, following in Lord Byron's footsteps. On the train from Florence to Venice, the two of them joined forces with a smartly turned out but rather threadbare Italian who seemed at once fairly congenial and not quite respectable. When Peggy Guggenheim came to fetch them from the station with her gondola, introductions were made. The Italian tagged along with their party. Finally, after paying him almost no attention for several days, Peggy Guggenheim took the Italian off with her and went to bed with him.

In writing about her illness, Mary had seen it as being "part of the baggage of provincial but resolute timidity that I took with me from New York." She was a timid tourist; Peggy Guggenheim, her skin tanned the color of chestnut, was "an explorer." Within hours of her arrival in Venice, she had stumbled upon the raw material for a story she would write two years later. For the moment, though, she was intent on writing a piece about Italy. But she had no intention of going further with this piece unless someone agreed to pay her well for her efforts.

Looking forward to going on to Rome, where she would eventually board a plane for New York, she wrote of her plans to Bernice Baumgarten. Although she was still feeling the effects of her illness, she sounded as if she were ready to stand up to any editor. Something had happened. Starting with her sale to *The New Yorker*, she had begun to recover her sense of vocation.

She had no teaching job to hurry back to, no apartment awaiting her in the city. Edmund Wilson could see to getting Reuel settled at St. Bernard's. Instead of taking that plane from Rome, she chose to return with Bowden by boat. Her second ocean crossing proved to be more convivial and more productive than her first. "On the troopship coming home there were Mary McCarthy and her about-to-be husband, Bowdoin [sic] Broadwater," observed the composer Virgil Thomson in a later memoir, "she writing every day and discussing every sentence with him as if he were a valued editor."

During her summer at Truro, she had attempted with little success to strike a balance between her son, her writing, and her social life. In Nova Scotia, where she had no son and no new friends to distract her, she had fared little better. At Bard a heavy teaching load had entered into the equation. There she had persisted in holding herself to the most rigorous standards. Even when it was clear it was eating into the time she might use for her writing, she had continued to pursue an active social life. By the end of the school year, she had in effect made herself sick. Without Wilson, she had lived as she pleased but she had not lived especially wisely. The strain of surviving on her own had taken a toll on her health and her work.

In Bowden Broadwater she had found someone who in every way seemed the antithesis of the overbearing older husband who had sat her down at a desk in a spare bedroom and shut the door for three hours every morning. As it turned out, in Bowden Broadwater she had found a

man who did not act like a monster but who nonetheless had it in him
to keep her at her desk. For that alone, friends who cared about her writing had cause to be grateful. The question was whether this slender
young man could offer anything like the kind of literary guidance
Edmund Wilson had provided. But, in the end, the most pressing question for anyone who cared at all about her was whether he could possibly make her happy.

# Chapter Eleven

# MRS. BOWDEN BROADWATER

On December 18, 1946, Mary McCarthy married Bowden Broadwater. The ceremony was small and the minister was Lutheran. This time the bride did not have to provide her own wedding breakfast or get through a long lunch shouting into the ear trumpet of a mother-in-law who looked to her like a "wart hog." Eunice Clark Jessup, McCarthy's Vassar classmate and sometime bridge partner, gave her a reception at her brownstone on East Eighty-third Street. In the thirteen years since graduating from Vassar, she had risked marriage three times.

Once again the wedding ceremony was followed by no traditional honeymoon, and once again there was no immediate change in either partner's living arrangements. The newlyweds returned with Reuel to the apartment at 206 East Fifty-seventh Street, which the groom had shared with his sister. There was no elevator. Just around the corner from the Third Avenue El, it was a railroad flat, with one room leading into another and the bathtub in the kitchen. The sister had not moved out.

Eight days earlier, Edmund Wilson had married Elena Mumm Thornton in Reno, Nevada. Intent on getting on with his life, Wilson had remarried as soon as he secured his divorce. Elena Thornton promised to be very different from her predecessor. Born in Germany and raised in France, she came from a family whose fortune was founded on the manufacture of champagne. Her first husband had been a rich Canadian playboy, but she had no real money of her own. Slender and fair, with lovely hands and feet, she had met Wilson while working for Harry Bull at *Town and Country*. Now she was giving up her job to take care of her new husband full-time.

That fall Wilson had signed a final separation agreement holding him to a payment of sixty dollars per week and giving him limited authority over Reuel's schooling, dependent on Reuel's mother's living arrangements. In the end, the judge had awarded McCarthy custody not only for the entire school year but for half of Christmas and Easter vacation and all of Christmas day, so that she would be with her son to celebrate his birthday.

Unfortunately, when there is a child to consider, it is not always possible to put the past behind you. Visiting the Fifty-seventh Street apartment in October, Wilson had been appalled by the "combined kitchen and bathroom" and the lack of heat for the bedrooms. "Even electric heaters won't help much," he had written in the letter announcing his marriage. He had been particularly upset by the location of Reuel's bedroom—by the fact that "Miss Broadwater will have to go back and forth through it." Writing Wilson of her own impending marriage, McCarthy had been careful to let him know that although Reuel seemed to have caught a cold, it was his first illness of the winter and he hadn't "even had a temperature." She had found an electric heater for his bedroom "that almost overdoes it." She had not been able to find a better apartment. "None exist under $500 a month."

At first glance it would seem that with a town house on Henderson Place and a substantial nineteenth-century house in Wellfleet, Wilson was far better situated than his former wife was. But for all that he was pleased with his new marriage, he had suffered a serious reversal. That October, a New York judge had ruled *Memoirs of Hecate County* obscene, immediately putting a halt to its publication, distribution, and sales. As quickly and miraculously as Wilson's royalty payments had begun pouring in, they were now cut off. He was reduced to relying solely on his *New Yorker* money. More than once in the next two years he was forced to apologize for being in arrears with his alimony payments. One time he had to reduce the sixty to forty because he was still paying off Reuel's school bill.

Wilson was not the only one short of funds. McCarthy had left New York just as the war was drawing to an end, with the city in a mood of elation and enjoying the spillover of all the wartime spending. She returned to face the consequences of this new prosperity—a housing shortage and rising rents. Matters weren't helped any by the fact that her new husband was bringing in no regular income. Before setting off for Europe Bowden Broadwater had given up his full-time job at *The New Yorker*. For the jobs that were now available to him, he invariably proved to be overqualified. His dilemma, though real enough, was by no means typical. Suddenly there were jobs to be had in factories as well as jobs in colleges and universities, which were expanding to accommodate veterans on the GI Bill. Thanks to a favorable exchange rate or the windfall of a Guggenheim Fellowship, intellectuals were suddenly finding it attractive to live abroad.

Among the intellectuals around *Partisan Review* you heard no further talk of the pressing need for a Marxist revolution. Marxism had become inextricably entangled with Joseph Stalin and his totalitarian regime in the Soviet Union. With Trotsky's assassination in 1940, there had ceased to be a radical-left alternative to Stalin, and with the new prosperity, a program for toppling America's political and economic structure had ceased to be an urgent priority—or even a plausible topic for discussion.

"Actually, as I remember, after the war was the very best period, politically, that I've been through," Mary McCarthy would later tell an interviewer. "At that time, it seemed to me there was a lot of hope around. The war was over! Certain—perhaps—mistakes had been recognized. The bomb had been dropped on Hiroshima, and there was a kind of general repentance of this fact." Without question there was a sense that the world was not the same. At *Partisan Review* there was a growing fear that Stalin's Russia might pose a real threat to a newly prosperous America. At *politics*, on the other hand, there was a steadfast refusal to let this fear degenerate into paranoia. A refusal to rule out hope.

For Mary McCarthy the years immediately after the war were a time of promise. She was back in New York with her young son and the young man she had wanted very much to marry, and she was back at the center of a group of people whose company she valued and sought out. Above all, she was back writing. In October *The New Yorker* published "The Blackguard," the first of her childhood stories that the magazine would take. With its publication, it was clear that she had found her way to a form that was natural to her. Part essay and part fiction, the memoir form was a hybrid particularly suited to the author of *The Company She Keeps*. Once again she was at the center of the story she was telling. And once again she was free to scrutinize her characters with detachment and amusement.

She was not only back writing fiction but she was soon back writing her "Theater Chronicle" on a regular basis. (For five of the seven years she had been legally married to Wilson she had managed to write only one review a year.) In the late 1940s *Partisan Review*'s influence on the intellectual world was all that its editors believed it to be. Its critics' opinions and judgments carried authority, even though they reached too small an audience to have any real financial clout. In the years she had been writing her "Theater Chronicle," she had inevitably grown more confident. At the same time, there had been changes in New York theater and at *Partisan Review*. On Broadway, along with a new play by Eugene O'Neill and an abundance of musicals and revivals, you were seeing a new generation of playwrights. The social realists like Clifford Odets were giving way to realists with very different styles and agendas.

Meanwhile, at *Partisan Review*, the editors' growing disenchantment

with Marxism had resulted in a magazine more concerned with literature and art than with politics. This triumph of modernism over Marxism had made possible an uneasy alliance with Allen Tate and the
conservative Southern agrarians. For McCarthy it made possible greater
critical freedom. When reviewing a play, she no longer felt any obligation to write from a political perspective. Listening first to the playwright's language, she had only to address his intentions and then
determine whether he and the director and the actors came close to real-
izing them. Having jettisoned any pretense to a Marxist point of view,
she was free to relax.

Once she was back in New York, living with Bowden Broadwater, her
only nagging worry was lack of money. She could devote all her time to
her writing and accept any invitation that appealed to her. In Bowden
Broadwater she had found a husband who would never prevent her from
leading the life she liked living, if only because he very much enjoyed
taking part in that life. At the same time, she had found a husband who
could be guaranteed to provoke consternation and speculation among
her dearest friends and the most casual of acquaintances. By the time
she married him, she had every reason to know that as a couple they
would be a source of endless curiosity.

In *A Charmed Life*, published in 1955, she did not forbear from making use of certain aspects of her third marriage. In this novel she gave
her heroine, Martha Sinnott, a conventionally handsome husband, "tall
and small-boned, with high coloring, neatly inscribed features, and dark-
brown, stiffly curling hair," who might pass for Bowden Broadwater
without the affectations and the edge. "He had stern faith in Martha," she
wrote. "He had seen her through three years during which she acted on
Broadway while studying for her Ph.D. in philosophy[. . . .] He had stuck
to a dullish job in the Historical Society, six days a week, so that Martha
could be free not to work on radio or television. He had done this vol-
untarily and over Martha's protest—she did not altogether like to be
believed in."

But without the affectations and the edge, what have you got? An all-
purpose secondary character who hovers on the fringes of the action.
Years later, after their marriage had ended, Bowden Broadwater wrote a
story in which he provided an account of a weekday morning—an account
that was at once highly stylized and finely detailed, and practically
begged to be taken as a typical morning on East Fifty-seventh Street.

### FROM "CIAO," BY BOWDEN BROADWATER, *PARIS REVIEW*, WINTER–SPRING 1961

The morning of February 18, 1947, three months to the day after my
marriage, found me stumbling through the Want-Ads in the *Times*. I

had been reading them daily for some time in order to give the impression to a certain person that I still believed that someone would hire me. The dripolator—a second pot—was dripping at my elbow. Across from me at the bridge-table at which we were breakfasting in the sitting-room, and would in time dine, my dear wife had her assured grip on the front page of the first section of our paper[. . . .]

As soon as I finished the formality of my one-way correspondence with the Classified, I could be free for the day. The sky above the d.w.'s red geraniums on the window-sill was a Roman blue. Wearing my gray suit, I could walk in the sun down Park Avenue and over to my hideaway, the quiet library of the Harvard Club, where I have cautiously managed to preserve a membership, acquired in the prosperous war years when my 4-F status had induced several employers to breach their form of never hiring, for just such an occasion as this. There, smoking a light cigar while the clock advanced the hour without comment, I could stretch out in a comfortable armchair with the ease of the deliberately unemployed, reading more of the novel I had begun the week before, or even dozing.

The narrator in "Ciao," who carries off his unhappy predicament with considerable brio, is possessed of no "stern faith" and sticks to no "dullish job." Self-sacrifice is hardly his line. But these passages, too, are misleading. Mary McCarthy was not just any "d.w.," Bowden Broadwater was not just any overqualified unemployed husband, and their apartment, for all that it was cheek by jowl with the El, was not without a certain style.

**EVE GASSLER STWERTKA**   Back then I thought it was Bowden who decorated the apartment. But later I saw Mary also decorated exquisitely. Black and white and gray was the scheme. Very austere but very charming nevertheless. A horsehair sofa covered in gray. And Mary had Roman busts in plaster or marble, I'm not sure which. The floor was black. Very original.

**JASON EPSTEIN**   The apartment had those dark green walls that everybody had in those days, and ivory enamel trim. I was in graduate school, just out of college, and I remember there was a big ham—a big Virginia ham hanging in the window—rather self-consciously, I thought.

Memory of course has a way of playing tricks with size and scale as well as paint color. In the eighties, when Mary McCarthy was once again teaching at Bard, Reuel Wilson returned with his mother to the house they had rented and found "it wasn't a mansion or an especially large house—it was a family house." All the same, after Upper Red Hook the apartment on Fifty-seventh Street was cramped and confining. Soon they were all calling it "the anthill."

For visitors the apartment's public rooms had undeniable charm, but for family members its recesses harbored many a vestige of its tenement origins. There was an old-fashioned icebox instead of a refrigerator, and there was the bathtub in the kitchen that had bothered Reuel's father. The bathtub had a cover that fitted over it when it was not in use. "I don't remember if you had to pour in the hot water or if it came from the tap," says Reuel. "The iceman would come in the morning and I remember him as terrifying. He would bang around and speak in a loud voice and make a lot of noise." Nonetheless, there were advantages to living at East Fifty-seventh Street. It was easy to see old friends, like Mike Macdonald. Across the street was a new Schrafft's, where Reuel and his mother could have breakfast. Then there were the double-decker buses, where the two of them were able to ride on top and see everything. And, above all, according to Reuel, there was Bowden Broadwater: "Bowden says he's not especially good with children, but he is. He takes an interest in what they're doing and what they have to say. He's easy to be with and he's fun."

From 206 East Fifty-seventh Street, Mary McCarthy set forth every day, sometimes on her own and sometimes in the company of her husband or son, to resume her old life in the city. Seeing her on the street, no one would suspect that she was living in a tenement. Like the young man in "Ciao," she dressed with great care. Fashion had always been of interest to her. But, unlike the young man in "Ciao," she was rarely, if ever, at loose ends. Invariably, as she sallied forth, she created a strong impression. In time, as the shoulder-length hair was drawn back in a tight knot, this impression was both altered and enhanced.

**ISAIAH BERLIN**   I remember seeing her for the first time walking on a street in New York. It was before I had met her, and I realized that we were going to the same luncheon. It's a terrible thing to say but I thought she looked exactly like a prostitute. Her clothes. Her shoes. Her way of dressing. Her gait. She had these sort of open shoes with her feet showing through and she had a particular way of walking. The skirt she wore. It seemed to me that was exactly what those people wore. But nobody was further from it.

**LUCILLE FLETCHER WALLOP**   I met Mary McCarthy again when she was married to Bowden Broadwater. I saw them walking down the street in the pouring rain under a huge black umbrella. He was tall and he was bending over her. She had a long black satin skirt on, to her ankles, flats, and a great big black velvet hat and a black shawl. They looked just like a couple out of literary legend.

**ROGER STRAUS**   I can remember a New Year's night at Philip Rahv's in the country. It was to be black tie and we were told to schlepp our clothes with us. There was Philip and his then wife Nathalie, and Bowdie, who was a pain in the ass, and my wife Dorothea and I. Philip was of course terribly pleased to have been Mary's lover and liked to show her off. So here we were in this freezing fucking house on the wrong side of the tracks in Millbrook. We all came down to dinner except Bowdie and Mary. Then Bowdie came downstairs and said, "I've just hooked her up." And then she came. She made an entrance at the top of the stairs and came down in a Balenciaga with one shoulder exposed. She looked absolutely beautiful.

**MARGARET SHAFER**  There was a period when she was married to Bowden when she seemed to me to be cultivating a sort of George Eliot plain look. Of course, Mary admired Eliot enormously, but it seemed odd that she would model *herself* on Eliot. I just had the feeling that Mary was aiming for an image that was not the glamorous image she projected at Bard. When we saw her in New York it seemed she was putting her hair up more and wearing scratchy looking tweeds.

**BRENDAN GILL**  When I first knew her she chose to have a fairly intimidating appearance. It seemed to me that it solved problems for her.

One problem this new severe style solved rather neatly was how to make sure that you and your ideas will be taken seriously by a band of intellectuals who confuse good manners and a pretty face with weakness. In 1941 Jean Stafford, newly arrived in the city, had been invited with her husband, Robert Lowell, to dinner at the Philip Rahvs' and found both Rahvs "very nice." Two years later, Lowell was serving time in prison as a conscientious objector and Stafford's view of the Rahvs and their parties had altered considerably. "[T]he greatest snobs in the world are bright New York literary Jews," she wrote her friend Peter Taylor. Stafford's response, for all that it was extreme, was by no means unique. Not everyone found *Partisan Review* parties congenial. And not everyone was able to shine at them.

### FROM *THE BEGINNING OF THE JOURNEY*, BY DIANA TRILLING

They were torturing affairs for any woman who attended them as a marital appendage rather than in her own literary right; both Edna Phillips and Nathalie Rahv, who had to act as hostesses for their editor husbands, would one day confess to me that in order to get through these evenings they had to fortify themselves with several stiff drinks.

### FROM ELIZABETH HARDWICK'S FOREWORD TO
### *INTELLECTUAL MEMOIRS*

An evening at the Rahvs was to enter a ring of bullies, each one bullying the other. In that way it was different from the boarding school accounts of the type, since no one was in ascendance. Instead there was an equality of vehemence that exhausted itself and the wicked bottles of Four Roses whiskey around midnight—until the next time.

To expect these gatherings to subscribe to the rules of polite society was to totally misunderstand their purpose. To make your way at one of them—indeed, to navigate the treacherous shoals of the New York intellectual world—it helped to be aggressive or argumentative. If you had no interest in romantic entanglements, it did no harm to have a forbidding appearance.

## FROM *THE TRUANTS*, BY WILLIAM BARRETT

One writer whom the circle could not intimidate in any way was Mary McCarthy[. . . .] I see her indeed in the image of a Valkyrie maiden, riding her steed into the circle, amid thunder and lightning, and out again, bearing the body of some dead hero across her saddle—herself unscathed and headed promptly for her typewriter.

**SAUL BELLOW**   I don't remember meeting her actually until I began to attend *Partisan Review* parties toward the end of the forties. I was interested in her. I had read "The Man in the Brooks Brothers Shirt" and some of the theater criticism. I thought she was a most beautiful woman. But she was beautiful in a sort of enameled way. I mean, she had a perfect exterior finish. It was a little unnatural. At the same time that she was charming, she was also very snappish. I was a little too timid for that sort of thing.

**ISAIAH BERLIN**   What I admired particularly was the sort of masculine quality of Mary's mind. Her strong, direct, cutting intellect. Mary would talk a certain amount of nonsense and she was sometimes deceived by quite inferior people—funnily enough, she was a little gullible in some ways. But she was a very good writer. She was very observant. She was tough and clear and utterly honest. And quite brave. She didn't compromise and she didn't suck up to anybody. She was not anxious to please. But there was considerable sweetness, too, behind all that harshness.

**ELIZABETH HARDWICK**   Mary never was harsh, even when she was young. She never was as harsh as her reputation. Not at all. I mean, not in her social life. There she was always very gay and charming, but not giving an inch.

Back in 1945, Mary McCarthy had barely had time to take Jean Stafford's measure and decide she did not care for her, when Elizabeth Hardwick, a young writer from Kentucky, had caught her attention. The author of a novel called *The Ghostly Lover*, Hardwick had been enlisted by Rahv to write the magazine's "Fiction Chronicle." Both Stafford and Hardwick shared McCarthy's love of gossip, her way with words, and a tartness of tongue that could be experienced as venomous. Stafford's lovely face had been badly damaged in a car crash, while Hardwick was at the height of her beauty. Stafford, drinking heavily and struggling to salvage her marriage to Robert Lowell, seemed to be out of her element. Hardwick seemed to be managing to keep afloat. Before too long, McCarthy was making room in her life for this talented young writer, who was attractive and amusing and prepared to have a good time.

**ELIZABETH HARDWICK**   When I met Mary, she didn't pay any attention to me at first. However, she had just taken up with Bowden Broadwater, and I was unmarried. All couples like unmarried friends. You don't have two of them. It's easier, and it's fun, and you can include them and you can go places. So when I first knew Mary and Bowden, before I got married, I saw a lot of them. And I went places with them. It was kind of hard to make the grade with Mary, but if you did she was a loyal friend.

**ISAIAH BERLIN**  Mary wasn't the cleverest woman I ever met. I think the cleverest woman I ever met is probably one of the editors of *The New York Review of Books*: Elizabeth Hardwick. Elizabeth Hardwick has a feminine mind. Much more bitchy than Mary's, but sharper and more original.

**ELIZABETH HARDWICK**  Mary used to find me sometimes quite out of line. She would say, "Why did you say to that woman that you liked the dress she was wearing when I know perfectly well you didn't?" I said, "Because I couldn't think of anything else to say." "Well," she said, "you just deliberately told a lie." I said, "Well, Mary, that's my style."

Hardwick's style, different as it was from her own, seemed to suit the new Mrs. Broadwater fine. It may have helped that Hardwick was single and loved pretty clothes and gossip and that she was sufficiently young and sufficiently unknown to be eager to "make the grade." Later on, it may have helped that she was having a not altogether satisfactory love affair with Philip Rahv. By the winter of 1946, the two women had become fast friends.

Cramped as the Broadwaters' apartment on East Fifty-seventh Street might be, there was always ample room for friends and family and for passing visitors. Along with old friends like the Macdonalds and the Chiaromontes and new ones like Elizabeth Hardwick and Eve Stwertka, you could find Kevin McCarthy, who was living with his wife, Augusta, in a nearby apartment. In the spring of 1947, you could also find a famous foreign visitor who had washed up upon the shores of *Partisan Review*. Handsome and opinionated but not quite as dashing and not nearly as agreeable as the writer Albert Camus, who had made a great success in New York the previous year, this much fêted French intellectual recorded her impressions of the Bowden Broadwaters in a letter to her lover in Paris.

**FROM *LETTERS TO SARTRE*, BY SIMONE DE BEAUVOIR**
[The charming American from Berne] took me to visit a young American novelist called Mary McCarthy, who's the rising star of *Partisan Review*. She's very beautiful and seems intelligent, but without the least charm or interest other than documentary (and as such she fascinated me), being so typically the American intellectual woman—I could write pages about her. She has a very insignificant husband (No. 3, not counting two official lovers). The four of us went to a restaurant called Lindy's—I'd wanted one that was typically American, and it really was.

Bowden Broadwater might not be every woman's dream, but anyone who had anything to do with him was not about to write him off as "insignificant." All the same, Simone de Beauvoir was neither the first nor the last person to take note of the seeming inequality of the Broadwater match. More than one member of the New York literary world was puzzled by the sheer improbability of their union. To Bowden's supporters as well as his detractors, the marriage had come as something of a shock.

**WILLIAM ABRAHAMS**   I'd never met Mary McCarthy, but on *The Company She Keeps* there was this ravishing picture of this very beautiful woman, sort of atilt. If you were to make a movie of Mary McCarthy's life, Grace Kelly could have played the part. During the war I had seen a bit of Bowden. Now somebody I knew said to me, "Did you know that Bowden Broadwater had married Mary McCarthy?" Well, I gave a hoot. I mean, it was the *most* improbable marriage to think about on either side. One couldn't believe it.

**NORMAN MAILER**   Bowden was a year ahead of me at school and our senior year, we heard that he was working at *The New Yorker*. We thought, Oh Lord, look at that. Then we heard he'd married Mary McCarthy. We thought he had it all.

**KEVIN MCCARTHY**   When Mary first brought Bowden around to our little apartment on East Fifty-sixth Street, Augusta and I became aware of Bowden's rather bizarre or uncommon deportment: Bowden would be sprawled on the floor sucking his thumb and pulling his forelock. And you thought, Wait a second. What is this? Am I being conventional in taking note of that? Or am I being observant? I had never seen a grown man—incidentally, a very bright and interesting man—suck his thumb and pull at his hair. And he was, I suppose, thirty years old at the time. I always liked him. I guess he felt comfortable with us.

**ROBERT GIROUX**   Peter Taylor, Randall Jarrell, and Robert Lowell all expressed the opinion that Mary married Bowden because she couldn't handle Wilson and decided on someone totally different. Bowden was a gentleman and really a gentle and cultivated person. He admired Mary enormously, you could see that. I did not know him intimately. The poets I knew were hard on Bowden, particularly Jarrell, who had a wicked tongue.

In the fall of 1946 and spring of 1947 Randall Jarrell was living in New York, teaching at Sarah Lawrence and standing in for Margaret Marshall as literary editor at *The Nation*. During this time he had an opportunity to observe Mary McCarthy and Bowden Broadwater at some length.

**FROM *PICTURES FROM AN INSTITUTION*, BY RANDALL JARRELL**
People were fond of wondering why Gertrude had married Sidney. (Nobody ever wondered why Sidney had married Gertrude.)
. . . .As she read, Sidney listened; as she wrote, Sidney waited to listen; and Homer himself never had a better listener than Sidney[. . . .]
Sidney went behind her like a shadow, useless and waiting to be used. If people could have remembered him they would have called him Mr. Johnson. He was—to identify him from the covers of her novels—"at

present engaged in research on documentary films"; last year he had been "a member of a public opinion survey"; the year before—how could anybody remember what Sidney had done the year before? Some people live; some people exist; he subsisted[. . . .]

Gertrude would say to him, "Don't interrupt me, Sidney!"—but then quickly, sometimes: "I'm sorry, Sidney." She betrayed toward Sidney, alone among mortals, a rudimentary and anomalous good-nature; one could see that, to her, there were people and Sidney. It was absurd of her to waste herself on Sidney, but as she said to herself, "Sidney needs me."

**ROBERT GIROUX**   Jarrell's novel, *Pictures from an Institution*, is based on Mary—no question. It was one of Jean Stafford's favorite novels and a brilliant piece of satire. It's undeniably about Mary and cruel about Bowden. Jarrell's metaphor for the marriage in the novel is the husband's picture painted on a bed pillow.

Describing Gertrude Johnson, Jarrell was careful to fudge certain details—the writer he gives us is small and plain, with reddish hair, a Southern accent, and no flair whatsoever for cooking and decorating. At the same time, he left other salient McCarthy features intact. Tone-deaf and possessed of a smile like a "skull's grin," Gertrude Johnson is at once feared and admired for her passion for hard facts and for her ability to see to the heart of the matter and then straight through it. "Torn animals were removed at sunset from that smile," we are told.

Because the novel is set at a college that bears some resemblance to Sarah Lawrence, a school where she later taught for a term, readers tend to assume that Randall Jarrell and Mary McCarthy taught there together. However, not until the spring of 1948 would she come to Sarah Lawrence. Still, the confusion lingers in the minds of casual readers and well-informed critics. For one thing, the narrator presents himself as a colleague of Gertrude Johnson's. For another, the portrait he paints suggests a long-standing familiarity. Jarrell was not the only observer to grant that the Broadwater marriage made a certain sense. But not everyone was so quick to conclude that Bowden Broadwater was only a face on the pillow.

**WILLIAM ABRAHAMS**   My first meeting with Mary McCarthy was in 1946 or early '47. He, Bowden, was essentially the same. But she was wearing a rather plain—I won't say frumpy—little dress. After that picture on *The Company She Keeps*, it was not the experience I was hoping for. They were in a plain little apartment and we sat facing the plain little coffee table. They were on a sofa, and I was across. The conversation was extraordinary. In a sense she did a very clever thing to marry Bowden because I don't know who else could have tolerated this consummate bitchiness that was going on between the two of them. They were like a brother and sister going at it. There was no name that was brought up that the two of them didn't exchange a look and shriek and giggle. "Oh, Bowdie," she called him continually. It was finally rather repulsive and deeply disappointing. We met again—it must have been at most a year later—this time at Cambridge. We had lunch and a mammoth martini. It was fun and I liked her rather more. First of all, I liked her more because she was out of that house dress.

**ALISON LURIE**    I remember going to dinner or a party at their apartment. Old valentines that she had sent him were framed and hanging on the walls of the flat. I know that she told people how beautiful he was. He was beautiful in a sort of soft, boyish, Renaissance angel way, I suppose, at that point.

**DAPHNE HELLMAN**    I think Mary did love him at first. She'd say, "Bowdie, what would you like to do?" "What do you think of this?" He sort of ruled the roost emotionally. And when it came to judgments on people.

**LIONEL ABEL**    I think she realized that what she wanted was not a husband but a wife in a male form. Which he was. And she realized that's what she needed for a lot of reasons: for her career and for her happiness. I don't think she formulated that to herself. Nobody acts that way. She was like the man who marries a steady girl and has affairs on the side.

**KEVIN MCCARTHY**    He was certainly 180 degrees different than Edmund Wilson—possibly a relief from that formidable personage. But he was more than a rest. I came to feel that this unusual but intriguing Bowden was very valuable to Mary.

**BARBARA KERR**    I don't think Mary was ever bored by Bowden. He managed to keep her entertained. Rather than confront Mary directly, Bowden was able to maneuver her. They were both keenly interested in their surroundings. You could use the word "intensity" about their approach to life. Mary had to have Bowden's concurrence about the smallest details. They worked it out together. They gnawed at the problem until both parties were satisfied with whatever the decision was.

**MIKE MACDONALD**    Riding back from Long Island on a bus in 1972, my father and I agreed that Bowdie—for all his cattiness and gossip—was paradoxically, the one man we'd trust with the deepest of secrets, a true confidant and a sympathetic listener and counselor.

Over the next eight years Bowden Broadwater would hold only one job for any length of time. All the same, his life could hardly be called idle. He joined his wife in writing letters and catalog copy for an ever more successful Mannie Rousuck. He sometimes found work as a freelance copy editor. At home, he gradually took over much of the cooking and cleaning. More important, he gradually took over the care of Reuel. Some observers credited the endurance of the Broadwater marriage to his willingness to perform these tasks, thereby freeing his wife to get on with her career. But to regard the marriage as a rest period or Bowden Broadwater as a wife in male form seems unfair to two consenting adults, one of whom showed every evidence in her letters from Bard of being very much in love.

With her favorite students at Bard, McCarthy had fallen back on recollections of long ago afternoons in Poughkeepsie, sipping tea on a small sunporch with Miss Sandison and Miss Kitchel. With the young Reuel she could fall back on her early years with Tess and Roy McCarthy. Indeed, the worst that could be said of her as a young mother was that she appeared sometimes to be trying too hard. Reuel would later say, "My mother was not good with children, but I can't say that she was not good with me. I was her child, after all."

But if Mary carried with her from her earliest years in Seattle the pattern of a child's paradise, that pattern served her only until her son reached the age of six. By the time Reuel turned eight she lacked any memories she cared to draw on. At eight she had been living with her brothers in a squalid house on Blaisdell Avenue, making a meal off turnips and a chicken's neck and running the risk of a beating every time she got above herself.

To gradually cede her new husband responsibility for Reuel may not have been her original intention, but once they were living together it may have been the better part of wisdom. Just as it may have seemed the better part of wisdom to rely on her new husband's advice when it came to other aspects of her life. When one partner is intent on doing away with any lingering difference of opinion (to leave no traces of any "positive and negative elements"), it's hard to later determine where one leaves off and the other begins—to know, for instance, if the decoration of the apartment on East Fifty-seventh Street was all Bowden's doing or if it represented a joint effort. To know how much in the way of suggestions he contributed to her writing. Whether he was an editor or merely a concerned reader. Whether he began to take an active hand in matters pertaining to her career.

At her desk at that small East Fifty-seventh Street apartment, starting in the fall of 1946, Mary McCarthy began producing the personal essays that would do much to ensure her place in American letters. Simone de Beauvoir had not been the only one passing judgment during her visit to New York City. De Beauvoir's questions and comments prompted her to take a careful look at America and then to take de Beauvoir's measure twice in print. The first time McCarthy wrote about Simone de Beauvoir, the "visiting Existentialist" went unnamed, and while her request to be taken to a restaurant that was "really American" was presented as patently absurd, there was no personal attack.

The second time she wrote about Simone de Beauvoir she did not hesitate to call her by name or to make her the subject of the essay. By then she had had a chance to take a look at *America Day By Day,* in which de Beauvoir had not identified her by name but had made mention, in passing, of a "cold and beautiful novelist who devoured three husbands and a crowd of lovers in the course of a neatly-managed career."

## FROM "MLLE. GULLIVER EN AMERIQUE," *THE REPORTER,* JANUARY 1952

In January, 1947, Simone de Beauvoir, the leading French *femme savante,* alighted from an airplane at LaGuardia Field for a four months' stay in the United States. In her own eyes, this trip had something fabulous about it, of a balloonist's expedition or a descent in a diving bell. Where to Frenchmen of an earlier generation, America was the incredible country of *les peaux rouges* and the novels of Fenimore Cooper, to Mlle. de Beauvoir America was, very simply, movieland—she came to verify for herself the existence of violence, drugstore stools, boy-meets-girl, that she had seen depicted on the screen.

Giving every evidence of a stunning self-assurance, Simone de Beauvoir had arrived in America with a tentative grasp of the English language and a firm attachment to Marxist analysis. As the consort of Jean-Paul Sartre and a ranking French intellectual, she had demanded attention. With her battery of preconceptions, she was everything a good reporter ought not to be. By the time McCarthy wrote "Mlle. Gulliver en Amerique," her amusement at de Beauvoir's blind arrogance had turned to outright dislike.

Between Simone de Beauvoir and Mary McCarthy, two good looking and unbending women, each of whom saw herself as unique, there was no love lost. In 1962, McCarthy, interviewed by the young Elisabeth Niebuhr for the *Paris Review,* said, "I think she's odious. A mind totally bourgeois turned inside out." Asked in 1985 what she meant by this, she answered, "Did I say that? I always thought she had the mind of an athletic nun." Only the year before, McCarthy had been quoted by Carol Brightman in *The Nation* as saying, "She's not utterly stupid; she would be a good 'B' student somewhere in the intellectual world, maybe not even a 'B' student." But the thing that seemed to bother her finally was not the limitations of de Beauvoir's intelligence but the way de Beauvoir had built *her* career.

## MARY MCCARTHY AT CITY ARTS & LECTURES, SAN FRANCISCO, MAY 10, 1985

I always felt that she did a tremendous amount of riding on Sartre's coattails, which is a very peculiar place for somebody to be who claims to be a feminist. That is, I think that "*Sartre et moi*" made her and that she used Sartre's genuine gift for some kind of mutual promotion, let's say. I don't think that there is anything crafty about that woman. I don't think she planned it that way, but that's how it happened, I believe.

To ride on a powerful man's coattails had come, with time, to be anathema to her. By marrying Bowden Broadwater she had seen to it that she herself could not be charged with such a crime. During her visit to Paris in the summer of 1946, she had been spared the special treatment of a visiting dignitary—indeed, no one had made the slightest fuss over her. Without Edmund Wilson, she had no name to speak of outside a small circle. What she had, thanks to Bowden Broadwater, was the time and the means to build upon the by no means negligible foundations of what de Beauvoir chose to called her "neatly-managed career."

"America the Beautiful" was not the first essay Mary McCarthy wrote in the years following her return to New York and it was not the first essay in which she chose to regard with skepticism the latest cultural hero or the latest popular idea. In November 1946, she had written a long letter to *politics* pointing out how misguided *The New Yorker* had been to devote a single issue to John Hersey's "Hiroshima." In April 1947, in a lighter vein, she went on to review a book called *Modern Woman, the Lost Sex*, and use it as a chance to take a hard look at the findings of Dr. Alfred Kinsey, who was claiming to have "discovered that from 50 to 85 per cent of American women college graduates had never experienced an orgasm." And, in the winter of 1949, along with Nicola Chiaromonte and George Orwell and just about every self-respecting intellectual, she addressed the death of Mahatma Gandhi—contrasting the grave distress of her elderly housekeeper and her young son with the responses of her fellow teachers at Sarah Lawrence.

By fixing her gaze upon contemporary politics and culture, she was venturing into areas that were at once more ambitious and more likely to capture the general reader's interest. To this new form of criticism she was bringing both her customary precision and her inveterate wayward-ness. Her personal essays were a natural extension of her literary criti-cism. Whether she was writing about sex or sociology or the murder of Mahatma Gandhi, she was not about to accept on faith any commonly held belief. If she had any faith at all, it was in her powers of observa-tion, her ability to tell right from wrong, and her good common sense.

Hers was the faith of the Enlightenment and it was, above all, a faith in the power of reason. It is everywhere evident in the writing of Samuel Johnson and Edmund Wilson. One can also find it in the essays of George Orwell—essays that, with the postwar publication of *Animal Farm*, were receiving increased attention both in England and America. Wilson's voice at its most characteristic is the voice of a gentleman scholar possessed of a sense of entitlement befitting a country squire, but Orwell does not speak with that kind of authority. Lucid and precise and above all sensible, his is the voice of a self-proclaimed outsider.

In McCarthy's personal essays, for all the occasional stylistic flourishes, the striking of poses that run the risk of sounding silly, you can make out echoes of Orwell. (In the early writing of James Baldwin this voice also comes through loud and clear.) This voice is subjective and it is willing to be cranky. It is also ready to resort to the devices of fiction when necessary. Above all, it is prepared to admit to fallibility. In "Shooting an Elephant," Orwell writes of killing a dumb beast before a crowd of some two thousand Burmese natives for no good reason other than to keep them from laughing at him. In "Artists in Uniform" McCarthy writes of the time when, caught between trains in the company of an anti-Semitic army colonel, she tried with some success to argue the colonel out of his prejudices, never once mentioning that she herself was part Jewish. In the end she loses all credibility and is made to feel a fool when he discovers (falsely, but in a sense correctly) that she is Jewish after all.

### FROM "ARTISTS IN UNIFORM," HARPER'S, MARCH 1953

We both glanced at our watches. "See you some time," he called. "What's your married name?" "Broadwater," I called back. The whistle blew again. "Broadwater?" shouted the colonel, with a dazed look of unbelief and growing enlightenment; he was not the first person to hear it as a Jewish name, on the model of Goldwater. "B-r-o-a-d," I began, automatically, but then I stopped. I disdained to spell it out for him, the victory was his.

If Mary McCarthy was sometimes prepared to assume a guise of fallibility in her personal essays, she saw no place for this in her theater criticism. Early on in their relations, Wilson had pointed out to her that her impulse as a reviewer was to draw up a brief against a play. Ten years later, while she was not quite so intent on building an airtight case, she had softened not at all. Her column continued to bear traces of the precocious and demanding Vassar graduate who in her first "Theater Chronicle" had made Maxwell Anderson out to be full of stale hot air.

During the years after the war, when she was living in the city with Bowden Broadwater and going to the theater regularly, she wrote two reviews that would ensure her reputation as a critic. Faced with *The Iceman Cometh*, a new play by Eugene O'Neill that was being greeted as another masterpiece, she was not about to be cowed. (But of course, living in a cold-water flat, she was familiar with the old joke about the housewife and the iceman—a familiarity she was not reluctant to use to O'Neill's disadvantage, omitting any hint of how she came by it.)

### FROM "EUGENE O'NEILL—DRY ICE," *PARTISAN REVIEW*, NOVEMBER–DECEMBER 1946

To audiences accustomed to the oily virtuosity of George Kaufman, George Abbott, Lillian Hellman, Odets, Saroyan, the return of a playwright who—to be frank—cannot write is a solemn and sentimental occasion[. . . .]

Yet it must be said for O'Neill that he is probably the only man in the world who is still laughing at the iceman joke or pondering its implications[. . . .]

What disturbs one here, however, as in so many of O'Neill's plays, is the question of how far the author himself is a victim of the same sentimentality and self-pity that is exhibited clinically in the characters.

Reviewing a play acclaimed as the play of the decade starring the young Marlon Brando, being touted as the greatest actor of his generation, she refused to be impressed.

### FROM "A STREETCAR CALLED SUCCESS," *PARTISAN REVIEW*, MARCH 1948

You are an ordinary guy and your wife's sister comes to stay with you. Whenever you want to go to the toilet, there she is in the bathroom, primping or having a bath or giving herself a shampoo and taking her time about it. You go and hammer on the door ("For Christ's sake, aren't you through yet?"), and your wife shushes you frowningly: Blanche is very sensitive and you must be careful of her feelings. You get sore at your wife; your kidneys are sensitive too[. . . .]

[Tennessee Williams'] work reeks of literary ambition as the apartment reeks of cheap perfume; it is impossible to witness one of Mr. Williams' plays without being aware of the pervading smell of careerism.

Several years later, trying to put her finger on the fatal flaw of *Death of a Salesman*, a play considered by many to be a masterpiece of the American theater by a playwright who was not only a friend of her brother but had cast him in several choice roles, she would not waver. So long as she was in the theater she was polite and courteous, but once she stepped outside she did not mince words.

### FROM THE INTRODUCTION TO *SIGHTS AND SPECTACLES*

"Attention must be paid," intones the shrill, singsong voice of the mother, ordering her sons to take notice of their father's plight. "Attention, attention, must finally be paid to such a person." She is really admonishing the audience that Willy is, as she says, "a human being." But that is just it: he is a capitalized Human Being without being anyone, a suffering animal who commands a helpless pity. The mother's voice raised in the age-old Jewish rhythms ("Attention must be paid," is not a normal English locution, nor is "finally" as it is used, nor is "such a person") seems to have drifted in from some other play that was about particular people. But Willy is only a type, demanding a statistical attention and generalized, impersonal condolence, like that of the editorial page.

**BRENDAN GILL**   People now accept as a matter of course the comparative savagery of her play reviews, but at the time they were much more breathtaking than anything John Simon says. They're very harsh and manly. We don't talk about gender anymore but in point of fact if they didn't say Mary McCarthy there would be no clue that the reviewer was a woman. She was trying to impress Rahv and all these guys and she was giving as good as she got.

Her pieces were strong and so were readers' responses. On occasion the response may have owed something to a personal tie to her target, but that did not necessarily make it any less valid.

**LIONEL ABEL**   My first falling out with her was when she said that O'Neill couldn't write a sentence. She denied the worth of *The Iceman Cometh*, which is probably the best American play ever. She said it was worthless because he couldn't write a sentence. Now, he isn't a good writer. Neither is Dreiser a good writer. But they're *great* writers. So I had that against her. Once Phil Rahv and I were talking about the theater, and I said, "She writes so much about the theater, I wish she knew something about it; she'd learn if she wrote a play herself." And Phil said, "Don't ever suggest that to her. She'll do it and it'll be a big success."

**ELLEN ADLER OPPENHEIM**   When Brando walked on the stage, it was just like electricity. There's not an actor, including Olivier or Redgrave, who didn't say there went the greatest talent of them all. You'd have to be a first-class shnorrer not to have noticed him. To have gone to see *A Streetcar Named Desire* and not have mentioned his performance—that has a grandeur about it of a certain sort. It's like going to the opera and being tone-deaf. I'm sure she has very good things to say and I'm sure a lot of it is very true. But if you're not interested in the performer, you're not really supposed to be a theater critic.

**GORE VIDAL**   Mary's great fault—I think her debilitating one—was envy. It was her most spontaneous emotion. She'd envy the shoes you were wearing. You see that envy in her piece about Tennessee Williams, in which she attacks perhaps the only great American play ever written. For Mary the very fact of its commercial success meant it must be bad. But when Mary dismissed Tennessee Williams it wasn't merely envy. She was deeply anti-fag. With Tennessee Williams her hatred would have been that a fag had made such a success in the theater. It was as basic as that. She wouldn't hear the writing. She would just hear a screaming queen who should be driven into the sea.

**PAULINE KAEL**   I'm interested in what's left out of Mary McCarthy's theater criticism. Her reviews are so precise and unloving in terms of performers, it's as if she had just read the play and hadn't attended the performance. There was nothing of a personal reaction to what went on on the stage.

### FROM A REVIEW OF *SIGHT AND SPECTACLES*, BY KENNETH TYNAN, *THE OBSERVER*, MAY 10, 1959

As a detector of phoneyness, she is one of the most highly sensitised instruments to which the drama has ever been exposed. No artistic concession escapes her, no trace of sentimentality, cliché, or pretentiousness. With a critical equipment as surgical, and a prose style as vivacious as Miss McCarthy's, almost any play ever written could be demolished in a few pages. My difficulty in picturing her as a playgoer is probably linked with my inability to imagine her as a member of any crowd, anywhere. There is something antiseptic about her intelligence that would always resist the contagion of multitudes. She is a born separatist, a cat that walks either by itself or with a pedigree *élite*. Yet one of the basic conditions of drama is (to use a word she would hate) togetherness.

But even when you did not go along with her fastidious approach to the theater, it could not be dismissed out of hand.

**GORE VIDAL**   I see Mary as having a very reliable voice. She was a first-rate critic and first-rate at anything she observed and wrote about. She could be very perverse. But she was a fearless voice. I think she did care that so many people disliked her. I once asked Kevin, "How does Mary think she can get away with saying those things?" "Mary thinks she has a cloak of invisibility," Kevin said. She would smile that smile of hers and it was as if she wasn't there.

In 1948, Mary McCarthy published two pieces of fiction, "Yonder Peasant, Who Is He?," a childhood memoir portraying her years as an orphan in Minneapolis, and a short story called "The Cicerone," which was a fictionalized account of her Venice reunion with Peggy Guggenheim. Both pieces of fiction were hardly fiction at all. Each had the potential for causing consternation among her real-life subjects or their survivors.

Although "Yonder Peasant, Who Is He?" was her third memoir, it marked a departure for her. Her two earlier memoirs, "C.Y.E." and "The Blackguard," belong to a genteel Anglo-American tradition of girls' boarding school novels. With "Yonder Peasant, Who Is He?," she was venturing into new territory and coming up against material of a different order.

### FROM "YONDER PEASANT, WHO IS HE?"

Whenever we children came to stay at my grandmother's house, we were put to sleep in the sewing room, a bleak, shabby, utilitarian rectangle, more office than bedroom, more attic than office, that played to the hierarchy of chambers the role of a poor relation. It was a room seldom entered by the other members of the family, seldom swept by the maid, a room without pride; the old sewing machine, some cast-off chairs, a shadeless lamp, rolls of wrapping paper, piles of cardboard boxes that might someday come in handy, papers of pins, and remnants of material united with the iron folding cots put out for our use and the bare floor boards to give an impression of intense and ruthless tempo-rality. Thin white spreads, of the kind used in hospitals and charity institutions, and naked blinds at the windows reminded us of our orphaned condition and of the ephemeral character of our visit; there was nothing here to encourage us to consider this our home.

In the course of two years, she had moved from a world of privileged young ladies vying for pretty pastel ribbons to a world of watery parsnips and mouths taped shut with adhesive. In the process she had found her way to a voice that was spare and harsh but not dispiriting. And she had found her way to the family tragedy that would make her memoirs unique. Perhaps because she herself wished to believe it, she managed to make her readers believe that through her faithful depiction of the most sordid details of her childhood she had discovered the possibility of a redeem-ing laughter.

With "Yonder Peasant, Who Is He?," she was proclaiming herself free of the McCarthys in Minneapolis, and the righteous anger behind her ela-tion at having made good her escape was everywhere evident. For her-self and her brothers—hapless orphans and thwarted runaways—she reserved her charity and goodwill. In the process, she earned the sym-pathy of readers who had written her off as cold or heartless. But she also earned the anger of her grandmother's oldest son, her uncle Harry, who came barreling up to New York from his retirement in Florida, accusing her of slandering his mother and getting all her facts wrong. Certainly it could not be called a flattering portrait.

### FROM "YONDER PEASANT, WHO IS HE?"

White hair, glasses, soft skin, wrinkles, needlework—all the parapher-nalia of motherliness were hers; yet it was a cold, grudging, disputa-tious old woman who sat all day in her sunroom making tapestries from a pattern, scanning religious periodicals, and setting her iron jaw against any infraction of her ways. Combativeness was, I suppose, the dominant trait in my grandmother's nature. An aggressive churchgoer, she was quite without Christian feeling; the mercy of the Lord Jesus had never entered her heart.

Harry McCarthy's visit with his wife, Zula—a visit that was fueled by alcohol and punctuated by outbursts of unrepentant anti-Semitism—ended with his niece saying something to Zula that led Harry and Zula to believe she had promised to stop writing about the family. Four years later she would allow as how she may have said something of the sort "in a less categorical form." When it came down to it, she could no more honor such a promise than she could deny her memories or bowdlerize her material.

"The Cicerone" was no less likely to give offense. But, unlike "Yonder Peasant, Who Is He?," it did not mark a true departure for her. Writing the stories in *The Company She Keeps*, she had felt free to use real people and to barely disguise them. After all, nothing she said about these men and women was any worse than what she said about her protagonist, Margaret Sargent.

With "The Cicerone" she had started to write a story in the manner of Henry James—a tale of two American innocents who brush up against a corrupt Europe and are changed in some way. In the end, Europe in the guise of Mr. Sciarappa is too wan and too shabby to merit much thought. Miss Grabbe, a loud and travel-hardened American heiress, takes over the story. Polly Herkimer Grabbe is clearly Peggy Guggenheim.

### From "The Cicerone"

Sexual intercourse, someone had taught [Miss Grabbe], was a quick transaction with the beautiful, and she proceeded to make love, whenever she traveled, as ingenuously as she trotted into a cathedral: men were a continental commodity of which one naturally took advantage, along with the wine and the olives, the bitter coffee and the crusty bread. Miss Grabbe, despite her boldness, was not an original woman, and her boldness, in fact, consisted in taking everything literally. She made love in Europe because it was the thing to do, because European lovers were superior to American lovers ("My dear," she told the young lady, "there's all the difference in the *world*—it's like comparing the very best California claret to the simplest little *vin du pays*"), because she believed it was good for her, especially in hot climates, and because one was said to learn languages a great deal more readily in bed.

Not all that long ago Peggy Guggenheim had shown herself to be a generous friend and a devoted one—staying on with her in Lausanne and finding her a good doctor. But, then, Manny Rousuck, the model for Mr. Sheer in "Rogue's Gallery," had also been a generous friend and, according to Brendan Gill, a lover. The difference was that Manny Rousuck was neither as notorious nor as trusting as Peggy Guggenheim, who had been satisfied to let her friend Mary read the manuscript aloud to her and had never asked to see the galleys. When the story came out in *Partisan Review*, Guggenheim was furious. Later she claimed to have nodded off and missed most of the reading.

**MARY MCCARTHY, IN AN INTERVIEW WITH JACQUELINE BOGRAD WELD IN *PEGGY: THE WAYWARD GUGGENHEIM***

I read [it] to her in my apartment, and she was on the sofa. She may have nodded. She behaved very well about it. But later they listen to what their friends say. When I read her the story, I left out her neck wrinkles like a travelling bag, and her name, Miss Grabbe. The name was mean. I had intended another name, but the publisher felt it was too close to the name of a socialite, that another one would be better. . . . Later, I regretted it.

A life devoted to letters may be challenging and may even permit an occasional brief flirtation with danger, but it does not pay the rent. In the spring of 1947 Bowden Broadwater managed to secure a job at *Medical Digest*, which had offices in New Jersey. The pay was good, but it would mean enduring a steamy New York summer without benefit of air-conditioning. When the *Medical Digest* job did not work out, the Broadwaters were free to spend their summer in Pawlet, Vermont.

That fall, Bowden took a job as an assistant production editor at *Partisan Review*. Thanks to the generous funding of a new backer, the magazine had expanded its staff, moved its offices uptown, and started putting out twelve issues a year. Unfortunately, by the end of the fall, Bowden had left the magazine. Later, in his memoirs, William Phillips would assess Bowden's time there favorably, though with some asperity: "He had a sharp tongue but was very competent and efficient. I have never been very astute in hiring people, but Bowden was by far the best of the staff we chose." Later, Bowden's former wife would attribute his precipitate departure to the fact that the editors had voted themselves generous salary increases while granting him a five-dollar raise. "I think it was intended to keep me in my place," she told Carol Brightman. But there would seem to have been less to it than that.

**WILLIAM PHILLIPS**   First of all, it's not true that we got big raises. We didn't get any raises. This is all made up. As I recall, and I'm absolutely certain of this, we were cutting down on expenses and cutting down on our staff and we let him go.

When Bowden left *Partisan Review*, McCarthy asked Philip Rahv if Eve Gassler could take his place. Gassler was hired at once. In February 1948, McCarthy herself took a job, filling in for the spring term at Sarah Lawrence while a teacher in the English department went on maternity leave. Although she lasted until the end of the term, her time there was not happy. At Sarah Lawrence there were no exams and no grades. The school had been founded in 1926 as a two-year college for young women. Like Bennington, Sarah Lawrence was known for teaching the creative arts. There was an open admissions policy, but tuition was high, owing to a meager endowment. The students, in McCarthy's view, were not of the caliber of the students at Bard. Harold Taylor, the president—tall and youthful and proud of his reputation as a first-rate tennis player as well as a progressive administrator—was no more to her liking than the students. As it happened, she had little to do with Taylor or his students. Her class met only twice a week. With its campus on the fringes of Bronxville, Sarah Lawrence was within easy commuting distance of East Fifty-seventh Street and less than an hour's train ride from Grand Central. Unfortunately, it was also within earshot.

**HAROLD TAYLOR**  Tales would come back of her telling stories about her students to people in New York. In those days at Sarah Lawrence, we took pains to help students who weren't doing well—whatever their weaknesses were, we tended to try to help them. Mary would also talk about her students with other students. It tended to undermine the confidence of the students in a way. She made fun of the college. For certain students who were prone to take the same posture, she worked out very well. She liked bright lively young people. Whereas the philosophy at Sarah Lawrence was you take them as they come. Her psychological distance from the college, her wish not to be identified with its sloppy progressivism, her seeing it as something to be made fun of along with the students and president, were all apparent.

Its proximity to the city made Sarah Lawrence attractive to poets and writers and anyone interested in drama. Vida Ginsberg, McCarthy's young colleague from Bard, was now teaching there. The year before, Randall Jarrell had taught there part-time. Unlike Jarrell, Mary McCarthy did not get an entire novel out of her term at Sarah Lawrence, but she did not leave empty-handed.

**VIDA GINSBERG DEMING**  There was a poetry weekend I remember at Sarah Lawrence and Mary was the roommate of Marianne Moore. She was utterly enchanted and awed by her. And was most impressed by Marianne Moore's bloomers.

McCarthy left Sarah Lawrence with some splendid details for the poetry conference that would provide the climax for *The Groves of Academe*. And she, like Jarrell, left with a model for her college president—one whom she would call Maynard Hoar and describe with some asperity as a guitar-playing "gadfly of the philosophical journals," and a "photogenic, curly-haired evangelist of the right to teach."

In Harold Taylor she found neither a friend nor an admirer. In Stephen Spender, who was also teaching at Sarah Lawrence that semester, she found a friend for life. And that winter, owing to her candor rather than to anything she'd written, she managed to make an enemy for life in the playwright Lillian Hellman. As she later remembered it, Hellman came to Sarah Lawrence to speak to the students at the invitation of Harold Taylor and an exchange took place in the sun parlor of the president's house, ending with her putting Hellman to rout. For decades the scene lay buried, only to reemerge in 1980. Stephen Spender, who witnessed such a scene, later remembered it as taking place at the house he and his wife, Natasha, were renting—a house that had no sun parlor.

### FROM MARY McCARTHY'S LETTER TO BEN O'SULLIVAN, FEBRUARY 26, 1980

[Hellman] was telling a group of bemused girl students that Dos Passos had "turned against" the Spanish Loyalists "because of his stomach—he was disappointed by the food in Madrid! She was alone in Taylor's sun parlor with her wide-eyed converts and, when I came in, she paid no attention to me, taking me (I supposed) for a student, because I looked quite young then, or for a younger faculty person of no importance. At any rate she went on talking to the girls, as though she could not guess that there was anyone in the room capable of giving her the lie. Which I then did, suggesting that if the girls wanted to know his real views, they should read *Adventures of a Young Man* on the subject, published nine years before. He had not "turned against the Loyalists" then, only against the Communists who were running the show and murdering Trotskyites, Poumists, and Anarchists. His immediate motive (I think I may have said) was not the food in war-time Madrid but the murder of Andrés Nin, who had been his friend[. . . .] I remember that on her bare shriveled arms she had a great many bracelets, gold and silver, and that they began to tremble—in her fury and surprise, I assumed, at being caught red-handed in a brain-washing job.

**STEPHEN SPENDER**   What happened was that the room divided at once into two little groups—one of which was around Lillian and one of which was around Mary. I think they probably rather hurled insults at each other across the two groups—I can't remember quite. I think that a student actually in order to ingratiate herself with Lillian went to see her afterward and said we'd arranged it knowing it was going to cause trouble. Which of course is absolutely untrue. But Lillian never forgot this, and about twenty-five years after it happened I sat next to her at the American Academy of Arts and Letters dinner and she said, "It would be my luck to sit next to you." And then she came out with all this. She'd been saving it up. She just had a memory like an elephant for any kind of grievance.

Needless to say, there was no suggestion from Harold Taylor that Mary McCarthy come back the following year. But even though her term at Sarah Lawrence ended as a sorry footnote to her year of teaching at Bard, she left knowing that she would not soon again be reduced to taking another job in academia. She could afford to thumb her nose at Harold Taylor. Or the boys at *Partisan Review*, if it came to that. In 1947, her uncle

Louis McCarthy had received a generous offer for the family's grain elevator business—an offer he felt he could not refuse. As soon as the sale for Capital Elevator went through, the McCarthy trust was broken up, leaving her with a lump sum of $23,250.

With the lump sum came a hidden dividend, one that was hardly negligible, even if she never saw fit to discuss it: she would henceforth be at liberty to write about her years on Blaisdell Avenue without so much as a thought about biting the hand that was helping put food on her table.

While the lump sum she received was no fortune, it was of more use to her than the annual dividend of $2000 she had been receiving from Capital Elevator—a dividend that had dwindled down to almost nothing during the Depression. With this extra money she would cease to be at the mercy of erratic payments from Edmund Wilson, who was still awaiting a final decision from the courts on *Memoirs of Hecate County*.

In her two years in New York she had written a respectable number of essays, reviews, and stories, but she had not acquired Wilson's knack of producing occasional pieces with some underlying connection, which could later be gathered into self-contained books. With no pressing need to earn money to pay the rent, she was suddenly free to devote as much time to her writing as she cared to. She could think about starting another novel, or she could try to finish off a collection of stories—a full-fledged book to make reviewers sit up and take notice. It had been five years since the publication of *The Company She Keeps*.

A lump sum, no matter what its size, can feel like a windfall. A fortune that has come out of the blue. Now, if she wished, she could devote all her time to her writing *and* take a better house for the summer. She could buy herself an entire new wardrobe. She could make a special expedition with Bowden to Brooks Brothers. She could set about planning another trip to Europe. She could begin to think about having another child. She could put all the money away in the bank and save it. Or she could set in motion a project that was dear to her heart.

# Chapter Twelve

# THE OASIS

In the early days of their courtship, Edmund Wilson had taken it upon himself to set Mary McCarthy straight about her hero George Gordon, Lord Byron. "Byron was always on the side of the rebel," wrote Wilson, "but had no politics properly speaking." The same might be said of his impetuous admirer. Writing for *Town and Country* in the summer of 1946 she had seemed almost oblivious to the damage everywhere in Europe. The continent seemed to touch her imagination first as a traveler's mecca long unavailable to her and then as the beautifully landscaped but ultimately fatal stomping grounds of literary figures both real and imaginary. To judge by her account of her nightmarish journey to Lausanne, the most significant transformation brought about by the defeat of Mussolini and Hitler was that *none* of the trains now ran on time.

In the fall of 1946, she returned from her travels to find her old friends on the Left taking a very different view of Europe. For them, the international situation was increasingly alarming. For the four years the United States had fought in the war, the Soviet Union had been America's most powerful ally. As long as the Russians were brave comrades in arms, questions about Stalin's police state had been pushed aside as irrelevant or impolitic. For a great many Americans—particularly those who had previously paid little attention to the Communist regime in Russia—Stalin had become "Uncle Joe." Now, with the war at an end and Soviet troops occupying and annexing much of Eastern Europe, Uncle Joe was fast shedding the guise of a kindly older relative.

Among the first to point out the potential menace lurking in postwar Russia were the editors of *Partisan Review*. To the world at large the magazine's two founding editors presented a united, and often terrifying, front, but it had reached the point where Philip Rahv and William Phillips could barely endure the sight of each other. Phillips continued to handle the business side of the magazine, while Rahv took the credit for editorial decisions. Delmore Schwartz and William Barrett tended to see Phillips as long suffering and underrated. Irving Howe, a new postwar contributor, saw Phillips as "the weak link," a view in which he was not unique. Dwight Macdonald, remarking on the growing tension between the two editors, liked to say that theirs was a marriage kept together by a magazine. But for all their domestic discord, when it came to international politics the two editors were in complete agreement.

In the summer of 1946 *Partisan Review* ran a piece by William Barrett called "The 'Liberal' Fifth Column," lashing out at liberals who had not yet shaken off their wartime infatuation with Stalin—fellow travelers at *PM*, *The New Republic*, and *The Nation*. These self-styled liberals were not merely fellow travelers, he declared, but a potential fifth column, providing aid and comfort to an enemy of the United States. According to *Partisan Review*, Soviet-backed regimes were proliferating in Eastern Europe and Stalin's next big assault would be on the ravaged countries of the West. For the United States to look the other way was no better than appeasement. Because appeasement was tantamount to surrender, it was important for Americans at home to resume the vigilance of seasoned anti-Stalinists and for their government to fill the leadership vacuum abroad.

Inevitably, *Partisan Review*'s appraisal of the international situation, with its sense of urgency and appeal to pragmatism, was destined to carry weight—far greater weight than any analysis of the international situation to be found in Dwight Macdonald's *politics*. Macdonald had been disgusted by the ease with which Stalin had outbluffed an ailing Roosevelt at Yalta, but he tended to take a sanguine view of human nature, even when it manifested itself along the banks of the Volga. For Macdonald, the Russian people and the Russian government were not one and the same. In the spring of 1946, he came out with a two-part piece called "The Root Is Man," borrowing a good many of his ideas from his friend Nicola Chiaromonte and his title from an early statement by Karl Marx. Placing his faith in individuals rather than in sweeping political theories or government bureaucracies, Macdonald urged upon his readers a return to modest empirical solutions, with an emphasis on morality and on "what ought to be" rather than what is.

Throughout his life Dwight Macdonald would veer wildly from one political ideology to another, embracing even moments of apostasy with all his heart. Almost invariably Mary McCarthy would follow him in his political migrations, but her heart, for all that it had every claim to being in the right place, did not always seem to be fully engaged. Her political views would always owe much to a complicated tangle of emotion, personal loyalty, and the facts as she saw them. She could rise to the occasion, but left to her own devices political theory did not much occupy her. In New York, during the thirties she had found herself living among men who took their politics seriously. With her return to New York, politics began once again to figure large in her life.

In 1947, the editors at *Partisan Review* could take some satisfaction in the news that the United States government was finally taking steps to fill the leadership vacuum in Europe. With the Truman Doctrine, the United States put Stalin on notice that it would support all free people resisting communism. This fine-sounding promise was soon followed by a program allocating more than $12 billion to help stabilize the shaky economies of the West. As American dollars began to make their way to the bombed-out factories of Europe, crates of heavy machinery and manufactured goods began to find their way to European docks.

But while the Marshall Plan represented a first practical step toward offsetting the allure of communism, money and material goods alone were not going to secure victory against Stalin. In the spring of 1947, Nicola Chiaromonte set off for a first postwar visit to France and Italy, only to find his old friends no more mistrustful of the Soviet Union than they were of the United States. Although a great deal of money was being spent, little effort was being made to sell American democracy to writers and intellectuals. It was Chiaromonte's belief that a way must be found to give nonaligned intellectuals of the Left the means to get together, to work out their differences, and to resist the blandishments of Russian propagandists.

Chiaromonte came back to New York that fall having made up his mind to return to Europe for good. It was his hope to do something about the deteriorating situation he had encountered and it was his belief that, compared to the money spent on the Marshall Plan, it would cost very little. For Mary McCarthy, Chiaromonte's decision represented a great personal loss. While he might harbor reservations about *her*, she had none whatsoever about him. In the years she had known him, she had come to respect his learning and to rely on his integrity and judgment, much as she had once relied on her two favorite teachers at Vassar. A gentle man as well as a scholar, he was the mentor she had hoped to find in Edmund Wilson.

Chiaromonte was returning to Europe lacking both a job and any official connection. Rather than dwell on her dear friend's departure, Mary McCarthy began to turn her thoughts to helping him once he arrived at his destination. To do this she set up an organization called Europe-America Groups and got Dwight Macdonald and Chiaromonte to join her. To help get Europe-America Groups on its feet, she contributed five hundred dollars to its treasury. To raise more money, she recruited a small nucleus of like-minded friends, which included her brother Kevin; his friend, the actor Montgomery Clift; her best friend, Elizabeth Hardwick; the writer Niccolò Tucci; and her fellow teacher at Sarah Lawrence, Vida Ginsberg. Part of the group's treasury was to be used to ship periodicals and books to Europe. But three quarters of it was to be put in the hands of Chiaromonte, who would make contact with like-minded intellectuals and provide material assistance wherever it was needed, distributing the money as he saw fit.

Freed by her inheritance to devote herself full-time to her writing, she chose instead to plunge into a freewheeling political debate, which might with little exaggeration be called a maelstrom. With some justice, Edmund Wilson might again have accused his former wife of acting out a drama when she ought to be writing one. This time, however, her flare for the dramatic produced tangible results and some rather depressing conclusions.

In later years she would speak of Europe-America Groups as a collaborative effort. Always she was quick to insist that this short-lived organization had its roots in a general mood of postwar optimism. There was a time, she explained, when it seemed easy to believe in "small libertarian movements" and easy to believe that it was possible "to change the world on a small scale." The guiding spirit, she said, had been Chiaromonte. She had merely provided the seed money.

But at the end of her life, talking off the cuff to Dwight Macdonald's biographer, Michael Wreszin, McCarthy seemed to suggest that the idea for Europe-America Groups (EAG) had been hers alone and it had been a face-saving device—a way to get Nicola Chiaromonte to take money she knew he very much wanted and needed. Certainly it seems fair to say that if there had been no lump sum from Capital Elevator there would have been no Europe-America Groups. Five hundred dollars was a substantial amount of money in 1948. With this generous contribution, she learned a bitter lesson: a well-meaning face-saving device can easily backfire.

At the start, to be sure, there was cause for elation. Even when EAG's early meetings were little more than the coming together of like-minded friends intent on doing some good, the talk was exhilarating and the company congenial. If the evenings dragged on longer than was desirable, they were not without their lighter moments.

**KEVIN MCCARTHY**    It was really during the days of the Europe-America Groups that Mary and I got to know each other. After the war Mary was living with Bowden across the street from the Sutton Theatre, on the second floor, and that was where those photographs I took of the Europe-America Groups were made. I set the camera up and ran over and we all got in.

**VIDA GINSBERG DEMING**    I was there for a few of the early meetings because I knew Kevin through Monty Clift. There would be about eight of us. The meetings were kind of . . .what could one say . . . *amateur*. They would bog down. Those of us there didn't have any political ideas really. We didn't know exactly what we wanted to do except to make a statement, which I felt was an important statement: That we were all in the same boat—literally looking for a boat to rescue people.

If you are serious about rescuing people and serious about raising money to make this rescue possible, you would do well to draw on as broad a community as possible. Niccolò Tucci and Saul Steinberg, who had been helping out with Nancy Macdonald's project to send bundles of clothing and food to refugees in Europe, agreed to lend their names. Even Alfred Kazin signed up. Sidney Hook and the editors of *Partisan Review* joined without ever contributing a penny. However, most new members were more forthcoming. From Richard Rovere and Arthur Schlesinger she received twenty-five dollars, contributions that neither man could comfortably afford and for which she would be everlastingly grateful. No less generous were friends like Elizabeth Hardwick, Vida Ginsberg, and Montgomery Clift. Drawing on the Right as well as the Left, she got support from her old friend Mannie Rousuck, no longer one step ahead of the sheriff and now an aspiring plutocrat.

Lionel Abel hung around long enough to be captured in Kevin McCarthy's photographs but apparently refused to join. "There was too much 'goodness' in the thing," he would later say. But she was not about to be stopped by such demurrals. Meetings that had at one time been bogged down by discussions of EAG's overseas mission were now devoted to planning a round of spring lectures, cocktail parties, and art lotteries—an ambitious series of fund-raising activities of the sort beloved by both the radical Left and the Junior League. On a more serious note, there were to be three debates in which well-known speakers would address timely political issues like the ill-fated campaign of Henry Wallace for the presidency of the United States. Later she would recall how one of these speakers stuttered so badly he drew the word "totalitarianism" out into twenty-four syllables.

The original manifesto was drafted some time in early 1948 and mailed to prospective members, along with a covering letter asking for a contribution of ten dollars. The founding members wanted to make it clear that EAG wished to keep alive a radicalism that had nothing to do with Stalinism but that EAG was *not* supporting the capitalist governments of the West against Stalin. It was decided that McCarthy would work on the final draft with Alfred Kazin.

**MARY MCCARTHY, IN AN INTERVIEW WITH MICHAEL WRESZIN**
We worked through an afternoon getting out a statement. He was always for the most rhetorical formulations and naturally I was against

any sentimental rhetorical formulation. And he was against whatever I said. So finally at the end of the afternoon he threw up his hands and said, "Never mind, do it your way. I'll sign." He departed and after he left we found among this paper on the dining table Alfred's note, which said, "the daily struggle." It was something he wanted to say. He wanted them to know that we were with them in the daily struggle.

By her own account, she won all the rhetorical skirmishes. Missing from the statement's opening were the worst of Alfred Kazin's flourishes. But while she could claim victory in the battle of polemical rhetoric, she had, without taking note of it, lost the war of ideas.

### FROM THE STATEMENT OF THE EUROPE-AMERICA GROUPS

We came together on the following basis:

1. We regard Stalinism as the main enemy in Europe.

2. We want to help any tendencies toward the formation of a new "left" which is independent of both the Soviet and American governments.

3. Our main emphasis is on free communication between American and European intellectuals—i.e., the creation of what Albert Camus calls a "community of dialogue." What we support in Europe today is not any specific program but the reexamination of political questions through controversy and discussion.

Somehow a strident anti-Stalinist plank had crept into the committee's platform. The fact was, members like Sidney Hook, William Barrett, Philip Rahv, William Phillips, and Nicholas Nabokov, were beginning to harbor views that were in many ways identical with those of the U.S. State Department. They had no real interest in an organization that was going to limit itself to a vague program of promoting "a community of dialogue" among intellectuals troubled by the way the world was going.

Certainly to ask Sidney Hook and company to join EAG made practical sense: with their names on the letterhead, EAG could never be accused of being soft on communism. In addition, once Hook and the boys took the first step, it might be possible to convert them. For the moralist in Mary McCarthy this argument would always hold considerable sway. By all accounts, however, Hook possessed debating skills unmatched by any of his contemporaries. Taking Hook on was not only the right thing to do, but a brave thing to do—so brave as to be almost foolhardy.

A dapper little man with a big mustache, Sidney Hook was hardly a formidable-looking figure, but in a group of "bullies" he went unmolested. In the late twenties, he had been William Phillips's philosophy professor at NYU and had been in large part responsible for introducing him to Marxism. In the thirties, he had been among the first important members of the American Communist Party to turn against Stalin. He was

regarded by many, including Irving Howe, as "the main political-intellectual figure" of the young *Partisan Review*. In the late forties, along with
Lionel Trilling, he was a member of *Partisan Review*'s five-member editorial board. But by the late forties, Hook's anti-Stalinism was such that
even his cohorts sometimes felt he went too far.

**IRVING HOWE**   He was fearless. I've had all kinds of disagreements with
him, but admire him. He was always ready for a fight, even when there was
nothing to fight about.

### FROM *THE TRUANTS*, BY WILLIAM BARRETT

Hook, they felt, had become a kind of Johnny One-note, clear and
forceful but also monotonous on the one issue he was always pursuing.
When the question came up one day of Hook's possibly doing an article that was then needed, Rahv rejected the suggestion in his usual cor-
rosive and reductive way: "No. Sidney will only tell you once again that
Stalin stinks."

Hook, Mary McCarthy liked to say, had been responsible for her education in Marxism. The two of them enjoyed a civilized, if not especially
warm, relationship. Defending her to Delmore Schwartz, Hook noted,
"People do what they want to do, anyway. She at least admits it." Indeed,
during the spring of 1948, when McCarthy was working hard to set up
Europe-America Groups, it would seem that Hook was not indifferent to
her charms. According to William Phillips, he was more than disposed to
show off for her benefit at a small dinner party Phillips had organized
that spring to welcome Arthur Koestler, who like many another famous
foreign visitor was eager to have a first-hand look at the leading intellectuals of New York. Invited to this dinner at the request of the dashing and
sinister looking Hungarian-born author of *Darkness at Noon* were Delmore Schwartz, Hannah Arendt, Elizabeth Hardwick, Dwight Macdonald, William Barrett, Sidney Hook, and Mary McCarthy, who was looking
her very best. Before the evening was over, those at the table had a chance
to see two Cold War warriors battle it out for McCarthy's benefit.

### FROM *A PARTISAN VIEW*, BY WILLIAM PHILLIPS

I have never seen her so handsome and youthful. She has always had
a miraculous ability to rise to an occasion and this time she was alive
to all the possibilities of the situation. I do not think she was excited so
much by the idea of meeting Koestler, who was not one of her heroes,
as she was by the social requirements and expectations of meeting a
famous European writer[. . . .]
Koestler, with his flair for drama, particularly for sexual drama,
almost immediately made a play for Mary McCarthy. But he had too
many bridges to cross[. . . .] Koestler, however, either knew or was
shrewd enough to discern where Mary's interests lay, and he pro-

ceeded to talk about Eastern philosophies, passive resistance, and personal morality as a political force[. . . .] The only trouble was this brought him into conflict with Sidney Hook, the super-rationalist and hard anti-Communist, who never let social considerations stand in the way of his intellectual principles. They got into a sharp argument—whose ostensible subject was philosophical and political but whose real subject was Mary McCarthy—which ended when Koestler said to Hook, "I didn't come three thousand miles to hear this nonsense."

Although Koestler could not in fairness be declared the victor, when the evening was over Mary McCarthy made a date to meet him alone at his hotel room at One Fifth Avenue—with the stipulation that the visit was to be limited to further discussion. Afterward, she let it be known that Koestler had gone back on his word. He had made a pass, she reported, and she had turned him down. In time-honored fashion, Koestler then went on to seek consolation with Elizabeth Hardwick, her best friend, where he apparently met with greater success.

In later years McCarthy would say that she had turned Koestler down because she was happy in her new marriage. By saying no to him, she managed to enjoy the benefits of a public flirtation with none of the risks, while at the same time enhancing her reputation as Delmore Schwartz's "complete adventuress." With Koestler in his hotel room she was in her element, but with Sidney Hook in her own living room she was venturing into new territory. In recruiting this new member, she seems to have betrayed a startling political innocence. In the early days, the EAG meetings had lacked a clear focus. Before long, they were mired in misunderstandings and arguments.

**VIDA GINSBERG DEMING**   Sidney Hook was unbearable. As Hook became more and more of a presence, some of the people I knew dropped out. Late that spring I left on a trip west and sort of drifted away.

In the end, the arguments at meetings proved to be the least of her troubles. That spring, with the Chiaromontes in Europe and Elizabeth Hardwick out of town, she received some disquieting news.

**MARY MCCARTHY, IN AN INTERVIEW WITH MICHAEL WRESZIN**
We were tipped off that there was going to be a meeting at Rahv's apartment of Europe-America Groups not convened by me but spontaneously convened by the Hook faction and they were planning to vote to take away the treasury[. . . .] They were going to turn the whole thing over to the custody of Sidney Hook, we were told. I pulled myself together and telephoned and got hold of anyone I could who was on my side, including my brother Kevin, and told them to come to the meeting at Rahv's. Rahv had invited Saul Bellow—that was the first

time I ever saw Saul Bellow and perhaps that left a stain on his image as far as I was concerned. And Kappy, Harold Kaplan, who was living in Paris and who was the *PR* correspondent and wrote the "Paris Letter." Of course they hadn't been members of the group or anything, much less given us a contribution. My friends were very good at their footwork, so that we had obviously gotten more people. Hook and company had only to look to see that they'd be outvoted. So they abandoned what was supposed to be their attack to steal our treasury. Of course maybe they weren't planning to steal our treasury. But in that case why had they called the meeting without my knowledge? None of these people ever forgave me. They thought we were trying to send money to Europe to subversives.

The rout of Sidney Hook and the "boys" would become with time one of her most cherished stories. Unfortunately, because the enemy backed off without putting up a fight, it was impossible to know precisely what they were planning to pull off. By the end of her life, she was sounding not all that sure as to how much she had to fear from them. That they were up to something that day in Rahv's living room there was little question. "The *PR* boys made a little trouble, but it fizzled out," wrote Macdonald to Chiaromonte that July.

EAG broke up for the summer, with plans to meet again in the fall. Sidney Hook left for Paris and the Broadwaters set off for Cornwall, a small village in the northwest corner of Connecticut, which boasted a covered bridge and no pretensions whatsoever to being an artist's colony. In early July, Mary McCarthy received her first long letter from Chiaromonte, telling of the contacts he had made in Paris and the money he had paid out. In addition he had some disquieting news. The plan had been for Camus to be her opposite number in France. But while Camus had put Chiaromonte in touch with "good" people, and had agreed to assist with the distribution of financial aid, he was prepared to do no more than that. "I think this side of the Atlantic seemed very unreal to Camus, who was also more interested in his love affairs than in much else," she would later say.

One of the "good" people Camus had put Chiaromonte in touch with was a young man who did not mince words. "He told me frankly," wrote Chiaromonte, "that our statement seemed to him extremely vague, however well meaning." The young man had also told him that the part about Stalinism being "the main enemy" would not sit well with the French. To avoid "misinterpretation," he had advised that "the point must be made more specific, so as not to leave any doubt about the fact that the Groups have nothing to do with official or semi-official projects."

Chiaromonte had been shaken by the young man's words, but EAG's founder remained undaunted. To Macdonald, she wrote of starting up a newsletter to be called *The Situation*. If Camus was not going to pull his weight, she would take up the slack. Rather than admit defeat she was inclined to push harder. If she felt anything, it was that she had not done enough:

### FROM MARY MCCARTHY'S LETTER TO DWIGHT MACDONALD, N.D. [C. JULY 1948]

[M]y preliminary impression is one of almost shame at the seriousness of the European response to our very trivial and muddling efforts. I feel as if I had gotten somebody with child in the course of an innocent flirtation[. . . .] I hate to postpone this till fall; it seems shameful that they should be so poor while all of us are in relative comfort (to say the least in our case; we have a luxuriant summer with vegetable gardens and fresh eggs and milk and chickens and cheap heavy cream and all the scenery thrown in).

Writing to Macdonald in July she could hardly wait to get started on her newsletter, but already she had more pressing business to occupy her. Inspired by the events of the spring, she had arrived at Cornwall with the opening pages of a short satirical novel that she had started while still teaching at Sarah Lawrence. The title, she would later tell interviewers, had come from some writings by Koestler that explored the possibility of setting up small libertarian "oases." It would seem that she had emerged from that hotel room at One Fifth Avenue not only intact but with material for her next work of fiction. If nothing else, this short novel could be used to complete and give weight to a collection of stories that both Hardwick Moseley at Houghton Mifflin and Bob Linscott, now at Random House, seemed to regard with little enthusiasm.

Inspired by a sense of outrage more potent than any mere social slight, she had gotten much farther with *The Oasis* than she had managed to get with "The Lost Week." She was well into her narrative when she caught sight of a flyer from England advertising a contest to find a new unpublished short novel. The contest was being run by Cyril Connolly, the editor of the estimable British quarterly *Horizon*, who had been inspired by the success of Evelyn Waugh's *The Loved One*, which had taken over *Horizon*'s entire February issue. The contestants could be "old and famous" or "young and unknown." All they had to do was "keep within the word limits and send in something perfectly constructed, perfectly moving, and word-perfect." The deadline was September 15 and the prize was £125.

There was no way she could make that deadline, but she had every intention of getting a completed manuscript to Cyril Connolly by early October. Understandably, she had no time to spare for a newsletter for EAG or for a letter to the friend who had inspired it. By the end of the summer, Chiaromonte had given away almost all of the $1200 in his purse. Writing from Rome, he closed a long letter to Dwight Macdonald with an urgent question, "Why hasn't Mary written me one single word?" Almost immediately, he received an answer.

### FROM DWIGHT MACDONALD'S LETTER TO NICOLA CHIAROMONTE, SEPTEMBER 14, 1948

Yesterday had a reply from Bowden to the effect that Mary has been so immersed in a short novel which she MUST have finished by next month that she has had no time or energy for letters. He asks me to explain to you, and he adds that her relationship to you "is such that any communication would take her no less than a week to compose, so she puts it off, though SHE SAYS every night she's just about to write him. . . . Assure him of her complete sympathy and appreciation for his splendid work." So, hereby. Myself, I'm not completely appeased— still think it was very irresponsible and flighty of her. I'd assumed she was in much closer touch with you than I was. After all, EAG is HER baby, not mine (primarily).

For her to turn from EAG to her novel was not necessarily flighty. EAG may have been her "baby," but she had been caught between Hook and Chiaromonte, two men who had greater ambitions for this baby than she did. When Hook and the boys had first started making trouble, she had wanted to throw them out, but had been persuaded by Chiaromonte and Macdonald to let them leave under their own steam. That October, Hook and the boys returned in full force. Vida Ginsberg and her friends did not. To attract new members and fill the organization's depleted coffers a revised statement was drafted. Weeks were devoted to getting the wording right, so as to allay the fears of European leftists while satisfying the demands of Hook. Reflecting both the trust of a gentler age and the reduced circumstances of EAG, the statement's covering letter asked prospective members to contact Mary McCarthy, 206 East 57th Street, N.Y.C. Tel. PL 9-2155.

### FROM DWIGHT MACDONALD'S LETTER TO NICOLA CHIAROMONTE, DECEMBER 10, 1948

We (Mary and I, who, so far, *are* EAG for all practical purposes) are now sitting back and waiting to see what the response will be. (So far, 7 replies, of which 5 have joined, 2 refused—one being Dorothy Thompson, who wants more anti-USSR less anti-rightwing attitude, the other being [Lionel] Abel, who wrote a snotty postcard saying it was all dull, philistine and equivocal.)

In the end, like most hard-won compromises, the revised statement satisfied no one. Chiaromonte found it "better than the first in certain respects, worse on the whole." Macdonald found it "unexceptional if a bit on the dull side." But for Macdonald its dullness hardly mattered, since in his view EAG was on its last legs. The reason was simple enough. The following April EAG was finally put to rest.

### FROM DWIGHT MACDONALD'S LETTER TO NICOLA CHIAROMONTE, DECEMBER 10, 1948

EAG has always depended—as all such things do—on one person keeping it going, doing the dirty work; Mary has been the person; the whole fall was wasted in a series of talky-talk meetings of the in-group where action was stymied by differences between Mary-me and *PR*-Hook factions[. . . .] [A]nyway, Mary, the sparkplug, has been mostly sparkless and lethargic (partly because of the dreary tension with the *PR* get-Russia-at-all-costs attitude).

**MIRIAM CHIAROMONTE**   Mary was the last one to get discouraged. She held out to the end, but people just gave up. There were too many other things that they were interested in. Europe was far away.

**WILLIAM PHILLIPS**   I never had any hope for the EAG. They fitted Mary's needs. They were too moralistic. They were politically vague. My main criticism was that they substituted morality for politics. That was Mary and Chiaromonte.

The news from abroad had done nothing to make the aims and ambitions of Europe-America Groups seem more practical or realistic. In the summer of 1948 the Russians had started a blockade of Berlin and the United States had responded with an airlift. The newspapers were full of news of the blockade as well as news of a Communist takeover in Czechoslovakia. Any minute the Communists were expected to achieve victory in China.

By the time Macdonald wrote Chiaromonte, he and McCarthy had gone on to join Friends of Russian Freedom, an organization whose goals were limited to providing aid to dissidents within the Soviet Union.

In the meantime, Chiaromonte was thinking of taking a job with UNESCO in Paris, and was trying to reconcile himself to the life of a United Nations bureaucrat. And Sidney Hook had taken charge of a group called the Committee for Intellectual Freedom. For Nicholas Nabokov and Sidney Hook, EAG proved to be little more than a dress rehearsal for organizations less idealistic, better funded, and far better equipped to seduce those European dissidents who had been suspicious of EAG's good-hearted overtures.

By the time EAG was put to rest, its demise was long overdue, and its founder had already commemorated its passing. She had not only written its fictional epitaph but had enjoyed the satisfaction of seeing this epitaph—her short novel *The Oasis*—published in its entirety in the February 1949 issue of *Horizon*. That fall, when she had been laboring "sparkless and lethargic" over the revised manifesto, Cyril Connolly had written from London to say that her novel had caught the fancy of "the carefully selected jury who happen to coincide with the editors of *Horizon*." The original purse for the Horizon Prize had grown to £200, thanks to a generous contribution from Evelyn Waugh. With the prize money came a dozen bottles of dry sherry. In his letter telling her she had won, Connolly did not hesitate to wax enthusiastic, calling the novel "brilliant and true and funny and beautifully written and intelligently thought and felt." Nor did he hesitate to presume on an earlier acquaintance, starting off by asking her permission to call her "Mary" and concluding by saying that Bowden was "a lucky man." All the same, he felt the need to offer a word of caution.

### From Cyril Connolly's Letter to Mary McCarthy, n.d. [c. late 1948]

[*The Oasis*] won't have anything like the popular success of *The Loved One*, because *The Loved One* had a universal appeal and this has an avant-garde appeal—most of our readers won't know what you are talking about half the time, but this won't matter in the least because we do not expect things we print to go bowling down the hill to Hollywood.

What Connolly did not say was that *The Oasis* was coming on the heels of a spate of well-regarded but little read political satires. Starting with the publication of George Orwell's *Animal Farm* in 1945, short political satires had been enjoying something of a literary vogue. To bring to bear a distorting mirror on some portion of society with the aim of reforming it was one way to grapple with a world that was running hopelessly amok. But it was not a sure way to produce a best-seller. *The Loved One*, which took California's increasingly bizarre funerary practices as its subject, turned out to be the only satire published immediately after *Animal Farm* to capture the general public's attention.

With *The Oasis*, Mary McCarthy did not seek out a barnyard or a Los Angeles cemetery but stayed close to home—sending a convoy of urban intellectuals off to establish a Utopian community on a New England mountaintop, where they expect to find safety from a threatened atomic war and a chance to test their ideals. This motley crew of colonists sets up camp in the ruins of an abandoned turn-of-the-century summer resort. They actually call their little colony "Utopia." Almost all are disciples of a saintly and modest Founder, who has disappeared on a trip to Europe and is feared to be dead. Among the would-be Utopians are several former Communists, a family of anarchists, a news editor, a poet, a minister, a girl student, a college teacher, a veteran, a printer, a novelist, a businessman, and a good-looking short story writer named Katy Norrell, possessed of dark hair and a slender young husband and a plethora of moral scruples.

On the mountaintop there will be no electricity and no labor-saving devices. Here the colonists will bake their own bread, harvest their own crops, realize their dreams, and live cheek by jowl in perfect harmony. But along with their children and their most valued possessions, they have brought with them decades of habits and prejudices. Even before they set off in their cars for the mountains, they cannot agree on whether the businessman Joe Loucheim, a retired factory owner, should be permitted to join them.

Early on the colonists divide into Purists and Realists. But, then, the lines are smudged. Macdougal Macdermott, the leader of the Purists, starts off as Loucheim's most outspoken opponent and quickly succumbs to second thoughts. "Tall, red-bearded, gregarious, susceptible to a liver complaint, puritanical, disputatious, hard-working, monogamous, a good father and a good friend," Macdermott is a twin for Dwight Macdonald. He and the other Purists have come to Utopia looking for "the reign of justice and happiness." The Realists have come looking for a new summer colony safe from atomic fall out. Disaffected Marxists, the Realists are now successful businessmen who retain "a notion of themselves as a revolutionary *élite*"—an elite deserving of the "the widest latitude in personal practice" both at home and at the office. They know the Purists are hoping to reform them and look forward to thwarting them. Above all, they look forward to seeing the colony fail.

The head of the Realist faction is Will Taub, who with his love of "confidences, closed rooms, low voices" and his "dark features" and "peculiar short harsh laugh" is a double for Philip Rahv. Seeing no need to hold his tongue or to indulge in any physical labor, Taub roves about the colony with a pretty young woman in tow. Seeing no need to hold *her* tongue, the author of *The Oasis* does not draw back from anatomizing Taub's marriage or the sorry need that binds him to the "reserved" wife who has a career as a clothing designer.

## FROM *THE OASIS*

A kind of helplessness came over him when he became conscious of his Jewishness, a thing about himself which he was powerless to alter and which seemed to reduce him therefore to a curious dependency on the given[. . . .] He began suddenly, as he always did on these occasions, to long for his wife, a Gentile woman who alone understood what he suffered on this score, and who had never, during all their years together, alluded to it unsolicited. For this tact he felt a gratitude toward her that was mingled with surprise and reverence. She held a unique place in his heart, though he consulted her convenience seldom, was brusque and out-of-sorts with her when she tried to think about social problems.

The plot of *The Oasis* reaches its climax so swiftly it can leave readers wondering if they have missed something. Having been led to expect a conflict between the Realists and the Purists, they must make do with a deus ex machina in the form of a family of trespassing local bumpkins and then accept as final and irrevocable pretty dark-haired Katy Norell's realization that the colony is doomed to failure and all her good intentions are no less doomed. Having waded through pages of character analysis and the skimpiest of plots, readers are rewarded with some fairly dispiriting insights. The potential for disappointment was not lost on Connolly, who in his letter to McCarthy let her know that the manuscript could do with "one or two improvements":

### FROM CYRIL CONNOLLY'S LETTER TO MARY MCCARTHY, N.D. [C. LATE 1948]

I am not quite happy about the ending which is a little too abrupt as if you had got bored with it or finished it in too much of a hurry because of the time limit[. . . .] You trust your powers in the analysis of your characters, but not in providing them with appropriate actions[. . . .] Do you think there is enough sex in the story? With all those contraceptives they seem to make precious little use of them.

Normally amenable to editorial suggestions from readers she respected, McCarthy seems this time to have turned a deaf ear. Possibly she had no choice. Hard at work in Cornwall, she'd had the contest to keep her going and Bowden at her side, egging her on, and feeding her with details from his brief unhappy tenure at *Partisan Review*. By late fall, when she heard from Connolly, she was no longer living a rural idyll in Connecticut but was back in New York, struggling with the real-life Realists and by all accounts worn out. In addition, she was under the gun, with a publication date that could not be put off.

*The Oasis* came out on schedule in the February issue of *Horizon*, causing enough of a sensation for Bob Linscott at Random House to decide to publish it as a small self-contained book. Without a whisper of sex, Mary McCarthy had once again managed a critical success that also stirred up a bit of a scandal. The novel was touted as a *roman philosophique*. In a generous introduction, Connolly placed its author firmly in the ranks of such writers as William Congreve and Benjamin Constant, Elizabeth Bowen and Ivy Compton-Burnett. Then, seemingly intent on taking away with one hand what he had bestowed with the other, he noted "she perhaps lacks narrative power" and "[t]he writing may at times seem a little strained." Indeed, that was the least of it.

**FROM CYRIL CONNOLLY'S INTRODUCTION TO *THE OASIS***

English readers may have to contend with two difficulties: they may be unused to the alert political-minded rootless urban intelligentsia of New York from which her characters are drawn, though it is really very like our own, and they may be alarmed by what seems a certain coldness and inhumanity in the writer which is sometimes a by-product of brilliance.

Connolly's prizewinner had produced a *roman à clef* for which the average English reader possessed no key. Connolly naturally made no mention of the fact that he himself was in possession of such an instrument, having been among the earliest of the postwar visitors to be wined and dined by the circle around *Partisan Review*. At lunch with the Lionel Trillings he had mortally offended his hostess by flicking ashes of his cigar into a rich chocolate cream prepared expressly for his benefit. Now with *The Oasis* he could count on provoking rage and consternation among a myriad of his former New York hosts. Because only a limited number of copies of *Horizon* could be shipped to New York, the anticipated uproar was at first little more than a murmur.

Dwight Macdonald, who had been painted as a good-hearted philistine and whose wife had been given a silver spoon that "tinkled in her mouth whenever she spoke against privilege," chose to take the whole thing in good part. After all, there were some consoling touches to be found in the portrait of Macdougal Macdermott. If he was sometimes foolish he was also generous. "The targets of his satire could never truly dislike Macdermott," readers were told, "for they found themselves endowed by it with a larger and more fabulous life." Making no mention of his own appearance in the book, Macdonald wrote Chiaromonte in Paris.

**FROM DWIGHT MACDONALD'S LETTER TO NICOLA CHIAROMONTE, APRIL 7, 1949**

Have you read *The Oasis* yet? Almost no one likes it around here except me. And I didn't like it the second time I read it anywhere near as much as when I heard Mary read it originally. Do you think it is vicious, malicious and nasty? (I won't pass on your remarks to Mary, so write freely.)

**FROM CHIAROMONTE'S LETTER TO MACDONALD, APRIL 11, 1949**

Mary's story has caused quite a stir over here[. . .] the aforementioned stir being on the whole negative, I am sorry to say. I myself should have liked to be enthusiastic about the story, but alas I am unable to do so. Mary is certainly a brilliant girl, but why she should be so hopelessly literal I can't understand.

The first hint of trouble came from a completely unexpected quarter.

McCarthy had called her businessman Joe Loucheim and now the husband of someone she knew from Vassar—a businessman with the name Joe Louchheim—was threatening to take her to court. It wasn't long, though, before legal action was threatened from a quarter that was not unanticipated. Alleging some 132 violations of his rights, Philip Rahv went to court to try to stop Random House from publishing *The Oasis*. Only after Dwight Macdonald convinced him that to win this suit he would have to prove that he was in every respect like Will Taub did Rahv back off. Decades later the author was prepared to acknowledge that there might have been some justice to Rahv's grievance.

### MARY McCARTHY AT CITY ARTS & LECTURES, SAN FRANCISCO, MAY 10, 1985

[He] had a legitimate cause, I suppose, to sue me. [. . .] There were many points of resemblance; in fact I wanted him to recognize himself. I thought, See how you look. But I do think that's often a motive for a certain kind of satire: See how you look to others. It's intended—obviously, in this case it was intended—for the reform of that person.

There is a story that Saul Bellow takes pleasure in telling whenever the subject of Mary McCarthy comes up. The story may be apocryphal but it has the ring of authority if not necessarily the ring of truth. As Bellow tells it, he ran into a friend one day in the Village. Sometimes in the telling the friend is Nicola Chiaromonte, sometimes not. Bellow goes on to say that when he asked the friend why he was grinning the friend told him, "I just ran into Mary and she looked wonderful, she was blooming. I asked her, 'How come, Mary, you're looking so well and so happy?' And she said, 'Well, I kicked the hell out of So-and-So and I tore the stuffing out of So-and-So and now I'm going to murder So-and-So.'"

Bellow's story owes something to "The Cicerone" and *The Company She Keeps*, but it has its roots in *The Oasis*. The fact is, reformation did not seem to be the only thing on her mind when she was writing this short novel. Talking to Doris Grumbach in the 1960s, she appeared to be speaking from personal experience when she said, "The best satire seems to spring from hatred and repugnance: Swift, Juvenal, Martial, Pope[. . . .] Satire, I suspect, is usually written by powerless people; it is an act of revenge."

**LIONEL ABEL**   Phil Rahv got wind that she had sent the story to *Horizon*, which was edited by Cyril Connolly and Sonia Orwell, who was then Sonia Brownell. I knew Sonia later in Paris and she said that a letter came in from Philip to Cyril, asking him not to publish Mary's story. And she said you can't imagine how delighted Cyril was to get that letter and to be able to answer it in the way that he did. You know what he wrote? He wrote, "We must all suffer for the sake of literature."

**ALFRED KAZIN**  Rahv was wounded in his sexual *amour propre*, which meant a great deal to him (he was a fantastic Don Juan). Mary's book had an element of putting down your old bed partner. So he called this meeting— he called the group together to discuss what they could do. This was typical. And he went on railing against Mary. Finally, William Barrett, who was the only non-Jewish member of this group, said, "Now look, Philip, let's be honest, we've attacked a lot of people ourselves." Whereupon, according to the story (I wasn't there), Rahv got up and shrieked, "Who did we attack? Who? Who?" Barrett said, "Remember we did a terrible thing on Peggy Guggenheim?" This remark only inflamed him more. He got up, reared back his head. "Peggy Guggenheim," he said. "Fuck Peggy Guggenheim." That became the great line.

*Schadenfreude* was an emotion not unknown among *Partisan Review*'s circle. But for a time the novel had the effect of bringing the magazine's editors and writers closer together.

### FROM *THE TRUANTS*, BY WILLIAM BARRETT
The circle gathered around like a group of mourners. "That woman is a thug," Diana Trilling said. Neither she nor her husband, Lionel Trilling, had been lampooned in McCarthy's story, but Mrs. Trilling felt it necessary to deliver her disinterested moral judgment.

**WILLIAM PHILLIPS**  The only one who really got off badly was Philip Rahv. The rest of us just reacted on a question of principle. Maybe also to forestall her taking us on in later fiction. There was a little bit of anger that she used her personal friendships and relations as fodder for her fiction. I remember Sidney Hook was terribly annoyed. He got angry at Mary for doing it. Everyone eventually spoke to her again. But *The Oasis* was terrible. It caused a lot of pain to Nathalie Rahv.

Philip Rahv wanted his former lover to know that she had not only caused unnecessary pain but had produced a bad novel, and he wanted her to know how others in their circle felt. To Dwight Macdonald he sent a "relevant passage" from a letter he had received from Harold Kaplan in Paris, who had stayed up half the night reading the novel with his friend Saul Bellow. "It might be a good thing to show this to Mary," wrote Rahv. "Perhaps it will wake her up from the miasmic dreams in which she has been moving of late."

### FROM H. J. KAPLAN'S LETTER, QUOTED IN PHILIP RAHV'S LETTER TO DWIGHT MACDONALD, MARCH 24, 1949
[W]e believe this thing is so vile, so perfect an example of everything that is nasty in New York and everything that is sterile in recent Amer-

ican writing, that we came to the conclusion that something should be
done about it. The worst of it is not her stupid caricature of you but the
utter cadaverous deadness of the whole thing; no more life, no talent,
no movement; the jokes are gruesomely flat, the story has no point,
there is no literary (and hence—this is our great grief—no moral) justification for the whole thing, except a bewildered and rather pathological vengefulness.

Not a few members of Rahv's circle took it on themselves to damn the
novel and shun its author. However, the *Partisan Review* crowd did not,
for all they might choose to believe otherwise, constitute the entire New
York intellectual world. Even among the magazine's stalwarts, there
were those who broke ranks. Trained as a lawyer, the critic Harold
Rosenberg, an old friend of McCarthy's who was believed by many to be
a former lover, offered to take his bar exams so that he could defend her
in court. But before there was any question of legal action, almost on the
heels of the novel's appearance in print, one member in good standing
of Rahv's circle took it upon herself to write the author a note to say how
much she admired what she had done.

### HANNAH ARENDT'S LETTER TO MARY MCCARTHY, MARCH 10, 1949
I just read *The Oasis* and must tell you that it was pure delight. You
have written a veritable little masterpiece. May I say without offense that
it is not simply better than *The Company She Keeps*, but on an all
together [*sic*] different level.

Signing the note "very cordially yours," Hannah Arendt cemented a
friendship that had gotten off to a rocky, not to say disastrous, start. When
the two women had met in the spring of 1944, Arendt had been working
as an editor at Schocken Books and living in a small apartment in the
West Nineties with her mother and her husband, the philosopher Heinrich Blücher.

Hannah Arendt had trained as a philosopher, studying with Martin
Heidegger at Marburg and Karl Jaspers at Heidelberg. In 1933, when
Hitler began his persecution of German Jews, she had fled with her
mother to Paris, where she shed her first husband and married Blücher,
a former Communist. Just before the Nazis invaded France, Arendt and
Blücher were arrested as "enemy aliens" and placed in separate detention camps, from which they both managed to escape.

When Arendt was later asked by Lionel Abel why she had come to
America and then stayed, she replied that in the first place she was "welcomed in America." She then said something that took him aback. She
said that she met Philip Rahv and William Phillips and "never in her life
had she met two such good people." When Abel asked what she meant

by "good," she told him she meant "virtue." Certainly Arendt had cause
to be grateful. Even though her written English was far from perfect, her
writing was published and championed by the two founding editors of
*Partisan Review*. Indeed, it was at one of the regular Friday gatherings at
Philip Rahv's apartment that Arendt and Mary McCarthy had had their
big run-in. Like the purloined EAG treasury, it became a staple of
McCarthy's repertoire, embellished and enriched with the passage of
time. Even at the end of her life she was still recounting it.

### MARY McCARTHY AT CITY ARTS & LECTURES, SAN FRANCISCO, MAY 10, 1985

There had been a number of anti-Nazi incidents in [Occupied] France
and the population had showed itself quite evidently to be on the whole
hostile, very hostile, and I had the sense that Hitler was terribly disappointed. He expected the French to love him! Very characteristic of
such mentalities. So, I said that night at Philip Rahv's, "You know, I feel
sorry for Hitler, because he'll never achieve this dream of his of being
loved by all these people that he's conquered." There was a terrible sort
of explosive sound, which was Hannah Arendt going off like a machine
gun. She turned to Philip and she said, "Rahv! Must I come to America
to hear this kind of talk in the house of you, a Jew." She went on to say
that she had been in a concentration camp[. . . .] Rahv knew me and did
not take my remark seriously—he knew that it didn't express any sympathy for Hitler on my part but a kind of amusement on my part at his
predicament. I think I left first, and she didn't speak to me for two years.

According to Hannah Arendt, this was no exaggeration. By her reckoning she had cut Mary McCarthy for six years.

### HANNAH ARENDT IN "MARY McCARTHYISM," BY BROCK BROWER, *ESQUIRE*, JULY 1962

She was being so deliberately naughty. I counted to one hundred and
twenty to let Rahv—who is not the greatest hero of the age—say something to her, and when he didn't, it was just too much. I had to do something about it.

Following this rupture the two women kept running into each other.
After all, they wrote for some of the same magazines and served on
some of the same committees. Both were on the editorial board of *politics* and helped Nancy Macdonald with her refugee aid. Over time they
noticed that they tended to share the same ideas.

### MARY McCARTHY AT CITY ARTS & LECTURES, SAN FRANCISCO, MAY 10, 1985

There'd be other people there and differences, but we always agreed.
We did not speak. We spoke across people. Finally[. . .] we left such a

meeting one night and walked down to the subway station at Astor Place. We walked side by side and we got to the station and were standing on the platform—silent—and she said, "This is nonsense. Let us forget it. Let us be friends. And to start with, let me tell you that I was never in a concentration camp."

By March 1949 Hannah Arendt and Mary McCarthy were well on their way to becoming friends, but with the friendship still tentative, Arendt seized an opportunity to strengthen this fragile bond. Not only did she write to show her enthusiasm for *The Oasis* but she went on to extend an invitation for dinner. Such interest and support could only have been welcome. In a year's time Mary McCarthy had lost Nicola Chiaromonte to Europe and Elizabeth Hardwick to a relationship that was totally absorbing.

Hardwick had become embroiled in a love affair with the poet Robert Lowell. Handsome, newly divorced from Jean Stafford, and recent winner of the Pulitzer Prize for *Lord Weary's Castle*, Lowell had attracted Hardwick's notice at a Bard poetry conference in November 1948—a conference which, along with the one at Sarah Lawrence, would later contribute memorable details to *The Groves of Academe*.

The previous summer, while she was hard at work at Cornwall, Mary McCarthy had been aware that she could not count on Hardwick's support in EAG battles. "Elizabeth, nice as she is, doesn't seem to take much *interest* in these matters; she is afraid if she started thinking she would disagree with the *P.R.* line—at least that is my diagnosis," she had written Macdonald in July. At the very least Hardwick was preoccupied.

That winter, Hardwick was happily ensconced at Yaddo with Lowell when, on February 11, 1949, *The New York Times* ran a front-page story proclaiming "Tokyo War Secrets Stolen by Soviet Spy Ring," stating that Agnes Smedley, the good friend of Yaddo's resident director Elizabeth Ames, was a Soviet agent and spy. Within a few days a correction was printed. Nonetheless, in late February, FBI agents were dispatched to Yaddo, where Hardwick and Lowell were still in residence, along with a young Southerner by the name of Flannery O'Connor. Inflamed by the *Times* story and by the FBI inquiry, Lowell called a meeting of the Yaddo board and demanded that Elizabeth Ames be removed as director. In the end, Ames stayed on and Lowell, Hardwick, and O'Connor left for New York.

Given the climate of the times, Lowell's actions seemed extreme but not wildly so. In Washington, Communist Party leaders were being brought to trial under the Smith Act, and subversive left-wing groups were being subpoenaed by the House Committee on Un-American Activities. A *Time* writer and former Party member named Whittaker Chambers had accused Alger Hiss, a high-ranking State Department official, of leaking sensitive information to the Soviet Union. Everywhere you turned someone was being accused of spying.

On March 21, when the Yaddo board met again, Elizabeth Ames was cleared of all charges. But by then Hardwick and Lowell, who was beginning to suffer increasingly from manic delusions as well as excessive political fervor, were engaged in an equally dramatic but altogether more lighthearted bit of anti-Communist activity in the company of Hardwick's good friend Mary—a bit of political activity which in its more exuberant moments recalled the 1934 dustup at the Waldorf, when she and *her* friends had dressed in their finest and held a demonstration in support of the hotel's striking waiters.

With the publication of *The Oasis* in *Horizon*, Mary McCarthy was learning that it is one thing to enjoy the satisfaction of getting your own back, but another to enrage your old friends to the point where they want nothing further to do with you. That winter, she'd learned that the Communist Party was sponsoring a gathering at the Waldorf being touted as a "Cultural and Scientific Conference for World Peace." The conference, which was to be held the last weekend of March, would be the first big Communist rally since the debacle of the Wallace campaign.

Already Sidney Hook, whose application to deliver a paper at the conference had been turned down, was mounting a counteroffensive. At a meeting at Dwight Macdonald's apartment, he had set about forming an ad-hoc group, which came to be called Americans for Intellectual Freedom. In no time at all this committee was making plans not only to stage a counterrally but also to take a suite at the Waldorf, which would serve as a base of operations for issuing bulletins and press releases discrediting the proceedings—and for perpetrating a few dirty tricks.

Mary McCarthy had not been invited to the original meeting at Dwight Macdonald's. Nor had she been asked to join the committee. If she wished to take part in the battle at the Waldorf, she was going to have to find some other way to do so. In time she learned that you could get into the conference by registering as a delegate. By then, Dwight Macdonald had dropped off Hook's committee; Lowell's excitement, while palpable, was not yet unbridled; and Elizabeth Hardwick was game. When invited, they were all delighted to join her for a foray into what looked to be the very heart of the Communist camp. Hook and his group predicted that they would never get their tickets. She said they would. And they did.

**MARY MCCARTHY, IN AN INTERVIEW WITH MICHAEL WRESZIN**
[W]e got the tickets[. . . .] We registered. Then I had an attack of conscience. By this time I'm not speaking to Rahv and Phillips and Hook

and the whole gang because of my book *The Oasis*[. . . .] [N]onetheless I thought I ought to give them a chance of getting into this[. . . .] So I called up Sidney Hook and I told him[. . . .] And he said, "Well, that just shows how little you know about politics."

### DWIGHT MACDONALD, IN A 1979 INTERVIEW WITH DIANA TRILLING, PARTISAN REVIEW, FALL 1984

They said that this was not a good idea at all; we would make fools of ourselves. We would also give the Stalinists a talking point; it was rude to go to their functions.

### MARY MCCARTHY, IN AN INTERVIEW WITH MICHAEL WRESZIN

Hook simply turned his back on me. Afterwards, he must have regretted it. I know he regretted it[. . . .] He said, "We know you're in the meeting and we'd like to brief you on what you should say." So we were led up to some quiet little room in the Waldorf and there was some goon from the freedom committee[. . . .] [He said,] "Assuming that your tickets are honored, they'll let you in the door. They'll start hazing you the minute you try to open your mouth. What you must do is go in there with chains or ropes or something to tie yourself to your chair so that they can't remove you. You tie yourself to your chair and in the meantime you've got a copy of your remarks—which we'll mimeograph for you—that you're going to make. If they throw you out of the meeting hall, you'll distribute these remarks to the press"[. . . .] I said I had no intention of doing it. And that these things weren't going to happen. We agreed to go home and write up our remarks[. . . .] I don't think we ever agreed to take any chains or rope or anything to tie ourselves to our chairs. But I remember Dwight was given the question about Anna Akhmatova. He was supposed to ask "Where is Anna Akhmatova?"

On March 26–27, 1949, three thousand Communists and fellow travelers from all over the world came together in New York for the much anticipated Cultural and Scientific Conference for World Peace sponsored by the National Council of the Arts, Sciences and Professions. Outside there were Catholic war veterans picketing. Inside were such literary luminaries as Norman Mailer, Lillian Hellman, Howard Fast, and Harvard literature professor F. O. Matthiessen. The composer Dmitry Shostakovich was the star of the Russian contingent. A. A. Fadeyev, secretary of the Union of Soviet Writers and an unabashed bureaucrat, was the most prominent Russian literary figure. Dwight Macdonald covered the conference for *politics*. Irving Howe wrote it up for *Partisan Review*. Both noted that if this conference was larger by far than anything New York had seen in the thirties, it was, by their standards, a comparatively lackluster affair.

### FROM "THE WALDORF CONFERENCE," BY DWIGHT MACDONALD, POLITICS, WINTER 1949

The Conference had little to do with either culture, science or peace but it was nevertheless of great significance. It was strictly a Stalinoid affair: the NCASP is a Communist-front organization[. . . .] The "call" to the Conference followed the same lines: it denounced at length the State Department's "cold war" policy but had not one word criticising the Russian power-moves to which this policy is a reaction[. . . .] The Waldorf Conference showed one thing very clearly: the Communists are on the defensive, in this country at least.

The writers panel met at the Starlight Roof on Saturday afternoon. By all accounts, Norman Mailer, the author of *The Naked and the Dead*, was the only young writer of any distinction. To this session McCarthy and her contingent came, with their mimeographed speeches in hand.

### MARY MCCARTHY, IN AN INTERVIEW WITH MICHAEL WRESZIN

[W]e took the precaution of bringing umbrellas. That is, Lizzie and Lowell and I. I think Nancy was there, but somehow she and Dwight were separated from us in the hall. I don't know why. We got in and we got to our places, no problem. We brought our umbrellas in order to make a demonstration and possibly as a weapon if we had to. As soon as the proceedings started we began banging on the floor with our umbrellas. I'm ashamed of it to this day that we behaved that way. But we did. Louis Untermeyer was the chairman and he looked like he recognized a number of us. He nearly fainted away with ecstasy when he saw Robert Lowell. And I think he even recognized me[. . . .] He made a little speech saying, "You are going to be allowed two minutes each to ask any questions and make any statements. Please keep silent until your time comes."

Three panel members made speeches, but the panelist who struck a raw nerve was F. O. Matthiessen, who spoke of Thoreau, Emerson, Whitman, and Melville as the Henry Wallaces of their day. At last the chairman recognized speakers from the floor.

### MARY MCCARTHY, IN AN INTERVIEW WITH MICHAEL WRESZIN

We did have our at least two minutes and we did ask our questions[. . . .] I think all of us were not very good.

Dwight Macdonald managed to ask Fadeyev, the Soviet bureaucrat, what had become of six internationally acclaimed writers, among them Anna Akhmatova. McCarthy asked F. O. Matthiessen whether he thought Fadeyev had answered Macdonald's questions adequately. Then she asked how he thought Emerson might "go about 'organizing liberty'" in the Soviet Union and how Thoreau might fare practicing civil disobedience there. Lowell, the last of the group to speak, asked Shostakovich how his government's criticism had "helped his own work."

Afterward, in his report in *politics*, Macdonald devoted two passages to the dissenting group at the Starlight Roof. Howe passed over their protest fairly quickly, noting that "it takes considerable skill to be able to express a political opinion in two minutes, and most intellectuals, accustomed to more indulgent audiences, lack that skill." William Phillips, decades later, remained unimpressed.

**WILLIAM PHILLIPS** I thought that was all rather childish. I didn't think they could get anywhere. It was their idea of standing up and being courageous. Again, courage and truth. I thought it was hopeless. You're going into a stacked meeting and nobody is going to pay any attention to you. You're going to have no effect whatsoever. It was naïve. Romantic. Elizabeth Hardwick was much less that way. She went along with it, but she was much less romantic.

Decades later, Norman Mailer, who had been seated on the platform, recalled the scene that played out before his eyes with precision and no little elation.

**NORMAN MAILER** The room where the session was held was wider than it was deep and there were about sixteen rows of seats. There were maybe two hundred people there and Mary and some of her group were more or less fourth row center. The rest were scattered around the room. From the dais I could see their faces clearly. Mary was the play caller for the group—the quarterback. She'd turn or point or nod to one or the other of them, signaling them to speak. I guess she was more like a conductor. I don't think she spoke at length. She may have asked a nasty question or two.

McCarthy and her team had made exactly the sort of impression they had envisioned. But there was more to come. At the end of the session Mailer himself left his seat on the dais and went up to the lectern to speak. For Jean Malaquais, Mailer's French translator and the man responsible for what transpired, the speech came as no surprise. For Dwight Macdonald the speech was "the most moving and sincere of the afternoon." Even in Irving Howe it struck a responsive chord. Decades later, Macdonald would tell Diana Trilling, "But of course the sensation was Mailer's speech." Mary McCarthy would marvel over what he had done. But in fact she and her friends had made it easier for him.

**MARY MCCARTHY, IN AN INTERVIEW WITH MICHAEL WRESZIN**
They gave him the floor and he embarked on a masterly sort of Ciceronian speech—soon it became apparent that all these things that

he wasn't going to speak of were the real matter of his address. And right there from the platform he attacked Stalinism. Well, you just can't imagine the nerve of it. Nothing could happen to him of course physically. And nothing did. But it takes a certain amount of cool I would say to do that.

"The conference, on the whole, was a failure," Irving Howe concluded in *Partisan Review*, reflecting the consensus among most observers. In America, there would never be another like it. But not entirely because of what had transpired in the halls and suites and ballrooms of the Waldorf. Within a year the Russians would explode their first atom bomb, the United States would send troops to South Korea to fight a Communist invasion, and Party members and fellow travelers would be scrambling underground.

With the culture conference behind her, Mary McCarthy could take some satisfaction in having shown Sidney Hook how little *he* understood about politics, but she could share this satisfaction with few of their mutual friends. For most of the *PR* crowd she was still persona non grata. Her last "Theater Chronicle," a long discussion of Olivier's Hamlet, had come out in January. With the publication of *The Oasis* in February, she had effectively cut off the major outlet for her criticism. Worse, without Rahv's protection and interest, she was vulnerable in ways she could never have anticipated. Vulnerable not only to gossip but to slander and ridicule and an attack from an unanticipated quarter.

"Tidings from the Whore," Delmore Schwartz would cry upon opening *Partisan Review* and seeing the latest piece by Mary McCarthy. His friends knew only too well how prudish Schwartz was about sexual matters. But at some point in the spring of 1949 Delmore Schwartz and Mary McCarthy were caught by Bowden Broadwater in a compromising embrace. The embrace took place in the entrance hall to the Fifty-seventh Street walk-up, after a cocktail party. According to her, it was Delmore who pounced. Without waiting for her to explain, Bowden ran off into the night.

Her first fear was that Bowden would throw himself in the river. Her next fear was that when he showed up again he would not believe her. She made Delmore go upstairs and wait so that on Bowden's return he could explain that he was at fault and "had forced himself on her." When Bowden finally showed up, Delmore did as he was told; Bowden was satisfied and peace was restored. But that was not the end of it. She would later say, "[Delmore] went around and told all these little boys, including Philip, that I had made a pass at him! Philip, of course, didn't believe him, but the others probably did." As it turns out, she was mistaken on both counts. The "little boys" were not quite so ready to believe Delmore.

And Philip Rahv, having read his copy of *Horizon*, was not quite so ready to dismiss Delmore's story out of hand.

**WILLIAM PHILLIPS**   Mary claimed that Delmore made a pass at her, and he denied it. I never could make that out. I was surprised that Delmore would go for her—it didn't seem the sort of thing that Delmore would do. This kind of behavior didn't belong to Delmore in my mind. He made passes at a different kind of person. Younger. Less formidable. Of course when he got drunk, who knows what he did.

### FROM *PORTRAIT OF DELMORE: JOURNALS AND NOTES OF DELMORE SCHWARTZ, 1939–1959*

P[hilip] R[ahv] observed to Wm. [Phillips]: "We're not criticizing you, Delmore," they said as I tried to defend myself—half falsely—that Bowden must have known what occurred. "If a girl does not want a pass made at her, she does not act like that."

In August 1949 Random House brought out three thousand copies of *The Oasis*. On the back of the novel's dust jacket was a picture of Mary McCarthy looking a good deal less glamorous than she had on the jacket of *The Company She Keeps*. This time, in the author's biography there was no name dropping, but, then, the author was no longer married to Edmund Wilson or seeing much of Elizabeth Bishop. Instead, there was a brief *curriculum vitae* and the information that the author was "married, and lives in New York with her husband and her young son in an apartment which they wish were larger. She can cook and sew."

Gracing the inside flap of the dust jacket was a blurb lifted from Cyril Connolly's letter, announcing that Mary McCarthy observed "like the devil" and recorded "like the recording Angel." Faced with the author's reputation and Connolly's hyperbole, few reviewers had the courage to disparage the novel's writing, but they were not quite so reluctant to question the success of her satire.

On the whole, the novel fared better with men than with women. In the *New York Post*, Dawn Powell, the writer Rosalind Wilson would have infinitely preferred as a stepmother, said that readers would find in its pages "the mothball odor of old prize essays." In *The Nation*, McCarthy's old collaborator Margaret Marshall did not refrain from letting readers know that while the author had based her characters on real people, their portraits were no better than "caricatures."

### FROM DONALD BARR'S REVIEW IN *THE NEW YORK TIMES*, AUGUST 14, 1949

The author's failure—it is a distinguished failure—is due to the lack of a story. We simply do not care whether Utopia fails or succeeds.

### FROM MARGARET MARSHALL'S REVIEW IN *THE NATION*, SEPTEMBER 17, 1949

> She has wit and gusto; she also has a bent for fastening upon some ridiculous or petty or pathetic aspect of a personality and she takes delight not only in exposing this defect but in making it central[. . . .] And since she has no qualms about using her best friends and closest associates as material for her fiction, it is small wonder that *The Oasis* has been one of the lesser scandals of 1949.

With *The Oasis* Mary McCarthy learned a bitter lesson: to take your revenge in the pages of a literary magazine is one thing—there the response is either private or limited to a small number of readers—but a book is something else again. By the time the novel was published, Rahv's friends and her enemies had had a chance to muster their artillery. On August 22, she wrote Bernice Baumgarten, "Did you see Dawn Powell's review?!!!! Dear friends have thoughtfully supplied me with three copies of it. Reuel says he is telling his father that he needn't expect him to come in and make his bows when Miss Powell is calling." On September 23, she wrote Elizabeth Hardwick, "Did you see Margaret Marshall's piece? I felt like writing her a letter and saying: my literary position must be even worse than I had imagined if *you* have the courage to attack me."

She was posting these letters not from the cramped walk-up on Fifty-seventh Street that she and her young husband and her ten-year-old son had long since outgrown but from a spacious nineteenth-century farm-house in Portsmouth, Rhode Island. In June 1949 the Broadwaters had packed up and left New York. To many observers, their departure had seemed precipitate and their choice of Portsmouth surprising. But for the two adults involved, this move may have seemed both sensible and wise. For one thing, the lump sum was rapidly shrinking to the size of a pebble: to live a stylish life in New York can be costly, particularly when you have a child. For another, New York was rapidly losing much of its special appeal. Not until 1954 would another story by Mary McCarthy run in the pages of *Partisan Review*. Not until 1955 would she write another "Theater Chronicle" for the magazine.

Looking back, Mary McCarthy tended to credit Philip Rahv's fury to troublemakers like Delmore Schwartz—friends and acquaintances who had suffered at his hands and were now seizing this opportunity to pay him back. With *The Oasis* she had exposed an aching wound, which any-one who had access to Rahv was free to probe. She had also created a rift that threatened to become a chasm. After the damage was done, either she could sit back and bide her time and wait for Rahv's hurt feelings to mend, or she could cut her losses and move on.

From earliest childhood, patience had never been her strong suit. As soon as Reuel's term at St. Bernard's ended, she and Bowden Broadwater took their leave of the city. Once again, she had rushed to have the last word in print and ended by writing herself out of a relationship without ever quite intending to do so. Once again she had won a skirmish but somehow lost the war. This time, with some justice, Sidney Hook might have pointed out to her that it all went to show how little she understood about politics—at least politics as practiced in the increasingly acrimonious and contentious world of New York intellectuals. But Sidney Hook was not speaking to her.

# Chapter Thirteen

# NEWPORT

On June 24, 1949, three days after her thirty-seventh birthday, Mary McCarthy wrote Elizabeth Hardwick from Portsmouth, Rhode Island, where she and Bowden were living "like campers" in their new home. "There are of course all sorts of repairs we hadn't counted on, including those made necessary by the workmen themselves," she wrote. "The first day the movers drove in and took a branch off a tree; the plumber followed with an estimate of $270 to put in hot water, and backing out, ran into Bowden's car (much laughter), wrecking the rear fender and the taillight[. . . .] Yesterday a tattooed youth who was laying the linoleum in the kitchen managed to fall through two windows, on opposite sides of the room, so today the glazier is here[. . . .] Despite the havoc, I am very happy, Bowden too."

For sixteen thousand dollars, three quarters of it on mortgage, they had bought thirty acres of land, bounded by a low stone wall, and a white clapboard farmhouse that she would describe to her editor Katharine White as "four-square" and "frugal." In the process she had put Sidney Hook and the boys behind her, and found paradise. The farmhouse dated from the mid-nineteenth century. Of the thirty acres, fifteen were leased to a local dairy farmer, who had plowed them a vegetable garden. In a shaded grove on the property was an old family cemetery. Recently they had discovered the ruins of a formal garden, with two climbing white roses, myrtle, and one blooming peony.

Writing Hardwick from the one finished downstairs room, she was enjoying a brief interlude of sloth while Bowden attacked the lawn with a mower and scythe. There was work to do everywhere she looked. But seated in her "royal blue" kitchen with its "white wainscoting and woodwork" and "dark blue linoleum floor," she was lord of all she surveyed. "The red table is in the kitchen," she wrote, "and we have eaten our first regular meal, looking out on Mr. Lacerda's cows and the pond turned pink in the sunset."

The occasion for this ebullient letter was an announcement that Elizabeth Hardwick was engaged to marry Robert Lowell. Expressing her delight, McCarthy extended an invitation to the new couple to come see them "at once, next week, whenever Cal can leave." If they preferred, the two of them could stay at a "beautiful rooming place" nearby. Lowell, whose extreme agitation had turned to a full-blown mania necessitating shock treatments, was about to be released from a private mental hospital outside Boston. As if to dispel any doubts Hardwick might have as to the suitability of such a visit, she added, "Everything is incomparably beautiful and serene here."

An hour from Providence and some two hours from Boston, the village of Portsmouth was light years away from the Waldorf Conference and Europe-America Groups. Situated on the northern end of an island not much larger than Manhattan, overlooking the blue waters of Narragansett Bay, it was best known for the Priory, a Catholic boys' school run by the Benedictine Order very much along the lines of a well-established Episcopal church school. It was also known for Green Animals, a beautifully manicured estate directly across the road from the Priory, where you could find a menagerie of giant topiary animals and the menagerie's indefatigable guardian and owner, Miss Alice Brayton. Born in Fall River and just under five feet tall, this New England spinster made no apologies for her elitist opinions or for the arcane customs and ceremonies with which she conducted her relations with the world. On the Broadwaters' very first day, she had come to call, bringing a bouquet of sweet peas.

Portsmouth, for all its old-fashioned charm, was no rural backwater. Newport was a ten-minute drive from their door. Before the first great crop of millionaires thought to build monuments to their bottomless pockets, the young Henry James had summered there with his father and his sister Alice. The young Edith Wharton, too, had summered at Newport: among the more literary dowagers you could still find some who referred to her as "Pussy Jones."

Before taking leave of New York, Mary McCarthy had given her new Rhode Island address to the handful of friends still speaking to her. The two-line address was simple enough: Union Street, Portsmouth, Rhode Island. Unfortunately, with her very first letter to Elizabeth Hardwick she had to explain that as far as the postal service was concerned this address was "incorrect": "As you see, Newport is the address fated for us; Bowden has decided to take this as a mark of distinction."

"Fate" may have had a hand in it, but the Broadwaters had landed in Newport by no accident. The previous September, when the lease on the house in Cornwall was up and *The Oasis* was still unfinished, she and Bowden had moved on to Newport, where they had reserved a room at the very boarding house that she was recommending so warmly to Hardwick. Evidently they liked what they saw. A friend in New York had put them in touch with Nicholas King, recently graduated from Harvard and a member in good standing of an old Newport family, now working on the Newport paper. King, whose father was a cousin of Edith Wharton's, had been taken as a boy to visit the great lady of American letters at her house outside Paris. It was King who introduced the Broadwaters to Miss Brayton and it was King who helped find them a house.

In August 1948, just before Mary and Bowden first set off to test the waters, "American Town," a profile of Newport by Jean Stafford, had appeared in *The New Yorker*. When Stafford examined the monumental edifices and lush green lawns on Ocean Drive she was at once fascinated and repelled. For the Redwood Library, with its portraits of "local and national worthies" and its capacious reading room, Stafford had only praise. But when she wrote of Bailey's Beach—"where it costs something like fifteen hundred dollars to maintain a cabaña for the season and where only thoroughbreds can go (you will hear fifty times, if you hear once, that photographers and journalists with fountain pens are relentlessly kept out)"—she found little to please her.

It was old Newport—with its library and venerable synagogue and shabby eighteenth-century row houses—that Stafford found most congenial. But old Newport was about to undergo a metamorphosis. A preservation society had been established. The row houses were in the process of being restored. Long shuttered mansions were being turned into self-sustaining tourist attractions. New money was pouring in. None of this was really revolutionary, Stafford wrote. "This place has always been vigorous, because it has always attracted new blood and new money."

From the Broadwaters the town of Newport could hope to get no "new money." But it would be getting several quarts of new blood. With Miss Brayton and Nicholas King to take them around and vouch for them, they were made welcome by whole sectors of Newport society. They were made welcome with some hesitation, for it was known of course that Mrs. Broadwater was a writer with a gift for social satire. All the same, in a relatively short time, they were granted admission to some of Newport's more notable strongholds. Their first summer, they even made it to Bailey's Beach.

**GORE VIDAL** I remember getting reports directly or indirectly of her talking casually of the great figures she had met—many of them related to me, which she never knew. As Henry James pointed out, a social career is a career like any other. And quite as serious a career as any other. She had hit a point in life where social climbing was all-important to her. She felt that having conquered literature hands down—and she had in a way with Philip Rahv and Edmund Wilson and that entire issue of *Horizon* devoted to *The Oasis*—she must now leap into greater, or at least very different, glittering worlds. For someone who has read Henry James and has begun to see herself in that great line, what is next? Newport. And the gentry. Bowden was her introduction to that.

#### FROM MARY MCCARTHY'S LETTER TO ELIZABETH HARDWICK, AUGUST 22, 1949

This neighborhood, or perhaps its money, has in some way promoted the real proliferation of character. Everyone is strange, but not impotently so; these creatures have *realized* themselves in a positively tropical fashion. Middle-class suburbia in Westport, Westchester, Vermont, the Walshes, etc. in Red Hook, don't prepare one at all for the startling fact that one isn't bored outside of the *Partisan Review* circle. One feels on the edge of some exhilarating discovery, perhaps an illusion, but still. . . .

**CANDACE VAN ALEN**   My husband and I live in Newport. A neighbor who had a connection to St. George's Preparatory School asked me to a tea party. When I walked onto the terrace, there was a new Mary McCarthy, draped on a Recamier sofa, wearing a large picture hat and a flowing long chiffon gown. She languidly waved an arm at me—what a change from the Mary McCarthy at Vassar. There she had often seemed ill at ease, awkward, with unkempt hair and messily dressed. She obviously wanted to be noticed, so she made many startling statements that one could not ignore. At Newport all was different—and she went out of her way to act charmingly. It turned out that her son had just enrolled at St. George's summer school.

Mary McCarthy never quite made it into Newport society, but in the course of her Newport adventures she made two close friends: Mary Meigs, a shy young painter from an old Philadelphia family, and Nicholas King, Edith Wharton's tall young cousin, whom she would later say reminded her of Pierre in *War and Peace*. Neither was a newcomer to the area, and neither had ever come across anyone like this handsome and outspoken writer from New York. In time each would come to see her assault on Newport according to his own lights.

**MARY MEIGS**   When I first met Mary, I was terrified of her. She fascinated me in the way that keen-minded and sharp-tongued people always do. She was warm and friendly but seemed to observe and test people according to her high standards of good taste. I felt that I failed her tests again and again. At Newport, Mary loved going to parties in the impressive mansions of very rich people. Perhaps because I came from an old Philadelphia family, she was puzzled by my dislike for her Newport friends, whom she seemed to admire. Perhaps she was interested in them as a novelist, though they don't seem to have made it into any of her books.

**Nicholas King**  She and Bowden were both attractive and amusing and very sophisticated. They were bohemian in quotation marks, just as she was a Communist in quotation marks. I introduced them to some friends and relations and they made their way. I never thought twice about introducing Mary to my friends. The world of Newport is built on nastiness of tongue. It's a social place with a lot of rich people and of course they talk. People were supposed to be scared that Mary was going to write a novel about them, although I don't think they entertained that seriously. I don't think they were really scared. They were in fact disappointed that she never did, I think. Rather wistful that she hadn't made use of what they thought was a rich store of material.

About one thing everyone is in agreement: defying all expectations, she never made use of Newport in her fiction. Not until 1983 would she write directly about Newport, and then only in a memoir of Miss Brayton. As to her moving to Newport in order to conquer new worlds, one can with equal justice argue that she was beating a hasty retreat. Certainly, there were reasons other than social for the Broadwaters to choose the area. Bowden Broadwater—who, according to Gore Vidal, made it possible for her to contemplate such a campaign—would later say that they moved to Newport because it had an excellent library, easy shopping, and a school for Reuel.

Their first summer, the Broadwaters had little time to use this excellent library for much more than its reading room, which was stocked with every magazine the most fastidious of hearts might desire. In the fall they planned to make use of one of the little island's three first-rate private schools. The one they had chosen for Reuel, who would turn eleven that Christmas, was a conservative Episcopal school called St. Michael's in the town of Newport itself.

If Mary's letters that summer are to be trusted, she was mad for her new house. In a letter addressed to Reuel at Wellfleet, where he was spending all of June and July with his father, she wrote apprising him of the hard work they were doing and of two of the treats they had in store for him.

## From Mary McCarthy's Letter to Reuel Wilson,
### n.d. [c. July 1949]

We have been working so hard that we haven't had time to go in the water for weeks—Bowden has learned to be a 1st class painter, like a professional. Our bedroom has an all-white floor; yours will be a sturdy grey. There are millions of butterflies here. Is your net still in one piece? We miss you and talk about you a lot. Do ask your father if he knows where you can get a puppy.

In the end, Reuel would have not one dog but two, Blackie and Brownie. He would have ample room for old friends like Mike Macdonald to stay over. He would have a big backyard and acres of fields. He would have Upton Brady, a son of the assistant headmaster at the Portsmouth Priory, for a playmate. And he would have Ellen Brady, Upton's older sister, to baby-sit him when it was needed.

Still, the house was not without drawbacks. Unlike the house in Upper Red Hook, it had not come furnished. For the time being they would have to make do with country auctions and a loan from Nancy Macdonald, who had inherited some pieces she had no use for. Responding to an inquiry from Dwight Macdonald in early July, Mary wrote to apologize for not acknowledging sooner the delivery of a spool bed, a good assortment of fireplace utensils and andirons, some barrels of china, a desk chair, a gilt shelf she planned to refinish, and a fine eighteenth-century cherry wood desk she had placed in a prominent corner.

The Macdonalds did not make it to Portsmouth that first summer. Just as the Broadwaters' domestic life seemed to be growing ever more settled, theirs seemed to be coming apart. In 1948 Dwight Macdonald had announced to subscribers that henceforth *politics* would be a quarterly. Now he decided to call it quits. Having used up all their savings, the Macdonalds had been eating into Nancy's capital. But in every respect their resources were depleted. Nancy Macdonald had started seeing a psychoanalyst; Dwight had followed suit; and the two of them had embarked on a series of casual affairs. That fall Dwight would take a writing job at *The New Yorker*, joining the staff of the magazine he had taken down a peg or two in the first issue of *Partisan Review*.

Elizabeth Hardwick and Robert Lowell also never made it to Portsmouth. Instead, Mary McCarthy went up to Boston to serve as matron of honor at their wedding, lending the bride a hat to wear and lending the ceremony an air of festivity by wearing her black-lace Balenciaga. The groom had six hundred dollars to his name. After the wedding, Hardwick and Lowell went on to Red Hook, where they had sublet Fred Dupee's house. (But, by the end of the summer, Lowell was back in the hospital again, this time at Payne Whitney. A year later, he and Hardwick would be in Florence, on a Fulbright Fellowship.)

Fourth of July, Eve Gassler, who had replaced Bowden at *Partisan Review, did* come for the weekend with her fiancé, Al Stwertka. The two young people were soon put to work painting furniture and raking and scything the neglected garden, which in time would provide the setting for *their* small wedding. However, the talk was not of gardening that weekend but of current events—particularly of the Hiss trial, which was finally drawing to a close. When they were not debating whether Judge Kaufman was in fact a member of the Party or whether Mrs. Hiss was having an affair with Whittaker Chambers, they discussed the latest atrocities perpetrated by the *PR* boys. At one point they managed to touch on both topics simultaneously: "Wm. Phillips says Chambers is a saint, a man who (like himself) has sacrificed everything to principles," McCarthy reported to Elizabeth Hardwick.

Eve and her fiancé were not the only visitors. In August, Bob Linscott of Random House stopped by on his way north. Then Harold Rosenberg and his wife came to stay. The Rosenbergs were later joined by a young Belgian refugee by the name of Paul De Man, who had caught McCarthy's eye one evening at a party at the Dwight Macdonalds. In late August, Edmund Wilson personally dropped Reuel off. Apparently he found the Broadwaters' new arrangements satisfactory. He returned in September and stayed on for lunch, solidifying a rapprochement that had begun with *The Oasis*.

Over the course of the next three years, the Broadwaters would again receive Edmund Wilson, along with a stream of old friends and new acquaintances. Some, like Ellen Brady, lived just down the road. But the bulk of their visitors would come from farther afield—not only the Shafers from Bard, but Frani Blough Muser, McCarthy's best friend from Vassar, whose parents had a summer house close by. To all who spent any time with Mary and Bowden, it was clear that Mary was reveling in this gentle rural domesticity. But while she might savor her life as a Portsmouth housewife, she had not entirely lost her desire to shock.

**ELLEN BRADY FINN**   Remember those plastic bubble pipes you filled with water and they whistled like a bird. One of us in the family got one in our Christmas stocking and it was sitting on the coffee table. Mary and Bowden were on the sofa and Mary said, "What's that?" She picked it up and I showed her how it whistled like a bird. She said, "Oh, I thought it was a condom." That was not a word you dropped in a household like ours in 1950.

To sustain and maintain the Union Street household was going to take money. Bowden would eventually find a job writing book reviews for the *Providence Journal*, but the work he was seeking would never meet the mortgage payments or put food on the table. To support the family was up to the lady of the house. Much as she may have hoped for a different outcome, it was clear by their first fall that she could not look for much help from *The Oasis*. Even at their best, the reviews were not what publishers call "selling." But for the book's poor sales she also blamed Random House, which had disappointed her with an author's photo she felt made her look like "a mental defective" and with a first printing of only three thousand. Furthermore, she blamed Bob Linscott for declining, for the moment, to follow up *The Oasis* with a collection of her stories—a reluctance on his part that prompted her to write, but not mail, an angry letter, which she left for safekeeping with her agent until the fate of the stories was settled.

### From Mary McCarthy's Letter to Robert Linscott, October 6, 1949

> I must say I am extremely angry and offended with your disposition of the volume of short stories[. . . .] I am interested in a publisher who wants to publish me, mistakes and all, if they happen, and not in being "protected" so successfully from the consequences of error or failure that I cease to appear at all. The over-protective publisher is as bad as the over-protective mother, worse in that the author is not a child[. . . .] An author may not be the best judge of his work, but he is committed to it, and an editor who does not wish to be involved in this commitment would be wiser to relinquish any pretense at collaboration.

Bernice Baumgarten, like the good agent she was, began shopping the collection around to other houses. Whoever bought the collection would also be getting the author's next novel—a novel for which she had in hand a completed first chapter. At Harcourt Brace and Company she found a potential buyer in Robert Giroux, who was not only editor in chief but the editor of Jean Stafford and Robert Lowell. All was settled to everyone's satisfaction, until a week after the book was signed up, when Giroux had lunch with Jean Stafford.

**Robert Giroux**   Bernice Baumgarten, my favorite literary agent, told me Mary was unhappy at Random House, disappointed with the poor sales figures of *The Oasis*, a complaint familiar to all editors. When Bernice asked if I would like to see the new book, I said, "Yes, she's a good writer." She sent *Cast a Cold Eye* and I liked it and Harcourt Brace acquired a new writer. I had met Mary at cocktail parties but did not know her then as well as I did later. Jean Stafford was one of my closest friends and I was young. Naïvely I said, "Jean, we've signed up Mary McCarthy," and she froze. *"Who is her editor going to be?"* I said, "I suppose I'll be her editor." Jean said, "Well, you're not going to be *my* editor if you're hers." It was as if I'd been hit with a wet fish. That there might be a problem had never crossed my mind. After all, as writers Jean and Mary McCarthy were not in the least alike. I asked Denver Lindley, whom I had recently hired, to take on Mary's books and he was delighted to do so.

The move to Harcourt, with its false starts and hidden snags, would not be completed until midwinter. In the meantime, she was short of cash. Setting up a new house, like teaching, does not leave much time or energy for writing fiction. Although Katharine White at *The New Yorker* was always eager to see her stories and pay handsomely for them, publishable stories cannot necessarily be produced on demand. Fortunately,

Katharine White was not the only magazine editor eager to see her writing—or to pay for it.

In October 1949, twenty years after she had first passed through Taylor Gate, Mary McCarthy set off to research a piece for *Holiday* on the current state of Vassar's students and faculty. Her plan was to stay for at least a week at Alumnae House. She arrived to find Miss Sandison older and frailer and about to step down as chairman of the English Department. In a letter written after she had been at Vassar a week, she told Bowden of her pleasure in sharing with Miss Sandison their "secret." At the age of thirty-seven, she was again looking forward to the birth of a child. Miss Sandison had "instantly decided it would be a little girl."

In the same letter she also wrote of how she had taken herself to Bard for the weekend and run into a newly arrived Paul De Man, who, thanks entirely to her glowing recommendation, had been hired by Artine Artinian to take his place while he was on a year's sabbatical. (That Artinian would return to find the house he had rented to De Man a shambles and his favorite student pregnant by De Man, no one could foresee that weekend. That De Man had been a Nazi collaborator and had a wife and two sons in Argentina, no one had the slightest inkling. His less than exemplary behavior would not become general knowledge for three decades, by which time he was famous as a leading exponent of deconstructionism and safely dead.) At Bard, Mary saw Paul De Man both Saturday and Sunday. On Saturday, they had dinner together.

#### FROM MCCARTHY'S LETTER TO BOWDEN BROADWATER, OCTOBER 18, 1949

> Then P. read me in French his article on *The Oasis*, not a bad one, really, but like Cyril he felt he had to modulate his praises in deference to his audience—why? Off the record, he told me that he had read it a second time and that it was a work of exquisite craftsmanship, a perfect *conte philosophique* and even better than I realized (this I refuted by joining in the eulogy myself).

Ever after, she would refer to *The Oasis* as a "*conte philosophique*." If anything further passed between her and Paul De Man, it went unreported. The letter to Bowden closed on a less heady and emphatically gravid note:

> I've begun to feel a little uncomfortable; the second drink is all or perhaps slightly more than I can take. This place is rather spooky and nonconvivial, creaking with old ladies. The *emeritae* (wonderful word—like butterflies) have become a terrible problem to the college, on account of penicillin[. . . .] I miss you so much, maybe I'll call you up on the expense account, tonight after dinner with the Dean.

Confronted with the Vassar of 1949, Mary McCarthy found little to please her. Compared with the place she had known, the college seemed sadly lacking in distinction. Its students, with their pageboys and knitting and ready acceptance of the information fed to them, struck her as ordinary. Its new curriculum included a smattering of courses in the social sciences. Its teachers, many of them married with children, seemed to her lacking in the dedication that inspires a love of learning—a dedication to be found in the spinsters, now almost all of them *emeritae*, who had so diligently taught her. The school, for all that it appeared to be flourishing, was suffering from the same slackening and falling off she saw everywhere around her, the same incursions of the new postwar homogenization she had hoped to escape by moving to Portsmouth. Vassar was educating career women, club women, and suburban matrons. But, then, looking back on her own experience and those of her classmates, she had to conclude that Vassar's graduates had rarely lived up to the romantic ideal of Edna St. Vincent Millay, Vassar '17.

### From "The Vassar Girl"

[The] older Vassar career woman is nearly as familiar to American folklore as the intrepid Portia or Rosalind she may at one time have passed for. Conscious of being set apart by a superior education, confident of her powers in her own field of enterprise, she is impervious to the universe, which she dominates, both mentally and materially. On the campus, she is found at vocational conferences, panel discussions, committee meetings—she is one of those women who are always dominating, in an advisory capacity. In the world, she is met in political-action groups, consumers' leagues, on school boards, and in charitable drives, at forums and round-tables. Married, almost professionally so, the mother of children, she is regarded as a force in her community or business, is respected and not always liked.

The Vassar visit, with its interludes of solitude, forced her to take stock, something she rarely allowed herself to do. Unfortunately, it concluded with the disturbing discovery that the whole time of her visit she had been the object of a highly effective campaign of slander and innuendo.

### From Mary McCarthy's Letter To Bernice Baumgarten, February 8, 1951

[T]he story was circulated, within a day after my arrival, that I was another Elizabeth Bentley, an ex-Trotskyite converted to Catholicism, whose purpose was to expose Communism at Vassar, that two hours after my arrival I was closeted with the Catholic priest in Poughkeepsie, that I was an anti-Semite and was heard to say something about the "Jew teacher" in philosophy. This story was being spread by people I was seeing constantly, even eating meals at their houses, and was run to earth by one of my old teachers, the retiring head of the English department, who had forced certain people to deny it and who told me of it finally the night before I left.

"The Vassar Girl" would go on to enjoy a great success and to mark the beginning of her public disaffection with her alma mater, but it would not run for more than a year. Highly personal and indisputably controversial, it was much longer than the reporting ordinarily found in *Holiday*. It was also full of observations guaranteed to cause consternation among Vassar's alumnae and faculty—consternation that, she felt, had an effect on *Holiday*'s handling of the piece. Before long, the editing degenerated into a lengthy process of negotiation and compromise, which ended with her holding in her hands a set of galleys she found mysteriously altered. "The whole thing is very disturbing and these seemingly covert changes are the final nightmare touch," she would write Bernice Baumgarten.

But months before this protracted battle began, the writing of "The Vassar Girl" was attended by a *first* "nightmare touch." To celebrate their first Thanksgiving at Portsmouth she and Bowden were planning to have the Arthur Schlesingers and Macdonalds come stay for the holiday. Reuel, too, was to be there to take part in the festivities. It would be their first big family celebration in the house. She finally finished writing her original draft the Thursday before Thanksgiving. That same day, she suffered a miscarriage and had to go into the local hospital for a D & C.

### FROM MARY MCCARTHY'S LETTER TO
### DWIGHT AND NANCY MACDONALD, NOVEMBER 20, 1949

This letter is just a premonition. I'm writing it from Newport Hospital, where I've been since yesterday morning—a miscarriage, alas, rather long-drawn-out. I think I'll be out Monday and consequently should be well enough to have you for Thanksgiving, but in case it doesn't turn out that way, I thought I'd better warn you[. . . .] I'm taking a hopeful attitude. But there may be complications. The classic fall on the stairs Thursday morning brought this dismal result, just after, fortunately, I'd at last got my *Holiday* piece in the mail.

She had lost a baby she very much wanted and for a while it looked as if all their elaborate holiday plans would have to be canceled. In the end, Thanksgiving was celebrated as planned and in style. Nonetheless, for both Broadwaters the miscarriage was a loss that could not be brushed off easily. It was also a terrible drain on their budget. The money from *Holiday* would be gobbled up by her hospital bills. In time friends would help out. Arthur Schlesinger would tell James Wechsler, the editor of the

*New York Post,* that she was in need of money and Wechsler would commission her to write a long piece on night life in Greenwich Village, an assignment she would happily accept.

That first Thanksgiving at Portsmouth marked the first of many visits from the Macdonalds and the Schlesingers. Indeed the Macdonalds would make it a point to stop off whenever they drove to the Cape. Gradually Dwight Macdonald would see enough of this household, with its pretty rooms and carefully prepared dinners, to feel no compunction about labeling his old friend and her husband as frivolous. His own financial predicament may have blinded him to the underlying desperation. In any case, he saw her scramble to make money as being purely a matter of choice. For all that he was a loyal friend, he was not a tactful one. Nor was his hostess, who was not loath to tell him she very much regretted his killing off *politics*. With all this honesty, it wasn't long before the friendship began to show signs of strain.

### FROM DWIGHT MACDONALD'S LETTER TO NICOLA CHIAROMONTE, DECEMBER 21, 1950

Saw Mary once this fall en route from the Cape [. . .] she has made money by writing piece on Vassar for *Holiday* ($1,000), by selling two stories to *NYorker* (probably $2,000 to $3,000), and by doing a reportage series on Greenwich Village night life (VERY bad) last spring for the *N.Y. Post* ($800); Bowden doesn't do much of anything so far as I can make out—maybe he writes—but no one will take his stuff apparently; Mary is working on a novel about college life; she finds life in country boring, wants to revive *Politics* with me so as to Get In Touch again— she and Bowden would put it through a cheap local press there, Bowden would raise the dough, Mary and I would edit it—don't know, rather prefer to do it all myself if it is to be done—very fond of Mary but nervous about a certain frivolity, lack of responsibility, eccentricity there, esp. with Bowden around.

### FROM MARY MCCARTHY'S LETTER TO ELIZABETH HARDWICK, NOVEMBER 28, 1950

Dwight was here and we discussed reviving *politics*, but nothing came of it. He seems too dispirited and scattered to work. There is a sort of floating hatred in the air, like clouds ready to precipitate. One feels really that one dislikes nearly everyone and vice versa. Personal relations have become too sharp to be tolerated.

Dwight Macdonald's assessment of the ten-part Greenwich Village series was hardly unjust. In a letter to Arthur Schlesinger, the author herself referred to the series as "the Lesbian in the Brooks Brothers Suit." The joke was not far from the truth. In January 1950 she had spent two weeks in the city. On weekends Bowden came down from Portsmouth to join her. Weeknights, in the company of good friends like Eve and Al

Stwertka and the Macdonalds, she set off to explore the more notorious homosexual nightclubs and bars.

### From the Draft of "Greenwich Village by Night"

A blue-eyed, marcelled, white fag behind us suddenly begins to camp excruciatingly when we sit down at a table; the expletive, *tourist*, is trilled out with gestures, but this is the only open breach of the prevailing butch style[. . . .] With a new start, I recognize the handsome virile youth who in a different environment, with different associates, was proclaiming the other night that he was going to get laid.

Time has not been kind to "Greenwich Village at Night," which too often sounds as if it had been written by one of those disappointed Vassar graduates who lives with her husband and children in an expensive suburb and has no experience whatsoever with homosexuals. But these failures in tone did her no harm in Newport, where, according to Nicholas King, "everybody rushed to buy the *Post*." Sadly, time has not been appreciably kinder to another piece of writing which ran soon afterward and also caused a sensation in Newport—a *New Yorker* story called "The Old Men," which tells of a slender and fastidious young Harvard graduate, who has fallen off a ladder in the midst of kissing his host's wife, and is confined to a private room in a small New England hospital with a badly fractured arm. The young man and the hospital remain nameless. The story ends on the morning of his fifth day, when the young man is taken down to the operating room and dies on the table before his doctor, Dr. Z., makes his first cut.

**Ellen Brady Finn**  After her miscarriage, Mrs. Broadwater had to go into the Newport Hospital for a D & C. She went with Dr. Zelinski. He's Dr. Z in her story "The Old Men." She used to call the story "Bowdie's Curettage," and she said she wrote it to pay the hospital bills.

Vaguely surreal and almost allegorical, seeming to lay claim to some larger meaning it never quite earns, "The Old Men" at least provided McCarthy with a title for *Cast a Cold Eye*, her first official short story collection. "Cast a cold eye on life, on death, Horseman pass by" are the first words with which the young man greets his last day in the hospital. The words, the reader is told, come from the tombstone of William Butler Yeats.

The collection was brought out by Harcourt Brace and Company in late 1950 and was dedicated to Bernice Baumgarten, who had shepherded it from Houghton Mifflin, to Random House, and on to its final home at Harcourt, while listening patiently to its author's hesitations and second thoughts. At a low point during the summer of 1948, McCarthy had been eager to jettison the lead story, "The Weeds." Evidently it was the confessional nature of the story that most troubled her and, more to the point, troubled Bowden.

### FROM MARY MCCARTHY'S LETTER TO BERNICE BAUMGARTEN, OCTOBER 19, 1948

It seems to me to have dated horribly since its publication, to be over-literary, gushy, and (frankly) hysterical. If I had it to do over again, I should turn the story into a rather gruesome comedy, objectify both the heroine and the husband more, and make the whole thing a study in absurdity[. . . .] I am sensible, of course to the fact that "The Weeds" is, or was, the most popular of the stories[. . . .] Bowden thinks as I do, in fact even more strongly; he calls it a waterfall or a running faucet and cannot imagine that any treatment would have made it better.

The collection's title had also owed something to Bowden. Etching the letters of the title on the pale blue of the jacket so as to suggest a tomb-stone was his idea, too. The story he had dubbed a "running faucet" was followed by "The Friend of the Family," "The Cicerone," and "The Old Men" and three childhood memoirs, "Yonder Peasant, Who Is He?," "The Blackguard," and "C.Y.E." The jacket photograph of the author standing in front of an optometrist's eye chart no doubt seemed amusing at the time. "They'd gone down to New York and Mary had gone and bought a dress for the back cover and there was much discussion of that," Nicholas King later recalled. Robert Lowell had advised against the title, warning that reviewers would turn it against her ever after. He was proven right. Even in favorable reviews, the title came up.

### FROM DUDLEY FITTS'S REVIEW IN
### *THE NEW YORK TIMES BOOK REVIEW*, SEPTEMBER 24, 1950

Miss McCarthy's eye is cold indeed and almost surgically sharp; and while the object of its merciless contemplation may be a fictional Fran-cis Cleary or an actual grandmother remembered, the reader has a feeling of being watched, and just as coldly, himself.

### FROM ROBERT HALSBAND'S REVIEW IN
### *SATURDAY REVIEW OF LITERATURE*, OCTOBER 7, 1950

Whoever thought the Yeats quotation appropriate is guilty of an understatement, for Miss McCarthy casts a distinctly jaundiced eye on all the characters who pass before her, including—and this is her sav-ing grace—herself.

### FROM LOUISE BOGAN'S REVIEW IN *THE NEW REPUBLIC*, NOVEMBER 27, 1950

The title, borrowed from Yeats's epitaph, part of the later, rather the-atrical, pose of an old poet who never cast a cold eye at anything in his life, is not fitting, affixed to the work of a young woman part of whose maturing equipment should be warmth. An emotional factor, by a paradox, must exist even in satire, lest analysis become so neat, and rational judgment so detached, that they shrink to rather mean proportions everything they touch.

In 1950, still young, if increasingly fixed in reviewers' minds as the possessor of a rational judgment that lacked emotion or warmth, Mary McCarthy received a fellowship from the Guggenheim Foundation. The grant relieved her of the worst of her financial pressures and freed her to work full-time on the novel she had promised Harcourt. At Portsmouth, she had a room of her own and Bowden to do the cleaning and field all the small daily intrusions that eat up time and energy. She also had Bowden to help her with her work.

**ADELAIDE WALKER**   I don't think I ever had a letter from Mary once she was with Bowden. Not I mean a long letter or one with something really to say. He really acted as her secretary.

**NICHOLAS KING**   If he didn't in fact edit her, he certainly advised her in many ways. And, I would say, managed her. And his contribution was considerable. His taste. They talked constantly. I'm sure that he was of great importance in her life. She was very disciplined about her writing, although at one point she said she had to beg Bowden to lock her in.

In Portsmouth, if nothing else, she had found a community where she would not have to constantly be begging Bowden to keep her at her desk. Whether she had intended it or not, she had replicated on a more modest scale her off-season life with Wilson on the Cape. However, at Portsmouth, when she craved diversion on an off-season weekend there was no motley assortment of artists and writers to fall back on. Here she found herself among a small circle of New England Catholics and Protestants who hovered close by the gates of the Portsmouth Priory.

Very much a part of this circle, although her memory would relegate them to oblivion, were the Bradys, who lived in an eighteenth-century house on the grounds of the Priory. At its center was Miss Alice Brayton, who recognized no Lowell since James Russell and who struck Mary McCarthy during her first summer at Portsmouth as being "like some queer topiary animal herself." Writing at the end of her own life about Miss Brayton's successful assault on Newport society, she could only delight in her old neighbor's audacity. The assault had begun with the death of Miss Brayton's father in 1939.

### FROM "THE VERY UNFORGETTABLE MISS BRAYTON," BY MARY MCCARTHY

Despite the late start, when I met her ten years later, she had made it. Her social strategy, as carefully worked out as a Napoleonic battle plan, was based on reaching the child that she counted on finding in every Newport dowager and tycoon. After Father was gone, she started giving her lawn parties, featuring a big rented merry-go-round near the gate on the Priory side and a clambake on the beach below the railroad tracks, with well-stocked bars dotted about in between. These parties were an instant success[. . . .]

It was the child in Miss Brayton who knew that to succeed you must make a party an adventure or a treat. Even an ordinary afternoon visit to her garden, ending with a tray of strong martinis, obeyed a canonical rule of children's parties; each guest must get a present to take home.

Miss Brayton, for all that she prided herself on her plain speaking, was anything but plain or direct when discussing her own history. Sometimes she seemed to want to take credit for inventing her green animals and decorating the house, and other times she wanted her guests to believe that all of this had existed for centuries. By 1983, it was clear to Mary McCarthy that Miss Brayton was a "fabulist," a braggart, and a snob. But in 1949 her allure was considerable. From the tiny doyenne of Green Animals McCarthy learned the importance of serving the perfect martini at exactly the right temperature. She learned the value of domestic ritual and of homemade mayonnaise. And she learned that by laying a strip of tan canvas on your front steps you can achieve twice the effect of a fine antique runner at a fraction of the cost. Not least of all, she learned how to celebrate Christmas with panache.

**ELLEN BRADY FINN**   The Broadwaters' first Christmas there was a little auction and the children were given ten pennies to bid on presents. Miss Alice auctioned the presents herself. Reuel was a chubby little boy and he spent all his money on this great big gorgeous tinselly stocking full of candy. It was eleven o'clock in the morning and Reuel was hungry. The rest of us were biding our time and getting wonderful presents. Miss Alice was like a fairy godmother. You could get your heart's desire, if you waited. I remember I got an English teapot. For some reason Mary and Bowden were terribly upset by all this. I think they wanted Reuel to make an impression as a tasteful little boy. Afterward they came to our house—we had a party after Miss Brayton's every year—and Mary said that Miss Brayton had "cruelly psychoanalyzed her guests."

After Christmas, when the fog settled in and the cold would come off the bay, Miss Brayton headed south for New York, not to return to Newport until Easter. At the Bradys' they kept four fireplaces going and pleurisy was routine. Ice and snow made the roads precarious, but Mary and Bowden did not let this put a crimp in their weekend entertaining. One Sunday, when the Harry Levins came down from Boston with their daughter Masha, a sudden snow flurry resulted in an accident that promised to have a lasting effect on the friendship. Oddly enough, it was not the effect that the Broadwaters anticipated.

### FROM MARY MCCARTHY'S LETTER TO ELIZABETH HARDWICK, JANUARY 25, 1951

A terrible thing, on the Mount Hope Bridge, covered with ice, Bowden was involved in a three-car collision that knocked out Masha's six front teeth (nobody else hurt) while the Levin family was being driven back from a day in the country here. Awful; insurance very slightly mitigates one's feelings and (I hope) theirs. It seems a sort of judgment on us for buying a new Studebaker convertible—second-hand but completely redone and luxurious[. . . .] She didn't shed a tear or utter a sound during the whole thing. She's still in bed and apparently will have to be hospitalized to have the roots extracted. Naturally, this leaves us linked with the Levins for life—a strange outcome to a Sunday invitation.

**ELENA LEVIN**   What happened was I couldn't stand being with them after that. I knew it wasn't their fault, but I just couldn't stand seeing them.

The eventual outcome of that terrible accident may have owed little to the crash itself. From the start of the day's visit, Mary had been talking exclusively to Harry Levin. As the snow got heavier and it was past time for her guests to depart, she was deep in conversation with him. When, at last, she was ready to see her guests to the car, the roads were hazardous. As Elena Levin saw it, they were lucky they didn't die.

The Levins were not the only couple who chose to see no more of the Broadwaters. And Elena Levin was not the only wife to find her husband's attention monopolized by Mary McCarthy. On visits to Portsmouth, Arthur Schlesinger's wife, Marian, simply put up with being "always sort of on the sidelines." But Diana Trilling, who prided herself on having "something of a reputation" as book critic for *The Nation*, would have none of it. Having endured one dinner on Fifty-seventh Street, during which her hostess concentrated all her attention on Lionel, she was not about to subject herself to a repeat performance. As she later told it, Lionel agreed with her completely: "When we got out the door the very first thing my husband said was 'How can an intelligent woman suppose that the way to charm a man is to be publicly rude to his wife?'"

Sad to say, when it came to friendship Mary McCarthy could be accused of operating by a double standard. If you were a woman friend she had made on her own—Elizabeth Hardwick or Hannah Arendt, Eve Gassler or Margaret Shafer—she was delighted to welcome you. If you were merely the wife of a male friend, you received short shrift. The striking exception to this rule was Augusta Dabney, Kevin's wife. To win McCarthy's affection you did not have to be a writer or intellectual. But you had to possess—at least in her view—no pretensions of being anything other than exactly what you were. Finally, honesty counted for as much as sheer accomplishment. When at last she found both qualities united in one person, as she did in Hannah Arendt, the friendship grew into something akin to love.

Arendt had been traveling in Europe at the time of the move to Portsmouth, but, thanks in large part to the efforts of Dwight Macdonald, the two women stayed in touch. The friendship, which had started up in 1949 with Arendt's enthusiastic response to *The Oasis*, was cemented in 1951 when Mary wrote to say how much she admired *The Origins of Totalitarianism*, Arendt's magisterial and highly original first book in English—an instant classic, which first searched out and then located the roots of twentieth-century totalitarian systems in the preceding century and went on to declare that, impossible as it might seem, Nazism and Stalinism were in crucial ways virtually identical.

### FROM MARY MCCARTHY'S LETTER TO HANNAH ARENDT, APRIL 26, 1951

> I've read your book, absorbed, for the past two weeks, in the bathtub, riding in the car, waiting in line in the grocery. It seems to me a truly extraordinary piece of work, an advance in human thought of, at the very least, a decade, and also engrossing and fascinating in the way that a novel is: i.e., that it says something on nearly every page that is novel, that one could not have anticipated from what went before but that one then recognizes as inevitable and foreshadowed by the underlying plot of ideas.

By the time she wrote of her passion for Arendt's big new book, the friendship was on a sound footing. But *The Origins of Totalitarianism* may well have altered the balance, if ever so slightly, by transforming Hannah Arendt from just another brilliant German Jewish refugee to a world-famous intellectual. In addition, the book's success made it possible for Arendt to move to a spacious apartment on Morningside Drive, where there would always be a guest room available for her friend in Rhode Island.

Before long, McCarthy would be availing herself of that guest room with pleasure. For the moment, though, she was committed to finishing as quickly as possible the novel she was writing for Harcourt. The political situation on the mainland had not improved since her vexed stay at Vassar. In "The Vassar Girl" she had not gone into the whispering campaign that had been started against her. However, the question of whether a member of the Communist Party has the right to teach—a question very much in the air during the two-week period when she was being called a Communist turncoat—had become the linchpin of the ingenious plot for a novel she had begun working on full-time once she received her Guggenheim.

The novel was called *The Groves of Academe*. With an ironic nod to Horace, whose second epistle provides the epigraph for the novel—"*Atque inter silvas academi quaerere verum*" (And go seek for truth in the groves of academe)—she set out to show that truth was a very rare commodity among the denizens of academia. During the early spring of 1951, the first chapter came out in *The New Yorker*, setting the scene for the amusing contretemps that would give the novel both its zest and its plot. In the very first paragraph Henry Mulcahy, a Joyce scholar and well-known campus radical, receives the news that his one-year contract at Jocelyn College has not been renewed by Maynard Hoar, the college president. The chapter reaches its climax with Mulcahy's choosing a weapon that will leave Jocelyn's president with no defense. Mulcahy will let it be known that his wife is desperately ill, that he has been hired with the promise of tenure, and that the president, an avowed liberal and champion of political freedom, has fired him solely because of his left-wing politics.

The book came out in February 1952, not quite a year later. (The last third of the manuscript had been completed in one great spurt, by dint of her writing as many as eighteen hours a day.) She had sprung *The Oasis* on Philip Rahv with no warning—giving troublemakers around *Partisan Review* a chance to poison Rahv against her. That February, she wrote Fred Dupee to say she had asked Harcourt to send him a copy of *The Groves of Academe*. She also wrote to warn him not to imagine he saw himself in Howard Furness, the "deeply mistrustful" chairman of the Jocelyn literature department, who has a "sharp, dapper mind," "bright delft-blue eyes" and "flat, rather wooden features," and who refuses to join his colleagues in supporting Henry Mulcahy. This warning may have prevented a complete break with Fred Dupee, but it did not make him like her or her book any better.

### From Mary McCarthy's Letter to Fred Dupee, February 2, 1952

In lieu of an inscription ( which I can't do from here), let me send love and warmest wishes to you and Andy. Also the assurance that no character in the book is based on my idea of you. You said to me last summer, "You've got all of us in it," but, as you will perceive, I haven't; the design of the book, if nothing else, precluded individual portraiture. In a way, I should have liked to have made a drawing of you, just for the challenge of it but this was not the occasion for it: characters in motion make certain functional demands.

Three months later she was still trying to explain what she had done.

### FROM MARY MCCARTHY'S LETTER TO FRED DUPEE,
### MAY 19, 1952

Furness, now that we mention it, is a cow-country version of one
salient of yourself, mixed with some people at Sarah Lawrence and
elsewhere. He could not have written the James book and must remain
a fixture at Jocelyn. He is right, of course, all along about Mulcahy and
the other people, and it is not a case of "right for the wrong reasons,"
horrid modern cliché, but right with insufficient aplomb, right with a
touch of grievance; here he becomes related to Mulcahy. I hope the
book is not too spiritualized, as you hint. The intention was a certain
even-handed justice, which of course remains beyond human grasp.

*The Groves of Academe* came out to generally positive reviews. As a
novelist she had grown more skillful and she had chosen a target that a
fairly wide audience could appreciate. Her talent was never in question.
But some reviewers had reservations about the way she treated some of
her characters.

### FROM ALICE MORRIS'S REVIEW IN *THE NEW YORK TIMES*,
### FEBRUARY 24, 1952

Miss McCarthy's satiric manner is based on a stunning, narrowly
aimed accuracy rather than on exaggeration. While she provides her
specimens of men and women with few softening extra-curriculum
features, neither does she deny them their humanity by making caricatures of them.

### FROM BRENDAN GILL'S REVIEW IN *THE NEW YORKER*,
### FEBRUARY 23, 1952

We see from the first page that Miss McCarthy is savagely at home
in academic life. Without wasting a gesture, she ransacks the desk of
the faculty and picks their pockets as they sit unwitting in department
meetings[. . . .] Their pretensions and fears, their shabby lust for
tenure—she thrusts it all out to us as if at the end of bare, strong fingers[. . . .] Putting down the book, so bristling with life, so crammed
with talent, and yet so cold, we cannot help thinking how much greater
an artist Miss McCarthy might be if she would only take things less
hard, if she would sweeten her astringency a little. Her standards of
conduct are so high that they are practically out of sight.

### FROM DELMORE SCHWARTZ'S REVIEW IN *PARTISAN REVIEW*,
### MAY–JUNE 1952

Miss McCarthy, as a friend of mine observed, writes intellectual journalism masquerading as fiction and asking to be unmasked. She is, I
think, one of the cleverest women around; but there is an ancient and
little remembered maxim that to be entirely clever is to be half a fool.

In 1952, depending on your perspective, *The Groves of Academe* was
wonderfully droll or terribly mean-spirited, her best book or a falling off.

If you'd had your fill of loyalty oaths and witch-hunts, you could only admire the novel's audacity—the way Henry Mulcahy saves himself by pretending to be a Communist. If you had a passing acquaintance with Harold Taylor, you immediately recognized him as the model for Maynard Hoar, the good-looking college president who makes the mistake of granting Henry Mulcahy an extra year without believing for a minute that he was ever a Communist and then fatally compromises his own integrity by getting caught questioning a visiting poet about Mulcahy's purported Party membership.

If you had spent some time at Annandale-on-Hudson, you spotted Lincoln Reis, the bane of Bard's philosophy department, as the inspiration for Henry Mulcahy. You spotted Fred Dupee as Howard Furness, the chairman of the literature department who is a little sweet on Domna Rejnev, the Russian bluestocking and deluded Mulcahy supporter. You recognized Irma Brandeis in Alma Fortune, the lover of Goethe and Jane Austen who tenders her resignation in support of Mulcahy. You recognized Fritz Shafer in John Bentkoop, the wholesome and upright teacher of Philosophy who joins Domna and Alma in Mulcahy's support. And you spotted Artine Artinian as the model for Aristide Poncy, the temporizing chairman of the literature and languages division who has a "taste for colonial or, as it were, secondary sources of a language" in the teachers he hires and little taste for chaperoning the students he takes abroad.

At the end of his life, Harold Taylor, who believed that not only Jocelyn's president but Jocelyn itself owed as much to McCarthy's teaching stint at Sarah Lawrence as it did to Bard, had the grace to credit her with a job well done.

**HAROLD TAYLOR**    I was looking at *Groves of Academe* last summer because I'm doing my autobiography. I was redoing the chapter on Randall and Mary. I read the book again and it's very good. It's packed with authentic detail. She's caught the attitude of the softhearted liberal. Randall Jarrell's book doesn't have the intricacy of Mary's observations about the liberal faculty members in a progressive environment. I don't think there's anybody who has better caught the flavor of an intellectual community where everything is permitted.

Looking back, it was possible for Harold Taylor to see that some of her observations about her characters had actually been quite accurate. When the book came out, he naturally lacked that sort of perspective. But you didn't have to see yourself in the book to object to the way that she treated her characters. What she saw as "even-handed justice," Dwight Macdonald saw as condescension. While his not liking the book reflected, to some degree, the state of his relations with its author, that did not make his critical assessment any less valid.

**FROM DWIGHT MACDONALD'S LETTER TO NICOLA CHIAROMONTE, FEBRUARY 14, 1952**

Mary's new novel, *The Groves of Academe*, is out and she sent me a copy. Alas, me no like. The trouble is she is so damned SUPERIOR to her characters, sneers at some of them and patronizes the rest. Also, usual static quality, even worse than in *Oasis*, acres of intellectual arguments, back and forth, like a tennis match[. . . .] WHY does she have to be so goddamned snooty, is she god or something? You begin to feel sorry for her poor characters, who are always so absurd or rascally or just inferior and damned—she's always telling them their slip's showing. She doesn't *love* them, that's [the] trouble, in sense of not feeling a human solidarity and sympathy with them—can't create real characters without love, or hate which is also a human feeling; she has just contempt and her poor puppets just wither on the page. Is she really like that? She doesn't seem so when I see her. Or is she just kidding *me* along too, and making all kinds of snooty little footnotes in her head as we talk?

**FROM CHIAROMONTE'S LETTER TO MACDONALD, APRIL 24, 1952**

Miriam has read *The Groves of Academe* and didn't like it. I have read only one chapter (on advise [*sic*] from Hannah Arendt), the one on the College setup. I found it very clever and confused. If Mary only learnt to stick to some line of consistent development, instead of showing off in all directions. She has a genuine talent for satire, and she is really intelligent. But she should make up her mind about some conclusion— nihilistic satire, or just play. But not both at the same time[. . . .] The trouble with so many intelligent Americans, it seems to me, is formlessness, not knowing where to stop, and wanting it both ways[. . . .] However, I like Mary's mind very much. There is something really generous and passionate about it, for all her smartness.

From Chiaromonte's letter we know that Hannah Arendt advised him to read the opening chapter of *The Groves of Academe* but we have no written record of what Arendt herself said to the author. Whatever she said was said in person—and, one can safely assume, laced with warmth and affection. By 1952, Mary McCarthy was staying in that spare room on Morningside Drive with some frequency.

The loyalty oaths and witch-hunts she had portrayed in her new novel could hardly be dismissed as a thing of the past. Indeed, the world of *The Groves of Academe* was rather pallid compared with what you could come across in the real world. Thanks to the McCarran Act, foreigners who were known Communists or who possessed suspect political pasts could not enter the United States. In the U.S. Senate, leading a rapidly swelling army of right-wing senators from both major political parties was a florid and unattractive demagogue from Wisconsin with the unfortunate surname of McCarthy. Having turned his Senate committee meetings into a public sideshow, this red-baiting populist was going after Communists in the highest reaches of the State Department—particularly those who belonged to what was now commonly referred to as "the Eastern establishment." Unabashedly xenophobic and anti-intellectual, Joseph R. McCarthy's brand of anticommunism was fast becoming an instrument of class aggression. Faced with Joe McCarthy and an increasingly vocal and militant band of right-wing anti-Communists, the anti-Communists of the Left were temporizing and arguing that Stalin posed a more serious threat to civil liberties than any obstreporous U.S. senator.

### FROM MARY MCCARTHY'S LETTER TO HANNAH ARENDT, MARCH 14, 1952

I can't believe that these people seriously think that stalinism on a large scale is latent here, ready to revive at the slightest summons; but if they don't think this what *do* they "really" think or are they simply the victims of momentum? My impression is that the fear is genuine, but so to speak localized. They live in terror of a revival of the situation that prevailed in the Thirties, when the fellow-travelers were powerful in teaching, publishing, the theatre, etc., when stalinism was the gravy-train and these people were off it and became the object of social slights, small economic deprivations, gossip and backbiting.

Sidney Hook, as the chairman for the Committee for Cultural Freedom, was perhaps the most visible anti-Stalinist to refrain from speaking out against Joe McCarthy. The committee he chaired was no more intrepid than he was. With loose ties to the better funded and far more influential Congress for Cultural Freedom in Europe, the Committee for Cultural Freedom boasted a catholic membership embracing liberals like Lionel and Diana Trilling, the grand old man of radical politics Max Eastman, the former Trotskyist James Burnham, and militant anti-Communists like William Barrett. In its size and in the breadth of its membership, the Committee for Cultural Freedom bore little resemblance to the core group that had formed at Dwight Macdonald's apartment in response to the Waldorf Conference. But size apparently did not confer courage, and diversity did nothing to dispel discord.

On March 29, almost three years to the day after the big Waldorf Conference of 1949, the Committee for Cultural Freedom held a conference of its own at the very same place. Mary McCarthy returned to the Waldorf, not as an umbrella-wielding member of the audience but as an invited dignitary seated on the platform, the author of a new novel that addressed, albeit somewhat irreverently, the very topic she had been invited to discuss: "Who Threatens Cultural Freedom in America Today?" The only woman on a five-member panel, she was slated to speak in the morning, after Elmer Rice and her friend Richard Rovere. As a public speaker, she was at her best fielding questions from the audience. But the speech she gave that morning was such that no one in the audience was likely to nod off. "Cultural freedom" in its *narrowest* sense was alive and well in America, she announced. Seditious ideas and books were free to circulate. Unfortunately, the men who gave voice to these ideas and the authors of these books were not.

### FROM "NO NEWS, OR, WHAT KILLED THE DOG," BY MARY MCCARTHY, *THE REPORTER*, JULY 1952

The ideas circulate and the individual is imprisoned—this, I fear, is the paradox toward which our society is floating, almost against its will. I have heard it said in all innocent plausibility that the Committee for Cultural Freedom ought not to criticize Senator McCarthy because McCarthyism is not a cultural phenomenon but an "event" in the sphere of politics, quite independent of culture, i.e., of books and statuary[. . . .]

What we will do, however, if we persist in our demands for loyalty, a positive citizenship, testimonials, confessions of error, in the investigative methods of McCarthy and McCarran, will be to create new underground men behind the façade of conformity, new lies, new evasions, new human beings who float like glittering icebergs on the surface of society, with the perilous eight-ninths submerged. We will live in a society of surfaces, where papers and books circulate freely, like so many phantom abstractions, while their human authors and readers have been suppressed or excluded from the country.

In his notes, Dwight Macdonald credited her talk with making "the deepest impression intellectually" of all the speeches given. But it would seem that a deep intellectual impression was not what was called for that day. The last speaker on the panel was Max Eastman, who had taken a sharp turn right. He created a sensation by announcing that the witch-hunts of the day were nothing compared to what he had witnessed before World War I. "The real threat to cultural freedom," announced Eastman, "is the worldwide Communist conspiracy."

On April 23, when the committee's board met to approve a final draft of an official policy statement, Macdonald made one last try to turn its members around. He argued that it was not enough to speak out against the use of "half-truths, insinuations and outright lies as a political technique" or to condemn "the amoral doctrine that the ends justifies the means." He argued that *they*, too, had to name names: that is, they had to say, "The chief current exponent of this doctrine on the American scene is Senator McCarthy."

Macdonald's motion for speaking out against the most visible source of "half-truths, insinuations and outright lies" was quickly voted down. In the small band voting with him were Philip Rahv and Arthur Schlesinger. Rahv, Macdonald noted, accepted the defeat "with the air of a veteran crusader for lost causes." Arthur Schlesinger, not yet inured to such setbacks, slipped off to devote his energies to getting Adlai Stevenson elected president.

Mary McCarthy was not present. But having taken the measure of both the right-wing anti-Communists and their counterparts on the Left, she was not ready to hold her tongue. Within months of the Cultural Freedom Conference, she delivered a second speech at a teachers' convention in the Midwest.

### FROM "THE CONTAGION OF IDEAS"

The initiated anti-Communists subscribe to a doctrine that one might call Gresham's Law as transferred to the field of ideas—the notion that bad ideas drive out good. According to this notion, Communism is an idea that is peculiarly contagious. The Communists may be few in number, but their ideas are felt to have a mysterious potency that other ideas do not possess[. . . .] Everyone who has had any experience of teaching knows how difficult it is to indoctrinate a pupil with anything—with the use of algebraic symbols, the rules of punctuation, the dates of American history; yet a Communist teacher, presumably, can "infect" *her* pupils with Marxism-Leninism-Stalinism by, to quote one writer, "the tone of her voice"[. . . .]

The proof that we do not regard Communists as lunatics is precisely this fear we have that their ideas may be catching, this fear, as I say, of the "germ" of truth.

Speaking out as a private citizen was satisfying. But to make a real difference she would have to take direct action. That summer, she seriously considered putting aside her writing to go to Harvard Law School. It was her plan to use her law degree to argue civil liberties cases in the courts. She was talked out of this quixotic return to academia by an old friend of Edmund Wilson's, a federal judge of the Court of Appeals who made the trip up from Delaware to point out to her that by the time she was qualified to defend the Constitution of the United States in the courts she would be almost fifty.

Whether it was owing to this setback or to influences more complicated, a new novel she had started—which had as its inspiration her stay at Vassar and had as its subject eight Vassar graduates from the class of '33—was not going well. Finally, she put the novel aside. Later, she would tell interviewers, that she had felt that she was beating up on those poor Vassar girls. But it would seem that politics had as much to do with her flagging interest as compassion. Added to this there may have been a touch of exhaustion. During her three years at Portsmouth she had pushed herself to the limit. As early as March, when the political situation was first beginning to absorb all her attention, she was already sounding like a fiction writer who would like nothing better than to escape from her typewriter.

### From Mary McCarthy's Letter to Hannah Arendt, March 14, 1952

> I so envy your going to Greece, or, rather, I wish that we too could be there this summer. What has happened about the magazine? In my desk drawer, I have dozens of suggestions for articles, drawn up on previous occasions, for a new magazine. They're mostly all still good; they remain to be done by someone. Doubtless, Dwight has a regular morgue of them too.

By the summer of 1952, she was over her infatuation with Newport. The move to Rhode Island had been made in large part to provide Reuel with a better place to live and a pool of three first-rate schools. Reuel was now thirteen years old. He had made new friends and had started seeing a bit of the daughter of the editor of the local paper, but the schools had not been all that she had hoped for. That fall, Reuel was slated to set off for Brooks, a prep school in Massachusetts with strong connections to Harvard.

The move to Newport had been made for Reuel but it had also been made to free both Mary and Bowden to write fiction. While she had done more than her fair share of writing, she was now experiencing a bad case of writer's block. For her, Newport itself had never been a source of inspiration. For Bowden, however, it had been—at least for a time. In December 1949 she had informed Elizabeth Hardwick that Bowden had written a Newport story "which, if published, will leave us in no decision as to what our proper sphere is." Two years later, she was writing Hardwick that he had finished another Newport story called "The Last Resort," which was "a poem to the social forms and longevity." Neither story ever found a publisher.

The summer of 1952, she returned from a visit to an ailing and senile Augusta Preston to find that Bowden Broadwater was intent on putting their carefully restored house on the market. A developer had bought the property across the road from them and was in the process of subdividing it. Their rural retreat was about to become a suburb, and not a very elegant one at that. No longer would Miss Brayton be able to introduce them to Newport socialites as the young couple who kept a "real farm" in Portsmouth. As Bowden saw it, they would do well to get out while the going was good.

Fortunately, leaving her pretty white clapboard farmhouse was not going to be the hardship it might once have been. In 1951 Nicholas King had left to take a job with Reuters in London. And while she continued to savor Miss Brayton's hospitality, she was having increasing difficulty with some of the views she heard her diminutive friend express. She was also having increasing difficulty brushing off the opinions she heard expressed at Newport dinner parties. From the mouths of dowagers and walruses she was hearing the same sentiments that were being voiced by the likes of Joe McCarthy. Her hosts' fine china and silver did not make these sentiments any more palatable. At forty she was no longer the brash young rebel who gleefully told the stuffy guests at John Peale Bishop's dinner party that her maiden name was Katz. All the same, at the podium and at the dinner table she did not hesitate to call a spade a spade.

"Crushed between the millstones of the proletariat—the proliferating little houses across the street here that breed like slum populations—and the plutocracy in Newport, we're selling our house. In fact, we've sold it," she announced to Dwight Macdonald in October 1952. Once the house was sold she and Bowden had two options available to them. They could return to New York, or they could pack their bags and go abroad. Back in the city, she would be forced to look for another cheap apartment and to deal once again with the boys at *Partisan Review*. Abroad, she would have the Chiaromontes in Rome, Nicholas King in London, and the Lowells in Amsterdam, where they had settled after their Fulbright year in Florence. Living abroad, her money would go further and she would not be without friends. But she and Bowden would be without a place for their books and silver and furniture.

"I liked living in Portsmouth. I was sorry when they sold that house," Reuel Wilson would later say. The house was sold with the stipulation that they could stay on until the day after Christmas so that Reuel would have, at least for the moment, some vestige of a mooring. As a family the Broadwaters celebrated one last big Thanksgiving in Portsmouth. After that, they prepared to take their leave of the cows and the dogs and Miss Brayton. By Christmas, the pretty linen curtains and Nancy Macdonald's fine cherry desk were bundled away in storage. Soon there was nothing tethering them to Rhode Island—or to America for that matter. Once the sale went through, Reuel was not the only member of the family to be cut adrift.

# Chapter Fourteen

# New York

If you don't like the way things are going, you can stand and fight or you can pick up and leave. Or, when all else fails, you can try to turn back the clock. On October 7, 1952, intent on putting behind her the first house she could call her own, Mary McCarthy sent Hannah Arendt a double-spaced typed letter from the temporary haven she had found at Dwight Macdonald's house in Wellfleet, on the Cape. "[I]t's extraordinarily beautiful," she wrote, "wild and woodsy, with steel-blue ponds mirroring each other and the pine trees—an arcadia at this season when the summer Pans have fled. This rustic life is a sort of consolation for the real estate we're losing, an assurance that far fields are greener. Perhaps we shall end by buying something here, for when we come back from Europe."

Never one to put off for tomorrow what she could do today, she did not wait to see how much greener those "far fields" might be. Within a week she had set her heart on a pretty red eighteenth-century farmhouse on Pamet Point Road and made an offer. The house was nothing like as grand as the house off Route 6 where she had lived with Edmund Wilson, nor was it as substantial as the house she was selling in Newport. It was not winterized, but it appeared to be within their means. When they tired of living abroad they would have a place to come back to. A place where Reuel could join them for the August weeks his father made his annual pilgrimage to Tanglewood. The house would provide some semblance of a mooring and a place to store their furniture and books.

That it was only minutes away from Wilson and his new family seemed to be of no consequence to her. In the letter to Hannah Arendt her attention was focused on the current presidential campaign: the Democratic candidate, Adlai Stevenson, she declared to be "the only political figure who's awakened my curiosity in years." Once again she was talking of starting up a new magazine—one that would concentrate on political analysis and social criticism and provide a forum for writers to make sense of what was going on. This new magazine, unencumbered and clear in its vision, would stay clear, very much the way *politics* and the old *Partisan Review* once had, of all cant and received opinion.

That there was a need for such a magazine she herself never questioned. Certainly as a writer she had experienced such a need firsthand. *Politics* was long dead and *Partisan Review* was closed to her, at least for the moment. In any case, *Partisan Review* had moved so far to the right she was completely out of sympathy with it. Under the title "No News, *or*, What Killed the Dog," her March talk at the Waldorf had finally found a home at Max Ascoli's *The Reporter*, a liberal fortnightly which her friends Arthur Schlesinger and Richard Rovere sometimes wrote for. It had been her third piece for Ascoli. The trouble was, she didn't much like him. Later she would call him a coward. More important, almost no one she cared about read *The Reporter*. Its pages lacked intellectual cachet.

As early as 1950, she had tried to persuade Dwight Macdonald to resurrect *politics*. In the process she had let him know what she thought of his joining *The New Yorker*, and relations between the two of them had never fully recovered. In 1951 she had reproached Macdonald for not doing justice to *The Origins of Totalitarianism* in a review he had written. In 1952, having taken advantage of his generous offer of the Cape cottage, she called him up short for accepting a trip to Europe from a wealthy admirer who was also a supporter of Senator McCarthy. "I believe there are some things which are absolutely false and evil, while you, I think, have a more relative view," she announced, letting him know that both Simone Weil and Leo Tolstoy saw things precisely as she did.

By enlisting Hannah Arendt's support, she was able to persuade Dwight Macdonald to at least consider the possibility of a new magazine, but he held firm in refusing to serve as its guiding force. In time she invited Richard Rovere and Arthur Schlesinger to join them. But as the fall drew to a close she was no longer content to limit herself to the pleasures of an occasional postprandial planning session. On December 2, she took time off from packing up the Portsmouth house to let Hannah Arendt know how things stood with her in the wake of Stevenson's crushing defeat by Eisenhower. "The election results have held me in a state of bitter exaltation for nearly a month; it was a queer abrading experience to get them at Arthur Schlesinger's and feel almost treacherous for having anticipated them," she wrote. Prompted by these election results, she and Rovere and Schlesinger had come up with a plan to assemble a group of six to ten writers and move in on *The Reporter*, where they would "concentrate fire," and mount a "concerted attack" on the new intellectual Right. "Ascoli, they say, is desperate—mainly for money reasons— and will listen to any proposal," she wrote.

Still, she was far from reconciled to a plan she believed to be "defi-

nitely second-best." Two days later, she was writing Schlesinger and
Rovere, trying to spell out what it was each of them really wanted from
the magazine they had discussed starting from scratch. She had concluded that Schlesinger and Rovere wanted a weekly or fortnightly somewhat like the old *Nation* and not unlike the current *Reporter*. She, on the
other hand, wanted a monthly "with no ideal of coverage, no consumer-
angle, analytic and satirical rather than newsy or crusading."

What she wanted, though she was not prepared to admit it even to
herself, was *politics* with an editor at the helm who believed that there
were "some things which are absolutely false and evil." But to edit such
a magazine would mean living much of the year in New York and giving
up her plans to go to Europe. Even though she would be joining forces
with Hannah Arendt, whom she had described to Elizabeth Hardwick as
"the only person I see regularly with whom one can have a 'normal' conversation," she would not be able to limit her time to company so congenial. To get financial backing for the magazine she would have to look
to rich businessmen and foundations. To enlist contributors she would
have to make peace with the men and women she had alienated with
*The Oasis*, including Philip Rahv.

Writing Hannah at the beginning of December, she had to confess
that her plans were still in flux. One thing, however, seemed settled: she
and Bowden had tickets to depart on the *Ile de France* on January 14.
Forced to leave Newport the day after Christmas, they were taking an
apartment in New York for three weeks. She was trying to get Isaiah Berlin
to secure a speaking engagement for her at Oxford. She had plans to come
down to the city on December 9 to meet George Orwell's widow and to
talk further with Richard Rovere. "Too many irons and not enough fire,"
she noted with some asperity. She was still planning to go to Europe. "But
I'd give it up like a shot if there were any hope of doing anything here
that required my presence," she wrote.

With no child to care for, no novel to finish, and no house to maintain,
Mary McCarthy at age forty, was not quite ready to conquer new worlds.
The tickets on the *Ile de France* were traded for a February 26 sailing and
then traded again for a sailing on April 14. By mid-January, she and Bowden Broadwater had taken up residence in a furnished apartment at the
Hotel Chelsea, just off Seventh Avenue on West Twenty-third Street,
making the best of a neighborhood not quite so prestigious as their former one and making do with accommodations that had seen better days.
Ascoli had turned down her proposal, so there would be no takeover of
*The Reporter*. But in the end something had come of all that talk of a need
for a new magazine.

By mid-February, she and her little group had managed to put
together a detailed plan for a new monthly that purported to be modeled

not on the old *politics* but on the conservative and highly respectable London *Economist*. Tentatively it was called *Critic*. She, Macdonald, Rovere, Schlesinger, and Arendt would serve as the board of editors. Macdonald would have the task of overseeing the opening pages devoted to "Comment," a section of short paragraphs addressing recent events. "Comment," which was to be "lively and miscellaneous," would come to no more than fifteen hundred words; the magazine would be thirty-two pages long. In essence, it would be the magazine she had envisioned. She helped put together and then revised two detailed prospectuses, one for potential contributors and one for potential investors. Both boasted an impressive roster of writers and a no less impressive list of projected articles. In both she was listed as the sole "working editor."

"I've always had quite an attraction to communal enterprises and things guided by friendship, or I used to have anyway. And I thought we were going to have an awful lot of fun doing it," she told Carol Brightman in 1980. On the list of contributors were James Agee, Nicola Chiaromonte, James T. Farrell, John Kenneth Galbraith, Geoffrey Hellman, Richard Hofstadter, Alfred Kazin, Philip Rahv, David Riesman, Saul Steinberg, Niccolò Tucci, and James Wechsler, among others. Kazin was going to write a piece about "The Marketplace and the Academy"; Richard Rovere was to write on "The Scruples of Senator Taft"; Chiaromonte on "Catholicism and Mass Politics in Italy." She herself planned to write on "the changed diet of the American poorer classes, based on observations in the Supermarkets." The piece was titled "Let Them Eat Cake" and would also address: "Hidden hunger. New class patterns in consumption and entertainment. Television, the mental marshmallow-fluff of the lower income brackets."

To persuade writers of the need for a new magazine was not going to be difficult. But to persuade investors that this need would be reflected in profits was another matter entirely. People who knew about such things said that they needed cash reserves to cover operating expenses for at least one year. Somehow they were going to have to raise $100,000. One likely possibility was Raoul Fleischmann, the owner of *The New Yorker*. Rather than go to Fleischmann directly, she decided to put a feeler out to her editor Katharine White.

## FROM MARY MCCARTHY'S LETTER TO KATHARINE WHITE, FEBRUARY 18, 1953

Here is the prospectus. The name is being criticized as too negative, hence un-American etc. I myself don't think it's ideal and wish we could find something better. Have you and Andy [E. B. White] any suggestions?[. . . .] I do think such a magazine *has* to be done, if any concerted political fight is to be put up against McCarthy and his friends[. . . .] If there were anybody else ready to start such a venture, I'd be happy to let them do it. But I don't see or hear of anybody[. . . .] I'm heartening myself with the examples of Dickens, Dostoievsky, Victor Hugo, all of whom practiced political journalism or edited magazines during their careers. I feel, quite selfishly too, that the fiction-writer, or at least my kind of fiction-writer, needs the experience of practical life if their work isn't to become too arcane and literary.

Wooing investors from the Chelsea, where memories of Mark Twain and Dylan Thomas added a much needed luster to the seedy public rooms, she had Virgil Thomson as a neighbor, a small kitchen that she deemed adequate, and as thoroughgoing an introduction to the world of practical affairs as anyone could ask for. While her books languished in the house on Pamet Point Road, waiting to be unpacked by Bowden come spring, her portable typewriter stood increasingly idle. The Vassar novel was permanently on hold. With Arthur Schlesinger teaching in Cambridge, the search for New York financial backers fell inevitably to the magazine's working editor. Sometimes Hannah Arendt would pitch in. Occasionally Arendt's friend Alfred Kazin would join them.

**ALFRED KAZIN**   We got together because we were both friends of Hannah and also because all through the McCarthy period—this was a very noble side of Mary and a much appreciated side on my part—she was really shocked by what was going on. Hannah and her husband were sort of absurd because they thought fascism was coming to America and we would try to reassure them.

For the most part, though, McCarthy bore the brunt of the fund-raising alone. When support came, she would later remember, it was not from any quarter she had reason to expect it to come from. The Republicans were often helpful; the Democrats were not. One Democrat who did help was Eve Auchincloss, married to a young *Time* editor. Another was Barbara Kerr, a friend of Arthur Schlesinger and active participant in Adlai Stevenson's campaign, who worked by day as a magazine editor and who presided at night over a small but by no means unimportant salon at her town house in the East Nineties.

On March 6, 1953, McCarthy wrote Schlesinger in Cambridge, bringing him up to date on the fund-raising and informing him, "I went to see your friend, Barbara Kerr, who promised to talk to Betty Hines and to talk to Lloyd Garrison." This lead, like virtually all that came her way that winter and spring, came to nothing. On April 14, the ship that she and Bowden had booked for Portugal left New York harbor without them. They wouldn't make the trip until the following spring. For much of April Bowden was in South Carolina trying to track down a job, leaving his wife to carry on alone. After an endless round of business lunches and dinners, the suits and dresses hanging in her closet at the Chelsea were beginning to show signs of wear. If the new magazine ever found a backer with deep pockets, it would be owing to her insistence on doing nothing by halves. Unfortunately, by mid-April she was beginning to lose patience. Of one thing she was certain: the blame for their failure to raise money did not reside with her or her cohorts.

### FROM MARY McCARTHY'S LETTER TO ARTHUR SCHLESINGER, APRIL 17, 1953

Jack Kaplan is very much interested; we've all been lunching and dining with him. He thinks he'll make up his mind up definitely next week; his eldest daughter is his consultant—a rather nice girl, whom, I gather, he'd like to see on the editorial staff[. . . .] A lunch with Dan Bell and somebody named Lou Harris, who was finally persuaded that the magazine was "in the mainstream of American politics," and is going to give the new prospectus to Oren Lehman and Bobby Straus, Jr. Mrs. Douglas Auchincloss (back of the book *Time*) is giving a dinner-party Monday night for me to meet Just Lunning and a rich maniac named Jack Burling. I'm drowning in floods of bernaise sauce.

### FROM McCARTHY'S LETTER TO SCHLESINGER, APRIL 21, 1953

Arthur, it isn't you or your letters that are the trouble it's the recipients. Almost all of them, except Miss [Lauren] Bacall, are intensely conformist people, if *their* letters reveal them correctly. Almost all of them even have the same typewriter, the most expensive electric model. (Perhaps I'm exaggerating here; all the worst brush-off letters *I* got were written on that same typewriter.)

Decades later, when those typewriters were being replaced in every self-respecting office by a word processor or computer, she would continue to speak of them with the deep and abiding scorn she reserved for her worst enemies. In the end, she managed to secure a promise of $50,000, contingent on raising another $50,000 to match it. Unfortunately, with that promise in hand, she could not seem to scare up a single new backer. With summer fast approaching, the "backer season" was drawing to a close. A professional fund-raiser she ran into warned her that the last $50,000 was always the hardest. On June 3, rested from a May visit to the Cape, where Bowden was putting the Pamet Point house in order, she announced to Arthur Schlesinger that she was "getting a new head of steam on." But six days later she had to confess that the head of steam had brought no palpable results. To help meet expenses she and Bowden had rented their new house to Kevin's friend Montgomery Clift for the summer, and were enduring a New York heat wave at the Chelsea, without benefit of air-conditioning.

### FROM MARY MCCARTHY'S LETTER TO ARTHUR SCHLESINGER, JUNE 9, 1953

[E]verything is in a sort of torpor. I sent out a lot of stuff last week, but so far nothing. B. and I have just been offered a house in East Montpelier, Vermont, starting next Tuesday till the 6th or 7th of July. We've decided to go, probably Monday; I have to have some solitude or I shall be destitute. Before then, we'll have some sort of magazine-meeting to decide what's to be done next[. . . .] Forgive this rather flaccid letter; it's so terribly hot and damp here that my brain feels like wet absorbent cotton.

In Vermont away from the New York heat, she quickly revived. By the end of the summer she had produced a considerable body of work. She not only finished a two-part piece for Ascoli but gave a long talk at Breadloaf, which would be published as "Settling The Colonel's Hash," deploring the new and pernicious tendency to look for symbols and hidden meanings in a novel or story with no regard whatsoever for what the writer is trying to say on the page. She urged the writers and readers in the audience to have no truck with such nonsense and to trust instead to common sense and to plain hard facts.

### FROM "SETTLING THE COLONEL'S HASH"

[T]he writer must be, first of all, a listener and observer, who can pay attention to reality, like an obedient pupil, and who is willing, always, to be surprised by the messages reality is sending through to him. And if he gets the messages correctly he will not have to go back and put in the symbols; he will find that the symbols are there, staring at him significantly from the commonplace.

By the end of her Vermont stay, she was back writing fiction. At Wellfleet that fall she finished a new childhood memoir for Katharine White and started a story that focused almost exclusively on another question of pressing concern to her: how to reconcile a belief in democracy with a wish to protect a treasured and hitherto exclusive preserve. It was a question she had raised before. In *The Oasis* she had written of a field of wild strawberries about to be picked clean by a band of local bumpkins. Now, in "The Appalachian Revolution" she wrote of a Vermont pond threatened by an influx of new summer people. Here the marauders were not a band of locals but two families of loud and unattractive New York psychiatrists. And the defenders were not failed Utopians but nervous young mothers, caught between their very real desire for privacy and the social scruples they had acquired at schools like Vassar and Bryn Mawr. From Wellfleet, she also wrote Hannah Arendt, making it clear that her life was not all work and no play and bringing her up to date on her travails as a free-lance writer and on her plans for the magazine.

### FROM MARY MCCARTHY'S LETTER TO HANNAH ARENDT, OCTOBER 4, 1953

The weather is so enchanting (in the daytime) that we don't leave. We swim and walk and go mushrooming in the afternoons and pick wild grapes and even get sunburned[. . . .] I've been having a long tussle with *Harper's* about the memoir, which I've renamed "My Confession," courtesy you. They wanted to publish it, with cuts that made it into a sort of bloomer-joke about the thirties. I refused and cut it my own way, repossessing the manuscript; now they want it back. This affair has consumed over a month[. . . .]

I'm becoming very dubious about the magazine, or perhaps hopeless is the word[. . . .] For myself, I can't give time to the magazine, in any form, until my finances are replenished. If the *New Yorker* takes my new story, I'll be all right for a little while; otherwise, I shall have to keep writing commercially until something sells. What I'd *really* like to do, I think, is start a new novel or start afresh on my old one. But that would mean goodbye magazine.

She had lost hope and she had lost valuable income. Like it or not, she was embroiled in a round of wheedling and cajoling, arguing and threatening, and playing one magazine editor off against the other. Later that year she placed "My Confession" with *The Reporter*, where it ran more or less as she had written it, but this would not keep her from returning to *Harper's* in 1954, when she was desperate to salvage a huge chunk cut from a *New Yorker* piece on Portugal. If she was going to get back to the serious business of novel writing, she was going to have to find a better way to make ends meet.

By the end of October, the Broadwaters were back in New York subletting Alfred Kazin's apartment on West 111th Street. In a letter to Elizabeth Hardwick, now living with Robert Lowell outside Boston, she was ready not only to confess that she had lost interest in the new magazine but to speculate about why it had gone wrong.

### FROM MARY MCCARTHY'S LETTER TO ELIZABETH HARDWICK, OCTOBER 27, 1953

In theory I could resume activities after I'd gotten out of debt—say in January—but my heart isn't in it any more. Nobody really wants such a magazine, except a few writers, who are all highly critical of each other; the rich people were uneasy about it, not, I think, politically, but afraid of being identified with a folly. Culture isn't looked on as a folly; it's an accepted way of dropping money, like keeping chorus girls or losing at the races. But politics and social criticism are too tricky; a magazine devoted to them is supposed to succeed.

Once the working editor dropped out, no one expressed any desire to continue with *Critic*. Like Europe-America Groups, the new magazine was very much her idea and very much of the moment. Long before she left for Vermont, Stalin's sudden death in March had already made the need for a new independent anti-Communist, anti-McCarthy bimonthly seem a little less urgent. By October, she was able to joke to Arendt that the recent marriage of Joe McCarthy was "like a warrior's ritual purification." By the end of the following May, a significant number of Americans would be ranged in front of those televisions she had been so quick to accuse of dispensing marshmallow-fluff, watching the senator from Wisconsin take on the army and begin to self-destruct.

Even though the failure to launch *Critic* was dispiriting, the launching itself had had its share of lighter moments. For Mary McCarthy, it cemented friendships with Hannah Arendt and Arthur Schlesinger. For Dwight Macdonald, it became an important part of their personal history, emblematic of what he valued most in her.

### FROM DWIGHT MACDONALD'S INTRODUCTION OF MARY MCCARTHY AT THE 92ND STREET Y, NEW YORK CITY, NOVEMBER 10, 1963

Mary and I have been together through a good deal of history. You know in Grant's Tomb there are those silk banners hanging in the rotunda— "Antietam," "Chancellorsville," "Vicksburg," "The Wilderness." Well, we have our own set of tattered dusty silk banners, but they're labeled "Trotsky Defense Committee," "Wars at the *Partisan Review*," "Europe-America Groups," which is such an obscure thing that it never really produced anything except a novel called *The Oasis* by Mary, "Spanish Refugee Aid," and finally something called "*Critic*," which was an abortive attempt, mostly by Mary, to raise funds to do something somewhat such as is being done now by *The New York Review of Books*. I might add that we've both been through *The New Yorker*, but that's a silk banner that is not dusty or tattered[. . . .] Mary McCarthy has been a close friend and a loyal friend of mine—the two things are not always the same—for almost thirty years.

But for Mary McCarthy and Alfred Kazin, the failure of *Critic* left a reservoir of bad feeling. The following summer she would complain to Hannah Arendt that Kazin was snubbing her in Wellfleet. Although relations between the two of them never recovered, their mutual dislike did not erupt into print until decades later, when Kazin attacked her first in *Starting Out in the Thirties* and then in *New York Jew*, while disparaging her novels in *Bright Book of Life*. Not long afterward, in the midst of describing her ill-fated hopes for *Critic* to an interviewer, she took the opportunity to pay him in kind. Her words did not go unnoticed.

### MARY MCCARTHY IN AN INTERVIEW WITH CAROL BRIGHTMAN, *THE NATION*, MAY 19, 1984

I thought we were going to have an awful lot of fun doing it. Then the usual thing developed, people became very hateful. I got word from

Alfred Kazin that my quitting had been a betrayal. He hadn't done one thing; he hadn't given us the price of a postage stamp.

**ALFRED KAZIN**  *The New York Review of Books* took an advance part of *Bright Book of Life* and she got very mad and wrote the *Review* a letter, which of course I answered. In the letter she said I was a sick man and should see a doctor. That was her rejoinder to my literary criticism. So I thought, Okay, nothing ever changes. Later on, she wrote a piece in *The Nation* condemning me for having dropped this anti-McCarthy magazine. I was actually baffled by this because I never felt they had raised enough money for the magazine. She really hated my guts.

As McCarthy saw it, the magazine had failed because no one had had the courage to put their money behind it. Someone else might argue that the magazine failed because its founding editors were not entirely honest with themselves or with each other. As she suspected, Schlesinger and Rovere were not all that dissatisfied with *The Reporter*. Macdonald was resigned to writing for *The New Yorker*. Irving Howe, who had been invited to take part in the early planning sessions and then gone on to start up a magazine of his own, believed that *Critic* was doomed from the start.

**IRVING HOWE**  We had one or two meetings. Mary was quiet, didn't say much. I think she felt that she was in with a lot of heavy politicos. She never felt terribly secure, I think, about political, ideological talk. Those meetings were desultory. It was clear nothing was going to come of that. What I've learned about a magazine—unless it's a big commercial venture—is that it depends on one person. One person who's willing to sacrifice him or herself to be the editor and carry the burden. I remember when we started *Dissent*, Meyer Schapiro wrote me a note of warning. And boy, was he right.

She had been willing to sacrifice herself, but only to a point. "On the one hand, I have a desire to be an activist, and on the other hand, *I don't*," she confessed to Brock Brower in 1962. While her first ill-fated adventure as an activist had spurred her to write *The Oasis*, this second disappointment did not produce any immediate fictional results. Still, there was a payoff of sorts. For the sake of the new magazine, at the urging of Hannah Arendt, she agreed to make peace with Philip Rahv. The tale of their reconciliation was one she delighted in telling, altering the details ever so slightly with the passing of time. To Brower, in 1962, she gave a version in which she appeared as a conquering heroine, unchastened and unbowed.

**MARY MCCARTHY, IN "MARY MCCARTHYISM," BY BROCK BROWER,** *ESQUIRE*, **JULY 1962**
Hannah convinced me that the magazine had to have Philip Rahv. So I finally got up my courage and telephoned him. He still wanted me

to say I was sorry, and I still wasn't going to say I was, but I finally invited him to a long peace luncheon at the Charles. When we came out of the restaurant, all smiles, one of the *PR* gang saw us and actually blanched.

To Carol Brightman, in 1985, she admitted that she had in fact apologized. "I didn't feel terribly happy about swallowing my pride," she confessed, and then went on to describe meeting with Rahv alone, at his invitation, at his apartment one night. There had been no witnesses to the meeting—Nathalie Rahv having been sent away by her husband in a fashion that no one apparently saw as high-handed. But there *had* been a verbal apology delivered. "I told him what was true, that I was very, very sorry that I had hurt him and that it had not been my intention to hurt him and that I was well aware by now that I had and that I felt badly about it."

Rahv had been "delighted" and "jubilant" and had cut short her apology. The lunch had been held the next day and it had been Rahv who issued the invitation. Afterward, as the two of them were walking up Sixth Avenue, they were spotted not by just any member of the *PR* gang but by none other than Delmore Schwartz, who did not "blanch" but, instead, "turned all the colors" and then ran off to tell "the boys." Delmore was chagrined that Rahv would have someone to take his side in future battles at the magazine, she explained. Once Rahv had an "ally," it meant that "their whole strategy had fallen into pieces."

Leaving the boys' strategy in pieces was a notion that appealed to her, but, in truth, she had played no active part at the magazine since the late thirties. Possibly Schwartz's chagrin had less to do with any potential foundering of their anti-Rahv strategy than with a dawning recognition that once again Rahv was about to declare black to be white and leave it to the rest of them to scramble to catch up.

**WILLIAM PHILLIPS** I remember Sidney Hook said, "That son of a bitch Rahv, he becomes friends with her while we all remain angry." Mary and I finally had a reconciliation several years later in Florence. We made a date and I said to her, "I guess we ought to make up. After all, you made up with Rahv, who was the real victim. I don't know why I have to carry on a feud on principle, so let's be friends again." She put on that knowing ironic smile and we became friends again—not intimate friends, but friends.

She and Rahv were no longer feuding, but sometimes she found her former lover hard going. That August, she informed Hannah Arendt that having entertained Rahv as a houseguest she could not agree with Arendt that he was "interesting on the subject of politics."

### FROM MARY MCCARTHY'S LETTER TO HANNAH ARENDT, AUGUST 10, 1954

Rahv's Marxist assurance strikes me as antedulivian [*sic*]; it's like talking with some fossilized mammoth[. . . .] I like him best when he's soliloquizing about literature, not current writing, which he regards from a polemical or strategic standpoint, but the old authors, Russian and German, who thrill his imagination. On all other topics, he made me horribly nervous, as if we were screaming at each other on the Tower of Babel. Nor unfriendly; just estranged and mutually watchful. Probably it was my fault.

By the mid-1980s, Rahv was long dead and she was remembering him with an affection that left many of their old friends reeling. She was charged with rewriting history or, at the very least, putting her own spin on it. To Carol Brightman, she pointed out that Rahv had published articles in *Partisan Review* and *Commentary* during the spring of 1952, in which he had attacked Joe McCarthy by name. Here, she said, was the reason she could bring herself to ask his forgiveness. "He was the only one of the group who had stuck his neck out." To put it another way, "[H]e was getting our friendship back because of his wonderful behavior about Senator McCarthy." But if Rahv had stuck his neck out, not everyone was convinced he had stuck it out far enough or long enough to justify talk of a reward.

IRVING HOWE   Rahv was not heroic in the McCarthy days. He conked out. He went underground. He didn't do anything wrong, but he didn't do anything right.

Over the years, at least one important detail of this tale of the great Rahv-McCarthy reconciliation never varied: always it was Hannah Arendt who was credited with persuading her to risk a step she professed to have no wish to take. That her reconciliation with Rahv was so startling gives some indication of the power it took to promote it. By the time she joined forces with Arendt on *Critic*, she was ready to defer to her judgment, not only to speak of her as her best friend but to regard her as her "wise counselor."

In photographs taken during this period, Hannah Arendt looks old enough to be her mother, but in age the two women were only six years apart. That their friendship was charged with feeling there is no question. That it affected the course of Mary McCarthy's life no one would argue. That it was the best thing that ever happened to her is open to debate. How you came to view it would always depend in large part on how you felt about McCarthy and on how willing you were to subscribe to her belief that Arendt was both truly good and truly brilliant.

**ALFRED KAZIN**   After the war, I met Hannah Arendt, to whom I became utterly devoted. I like Europeans. I was brought up, after all, by European parents. I always feel uneducated by comparison with them. And Hannah was tremendously learned. And very womanly. The attraction that she exuded (which Robert Lowell felt and others), while a lot of it was based on her fantastic knowledge, it was not lacking in eroticism. She was very German. But she was very womanly and she had a great gift for friendship. I was Hannah's witness for her citizenship and very proud to be that.

**ISAIAH BERLIN**   She was a typical Berlin bluestocking. I found her arrogant and dry. I think she impressed people in New York as being European culture, which they knew nothing about and which seemed to them should have represented a rich tradition. The book on totalitarianism is quite good on Germany and no good on Russia. Just no good on Russia. She got it all wrong. When I read her books I found there was no argument in them ever. Just metaphysical free association. One idea after another. One thing suggested another, but there was no logical structure.

**WILLIAM PHILLIPS**   Isaiah Berlin wouldn't be impressed with her. He had too much of a systematic education and mind to like her. I liked Hannah personally. She had for me a certain amount of charm and force. She was to some extent frightening—she was so forceful. She had some wit, but I don't think that was her outstanding characteristic. She was much more formidable than Mary. She was a strong woman, intellectually and personally. I edited Hannah and rewrote her too. She was all right to work with. At the beginning she thought she knew English. She really didn't. She had to be put into English. Later she learned. Her spoken English had charm. She was charming in a forceful way. Not charming in a sweet way. There was a little bit of a mother in her, when you had dinner in her house. But that was not the essential Hannah.

**SAUL BELLOW**   I remember one day she came to see me in Chicago and there were some hard water biscuits on the table, I said, "Hannah, don't eat those." But she was in the middle of a sentence and so she picked one up and started to bite into it and her teeth wobbled in all directions. Hannah was long in the teeth. You can't think of a woman who looks like that as a sex object. She looked like George Arliss playing Disraeli.

Depending on how you felt about the two principals, their friendship was a source of delight or a source of amusement, something to be grateful for or something to be deplored. That there was loyalty and affection there was no question. When it came to the precise nature of this affection, however, there was no unanimity of opinion.

**ALFRED KAZIN**   Would I have predicted the great friendship with Hannah Arendt? Can I explain it? No. To me it will always be a mystery. Mary was not my kind of woman. But since, on the other hand, we were both crazy about Hannah Arendt, there was obviously something there. I've never understood it. Not only would I not have foreseen it, but I didn't understand it while it was taking place. With Hannah, Mary was fantastically submissive. Hannah could be like a queen. I do believe that with Hannah there was no barbed wire, there was nothing but respect and ease because she was dealing with a woman rather than a man. I had the feeling she was more comfortable with women.

**HELEN WOLFF**   I don't think Miss McCarthy had much compassion in her makeup. She was not kind. I came to know her through Hannah, and with Hannah she was different. She stood in absolute awe of her and was totally devoted to her and always willing to come to her. I know that Hannah enormously appreciated her intelligence. She said once to me, "Mary understands everything immediately. She has this capacity of entering another person's mind."

**BARBARA DUPEE**   I think Mary really loved her. And I think that she was much more worthy of Mary's love than many of the men in Mary's life.

**ISAIAH BERLIN**   Hannah was beyond criticism, and regarded by Mary as the most wonderful woman she'd ever met. She adored her and respected her and was influenced by her in some ways. Mary could be harsh. She had a powerful mind, but Hannah took her in. With Hannah Arendt only litterateurs were taken in. Thinkers were not. Mind you, Auden liked Hannah very much. Lowell thought she was marvelous. Mary was completely bamboozled by Hannah. I asked Meyer Schapiro why. He said, "Oh, she's her Jewish grandmother."

**WILLIAM PHILLIPS**   They were like sisters. But there was enormous devotion—the source and cause of which I couldn't begin to speculate on. They were very different, but they were tied together maybe by a sense of "truth" and "morality" and "honesty" and "bravery" and "intellectual courage."

**LOTTE KOHLER** [Hannah's executor]   Mary was almost like a student to Hannah, but it's a little more involved. Hannah was really in love with Mary. It was Mary who somehow captured her heart and soul. If Mary was coming, all prior plans were dropped. She would say, "Mary is coming, Mary is coming." And you knew that this was a very special person. Fortunately Heinrich also liked Mary. He liked her no-nonsense directness. And Bowden liked Hannah.

**IRVING HOWE**   Mary was absolutely stricken with Hannah. It had a kind of schoolgirl element to it. It wasn't just intellectual admiration. She really had a crush on Hannah. And Hannah was very domineering, very dominating, but with great charm. She was tremendously seductive. She wasn't a good-looking woman but she had great presence, so it really didn't matter. And she and Mary became, I gather, very very friendly.

On at least one occasion Hannah Arendt and Mary McCarthy showed a taste for mischief of a somewhat ambiguous sort. One spring day, on the way back to New York from attending one of the Gauss lectures at Princeton the two of them suggested to William Phillips, notoriously timorous when it came to matters affecting his personal health and well-being, that they pull into a motel. Phillips turned them down flat and lived to tell the tale—a tale that he later disowned when confronted with it by an interviewer, saying he didn't want it printed, so he was going to deny it. When asked what this tale he was bent on denying said about Mary and Hannah, he paused only an instant. Mary was an adventurer, he answered, whereas Hannah wasn't afraid of anything and might be pulled along.

Mary was an adventurer and a rebel and a natural outsider, but she had no liking for the life of a pariah. Thanks to *Critic* and Hannah Arendt, she was once again invited to the big crushes at *Partisan Review* and to dinners at Philip Rahv's. Not until 1955 would *Partisan Review* run another "Theater Chronicle" but in the fall of 1954 the magazine published a short story, one that could not by any stretch of the imagination be edited to a point where it was acceptable for *The New Yorker*.

The story, which was called "Dottie Makes an Honest Woman of Herself," was made up mostly of an early section from the Vassar novel she had scrapped two years earlier. The story described in clinical detail how Dottie Renfrew, a shy and slender girl from Boston, given to respiratory ailments and eczema, loses her heart and her virginity to a sardonic Village painter, who first suggests that she go be fitted for a pessary, or diaphragm, and then leaves her to languish with that diaphragm on a park bench.

### FROM "DOTTIE MAKES AN HONEST WOMAN OF HERSELF," *PARTISAN REVIEW*, FALL 1954

Dottie did not mind the pelvic examination or the fitting. Her bad moment came when she was learning how to insert the pessary by herself. Though she was usually good with her hands and well co-ordinated, she felt suddenly unnerved by the scrutiny of the doctor and the nurse, so exploratory and impersonal, like the doctor's rubber glove. As she was trying to fold the pessary, the slippery thing, all covered with jelly, jumped out of her hand and shot across the room and hit the sterilizer[. . . .]

"Medical instruction," said the doctor kindly, with a thoughtful look at Dottie, "can often help the patient to the fullest sexual enjoyment. The young women who come to me, Dorothy, have the right to expect the deepest satisfaction from the sexual act." Dottie scratched her jaw; the skin on her upper chest mottled. What she especially wanted to ask was something a doctor might know, above all, a married doctor. She had of course not confided in Kay the thing that was still troubling her: what did it mean if a man made love to you and didn't kiss you once, not even at the most thrilling moment?

Having faulted her for her childhood memoirs, Rahv and the boys were prepared to print the pessary story and run the risk of coming up against the postal authorities. In 1954 no other literary writer in America would have attempted to tell such a story. But more important, no other magazine which prided itself on its seriousness or regarded itself as respectable would have gone ahead and printed it. Attention was paid to the story by a wide range of readers, including the young Philip Roth. In 1959, in *Goodbye, Columbus*, he would have Neil Klugman urge his girlfriend Brenda Patimkin to get herself fitted for a diaphragm at the Margaret Sanger Clinic, prompting Brenda to turn on him with an immediate question.

### FROM *GOODBYE COLUMBUS,* BY PHILIP ROTH
"You've done this before?"

"No," I said. "I just know. I read Mary McCarthy."

"That's exactly right. That's just what I'd feel like, somebody out of *her.*"

On her return to New York in the fall of 1953, Mary McCarthy had not only once again been treated to the kind of brusque scrutiny and uncompromising support she had learned to count on from the editors of *Partisan Review* but she'd had a chance to observe firsthand the game of literary politics as it was played behind discreetly closed doors. She had been asked to serve on the fiction committee for the National Book Award. The year before, Ralph Ellison's *Invisible Man* had been honored. Of the current batch of novels nominated, *The Adventures of Augie March* by Saul Bellow seemed to her to be far and away the best. Not easily waylaid by ambivalence, or inclined to waste time from sheer politeness, she was not slow in letting her fellow committee members know exactly how she felt.

**LEON EDEL**   This was our first meeting and it was not a happy one. She breezed in and she said, "It's *Augie*. It's obvious. There's not another thing on the list as good." As far as she was concerned, there was no need for any further discussion. There were two or three other people on the committee and we said, "Well, that may be, but there still are some other books that have been nominated." We made her sit there almost two hours as we went over each book. Remember that was the period of her involvement with *Partisan Review*. Bellow was part of *Partisan Review*. We went through all the novels and then we had a vote and finally got it down to Wright Morris and Bellow. Now, Bellow was a friend of mine and I was all for his getting the award. I was only arguing for fair play. I suggested that there be a final vote, so we could see how we stood. There was clearly a majority for *Augie*, so I said, "Now that we've had our discussion, why don't we make it unanimous?" The interesting part of the story is that she must have let it out that Wright had been a contender, because various people spoke to me afterward and seemed to think that I had voted against *Augie*. The next time I met Saul he cut me dead. Turned on his heel and walked away. He was cold to me for a number of years.

Leon Edel was not the only one to be cut by Bellow. The following summer Mary McCarthy would complain to Hannah Arendt that Bellow was "not very friendly" when he ran into her at Wellfleet. But if her brush with literary lobbying left a residue of bitterness, this did not deter her from indulging in it on occasion. She had no gift for literary politics, nor did she have the patience. Some of her best friends, however, showed a surprising aptitude. Within a few years, Robert Lowell would be trying to enlist Elizabeth Bishop in a scheme to get three of their candidates into the National Institute of Arts and Letters.

### FROM ROBERT LOWELL'S LETTER TO ELIZABETH BISHOP, APRIL 19, 1959

I think we are each allowed one *nomination.* I am nominating Randall. If you'll nominate Flannery, I'll second. I am trying to get [poet R. P.] Blackmur to nominate Mary. Then we can all second each other's candidates, I doubt if any of them except Flannery have a chance. Such disgusting fluff is proposed and elected most of the time that one hesitates to raise one's voice. I think we must, though.

Never did such machinations come naturally to Mary McCarthy and rarely did they make her comfortable. At a dinner party at Barbara Kerr's Upper East Side town house, a mild-mannered staff writer at *The New Yorker* came upon her in a corner, divvying up the year's awards and prizes with Dwight Macdonald. Caught red-handed, she turned on the writer and gave him a tongue-lashing so harsh that her hostess and fellow guests would remember the incident long after they could recollect a word that was uttered. "I made a joke and it hit a nerve obviously," the *New Yorker* writer later recalled. "I said, 'You people should be in some line of work where you can be handing out trophies, like basketball.'" Of course, delivering a tongue-lashing at a party was not unheard of for her. In February 1952, she had taken Brendan Gill, another *New Yorker* writer, to task for his *Groves of Academe* review.

### FROM MARY MCCARTHY'S LETTER TO BERNICE BAUMGARTEN, MARCH 5, 1952

I also had a little discussion with Brendan Gill at the *New Yorker* party, nothing acrimonious. But I think he was rather miffed. He told Bowden, after our conversation, "Hereafter I'll have a separate standard for Dostoievsky, Tolstoy, and Miss McCarthy." (I'd pointed out to him that reviewers didn't seem to object to unpleasant characters, once their creator was dead.) Such conversations, I admit, are absolutely futile, but there he was and I couldn't see talking about the weather with him.

The "discussion" with Brendan Gill had taken place at an office cocktail party in a large hotel, where it was not likely to spoil the evening, but the tongue-lashing took place at a small dinner, at the home of a good friend. For more than a decade, Mary McCarthy would be a frequent guest at Barbara Kerr's dinner parties. At the fine old mahogany table that had come down to Kerr through her family, you could find novelists and poets, working journalists, foreign visitors, captains of industry, members in good standing of the social register, and a generous sprinkling of Stevenson Democrats.

**BARBARA KERR**   I am what is known as "a proper Bostonian" and Mary liked that. I was quite aware that this was a large part of my appeal for her. She was very acutely aware of social conventions. Mary was a very loyal friend for many years. I particularly remember one incident that touched me deeply. I was an editor of *The Woman's Home Companion* when Crowell Collier [the magazine's corporate owner] failed—it was almost Christmas Eve—and Mary was the first to telephone me out of all the people I knew, ahead of my aunts and uncles, and ask if I had enough money. "Are you going to be all right?" she asked. "We'd be glad to give you some money."

**AL ALVAREZ**   I used to see Mary and Bowden at Barbara's dinners. I loved Bowden's sly wit, but Mary was too much spun steel for my taste. I prefer someone a little more yielding. But she was a commanding woman, strikingly handsome and very funny. And she had that famous smile. Someone once said, "Mary can do anything with that smile—even smile with it."

**LOUIS AUCHINCLOSS**   She was not a tiger in my presence, though I think she could rend people to pieces.

**BARBARA KERR**   At a party, if she was interested in a man, God help anybody who wanted to talk to him. She would zero in on him and buttonhole him so that he had no possible chance of escape. I think Mary would have been absolutely ruthless if she had wanted your man for an evening—or a week. Friendship would not have stood in the way. In fact, I took great care never to expose her to any man I was interested in.

She might be prepared to rend someone to pieces at a dinner table or a cocktail party, but she could not possibly cover herself on every front. To one sort of attack she was potentially vulnerable: having turned her husbands, friends, and lovers into characters in her fiction, it was only a matter of time before someone returned the favor. As luck would have it, when the attack finally came in 1954 it arrived from the poet and critic Randall Jarrell, whom she had let off lightly in *The Groves of Academe*, by simply naming him in passing.

Back in the early forties, Jarrell had courted Edmund Wilson with letters, which more than once made favorable mention of some new work of fiction by Wilson's gifted young wife. (Not only did he praise "The Man in the Brooks Brothers Shirt" and "Ghostly Father, I Confess," but in November 1942 he wrote, "I tried hard to get [*The Company She Keeps*] to review, but nobody would give it to me.") Jarrell had then gone on to pay a visit to the Wilsons at Wellfleet. The visit, which coincided with a visit from the Nabokovs, had not been a success. Jarrell, McCarthy later recalled, had trailed after her "screeching in a whisper," asking why she bothered with "these people." By the time the two of them started running into each other in New York in the late forties, it was clear that they were never going to be friends. Still, they had no way of avoiding each other. Jarrell was a good friend of Robert Lowell. More to the point, he was devoted to Hannah Arendt. In their worst moments, she and Jarrell were each capable of the sort of behavior one expects from a willful and precocious child. That there was a similarity in their makeup was not lost on at least one of their friends.

### FROM ROBERT LOWELL'S LETTER TO ELIZABETH BISHOP, JULY 30, 1968

I find Mary a bit hard (how shall I put it?) to get at[. . . .] [T]he mind, as Hannah Arendt puts it, that wants to be ninety per cent right, times when nothing seems addressed to me, and nothing I say is heard— maddening when you think what you said is quite good, or the subject is one you feel could be referred to you. At times I think of Randall in his off-moods, though Mary is never discourteous.

In *Pictures from an Institution*, the novel inspired by Jarrell's teaching stint at Sarah Lawrence, Mary McCarthy was immediately recognizable as the model for the writer Gertrude Johnson. Jarrell's altering certain key details fooled no one. Everywhere you looked there were salient McCarthy characteristics. Broadly drawn and thoroughly incorrigible, Gertrude Johnson was the butt of the author's best jokes.

Jarrell dedicated his novel "to Mary and Hannah." "Mary" was Jarrell's wife, the former Mary von Shrader, and "Hannah" was Hannah Arendt. When the book came out in 1954, it received glowing reviews and enjoyed respectable sales. Jean Stafford had been happy to give Jarrell a blurb saying, "I can't think when I've read anything with so much relish." But not everyone who was asked for a blurb shared her unmitigated delight. Elizabeth Bishop responded with some hesitation. For Bishop the portrait of Gertrude Johnson had an aspect of meanness—if not of meanness, then of dismaying accuracy. In addition, she found the novel to be flawed.

### FROM ELIZABETH BISHOP'S LETTER TO PEARL KAZIN, FEBRUARY 22, 1954

I'm getting off a blurb—my first—for *Pictures from an Institution*[. . . .] [H]e *is* funny, but this book affects me like an overlong visit. It's too incessant and hysterical, and then when he isn't being mean about Mary, he gets sentimental about Germans, etc. Well maybe one shouldn't say "mean." I haven't seen much of Mary for years and years, but it's *her*. She's still saying some of the same things she said at college, apparently. Oh poor girl, really. You know, I think she's never felt very real, and that's been her trouble. She's always pretending to be something-or-other and never quite convincing herself or other people. When I knew her well I was always torn between being furious with her and being very touched by her—because in those days her pretensions were so romantic and sad. Now that they're so grandiose, I suppose it's much harder to take. And I still feel mean about writing a blurb for a book about her.

Delmore Schwartz simply declined to give a blurb. While he was not made uneasy by Gertrude Johnson, he questioned the validity of Jarrell's satirizing a writer for writing exactly the kind of *roman à clef* that he himself was attempting to pull off. Schwartz was in fact the second member of the *Partisan Review* circle to refuse support for the book and register his disapproval. In the summer of 1953 Philip Rahv had turned down a chapter because of the McCarthy satire, prompting Jarrell to write a long letter of disclaimer.

### FROM RANDALL JARRELL'S LETTER TO PHILIP RAHV, AUGUST 1953

Gertrude is so large and real to me (I can make up in my sleep a sentence for her to say about anything) that it seems funny to have her confused with Mary McCarthy, whom I know slightly and don't know too much about: but she *is* the same general type as Mary McCarthy, her books are like, and I got five or six happenings or pictures from M.M. But the readers who know Jean Stafford best think *she's* Gertrude, and the ones who know—but I won't go on with this list of Lady Writers. I hope (this is said in a grandiloquent tone) that Gertrude will survive when all of them are forgotten.

Rahv returned the manuscript with apologies and Jarrell never again offered *Partisan Review* his reviews or his poems. (Of course if Jarrell had finished *Pictures from an Institution* three years earlier, he might have met with a very different reception.) As it was, the real-life model for Gertrude Johnson had only to ignore the novel as much as was decently possible and let it be known that she had naturally assumed that Jarrell's source of inspiration was Jean Stafford or Elizabeth Hardwick. If she could not stop the book, she could at least control the damage.

Ever after, she maintained cordial but distant relations with Jarrell. She never exacted a particle of revenge. Possibly the mildness of her response owed something to Jarrell's close tie to Hannah Arendt, who, with Heinrich Blücher, had served as the inspiration for the Rosenbaums, the German couple Jarrell so idealized in his book. This response, which amounted to a strategy, may have been made easier by the fact that for much of 1954 she was living out of New York. It may have also been made easier by the fact that Gertrude, for all her many flaws, is a formidable figure. For Bowden Broadwater there was no such consolation when he looked at Gertrude's husband, poor Sidney. But, then, no one was asking Bowden what he thought.

In the fall of 1954, when Jarrell's book was the talk of literary New York, Mary McCarthy and Bowden Broadwater were living in a large, well-heated house near Newport. (The Wellfleet house had no furnace.) There McCarthy was struggling to finish a novel set in Wellfleet that would have done Gertrude Johnson proud, while trying to earn some much needed cash. Her finances had not recovered from the months spent on *Critic*. To raise money she was putting together a collection of her old "Theater Chronicles."

In 1954 publishers were no more inclined to undertake collections of out-of-date theater reviews than they are today. But when Harcourt passed on the collection, deeming it unlikely to attract sufficient readers to make it worth their while, Roger Straus, an editorial advisor to *Partisan Review* and a close friend of Philip Rahv, expressed an interest in bringing it out at his publishing house, Farrar, Straus, and Cudahy. In taking on these pieces, Straus was no doubt hoping to one day get hold of McCarthy's fiction. Bernice Baumgarten stayed clear of the project, leaving it to her client to strike a deal with Straus, who in his short time as a publisher had already acquired a reputation for the stellar quality of his list and the meager advances he paid his authors. But by bringing to the table a hint of flirtation and more than a hint of desperation, McCarthy was able to get her $500 advance paid in full, up front.

### FROM MARY MCCARTHY'S LETTER TO ROGER STRAUS, NOVEMBER 12, 1954

I'd like to be able to have it in toto, now, when and if the contract is signed. The sum isn't very large (I'm not complaining about that), but it's larger to me than it is to you. I'm not earning any money at the moment and won't be till I finish my novel, and I'm eager not to have to break off and do a piece for the *New Yorker* to keep myself alive. Moreover, even when I finish the novel, I'll have to do the final theatre pieces for *Partisan Review*, which isn't very lucrative. And practically I don't suppose you're worried about getting the book; I'm not a collector of advances on daydreams, as any of our friends can tell you.

It was her plan to give readers a sense of what New York theater had been like when she had done the bulk of her reviewing, and to make it clear how she had come to do theater reviewing in the first place—to start off by telling the story of the founding of *Partisan Review*. It was also her plan to call the collection *Sights and Spectacles*, a title that would have a familiar echo for certain readers.

## FROM MARY MCCARTHY'S LETTER TO ROGER STRAUS, OCTOBER 22, 1954

The model, I think, should be Edmund's *Classics and Commercials*, which was not a complete record either. The title—mine, I mean (*Sights and Spectacles*)—I thought of a few years ago, before his came out, but perhaps it's too much like it. If so, I can think of something new and not alliterative.

By the fall of 1954 Mary McCarthy was an established figure on the literary scene. She was not as famous as Edmund Wilson had been when she married him, but, owing to her theater chronicles and her novels, she was now probably better known to the general reading public than he was. Certainly she was better known than Elizabeth Hardwick or Jean Stafford. She had not written a best-selling novel like Stafford, but by dint of sheer fortitude and productivity and force of personality—reading at the Y, holding forth at the dinner table, conferring the favor of her attention upon the occasional eager young writer—she had made a name for herself. The title stayed in place.

In the introduction she would write for the collection, she got a fact wrong here and there—such as locating the first *Partisan Review* offices at the old Bible House on Astor Place, instead of on Seventeenth Street, just off Union Square—but with her introduction she provided the first published account of the early days of a magazine that was well on its way to becoming an institution. Others would come after her, differing in their facts and interpretations. Nonetheless, she set the standard. If she could never again be one of the boys, she brought to her introduction the cheek and insouciance of a writer who is assured of her place as one of the boys' favorite girls.

Finally, McCarthy's efforts on behalf of *Critic* cannot be called wasted, if only because they led her to swallow her pride and make peace with Philip Rahv. The immediate effect of her return was to make possible the publication of the pessary story. A delayed, but longer lasting effect, was to set in motion the publication in book form of her nonfiction. *Sights and Spectacles* was followed by *On The Contrary*, a collection of the best of the pieces she had been forced to place, catch as catch can, with magazines of dubious merit or limited readership. Bound between hard covers, with the ideas of one thrown into relief by those of its companions, these pieces showed to advantage—to far better advantage than they could ever have shown in *Critic*, for instance. Here the whole was indeed greater than the sum of its parts.

Together, the two essay collections would form one of the enduring cornerstones of her reputation. So in the end her brief but discouraging "experience of practical life" did prove of benefit to her writing career. But she had hoped for something more than that. To Roger Straus she had confided, "People still keep asking me, 'When are you going to do those theatre pieces again?' when I'd prefer an inquiry about my new novel."

# Chapter Fifteen

# THE CAPE

When you try to turn back the clock, you do so at your own risk. Back in October 1952, Mary McCarthy had written Dwight Macdonald to thank him for her "lyric stay" at his house in Wellfleet and to tell him that she and Bowden had decided to buy "the Sayre place" on Pamet Point Road. To Macdonald, who had witnessed her sorry Cape history as Mrs. Edmund Wilson, she made no mention of the "arcadia" or "steel-blue ponds" she had raved about in her letter to Hannah Arendt. She wrote, instead, of the sole reservation she had about their decision: "I've long felt that the Cape is an impossible place to work, but I'm going in the teeth of this conviction; at this time of year, it's so beautiful that one can't bear not to possess a part of it." That was all.

The red eighteenth-century saltbox she and Bowden bought had never been grand enough to house any sea captain, but it enjoyed a modest place in Wellfleet history. In the days when itinerant preachers journeyed to the far reaches of the Cape on horseback, its owners had put up visiting clergymen in the pretty front parlor. Unfortunately, in the intervening years no owner had thought to put in central heating. Still, it had advantages. Set on a hill amid a stand of oaks and pines and locusts, the house was well away from the main highway and came with a barn that would serve nicely as a studio. At the front door was a large box bush; by the kitchen door was a quince. Close by, just down the hill, hidden by a thicket of wild roses and blackberries, was a smaller yellow house that shared the same well.

The red house was within their means, and once they persuaded their Newport friend Mary Meigs to purchase the yellow house down the hill, their privacy was ensured. They would have a pretty garden, and they would have small but well-proportioned rooms suited to their furniture. More important, they would have a place to retreat to when they tired of

Europe. The only possible drawback was, living on Pamet Point Road would put them only minutes away from Edmund Wilson.

In her stillborn novelette "The Lost Week" Mary McCarthy had written, "A painter might run away with his neighbor's wife [. . .] and out of a feeling of propriety the guilty pair might wander desolately from summer colony to summer colony for one year or even two; at the end of that time, they would return and settle down a mile or two from the house of the wronged husband—it was not that they were brazen; they had nowhere else to go." By her own reckoning, she was, if anything, a good six years overdue.

Writing "The Lost Week" in the summer of 1945, bitter at the treatment she had been receiving at the hands of Wilson loyalists, she had described her fictional Wellfleet as an "asylum for derelicts of the American creative life," its denizens no better than "walking case-histories of all the literary diseases." Eight years later, these derelicts and walking case histories did not look quite so unappetizing. Neither did Edmund Wilson. Indeed their first lunch at Portsmouth had marked the end of their protracted and acrimonious divorce.

After that lunch Edmund Wilson had continued to look over his former wife's shoulder and fault her for the way she was raising their son, and she and Bowden Broadwater had continued to refer to Wilson as "the Monster"—finally driving Elena Wilson to suggest that it would be best if Reuel's mother did not try to set Reuel against his father. But when it came to matters that had nothing to do with child rearing, McCarthy had shown she could be remarkably forbearing. In the summer of 1950, when a play by Wilson called *The Little Blue Light* debuted at a small theater in Cambridge with Jessica Tandy starring as a difficult and good-looking young woman named Judith who lives in the country with her husband, a long suffering magazine editor, she made no mention of it. When the play went on to enjoy a brief New York run with Arlene Francis as Judith, she continued to ignore it.

In the stage directions for *The Little Blue Light,* Judith is described as "a handsome brunette, in her early thirties." She wears her hair "parted straight in the middle" and "tightly stretched back and done up in a bun." At one point her husband's male secretary is moved to say, "You're the only girl I ever knew who had the same kind of brains as a man and yet at the same time was perfectly beautiful." The secretary is Judith's lover. She is chronically unfaithful to her older husband, who shows every sign of being at once chronically jealous and the innocent victim of her unhappy past. Judith's bad temper, we are told, is the product of her tragic childhood: her father killed her mother and then shot himself after losing his money in the crash of 1929.

The play's action takes place in the not too distant future, a time when people are found mysteriously incinerated by a device triggered by a little blue light—a device that would seem to owe more to the Prince of Darkness, whose demonic presence had been very much a factor in Wilson's *Memoirs of Hecate County*, than to any atom bomb. The play, which ends with a literal explosion brought on by Judith's bad temper, is not very good.

*The Little Blue Light* was first mounted in 1950, but it feels like something written in the years immediately following the divorce. Whether or not this was in fact the case, Wilson's former wife seems to have decided to give Wilson the benefit of the doubt. While she was at Newport, her relations with Wilson remained resolutely cordial and, when it came to literary matters, positively amiable. Wilson, for his part, was once again staunch in his support of her fiction—not only describing *The Groves of Academe* to Vladimir Nabokov as "in some ways, the best thing she has done" but urging him to read it. Soon she was trying to get Wilson to join the list of contributors for *Critic*.

As far as anyone could tell, Mary McCarthy and Edmund Wilson had finally mastered the art of conducting a civilized divorce. But in moving to a house where she would be only minutes away from her former husband, she was putting their fragile relations to the test. Not surprisingly, writing Dwight Macdonald in October of her decision, she was on the defensive. Forestalling any attempt he might make to dissuade her, she made it clear just how desperate her current situation was. "Newport, or rather the island," she had written in the fall of 1952, "is in the process of being ruined by industrialization; war-workers are moving in so fast that it's like some monstrous fairy-tale; goblin houses spring up overnight."

In the real world, as in fairy tales, memory can be astonishingly short. Eight years after making good her escape from Wellfleet, she gave every appearance of being eager to return to the scene of her former entrapment, a New England village that continued to harbor a fair number of goblins and one full-fledged monster, or minotaur.

**ADELAIDE WALKER**   Mary and Bowden Broadwater made a terrible mistake. They bought a house up here, which they never should have done. Everybody thought it was a great mistake for them to come back here. I think it was mostly hard on Elena. She'd been very good to Reuel and was trying to continue to be, and she was also trying to be a good wife to Edmund, which wasn't easy.

**MARIAN SCHLESINGER**   There was a side of Mary that was very reckless.

In the fall of 1953, Mary McCarthy officially returned to Wellfleet, but from the moment she arrived, it was clear that she was not going to have an easy time of it. To help meet expenses, she had rented the red house that summer to Montgomery Clift, who was no longer the affable young Broadway actor who had contributed his support to Europe-America Groups but a world-famous movie star with a growing fondness for pills and alcohol. Montgomery Clift had joined Augusta Dabney and her two children in Wellfleet almost immediately after filming *From Here To Eternity*. Weekends Kevin had joined the household, but in the end neither his presence nor Augusta's had served to keep his sister's tenant in line. Grilling a large steak in the fireplace grate, Clift somehow flipped the steak onto a white shag rug and proceeded then and there to hack it apart. Another time he managed to drive a car over his landlady's newly planted herb garden, destroying it entirely while retaining no memory of what he had done.

Although her new house had been thoroughly trashed, McCarthy omitted any mention of this when writing friends like Hannah. Instead, she wrote once again of the pleasures to be discovered during the off-season on the Cape. Making this easier was the fact that her new house was, in at least one important respect, a success. Seated at her desk in the front parlor, within easy reach of a small revolving bookcase stocked with just about any reference book she might need, she was finding it not only possible to work but possible to work well. When she craved company, she had Mary Meigs a short walk down the hill. Not to be discounted was the fact that the house itself was lovely. Mary Meigs, who for a time shared not only the Broadwaters' well but the ancient pump in their cellar whose "indiscreet hawking and belching" let them know every time she "took a bath or flushed the toilet," would go on to publish a precise and detailed portrait of the red house and the life they led in it.

**MARY MEIGS**   I felt as if Bowden and Mary were my parents and I was their child who needed guidance. Mary was five years older than I, but her authority over me came less from age than from intellect. I think that she genuinely liked me but I was too wary of her to allow myself to believe it. I myself was in that state of fear and admiration that's close to being in love.

### FROM *LILY BRISCOE: A SELF-PORTRAIT*, BY **MARY MEIGS**

Mary and Bowden painted the panelling white, like fresh cake icing, and the walls, pale pink and the ghost of lemon yellow. They filled the rooms with graceful and formal antique furniture and fresh flowers—exotic flowers like ronunculas and anemones and freesia, which came from heaven knows where[. . . .] [The house] became a dwelling worthy of Mary and Bowden, who made a work of art of their life, with *fêtes champêtres* and dinner parties which they spent days creating, and over which they presided brilliantly, often dressed in matching black and white.

Lulled by the fine autumn days, Mary and Bowden stayed on past the date scheduled for their departure, leaving empty a New York apartment they were paying rent on and waxing rhapsodic. Mary was so delighted with her first months on the Cape that she set about talking Arthur Schlesinger into taking a cottage at Wellfleet for the following summer. At the same time, she and Bowden made plans to stay on for the full summer season. That way, there would be no unreliable tenant wreaking havoc when her back was turned. But there would also be no keeping a discreet distance from Edmund Wilson during Reuel's annual summer visit.

In May 1954, having made good on their promise of a serious trip abroad, with a three-month stay in Lisbon and a long stopover in London, she and Bowden were once again back in Wellfleet. By the time the Schlesingers arrived with their four young children at the small cottage they had rented, she was already hard at work, absorbed in a new novel, whose subject she was hoping to keep secret at least for the time being. She was not so absorbed in her writing, however, as to forget that other writers, too, might need a quiet place to work. She immediately invited Arthur Schlesinger to come over in the mornings and work in her barn on what would later become the first volume of *The Age of Roosevelt*. With the offer of the barn came the offer to later read what was written in it.

### FROM ARTHUR SCHLESINGER'S REMARKS AT MARY MCCARTHY'S MEMORIAL SERVICE, NOVEMBER 8, 1989

Later she read the manuscript and returned it with a series of acute, indeed rather devastating, criticisms. I remember her remark about the prologue, a portentous account of FDR's first inauguration—almost pre-Raphaelite, she said. She was absolutely correct. This was shortly after Adlai Stevenson's 1952 campaign, and I was writing history as if I were still writing political speeches. Her comments shifted my whole perspective on the text. I withdrew the manuscript from the publisher and spent a month going over it sentence by sentence and purging it of its flourishes and excesses. This was typical of Mary—both of her generosity in giving time to her friends and her absolute fidelity to her exacting standards.

In life and in art, her high standards were everywhere evident.

**BARBARA KERR**   I remember when I stayed with them at Wellfleet Bowden had to drive to Boston—over a hundred miles to get some vanilla beans to make some vanilla ice cream. Vanilla extract wouldn't do.

**MARIAN SCHLESINGER**   For a picnic on the beach, I would pack some cheese or sandwiches, but everything was a production with her.

**CHARLES JENCKS**   She was like a black-haired Grace Kelly. On the Cape everyone is laid-back and disheveled and she was so well manicured. I mean, not a hair was wrong.

At the same time, she was not above participating in one pastime beloved by thirties radicals and fifties Cape bohemians.

**BARBARA KERR**   One day, we went over to the Macdonalds and we all went swimming nude. Nancy had decamped and Dwight was between wives. Being Bostonian, I went in sheepishly and stayed face down, but Mary was totally unconcerned. She had a rather earthy figure. I mean she had haunches—a remark that one isn't inclined to make about most women today. She looked primeval like the Venus de Milo. And I think she was not unaware of that. She didn't rush in or out of the water with any particular alacrity.

She was a strong and fearless swimmer and any hesitation on her part owed nothing to a lack of courage. For instance, when Wilson was in residence, she did nothing to avoid him. On the contrary, she was known to sometimes seek him out—to haunt, as it were, the big white house she had once lived in so unhappily. In the morgue of *Time-Life,* there is an interview with Pearl Kazin, Alfred's baby sister, from the fall of 1955 which states that it is well-known that "Mary goes into Wilson's house in Wellfleet unannounced and without knocking, a practice that infuriates the new Mrs. Wilson."

Proximity made for problems. But if there was cause for distress in the Wilson and Broadwater households, this distress may also have had roots in the past. Given the slightest opportunity, Wilson had always been quick to credit any deficiencies in Reuel's education or deportment to lapses on the part of Reuel's mother. Back in the summer of 1948, Wilson had written, "Reuel's lessons so far have amounted to nothing more than learning a few stanzas of poetry and identifying the rhymes and the beat of the verse. I had him learn some Omar Khayam because he is very much steamed up about Persia and demanded to read some Persian poetry."

Margaret Shafer would later remember Mary and Bowden's teaching Reuel "Under the Bamboo Tree" that same summer in Cornwall, so he would have it to recite for his father when he picked him up at the train station to take him to Wellfleet. Bowden had dropped Reuel off and was back at the house when Reuel called, panicked because he'd forgotten a couple of lines. "Mary very patiently recited the lines to him," Shafer recalled, "She was very calm, but you could tell it was important that Reuel not go to Edmund Wilson without some Eliot poem committed to memory. Edmund, it seemed, had complained that Reuel was not getting sufficient intellectual fare from Mary."

During the summer of 1954, Reuel was no longer a frightened little boy, trying to please and mollify two warring parents. He was fifteen years old and beginning to go to dances and to date girls. Still, there were moments when a friend would catch his parents reverting to their old roles.

**GALEN WILLIAMS**  As often happens in those cases, Reuel was the weapon they used between them. I can remember being over there one Sunday with Reuel when Edmund Wilson and Mary McCarthy were fighting. She had stopped by and wanted to take Reuel off to a picnic, but Edmund and Elena were about to sit down to lunch and Edmund insisted Reuel stay home for the meal. Elena was watching and listening, I remember. She had a way of fading into the background at times like that. Reuel turned to me and said, "Let's go for a swim." So we slipped off to Slough Pond. Needless to say, he later went on the picnic. Mary always won those fights.

**REUEL WILSON**  When my mother and Bowden were living at Wellfleet, I sometimes stayed with them and I don't remember noticing any special tension. But it couldn't have been easy for my stepmother. And it must have been a problem for some of the Wellfleet hostesses, though it seems to me there were parties at which everyone was present.

For the Broadwaters their second stay at Wellfleet did not live up to the promise of the previous autumn. Dwight Macdonald was not around to invite them over for an afternoon of nude swimming or to offer his loud and very vocal protection. With the final dissolution of the marriage, Nancy Macdonald had taken herself off to Europe and Dwight was keeping his new wife, Gloria, at a safe distance from the Wellfleet gossips. Without his presence the cocktail parties and communal beach picnics took on a less genial aspect. Mary McCarthy could fall back on Mary Meigs and the Schlesingers for support, but the three of them were all newcomers to the Cape. Among Wellfleet veterans, she could count on Gardner and Ruth Jencks, and she would always have a friend, albeit a distant one, in Adelaide Walker. Still, when it came down to it, she was as vulnerable as she had ever been to the buffeting that invariably attended the height of the Wellfleet summer season.

### FROM MARY MCCARTHY'S LETTER TO HANNAH ARENDT, AUGUST 10, 1954

Alfred [Kazin] was here and cutting me dead, for some reason. It upset me at the time, quite unjustly, since I don't like him. On the other hand, I don't dislike him so *totally*. Saul Bellow was here too, with son and dog, not very friendly, either. In short, last month was rather paranoid, which got me rattled. That's the worst of places like this; your value is continually being called into question and you shiver at social slights, even from people you don't care for. And all your friends are eager to tell you, on the beach, about parties you aren't invited to. You can't avoid knowing just what your current status is, unless you stay in the house with the door locked[. . . .] I miss Dwight, I must say.

She had set herself a January 1 deadline to finish the novel she was writing. But by mid-September she was feeling very much under the weather—confined to the house by a major hurricane, which had brought a succession of bad squalls in its wake, and confined to bed by a respiratory infection, which had lodged in her chest and threatened to turn into pneumonia. However, sick as she was, she enjoyed sufficient strength to receive Dwight Macdonald and Gloria, his "flirtatious" and "lively" new wife. "The contrast with poor Nancy is very striking," she wrote Hannah Arendt.

To both Arendt and Bernice Baumgarten she wrote of her plan to move from the "cold and gloomy" Cape to a large, well-heated house near Newport, where things promised to be better. Not only did this fall rental have the advantage of being located in a bird sanctuary but it was an "eighteenth century" house with "quantities of twentieth century bathrooms." To Baumgarten she also wrote of her own ill temper.

### FROM MARY MCCARTHY'S LETTER TO BERNICE BAUMGARTEN, SEPTEMBER 16, 1954

The summer has been vile in nearly every respect, except that I got a little work done. The weather, the people, the boredom—I've never been so tired and misanthropic.

Without question, by mid-September of 1954 she had soured on the Cape. But the letter to Baumgarten contained good news as well. She had completed a sizable chunk of a new novel, which was going to make it difficult, if not impossible, for her to remain in Wellfleet. The novel was called *A Charmed Life* and told the story of Martha Sinnott, a pretty young actress and aspiring playwright who returns with her young husband to the scene of her disastrous first marriage. Seven years have passed since Martha's scandalous departure, in her nightgown, in the dead of night. Miles Murphy, Martha's former husband, is living fifteen miles down the road, with a new wife and baby. A sometime philosopher and lay analyst, older and overbearing, Miles Murphy is the author of one highly successful commercial play.

At the same time Mary wrote Bernice Baumgarten of her plans, she packed up and mailed Baumgarten five chapters, with the hope that her agent would be able to persuade Harcourt to commit to a contract. As usual, she and Bowden were short of cash. Although it would have been wiser to hold off showing her hand, she had already sold the first chapter of the novel to *The New Yorker*. Proofs had arrived from the magazine on August 9. The minute the chapter appeared, her Wellfleet readers would see that she was up to her old tricks again, borrowing from her own life in the very first paragraph, while indulging in a bit of artistic license when real life threatened to fall short of the drama she needed to wrest from it. But not only Wellfleet readers would recognize the curious mixture of perversity and trepidation that had brought the Sinnotts back to New Leeds.

## FROM *A CHARMED LIFE*

[John and Martha] liked to be brave; dauntlessness was their medium. The fact that Martha trembled gave a shimmer to their exploits. They had bought the house because, as Martha explained to sundry perplexed listeners, they were afraid of being afraid to buy it[. . . .]

John Sinnott cut his hand trying to raise a stuck window in the downstairs bathroom. They had been established in their new-bought house a month, and John was still doing minor repairs. The summer tenant had left a row of cigarette burns on the upstairs-bathroom mantel, a big grease spot on the rug in the dining room (where he had spilled a platter of steak), a broken windowpane, an ink-stain worthy, as Martha Sinnott said, of Martin Luther on her white writing desk. The tenant was a bachelor lawyer from New York, with a theatrical clientele; and he had paid a very good rent, Martha reminded John, who was inclined to fly into tempers and feel himself misused. You had to expect some breakage, Martha said virtuously. They, too, had broken things in their day, she pointed out, reciting an inventory of their own sins as tenants. But for John it was not the same thing.

By the fall of 1954 Mary McCarthy was an old hand at dealing with the fallout from her fiction. Sometimes she seemed even to relish it. But when she was in the midst of working on her new novel, she did not want her friends and neighbors or her former husband suddenly getting the wind up. Rightly or wrongly, she believed that the novel's subject was a closely guarded secret.

## FROM MARY MCCARTHY'S LETTER TO BERNICE BAUMGARTEN, SEPTEMBER 16, 1954

By the way, don't tell anybody the subject of this novel. There's no sense in *borrowing* trouble. The first chapter, when it comes out in *The New Yorker*, is going to be described by me as a *short story*; I don't think it will offend anybody, especially; this region has no Chamber of Commerce, and there are no portraits of individuals, except the hero and heroine, who are very broadminded about that sort of thing.

With *A Charmed Life* Mary McCarthy finally got right the Cape satire she had started to write in the summer of 1945. By stating at the very outset that the villagers of New Leeds were living under a strange enchantment, she immediately darkened her fictional landscape. This time, failed writers were not the sole subject of her scrutiny. Her eye lingered long over Warren Coe, a former art instructor who is trying to introduce fission into his painting and who has a fatal fascination with the life of the mind, a fascination that takes the form of constantly asking "Why not?" and "Why?" She made fast work of Coe's rich and lazy but imperious wife, who serves guests their drinks in paper cups, substitutes toilet paper for napkins, and withholds the news of the death of her husband's mother when it threatens to interfere with a dinner party. In her spare time, McCarthy literally brought before the bar the incorrigible Sandy Gray, a sometime art critic and full-time philanderer, who fancies himself a free spirit and refuses to pay a penny of child support. (The hapless Coes owed not a little to Gardner and Ruth Jencks, loyal friends whose son, Charlie, was close to Reuel; Sandy Gray bore a passing resemblance to a dashing local by the name of Jack Phillips.)

The author's victims were dispatched with scarcely a whimper and with no little merriment. If her touch was light, it could not be said to be kind. Writing of Dolly Lamb, the shy and unmarried painter who lives down the hill from the Sinnotts, she described her as "curiously flattened out, like a cloth doll that had been dressed and redressed by many imperious mistresses." When Sandy Gray dismisses the delicate still lifes Dolly Lamb paints, he says, "It's your own shit you're assembling there, in neat, constipated little packages." (Dolly Lamb, of course, was Mary Meigs.)

At its best, McCarthy's Cape novel feels as if she has transported the cast of *The School for Scandal* to a dark New England forest where Hawthorne himself might not feel ill at ease. For much of the time, her characters, with their self-delusions and social pretensions, float clear of her sinister setting. Of all her novels, *A Charmed Life* seemed to best reflect the spirit, if not the direct influence, of Bowden Broadwater.

**NICHOLAS KING** Bowden's satiric point of view may have tempered Mary's rather rigorous tendency to draw a moral judgment. I think that the element of satire and amusement in novels like *A Charmed Life* may have come from him. Certainly he contributed to it.

*A Charmed Life* has the verve or the delicious bitchiness of social satire, but, above all, it is the story of Martha Sinnott's undoing. Martha believes that she is different. Hubris has brought her back to the village where she lived with her former husband. Hubris, bad luck, and a bit too much alcohol land her in the arms of Miles Murphy. Sheer momentum carries the narrative through the reading of Racine's *Bérénice* and on to a rape that is at once brutal and comic when seen through Murphy's small green bloodshot eyes.

### FROM *A CHARMED LIFE*
An hour and a half later, he was making love to her on the Empire sofa in her parlor. She would not let him carry her into the bedroom,

where they could have done their business in comfort. Straining at a gnat and swallowing a camel, as the Good Book said—that was milady Martha. He settled a small sofa pillow firmly under her hips, but the position was still not right[. . . .]

He began to get the idea. The thing was to respect her scruples. She did not seem to mind if he kissed her arms and shoulders; it was her breasts and mouth she was protecting, out of some peculiar pedantry[. . . .] She did not scream or try to hit him or scratch him, as she might have, and he, on his side, did not try to raise her skirt[. . . .] They made him think of a pair of wrestlers, heaving and gasping, while taking care to obey the rules. A string of beads she was wearing broke and clattered to the floor. "Sorry," he muttered, as he dove for her left breast. He heard Martha laugh faintly as she pushed his head away from her tit.

**JOHN UPDIKE** I remember a long scene where they are reading Racine in French, and again a kind of *Hecate County* moment when this husband-figure compels her to have intercourse and she more or less shrugs and goes along with it. A sort of insouciant piece of date rape.

With this rape on a sofa much like the one she herself owned, she seemed to have strayed into her former husband's fictional territory and then, not content with that, slipped into his very shoes. If you remember nothing else from the novel, you will remember Martha on that Empire sofa. The trouble is, even at the moment of Martha's undoing, the writer's tone is so insouciant that later, when Martha discovers that she is pregnant and has no idea whether Murphy or Sinnott is the father, it seems at first no more than another twist in the increasingly complicated plot. It is hard to believe that Martha is seriously debating whether to pass the baby off as her husband's or to get an abortion. In New Leeds, after all, it is so easy to say, "Why not?" And when Martha chooses the abortion and the sinister forces that lurk in the dark woods of New Leeds are at last unleashed, the reader is taken aback.

### FROM *A CHARMED LIFE*

Around a blind curve ahead, she saw the faint reflection of the headlights of a car, coming rapidly toward her: Eleanor Considine, doubtless. Martha slowed down and hugged her own side of the road. As the car crashed into her and she heard a shower of glass, she knew, in a wild flash of humor, that she had made a fatal mistake: in New Leeds, after sundown, she would have been safer on the wrong side of the road. "Killed instantly," she said to herself, regretfully, as she lost consciousness. This succinct appraisal, in the wavy blackness, became a point of light receding until she could find it no more.

**JOHN UPDIKE** I am offended by most novels that end with the violent death of the central figure. Maybe the Russians could pull that off, but in Mary McCarthy's world somehow heroines don't die that way.

Martha's death in a senseless car crash on her way to the abortionist can seem less like some terrible cosmic irony or the end of a dark modern fairy tale than a writer working against her own grain.

**JAMES MERRILL**   She wouldn't ever, even as a novelist I guess, begin to envision what it might be like to die. If she killed someone off, it was fast. The end of *A Charmed Life* is a sort of Nabokovian stroke—the lady novelist, advancing on the last page, kills the heroine.

At one point she had contemplated killing Martha off on the abortionist's table. After she sent the book on to her publisher, she was still having second thoughts.

### FROM MARY MCCARTHY'S LETTER TO BERNICE BAUMGARTEN, MAY 1, 1955

Is it very unsatisfactory to say that I don't know what happens to Martha? She might be killed and on the other hand she might have a miscarriage, simply. I think she's probably killed. This would prove she's not (what she fears) a New Leedsian, since she is mortal. See Chapter One. The end is a sort of joke or rug pulled out from under the reader. Perhaps no one will like that. The original idea was to have her die or made sterile by the abortion. I prefer this comic twist, which carries a similar idea but without sentimentality.

Forever after, Mary McCarthy would present the argument that Martha's death proves that Martha is mortal and not living under an enchantment. But for some readers she could never dispel a lingering sense that her ending was improvised or high-handed. She was no Russian and Martha Sinnott was no Anna Karenina. If her letters to Hannah Arendt are to be taken at face value, at the time she was writing the novel, she was devoting more of her attention to the poor excuse for thinking endemic to the natives of New Leeds than to the fate of her poor heroine.

### FROM MARY MCCARTHY'S LETTER TO HANNAH ARENDT, AUGUST 10, 1954

One thing I'm anxious to talk to you about is a problem connected with the novel[. . . .] "How do you *know* that?" one of the characters keeps babbling about any statement in the realm of fact or aesthetics. In morals, the reiterated question is "Why not?" "Why shouldn't I murder my grandfather if I want to? Give me one good reason," another character pleads. This is Raskolnikov's old problem, but in a kind of grotesque parody; the questioner is not serious but in a kind of mental fret, like a child begging for answers, which it doesn't expect to understand[. . . .] When did this ritualistic doubting begin to permeate, first, philosophy and then popular thinking? I presume that in its modern form it goes back to Kant. Or would you say Hume?

That this battery of questions was brought forth with some intention of currying favor with the recipient of the letter is quite possible. If so, it had its intended effect. For Arendt the questions were "a real joy," sending her off to her typewriter to compose the first long letter of their burgeoning correspondence—a three-page single-spaced disquisition that moved from a lengthy history of skepticism to subjects more mundane, including a proposed visit to Wellfleet. In passing, Arendt took time to sound an epistemological warning.

### FROM HANNAH ARENDT'S LETTER TO MARY MCCARTHY, AUGUST 20, 1954

The chief fallacy is to believe that Truth is a result which comes at the end of a thought-process. Truth, on the contrary, is always the beginning of thought; thinking is always result-less.

But if there was an element of flattery in McCarthy's queries, there was also some attempt to deflect potential criticism. Four months later, when she again broached the subject of the novel, it was clear to her that the book would never be finished by the beginning of January. It was also clear to her that Arendt was never going to be happy with at least one important aspect of it.

### FROM MARY MCCARTHY'S LETTER TO HANNAH ARENDT, DECEMBER 8, 1954

My novel is going ahead, but I have you horribly on my conscience every time sex appears. You are tugging at my elbow saying "Stop" during a seduction scene I've just been writing. And your imagined remonstrances have been so effective that I've rewritten it to have it seen from the man's point of view, instead of the heroine's. But you still won't like it, I'm afraid. I'm not joking, altogether; I have misgivings about the taste of this novel, which localize around your anticipated or feared reaction. It has a "personal" note that troubles me, even though I assure myself that many of the great novels had that too[. . . .] Well, one doesn't have to rehearse the history of literature to know that there are precedents, but precedent is a poor rallying-point for works of art.

Knowing that this novel was going to be closer in spirit to *The Company She Keeps* than to *The Oasis*, she had continued to work on it. She continued, knowing all the while that Hannah Arendt was not going to like it. And she continued, knowing how much Bowden had disliked "The Weeds," the last work of fiction to rely for its titillation as well as its energy on exploring the horrors of her marriage to Wilson.

As her first reader and husband, Bowden Broadwater continued to enjoy much sway with her. If she was prepared to put Wellfleet behind her, she had no wish to walk away from her third marriage. In the end, the first chapter she sold to *The New Yorker*, with its anatomy of the pressures and tensions that threaten the Sinnott marriage, would be as personal as *A Charmed Life* would ever get. By turning the focus of the novel outward and emphasizing the earlier satirical premise of "The Lost Week," she managed to skirt some, if not all, of the intimate details that were bound to displease her husband and her best friend.

John Sinnott—so closely observed at the novel's beginning—was gradually but ineluctably pushed from the foreground. The trouble is, in art and in life, nature abhors a vacuum. Whether he was destined for this role or not, the terrible Miles Murphy gradually began to take John Sinnott's place on the page. By the time Miles Murphy rapes Martha on the Empire sofa, John Sinnott seems continents away rather than just a few dozen miles down the road. For all that he is Martha's husband, he has less substance than Warren Coe or Sandy Gray—less substance certainly than the man who is tearing the dress off his wife. Only afterward, when she has sent Miles home, does Martha stop to think about her husband:

### FROM *A CHARMED LIFE*

She made a face and proceeded unsteadily to the bathroom. But as she stood there, brushing her teeth, her sensuality relived those few moments, and she longed for John to come home. Disgusted with herself, she rinsed out her mouth and spat into the basin. Nothing, she thought, angrily, could be more immoral than utilizing your husband, whom you loved, to slake the desires kindled by another man, whom you detested. Moreover, her practical side added, she would be very unattractive to him in her present condition, still half-tight, swaying a little, and smelling of stale alcohol.

That there had been an actual rape by Edmund Wilson seems unlikely. Indeed the scene on the Empire sofa has the antic authority and chilling power of fully imagined fiction. But even if Wilson did not lay a hand on her it is very possible that she felt as if she had been taken over, or overwhelmed. Autocratic and seductive, Wilson the critic, like Wilson the man, tended to carry all before him. His opinions were delivered with the resounding force of final judgments. To make matters worse, she had somehow brought this all on herself.

In the fall of 1954, Edmund Wilson cast a long shadow. Negotiating with Roger Straus over the collection of her "Theater Chronicles," she felt a need to deny that she had been influenced by his *Classics and Commercials* when she decided on her proposed title. Later that fall, her opinion of the manuscript of Nabokov's *Lolita* became bound up—though it was not her intention—with Wilson's.

By mid-November both she and Roger Straus had read a good portion of *Lolita* at the behest of Philip Rahv, who was thinking of taking a portion for *Partisan Review*. Rahv had brought to the book the special sympathy of someone born and partly raised in Russia. For their part, both she and Straus were not quite so enamored of the manuscript. Characteristically, she was troubled by a lack of clarity in the last section and by an annoying sense that she had missed something. Still, she found a good deal to like. More to like, she was quick to say, than Straus did, although both readers were hardly oblivious to the book's special power.

## FROM MARY MCCARTHY'S LETTER TO ROGER STRAUS, NOVEMBER 11, 1954

I got within forty pages of finishing Vladimir Nabokov. I don't exactly see it as you did. The second volume didn't bore me; I liked the motels and the awful American scene and the desolation of the whole business. What troubled me was that I didn't understand the latter part; it seemed to be turning into some sort of myth or allegory, but what it was I couldn't make out. Everybody began to get very symbolic or was it supposed to be merely sinister: I missed the end, which might have cleared things up; we had to leave before I could finish. The other thing that made me wonder was that the writing got awfully hit-or-miss toward the end. But was that supposed to be part of the idea? What I do feel sure of is that anybody who published it would be prosecuted. He makes nympholepsy or whatever it is too seductive, like an actual temptation. Is Philip going to dare it?

## FROM STRAUS'S LETTER TO MCCARTHY, NOVEMBER 15, 1954

As to Nabokov's book, I agree with you that nobody will dare touch this, leaving out its literary merits or demerits. I did talk to Philip about it and he does want to play around with the idea of publishing a section of it. He seems to like it the best of all, excepting perhaps Elana [*sic*] Wilson, who really likes it. It is the damnedest book, and as I walk down Madison Avenue I can now see a nymphet or a juvenile nymphet or an overage nymphet at least three blocks away.

Edmund Wilson, however, remained thoroughly impervious to any seduction by "nymphets." At the end of November he wrote Nabokov to let him know that he did not much care for *Lolita* and neither did Mary. "Nasty subjects may make fine books," he wrote, "but I don't feel you have got away with this." To supplement his letter he enclosed a warm note to Nabokov from Elena and an extract from a letter sent him by Mary.

Putting together this little packet for Nabokov, Wilson had availed himself of a virtual harem of second readers. As in any harem, there was a favorite. Whereas he was pleased to pass on his current wife's words of praise for *Lolita*, he did not give her words quite the same weight as the

more negative opinion offered up by his former wife. Elena might be of
Russian extraction and European in her upbringing, but when it came to
the fine art of literary criticism she was in his eyes a rank amateur. His
former wife, of course, was a pro. Writing to Wilson, whose opinion of
the manuscript was no secret to anyone, she had managed to raise again
the specific objections she had raised in her letter to Straus while sounding a note that was at once a shade more tentative and a shade less positive.

### FROM MARY MCCARTHY'S LETTER, QUOTED IN EDMUND WILSON'S LETTER TO VLADIMIR NABOKOV, NOVEMBER 30, 1954

About Vladimir's book—I think I have a midway position. I say think
because I didn't quite finish it[. . . .] I don't agree with you that the second volume was boring. Mystifying, rather, it seemed to me; I felt it
had escaped into some elaborate allegory or series of symbols that I
couldn't grasp[. . . .] [A]ll the characters had a kite of meaning tugging
at them from above, in Vladimir's enigmatic empyrean[. . . .] I thought
the writing was terribly sloppy all through, perhaps worse in the second volume. It was full of what teachers call *haziness*, and all of
Vladimir's hollowest jokes and puns. I almost wondered whether this
wasn't deliberate—part of the idea.

Mary McCarthy was well away from Edmund Wilson when *A
Charmed Life,* sporting a full-page jacket photograph by Cecil Beaton,
came out in the fall of 1955. From *The New York Times* it received a
splendid daily review. From the bulk of the critics, however, it received
the sort of mixed but slightly acid response that she had grown to expect.
Even John Chamberlain, who had always made it a point to give her the
benefit of the doubt, did not see fit to spare her this time round.

### FROM CHARLES POORE'S REVIEW IN *THE NEW YORK TIMES*, NOVEMBER 3, 1955

The stuff that Noel Coward made into a glittering comedy in *Private
Lives* Mary McCarthy makes into a glittering tragedy in *A Charmed
Life*[. . . .] Both embody dire warnings of the perilous effects that first
husbands are likely to exert if they are allowed to come horsing around
second marriages. The greatest love affair in the lives of Miss
McCarthy's heroines is always the courtship of disaster. They hate
what they want when they get it.

### FROM VIRGILIA PETERSON'S REVIEW IN THE *NEW YORK HERALD TRIBUNE BOOK REVIEW*, NOVEMBER 13, 1955

Does Martha still love her second husband? Does she still hate her first
one? Or does she perhaps still love and hate—in her thirties—only herself? Those who can lend themselves to Mary McCarthy's brilliant
sophistication, relentless wit, and curious mixture of respect for the

mind and disrespect for the soul, will want to know[. . . .] [But] the book will leave most readers quite unmoved.

## FROM JOHN CHAMBERLAIN'S REVIEW IN *NATIONAL REVIEW*, DECEMBER 21, 1955

Miss McCarthy once praised her own education in a very revealing piece about Vassar. Yet she is a living example of what happens when an artist of potentiality is deprived of knowledge for lack of immersion in the ordinary world. Miss McCarthy should have lived in suburbia, or married a politician, or joined the Waves or the Wacs, or done something else that would have brought more important material into contact with her extraordinary sensibility. As it is, she is wasting a ten-inch gun on gnats, and paying off old scores by striking at people she might as well forget.

By now not only intimates but reviewers were well aware that they could count on finding real-life models for the better part of McCarthy's characters. A review in the *Boston Globe* was devoted almost entirely to the question of whether Wellfleet, which had no ferry, could possibly be the model for New Leeds. At more or less the same time, Louise Bogan was expressing her horror to May Sarton at what Mary McCarthy had done to her good friend and Wellfleet's most prominent citizen. Indeed, the effect of the book on Edmund Wilson and his immediate family seemed to be on more than one mind that fall and winter.

## FROM LOUISE BOGAN'S LETTER TO MAY SARTON, DECEMBER 1, 1955

[I]t's a pity she had to disguise Edmund into such a *caricature*—with a *Jesuit* education: he who is the most early American Protestant character I have ever known[. . . .] Well, she is a strange one—from the *Partisan Review* to Cecil Beaton in less than 20 years takes some doing. If someone could break through her veneer, she might write a fine novel. But surely that cannot happen, now that she is in her middle-forties (she is a perennial 32 in the book, you will notice).

**GLORIA MACDONALD**  One night in New York at our apartment, soon after *A Charmed Life* had come out, she called Reuel, who was in school then, and after talking to him for a while she came back from the telephone and she said, "I don't know why Reuel was so cold to me." Dwight said, "Don't you think it might have been because of what you wrote about his father?" And she said, "What do you mean his father? That wasn't supposed to be Edmund. Edmund never painted."

**REUEL WILSON**  I don't remember being upset by the book. So I'm sure that any coldness to my mother on the phone had nothing to do with that. My father claimed he never read the book.

When Edmund Wilson claimed never to have read the book, some people took him at his word, while others, like Mary Meigs, found this hard to credit. In public Mary McCarthy would continue to claim that she had never been thinking of Wilson—after all, his nose was not long and he was not by any stretch of the imagination Irish—but to Arthur Schlesinger she admitted in private that while Miles Murphy was not intended to be Wilson, her former husband had been a source of inspiration.

### FROM MARY MCCARTHY'S LETTER TO ARTHUR SCHLESINGER, NOVEMBER 13, 1955

> He's not really meant to be Edmund, but a modern type of "compleat" man who is always a four-flusher like a piece of imitation Renaissance architecture. To the extent that Edmund is a boor and a four-flusher[. . . ], Miles is a kind of joke extrapolation of him—minus the talent, minus the pathos[. . . .] Edmund has in common with Miles a capacity for behaving *incredibly*. But I'm not under the illusion that he would buy a portrait of me by Warren Coe or by Titian; or that he would bluster into my house and make a pass at me. Nothing could be farther from his character, which is that of a bourgeois family man; he has extremely strong notions of propriety.

After the publication of *A Charmed Life*, relations with Wilson grew ever more distant but that may have had more to do with geography than with anything she had done to him. If Wilson did at some point take a look at a few choice pages, he may have regarded Miles Murphy as fair repayment for Judith in *The Little Blue Light*. He was a difficult man but he was a generous man. Taking his lead from his former wife's response to his play, he may have decided to bide his time. He may have also concluded it was hardly worth his raising a fuss.

Not every resident of Wellfleet was so forbearing. But for the most part, friends who found their likenesses in the book bore up with style. On the eve of the novel's publication, Ruth Jencks wrote Bowden Broadwater to say how much she and Gardner admired what Mary had done.

### FROM RUTH JENCKS'S LETTER TO BOWDEN BROADWATER, N.D. [C. LATE 1955]

> We have finished *The Charmed Life* [sic] with much laughter and sadness to be through and Gardner with many a Warren Coe question, and me with some too. Your anxieties about our reactions were quite unnecessary—we loved every minute of the book and didn't feel the least big angry at all. It often seemed as if Mary were really writing just for us[. . . .] Of course I don't feel G. is quite such a fatuous fool as Warren Coe, but I can't seem to feel any resentment, only real pleasure that so much of Gardner's wonderful qualities were also perceived.

Of course laughter and pleasure on paper do not preclude the possibility of other, less becoming, responses in private.

**NANCY MACDONALD**   The following summer Ruth Jencks and I decided we were going to write an anti-Mary novel, but we never did anything about it. In the end everyone forgave Mary.

**CHARLES JENCKS**   My mother would be upset, but she would never let it fester. She would forgive and forget.

**GLORIA MACDONALD**   After the book came out, I was afraid to mention Mary's name, I thought the Jenckses would be so horrified. Instead, it was their apotheosis. They talked about it all the time. In fact, they were in New York a bit and staying at the Hotel Chelsea and Ruth had us over for drinks, and she said, "See, jelly glasses," holding up the glass in her hand.

**MARY MEIGS**   Nobody in the book was pleased, particularly Gardner Jencks. I know this because we talked to each other about it. Gardner was struck to the heart by this image of him as a kind of holy fool, brimming with improbable ideas and anxious to talk about them. He thought that Mary's image of him made him seem ridiculous.

For decades Mary Meigs said nothing, and then in 1982, she published her autobiography, letting McCarthy know just how painful the portrait of Dolly Lamb had been for her.

#### FROM *LILY BRISCOE*, BY MARY MEIGS
> It was as though all of Mary's victims in Wellfleet had been struck down with a wasting disease. I saw them, pale and shaken, unsure of themselves, unsure of everybody else (for this awful image of themselves might now be accepted as the true one), and I dragged myself about in a state of doubt and self-loathing for a long time[. . . .] It meant nothing to me that Dolly Lamb was the nicest person in the book [. . .] and that Martha says to her, "I love you, Dolly." This "I love you, Dolly" was propitiatory, like Mary's smiles—either that or it was supposed to give her the right to be cruel.

The author of *A Charmed Life* responded with a long letter, explaining how she had been using the "*style indirect libre*" beloved by Flaubert and had never expected Sandy Gray's words to be mistaken for her own. Mary Meigs was not entirely mollified. She wrote back, "Of all my friends who've read both *A Charmed Life* and my book not one of them [. . .] has either spoken of your use of the *style indirect libre* nor has pointed out to me that my interpretation was wrong." Even so, the two women remained on good terms. In her letter McCarthy had written of her fondness for Mary Meigs, signing it, "My love to you, as always." Furthermore, she had apologized for the pain she had caused.

#### FROM MARY MCCARTHY'S LETTER TO MARY MEIGS, JANUARY 20, 1982
> [B]y the invention of Dolly I grossly invaded your privacy, and that I

am sorry for, even though I don't know how to rectify it and never did. I cannot stop using real people in my fiction. Hannah, as so often, had the explanation: "You are a critic, and so you must quote." As you see, it's a kindly explanation.

In *Lily Briscoe* Mary Meigs had also written about Bowden Broadwater—about his information gathering, about his visits to her cabin, and about his attempt to cure her of her homosexuality.

### FROM *LILY BRISCOE*

He was like a pelican digesting its fish and making a savoury mess of it, which it then regurgitates for the infant bird—in this case, Mary. Bowden acted as an extra pair of eyes and ears for Mary, I thought[. . . .] While Bowden, with his eyes on me, talked lazily about heterosexual love, I found myself sliding toward one of my ritual tests, for he proposed himself as a mentor one night when Mary was away and we were having dinner together at my house. I prepared myself for the ordeal with two dry martinis and we went to bed. For me it was over in seconds and I proved, at least to myself, that I wasn't frigid[. . . .] Oddly enough, I had no feeling of having betrayed my friend. My experience with Bowden, I thought, could only have made Mary laugh the laugh that I liked and feared.

In her letter McCarthy was quick to correct Meigs on the subject of Bowden's being her eyes and ears. But when it came to the second, and more shocking, bit of information, she showed no such readiness to pursue the discussion.

**MARY MEIGS** Mary didn't know until she read my book that I'd gone to bed with Bowden. But she didn't say anything about it in her letter and never brought it up later. When I wrote the book I didn't worry about whether Mary knew or not. Our going to bed wasn't important to me. And I didn't think it was important to Bowden, either.

How Bowden felt about *A Charmed Life* no one seemed to know. But Philip Rahv, who had told a *Time* interviewer he saw no reason for Wilson to be upset by the portrait of Miles Murphy since it wasn't much like him, was not so sanguine about the fate that Bowden Broadwater had met. As he saw it, by making John Sinnott so bland in the novel the writer presented no possible reason that anyone would want to be married to him. In this opinion Rahv was not alone, but if Bowden Broadwater found fault with the portrait of John Sinnott—or was hurt by it—he did not let on.

**REUEL WILSON**   I remember teasing Bowden about John Sinnott, but I don't think it bothered him. I don't think he had any reason to be upset. He wasn't anything like John Sinnott.

Even if Bowden Broadwater had in fact been like John Sinnott, this fictional portrait was not of a sort to send you off screaming into the night. Compared to the portrait of poor Sidney in *Pictures from an Institution*, it was positively flattering. If John Sinnott was a pale character, he was nonetheless Martha's equal. And if the author of *A Charmed Life* had done him a disservice, she had not done it deliberately. Unfortunately, the life the Broadwaters were living in Wellfleet was beginning to conform more than was comfortable to the life Jarrell had mocked on the page.

At Newport, Bowden had been a full partner in the marriage. Indeed when it came to Newport society he had enjoyed a decided advantage. Once they were back in New York and his wife had made her peace with Philip Rahv, he was left to make the best of it. For Bowden, his wife's return to the fold was hardly a victory. In New York, with no job in the offing and Reuel away at boarding school, he had nothing to occupy him. In Wellfleet, with his fine manners and fine clothes, he risked being taken at less than his worth or being dismissed as faintly ridiculous. At most, he seemed like a useful appendage—Mary's eyes and ears. Finally, along with the rest of his wife's circle, he had become grist for her fictional mill.

**CHARLES JENCKS**   I guess she thought her duty was to her art and not to her friends. It was the reverse of Forster, who said, "I'd rather betray my country than my friend."

Whether Mary McCarthy had intended it or not, the writing of *A Charmed Life* marked a turning point in her career and in her life. Despite the working fireplaces and the central heating in the rented Newport house she and Bowden had been living in as she struggled to finish her novel, she had succumbed to pneumonia in January 1955. In March, with *A Charmed Life* still unfinished and spring a distant promise, she and Bowden had taken a friend up on his offer to lend them his villa on Capri.

On the island of Capri, like centuries of visitors before them, they had found warmth and sunshine and a sufficient number of curiosities to amuse them for five weeks. By the time they had left the island in late April, she had finished her novel and she and Bowden were not getting on. Why they were fighting she would later declare to be a mystery. Why she did not pack up and return to the Cape was simple enough: she and

Bowden had once again rented their house out. In any case, their money, such as it was, would go farther in Europe. Already they had promised themselves an economy version of a "grand tour." With Bowden's old friend Carmen Angleton they planned to buy a Jeep and drive through southern Italy and then take a ferry to Greece, where at last she would set foot on the soil where Lord Byron had lost his life fighting for democracy and independence against the Turks.

Once again, by following in Byron's footsteps, Mary McCarthy ended up confined to her bed. "A writer's witchcraft is at work," Mary Meigs would later write, describing what she had wrought by creating the character Dolly Lamb. But the witchcraft was apparently beyond the writer's control. For Martha's creator, life very soon began to imitate art, and then to improve on art with a vengeance. Upon her arrival in Greece, having long since abandoned the Jeep, she discovered that she, like poor Martha Sinnott, was pregnant. The time could not have been more inconvenient.

Unlike the heroine of *A Charmed Life,* she chose to keep the baby. But she had no more influence over her fate than Martha Sinnott had. She had begun to bleed. Permitted no sight-seeing and only the briefest of excursions to the Acropolis—where she "literally crawled over it and up the steps of the Parthenon"—she spent most of her time in Athens and her ten-day stay on Mykonos confined to bed. Having staved off a threatened miscarriage long enough to depart for parts more civilized, she lost the baby on the plane to Paris. All her pain and suffering had been for nothing.

By the time *A Charmed Life* came out, she was renting a room in an apartment in Venice, and Bowden Broadwater was back in New York looking once again for a job and a permanent place to live. The Wellfleet house had been sold to Mary Meigs. Touring the south of France in the company of Reuel, the Broadwaters had barely spoken to each other. In mid-August they had separated. For months they had been living apart. If she and Bowden were once again exchanging letters, it was owing to her persistence. While she was ready to put Wilson and Wellfleet behind her, she was not yet ready to turn her back on her marriage. In important respects Bowden suited her. This time, though, the decision might not be hers to make.

On the back of the dust jacket of *A Charmed Life* is a photograph worthy of Greta Garbo, credited to Cecil Beaton, where the author is shown leaning against a pillar. Her head is in profile, the lid of her one visible eye lowered, as though in reverie. She looks at once beautiful and serene. Below the photograph is her name, Mary McCarthy. Nothing more. Nowhere on the dust jacket or within the body of the book is there any personal history. Recognition is taken for granted. The writer has reached a point where she does not have to explain who she is.

For some readers *A Charmed Life* would be McCarthy's most perfect novel. For others it would be the last of her novels to hold out the promise that one day she might rise to the level of a Jane Austen or George Eliot. In the next decade she would go on to become an international celebrity, but never again would she occupy the enviable if daunting position of a writer at the height of her powers poised to take on the world.

# Chapter Sixteen

# VENICE

During the 1950s, when television was just beginning to present a threat to print journalism, Henry Luce's *Time* could be found in virtually every self-respecting middle-class household in America. With its Republican politics and its snide sentences that ran backward, it was something of a standing joke in the circle the Broadwaters traveled in. Yet its lack of literary cachet did not keep Bowden Broadwater from moonlighting there as a free-lance proofreader. For writers and intellectuals it had always been the employer of last resort.

Like it or not, the magazine's power was undeniable: to make the cover of *Time* was to know you had truly arrived. In the early fall of 1955 *Time*'s editors began preparing a full-scale piece to mark the November publication of *A Charmed Life*. If such attention was flattering, it was also fraught with peril. Living on her own in Venice, a nervous Mary McCarthy found she could neither deflect *Time*'s assiduous researchers nor totally ignore them. Finally, against her better judgment, she consented to be interviewed by the director of the magazine's Rome bureau.

She did not make the cover of *Time*. Instead, a personal profile masquerading as a three-column book review ran in the issue of November 14. "Among those puffing their way up the descending escalator of intellectual fashion, many have cause to remember the shrewdly placed elbow and deft umbrella of a comparative shopper in ideas called Mary McCarthy," *Time* announced right off. Having made it clear that the handsome dark-haired novelist in the accompanying Cecil Beaton photograph had no lock on impudence or free-floating bitchiness, the editors proceeded to rely on sly insinuation, unattributed quotes, and outright gossip. Having lingered long over her years as a Sacred Heart misfit and Vassar outsider, they concluded that the "Clever Young Egg" of her memoir "C.Y.E." had hatched into "a pretty bird of prey" whose natural habitat was the world of little magazines and whose "far-from-secret weapon is to write her enemies—and friends—into her books." Her new book, readers were told, was no exception.

All the same, for the pretty bird of prey there was some consolation. *Time* let it be known that Mary McCarthy was someone educated readers could not afford to ignore. "She is," the magazine proclaimed, "quite possibly the cleverest writer the U.S. has ever produced." Overheated and hyperbolic and ultimately ambiguous, *Time*'s imprimatur would stick to McCarthy, and remain fixed to her, for the rest of her writing life. For the bulk of readers, these fine-sounding words would pass as a glowing recommendation—fodder for more than one dust jacket and for untold future profiles. But for McCarthy and her friends, they carried an implication that was hardly complimentary. For anyone who chose his words with care, "clever" would always carry the unhappy connotation of "lacking in depth and soundness."

That November, *Time* did not stint on ambiguous superlatives. She was not only lauded for her cleverness but also declared to be "the most enviable of women." Readers were told that she was enviable because she was "remarkably handsome at forty-three," because she was "renowned among her friends both as a wit and a cook," and because she was "currently in Venice," working on a book on the city that was "already commissioned."

In fact, by the time the *Time* profile came out, she could be found beating a hasty retreat from a city in which she had landed by pure accident and in which she had never felt completely at ease. She was about to return to Manhattan, to mixed reviews of *A Charmed Life* and the Hotel Chelsea. No suitable apartment had materialized. Any place Bowden Broadwater could afford to purchase with the proceeds from the sale of the Wellfleet house had fallen short of her exacting standards—and of his, for that matter. Indeed, after a spate of letters in which she had made every effort to repair the rupture that had led them to part company at the end of the summer, there was some question as to whether they were going to get back together at all.

Certainly shrewdness and calculation had played little part in getting her to Venice in the first place. By mid-August not only were she and Bowden barely speaking but they were terribly short of funds. They were in Paris, preparing to return to America, when forty-eight hours before they were due to board a ship for New York, a "freak hurricane" blew up. A message arrived at their hotel from Georges and Rosamond Bernier, a couple known to them only as the editors of a stylish new French art magazine called *L'Oeil*.

The Berniers were in Switzerland, meeting with their printer, final-izing plans for a book on Venice—a book to be lavishly produced, with splendid new color photographs of the finest Venetian sights and splendid color plates of the more celebrated works of art. They wanted McCarthy to write the text. If all went well, it would be the start of a series. For her efforts they promised to pay an advance of three thousand dollars and a royalty of 7½ percent on a projected printing of thirty thousand copies. Half of the books were to be in English and half in French and they would sell for about twelve dollars each.

Her name had been suggested by a mutual friend who was privy to the recent discord in the Broadwater marriage and had reason to believe that a temporary separation might be welcome. Georges Bernier had read *The Company She Keeps* and admired it. In addition, he knew that she sometimes earned extra money as a ghostwriter, penning letters and catalog copy for Mannie Rousuck, who had risen through the ranks of Wildenstein's to become the head of the gallery's department of European painting and a good friend of the collector Paul Mellon.

When it came time to set sail for America, Bowden Broadwater took Reuel back with him to New York and Mary McCarthy turned in her ticket and prepared to join the Berniers in Lausanne. As yet she had not laid eyes on either of them. All she had to go on was their promise that they would be waiting at the train station to meet her.

As it turned out, she and the Berniers had quite a number of friends in common, not least of them Cyril Connolly. Rosamond Bernier, an American whose friends called her Peggy, had been born in Philadelphia and educated first in England and then at Sarah Lawrence. She had worked as an editor at *Vogue* and was bright and ambitious and "open in her manners." Her husband, however, was another matter. Older than his wife, Bernier was dark, possessed of "an 'interesting' profile," and hard to read. On her second day in Switzerland, when the Berniers were late sending half of her promised advance to her bank in America, she began to wonder if she could trust them. She was not quite sure what to make of them. More to the point, she was not sure what they made of her.

The Berniers had put her up at the Hotel Victoria, not an obvious choice but one that had special meaning for her. It was the same hotel where nine years earlier she had nearly succumbed to pneumonia and the ministrations of a Swiss doctor. In 1946, she had been very much in love and very much afraid she would lose Bowden Broadwater to Carmen Angleton. In due time, she had recovered her health sufficiently to follow Peggy Guggenheim to Venice, before returning to America with Bowden Broadwater safely at her side. In 1955, Carmen Angleton was once again playing an important part in her life, having just accompanied her and Bowden on their ill-fated trip to Greece.

Her second day in Lausanne, with nothing to do but sit in her hotel room awaiting final confirmation that the money the Berniers sent to her bank had arrived safely, Mary wrote Bowden a three-page typed letter. She wrote of arriving to find their old hotel suddenly "plate glass and blond woods"; of getting to know the Berniers, who reminded her "somehow of people in the theatre or Hollywood people"; of running into James Laughlin before she left Paris and finding him "more ox-like than ever"; and of then going to Chartres for a day trip with Carmen Angleton, who "wanted to know the legend of every tiny pane of stained glass." But she was not able to sustain this blithe gossipy tone for long. "I miss you terribly," she confessed. "It feels so weirdly unreal to have you gone. When I wake up in the mornings my eyes feel and look swollen, as if I'd been crying in my dreams."

The third day, when she was certain her advance had been paid in full, she wrote Bernice Baumgarten. Informing her agent of her sudden change of plans and of the financial deal she had struck, she sounded at once confident and very pleased with herself. She made no mention of any personal reasons for her sudden decision to stay on in Europe. But at the end of the letter, having sent her "warm regards" and promised to write soon, she once again confessed to distress. "Between ourselves, I'm scared to death by this dreamlike situation, which has the added oddity of retracing for me step by step my trip in '46, so that I feel: this is where I came in."

Later that same afternoon, she set off with the Berniers in their convertible for Venice, where Georges Bernier booked rooms for nine days at the Bauer Grunwald, the one luxury hotel on the Grand Canal where you did not have to reserve in advance. Ostensibly the Berniers were there to see that she got her bearings—to introduce her to the libraries she would need for her research, to show her the major points they wanted covered, to make some necessary introductions, and to help her find a place to stay for the next three months. But the Berniers' presence was a mixed blessing. The more the three of them talked, the more it became apparent to her that the book that had been commissioned was not "something impressionistic" but "something very solid and packed with documentation." Something with "a rapport between the pictures and the text."

To Bowden, who had written in response to her Lausanne letter, she confided how bad things were. With friends who stopped by for drinks or dinner, the Berniers spoke French and Italian. Her spoken French was not fluent; her Italian was nonexistent. Whenever she crossed the threshold of the Galleria dell'Accademia, it was evident she had only the haziest idea of what she was seeing. She was no art critic. Venetian history was no more than a confused jumble to her. Though the editors at *Time* might choose to call her clever, from the outset of her stay in Venice she felt "completely overwhelmed."

### FROM MARY MCCARTHY'S LETTER TO BOWDEN BROADWATER, AUGUST, 29, 1955

"You will want, perhaps," says Georges Bernier, "to give ten pages to Tiepolo. . . ." !!! And of course I know absolutely nothing of the three Vivarinis and the three Bellinis, Jacopo, Giovanni, Gentile, or of the vast distinction between Lorenzo Veneziano and Paolo ditto. All this has produced the most intense symptoms of Feelings of Personal Inadequacy, so that I make the most awful mistakes, like talking of Pierre Matisse when I mean Henri but really mean Piet Mondrian. I can no longer tell Gothic from Romanesque or Renaissance from eighteenth century or eighteenth century from ottocento, and I'm afraid to open my mouth for fear of what monstrous toad of error may come out and frighten the Berniers out of their wits.

If the Berniers were alarmed, they were careful not to show it during the nine days they stayed with her. By the time they took their leave on August 30, it was settled that Rosamond Bernier would return to check on how she was getting along. All the same, certain unspoken questions seemed to linger in the air. First, how was she going to survive without a guide or interpreter? Second, how was she going to turn in a finished book by her March deadline without disgracing herself and these two cosmopolitan publishing entrepreneurs? Finally, how had two such shrewd and ambitious people made such a terrible mistake?

**GEORGES BERNIER**  I knew somehow that she had worked and done research for Wildenstein, so I thought that this very talented author who had some knowledge of art history might be interesting to contact. I wanted somebody who was out of this perpetual thing, you know, of twenty-five art writers who dance a ballet between Europe and America. It was a gamble.

**ROSAMOND BERNIER**  In a nutshell, she was commissioned to write the equivalent of a profile of Venice. Not an art book.

The apartment the Berniers helped her find was situated on the Campo San Lorenzo, within easy walking distance of St. Mark's Square and the Correr Library. Like all the places she had looked at, it was expensive. And, like all of them, it was far from perfect. She would have to share a bath with the chic blonde signora who owned it plus her teenage son and daughter, all of whom were moving to a smaller apartment upstairs. But for her eighty thousand lire she would be getting a telephone, gas and electricity, and a "glorious gold Florentine bed with life-size cupids."

By the time the Berniers were ready to go back to Paris, she had agreed to take the signora's apartment. She had also concluded that Rosamond was "very straight, very sweet, hard-working and delicate at the same time," while Georges was simply "*autre chose,*" but "kept up to the mark" by his wife. Unfortunately, Rosamond did not have a chance to impose her rigorous standards on the signora, who from the start showed no inclination to honor her promise to move out.

Before the new tenant had passed her first full night in that glorious Florentine bed on the Campo San Lorenzo, it was apparent that she was never going to have the apartment entirely to herself. Not only had the family "retained a hold on half the icebox and half the bathroom" but the family cat was "laying siege" at her window. Still, there were practical reasons for staying—the rent was lower than she had remembered and the kitchen was large and modern. More compelling were reasons that were not so practical.

### FROM MARY McCARTHY'S LETTER TO BOWDEN BROADWATER, AUGUST 31, 1955

> It has a romantic view of the cypressy gardens of a palazzo next door, lots of light, and furniture I rather like—blue and white striped cushions on Louis Quinze style chairs, painted tables and cabinets all in blue and white and pink, with Tiepolo motifs, pretty china on display everywhere, waiting for *il gatto* to break, and the huge gilt Florentine bed I think I wrote you about. The signora has allowed that I am *come una bella donna fiorentina del quattrocento.*

Unfortunately, her one contact in Venice was problematic at best. When the Berniers were still in residence, Peggy Guggenheim had invited the three of them to dinner and served them "awful food, a stingy peppery goulash prepared with her own hands." She had lent the three of them her gondola for an afternoon and then gone on to lend her Ruskin's book on Venice and a "delightful" book by William Dean Howells. But Guggenheim had not really forgiven her for "The Cicerone." She kept "coming back to the topic of 'Why did you put such awful things about me in your book?'"

Moreover, the research was not going well. Seated at a long table at the Correr Library, exploring the farthest reaches of the lagoon, or slipping into a poorly lit chapel one step ahead of an eager sacristan, she was constantly aware of the myriad writers who had preceded her—not only Howells and Ruskin but Casanova and James and Pater. Of all the art she saw at the Accademia she liked best the Tintorettos and the St. Ursula series by Carpaccio. Best of all she liked the Carpaccios at San Giorgio degli Schiavoni—the most famous of them depicting the encounter between St.

George and the Dragon. Unfortunately, her judgments seemed to "coincide precisely with Ruskin's judgment." There was nothing fresh to say.

She could not tell one doge from another. She could find no history of Venice in English. The eighteenth-century comedies of Goldoni, Venice's sole stellar literary figure, she could find only in Italian. For reproductions of the art she was seeing, she was reduced to picture postcards. At the end of the day, when she had a few precious hours of liberty, she was not really free to enjoy them. She liked living by herself little better than she had twenty years earlier, when she had rushed from her marriage to Harold Johnsrud to embrace the bohemian life on Gay Street.

### FROM MARY MCCARTHY'S LETTER TO BOWDEN BROADWATER, SEPTEMBER 2, 1955

This is *no place* to be solitary—a spectre at the feast. The very waiters in the restaurants shrink from me (or so I think) when I creep in begging a table for one. I find myself lying (in Italian) to the landlady, pretending to be going out to a social engagement.

Her Italian might be adequate to put off her landlady, but it was not good enough for her to strike out and make Venetian friends on her own. At the same time, her spirits were not up to approaching the various English-speaking expatriates whose addresses and phone numbers she had been given. The last week in August, when Arthur Schlesinger had been in town, staying at a rented *palazzo* with Ronald and Marietta Tree, she had been convinced he had invited her to join them for lunch out of democratic feelings, not because he had any real desire to see her. Talking to Rosamond Bernier, she dared not confide how bad things were, but writing to Carmen Angleton, who was not her employer and who might be cajoled into keeping her company, she saw no reason to hold back.

**ROSAMOND BERNIER**   She really was quite lonely. I mean, she was a foreigner in a strange city. From the beginning I sensed the vulnerability there, including a great social vulnerability. She would worry about how you were supposed to dress to go to So-and-So's. She would have liked to be chic. You see, the confidence was all intellectual, but when it came to going to a dinner party or what to wear, she was not Rebecca West, let's say, who just strode over everything. She was lonely and insecure. I don't think she ever confided in me, but I could see it.

### FROM MARY MCCARTHY'S LETTER TO CARMEN ANGLETON, SEPTEMBER 2, 1955

The fact is I've been having a perfectly wretched time in Venice; I can't stand the conspicuous solitude I feel myself to be in. I've been holding you up to myself as an example of composure and dignity under such conditions, but I don't really see how you bear it. It would be bad enough anywhere, but Italy (and Venice!) seem a subtly contrived torture for the solitary individual; everybody stares and accosts and pities and contemns.

In Venice she was almost totally without resources, an object of pity, but had the Berniers asked her to write a book on London her situation would have been very different. There, from the day Cyril Connolly awarded her the Horizon Prize, she had cut something of a figure—not only welcomed by friends like Stephen Spender, Isaiah Berlin, and Terence Kilmartin but courted by *The Observer*, the BBC, and her publisher, Heinemann. Here, however, she was just another American tourist. Only the English-speaking expatriates had any idea who she was. Italians did not read her, in English or in translation. Her closest friends, the Chiaromontes, were hours away in Rome. Waking each morning in her gilded matrimonial bed, she had nothing to look forward to but a three-day holiday in mid-September, when the Congress for Cultural Freedom was to meet in Milan. She could ill afford to take time off from her research, but she could not bear to forgo the opportunity to see old friends from New York.

Just as she was beginning to fear that she was not going to be able to bear her solitude, she was saved. "[O]ut of the blue," a letter turned up at American Express from Hannah Arendt, announcing that she would arrive in Venice on September 3 and would spend an entire week there before proceeding to the conference in Milan. The letter may have come out of the blue but the change in Arendt's itinerary had not: Bowden Broadwater, who had taken up temporary residence at the Chelsea, had let her know how things stood on the Adriatic. Still, to Mary this sudden detour seemed little short of miraculous. "I feel as if God at least has remembered my existence," she wrote Carmen Angleton.

On the eve of Hannah Arendt's arrival, her languishing social life picked up. Indeed the very first night, she had to leave her good friend behind while she set off for a dinner party. For her part, Hannah was full of bracing advice—first breaking out well-thumbed guidebooks and then urging her to get to know *"le peuple."* Together the two of them toured the churches of Venice. In the company of a young British expatriate they drove for the day to Ravenna, to study the mosaics. While she might claim to feel like a "spectre at the feast," she could no longer claim to be "festering with loneliness." But after sharing close quarters with Arendt for a week, she had gradually come to see her good friend in a less rapturous light.

## FROM MARY MCCARTHY'S LETTER TO BOWDEN BROADWATER, SEPTEMBER 9, 1955

Hannah seems tired and a little Germanic about her sightseeing; we're on each other's nerves a little, but not (I hope) seriously. She makes me tinny and I make her doctrinaire.

All the same, she did not hesitate to follow Hannah Arendt to Milan, where anti-Communist writers and intellectuals had gathered from the far corners of the earth, enticed by free first-class tickets and the promise of deluxe rooms and all they could eat and drink. At the last minute Nicholas Nabokov, who was running the conference, had booked her a room at the Continentale. In Milan, Arendt was very different from the guest who had gotten on her nerves—ordering flowers for her hotel room, buying her an evening bag, showering her with little notes. But to the organizers of the congress, Arendt showed a less tender side—treating them with an "almost good-natured contempt" and refusing to let them pay for *her* hotel room. This at a time when no one was willing to ask publicly who might be funding this gravy train. When no one was so much as whispering, "CIA."

In Milan, watching Sidney Hook preside over the endlessly prolifer-ating factions of the anti-Communist Left, she might as well have been back at the Waldorf. For company there was a large party of old friends. Isaiah Berlin and Dwight Macdonald had come down from England. The Chiaromontes had come up from Rome. Then there were new friends like the Polish writer Czesław Miłosz, who had cashed in his first-class ticket and taken a coach down from Paris, sitting up all night. Miłosz had gone out of his way to tell her how impressed he had been by her per-formance at the Waldorf's Starlight Roof back in 1949. Impressed by his fine discernment, she helped him find a present for his wife.

**CZESŁAW MIŁOSZ**  She was very friendly and very generous. It may be because I looked at her with a certain admiration for her beauty. I didn't make any passes, but she knew that I appreciated her.

Appreciated and well cared for, she returned to the signora's sound-ing more like her old self. This time she was not lacking for company. Stragglers from the congress had drifted on to Venice. Now it was her turn to minister to an old friend. Dwight Macdonald had just learned that the directors of the congress were not making good on a promise to make him co-editor with Stephen Spender of their British magazine, *Encounter.* Instead, they were offering him a salaried sop: the job of general con-sultant for all congress magazines, to be based in London. All was not lost, but all was not right. Macdonald, who only two years before had seemed saved by his new marriage, looked to be in a bad way. In Milan, with Gloria back in England, he had been drinking heavily. He had come across as "naive, crude, bumptious, like a peasant from some Slovenian province hitting the capital city for the first time." On his arrival in Venice, he had improved not at all.

**FROM MARY MCCARTHY'S LETTER TO BOWDEN BROADWATER,
SEPTEMBER 23, 1955**

His first remark on arriving in Venice was "Why don't the gondolas have outboard motors?" a thought which he revolved in his head and repeated daily until I quoted him to himself, satirically, which reduced him to silence but not submission[. . . .] He was the opposite of Hannah, very inert as to sightseeing; I don't think he ever consciously looked at the Doge's Palace though he passed it a dozen times.

To look long and hard at the world around her was second nature. It was both a source of pleasure and a source of income. Her much celebrated cold eye had brought the Berniers to her in the first place. But scrutinizing the sights of Venice, with no one hovering at her elbow, eager to hear what she had to say, was proving to be a pretty dry business. Dwight Macdonald, with his indifference to the sights around him, was no use to her. Hannah Arendt's brusque and active approach to Venice had suited her little better. For praise and criticism—and, when necessary, a dissenting opinion—she had grown to count on Bowden Broadwater. In lieu of his company, for much of her stay she was forced to make do with a hurried visit from Rosamond Bernier and an occasional meeting with Inge Morath, the young photographer the Berniers had hired to work with her.

**INGE MORATH**    This was my first major book and everybody told me, "She's the most difficult woman." We made a rendezvous at one of the two cafés at St. Mark's—Florian's, I think. I was really quite terrified. I was so worked up that, by the time I finally saw her, I said, "Look, you can just tell me what you want from me. But I'm not going to see you until I've done what *I* want." I think this intrigued her, this absolute independence. I was very candid. For a week I did not see her. I just went around and photographed what I thought should be in the book. Then she rang up and had me come to her apartment. I was still very defiant. I think she was kind of breaking down my resistance. At first she said absolutely nothing, but when she caught on that I really knew who painted what, she became very open and said, "Look, we should help each other." And then she left me alone. She trusted me, which I liked.

Although Bowden was an ocean away, his tastes and opinions remained very much on her mind.

**ROSAMOND BERNIER**    In Venice there are endless shops. Lots of men's shops. We had never met Bowden, but walking around as we did we would go by some shop and Mary would say, "That would be perfect for Bowden" or "Now, that's the kind of thing Bowden would like." No one had ever described Bowden to us. Bernier and I built up this picture of this marvelously handsome, elegant man. We were quite surprised when we met him.

She had arrived with the Berniers to a fairy-tale city blessed with soft golden days and warm festive evenings and with enough tourists to suggest to anyone who didn't know better that it was still the height of the season. Through most of September, for all that there was a hint of fall in the air, the city had felt as if it was on holiday. Visitors still came to see the season's big Giorgione exhibition, to debate which paintings were done by the master and which were falsely attributed. To take in a concert at La Fenice. To make one last trip to the Lido.

After her return from Milan, all that changed. At some point every day there was a downpour. Everywhere she went she had to carry an umbrella, even when she went with an acquaintance to the Ghetto, to watch the Yom Kippur service from the women's balcony. With the rain came the high water, or *agua alta*, spilling over onto the quays by the Grand Canal and necessitating the laying of a wooden boardwalk along the rim of the big square at St. Mark's. As the days shortened, the Accademia, which depended on natural light, closed earlier and earlier. The number of scholars dwindled. Finally, she and a young Cambridge art historian researching a book on painters and patrons of the eighteenth century had the place more or less to themselves.

**FRANCIS HASKELL**   In those days there were a series of libraries—the first opened at half past eight in the morning and one went on until about half past eleven at night. If you wanted to work very hard, you started at one and went on to another. At each one you could reserve books to read. I found after about a week that there was one person who was following roughly the same routine I was. We'd walk out together when the library would close. We got chatting as we went out. And then from time to time we'd go to a café and have a coffee or a drink. She didn't read Italian properly, and I'd recommended a book by an Italian historian who was alive then, Roberto Longhi, who wrote a very brilliant, highly controversial provocative book about Venetian painting. She was immensely fascinated by this. I didn't know her name or anything and I don't think she knew mine.

Mary McCarthy and the young Cambridge scholar had still not exchanged names when in early October Bernard Berenson, the great art expert, arrived with his entourage for his annual visit from I Tatti, his estate just outside Florence. With him he brought his companion Nicky Mariano (who with her sister saw to the running of I Tatti) and his young British secretary, William Mostyn-Owen. Berenson was fast approaching ninety but retained his curiosity. In his honor the Countess Anna Maria Cicogna, one of the great hostesses of Venice, took it on herself to give a luncheon. To this luncheon she invited not only friends and resident notables she thought suitable but a visiting American writer, recently recommended to her by Isaiah Berlin's fiancée.

An excited Mary McCarthy wrote Bowden of how the countess had called to invite her to lunch with Berenson, whom the countess called "B.B." To this first meeting with B.B., the ragpicker's son from Boston who had gone on to Harvard and international glory, there were at least two witnesses who showed a keen interest. One was his secretary and the other was the young scholar from Cambridge.

**WILLIAM MOSTYN-OWEN** Berenson was staying at the Hotel Europa, where he always stayed. I believe he had recently read a story by Mary that appeared in *Partisan Review*. She arrived by boat. There we were in the hall of the Europa when she came in off this boat. She was wearing a pale color. Very nice. Of course she was speaking to B.B. I was observing. She was very beautiful—very black hair—and she towered over the other women. She was fairly casual about her appearance. But I think she was loveliest when she was in Venice, when she was in disarray a bit. Afterward she told me that the first thing Berenson said to her was "Have you brought your pessary with you?" She laughed, though she was slightly taken aback.

**FRANCIS HASKELL** When Berenson came to Venice, I must have been invited to lunch by him or Anna Maria Cicogna. At that lunch, in the room, also shaking hands with Berenson, was my library friend. As soon as I was introduced to her, I recognized the name. I'd read *The Groves of Academe* and I'd liked it very much indeed.

Berenson, like Francis Haskell, had read *The Groves of Academe,* but it had created nothing like the impression of her pessary story. In the course of that luncheon, Berenson created no little impression himself. To Hannah Arendt she admitted to having been shocked by his behavior, but by the time she wrote Bowden a week later, her shock had given way to emotions more complicated.

**FROM MARY MCCARTHY'S LETTER TO HANNAH ARENDT, SEPTEMBER 29, 1955**

[I met] Bernard Berenson, whom I'm to dine with again tomorrow night—a regular old Volpone of ninety summers, with a glistening gold smile, more like a puma, really, than a fox. As a case of sheer preservation, he's extraordinary; he keeps his prodigious memory and all his faculties and appetites. He was familiar with my work, greeted me with an apt and naughty quotation from the one about the pessary—imagine! I felt quite shocked.

**FROM MARY MCCARTHY'S LETTER TO BOWDEN BROADWATER, OCTOBER 7, 1955**

B.B., who met me at the Countess's motor boat, had a remark about Dottie and the pessary on his dry old lips. I was so shocked and startled that I pretended to think he was talking about Pesaro[. . . .] Since then he's invited me to dinner once (I had to back out at the last minute for fear of causing his death by my cold), sent me the new edition of his book on Lotto, inscribed "With admiration and sympathy," invited me to dinner again, which I took with him *à deux* in his sitting-room upstairs in the Hotel Europa, and told me the story of his life, with particular reference to the amatory side of it[. . . .] He has asked me to visit him in Florence (which I won't). I don't know quite what to make of him. There's so much of the actor in all this that it leaves me fogged-up and confused.

Not only was she confused by Berenson's attentions but she feared that Anna Maria Cicogna was annoyed with her. After the luncheon, she had heard nothing further from the countess, who, she told Bowden, "perhaps didn't like the way B.B. monopolized me, which meant, in effect, my monopolizing him." B.B. continued to monopolize her, but for all that she continued to shrink from his advances, she did not shrink from telling of them.

### FROM MARY MCCARTHY'S LETTER TO BOWDEN BROADWATER, OCTOBER 8, 1955

B.B., appalling to say, has begun to make tremulous passes at me, confined as yet to hand-holding and a kiss on each cheek and declarations: "If I had known you sooner, I should never have let you go." "But now you must be my friend, my *intimate* friend." Don't, I beg you, repeat this to anyone; I find it somehow humiliating, to be a chill morsel on a nonagenarian's plate.

She was spared further "humiliating" declarations only when her nonagenarian admirer succumbed to a cold and had to retire to his bed. Still, the visit seems to have marked a turning point. She had come to reconsider her initial impression of Venice and its denizens.

### FROM MARY MCCARTHY'S LETTER TO BOWDEN BROADWATER, OCTOBER 10, 1955

Did I ever say I like the Venetians? They're very quick and dry and somehow strict, as well as droll and ironic. And everything is said and done with an exquisite grace and courtesy; buying a stamp, even. Their dialect sounds like the singing of the daintiest birds. They don't have the oil and treacle of other Italians. The young gondoliers are so straight and almost severe, like trained acrobats of the highest caliber[. . . .] And everyone, everyone, is extremely kind.

Foremost among those who had been kind was the Countess Cicogna, who had called to invite her to a second luncheon, this time to honor the political pundit Walter Lippmann. The countess, it turned out, read *The New Yorker*. Growing up, she'd had an English nanny. When they were alone together, the two new friends spoke English. In the countess's motor launch there had been a long discussion of how best to translate the title of *A Charmed Life.*

By the time B.B. returned to Florence, Mary could not claim to be lonely, although there were times when she was depressed. No small part of her depression had to do with her tenuous relations with Bowden. She had received a letter from him that let her know how little he saw to like in her. Ready to acknowledge the validity of his charges, she went on, characteristically, to question her own protestations of remorse.

### FROM MARY MCCARTHY'S LETTER TO BOWDEN BROADWATER, OCTOBER 8, 1955

That you don't like me, or have "seen through" me, I find bitter but wholly natural. It's the same, I think with Reuel. I don't expect that anyone will ever like me again[. . . .] It's not that I am so bad—there are far worse people, God knows. It's simply that I'm so hollow, tinny, unstable, insecure, dependent on admiration, affection. And, of course, selfish. I've used you selfishly, without exactly wanting to; that's the trouble, I suppose—neither fish nor fowl. For I want my own admiration as well as other people's, and that is an excessive demand—greediness[. . . .] As for now, I think I would like you to save your soul, whatever else befalls. But there's an element of vanity in this, a desire to behave nobly[. . . .] I haven't even shed a tear since you left, though a few have moistened my eyes. But what, I ask myself, practically, is the use of crying with no one to tell you to stop?

There was no one in Venice to tell a penitent wife to dry her tears, but there were pleasing distractions. Although she did agree to write to B.B., she remained true to her word and did not visit him in Florence. However, she continued to see his secretary, William Mostyn-Owen, a very tall and very blond Scottish lord who managed to break away from Florence on occasion and who, she told Bowden, reminded her not a little of her brother Kevin. In the company of Anna Maria Cicogna, William Mostyn-Owen, and Francis Haskell—sometimes together and sometimes separately—she ventured into the back alleys and byways of Venice, explored the Palladian villas of the Veneto, and wandered as far afield as Bologna.

**WILLIAM MOSTYN-OWEN**   We went out to the country. First, we went to Treviso. We all went together with Walter Lippmann to see some recently restored Bassano frescoes. There was such a long procession of cars that Francis was reminded of the picnic in *Citizen Kane.* You always knew when Mary was observing people. There would be a little sort of hmm, hmm. A little noise that indicated that something had caught her fancy and amused her. She was staying in an extraordinary flat with a huge bedroom and a huge, gilded, elaborate baroque bed. Of course Mary at that time was still, technically speaking, married to Bowden Broadwater. Bowden was in the States and Mary was leading a very sort of free life.

**FRANCIS HASKELL**  From time to time I would go with Mary to look at paintings—especially Cima. She was fond of his work and I remember she wrote a very beautiful piece about autumn and Venice and the fruits piling high in the marketplace and she associated Cima with all that. Mary was enormous fun to be with. She was also a bit alarming. She was very . . . if I say "censorious," it sounds nasty and I don't quite mean that. But if we were talking about literature and I would say I liked some book, Mary would sometimes say, "You can't like that. Don't you see how badly written it is, how phony it is." And I'd back off.

By the end of October, when she could no longer claim to be lacking for company, Carmen Angleton came to stay. With her craving to know the legend behind every pane of stained glass, Carmen Angleton proved to be the companion most to her taste.

**CARMEN ANGLETON**  Mary and I didn't fatigue each other. We liked to go along together looking at things—we liked looking at particulars. She was fascinated by Italian art, which she hadn't known before. It was all quite a revelation to her. I think Mary was very happy then. She had a small circle of intelligent friends in Venice, who were very informative. She became supremely confident about Venice. She would move around as though she were a native, you might say. She took delight in mastering Venice and in mastering Italian. We were reading an extremely difficult book by Roberto Longhi—a marvelous writer, but very intricate—which was full of metaphors, similes, and allegories. She got the meaning immediately—almost intuitively, I would say, except there was a great deal of intellect in it. She had an excellent mind. Her Italian wasn't then perfect. She often corrected herself as we spoke. She would hear what she had said and then she would say, "No, you can't say that, I should put it this way." She was both the teacher and the pupil.

When she had the opportunity, the teacher in her made sure that the pupil's hard work was rewarded. On the worst of the cold days Francis Haskell would come over with his books and the three of them would study in her sitting room, getting what warmth they could from the signora's electric heater. When the day's work was done, her visitor would sometimes stay on.

**FRANCIS HASKELL**  Mary organized an Italian play-reading society. We used to sit together reading these Goldoni plays in which each of us would take several parts. There weren't nearly enough of us. And then we'd have an absolutely delicious dinner, which Mary cooked. I remember this huge, marvelous fish risotto.

**CARMEN ANGLETON** She was cooking and inviting people and putting up with her landlady. It pleased her because she overcame all these problems. And there were many problems. I remember, one time, the landlady inspected my clothes and wanted to buy them for her daughter. There were many episodes. I didn't stay with her too long, because I had to return to Milan.

On the heels of Carmen Angleton's departure, Francis Haskell, too, moved on, leaving her once again to her own devices and the kindness of casual acquaintances. Increasingly her thoughts were directed over-seas. Now that the Pamet Point house had been sold to Mary Meigs, Bowden was looking for an apartment for the two of them. But how per-manent an apartment did they want? Was Bowden ever going to find a job? And what kind of fate was *A Charmed Life* going to meet with the critics?

By this time she was capable of translating five pages of Roberto Longhi a day. Originally she had hoped to be in Paris in early November, to meet one last time with the Berniers, before boarding a ship for New York. Now Thanksgiving was her deadline: Harcourt was throwing a big party for *A Charmed Life* in early December. The heater the signora had provided broke down. She was making her solitary rounds of the libraries, writing a first letter to Berenson, trying to make the best of her solitary drinks and coffees, when the episodes with the signora ceased to be a joke. No longer was it a question of objects admired and objects borrowed. Objects were borrowed and never returned. Accusations were leveled. Her last week, a bill was presented for charges never mentioned in the original agreement. After that, there was nothing to do but flee into the night and take shelter with an acquaintance who was kind enough to take her in. The acquaintance was unabashedly homosexual, but she was hardly looking for romance. For the moment at least, she and Bowden had decided to try to get back together. She had publishers to deal with and a deadline to meet.

Never one to waste her time when nothing better offered, she set about writing her book for the Berniers during her voyage home from Paris on the *Liberté*. The most upsetting news that met her on her arrival was that Katharine White was retiring to Maine, leaving her, she believed, with no strong supporter at *The New Yorker* other than William Maxwell. Fortunately, the domestic scene she returned to was happier than she had anticipated. Bowden had secured a job running the library at Reuel's old school, St. Bernard's. Although they decided not to tie up their Wellfleet profits in an apartment, they did not have to stay at the Chelsea for long. By April, they were living in a walk-up with a small ter-race in a well-maintained town house on Ninety-fourth Street, close by

Barbara Kerr, just off Fifth Avenue, and only four blocks from Bowden's new job. Best of all, she had turned in a finished manuscript to the Berniers.

In later years, she would make it sound as if the commission for *Venice Observed* had come to her simply because she had been at the right place at the right time. She would also imply that she had been only minimally equipped for this project. But just as she had not been a complete novice when Philip Rahv had asked her to write *Partisan Review*'s "Theater Chronicle," she was not totally inexperienced when the Berniers approached her to do a bit of well-paid travel writing.

Besides the *Town and Country* piece from her first trip to Europe, she had recently published two substantial articles in well-regarded periodicals. The first, a "Letter from Portugal," had appeared in *The New Yorker* in February 1955. The second, a portrait of a bustling bureaucrat in charge of public housing for the Salazar regime (cut, despite her strenuous objections, from the *New Yorker* piece), had come out in *Harper's* that August. In *The New Yorker*, she had made much of the picturesque setting and cheap prices that drew Americans to live in Lisbon, only to show the real poverty peeping out from behind the city's pretty façade. In *Harper's* she had simply described a private tour of the city's much vaunted public housing, during which she couldn't help noting that houses said to be designated for low-income families were frequently in the hands of the middle class.

In her previous travel writing she had shown no reluctance to pass judgment on a country or its citizens, even when they were new to her. She might linger over some insight or detail, but she did not stop short of placing it in some larger context. When necessary she could summon up a relevant bit of history. As an inveterate satirist, she saw no reason to leave the sharper tools of her trade at home. Where others might fall back on a visitor's diffidence, she continued to rely on her fierce and intrepid truthfulness. When all else failed, she trusted to common sense.

With Venice, of course, she had a special case. Venice was no ordinary city. Its coffers had overflowed with the treasures of Byzantium; its churches and palaces had been bedecked by artists and artisans from all over the world. With its splendor reflected and enhanced by the water that was everywhere, the Republic of Venice had been the Wonder of the World. Settled by outcasts, marked by a love of opulence and a deep mistrust of tyrants, Venice had survived for twelve centuries through a combination of shrewdness and guile. By the eighteenth century the republic could no longer be counted a great power but its gilded splendor, for all that it was visibly tarnished, remained the stuff of dreams. Visitors, drawn by a reputation for masked licentiousness, swarmed to its pre-Lenten Carnival. After the fall of the republic, it had ceded its independence in exchange for protection from the emperor of Austria. But even after its more portable treasures had been carted off to Paris by Napoleon, Venice did not cease to seduce and beguile.

To dazzle the world is no easy matter. To capture its attention is difficult enough. When it came time to write her book for the Berniers, McCarthy met this challenge very much in the spirit of the city that had been set her as a subject. She did not make light of the dismaying task facing any writer who presumes to come up with anything fresh to say about Venice. On the contrary, she made much of it.

**FROM *VENICE OBSERVED***

"I envy you, writing about Venice," says the newcomer. "I pity you," says the old hand. One thing is certain. Sophistication, that modern kind of sophistication that begs to differ, to be paradoxical, to invert, is not a possible attitude in Venice. In time, this becomes the beauty of the place. One gives up the struggle and submits to a classic experience. One accepts the fact that what one is about to feel or say has not only been said before by Goethe or Musset but is on the tip of the tongue of the tourist from Iowa who is alighting in the Piazzetta with his wife in her furpiece and jewelled pin.

Above all, she made use of her skills as a writer of fiction to portray the particular corner of Venice presided over by her incorrigible landlady.

My shrewd, clowning signora and her family have slowly, like cats, repossessed their apartment, corner by corner, room by room. Hairpins and a hair-dryer have appeared in the bathroom that is supposedly "mine." Next, it is nylon underwear hanging in the bathroom window[. . . .] One day, the bathtub is full of laundry[. . . .] My toilet soap vanishes, as if by magic. I buy a new cake, and in a day or so it is a sliver[. . . .] As soon as I leave the apartment, the whole family frisks about among my possessions, touching, tasting, sniffing. "Your glasses exactly fit my eyesight," confides the signora.

Although the signora came across as larger than life, it would seem that artistic license played little part in this.

**CARMEN ANGLETON**   Mary was not exaggerating. If anything it was worse. There were many episodes, which she didn't emphasize or put in.

Not only was the signora shrewd and cunning, wrote McCarthy, but she was the possessor of uncanny powers—not least of them, the power to provide sustenance where there appears to be none. For two years two pallid goldfish had lingered on in the signora's kitchen, with no visible source of nourishment other than the coins placed at the bottom of their pretty blue and white bowl. Having spent weeks observing these poor "blanched creatures," the signora's tenant had come to see a special meaning in their survival. In case the reader missed the point, she spelled it out.

### FROM *VENICE OBSERVED*

[I] take them as an allegory on Venice, a society which lived in a bowl and drew its sustenance from the filth of lucre. Once flame-coloured, today it is a little pale and moribund, like the fish after two years of the signora's regimen.

As a student Mary McCarthy had always been a quick study. In a matter of months she had managed to master not only the allegory in the signora's kitchen but twelve centuries of Venetian history—a history punctuated by a dreary succession of aged doges who were little more than puppets of a powerful clique of nobles. In this she found an enlivening paradox. Gray men devoid of any of the glamour of a proper royal dynasty, the doges presided over a republic whose celebrated imperialism stemmed not from any thirst for dominion but from a desire to protect its markets. The gilded Queen of the Adriatic was a city of cautious businessmen.

To make short work of the doges and their countinghouse mentality came naturally to a writer who from childhood had dreamed of fighting at the side of Bonnie Prince Charles. To do justice to Venetian art was something else again. Here she was forced back on a deep and enduring fondness for the details of the material world and an abiding mistrust of anything that smacked of extravagant emotion or mysticism.

For Carpaccio, Bellini, and Veronese—painters who appeared to share her preoccupation with the quotidian—she had an immediate sympathy. For Carpaccio—who painted St. Jerome a little white dog to keep him company while awaiting a vision in his study and painted St. Ursula a pretty pair of mules to rest by her virginal bed—she had an especial fondness, seeing in him a kindred spirit and fellow ironist.

But in trusting to her own prejudices, she was not all that different from the tourist from Iowa who flatly declares that he knows what he likes. Luckily, she *had* done her reading. And, thanks to her little flirtation with Berenson, she did not need to rely solely on dead critics she knew only from their writing. When she found she had no use for Berenson's judgments, she had younger critics she could call on. Writing about Cima, a contemporary of Bernini, she made use not only of Roberto Longhi but of Francis Haskell, William Mostyn-Owen, and their glorious October outing to Treviso.

### FROM *VENICE OBSERVED*

Earth is the primal matter of Cima, the son of a hides-dealer from hilly Conegliano in the rustic Veneto. His square-jawed peasant

Madonnas reveal their natural origin in the peculiar whitish clayey tones of their complexions, hard baked from the Maker's kiln. This sweet shepherd among Venetian painters ("Virgilian," Longhi calls him, likening his countryside to the classic *rus* of the Georgics) turns the pure mountain light on the Bellini landscape and figures, which seem to jump forward as if in a stereopticon. Cima's golden, crystal light is that of the Veneto in the autumnal days when the foliage is just turning and the walnuts and funghi and white soft cheeses are coming down from the mountains to the markets in the Rialto and Santa Maria Formosa.

Unfortunately, when writing about Tintoretto—a painter whose work did not recall the crystal light and ripe cheeses of any landscape to be found on this earth—she had no such sunny memories to call on. Worse, her own outspoken prejudices were effectively blunted by ambivalence, leaving her to fall back on such statements as "Tintoretto is certainly inferior to the great Venetians—Carpaccio, Bellini, Cima, Giorgione, Veronese, Titian[. . . .] But the force of this genius takes the breath away." Or: "One's admiration is given more, possibly, to the *conception* of a Tintoretto than to its realization. He writes large what he means to convey; that is why we amateurs respond to the 'terrific' effects of *The Last Supper, The Crucifixion, The Manger, The Annunciation.*"

To skip Tintoretto entirely might have been wiser. But it was her intention to give the Berniers the solid book she believed they wanted—to cover the painting of the eighteenth century, to write a bit about the music, to try one last time to capture the spirit of modern Venice. As she approached her finale, she was beginning to sound a little breathless. But by the very end she was herself again.

**FROM *VENICE OBSERVED***

When I go, it will have to be by gondola because I have so much baggage. Some private Charon of the signora's will ferry me down to the station in his shabby funeral bark. That is how the Allies took Venice, arriving from the mainland, at the end of the second World War. There was a petrol shortage, and the Allied command, having made secret contact with the gondoliers' co-operative, officially "captured" Venice with a fleet of gondolas. Even war in Venice evokes a disbelieving smile.

Thanks to the kindness of two old friends, four relative strangers, and one benighted landlady, she had succeeded in getting a purchase on the dismaying mountain of material she must master so as not to disgrace herself. In the process, she managed to give the Berniers what they wanted. And then some.

**ROSAMOND BERNIER**   Once she was in Venice and she'd been there for some time, she then sent back a section on Titian and a section on Tintoretto—which was not at all what we wanted. Nor did we find it really valid. With Mary if you changed a comma you heard at once, so it was either a question of dropping the entire project or compensating for the fact that what she wrote was not valid from an art historical point of view. So we asked André Chastel, an outstanding though rather pontificating specialist in the Italian Renaissance, to write extensive notes on the illustrations.

**GEORGES BERNIER**   We always intended to have that section by André Chastel as a separate part of the book because I knew very well that Mary could do an interesting, sensitive, intelligent *souvenir de tourisme* or *journal de voyage,* but not a study of Venetian art.

**ROSAMOND BERNIER**   I simply couldn't tell you at what point Bernier told Mary about this. Did he not tell her until she saw the proofs? He was very devious and quite unscrupulous. So it is possible that she felt that she was somehow misled about this. I do remember that she wished to dedicate the book to Carmen Angleton. And Bernier wouldn't hear of it. He said, "This is a cooperative venture. This is not one person's book."

Georges Bernier did not breathe a word to her about hiring André Chastel until September 1956, when the two of them met in Paris to go over the galleys. By then it was too late for her to kick up a fuss: the book was due out in November. But by then she had already found thousands of readers delighted to defer to her opinions on art. They had come to her thanks to *The New Yorker,* the very place where she had imagined herself so bereft of friends and supporters. The previous spring, William Shawn had purchased the first serial rights of her newly completed Venice manuscript. Jettisoning the signora and the side trips to Murano, Burano, Torcello, and Chioggia, he had pared the piece down so that it could run in two parts. *The New Yorker* paid on a word rate. Although they were not taking the entire book, they were taking a lot of it. Thanks to this windfall, she was in Milan when it came time to read the final galleys. Always before she had counted on Katharine White to defend her from the worst assaults on her writing by *The New Yorker*'s proofreaders and fact checkers. This time, she had to rely on William Shawn, whom she knew only from casual meetings at *New Yorker* parties. In later years Shawn would recall their collaboration as a happy one.

**WILLIAM SHAWN**   At her best she wrote beautifully. She was a very forceful writer of prose. What made for that was the clarity of her thinking. She was well educated, she knew a lot, but mostly she had an original turn of mind. There aren't so many people you could mention in connection with Samuel Johnson, but you could mention Mary McCarthy.

She might accept Shawn's editing, but that did not mean she necessarily liked it. Or liked it for long.

## FROM MARY MCCARTHY'S LETTER TO BERNICE BAUMGARTEN, JUNE 22, 1956

Our Italian trip has been halted here in Milan by Shawn's proofs, which have been pouring in very rapidly[. . . .] The checker is an absolute cretin, and the answering of foolish, ruminative questions has made the process a little slower than it should have been. I thought Shawn's own cutting and re-arranging very good, almost miraculous in parts.

## FROM MARY MCCARTHY'S LETTER TO HANNAH ARENDT, AUGUST 1956

I've done no writing, except struggling with the *New Yorker* proofs of the Venice pieces[. . . .] Don't judge the book too much by them. *The New Yorker*, in cutting (they used only about a third), excised nearly everything except facts and figures. The editor, Shawn, is really a curious person; he's a self-educated man and he assumes that everybody, like his own former untaught self, is eager to be crammed with information. A sentence larded with dates and proper names fills him with gluttonous delight—like a *boeuf à la mode*.

The two-part piece ran the first two weeks in July as "The Revel of the Earth," borrowing its title from Lord Byron, who had discovered in Venice "the revel of the earth, the masque of Italy." For *The New Yorker* it was a first.

**BRENDAN GILL**   We never had anything like *Venice Observed*. Now it would be a commonplace. I remember the opening page had a reference to a *ridotto* in sixteenth-century Venice and I went to Shawn in protest to say, "You know perfectly well you never knew what a *ridotto* was and none of our readers is going to know what it means." Shawn just said, "I know now." It was a gambler's place or casino. In any event, that was a startling piece. More and more the magazine was becoming something other than what Ross had intended it to be—Ross trying desperately always to keep everything in New York, reluctantly admitting Washington. We'd had Paris from the beginning because of Jane Grant, who was a friend of Janet Flanner. He couldn't do anything about that. Shawn was the person who felt that a wonderful piece of writing existed in *The New Yorker* because it was the kind of place that should have a wonderful piece of writing.

If some readers were bothered by the heavily larded sentences, for most readers the wonderful writing carried the day. And the writer herself could always look forward to November, when the book would come out with her verbal portrait of Venice intact. But here too she was destined for disappointment. André Chastel's appendix was only the first surprise that Georges Bernier had in store for her. To know that you are part of a deluxe picture book is one thing. To hold this glossy volume in your hands is quite another, particularly when you have enemies as fastidious as you are and as quick to pick up a pen and put their opinions on record.

**FROM DAWN POWELL'S REVIEW IN *THE NATION*, DECEMBER 22, 1956**

    Here is one of those synthetic spectaculars produced by publishers at this season, not quite literature, not quite art, not quite travel, but definitely Gift-Book. Rich aunt, neglected old friend, potential customer or boss are bound to be appeased by the printed price if they are not stupefied by the lavish beauty.

If she had wound up with a book perfect for a Vassar graduate living in some Westchester suburb, she was nonetheless proud of what she herself had done and ready to defend her portrait of Venice against all comers—even Berenson himself, who a year and a half after their first meeting no longer sounded quite so smitten. But she was less ready to defend the Berniers' packaging.

**FROM MARY MCCARTHY'S LETTER TO BERNARD BERENSON, FEBRUARY 25, 1957**

    You are wrong, I think, about the Venice book. I don't propose to put it behind me or turn over a new leaf. On the contrary, I feel quite proud of it and some time (not now), I want to try something else in a similar vein. It seems to me original; I don't know of anything like it. What its quality is, if one can be objective about one's own work, is a certain intensity of *thought*, a revolving of Venice in the mind, as though to hold it up and ask, "What is it?" Even if such an effort failed, it would not be unworthy of my standard. And I don't think it fails. It ripples along rather merrily and this may be misleading, though I should think more so to those who know little about the literature of Venice than to those who know a great deal. Those who know little might assume, from the easy tone, that all this is familiar stuff—the facts, of course, are familiar, but the discovery of a pattern in them is, so far as I know, completely new. No other writer I could find has even tried to look into the facts for a pattern or a symmetry, though Venice, uniquely among cities, seems to solicit just such an act of recognition[. . . .]

    The presentation is a different matter. I now feel rather sorry that I lent myself to what seems mainly a fashion enterprise. I ought to have foreseen this, but I didn't. The text is simply buried in chic and folderols[. . . .] The book looks cynical; that's the only way I can describe it. My hope is that some time, when this market has been exploited to the limit by the publishers, the text can be reprinted in a plain small volume, with perhaps a few black-and-white illustrations in the back.

In time Mary McCarthy would get her heart's desire—a small volume designed to let the text speak for itself. For Georges Bernier she would never have much use. For Rosamond, she would always have affection, persisting in giving her credit for being fundamentally straight. Fortunately, most reviewers did not see the book as "cynical." The bulk of

25. Bernard Berenson at I Tatti, 1952 (Corbiss/ Bettman-UPI)

26. Peggy Guggenheim in Venice (Owen/Black Star)

27. Hannah Arendt

28. John Davenport
among his books
(Frank Monaco)

29. Mary and Kevin McCarthy, 1956 (Inge Morath/Magnum)

30. Mary McCarthy with Miriam Chiaromonte in Italy

31. The new Mr. and Mrs. James West cross the Atlantic, early 1960s.

32. At work in Paris (Gisele Freund/John Hillelson)

33. Mary and Reuel, 1961

34. Deborah Pease, Niccolò Tucci, and Mary in France

35. Daniel, Alison, and Jonathan West, accompanied by their nurse Maria Fourrier, at the Leaning Tower of Pisa. (James West)

36. A gathering of old friends, New York, 1966: Nicola Chiaromonte, Mary McCarthy, and Robert Lowell are seated, while Heinrich Blücher, Hannah Arendt, Dwight Macdonald, and Gloria Macdonald stand behind them.

37. Arriving in North Vietnam, 1968

38. Visiting the North Vietnamese countryside

39. The Wests in Castine (Hannah Arendt)

40. Susan Sontag, 1978 (Thomas Victor/Harriet Spurlin)

41. Carmen Angleton and Mary McCarthy consulting a guide book (James West)

42. Lillian Hellman, 1979 (R. Howard/Black Star)

43. Reuel Wilson, Mary McCarthy, and Thomas Mallon at Vassar, 1982 (Robert Pounder)

44. Mary McCarthy and Elizabeth Hardwick at Castine (Alison West)

45. Mary McCarthy with summer visitors (from left) Eve and Al Stwertka, Reuel Wilson, Alison West, Sophie Wilson, and Natsuko Murase, Castine, 1989. (James West)

them gave her credit for a lively and entertaining portrait and showed no surprise that this portrait was embedded in an oversized, brightly colored artifact designed as the perfect gift for anyone with a large disposable income and an interest in travel and art. In short, it was the perfect coffee-table book. Indeed, with the average reviewer, the book fared slightly better than most of her fiction, if only because it was clear that she had taken so much trouble. As far as *Time* was concerned, she had lived up to her advance billing. With reviewers who felt protective of Venice she sometimes ran into difficulty.

### FROM "THE FLOATING CITY," *TIME*, NOVEMBER 26, 1956

More than a century has passed since Byron swam from the Lido to Venice and through the Grand Canal (four miles) and nearly two since Napoleon pronounced the pigeon-swept square of St. Mark's "the best drawing-room in Europe." But the destiny of Venice remains constant, to be "the observed of all observers." The latest to succumb to the spell of the floating city is Critic and Novelist Mary McCarthy (*Time*, Nov. 14, 1955), who has fashioned the spectacle of Venice into a handsome and intelligent mosaic of art, history and personal impressions.

### FROM SACHEVERELL SITWELL'S REVIEW IN *THE NEW YORK TIMES*, NOVEMBER 18, 1956

This is a first rate piece of reporting and ably written. But its title could be improved to *Venice Observed, Marked, Learned and Indigested* for it leaves a sour taste in the mouth which lingers till next morning.

Rosamond Bernier would later recall that *Venice Observed* was the best-selling art book of the 1956 Christmas season. For the general reader it provided a lively, if occasionally taxing, introduction to the special virtues of Mary McCarthy's writing. For friends and acquaintances the book seemed to reveal as much about the author as it did about Venice. For Eleanor Clark, whose pieces on Rome had been published in *Partisan Review* and various quarterlies and then brought out in book form three years before, *Venice Observed* was an act of rivalry so presumptuous as to be beyond forgiveness.

**WILLIAM MOSTYN-OWEN**   I found the Venice book mischievous. It's got some wonderful observations in it because she has that power of solidifying some idea, theme, or characterization of people. She makes very sweeping historical generalizations about the doges which don't really hold up. But maybe she's having a good tongue-in-cheek. I mean, Cyril Connolly's "Mary Mary quite contrary" was not without foundation.

**INGE MORATH**   She was having a good time in Venice. It suited her at that point. I like the freshness of the book. It's admittedly an outsider looking at the city. It doesn't pretend to be more than it is. That's what's good about it.

**ELEANOR CLARK**   Mary just got onto Italy because I was. I damn well think that. She knows nothing about Italy. Her Italian was atrocious. She didn't know a goddamn thing about Italian history, Italian art, Italian anything. It was pathetic. She was highly competitive. It was as complicated as that. When I was doing *The Oysters of Locmariaquer* years later, I said to somebody, "Don't tell Mary, she'll do a book on clams."

Mary McCarthy did not go on to do a book on clams, but she was falling back on no idle threat when she wrote Berenson that she might well do another book in the same vein. Sales for the Venice book had been brisk. In the eyes of the general public she was now an authority. In the eyes of the Berniers she was once again desirable. Whether she chose to stay with them or not, she would have no difficulty finding a publisher. Her chief difficulty was finding the right subject.

She had not initiated the Venice project, but she had embraced the idea immediately because it was expedient. Her situation in the spring of 1956, once she turned in her manuscript, was no longer desperate. On the one hand, this situation looked to be reasonably comfortable. On the other hand, it was not ideal. To their walk-up on East Ninety-fourth Street she and Bowden had brought none of the dreams and aspirations they had brought to Portsmouth—or to Wellfleet, for that matter. The apartment was pleasant and well situated but by no means spacious. The Empire sofa had been recovered in ticking. On their tiny terrace they had planted an herb garden. The second bedroom did double duty as a study. Unfortunately, the study had to be relinquished when Reuel came down from school.

In this study Mary had completed the Venice book and then finished compiling the collection of theater pieces she had promised Roger Straus back in 1954. Taking her lead from Edmund Wilson, she was contemplating putting together still another collection of published writing. This one would be at once more ambitious and more personal—a collection of her childhood memoirs, which would end with a memoir of her Jewish grandmother, no longer alive to read and disapprove of what she had written. None of this required isolation or extended periods of concentration. For the moment at least, the Vassar novel, with the pessary chapter that had so tantalized Berenson, remained on hold.

She and Bowden Broadwater had reconciled, but the balance of their relations had once again altered. Even though she had practically begged to return to him, she gave little evidence of adoring him. Words had been exchanged that could not be recalled. There was no hope now of another child, no serious hope any longer of a writing career for Bowden. Five days a week he was working at St. Bernard's. He was also doing some writing for Mannie Rousuck and continuing to moonlight at *Time*. While he was tied to New York until school let out, she herself had little to hold her once she turned in her two manuscripts. Reuel was away at Brooks until the end of the term. Next year he would be starting at Harvard. Elizabeth Hardwick and Robert Lowell were living in Boston. Dwight Macdonald was in London. Hannah Arendt was teaching at Chicago and traveling more than ever.

The previous summer, Venice had provided her with a face-saving solution to her marital problems. By the end of her stay at the signora's, she had grown sufficiently accustomed to her solitary state to begin to savor her separation and make use of the freedom it conferred. The favorable exchange rate made it easy to live well in Italy on relatively little money. She had come to like the art, the food, and the language. She had even made a few friends.

That spring, she returned to Italy. Thanks to William Shawn and *The New Yorker,* she could look forward to a summer free of financial worries. Upon further reflection, she had decided to take Berenson up on his invitation to come visit him outside Florence. Having left Bowden behind to finish up the school term, she was counting on joining him later in Milan. This time it might with some justice be said that her position was enviable. Certainly it owed something to her own exertions—or, as *Time* magazine would have it, her own unparalleled and undeniable cleverness. Having had a first taste of independence and survived it, she was going back to take a try at independence on her own terms.

# Chapter Seventeen

# B.B. AND J.D.

"Well, here I am in 'Mary's Room' with its own library and bath, its paintings catalogued in a neat folder," wrote Mary McCarthy in a fine spidery hand, safely past the most recent contretemps in a brand-new European adventure of her own making. "Servant unpacked, disinterring old wads of Kleenex from briefcase. Dinner is at nine; a short period of panic has just ended, during which I couldn't find where the maid had hung my dresses. Located them in an *armoire*." She was writing Bowden Broadwater from I Tatti, Bernard Berenson's villa in Settignano, on May 16, 1956. To dispel any confusion, she took care to insert the briefest of notes, up by the date: "'Mary' was Mrs. B.B."

She had arrived with a sore throat and cough and a "sense of utter misery" but with a clean bill of health from a Rome doctor, who had sent her on her way with a "bumper" of penicillin and his assurance that she would not be carrying a fatal case of German measles to her aged host. Berenson himself she had found to be in fine form: "splendid, small, frail, and witty—a brittle vase of nineties memories." House and owner were very much of a piece. The rooms of I Tatti were "dark and esthetic, in the nineties taste." But the grounds were something else again, "full of lemons and azaleas, cypresses, and vistas, great tubs of white blooming plants and classic statuary." About Berenson she continued to harbor reservations, but about I Tatti she had none.

The following morning she was to be given a special tour of Berenson's private collection of paintings. But how was that tour to be accomplished? No one had ever said. The prospect of going downstairs and waiting among the empty rooms and corridors was dismaying. Would she do better, she wondered, to wait in the garden and "linger, smelling a rose until discovered." Like Isabel Archer, she had crossed the ocean and slipped into a setting that was appealing in its refinement but resistant to her every effort to fathom its secrets. To this household whose corridors vibrated with veiled motives and inscrutable meanings she had come well prepared by literature, but not by temperament. Or taste. She had never been an admirer of Henry James.

On May 2 she had set sail for Italy on the *Cristoforo Colombo*. Upon learning that she was on board, the well-known theologian Paul Tillich, a friend of Hannah Arendt, had invited her to join his table. In no time at all the sixty-nine-year-old Tillich was squeezing her hand and stealing a kiss on the cheek and turning the conversation to "sadism, beatings, and biting and Greek gods with little scourges made of willow twigs." To make matters worse, she wrote Bowden from her cramped cabin, Tillich's wife had taken against her. "She doesn't like me, but not, I think, because of the Reverend's behavior, which at least has taken place out of her sight though not out of sight of the astonished waiters and passengers."

Because Bowden would be making the trip by plane, she was solely responsible for conveying to Italy their transportation for the summer. In the ship's hold was a black Chevrolet, a big monster of a car, which she was hoping Carmen Angleton would help her drive first to Rome and then on to I Tatti. At Naples, Carmen Angleton failed to meet her at the dock. Driving the black sedan through the congested streets of this crowded city, she struck two pedestrians. The car's speedometer had registered no more than five miles per hour and neither pedestrian had been seriously injured, but fists were raised and insults were hurled. It was not an auspicious start to her summer abroad.

At I Tatti, she fared better. Her two-part Venice piece would not appear in *The New Yorker* until July and having yet to catch her trespassing on his territory, Berenson was free to enjoy his good-looking guest's company. For his guest, too, this stay at I Tatti was a pleasant diversion. Mrs. B.B. was long dead, and Nicky Mariano, who had long ago replaced Mrs. B.B. in Berenson's affections, was indulgent toward his flirtations. But, much as she liked being part of the little family that Berenson and Mariano formed with William Mostyn-Owen, she could not linger with them indefinitely.

Through Nicky Mariano she found a place to stay at the Albergo della Signoria, a small hotel in Florence. Living there, she need answer to no one. On the other hand, she could count on no one to join her for meals. In Venice this had been a source of enduring misery. But in Florence she began to turn it to her advantage. "I have been having quite a good time, existing on the principle of skipping one meal a day," she wrote Bowden. "I'm usually invited out to at least one meal, generally lunch, and I eat it for two, so to speak[. . . .] This system has many advantages: it saves money; it keeps you from getting fat; and it keeps me from having to go into restaurants alone. . . ."

Florence, unfortunately, was not quite as she remembered it from their 1946 trip. The chandeliers lighting the Duomo had been removed, leaving it looking "almost too cold and bare." The Baptistry was still wonderful, but you could no longer sit in the Piazza del Duomo "because of the whirring traffic." Owing to a local election there were loudspeakers "blaring speeches at every main corner." When it came to Florentine painting she was far from enthusiastic. "I haven't yet got the feeling for Florentine painting that I have for Venetian: I like Baldovinetti, Andrea del Castagno, Polliouollo [Pollaiuolo], and Giotto—that is about it," she wrote.

At this point, of course, she had no vested interest in the paintings, the Duomo, or the traffic. She was simply another American tourist. On a bad day, she was fair game for every self-styled lothario. On a good day, if she played her cards right, William Mostyn-Owen might take her for a private tour of the Sitwells' unoccupied villa, where you could find "a suit of chain mail hanging on a cheap wooden clothes-hanger in the entrance hall," or for a visit to La Pietra, Harold Acton's fifty-six-room Renaissance villa, where "martinis were concocted" by Acton's eighty-four-year-old mother, decked out in "something Chinese" and looking precisely like "*every* homosexual's mother." Best of all, however, was to be invited to come to lunch at I Tatti.

Berenson's pretty stucco villa, just north of Florence, had become a mecca for traveling celebrities. A deep and abiding curiosity played some part in Berenson's hospitality, but this curiosity could hardly be said to be one-sided. At lunch at I Tatti you could find everyone from Harry Truman to Laurence Olivier.

**WILLIAM MOSTYN-OWEN**　I Tatti was a house of unbelievable grandeur and comfort, but, mind you, everything was very old-fashioned. The plumbing had been put in in 1910. It was beginning to show its age. Mary said that the day seemed twice as long as anywhere else because the timetable was so rigid. If you were going for a walk with Berenson it was 12 o'clock. Lunch was at 1:30. Then you went up at 3:00 to rest or whatever. And then he would like to go for a walk again. In the summer the walk would be at about 5:00. Berenson was known to be wolfish toward life and toward women. If you were someone he really liked, he would ask you to go for a walk with him. On his walk he would take just one person. On his walks with Mary I think they talked a lot about writing, literature, and history, and a bit about art, though he hated talking about art usually. He used to say, "I want to find out what goes on in other people's minds. I know quite enough about art as it is."

**LUISA VERTOVA NICOLSON** [*Art historian who worked as Berenson's assistant from 1945 until his death and translated his books into Italian*]　Mary McCarthy was very much playing up to him. She was trying to seduce him almost. She would show off having read something. Instead of being humble and trying to make sure what she understood was correct, she almost wanted to teach Berenson. I never spent any time alone with her, but for someone like myself who belonged to an old Florence family and was raised with art history, she appeared presumptuous. Berenson felt his conversations with her were a bit of a joke.

During her first visit to I Tatti, she had no serious thought of writing a book on Florence. She was in Italy on vacation. Berenson had gone so far as to invite her and Bowden to come visit him at his summer retreat at Vallombrosa. He had expressed a great wish to meet her husband. William Mostyn-Owen was no less eager. And she, for her part, was eager to hear what Bowden made of the two of them.

In May 1956, the only pressing matter she had to attend to was seeing her Venice chapters safely through the editing process at *The New Yorker*. Once that was taken care of, she was planning to devote a few hours a day to finishing a memoir of her Jewish grandmother—a subject of interest to Berenson, who for all his dabbling with Catholicism had not forgotten he was the son of a Jewish peddler. Already there had been a few false starts. From the *Cristoforo Colombo* she had written Bowden: "[T]he entry to the subject is surprisingly hard to find, as though my grandmother were standing at the door, barring the way."

On May 30, with Carmen Angleton at the wheel of the black sedan, she headed south to Rome, where she could count on the Chiaromontes for company. For the past year Nicola Chiaromonte had been working with Ignazio Silone as co-editor of *Tempo Presente*, the last of the European periodicals to be set up and funded by the Congress for Cultural Freedom. Now editors from three longer established congress publications had descended on Rome for a conference, most of which seemed to take place, she wrote Bowden, "all day long and half the night too in the cafes of the Via Veneto and Trastevere trattorias."

The Old World might be at once more civilized and more complicated than the New, but it was increasingly susceptible to its incursions. At the very last big "cocktail" of this "continuous public event" she ran into Robert Penn Warren and his wife, her former Vassar schoolmate and fellow chronicler of Italy, Eleanor Clark. Invited by Silone to join him and the Penn Warrens for dinner, she accepted against her better judgment. Decades later, Clark would still be relishing her rival's rout.

**ELEANOR CLARK**   I was sitting on one side with Silone and my poor husband, Red, had to sit with Mary on the other side. She bored the daylights out of him—she was just running down everybody in the literary world. That was the way he described it. Everybody who got mentioned, she had some bad thing to say about him. On our side of the table Silone and I spoke Italian. Her Italian was atrocious.

All the same, her stay in Rome was not without its pleasures. A room had been reserved for her on the top floor of the Hotel d'Inghilterra. This room, with its panorama of chimney pots and tiled roofs, was nothing like "Mary's Room," but it was by no means lacking in charm. The Inghilterra provided her with a freedom she would never find within the seductive confines of Berenson's beautifully regulated household and with her one great European romance, in the form of a fellow guest.

The hero of this romance was no handsome Italian count but a short, powerfully built English critic eight years her senior by the name of John Davenport. The lead fiction reviewer for *The Observer*, Davenport was a friend and supporter of Malcolm Lowry, an early advocate of the novels of Patrick White, and a great admirer of Isak Dinesen. He had briefly earned his living as a teacher and as a Hollywood screenwriter. A graduate of Cambridge and a close friend of the late Dylan Thomas, he was more likely to be taken for a heavyweight boxer than a man of letters. Later that year, he would describe himself to the young writer Nora Sayre, about to meet him for the first time at a London pub, as looking like an overgrown dwarf.

In introducing himself to McCarthy, Davenport sounded a less self-deprecating note. In time-honored fashion he slipped a brief message into her mailbox, inviting her to join him for drinks at the hotel bar: "My excuse, apart from being a great admirer of your writing, is that we have many friends in common in New York." He immediately made it clear that any obligation on her part would be slight: he was scheduled to leave Rome the following day.

The drinks multiplied and drifted from the Inghilterra bar to one of the Inghilterra's top floors and by the time Davenport departed for England the two of them had seen enough of each other to know that they wanted very much to see each other again. John Davenport had a wife and two sons to return to, not to mention a previous wife and two daughters. The current wife, by his own account, was quite possibly mad. Mary McCarthy, for her part, had Bowden joining her for the summer, with Reuel scheduled to meet them later on.

To Bowden she had written at great length of her ongoing flirtation with Berenson, of her brush with Tillich, and of a red-haired reader of Faulkner who had picked her up at a café in Florence and taken her for a long drive in a second-rate sports car he claimed to be driving only because his own car was in the shop. But in writing of her meeting with Davenport she took a somewhat different tack.

### FROM MARY McCARTHY'S LETTER TO BOWDEN BROADWATER, JUNE 9, 1956

He is a very, very heavy drinker, socially impossible and dangerously combative, according to Sonia Orwell, but I liked him extremely and we spent a long strange evening, a large part of it on the top terraces of the Inghilterra. The next morning (after about two hours sleep) he called me to have breakfast with him—he was off on a morning plane for Paris—and *his* breakfast consisted of a Negrone.

She described Davenport as "a fat, romantic man, with some Danish ancestry and something of Cyril [Connolly] in his appearance." On parting, she told Bowden, Davenport had promised to send her some of his writing. "He had a parody of Cyril (not worth sending, he thinks) called "Peel Those Medlars" in the *New Statesman*. Did you see it?" If she told Bowden more than was wise, she did not, at this point, tell all. She ended by making a point of assuring him of how eager she was for his arrival.

Bowden was due on June 13. Carmen Angleton saw to it that she was not left to await his arrival alone. By now she and Angleton were comfortable travel companions, sharing a taste for rigorous sight-seeing and a healthy respect for guidebooks. If Angleton was an ideal companion in most ways, she fell short in one important respect: she was not John Davenport.

Two days after Davenport boarded his plane, a postcard from him arrived from Paris. With no address for him in that city, she sent off a card in care of *The Observer* saying, "I miss you in Rome." Four days later, on June 10, she sent a card to his home address in London, informing him she was leaving for Milan. All summer she wrote Davenport, first from Milan and then from Lake Garda and Venice, sending off letters and postcards long on local news and short on reproaches, bent on entertaining the recipient while letting him know she was dead serious about him.

### FROM MARY MCCARTHY'S LETTER TO JOHN DAVENPORT, JULY 3, 1956

The most alarming thoughts are coursing through my mind; ideas of letters intercepted, a conspiracy "for our own good," illness, accident, death. This is a pretty, rustic place on Lake Garda, with wonderful icy swimming, but my inner agitation gives me the keenest sensation of imprisonment. Aside from this, everything is tranquil, amiable, delightful.

By the time Mary and Bowden left Milan, Davenport had shown himself to be no faithful correspondent. If she was beginning to experience doubts about Davenport, she did not let this keep her from telling her husband of her new lover. In no time at all they were openly quarreling. At some point Carmen Angleton left for Rome. Decades later, only months before her death, McCarthy confided to Carol Brightman that on being told of the affair with Davenport, Bowden let her know that he had been conducting an affair with Carmen all the while she had been suf-

fering through her protracted miscarriage in Greece. To her news of
Bowden's revelation Davenport *did* respond, wanting to know more
about Carmen Angleton, whom she continued to regard as a dear
friend.

### FROM MARY MCCARTHY'S LETTER TO JOHN DAVENPORT, JULY 21, 1956

> *So . . .* Now you're interested in Carmen. I tried to tell you about her
> in Rome, but *then* you wouldn't listen. An exotically beautiful girl
> (woman?), 35 years old, dark Indian-straight hair, white skin, green
> eyes[. . .] solitary, pensive, highly perishable, one thinks, like a garde-
> nia in a florist's box. I love her—in a normal way. In Rome, one night,
> with Nicola Chiaromonte, we were relating our childish dreams. I said
> I wanted to marry the French pretender and conquer back the throne
> with him. *She* said, "I wanted to be a page and die for my king." There
> was the transfixing difference.

In the end, neither revelation kept the Broadwaters from continuing
on together to Venice. On August 1, she and Bowden were ensconced in
a large apartment as charming as the one belonging to the Ur-signora but
better equipped and free of its complications. In addition it overlooked
the Grand Canal. Reuel joined them at the apartment. Nancy Macdonald
was also in Venice, with her sons, Mike and Nicholas. At times she felt
as if she "might as well be in New York," she confided to Hannah Arendt.

The good news was that Anna Maria Cicogna was happy to see her. To
Berenson, who was never far from her thoughts and who had invited her
to become his faithful correspondent, she wrote of the fuss Anna Maria
Cicogna had made over them, "giving a lot of dazzling parties with wonderful food." She also wrote of Peggy Guggenheim, who had put them up
for a few nights and was suddenly free of all resentment. "Why is she
ostracized?" she asked. "Her morals are no worse than the next Venetians. At her best, she is rather fresh and amusing, like a naughty child."

As the summer drew to an end, the onslaught of American visitors did
not let up. Nancy Macdonald and her two sons were followed by Dwight
Macdonald, who returned for a second visit to find that the gondoliers
persisted in plying the canals with long poles instead of outboard motors.
He and his new wife, Gloria, arrived not long after the two-part Venice
piece appeared in *The New Yorker* and were there when she received a
disturbing postcard from Berenson telling her just what he thought of it.

**GLORIA MACDONALD**   Mary had been at I Tatti with Berenson and she
thought she'd worked a lot with him. Anyway, she got this card from him
saying something like she certainly was fearless and had a lot of nerve. Later
we were in Florence, when she and Bowden were there. We went around
together. She sopped up knowledge, you know. We'd stand in front of a paint-

ing and she'd give us the whole background history—sort of like a tone-deaf person listening to music.

To the casual observer, the Broadwaters looked like a settled family. But if that earlier bout of mutual confessions did not make for an immediate rupture, it seemed to set each partner in the marriage more firmly on an independent path. Certainly it seemed to strengthen Mary's resolve to again see John Davenport (or J.D. as she had taken to calling him). Instead of irritation, his long silences continued to elicit only fond concern.

### FROM MARY MCCARTHY'S LETTER TO JOHN DAVENPORT, SEPTEMBER 18, 1956

Nothing special here—solitude, walking, reading, climbing the stairs to the library. It's a repetition of last year, except that now I welcome this lorn state in which everything seems poignant and transfixing[. . . .] And you? Will I hear tomorrow?

It had always been her intention to linger on in Venice after Bowden set off for the fall semester at St. Bernard's. Before returning to America, she planned to go to Paris, making a side trip to Holland to catch in a bit of sight-seeing with Hannah Arendt. At the end of her stay in Paris she would return first-class on the *Queen Elizabeth*.

The journey from Venice to Paris was ordinarily a mere train ride, but once again Bowden had left her in charge of the black Chevrolet. The sedan was to be shipped back home. After a summer of misadventures, she had good reason to know that driving the sedan was beyond her. An acquaintance had agreed to take her from Padua to Paris. Somehow, though, she would have to make it to Padua on her own. The morning of her departure, she was about to set forth, when salvation arrived in the form of Peggy Guggenheim.

### FROM MARY MCCARTHY'S LETTER TO BOWDEN BROADWATER, SEPTEMBER 28, 1956

She discerned (yes, discerned, incredibly, for I didn't tell her) that I was afraid to drive to Padua, and volunteered her services, appearing at San Gregorio with the gondola and Rino. She herself was dressed in an orange suit and red shoes, looking very gallant and cute really. She drove me to the station and hopped on the train back to Venice[. . . .] All this was done in a spirit of gayety. "I couldn't let you go alone," she remarked, "especially after I remembered the ending of *A Charmed Life*."

Fortunate enough to arrive intact at her hotel in Paris, Mary had every reason to avoid putting her luck to a further test. On the contrary, she set off on an adventure which might have been dismissed as foolhardy if it had not been undertaken by someone known for her clear thinking and good common sense. At the last minute, she scrapped her original plan to meet Hannah Arendt in Amsterdam so that she could take a secret week in London with John Davenport. From this hazardous escapade she also emerged unscathed—not only unscathed but ecstatic.

### FROM MARY MCCARTHY'S LETTER TO HANNAH ARENDT
### N.D. [C. EARLY OCTOBER 1956]

Dear Hannah, it's been wonderful, more so than I could conceive, abstractly. The apartment is above a green square, and I stay here most of the day like a captive canary, high up, but we've ventured out a little and I've seen a new side of London, a side I love. Last night, we went to Hampstead and I waited in two pubs while he visited his daughter, who'd just had her appendix out, in the hospital[. . . .] This has all gone very deep, on both sides. I no longer see a terminal point when I leave London. I told him you'd said, "This can go on for twenty years," and *he* said, agreeing with you, "She's a European."

How Davenport felt she had no way of knowing. On her side, certainly, it had gone very deep. For the moment, she was keeping Bowden in the dark about this London visit while enlisting Hannah Arendt in an elaborate bit of subterfuge. Enclosed with her London letter were two picture postcards to be mailed to Bowden, the first regaling him with a tale of waiting for Hannah at the Amsterdam airport and the second giving some hint of the arduous nature of their initial sight-seeing.

By the time she set sail from Cherbourg on the *Queen Elizabeth*, with the perfidious black sedan safely stowed in the liner's hold, she was fairly certain that she wanted John Davenport to be a permanent part of a new life. By November—having resumed her old life on East Ninety-fourth Street, seen the publication of *Venice Observed*, and made a trip to Boston to visit the Lowells—she was absolutely convinced of it. She was convinced as well of the importance of dispensing with all compromise. But Davenport, it seems, knew himself better than she did.

### FROM JOHN DAVENPORT'S LETTER TO MARY MCCARTHY,
### NOVEMBER 15, 1956

The part of your letter that most demands answering I must ponder over. No deceits, no *maris complaisants*[. . . .] By "pondering," I mean that I don't want to agree too quickly with or press against your "intuitions." One dreary fact is that if you burn your boats (to use H[annah]'s phrase) I am not even a jetty, practically speaking.

**PEREGRINE WORSTHORNE**   One of the last times I saw him he came into El Vino's, a wine bar at Fleet Street where everyone used to go. He came rolling in, a sad figure. He had a high, squeaky voice, which didn't go with the figure he cut. He was a tiny pugilist, short and enormously strong. "I was talking to the Pope only last week," he said, "and the Pope told me how much he admired your articles." He was an appalling drunk, a liar, and a fantasist. He was also a tremendously stimulating and sophisticated companion. That she liked him doesn't surprise me. It surprises me that she would have thought of living with him or marrying him.

**ANTHONY SAMPSON**    At *The Observer* he was regarded as a very good writer who drank his talent away. He would arrive at the office on Friday very drunk, with his review copy in hand. His arrival was spectacular. There was always a question of whether Port would make it or not. "Port is on the way," they'd say. "Port has reached El Vino's bar." He was incredibly strong, having been a boxer. There was a story about Port and the Lord Chancellor, Somerset Maugham's brother, who was quite short. Port was having a row with him at the Savile Club and he'd had enough. He picked him up and set him on the mantelpiece, saying, "Sit there like a good boy and tick like a clock."

Davenport's escapades made for good stories and he was as colorful as any character in fiction. Indeed Muriel Spark would later confide to Nora Sayre that he had provided her with the inspiration for a secondary character in *The Bachelors*—a bibulous and boisterous art critic given to denouncing those who fail to live up to his high standards as "common little creatures."

**NORA SAYRE**    I met John Davenport in London in 1956. After my first book reviews were published in the *New Statesman*, he rang, saying he'd known my parents in California when I was three. "I used to play bears with you in Hollywood," he said, "and I once gave you a bath." His language was a feast and he was marvelously witty. Also a wonderful galvanizer and stimulator: you'd be talking about something and he'd say, "I think you should write about that." John made you feel like going home and writing. He never made a pass. He did talk about his affair with Mary. He was so indiscreet that one thought his wife, Marjorie, would have realized about the affair. Many of his London friends knew.

**PEREGRINE WORSTHORNE**    He had no real application. There's a sad story of John's standing at the bus stop browsing through Cyril Connolly's *Unquiet Grave*. It was of course the book he was meant to write. He could have done it as well if not better.

For Davenport, Cyril Connolly had long figured as a *bête noire*, arousing, in almost equal measure, the keenest envy and the most damning disapproval. "Whom the gods wish to destroy they first call promising," Cyril Connolly had written when he made his first great literary splash in 1939. As Mary McCarthy had been quick to note, Davenport resembled Connolly. He resembled him not only in his physical appearance and his reputation for irascibility but in his failure to live up to early promise. But, as she had not seen fit to note, he also bore a certain resemblance to Edmund Wilson. Both were short and stout. Both were heavy drinkers. Both possessed in abundance qualities that had drawn her to her favorite teachers—a love of learning, a breadth of knowledge, and a belief that what one set out to do in life really mattered. Of course there were differences: Davenport was a great teacher and talker, while Wilson was a disaster in a classroom or a lecture hall. Davenport never managed to publish one book of his own, while Wilson turned them out with seemingly no effort. However, Davenport at his best, like Wilson at his best, had a gift for inspiring and pushing the people he cared about.

As Mary had been preparing to take her leave of Venice, she let Bowden know that she was making good progress with her memoir of her Jewish grandmother but was still lacking an ending. "[I]t needs some new turn, some new inspiration, to bring it off," she wrote. Not long after she returned to New York, she submitted a finished manuscript to *The New Yorker* of "Ask Me No Questions," which ended with her grandmother, bedridden and cared for by nurses, no longer capable of remembering the word for mirror. "At that moment, the fact that my grandmother was senile became real to me," she wrote. Of all her childhood memoirs, "Ask Me No Questions" is the densest and most ambitious. For many readers it is her best. This may be owing to some suggestion—some "new inspiration"—from Davenport. Or merely to the heady excitement of being in love.

From the start Davenport had made clear to her that he was no one to pin her hopes on. She, for her part, seemed not to hear him. For some months, though, she had little time to spare for daydreams about a future together. Having sold this last memoir to *The New Yorker*, she was soon hard at work weaving together all eight childhood memoirs in such a way as to make a satisfying book. What she was aiming for was not just a random collection of related pieces but a coherent autobiography that built to a dramatic climax. To accomplish this she set about writing an overall introduction and then a series of postscripts. With her introduction she immediately addressed the question of whether these stories of her childhood had all been made up.

### From "To the Reader" in *Memories of a Catholic Girlhood*

These memories of mine have been collected slowly, over a period of years. Some readers, finding them in a magazine, have taken them for stories. The assumption that I have "made them up" is surprisingly prevalent, even among people who know me[. . . .] Can it be that the public takes for granted that anything written by a professional writer is *eo ipso* untrue? The professional writer is looked on perhaps as a "storyteller," like a child who has fallen into that habit and is mechanically chidden by his parents even when he protests that *this* time he is telling the truth.

Many a time, in the course of doing these memoirs, I have wished that I *were* writing fiction. The temptation to invent has been very strong, particularly when recollection is hazy and I remember the substance of an event but not the details—the color of a dress, the pattern of a carpet, the placing of a picture. Sometimes I have yielded, as in the case of the conversations.

To this matter-of-fact approach she brought something of the spirit, if not the actual prose, of George Orwell, whose gritty memoir of boarding school days, "Such, Such Were the Joys," had appeared posthumously in *Partisan Review* only two years before. It was an approach first tried by Cyril Connolly in "A Georgian Boyhood." Frank and analytic, this approach came naturally to her. Moreover, it allowed her to satisfy the objections of critics like Delmore Schwartz, who had argued that *The New Yorker's* memoir form did not make for intellectual rigor. Now, as she looked back at the real events she had portrayed in her original memoirs—noting where she had diverged, whether by accident or intention, from the facts of the case—she was free to take time to ponder the motives lurking behind the curious actions and reticences of the leading characters in her tale.

*Memories of a Catholic Girlhood* came out in late spring of 1957 to reviews of a kind she was not accustomed to seeing. In love with Davenport, unsure about her future with Bowden, not knowing where she would be living next, she had pieced together a book that seemed almost serene in its self-assurance. Somehow she succeeded in portraying the sorrows and upheavals of her troubled girlhood while suggesting, without ever quite saying it, that she had put such sorrows behind her. If there was anger, there was also humor and intelligence and an attempt at fairness. With her insistence on getting at the truth and her refusal to see herself as a victim, she touched the hearts of critics who had long since categorized her as a writer so clear-sighted as to be lacking in all feeling. On balance, men were more smitten than women. And Protestants and Jews were more sympathetic than Catholics.

### FROM W. T. SCOTT'S REVIEW IN THE *NEW YORK HERALD TRIBUNE*, MAY 26, 1957

Miss McCarthy, who writes better than most people, here writes better than herself. In this slow-grown book there is almost none of her dismaying heartless, though brilliant, satire. She records with her customary sensibility, but not with the eye cast coldly; rather, at last, with passion and compassion, with commitment of herself.

### FROM VICTOR LANGE'S REVIEW IN *THE NEW REPUBLIC,* JUNE 24, 1957

Miss McCarthy's new book has a quality of gentleness and warmth for which her earlier fiction scarcely prepared us.

### FROM PHYLLIS MCGINLEY'S REVIEW IN *SATURDAY REVIEW,* JUNE 8, 1957

No virtue is more intimidating than truth-telling[. . . .] Fortunately, it is nearly impossible of accomplishment. For truth, no matter how plain or unvarnished, is also so multiple-faced that few can see it whole. Mary McCarthy has had a try at it in the latest of her brilliant books [. . .] and it is a highly talented try. Whether she has succeeded or not no one can say for a certainty.

### FROM N. W. LOGAL'S REVIEW IN *CATHOLIC WORLD,* NOVEMBER 1957

Mary McCarthy's *Memories* should take this year's Pulitzer Prize for being the Number 1 Cry-Baby-Book of the year. Her stylish profiles, etched in bitter acid, prove that this woman who should have reached maturity a long time ago, is still the pouting child, the youthful rebel, the adolescent skeptic, and the cute exhibitionist of her earlier years.

The response to *Memories of a Catholic Girlhood* was strong and immediate. Letters poured in from readers—not only readers who'd had some brush with the Prestons or McCarthys but total strangers who felt the need to reach out to the author of this book. Unfortunately, she was not in America to read those reviews or answer those letters. When the book came out, she was in Florence, recovering from a bad bout of pneumonia.

It had been her intention to spend a second summer in Italy. And it had been Bowden's intention once again to join her there as soon as St. Bernard's let out. But the first week of May, instead of sailing directly to Italy, she set off for England, to track down John Davenport. Troubled by his long silence and by reports that he had gone around London bragging about her, she was intent on forcing their sputtering affair to a resolution. To get hold of her errant lover she turned to the only friend of his she'd had any dealings with, a lawyer in his middle forties with a flat in Belgravia named William Hughes. Having been told by her lover that Hughes was both a cousin and a friend, she had felt free to use him as a mail drop.

The plan she worked out with Hughes was simple enough: making no mention of her name, Hughes was to ask Davenport for a drink at his Belgravia flat at a quarter of six. Once the two of them were together, Hughes would retire discreetly, leaving her to find out exactly where she stood. To this end, pubs were searched and a telegram was dispatched. (Davenport's phone had been shut off for lack of payment.) At the appointed hour, she arrived at the Belgravia flat, ready to forgive and forget. But there was no sign of Davenport. Hughes, who was wearing white tie and tails, had to leave for a dinner promptly at six fifteen. As a last resort, he sent his housekeeper in a taxi to Davenport's lodgings with instructions to rouse him. Davenport was not to be found. There was no scene, no confrontation. But in that half hour before he went on to dinner, Hughes took it on himself to tell her something of the man she had sought out.

### From Mary McCarthy's Letter to Bowden Broadwater, May 9, 1957

Mr. Hughes is not his cousin or "kinsman"; he is not related to him in any fashion ("Thank God! added Mr. Hughes, piously crossing himself or the next thing to it). "You ought to know," he went on, after a short hesitation, "that John is a pathological liar." His father was a writer of light lyrics for musicales, a drunken half-literary man; his mother was an actress who played chars[. . . .]

After we'd talked about twenty minutes, I said I didn't think I wanted to see John, after all. Mr. Hughes said to think it over and that he would call me in the morning: if I still wanted to, he would arrange it. He called this morning and I said no[. . . .] He suggested that I might write John a letter, just before I left London, saying that I'd heard that he was talking about me and telling him to stop it. I said that that would only bring out the worst in him, I should think, and make him talk more. Mr. Hughes said he thought probably I was right and that, in any case, John's punishment for being a liar was that no one would believe him even when he was telling, as it happened, the truth[. . . .]

I said: "In a way, I'm not absolutely surprised by all this, and yet it has no connection with what he was when I saw him or in his letters." He said: "Well, he's a deeply mysterious person." The part about the wife's breakdown is true, but he attributes it, naturally, to what she's been put through, with the drinking, no money, two children, etc. "But he goes around, damn it, saying she's mad."

To put it kindly, Davenport was a deeply mysterious person. To put it bluntly, Davenport was a liar of epic proportions.

The only true part of him, according to Mr. Hughes, is his love of books and knowledge of them; that is why he has liked him, he says, in spite of everything[. . . .] I asked him what he thought had happened to J.D. about me, and we agreed that it was possibly a case of his becoming exhausted by the illusion he was maintaining (to himself too) of being a different man from what everyone else knew him to be.

There was a relief of sorts in knowing the truth, but she was suffering— from a broken heart and from having made such a fool of herself.

You are entitled to leave me forever for my colossal folly. I shan't blame you if you want to. I am afraid you will feel literally *disgraced* by it, even if no one believes it. The fact, indeed, that no one would believe it makes matters worse. It is a horribly *private* stigma. What I'm most ashamed of—the only thing, in a way, I'm ashamed of—are my tears.

One thing was certain: she must avoid Davenport at all costs. For Davenport any such meeting would be an embarrassment. But for her it would be nothing short of torture. Unfortunately, she had made plans to stay in London for a week. She had made these plans, believing that if things turned out badly she could always fall back on the company of Dwight Macdonald. As luck would have it, Macdonald was out of town. Most of her other London friends had ties to *The Observer*. When she saw them, it was going to be hard, if not impossible, to avoid stumbling upon *The Observer*'s lead fiction reviewer. And hard, if not impossible, to avoid rumors of their affair.

In her next letter to Bowden, written three days later, as she was about to leave early for Florence, she sounded a good deal less relieved. For one thing, there had been no word from Bowden. For another, she had a bad cold: "a physical reaction, no doubt to the news contained in my last letter." One last time she had gone on to meet Billy Hughes—for drinks at the Ritz, where he had told her that Davenport had "a great deal of feeling and heart"; that he wrote some of his reviews when drunk, because he had come to writing late and had no disciplined work habits; and that if he was violent on occasion, the violence was directed toward "rather awful people" and "not against men he likes or against women."

### FROM MARY MCCARTHY'S LETTER TO BOWDEN BROADWATER, MAY 12, 1957

He said that when we'd had our first conversation he was presenting, so to speak, the case for the crown. At the Ritz, he presented the defense and we both became very, very sad[. . . .] Billy Hughes' view is that a kind of salvation presented itself in the shape of me, and that [J.D.] had a compulsion to push aside the only thing that could save him.

To be pushed aside is never pleasant, whatever the reason. By the time she reached her hotel in Florence her physical reaction to the news had developed into bronchial pneumonia. Sick in bed and still feeling "morbidly sad," she did not hear from Bowden until May 20, when, after almost three weeks of silence two letters from him turned up in the mail. The letters, which touched lightly on his preparations for a St. Bernard's field day and the latest New York gossip, made no mention of

John Davenport. With both he included reviews for *Memories of a Catholic Girlhood*.

Although it was a relief to get these letters from Bowden, they were not what Mary was hoping for. "[A]las, they sound terse and cold. *What* are you angry at now? Or do I imagine?" she wrote. That Bowden would not feel all that sorry for her seems not to have occurred to her. The next day she turned to a correspondent more likely to offer the sort of sympathy she required. On May 21, in a letter to Hannah Arendt, she repeated the story of her miserable half hour in Billy Hughes's flat. She varied the telling hardly at all. If anything, she made Davenport's failings sound worse this time around. As an experienced writer she knew how to polish her narrative. She knew also to keep in mind the special needs of her audience. To her best friend and confidante she did not disguise how much she had been made to suffer first by Davenport's defection and then by her decision never again to see him.

### FROM MARY MCCARTHY'S LETTER TO HANNAH ARENDT, MAY 21, 1957

[I] had given up the idea of a meeting, for what was the point? We couldn't make love, thanks to the publicity he, John, had given the affair, and if we talked simply, I wouldn't be able to dissemble the knowledge I now had. This, it seemed to me, would be horrible for *him*, and he would probably edge out of it by lying or bad temper. It also struck me that *he* would rather not see *me*. Who knows whether I was right or wrong? I repented the decision terribly before I left London[. . . .] What troubled me most was my staying there and so publicly *not* seeing him, as if giving him the lie, which seems cruel. The truth is, I still care about him, just as much as ever.

By the time she wrote Hannah Arendt she was well on her way to recovery. In her choice of hotel, if nothing else, she had been fortunate. From the moment she was confined to bed the *padrona*'s "own cook" had been sending up trays laden with "delicate broths; *verdura*, cooked; chicken breasts; scraped apple; cooked apple and lemon peel; a morsel of snowy white fish with oil and lemon." From a local doctor recommended by the *padrona* she had been receiving shots of penicillin. Owing to these ministrations, her lungs had almost cleared. But hearts are not so easily mended.

She did not hear from Hannah for two weeks. When the letter finally arrived it opened not with words of sympathy but with praise for *Memories of a Catholic Girlhood*: "Of all your books, I feel this is most as you are yourself—which is not a 'value-judgment.' [. . .] [T]here is a cheerfulness in the very relentlessness with which you separate factual truth from the distortions of memory." Only then did Arendt offer up a gratifying bit of information. Bowden had come to Sunday dinner and "made one little gesture which was quite telling." Arendt had taken care to show no reaction but she could see he was "delighted about the outcome of the London affair." Finally, when the letter was well under way, Arendt dispensed the words of solace she craved. And a much needed bit of balm for her poor wounded heart.

### FROM HANNAH ARENDT'S LETTER TO MARY MCCARTHY, JUNE 7, 1957

> Mary, dear, I am afraid you came into too close a contact with the English variety of the "lost generation"—which apart from being a cliché is a reality. They are always the best and the worst, but in such a way that every single one of them is both at the same time[. . . .]
>
> [T]o destroy oneself and become "self-destructive" can be a time-consuming and rather honorable job. More honorable and less boring than to save oneself. The only thing which is really not permissible is to drag other people into one's own amusements. So, you had to be frightened away; and he must have known that it would take rather drastic measures to achieve this. Certainly, there is a great deal of cruelty in all this; but then you can't expect somebody who loves you to treat you less cruelly than he would treat himself.

From her earliest years, work had seen Mary McCarthy through the worst of her personal crises. With Edmund Wilson it had been her salvation. With Bowden Broadwater it had invariably made a great difference. Unfortunately, recovering from John Davenport, she had no compelling project to occupy her. The Vassar novel was still out of the question. There was no other novel she wished to start.

In April she had written Berenson of how she was thinking of doing a book on Florence, Bologna, and Mantua. After the great success of her Venice book the previous winter a second book on Italy seemed a good idea. *The New Yorker* had already expressed interest, and the Berniers were making overtures. Berenson's criticism of the Venice book may have chastened her, but it had not deterred her. She had received no direct response to her April letter. By the time she arrived in Florence she had heard from friends that Berenson was feebler and deafer. He had suffered a hemorrhage that left him blind in one eye and was no longer able to work.

Nonetheless, when she was feeling more like herself again, she took Berenson up on an invitation to come visit. Berenson was not about to deny himself the pleasure of her company simply because he disapproved of her new project. And she was in great need of distraction. She found her host better than expected, but a visit to I Tatti was not what it had once been.

## FROM MARY MCCARTHY'S LETTER TO BOWDEN BROADWATER, MAY 25, 1957

He entered, wearing a pair of sapphire-blue glasses and said: "You've changed a great deal in the last year; your face has elongated." He was very lively [. . .] but after dinner, he kept falling asleep. None of us were in good form; Willy and I both very shaky, from recent illness; Nicky tired. This morning, on my tray, instead of the usual rose, there were 3 bachelor buttons; I seem to be going the way of Mrs. Berenson.

The flowers for all breakfast trays were in fact chosen by the gardener. And Berenson was beginning to fail so rapidly it was hard to tell which slights were owing to intention and which were simply owing to ill health. Things had reached such a pass that Berenson was departing from his time-honored summer itinerary and was leaving Florence in early June, taking his old bones down to Naples, where he would not be plagued by the hay fever that seemed to be making his eye heal so slowly.

She, on the other hand, was committed to Florence until mid-July. Nicky Mariano had found her and Bowden an apartment for the summer, across the Arno by the Boboli Gardens, and she had taken it for six weeks, starting on June 3. The apartment boasted a terrace and four bedrooms. She and Bowden could keep it longer if they wished. While the apartment was costly and short on closet space, it came with a maid and with the recommendation of having met the exacting standards of the art historian John Pope-Hennessy the previous summer. When it came down to it, finding a place to stay was a good deal easier than finding a place among the city's more glamorous residents. Once again she was being treated as a tourist and outsider.

Without Berenson in residence, she was having to make do with no promise of a lunch or an overnight stay at I Tatti and no William Mostyn-Owen for company. But before long she was writing letters that sounded more or less like her old self. She was able to do this because she knew that in no time at all Bowden would be joining her and because her social life was picking up. She had met one of the more aged pillars of the Anglo-Florentine community, Violet Trefusis, Vita Sackville-West's old lover, who lived in a villa said to have housed Galileo. She had run into William Phillips and at long last made peace with him over *The Oasis*. And she had met Roberto Papi and Cristina Rucellai, two members in good standing of the Florentine aristocracy.

Cristina Rucellai's annual ball was the high point of the Florence social season. Her salon was frequented by foreign visitors and members of the city's oldest families. She was known for her beautiful legs and for having very little use for women. The Palazzo Rucellai was one of the great houses of Florence. (A photograph of its façade would eventually grace the cover of the paperback edition of *The Stones of Florence*.)

Roberto Papi was married to a member of the Contini Bonacossi family, at one time possessors of one of the finest collections of Renaissance paintings in Italy. Indeed, it was said by some that the art holdings of his wife's family had gained him entree to Berenson's court. Charming and well spoken, he had an aura of authority. During the war he had been imprisoned by the Germans. Not long before she met him, his best friend from the war had died, leaving him, by his own account, depressed and lonely for company.

The previous summer, Mary had written Berenson at Vallombrosa, wanting to know why Peggy Guggenheim was ostracized. Once again, she chose to consult him. In a letter to Naples, she told him of her two new acquaintances.

### FROM MARY MCCARTHY'S LETTER TO BERNARD BERENSON, JUNE 7, 1957

Countess Rucellai strikes me as a person who is trying to be the local Anna Maria Cicogna. But something has given her the idea that it is clever and "original" to be rude. Or am I wrong and is she merely stupid and shy and I should feel sorry for her, etc, etc?[. . .] The person I keep meeting, and the only person I seem to be able to talk to, is Roberto Pappi [*sic*], but here there's a language barrier, and I have to discontinue conversation, in a sweat of exhaustion, after 15 minutes of hard-breathing French or Italian[. . . .] Oh dear, don't repeat any of this. I've just been reading how the best people in Florence, including the Brownings, didn't want to receive Mrs. Trollope on account of her sharp tongue.

### FROM BERENSON'S LETTER TO MCCARTHY, JUNE 11, 1957

The aspiring Countess Rucellai I do not know—is she the American born Higginson?[. . .] *Real Florentines are the least hospitable of people.*

If Berenson did not know the countess, he did know Florentine society, where a name, a fortune, or a fifty-six-room villa will not gain you entrée unless the old families find you *simpatico*.

CRISTINA RUCELLAI   I don't remember who brought her to me. The person who introduced us told me she was an American writer. I had no idea who she was. I had never read her books. I did not find her beautiful. I did not find her well dressed and certainly not chic. She used to come here very often. We spoke in English. Never in Italian. I did not see her socially at all. I never saw her anywhere else, other than in my house. She was one of the foreigners that every now and then I invited over, mostly because of her friendship with Roberto Papi. With Anna Maria Cicogna certainly she succeeded in making friends. Why? Because Anna Maria Cicogna flattered her.

She really believed that perhaps Mary McCarthy was a great writer. Anna Maria is easily impressed.

For Cristina Rucellai this poorly dressed American writer was not and never would be *"simpatico."* Bowden Broadwater, however, was another matter.

**CRISTINA RUCELLAI**  Bowden was fantastic. Bowden I loved. Really loved. I continued to see him for many years. He was one of the most pleasant men I've ever met. Wonderful company. They were so different one from the other that one wouldn't even match them.

The Broadwaters' plan was to use Florence as a base of operations, while Mary began serious research for her Florence–Bologna–Mantua book. On their forays into the countryside, they would take time for an occasional *fête champêtre* (she had asked Bowden to bring calling cards and their treasured set of picnic knives and forks as well as her beaded evening sweater). By midsummer, however, the Arno valley was hot and humid and plagued by mosquitoes. The Pitti Palace and the Uffizi were swarming with German tourists in shorts, while the palaces of its first citizens were shuttered and empty. Sweaters and calling cards were the last things they needed.

In August, after a stay in Venice, where they could always count on a welcome, the Broadwaters finally paid a visit to Berenson at Vallombrosa, staying at a nearby hotel. Berenson, who could not embrace her writing wholeheartedly, proceeded to embrace her choice in husband. Despite everything, Berenson's approval continued to matter to her. Known for dressing down any critic foolish enough to give her a bad review and then to greet her at a cocktail party, she could not quite bring herself to turn her back on this frail nonagenarian. Of course to turn her back on him would have been to turn her back on the pleasures of life at I Tatti. Still, there was more to it than that.

Berenson had read "Ask Me No Questions" in *The New Yorker* in April and had written her in New York of his admiration of "that fabulous odalisque, your Jewish grandmother." Because of the hemorrhage in his eye he had not been able to read the copy of *Memories of a Catholic Girlhood* she placed in his hands that May, but Nicky Mariano, ever devoted, had read chapters aloud to him. Much as he admired these chapters, he could not resist probing an area where she admittedly felt vulnerable.

**FROM BERNARD BERENSON'S LETTER TO MARY MCCARTHY, JUNE 11, 1957**
I am still under the impression of your Catholic girlhood. The wealth of detail, the theological discussions *à la* Compton Burnett [*sic*], keep

me wandering how much is *Wahrheit* [fact] and how much *Dichtung* [fiction].

Among those who could see no earthly reason for Mary McCarthy's great attachment to Hannah Arendt, not a few had been moved to hypothesize that Arendt was her Jewish grandmother. Certainly her friendship with Arendt helped make it possible for her to scrutinize her Jewish grandmother with curiosity rather than embarrassment. And her acceptance by Arendt may well have helped make it possible to come to some sort of peace with that elusive but endlessly seductive figure. At the same time, it could be argued that Berenson with his carefully maintained schedule, his nineteenth-century house with its closed doors and silent corridors, his love of luxury, and his persistence in withholding both the information she wanted and his full approval, was a truer incarnation of Augusta Preston. As such, his power was considerable.

**CRISTINA RUCELLAI**   Berenson treated Mary McCarthy very badly. This I heard from Roberto Papi. Berenson did not like these people who would arrive and have the pretension to write a book on Venice or Florence, knowing nothing about these cities in a real way and expecting everybody to give them information. He had no real liking for people who were like vacuum cleaners, sucking up the information from other people. Berenson would play with these people and he would play with Mary McCarthy. She would go up there and he'd give her a dribble of information. A drop here, a drop there. Never the whole thing.

In late August, when Bowden left for England before going back to his job at St. Bernard's, she returned to their rented apartment in Florence, to discover that there was no running water for much of the day, owing to a bad drought. On the surface this second Italian summer had been pleasant and even tranquil. Only once had she faltered, when on the eve of Bowden's departure she had blamed him for the life they had been leading. By the time she wrote to apologize for this lapse, she was beginning to have second thoughts about her new Italian project:

**FROM MARY MCCARTHY'S LETTER TO BOWDEN BROADWATER, SEPTEMBER 14, 1957**
Forgive me for blaming you at the Taverna. It's just that I feel such loathing for the life we keep being pulled into, the life everyone seems to be leading and this includes nearly everyone[. . . .] So perhaps, as you say, we had better stay home next summer, maybe longer[. . . .] I see that these Florence-Venice pieces are an irrelevancy, a bore even (for others), too much of an artifice or a manufactured product[. . . .] If I'm lucky, I might be finished by Christmas.

She had no time to dwell on her doubts about her new project or on the apartment's deficiencies. Or to wonder what had ever become of John Davenport. She was spending long hours at the German Institute, reading first Kenneth Clark and then John Pope-Hennessy on Italian Renaissance painting. Berenson on Florentine drawing she found "godawful" and "pure treacle." John Pope-Hennessy, the former tenant of the apartment, she found more to her taste. "[H]e would make a good teacher," she wrote.

In mid-September, while Bowden was entertaining Cristina Rucellai and her husband in New York, taking them to the theater and out to dinner, she was suddenly swept up by Roberto Papi, who had assigned *himself* the full-time role of teacher, guide, and muse.

**Cristina Rucellai**   Mary and Roberto Papi got along very well, because Roberto had a heart of gold and wouldn't even realize that she was taking advantage of him. He was a very cultivated man. He knew everything about Florence. He would go stand in front of the Duomo and tell her this is what happened here. He loved telling stories. Mary liked to make people believe that there was some kind of affair going on with Roberto Papi. She liked to suggest that, but truly it was not the case.

**Luisa Vertova Nicolson**   Roberto Papi was very handsome and very spoiled by everybody. He had married a very rich woman and he sang for his supper. He was not particularly knowledgeable about art. He was very worldly. Today there is hardly any salon life, but in the old days there was this kind of salon life in Florence. Hostesses were happy to have him. He was the ideal person to have to dinner or tea. He was a young man about town, only he was not young anymore.

Cristina Rucellai had her own reasons for feeling protective of Roberto Papi. Some years before, she and Roberto Papi had been lovers. Although the affair had ended, they remained close friends. Their story was common knowledge, but it never occurred to Mary McCarthy to keep her hands off Roberto Papi when Cristina Rucellai was around. All she understood was that Roberto Papi was "not in a mind to make a pass." As it happened, she was not in a mood to encourage him. It was enough that when they were deep in conversation at lunch at the Cave di Maiano she saw the essence of Florence with a startling clarity. Florence, she suddenly realized, was "a mountain city, like ancient Athens," a city of which one could truly say "there *is* a continuity with Nature."

Coming so soon after a failed love affair, Papi's faith in her was the sweetest of elixirs. What could be better than to be sought out by a charming and attractive admirer so intent on taking her on the highest terms. To be brought as an honored guest to share a quiet dinner or a country weekend with his wife and children. To be shepherded to a quiet hillside *taverna*, where over lunch and wine he felt free to talk of his disappointments and dreams. Like John Davenport, Papi was a great talker.

When he persisted in speaking no English, she was almost always able
to catch his meaning.

### FROM MARY MCCARTHY'S LETTER TO BOWDEN BROADWATER, OCTOBER 3, 1957

> There was also a good bit about the relation I was trying to make with
> history or that he thought I was trying to make with history, and this
> part I did not understand very well. But the idea, I think, was that his-
> tory is a tissue of lies.

By the time Mary was ready to take her leave of Florence, she had
decided to scrap her original plan and to make the city of Florence the
sole subject of her second Italian book. *The New Yorker* had let her know
that the magazine was eager to run anything she wrote on Italy. But
rather than labor long and hard to produce another article for *The New
Yorker*—an article that would be subject to the red pencil of Mr. Shawn
and his meddling fact checkers—she decided to do another picture book.
This time, however, on the advice of Berenson, she would stay clear of
the Berniers, with their sleek production values and their last-minute
notes from someone they regarded as a higher authority.

Harcourt, when approached, was more than willing to go ahead with
the project. Picture books are expensive to produce, but the Venice book
had sold better than anyone had expected. Clearly there was an audience
for this sort of thing. Harcourt agreed that she would have approval of
the photographer, the layout, and the paper. She would not only have
approval of all the photographs but would have a say in matching the
photographs to the text. By staying with a house that had seen her through
the publication of four books, she had a reasonable chance of ensuring
that there would be no last-minute surprises.

Back in New York, it soon became apparent, however, that she was not
to have total control. When she suggested Cecil Beaton as the book's photographer, Harcourt rejected him, saying that he would turn it into a
"Beaton book." What they omitted to say was that he would have rightly
expected to be very well paid. But she did not let this setback discourage
her. On the advice of a mutual friend, she decided to try her luck with
Evelyn Hofer, a younger, relatively unknown photographer who, like
Inge Morath, had been born and educated in Europe.

The Florence book was harder to do than the Venice book in large part
because she took it so seriously. She was trying to make it an insider's
view of Florence, but, above all, she was trying to make it a portrait of a
Renaissance city rather than the "tooled-leather" portrait of "a dear bit of
the Old World" made popular by the Brownings and their nineteenth-
century contemporaries.

She failed to meet a deadline of Christmas 1957. In late winter, she collapsed from exhaustion and was ordered to bed by her doctor. For the moment there was no further talk of spending the following summer in America. In May she set off for Florence with plans to meet up with Evelyn Hofer and to write the book's final chapters. Once she got Hofer settled, she would shepherd her around, pointing out to her the palaces, churches, streets, and squares she wanted to use. Like most plans of this sort, it made no allowances for two very different personalities.

### FROM MARY MCCARTHY'S LETTER TO HANNAH ARENDT, JUNE 14, 1958

I ought to have written sooner, but you know me and besides everything has been in a wobble of indecision until a few days ago, when I cabled Bowden to come here, *aux secours*. The photography hasn't been going well; everything I wanted photographed turns out to be unphotographable or so the camera-artist declares. And she herself turns out to be a handful, a dark bird all a-flutter, fearful and obstinate, with as much temperament as twenty divas.

**EVELYN HOFER**   My feeling was that I wasn't illustrating her book but was taking my own photographs, which would be running parallel to her text and would be complementary to it. At first Mary and I walked around together. It was her idea that when she saw something she liked, she would exclaim, "Oh, Evelyn, that's pretty—take a snap." But that wasn't the way I worked. I used a large 4-x-5 camera on a heavy tripod. Each picture took a long time, sometimes days, waiting for the sun and shadows to be at their best. This moment lasts only a few minutes and if a cloud appeared I had to return the next day.

Nervous as Evelyn Hofer made her, once Bowden arrived, Mary felt free to cease going around with her. Not only did Bowden provide help on a technical basis but he was able to drive Hofer and her camera from one location to another. Bowden later acknowledged that it had been tricky but Hofer delivered the goods. The trouble was, amassing a first-rate collection of photographs was only the beginning.

When at last they all returned to New York in the fall of 1958, there was no slapdash collaboration like the one that had produced the Venice book. This was in part owing to her desire to do well by this city presided over by Berenson and beloved by Roberto Papi and in part owing to the fact that Harcourt was making every effort to please her. Harcourt was making this effort not merely out of a longstanding regard for her but also out of a mixture of pragmatism and desperation. At this point her editor, Denver Lindley, had left for Viking and Bob Giroux, the editor who had brought her there, had gone to Farrar Straus. Gerry Gross, the head of the design department, was on his way out. The book's designer was a young woman she had never met. She knew William Jovanovich, the new head of the Trade Division, only from hearsay. What she had heard did not necessarily dispose her in his favor. Having started out selling textbooks, Jovanovich had in a relatively short time pushed his way to the top of the company, leaving not a few mangled bodies in his wake. To most eyes he looked like a businessman pure and simple—and a none too fastidious one at that. Already more than one Harcourt author had jumped ship.

**WILLIAM JOVANOVICH**   We met in Gerry Gross's office. I believe that others were more concerned about Mary McCarthy's leaving us than I was. But the fact is that the first meeting did not go smoothly. Mary McCarthy talked very little. I probably talked too much. In any event, a new beginning was made within a fortnight at her small apartment on the East Side. Gerry Gross accompanied me. Mary McCarthy and I hit it off very well indeed. [We] met alone soon after this in my office and at the Brussels Restaurant.

**JANET HALVERSON**   I had been warned that Mary McCarthy was difficult before my first meeting with her at Evelyn Hofer's studio. There Mary conveyed her vision of the book; and the early sample pages I showed her suited that vision. I was familiar with the book arts of *quattrocento* northern Italy, and easily selected a beautiful typeface, Bembo, available from our Swiss printer and appropriate to Mary's vision. (Bembo was derived from a Venetian type of the period when much of her Florentine action was going on.) Eventually I could almost anticipate what Mary would like—it seemed to be what I liked—but she was bolder. I'd say, "I don't know, maybe this isn't *pretty* enough." And she'd say, "It's not *supposed* to be pretty." Mary knew what she wanted and kept it in mind. It was to do the best book possible. It was a pleasure to do Mary's will.

**ROBERTA LEIGHTON**   The thing I remember about Mary—and maybe that's why I loved her forever—was that when I was brought in as copy editor she said, "I'll do the index." And she did it. She wanted that book to be perfect and she knew the way to get it perfect was to do it herself.

*The Stones of Florence* came out in *The New Yorker* in August 1959, the first summer in four years that the Broadwaters had not made the journey to Europe. Finally, she and Bowden made good on their vow to stay home. They had taken a small house near Pawlet, Vermont, where they were living on a hillside in what she described as "almost total solitude."

Even after the customary cutting and rearranging by William Shawn, *The New Yorker*'s piece on Florence stretched on into three parts. The erratic summer mails played havoc with this serialization, but two intrepid readers refused to admit defeat. Hannah Arendt wrote from the Catskills to say that she had read the third part, having missed the first two parts, and found it "superb." Elizabeth Hardwick wrote from Castine, Maine, to say that she and Lowell had read the first two parts—having almost tossed out the first by mistake—and so far they found it to be "a brilliant, wonderful work, marvelously written, completely interesting, and miraculously real and tangible."

The book came out in late fall, bearing a dedication to Roberto Papi. It was clearly far more ambitious than her book on Venice. For one thing it was longer; for another, it made greater claims for its subject. Extolling the virtues of the republic under the early Medicis, she credited *quattrocento* Florence with being a city-state in the great tradition of Athens. But that was not the end of it: "The Florentines, in fact, invented the Renaissance," she proclaimed, "which is the same as saying that they invented the modern world—not, of course, an unmixed good." She began her first chapter by giving readers a taste of the modern world those early Florentines had wrought.

## FROM *THE STONES OF FLORENCE*

"How can you stand it?" This is the first thing the transient visitor to Florence, in summer, wants to know, and the last thing too—the eschatological question he leaves echoing in the air as he speeds on to Venice. He means the noise, the traffic, and the heat, and something else besides, something he hesitates to mention, in view of former raptures: the fact that Florence seems to him dull, drab, provincial.

Cities, she asserted, were either masculine or feminine. Venice and Siena, perennially popular with tourists, were both feminine. Florence, a masculine city to its core, made no concessions to pleasure. There were no smart cafés, no memorable restaurants, no broad boulevards. From the street its *palazzi* looked more like fortresses than palaces. "Dry," "proud," "terse," "thrifty" were the adjectives she favored when writing of both the present and the past. Florence, she said, had always been a city of stone, and its great artists had almost all been sculptors or architects, and bachelors. In the course of writing the book, she had arrived at an idea that made it possible to better appreciate the statues in Florence. Having tested this idea on Hannah Arendt—and met with no resistance—she gave it a prominent place in her second chapter:

The statuary of Florence is its genius or attendant spirit, compelling awe not only because it is better than any other statuary done since ancient Greece, a categorical statement, but because, good and bad alike, it is part of the very fabric of the city—the *respublica* or public thing. It belongs to a citizenry, stubborn and independent, and to a geography, like that of Athens, of towering rock and stone.

In the republic, as in ancient Athens, homosexuals had enjoyed great influence in both politics and the arts. Whether homosexual or married, the artists tended to be puritanical. In the *quattrocento* they had produced some of the world's greatest art: Uccello, who had given the world the science of drawing from perspective; Brunelleschi, the architect who designed the dome for the cathedral; and Donatello, whose *David* she found infinitely preferable to Michelangelo's. For Michelangelo—who outlived his fellow bachelors and survived the fall of the republic—her admiration was grudging at best. For the artists who came after the republic she had no natural sympathy. For Botticelli her tolerance was limited and for Pontormo it was so limited as to verge on contempt.

Florence was the city of Petrarch, Boccaccio, Dante, and Machiavelli, but she chose to write a book that focused almost exclusively on the visual arts and on what she could see with her own eyes. In order to do this she concentrated on an area where she had no real expertise and where her previous publisher had felt she was in need of a scholar's help. Inevitably, she ran the risk of seeing only what she wanted to see. In the end, she produced a striking and highly personal portrait, in which the text and illustrations were closely intertwined.

With *The Stones of Florence* she managed to please not only Elizabeth Hardwick but most of the critics. In *The New York Times* Charles Poore wrote, "No one has ever written about the town with quite her combination of fierce partisanship and measured detachment." Lincoln Kirstein in *The Nation* wrote, "[A]greement or disagreement is beside the point. She may be writing the most stimulating guidebooks of our time." A few reviews were mixed, but almost all the reviewers loved Hofer's photographs. In the end, there was only one outright attack: an unsigned review in London's *Times Literary Supplement.*

**FROM *THE TIMES LITERARY SUPPLEMENT*, NOVEMBER 13, 1959**
> By temperament Miss McCarthy is a reporter. But works of art are scarcely ever susceptible of the normal technique of reporting, and nothing in the book suggests that her aesthetic receiving apparatus is anything but commonplace. Many of her difficulties stem from a failure to admit that this is so. She is prepared to write that "the cruel tower of Palazzo Vecchio pierces the sky like a stone hypodermic needle," though she must be perfectly aware that it does nothing of the kind. For her Donatello's *David* "wearing nothing but a pair of fancy polished tall boots is a transvestite's and fetishist's dream of alluring ambiguity." For her Michelangelo's *Victory* is "an inane-looking young man crushing the back of an old one," and Pontormo's infinitely moving *Deposition* "as though Cecil Beaton had done the costumes for a requiem ballet on Golgotha." All these are supreme works of art, and Miss McCarthy's comments are vulgar and irrelevant.

**JOHN RICHARDSON**  Bowden said to me, "Who on earth could have written this?" In the end I broke down and said, "It was John Pope-Hennessy." Bowden said, "It can't be. A lot of that material came from John Pope-Hennessy. He's a great friend of Mary's." I said, "Exactly."

From Florentines who read the book, and from those who didn't, she met with a response not unlike John Pope-Hennessy's. The book suffered from a fundamental schizophrenia: there was the partisan and there was the critic, and for Florentines the more memorable of the two voices was the one that described the heat, the Vespas, and the dowdiness.

**CRISTINA RUCELLAI**  At the end the overall effect—and this was not Roberto Papi—was extremely negative. It is not a positive book about the city. The reason for that is simply because nobody liked her. The result is she cannot be positive because her experience was not positive.

**LUISA VERTOVA NICOLSON**  I didn't read the Florence book. As an art historian I wasn't interested. It was difficult to take her seriously. She got things so wrong. For instance, she complained to me that the flat that Nicky Mariano had found for her had no closet in the bedrooms. Instead, there were large wardrobes, which she found monstrous. Anyone could have told her that they were masterpieces, chests made in the Middle Ages by master carpenters. At Christie's they would fetch a fortune. How can you pretend to write about Florence and not have the curiosity to ask about such things?

From Roberto Papi she received an effusive telegram in Italian, but when she saw him in Florence that winter it was apparent that poor Papi had been made to suffer for her sins.

**FROM MARY MCCARTHY'S LETTER TO BOWDEN BROADWATER, DECEMBER 12, 1959**
> Roberto looks older; he hasn't been well and, incidentally, he has really suffered over my book. Because it has been violently attacked here and he does not know what to say.

Francis Haskell gave the book a positive review in *The Spectator*, but he liked the book less well than her Venice book. William Mostyn-Owen felt as he did and believed he knew what had gone wrong.

**FRANCIS HASKELL**  She was doing this thing which people like Ruskin have done, which is to put forth a moral stance of her own about life as it were. I recognize that seventeenth-century Florence was a falling off after the early Renaissance, but I thought she misunderstood all that.

**WILLIAM MOSTYN-OWEN**  She got a little bit too involved with Berenson's courtiers and with Roberto Papi in particular. I think he gave her quite a lot of ideas. And sometimes they were crackbrained. Her fondness for Florence was willed, I think. I don't think she really was as fond of the Florentines as she claimed to be. I don't think she really liked them. It's terribly difficult to like the Florentines anyway.

While Dwight Macdonald faulted her for "far too much insider snobbishness, far too many Facts and far too little feeling," Chiaromonte allowed as how there might be "[m]any questionable ideas or cracks, as usual," but gave her credit for doing her homework and producing a book that was "quite readable, too."

### FROM NICOLA CHIAROMONTE'S LETTER TO DWIGHT MACDONALD, NOVEMBER 15, 1959

Of course, it is dry. But that is Mary, an overly intelligent woman, with a streak of foolishness[. . . .] In any case, as you know, I like her very much; not only is she extremely intelligent, and a good woman, but she has real character and moral stamina.

Back in March 1958, Berenson had written, "I am wild with curiosity to see what you are making of your book on Florence. I flatter myself to think that if I had the leisure and the energy, of course, I could make a very readable book about fifteenth and sixteenth century Florence—'*quattrocento*' in particular." That May, when she had arrived for her third consecutive summer in Florence with Evelyn Hofer and a nearly completed manuscript, she found Berenson suffering from severe back pain and "in a very bad state." After a visit to I Tatti she wrote Bowden, "He's so shrunken and silent that one actually feels, sometimes, that he is gone and that his little ghost is sitting there, watching and nodding to itself."

But Berenson was not in such a bad state that he could not make his guest's life hell. Tales of her outings with Evelyn Hofer were greeted with narrowed eyes and total silence. His jealousy of the Florence book was impossible to ignore. Diverted by her company, Berenson had brought himself to forgive her for her Venice book. He had been willing to forgive her because he believed she knew no better and because he had a real admiration for her abilities as a writer. After taking her for a drive during her first visit, he had written in his diary, "Mary scarcely opened her eyes to all this beauty. Yet she will write about it, and be evocative and give readers the longing to come and experience for themselves, as I never, never could." But the Florence book promised to tax his powers of forgiveness beyond the breaking point.

Old habits die hard. All her life she had believed that when all else fails the truth will set you free. "The only way, I think, to exorcise this demon is to read him a little of it," she wrote Bowden. Unfortunately, the reading was not the exorcism she had hoped it would be. Berenson did not like her characterizing Florence as a virile city. And he did not like her making such a fuss about the Vespas and all the traffic and noise. Friends who saw her immediately after the reading found her badly shaken. She might make fun of his "treacle" but there was something in him she respected and admired. And something she could not bring herself to pull away from. By the end of June Berenson had broken out in boils. If he had Job's affliction, he did not have Job's patience.

### FROM MARY MCCARTHY'S LETTER TO HANNAH ARENDT, JUNE 23, 1958

> Poor old Berenson is now like some specimen preserved in a bottle and a fearful atmosphere proceeds from his house—of hate and fury—that leaves one feeling poisoned[. . . .] Anyway, there is something *wrong* and dead somewhere in the immediate milieu, which may pass off, like the smell of a rat that has died in the walls; at least, I hope it will.

As the months passed, she continued to hope that the smell would "pass off" and she continued to hold up her end of their three-year correspondence. In August 1959, when the Florence pieces were about to come out in *The New Yorker*, she sent a letter to Vallombrosa from Pawlet, Vermont. She sent the letter to Nicky Mariano rather than to Berenson, who at this point was confined to a Bath chair and had lost all interest in current events. More fortunate than Augusta Preston in her dotage, Berenson had good days as well as bad, but it was clear that the end was near.

"We've thought about you a great deal, and with affection; indeed, you're always in our minds because this place, on a Vermont mountainside, is hauntingly like Vallombrosa," she wrote Mariano and then went on to say, "I've been working on the novel about 8 Vassar girls, of which B.B. and you read the chapter about the pessary. With a long harrowing interruption of struggling with *New Yorker* proofs of their extracts from the Florence book, which is coming out in October. Poor B.B.—how he disliked it! It is a merciful thing, I guess, that he will be spared any more of it." A merciful thing for both of them perhaps.

The adventures that had begun with such promise three years earlier in "Mary's Room" had taken turns she could only regard with regret, if not sadness. The terrible visit to London in May 1957 had not marked the end of her relations with John Davenport. That December, after more than half a year of no word from him, she had received a short note. "[B]y now friends will have explained my silence," wrote Davenport. "Not due to lack of love, as you should know." He closed by saying that he longed to hear from her. The explanation he alluded to was simple enough: on July 17, 1957, Marjorie Davenport had "fallen" from a window at the Strand Hotel. His wife's depression, or madness, had ended in suicide. Four months later, in March 1958, Davenport followed up on this note with a full-fledged letter, filling her in on such details as he felt she should know. Again he apologized for his silence. "It would not have been fair to burden you with any of it. You were terribly involved in it all and were not to blame. Entirely my fault. That was why I waited six months before writing. I'm so glad you knew nothing about it at the time."

Davenport had explained his long silence without ever quite explaining why in May, a good two months before his wife's death, he had done everything possible to avoid her. She, on her part, gave no indication that any explanation was necessary. Toward the end of that summer, when she and Bowden were finishing up in Florence with Evelyn Hofer and about to go to London to attend Sonia Orwell's wedding to Michael Pitt-Rivers, she sent Davenport a postcard telling of her impending visit and saying "I should like to see *you*." He wrote back, "Of course I must see you." Unfortunately, her postcard arrived late and omitted any mention of where she would be staying. This time, however, Davenport managed to find her. They met and they talked.

But if tragedy had chastened John Davenport it had not changed him. In late September 1958, when she was back in New York embarking on the formidable task of putting together the Florence book, she was pleading with him, "Please write. Why don't you write?" This letter, which was to be her last to him, came to no more than five very brief typewritten paragraphs. It began as if she was simply picking up their last conversation where it had left off. Having nailed down a fact, she was passing it along to him. "The quotation from Isak Dinesen in Hannah's new book is: 'All sorrows can be borne if you put them into a story or tell a story about them.' That, it seems, was the source of Hannah's consoling prophecy to me—remember? But I am not consoled." She signed the letter, "Much, much love."

# Chapter Eighteen

## JIM WEST

On June 28, 1959, Mary McCarthy wrote Hannah Arendt from Vermont to let her know her work on the Vassar novel was "going pretty well." Bowden, however, had suffered "an awful blow." Having planned to spend his summer translating a book for Harcourt, he had suddenly been informed that his services were no longer needed. "Jovanovich, cabling for rights, discovered that an English publisher had already commissioned another translation. So that was that. He went on translating for a few days like a chicken that keeps on having reflexes when its head has been cut off."

Not a promising start to their summer. And not the best metaphor to describe the stricken state of a devoted husband. Gone was the tender optimism of letters posted from Cornwall and Portsmouth a decade earlier. And gone was all effort to persuade an old friend of Bowden's brilliance. This time, she could not even summon a "poor Bowden." The best she could come up with was: "So far, no substitute has been thought of."

That a substitute was necessary she seemed to regard as self-evident. During their three summers in Italy it had never mattered that Bowden had no work of his own. When he wasn't rushing to her rescue or seeing to it that their life ran smoothly, he had more than enough to occupy him. When she was at her desk for three hours in the morning, there was always someone like Cristina Rucellai delighted to carry him off for a tour of her estates. In Vermont, on the other hand, there promised to be no need for his services: Reuel was in Europe for the summer and the worst they could look forward to were queries on her Florence piece from *The New Yorker*'s fact checkers. More important, there promised to be no diversions: they were living like hermits.

It is one thing to plan a solitary summer and quite another to pull it off. In mid-August she wrote Hannah Arendt to say that she had seen more in the way of human society than she had planned on. Not only a teacher from St. Bernard's but her brother Kevin had come to stay, bring-ing with him two children and a maid. At the same time, her skirmishes with the checkers escalated into a full-scale war.

In the end there had been no need to think up a substitute for Bow-den. When he was not helping out with the visitors, he was helping her deal with *The New Yorker*. Indeed, *The New Yorker* wrought havoc with her peace of mind another time that summer. Better pleased than his checkers with her portrait of Florence, William Shawn had asked her to write a profile of the city of Jerusalem—a profile which would empha-size the historical nature of the city and which in all likelihood would take two years to complete.

Knowing only too well the trials and tribulations of writing a factual piece for *The New Yorker*, she confessed to Arendt that she was nonethe-less "flattered." She was also tempted by the "money," by the "glamour," and, most of all, by "the idea of learning something new." Bowden, how-ever, was very much against the project. "He says that these years, the next ten, are the best years of a novelist's creative activity, and that it would be wicked to squander them on journalism, even very high-class journalism. He is right about 'the best years'—at least for most novelists of the past, and he's thinking, I imagine, chiefly of George Eliot, who began writing fiction at about thirty-seven and reached her peak in her early fifties[. . . .] Anyway, tell me, if you will, what you think."

If she was hoping Arendt would take her part against her practical-minded husband, she was destined for disappointment. Arendt, wise in the ways of the world and of marriages, chose to go along with Bowden on the Jerusalem profile, though she did not go so far as to concede that he was right in *principle*.

If this was not exactly the advice she was hoping for, she could at least take it to heart. She decided against doing the piece. By behaving sensi-bly she had gotten through the worst of her pain and disappointment over John Davenport. And by behaving sensibly she had kept her mar-riage intact. Still, one could argue that the marriage, like that poor chicken with its head lopped off, was being propelled by little more than reflexes. And not the best reflexes at that.

**ROGER ANGELL**    I was out at Idlewild Airport one day and I saw Mary and Bowden sitting together waiting for a plane. I was sitting directly behind them and I could hear what they were saying. Mary was reading the newspaper. Bowden kept saying that he wanted to do this, he wanted to do that, he wanted to go here, he wanted to go there. Her response was always to say nothing at all.

**JOHN RICHARDSON**    I remember going to a dinner at the apartment, when it was just Mary and Bowden and Eve Auchincloss and myself. That must have been late 1958 or early 1959, when I first came to New York. Bowden and Mary had evidently decided that they had too many friends and would say things like "Well, we can certainly do without the So-and-so's." I didn't know who half these people were, but I thought, God, how frightening. Bowden is the kindest of men, but he likes to hide this side of his nature and come across as more sardonic than he really is. This was especially true when Mary was around. She brought out his *méchanceté* and he brought out hers. To this extent they were a *folie à deux*.

EVE AUCHINCLOSS  I can remember sitting around after everybody had had a lot to drink and we were having a wonderful time just cutting everybody up. We were being so mean. And the next morning—or maybe even at the time—I remember thinking, How awful. And feeling rather ashamed of myself.

That fall, when the Broadwaters returned from Vermont there was little time to spare for character assassination. Almost immediately, Mary began to repack her bags. Thanks in part to Hannah Arendt's letter of recommendation, she had received a grant from the Guggenheim Foundation, freeing her to work on the novel full-time. The study in their small apartment was cramped. It simply was not possible to live a hermit's life in New York. For a while she had dabbled with the idea of spending the fall in Newport. In the end she wrote Anna Maria Cicogna, asking if she knew of an apartment to rent in Venice. Anna Maria Cicogna responded with a counterproposal: Why not join her at her villa in Tripoli?

In early October, she arrived in Tripoli with the manuscript of her novel and a book she had brought along for her research, a copy of Veblen's *The Theory of the Leisure Class*. For seven weeks she remained at Anna Maria Cicogna's villa, keeping to her room until lunchtime and working as many as eight hours a day so as to have two new chapters to send to Bowden. Not all of these hours were devoted to the novel. As always when she was lonely, she fell back on her husband and friends. To Katharine White, to the Lowells, to Hannah Arendt, and to Bowden she wrote long letters cast from the same boilerplate, but tailoring each in such a way as to emphasize those aspects of life in Tripoli most certain to appeal to the recipient.

With Katharine White she was fairly circumspect, letting her know she was hard at work on the novel while giving her a brief sketch of her sojourn among the Italian leisured class—a sojourn that showed every sign of being colored, if not enriched, by the insights of Thorstein Veblen. With Cal Lowell and Elizabeth Hardwick she went a bit farther— portraying, for their delectation, the endless hours expended by her hostess and her fellow guests on antiquing an old mirror and painting a wall of plate glass. With Hannah Arendt she was more forthcoming about her sense of isolation. "No one has the slightest interest in me, including the hostess," she wrote. And with Bowden she was quite frank about how unhappy she was.

### FROM MARY McCARTHY'S LETTER TO BOWDEN BROADWATER, OCTOBER 27, 1959

> I feel rather a lump, and they mostly ignore me, which is probably a form of tact but makes me feel still more like an excrescence[. . . .] As for feeling left out and clumsy, this is only my vanity, I suppose. And it will either become more painful or I will cease to feel it. I've been in these positions before and generally something happens to ease them: the first days in the convent; the first days at Vassar; the first days alone in Florence, being snubbed by Cristina. Do you think the first days in Heaven would feel like that too?

On December 1, she left the villa a week early, to visit friends in Italy and then join up with Bowden in Vienna, where with Reuel they were going to celebrate a gala Christmas abroad, all thanks to the Guggenheim Foundation, Arthur Schlesinger, and the United States government.

In the waning years of the Eisenhower presidency, the State Department was beginning to show signs of a more pragmatic approach to the Cold War. Schlesinger, who had been part of a first delegation of writers to be ushered behind the Iron Curtain, had proposed her name for the second. Unlikely as it might have seemed a decade earlier, she had been approved and invited. And unlikely as it might have seemed a decade earlier, she had accepted with pleasure.

The plan was to do a bit of sight-seeing in Vienna and Prague and then go on as a family to Warsaw, where her official State Department work would begin. At the end of the Christmas holidays Reuel and Bowden would return to America and she would fulfill her remaining obligations in Poland before going on to Yugoslavia. In both Poland and Yugoslavia there would be a second touring American writer—Saul Bellow, author of *The Adventures of Augie March*, the novel she had so strenuously supported for the National Book Award.

As "visiting specialists" she and Bellow were expected to meet with students and intellectuals, to give prepared lectures and informal talks, to attend embassy dinners and cocktail parties, to grant interviews and be available for any last-minute engagements. By the time she was ready to leave for Poland she had the rudiments of three talks: one on the current state of American theater; one on the difficulties facing contemporary writers who wanted to write realistic novels in the tradition of Balzac or Tolstoy; and one on the difficulties facing any novelist who, instead of giving readers a quivering mass of sensibility, attempted to portray fully rounded characters in a richly detailed social setting.

Although she had chosen three broad topics, the talks dealt with matters she had been grappling with for years. And although she was not at ease at a lectern, she could always fall back on her early training, when she had entertained thoughts of a career on the stage. Still, the role of cultural ambassador was altogether new to her. To ensure that her stay in Poland went off without a hitch, she, like all visiting specialists, was placed in the hands of a member of the Foreign Service who was not merely qualified to book a good hotel room or secure a reliable driver but was prepared to steer her safely through official protocol and past the blandishments of any number of black marketeers and double agents.

**JAMES WEST**  I remember first hearing her. She was calling from a little town en route to Warsaw, traveling with her husband and son. "Mr. West, this is Mary McCarthy. I believe you're supposed to look after me while I'm in Poland." "Miss McCarthy," I said, "I will."

The Warsaw airport was fogged in and her plane had to land at a provincial airport, miles distant. The remainder of the journey was made by bus. Not until midmorning of the day after she was scheduled to arrive did she and her two traveling companions check into rooms reserved for them at Warsaw's Grand Hotel. Before she had time to unpack, she was greeted by Yale Richmond, who worked under James West, the public affairs officer at the American embassy. Richmond found her to be "bright, energetic, and a good trouper." To West he reported that he was "smitten." Soon he was not the only one.

**JAMES WEST**  I invited her and her son and husband to dinner and a fun evening. I took them to a club in the old city that was three floors down—it used to be a bakery—called the Krokodil. We had a nice dinner and lots of fun and I liked her husband fine and I certainly liked Reuel. I was quite interested in Miss McCarthy as well. I don't care for dancing much, but I said, "Miss McCarthy, would you care to dance?" Mary was no great dancer either, but we had a wonderful dance. In the middle of it I looked at her and said, "I'm going to marry you." She practically stopped in middance and she looked at me with amused astonishment, mildly concealed, and then we danced on and went back and sat down.

**REUEL WILSON**  Jim West was cheerful and competent and very much the way you'd expect someone in that position to be. In those days, Jim was very straight and serious, his hair clipped short in a brush cut. I didn't notice anything going on at that first meeting. I didn't think twice about it. I don't know that Bowden did. What I did notice was that Jim West and his wife didn't disguise the fact that they were not getting along. They would say things to each other in front of everyone. I had the impression that they didn't see much of each other except for public occasions.

**SAUL BELLOW**  I was unaware that there was any flirtation going on. First of all, I wouldn't have predicted her interest in him. He was so meek. He was married to a rather buxom, dark-haired, heavily made up, but nevertheless attractive lady. Much younger and with a house full of kids. What did he fall for? The witch of Endor. He fell for the glamour.

Certainly Mary McCarthy had a reputation for glamour. As to whether or not she lived up to that reputation, there was some disagreement. To at least one embassy wife she seemed surprisingly ordinary, even dowdy. With that severe hairstyle she looked like an old-fashioned blue-stocking. There were strands of gray in her hair and she did nothing to disguise it. Nor did she disguise her lack of interest in the embassy wives. When they were brought over to meet her at lunch, or at tea, she was perfectly polite, but that was the end of it. She wasn't cold exactly, but she was distant.

Of course when she chose to be, she could be thoroughly charming. With Yale Richmond she was always "a good trouper." On the two occasions he accompanied her to lectures he found her to be an impressive speaker. But he did not have much of a chance to see her. Gradually Jim West took over as her programmer, making good on his promise to take care of her.

**JAMES WEST**   Now, I'll tell you something you won't believe and no one ever does, but one day long ago I had a copy of *The New Republic*—I was living in a miserable hut, so to speak, in New York on Bank Street and was going to write the Great American Novel and did nothing but enjoy New York for a year and have a wonderful time—and one day I took the magazine and then on it put the name "Mary McCarthy" on the top of the margin and I drew a straight line to "West." Then I drew a curved line, so the thing looked like a bow, but with the same result. That was around 1936. I had seen, read, or heard, or felt something about her that slipped into place forever. So I did look after her. It took a while. I had a wife and she had a husband, but it worked out all right.

An only child and, by his own account, his mother's darling, James Raymond West was two years younger than Mary Therese McCarthy. His parents had divorced when he was very young and his mother had married a rich man who liked to travel and, moreover, had little use for children. For much of his childhood he stayed with his mother's parents in Maine. Born in Old Town, he attended Bowdoin College. After college, he had taken his time settling down. Along with the year in New York, there was time spent working on *Babson's Reports* and a summer managing the Wharf Theater in Provincetown. The war brought an end to further experimentation with the arts. He joined the Air Corps, taught celestial navigation to cadets, flew out of Italy, and was demobilized in 1947 with the rank of major. Almost immediately he took a job in Paris

with the Foreign Operations Administration, one of the newly minted
State Department agencies whose purpose was to promote economic
recovery in Europe. In 1954 he joined the United States Information
Agency in Washington. After his first marriage ended in divorce, he married a woman some fifteen years his junior. In June 1959, he was posted
to Warsaw, to serve as the embassy's chief information officer.

At the time he met Mary McCarthy, Jim West was forty-five years old—
his hair had turned silver, his features were regular, his tailoring impeccable—and it was apparent to more than an occasional visitor that he and
his wife were not getting on. Some of this may have had to do with the
difference in their ages, some with the fact that in rapid succession Margaret West had given birth to three children. Danny, the older boy, was
seven; Alison, the only girl, was six; and Jonny, the baby, was four.

Before it could work out "all right" between Jim West and Miss
McCarthy, or even work out at all, West was going to have to make provisions for those children and their mother. And Miss McCarthy, for her
part, was going to have to come to some agreement with her husband of
thirteen years. But first of all she had to honor her commitments to the
State Department, which did not cut its "visiting specialists" much slack.

### FROM MARY McCARTHY'S LETTER TO NICKY MARIANO, APRIL 21, 1960

Saul Bellow and I were together off and on in Poland and Jugoslavia,
and we felt like barnstorming actors of the old days; we were the first
American writers to see most of the places we went and of course had
to be seen too. We were both exhilarated by Poland and somewhat
depressed by Jugoslavia, which made us think of the American Stalinist movement in the thirties.

The taxpayer certainly gets his money's worth from these State
Department touring specialists; as Saul said, in Jugoslavia there was
not even time to spit.

Still, there was sufficient leisure for the two visiting specialists to take
each other's measure.

### FROM MARY McCARTHY'S LETTER TO BOWDEN BROADWATER, FEBRUARY 4, 1960

Saul and I parted good friends, though he is too wary and raw-nerved
to be friends, really, even with people he decides to like. He is in better shape than he was in Poland, yet I felt sorry for him when I saw
him go off yesterday, all alone, on his way to Italy, like Augie with a
cocky sad smile disappearing into the distance.

**SAUL BELLOW** She had such an easy way with top officials. I remember
when we were received by the ambassador in Belgrade and you almost felt

she was buttonholing him. Interrogating him. She took charge. I was sort of an observer—the cat in the corner—which is my favorite position as a novelist. She marched me around Belgrade several days in a row. It was very cold and I was talking a mile a minute. She wanted to know the story of my life. Her way of obtaining the truth was inquisitional. There was a battery of questions. I never connected it with any sexual motive she might have. She did take up with some Serb or other in Belgrade briefly. She was good company, except that she was rigid in her views. She had a line and she was inflexible about it. You couldn't have a real discussion.

Talking a mile a minute, Saul Bellow saw what he wanted to see and managed to disarm his Belgrade interlocutor. Having been subjected to the sort of scrutiny that many a man had found beguiling, Bellow (at least in retrospect) refused to be charmed or beguiled.

**SAUL BELLOW**   You would never be bored in her company, but you could get tired of her antics, as I sometimes did. There was not a relaxing moment with Mary. I can imagine what it would be like to go to bed with her—she'd put you through your paces. I didn't feel like going through hoops for Mary or anybody else. I'd had that.

As it happened, she was not in fact seeing a Serb in Belgrade. She was seeing the silver-haired public affairs officer from the embassy in Warsaw. After a few long walks with Saul Bellow in Belgrade, Jim West, with his courtly manners and frank adoration, may have looked especially appealing. Unfortunately, in the brief time they were together there was little opportunity to ascertain just what kind of man he was. Still, there was time enough to know that she very much wanted to see more of him. To get what she wanted, she, who had all her adult life prided herself on her candor, had to be less than honest with her husband. It was not a dilemma entirely new to her—in certain ways, it resembled her last weeks with Philip Rahv.

The best lies, of course, are those of omission. After Bowden and Reuel's departure for the States, she and Bowden wrote each other long news-filled letters. Or, rather, Bowden wrote *her* long news-filled letters and she responded at most three times. He wrote of his work at St. Bernard's, of his frenetic social life, and of Carmen Angleton, who had come to New York for ulcer surgery and was convalescing in their apartment. His first letter was mailed to her in Poland c/o Jim West.

Her obligations to the State Department did not end with Yugoslavia and by mid-February she was on her own in Britain. In the north of England, she gave six lectures in ten days, including stops in Manchester, Nottingham, and Leeds. In London, in the midst of granting a series of interviews and making herself available for teas and lectures, she tried to see something of her old friends. She made no attempt to see John Davenport. But when her work in England was finished, she did not go back to New York. On March 3, she went on to Paris, where she had agreed to give one last lecture and where the State Department had booked her a room for ten days.

**SAUL BELLOW**   I was in Paris, sitting in the Brasserie Lipp, on my way home, peacefully eating my steak, and in came Mary with Jim West. She put her finger to her lips and she looked exceedingly mischievous. I needed no more than that to understand what had happened.

A taste for mischief and a talent for subterfuge would seem to be fundamentally incompatible. On arriving at the hotel where the State Department had booked her a room, she checked out immediately, saying she preferred to stay with a "friend." She made sure, however, to leave Bowden a phone number where she could be reached. Inevitably Bowden made use of that number, and inevitably Jim West answered the phone. After that, there was no question of keeping the liaison secret. All she could do was try to hide the identity of the man in her room.

To Bowden she said that she was with someone she had met during the tour. That was all. Briefly Saul Bellow was privy to more information than her husband was. But it was only a matter of time before the name of the man staying with her reached her husband. Apparently it had not occurred to him that it might be the public affairs officer from Warsaw. But, then, apparently, it had not occurred to him that there might be serious cause for worry. Or if it had occurred to him, Bowden, like many a man before him, had been able to entertain two views of the marriage simultaneously.

**MARGARET SHAFER**   Bowden was on his way to Poland when he came up for a weekend and brought *The Stones of Florence*. He started to inscribe a copy "From the author's . . ." and then he said, "Perhaps I should write '*third* husband.'" And I said, "What a thing to say!" He replied, "Oh, I think it's the right thing to say." So I guess that he knew even then that it was over.

**WILLIAM ABRAHAMS**   In 1960 I finally sat down one night to read *Memories of a Catholic Girlhood* and I wrote Bowden and Mary to say I thought it was marvelous. Back comes a letter from Bowden saying, "Thank you so much for writing. Mary is in Paris, but I'll let her know about your letter. When she comes back in the spring, come and see us."

The marriage was in fact over and if she was coming back it was only to pack up her belongings. During those ten days in Paris she not only made up her mind to see more of Jim West but she made up her mind to become *his* third wife. From Paris she wrote Bowden, asking for a divorce.

**GLORIA MACDONALD**   How long were they married? For twelve years? I think they were happy together. And then comes this terrible bombshell of a letter from Mary saying she is in love for the first time. Bowden was furious. He was in a rage. It would have been quite easy to put it a little differently. When I met Mary and Bowden, they seemed to me a happy couple. Very. She was infatuated with Bowden. I think she was in love with him. I think she must have forgotten the past.

For the moment, all she wished to see, or was capable of seeing, was the possibility for a rosy future with Jim West, whom she believed she loved in a way she had never loved before. Hoping to get a jump on the gossip, she and Jim West set about extricating themselves from their marriages. For Jim West, secrecy was of prime importance. Once he was back in Warsaw, he did not say to his wife that he had found someone he much preferred to her, or that he was in love for the first time. He simply said he wanted a divorce because the two of them were incompatible—a fact that was undeniable. That Margaret West did not see things as he did was soon undeniable as well. The Foreign Service adhered to a strict behavioral code. Until such time as his wife agreed to a divorce, Jim West wanted not a whisper about his affair with Miss McCarthy to reach her ears or the ears of his immediate superior, Ambassador Jacob Beam, or the ears of any member of the international diplomatic community.

For Mary McCarthy, speed not secrecy was the foremost priority. In early April she went back to New York to say good-bye to old friends, to sort through her possessions, and to get Bowden to consent to a quick divorce. Her plan was to return to Europe as soon as possible. Bowden was now sounding forlorn rather than angry. Certainly he was taking a more conciliatory tack. As he saw it, this new lover promised to be just another John Davenport. Seeing things this way, he was inclined to let his wife take from the apartment those items she said she wished to keep.

Common sense dictated that she not stay with Bowden at East Ninety-fourth Street. Instead, she went to stay with Hannah Arendt, who had moved from Morningside Heights to an apartment on Riverside Drive overlooking the river. The trouble was, her best friend, like her husband, was urging her to exercise caution—to try to get to know Jim West better before throwing over her old life for good.

**CARMEN ANGLETON**   I was in New York at the time when Mary came to pack up. It was all very sad and uncomfortable because I had known about it before Bowden did. This gave me a sense of guilt. He knew there was somebody and I couldn't tell him because I'd promised not to. When you're in love with somebody else, you don't think too much about the feelings of the person you're leaving behind.

Having no wish to disrupt Bowden's life more than was necessary, she took none of the paintings and furnishings which together they had chosen and refurbished with infinite care. She did take her grandmother's silver along with her old books. She tried to be fair and do what was right, but she was under duress. She could not return to Poland. She had no place to stay in Paris. In the end she settled on Rome, where Carmen Angleton, who was still convalescing in New York, had a perfectly good apartment that was standing vacant.

But while Carmen Angleton was happy to offer her a place to stay and insisted on taking no payment, that was the extent of what she was willing to do to help out a good friend. At one time she might have been willing to take Bowden off her hands and Bowden might have been willing to go along with it. But in the spring of 1960 Bowden was occupied with a newfound passion for his wife and Carmen was occupied with a love affair of her own.

Unfortunately not every household was so easily dismantled and packed up as the one on Ninety-fourth Street. In Vienna, where she met Jim West for a long Easter weekend, she learned that Margaret West had no wish to relinquish the life of a diplomat's wife. For the moment, Jim West was sleeping on the "divan," working long hours, and trying to snatch time with the children when Margaret was not around. It looked as if the best he could hope for was to meet his new love every two or three weeks for a long weekend. Even that would not be easy. The embassy was understaffed and Margaret was on her guard. In order to get away to Vienna he'd had to say he absolutely had to see his dentist.

To Hannah Arendt, who, like it or not, had replaced Bowden as her chief confidante, Mary wrote what she called an "arrived safe" letter from Rome, passing along all this dispiriting news while trying to make it clear once and for all that Jim West was not about to let his wife, or anyone for that matter, interfere with their plans for a life together.

### From Mary McCarthy's Letter to Hannah Arendt, April 20, 1960

What he has been doing in Warsaw, is confront, very grimly, the price, and the price is the children, whom he loves. He insists on seeing this clearly, without softening it[. . . .] On the other hand, he *will* not live with her, the damage to the children, some of it, has already been done or was done at their birth. "I keep reminding myself," he says, sadly laughing, "that *I* asked that girl to marry me."

Over Easter weekend, the two lovers drew up a plan. West would offer his wife an extremely generous settlement if she would agree to leave Warsaw in June and move with the children to Washington, where he owned a house and where she would have her parents nearby. If she did not deem Washington acceptable, he was prepared to offer her Paris. There, thanks to the favorable exchange rate, living was less expensive. And there he would have his children within reach.

Either way, this divorce was going to be costly. But the cost did not seem to trouble Jim West. "If I do this, I'm going to pay for it," she reported him as saying. Not only was he prepared to shoulder the burden of Margaret and the children, but he was prepared to support the woman he loved in a style to which she had never had a chance to grow accustomed. Once married, she would be permitted to pay for clothing and books and luxuries and perhaps a new car. That was all.

### FROM MARY McCARTHY'S LETTER TO HANNAH ARENDT, APRIL 20, 1960

He's the most wholly serious person I've ever known, anywhere; I don't mean lacking in gayety or human or wild high spirits[. . . .] But I'm alarmed, for him, for his nerves and stamina, by what's going on in Warsaw; it's as though, here, I were living an ordinary life (or will be) while someone was being tortured white, just out of view.

That she loved Jim West was simply a fact. That she was concerned about him was a fact as well. But it was not Jim West that Hannah Arendt was concerned about. She was worried about her friend: "You know that I am frightened that you might get hurt and you know also that I am quite aware that this is nonsense," she wrote. "Is there any chance of spending a few weeks together during vacation?" Moreover, Arendt was worried about Jim West's children, the two oldest of whom his wife was threatening to send off to boarding school: "To add to the shock of parental separation the shock of separating them from each other seems a bit unwise," she wrote. "Can't you simply take the children—which, after all, also will be cheaper when it comes to divorce proceedings."

In 1960 there was no hope of taking the children—the mother always had the right to them in such cases. And there was no getting Mary McCarthy to proceed more slowly on this perilous path she had chosen. If anything, the rumors, the need for secrecy, and the lack of security seemed—at least at the beginning—to add a certain zest to what might otherwise be just another rather staid September romance.

### FROM MARY McCARTHY'S LETTER TO NICKY MARIANO, APRIL 21, 1960

We're living meanwhile in a harrowing suspense and meeting every other weekend at some midway point: Vienna, Geneva, Copenhagen, though that isn't midway for me[. . . .] This is a 19th-century situation with mid-20th century stage accessories (airplanes and telephones) and the far-off promise of a twenty-four hour Mexican divorce—the equivalent of jet travel.

Once Carmen Angleton's apartment was dusted and set to rights and her crates and boxes were safely stored away in the "cantina" in the basement, she had nothing to do but maintain a reasonable discretion and wait for her lover to break free. While she waited, she was not lacking in friends or entertainment. Jim West, on the other hand, was being made to suffer. At the end of May, he told his wife the whole truth.

Confronted with the facts, Margaret West agreed to a divorce. She found Paris preferable to Washington. And a September divorce preferable to June. In June she would go to Paris, to meet with a lawyer and start looking for an apartment. All she asked was that West stay on with her through August, when her parents were due to visit. Come October she promised to leave Warsaw for good.

But October was a long way off and Mary McCarthy at forty-eight was no more patient than she had been as a young woman. And no better at living alone. In the midst of her affair with Davenport, writing had provided a respite and distraction. This time, however, she was finding it impossible to get back to the novel. For one thing, Bowden was showering her with letters, telling her he now realized how much he loved her. Faced with a sheaf of Bowden's letters, she found it impossible not to respond. And she found it no less impossible to spare his feelings, for all that she was touched by his words.

### FROM MARY MCCARTHY'S LETTER TO BOWDEN BROADWATER, APRIL 25, 1960

Dear Bowden, what shall I say to you? I know very well (I was thinking about it yesterday) that there are two yous. One, your attitudinizing and social self and the other a primary self, very fine, brave, gentle, intelligent. Perhaps in everybody there is that, so to speak, concealed drawer which opens only to certain touches. Or not in everybody, after a certain age. I don't know. But in the last few years that drawer in you has been closed tight, and I've been left with your social self, whose company (I'll be truthful) has been a little wearying. That is the explanation, I think, of my friendship with Roberto and my affair with J.D.: a sense of being shriveled, prematurely, by prolonged contact with a dry and withering element.

"I grow fonder of him as he recedes a little into the distance and all the memories become good ones," she wrote Hannah Arendt. Although she recognized that there might be "an element of dramatization" in Bowden's letters, she could not help but be touched by his suffering.

"[T]his picture of a morally re-educated, redeemed, christened, so to speak, Bowden, makes me smile as one would at a dear child."

She might smile at the Bowden of these letters but she believed that she saw both him and their marriage clearly. She now saw that the marriage was no better than "two people playing house, like congenial children." In all this she did not spare herself. "I slowly realize that all my love affairs and marriages have been little games like that—and snug, sheltered games." She paused in this bout of clearsighted analysis only long enough to say, "Perhaps I am sounding like the redeemed, christened Bowden." Perhaps she was. But that spring the new Bowden was touching more than one heart.

### FROM HANNAH ARENDT'S LETTER TO MARY MCCARTHY, MAY 18, 1960

> He was never so nice before, never. As though something had happened to wake him up. I told him rather bluntly he had lived so far in a kind of fairy-tale land, and he replied: are you sure I am fit to live in any other kind of land?[. . .] By and large, I think this is a catastrophe for him, and it is still better than no catastrophe ever.

Bitter as her leaving was for him, Bowden was behaving like a gentleman. But as time passed his wife got more than she bargained for. For one thing, Bowden showed no willingness whatsoever to accept her assessment of Jim West as a fundamentally good man tied to a monster. Worse, he insisted on telling her that he knew her better than anyone else did. Better certainly than her new lover. Indeed better than she knew herself. Although she now believed that she would love Jim West always, that was not in her nature, he argued. But Bowden was not content to rest his case there. Like some sorcerer in a fairy tale, he felt impelled to predict the future. She might regard Jim West as the most wonderful man in the world, he warned her, but the day would come when she would awaken from the spell she was under, only to see him as he actually was.

She might tell Bowden that he had it all wrong, but she could not make him take back his words or stop him from believing that it was only a matter of time before she came back to him. With these letters she was getting in deeper and deeper. Finally she decided to call a halt.

### FROM MARY MCCARTHY'S LETTER TO HANNAH ARENDT, MAY 15, 1960

> [Bowden] has written three times in response to my last letter, and so I've purposely slowed down a little on answering, not to keep up a fevered correspondence with him, which would awaken all sorts of hopes. Indeed, they *are* awake.

Bowden was not the only reason she was finding it difficult to concentrate on her novel. By late spring she had come to see that she had fallen in love with a man who was ardent in ways she had never encountered and difficult in ways she could never have anticipated. The Easter weekend in Vienna had been checkered and somber, but when she joined Jim West for a long weekend in Zurich she saw a side of him that left her shaken.

### FROM MARY McCARTHY'S LETTER TO HANNAH ARENDT, MAY 9, 1960

I *got* hurt this time, and we both lay awake in a single bed while I wept slowly and steadily as we listened to the churches ring the quarter hours from three a.m. till six, and my chest hurt so it felt as though my heart were breaking. The occasion, weirdly, was Clem Greenberg. I'd engaged in over-exuberant reminiscence earlier and told about my affair with him, together with a *description* of his appearance, slothful habits, and general character. This produced an angry and totally uncomprehending reaction: "How *could* you go to bed with a man like that?" Over and over, and all I could say was, "I don't know." I felt as if I was being examined by some cruel magistrate who was going to be grilling me for the rest of my life and picking flaws in my story.

In retrospect, she could see that the suffering she had set in motion had not been wasted. That terrible night had been a source of mutual joy and edification.

### FROM MARY McCARTHY'S LETTER TO HANNAH ARENDT, MAY 9, 1960

I felt it was better, since he has what he calls this "wicked strain" in his nature, to have had it shown me or shown both of us, for examination and perhaps, if we're fortunate, repair. (I don't imply there was any physical roughness, just harsh words and skepticism.) In the end, we were wildly happy again, and he did not *indulge* himself in remorse. I think this trait or habit can be cured; it is more a habit than a trait.

Arendt, who had spent much of her adult life finding reasons to love and support Martin Heidegger, a man who had habits or traits that the majority of right-thinking people could neither forgive nor tolerate, did not think this kind of "getting hurt" was anything to worry about but "only another way of being alive." If anything, she was amused by "how long some chickens take to come home to roost." At the same time, she felt the need to offer a word to the wise.

### FROM HANNAH ARENDT'S LETTER TO MARY MCCARTHY, MAY 18, 1960

[P]lease don't fool yourself: nobody ever was cured of anything, trait or habit, by a mere woman, though this is precisely what all girls think they can do. Either you are willing to take him "as is" or you better leave well enough alone.

People in love tend to hear what they want to hear and Mary McCarthy was not about to "leave well enough alone." That the man she loved was jealous she saw as being in some way to his credit. That he made her suffer was in some way fitting. Certainly it fit in with a belief, at one time accepted as a given, that one must do penance if one is to earn a chance at future happiness. All the same, she took care not to suffer unduly.

In June, when Margaret West left for Paris and Jim West was unable to get away for the vacation they had been planning, Mary joined Ignazio Silone, the Chiaromontes, and a host of old friends and enemies at a giant convocation of the Congress for Cultural Freedom in Berlin. From Berlin it was no distance to Warsaw. For two weeks, while Margaret West was in Paris consulting with a lawyer, Mary stayed at the Hotel Bristol, the one Warsaw hotel with some claim to charm, savoring a semiclandestine existence, which recalled, if it did not precisely replicate, her London tryst with John Davenport in the fall of 1956.

### FROM MARY MCCARTHY'S LETTER TO HANNAH ARENDT, JUNE 29, 1960

My presence here is probably the height of recklessness, but he wanted me to come and so I came[. . . .] [Warsaw] seems real, pretty, and almost pastoral, shimmering in a deep summer green of thick vines, with pots of red and white geraniums lining the streets and the window boxes of houses[. . . .] I feel so comfortable, strangely, as if I belonged here; he comes at lunch-time and brings me whatever is interesting in the mail and the paper and the office gossip and the magazines that have come in; then at five-fifteen, again very domestically.

But Warsaw was not London. Despite its pretty churches and increasingly Western orientation, it sat behind the Iron Curtain. For Jim West exposure could have serious, if not devastating, consequences.

**JAMES WEST** In the beginning of our being together, before marriage, our life was cops and robbers or something. It was very strange in Warsaw, where you're not really very sure of everything and you're quite sure there's someone on your tail that would like to have a little information that might do you damage.

**MARY BRADY** *[The young wife of a Foreign Service contemporary of Jim West's who would later go on to become McCarthy's secretary in Paris but who,*

*at this point, was merely stationed with her husband at the Moscow embassy]*
This is not the way you want to run your embassy at the height of the Cold
War—to have everyone skulking around talking about Warsaw and Mary and
Margaret and Jim West. Mary was oblivious to the whole business of Eastern
Europe and the Cold War, which I think was one of her less attractive quali-
ties. Everything was an occasion for Mary. She was self-dramatizing.

For both lovers the potential danger seemed to present no serious deterrent. For Jim West it seemed to act as a spur to follow his heart rather
than the dictates of common sense. For her it seemed only to add to her
sense of exaltation.

### FROM MARY MCCARTHY'S LETTER TO HANNAH ARENDT, JUNE 29, 1960

Yesterday we drove out in the early evening to see the children, who
are living in a summer hut with their nurse on a bluff by a broad river.
A wonderful place, deep in peasant life, and wonderful children. He
sat down on a stool outside the cook house, took a manicure scissors,
and proceeded to cut the children's toenails and the hair around the
youngest one's ears, very competent, concentrated and yet laughing.
We brought them provisions from Warsaw and presents from Vienna,
and everyone was gay and buoyant, including the driver and the
nurse, a handsome young woman, who brought me a big pink rose and
set out a dish of fresh cherries. He is sacrificing these children and he
knows it (he thinks there's really very little chance of his having them,
except for summers and vacations) and everyone, perhaps even the
children, must know it, and yet everyone was, somehow, rejoicing, as
if only good could come of this occasion, which of course is not true.

That there was pathos and even tragedy in the children's situation
was not lost on her. But by contemplating those children and their
predicament from the perspective of a pretty scene out of Tolstoy, she
was able to make light of it. "I can't see it in any traditional way, as a conflict between love and duty or something of the sort," she wrote. "[T]he
very idea of a conflict seems implausible, and the fact that the children
will undoubtedly suffer does not appear as a fact."

That summer, she was finally able to spend sufficient time with Jim
West to give love an opportunity to take precedence over duty. All in all
they were together for forty-seven days. If there were any further scenes
like the one in Zurich, she chose not to report them. From Warsaw the
two of them drove to France, where they were greeted by three weeks of
almost incessant rain and a series of highway breakdowns. But in spite
of the faulty car and the foul weather, their first extended period of time
together was deemed a success.

In August, when Jim West returned to Warsaw, to do his duty by Margaret and her parents, she took the Chiaromontes up on their invitation

to join them at Bocca di Magra, a fishing village on the Ligurian Sea. At Bocca di Magra she was free to write in the mornings, to swim at a beautiful white marble beach, and to spend her evenings waiting at the outdoor café with the rest of the village for a call to come in from Jim West on one of the two working telephones. But by the time she returned to Rome in mid-September the stress of conducting a nineteenth-century romance with twentieth-century spouses was beginning to take its toll. Certainly she was fast losing patience with Bowden, who seemed intent on thwarting her every move.

She had written Bowden one last time in June, before setting off with the Chiaromontes for Berlin. In her letter she had apologized for disturbing him when she knew he was convalescing from mumps and then had quickly gone on to tell him that she was going to go ahead with her plans to marry Jim West. She was writing, she said, because she had heard that he was planning to spend his summer in Italy and perhaps stay on there indefinitely, closing down the apartment and giving up his job at St. Bernard's. Before she lost track of him, she wanted him to agree in writing to a divorce.

To her request she received no answer. When Bowden finally wrote her from Venice, in August, it was not a letter intended to please. He began by saying it was his understanding that she was still enchanted with her new lover, whom he now called "the Old Pretender." He then warned her that judging from certain reports he had been hearing, she might soon feel very differently.

Finally, after attacking the man she wanted very much to marry, Bowden let her know that he had no intention of granting her a divorce—certainly not before he, too, found someone to love. That, he estimated, would take two years. Armed with this letter from Bowden and a report from Carmen Angleton, who had also spent *her* summer in Venice, she wrote Hannah Arendt to let her know that the redeemed, christened Bowden was no more.

### FROM MARY McCARTHY'S LETTER TO HANNAH ARENDT, AUGUST 30, 1960

[Carmen] reports such details about him as that he has started lying about his age[. . . .] He was living with one of the poets of the Beat Generation—Gregory Corso (not a homosexual) and was very active socially, very malicious. He and his whole set—all younger people, in their twenties, mostly—drank a great deal[. . . .] She thinks he may have begun (or will soon begin) to sleep with casual women, and that he will try to keep this secret from me because it's inconsistent with his line of not giving a divorce because of his belief in monogamy. I said, "But that's very unprincipled." And she said, "But that's the way he is."

Any hopes that this report would turn Hannah Arendt against Bowden were doomed to disappointment.

### FROM HANNAH ARENDT'S LETTER TO MARY MCCARTHY, SEPTEMBER 16, 1960

He is under the impression that he is being treated as a *quantité négligeable* and though he will finally give in (about this, there is no doubt in his or in my mind), he will do whatever is in his power to make you aware of his existence. Maybe, it would be wiser to answer his letters and to keep up some kind of relation. I am on very good terms with him and I must say that he makes it easy for me[. . . .] I do not believe Carmen's gossip and, as far as I know, Corso is a homosexual. Bowden did not talk to me about this at all, but if I had suspicions in this direction, it certainly would not be in "the casual women" line[. . . .] The sad truth of the matter is that he loves you.

Bowden was not about to hand her over to Jim West without a whimper—of that there was no question. As far as the gossip about "casual women" was concerned, she was more on the mark than Hannah Arendt—at least for the moment. While Bowden might look like a cross between Caspar Milquetoast and an American Mr. Chips, he was anything but. He was strong and he was muscular and he confided to at least one friend that the only way to really know someone was to go to bed with them.

**EVE AUCHINCLOSS**  The fall Mary decided not to come home, Bowden and I were having dinner with some other people at Ninety-fourth Street and after they left, Bowden said, "Well, let's hit the hay." I couldn't believe it, but we did. And we went on doing that for a few months. I think it was some consolation to Bowden at this painful time in his life.

In September 1960 Bowden was back at St. Bernard's, his dreams of a life in Italy having come to nothing. Hoping to test the waters, she wrote him a dry matter-of-fact letter, letting him know that she had been invited to give the Harcourt Brace Lecture at Columbia in October and would like to take the opportunity to slip down to Alabama for a quick divorce. Put to the test, Bowden refused to release her at her convenience. "This is not a game," she wrote back. Game or not, Bowden had some justification for feeling he'd been mistreated. In addition, he had the advantage.

**BARBARA KERR**  It was Bowden who kept the house running. If Mary was working, Bowden would do the shopping. Bowden was sort of secretary of state for foreign affairs. Being Mary's husband was a full-time occupation. I don't think it would have been possible for Mary's husband to have an independent career, really. And for years Bowden didn't. He simply accommodated to her existence. And did it very well. What he did was build a protective wall around her, so she could work undisturbed. It was an unusually close relationship. But when the teaching job developed at St. Bernard's he began to have a life of his own. They liked him there. Suddenly he was not at Mary's beck and call every minute; suddenly he was standing on his own feet. This would have made him less desirable in Mary's eyes. She wouldn't have acknowledged this verbally, but nevertheless it made an impression on her. He wasn't *there* anymore. And she really didn't like that. Mary ran through men—and tended to discard them like used Kleenex if another one caught her eye.

Left behind while his wife went on to make this exciting and unexpected new conquest, Bowden had discovered what Margaret West had known from the very start: when your world is being blown apart, there is not much to be said for good form. Forced to wait upon Bowden's pleasure, his wife was in no mood to understand this, nor could she ignore a growing suspicion that she was being poorly served by the friend she had enlisted as a go-between. "It strikes me (and I may as well say this) that he has somehow persuaded you that he is right. Or at least reasonable," she wrote Hannah Arendt. "Perhaps I am getting paranoid to imagine this, but it is a suspicion that creeps over me. If he has, *how?*" She received no reply for more than a month, and when she did, it was because she had written first to explain at some length why she was accusing Arendt of "seeming to condone" Bowden's delaying her divorce.

### From Hannah Arendt's Letter to Mary McCarthy, November 11, 1960

As I see it Bowden has not delayed, was not even in a position to delay your marriage[. . . .] Since I wanted to persuade him, I have seen quite a bit of him during the last few weeks[. . . .] I talked to him as a friend and I did not lie[. . . .] You say you cannot trust him. Perhaps you are right, perhaps you are wrong, I have no idea. But it strikes me that you can forget so easily that you trusted him enough to be married to him for fifteen [*sic*] years.

By the time she received Arendt's letter, she was better prepared to listen to reason. But in October she had been desperate. The lease on Carmen Angleton's apartment was due to end in the middle of October and soon she would be homeless. In New York everything was conspiring against her, while in Poland everything seemed to be proceeding according to plan. Jim West had told the ambassador that he was divorcing his wife and marrying the writer Mary McCarthy. Margaret West had set off, as promised, for Paris to finalize arrangements with her lawyer and to rent an apartment.

In the end, Mary McCarthy did not deliver the Harcourt Lecture at

Columbia. Instead, she applied for a thirty-day visa to visit her son in Poland. Reuel, having graduated cum laude from Harvard, had received a Fulbright Fellowship to pursue his study of Slavic languages in Cracow. By late October, for the third time in less than a year, she was back in Warsaw. This time, she was forced to make do with a room at the Grand Hotel, which lacked the charm of the Bristol but which was only rarely frequented by embassy staff. If her accommodations were not to her liking, they had one decided advantage: Jim West, who had finally moved out of the apartment he shared with Margaret and the children, was secretly staying in a room across the hall.

On this visit, Margaret West was still very much in evidence. Having rented an apartment in Paris, she seemed to believe that she had done more than enough. Although her lover's wife was making no move to vacate the premises, at the start of her visit Mary could see the marital muddle in Warsaw as "a marvelous comedy of modern life." It was easier to see it this way because, just as Hannah Arendt had always predicted, Bowden Broadwater, faced with the inevitable, had agreed to put an end to the marriage.

**CARMEN ANGLETON** Before we knew it, Bowden had given Mary a divorce, so she could marry. At first he refused on principle—which is very Bowden—and then condescended. But he did it very elegantly—with grace and dignity, to my knowledge.

Not only had Bowden come round but the ambassador had gone so far as to allocate his chief public affairs officer a house with a pretty garden. Jim West would be able to renovate and furnish the house at government expense but he would not be able to occupy it until he was officially remarried. The renovation was proceeding nicely when he was told that if he wished to have any say about the furnishings he would have to see to them immediately—otherwise, the U.S. government would do the decorating for him. Faced with this prospect, he and his prospective wife set off for Copenhagen, the best source for the sort of things the State Department approved of (old furniture and antiques were deemed unacceptable).

### FROM MARY MCCARTHY'S LETTER TO HANNAH ARENDT, OCTOBER 26, 1960

I've had to pick out every item down to the last toilet-paper holder and soap dish[. . . .] You can't imagine how difficult it is in Denmark to find chairs and sofas to sit down on that don't look like manifestoes.

During her third stay in Poland, Mary McCarthy was virtually confined to her hotel room, save for the trip to Copenhagen and for ten days she went to stay with Reuel in Cracow. For want of anything better to do, she was back working on her novel. She could take some satisfaction in the fact that the novel was coming along, and in the bond she believed she saw forming between her lover and her son.

### FROM MARY MCCARTHY'S LETTER TO HANNAH ARENDT, NOVEMBER 23, 1960

> Reuel seems to be extremely attracted by Jim; I think he feels the lack of a virile and straightforward man in his family. Bowden is a child, and Edmund is an old woman.

Weeks had passed, and Margaret West not only remained fixed in the Warsaw apartment but began talking about leaving some time in February. The "modern marital comedy" had ceased to be amusing. In November there was no golden light on the churches; there were no geraniums in the window boxes; and the listening device planted in the ceiling light of her room was hard to overlook.

### FROM MARY MCCARTHY'S LETTER TO HANNAH ARENDT, NOVEMBER 23, 1960

> [T]he business with Margaret (into which the Embassy has now entered) has been so depressing that we've come to look on my hideous room with flowered bedspreads and curtains decorated with Red stars and the listening device in the lighting fixture as a tenderly loved home and refuge. As though we were living a peculiar modern idyl: intense love in extreme conditions, to be transcribed by the Secret Police.

The modern stage trappings had taken on a decidedly totalitarian cast. At the end of November, when her visa was about to expire, she packed her bags and retreated to Paris—to the very apartment Margaret West had rented and then chosen to leave vacant. But difficult as her stay in Warsaw had been, it had brought matters to a head.

In mid-November, the ambassador had delivered an ultimatum: So long as the Wests were officially married and Margaret remained in Warsaw, they were going to have to attend embassy functions as a couple. After briefly trying to comply with this order, Jim West went to the ambassador and offered to resign. Upon hearing him out, the ambassador delivered a second ultimatum: Unless Margaret West agreed to leave at the end of December and proved to his satisfaction that she was really going to do this, Jim West would have to leave his post in Warsaw at the end of the week. A departure so abrupt would create an immediate scandal, making it difficult, if not impossible, for Jim West to find another position in the Foreign Service—impossible certainly to find a high-paying position behind the Iron Curtain. Faced with the immediate loss of her husband's hardship pay and the distinct possibility that he might very soon be unemployed, Margaret West finally gave in.

In the end Mary McCarthy made the trip to Alabama. A wedding date was set for Paris, on April 14, 1961. To Edmund Wilson and Katharine White she wrote, the way she might to two parents, filling them in on Jim West's family background and making it clear that this was not some feckless infatuation. To Wilson, who had never quite approved of Bowden, she wrote, "I give you all these biographical details because I know you like that kind of thing." As it happened, she, too, liked that kind of thing. But she also liked the idea that this time she was finally marrying the kind of man he approved of. And the kind of man her friends would approve of as well. As it turned out, her choice took not a few friends by surprise.

### From Mary McCarthy's Letter to Edmund Wilson, March 30, 1961

[H]e's a very nice man, different from all my other husbands, though he seems to feel a certain kinship with you. For me, he is more like the McCarthy men—not any one of them but all of them; that is, with a certain wild solitary streak combined with an engaging air, combined with a kind of solidity. But maybe it's only that like my father and my grandfather and Uncle Harry he has prematurely grey hair.

### From Robert Lowell's Letter to Elizabeth Bishop, February 15, 1961

Mary McCarthy was here last night *fresh* from her Alabama divorce. Her new man in photographs looks like a combination of Lionel Trilling and Jim Farley—though a year or two younger than Mary, he looks of an older generation[. . . .] Mary's more at ease and more generous than we've ever seen her—no more nervous Broadwater rundowns of everyone under the sun.

### From Dwight Macdonald's Letter to Nicola Chiaromonte, April 6, 1961

I think, as I told [Mary] with my usual tactfulness, that after 30 years of experiment, she has found Mr. Right[. . . .] [A] gentle, sweet, responsible family-man type, who may be able to give Mary just the combination of lover and father she needs.

**Carmen Angleton** I first met Jim West when he came to stay with Mary at my little apartment. He was very handsome and she thought until the day she died that he became more and more so. She was really madly in love with him. And he with her. It's not something that I can explain.

This might be her fourth marriage and her bank account might be alarmingly low, but Mary McCarthy had every intention of celebrating in style. Almost at once she settled on a green and white silk dress which she'd bought in Italy the previous summer. Jim West had first suggested a wedding breakfast at the Crillon, but she was hoping for something less formal and more economical. Both of them agreed that a civil ceremony was appropriate.

Through no fault of their own, her two dearest friends were absent. Nicola Chiaromonte was in Rome, recovering from a heart attack and forbidden all travel by his doctors. Hannah Arendt was in Jerusalem on assignment for *The New Yorker* covering the trial of Adolf Eichmann. But Carmen Angleton made the trip from Rome, bearing four kilos of green coffee beans, olive oil, and two kilos of Parmesan cheese for the bride to carry back to her new home in Poland. Dwight and Gloria Macdonald came over from London. Reuel, looking thin and handsome, arrived two weeks ahead of time from Cracow.

In the end the reception was held at the home of Peter Harnden, Jim West's best man, where the garden promised to provide the perfect setting for a simple wedding breakfast. When the mayor of the Eighth Arrondissement delivered a lecture to the newlyweds appropriate for a couple in their twenties, these two veterans of multiple marriages chose to greet it as a delicious gaffe. Although the wedding went off with scarcely a hitch, it provided Dwight Macdonald and Nicola Chiaromonte with food for thought.

### FROM DWIGHT MACDONALD'S LETTER TO NICOLA CHIAROMONTE, APRIL 23, 1961

Mary's wedding, of which you will doubtless have heard from Carmen, was very grand. Even the simple ceremony in the mayor's office turned out grand (typically of Mary)—for it was the *mairie* of the VIII arrondissement, the President's one, most elegant in Paris. Mary had written me she was getting married in an old dress, for economy (it turned out to be a lovely green chiffon creation with a fantastic matching hat) and was toying with idea of "a real workers' wedding breakfast, like in *L'Assomoir* (this turned out to be a *fête champêtre*, 30 or so people, five tables, waiters in white gloves, champagne, fish mayonnaise, roast duck, strawberries and cream—all transported to house of friend an hour out of Paris). But it was all very nice (though slightly stiff, don't know just why)[. . . .] On sense of strain, stiffness, unspontaneity at wedding breakfast—might have been partly due to Mary. I love and respect her, she's my oldest friend, I'm devoted to her but I never feel easy with her; the vivacious passages in talking with her are superb but there are no lower tones—burn this letter!—all highlights and almost no chiaroscuro; if only she were less clever; or more. But so she is and it is a great deal—and there's always that sense of life and interest and control.

### FROM CHIAROMONTE'S LETTER TO MACDONALD, MAY 9, 1961

I had no doubt that Mary's wedding would be "grand." That's her style—a fairy-tale style, I should say. Occasions are to Mary challenges to the imagination, which is one of her most charming sides—probably the most charming, since her wonderful generosity is part of it. But I understand your feeling well. Mary acted all through the period of her "engagement" as if this was her first love, and was going to be her first marriage. Sweet, but slightly false, nevertheless more than false, unreal and unconvincing, like some of the psychological cracks in her novels. But maybe Jim is going to have a "humanizing" effect on M. Although, I doubt it. She is going to be the Queen again—and he the Prince Consort.

In a fairy tale the bride and groom go off and live happily ever after. In Jim West's new car, the newlyweds set off for a week's honeymoon in Switzerland, loaded down with Carmen Angleton's olive oil, green coffee beans, and Parmesan; a roaster and grinder for the coffee beans; and pots of chives, tarragon, thyme, and rosemary from the Marché des Fleurs. From Interlaken Jim West called his office, only to learn that Margaret had refused to vacate the Warsaw apartment, claiming that her daughter had come down with chicken pox. The honeymoon couple drove on to Vienna, hoping to wait Margaret out. For the new Mrs. James Raymond West to proceed to Warsaw would be awkward. But for West to remain out of the country any longer was out of the question. He had to get back to work.

When her hard-pressed husband repaired to Poland, Mary accompanied him to the border. It was her hope to join Reuel in Cracow. When she couldn't find Reuel, she returned to Vienna, giving out the story that she lacked a proper visa. Unfortunately, her handbags and umbrella went off in the car with Jim West. In a letter to Carmen Angleton she tried to make light of what had happened, but she had seen enough of the Foreign Service to be less than optimistic.

### FROM MARY MCCARTHY'S LETTER TO CARMEN ANGLETON, MAY 1, 1961

Jim's goose, we both think, is probably cooked anyway, as a result of her return. I.e., he will be transferred in August, if not (and I fear this privately) sooner.

She had barely sent off this letter, when she was felled by excruciating back pain. For two and a half weeks she was confined to a clinic in Vienna. All her adult life, whenever things had gone terribly wrong, her health had broken down. This time, the doctors diagnosed a slipped disc. By the time Margaret West finally left for Paris, the damage had been done. Arriving in Warsaw, Jim West's new wife had to be carried off the plane in a wheelchair, wearing a cervical collar. Her first weeks in the house she and Jim West had furnished with such care were spent in bed. Not only were they spent in bed but they were spent in the company of the three West children. Believing that her husband's goose was cooked, she tried to make the best of it.

### From Mary McCarthy's Letter to Hannah Arendt, May 24, 1961

My arm and hand (and neck) seem to be worse again, it comes and goes, quite arbitrarily. But Jim says I'm getting better[. . . .] What most irritates me is the sense of how tiresome this is for the children. An adventure at first—a strange lady in a bandage—but soon merely a tedious presence in the bed. Or so I fear. They are here for a week before going to Paris to their mother, and I should like to be better and have my neck uncorseted at least one day before then. Jim is wonderful.

Every three years Foreign Service officers had to return to the States for two months of home leave. Jim West was due to return on August 1. If he was lucky, after reporting to Washington, he would be sent back to Warsaw (or "round-tripped") for another two years. He loved Poland and his new wife showed every sign of loving it, too. Together they were beginning to entertain select friends in their new house. But this time Jim West's luck had run out. Orders came from Washington to pack up all their belongings and put them in storage.

**Mary Brady**   There are things you don't do in the Foreign Service. One of them is marry a woman who is (a) famous and (b) been rattling around the world doing all the things Mary had been doing. Another is dump your wife, who is still holed up in your apartment. It all was just too much for everybody. Word traveled all over the Eastern European circuit. Everybody who came to Moscow via Warsaw brought one more hot tale of what was going on in that embassy. It consumed us all.

Faced with the scandal of two Mrs. Wests residing in Poland with diplomatic passports, the State Department declared that enough was enough. Before the Wests had a chance to finish sorting through all the cartons from Rome and Copenhagen, they had to pack everything up again. Where they would unpack their cartons next was anyone's guess.

Rather than wait to the bitter end, the Wests left Warsaw for Bocca di Magra the third week in July. There they were joined first by the children and their nurse, Maria, and then by Reuel and a young woman he was thinking of marrying. Money was tight and the future uncertain. At the end of the summer, when the children returned to their mother in Paris, the Wests made the requisite journey back to America. While Jim West waited for reassignment, they rented a small house in the Portuguese section of Stonington, a fishing village on the Connecticut coast, within a reasonable distance from Washington and almost within commuting distance from New York.

Two months of home leave dragged on into three and then four. For a time it looked as if Jim West was going to be sent to Vienna. Mary McCarthy hated the idea. She had been to Vienna twice in the past year, most recently during her unhappy stay in the clinic, and felt qualified to describe the city as restricting, narrow, and petty. Fortunately, she was not lacking in friends who had influence with the State Department. By the start of the new year there was talk of assigning Jim West to the newly established Organization for Economic Cooperation and Development (OECD), an outgrowth of the Marshall Plan with eighteen member countries and offices in Paris.

Just as it was becoming clear that Jim West's goose had not been cooked to a crisp, she chose the occasion of a visit by Sonia Orwell to serve up a cassoulet to more than seventy-five friends at a party she gave with Kevin and Augusta at their house in Dobbs Ferry, New York. The cassoulet was three days in the making, with Augusta assisting as *sous*-chef and some of the rarer ingredients imported from the city. In large earthenware pots she layered the traditional onions and garlic and tomatoes and bacon, the white beans and sausage and bread crumbs. In place of preserved goose she substituted duck.

For decades the party at Dobbs Ferry would be remembered for its daring, its originality, and for its delicious food. There were readings by Zero Mostel and E. G. Marshall. There were potential fistfights that came to nothing. Tables with place cards were set up both upstairs and down. The guest list included friends of Kevin's from the theater, the old *Partisan Review* crowd, her publisher William Jovanovich, the photographer Inge Morath and her fiancé Arthur Miller, and friends from Stonington, like James Merrill and Eleanor Perényi.

The party was at once a triumph of imagination and the wedding reception she was finally able to get right. It was also a farewell to her former life. By the end of February, the Paris billet was definite. This time she was not moving to Stamford or Newport or the Cape. She would be crossing the Atlantic to make her home in a country that placed little value on the English language and had little liking for Americans.

To her fairy-tale romance she was granted a happy ending. But, for all the power of her imagination, it was not precisely the ending she had counted on. In this new life there would be holdovers like Hannah Arendt and the Lowells and the Chiaromontes. But there would be dear friends she rarely saw anymore. In time the circle around *Partisan Review* would grow ever more distant. As Mrs. James West, she would entertain more frequently, more formally, and more extensively than she ever had as Mrs. Bowden Broadwater. But as Mrs. James West she would have to contend with the French.

# Chapter Nineteen

# LADY OF LETTERS

By marrying Jim West, Mary McCarthy had sacrificed a husband of fourteen years and a life which on balance suited her quite nicely. For this chance at perfect happiness she had been prepared to let romance take precedence over a carefully orchestrated career. She believed she was prepared to accept the consequences of the bargain she was striking. What she had forgotten was that both in her life and in her work paradox had often figured large.

On May 4, 1962, after passing her first month in Paris making the best of still another hotel room, she wrote Hannah Arendt to apologize for her long silence. "I've been half sick since we got here [. . .] in bed one day, up the next, and for some reason very depressed and toneless. Perhaps this is a characteristic of the germ or perhaps it's change of life or still something else—I don't know. I've never felt depression as a physical thing before, like a heavy poison in one's veins."

Confessing the extent of her misery to the friend who had continually urged restraint and caution may have been made easier by the fact that Hannah herself was in a bad way. For weeks she had been laid up with nine broken ribs and a splintered wrist, a bad concussion and damage to the muscles in both eyes, having nearly been killed when a taxi she was taking was sideswiped crossing Central Park. Later it would turn out that there had been damage to the muscle of her heart.

In spite of her depression, McCarthy's life in Paris was beginning to look more promising. She had sublet a furnished apartment belonging to Inge Morath, who had married Arthur Miller and was living full-time in America. The sublet, though small, was located in a chic neighborhood and came with an adequate kitchen and a very good maid. Then, after weeks of searching, she had found a permanent Paris apartment she both liked and could afford.

The apartment was on the rue de Rennes, a short walk from St. Germain des Pres. It was not grand and it was not in good condition but it had one large bedroom and two small ones, a large old-fashioned kitchen, a good-size dining room, an ample living room, and a long curved entrance hall. One of the bedrooms would make a perfect study. The other would serve for a single visitor. There were two fireplaces. The back of the apartment looked out over a convent garden and the front had a small balcony with an ironwork rail.

Because the rue de Rennes apartment was high up, on the sixth floor, even on an overcast Paris day it could be described as "gay." Its location made for good light and a modest asking price of $31,000: the building's elevator was broken and to pay for a new one each tenant was going to be assessed an additional $2,000. "[T]he agreement of the other tenants is necessary, and one is holding out (the one on the second floor, naturally)," she wrote Arendt.

In the early days of their courtship, Jim West had announced his intention of paying for everything but the occasional luxury, but a divorce can wreak havoc with the most impressive incomes. To come up with the money to buy what amounted to a sixth-floor walk-up Mary was once again going to have to sell stock—this time, stock inherited from her Jewish grandmother. To make this new home livable was going to require a good deal of money and a good deal of work. All the same, she refused to be daunted. She did not question the real estate agent who assured her that there was a law on the books stating that where once there had been an elevator there must always be one. And she did not question the workmen who promised that she would be able to move into the apartment by September.

From a good friend one looks for sympathy and support, and for tact. In her letter to Arendt, she chose to dwell on the necessity of Arendt's finding a good hairdresser to cover patches of scalp the surgeons had shaved rather than on the damage wrought by a potentially fatal car crash. In *her* letter, Arendt chose not to question McCarthy's faith in the promises of builders and real estate agents. She also chose to attribute this poisonous Paris depression to menopause rather than to any reversals and upheavals attending the new marriage. "[D]o you have a good doctor there" Arendt asked, before going on to confess, "I had the same thing about 3 years ago, clearly change of age, and did not go to the doctor because I hated to admit that I had a depression. Whereupon I lost it—after about 6 months."

Her month of feeling "half sick" may have owed something to what Hannah called "change of age" and something to the letdown that comes with getting through a terrible ordeal. However, it would seem to have owed nothing whatsoever to any disappointment with her new husband. During the worst of their troubles, on this point she had never wavered.

That she had made the right choice when she married Jim West she believed with all her heart.

### FROM MARY MCCARTHY'S LETTER TO HANNAH ARENDT, JANUARY 11, 1962

He's an intensely lovable man, the most so, by far, I've ever been close to, and he seems to be getting happier all the time, which is odd to see since when I first knew him he was indifferent to the whole idea of Happiness and cared only for something narrow and very personal and private called Experience.

While she might believe that her love was strong and enduring, there was good reason, given her history, to be less than sanguine about Jim West's prospects.

**YALE RICHMOND**   I never thought it was going to last. Nobody in Warsaw thought it was going to last. Everybody thought that this was just another husband for Mary McCarthy. I remember one American woman there saying, "She collects men's scalps."

From the earliest days of the marriage, she and her new husband had been the subject of speculation, analysis, and intense scrutiny. By the time they had found shelter in a renovated fisherman's cottage at Stonington, it was evident that Jim West was not about to live in his wife's shadow. By the time she moved on to Washington, to baby-sit for the Schlesinger children while awaiting Jim West's next assignment, it was clear that the two of them were supremely well matched.

**JAMES MERRILL**   There was an evening at Eleanor Perényi's when Eleanor and Mary began talking about that woman who married Gorky and they began a little antiphon of snideness. Jim cleared his throat and said, "I've always liked her myself, and, especially now that she's down on her luck, I don't think she needs to be trampled all over by hot little high heels." Mary blushed—a real pink blush by candlelight—and that was that. When I came to know her, I saw that there was a lot of the chameleon in Mary. She took on the aspect—the psychological aspect—of the husband at the time. Bowden encouraged a certain bitchiness in Mary, whereas Jim had no use for it. And Mary cut it right out.

**CHRISTINA SCHLESINGER**   At night we'd sit at the long candlelit dinner table, and they would be at either end and my brother Andy and I would be across from each other and they would lift their glasses of wine up at each other and hold them there and with huge smiles lock eyes for what seemed an embarrassing eternity to us, adolescents unused to such lovey-dovey behavior at home.

Jim West was very much in love and not afraid to show it, but not all of the changes in Mary's life were for the better. Paris might be preferable to Vienna, but it was hardly ideal. De Gaulle was about to cut loose Algeria, and Parisians, faced with the end to any lingering dreams of *la gloire*, were in a particularly "ugly mood." Americans were the last to be spared their rage and resentment—particularly Americans of a certain age and class.

**ROSAMOND BERNIER**   Later on, she made a film for the BBC about Paris. In it she walks around Paris and you really get her dislike of the French.

**TERENCE KILMARTIN**   The French irritated her. Although she was not a great American patriot, she would have been irritated by intellectual French anti-Americanism. If someone was going to attack America, it was going to be Mary.

Much of the time, that first spring, she was lonely for company.

### FROM MARY MCCARTHY'S LETTER TO HANNAH ARENDT, JUNE 1, 1962

For my part, I rather miss having a circle in Paris, i.e., a group of friends who all know each other, as I had in Rome or as we all have in New York. Here our friends seem to come in isolated pairs, as in the Ark. There is an American semi-Bohemian circle but of rather low quality, frankly: they're to be found usually at art-openings. The only French person I'd really *like* to meet is Nathalie Sarraute.

**INGE MORATH**   There were the Americans in Paris and the French in Paris and they didn't really mingle. The French can be very difficult in accepting people. Americans would be invited to big parties and not the small dinners. Mary spoke French, but from what I heard it sounded dreadful to the ear. If you don't speak very well, you are not going to be accepted.

**ALISON WEST**   To us, her accent in foreign languages was almost comical. We knew even as children our phonetic gift was far greater than Mary's. I remember we were pulling up at a gas station near Bocca di Magra one Sunday and Mary's asking for directions. The man just leaned over and said, "Oh, so you're American." Mary looked at my father and said, "How did he know that?" She appeared genuinely puzzled.

On weekends she was obliged to share her husband with three small children who were capable of judging a stepmother and finding her wanting. During the week she had her husband to herself, but he was working long hours at a job he did not much care for—a job that called for him to whip into shape a staff firmly set in its ways and then make comprehensible "a flood of publications which could not be understood by a professional economist." While the job promised to become easier with time, it did not promise to become more satisfying.

**MARY BRADY**   As public affairs officer for the OECD you really don't have to do much. Once in a while someone comes up with a report and then you have to fiddle around with it. The job is famous in the Foreign Service for being very cushy and it's tax free. When he first got the slot at the OECD, I'm sure it was welcomed by Jim. After all, Paris is Paris. But it was a side rail for Jim in terms of his career. He was not going to go any further.

There was no way, given her lack of experience with the diplomatic community, that Mary McCarthy could have anticipated the disarray of an international organization barely one year old. No way that she could have imagined the strain of trying to win over three small children whose mother made no secret of loathing her. And no way, given all her years with Bowden, that she could have foreseen the difficulty of trying to set up a new home with a husband who was not free to step in when she needed time off to write.

However, on one front, at least, she arrived fully prepared. Long before Jim West was assigned to Paris, back when she was waiting out the final weeks there before her wedding and looking forward to returning as a happy bride to Warsaw, she'd had a taste of what life among the French could be like.

Now that her stay in Paris was no longer temporary, it was abundantly evident that the average French writer or intellectual was every bit as xenophobic as the average man on the street. It did not help that she saw no reason to keep to herself her reservations about Jean-Paul Sartre or her low opinion of Simone de Beauvoir. But for an American, no matter how circumspect, life in the City of Light in the spring of 1962 was not all that different from life on the Cape in the winter of 1939. Within the expatriate community, there was the sort of intimacy that comes from living in an igloo. Occasionally, with luck, there was a true meeting of minds.

**GLORIA JONES**   When my husband, Jim, and I first met Mary, she needed us because she was alone in France and had fallen in love. She wanted friends and was pleased that we were friends with her son. My husband was very fond of her. She had a good sense of humor. She didn't take me seriously but she liked me. She had a wonderful way of looking at you. I could always see her thinking. In her eyes.

Through Reuel, back in 1960, she had gotten to know the author of *From Here to Eternity*, and his beautiful young wife, Gloria. Unfortunately, she returned to discover that Jim and Gloria Jones were in Jamaica for a year. Still, she was not without resources. At their dinner table she had met Thomas Quinn Curtiss, who wrote theater reviews for the *International Herald Tribune* and lived in an apartment just above the Tour d'Argent. Back in 1946, on her very first trip to Europe, she had met Janet Flanner, who wrote *The New Yorker*'s "Letter from Paris."

Her first encounter with Flanner had not been a success: Flanner had referred to Edmund Wilson as a Communist, and she had felt obliged to dismiss this characterization of her estranged husband as a gross oversimplification. With time, however, she had come to better appreciate Flanner, who continued to turn out Paris letters from a cluttered apartment on the top floor at the Hotel Continental and who had on more than one occasion expressed unmitigated admiration for her prose style, well-furnished mind, and beautifully shaped head.

**NATALIA DANESI MURRAY**   [*close friend and sometime companion of Janet Flanner*] When Mary came to live in Paris she saw a lot of Janet and Janet very much enjoyed that. Janet admired her essays enormously. She admired her discipline. If Mary hadn't been good to Janet, Janet wouldn't have taken it.

**BRENDAN GILL**   I don't think Mary's relations with Janet were ever easy. This is pure speculation on my part, but I think in the beginning with Mary in Paris Janet was a little afraid of having her turf invaded. It was a time when she was feeling that she was losing her own *puissance*. She had governed a whole underworld and some overworld in Paris and here came this star turn—young, vigorous, and so on. And I think that may have made her skeptical of Mary's presence there. Janet in Paris became an increasingly sad figure. She grew old and lonely as all her contemporaries died off.

Working on *Venice Observed* Mary McCarthy had come to know Rosamond Bernier, whose husband and business partner had so thoroughly disappointed her. Although there had been a breach, it did not prove to be irreparable. Rosamond was good company and a good cook and at the Berniers' table you could find everyone of importance in the arts, even the French.

**ROSAMOND BERNIER**   In those dear departed days you kept a book of menus and seating plans for dinner parties. Recently I found this little book and was surprised to see how many times Mary and Jim came for dinner. She was known as this very formidable intellect, and also she could be quite terrifying in her sharpness, her humor, her dryness. But I think I saw another side—real staunchness, kindness, loyalty, and a sense of decency. With Mary I think either friends had to be on her level—a Hannah Arendt— or they provided a certain coziness she needed.

Her modest collection of Paris friends soon expanded to include Eileen Simpson, the former wife of John Berryman, who was now living in Paris with her second husband.

**EILEEN SIMPSON**   In Paris I thought she had softened. But, then, I had never before seen the domestic side of her. And we had more things in common—Paris and the struggles. It wasn't easy.

The apartment she had sublet from Inge Morath was dark and cramped and not really suited to serious entertaining. All the same, she was lucky to have it while she waited for the work on her new apartment to be completed. And lucky that Morath was willing to look the other way when it came to her tenant's less than flattering comments about her new husband's gifts as a playwright.

**INGE MORATH**   She had said a lot of bitchy things about Arthur before we married. I don't know how much she said after—I think she cooled it. When I saw her with Arthur she was always very nice. She was a hard worker and she had a gallantry to her that I liked. That kind of standing up for things. She was a true artist in that she didn't have a small mind. She was like a young chevalier with his sword. You know gallant soldiers don't always defend the right side.

Experienced in making do with living quarters that were less than ideal, she did not let the apartment's deficiencies curtail her social life. She let a month lapse between her letters to Hannah the spring of 1962—not because she was too depressed to show her face but because suddenly she had no time to write. Like a good diplomat's wife, she was going to "too many official parties," trying to help win over the "vegetating" staff her husband was trying to whip into shape. She was also receiving and entertaining company more to her liking. During her last stay in Paris, back when she was waiting for Jim West to leave his wife, she had not let her solitary circumstances dull her appetite for entertaining. With no husband to toast her across the table, she had given full sit-down dinners, which bore more than a passing resemblance to the dinners she had given with Bowden in their glory days. To one such dinner Reuel had brought Elisabeth Niebuhr, an old Harvard acquaintance who was living in Paris on a Fulbright Fellowship.

**ELISABETH NIEBUHR SIFTON**   I remember her as being a wonderful hostess. She was warm, funny, and witty. There was Reuel, of course, and a Pole, a French couple, and Jim and Gloria Jones. She made roast lamb, with oysters to begin. Food matters, as she well understood, bless her heart. Toward the end, she and Jim Jones got into an argument about how to put a novel together. It was so exciting to hear them—just bliss.

Now that she was actually living full-time in Paris her dinners were no less spirited. Her new husband shared her belief that food mattered and he believed in good wine. If there were fewer heated arguments on the subject of how to put together a novel, this was not necessarily regarded as a loss. By all accounts, she had finally found Mr. Right.

**EILEEN SIMPSON**    Elizabeth Hardwick once said that Jim was "a husband-type husband." And he was. There's no question that Mary was happier after she married him. I think Jim was a good balance for Mary. He was really there, very attentive. But there was nothing timid about him. On occasion he could be severe with her.

**ROSAMOND BERNIER**    I think very definitely Jim made a difference. I knew Mary before Jim and after Jim, and I think that Mary felt before that she could not allow herself to express any kind of sentimentality. They hadn't been married so very long—she was in another country—and I was having dinner with Jim in their Paris apartment, and Mary telephoned. They talked and then I couldn't help but hear Jim say, "Say 'I love you.' Say it, Mary." He was forcing her to be what she could be.

**SYBILLE BEDFORD**    Mary was radiant (I think it was the beginning of the life with her last husband) and one responded to her glow. I was going out to a dinner and Mary offered to drive me there in *his* car. And there in the narrow Left Bank street stood a long, gleaming, open car. "Look at this beautiful car," Mary said, and we took what felt like a joyride through the Paris summer evening streets. No trace then of the *femme fatale* and the literary prodigy of those New York days.

With no apparent struggle and no apparent fuss, Jim was managing to alter the face Mary turned to the world. He was attentive and loving and he satisfied a need for stability—but from her husbands she had learned to look for more than that. Writing Nicky Mariano back in April 1960, she had not been so blinded by the excitement of embarking on a great love affair as to disregard entirely the possibility that this change of partners could damage her writing career.

## FROM MARY MCCARTHY'S LETTER TO NICKY MARIANO,
## APRIL 21, 1960

I wonder what B.B. would have thought of all this. Probably he would have disapproved. I know he thought Bowden a very good husband for me as a writer or literary lady, and that is true. But I do not want to be only a writer or literary lady and have been rebelling from it more and more these last years.

Always her husbands had been her first readers. With the Florence book Bowden had been more than that—interceding when there was a crisis and making it possible for her to play the role of the exacting lady author who is fundamentally a good sport. But Bowden's assistance had never been limited to reading manuscripts or crisis management. From the beginning, when plotting the trajectory of her career, she had relied on his taste and judgment, just as she had relied on Edmund Wilson's.

She might claim to desire to be more than a literary lady, but old dreams, like old habits, die hard. And good first readers are hard to find. During the early days of her romance she as much as acknowledged this. Having written up her talk from the State Department tour on the importance of facts in fiction and shepherded it through publication at *Partisan Review* with only Jim West to read the manuscript, she wrote Hannah Arendt to say how reassuring it was to receive *her* words of praise. During the harried months that followed, it began to look as if her romance with Jim West might well wreak havoc with her writing.

### FROM MARY MCCARTHY'S LETTER TO HANNAH ARENDT, AUGUST 30, 1960

The only other person who had read it (not counting William Phillips, who niggled rather) was Jim; he liked it but then he is not literary, besides being in love.

### FROM MARY MCCARTHY'S LETTER TO KATHARINE WHITE, N.D. [C. DECEMBER 1960]

To do any sustained work in the midst of moving about and being uncertain about the future has been slightly difficult[. . . .] At the moment I'm doing a scissors and paste job on a book of essays that Farrar Straus is going to bring out in the spring, but this is more or less Occupational Therapy to get me through the shock of another move.

By the spring of 1962 one thing was clear: her writing career had not suffered, after all. That bit of occupational therapy had produced the manuscript for *On the Contrary*, a collection of essays, which was immediately greeted by critics as her most important work to date. Published in the fall of 1961, just as she and Jim West were settling in at Stonington, the collection led off with her 1946 attack on John Hersey's *New Yorker* piece on Hiroshima and concluded with her three State Department talks: "The Fact in Fiction," "Characters in Fiction," and "The American Realist Playwrights." Whether she was writing about Simone de Beauvoir, Dr. Kinsey, the future of the novel, or her own brush with a full-blown anti-Semite, each essay partook of the chronic skepticism promised by the title.

Almost all the reviews had been positive. Even the rare reviewer who found her standards too high or her tone too elitist had taken the collection seriously. Occupied with the joys and vicissitudes of her great love affair, she had not at first understood the implications of this response. Her life might still be in disarray, but with a pair of scissors and a pot of paste she had secured for herself the stature of a full-fledged lady of letters.

### FROM VIRGILIA PETERSON'S REVIEW IN *NEW YORK HERALD TRIBUNE BOOKS*, SEPTEMBER 24, 1961

There has probably never been a "Mary" more "contrary" than Mary McCarthy. But whether or not her intellectual fireworks are enkindled by a wicked *esprit de contradiction*, the case she builds for them is not only as brilliant as her coldly brilliant novels have led us to expect but, surprisingly, not wicked at all. On the contrary [. . .] she emerges from this highly opinionated set of opinions as a moralist.

Perverse and opinionated she might be, but suddenly it was possible to perceive that, coupled with an unregenerate contrariness, there was a steady and unflagging devotion to what was solid, enduring, and resistant to changes in fashion. As a novelist she had rarely been able to please everyone, even close friends. With this collection of essays it seemed she could do little wrong.

### FROM ROBERT LOWELL'S LETTER TO ELIZABETH BISHOP, AUGUST 31, 1961

Mary McCarthy will be in New York this fall to display her new husband. Her essays are out and have a lovely naive, very intelligent dissenter's springiness to them.

### FROM JANET FLANNER'S LETTER TO NATALIA DANESI MURRAY, MARCH 9, 1962

I have been greatly impressed by Mary McCarthy's book of essays, *On the Contrary* I think it is called. The most educated female mind of our time in both America and England, I believe, as biased as Rebecca West in some directions, but more truly literary, which to me is more truly interesting, for she is a more conscious writer than Rebecca who lashed out with words like someone swimming or skating. Mary, on the other hand, flew on them somehow.

### FROM NICOLA CHIAROMONTE'S LETTER TO MARY McCARTHY, SEPTEMBER 16, 1961

I just *must* tell you with what enormous pleasure I have been reading those essays of *On the Contrary* which I did not know—what a sharp, brilliant, "radical" intelligence, and united to what grace and imagination! I simply cannot think of any contemporary writer who can be compared to you as a commentator on present-day mores. The artist is ever present in these writings—which are in fact just the *other side* of your talent as a novelist, I feel.

Nicola Chiaromonte might speak of her talent as a novelist, but in the spring of 1962 that talent was not much in evidence. For one thing, her marriage had yet to provide the sort of tranquillity that might encourage her to pick up her novel again. For another, only her editors were urging her to hurry and get back to it. Virtually every friend and critic was pointing to her essays as being somehow finer and nobler than her fiction. Independent minded she might be, but it is the rare writer who can remain impervious to that kind of consensus.

*On the Contrary* was soon followed by a string of striking essays published in places like *The Observer, Harper's, Partisan Review*, and *The New Republic*—a jaundiced look at a collection of theater pieces by a much admired critic; an evisceration of a sacred cow much beloved by young readers; a cutting down to size of one of Shakespeare's great tragic heroes: and a passionate critical study of a new novel by an old friend. If her marriage to Jim West had softened her, it had done little to take the edge off her published criticism.

### FROM "CURTAINS FOR TYNAN," *THE OBSERVER*, OCTOBER 22, 1961

Rational discourse is not [Kenneth] Tynan's strong point[. . . .] Like most of the humorists who have written about the theatre, Tynan is less a critic than a performer and mime in his own right; his reviews are excited performances. He can make you see and hear an actor, sometimes a whole play or rather its production; he can spot a defect or a virtue, but he cannot reason or analyze.

Two years earlier, in a review of *Sights and Spectacles*, Kenneth Tynan had accused *her* of being too fastidious to be a first-rate critic. He had even gone so far as to call her "the queen of the patrician *bas bleus*." That she was aware of Tynan's review there is no question. Just in case it escaped her notice, Dwight Macdonald had been quick to bring it to her attention. Whether the piece she wrote for Terence Kilmartin, *The Observer's* literary editor, was prompted by a failure to appreciate Tynan's virtues as a critic or by pure unadulterated revenge, she did not hesitate to add insult to injury by launching her attack from the pages of a publication Tynan had every right to expect to be friendly to him.

**TERENCE KILMARTIN** It caused me the most acute embarrassment because not only was I a friend of Ken but I employed him. You know, he was *The Observer's* drama critic. I had a terrible time. I had to tell Ken it was going to appear and that I couldn't censor it. I came to be very, very fond of Mary. She became a good friend. But there was a streak of cruelty in her. I think she rather liked giving intellectual pain. I don't mean she didn't believe what she said. She wasn't ever in the business of making concessions for the sake of friendship.

Having seen the piece provoke an uproar in London, she did not scruple to let *Partisan Review* bring it out in New York. Tynan was not the only writer with a stellar reputation and an editorial family in common to get a swipe from her that year. The following spring, inspired by the appearance of *Franny and Zooey*, she took out after J. D. Salinger. Once again her attack did not go unremarked.

#### FROM "J. D. SALINGER'S CLOSED CIRCUIT,"
#### THE OBSERVER, JUNE 1962

Who is to inherit the mantle of Papa Hemingway? Who if not J. D. Salinger?[. . .] [T]he very image of the hero as pitiless phony-detector comes from Hemingway[. . . .] Like Hemingway, Salinger sees the world in terms of allies and enemies[. . . .] *The Catcher in the Rye*, like Hemingway's books, is based on a scheme of exclusiveness. The characters are divided into those who belong to the club and those who don't.

#### FROM JANET FLANNER'S LETTER TO MARY MCCARTHY,
#### N.D. [C. 1962]

Mary Darling, [. . . .] Your *Observer* piece on Salinger must have shaken *The New Yorker* from the 19th Floor to the basement. Love always, Janet.

To Hannah Arendt she explained at some length that writing this piece on Salinger had given her "no pleasure, except to get it out of the way." But long after the fuss had died down, one *New Yorker* staff member would beg to differ with her.

**WILLIAM MAXWELL**    That piece is totally unjust. If not totally, then so unjust as to make one think, Oh, God, there's too much blood in the water. His virtues were not of a kind she would have appreciated—the charm of his dialogue and economy and a total absence of intellectual pretense at that point. The Glass stories are not intellectual. They're mystical. And that might have made her uneasy. And annoyed her. I can't say what prompted it. All I can say is that the water's full of blood.

The best that could be said for her Salinger attack was that it did not run first in *The New Yorker*. All the same, she was sufficiently aware of the magnitude of what she had done to one of the magazine's great stars and two of its writers (Tynan had served as drama critic in 1958 and 1959) to wonder why for the first time in years she had received no first-reading agreement from the magazine. Writing William Maxwell, she professed to believe it was an oversight, while acknowledging that it might well have been nothing of the sort.

#### FROM MARY MCCARTHY'S LETTER TO WILLIAM MAXWELL,
#### JUNE 16, 1962

I did hear [. . .] from some *New Yorker* writer (I can't remember who—not Dwight or Tucci), that Shawn was very upset by what he regarded as a series of attacks by me on the magazine. E.g., the Tynan review and a fifteen-year-old piece on the Hersey *Hiroshima* that I republished in my last book. He will feel this even more strongly, I fear, if he sees a thing of mine on Salinger that just appeared in *The Observer*. I myself don't think this is a "pattern"; there's a side of *The New Yorker*

I've never cared for and have told Shawn so in a friendly dispute. But there's also a side I like and defend (though not in print, I confess).

Her confession, such as it was, proved to be beside the point. During the past year she had changed addresses so many times that the magazine had simply lost track of her whereabouts. Nonetheless, it was just as well that the next time she went on the attack she was not once again putting this long-standing relationship at risk. With "General Macbeth" she was merely providing a totally unexpected reading for a classic so familiar to theatergoers that there seemed to be nothing new to say on the subject—turning the Thane of Cawdor into a second-rate Eisenhower Republican, "a commonplace man who talks in commonplaces, a golfer, one might guess, on the Scottish fairways."

With this new batch of criticism Mary McCarthy was betraying only occasional hints of the born-again moralist admirers had discovered in *On the Contrary*. At the same time, she was displaying little in the way of generosity or grace. Such generosity as she showed she reserved for a lengthy consideration of Vladimir Nabokov's *Pale Fire*, a book that did much to lift the depression she'd had such difficulty throwing off.

#### FROM "A BOLT FROM THE BLUE"

*Pale Fire* is a Jack-in-the-box, a Fabergé gem, a clockwork toy, a chess problem, an infernal machine, a trap to catch reviewers, a cat-and-mouse game, a do-it-yourself kit[. . . .] [T]his centaur-work of Nabokov's, half-poem, half-prose, this merman of the deep, is a creature of perfect beauty, symmetry, strangeness, originality, and moral truth. Pretending to be a curio, it cannot disguise the fact that it is one of the great works of art of this century, the modern novel that everyone thought was dead and that was only playing possum.

#### FROM MARY MCCARTHY'S LETTER TO HANNAH ARENDT, JUNE 1, 1962

I really fell in love with the Nabokov book and worked very hard on it, with pure joy. I'm very curious to know what you'll think of the book if you read it; to me it's one of the gems of this century[. . . .] [I]t's the first book I know to turn this weird new civilization into a work of art, as though he'd engraved it all on the head of a pin, like the Lord's Prayer.

A great work for some, a curio for others, *Pale Fire* elicited from her an unprecedented sympathetic understanding. It also elicited a rigorous gloss on the text, which at times recalled the benighted gloss that Kinbote, the novel's insane narrator, provides for the 999-line epic left behind by the poet John Shade. Reading the book on the heels of her impassioned advocacy, Hannah Arendt and Nicola Chiaromonte remained unimpressed. For Edmund Wilson, Nabokov's longtime friend and supporter, her dissection of the text was overzealous at best.

### FROM EDMUND WILSON'S LETTER TO MARY McCARTHY, JULY 7, 1962

About *Pale Fire*: your article was the only one I have seen which really grappled with the book. The other reviewers didn't even know what was supposed to be taking place. But I don't see how you can possibly think it is one of the great works of art of our time. I thought that—although the idea of the commentator's substituting himself for the poet is amusing in itself—the book as a whole was rather silly. I was irritated and bored by all his little tricks, and did not bother to try to figure everything out as you did. I believe that in some cases you attached to details a significance that he did not intend.

For all that dear friends and her former husband remained impervious to the book's charms, Mary McCarthy's review in *The New Republic* helped make the reputation of *Pale Fire*. (The review also marked the beginning of a desire to display learning, which would occasionally give subsequent pieces of criticism a less than engaging pedantic flavor.) As McCarthy herself was well aware, literary reputations are not necessarily enduring. As this most challenging of novels has fallen out of fashion, more than one reader has come to credit her passionate advocacy to second thoughts about failing to appreciate *Lolita*. Certainly a wish to make amends may have entered into her willingness to embrace *Pale Fire*. However, her first spring in Paris as Mrs. James West she had every reason to be receptive to a novel suffused with a sense of exile and loss.

Fortunately, that spring she had more than an old friend's new novel to lift her spirits. On the heels of the publication of *On the Contrary* she was suddenly very much in demand. *Esquire* had commissioned a full-scale profile for a special July issue devoted to prominent American women. Better yet, a very good "Writers at Work" interview had appeared in the Winter–Spring issue of *Paris Review*.

Only the year before, the editors of *Paris Review* had seen fit to take an old story by Bowden called "Ciao," which gave the titillating illusion of portraying a day in the life of the Broadwaters circa 1948. With this "Writers at Work" interview, they were going a long way toward making amends. From first to last they treated her as a writer of the first rank, worthy of the same sort of consideration accorded a Faulkner or a Hemingway or a Rebecca West. The interview, as it happened, had come about purely by chance.

**ELISABETH NIEBUHR SIFTON** I was having dinner with Nelson Aldrich, who was then Paris editor of *Paris Review*, and he asked, "How's life with

you?" I said life was terrible. Then I said, "Well, I'll tell you one nifty thing.
I met Mary McCarthy." I told him about the dinner with the Joneses. Desperate editor that he was, he said, "Why don't you do an interview? Everybody else in Paris is scared of her." I told him I couldn't do it. I'd never done
anything like that before and, anyway, I hadn't read all her books. "What are
libraries for?" he said. So I went and read all her books and then, shaking
with fear, I called her. She said that her first reaction was reluctance, but, on
the other hand, she had profited so greatly from the *Paris Review* interviews
with other writers that as a gesture of gratitude she would consent to do it.
She put it that way.

By choosing to be a good sport, she was rewarded with an introductory
portrait that noted every imperfection and yet managed to be flattering:

### FROM THE INTRODUCTION TO ELISABETH NIEBUHR'S
### INTERVIEW WITH MARY MCCARTHY, *PARIS REVIEW*,
### WINTER–SPRING 1962

> She is of medium height, dark, with straight hair combed back from a
> center part into a knot at the nape of her neck; this simple coiffure sets
> off a profile of beautiful, almost classic regularity[. . . .] She speaks not
> quickly, but with great animation and energy, gesturing seldom[. . . .]
> Her sentences are vigorously punctuated with emphatic verbal stresses
> and short though equally emphatic pauses[. . . .] [I]t is typical of her
> that she matches the tremendously elegant carriage of her arms and
> neck and handsomely poised head with a deliberate, almost jerky
> motion in taking a step.

Readers were rewarded with a cache of emphatic sentences setting forth
her views on everything from politics and writing to her own character—
a trove of treasures ready and waiting for anyone who set out to write
about her.

### MARY MCCARTHY IN AN INTERVIEW WITH
### ELISABETH NIEBUHR, *PARIS REVIEW*, WINTER–SPRING 1962

> What I really do [with my novels] is take real plums and put them in
> an imaginary cake. If you're interested in the cake, you get rather
> annoyed with people saying what species the real plum was[. . . .]
>
> I don't think the problem of social equality has ever been solved[. . . .]
> And yet once the concept of equality had entered the world, life
> becomes intolerable without it[. . . .]
>
> [T]here's a certain kind of woman writer who's a capital W, capital W.
> Virginia Woolf certainly was one, and Katherine Mansfield was one,
> And Elizabeth Bowen is one[. . . .] [T]hey become interested in
> décor[. . . .] Jane Austen was never a "Woman Writer," I don't think.
> The cult of Jane Austen pretends that she was, but I don't think she
> was. George Eliot *certainly* wasn't, and George Eliot is the kind of
> woman writer I admire. I was going to write a piece at some point

about this called "Sense and Sensibility," dividing women writers into these two. I *am* for the ones who represent sense, and so was Jane Austen[. . . .]

Something happens in my writing—I don't mean it to—a sort of distortion, a sort of writing on the bias, seeing things with a sort of swerve and swoop[. . . .]

I suppose in a sense I don't know any more today than I did in 1941 about what my identity is. But I've stopped looking for it. I must say, I believe much more in truth now than I did. I do believe in the solidity of truth much more. Yes. I believe there is a truth, and that it's knowable.

Unfortunately, by choosing to cooperate with the young man from *Esquire* for the July issue on American women, she was rewarded with a profile that seemed nothing short of a breach of faith. She had given the writer, Brock Brower, carte blanche—first talking to him herself and then providing him with introductions to her friends. He had repaid her by going down to the New York courts and copying out choice extracts from the Wilson divorce affidavits. From there he had moved on to her attack on Kenneth Tynan. Such sympathy as he expressed for her trials as an orphan or such admiration as he expressed for her groundbreaking work as a woman writer was more than offset by a heady blend of back stabbing and gossip. From the very start he was on the attack.

### FROM "MARY MCCARTHYISM," BY BROCK BROWER, *ESQUIRE,* JULY 1962

Mary McCarthy has the Nicest Smile. At the slightest social pressure, it springs open and automatically catches. She can hold it there—flicking its long, white upper blade of handsome, emphatic teeth this way, that way at every threatening conversational turn—for sometimes five, ten minutes at a stretch. Nothing cows it. She can smoke through it, argue through it, spill the beans through it, even *smile* through it[. . . .]

Many an intelligent young lady has declared fiercely for her sexual freedom [. . .] for the challenge of a heads-on competition with men [. . .] only to find herself disastrously undermined by feminine self-doubt, foolish shame, and a desperate need to be Told What to Do[. . . .] Mary has defined these contradictions almost too well, so exactly, in fact, that her hostile critics claim that what she has really defined, for all men to know, is the Modern American Bitch.

### FROM MARY MCCARTHY'S LETTER TO EDMUND WILSON, JULY 27, 1962

In case you saw a horrible thing about me in *Esquire*, I trust you gathered that I'm not responsible for unpleasant passages about you in it. The author must have dredged them out of the court files. I *am* responsible for being such a fool as to let this young man do the piece—see my friends, etc. The understanding was that it was to be "purely literary, and biographic only in that public sense, not a personality piece at all." I do not seem to live and learn.

### FROM WILLIAM JOVANOVICH'S LETTER TO MARY MCCARTHY, JULY 24, 1962

I read the *Esquire* article on you, with a fast burn, Kee-rist!

Brock Brower might conclude by saying "there is a secret admiration for her candor, her audacity, and her stupendous try for the woman's moon"—and go on to grant that at this stage in her life she could be said to have attained Margaret Sargent's celebrated wish to be her own woman *"wel at ese"*—but that was not about to fool anyone. Still, if one believes that there is no such thing as bad publicity, then the pain caused by the piece was more than offset by the attention it brought her. Not only did it place her in very heady company but it treated her fame as a fait accompli.

### FROM "MARY MCCARTHYISM," BY BROCK BROWER

[O]ne startling aspect of her present fame, a mark of her rather special position among other famous and intellectual women—is that she has accomplished it all *without a man*. Not that there haven't been men in her life. But as her own woman, she has never been bracketed with a man in the way that most other outstanding women have been, even in their eminence. Eleanor Roosevelt is *Mrs.* Roosevelt. Clare Boothe Luce may be playwright, Congresswoman, and ambassador, but she is still very much regarded as Mrs. *Luce*[. . . .] Even Simone de Beauvoir, despite her own outspoken championship of the Second Sex, is still the unwed existential bride of Jean Paul Sartre. But Mary is definitely *Miss* McCarthy, even though she may in private life be Mrs. Bowden Broadwater, or Mrs. James West.

To the world at large Mary McCarthy might be Miss McCarthy, but as Mrs. James West she had taken on her full share of responsibilities. Her new husband was steadfast and loyal and he was extremely proud of her accomplishments, but he was also the father of three young children. Like it or not, summer vacations were to be spent with the three children and their Polish nurse, Maria. Having been forced by the courts years before to give up Reuel to Edmund Wilson every summer, she was now getting a chance to see how this arrangement may have looked to Elena.

Her very first August at Bocca di Magra, back in 1960 when she had been waiting on her own for Jim West to leave his wife, she had gotten an enormous amount of work done. At eleven, when her writing for the morning was finished, she had merely walked down to the docks and hired a boat to take her to the beautiful white marble beach called Punta Bianca. She had shared a house with Anjo and Mario Levi, whom she had first met in Paris in 1946. Her midday meal had been taken with the Levis and their two children at a long table set up in the garden. At night she'd dined *en pension* at the hotel. That first summer, the chief excitement, aside from a nightly game of chess, had been a novel called *Naked Lunch*, which William Phillips was said to have pronounced brilliant and which Chiaromonte, when he got hold of it, declared to be very much like "action painting." Without fail she had been in bed before midnight.

Her second summer, she had arrived with her husband, his three children, and their nurse to find Reuel at the inn, accompanied by a handsome young woman he was thinking of marrying. Before long, Dwight and Gloria Macdonald had turned up at the inn for a first visit. At the house where she and Jim West and the Levis were staying, a separate apartment had been reserved for Jim's children so that she would be free to work in the mornings. Most mornings after eleven, she had little hope of getting back to her desk. Despite the demands on her time and attention, she found time to savor the pleasures of family life and of Bocca di Magra's beautiful white beach. She also found time to develop an even greater liking for the Levi family. Best of all, she had time to see a good deal of Nicola Chiaromonte, who was convalescing from the heart attack that had kept him from her wedding.

### FROM MARY MCCARTHY'S LETTER TO CARMEN ANGLETON, AUGUST 29, 1961

> Life this year at Bocca di Magra simply devours time, chewing it up bit by bit. The major undertaking is getting to Punta Bianca and back[. . . .] [T]he afternoon—after the morning spent in the water and getting to and from it—is usually devoted to a trip or games or a walk[. . . .] Reuel was here himself, with a thin, rather Biblical-looking Jewish girl friend named Renata whom he met last spring in Paris and who is either quite homely or a beauty, according to taste[. . . .]
>
> It's the third day (oh, dear) since I started this. I write a paragraph and then there's an interruption[. . . .] Sorry no signature. The children have taken my last pencil.

**JAMES WEST**   At Bocca di Magra the children liked to draw, to paint. In the afternoon we went on picnics and into the mountains. Beautiful quarries at Carrara. They loved the old boatman, who really belonged in a Hemingway novel and was the skipper of the little boat that took us to the beach. He had a nice deep voice and big brawny arms and the biggest big toe I ever saw in my life.

**ANGÉLIQUE LEVI**   I think she was always the same whether she was in Bocca di Magra or Paris. Always ceremonious. Precise. I very much liked her character. She played seriously at keeping house the way children play seriously. Everything was ritual—the meals, the picnics, the cooking, everything in its place. Children like that, too. It's comforting.

Though her patience was sometimes tried, she managed to keep her temper with Dwight Macdonald, who after years of hard drinking had, in her view, "taken on the look of an aged still or swollen wineskin." In addition she managed to make the best of Gloria, the second wife whom she—along with all of Dwight's old friends—chose to blame for his drinking and erratic behavior and his increasingly frequent bouts of writer's block. Forbearance had not been necessary, however, when dealing with another first-time Bocca di Magra visitor—Reuel's first serious girlfriend, a graduate of Bryn Mawr who was taking a degree in philosophy at Harvard.

**RENATA ADLER**   When I first met Mary I had never read her. I had taken a course with Edmund Wilson. I hardly ever read *The New Yorker*. I didn't really know what sort of writer Mary McCarthy was. Reuel and I arrived at Bocca di Magra, a few days before Mary and Jim. It didn't seem like a fishing village. Each morning, after Jim and Mary arrived, we went by boat, around the rocks, and swam at the white beach. I thought Mary was wonderful. I was shy in those days, and she was extraordinarily kind to me. Later, when I read her writing and recognized that critical intelligence to be feared, I was surprised. I loved and admired her. I remember Aldo Bruzzichelli and the Chiaromontes, and conversations I took to be wonderful.

In 1962, Mary returned to Bocca di Magra with Jim and the children to find that there was a gasoline pump by the water, a new pizzeria with a "hideous" flagstone terrace, and Germans in the neighboring town of Sans Façons. "But still it is delightful and somehow fresh," she wrote Carmen Angleton, trying to make the best of it. The invaders were not yet something to be taken seriously and Nicola Chiaromonte was more like his old self.

That summer she was looking forward to getting to work on a short story she had long had it in mind to write—a story set in a modest Italian village called Porto Quaglia, which, for all that it was "populated by fishermen whose thin brown nets like hair nets were spread out to dry in the sun behind the whitewashed houses," was totally lacking in the chic and charm one associates with summer resorts that go by the name "fishing village." But once again her time was not entirely her own. In the mornings Jim West might try to keep the children occupied with pencils and crayons, but after eleven it fell to her to help see to their care.

**ALISON WEST**   Mary loved to share pleasure and she loved to give gifts. We very much appreciated the intellectual nature of some of these gifts. For example, the books that she read us, like Pyle's King Arthur with its antiquated English—those were things we loved. She made a special effort in that direction. But as children we felt a pronounced lack of freedom. Everything seemed orchestrated and planned. Still, the summers in Italy were marvelous. There would be a trip to Venice or to Rome or to Florence. All of these things we appreciated, but at the same time it was always rather stressful. There was no real joy or lightheartedness because my stepmother was just not good with children. I have no memory of a hug ever from Mary. She was simply not capable of it.

**ANGÉLIQUE LEVI**  I don't think she was very fond of little children. Why I don't know. She pretended to be. She tried. But her heart was not in it. She was very kind to *my* two children, but they were great children and they were twelve years old.

**MIRIAM CHIAROMONTE**  Mary did everything she could for Jim's children, but she was in a very difficult position. They all seemed like perfect ladies and gentlemen but I think they must have had very strange feelings about Mary and their mother. They must have been uncomfortable. Mary read them stories at night and had parties for them and brought Alison, I remember, a beautiful velvet dress from Venice. She did all these things that a good stepmother should do. At Bocca di Magra one summer, Jim and Mary had to leave a couple of days before the children, and Jim asked me to take the children to the station to put them on the train for Paris, to go back to their mother. And I remember on the platform—we were there very early—I asked, "Do you want anything, should we go inside and get some chocolates?" and Alison very provocatively said, "I want to get something for my mother." She made it clear.

If sometimes it seemed as if she was making little headway with her three stepchildren, Mary McCarthy could console herself with the knowledge that she was making every effort. Moreover, when it came down to it, the rearing of another woman's children was not the main concern of her life. As a lady writer married to a diplomat with a young family she was doing very nicely, thank you. Not only interviewers were eager to hear what she had to say. Indeed, soon after arriving at Bocca di Magra that August, she had to leave behind her husband and his young children in order to attend a five-day conference at Edinburgh on the future of the novel.

She was cutting short her family vacation at the behest of one of the conference's organizers, Sonia Orwell, who had provided the occasion for the big party at Dobbs Ferry. The fact was, with her two long essays on the art of fiction she had become something of an authority. Because the children's Polish nurse had once again accompanied them to Bocca di Magra she did not have to feel unduly guilty about deserting Jim West.

At Edinburgh, she was slated to be the sole woman writer on an American delegation that also included Norman Mailer, William Burroughs, and Henry Miller, three men known to show little respect for women, whether on a public platform or in the privacy of a bedroom. If her compatriots were not to her liking, she was not going to lack for company. On the British delegation she would have two good friends, Stephen Spender and Malcolm Muggeridge, and one new acquaintance, Rebecca

West, who had unbent sufficiently while crossing the Atlantic that spring to grace her with a personal photograph complete with husband and dog.

Dame Rebecca's husband was a sensitive businessman and the dog was the sort of dog appropriate to a dowager who was a member in good standing of the Conservative Party and kept a large establishment in the country. At seventy the dashing rebel of McCarthy's Vassar years was a fascinating, if dismaying, monitory figure—a "good talker" but "cracked" and "paranoid," the long, thick dark hair now short and grizzled, the handsome face twisted and contorted at the jaw.

All told, some seventy writers from all over the world had flocked to Edinburgh. Thanks to the microphones and simultaneous translations in three languages, the conference soon took on something of the aspect of a plenary session of the United Nations. Unlike the United Nations, it was run for profit. In the vast auditorium sat some two thousand listeners who had paid good money to be entertained as well as informed. The panelists made sure to give them their money's worth, speaking out on everything from sex and censorship and the advertising industry to the fate of Western civilization. Before the first day was over, the proceedings had begun to resemble a three-ring circus, complete with freak show.

### From Mary McCarthy's Letter to Hannah Arendt, September 28, 1962

People jumping up to confess they were homosexuals or heterosexuals; a Registered Heroin Addict leading the young Scottish opposition to the literary tyranny of the Communist Hugh MacDiarmid [. . .] an English woman novelist describing her communications with her dead daughter; a Dutch homosexual, former male nurse, now a Catholic convert, seeking someone to baptise him; a bearded Sikh with hair down to his waist declaring on the platform that homosexuals were incapable of love, just as (he said) hermaphrodites were incapable of orgasm (Stephen Spender, in the chair, murmured that he should have thought they could have *two*)[. . . .] I confess I enjoyed it enormously.

From the very start of the conference Mary McCarthy had star billing in the dazzling high-wire act that held sway over the big center ring. The first morning, taking part in a platform discussion on the topic "How does the novel form stand today?," she gave a brief talk guaranteed to jolt the average dozing listener awake. The nation-state was dying, she asserted, and so was the novel. For the nation-state she saw little hope. But for the novel she saw possible salvation in works by two writers that addressed this stateless condition. The first writer was Vladimir Nabokov, author of books she "personally [had] gone overboard for." The second was William

Burroughs, who was the author of *Naked Lunch*, the novel which had made the rounds at Bocca di Magra in 1960. Burroughs, she informed the audience, was "here now."

Although *Naked Lunch* was not as well-known to her average listener as *Lolita*, it promised to be no less infamous. Brought out in Paris by Maurice Girodias, publisher of *Lady Chatterley's Lover*, it dared to depict a drug addict's surreal and at times hilarious flirtation with death by means of a dizzying array of scenes sufficiently pornographic to render it unlikely that it would soon find a publisher in the United States. As if none of this was at issue, she proceeded to explain to her listeners why, to her mind, it was the quintessential stateless novel.

### FROM MARY MCCARTHY'S TALK AT EDINBURGH

The *Naked Lunch* is laid everywhere and is sort of speeded up like jet travel and it has that somewhat supersonic quality. It also has some of the qualities of Action Painting. It is a kind of action novel. And you could not possibly consider this as a description of American life.

Burroughs was a literary outlaw, a self-confessed former heroin addict, who had accidentally shot and killed his own wife. In his dark suit he might look more like a businessman than a writer, but he was hardly respectable. By placing him alongside Vladimir Nabokov in a newly created corner of her personal literary pantheon, she had the pleasure of causing a sensation. She also had the pleasure of taking by surprise the preternaturally unflappable writer she chose to cite. In a matter of days, news of the stir she had created would reach Paris. In a matter of months, it would reach as far as Tangiers. Decades later, when they had lost her power to shock, her remarks would continue to reverberate.

**WILLIAM BURROUGHS** I'd met her once before in Venice, with Alan Ansen, at lunch or drinks in 1956. She was married to Bowden Broadwater and she described me to Alan as "a cynical old newspaperman." We got along very well. I probably first learned at Edinburgh that she liked *Naked Lunch*. I have no idea how she encountered it. I felt she did full justice to the book— full enough, for her. Her remarks make sense enough.

### FROM JANET FLANNER'S LETTER TO NATALIA DANESI MURRAY, AUGUST 8, 1962

Mary McCarthy was the queen of the International Literary Caucus at the Edinburgh Festival according to the London *Times*[. . . .] She said *Naked Lunch* by a writer named Burroughs of whom I never even heard and *Lolita* are the focal works of our century. I shall ask *The New Yorker* to send me the nude luncheon affair. If I like it no better than *Lolita* as a major work, I shall find myself *démodée* indeed.

**FROM PAUL BOWLES'S LETTER TO ALLEN GINSBERG, OCTOBER 30, 1962**

Of course everyone's excited over Mary McCarthy's espousing of Bill B. The bitchy ones say: A kiss from the Angel of Death, and so on.

**SUSAN SONTAG**   The world Burroughs depicts is so remote from anything she could identify with or imagine, how could she possibly have liked it? I mean, I *can* imagine it, and it fills me with horror and revulsion. But I actually knew all these people socially, knew them well. I knew Burroughs. I knew Ginsberg. I knew Peter Orlovsky. I knew Gregory Corso. I knew them just at the point when all this was happening. I, too, thought I *ought* to like Burroughs's work. Not because anybody told me to but because I had a conventional idea of the worthiness of literary experimentalism. It was no deeper than that. . . . I felt that there was a place for that kind of thing and I should be respectful of it. But at least I *did* understand what Burroughs was doing and that's why I *couldn't* like it. *Naked Lunch* is about cruelty. It's a very cruel work about emotional deadness. And it's about the pleasure of thinking about cruel situations.

By speaking out on behalf of Burroughs, she leapt onto that center-ring high wire and executed a neat pirouette, leaving poor Dame Rebecca down below among the bleachers and sawdust. Having assumed as if by right the mantle of Edinburgh's dark lady of letters, she had the pleasure of confounding all those who thought they could predict what she would say and do next.

**NORMAN MAILER**   The first time Mary was ever friendly was at the Edinburgh conference and it was because we both liked *Naked Lunch*. That was the first hint of collegiality we ever felt. At Edinburgh you would have seen Mary's and my faces together a few times, but I don't think Mary much cared for drinking and I was drinking like a fiend—my daughter Kate was about five days old when I left for Edinburgh and that may have had something to do with it. At one point I threw someone down the stairs. There was a remoteness about Mary. An element of *noli me tangere*. She was eleven years older than I was and there was always an element of the older sister.

**NICCOLÒ TUCCI**   I represented the Italian writers and everywhere I went there was Norman Mailer, who was always drunk and very proud because he had married the daughter of a lord. Mary was so impressed by Norman Mailer. When Mary, who had praised my writing very much, was asked who were the good writers in America, she didn't mention my name. I was furious. I went to her and said, "Mary, what is that?" "Oh," she said, "I had forgotten. I thought you were not an American citizen."

While she left her old friend Niccolò Tucci believing she had deserted him for a drunken social climber, she managed to leave a young Dutch writer she met on a day's outing to Loch Lomond feeling singularly blessed. Tucci would in time forgive her. And the young Dutch writer,

Cees Nooteboom, would go on to become so close a friend that two decades later more than one observer would speculate about the precise nature of the special bond between them.

**CEES NOOTEBOOM**  She was at the apogee of her fame and had just turned fifty and I was twenty-nine, with nothing in my hands that I could show her. Nothing of mine had been translated into English. I knew her reputation as a merciless critic and had read her fiction and *On the Contrary*. I didn't know anybody who wrote like that—rational and rhetorical at the same time. I felt clumsy and young, frivolous and quite often stupid. I was in bad shape and there were things I never told her. But when I was with her I had the feeling she helped to put my mind in order. You always wonder what it was that made for a relationship. Was it amusement or conversation or what? I decided to accept the riddle or enigma of this sudden friendship. It would, with all its ups and downs and with all the severity and humor that belonged to her character, become the most important and dearest friendship of my life.

When her stay in Edinburgh came to a close, she had to exchange all the attention and excitement for a quiet family life at Bocca di Magra. Still, there were compensations. And, at the end of August, when it came time for Jim West and his children to leave for Paris, she stayed on for two weeks. With only the Chiaromontes and the Levis for company, she easily completed her tale of Porto Quaglia—that fishing village uncannily like Bocca di Magra.

In this tale she wrote of a small group of friends who find their cherished summer retreat besieged by a horde of invaders. The friends were English, Italian, French, and American and the invaders were a pack of vulgarians headed by some red-faced Germans. Although her new cast of characters was international, the story's concerns were familiar to anyone who had read "The Appalachian Revolution" or *The Oasis*.

Once again she was portraying the moral conflict that arises when the best of all possible worlds can continue to exist only at the expense of a democratic ideal. Once again she was writing about loss. And once again she was writing directly from life. The French family at the center of her story was clearly based on the Levis. Mike, the bewhiskered American all the children mistake for Uncle Sam, was immediately recognizable as Dwight Macdonald. And Mike's wife, Irene, who is disappointed to discover that the village attracts "no real intellectuals, like Sartre or Françoise Sagan," was unmistakably Dwight's wife, Gloria.

But save for Mike and Irene, "The Hounds of Summer" marked a departure. Although the writer might be exaggerating the threat to her beleaguered fishing village, she was not coming at most of her characters with a swerve and a swoop. Indeed she was scarcely coming at them at all. Together they formed a sort of international chorus. It was their situation that pricked her interest rather than their individual weaknesses.

For better or worse, the story did not concern itself with any of the scandalous events of her recent history. It did not partake of any enlivening infusion of gossip. For all that she could not resist giving Gloria Macdonald a passing swipe, she was not writing satire. After reading the story, no one was going to accuse her of unfairness. (Certainly not Dwight Macdonald's old friends.) No one was going to threaten her with a lawsuit. Family members were not going to cease speaking to her. And Jim West was not going to call her up short. Decades later it would remain one of Reuel's favorite stories. Anjo Levi would smile as she called attention to the fact that it contained portraits of her father and her children. Immediately upon its publication Hannah Arendt informed her, "That is one of your very very very best short stories" and Katharine White wrote from her retirement in Maine, "I hope you have several more short stories up your sleeve for the near future."

"The Hounds of Summer" was in fact the last short story Mary McCarthy would write. What gave the story freshness was not its theme or its depiction of character but its atmosphere. From start to finish it captured the flavor of her new expatriate life—a "stateless" life in which, like it or not, the lingua franca was French, a language that put her at a disadvantage. The story was elegiac, irreproachable, and perfectly suited to *The New Yorker*, which paid her handsomely for it. To William Jovanovich, she allowed as how she had written it with the magazine's generous rates in mind. Renovating and furnishing an apartment in Paris was costly and she and Jim West did not have much money.

However, her need of money did not keep her from jeopardizing the story's purchase when she felt that its special flavor was being compromised. She refused to make further adjustments to the text in order to make her generous smattering of French idioms and phrases totally intelligible to the average reader. "I don't want you to think I regard this story as Holy Writ, but I can't help feeling alarmed at the vision of a running translation," she wrote William Maxwell.

By the time she wrote William Maxwell in defense of her new story, it was fall and she was back in Paris, trying to complete a novel that was in no respect international—the novel she had started working on back in 1952. Much to her dismay, she was back in the small apartment that she had sublet from Inge Morath. The renovations on the rue de Rennes apartment were taking far longer than she had anticipated. Moreover, having lived among the French for more than half a year, she found that she liked them no better than she had upon her arrival. If anything she liked them less.

**EILEEN SIMPSON**  Mary said she would have preferred to be in Poland. *She would have picked some unfashionable place to be.* Over dinner, either at the Wests' apartment or at ours, we would swap horror stories about the difficulties we were having setting up our households. Before the Wests moved into their flat on the rue de Rennes, workmen burned the shelves of an eighteenth-century bookcase Jim had given Mary for her birthday. The excuse for this vandalism? They needed the wood for fuel to supplement the stingy supply of heat.

### FROM MARY MCCARTHY'S LETTER TO CARMEN ANGLETON, DECEMBER 14, 1962

[P]hysical conditions in Paris are frightful—the traffic, the parking problem, the fact that something—the telephone, the heating, the hot water, the electricity—is always out of order, and you can't get anyone to come and fix it for days. Apparently it is "not done" to die in Paris, for example, on a Thursday or a Friday—you can't get an undertaker and you lie in your apartment decomposing. This has happened recently with two old ladies—Sylvia Beach and poor Esther Arthur, who had a heart attack[. . . .] I'm coming to hate most of the French, who are so rude and unpleasant that any one of them who is normally polite—nothing extra—appears to you as a good angel. And their chronic bad humor, of course, is catching.

Six months had passed and the promise held out by Hannah Arendt had failed to materialize. The heavy poison in her veins had returned.

### FROM MARY MCCARTHY'S LETTER TO CARMEN ANGLETON, DECEMBER 14, 1962

I've been fearfully depressed. And this is unnerving because one of the things about me is that I don't get depressed, for more than a few minutes at a time, so that I feel I have migrated, like a soul, into the body of another person, a rather inert body. Jim, I think, is depressed too, though we don't talk about it, or at least he doesn't and I very little (I hope). His work is difficult and oppressive; he has an inadequate staff that he inherited and can't get rid of—the typical bureaucratic problem. Then the apartment has been harassing him too.

She had not lost her depression. Indeed, at times it seemed to be contagious. For weeks at a stretch her mood had lightened, only to have the lassitude and tonelessness return with a vengeance. She had struck up a friendship with Nathalie Sarraute, the one French writer she had wanted to meet, but that seemed to offer little comfort. Her stepchildren were beginning to fit into their new life—at Bocca di Magra they had grown attached to the Levis *and* the Chiaromontes—but that did not seem to make much difference. For every gain there was a loss.

The very good maid that came with their sublet apartment had defected to America. She and Jim West were having to deal with the cleaning and laundry by themselves. Writing, when she could find time for it, had ceased to be a joy. The best she could bring herself to do was look to the future. "[I]n the new apartment you can at least see the clouds moving across the sky," she wrote Carmen Angleton, "I keep telling myself and Jim that a new life is going to begin as soon as we have moved in—a tranquil, airy life."

She might tell herself that this "tranquil, airy life" was soon to begin but she did not sound as if she believed such a life was anywhere within reach. Yet to most observers she looked as if she had already attained it. At the age of fifty, after a host of trials and tribulations, the poor orphan from Minneapolis had, by all accounts, been granted her every wish. She numbered among her friends some of the most celebrated intellectuals of her day. For a husband she had a man she believed to be not only truly handsome but truly good. To marry her he had left a woman almost half her age. She was living in a city most people considered the most beautiful in the world.

In the course of three decades she had produced a body of work that almost anyone would be proud to lay claim to. In the company of the great Rebecca West she had no need to make apologies. Even when they had a bone to pick, readers whose opinions she valued approached her writing with care and respect: you did not dismiss a book by Mary McCarthy without thinking twice about it. If she lacked the means to afford a first-rate apartment in move-in condition, or lacked the circle of friends whose company she'd long delighted in, she could take pride in a reputation which seemed likely only to acquire greater luster with time.

# Chapter Twenty

# THE GROUP

"I'm not a collector of advances on daydreams," Mary McCarthy had told Roger Straus in 1954, when he was about to become her publisher. In life she was a romantic, a champion of lost causes, eager to prevail against the most daunting of adversaries. When it came to her work, she was anything but. Since graduating college she had earned her living as a professional writer and she prided herself on making good on her promises. Over the years she had learned to cut her losses—to jettison any project that resisted her best efforts. Nevertheless, early in 1963, when another writer might long ago have given up on it (and she herself had more than once declared it to be hopeless), she made one final assault on her Vassar novel. She had been working on the book for eleven years.

This vexed novel, which now bore the title *The Group*, had been conceived in Portsmouth, Rhode Island, the year Eisenhower first defeated Stevenson. Her final assault was made in Paris, when Kennedy had been president long enough for her to be thoroughly dissatisfied with him. Along the way she had shed one husband for another and put first Portsmouth and then all of America behind her. She had watched her son go off to prep school and college and then on to graduate school at Berkeley. At one point the book had lost its original editor and acquired another. By the time she made this last attempt to get it right, an improbably youthful author of forty had become a handsome matron of fifty.

Back in 1952, the plan had been to take eight graduates from the class of '33 and follow them through the Depression, the Second World War, and on into the present—a period when television sets and subdivisions were turning up everywhere in America and Congress was doing everything in its power to ensure that both remained safe from Stalinists and fellow travelers. Having published two novels and two collections of stories, she could hardly be called a novice. However, with this new book she was no longer limiting herself to a narrow time frame or a single finely detailed milieu. Nor was she limiting herself to a single heroine or villain. In the company of her eight Vassar girls she was embarking on a postgraduate novel that promised to take on something of the aspect of a midcentury saga.

In 1953, barely a year after she'd started writing, she put the novel aside—first to pursue the possibility of going to law school and then to pursue backers for *Critic*. When plans for the magazine came to nothing, she went back to writing full-time. She did not, however, go back to writing *The Group*. By the end of 1954, when she announced to Roger Straus that she was not a collector of advances on daydreams, she had shelved the manuscript.

Salvaging what she could, she sold the third and last completed chapter to *Partisan Review*, which ran it in 1954 as "Dottie Makes an Honest Woman of Herself." The story of Dottie's getting herself fitted for a diaphragm created a sensation. It also created a strong desire to see what befell Dottie's seven classmates. Over the next few years—as she brought out a third novel, a book on Venice, a book on Florence, a childhood memoir, and two collections of essays—this desire did not abate.

There are few things more seductive than the knowledge that you have it in your power to please a fastidious reader. In the spring of 1959, buoyed up by a Guggenheim Fellowship and strong encouragement from Hannah Arendt, she resumed work on the manuscript. Further heartened by the reception her opening chapter received from a packed audience at the 92nd Street Y, she took the manuscript off to a retreat in Vermont. The trouble was, she brought with her no fresh inspiration. From her rented house she wrote William Maxwell, "I'm working on my novel and feeling like a carthorse. No wings."

That fall, at Tripoli, by dint of spending long hours in seclusion, she completed two passable chapters to send back to Bowden. But the following summer, absorbed in her great romance with Jim West, she was telling Bowden she had reread those chapters and started revising again. "It's rather like a certain kind of embroidery stitch where you go back with your needle each time before advancing."

Indeed, from the moment she became intent on marrying Jim West, her novel began to take on the aspect of an elaborate piece of handiwork—something to be carted from one hotel to another and picked up in moments of leisure. In any skirmish between love and art, the demands of love inevitably took precedence. In fact, there was no real contest. Of course, if the novel had been going better, she might not have been so quick to give it short shrift—or so quick to talk about it.

In her letters during the early sixties she did not scruple to make mention of her irritation with this book. To interviewers who questioned her, she showed no reluctance to lay bare her plan for it or discuss the challenges this plan presented. The novel was "about the idea of progress, really," she told Elisabeth Niebuhr, her *Paris Review* interviewer. "The idea of progress seen in the feminine sphere. You know, home economics, architecture, domestic technology, contraception, childbearing; the study of technology in the home, in the playpen, in the bed." Her plan was to show a gradual "loss of faith" in the whole notion of progress. The challenge she faced was in portraying the Vassar girls who were destined to lose their faith. "These girls are essentially comic figures, and it's awfully hard to make anything happen to them[. . . .] [T]hey really can't develop."

One year later, when talking to Brock Brower from *Esquire*, she was equally forthcoming. To Brower she confided that back in 1954 she had stopped working on the novel because she had become "too depressed" by the ending implicit in its early chapters. "The fates of these girls were going to be too cruel for me to go on. I mean, to humanity—not just the girls."

Oddly enough, these public admissions of doubt and failure seemed to whet the appetites of her readers, her *New Yorker* editor, and her publisher. For William Jovanovich, who had stepped in and seen her through the publication of her Florence book at Harcourt, the novel was an object of abiding fascination. By 1962 there had been a rash of best-sellers from "literary" authors. In 1955, Vladimir Nabokov had caused a sensation with *Lolita*. In 1957, after a career of respectful reviews and disappointing sales figures, Harcourt's own James Gould Cozzens had surprised everyone with *By Love Possessed*. Then, in 1962, after twenty years of labor, Katherine Anne Porter had brought out *Ship of Fools* to universal acclaim and unprecedented sales.

For both author and publisher, there was a real financial incentive to get *The Group* out into the world. In early August 1962, William Jovanovich wrote to say that the prestigious London publisher Rupert Hart-Davis was eager to pay $7,500 for the privilege of bringing the book out in Great Britain. "[A] *very* strong display of confidence," he noted, adding that he himself would be happy to increase his *own* advance "in order to help you keep at the book until it is finished." Later that month, Jovanovich was back harping on the same subject. "Is there any way you can give me a hint of a shadow of a suggestion of when *The Group* will be ready?" he asked. He had it listed in the catalog for spring.

In early February 1963, when it was clear that a spring publication was out of the question, Jovanovich wrote to say that he and his marketing people were hoping to bring the book out at the end of August. That way it would "get a jump on the flood of Fall books." On this one point he was adamant. "If we can get it started early enough, we think it will build and build right up to Christmastime and then have the momentum to carry over into 1964. This is not a pep talk, I assure you. We're now planning a 50,000-copy first printing!"

By February she was finally settled in the new rue de Rennes apartment. If her life was neither peaceful nor airy, she had a study all to herself and only the occasional straggling workman to break her concentration. On every front, things seemed to be looking up. First, having grappled to no avail with following her girls all the way into middle age, she was simply ending the novel at the outbreak of World War II. Then William Maxwell had notified her that *The New Yorker* was taking two chapters and running them as a story.

Best of all, William Jovanovich had at last found a way to speed up her pace. As soon as it looked as if the end was in sight, he announced that he had started setting the book in type. "I rather like the idea," she wrote William Maxwell. "I've always felt that the novelist was probably most novelistic when, like Dickens and Dostoievsky, he was still writing the book which his readers were gobbling the first chapters in serial form."

Jovanovich's appeal to both her competitive spirit and her romantic imagination produced the desired result. In early April, he had in hand a finished manuscript, which pleased him sufficiently to announce he was raising the book's first printing to 75,000 copies. At last, she was free to enjoy a holiday in Rome. She had completed the novel in a last desperate two-week sprint, often staying at her desk from seven in the morning until nightfall. While she had every reason to be pleased with the results, she did not have the constitution of a Dickens or Dostoyevsky. In Rome, she came down with hepatitis. Upon her return, she consented to stay for a week at the American Hospital at Neuilly before returning to work.

**EILEEN SIMPSON**   Mary didn't have hepatitis like anyone else. She was suffering from nausea and malaise, but these symptoms didn't prevent her from dragging herself from the bed to her desk. She was working with her translator on the Italian edition of *The Group* and couldn't afford the luxury of a convalescence. Her attitude was: I'm not going to let this illness slow me down.

The novel was eventually sold to twenty-three countries—not only to such likely markets as Italy and Germany but to Iceland and Japan. By late June, when the excerpt called "Polly Andrews, Class of '33" appeared in *The New Yorker*, it was beginning to look as if all her effort would be well rewarded. There was talk of a sale to the movies (Otto Preminger was said to be seriously interested). Already Avon had agreed to pay $100,000 for the right to bring the book out in paperback. (At a time when $20,000 could buy a fine New York co-op, this was a sum to be reckoned with.) For mass market writers, huge advances and paperback sales had yet to become commonplace. For literary writers, such sums were unheard of. For a writer whose most popular book had sold no more than seventeen thousand copies, Avon's offer was astonishing. However, not quite so astonishing if you believed the rumors about the novel's contents.

### FROM NICOLA CHIAROMONTE'S LETTER TO DWIGHT MACDONALD, JUNE 15, 1963

I hear Mary's book will be the most obscene ever published[. . . .] Apparently, obscenity pays a lot, too. Mary says she has become rich just on the sale of the book for the paperback edition. Rich, and, I am afraid, also very very full of her own importance as a writer. Let's hope not too much. . .

To Nicola Chiaromonte it looked as if all this money and attention might prove to be a mixed blessing. To Robert Lowell, who spent several golden days with her in Paris, assessing at his leisure her new home and her new husband, it looked as if she ran the risk of getting more than she'd bargained on.

### FROM ROBERT LOWELL'S LETTER TO ELIZABETH BISHOP, AUGUST 12, 1963

A lovely apartment, William Morris wall-paper, every item clean as a ship, and mostly brought over from England, meals planned and worked on for days, elevating, industrious trips to churches and museums, everything performed and executed to the last inch, though Mary had just gotten over a bad attack of jaundice. Jim doesn't gossip, and Mary really seems to have become a remarkably kind, generous person, and as happily married as anyone I know. All real, I think, but there is a bubble or two. One is Mary's new novel, which will bring her maybe a quarter of a million (she is already planning to set up a foundation for peace or something with it, though they really don't have much money)[. . . .] But no one in the know likes the book, and I dread what will happen to it in the *New York Book Review*.

Lowell's fears may have been exaggerated but they were anything but groundless. Earlier he had written Bishop that Elizabeth Hardwick had declared it to be "an awful fatuous superficial book." Knowing what he knew, and seeing the book the way he did, he wanted to believe that the author herself did not think much of it.

I've now read it through, and in my usual see-sawing, indecisive way, have formed two opinions: 1) bad, that it is a very labored, somehow silly Vassar affair [. . .] 2) good, a kind of clearness and innocence, trying to be kind to the characters—one feels she often made them dull so as not to resemble any of her real class-mates[. . . .] I doubt if she feels it's much of a masterpiece, still the excitement of a first commercial success is intoxicating.

Rarely, if ever, had Mary seen the novel as a masterpiece. But such reservations as she harbored had quickly evaporated, as they tend to evaporate for most writers in the excitement of finally reaching the finish. For the moment this problem child of her imagination was a favorite. What, then, was this problem child like? For one thing, it purported to tell the story of eight young women who roomed together their last year at Vassar in a large suite in the South Tower of Main—a suite identical, as it happened, to the one in which she herself had lived with her group as a senior. For another, it told this story from multiple points of view. Rich in period details, the novel opened with a gabble of voices, one week after commencement, at the wedding of Kay Strong to the actor Harald Petersen.

### FROM *THE GROUP*

Paying the driver, smoothing out their gloves, the pairs and trios of young women, Kay's classmates, stared about them curiously, as though they were in a foreign city. They were in the throes of discovering New York, imagine it, when some of them had actually lived here all their lives, in tiresome Georgian houses full of waste space in the Eighties or Park Avenue apartment buildings, and they delighted in such out-of-the-way corners as this, with its greenery and Quaker meeting-house in red brick, polished brass, and white trim next to the wine-purple Episcopal church.

In alternating chapters the novel follows the eight members of the group through the greater part of a decade notorious for economic and political upheaval, all the while focusing on matters romantic or domestic. Although some girls receive more attention than others, this is not necessarily a reflection of the novelist's goodwill.

**Kay Strong**, whose wedding opens the novel, has never been fully accepted by the fancy easterners she has invited to attend it. Kay, who looks "like a country lass on some old tinted post card," is the character whose life most closely resembles her creator's, but she is far too crass and fallible to be a stand-in for the author. In the end she proves no match for her actor husband, who mocks her, betrays her, beats her up, and checks her into Payne Whitney.

**Dottie Renfrew**, who was always teased at school "for her decorum and staid habits and mufflers and medicines," is handsomer than she realizes and more sensual than anyone has guessed. It is Dottie who gets fitted for the infamous pessary and who abandons it when the self-professed bounder who has seduced her leaves her to wait alone on a park bench.

**Norine Schmittlapp**, a slattern and sexual adventurer, has never been a part of the group. Because she is everything the group is not, she helps define it. "You people were the aesthetes. We were the politicals," she tells one of its members. "We eyed each other across the barricades." Married to an impotent Yale man named Putman Blake who edits a populist monthly, she takes up with Kay's husband and exacts her revenge.

**Helena Davison**, described by Kay as "a neuter, like a little mule," is "the droll member of the group." She is the class correspondent, and, to some degree, its conscience—bearding Norine in her squalid basement den and ordering her to end her affair with Harald Petersen. Helena's moral fiber derives from her mother, who did not go to Vassar—or any college for that matter.

**Pokey Prothero**, "a fat cheerful New York society girl," is the group's "problem child" and the richest of them all. Pokey managed to make it through Vassar by being "coached in her subjects, cribbing in examinations, sneaking weekends, stealing library books." Her dream is to become a veterinarian. With money anything is possible: she flies to her classes at Cornell Agricultural School in her own two-seater plane.

**Libby MacAusland**, who sees herself as "a high-bred tempestuous creature," uses every available wile to get a full-time job in book publishing and, when that fails, settles for becoming a literary agent. Flirtatious but frigid, she runs into trouble when a handsome German ski instructor pounces and, upon meeting her furious resistance, leaves her with a black eye and a badly torn dress.

**Polly Andrews**, "one of those 'gentle ray of sunshine' girls," is a model of renunciation. From a fine old family fallen on hard times, she gives up her dream of becoming a doctor and takes a job as a laboratory technician. When her married lover's psychiatrist insists that stability is crucial for his analysis, she sends her lover back to a faithless wife and takes in her manic-depressive father. At the end, when she settles down with a handsome doctor, it seems to have happened without her volition.

**Priss Hartshorn**, small breasted and "rather colorless," is the group's one "dyed-in-the-wool liberal." When the Supreme Court declares Roosevelt's National Recovery Administration unconstitutional, she loses her first job. But her real troubles begin after she becomes pregnant. Her husband, a society pediatrician eager to test his latest theories, insists she breast feed on a strict schedule, even though her small breasts don't provide their newborn son with sufficient nourishment.

**Lakey**, born **Elinor Eastlake** to a fine Lake Forest family, is "the taciturn brunette beauty of the group." She is "intellectual, impeccable, disdainful" and almost as rich as Pokey. Immediately after Kay's wedding, which she can view only with dismay, she sets sail for Europe to study art. When she returns in the last chapter, forced home by the impending war, she arrives in the company of a thickset German baroness. Lakey is a lesbian.

The novel, which starts off with Kay's wedding, concludes with her funeral in the spring of 1940. By this time we have seen what a frail implement a Vassar diploma may provide for making one's way in the world. Although we have never seen these girls at school, the college has played so crucial a role in their lives it might almost be another character. Divorced from Harald Petersen and obsessed by the notion that the Luftwaffe is about to bomb New York, Kay tumbles (whether by choice or by accident there is no way of knowing) from her bedroom window at the Vassar Club. Finally, it is not Kay's family but her old classmates who see to it that she has a fitting funeral.

### FROM *THE GROUP*

At college the group had had long discussions of how you would like to be buried. Pokey had voted for cremation with no service at all, and Libby had wanted her ashes scattered over New York Harbor. But Kay, like the rest, had been for regular burial in the ground, with a minister reading the funeral service over her—she loved the "I am the Resurrection and the Life" part (actually that came in the service, not at the open grave), which she used to recite, having played Sidney Carton in a school dramatization of *A Tale of Two Cities*. And she hated embalming; she did not want to be pumped full of fluid[. . . .] How like Kay it was to have such violent preferences, her friends agreed. After all these years [. . .] the group could still remember exactly what she liked and what she despised. And she had never grown older and wiser. This had made it easy for them—sad to say—to get her ready for the funeral.

In its tone and in its subject matter, *The Group* was nothing like the novels that had preceded it. Here were no intellectuals or artists, no attempt to reconcile individual morality with the demands of society. Reading it in manuscript, Robert Lowell had cause for confusion, and time to waver between qualified respect and outright disapproval. The author, however, had no time for second thoughts. Down to the wire, she was caught up in the details of production—suggesting a chain of eight daisies for the front of the dust jacket; approving a full-length photograph for the back which showed her gazing out over a Paris skyline; spending hours on the telephone, going over reams of page proofs with the copy editor, attempting to make the text perfect within the restricted space allotted for last-minute adjustments.

Once there was nothing further she could do to assist with editing or production, she was caught up in the publicity that was to herald the novel's publication. *Life* sent a staff reporter to sit with her for hours and record her opinions on anything that caught her fancy. The reporter was young and personable and she found she had a lot to speak out about.

That August at Bocca di Magra she was soon meeting with a photographer and reporter from *Newsweek*, which had promised her its cover. A summer vacation might seem to guarantee a respite from the excitement attending the book's publication, but even though she was convalescing from hepatitis and was very much occupied with providing care and entertainment for three active children, she could not always bring herself to say no.

**MIRIAM CHIAROMONTE**   I remember reading reviews on the beach at Bocca di Magra with her and Mary's being pleased with some and not with others. *The Group* did not give her the kind of success she especially wanted. But she enjoyed having a public life. I know that there were reporters who came around and took pictures for two days and followed her everywhere, and Mary was enjoying it. She loved performing. She loved interviews. When did she sell the movie rights? I remember she got a lot of money and made marvelous presents to everybody. She got me the most beautiful white bathing suit.

The most expensive present she bought was for Jim West—a white Mercedes convertible coupe so magnificent he would hold on to it long after it had outlived its usefulness. For the children, she rented a house in the country where they could all be together for weekends. For herself, she made do with some additions to her wardrobe.

**EILEEN SIMPSON**   As the money began to roll in, Mary went on a shopping spree. Until then I had thought that, like many intellectual women I knew, she cared little about clothes. How wrong I was I saw when she returned from the couturier houses with Chanel suits and Balenciaga coats. When I admired a pair of espadrilles she was wearing, she said, laughing at the fun of it, that she had bought three pairs at Lanvin.

**ROSAMOND BERNIER**   Now that she had more money she would go to the boutiques. She wanted to be smart. But she had no notion really.

*The Group* sold to the movies that fall, for the astonishing sum of $162,500. When Otto Preminger finally decided to pass, it was optioned by Charles Feldman, a former agent, who hired as his director Sidney Lumet, a former television director whose first film had been *Twelve Angry Men*. To protect his investment Feldman went on to spend $50,000 on promoting the book. But already on Sunday, September 8, *The Group* was popping up on *The New York Times* best-seller list. By September 22 it had climbed to number three. In early October an elated Jovanovich was cabling her in Paris: "THE GROUP NUMBER ONE ON TIMES BESTSELLER LIST SUNDAY NEXT WEEK. THERE WILL BE 95,000 COPIES IN PRINT." Contributing no doubt to Jovanovich's elation was the knowledge that from their very first meeting he'd had his eye on this property and its possibilities. Although he'd had no idea where the novel was headed, he had never lost faith in its creator's ability to carry it to a satisfactory conclusion.

**WILLIAM JOVANOVICH**   I'd not read a contemporary book quite like it. Here was the narrative, an absorbing story, that managed to convey several points of view that mixed wit with sympathy, that treated women as individuals whose friendship was not inevitably dispoiled by the men in their lives. Now, I didn't think *The Group* unique. Obviously, many issues in the book can be found in other fiction of its time. But Mary McCarthy had pulled off a most difficult aspect of fiction, which was to treat at once the times and the person, the context and the event, and to do so without the reader's hearing the creaks of some deus ex machina.

With the public, *The Group* was an immediate success. With the critics, too, it did well at first—particularly with those who wrote for the newspapers and magazines the general reader was likely to see. Even when the reviews failed to agree that McCarthy had in fact pulled off a most difficult aspect of fiction, they respected her skill and ambition. More important, they acknowledged the book's importance. A week ahead of its official publication date, the *Times Book Review* gave the novel its front page. The *Saturday Review* went on to give *The Group* its cover and treat its publication as an occasion of far greater consequence than the appearance of Jessica Mitford's *The American Way of Death* or the posthumous publication of Camus's early notebooks.

### FROM ARTHUR MIZENER'S REVIEW IN *THE NEW YORK TIMES BOOK REVIEW*, AUGUST 25, 1963

In her persistently reasonable, acutely amused way, Miss McCarthy knows everything about these girls. If they seem to some readers grotesque, it is because we are made to see them, with unsentimental clarity, as all too human. Perhaps, as Miss McCarthy has implied, *The Group* is not, in the conventional sense of the word, a novel. But whatever we may call it, it is, in its own way, something pretty good.

### FROM GRANVILLE HICKS'S REVIEW IN *SATURDAY REVIEW*, AUGUST 31, 1963

*The Group* is in many ways an admirable piece of fiction and the best book [Miss McCarthy] has written[. . . .] It is perhaps as social history that the novel will chiefly be remembered: but over and above its sensitive observations it has a quality that one has not come to expect from this particular author and that is compassion.

While none of *The Group*'s early reviews could be said to be wildly enthusiastic, or particularly enlightening, they were what publishers like to call "selling." The books were in the stores and the articles and reviews were evidently doing their job, prompting even those who had never had much use for Miss McCarthy to lay out their money for a copy.

**FROM LOUISE BOGAN'S LETTER TO RUTH LIMMER, SEPTEMBER 8, 1963**

Mary McCarthy's *The Group* showed up in the little paper and book store, downtown, so I *bought* it. I'll send it on to you, as soon as you get settled. Women's secrets again, told in clinical detail: a seduction, told as though by slides in a microscope, is the best; also, various involve-ments of high-minded girls with low-minded men are wittily put forth. M.'s style has become v. sharp and economical, too. But the semi-Mary protagonist gets killed again (suicide?); while her *other* half (rich, soignée, onto everything) turns out to have been a corrupt and cor-rupting *Lesbian*, all along. V. strange! Meanwhile, there's the usual pic-ture of Mary, looking just the same as always—neat, clear featured and pulled together—gazing out over a Parisian suburb, this time.

In its September 2 issue, *Newsweek* reported that booksellers were order-ing copies of *The Group* at the rate of five thousand per day. Already it was looking as if Jovanovich possessed a gift for prophesy.

**WILLIAM JOVANOVICH**   I cannot claim great prescience. I've missed on my guesses as often as I've made them! There is a phenomenon in publish-ing: once a book gets going strongly, it picks up more and more favorable reviews, as if no one wanted to be left off the record of a success story. This applies less to nonfiction than to fiction. But success brings reaction.

The first overt sign of a reaction—or backlash—came from *Newsweek*, which had bumped McCarthy from its cover in order to make way for a long piece on the big civil rights march in Washington. The profile they ran paid due deference to her impressive sales figures and her position as America's "only real woman of letters," while portraying her as a scold whose upper lip sported a "mustache of middle age" and whose latest effort was no better than a potboiler.

**"CONTRARY MARY—VASSAR '33," *NEWSWEEK*, SEPTEMBER 2, 1963**

[T]he reader who approaches the book without the benefit of the author's indoctrination lecture gets the uneasy feeling that this is the kind of thing Rona Jaffe might have written with a better education.

The piece that ran in *Life* later that month was only marginally better. While it gave the not altogether accurate impression that she was pre-siding over a bustling Paris salon, the accompanying "Gingery Sample of McCarthy Views," presented under the heading "Lady with a Switch-blade," suggested that even in Paris the switchblade was never far from her side.

Mary McCarthy was familiar with ambitious young reporters out to do a sharp-tongued woman of letters one better. Annoying as such pieces might be, she could tell herself they held no sway with the readers who mattered to her. On the other hand, broadsides from members in good standing of the New York intellectual world were not so easily shrugged off.

The first salvo came at the end of September from Norman Podhoretz, a frequent contributor to *Partisan Review* and a sometime friend of Hannah Arendt. If there was one saving grace it was that the attack was launched from the glossy pages of Huntington Hartford's magazine *Show*, not at all the sort of place where one would expect to find it.

### FROM "MARY MCCARTHY AND THE LEOPARD'S SPOTS," BY NORMAN PODHORETZ, *SHOW*, OCTOBER 1963

A somewhat cynical critic I used to know once remarked that if writers of fiction were forbidden to indulge themselves in elaborate descriptions of dress, furniture and food—the way freshmen in composition courses are forbidden to use too many adjectives—virtually the whole tribe of contemporary lady novelists would instantly be forced out of business. He had a point, I said, but what about Mary McCarthy? Surely she was different, surely she was better than that. He snorted: an intellectual on the surface, a furniture describer at heart.

Far more devastating was a short satire credited to one "Xavier Prynne," which appeared in *The New York Review of Books*, a biweekly periodical started the previous February by Robert Silvers, Elizabeth Hardwick, and Barbara Epstein. Originally launched as a response to a long newspaper strike that had knocked out most major book coverage, the *Review* had gone on, after a brief hiatus, to enjoy an increasingly healthy circulation.

### FROM "THE GANG," BY XAVIER PRYNNE, *THE NEW YORK REVIEW OF BOOKS*, SEPTEMBER 26, 1963

Maisie had always, rather demurely, thought of the great event as a "defloration," from the Late Latin, *defloratio*. (To everyone's surprise, this sociology major had been a whiz in Latin at St. Tim's.) The funny thing was that never in the world would she have expected it to happen *this* way: on a rather tacky, flowered couch that opened out into a day bed. (Mother would somehow have minded the odious couch more than the "event.") But demure, rather strait-laced as Maisie was, now that she was here in the cold-water flat she was determined to go through with it, like Kierkegaard through clerical ordination. For this squinty, pink-cheeked girl, *it* was a duty and the old American stock in her (along with the industriousness of Mother's Chicago meat-money parents) stood her in good stead as the evening wore on. Of course she was thrilled, too.

Having taken time from her work on the novel to contribute a piece on William Burroughs for the *Review*'s first issue, she might have expected its editors to greet her latest effort with a modicum of charity. Two of the editors were casual friends and one was a close friend. In the past months they had not scrupled to solicit further pieces from her. Nonetheless, on the heels of "The Gang" there came a long review from Norman Mailer, who had not taken it kindly when she refused to participate in a public debate with him after her star turn at Edinburgh. Mailer's assessment of the book made Podhoretz's review pale in comparison. After paying mock obeisance to "our saint, our umpire, our lit arbiter, our broadsword, our Barrymore (Ethel), our Dame (dowager), our mistress (Head), our Joan of Arc," Mailer announced that McCarthy's new novel was "not nearly good enough."

### FROM "THE MARY MCCARTHY CASE," NORMAN MAILER, *THE NEW YORK REVIEW OF BOOKS*, OCTOBER 17, 1963

> She is simply not a good enough woman to write a major novel; not yet: she has failed, she has failed from the center out, she failed out of vanity, the accumulated vanity of being over-praised through the years for too little and so being pleased with herself for too little.

Not content with faulting McCarthy for a failure of nerve—"Her eye sees with a knife's edge, but her hand, overwary of drama and surprise, blunts the stroke"—Mailer faulted her for letting background details overwhelm her story. "The real interplay of the novel exists between the characters and the objects which surround them until the faces are swimming in a cold lava of anality." *The Group*, he concluded, was "the best novel the editors of the women's magazines ever conceived in *their* secret ambitions." The most he would say for its author was it was "possible now to conceive that McCarthy may finally get tough enough to go with the boys."

### FROM MARY MCCARTHY'S LETTER TO HANNAH ARENDT, OCTOBER 24, 1963

> I suppose you saw the Mailer piece and the parody that preceded it. I find it strange that people who are supposed to be my friends should solicit a review from an announced enemy but even stranger that they should have kept pestering me to write for them while hiding from me the fact that the Mailer review was coming. As for the parody, they have not mentioned it to this day, perhaps hoping that I would not notice it[. . . .] This leaves me bewildered and disoriented. I can't put myself in the place of Elizabeth Hardwick or even of Bob Silvers.

### FROM ARENDT'S LETTER TO MCCARTHY, N.D. [FALL 1963]

> I read Mailer's review only a couple of days ago—it is so full of personal and stupid invectives (stupid means vulgar) that I can't understand how or why they printed it.

It was Hannah Arendt's belief that it had been Elizabeth Hardwick who'd "had the brilliant idea" to get Mailer to write that review; in fact, it had been Robert Lowell, who had assumed, on the basis of all he'd heard and read, that she and Mailer had become great friends at Edinburgh. When *The Group*'s aggrieved author took the occasion of still another solicitation from Bob Silvers to lodge a protest, she was told by Silvers that Mailer was the most sympathetic reviewer he could find. For all that it may have sounded like a beleaguered editor's desperate equivocation, there is reason to believe that Silvers was not exaggerating.

**PAULINE KAEL**   I still lived on the West Coast when *The New York Review of Books* commissioned me to review *The Group*, so I don't really know what happened. They rejected my piece, but I don't know if that was because they'd got Mailer, or if they genuinely found my piece off the mark. I was rougher on her than Mailer was. But of course he had that condescending "now our Mary is running with the boys" attitude. I took her more seriously because I loved a lot of her earlier work. *The Group* was a real letdown. Particularly in her attitudes, which were, I thought, very snobbish. She beats up on those girls.

In two landmark essays and in two much publicized interviews McCarthy had set herself up as something of an authority on the novel. She had made much of the reliance of such writers as Dickens, Tolstoy, and Jane Austen on a heady blend of quotidian details and outright gossip to achieve their effects. Then, she had argued for the triumph of sense over sensibility. Finally, she had asserted that whereas the great novelists of the past had never held back from grappling with serious moral issues and the intricacies of a fully detailed cross-section of society, the modern novelist was a relativist, a miniaturist, and a ventriloquist, venturing no farther than the boundaries of an alien voice or consciousness.

Although she had taken care always to include herself among the ranks of the novel's modern practitioners, by merely making such pronouncements she immediately set herself apart. She also made herself vulnerable. Not only did reviewers dissatisfied with *The Group* quote her own words back to her, they proceeded to judge her by her own standards.

### FROM "CLASS OF '33," BY JOHN GROSS, *NEW STATESMAN,* NOVEMBER 15, 1963

Talking to the interviewer from *The Paris Review*, [McCarthy] divides women novelists into the schools of sense and sensibility, and brackets herself with Jane Austen as a novelist of sense. But without a firm moral basis the novel of sense soon degenerates into the novel of complacent, amused superiority. It is intriguing to speculate what Jane Austen would have made of the author of *The Group*. She might have given her the works.

Dwight Macdonald, who had recently brought out a collection of essays, saw in these attacks a paradox he had noted with the publication of his own book, *Against the American Grain*. "[T]he big dailies and weeklies have been respectful and even enthusiastic," he wrote Nicola Chiaromonte, "while the highbrow sheets have been the reverse." But for all that he sympathized with the author of *The Group*, Macdonald did not much care for the book. He liked the defloration scene but missed in the novel's gabble of well-bred voices the author's "own wellgroomed witty style." Chiaromonte felt that *The Group* was her best novel so far, but in fact he had little use for the novel as a genre.

Only in the pages of *Partisan Review* did the highbrows treat *The Group* with notable sympathy—a sympathy that may have owed as much to editorial pragmatism as to any latent generosity. Faced with the defection of longtime contributors to an increasingly formidable *New York Review of Books*, Philip Rahv and William Phillips had good reason to reach out to any writer who might be disposed to return to their ranks.

### FROM WILLIAM PHILLIPS'S LETTER TO MARY MCCARTHY, DECEMBER 12, 1963

This review of your book was not solicited. It had been written for the *Atlantic*, and for some reason, I think space, wasn't used. [Richard] Poirier and Rahv saw it and thought it should be used[. . . .] What do you think? If you're at all embarrassed by my sending it to you, it's really just plain courtesy.

### FROM "AFTER THE DAISY CHAIN," BY WILLIAM ABRAHAMS, *PARTISAN REVIEW*, WINTER 1964

Miss McCarthy's mastery of the intonations and vocabulary of what one might call "educated-banal" is a remarkable *tour de force*, sustained as it is for almost four hundred pages. Only very rarely does she falter in her discipline: then the *author* enters, and one hears: "Libby's red open mouth, continually gabbling, was like a running wound in the middle of her empty face." Or, describing Norine: "Her eyes, which were a light golden brown, were habitually narrowed, and her handsome blowzy face had a plethoric look, as though darkened by clots of thought." At such moments one is forcibly reminded of what has been sacrificed to obtain the virtuoso style-that-is-no-style of *The Group*.

Where William Abrahams saw a loss, or sacrifice, other readers no less sympathetic to the author had seen a dismaying misstep. That August, Elizabeth Hardwick, who within recent memory had written about McCarthy's fiction with great clarity in the pages of *Partisan Review*, had written a letter whose syntax seemed to betray more than bewildered admiration.

### From Elizabeth Hardwick's Letter to Mary McCarthy, August 3, 1963

I have a dozen impressions of [the novel]—at least a number of impressions. It's very interesting and very sad and as one reads along one remembers and says, Yes, that is the way it was[. . . .] All of this is done with great sympathy[. . . .] It is very full, very rich. The only thing I miss in it is YOU[. . . .] There are technical aspects that perplex me a little. I don't know always to whom the information is addressed. Is it the writer informing the reader, or is it the writer informing the girls, or the girls speaking to the reader[. . . .] All these fictional problems interest me[. . . .] What I want to say is Congratulations. I'm so happy to have this wonderful book finished and so happy that you will make money on it as we all "knew you would!"[. . .] It's a tremendous accomplishment, Mary.

In September, Katharine White chose to come out and say just how she felt about the book—a bit of truth telling which was received by the author, after a month's consideration, as a sign of genuine concern rather than an attack.

### From Katharine White's Letter to Mary McCarthy, September 23, 1963

I've always been honest with you and so I feel I have to admit that this is not my favorite among your books and for more reasons than my personal and perhaps old-fashioned opinion that in several places you went over that thin line of taste "between candor and shame"[. . . .] But this isn't my reason for not wholly liking the book so much as that I found it too much a social document and too little a novel about six or eight young women. Only one or two of the girls seemed to me really to come alive in the way most of your characters in other books and stories have.

### From McCarthy's Letter to White, October 26, 1963

This isn't a letter but a mere sign. If I don't write I'm afraid you'll think I'm angry or hurt. In fact your letter pleased me and filled me with affection for you. I love you for taking all these pains to tell me the truth. Is there any hope of seeing you in New York this next month?

Three thousand miles of ocean may cut you off from friends and family, but those miles can also provide a formidable buffer, particularly when you choose to avail yourself of one. For instance, when Rupert Hart-Davis went back on his offer to publish the book in Britain, leaving Jovanovich with no choice but to sell the contract to Weidenfeld, it was possible to remain happily ignorant of both the impetus behind the initial offer (Jovanovich had bought a majority share in Rupert Hart-Davis's publishing house) and the reason for the subsequent rejection (Rupert Hart-Davis loathed the book).

Unfortunately, once the author of *The Group* crossed the Atlantic that November, there ceased to be any barrier or cushion between her and those who had no use for her book. Because Jim West could not take two weeks off from his job in Paris, she was left to face a demanding schedule of interviews, television shows, and readings on her own. Because Hannah Arendt was teaching that semester at the University of Chicago, she had to put up in New York at a small hotel. Under the best of circumstances, her solitary state would have displeased her. Given the sort of reception she was meeting, it was particularly unfortunate. Not long after her arrival, on the eve of a sold-out reading at the 92nd Street Y, she was set upon at Dwight Macdonald's by a disappointed reader she had long numbered among her oldest friends.

**GORE VIDAL**  You've probably heard how Fred Dupee made her cry when *The Group* came out. I was not there, but I heard it from Fred. Fred said they were at the usual party and Mary did the unforgivable, saying to him, "I hear you don't like my book." It was rather unlike Mary to lead with her chin. And Fred, who was exquisitely polite, decorous, and noncombative, said, "Well, Mary, I don't like it." Then she made the second mistake. "Why don't you like it?" And he said, "Well, that's too much to go into, but you who have set such intolerably high standards for others must be ready to accept them as applied to you." With which she burst into tears.

**GLORIA MACDONALD**  She was on top of the world because she'd never had a best-seller before. She was so gay and happy. She'd come to see us for dinner. During the evening Bob Silvers called, and I'm afraid I answered the phone and said, "Mary's in and some people, would you like to come up?" And he said yes. And then it all began. Fred and Dwight were drinking and everyone was drinking, and Fred says to her, "That wasn't a very good book, you know, Mary." And she started to cry. Dwight was supposed to introduce her at the Y the next night, and she said she never wanted to see anyone again and she flew out of the apartment and ran down the street. They all ran after her. It was about 2:00 A.M. I was looking out the window. So they talked in the street, and the next morning there was this flurry of phone calls, and Dwight introduced her that night with the most loving introduction.

At one point while reading from her book at the Y, Mary laughed so hard she could barely go on. Still, a loving introduction and an overflowing auditorium could not take away the sting. She might tell herself that all that unexpected money had precipitated a backlash compounded of *schadenfreude* and envy. She might tell herself it was ultimately of little consequence. All the same, how was she to respond to the discovery that she could count on almost no one? Not only had Fred Dupee savaged her in front of a room full of listeners but "Xavier Prynne" turned out to be none other than Elizabeth Hardwick, nowhere visible during her stay in New York but nonetheless eager to make amends.

### FROM ELIZABETH HARDWICK'S LETTER TO MARY MCCARTHY, NOVEMBER 30, 1963

I am very much distressed that I didn't get to see you when you were here. I had thought that I would see you at Barbara Kerr's at least[. . . .] I am very sorry about the parody. That is what I wanted to say. It is hard to go back to the time it was done, but it was meant as simply a little trick, nothing more. I did Not mean to hurt you and I hope you will forgive it. I'm sure you know how much I value your friendship and your utterly exceptional company!

What made it all impossibly complicated was that Hardwick was married to Robert Lowell, who had done nothing to anger her and who looked as if he might again have to be hospitalized. How to turn her back on one without leaving behind the other? And how to give up a friendship of almost twenty years?

### FROM MARY MCCARTHY'S LETTER TO ROBERT LOWELL, JANUARY 9, 1964

Dear Cal, I was afraid when I left that you were on the verge of a break, and I felt as if I were contributing to it by all my own excitement and anger[. . . .] My equilibrium isn't very steady. It's mostly the success of *that book* and all its byproducts[. . . .] I welcome the sight of John O'Hara grappling up the best-seller list[. . . .] Please give Elizabeth my New Year's wishes, good ones, I mean, not bad. That's the best I can manage just now, but I will try for better. I think it's easier to forgive your enemies than to forgive your friends.

By January 1964, when she wrote Lowell of her dilemma, she was back in Paris, having had time to convalesce, if not completely recover, from the travails of her book tour, which had reached a climax with a talk at the Vassar Club in Washington, where she had announced to the assembled audience and any reporters who happened to be present that if she had a daughter she would definitely send her to Radcliffe. Unfortunately, excitement and anger were in the air and she was not the only one to see herself as an aggrieved party.

A decade earlier, when the pessary chapter had first been printed in *Partisan Review*, the official correspondent for the Vassar class of '33 reported to the *Alumnae News* that reading the story she had felt "nary a chill[. . .] no resemblance to anyone at all." Then in the summer of 1963, when the book was in manuscript, Robert Lowell had reported to Elizabeth Bishop, that it seemed to him that Mary had made her girls "dull" to ensure they would not resemble any of her real class-mates. However, by October of 1963 Bishop herself had taken a look.

FROM ELIZABETH BISHOP'S LETTER TO MAY SWENSON,
OCTOBER 3, 1963

Now I've just read *The Group*—felt I had to. Mary was a year ahead of me so I was not in her "group" (thank heavens) although we were friends. My oldest friend [Frani Blough Muser], with whom I went to school, camp, *and* college, is "Helena"—if you read it. Mary lets her off lightly! but doesn't bring her to life. I recognize . . . Mary's first husband and pieces of Mary herself, and Eunice Jessup and bits of the others— but it's too much like trying to remember a dream. . . . I admire her *gall*. I dislike the age we live in that makes that kind of writing seem necessary, though. We're all brutes.

Because Bishop did not spot herself in the novel and because she believed that its author had attempted to treat Frani Muser fairly, she was prepared to be tolerant. However, the majority of her fellow graduates could not bring themselves to be so generous. For them the book was a betrayal. In the most literal and immediate sense they believed its author to be a traitor to her class—not only to its individual members but to the class as a whole and to the entire college.

Where in these pages were the Elizabeth Bishops, the Muriel Rukeysers, the Eleanor Clarks? Why make her girls so fatuous? So in thrall to material objects? So preoccupied with sex? And why make the sex so explicit? Three decades later Mary McCarthy was dead and her classmates were still trying to answer these questions. For them the book's outrages and deficiencies remained a subject of perpetual interest, even when they could bring themselves to regard this subject with something approaching amusement. Or, if not amusement, then something akin to calm.

**MADDIE ALDRICH DE MOTT**   I was fond of Mary and I wasn't upset when *The Group* came out, though I thought it was unnecessarily unkind. I couldn't put it down, but I didn't know why it would be interesting to people who were not in our group. I always wondered why it was. It really isn't a good or deep novel. It wasn't really based on understanding people.

**HELEN DOWNES LIGHT**   *The Group* was obviously very well liked by the reading public. Before the days of credit cards, I used to keep seventy-five dollars of mad money in a book. We had *The Group* on the shelf in our guest room and I thought, I'll remember where it is if I put it in there. Every guest we had would come down the next morning and say, "Did you know you had money in that book?" After a while, I changed it to *The Oxford Book of Verse* and nobody ever brought it up again.

**ELINOR COLEMAN GUGGENHEIMER**   I always found it in a way astonishing that the book was so extremely popular. She totally failed to capture the feeling of the thirties. Totally. Look, the thirties got the kids to go over and fight in Franco's war. It created Communist cells on campuses. It was a period of ferment, much like the sixties, only a bit different. That was not the kind of world that she built.

**FRANI BLOUGH MUSER** In *The Group* Mary doesn't go on with any of those who went into serious work. For one thing, they usually were working so hard right after college they didn't make very lively material. They were getting further degrees or getting jobs that were fairly menial in their chosen profession. A case history would be different, but she was writing a novel. This was not a case history at all, though I think a lot of people read it that way.

For the most part, Vassar readers were sufficiently sophisticated to appreciate the difference between fact and fiction. While classmates faulted the book's author for portraying Vassar girls as frivolous or snobbish or preoccupied with sex, they faulted her, above all, for making no effort to disguise the nine real plums she had baked into her nasty fictional cake. Even before publication, there had been concern among three members of the original group in South Tower.

**HELEN KELLOGG EDEY** When we heard that Mary was writing *The Group*, Rosilla Hornblower, Maddie Aldrich, and I said, "Oh, God, we're going to be absolutely ripped apart." We took it for granted. We knew it was going to be a bitchy book. We were all extremely nervous. By then I'd read *The Company She Keeps* and *A Charmed Life*. In any case, when it came out, I said, "I don't think it's as bad as we thought." But Rosilla was infuriated. She said, "She's made me out to be this prissy prissy Priscilla." The thing that made us mad and still makes me mad is that we were absolutely clearly identifiable. And of course I'm in there. I was just plain stupid in this book. And I was *not* stupid. But Pokey's house was my house. Absolutely. There were my parents and there was our butler. Mary spent the weekend at least once. Maybe even twice. And this was how Mary repaid me.

**MADDIE ALDRICH DE MOTT** Both Mary and Helen, in totally different ways, were extremely bright. Helen was gifted at mathematics and science and I don't think Mary had a clue about such things. Helen majored in philosophy. She was absolutely brilliant. In the end she became a full-fledged doctor and then a child psychiatrist, and she didn't start until she was thirty-five.

**ROSILLA HORNBLOWER HAWES** Dottie Newton was my closest friend. Mary used Dottie's name and put her in this rather embarrassing position, and Dottie was the most fastidious, the nicest, kindest person imaginable. I thought what Mary did was rotten.

**JULIA DENISON RUMSEY** Dottie had the name and she had Boston, but, then, people would assume that the rest was true. Rosilla was furious. I think all of them were except me. I don't know about Kay McLean. I think she irritated Mary and Mary got back at her.

**KAY MCLEAN**   Mary didn't have any use for me and she could be ruthless. That was just the way she was. If you looked at the book with the idea that Mary had done all the things she has those girls do, then there was some truth to it. I have nothing to complain about with my portrait. But I think she was getting back at people. She meant to do harm.

**FRANI BLOUGH MUSER**   It was very foolish of Mary to use real names. I don't know why she did that. Always before Mary had made such a fuss about making up names for people in her books, but here she hadn't bothered. I think Mary had a naïve side. She was shocked when people like Dottie didn't like it.

**MADDIE ALDRICH DE MOTT**   There is a story Rosilla told me of how Dottie was having lunch at the Ritz Carlton in London and how Mary was there and came over to her table and made a big fuss over her and said she'd never said anything mean about her. Dottie couldn't understand all that. She was polite to her, but she was very hurt. I talked to Mary about this years later and Mary said, "She had no reason to be hurt. Nobody knew it was her."

The girls in the book were not the only ones to suffer at the hands of the author. With rare exception, the men from her past who turned up in its pages fared no better than their mates. Harald Petersen, who owed so much to Harold Johnsrud, was portrayed as a wife beater and closet homosexual, while Putnam Blake, who in just about every recognizable detail resembled Selden Rodman, was nothing short of a laughingstock.

**SELDEN RODMAN**   "Put is impotent" was her line. Obviously what she said was untrue with respect to me. Still, it was pretty cutting. I thought it was unfair. Until then I had no sense that she was angry with me. I hadn't particularly liked Mary when I first met her and Mary had been on the make for me at the time. She must have resented the fact that I didn't go for her. The last time I saw her was on the corner of Fifty-seventh Street and Madison and we were going in opposite directions. This would have been not too many years before *The Group* came out. She said, "What are you doing?" I said, "I'm writing a book about Beethoven." She said, "I never liked Beethoven." I said, "I wouldn't have expected you to."

To be fair, not everyone who provided aspects of himself or herself for the book was made to seem silly or ridiculous. Frani Blough Muser, who with her love of madrigals and her pale blue Paris policeman's cape was easily recognizable as Helena Davison, could console herself with the fact that the worst that was ever said of Helena was that she was a neuter. But if the book has a heroine it is not Helena Davison. Nor is it Kay Strong, Dottie Renfrew, Priss Hartshorn, or Pokey Prothero. For most readers the two characters who come off best in the book are Polly Andrews and Elinor Eastlake. One fair and one dark, one sweet and one tart, each is true to her nature and each, in her own way, ends up happily married. Later, Mary McCarthy would tell the critic Irvin Stock that she wrote of Polly Andrews with Martha McGahan in mind. But for Polly Andrews's physical attributes and family history she had also drawn on two members of the real-life group—Clover Benson and Julia Denison. For Elinor Eastlake there was no model that any member could spot, although that did not rule out a model in the class at large.

**JULIA DENISON RUMSEY**   I'll tell you one thing that is just an interesting sidelight. In *The Group* all these different girls are named and the one that she calls Polly Andrews I always thought was meant to be myself. She used to call me Pollyanna. She thought I was so naïve about things.

**HELEN DAWES WATERMULDER**   Nobody seems to realize it, but Mary put herself into all of the girls. For instance, Lakey is true Mary. Nobody seems to have caught on. They all think it's Kay. The description of Lakey is Mary as she saw herself. Black hair, white skin, long green eyes. It is pure Mary, and everything she did, except being a lesbian, is Mary. Lakey's life is Mary when she went abroad to live in Florence. And Lakey always has the last word.

Thirty years after the book's publication Dottie Newton was dead, as was Eunice Clark Jessup who had contributed so many identifiable features to Norine, the outsider who wreaks havoc in *The Group*. But that did not keep friends or family for speaking out on their behalf. Or from coming up with reasons why Mary McCarthy had done what she had.

**ELEANOR CLARK**   It's awkward to gabble about someone you didn't like. I didn't like Mary. I never liked her. My sister Eunice knew her a lot better, and for her pains and I must say in some cases extraordinary generosity, she got kicked in the teeth. In *The Group* she got pilloried along with everyone else. I never read *The Group* because I wouldn't read Mary at all, but I know my sister was in it.

**HELEN DAWES WATERMULDER**   Eunice never got over *The Group*. Never. It was a true likeness of her, including her untidiness but none of her brilliance and charm. The girl called Libby who goes into publishing was a friend of mine. It's not a coincidence that Eunice was the head of *The Miscellany News* and the other girl was head of the *Vassar Review*. I think Mary had a good deal of resentment and jealousy then.

**JULIA DENISON RUMSEY**   I had a funny feeling that what Mary was doing was trying to make up for the fact that she always felt socially inferior. In the social register way she was. But my goodness, she was so far ahead of us intellectually.

**HELEN DAWES WATERMULDER**   The people she used couldn't get back at her and she knew it. She picked on very conservative ladylike people who would never sue her. You would think that Mary, who was vulnerable under that hard exterior, would know how vulnerable these women were. After all, she had suffered abuse as a child. But, then, they always say that those who are abused as children go on to be child abusers themselves.

At the book's publication, some of the ladylike people who were used in *The Group did* get back at the author. To do this they did not resort to a lawsuit and they did not confront her directly. Instead, they took advantage of a generous offer from a *New York Herald Tribune* reporter, who promised them anonymity in exchange for a frank and uncensored discussion of what Miss McCarthy had wrought. By resorting to the printed page instead of the courts they spared themselves unnecessary legal costs and unwanted publicity. By consenting to have their opinions set forth in the book pages of a major newspaper they simultaneously invaded the author's territory and behaved in a way that was totally out of character.

"Miss McCarthy's Subjects Return the Compliments," by Sheila Tobias, ran on January 7, 1964, on the *Book Review*'s front page accompanied by a dramatic but far from flattering photograph of Miss McCarthy in profile. It would seem that Sheila Tobias had spoken to the real-life models for Libby, Pokey, Priss, and Norine. Almost to a woman, they expressed the opinion that the author of *The Group* had been out for revenge. After dissecting her methods and her motives at some length, they went on to pay Miss McCarthy back in kind.

FROM "MISS MCCARTHY'S SUBJECTS RETURN THE COMPLIMENTS,"
BY SHEILA TOBIAS, *NEW YORK HERALD TRIBUNE,* JANUARY 7, 1964
 "She had that harsh angular hair-do, the one she still wears today. She may, in fact, be the only Vassar girl not to have changed her hair style in 30 years. Perhaps she takes care of it now, but then there was always some clump of hair out of place." This from a woman who found important pieces of herself written into [. . .] the character of Libby MacAusland[. . . .]
 "Mary was sort of a beatnik," another member of The Group told me. "She appeared unwashed and unbrushed—always kind of gray. You certainly wouldn't have thought of her as a sex object." This from a New England woman who was close to the girl called Dottie Renfrew in the novel[. . . .]
 "A love affair with Vassar?" another classmate, a non-member of The Group and almost certainly the much-maligned Norine in the novel, said with a hearty laugh. "The only thing Mary learned to love at Vassar was the sound of her own voice."

There are two ways to respond to such an attack. You can keep silent and try to ignore it, hoping it will soon blow over, or you can mount a full counterassault. Unlike her classmates, the author of *The Group*

behaved perfectly in character. After waiting a month, she sent off a stinging two-page letter to the editor of the book review, letting her know that,
for her, reading the piece had been like "getting a collection of anonymous letters."

First off, she set about correcting the factual errors: she had *not*
received $500,000 for the screen rights to *The Group*; Hartshorn did not
have a final "e"; and *The Group* was *not* a *roman à clef*, since the girls in
the novel were "modest wallflowers unknown to the public," ruling out
the possibility of any "guessing game." More important, Polly Andrews
was *not*, as Miss Tobias suggested, a composite. She was "a real person,"
whose poverty had apparently "rendered her invisible to the classmates
Miss Tobias 'contacted.' "

Miss McCarthy, as it happened, had expected the "real" Dottie Renfrew and the "real" Priss Hartshorn to understand that "these characters
were fictions, gay improvisations on some theme, often a minor one, of
their natures." Where there had been an improvisation that was
unfriendly, there had been no real girl involved. But she did not leave it
at that. She went on to strike back at those classmates who had been so
bold as to take her to task before the whole world.

### FROM MARY MCCARTHY'S LETTER TO MISS ROSENBAUM, FEBRUARY 6, 1964

Libby is a blend of several ghastly girls, none of them members of my
group at Vassar, not all of them Vassar girls, and none of them close to
me. In fact I don't know where most of Libby comes from, though I
seem to have heard her voice all my life[. . . .] As for Norine, if I were
a person who recognized herself as Norine Schmittlapp, I would keep
quiet and decline to be interviewed. But it's the essence of Norine-ness
to talk for publication[. . . .]

I did not write [*The Group*] to pay off old scores, and if in the course
of writing it, I did pay off a score or two, this was only by the way. A
piece like Miss Tobias', I should think, must be much more embarrassing to the girls of the South Tower than my novel, since in her text
they appear so much more commonplace and disagreeable than the
girls in *The Group*.

Truth of course was what she was after. And the truth of the matter, as
she saw it, was that she had written the book to get back at no one. But
her letter to Miss Rosenbaum had not always ended with this ringing
declaration. Originally she had gone on for two more pages, trying to
explain why the "notion" that she was "still wincing from a sense of
social inferiority" was "improbable": Although freshman year she had
"*hated* the group" or at least those members of it she knew, by senior year
she had been "delighted" to join the group in South Tower even though

she recognized that she was "not really" a member but only "a sort of guest."

## FROM THE DRAFT OF MARY McCARTHY'S LETTER TO MISS ROSENBAUM, FEBRUARY 6, 1964

[T]he group and my position in it were not a source of great emotional concern to me then[. . . .] Only one time I remember caring acutely, and that was during Christmas vacation. As a girl from the West Coast, I had the usual problem of where to spend the holidays[. . . .] In previous years I had been invited to stay with one or another classmate or I had stayed with the man I was engaged to, signing out with a fictitious address. But this year he was not in New York, and no one invited me to stay with them[. . . .] I don't know how this happened[. . . .] But to me this was the most horrible thing that had ever happened—to have [to] stay on at Vassar, where a skeleton building was kept open for the few pariahs that had to remain. It was as public as being in a pillory[. . . .] I think the group had decided jointly to be hard, not to let themselves be "used"; society people are capable of this deaf hardness; it is part of their "training." Anyway, the day came; everyone left, very gaily, and I was alone[. . . .] Then, at the last minute, someone relented toward me.

Having gone this far, McCarthy went on to say, "Reading this over, I wonder whether I have forgiven this—I mean, the original decision to leave me to my fate in Main Hall. Could I have written *The Group* to show them? Maybe? Who knows? They don't, certainly. But at the time I didn't blame any of them individually. Perhaps I did not dare. To blame them would have been to accept the thing that was happening to me as real." Long ago she had put the church and psychoanalysis behind her. Both, she believed, fostered a form of personal scrutiny that mistook confession for a true moral reckoning. Both offered a form of cut-rate absolution. Psychiatry, she would sometimes say, tended to foster self-pity. It would seem that she spoke from experience. Here, by pausing to take a second look at her motives, she sank into a quagmire. Wisely, she put the final two pages aside. All the same, she saved them. They, too, after all, were part of the truth.

Seeing the truncated version of her response published provided some satisfaction, but it did not put the matter to rest. As late as 1979 she would be writing Elizabeth Bishop a two-page letter, trying to mend a rupture in a friendship that mattered a great deal to her. Bishop, who had initially greeted the book's publication with restrained amusement, had gradually been persuaded by friends that she was the model for the lesbian in the book. Not only was she the model for Lakey, friends told her, but Lota de Macedo Soares, her Brazilian lover, was the model for the baroness.

### FROM MARY MCCARTHY'S LETTER TO ELIZABETH BISHOP, OCTOBER 28, 1979

> Lying isn't one of my faults, and I promise you that no thought of you, or of Lotta [*sic*], even grazed my mind when I was writing *The Group*. The character Lakey owed a little something to Margaret Miller but only in her appearance—the Indian eyes and the dark hair—and in her Fine Arts studies. There was also something of Nathalie in her—a kind of hauteur or fine anger maybe or fathomless scorn. As for the Baroness, I can't remember where I got her if she came from real life at all[. . . .] I can see how someone could imagine that you, as a Vassar contemporary, might be expected to figure in *The Group*. It's perhaps even strange that you didn't, but that is the fact[. . . .] Well, this is a bore for you, and I won't say more. But please do believe me.

Even in old age, the author of *The Group* continued to believe that the truth will set you free. If she could nail down the facts of the case, all might be well again. The trouble was, Bishop was dead by the time the letter arrived, felled by a cerebral hemorrhage. But back in 1964, her letter writing had met with better success. After the *Herald Tribune* printed her response to Miss Tobias, she heard at once from a "real" member of the group who had contributed attributes to Polly Andrews.

### FROM JULIA DENISON RUMSEY'S LETTER TO MARY MCCARTHY, MARCH 8, 1964

> While I couldn't have written you my subjective criticism of your book, *The Group* (I could only *tell* you face to face if we ran into each other), I can and must write you my entire—sub and objective—agreement with your letter finishing off the parastic, dishonest, sensation hunting Miss Tobias! Only: you shouldn't have answered her, even this indirectly[. . . .] So, Mary dear, this is to congratulate you on (I hope) putting Miss T. in her rightful *low* place. I'm mad at *you*, of course; but for totally different reasons. You have intellectual integrity to the nth degree . . . in fact, that may be the trouble—you were too bright for us (and the "us" includes yourself). Yet I think of you, always, with fondness—no matter that surprise has recently been mixed with that.

She also heard from the "real" Helena Davison, who had for some years been sadly absent from her life. Reading the book, Frani Blough Muser had not only "laughed out loud" but had experienced some difficulty wrenching herself back to the present. The bad news was that a detail she had used about Helena's mother's sitting and washing the family china in a little basin at the breakfast table was a mistaken attribution: Mrs. Blough had never done such a thing in her life. "I'm relieved to hear she hasn't read it," Mary wrote Frani, "for I doubt whether she would have recognized that Mrs. Davison was the book's Heroine."

Precisely one year after she had turned in the finished manuscript of *The Group*, Mary McCarthy was announcing with evident sincerity that the only character she was prepared to see as a heroine was a woman who had not gone to Vassar and had not even attended college. But that January, writing to Lowell, she'd already had intimations that the book was a big mistake. And while John O'Hara might in time supplant her at the top of the *New York Times* best-seller list, it was never going to obliterate from memory the painful incidents of the past months.

### FROM "ODE TO A WOMAN WELL AT EASE," BY EILEEN SIMPSON, *LEAR'S,* APRIL 1990

During this time of excitement about *The Group* I met Mary coming out of Elizabeth Arden's one day and was stunned to see that she had had her hair bobbed. She made little of the radical change, saying she'd simply grown tired of the old way. Since, as she herself said, she didn't change her habits easily—she never accepted synthetic fabrics, still smoked, drank martinis, and wore her stockings rolled—I wondered if the haircut had been Jim's idea. No, no, she said impatiently. It had been her idea and hers alone. Fifteen years later when I was in London I discovered the real explanation. In an *Observer* interview she was quoted as saying, "I hated it when *The Group* got the best-seller treatment; there was a time when I thought it had ruined my life. I didn't like the exposure; it made me into a different kind of person. I had to change my hairdo; I couldn't stand the sight of that bun in photographs. And I hated the whole business of interviews and TV. I felt I'd been corrupted . . . I had been corroded perhaps more than corrupted."

With a simple trip to a good hairdresser she could rid herself of that bun. However, there was no way she could rid herself of *The Group*, which continued to linger on the best-seller list through the summer of 1964, just as Jovanovich had plotted and planned for it to. And she could not rid herself of the memory of what her classmates had said.

**WILLIAM JOVANOVICH** It perhaps speaks of our trust in each other that once, in Stonington, Connecticut (where she and Jim rented a summer place not far from James Merrill), she said to me, "Few things have hurt me so much as being called 'dirty' in my appearance" by some of her Vassar classmates.

That summer, she and Jim West decided to bring the children back with them to Stonington for the second mandated home leave of their marriage. They were living in a small fishing village more than two hours north of New York. Even so, she could not escape the fallout from *The Group*.

**KAY MCLEAN**   There was a big hullabaloo at the club as to whether they would let Mary and her husband have guest privileges. I was at the meeting when it was brought up and I did nothing one way or the other. I always felt a little guilty that I hadn't done anything, but I didn't want to get my mother all upset. My mother, who was a Vassar graduate, got hold of the book and read it and was so horrified she didn't think it ought to be sent through the mail.

Without the help of Kay McLean, she was able to secure guest privileges for her husband's children. But while she could easily dispense with most of her old classmates, she was finding that there were some people she could not manage to live without. Before long she was once again subscribing to *The New York Review of Books* and corresponding with Elizabeth Hardwick and Bob Silvers. At the age of six she had lost the two people she loved best. For all her reputation for intransigence, she was reluctant to lose people she cared about.

*The Group* would go on to stay on the best-seller list for almost two years. It would be banned for obscenity in Ireland, Australia, and Italy. As *Die Clique* it would sell a quarter of a million copies in Germany. By 1991 sales would total more than 5 million copies worldwide. However, by the fall of 1964, *The Group* was no longer the only novel by a literary writer to make the best-seller list. That September, when she was back in Paris, William Jovanovich wrote to say that Saul Bellow had joined her there.

A decade earlier McCarthy had done everything possible to secure Bellow a National Book Award. Now, little as she happened to like this new novel, she did her best to provide the sort of support she herself might have appreciated. At Cap d'Antibes, in the spring of 1965, she helped secure for *Herzog* the Prix Formentor, an award underwritten in part by her current London publisher, George Weidenfeld.

At Cap d'Antibes, she was once again the queen of a conference. But she could not escape all memory of the unpleasant critical reception of her own most recent novel or shrug off the news she had received earlier that spring that back in America there was a dark princess waiting in the wings, ready to take center stage.

**JOHN GROSS**   Our meeting there was somewhat handicapped by the fact that I'd written an essentially adverse review of *The Group* in England. It was quite clear from the review, I hope, that I admired her in general, but I wouldn't have been pleased to read it as an author. I don't know if she ever directly alluded to the review, but she didn't have to tell me. There was a constraint—which I suspect may have been more in my head than hers, but I think that's partly because Mary took a decision on me. She took a great shine to my wife, Miriam. She could be very emotional, but she was a very hardheaded and cut-and-dried person in many ways. I remember her saying to me at that same meeting of Susan Sontag, then a new name, "She doesn't sound very good news." Susan Sontag was my generation and she was just coming over the horizon. I think that made me think, Well, if she feels that way about Susan Sontag, what can she feel about me?

As it happened, Mary McCarthy *had* a copy of the John Gross review in her files, but she could not go on quarreling with everyone who attacked the book. And she could not completely ignore Susan Sontag, a striking young writer from California who had published a novel called *The Bene-factor* and written a couple of theater chronicles for *Partisan Review* and who, with the publication of a piece called "Notes on 'Camp' " in *Partisan Review*, was suddenly being touted as the new Mary McCarthy. Indeed there had been a piece by Susan Sontag in the issue of *The New York Review of Books* that featured the parody of *The Group*. In case she failed to take note of the attention Sontag was receiving, Philip Rahv had taken care to apprise her of it, with predictable results.

**FROM PHILIP RAHV'S LETTER TO MARY McCARTHY, APRIL 9, 1965**
I find New York quite different from what it was three years ago, when I lived here last. Susan Sontag's "Camp" style is very much in fashion, and every kind of perversion is regarded as avant-garde. The homo-sexuals and pornographers, male and female, dominate the scene. But Susan herself, who is she?—in my opinion, above the girdle the girl is a square. The faggots love her because she is providing an intellectual rationale for their frivolity. She, in turn, calls me a conventional moral-ist, or so I am told.

**SUSAN SONTAG**   "She's the imitation me," or "she's the ersatz me," Mary McCarthy is reported to have said, though no one has been able to pin down when she said it or to whom. Mary McCarthy was, with the exception of one waspish remark, unfailingly polite and friendly to me.

As critics, the two writers' styles were totally different. Sontag, like the French intellectuals she admired, made it her mission to analyze, expli-cate, and place in a larger context writing she believed to be important. Mary McCarthy, on the other hand, was almost always on the attack. Nonetheless, in their early careers there were certain similarities. Both could count on being the smartest and most beautiful girl in the room. Both were from the west and were in the process of self-creation when they met up with an established eastern intellectual. Both took up with these powerful older men and had sons by them.

Naturally, neither Sontag nor McCarthy was inclined to see such com-parisons as flattering. If anything, Sontag viewed the whole business as a bit of troublemaking by the boys. In the interests of this troublemak-ing, she had been asked to write a review of *The Group* by one of the big periodicals, an offer she immediately declined. No one had gone so far as to approach McCarthy to review *The Benefactor*. Still, there was no avoiding its much discussed author. But while there was no avoiding Sontag in print or at the home of mutual friends, she saw no reason to get to know her better.

**SUSAN SONTAG**  Mary came into the room like an aircraft carrier. She wasn't folks. I mean, she behaved like a society matron. There was Mary and there was a space that was cleared around her. You felt that if you sat next to Mary and said, "Hello, Mary. How nice to see you," she'd say, "Really?" She wasn't contentious, but there was a barrier. It was sort of: Prove that I should be friendly. She was twenty-one years older than I was. She was a dowager. I didn't think she was beautiful, but she was attention grabbing. Not because of her manner but because of a kind of intensity she had. I must have met Mary at the Lowells. That would have been the connection. The first time we met, I remember she said to me, "Oh, you're not from New York." She obviously knew nothing about me, but she had some idea that I was this up-and-coming New York whatever. I said "No, actually I'm not. Although I've always wanted to live here, I feel very much I'm not from here. But *how* did you know?" She said, "Because you smile too much."

Mary McCarthy knew another bright and ambitious girl from the west when she saw her, but that did not mean she was about to reach out to her. And she was not about to accept with good grace the fact that when it came to sexually explicit best-selling novels by literary writers there seemed to be a double standard. Her big best-seller had been given at best a grudging respect for craftsmanship. Bellow's best-seller was treated as a major literary breakthrough, even by those who did not much care for it. Of course Bellow had not written a book that appealed primarily to women and Bellow had not received quite the media attention she had. In addition, he had not sold the rights to his book to Hollywood.

In 1966, just when the public exposure from *The Group* promised to subside, the big-budget Technicolor movie made by Sidney Lumet came out with great fanfare. Along with Joan Hackett as Dottie, the movie had Shirley Knight as Polly and an astonishingly beautiful Candice Bergen making her acting debut as the lesbian Lakey. Back when the rights had been sold, Mary had agreed to meet with the screenwriter, Sidney Buchman. After one brief meeting, neither Buchman nor Lumet had deemed it necessary to consult her again. Despite this, the two Sidneys' script was remarkably faithful to the book's words. It was the book's satiric spirit that seemed to elude them. But by 1966 its author had learned not to expect too much from anything having to do with *The Group*.

**NICHOLAS KING**  I went with Mary to the first showing of *The Group* in Paris. It was in a small screening place. She'd invited us. She didn't like when they kept saying, "Who'd have thunk it," but she liked it visually. Inevitably the movie boosted her into the limelight. And on the whole it wasn't bad. At the end, at the funeral, I heard her say, "It'll do."

Although she tried to view the movie with detachment, she struck a very different note a few years later, when William Abrahams thought to send her a new collection of pieces by Pauline Kael, which contained a sobering account of how *The Group* had been dismissed as soap opera by the film's director and young actresses, all of whom seemed to have no "notion" that the author of *The Group* was both a great literary figure and a great "culture heroine." It also contained a brief critique of the novel, which gave some indication of the tenor of the review turned down by *The New York Review of Books*. Rather than reply to William Abrahams, she wrote directly to Kael, correcting factual errors and setting her straight on one important point.

### FROM "THE MAKING OF *THE GROUP*," BY PAULINE KAEL

Mary McCarthy has always satirized women. We all do, and men are happy to join us in it, and this is, I think, a terrible feminine weakness—our coquettish way of ridiculing ourselves, hoping perhaps that we can thus be accepted[. . . .]

The most condescending, most sanctimonious, the phoniest dialogue in the movie (and it's right out of the book) is uttered by dear little Polly and is intended to show what a fine girl she is. She tells Gus LeRoy that she set out to be a doctor. And he says, "Too late now?" and she says, "Well, not if I had Libby's drive, I suppose—or Kay's." Gus says, "You think you haven't?" and she answers, "Worse, in college, I never cared particularly for people with drive—or those most likely to succeed. The truth is, the only way I could like assured, aggressive girls was to feel sorry for them"[. . . .] I don't think there's any doubt that Polly is here speaking for the author because the structure of the book says the same thing: that the quiet girls who don't come on strong come off best as human beings. Although at the time she was writing *The Group*, she may have believed in this quietism and imagined that as the author of *Venice Observed* and *The Stones of Florence* she had become an elegant aesthete like Lakey, it is her inability to endow Polly and Lakey with the hideous believability of the others that gives the lie to the structure of the book.

### FROM MARY MCCARTHY'S LETTER TO PAULINE KAEL, MARCH 24, 1970

This is not a question of strict factuality, but you are mistaken if you happen to think that Lakey, the "elegant esthete" is an object of my admiration or that I "identify" with her. To me Lakey is a rather unpleasant person and just the right disdainful goddess for the poor Group.

**PAULINE KAEL**   She objected to my having suggested that Lakey was part of her, and she complained that she hadn't seen the piece before—as if I'd been keeping it from her. She was so crabby I didn't know any way to answer that wouldn't infuriate her. So I didn't. I was especially surprised and shaken because when I first published it—in San Francisco's *City Lights*—she had written the editor and among other comments on the magazine congratulated him on finding me.

If almost every mention of *The Group* made Mary McCarthy crabby, she had her reasons. She was still receiving letters from irate readers attacking her for her "perverted outlook on life" and accusing her of wasting her "God-given talents" writing "such filth." She was still being shunned by most of her Vassar classmates.

Seven years had passed and she had not yet put her big best-seller behind her, even though she was close to finishing the novel that was to be its successor. Much as she might like to believe otherwise, *The Group* had affected her as a writer. With its publication she had ceased once and for all to retain any vestige of the enviable literary halo of a gifted young tyro. For the playwright Lillian Hellman, whom she had once faulted for her "oily virtuosity," it was suddenly possible to say, "I think Miss McCarthy is often brilliant and sometimes even sound. But, in fiction, she is a lady writer, a lady magazine writer."

Although *The Group* had brought her a vastly larger audience, it had done her little good with the readers who mattered most to her. For the *Partisan Review* crowd her prose had lost some of the sheen that had once dazzled them. Not a few in that crowd seemed to see that sheen in the prose of a new dark-haired lady of letters who favored leather and black turtleneck sweaters. For them, and for the younger critics who were first breaking into print, the author of *The Group* was revealed as a Saint Joan who had traded her sword and armor for a tailored Chanel suit.

Indeed, suddenly there was some question as to the quality of that celebrated sword and armor. After all, if *The Group* was to be viewed as a fulfillment of her early promise, it was only natural for readers to take a second look at the work that had preceded it. Seeing this happen first with long-standing enemies and then with friends whose admiration she had come to take for granted, she could not remain unaffected. Under the circumstances it became doubly important that she follow *The Group* with a novel that demanded to be taken seriously.

That the new novel must mark a departure from her big best-seller was self-evident. Just what kind of departure was another matter. *The Group* had been written, as had all her fiction, for a coterie—a far from sizable cluster of well-educated readers who, for better or worse, had always responded to her work. But now she had to contend with an audience that numbered in the hundreds of thousands. She also had to contend with her own very natural desire to write another "big" book.

Mary McCarthy liked being recognized and fussed over. She liked having money, and at the rate she and Jim West were living, she was going to need a lot more money soon. Directly or indirectly, *The Group* affected more than her hairstyle. Once it hopped onto all those bestseller lists, there was no looking back.

# Chapter Twenty-one

# FAME

"Yes, fame is very tiresome and very tiring," Hannah Arendt wrote Mary McCarthy in the fall of 1963, when the author of *The Group* was licking her wounds from a stinging barrage of negative reviews. From the sound of it, Arendt knew whereof she spoke. For both women 1963 marked a turning point. Having learned to take for granted the esteem that comes with a well-established career in the world of letters, both suddenly found themselves in the anomalous position of being at once celebrated and vilified because of a book.

In May 1963, the Jerusalem reporting that had kept Arendt from McCarthy's Paris wedding had been published as *Eichmann in Jerusalem*. Although it purported to be nothing more than an objective examination of the trial of a Nazi official whose proudest achievement had been to ensure that the trains to Auschwitz ran on schedule, it was far more than that. Not only did it present a subversive and highly subjective portrait of Adolf Eichmann, it also offered a graphic, highly controversial history of Hitler's extermination of the Jews of Western Europe.

Back in February, when the Eichmann report had first appeared in five parts in *The New Yorker* under the title "The Banality of Evil," Mary McCarthy had been in the midst of her desperate last-minute sprint to get the final portions of *The Group* to the printers. Nonetheless, she had taken time to say to William Maxwell, her editor at *The New Yorker*, "to find it in a large-circulation magazine is startling, like some kind of white hind or an angel. As you read it, you keep rubbing your eyes."

Already, however, those five pieces were causing great consternation in the Jewish community. First of all, Arendt was being attacked for portraying Adolf Eichmann as no monster but, rather, a pathetic little bureaucrat whose cliché-ridden speech rendered him incapable of real thought. But above all, she was attacked for suggesting that by handing over detailed lists of the men, women, and children under their jurisdiction, and by urging them to cooperate fully with the Nazis, the Jewish Councils of western Europe had made it easier for Hitler. "To a Jew this role of the Jewish leaders in the destruction of their own people is undoubtedly the darkest chapter of the whole dark history," Arendt had written. But she had not left it at that. "The whole truth was that if the Jewish people had really been unorganized and leaderless there would have been chaos and plenty of misery but the total number of victims would hardly have been between five and six million."

When the *New Yorker* pieces came out in book form, disapproval of what she had done was given immediate voice in print. In *Dissent*, Marie Syrkin wrote of Arendt's depiction of the trial, "[T]he only one who comes out better than when he came in is the defendant." In *The New York Times Book Review*, Michael Musmanno, a non-Jew who had served as a judge at the Nuremberg trials, wrote, "The disparity between what Miss Arendt states, and what the ascertained facts are, occurs with such disturbing frequency in her book that it can hardly be accepted as an authoritative historical work."

What Arendt was saying, according to those who denounced her, was that the Jews had been complicit in their own extermination. Hitler's minions, on the other hand, had only been doing their jobs. In late spring, when these attacks began in full force, Mary McCarthy was in Paris, recovering from hepatitis, going over galleys, and helping with prepublication publicity for *The Group*. Understandably, while she might sympathize with Arendt's troubles, those troubles were hardly foremost on her mind. But all that changed when *Eichmann in Jerusalem* was slashed to ribbons by Lionel Abel in the summer issue of *Partisan Review*.

Arendt had been made to suffer at the hands of those she'd assumed to be trusted friends. With dozens of candidates to choose from, Philip Rahv and William Phillips had selected Lionel Abel, who had given a bad review to a previous book of hers and who now charged her with omitting and altering facts that did not suit her thesis. Above all, he charged her with placing aesthetics above morality. "If a man holds a gun at the head of another and forces him to kill his friend," Abel wrote, "the man with the gun will be aesthetically less ugly than the one who out of fear of death has killed his friend and perhaps did not even save his own life."

From the first Hannah Arendt had refused to defend herself against what she called "a political campaign," arguing, "The criticism is directed at an 'image' and that image has been substituted for the book I wrote." She did, however, provide close friends like Mary McCarthy with a four-page single-spaced memorandum, to use in any defense they cared to mount on her behalf. In September, drawing on her copy, McCarthy started to compose a response to Abel to run in the pages of *Partisan Review*. Not satisfied with her first draft, she wrote a long letter to Rahv and Phillips accusing them of taking part in what she went so far as to call "a pogrom." "As things are going now," she wrote, "I expect to open the next number of *PR* and find [*The Group*] reviewed by Lionel. Or by Eleanor Clark."

Polemical writing had always come easily to her. Moreover, she enjoyed it. It was her plan to join Robert Lowell and Dwight Macdonald in defending Arendt in the winter issue of *Partisan Review*. Unfortunately, with *The Group* at the top of every best-seller list, there was little time to spare and every reason to see the world as essentially benign. All that changed, however, once she returned from a writers conference in Madrid to find a stack of reviews attacking *The Group*—among them Norman Mailer's assault in *The New York Review of Books*, which was coming on the heels of the "Xavier Prynne" parody. Reeling from what she saw to be a two-pronged attack from editors she had believed to be *her* trusted friends, she wrote the one person she knew for certain would have no trouble understanding just how she felt.

### FROM MARY MCCARTHY'S LETTER TO HANNAH ARENDT, OCTOBER 24, 1963

It occurs to me that a desire to make a sensation has taken precedence in New York over everything else[. . . .] If I am upset, I can imagine what you must be. And combining being upset for you and upset for myself has made my head spin. In this revolving door one is caught without an exit, and in this multiple vision—like a Picasso image—there is no cheek left to turn.

### FROM ARENDT'S LETTER TO MCCARTHY, N.D. [FALL 1963]

I am afraid that Elisabeth [*sic*] had the brilliant idea to ask [Mailer]—just as she had the brilliant idea to ask Abel to do the *PR* piece. I asked her and she said "yes"—so no doubt about *PR*. But she probably would not have done either if there had not been fertile ground for precisely this kind of stab-in-the-back. And what surprises and shocks me most of all is the tremendous amount of hatred and hostility lying around and waiting only for a chance to break out.

At the beginning of November, with her response to Abel still unwritten, McCarthy went on to New York to do the interviews and readings and book signings that help keep a book on the *Times* best-seller list and to experience, in person, what it feels like to be treated to the "honest" criticism of friends over dinner or drinks. She was more than happy to leave all this behind and join Hannah Arendt in Chicago, where Arendt was teaching philosophy at the University of Chicago. Although the two friends had had their share of difficult moments during the breakup with Bowden Broadwater, this visit was a success.

On her return to Paris, she finished her "attack" on Abel before Christmas, ignoring William Phillips's warning that many people in New York thought *Eichmann in Jerusalem* was not merely "bad" but "full of errors and quite biased." Speaking no German, she made no effort to consult primary sources or the trial transcript. Moreover, she took her friend's position on the culpability of the Jewish Councils as a given—something most Jewish intellectuals were not prepared to do then, or decades later.

**SAUL BELLOW**   I believed that what Hannah said about the Jewish Councils was probably true. But the idea that it was possible to resist the kind of brilliant total organization of the death squads and the SS and all the rest of that . . . In reading German romantic literature Hannah had absorbed a certain amount of heroics. I think she felt it should have been possible for the Jews to organize more resistance and not fall so readily to the Nazis. But then everybody fell. And these were nations. Once they were in the clutches of this tremendous organization there was no chance for them.

**ISAIAH BERLIN**   Saul Bellow is rightfully angry with Hannah. My position is that anything they did is fine. You can't judge them at all. Whatever they did they did. Moral philosophy was not invented for this purpose. It's a case of horror. And the idea of lecturing them afterward from New York—saying they should have died, they should have committed suicide—the arrogance. If you saved a few lives, why not. Sixty people are alive who might have been dead. That's quite a good thing.

Well aware that the best defense is a strong offense, Mary McCarthy began her piece by stating uncategorically that it was a special breed of reader who failed to see the beauty of *Eichmann in Jerusalem*. She then went on to get in a few licks on Hannah Arendt's behalf.

### FROM "THE HUE AND CRY" BY MARY McCARTHY, *PARTISAN REVIEW*, WINTER 1964

When I read *Eichmann in Jerusalem* in *The New Yorker* last winter I thought it splendid and extraordinary. I still do. But apparently this is because I am a Gentile. As a Gentile, I don't "understand." Neither do any of my Gentile friends and relations, who speak about it to me in lowered voices[. . . .] It is as if *Eichmann in Jerusalem* had required a special pair of Jewish spectacles to make its "true purport" visible[. . . .]

As a reader, Abel claims to feel that Eichmann "comes off so much better in the book than his victims." This is given a priori, though it is also his conclusion, which is arrived at by a vicious circle—the term never sounded more apt. "Eichmann is aesthetically palatable, and his victims are aesthetically repulsive," he finishes, as he began. He offers no evidence on behalf of this idea. He can defend it, if he wishes, as his personal impression. But this is more of a judgment of Abel than of Miss Arendt: reading her book, he liked Eichmann better than the Jews who died in the crematoriums. Each to his own taste.

Revenge was not her only objective. She wished to convey the splendor and generosity of her friend's intentions. Above all, she wished to convey how much her friend's book had meant to her.

> I took the book as a parable for the Gentiles in the widest sense of the word, *i.e.*, the innumerable "others," a lesson in what was possible for the average man, the neighbor, who is not *forced* to look the other way when the police cars come for the "Jews"[. . . .] Miss Arendt is not interested in the safety of the Jews but in the safety of humanity. Trying to learn from history, she is thinking ahead on behalf of other "superfluous" people who may be the next "Jews" on someone's list for "resettlement in the east."
>
> To me, *Eichmann in Jerusalem*, despite all the horrors in it, was morally exhilarating. I freely confess that it gave me joy and I too heard a paean in it—not a hate-paean to totalitarianism but a paean of transcendence, heavenly music, like that of the final chorus of *Figaro* or the *Messiah*. As in these choruses, a pardon or redemption of some sort was taking place. The reader "rose above" the terrible material of the trial or was borne aloft to survey it with his intelligence. No person was pardoned, but the whole experience was bought back, redeemed, as in the harrowing of hell.

With Hannah Arendt, one of their best-known writers, lost to them, and with *The New York Review of Books* breathing down their necks, Philip Rahv and William Phillips were making every effort to be agreeable. Nonetheless, Phillips felt a need to tell McCarthy that he found her argument about the gentile response less than persuasive and some of her remarks about Abel to be "not in the best taste." She herself was not entirely happy with what she had done. "Polemics ought to be gay, but this couldn't be gay," she wrote Robert Lowell. But feeling as she did, she did not withdraw the piece. And feeling as he did, Phillips went on to publish it pretty much as written. Indeed he brought it out in the same issue as William Abrahams's positive review of *The Group*. From the one reader in the world she cared most about the response was both immediate and gratifying. From a second reader she cared deeply about the response was almost as gratifying. But not *every* response was quite so satisfactory.

### FROM HANNAH ARENDT'S LETTER TO MARY MCCARTHY, FEBRUARY 2, 1964

> Your piece, I think, is splendid—or shall I join the chorus and say: Who am I to judge? The beginning quite funny and then of such a calm sharp and, as it ought to be, essentially simple intelligence that it was a pleasure. I liked especially the paragraph about being *forced* to kill one's friend. This kind of moral turpitude, for this is what it is, seems to me the almost general characteristic of all this kind of stuff. But it

also shows how "innocent" people are when they condemn as "arrogance" every attempt at moral judgment.

### FROM NICOLA CHIAROMONTE'S LETTER TO MARY MCCARTHY, FEBRUARY 29, 1964

I have just received *PR*, and read your defense of Hannah. I want to tell you that I think it is the best it could be offered, short of an intervention by the Author herself. (What I mean is that you obviously had to slide over some insufficiently documented points . . .) Your best points, I feel, are the one about the Gentiles and the Jews. That had to be said. Also excellent is your frank statement about Hannah's not being especially interested in the state of Israel, but rather in the future of mankind.

### FROM PHILIP RAHV'S LETTER TO MARY MCCARTHY, APRIL 14, 1964

You have not answered my letter of some months back. I suppose you are angry because of my attitude to Hannah. Well, I don't think you have any reason to be so one-sidedly fanatical on the subject. There are not a few things exasperating to me in your defence of her in your article in *PR*; but that sort of thing is an intellectual question primarily and you should not let it come between us.

In the spring issue of *Partisan Review*, Lionel Abel and Marie Syrkin presented impassioned rebuttals and William Phillips faulted her for scoring "debaters' points." It was the rebuttal from Marie Syrkin which most upset her. First, Syrkin addressed the question of why so many Jews had attacked the book. Then she went on to address the "paean of transcendence." Syrkin, no mean polemicist herself, knew a soft underbelly when she saw one.

### FROM "MORE ON EICHMANN," BY MARIE SYRKIN, *PARTISAN REVIEW*, SPRING 1964

Till Miss McCarthy's sally into the field the reason for this difference seemed fairly obvious. Jewish reviewers were for the most part specialists in the areas discussed by Miss Arendt and able to challenge those errors in fact on which interpretation depended[. . . .]

[Miss McCarthy] tells us that she found Miss Arendt's account of the extermination of six million Jews "morally exhilarating" and that she heard in it "heavenly music, like that of the final chorus of *Figaro* or the *Messiah*," because of the "happy endings," the episodes in which a few Jews were saved. Miss McCarthy's acoustics are, to say the least, remarkable. She would probably suggest that a special Gentile hearing aid is required for the reception of these higher registers. Jews are too deafened by the cries of a million shot and gassed children to appreciate the full angelic orchestration enjoyed by Miss McCarthy.

To Syrkin's last point she responded at once. Precision, after all, was something she prided herself on. But she did not feel quite as confident as she sounded. Having resorted to a trope completely out of keeping with her nature, she went on to strike a penitent note no less out of keeping with her customary behavior.

### FROM "MORE ON EICHMANN," BY MARY MCCARTHY, *PARTISAN REVIEW*, SPRING 1964

If anyone is willing to turn back to the last number of *PR*, he will see that I did not find "Miss Arendt's account of the extermination of six million Jews" morally exhilarating. What I found morally exhilarating was her book, which is an account of the Eichmann trial. Nor did I say that the extermination of the Jews "made sense." One of the functions of a work of art is to give sense to suffering, such as the blinding of Oedipus. I felt that Miss Arendt's book had given sense, through form, to Jewish *suffering*; in that respect, it resembled a work of art.

### FROM MARY MCCARTHY'S LETTER TO HANNAH ARENDT, JUNE 9, 1964

Hannah, let me tell you how I regret putting in Mozart and Handel. Jim warned me, and my internal alert system warned me too. But just because of that I left it in[. . . .] Jim said I sounded too girlish in that passage, and I agreed, but I said to myself, "All right, I won't hide it." But neither he nor I ever thought that anybody would use it to show that I was exulting over the mass murder of the Jews. I don't even mind that; what I do mind is that they have used it to compromise *you*. That's why I should have shown more caution. Please forgive me, if you can.

### FROM ARENDT'S LETTER TO MCCARTHY, JUNE 23, 1964

Just one word about the Mozart business. I agree with Jim—not that it matters!—primarily because the comparison even of effects is too high. But I always loved the sentence because you were the only reader to understand what otherwise I have never admitted—namely that I wrote this book in a curious state of euphoria.

If she had erred, it had been out of love. This fact was not lost on Hannah, and it was not lost on many of those who had lined up against her.

**LIONEL ABEL**   Mary's friendship with Hannah was a very nice friendship. They were both brilliant women. But then when the controversy began over Hannah's *Eichmann in Jerusalem*, Mary felt she was going to defend her deep friendship with Hannah. And really Hannah verged on anti-Semitism.

**IRVING HOWE**   Mary had an intense loyalty and admiration for Hannah. She really worshiped her. I think Mary was pretty silly in what she wrote. It was all based on personal loyalty. It became overheated on both sides, to be fair. It was ferocious. Mary felt that we had ganged up on Hannah, although no one ganged up on Hannah very easily.

**ISAIAH BERLIN** Mary was devoted to Hannah and she was completely dominated by her. She had a powerful mind, but Hannah took her in. Sometimes these things happen. Somebody becomes completely infatuated. Like a love affair.

In rushing to Hannah's defense, she had been acting out of a conviction so strong that it could be said to be a passion. Stung by the reception for *The Group*, she had gone on to cry more on Hannah's behalf than she could ever permit herself to cry on her own. Decades later the wound would be as raw as ever.

**SAUL BELLOW** Most of the difference between Mary and me was over Hannah's Eichmann book. Mary didn't like the fact that I had criticized Hannah. Hannah and her husband, Heinrich Blücher, used to sit around and between them they would dope everything out and I think "the banality of evil" was his suggestion. Anyway, I took exception to that later on in print and Mary was furious with me. Mary didn't know beans about it. She only knew this was a cause, her late friend Hannah. As if it was a personal question between Hannah and me. And it wasn't. She wrote me a wicked letter about four or five years before she died, saying, "Hannah is in the grave and can't defend herself and you speak ill of her." At the bottom there was a note: cc to Bob Silvers. She hoped that I would reply and then she could tear me up in *The New York Review of Books*. I had no intention of getting myself into that.

**ISAIAH BERLIN** One time, after Hannah's death the *TLS* had everybody write what was the most overestimated and underestimated book and I said the most overrated book was *The Human Condition*. What happened then was Mary wrote me from Paris: "Your opinion about Hannah is reciprocal." I wrote to Paris and said, "Maybe we're both right." She wrote back, "Could I print that in the *TLS*?" I said no. I wouldn't have written it if Hannah was alive. I didn't write that to cause pain. I wrote it because Hannah was no good. The only pain of course was Mary's.

Fame can leave you feeling bruised and battered, and it can also leave you feeling cut off from your old self. In the spring of 1964, when the Eichmann business was still very much on her mind and Hannah was still very much alive, Mary McCarthy decided that the time had come to start a new novel. She wrote her dear friend to tell her the news. "And yet when, yesterday, I finally sat down to contemplate this," she wrote, "a horrible blank faced me, as when in the middle of a lecture you realize that you have forgotten the next point you want to make. It struck me there was *nothing* I wanted to say. Or more accurately, that I could not remember the person (me) who had been wanting to say something."

This most confident of writers was in trouble, and it would seem that the trouble was no mere block to be faced down with long hours before the Olivetti. Some of it may have had to do with her new celebrity. For Nicola Chiaromonte she was "the same lovable woman," but a lovable

woman who was developing a " 'literary' personality." To Dwight Macdonald he wrote of catching her one evening in Paris "literally *posing* as
a very superior 'femme de lettres.' " For him, the effect was "most disagreeable, but fortunately also comical."

Even before all the furor attending the publication of *The Group*, she'd
had reason to feel cut off from her old self. By marrying Jim West she
had become a second-class citizen in a country where she did not speak
the language with any great fluency and where her position as a writer
seemed marginal at best. *The Group*, conceived when she was a member
in good standing of the New York literary world, had been a burden and
a source of consternation, but it had also been a bridge to her former life.
So had the Eichmann controversy, in its way.

By the spring of 1964 these bridges were fast disappearing. All the
same, in England, Germany, and America—in just about everywhere but
France—there was an audience numbering in the hundreds of thousands
eager to read what she wrote next. Unfortunately, there was nothing she
herself was eager to write. A possible solution was to dash off a quick
essay or piece of reporting, but, as she saw it, an article was at most "an
evasion or distraction," no better than "loud chatter to cover up a social
silence."

For this blocked writer it was going to be a novel or nothing. As it happened, she believed she had come up with precisely the sort of novel it
was incumbent upon her to write. Always, she liked to say, her novels
started with an idea. With this new novel she was hoping to address a
question that had troubled her as far back as *The Oasis* and as recently
as "The Hounds of Summer": How to reconcile a belief in democracy
with a desire to protect what is fundamentally exclusive and elitist. In
the process she would also address the more mundane question of how
to make a life in Paris when you find yourself cut off from your friends,
your family, and your homeland.

The new novel was to be at once a way back and a departure. Instead
of placing at its center some older and wiser version of Margaret Sargent,
she planned to have a shy and awkward nineteen-year-old boy. Instead
of placing this boy in a society whose rules were familiar, she was sending him off to study in a city where he had no ties to anchor or chafe him.
More important, instead of coming at this boy aslant, she was making
every effort to approach him head-on. "The book won't be a satire, at least
not on the hero, though he has a vein of self-satire connected with his
shyness," she announced to Arendt. Still, she had some lingering doubts:
"Excuse me, Hannah, if I'm boring you with all this and tell me, please,
that it won't come out like *The Catcher in the Rye*!"

She need not have worried about *The Catcher in the Rye*. When *Birds
of America* was published seven years later, no reader would point out

that the fifteen-year-old Holden Caulfield and the nineteen-year-old Peter Levi share an obsession with lost birds: Holden with the ducks who have vanished from the little pond at the foot of Central Park and Peter with the great horned owl. No reader would point to Holden and Peter's shared longing for a golden age forever lost to them or the similarity of their fates: Holden, having nearly succumbed to pneumonia, ends up convalescing in a California sanitarium; Peter, bitten by a swan, ends up conversing with Immanuel Kant from his bed at the American Hospital at Neuilly.

If she was hoping to show up a writer she had more than once declared to be overrated, she was destined for disappointment. Salinger's triumph is to tell Holden Caulfield's story in Holden's voice and make him both appealing and believable. The one time his creator has Peter Levi put pen to paper and write his mother, Rosamund, he sounds like no nineteen-year-old known to man. Half Jewish and half Protestant, half American and half Italian, plagued by oedipal trepidations and scruples about masturbation, camping out in a series of seedy Paris hotel rooms and turning up for an occasional lecture at the Sorbonne, desperate to lose his virginity and intent on taking his spindly potted fatshedera for a weekly walk in the sun, poor Peter Levi threatens to turn into a woefully self-conscious mass of fastidious notions and high-flown ideas.

Why, one wonders, did a writer so shrewd and accomplished set out to write a novel lacking in irony and social context and virtually all the qualities that had given her best fiction its bite. She may have done it simply to see if she could do it. Or she may have done it to confound the critics who thought they knew her. She may have done it because she had a husband who had three young children to support and a highly sensitive position with an international organization—a husband who had no great liking for a slashing attack, even when it was served up with a dollop of dinner table gossip. Or she may have done it to please Hannah Arendt (to whom the book would be dedicated) and Nicola Chiaromonte, both of whom preferred her writing when it was at its most thoughtful and earnest.

As she saw it, she did it because she had no choice. In an interview that ran in the spring of 1971, alongside a front-page Sunday *New York Times* review of *Birds of America*, she confided to her friend Jean-François Revel, "I couldn't do a novel about French people, because they'd have to talk French. I couldn't even write about English people. I'm incapable of writing at length about anybody except an American, so it's not only a question of being out of touch with the native speech but of being out of touch with the native subject matter."

Despite her protestations to Revel, her life in Paris might in fact have provided material for a good half dozen novels. But, sadly, for all the pleasure she might appear to take in her new position as a "superior 'femme de lettres,' " she was not completely at ease with her new life. Her discomfort, unlike Peter Levi's, did not stem from isolation. Every August and every other weekend she had a family to attend to, and during the week she had a full social schedule. (Although she continued to make little headway with French intellectuals close to Jean-Paul Sartre, she was being asked to dine by the Rothschilds *and* by Nathalie Sarraute.) The fact was, although her days were no less vexed and varied than they had been back in America, she had little time or inclination to examine them with her legendary cold eye.

## FROM MARY MCCARTHY'S LETTER TO HANNAH ARENDT, JUNE 22, 1965

I am gasping, literally, for breath. Jim's office social life (at its height in June), mine, attempted work, family, income tax (due June 15 for foreign residents; I do our return myself); incredible pressure from publishers and journalists demanding interviews; a conference for French and African students near Mont St. Michel where I gave a lecture; the hairdresser; fittings. And worst of all the May–June American landings in Paris. Everyone I've ever known, I think, has been here, including my brother Kevin, Carmen, Tucci and girl friend, Nancy Macdonald and son Nick, the Rahvs, Arthur Schlesinger's oldest son[. . . .] The telephone shrills like an air raid siren.

Once a working elevator was finally installed at 141 rue de Rennes in the spring of 1964, she set about turning her new apartment, with its William Morris wallpaper and its carefully chosen pieces of furniture, into the sort of salon she had planned for herself all those years ago with Frani Blough.

**EILEEN SIMPSON**   It was a comparatively small apartment, but she had everything the way she wanted it—the curtains, the wallpaper, her desk. At her parties there were not crowds of people. There would be seats for everybody and you could really talk.

**ANGÉLIQUE LEVI**   It seemed to me to resemble a doll's house. In a doll's house you don't have white walls and everything is in its place—many small objects, no disorder, always ceremonious and precise. She would invite her friends to eat and feed them the way a child would feed her dolls.

Even before the elevator was installed she was inviting friends like Ivan Nabokov, and his wife, Claude, the Levis, Janet Flanner, and Sonia Orwell—along with one or two State Department couples—for a first Paris Christmas party, with eggnog and Virginia ham.

**IVAN NABOKOV** *[Moved back to Paris from New York in 1963]*   She would go to a lot of trouble for her Christmas parties. There would be about thirty people. She would buy little gifts for everybody, wrap them up, and then she'd tie them on the end of a ribbon. You would go in and she would be like a little girl and you'd have to take a ribbon and pull your gift. Chance gave you your gift.

Chance may have determined your gift at Christmas but little else was left to chance at 141 rue de Rennes.

**FRANCES FITZGERALD** *[Arrived in Paris in 1962, after finishing college]* It wasn't just that she was one of the world's great cooks. She loved to bring people together. It was more generous than just to see what would happen. It was fun. There are some people who create dinner parties like perfect flower arrangements. She didn't do that. It was more informal. She just wanted to see these people. When you got there, she acted as if she really wanted to know what was going on with you and what you thought about things. And she would never leave anyone out.

Within the expatriate community she now occupied a position much like that occupied by Jim Jones, looming larger than she might have elsewhere as an undeniably successful and generously rewarded American writer. If there were certain similarities, there were also crucial differences.

**JONATHAN AARON** *[Son of Daniel Aaron and a model for Peter Levi; took a year off from college in 1962–63 to live in Paris and take courses at the Sorbonne]* The Joneses and the Wests weren't intimate friends, but they saw a good deal of each other socially. Each household was a place where you might often find yourself amidst a richly international mix of writers and artists. Mary and Jim Jones were very different, but I think they genuinely respected each other. Jim, I remember, didn't like to be lionized or kowtowed to—he was immensely proud of his own work, proud to *be* a writer, but he didn't like being treated as a celebrity. When I first met him, I didn't dare ask him about his writing. Maybe that's why he more or less took me under his wing. Mary, on the other hand, was a touch more old-fashioned. She *did* like to be deferred to for her accomplishments. When she had people to dinner (she was a really good cook, by the way), she was too stylish to claim center stage in the conversation among her guests, but when someone would turn to her and say, "What do *you* think, Mary?," you could see her pleasure as she prepared to take command.

Although she was careful never to use Jim or Gloria Jones in a work of fiction, Jim Jones could not resist drawing a likeness of her for a short novel he set in Paris.

**FROM *THE MERRY MONTH OF MAY*, BY JAMES JONES**
I had met [Martine] at a literary cocktail at Magdalen McCaw's, a type of function she absolutely never went to. But Maggie's husband

George, who was with O.E.C.D., had had to pay off some social debts to minor Government people, and had invited Martine's, ah,—well, friend. God only knows why he brought Martine instead of his wife. Maybe he thought Maggie and George, Maggie being such a famous American lady writer, were Bohemians—which only shows how little he knew Maggie.

The model for Maggie McCaw had long ceased thinking of herself as a rebel or bohemian, but fueled by the martinis and scotch and the marvelous food and wine, one of her formal dinners might on occasion take an unexpected, if instructive, turn.

**GEORGE WEIDENFELD**   Mary was passionately interested in people's illicit relationships and clandestine affairs. She was a great gossip. She loved to analyze people's motives, particularly their ambitions climbing the social or intellectual ladders. She always wanted to know what her friends were doing and was lovingly malicious and indiscreet about them. Jim was a very good foil. Bowden was like an elegant wasp with his sting. Jim was the more staid accompaniment, the bass or counterpoint, a cello. With Jim it was better.

**MARY BRADY**   That first year we went to dinner a couple of times at Jim and Mary's. My husband did not like Mary. He was terrified of her. Because she could be so cutting. And she didn't understand a straitlaced Foreign Service officer. You never knew what tornado was going to fly across the table next.

For an American living in Paris and for a visitor from abroad, the occasional tornadoes flying across the dinner table were no deterrent. But for the average French writer or intellectual, her entertaining appeared to hold considerably less allure. The few French writers she knew spoke English and shared her feelings about Sartre and Simone de Beauvoir.

**IVAN NABOKOV**   She had a very peculiar bunch of French people that she knew. I mean, aside from Nathalie Sarraute and Calvino. A gathering at rue de Rennes always had very strange people and she could have actually known a tremendous number of interesting people. But she didn't. She could have known anybody she wanted to.

**FROM MARY MCCARTHY'S LETTER TO HANNAH ARENDT, JANUARY 18, 1965**

We had a party yesterday for Nicola and Miriam[. . . .] The whole evening made me feel that a disappointed minority was assembled here. What used to be called the anti-Communist Left—that is, the minority of a minority. And the impression was of the second-rate or also-rans; perhaps France does that to slightly marginal people.

## FROM NICOLA CHIAROMONTE'S LETTER TO DWIGHT MACDONALD, MARCH 9, 1965

All considered, I don't think living in Paris is very good for her. French literary people have snubbed her, and she has gone the wrong way about making inroads in their milieu. Too much show of money, parties, dresses, dinners, cocktails etc. Moreover, she has no real sensitivity for things French, except cooking and fashions. She would be much better off in Italy, where people care even less at bottom, but make a continuous show of cordiality. Not to count the fact that in Italy her being able to entertain lavishly would help her popularity.

**NICHOLAS KING** The French were the last people who could have appreciated her. They saw her only as someone who was an innovator and a revolutionary or whatever, fighting and battling. I was in Paris for six years when she was there. I was at the embassy and I saw a lot of her. She didn't have a French circle. She had a few people. Most of the people she saw were Americans who came through. In that way she was like Edith Wharton or Gertrude Stein. She didn't really fit in.

Much of her work during those years was on *Birds of America*, the greater part of it accomplished at an enormous partner's desk across from a framed poster of the young Franz Kafka. Sometimes, however, it was necessary to go out in the field. By this time Jim West had his job at the OECD under control and was free to walk every street of Paris with her, tracing Peter Levi's path. With Jim West she stayed close to home, but with Nicholas King she took a train out to Trappes to do a bit of bird watching with Les Jeunes Ornithologues de France. In the course of these weekend expeditions she and Nicholas King became good friends. For her King's appeal was in some respects like that of James Merrill, whom she had gotten to know during her two stays in Stonington. Cultivated and well-read, born into families with money, both men conformed to some ideal she had of an American aristocracy. Of course Merrill was a fine poet, but King was more than a mere journalist or press attaché at the embassy: he was a careful writer who knew a great deal not only about birds but about American history and the Episcopal Church, all subjects she found of particular interest. He, in turn, valued her for qualities he saw as setting *her* apart.

**NICHOLAS KING** Mary was a woman who was deferred to. She carried that with her. It's partly bearing, partly voice. She was born into a world where people were used to having their wishes obeyed. Her power and authority started from a base of assumptions. It's partly born and partly accreted. It seemed natural and inevitable in someone like Edith Wharton. But Mary had it all right. She knew what she was worth. Having met both women, I could see that similarity. The work is different, but both were in the French world living outside of it, thinking about America all the time. I don't think Mary wrote about anybody but Americans, even when she wrote about the North Vietnamese. It was her scale of justice.

Writing *The Groves of Academe*, *A Charmed Life*, and "The Cicerone," Mary had taken care to keep her efforts under wraps, but with the new novel she saw no cause to hide what she was about.

**ROSAMOND BERNIER**   One day I met Mary for lunch—she'd been working on *Birds of America* for some time—and she said, "I've just put you in my book." I thought, Oh, God. *Birds of America* is not Mary's best book, but a central character *is* called Rosamund. Instead of her last name being Bernier it's Brown. Mary didn't use my life, but I played the harp and this woman played the harpsichord. Mary told me this, you see, with that famous sharklike smile. Then she said the equivalent of "It's really about both of us." The cooking, for example. I also liked to cook very much. Then she said, "When I'm writing I have to think about your way of laughing, your way of listening." Of course the character is much more Mary than me.

## FROM MARY MCCARTHY'S LETTER TO HANNAH ARENDT, JUNE 9, 1964

> Models [for Peter Levi] are the sons of Miloscz [*sic*], a bit of Vieri Tucci, a bit of Reuel, a bit of a boy called Carlo Tagliacozzo, a bit of a *Life* reporter called Jordan Bonfante, and a boy who was at the Sorbonne called Jonathan Aaron—the son of Daniel Aaron. A charming detail about Jonathan is that he had a plant in his room, which was on a dark court, and he used to take the plant for a walk to give it light. This rueful oddity is going to be characteristic of my young hero, whose name will be Peter Bonfante. ("Bonfante" means "good soldier," though people think it means "good child.")

**JONATHAN AARON**   My parents gave me several names and addresses of people in Paris, among them Mary's. When I called her, after hesitating for a long time, she immediately invited me to dinner. She was very sweet, nothing like what, I already knew, some people had said about her. During my year in Paris, I saw her and her husband, Jim West, fairly often—maybe eight or nine times—mostly for dinner, sometimes for a party. Sometimes I'd arrive early, before Jim got home from work. A glass of wine in my hand, I'd hang out in the kitchen with her as she made dinner. I remember setting the table for her on some occasions. A couple of times, I simply dropped by without phoning her. I don't recall her ever being bothered by my presumption. I'd hear from others that she was difficult and challenging, but with me she was always quite jolly and warm. She wasn't gushy—there was always a touch of reserve in whatever she said—but she seemed interested in talking with me. She may have been conducting research, of course, but she was genuinely nice.

In the end Jonathan Aaron's contribution proved to be more long lasting than Jordan Bonfante's. But as late as 1967, her interest in talking with young men had not abated. Her eye and ear were as acute as ever. However, what she made of the information she gleaned was something else again.

**JOSEPH GIOVANNINI** *[Arrived in Paris in 1967 to do a master's degree in French.]* I met her at a party and I saw her on three separate occasions after that. I was twenty-two and I had read *The Group* and I was all impressed with meeting her. At some point—I'm not exactly sure when—she *did* tell me she was writing a book about a young American student of Italian background in Paris. We both realized that I happened to be a young American student of Italian background. There was a symmetry in the situation that was almost too obvious. But unless she was writing about an introvert I don't know that I would have offered much. Back then I was keen on observing rather than acting. I remember she told me she had kept this young American student in her book a virgin just to keep it simpler. I remember that quite vividly because *no* student at that time was a virgin.

**JONATHAN AARON** That year in Paris I had a potted geranium. I must have gotten it to decorate my room once I'd found a place to live. I went to her apartment one afternoon for tea (she told me that you should never make tea with *boiling* water). At one point, she asked me, "Jonathan, what do you do with yourself during the day?" I'd been reading the poems of Gérard de Nerval, known for walking his pet lobster on a leash in the Paris streets, so I made a joke. I said, "When I get home from school, I take my plant for a walk." She thought that was very funny and, as I found out later, she thought it was true.

It would be fair to say that *Birds of America* owed not a little to a fundamental misunderstanding. In 1971, when the book came out and she was crediting its sources of inspiration, she made much of Jonathan Aaron. At the same time, she omitted any mention of Reuel. This omission may have been prompted by a wish to preserve his privacy or by motives more complicated. As a child Reuel had played an important part in her life, but from the time he had left Portsmouth for prep school, her contacts with him had been limited mostly to vacations and holidays. Whenever she stayed long months abroad, it was Bowden who made a home for him.

Together she and Reuel had never shared an interlude like the months she gave the book's Rosamund and Peter at a New England village she called Rocky Port. The closest they had come had been a few days together first in Cracow and then in Paris when she was waiting for Jim West to leave his wife. Proud of his success at Harvard, she had taken to her heart Renata Adler, the young woman he brought to Bocca di Magra. But by 1967 Renata Adler was long gone and Reuel was now at the University of Chicago, where he was slowly finishing up his doctorate, married to a young woman she did not much care for and awaiting the birth of a child she believed he could ill afford.

**FROM MARY MCCARTHY'S LETTER TO HANNAH ARENDT,
SEPTEMBER 12, 1967**

The only other visit we have scheduled is from Reuel and Marcia on the 20th. I don't know yet how long they'll stay—rather briefly, I think. Did I tell you they're expecting a baby in January? Between ourselves, relations with them have been very strained, to say the least, during the last month. Both Jim and I are very much distressed and worried about what this portends. His relation with me is turning into that of an extremely hostile parasite. It's impossible to find out anything from him about the progress of his work [. . .] his statements on the subject are highly guarded and elliptical. I'll be glad to have your advice and good judgment about what is to be done. It's clear that the coming baby means increased support from me—with increased resentment on their part. Classic. His recent outbreaks of hatefulness may have something to do with her pregnancy. It's all directed on me; they are both beaming fondly on Edmund, who ceased his contributions several years ago.

**VIDA GINSBERG DEMING** I remember Mary and I were having drinks in the Ritz Bar and I asked about Reuel, whom I hadn't seen in years, and she started telling me that for some reason she didn't understand he was not talking to her. There had been a real schism and she really didn't know why this was. She cried bitterly. Crying was not something she did easily. And it wasn't the place for tears.

Easy irony was something Mary McCarthy had little use for. All the same, there was no question that in the course of her seven-year on-again-off-again infatuation with Peter Levi, her relations with Reuel deteriorated badly. Even when relations between them improved, they never fully recovered. Somehow, it seemed, she never found the time to put things right. In the first years of her marriage her time had been much in demand. In addition, she had a new family to occupy her. No matter what reservations she might harbor about her stepchildren she saw no reason to do things by halves. When Jim West had to take his second mandatory home leave, she spent the summer with him and his children at Stonington, where the children would have swimming and tennis and she would have Eleanor Perényi and her mother, the novelist Grace Zaring Stone, as well as James Merrill and his companion, David Jackson.

**JAMES MERRILL** Mary was very nice with Jim's children. Now, Eleanor has always had the feeling that the children—especially Alison—got a bum deal from them. But I didn't see any sign of it that summer. The climax of that summer was a huge picnic. Mary got this old Frenchwoman who lived out in the country to let us use her property. I think there must have been thirty people. Kevin and his family were there. Grace and Eleanor. Harry and Elizabeth Ford were up visiting for the weekend. There were about eight children. Wonderful wines. Rice salad and potato salad. Very elaborate hampers were packed. Those who wanted to could strip down to their suits and hop into a stream with a waterfall. It was just a lovely day. And this was her sense of showing the children something American. We didn't have flags and bunting, but it was a very grand moment.

At Stonington, she took care to show her husband's children the best of their homeland and when they returned to Paris, making use of her new riches, she rented a house in the village of Gourville, an hour from Paris, where they could all be together at least two weekends a month. Fridays Jim West would pick the children up from school and late on Sunday they would all drive back together. On more than one weekend they were snowed in. The house at Gourville was not grand but there was a separate building, a former bakery, which was well suited to the reading of everything from ghost stories to the legends of King Arthur and the adventures of Sherlock Holmes. Later on, she would rent a château in Verderone, which for all that it had "floods in the cellar, heat failures, power failures, plumbing problems, moles in the lawn, short circuits and telephone blackouts," was very grand indeed.

**DANIEL WEST**   Mary didn't laugh a lot. More than anything she appreciated other people's humor and wit. There was no idle, trivial thought. It wasn't relaxing. It woke you up to how to go about speaking or behaving but it was very formal. Breakfast, lunch, and dinner were eaten at a certain time. You didn't just go in and get a snack. Always Mary loved the idea of reading to us. This appealed to Mary as an aesthetic pursuit. I remember her reading King Arthur. Since we appreciated it, that made it all the better. She was reading for the language as much as for the story. As a child you don't ordinarily hear expressions like "bathing in tepid water."

In the summer of 1964, Maria Fourrier, who had accompanied the children to Bocca di Magra and who had been employed by Margaret West until recently, joined the family in Stonington. When word arrived from Poland of the death of Maria's father, Mary McCarthy arranged to have a mass said at the local church.

**MARIA FOURRIER**   It was then that I became aware of all her qualities. The following morning I went to the church and with me were the children and Monsieur and Madame West. We prayed for my father and there was such warmth and heart. It was something extraordinary. I wouldn't have believed it. When we returned to Paris, after I had said good-bye to the children, Monsieur West said to me, "Whenever you wish to come back to us, the door is always open." On reflection it seemed a good idea. It was easy to work for Madame McCarthy West. *Elle était très gentile. Elle était bonne et on peut dire très sensible aussi.* She was like no one I ever met. She was a person whom I adored always and admired enormously. And I think she was attached to me as well. Truly. With her there were none of the upsets you find in most households. Never. Care was taken that everything was in its place and I did my best to maintain order and peace. In that we were alike. Between us there was sympathy.

For the children, having their old nurse at rue de Rennes was a source of satisfaction and comfort. But there was no way Maria could make up for the lack of civility attending this particular divorce. Or alter the nature of her new mistress.

**DANIEL WEST**   I was never very close to Mary. She was rather formal. I felt a lot easier around my father. He was more at ease with children. We always knew we were his children. Mary was never really our mother.

**ALISON WEST**   I never heard Mary raise her voice the whole time I knew her. She pouted. She could be like an angry child. But she was also my father's strength. She was tough-minded in a way that our father was not. We always felt, even when we were little, that Mary was good for our father. And I'm sure that my father was good for her, in that he surrounded her with attention and devotion. They'd both had miserable childhoods. Neither of them had any idea of what a normal family life was like. *Their* relationship was more important than anything else, so that as children we knew that we would never be as important to them as they were to each other. They were devoted to each other.

Jim West encouraged his new wife to laugh at herself. He also encouraged her to think twice before laughing in public at anyone she regarded as her enemy. With the latter his success was mixed. In 1964, Mary McCarthy wrote a piece for *Le Nouvel Observateur*, in which she presented a matched set of unflattering portraits of Simone de Beauvoir and Jean-Paul Sartre. With great care she showed the world's most famous living existentialist and his official consort holding sway at a meeting of young Communists whose magazine had been denied further funding by the Party because its fiction was deemed too literary.

### FROM "CRUSHING A BUTTERFLY"
Simone de Beauvoir, sounding like a smiling, sharp school principal, read an existentialist lesson mixed with ordinary schoolteacher's bromides. Literature communicates a "vision of life." It is a remedy for solitude. It allows you to live in someone else's world. In one sense, she said, all writing was committed, whether the writer intended it or not, but there was passive commitment and active commitment. The bad, passive kind was when the writer shut himself up in his ivory tower. She did not really say what the good kind was. The audience applauded fervently, possibly because it was hearing familiar words.

Sartre gave an exhibition of dialectics[. . . .] As usual in his writings, he had a surprise opening or gambit. The others had talked about the *writer*; he, more democratic, would talk about the *reader*. For the advocates of "pure" literature, the reader was only a means, the work of art being an end in itself. For Sartre, he explained, the reader was an end, since the aim of literature was communication. Furthermore, the Sartrian reader is not just an end or target; he is the author's better half, his collaborator[. . . .] This, in my opinion, was clever demagogy, whose effect was to alert and flatter a mass of four thousand young readers who had not known, until then, that they too were creative.

She concluded the piece by saying that the students had asked "a serious question" and gotten "a very dusty answer," prompting one "young man" to sum up the evening by saying, "Those are the reactionary writers of the Left." Back in New York "Crushing a Butterfly" would have been regarded as part of the give-and-take of literary life. Certainly it paled in comparison with the attacks that had greeted *Eichmann in Jerusalem*—or *The Group*, for that matter. In Paris it made for consternation. For the moment at least, she ceased to be ignored.

### FROM MARY McCARTHY'S LETTER TO HANNAH ARENDT, DECEMBER 22, 1964

This has started a ten-day *cause célèbre*. The *Nouvel Observateur*, which had commissioned it, refused to print it without "softening"; they could not afford, they explained, to offend Sartre. It was then turned down with a rude note by the *Figaro Littéraire*. No one knows why, but it is thought that it was fear of Sartre again, unlikely as that seems. I finally gave it to [François] Bondy [editor of *Preuves*], who is printing it. The sad thing is that it's not even very good[. . . .] But now that it is an issue—one young writer resigned from the *Nouvel Observateur*, he claims because of this—it is going to be reprinted everywhere. In Italy, England, Germany[. . . .] Since it has become a document, I can't even rewrite it.

Faced with the perpetual adulation accorded the royal couple of the French Left, she had finally lost patience. But in a matter of months, crossing the Channel to appear on British television, she managed to practice both tolerance and forbearance when asked to debate Kenneth Tynan, who had let it be known that he could not imagine her unbending sufficiently to become part of any audience (a thrust she had repaid by asserting that rational discourse was totally beyond him). Indeed, having made up her mind about Kenneth Tynan, she showed herself to be fully prepared to change it when, in 1965, she agreed to join him on a BBC television panel on free speech (a subject about which they turned out to be in virtual agreement).

**KATHLEEN TYNAN**    That was the occasion when Ken said the famous four-letter word. When he was asked whether he would allow a play in which sexual intercourse took place to be put on at the National Theatre, Ken said,

"Oh, I think so, certainly. I doubt if there are very many rational people in this world to whom the word 'fuck' is particularly diabolical or revolting or totally forbidden." Mary was convinced he'd planned to say it. That he'd hoarded it, waiting. It amused her. She liked the drama. She came back to the apartment with Ken and we spent the evening together and immediately formed a social friendship. We saw quite a bit of her and Jim after that. I loved her company. She was tough but not mean. And I loved the getting high on ideas. It's very seductive. Ken was like that, so they were very good together. Having dinner with Mary would be an occasion. She performed. And Ken of course was a marvelous performer. There was this obligation to deliver to your friends—not just to be there. I don't know many people like that anymore who can really animate an event.

Cut off from the center of French intellectual life, Mary was not without resources. Having found satisfaction in helping more than one young man who was not her son, she was finding pleasure in helping young men who were no longer quite so young. One was Cees Nooteboom, the young writer from Holland she had first met at Edinburgh. Another was Vassilis Vassilikos, an exiled Greek writer married to an American, who had fled the military junta that had toppled his country's constitutional monarchy. Over time she introduced Cees Nooteboom to a life where hard work was well rewarded and where an impeccably dressed hostess could get up from her perfect dinner table, "go to bed and write a devastating piece on something"—a life he came to regard as nothing less than "a feat of imagination." Vassilikos she helped with the translation of his novel *Z*. But as she grew older, she was also finding satisfaction and even solace in a quarter she had rarely felt a pressing need to pay attention to before.

**EILEEN SIMPSON** I had a feeling that Mary had been teased about being always at the center of a circle of men. Or that at some point in her life she began to worry about not having enough women friends. Because from then on she made such a point of saying things like "my friend Carmen Angleton." Of course there had been Hannah and Elizabeth Hardwick, but they were not in Paris.

When introduced to Susan Sontag, she had shown a singular lack of interest, but when the right young woman came along, she was more than willing to put herself out. At the 1965 conference at Cap d'Antibes where she met John Gross, she also got to know his wife, Miriam, and her friend, Gaia Servadio, the beautiful young Italian wife of *her* old friend William Mostyn-Owen.

**GAIA SERVADIO** George Weidenfeld and I stopped at the Paris airport to pick her up. She got on the plane with this huge smile and enormous hat—very dashing. At Cap d'Antibes we had marvelous times. After that, whenever she came to London, I always gave her a big party. She and Jim came for Christmas at Aberuchill, our house in Scotland. When I was writing my first novel I remember her saying, "Gaia, when you write a book it has nothing to do with the spoken word." Of course she was right.

**MIRIAM GROSS**  Mary loved Gaia for her exuberance and her beauty. And also for the fact that she had lovely houses. And why not? I remember Mary swimming almost immediately upon our arrival at Cap d'Antibes. She didn't hang about. She was very direct and very energetic. Mary had a very strong set of ideas. I don't know quite what they were—they certainly weren't predictable—but one felt that one could easily put a foot wrong. In Mary's company it was very easy to become one's meeker self. I may be wrong about this, but I never felt that she quite understood that she had an inhibiting effect on younger people.

**KATHLEEN TYNAN**  She had this marvelous head-girl quality. There she was with her perfectly cut suit and one good brooch on the right lapel and she'd say things like "I'm going to take you to my *vendeuse* at Lanvin." I remember her taking me in hand just before I married Ken. Lanvin didn't suit me, nor I Lanvin, but I was terribly impressed that she had done this.

**FRANCES FITZGERALD**  I worried terribly about boring her. I would do anything to amuse her. This was my problem, not hers. And of course I felt, Who am I, this little college senior just graduated? I just wanted to sit at her feet.

If you were a certain kind of young woman, you did not have to actually know her to feel a great wish to sit at her feet.

**MARY GORDON**  Growing up I simply modeled myself after Mary McCarthy. For me she combined purity of style with a kind of rigorous moral honesty. A relentless moral perspective on the world. There was never anything that she did not look at morally. Since that was my particular tic, it enabled me to see that one could do that stylishly. I also identified with her very much because my father died when I was seven and I then went with my mother to live with my aunt and grandmother. My aunt was very like her aunt. It was very much that kind of denying, dour, who-do-you-think-you-are, joyless household. And then I was part Catholic and part Jewish. Before I met her, before I'd published anything, I often had a big fantasy about Mary McCarthy. I knew that she had a son, so I thought what I would try to do was marry her son and she could be my mother-in-law.

**DIANE JOHNSON**  I read *The Group* like everybody else when I was in college and I thought, This is my writer. And then I went on to read everything else. I loved the writing. I just felt, Oh, this is the way I want to write. I guess I saw Mary as that terrible, tiresome phrase "role model." The person I would like to be.

**FRANCES FITZGERALD**  She was generous toward young women—I don't quite know why that was so. It's an awfully nice quality and fairly rare. Most people in her position were men, and they would tend to have young male friends if they had any young people around them at all.

**DEBORAH PEASE**  When I was twenty-five I wrote a novel and she was so gracious. She read it and she wrote a little blurb for it. Such a busy woman and she took the time to do this.

Deborah Pease's book was not the only one by a young friend to receive her support. In 1966, she wrote a long and highly laudatory review for the English translation of *The Opoponax*, Monique Wittig's experimental novel of early childhood, a subject always of special interest to her. Both the book and its author had been brought to her attention by Nathalie Sarraute. Soon she was joining Wittig and Sarraute and some friends once a week for lunch.

**MONIQUE WITTIG**  At lunch she did not speak much. She was not some-one who would put herself forward. She did not like to speak French at all. She would sit there with a funny look in her eyes. She was amused by me and I was amused by her. She was conducting herself as though she were a queen, but she had also this shyness. Mary knew I was a feminist from the start. She would push me into a group of men, introduce me, and watch me fight battles that she would not have fought but she was not in disagreement with. When her support became too public, I told her I was a lesbian. I didn't want her to find herself in a false position. As an answer, two weeks later she invited me over and there was Marie-Claire Blais, the girlfriend of Mary Meigs.

As a teacher at Bard she had attracted a small but staunch group of young women students. In Paris, not only the young women but the demands on her time seemed to multiply geometrically. With each morning mail there were requests for rights and permissions, for blurbs and translations, for interviews and lectures, for financial support and recommendations.

**MARY BRADY**  In the spring of 1967 my husband and I went to dinner and Mary was in a twit because whoever was her secretary at the time was leaving. I was very, very bored being an embassy wife and in an odd moment I said to Mary, "I'd be happy to come and help you." She looked at me and then she said, "Well, *there's* an idea." The rule for the Foreign Service then was that no wife of a senior officer could work. You were supposed to spend your time giving dinner parties. So we had to keep it a secret. My pattern at Mary's was unvarying. Two afternoons a week I appear at one o'clock. I have a key and open the door and Maria comes and greets me. Mary calls out hello from her study and we have a lovely lunch served by Maria from one to two. Mary hears about the embassy from me—she is not welcome in embassy circles due to her position on Vietnam—and she's very curious. At two o'clock we promptly leave the table and proceed to the study or to the huge Empire sofa in the living room, where we sit with a folder and we start to do whatever project is at hand. I stay until between four and five. For her routine correspondence I draft most of the letters. She sometimes dictates letters and I use my sloppy speed writing. I typed them up on the old manual typewriter that sat on the desk. Most of her letters were on a kind of flimsy bluish paper. You try and erase that stuff. The first thing I did for her was organize her files, which was wonderful because I got to read everything. She was a better typist than I was. At one point I was really angry with my husband and I remember sitting there crying and Mary being very comforting and wise. We had in those years an extraordinarily close relationship. We were friends.

In 1969, when her husband was transferred, Mary Brady gave way to a secretary who had no contact with the embassy.

**MARGO VISCUSI**   I was invited to the apartment for tea. I remember there were little fruit tarts and I was too terrified to eat—I was afraid if I put a fork to one of them it would go flying across the room. Mary and her departing secretary, who had arranged the interview, talked mainly about trips to Italy, and I felt totally inadequate. Mary never asked what I could do or where I'd worked before. Then at the end, when we were at the door and I was thinking, Well, great, I've met her once, that's enough, she said, "When do you want to start?" I blubbered, "But you haven't really interviewed me. You haven't asked any questions." She got a little flustered. "I'm not a very good interviewer," she said.

**MARY BRADY**   Mary wrote me once soon after Margo started, "Margo is working out all right but she doesn't know who Linnaeus is. Wouldn't you think somebody would know that?" This was so typical of Mary's testing of people. Margo was supposed to know about this Swedish plant man, for heaven's sake. Mary had expectations of all of us and of our educations that fit her world but did not fit ours. In the end she forgave us.

**MARGO VISCUSI**   She was demanding, sometimes critical, but invariably gracious, and she organized her time very efficiently. It took about a year for her to get to know my husband, Anthony, and me and decide we were all right. She became extremely fond of Anthony. She loved all things Italian. With time we began to be invited to her dinner parties or to a restaurant. At that time they had a very lavish social life.

**MARY BRADY**   I learned a lot from Mary. First, I learned precision. The pencils were here and the typewriter was there and her desk was perfectly organized. Things just didn't get out of place. Even when she was having trouble with Peter Levi, the manuscript was still very precise. Second, I learned a lot about discipline. She would write in the mornings and you couldn't call her. I would never call her between nine and noon. Five days a week. And finally, I learned to think much better. I was changed by Mary and perhaps Margo was too.

**MARGO VISCUSI** She was a combination of older sister, which I do not have, and mother. She was all those close figures but without the threatening aspects of somebody who is a blood relation. In a sense she adopted Anthony and me, and as our kids grew older she became intensely interested in their lives as well. Any problem that was ours was hers—she'd take it very seriously.

Having found their way to her by force of will or sheer chance, a surprising number of these young women went on to become close friends. However, one not-so-young woman who sought Mary McCarthy out in Paris met a fate very different. Of course, with a respectable career as a novelist and literary critic, Doris Grumbach was in need of no role model. With a book-length critical study of McCarthy two thirds finished and a New York publisher eager to bring it out, she was a biographer in literal search of her Subject. If there were initial doubts and hesitations on the part of this Subject, Grumbach was sufficiently persuasive in her first letter to put them to rest.

### FROM DORIS GRUMBACH'S LETTER TO MARY MCCARTHY, OCTOBER 23, 1965

My policy has been to stay as far away from hearsay, gossip, and the usual tittle-tattle of friends and former friends as I could; in fact, I have spoken to no one who knows you or knew you[. . . .] I had thought it possible, and desirable, to avoid you, too, but the further into this project I go the more it seems difficult for a number of reasons[. . . .] There are purely factual questions I can settle or answer in no other way except to ask you[. . . .] I can think of no reason why you should agree—this sort of interview can be no more alluring than reviewing the contents of one's fluoroscope with one's surgeon—but I would be grateful if you do, and I will be quick, direct, and painless.

Against Jim West's advice, she agreed to an interview. Living in a city where her name and reputation counted for very little, she had reason to find Grumbach's request gratifying. Once she agreed to a meeting, Grumbach tentatively asked permission to make use of a tape recorder. With Elisabeth Niebuhr she had been reluctant to have the interview recorded. This time, she responded with a brief note, saying, "Thank you for writing. I don't mind a tape recorder; in fact I rather like them." Grumbach arrived in Paris one step ahead of a major snowstorm to find her Subject just back from a Christmas holiday with the children in Scotland. First impressions can be misleading, but, in both parties' view, the meeting was a success. The interview, conducted on the large Empire sofa that dominated the living room, went off without a hitch.

**DORIS GRUMBACH** When I first met her I liked her. We got on well—or seemed to. She had this wonderful smile, but it was an instant smile. It would flash on. It never lingered. I thought that meant pleasure. The only difficulty was I had just been in London, where the only vegetable I was able to get was brussels sprouts, which the English cooked very badly. In my first visit to her apartment she said, "We're having lunch here. I've just made a little lunch and I hope you like brussels sprouts. . . ." I did the taping in the course of two visits. Each day we worked for about three hours. She was a very good speaker, sprightly and alive and witty. When she wished to be, she could be wonderfully charming. She said that she was pleased that I was doing the book. She said that she had turned down other requests. I don't know how much she liked me, but she seemed to trust me. She got out a lot of pictures, some of which she allowed me to take back with me.

The first hint of trouble came barely a month later, when Grumbach wrote to say that she was sending along a typed transcript and a battery of questions. For someone who all her life had worked hard to make things as clear as possible, Grumbach's talk of "clarifications" and "verbatim" was alarming.

### FROM MARY MCCARTHY'S LETTER TO DORIS GRUMBACH, FEBRUARY 22, 1966

I must tell you that I am worried about the future destiny of this interview. My understanding was that we were doing it for background for your book. But *not for publication*. It's evident that if it were published, a number of people would sue me for libel (or is it slander on tape?) and in fact could sue you too and your publisher.

Having registered her alarm, she proceeded to compound the damage by providing four pages of densely packed remarks ranging from the highly indiscreet to potentially libelous. In the same packet she included a seven-page chronology, which noted, among other things: "lost virginity fall, 1926, in Marmon roadster; unpleasant experience."

Upon receiving this windfall, Grumbach wrote back to reassure her, "I have *no* intention of using verbatim (or even hinting at in the text) any of the portions which you feel might be libelous." In early spring Grumbach turned in her completed manuscript to her New York publisher, Coward-McCann. In early summer, McCarthy happened to stop by *her* London publisher, when they were considering the galleys of Grumbach's book, now called *The World of Mary McCarthy*. By then she had calmed down sufficiently to propose a better title ("I'm rather good on titles, not just my own.") and to also propose, albeit rather more gingerly, checking the galleys for errors.

Grumbach wisely agreed to take *The Company She Kept* as her title and not so wisely agreed to accept her Subject's offer to check for factual errors. The crisis came to a head when Grumbach's publisher sent galleys to *both* McCarthy and Edmund Wilson. After reading those portions that touched on their marriage, and finding not only statements that were libellous but at least two important errors of fact, Wilson wrote the head of Coward-McCann.

### FROM EDMUND WILSON'S LETTER TO JOHN J. GEOGHEGAN, SEPTEMBER 24, 1966

In regard to *The Company She Kept*, the important thing for Coward-McCann is not to let Miss Grumbach say that the inventions of Miss McCarthy's fiction are literally true of me and her relations with me. (I don't know about other people—I haven't read the whole thing.) On galley 24, she says that an incident in *The Group* "is an exact statement of what happened between Edmund Wilson and Mary McCarthy." This is not true. Miss Grumbach does not know what happened, and Mary, in the state she was in, did not know what was happening either[. . . .] Miss Grumbach ought to be on her guard against Miss McCarthy's constant tendency to distort and exaggerate, and her publishers should be on their guard against allowing to get into print statements that are potentially libellous[. . . .]

It might be brought to Miss Grumbach's attention that she misspells Morgenstern and, on galley 70, next to last paragraph, writes *disinterest* when she means *lack of interest*. I don't know what she means by saying that my son is a "student of sorts." He is a teacher as well as a student of Slavic languages and about to get a Ph.D.

Having spoken his mind, Wilson mailed a carbon copy of his letter to his ex-wife in Paris, scribbling a brief note at the bottom addressed to "Dear Mary" and signed "As ever, Edmund," saying, "I wonder if you have seen this book and approved it in its present form. If you haven't seen it, I think you should. The author is evidently an idiot." McCarthy, as it happened, was in Switzerland, traveling with Hannah Arendt. She, unlike Wilson, had read the galleys in their entirety and had found even less to like than he had. Rather than write the publisher, she had started a letter to the book's author, whom she continued to address as "Dear Doris."

### FROM MARY McCARTHY'S LETTER TO DORIS GRUMBACH, SEPTEMBER 26, 1966

Straight off, I don't like what you've done with me as a human being and with the other human beings associated with me. There has evidently been a serious misunderstanding. Our agreement was that the tapes you recorded were for "background," for your own enlightenment. You assured me that nothing would be quoted from them. Apparently, you must have felt at some point that this agreement no longer held[. . . .] I feel especially horrified by the lowdown you furnish on Edmund: the black eye, he got "drunk," etc. He is an old and distinguished literary man, who has been having, as everybody knows, serious troubles with taxes. He does not deserve to have a peephole applied to him, to be in short "exposed"[. . . .] For different reasons, I must ask you to cut your account of my love-affair with Jim. *In toto*, as it stands. You forget that his former wife is still very much around and that he has to deal with her all the time in connection with the children, whom he loves. Their future could be damaged, gravely, if she decided to use some of the material you have supplied against him in a legal action.

At this point Mary McCarthy was willing to concede that her biographer was not solely at fault here: "Unfortunately, I am not discreet and I do not seem to 'learn.' I enjoy talking." With the letter still unposted, she returned to Paris, only to be greeted by the carbon of Wilson's letter to Coward-McCann. Having read it, she added a typed postscript to Grumbach: "I am distressed he should have received the proofs before I did, which leads him to speculate as to whether I approved or did not." Before finally posting the letter, she also found time to set her biographer straight on one point: "He's mistaken about the spelling of my grandmother's name." She did not see any need to set her biographer straight about her son.

For years she and her second husband had been addressing each other with a civility that had been sadly lacking in their marriage. Now it looked as if he might never forgive her. As it turned out, her fears proved unwarranted. Rather than berate her further, Wilson chose to accept her protestations of innocence and devote himself to putting pressure on Coward-McCann. His behavior, under the circumstances, was exemplary. Unfortunately, Miss Grumbach did not respond in like fashion. In Paris, waiting to hear from Grumbach and fearing the worst, McCarthy turned again to Hannah Arendt.

### FROM MARY MCCARTHY'S LETTER TO HANNAH ARENDT, OCTOBER 11, 1966

I've not had a syllable in reply to the long letter I wrote her. Nor from her publisher[. . . .] Urged by Jim and Janet [Flanner], I called Jovanovich, who sounded quite pessimistic about the result of any legal action and even more pessimistic about the workings of grace in the hearts of the author and her publisher[. . . .] Jovanovich is worried about the legal position. I am not libeled, so far as I can see, in the book. And he thinks that invasion of privacy may not apply with a public figure. A spoken and written agreement has been violated, but it was not, of course, a contract. Anyway, he is now consulting a lawyer and has told me not to talk about it until I hear from him.

She herself had not been libeled and she had no written contract. However, she had the power to refuse permission to quote from her work. To reset galleys would be costly. But to remove offending passages would be nowhere near as costly as removing all quotations from her published writing. Publishers are businessmen and Coward-McCann was not inclined to throw away good money. Every effort was made to persuade their beleaguered author to remove those passages her Subject viewed as highly damaging. Eventually Grumbach gave in.

**DORIS GRUMBACH**   The parts that she struck out of the book, most completely, were the parts about her marriage to West and her affairs before that. I did hear from someone that Jim West's ex-wife wanted to go back to the United States with the children, but she couldn't do it because he had these visitation rights in Paris. And of course he had to stay in Paris. My private theory is that people read that galley, including Jim West, and decided that the ex-wife would be able to claim that Mary was not a fit person to have her children around.

The book that Coward-McCann brought out in the late spring of 1967 was guaranteed to please no one. By this time the battle between Grumbach and her Subject was common knowledge. Just below a long review in the *New York Times Book Review*, readers could find the author's account of how it had all gone sour.

### FROM "THE SUBJECT OBJECTED," BY DORIS GRUMBACH, *THE NEW YORK TIMES BOOK REVIEW*, JUNE 11, 1967

It all started so innocently, like the most medieval love affair[. . . .] So simple. So innocent. Such childlike faith in the unharassed procedures of scholarship[. . . .] The end of our affair, our final "misunderstanding," came when I realized how highly autobiographical a fiction-writer She was[. . . .] Ultimately, like a divorcing couple, all passion spent, who come separately into the judge's chambers for the final papers, we came to terms.

Although she had been given a chance to present her side of her doomed literary love affair, Grumbach was not given the sort of treatment from reviewers she was hoping for. From her Subject's point of view, this was hardly unjust. Announcing itself as "A Revealing Portrait," *The Company She Kept* portrayed Mary McCarthy as someone you would not want to meet in a dark alley. She is "the reformer who is willing to discard the baby in order to be permanently rid of the bath water," wrote Grumbach. "The worst-tempered woman in American letters," she quoted Katharine Anne Porter as saying. The reviewers in the *Times* and *The Washington Post* faulted Grumbach for being literal minded and mean-spirited. At the same time, these reviewers bestowed upon her Subject a respect and appreciation found only occasionally in reviews of her own published work.

### FROM "FICTIONS AND FACTS," BY ELLEN MOERS, *THE NEW YORK TIMES BOOK REVIEW*, JUNE 11, 1967

The urge to scribble on Mary McCarthy has now been given official standing by the publication of some McCarthy marginalia by Doris

Grumbach, herself, like her subject, a writer of fiction and criticism[. . . .] The fact is that one returns to Mary McCarthy not for her
gossip but for herself, or rather for herselves, those black shadows cast
by the fingers of a very gifted writer on the hard wall of experience.

## FROM "MARY, MARY," BY MARY ELLMANN,
### *WASHINGTON POST BOOK WEEK*, MAY 28, 1967

In discussing Mary McCarthy's life this book tries to be impertinent,
but in discussing her work it succeeds in being dull[. . . .] Still, Mary
McCarthy survives [Doris Grumbach's] examination. It is impossible
not to admire her rashness, her wit, her inimical curiosity[. . . .] How
awful if she should mellow, and go all balanced and long-suffering and
representative.

In the end, the tempest surrounding Grumbach's literary portrait
came to nothing. This was no *Eichmann in Jerusalem*. Nor was it anything
like *The Group*. Certainly the hint of scandal did little to boost sales. The
immediate effect on Mary McCarthy was to take time from *Birds of America*. "This novel is dragging along, constantly interrupted, and I sometimes feel I ought to give poor Peter Levi euthanasia," she wrote her *New
Yorker* editor not long after Grumbach's book came out.

When it came to the crunch, she did not kill off poor Peter Levi. Having had one brush with allegations of libel and invasion of privacy, she
had no wish for another round with the lawyers. Instead of giving him
euthanasia, she saw to it that he would never offend a living soul. Neither her present husband nor her second one would have anything to
worry about. Nor would their children.

Those close to Mary McCarthy tended to see her clash with Doris
Grumbach as the inevitable consequence of what they knew of her character. Mary Brady saw it as another instance of her propensity for self-
dramatization coupled with a refusal to take responsibility for her own
indiscretions. Jim West would later say that the taping with Grumbach
was one of only two occasions he recalled her ever changing her mind.
There would seem to be more to her anger, however, than a sense of personal embarrassment or personal betrayal. Doris Grumbach had made
serious trouble for her with Edmund Wilson and was prepared to make
serious trouble for Jim West. But Grumbach had done something far
harder to forgive: she had brought to bear on her Subject's life an intensity of gaze that she herself could no longer afford to bring to it.

"I am glad to see you on the best-seller list, and also that you get so
much money. That is the right thing for you, dear, enjoy it and be happy,"
Hannah Arendt had written back in 1963, just as it was becoming apparent that for the author of *The Group* nothing would ever be the same
again. While Hannah's blessing may have been welcome, it failed to take
one factor into account. Yes, she enjoyed being a best-selling author and

she enjoyed the fine clothes and the fine food and wine. But it was not in her nature to value any arrangement, no matter how comfortable, when it was sustained by a series of concessions and compromises.

By inviting Doris Grumbach to bring her tape recorder into her apartment, she had been playing with fire. Before long she would bring fire down on her head. Already, when her would-be biographer was preparing to visit her in Paris, she was steeling herself to put the world on notice that forces beyond her control were disrupting her settled life as the wife of a career diplomat, drawing her into political battles more ferocious and more perilous than any she had ever before engaged in and forcing her to temporarily put poor Peter Levi aside.

# Chapter Twenty-two

# VIETNAM

"What are you doing about Vietnam?" Mary McCarthy wrote Dwight Macdonald in February 1966, when Lyndon Johnson was shipping out battalion upon battalion of armed troops and it looked as if America's struggle to get the better of North Vietnam was about to result in a full-scale war. This was not the first time she had broached the subject of Vietnam to Macdonald. From the moment Johnson had started his bombing of the North she had been probing her friends in America with the passion of a longtime Kremlinologist relegated to the outermost reaches of Siberia.

When she was not writing Macdonald she could be found querying Hannah Arendt. "I read with slight relief the *New York Times* editorials and Walter Lippmann," she wrote in April 1965, asking whether there was "any movement of protest among private people." One month later, she was back again: "I've been reading about the teach-ins and about [Hans] Morgenthau; tell me more. Obviously some new alignment is being formed or perhaps just explored. Bobbie [Kennedy] would not attack U.S. policy if he were not confident of support. And I was struck by Schlesinger's role in the Washington teach-in; I would have expected him to take a straight official line."

With her marriage to a Foreign Service officer based in Paris, not only had she put herself at a distance from the writers and intellectuals who had provided the inspiration for her best fiction but she had cut herself off from the sort of political discourse she had come to rely on. Worse, she had put herself in a position where such political discourse was potentially reckless.

Her politics had always been up close and personal—not something reserved for a theoretic discussion but the stuff of everyday life. More than once she had spoken of how a passing encounter at a New York cocktail party had brought her to the Trotsky Defense Committee, and of how the friendships she had formed on that committee had helped keep her a committed anti-Stalinist for almost two decades. All this had led Doris Grumbach to speak with great assurance of the lack of seriousness of her politics, mistaking irony for pure confession and bravado for a lack of serious commitment.

Certainly, after the death of Stalin and the downfall of the senator from Wisconsin with the thoroughly dismaying last name of McCarthy, politics had begun to seem a good deal less urgent. Rather than work to change the system, she, like many another New York intellectual, had continued to vote for Norman Thomas while setting to work to make a better life for herself. She'd had no use for Dwight D. Eisenhower and she'd liked John F. Kennedy little better. But, then, Kennedy had made no effort to woo her with an invitation to a state dinner or a quiet evening of chamber music—the sort of invitation that sent Diana Trilling into a sartorial tailspin and prompted Robert Lowell to conceive a manic passion for Kennedy's beautiful young wife. In any case, she had been too busy with her own romantic life to take much interest in Camelot on the Potomac.

As it turned out, John F. Kennedy would be most compelling in his dying. By chance she happened to be with Hannah Arendt in Chicago, taking a break from touring for *The Group*, the day he was shot. Like most of America, she tried to make sense of the shocking events in Dallas. Unlike most of America, she went on to read the Warren Commission's report from cover to cover, the way she would a book she was about to review. To Dwight Macdonald she wrote, "I am not sure Oswald had accomplices. But I am sure that the Warren Commission, acting in 'good faith,' never let itself entertain for an instant the idea that he might have had. Any more than the average wife lets herself think that her husband might be cheating on her."

For her, the irreconcilable details surrounding the shooting at Dealey Plaza—the attempt on General Walker, the shooting of Officer Tippit, Oswald's unprepossessing marksmanship—were endlessly tantalizing. On the other hand, Lyndon Baines Johnson, the one person who had benefited directly from the assassination, was, in her view, the most tedious of open books. In the spring of 1964, felled by what looked to be a bad case of writer's block, she confided to Hannah Arendt that if the only alternative was to write about Johnson's campaign against Barry Goldwater, she preferred to remain idle.

Only by turning an ill-conceived armed intervention into a highly destructive and potentially disastrous war that she found personally distressing did Johnson finally get her attention. To learn from a newspaper headline at a Paris kiosk that Johnson had bombed North Vietnam was, for her, every bit as upsetting as first hearing of Truman's dropping

the atomic bomb on Hiroshima. It was, among other things, morally indefensible. The French, who had themselves been brought low by Vietnam,
might not speak in such terms, but they were not above pointing out the
*gaucherie* and sheer futility of such bad behavior. Suddenly, as a U.S. citizen living in Paris, she had much to apologize for.

All her life, when confronted with a challenge, she had found it
impossible to back off. Even when it went against her own best interests,
she could not leave well enough alone. For the next two years she lay
awake night after night trying to figure out which government official
close to Johnson might respond to an appeal from her and, failing that,
which political action on her part might help end this terrible war without jeopardizing her husband's job.

For a time she considered withholding all, or part, of her taxes and
making the government come after her. The trouble was, she and Jim
West filed a joint return. No less tempting was to write about the war.
Back when Joe McCarthy had been rooting out Communists in high
places, she, practically alone among her circle, had spoken out. But in
March 1966, when Bob Silvers sent a telegram proposing she go to Vietnam as correspondent for *The New York Review of Books*, she had to conclude, after much anguished debate with Jim West, that she must decline
this tempting offer. After all, with three children to support, Jim West
could not afford to antagonize the State Department.

From *Eichmann in Jerusalem* she had learned the importance of taking
direct political action in the face of moral failure. That December, with
nearly 400,000 American soldiers in Vietnam and the war escalating
exponentially, the lesson she had learned was very much on her mind.
In an interview taped for NBC television, she announced to Edwin Newman, "[T]he moment is past for signing manifestos[. . . .] I think if we don't
do something more serious and this whole thing continues on its course,
unarrested, if somehow we aren't able to reach the political conscience
of Washington, that we will really not be much better off than the German people under the Nazis."

Something had to be done and it was incumbent upon her to do it. Just
what that something was continued to elude her until the following January, when Robert Silvers, like some besotted suitor who refuses to take
no for an answer, approached her a second time. By then, not only had
the war worsened but her lack of credentials as a war correspondent had
come to seem less daunting. For one thing, her young friend Frankie
FitzGerald had just returned from a year in Saigon, where she had written articles exposing the futility of the American effort for *The Atlantic*
and *The New York Times Magazine*.

This time, she did not dismiss Silvers's invitation out of hand. Instead,
after she and Jim West had peered at the offer from every angle and

probed all the possible ramifications, they came to a decision, which had
nothing to do with common sense and caution and everything to do with
romance and adventure.

### FROM MARY McCARTHY'S LETTER TO CARMEN ANGLETON, JANUARY 7, 1967

[Jim] now feels that as a writer and a citizen I have the right to go and
see what is going on there, whether I am married to a foreign-service
officer or not. His patriotism and fighting spirit and sense of derring-
do have been stirred. I'm struck with admiration for his sudden deci-
siveness on this issue; Nicola was counseling prudence: "Don't go. You
are a *writer*, not a journalist. What can you do there?" The day before
yesterday, Jim and I met for a coffee after lunch at the Deux Magots to
make the fatal decision. It was like meeting in some coffee-house in
Poland when he was deciding to beard the ambassador. When I saw he
was going to say yes, I started to weep, from joy, nervous strain, relief,
and civic emotions.

Her letter to Carmen Angleton had actually begun in a less dramatic
vein. "I want to make you a proposal, which I expect, though, you'll have
to turn down because of your parents' health[. . . .] How would you like
to come with me? I would stay two or three weeks and come back stopping for a few days in Cambodia; if you came, we could dash up to Thai-
land and see Angkor Vat (sp?)."

Sadly, with neither Jim West nor Carmen Angleton free to accompany
her, she was destined to see Angkor Wat on her own. But even though he
was not going with her, her husband was standing firmly behind her. All
he asked was that she not go out on military patrols, where she would be
under direct fire. For this she gave him full credit, both at the time and
in retrospect. Laconic and courtly, West himself was not a man to use
words like "derring-do" and "fighting spirit." Nor was he inclined, three
decades later, to view his actions in quite so dramatic a light.

**JAMES WEST**   When we talked about Mary's wanting the first time to go to
Vietnam, I said, "Yes, go ahead. If you want to go, you might do some good."
In one of those books, I guess it says that I said something like "I don't care
if they fire me." That wasn't quite my language, but I did suggest that her
ability to do something useful outweighed the possibilities of my having a
coruscating experience with the State Department. I don't think they really
cared much anyway.

She was as much in love with Jim West as ever, but she was preparing to
set off for the other side of the globe without him. With the same zest she
had brought to setting up their first home in Warsaw, she made provisions for the disposal of her possessions.

### FROM "HOW IT WENT"

I had fun making my will, especially with the bequests of jewelry and art objects. Would the jacinthe and brown topazes be good with Hannah's eyes? And Carmen—the seed-pearl bracelet we had chosen together, with the little insets of sapphires and diamonds[. . . .] It was like picking out presents, which I love doing, and the men as usual were harder.

No less necessary, if nowhere near as amusing, was getting fixed up with the right visas and letters of introduction. Whether it was owing to her husband's position or her own not inconsiderable celebrity, she had only to pick up the telephone to arrange a meeting with Chip Bohlen, the American ambassador in Paris.

### FROM "HOW IT WENT"

[F]or an hour we debated about Vietnam. It reminded me of school, when you have to listen respectfully to the principal as she carries out her duty, which is to point out to you the errors of your thinking, even though she knows you will do what you have determined to do anyway. Having executed that formality, he became very nice.

If she had been spoiling for a fight, she was doomed to disappointment. Bohlen was well aware that there was more than one way to view the war in Vietnam.

**MARY BRADY** It's hard for people to recollect what a bitter event this was in the Foreign Service. In my own home it was a subject that we couldn't talk about. My husband was out there defending a policy that I totally disapproved of. If I'd been here in America, I would have been marching. There were other people who were opposed to the war, and we were all in this terrible position. It was divisive at the embassy. There were demonstrations. It was a very, very difficult time. Whereas other people bit their tongues, Mary's opinions of course were very well known. Everybody knew where she stood.

Having failed to budge her an inch, Chip Bohlen promised to get her the State Department's permission to travel to a country that was not on the department's "approved" list and advised her against using her diplomatic passport (the Vietnamese would assume she was a spy). He then passed her on to the embassy's Vietnam expert. If this expert was not quite so "nice" as the ambassador, he was prepared to make every effort to secure her the necessary visa and to provide her with introductions to useful contacts in Saigon. He was also prepared to present the government's position, which he proceeded to do for one full hour.

The sole argument that had given her pause came not from a Foreign Service officer but from Nicola Chiaromonte, who had felt obliged to point out that she would do far better to write a polemical essay and do her research at the library. As a reporter she would be expected to stick to the mechanical recording of pure facts and as an inexperienced reporter she would not know the right questions to ask, Chiaromonte warned her. It was a warning she chose to ignore.

Certainly she was lacking in journalistic experience. The last time she had tried her hand at this kind of thing had been back in 1954, writing about Portugal for *The New Yorker*. With this invitation to go to Vietnam as a correspondent for *The New York Review of Books*, Bob Silvers was offering her what no other editor was prepared to offer. He was also, in effect, making amends. He was giving her a chance to help stop an immoral war by turning to some profit the hundreds of thousands of readers she had attracted with *The Group*, the best-selling novel she had seen ridiculed and disparaged in his magazine's pages. Those readers, she believed, would be eager to hear what she had to say. "To hear from a novelist about a trip he has taken through a debated area is like getting a long letter from someone you know well," she would write in "How It Went," the introduction to her collected Vietnam writing.

Whether this conviction of hers was valid remains debatable. What is not debatable is that Bob Silvers was encouraging her to take a stance that most readers of best-sellers would hardly find congenial. Moreover, he was asking her to put her life at risk. As she prepared to set off for Saigon, none of this seemed to trouble her. According to one not entirely sympathetic observer, the reason for this was simple enough.

**LIONEL ABEL**   Her friends were all against the war. Well, so was I, although since then I've had some doubts. She relied on the political opinion of her friends. And as I say, they were all against it—Phil Rahv, Harold Rosenberg, and Dwight. We'd all written against it and so she assumed it was wrong. She felt she had behind her sophisticated opinion about the war. As far as I'm concerned, that's all that counted for Mary—and for Dwight. What's so bad about that? It's generally better than unsophisticated political opinion.

Of course as someone who had never had much use for fashions in opinion, she would have begged to differ. Indeed she would later say that she took Silvers up on his offer because she could not continue to write a novel about a young American of draft age unless she did her best to help stop a war that might cost him his life. To a fellow novelist, who was very much in favor of the war, this argument made a certain sense, even though he had no use for it. But it was hardly her style to be swayed by such sentiments.

**SAUL BELLOW**   Like so many people at that time, she felt a need to ally herself with the young. With the militants of the sixties. In a way it was not wanting to lose touch with the younger generation. It was partly nostalgia.

It was partly a nursing attitude—all these tender young things we've cherished are being sent off.

**WILLIAM PHILLIPS**   I don't think that Mary's position on the Vietnam War came from a misplaced sympathy for the young demonstrators or having a wish to relive the battles of her youth. Or as having had anything to do with the fact that at the time there was more sympathy for North Vietnam in Paris than there was here—she wasn't part of that milieu. I think that Mary decided that the brave and honest thing to do was to be for North Vietnam. That was Mary: figuring out what was brave and honest. Always.

**MARY BRADY**   Mary spent most of her life being very much Mary. She had her own agenda and her own view of the world—frequently somewhat mistaken. Everything was an occasion for Mary. Vietnam was very dramatic. It was a big number and Mary had to be there.

Although she was traveling to Saigon on a regular passport, she was traveling as a diplomat's wife, preceded by letters of introduction to officials in high places. She was also traveling with several suitcases packed with carefully folded dresses and jackets and at least one Chanel suit. This did not keep her, when she needed to, from putting aside her beautifully tailored wardrobe for an army cap, field jacket, and a pair of oversized trousers borrowed from a former colleague of her husband. Or from forsaking those officials in high places for younger company she found more to her taste.

**JONATHAN RANDAL** *[New York Times correspondent]*   The first time I met her was in Saigon. I was at the Hotel Continental and she knocked on the door and said, "I'm Mary McCarthy, may I come in?" I said of course. She asked if she could use my bath. It was an old colonial hotel and the rooms were very spacious, with high ceilings and fans. The bathroom was a separate and rather large room itself. Anyhow, we became friends. We enjoyed seeing each other. The terrace of the Continental was called the Continental Shelf and all the correspondents spent a lot of time there. She liked to drink and smoke. She was a very attractive woman and the fun was to be with somebody who had obviously seen a lot.

**WILLIAM TUOHY** *[Los Angeles Times correspondent who went to Vietnam in 1964 for Newsweek and switched to the Times in June 1966]*   I had seen the book jacket photographs of this sort of mysterious, elegant, dark-haired lady of the night and then she turns up on the Continental Shelf in a kind of costume—wearing what we used to call fatigues. She looked silly in fatigues. That's what you wear in the field. She didn't wear them to show off. I think she just didn't know what to wear. Yet she was marvelous once she started talking.

**JONATHAN RANDAL**   When she first met all of us, she told us exactly how she felt about the war. She never made a secret of being very much against it. I simply thought the war was unwinnable. I didn't see it as a moral crusade.

**TOM BUCKLEY** *[New York Times* correspondent, *who arrived in Saigon in November 1966]* She had already decided that she really and truly hated the war, but the circumstances would make any reasonable-minded person hate the war. Nonetheless, she did not impress one as having an absolutely closed mind. She wasn't argumentative. She really could listen, which came as a pleasant surprise. She was the exact opposite of a left-wing intellectual wiseass.

**WILLIAM TUOHY** Obviously at some point she must have taken those fatigues off when we were out to dinner, because I remember her at dinner in a Chanel suit. She had enormous charm, enormous intelligence. She lit up a table. She never went over the top. She never said, "This goddamn war is all wrong." I have the feeling she didn't want to get in a fight with us. I think she liked us all.

Knowing how she felt, she listened to an official from the Agency for International Development who was doing his best to win "the other war" while implementing policies uprooting hundreds of thousands of Vietnamese from their villages and farms. And knowing how she felt, she listened to a South Vietnamese major selling anyone who would listen on the stellar performance of the pajama-clad cadres in the government's own "revolutionary development" program. Although she kept her promise to Jim West not to go out on patrol, she made sure to strike out into the field, where she saw deserted villages and teeming refugee camps, a hospital run by the German Knights of Malta, and a scale model of a new village to be built in the hills north of Da Nang, the proud creation of Colonel Corson, a "witty and sardonic" Marine tank commander whom she would later give four pages in her book.

**WILLIAM TUOHY** Everybody was searching for ways to justify this enormous American commitment—in those days, construction companies were building ports. We were building everything, because that's what America knows how to do. We don't know how to rid a rural society of local insurgency. Colonel Corson was trying to address this. And rightly so. Mary cottoned onto him. He knew how to talk her language. He wasn't saying, "We're going out there and kill those bastard Viet Cong." He was saying, "We are here to strengthen democracy at the lowest level." She was susceptible to language. She liked him and he was a good spieler. She was looking for someone in this morass to say something positive. And she found in Corson at least one voice.

The three-part piece she wrote immediately upon her return to Paris made it clear that no one she met during her month-long stay in Saigon had tempted her to budge an inch from her original stance. With her very first sentence she put readers on notice. "I confess that when I went to Vietnam early last February I was looking for material damaging to the American interest," she began. And nothing that followed made any pretense of hiding her bias.

### From "Vietnam"

To an American, Saigon today is less exotic than Florence or the Place de la Concorde. New office buildings of cheap modern design, teeming with teazed, puffed secretaries and their Washington bosses, are surrounded by sandbags and guarded by M.P.'s; new, jerry-built villas in pastel tones, to rent to Americans, are under construction or already beginning to peel and discolor. Even removing the sandbags and the machine guns and restoring the trees that have been chopped down to widen the road to the airport, the mind cannot excavate what Saigon must have been like "before." Now it resembles a giant PX[. . . .]

The Filipinos were fairly dispassionate about their role in pacification[. . . .] The Americans, on the contrary, are zealots—above all, the blueprinters in the Saigon offices—although occasionally in the field, too, you meet a true believer—a sandy, crew-cut, keen-eyed army colonel who talks to you about "the nuts and bolts" of the program, which, he is glad to say, is finally getting the "grass roots" support it needs. It is impossible to find out from such a man what he is doing, concretely[. . . .] He cannot tell you whether there has been any land reform in his area—that is a strictly Vietnamese pigeon—in fact he has no idea of *how* the land in the area is owned[. . . .]

If you ask a junior officer what he thinks our war aims are in Vietnam, he usually replies without hesitation: "To punish aggression"[. . . .] He has been indoctrinated, just as much as the North Vietnamese P.O.W., who tells the interrogation team he is fighting to "liberate the native soil from the American aggressors"—maybe more. Only, the young American does not know it; he probably imagines that he is *thinking* when he produces that formula.

Having turned her cold eye on the corruption that had come with the American occupying forces, she went out of her way to show how language could be used to make light of the terrible things that were happening. A much touted "pacification program" was no better than wholesale dislocation and selective slaughter. A camp for "refugees" was no better than a concentration camp. But that was the least of it. As she saw it, this war to punish aggression promised not only to level everything worth saving in South Vietnam but to debase all that was best in the United States. "The worst thing that could happen to our country would be to win this war," she wrote.

We draw a long face over Viet Cong "terror," but no one stops to remember that the Viet Cong does not possess that superior instrument of terror, an air force, which in our case, over South Vietnam at least, is acting almost with impunity[. . . .]

To political scientists [. . .] the word "genocide" is quite unsuitable to describe what is happening. Genocide is *deliberate*. It is the same with bombs and mortars. If the Viet Cong plants a bomb in a theater, that is an atrocity, but if the Americans bomb a village that is "different." When you ask how it is different, the answer is that the VC action was deliberate, while the U.S. action was accidental. But in what way accidental if the fliers saw the village and could assume there were people in it and knew from experience that the bombs would go off?

Her three Vietnam pieces appeared in *The New York Review of Books* that spring. Nicola Chiaromonte, who had been so strongly opposed to her going, wrote at once.

### FROM NICOLA CHIAROMONTE'S LETTER TO MARY MCCARTHY, MARCH 31, 1967

May I say that it is simply masterful? Nothing (by a long shot) so devastatingly simple and direct has been written about Vietnam. And I do not know of anything at all that can be compared to your piece of *writing* in contemporary journalism. It was done through simplicity and *true* concern. Miriam thinks the same, and we both want to give you a very very special hug. Love to Jim (who has some merit in your achievement). P.S. I won't forget to eat some humble pie for having doubted your ability to come out of this victoriously.

Dwight Macdonald, caught up in a last-ditch effort to put together a list of prominent people to join *him* for tax refusal, mentioned in a brief postscript to a two-page letter that he had heard good things about the piece not only from Bob Silvers but from Bowden Broadwater, who had been moved, after all the bad blood between them, to declare her "a good person." While tax refusal had lost its special allure, that part of Macdonald's news was unexpectedly gratifying.

### FROM MARY MCCARTHY'S LETTER TO DWIGHT MACDONALD, APRIL 4, 1967

Thank you for telling me that Bowden said I am a good person. It is nice to hear that because I gathered he hated me. By the way, *he* would do [tax refusal], but I would shrink from asking him; maybe one shrinks from asking anybody who would be hurt by such a gesture.

A month later, when all three pieces were out, Macdonald wrote again.

### FROM DWIGHT MACDONALD'S LETTER TO MARY MCCARTHY, MAY 17, 1967

One of the best things you've ever done—everybody I meet talks about them, admires them, even some of your hitherto unfans—you realize you DO have some, don't you, Mary dear, as I do. God knows we've both tried hard enough to create them!

But as the spring of 1967 turned to summer, Dwight had some second thoughts about what she had done. To Chiaromonte, who had not only declared the pieces to be "splendid" but had gone on to translate and edit them for *Tempo Presente*, Macdonald confided the source of his misgivings.

### FROM DWIGHT MACDONALD'S LETTER TO NICOLA CHIAROMONTE, JULY 5, 1967

[R]ecently I've run across two *New Yorker* writers who have just come back from Vietnam and both, to my surprise, when I asked them what they thought of the pieces, were very critical—not on her ideas or her generalizations but on what I thought was the best aspect, the detailed reportage of facts and impressions. Both thought she was biassed [*sic*] and, worse, inaccurate, insubstantial!

As it happened, the accuracy of the "reportage" in those pieces was hardly foremost in Chiaromonte's thoughts that spring. A recent article in the counterculture monthly *Ramparts* had presented incontrovertible evidence that the Congress for Cultural Freedom, along with its many publications, had been funded from the very beginning by the CIA. At *Encounter*, Stephen Spender, claiming a total lack of knowledge of any of this nasty business, quickly resigned as co-editor. At *Tempo Presente*, Chiaromonte, claiming a lack of knowledge no less total, saw no reason to follow suit. Inclined to subscribe to the theory that "most likely the 'revelations' were started by the rightwing CIA to eliminate the 'leftwing,' " he was fighting to clear his name and to keep his magazine afloat. Even so, he found time to give his best friend's misgivings some thought.

### FROM NICOLA CHIAROMONTE'S LETTER TO DWIGHT MACDONALD, JULY 18, 1967

What Mary's articles contributed was a very clever and pitiless description of "The Americans in Vietnam"[. . . .] As for the "factual" side of Mary's articles, I know Mary well enough to be able to imagine that she got away with the few books she read and with whatever she got from the "briefings" she describes so well. But, as I said, this does not seem to me the point: the value of her articles consists entirely in the description of the Americans "at work" in Vietnam, as seen by a couple of bright American eyes. And the effect *is* devastating, I think.

For Chiaromonte her pitiless description of the American presence in Vietnam was a devastating condemnation. For Chip Bohlen, who had first done his part in counseling her and then done his best to assist her, this devastating condemnation was tantamount to a personal betrayal. Seven years later, his response would still sting.

### FROM "HOW IT WENT"

In June, when I met him at a cocktail party at the house of Bob McBride, the American minister, he seemed affronted and angry. He had just read my first article in *The Observer*. "What does that mean, you were 'looking for material damaging to the American interest'? What *is* the American 'interest'?" I had gone to the party, alone (Jim was away), thinking I must show myself in the official community and stand behind what I had written. But until Bohlen had caught sight of me, on the terrace, I had noticed no difference in my welcome. Now, as we confronted each other, a semi-circle formed, and tactful aides (or so it looked) stood ready to get between us. He had turned slightly red, and I had turned pale, I imagine. I do not remember what I answered, but my position, I knew, was shaky owing to a physical fact: the terrace was covered with several inches of ornamental gravel into which my high heels sank, causing me to lose footing each time I took a step backward or forward or shifted my weight in the course of the exchange. Bohlen, in flat shoes, did not have that disadvantage. After a minute or two, he walked off[. . . .] Once he was gone, a few of the Embassy people present came up to tell me they agreed with me and offer their congratulations.

On one level Bohlen's response was satisfying, if only because it suggested that her trip to Vietnam had ceased to be a source of official amusement. No less satisfying was the fact that both William Jovanovich and Roger Straus were vying for the privilege of bringing out her Vietnam report as a book. Both men had published her work before. Jovanovich, however, had not only made her a small fortune but had gone on to become a good friend. The problem was, Jovanovich was totally *for* the war. Roger Straus felt more or less the way she did. She was being wooed by two persuasive and eminently attractive suitors. Understandably, courtship was very much on her mind. And perhaps no less understandably, given the two men involved, there was an undeniable frisson.

### FROM MARY MCCARTHY'S LETTER TO WILLIAM JOVANOVICH, MAY 11, 1967

It's true, I suppose, that I do have a sort of publishing flirtation with Roger, but there's never been any thought, and you know this, of my giving him a work of fiction, which would be the equivalent, I guess, of the "final favor."

Protesting that he knew what he was getting into, Jovanovich replied in kind: "As for another publisher's pleasure, I count my own before his, which is natural enough." She stayed at Harcourt. But having done everything in his power to keep her, Jovanovich was now obliged to do everything in his power to please her. And it was her expressed wish that Harcourt bring her report out as an oversized pamphlet rather than a hardcover book. That way, she argued, they would get it into the hands of tens of thousands of readers as quickly, and cheaply, as possible. And that way they would have a fair chance of turning the publication into a full-fledged event.

Dedicated "to Jim" and priced at a reasonable $1.95, *Vietnam* was in the hands of the wholesalers by early fall of 1967. To help make the report more attractive to those who had already read it, she had taken the step of adding a fourth, and final, section and then passed that section along to *The New York Review of Books.* Called "Solutions," it proposed the not entirely novel thesis that the only way to salvage anything from this moral and military disaster was for the United States to get out of Vietnam at once. Whatever the cost. To try to come up with some practical humanitarian "solution" was a waste of time and "a booby trap." Let the military men and politicians see to that.

As proposals go, it was anything but modest. As such, it elicited a strong response. At Christmas, Elizabeth Hardwick wrote her in Paris to say her "willingness to face all the implications" was nothing less than "the most moving, beautiful and reasonable thing I've seen in a long time." Hardwick of course was a founding editor of the *Review*. Diana Trilling—who for decades had viewed international communism as a serious threat to democratic freedom and who had no such connection— saw it differently. Not bothering to post a note to Paris, Trilling addressed a long letter to Bob Silvers. Never one to let an attack go unanswered, McCarthy quickly mailed off an angry rebuttal to be published in tandem with Trilling's letter.

## From Diana Trilling's Letter to *The New York Review of Books*, January 18, 1968

I too oppose this war and urge our withdrawal from Vietnam, on the well-explored ground that America cannot militarily win the third world from Communism without the gravest danger of thermonuclear war or, at the least, without conduct inconsistent with and damaging to the democratic principle and the principle of national sovereignty we would hope to protect and extend[. . . .] But even as I take this stand I confront the grim reality that in withdrawing from Vietnam we consign untold numbers of Southeast Asian opponents of Communism to their death and countless more to the abrogation of the right of protest which we American intellectuals hold so dear. And if, unhappily, I have no answer to the torturing question of what can be done to save these distant lives, I don't regard this as proof of my moral purity or as an escape from what Miss McCarthy calls the "booby-trap" of "solutions." I hope that everyone, including intellectuals, will keep on trying to find the answer I lack. For without this effort the moral intransigence for which Miss McCarthy speaks is its own kind of callousness.

### From Mary McCarthy's Letter to *The New York Review of Books*, January 18, 1968

Mrs. Trilling has the gift of prophecy. I have not. I do not know what will happen to millions of human beings in Southeast Asia if the Americans pull out[. . . .] It is perfectly true that many thousands of South Vietnamese have been compromised by working for the Americans, as interpreters, language teachers, nurses, drivers, construction workers, cleaning women, cooks, PX employees, and so on; there are at least 140,000 on the military payroll alone. No outsider can be long in Vietnam without feeling some misgivings as to what may happen to them "afterward"[. . . .] In exceptional cases, something *will* be done, on a person-to-person basis[. . . .] But the majority will be left to face the music; that is the tough luck of being a camp follower[. . . .]

Some sort of life will continue, as Pasternak, Solzhenitsyn, Sinyavsky, Daniel have discovered, and I would rather be on their letterhead, if they would allow me, than on that of the American Committee for Cultural Freedom, which in its days of glory, as Mrs. Trilling will recall, was eager to exercise its right of protest by condemning the issue of a U.S. visa to Graham Greene and was actually divided within its ranks on the question of whether Senator Joseph McCarthy was a friend or enemy of domestic liberty.

**DIANA TRILLING**   I'm not very comfortable about the idea of talking about somebody who is dead. It's not a comfortable feeling, especially when you're going to be critical, to speak about somebody who can't answer. But I'm relieved of that scruple because I just reread the exchange between Mary and me in *The New York Review of Books* and there's something so ugly about her tone—in addition to the total irresponsibility of the political position that she took—that I feel I was granted a dispensation from the scruples I had. In her letter to the *Review* she was trying to imply that no one who held my political position—that is, who was known for years and years as an anti-Communist—could be against the war. Or could be in any way a liberal. She was not alone in finding this very confusing—people can't take two ideas and hold them in their heads at the same time—but her tone was sly. Mary was trying slyly to suggest that I was one of the people who, because I'd been not only a member but an officer of the Committee for Cultural Freedom, had denied Graham Greene a passport. I never denied anybody a passport.

To defend her proposal Mary McCarthy had been willing to go to any length. While this was not unheard of in New York intellectual circles, it did not sit well with Jim West. Nor did it sit well with Hannah Arendt, for all that she herself had been known to snub Diana Trilling in front of a room full of people.

### From Mary McCarthy's Letter to Hannah Arendt, January 26, 1968

Jim is disgusted if he comes home and finds me typing out some screed on Diana instead of working on my novel. His view is that one shouldn't deign to answer; he says she's an example of brain drain without geographical displacement. But for me she has become an occasion for articles—like occasional poems.

### FROM ARENDT'S LETTER TO MCCARTHY, FEBRUARY 9, 1968

I read your answer to Diana Trilling and liked it, but generally incline to share Jim's opinion. It is a waste of time and brains.

While this was not the response Mary McCarthy was looking for, it was offset by a bit of good news. "The students all mentioned with great enthusiasm and warmth your book on Vietnam," Arendt wrote. Unfortunately, Arendt's students at the University of Chicago were the exception that proved the rule: Contrary to what the pamphlet's author had anticipated, virtually no readers in America—be they men or women, students or housewives—showed much interest in a book on Vietnam by the author of *The Group*. Worse, while *Vietnam*, with its handsome red, white, and black cover, was languishing in bookstores, Lyndon Johnson was bringing the troop level up to almost 500,000 and intensifying his bombing of the North.

From the very beginning it had been her hope to get an invitation to visit North Vietnam. Her reason for making such a visit was very much like her reason for visiting the South: to bear witness and take action. Nonetheless, there were important differences. Writing from Saigon, she had been one reporter among many; writing from Hanoi, she would virtually have the field to herself. The sole American correspondent of any stature to visit North Vietnam and write about it had been Harrison Salisbury of *The New York Times*.

By the time her special visa came through on March 1, 1968, America was reeling from a Viet Cong offensive that had left the city of Hue in ruins and a team of VC commandos inside the Saigon embassy for six hours. Another writer might have thought twice about making still another foray into Southeast Asia at this particular moment. Or thought twice about sticking fast with a publisher she'd had qualms about in the first place. Not only did she go ahead with preparations for a two-week Hanoi visit but she agreed to let Jovanovich underwrite it, with the understanding that if she chose to put together a Hanoi pamphlet he would sell first-serial rights to *The New York Review of Books*.

On her first visit to Vietnam she had set off from Paris as a credentialed reporter. This time she would be going as a guest of the Peace Commission of the Democratic Republic of Vietnam. During her trip to the South, the journalist Bernard Fall had been killed by a Viet Cong mine only days after she met him. This time, she would not have to worry about VC mines but she would be living under attack from American bombers. Before her first visit, she had been primarily concerned with the equitable distribution of her jewelry. This time, she was occupied with appointing Jim West and Elizabeth Hardwick as co-executors, with Hardwick to handle literary matters. Given what she knew, there was no way she could see her second journey to Vietnam as a lark.

**MARY BRADY**   When I got to the apartment the day she was due to leave, she was practically hysterical. I had never seen her so agitated. She finally had to ask me to finish packing her suitcase. There I was, looking at this unbelievable underwear. In those days we had garter belts, we didn't have panty hose, and Mary had drawers with beautiful Belgian lace. Not panties. And she had these gorgeous slips. It was all silk. She was taking this to Hanoi! The car came for her at about four and I was with her almost the whole day. She would say things like, "Oh, do you think I should go—should I be doing this to Jim?" I think she was deeply worried about him. And I think he was deeply worried about her going. Maybe she thought for once she had gone too far.

To get to Hanoi was no easy matter. Every two weeks, a single military plane—a nonpressurized Convair flying under the auspices of the International Control Commission—made the trip from Saigon. The plan was for her to meet the plane in Cambodia, at Phnom Penh. Owing to bad weather and a backlog of passengers, she had a three-day wait before boarding. Then, when the plane put down in Laos to pick up additional passengers, there was a further delay of four days. During all this time she had ample opportunity to get to know her three traveling companions—a China scholar from the University of California–Los Angeles, an eminent Japanese novelist, and a young Japanese journalist. And ample opportunity to get caught in a nasty dustup between the UCLA China scholar and the American ambassador to Laos, which put to shame her confrontation with Chip Bohlen. Contrary to all evidence from her recent sales figures, the author of *The Group was* news.

### FROM "PEOPLE," *TIME*, MARCH 29, 1968

All was clinking glasses and pleasant buzz at the French embassy party in Vientiane, Laos. That is, until U.S. Ambassador William H. Sullivan, 45, strolled up to a group of American pacifists, who had stopped long enough to wet their whistles before flying on to Hanoi. At the sight of Sullivan, U.C.L.A. Professor Franz Schurmann, 41, reelingly announced: "I'm a subversive." "I hope you enjoy your adolescent behavior," snapped the ambassador. "Say 'adolescent' again and I'll fight you!" roared Schurmann and put up his fists. It got no further, of course, as embassy aides and Novelist Mary McCarthy, a member of Shurmann's group, stepped between the two men. Next day Schurmann sent around a note of apology explaining that his tipsy condition was responsible for the silliness. "I think I could have taken him," mused Sullivan. "He's smaller than I am."

Later on, when writing about her trip to Hanoi, Mary McCarthy would omit the Schurmann incident entirely. Just as she would say nothing of how she used a precious cable to send a birthday greeting to Janet Flanner in Paris. "I don't know how she knew it was my fête day, but it lifted my spirits at midnight," Flanner wrote Natalia Murray. Instead she would make much of the terror and anxiety she suffered upon discovering, via the Thai newspapers, that Johnson was about to use F-111A bombers against the North.

To Eve Stwertka she had once confided that she herself never experienced anxiety. Certainly by cramming her days with every variety of literary and domestic activity she had left few opportunities for anxious reflection. At Vientiane, she had nothing to occupy her. Joining her companions for dinner at a restaurant, she was able to joke about how if things got bad they could all escape by hopping a Polish freighter at Haiphong. Back in her hotel room, she was at leisure to consider the implications of what she had done.

### FROM "HOW IT WENT"

What I saw was that I had no right to die: my stupid, silly life did not belong to me alone; it was in a joint account. Personally (I thought), I no longer cared whether I got killed; it would almost be a relief. I was only agonizing on Jim's behalf. Was this truthful or not? Then, at any rate, I was sure it was[. . . .] I sat on my bed. I cried. I got hold of myself and tried to read. A wave of panic would hit me, and I would moan. It hurt, like a real pain. I wrote [Jim] letters. But as soon as my pen touched paper, a censor interposed. "Careful, my friend. Watch yourself." I could not pour my heart out; that criminal relief was forbidden. If I told him I was sure I was going to be killed, that would finish him. Assuming he still cared about me, and perhaps even if he didn't. Maybe better not mention the F-111A's? Or touch upon them lightly, in a comical way?[. . .] Mention my idea about Haiphong and the Polish freighter. . . .

**JAMES WEST**    When I got that letter, I went through the roof. What is the matter with that woman? I thought. Polish freighters are just as much the targets of our bombing as anything else is. It wasn't until later I understood she had been joking.

In trying to sustain a facetious tone, she had lost sight of how the Polish freighter might play in Paris. Fortunately, after four days, the ICC plane was able to take her and her companions on to Hanoi, where, after landing in the dark, they were greeted by a delegation from the Vietnamese Peace Commission bearing a big bouquet for each of them. For the length of her stay, no matter how remote the village or hamlet and no matter how crowded the bomb shelter, she would be accompanied by an interpreter from the Peace Commission, who would think nothing of following her to the very door of a local privy, the bouquet having given way to a stack of folded toilet paper. Only when she was in her room writing would she have to fend for herself.

On the drive from the airport, when her car was forced to pull over for an air raid alert, she had her first encounter with life in North Vietnam. This time the American bombers turned back without dropping their load on Hanoi. However, by the time she resumed her journey, helmet at the ready, she was conducting herself very much the way she did in personal relations. Having been impressed by her hosts' courage under threat of attack, she was prepared to be charmed and beguiled.

The hotel where foreign visitors were put up did not have the high ceilings and elaborate moldings of the Continental, but it had hot water of a plenitude inconceivable in the South. Moreover, the food was good. On awakening the following morning, she saw a well-scrubbed but bomb-ravaged city, its gray streets dotted with lakes and parks and shaded by a canopy of tall trees. In Hanoi, you could still hear a cock crow. The civilian population relied on bicycles and motorbikes; automobiles were reserved for officials and visitors; trucks were reserved for transporting precious cargo.

Because of the constant bombing, serious travel had to take place at night. At the onset of the war all industry had been moved into the countryside. Scattered in remote hamlets you could find miniature factories and immaculate small clinics. Where the machinery was broken or inadequate, workers took up the slack. Where there was a shortage of medical supplies, doctors and nurses came up with surprisingly successful alternatives. Everything was neat and serviceable and evocative of a time long distant. Everything, that is, but the speech of her guides, which was laced with stock phrases like " 'the American aggressors,' 'the American imperialists,' 'the war of destruction,' 'the air pirates.' " As a good guest, she was prepared to give her hosts the benefit of the doubt. "[I]t has occurred to me that the set phrases of North Vietnamese diction are really Homeric epithets," she wrote. If need be, she was also prepared to hold her tongue.

#### FROM "HANOI"

Under the cover of darkness, the country was resupplying. Respecting that cover, I never asked exactly what was in the trucks or where the convoys were going. I did not want to feel like a spy[. . . .] I tried to restrict myself to innocent questions and speculations, such as "Was that thunder and lightning or a bomb?" This inhibition extended to observing my companions and attempting to study their attitudes and behavior, in the manner of a social scientist. A poor approach for a reporter, but I suspect it was rather general and dictated by courtesy to a people whose country was being invaded not only by fleets of bombers but also by reconnaissance planes, monitoring every pigsty and carp pond.

However, there were moments when her discomfort was palpable. One came at the War Crimes Museum, where she was presented with a metal ring made from the wing of a downed American bomber: having accepted the ring, she found it impossible to keep it on her finger. Another came when she was brought to meet two captured American pilots, fellow countrymen whom she found a good deal less sympathetic and companionable than her hosts.

> The Vietnamese, one hears, have been taken aback by the low mental attainments of the pilots, who have officer rank (the gaunt, squirrel-faced older man led in to see me was a lieutenant colonel) and usually college degrees, which must be leading their captors to wonder about American university education. I was taken aback myself by a stiffness of phraseology and naïve rote-thinking[. . . .] Far from being an élite or members of an "establishment," they were somewhat pathetic cases of mental malnutrition[. . . .] It *was* painful, because of the distance between being free and being under duress, between leaning forward on a comfortable sofa and sitting upright on a stool, but also because of another, unexpected distance—not a moral one, for I did not feel morally superior to those American strangers in prison pajamas, if anything the reverse, since they were "paying" and I wasn't, but a cultural distance so wide that I could see myself reflected in their puzzled, somewhat frightened eyes as a foreigner.

She had arrived in Hanoi with eight suitcases, she would later explain to a young antiwar activist who was trying to find some common ground in their Hanoi experiences. She had also arrived with a lifetime of assumptions. By the time she met Pham Van Dong, the North Vietnamese prime minister, she believed she was ready and eager to divest herself of every form of excess baggage she carried with her.

> Everybody knows that you cannot serve God and Mammon, but few can refrain from trying; each counts on being the exception, especially if, as in my case, it is Mammon who seems to be serving *us*, gratuitously, with no collusion on our part[. . . .] [L]ike most of the non-Communist Left, I was moving effortlessly into a higher and higher income bracket. The slight discomfort this caused me was outweighed by the freedom from any financial stringencies and the freedom to write exactly what I wished[. . . .] In Hanoi, for the first time in my travels, I found that this freedom and the material evidences of it, in the shape of clothes and possessions, were not regarded as enviable. The number of my suitcases (I have never learned to travel light) may have afforded some slight amusement; that was all. The license to criticize was just another capitalist luxury, a waste product of the system.

In South Vietnam she had made it a point to avoid generals and high-ranking government officials, but in the North she did not scruple to meet with the country's handsome and well-spoken prime minister or to take as a rare compliment his saying, *"Vous avez beaucoup de coeur, madame."* In Saigon she'd had the company of three seasoned correspondents, but in Hanoi she was left to see the error of her former ways unimpeded—to see that a good heart was preferable to a cold eye and that criticism was at once superfluous and suspect.

Leaving Saigon, she had firmly believed she was acting as a patriot. Leaving Hanoi, she was beginning to believe that she was simply there for her own peace of mind: if the war came to an end, she might once again sleep through the night. At the end of her stay in the North, she was heartened by Eugene McCarthy's nearly winning the New Hampshire primary and by Lyndon Johnson's decision not to seek a second term in office. Fortunately, she did not have to wait until she was back in Paris to celebrate all this good news with Jim West. Instead, she was able to join him in Osaka, where he was meeting with Japanese officials on OECD business and looking forward to her arrival with no notion that she regarded herself as a changed woman.

**JAMES WEST**   She was exhausted when she reached our hotel, but her eyes opened wide when she saw I'd taken a very nice suite and filled one of the closets with all her best evening clothes. There were matching shoes and the works. She was overwhelmed. The main thing I remember was the smile of complicity. I knew her very well. I knew she couldn't wait to get out of those fatigues.

**DAVID DUVIVIER**   When she went off to Vietnam the first time, we all had dinner at the airport—at Le Bourget—and she read us her will. Later, after she got back safely, I think she wanted to change her will and Jim said something pretty funny. He said, "It's like taking back Christmas."

Not only did her husband know her very well but he had a knack for putting her grander gestures in perspective. By the time she got back to Paris there was no question of shedding any material excess baggage or of holding back from writing a second Vietnam report. If the tone of her Saigon pieces had been sharp and ironic, writing about Hanoi she was inclined to wax rhapsodic. Once again, she made no effort to hide her bias. The first response from Hannah Arendt was particularly gratifying.

### FROM HANNAH ARENDT'S LETTER TO MARY MCCARTHY, JUNE 13, 1968

I wanted to write yesterday just after reading the third instalment of the Hanoi book. I rarely saw Heinrich so enthusiastic; I love it enormously. This still and beautiful pastoral of yours has the effect of showing the whole monstrosity of our enterprises in a harsher light than any denunciation or description of horror could. It is beautifully written, one of the very finest, most marvellous things you have done.

Unfortunately, Arendt did not much care for subsequent sections in which McCarthy took herself and her fellow intellectuals to task, while succumbing totally to the charms of Pham Van Dong. Arendt was not the only one to have problems with those sections. There was a notable demurral from a British friend, the foreign correspondent for *The Observer*, whom she had credited with producing some of the best reporting on the war.

**GAVIN YOUNG**   We were in Holland when she was writing *Hanoi* and she would sometimes ask me what I thought. I didn't really agree with what she came up with, frankly. I thought she took an overly strong unqualified line. When I said that to her at the time, she laughed it off by saying that she'd met a very handsome North Vietnamese officer who took her around—he was so handsome and so charming she had to believe every word he said, how could she not. I said, "Okay, Mary, if you're going to fall for a pretty face at your age I can't argue with you." It was futile to argue about the war— that's the way you make life enemies. I mean, why bother? And I'd grown to care for Mary, there was that.

Once again her pieces for *The New York Review of Books* were brought together and published as an oversized pamphlet. This time, however, there was a bit more review attention—most notably from *The Washington Post*, which ran a daily review by Ward Just, who had spent a year and a half in Saigon as the *Post*'s correspondent and who had the inspired notion of damning her with her own words.

**FROM WARD JUST'S REVIEW IN *THE WASHINGTON POST***
In the winter of 1968, Mary McCarthy, the leading American *femme savante*, alighted from an airplane at Gialam airport, Hanoi, for a three week stay in North Vietnam. In her own eyes, this trip had something fabulous about it, of a balloonist's expedition or an ascendancy into heaven. Where to Americans of an earlier generation North Vietnam was the incredible country of Ho Chi Minh, Vo Nguyen Giap and the hated Cong, to Miss McCarthy North Vietnam was, very simply, dreamland[. . . .]
The paragraph above, with necessary transpositions, is taken almost verbatim from a piece Miss McCarthy wrote about Simone de Beauvoir, the leading French *femme savante*, in January of 1952[. . . .] [T]he lady came to North Vietnam with a closed mind and an open notebook, and she believed everything they told her. It is only because North Vietnam and the attitudes of its people matter so much that the reader must mourn what this book might have been.

**WARD JUST**   I'm a great admirer of Mary McCarthy's work, both the essays and the novels. It's just the Vietnam stuff that I didn't like. She didn't understand Vietnam at all. It's a minor thing. She had a distinguished career, and Vietnam was just a blip on the chart.

**WILLIAM TUOHY**   Later on, not long before Mary died, I invited Ward and Mary both to lunch in Paris. They seemed to get on fine. I didn't know Ward had slammed her book. Ward, I think, thought she was a bit of a dilettante. If he had known Mary in Vietnam, I think he would have liked her, because they were two of a kind. They would have responded to each other instantaneously.

After being pressed into service by the *Post's Book World*, Tom Buckley, who *had* met her and liked her enormously, tried to temper his objections to *Hanoi* with admiration for her first Vietnam book. William Tuohy and Jonathan Randal tried not to take too hard a look at what she had done. Still, they couldn't help noticing.

### FROM TOM BUCKLEY'S REVIEW IN *WASHINGTON POST BOOK WORLD*, DECEMBER 1, 1968

[*Vietnam* was] a sharp, witty, angry look at some of the greater stupidities of the American war machine and its civilian auxiliaries[. . . .] [Here] the clear voice has been muted, indeed almost strangled, by rage and shame over the bombing of North Vietnam and by the author's compassion and admiration for its people and their leaders[. . . .] The author's protective, even maternal, attitude toward the North Vietnamese, her expressed concern to do or say nothing that might prove injurious to them, seem excessive to the needs of the world's toughest and most able revolutionaries.

**WILLIAM TUOHY**   I liked Mary enough that I didn't want to read her Vietnam books. I just figured, I like her for what she is here and if she writes something idiotic, I'm not going to lose sleep over this.

**JONATHAN RANDAL**   Remember, to go to North Vietnam meant it was difficult to do any reporting because you were taken around. They were at war and they were paranoid. All people at war tend to be paranoid. *But I think you can always ask questions.* Harrison Salisbury did, when he was there in 1966.

Why *hadn't* she asked questions? reviewers asked. Why here of all places did she insist on being the perfect guest? Within a few weeks Susan Sontag would go to Hanoi, following in her footsteps, though hesitating to tread on ground that threatened to be treacherous.

**SUSAN SONTAG**   I saw a lot of the things that she saw and I was taken to see the same prisoners. There we were in this room and there was a guard over to one side. I was really dumb in those days. But I still had my instincts and I thought, This is a terrible situation. I don't understand it and I don't know what's right. So I didn't deal with it in my book. I was also at the same hotel.

You can't imagine what it was like—with the bombs and these young women with bandoliers serving you in this most spartan of dining rooms, which was like a prison commissary or something. Then the sirens would go off and your waitress would rush off to the roof to fire at the American planes. When you left you were asked to sign a guest book. Of course I looked through to see who'd been there that I might recognize and I saw Mary's name a few pages back. She'd been there maybe two months before. What she said was something like, "I've had a wonderful stay in this hotel. The service is worthy of a hotel in Paris."

When Sontag's book was brought out by Farrar Straus, it made sense for Bob Silvers to ask Frances FitzGerald to review both volumes together. And it made sense, given their past history, for Silvers to send his Vietnam correspondent a brief note, preparing her for a response that was less than enthusiastic. He had reason to be anxious. Of the two titles, FitzGerald found Sontag's *Trip to Hanoi* "the more accurate," because "the subject of both books [was] not so much [North Vietnam] as the American encounter with it." Of the two authors, both of whom were ill prepared for their task, she found McCarthy the more fallible, if only because she seemed not to suspect how little she understood of her hosts. Three decades later, as far as FitzGerald was concerned, it was six of one, a half dozen of another.

### FROM FRANCES FITZGERALD'S REVIEW IN *THE NEW YORK REVIEW OF BOOKS*, MARCH 13, 1969

On the one hand [Miss McCarthy] does not do the work of a careful enthnologist, by keeping close watch over her evidence. From her account the reader might gather that the North Vietnamese have no acne, and the Southerners neither hot water nor classical music. On the other hand, she "excuses" the Vietnamese for what will not fit within her system of values. When she calls her guides' orthodoxy a sad result of the war, she is assuming that the Vietnamese would aspire to her definition of freedom if the war had not intervened.

**FRANCES FITZGERALD**   I can't remember which book I liked better. She and Sontag had done the same thing. The books were more or less travelogues. Neither of them understood the Vietnamese very well, I'm sorry to say. I think it was great that they both went and did this—that they both made the attempt. But looking at the books now you find them less than a huge contribution to one's knowledge of the Vietnamese.

Back in 1968, as far as Mary McCarthy was concerned, it was nothing for Silvers to lose sleep over. She had taken to Frances FitzGerald from their first meeting and she had made her peace with *The New York Review of Books*. Moreover, at this point any review attention was welcome. While *Hanoi* had gotten more coverage than *Vietnam*, it received no reviews from *The Nation*, *The New Republic*, *The New Yorker*, or *The New York Times*. Unfortunately, the timing of its publication was less than ideal. By December 1968 Robert Kennedy had been shot; Eugene McCarthy's children's crusade had come to nothing; Chicago's Mayor Richard Daley had let his police run riot; Hubert Humphrey had been handed the Democratic nomination; Richard Nixon had been elected president; and *Hanoi* looked to be old news. But there seemed to be more to it than that, particularly in retrospect.

**WILLIAM JOVANOVICH**   Why didn't the books sell? To this day, I am of several minds. I broke my back getting the books out, promoting them, talking them up with my colleagues. But they failed abysmally. At one early period, I thought that hardcover publication might make the books less like broadsheets (eighteenth century!), less like overnight-published Bantam books of the time. Then, I saw that *currency* overrode all and so put the books in paperback and rushed their production. I now doubt the hardcover—versus paperback—publication was an issue central to their poor reception. There's no doubt that the books exuded for some readers a strong sense of Mary McCarthy's hating her own country. She reinforced this adverse opinion by the act of receiving as a gift from Hanoi officials a ring made of the metal of a downed American airman. This was for most people a terrible thing to do; and her discussing it in *Hanoi* as if it were a philosophical question only made it worse.

Mary McCarthy did not hate her own country. On the contrary, she believed she loved it and wanted to save it from its worst self. Nonetheless, after the publication of *Hanoi* she had reason to believe her rescue attempts were unappreciated. She also had reason to believe further attempts might be unwarranted. When Nixon took office in January, the peace talks were well underway in Paris and there was every reason to expect that he would honor the wishes of the electorate that had pushed his predecessor out of office. Under the circumstances, it made sense to return to work on her novel.

In *her* Paris, as opposed to Peter Levi's, life was bustling and frequently amusing. While the novel lurched along in fits and starts, she continued to give dinners and to go out with friends and to make herself available to a certain number of young American dissidents who found their way to Paris. Regrettably, most of these dissidents were little more to her taste than the downed American pilots.

## FROM MARY McCARTHY'S LETTER TO ROBERT LOWELL, FEBRUARY 7, 1968

I too have been exposed to what you saw in your draft-resistance meetings. Here it was a half-hour "documentary" featuring a deserter named Philip Wagner[. . . .] Exactly as you say, a mixture of total incoherence and dead clichés. He was incapable of saying why he was against the war or in fact of saying what he felt about anything. He used "wilfully" twice when he meant "willingly": "I would wilfully give my life"[. . . .] They're all like that nowadays, [Jim Jones] said, whether they're for the war or against it. This is what education has done to them.

**MARY BRADY**  She met with a lot of underground people in Paris. They would come to the apartment. People who had left the country. People who were deeply involved in protesting. I didn't meet very many of them. The Weathermen you wouldn't find. Bernadine Dohrn was not her cup of tea. She met with the intellectuals.

Unfortunately, as Nixon settled into office, it became clear that the resisters were destined to be in Paris for a good long time. No president, however shrewd or cynical, wanted to be responsible for losing this war in Southeast Asia. Instead of bringing the fighting to an end, Nixon was bringing it to Laos and Cambodia. A rash of demonstrations within the United States did not deter him. Nor did the death of four students in the spring of 1970 at Kent State.

In the summer of 1971, when *Birds of America* was finished and safely, if not entirely satisfactorily, published, McCarthy was once again prepared to take on the mantle of a reporter. That spring, Lieutenant William Calley had been convicted and sentenced at an army court-martial for the murder of twenty-two Vietnamese civilians at My Lai in March 1968—most of them women and children. Occupied with her novel, she had let Calley's trial pass without written comment. But when Captain Ernest Medina, the commander of Charlie Company, was court-martialed for the deaths of those same civilians, she sent off a letter to William Shawn, offering to go to Georgia to cover the trial for *The New Yorker*.

This time, she was writing for a magazine where she would have access to some quarter of a million readers and a virtual guarantee of receiving serious review attention for her pieces when they were published in book form. By their very nature trials are dramatic: the proceedings in the Eichmann courtroom had provided Hannah Arendt with a narrative line strong enough to support the whole sorry story of Hitler's extermination of the Jews. As the granddaughter of a prominent Seattle lawyer, McCarthy knew her way around a courtroom. As a skilled polemicist, she had produced her fair share of closely reasoned arguments.

At Fort McPherson, however, she was operating with a handicap Arendt had never had to contend with. Coming on the heels of Calley's conviction, this trial promised to give off the stench of reheated bad news. Such excitement as there was seemed to reside with Medina's civilian defense counsel, the redoubtable F. Lee Bailey, with his bad-boy behavior and custom-made suits.

Having delayed her arrival one week in order to share a part of her husband's vacation, she had no difficulty in catching up. And no difficulty in catching on to the fact that the case against Medina was slowly unraveling. "It all seems like an exercise in futility," one spectator was reported as saying. Indeed the defendant and his counsel seemed thoroughly bored by the proceedings as they "yawned, stretched, doodled, slumped, whispered, rolled martyrs' eyes skyward, nudged neighboring ribs, cupped mouths to pass sardonic asides, like a pewful of restless schoolboys during a particularly dull and long-drawn-out chapel service."

It didn't help matters that everyone, save for the presiding judge, either manifested the weakest imaginable grip on English grammar or spoke like "a letter from a credit company." Nonetheless there were moments when the boredom lifted and a clear dissenting voice could be heard.

### FROM "MEDINA"

If there were American heroes at My Lai, they were the bubble-ship pilot, Chief Warrant Officer (now Capt.) Hugh Thompson, and his door gunner, Lawrence Colburn. The two were later decorated—with a misleading allusion to "cross fire"—for evacuating Vietnamese civilians they saw cowering in a bunker. Thompson and his crew made three rescue lifts, on their own, independently of any orders, and with rifles on the ready to shoot any man of Charlie Company who tried to interfere.

Thompson and Colburn had done all they could to put a stop to the killing and then refused to be silenced. In these two men she found her "good Germans." In the end, though, their testimony counted for little. One month after he was brought to trial Medina was found innocent. The army had gotten the verdict it wanted. Her report appeared in *The New Yorker* in the spring of 1972. By the time her book came out late that summer Medina was working as the foreman of F. Lee Bailey's helicopter plant; Calley's sentence to life imprisonment had been reduced to twenty years; and she'd had ample opportunity to reflect on what had gone wrong at My Lai.

Much of what had gone wrong, she believed, had to do with a fundamental misperception. In the courtroom, the men of Company C had spoken of earlier "casualties" they had taken as if they had been "atrocities inflicted on them by the enemy." In short: they saw themselves as "*civilians.*" "When a man in uniform, with a gun, makes no distinction between himself and a civilian, he will scarcely make a distinction between the military and civilians of the other side," she wrote.

But this failure to make important distinctions was not limited to the men of Company C—or to the military for that matter. As she saw it, by failing to understand why collective responsibility for the war need not preclude individual guilt, the American public (particularly members of the "counter-culture" who dismissed Calley's conviction as "hypocrisy" and "fake justice") had helped create a climate in which not only would the massacre at My Lai go unpunished but more massacres would inevitably take place.

At Fort McPherson she was no tourist. While much of what transpired in that courtroom could rightly be called boring, her reporting was nothing of the sort. Three months after coming out in *The New Yorker* the pieces, slightly altered and amplified, were published by William Jovanovich in hardcover and paperback. *Medina* did in fact receive more review attention than its predecessors. The attention, however, was not of a sort to please her. In *The Nation*, she was accused of being harder on the Left than she was on the Right. In *Time* she was accused of letting her "bitterness [lead] her into overstatement." And in *The New York Times Book Review* she was accused of skipping over material that did not buttress her conclusion—like the fact that, according to the *Times*' own reporter, when Medina was acquitted, his wife was in tears and he himself was "struggling to maintain his composure." She was also accused of being an intellectual snob.

### FROM GLORIA EMERSON'S REVIEW IN *THE NEW YORK TIMES BOOK REVIEW*, AUGUST 13, 1972

Miss McCarthy is quite rightly very opinionated about the war and the United States Army. So am I. Surely any American who still has a truly open mind about the war possesses almost no mind at all. So it gives me no pleasure at all to criticize Miss McCarthy for what appears to be a smart-aleck tone in her book, for letting a thin ribbon of upper-class contempt weave through it all. *Medina* is Miss McCarthy sizing up the dumb clods, the liars, the cowards, the dink-haters, and the 'lifers,' (the contemptuous G.I. term for career officers) who can't put into words what they want to say[. . . .] But who do you think was sucked into the Vietnam war, Miss McCarthy, our Harvard and Princeton boys?

She was still digesting these dispiriting assessments when just before Christmas of 1972, in an effort to force the enemy back to the bargaining table, Nixon ordered a massive bombing of the North. Unbowed and unchastened, she was as ready as ever to take action—to set off for Hanoi with a group of twenty prominent Americans and, if need be, to sit amid the rubble while the bombs fell all around her. At one point she considered enlisting the Pope. This time, it was not her husband but a fellow novelist who sought, with humor, to put things in perspective. Her own husband, as it turned out, was in no mood to joke.

**GLORIA JONES** We were there at dinner when she made up her mind to go to Hanoi to stop the bombing. To get other Americans to go with her and sit there. And she turned to my husband, the way she had done in the past with me—so there were ten people looking at you and you were supposed to give an opinion—and she said, "Jim, what do you think?" And he said, "If the bombs fall on you, Mary, keep a tight asshole."

**JAMES WEST** During the Nixon Christmas bombings of North Vietnam, when Mary wanted to go to Hanoi, I said no. It was one of the few times I said no, because I had spent years in the air force. They had this new plane and I thought, That's what's going to be bombing dear Mary, and I didn't like that idea at all.

Faced with the very real possibility of his wife's meeting her death in Hanoi, Jim West remained adamant. The debates in their Amsterdam hotel room threatened to ruin the Christmas holidays and even take a toll on the marriage, until, as she later remembered it, at some point West agreed to let her go so long as he could go with her.

Fortunately, there was no need to take Jim West up on this offer. When the North Vietnamese were approached in Paris, they let it be known that, with half the Hanoi airport destroyed and a large party of guests, including the singer Joan Baez, stranded for the duration, there was no room for additional bodies. In any case, before the holidays ended and before her fevered imagination could come up with still another way to test her husband's love, the North Vietnamese agreed to go back to the negotiating table and Nixon halted his bombing of the North.

**ELIZABETH HARDWICK** I was actually there when she was planning to go to Hanoi during the Christmas bombings. To sit and be bombed. The infinite romantic playacting, it's so different from what you see from other people in her world. Other people were more realistic. That she could be so analytical and so romantic is bizarre.

**HANS VAN MIERLO** She asked me to go over with her and other well-known Americans and I was flattered that Mary invited me. I would have gone. The North Vietnamese embassy here said that they would not allow us to do so. They said, "War is serious." Later, I thought, To imagine that Nixon would have stopped bombing because of a few people who were famous was absolutely madness. But for a little while we thought it was a good idea.

It may have looked like playacting, but for her it was no joking matter. It never had been. To be thwarted in her one last great effort to end the war was dismaying and infuriating. But no more infuriating than to see each one of her Vietnam books receive short shrift. Their lack of success was bearable so long as no other books were finding favor. But in

1972, while friends had searched in vain for *Medina* in their local book-stores, *Fire in the Lake,* a historical, political, and cultural analysis by Frances FitzGerald, was receiving both the lion's share of review attention and going on to win both the Pulitzer Prize and the National Book Award.

The following year would prove to be even more dispiriting, when she was forced to watch *The Best and the Brightest,* David Halberstam's attempt to fix blame for the war on a dazzling but benighted circle of Kennedy insiders, sell 60,000 copies in its first two weeks and become a number-one *New York Times* best-seller. FitzGerald's book she found in every way admirable. Halberstam's she found sloppy and portentous and lacking in any real ideas. Moreover, she found it unreadable. "I attribute my stupefied boredom partly to Halberstam's prose, which combines a fluency of cliché with deafness to idiom and grammatical incomprehensibility," she wrote in *The New York Review of Books.* She was evidently in the minority. At least one writer she was on record as having no use for (though she was not about to revoke his visa) had rallied to Halberstam's side.

**DAVID HALBERSTAM**  I got a letter from Graham Greene after I sent him an inscribed copy of *The Best and the Brightest.* It went something like this: "Thank you very much for the book with the dedication on the first page," and went on to say, "I could not understand that vicious review of Mary McCarthy's, not one of my favorite writers. I assume she was upset by your failure to take note of a weekend she spent in Hanoi."

In the spring of 1974, the war was winding down and a beleaguered Nixon was facing impeachment. At this point, another writer might have simply called it quits. Instead, she decided to bring together all three Vietnam pamphlets, along with her review of Halberstam's book and her exchange with Diana Trilling, in one oversized book to be called *The Seventeenth Degree.*

This time she was leaving reviewers no excuse to ignore her. The book would be published simultaneously in hardcover and paperback and virtually in conjunction with a timely collection of her Watergate reporting. Not only that, it would open with a fifty-four-page confessional memoir—her first memoir since *Memories of a Catholic Girlhood*—explaining why she had felt she must go to Vietnam in the first place.

The first sign of trouble came when she tried to place the memoir with *The New Yorker* and then with *The New York Review of Books.* William Shawn turned the memoir down out of hand and Bob Silvers, in rejecting it, let her know that it would do her no good with the average reader. Although there might be some merit in his argument, she was not about to back off. And she was not about to back off when Silvers then offered her a chance to respond to a new Random House book by the squirrel-faced lieutenant colonel she had met in North Vietnam. The colonel, it seemed, had been tortured most horribly by his captors, beaten, starved, and trussed like a chicken. Moreover, he had his own page-long version of their Hanoi encounter.

### FROM *THE PASSING OF THE NIGHT*, BY ROBINSON RISNER

I sat at the end of a coffee table, for this was supposed to be very informal. Mrs. McCarthy was on my right. She was a rather large woman and looked as though she might have been a sports enthusiast in her earlier years[. . . .] She said her husband was a diplomat in Paris. She asked me about myself, and told me she had requested the interview to be with me. She also talked a bit about Senator Eugene McCarthy and his chances for the presidential nomination, about which she was optimistic. Then she wanted to know what I missed the most. I told her a Bible[. . . .] She was a rather forceful woman. When she turned to the Cat [head officer] and said, "Can I send him a Bible?" it caused a big flap[. . . .] Then she asked, "What else do you miss?" I said, "Sweets." She said, "I'll send you a cake." Then she turned and asked the Cat, "Can I send him a cake?"[. . .]

Then she asked them a different kind of question. They began to circumvent it. Finally she looked at me and said, "You know, I don't think they understand me." I raised my eyebrows and said, "I think they do." Another time she mentioned hopes for an early end to the war. "We had better knock on wood," and she knocked three times on the table. I was in interrogation for three hours trying to convince the Dude [another interrogator] that raising eyebrows and knocking on wood were not secret signals. I sometimes wondered if Mrs. McCarthy was playing a dual role. I know I suffered because of her request to see me, and to my knowledge she did absolutely nothing to help our cause.

Before publishing *The Seventeenth Degree* she did make one last-minute change. She added a footnote to "Hanoi," identifying the squirrel-faced lieutenant colonel by name and adding some less than flattering details culled from her original notes.

This was Robinson ("Robbie") Risner, today a widely admired hardliner and Nixon zealot. From my notes: "tight lined face, wilted eyes, somewhat squirrely. Fawns on Vietnamese officers. Servile. Zealot. Has seen error of ways. Looks at Bananas. Grateful. 'Oh, gee, bananas too?' Speaks of his 'sweet tooth.' Loves the Vietnamese candy. Effusive about it. Perhaps ostracized by his fellow prisoners. Speaks English slowly, like a Vietnamese practicing the language. Stereotyped language."

But she was not content to leave it at that. Taking Bob Silvers up on his offer, she wrote a long response intended to accompany a piece by

Anthony Lewis, in which Lewis reviewed Risner's *The Passing of the Night* in tandem with a collection of interviews with other downed pilots. In the end, much as he might have wished to believe otherwise, Anthony Lewis had been forced to conclude that the North Vietnamese had indeed tortured their American prisoners. If he was dismayed, he was also prepared to give these former prisoners a fair hearing.

McCarthy could not bring herself to go quite that far. Acknowledging that Risner had probably been tortured, she tore into his description of their meeting, calling into question one detail after another.

### FROM "ON COLONEL RISNER," *THE NEW YORK REVIEW OF BOOKS*, MARCH 7, 1974

Although I am a devoted cake-baker, I bake them only for people I like and I did not like Lieutenant Colonel Risner and in fact was rather disgusted by his talk of his "sweet tooth"[. . . .]

I had never heard of Risner until that day. When he was led into the room, his name meant nothing to me[. . . .] A naïve sense of his own importance transpires from the book and this primitive vanity perhaps also explains the cake memory: "a cake just for *him!*"[. . .] I am sorry to hear he suffered, but it was not through my singling him out[. . . .]

In the proofs "large" was "tall." I am neither large nor particularly tall and I wonder who or what prompted him to make the change[. . . .]

I did write to Risner's wife and to the younger pilot's mother and fiancée, to say I had seen the captive men and that they had seemed to be in good health and spirits[. . . .] Mrs. Risner never answered. Peculiar. At the time I thought that political fanaticism directed toward me must have been more powerful than her interest in hearing about her husband, or else that she did not *want* to hear about him, having got word through the POW grapevine that in captivity he had become a North Vietnamese toady.

When Bob Silvers suggested that she comment on the immorality of the North Vietnamese using torture, she went along, but only to a point.

Looking back, I can see that Risner's behavior that day was consonant with his having been tortured. Had I thought so then, I hope I would have tried to do something about it. Published my impression or gone to the North Vietnamese to warn them that this had to stop, in the name of humanity and their own interests[. . . .] It is hard for me to believe that the North Vietnamese leaders (those I have seen anyway) would not find the abuse and degradation of captive men morally repugnant. Nor can I imagine Pham Van Dong, a highly perceptive and intelligent man, failing to be disgusted with the gross stupidity of the enterprise[. . . .] In my opinion, the full truth of what went on in the camps is not yet known[. . . .] Colonel Risner's book does not convince me that he is giving the full truth of his experience; instead, it persuades me that he is offering something less and something more.

In the spring of 1974 Robinson Risner was neither prepared nor inclined to rush to his own defense. Twenty years later, when he was living in Austin, Texas, with his Vietnam experience well behind him, he was pleased to inform this interviewer that Ballantine Books had sold hundreds of thousands of copies of the paperback edition of *The Passing of the Night* (mostly in places where you could find a large military base). To his knowledge, the paperback was still in print. When questioned about that Hanoi meeting, he, too, was inclined to dwell on certain salient details as if they might provide some clue as to why the two recollections of that stilted exchange did not jibe.

**ROBINSON RISNER**   Just because she says she didn't ask for me doesn't mean that she didn't. I never saw her standing. I sat to one side of her. She appeared to be tall because her eyes were about on my level and I'm five foot ten. I don't remember that conversation about sweets, but I had been prepped beforehand about what I could talk about and sweets would have been a safe thing to talk about. When we were talking she seemed to really be looking at me, but she didn't seem exactly sympathetic. I'm not saying she wasn't. But I just don't recall any sign that indicated that she was. I knew from the onset that the Vietnamese never forced me to see anyone unless it was a friend of theirs. I spoke slowly because I was carefully choosing my words, as you might understand, because I didn't want to be tortured.

Why had Risner gone and changed her physical description in his book? Someone at Random House had urged him to. And why had she failed to suspect that he was under severe constraint?

**ROBINSON RISNER**   I think the Vietnamese had told her that we were treated very well and she just believed them. Instead of her own American citizen, she chose to believe the Communist Vietnamese.

Risner's ability to recall her attack with equanimity may have owed something to his own book's impressive sales figures. But there seemed to be more to it than that.

**ROBINSON RISNER**   Some of her contemporaries, who allegedly were her friends and were liberals like she was, took her to task for what she had done and said that was not a book review on her part, it was a character assassination. I read that. The young man that helped me put the book in order sent it to me. I remember that more than one person responded to that piece very adversely.

Foremost among those contemporaries who took her to task was Doris Grumbach, who was now serving as literary editor of *The New Republic* and who accused her of writing a "review by insinuation, implication, sly suggestion." Just because Mary McCarthy found Robinson Risner "unlikable" didn't mean he hadn't suffered "years of mistreatment," concluded Grumbach. A more objective "contemporary" was James Fallows, fresh out of Harvard and doing his best to make a name for himself. Writing about her Vietnam and Watergate reporting for *The Washington Monthly*, Fallows gave her brush with Risner two pages of a twelve-page piece.

### FROM "MARY MCCARTHY—THE BLINDERS SHE WEARS," BY JAMES FALLOWS, *THE WASHINGTON MONTHLY*, MAY 1974

Mary McCarthy's hatchet has been bloodied before, and she counts such figures as J. D. Salinger, Truman Capote, and David Halberstam among her victims. But the Risner article was the first in which she'd attacked a defenseless victim, a man so ill at ease with words as to be in no condition for trading debating points with anybody. The case suggests some interesting questions about Mary McCarthy. She cannot be blamed for having missed the truth the first time, although she may have been mistaken to draw belittling conclusions from the evidence ("naive . . . childish") rather than withholding judgment[. . . .] But there are ugly implications in the fury with which she lashed back at Risner; she shows no awareness that missing the truth, whether innocently or not, is a matter of some gravity.

Fallows saw no reason "to fault her" for missing the signs of abuse. He faulted her for attacking the bearer of bad news. As he saw it, she had not only beaten up on a man who was no match for her but had failed dismally as a reporter.

She obviously enjoys being on the scene of the political story of the day, but she feels no compulsion to be there long enough to ask all the questions and find the answers[. . . .] In the preface to *The Seventeenth Degree*, she says: "The trouble with trying to be a reporter is that events either hurry ahead of you or lag behind. They do not sit still and wait for you to join them like the characters in a novel." Her attitude and performance realize the worst fears of the enemies of the "New Journalism," who predicted that writers who embellished the facts might fail to include the facts at all.

Of course *The Washington Monthly* was neither *The New York Times* nor *The Washington Post*. Nonetheless, it had a circulation of 25,000 and was read by people who cared about politics. Twenty years later, Fallows would be prepared to stand by what he had said. In so doing he would seem at times to be echoing Chiaromonte's original argument against her going to Saigon.

**JAMES FALLOWS**   In the great divide of those days—that of being for or against the war—I was certainly on her side. It was just the tone of unearned superiority that grated on me. Unearned not in the broadest literary sense, because she had certainly earned literary eminence. But when talking about these public matters she seemed unwilling to dirty her hands by actually finding out what had happened. She seemed to be just delivering these pronouncements. If it had been presented only as cultural criticism from Paris, that would be fine, but this sort of dilettante reporting really annoyed me. I think my outrage comes in a way from the fact that this was a failed opportunity.

William Shawn and Bob Silvers had been right to warn her about the preface. Although it would provide material for future biographers, it did her little good with any reviewer who wished to attack her credentials as a reporter. At the same time, it did nothing to garner her the sort of review attention she was looking for. *The Seventeenth Degree* was ignored by *The New York Times*, *The Nation*, *The New Republic*, and *The New Yorker* and called "a punishing chunk of lard" by Gloria Emerson in *The Washington Post Book World*. The most favorable attention it received was in *The New York Review of Books*, where any praise was immediately rendered suspect.

"I shall be glad to pay a reward to any reader of this volume who can explain to me what happened and why," she announced near the start of the preface, trying to find an answer to why, despite all her efforts, her Vietnam books had failed to find an audience. The reason, wrote Gloria Emerson, was that "better reporting and finer writing from Vietnam was done by others." Among those others, Emerson named and quoted her great and good friend David Halberstam, who had been there in 1962 and 1963.

Privately, McCarthy's publisher was compiling his own list of reasons. Inevitably, so were her friends and her enemies. Decades later there would be a feeling, even among those who had been all for her going to Vietnam in the first place, that with her writing about the war she had somehow fallen short of what she had hoped to achieve.

**JASON EPSTEIN** Mary had plenty of courage during the Vietnam War when she denounced the American interest there. Maybe even excessive courage. She never wrote a great essay on the subject, but she wrote good things. Her positions I thought were correct, and it was an occasion to write a great essay of an Orwellian kind, but she never got to do that. It would have been a wonderful time for her to reflect on the Stalinist issue. One hoped that she would, and that would have been her great piece.

**AL ALVAREZ** Even if you agreed with her about the war, there was something self-righteous about her manner that put you off. It's a thing that trendy lefties often do. They make you feel they aren't supporting these causes simply because they believe in them but because the causes give them a kind of moral edge.

The kindest explanation fixed some of the blame on bad timing. The most damning explanation was offered by the author of *The Best and the Brightest*.

**DAVID HALBERSTAM**   The fact is, when it came to Vietnam it didn't matter what you'd done in the past. Vietnam had its own body of writers. Its writers were people who paid the price. It was our generation—people in their twenties and thirties. People like Frankie FitzGerald who spent months and years there. They had nothing to unlearn. Mary McCarthy went as a famous writer and the wife of an American diplomat. They showed her what they showed Joe Alsop.

**ISAIAH BERLIN**   Her going to North Vietnam was a mistake I think. She was taken in a bit. She had a left-wing slant and didn't want to be on the side of the imperialists. Her pieces on North Vietnam were very unconvincing. She was very skillful as a reporter. The pieces were beautifully written. She painted a picture. But she was not good with ideas.

Unfortunately, subsequent events made her original assessment of the North seem misguided if not willfully blind.

**MARY MCCARTHY, IN AN INTERVIEW WITH MIRIAM GROSS,**
**THE OBSERVER, OCTOBER 14, 1979**
As for my current views on Vietnam, it's all rather daunting. I've several times contemplated writing a real letter to Pham Van Dong (I get a Christmas Card from him every year) asking him can't you stop this, how is it possible for men like you to permit what's going on? One can allow for a certain amount of ignorance at the top for what is executed at a lower level; that's true in any society. But this has gone past that point. I've never written that letter, though; it is still in my pending folder, so to speak. Of course it shouldn't have stayed there, but it did. I might have signed the Joan Baez protest about the boat people, but I was never asked.

**DIANA TRILLING**   Mary lived to see the boat people. This was what my piece was foretelling. Of course I didn't know the exact circumstances of people clinging to the sides of boats in their passion to get out of the country. It was horrendous. Many people drowned. Mary lived through that, and I don't think that it moved her to any correction of her position about the relation of the Viet Cong to its enemies—the relation of any Communist authority to its opponents. Mary continued to the end of her days, as I understand it, to be a friend of the Viet Cong.

**GAVIN YOUNG**   I thought that Mary should have gone back. I'd become very involved with a Vietnamese family, so I did go back and I did see what happened. They were taken off for eight years to re-education camps and finally they were let out, but they weren't purged of their sins, according to the Communists. They continued to be punished by not being able to get jobs and not being able to send their children to school. They found life absolutely intolerable. So they became boat people. I did talk to Mary about this. I thought that people like Mary, Jane Fonda, and Frankie FitzGerald should have gone back. They could have said, "America had to get out, but the sequel was this."

**ROBERT SILVERS**   I wonder what Mary would think now. Since the war, the behavior of the North Vietnamese government has been brutal and terrible. I think that she might well have changed some of her views. She was a woman who was capable of that. Very much so.

She was a woman who was capable of being a hard-hearted realist and a great romantic. At the same time, she was a woman incapable of doing anything by halves. With her Vietnam writing Mary McCarthy had set out to save America from disgracing itself, only to find that it was fast becoming a country she scarcely recognized. Those few readers and reviewers who took notice of what she was doing seemed only to resent her for it. By the end she was being attacked for her snobbishness, for her failure to separate the sheep from the goats, and, above all, for being a bad sport.

In some ways her predicament recalled that of Hannah Arendt after the publication of *Eichmann in Jerusalem*. She, like Arendt, was being lambasted for placing aesthetics above morality. And she, like Arendt, was being faulted for including only the facts that suited her. However, unlike Arendt, she could take no comfort in knowing she had made her case to tens of thousands of readers. Moreover, she could take no pleasure in seeing a sizable group of friends rush to defend her.

"It is not that I think *A* or *B* should have come to my support; what astonishes me is that no one did," she wrote Hannah Arendt in the fall of 1974, when she had cause to feel particularly low. As it turned out, the sole friend who came to her support was the same friend who years before had offered to represent her in court against an irate Philip Rahv. In a piece that ran in *The New York Review of Books* Harold Rosenberg gave her full credit for an "alert sensibility," an "ever-active mind," and, most of all, the kind of "good writing" rarely found in current reporting. He made no mention of Robinson Risner.

"I never dream of Vietnam, North or South," she'd written in her introduction to *The Seventeenth Degree*, back when she still had hopes of finally reaching more than a handful of readers, "but I have a recurrent nightmare *concerning* Vietnam but laid in Cambodia or, sometimes, Laos[. . . .] I have an important message to carry or a report to make to a court of law. It is something about a war crime I have witnessed, and these people swarming around may try to obstruct me. Then I realize I have forgotten the thing I need to report about. It has slipped my mind, and now—the frontier is closed or there is fighting—I cannot get back into Vietnam to find it."

For all that she had no use for Sigmund Freud, she went on to try and make sense of this dream. "Probably this is my secret assessment of how I carried out my Vietnam 'assignment.' Some essential was missing. But I do not know what it was, and indeed that is the plot of the dream: that, being the person I am, I am unable to recover that essential, find the master-switch that will give illumination. I had it once, apparently (in my youth?), and lost it, from sheer distraction."

By that fall, it was beginning to look to some observers as if more than one essential might be lost, or missing. After years of coming up against what she believed to be more than her fair share of incomprehension and disparagement and outright invective, she had stumbled badly. For a time it seemed as if she ran the risk of losing her balance entirely. Or, to put it another way, of losing all that might be called her best self.

Fortunately, she did not lose her balance for more than a minute and she did not come away from Vietnam empty-handed. If her efforts to stop the war were destined to bring her little appreciation, she was rewarded with something more tangible and altogether less fleeting. Thanks to the husband whose patriotism and fighting spirit had made it possible for her to take action in the first place, her Vietnam writing served, in the most literal way, to help bring her back to America—an America she was not only quick to recognize but, in time, was happy to call her own.

# Chapter Twenty-three

# CASTINE

In February 1968, when Mary McCarthy was in the throes of saving America from "disfiguring itself," Hannah Arendt was thinking of leaving America for good. She had her reasons. "I have the impression that Johnson is not just 'bad' or stupid but kind of insane," she wrote from New York, where she had recently joined the faculty of the New School. But that was just the half of it. "The 'activists' are in a mood of violence," she wrote, "and so, of course the Black Power people. Meanwhile, more crime in the streets, open defiance of laws by the Unions, and everywhere some inarticulate fear of mob rule."

In virtually every quarter, opposition to the war had unleashed unprecedented disorder. For Arendt it recalled the last days of the Weimar Republic. But you did not have to be a refugee from Hitler's Germany to see cause for alarm. "For the first time, I meet middle-aged, native-born Americans (colleagues, quite respectable) who think of emigration," Arendt confided. What she did not confide was that she and Heinrich Blücher had asked an old friend to be on the lookout for a place for them in Switzerland.

Mary McCarthy took no joy in seeing Lyndon Johnson's chickens come home to roost. Above all, she took no pleasure in hearing from a mutual friend that Arendt herself might emigrate. She wrote back to say, "I feel very strongly that you would be *wrong* to take such a step."

As she saw it, this was "a moment not to leave but to *come back*." Although her argument owed a good deal to principle, it could hardly be called objective. In the spring of 1967, she had chosen to come back, by purchasing a sizable chunk of real estate. The purchase had been made on the spur of the moment, but it had not been made lightly. For some time she and Jim West had been thinking of buying a place where they could spend summer vacations with the children and where they could spend the months of West's compulsory home leave.

Bocca di Magra, by virtue of its location, had been out of the question. The Cape had been ruled out for a number of reasons—not the least of them being a very real former husband in the person of Edmund Wilson and a host of real-life models for the characters in *A Charmed Life*. Newport, where Bowden Broadwater retained a wide circle of friends, was hardly an option. Finally, Stonington, where they had been made welcome during the early months of their marriage, had proven less congenial on a second visit.

In the summer of 1964, she had written Carmen Angleton, "[T]here's not a cake rack or a muffin tin in the village, as I've learned from trying to borrow them, and the bean pot I'm using had been accommodating an 'interesting' arrangement of dried grasses and weeds, since most people are too lazy to grow flowers, except the old perennials they can't stop from coming up. Everybody lives on 'gourmet' foods, frozen or tinned[. . . .] In the fish market all the fish is filleted, if not frozen as well; you can't buy a whole fish[. . . .] The children, who don't share the adult taste for frozen lasagne casseroles and canned lobster newburg with pre-saffroned rice, live on hamburgers and hot dogs, but in a year or so they will be eating dog or cat food, I think."

In the end, she and Jim West had headed farther north to the coast of Maine, where they settled on Castine, a sedate community of summer and full-time residents situated at the tip of a narrow peninsula jutting out into Penobscot Bay. At Castine, Jim West would be a short drive from places where he had been born and raised, and she would be within walking distance of Elizabeth Hardwick and Robert Lowell. (For the past decade the Lowells had been spending their summers in a house on the village Common belonging to Lowell's cousin Harriet Winslow, with Lowell going off to write every morning at a barn on the bay that he used as a studio.) Back when she had been smarting from Hardwick's parody of *The Group*, such a move would have been inconceivable. But four years had passed, and she and Hardwick were making every effort to put all that behind them.

Indeed, it was Robert Lowell who had first broached the subject of a possible house for them—a federal-style house belonging to a retired army general by the name of Gillette, which had been languishing on the market for some time. On learning that the Wests were eager to see it, Hardwick had followed up with a letter, letting them know she was "thrilled." Although she herself had never been inside the house, she did not hesitate to sing its praises. "I remember my friend Mary Thomas saying that it was noble! It's lovely from the outside and seems very large, with even new rooms over the garage."

But even while Hardwick waxed rhapsodic, she took care not to oversell the village. Castine, she warned, was "slow and quiet." It was also "tiny." And the swimming was poor. Trying to strike a happy balance, she allowed that they would have no trouble lining up tennis and sailing lessons for the children. "[I]t is absolutely lovely if one likes it. And most people do like it after they dig in," Hardwick promised.

That spring, when his wife was hard at work readying her Saigon report for *The New York Review of Books*, Jim West made a trip to Castine and liked what he saw. The village was not quite so fashionable as Blue Hill, its near neighbor, and not nearly so splendid as Bar Harbor, an hour and a half farther north, but it had its fair share of "noble" houses and carefully tended lawns. Established as a trading post in 1630, Castine had been a bustling port by the outbreak of the Revolution, when it had rapidly acquired a reputation as a Tory haven. After the Tories moved on to Canada and its days as a serious port were over, the village retained a vestige of its former glory in the form of a fully accredited maritime academy.

From the outside the Gillette house was indeed lovely. Built in 1805 by a prosperous local merchant, it was set well back from the street and shaded by a canopy of trees. Four large public rooms made it perfect for entertaining and the apartment over the garage made it perfect for their extended summer family. What made it irresistible was the property in back—an expanse of green surprisingly ample for a house at the center of a village, boasting the remnants of a formal garden that had seen better days.

Without waiting for his wife to come take a look at the house, Jim West made an offer. He got the house for $32,000. Although the price was right, it represented a considerable outlay of cash—particularly for a house that would ordinarily be occupied no more than six weeks a year. Certainly the house would add to the heavy financial burden the Wests were already carrying. Nonetheless, it seemed, on balance, well worth the money. For Jim West, it would be a place to bring the children, much like the place he'd grown up in.

For his wife, it would be a place she could call home. No less important, the Castine house promised to be of immediate strategic value. By securing a foothold in Maine, she was hoping to protect a weak flank. Indeed, the following winter, when a BBC interviewer noted that as an American living in Paris she was criticizing America from "a well known anti-American camp," he did not catch her off guard. "I am not an expatriate," she informed him. "I live in Paris because my husband works there." And when the interviewer went on to ask, "[D]o you wish you were back in the States committed to the scene, to your own people?," she was ready with her answer. "[W]e did have some such idea in mind when we went back to America last summer: we bought a house in Maine, feeling that if we are going to attack this country we have got to be there."

As it turned out, she would get little credit for her house in Maine from those who took exception to her Vietnam writing. What she got, instead, was Robert Lowell and Elizabeth Hardwick and a village full of new neighbors who showed themselves perfectly delighted to welcome her. In addition, she got a chance to renew ties with Katharine White, her first *New Yorker* editor, who was living in retirement less than an hour away in North Brooklin. Last but not least, she got a chance to see old friends she had not spent much time with in years.

On July 4, 1967, Jim West ushered her through the front door. Earlier, Elizabeth Hardwick had written, warning of the necessity for fires and sweaters on even the most glorious of summer evenings. That month the weather was consistently cold and damp. The house cried out for a thorough cleaning. The trees were in need of pruning, and the garden was in need of immediate attention. Her husband's two sons were in residence and his daughter was due by the end of the month. Frani Blough Muser, her best friend at Vassar, had taken a place with her family in Maine and was urging her to come visit. But everywhere she looked there was work to be done.

### FROM MARY McCARTHY'S LETTER TO FRANI BLOUGH MUSER, JULY 20, 1967

Painters are here (exterior only this year), and at this moment a lot of tree surgery is going on outside my window, as well as roto-tilling, mowing; I've been weeding and scattering annual seeds and putting in a few herbs (thinking with envy of your mother's creeping thyme) and wondering what would happen if I put some dark green draperies in the washing-machine with Javel water—Jim says it would wreck the machine.

Although the plan had been to paint only the exterior that first summer, by early August the white clapboard siding was a pretty lemon yellow and the painters were hard at work on the public rooms downstairs. This frenzy of refurbishing might have left another woman exhausted, but it wasn't long before she was sending off invitations, in which she took care, like Elizabeth Hardwick, to do justice to Castine's failings as well as its pleasures.

### FROM MARY McCARTHY'S LETTER TO DWIGHT MACDONALD, AUGUST 6, 1967

[C]an you come up and stay with us? You know the way. The Lowells would love to see you too. We have plenty of room, though there may be a certain confusion of painters and paperhangers. Jimmie Merrill, Eleanor Perenyi, Grace Stone are coming the weekend of the 19th; Bill Jovanovich is coming for one night on the 29th. But otherwise we're free[. . . .] Please do come. You know the drawbacks of Castine—the swimming situation, which I rather mind and keep having reveries of finding a hidden sunlit cove that nobody had thought to mention. We have, on the positive side, a little Cercle Francais that meets every Saturday night and at present is reading Pascal. Next Montaigne.

At the same time, she began taking a hard look at the quiet corner of America where she had fetched up.

> But I must say, America is a shock. Even to the children. There is this weird business of technology turning into its opposite, as if in some Midas fable: no trains, scarcely a bus, whereas forty years ago there were all sorts of carriers that took visitors to Castine, including a night boat from Boston that steamed into the harbor, loaded with summer trunks. No farming any more, except industrialized potato-growing, no fish, frozen bread; apparently people drive for miles to attend cake sales. It is all very pathetic. I must stop and go call up the paper-hanger—another all but extinct craft. We're going to have to import him from Bar Harbor. Practically like colonial times.

Castine had not been spared the sad decline she had witnessed earlier in Stonington, but the paper hanger proved to be adept and William Jovanovich and her Stonington friends all made the trip.

**JAMES MERRILL**   Stonington is smaller than Castine, and seems rather second-rate after you've seen it. I used to prepare for the Stonington summer by rereading some of the E. F. Benson novels. The Lucia books. But before I went to Castine I reread *Emma*.

**ELEANOR PERÉNYI**   Mary was a fabulous hostess—if that's the right word. There was the food, of course. Though she wasn't herself quite the cook she thought she was, she *provided* fine food via their Polish Maria, who cooked for them in Paris and came to Castine every summer. And Mary took all kinds of trouble. Getting up at dawn, for instance, to make blueberry muffins for breakfast before our long drive back to Stonington. She planned things to do— picnics (she adored picnics with elaborate food, lobsters and chocolate cake) and expeditions to places that might interest you. I've never known anyone who took more trouble over their friends.

Almost as soon as she moved in she caught the attention of her nearest neighbor—the poet Philip Booth, who spent summers with his wife, Margaret, and daughter, Margot, in a house that had been in his family for five generations. The Booths were hardly your average Castine natives. As a member in good standing of the Cercle Français, Philip Booth had been introduced to a fair number of visiting literary figures. But this new arrival was something else again.

**PHILIP BOOTH**   I think it was the fact of Mary McCarthy I noticed first, rather than the physical figure. It was the intellectual busyness that surrounded her—or that she surrounded herself with, more accurately. I think my strongest memories are of the people she all but immediately brought here. These were all people of whom she approved socially as well as intellectually. It was very gay, in the old sense of the word.

**MARGARET BOOTH**   Philip and I couldn't get over the way Mary entertained. Nothing like this had ever hit Castine. Certainly she was the major motivator for whatever was going on. It seemed to be absolutely necessary for Mary. I think she needed that constant contact—friends that she wanted to have here and be here.

**MARGOT BOOTH**   There was quite a buzz about Mary's moving to Castine. As a child, I was a little more frightened of her than I was of Lizzie. You never trotted around to the back. You went in the front door.

It wasn't long before she had painted the floors in clear blues and mustards and laid a tan duck runner up one side and down the other of the freestanding staircase. But that was just the beginning. A rose garden was planted to the right of the main garden and soon the vegetable beds put to shame any kitchen garden she'd had in the past.

**ELIZABETH HARDWICK**   At meals there were always lots of fresh vegetables—lettuce, beans, zucchini, all sorts of things. They had a dishwasher, but Mary wouldn't use it. To grind the coffee beans every morning she had a great big brown thing. She wouldn't have a little Braun like we all have.

**MARGARET BOOTH**   I'd drop in and she'd be in the kitchen preparing vegetables for dinner or lunch. Even when Maria was there, she did a lot of the work herself. I learned a lot about food from Mary. I once said to Jim something about Mary's being such a great cook and he said, "She certainly is, and one thing I've learned is to stay out of the kitchen."

In the kitchen, helping make everything go smoothly was Maria Fourrier, who did not speak a word of English and who was quietly counting the weeks until they would return to Paris.

**MARIA FOURRIER**   At 7:45 A.M., without fail, I served her breakfast in bed. Mostly she would have poached eggs on toast, orange juice and black coffee. And Monsieur West would have the same. After her breakfast Madame West would wash and get dressed. She would work until lunch in her study. Before she would go up to her study she would make phone calls. Then she would let nothing disturb her. Sometimes she would go to the garden before working. When they had friends to stay, she would always have breakfast at the table. She loved to make pancakes for her guests. She would stay at the table for one or two hours and there would always be some talk about books and subjects that interested her. When there were guests she didn't work the way she normally did. If the guests went off by themselves to sight-see or visit, Madame West would profit from their absence.

Always Mary tried to stick to a strict work schedule. Still, in a village that numbered among its residents a retired Episcopal bishop and a Nobel Prize–winning physicist, she managed to cut quite a swath.

**SALLY AUSTIN**    Castine had always been a place that was very low key. It was not Northeast Harbor. Mary was the first one who brought that kind of rather classy entertaining. I mean, you put on your best dress.

**ELIZABETH HARDWICK**    Mary never made the concessions the rest of us make. She had very beautiful linen place mats from Europe that required constant washing and ironing. And she always insisted on having a first course. There was always a soup or some kind of roasted peppers or something. I once said about her, "Mary treats the first course at dinner as if it were the Bill of Rights."

No matter who was staying with her, she ran her household by a strict set of rules. Breakfast was served at eight, lunch at one, drinks at seven, and dinner promptly at eight. Summers, when Reuel and his wife, Marcia, came to stay in the apartment over the garage, she made no adjustments. Even when Kevin came with his family, she remained unbending. (By 1967, Kevin and Augusta Dabney had divorced, and Kevin, often accompanied by one or more of their three teenage children, was a regular summer visitor. In 1979, he would remarry and start a second family.) Small children were not invited to sit down with the adults at the dining room table. The sole concession she made to her youngest guests was to provide a small black-and-white television for the apartment over the garage. Naturally enough, this mode of domestic management did not sit well with everyone. Sometimes it was hard to remember that the house had been purchased not only with a view toward entertaining but as a summer home for the three West children.

**DANIEL WEST**    My brother, Jonny, and I went to Castine for three months that first summer and Alison came later. We were delighted to be there, with the backyard and the trees. My father really loved it. There were virtually no friends our age. There was no relaxed playing around with the kids next door. What was remarkable was the intellectual and aesthetic level of the life you experienced.

**BARBARA DUPEE**    Fred and I were in Maine when Jim's younger son was there and there was this enormous correctness that I have not seen since I was a child and I would go to a family friend's house—the exact proper behavior, now it's time to do the puzzle, now we will have the nature walk, and so on. That isn't really the way children get raised nowadays.

**ALISON WEST**    At the end of the first and only summer that I spent in Castine as a child, I had a hideous conversation with my mother. I called her in Paris to ask if I might stay a little longer. My mother said, "If you plan to stay any longer, don't even think about coming back here." I cried with both shock and misery. That was the only time I can remember Mary vaguely putting her arms around me. Even then I felt the two of us were doing it because the situation seemed to require it. For a long time after that I saw my father and Mary on no more than a few rare occasions a year. My brothers were allowed to spend the summers with them, but I was not. My mother never offered an explanation. I didn't get back to Maine until I was eighteen and had returned to the United States for college. That first time I returned to Castine we were walking through the house and Kevin pointedly said to me, "Well, I guess you don't have your own room in this house, do you?" My brothers each had their own rooms, but my room had become a guest room.

When it came to spending time with the children, she got less than she'd hoped for. (In 1970 Danny wrote to say that rather than hang around Castine, where there were no good summer jobs, he preferred to earn some money during his school vacation. Jonny, rather than come to Maine on his own, soon followed suit.) With the Lowells, on the other hand, she got more than she'd bargained on. Living in each other's pockets, it was impossible to dismiss the dark side of Robert Lowell's brilliance.

### FROM MARY McCARTHY'S LETTER TO HANNAH ARENDT, SEPTEMBER 12, 1967

He is taking some new drug, a kind of salt, that is supposed to guarantee that he'll never have another manic seizure. But what it has disclosed, by keeping him "normal," is how mad he is all the time, even when on his good behavior[. . . .] He's very tense and, when he's drinking, quite grandiose; he oughtn't to drink and has stopped for the moment, but I don't think he can keep it up. It's as though the drugs were depriving him of his annual spree and he compensates for the deprivation rather cunningly by using the license given to drunkards. My opinion is that it would be better to let him be crazy once a year, be locked up, then emerge penitent, etc., than to have him subdued by this drug in a sort of private zoo—his home—with Lizzie as his keeper. But she prefers it that way. So long as he doesn't drink, she says.

The trouble was, lives were not so easily arranged as books and furniture. In 1970 Robert Lowell would leave Elizabeth Hardwick for the writer Caroline Blackwood. Faced with his defection, and with the loss of a reliable source of diversion and enlightenment as well as bad behavior, McCarthy would choose to regard it as a blessing for her friend Lizzie.

She herself would continue to find Castine the sort of place where it was not only possible but positively pleasurable to "dig in." She might have to drive to Bar Harbor for a first-rate butcher and import her guests from Connecticut or London, but Castine, with its sleepy harbor and its quiet shaded streets, possessed undeniable allure. (As it turned out, it even possessed a shaded fresh-water pond perfect for swimming and picnicking belonging to a cousin of Philip Booth.) Indeed, as long as this remote corner of New England persisted in presenting such a reassuring face, it was no real hardship to come back.

Life, however, has a way of calling one's bluff. Three months after hearing Hannah Arendt say she was thinking of leaving America for good, Mary McCarthy got a taste of the sort of tumult that had driven her best friend to contemplate forsaking her adopted homeland. In May 1968, she had returned from Hanoi to find actual fighting in the streets of Paris. With the workers out on strike and the students occupying the Sorbonne, words like "violence" and "mob rule" ceased to smack of hysteria. One fine spring day it looked as if the army was about to mow down a phalanx of students within blocks of her apartment. At one point the de Gaulle government seemed on the verge of toppling. Five stories above the fray, putting the finishing touches on the last of her Hanoi pieces, she took time out to type a letter to Hannah, who had written to say how much she had liked her "North Vietnamese Bucolic" and who seemed likely to understand what she was going through now.

### FROM MARY McCARTHY'S LETTER TO HANNAH ARENDT, JUNE 18, 1968

> I have the sense that I'm losing touch with my own writing, that I can't rely, with these articles, on my usual separate judging, critical self. But it may be partly the circumstances. It was weird, writing about North Vietnam during all the turmoil and passionate excitement here. Hanoi seemed so far away—several centuries[. . . .] I found the events here shaking. Hanoi was shaking too but this was more so because closer to home both figuratively and literally. All one's habits, possessions, way of life, set ideas were called into question, above all one's critical detachment.

Seeing the error of your ways is one thing. Actually changing those ways is quite another. Early on during the summer of 1968 there was a brief flurry of excitement when it looked as if Eugene McCarthy would pay a visit to the Lowells on a pre-Convention swing through Maine. (Robert Lowell's old friend Blair Clark was working as the senator's campaign manager, and Lowell and the senator had become good friends.) Unfortunately, time was short and the candidate had to cancel. But, even though she would have to wait to make the acquaintance of the one Senator McCarthy whose last name she did not mind sharing, her summer was not lacking in excitement. Sonia Orwell, who was recovering from a hysterectomy and the formidable task of putting together a four-volume collection of her late husband's letters and essays, came to stay for several weeks. This visit, which provided the occasion for a hectic round of dinners and receptions, expeditions and picnics guaranteed to fell a less resilient or less bibulous visitor, set the pace for many summers to come.

## FROM SONIA ORWELL'S LETTER TO MR. AND MRS. JAMES WEST, AUGUST 26, 1968

Oh my goodness me, HOW I miss Maine and life in your house! I go on thinking it over and over and the maddening thing is that the only people I really want to discuss it all with are you! It's easy to tell every-one how beautiful, what fun etc., but they haven't got it all inside their minds which is so boring of them. I shall never get over the shock of my arrival and all that architecture and the beauty of it all and your house and the curtains and the staircase and the blazing fires and *every-thing*. But there are so many things that started the very morning after that I'd like to discuss for hours. Mr. Hall (of course we say "period piece" not "of the period"!) and the auction, clam-bakes and all those trips, to "undecided" in Calais and Deer Island and Ram Island and the picnic in the Wildlife Reserve: in fact *all* the picnics were so glorious. (It's so nice that Mary has such a passion for them too!)

**EVE GASSLER STWERTKA** Mary had enormous stamina. People couldn't keep up with her. Andy Dupee told me quite recently about the time she went up to help Mary move into the house in Maine. They had crates to unpack—china and glass and all the pots and pans. Andy said they had a very good time together the first few days. I asked what happened after that. And Andy said something that I've always felt exactly. She said, "Well, Mary's a very clever woman and after a certain time you just can't keep up." You no longer have things to say that will really interest her. She's ready to go on and have more discussions and more news and more activities, and you're fading fast.

**ELIZABETH HARDWICK** A tremendous effort was put into birthdays and all that. Years ago I said to someone, or maybe someone said to me, that per-haps all of that came from being an orphan. But I don't know.

**MARGARET BOOTH** The whole town wanted to come to Mary's parties. And of course she and Jim were generous enough to invite the whole town—sometimes to their dismay. Some people never knew when to go home.

In time not only the poet next door but the poet on the Common tried his best to convey what it was like to partake of her uncompromising hospitality.

## FROM "FOR MARY McCARTHY 1," BY ROBERT LOWELL

Your eight-inch softwood, starblue floorboard, your house
sawn for some deadport Revolutionary squire. . . .
A friendly white horse doing small-point, smiling,
the weathered yeoman loveliness of a duchess,
enlightenment to our dark age though Irish,
our Diana, rash to awkwardness. . . .
Whose will-shot arrows sing cleaner through the pelt?
Have I said *will*, and not intelligence?

> Leaving you I hear your mind, mind, mind,
> stinging the foundation-termites, stinging
> insistently with a battering ram's brass head of brass. . . .
> I hide my shyness in bluster; you align
> words more fairly, eighty percent on target—
> we can only meet in the bare air.

### FROM "MARY'S, AFTER DINNER," BY PHILIP BOOTH

> Both hands talking, raised to shoulder height,
> the left uptilted with a Lucky Strike,
> the right still doubled down, inside of smoke,
> across an opposite heart:
> > *the argument is nothing,*
> *nothing after all . . .*
> > > . . . all August that we've drunk,
> made talk of, dined on, drawn back from,
> then come back to sip;
> > the evening settled,
> dearly, in your hands, the room
> moves to the logic of your smile[. . . .]

If the poet on the Common tended to regard that lucid smile with greater ambivalence than the poet next door, he'd had two decades to observe it. But by the middle of the second summer, writing Elizabeth Bishop of how Mary sometimes reminded him of Randall Jarrell, he was sounding like someone who'd had his fill of it.

### FROM ROBERT LOWELL'S LETTER TO ELIZABETH BISHOP, JULY 30, 1968

> I find Mary a bit hard (how shall I put it?) to get at. The beautiful big house, the beautiful big meals, the beautiful big guests, the mind, as Hannah Arendt puts it, that wants to be ninety per cent right, times when nothing seems addressed to me, and nothing I say is heard— maddening when you think what you said is quite good, or the subject is one you feel could be referred to you.

Of course it was Robert Lowell who had written Elizabeth Bishop back in 1962 of a dream in which Philip Rahv was "ascending the social ladder rung by rung" while he himself was making his descent. "Have you ever noticed how snobbish the old rebel bohemians are," he had written. "No one believes in society except Mary and Philip." Without question, Elizabeth Bishop's old schoolmate from Vassar believed in society. To some degree she always had.

**ROBERT SILVERS**   Mary was fascinated by the workings of American social life, and she was always placing people, very aware of who they were and where they came from.

**SAMUEL TAYLOR**   *[Playwright best known for* Sabrina Fair *who lived nearby in Blue Hill]* She liked being among these Maine people, social people, dull people, just ordinary people. She rarely said harsh things about them. They never bored her. She accepted them and they accepted her.

**THOMAS MALLON**   When it came to Castine, I think there was some of the same wide-eyed wonder that informed her Hanoi pastoral. She liked it for what it represented—for the old values she remembered from her child-hood. She might laugh at this tendency to see things with a rosy glow—there is unquestionably some irony in that title "North Vietnamese Bucolic"—but, all the same, she did see things that way.

As Mrs. James West she could be remarkably forbearing, but as the writer Mary McCarthy she held her friends to a high standard. Within months of Sonia Orwell's visit, she went out of her way to put truth before friendship when reviewing Sonia's collection of her first hus-band's letters and journalism—a collection brought out by William Jovanovich, her very own publisher. Taking a second look at a writer long held to be a giant of twentieth-century literature, she did not draw back from giving voice to conclusions guaranteed to please no one. After dismissing Orwell's socialism as sheer rant, she accused him of being anti-intellectual and antihomosexual. "What he really had against intel-lectuals, pansies, and rich swine was that they are all fashion-carriers—a true accusation," she wrote.

Having pointed out that in the entire collection there was only one letter to the young woman he had "married in his last illness," she went on to portray the great man himself as a self-destructive, self-denying crank who lacked "enough human weaknesses to be a real novelist." Not only did she fault him for being a closet conservative and an unabashed philistine, she faulted him for sins he never lived long enough to commit.

### FROM "THE WRITING ON THE WALL," *THE NEW YORK REVIEW OF BOOKS,* JANUARY 30, 1967

> Surely he would have opposed the trial and execution of Eichmann, but where would he be on the war in Vietnam? I wish I could be certain that he would not be with Kingsley Amis and Bernard Levin (who with John Osborne seem to be his main progeny), partly because of his bel-ligerent anti-Communism, which there is no use trying to discount, and partly because it is modish to oppose the war in Vietnam.

Ultimately, she could not bring herself to lament Orwell's early, and some might say tragic, death.

If he had lived, he might have been happiest on a desert island, and it was a blessing for him probably that he died[. . . .] His end had something macabre in it, like the end of some Victorian pathologist who tested his theories on his own organs, neglecting asepsis. In his last letters, he speaks of his appearance as being "frightening," of being "a death's head," but all along he had been something of a specter at the feast.

By her own admission she had not merely admired Orwell but actually modeled some of her best essays after his. What, then, had prompted her to be so "hard" on him? One Orwell defender who accosted her in person on behalf of the widow believed that she had been prompted by the same impulse that had led her to denounce America's involvement in Vietnam. A close friend of Sonia believed the piece owed more to irritation with Sonia than to intellectual fashion. And a fairly disinterested observer was inclined to agree.

**SAUL BELLOW**   Why did she say that about Orwell? She was being a little opportunistic. She thought she would dissociate herself from the old crew and get on board the youth vessel. Not the *Horst Wessel*. She felt nostalgia for the old *PR* days when she had been a rebellious young thing.

**MIRIAM GROSS**   Sonia was the sort of person who eventually fell out with many people. She was very emotional and grew very attached to her friends; then she would try too hard to enter their lives and she could become overbearing. She would often take the side of one or the other partner in a marriage. She drank a lot and, as a result, she could be rather trying. I've heard that on that visit to Maine, Sonia was heavily billed as the widow of George Orwell and perhaps she overplayed the part.

**PHILIP BOOTH**   Sonia overstayed her welcome, unfortunately.

The attack on Orwell may have owed something to Sonia's overstaying her welcome, but the reviewer herself had some reason to find fault with him. Back in the forties, when McCarthy had been writing those early essays, it had been possible to believe that she and Orwell were kindred spirits. She, too, had been an outsider—not exactly down and out, but living hand to mouth. But by the time she finished her bout of reading it was clear that she and Orwell had parted company long ago. The writer she discovered would never have preferred Pham Van Dong to Robinson Risner. And he most certainly would never have agreed that, having undergone a spiritual conversion in Hanoi, you could once again take up your role as the new doyenne of Castine. Unless she cut him down to size, Orwell threatened to become a specter at *her* feast.

"The Writing on the Wall," her controversial reassessment of George Orwell, was the title essay for a collection William Jovanovich brought out in the winter of 1970—a slender volume leading off with her forays against the Thane of Cawdor and the novels of J. D. Salinger and containing a decade's worth of nonfiction presented in strict chronological order. None of the essays written after 1964 addressed the work of an American writer. (Two were devoted to the works of Ivy Compton-Burnett, one to Flaubert's *Madame Bovary*, and one each to novels by her friends Nathalie Sarraute and Monique Wittig.) She might have put down roots in America, but her intellectual life seemed to be flourishing elsewhere. Interviewed not long after the collection came out, she would blithely admit that she had never read any novels by Walker Percy, John Barth, and Thomas Pynchon, or anything by Philip Roth.

When Harcourt published the collection, its author received the sort of treatment reserved for a pillar of the literary establishment. If her Vietnam books were being ignored by the critics, the same could not be said of her essays. In the Sunday *Times*, Anthony Burgess begged to differ with her on the subject of George Orwell—"It is never a blessing for anyone to die," Burgess noted—but took care to treat her as a critic of the first rank.

### FROM ANTHONY BURGESS'S REVIEW IN *THE NEW YORK TIMES BOOK REVIEW*, MARCH 8, 1970

The brand name tells all. Potential readers do not have to be informed by me of the excellence of this volume—the acumen, intelligence, clarity, wit and lack of bitchiness[. . . .] Mary McCarthy is excellent not only in the things she says but in her recognition of the excellence of things said by others[. . . .] She remains our best living mediator between the Anglo-American literary world and the French.

The French might fail to value her acumen as a lady of letters, but in the Anglo-American literary community she remained a presence to reckon with, eliciting sympathy in some quarters and pure venom in others.

**SYBILLE BEDFORD** When she used to come over to London to lecture at some PEN events, she and I and her husband, whom I liked very much, would be put at the same table for lunch. (At that very light large room at the Festival Hall by the river.) What I felt for Mary McCarthy then was affection, friendliness, respect. As for her, putting it, if I may, in an English way: "she was very nice to one." (Alas the lecture that followed would be rather college-girl academic: serious and long.)

### FROM THE DIARY OF JOHN RICHARDSON, VENICE, AUGUST 11, 1970

Peggy and Truman [Capote] got going on Mary McCarthy. Peggy, who has cause to resent Mary for the caricature of herself (Polly Grabb [*sic*]) in "The Cicerone," was relatively merciful. T.C. was merciless. Characteristically, he started on her looks; presumably this is where *he* feels most vulnerable. "That vapid grin she switches on and off, as if to prove what a nice open faced Vassar girl she is. Who does it convince? It wouldn't be so painful if she had a better dentist. And then all those hairs sticking out of her nose—like a potato that's been stored so long it's started to sprout. (I may say Truman's nostrils are conspicuous for their hairiness.) Poor Mary, she looks about as wholesome as the girls who murdered Sharon Tate." As for her work, T. came out with his usual indictment (the same goes for Gore Vidal or Norman Mailer): she's hopeless as a novelist—not bad for an essayist, or when she has a try at autobiography. *Memoirs of a Catholic Girlhood* [*sic*] is fascinating, because the portrait of her father is likewise a portrait of her present husband, Mr. West, "whose ability as a stud presumably compensates for his dreariness in every other respect." Truman was far kinder about Bowden—"he kept her straight, so far as her writing went. It was a real case of the fan marrying the star." "When I first knew Bowden," said Truman, "he was working on *The New Yorker*; he was very delicate and precious and totally star-struck by Mary. When they got married, Mary said it was to save him from homosexuality. . . . Bowden did his best, but what Mary really wanted was Daddy."

Essay collections rarely attract readers in large numbers. Indeed George Weidenfeld, her British publisher, had argued for piggybacking the essays onto her next novel. After some discussion Weidenfeld had been overruled. For the author, bringing out the collection was a way to ensure that she would once again be taken seriously as a lady of letters while bringing in some welcome money. Back in 1963 she had been advised, like many another best-selling author, to defer the bulk of her earnings—taking her royalties in annual installments of no more than $25,000, so that they would be taxed at a lower rate. At the time the dollar had been strong and her annual payment had been more than generous. But with the purchase of the house in Maine and the weakening of the American dollar, she was soon finding she had to borrow against future earnings. The two Vietnam books never made back their relatively modest advances, and by 1970 she was drawing on her capital at the rate of $30,000 a year.

**WILLIAM JOVANOVICH** She was a spender, no doubt. She felt at ease spending, as some people do not. She was not a bargain hunter, not much of a negotiator when it came to buying things. One incident summed up our mutual understanding of her treating money cavalierly. I took her to Idlewild to catch Air France. At the last moment she decided to upgrade her ticket to first class. The plane was on the runway and her delay in fact caused her to have to enter from the tail stairway—the regular passenger entrance was already closed. As she stood at the counter she decided to pay the extra fare in cash. Out of her capacious handbag came fifty-dollar bills, splaying onto the linoleum. She turned to me and said, "Don't look."

For her publisher, the collection was a way to bring one of his most prestigious writers back to the attention of readers who had first discovered her with *The Group*. Jovanovich wasn't thinking only of potential readers. He and his staff were hoping to take some of the heat off her next big book. "I'd just as soon interpose between your next novel and *The Group* a book of critical essays," he wrote in June 1969.

**JULIAN MULLER** [*for many years Harcourt's editor in chief and the editor who handled production for almost all of McCarthy's books*]   I don't mean to suggest that there weren't justified criticisms of Mary's work, but she was an extraordinary target. After *The Group* particularly. I tried to warn her about this. I said, "The next time round they're going to have the big guns out ready to shoot at you."

Early on, there were signs that Jovanovich believed her new novel might be headed for trouble. Instead of bringing *Birds of America* out with the big fall 1970 books, he chose to publish in the spring. Instead of starting off with a printing of 75,000, the way he had with *The Group*, he chose to ship 35,000 and then print another 15,000 to back that up. The best prepublication news he could muster was that *Birds of America* had been taken as a main selection by the Literary Guild.

When it came down to it, nothing was going to make *Birds of America* an easy sell. Not only did it lack the taint of sex and scandal, it lacked just about all the qualities that had won its author a devoted following. Back in 1963 this quiet and reflective story would have had difficulty finding an audience. In 1971 it was competing for the attention of readers battered by the Vietnam War, transformed by the "summer of love," and accustomed to the likes of *Couples*, *Myra Breckinridge*, and *Portnoy's Complaint*.

Making a virtue of what any sales department had to regard as a formidable handicap, Jovanovich chose to market the novel as a modern classic, very much in the spirit of Voltaire. Not only would this make it clear that Peter Levi was someone to take seriously but it would provide readers and reviewers with a most welcome handle on the book. Indeed, when it came to readers and reviewers, little was left to chance. First they were given a précis of the plot by Julian Muller and then told how to respond to it.

#### FROM THE DUST JACKET OF *BIRDS OF AMERICA*

*Birds of America* is the story of Peter Levi, an innocent abroad, who is Miss McCarthy's Candide. In the fall of 1964, he arrives in France to do his junior year at the Sorbonne[. . . .] He tries to live his daily student life according to Kant's dicta, hoping that his will may have the force of a natural law. The result is comedy, mild disaster, frustrated clashes with the police and other forces of order[. . . .] *Birds of America* is a witty and tender *Bildungsroman*. The reader will *like* Peter and his family and the other migratory birds he meets along his flyway, some of them his friends. They are seen by Mary McCarthy with a warm, though hardly moist, eye.

To the end of her days Mary McCarthy professed to love *Birds of America* best of all her novels. Of course from time immemorial writers have been known to harbor a special fondness for the frailest of their offspring. Henry James, for instance, had an abiding affection for his early, ill-fated plays. But more seemed to be going on here: from start to finish, *Birds of America* was a very personal book.

In *Birds of America*, the author's cherished beliefs and pet crotchets were everywhere visible. The reader first spots them in Rosamund, Peter's handsome harpsichord-playing mother, who is trying her best to provide her son with two brief but perfect idylls at a New England village bearing not a little resemblance to Stonington, Connecticut. Ready to speak out against the frozen food proliferating in the Rocky Port supermarket, to take a stand against the gaudy zinnias blazing in the village's deteriorating gardens, and to do battle over the new historic plaques gracing its oldest houses, Rosamund wants to give Peter the America of her youth and not some tarted-up version of it.

If Rosamund can be said to be Mary on the warpath, Peter is Mary plagued by doubts and second thoughts. As the reader watches a sorely beset Peter struggle to avoid self-pity while doing right by the well-intentioned and excruciatingly embarrassing Americans who cross his path, Peter may seem unduly fastidious, but for Peter's creator his dilemma was dismayingly real.

Unfortunately, a handful of real moments do not add up to a satisfying book. And a carefully orchestrated publishing campaign cannot compensate for this. If reviewers were prepared to make use of Harcourt's press kit when summarizing the plot, they were rarely prepared to go so far as to embrace the novel's hero. Not only did reviewers fail to warm to poor Peter, they showed an unhappy tendency to fall back on Norman Mailer. Even the best reviews could hardly be called selling.

### FROM HELEN VENDLER'S REVIEW IN *THE NEW YORK TIMES BOOK REVIEW*, MAY 16, 1971

[N]o creature more devoid of existential reality ever lived than this so-carefully-documented Peter Levi. Why a character "lives" or does not is often mysterious; perhaps here it is fairest to say that Peter has no passions and no contradictions. He worries, he is rueful, he is ironic, he is quixotic, he is awkwardly idealistic, he is solemn—or he is meant, by the fictional gestures being made, to be all these things—but he has no insides.

**FROM ANATOLE BROYARD'S REVIEW IN *THE NEW YORK TIMES*, MAY 19, 1971**

Forsaking the group and the groves, Miss McCarthy has elected to take us into the kitchen and nursery of her imagination. In many ways, it's a fascinating experience. (Can you imagine Julia Child writing a political novel?)

**FROM JOHN W. ALDRIDGE'S REVIEW IN *SATURDAY REVIEW*, MAY 8, 1971**

When the action lapses for Miss McCarthy, she starts making lists[. . . .] She begins to inventory the furniture, the books on the shelves, or the contents of the cupboards[. . . .] As Mailer has said on another occasion, "Lists and categories are always the predictable refuge of the passionless, the timid, and the bowel-bound."

With 50,000 copies in print something had to be done. At William Jovanovich's urging, she consented to come to New York, to talk to reporters and submit to at least one television interview. Here, too, she met with little success. For one thing, she could not always keep her novel free from attacks on her Vietnam books. When she appeared on *Firing Line* and William F. Buckley accused her of hating her own country, it was clear she was headed for trouble. When Buckley announced that it was his understanding that she had grossly exaggerated the lamentable state of cooking in "Rocky Port, Maine," much the way she had slanted her Vietnam reporting, it did her no good to point out that Rocky Port was not situated in Maine and that *Birds of America* was not set in 1971 but back in 1964. Nothing she said was likely to convince her television host that she did not hate her own country. By the time Buckley declared that as far as he was concerned *Hanoi* had merited more review attention than it got if only because it was "news" when Mary McCarthy wrote a bad book, she was so shell-shocked it took her a minute to see that her host intended this as a backhanded compliment.

Without question, the reception of *Birds of America* had taken its toll. It was not only the "bitchiness" but the poor "quality" of the reviewing that bothered her, she told an interviewer from *Publishers Weekly*, going so far as to add, "I'd rather have something like Norman Mailer's perceptive but unfavorable review of *The Group*, in *The New York Review of Books*, than what I've been getting."

She was hurt and disappointed and saw no reason to hide it. From old friends she was offered words of consolation. From Stonington friends she heard only praise, although so far as they could recall they'd had no difficulty getting whole fish and fresh produce back in 1964. Friends, for the most part, treated the book with tact and respect. If they were disappointed, they took care to make no mention of it. Among themselves, however, they were free to give voice to their reservations.

### From Hannah Arendt's Letter to Mary McCarthy, May 28, 1971

I am late in writing this letter, but there was neither typewriter nor that quiet hour available in England to sit down and write. Meanwhile I read as many of the reviews [as] I could lay my hands on and I am still rather speechless[. . . .] Some of the reasons [for] the reaction are clear—no one ever expected you to write this kind of book and the amount of malice that is floating around here in literary circles is enormous; you are an ideal object to crystallize it and this is an old story. The discrepancy between public image and actual person is greater in your case than in any other I know of. And in this book it is your whole person that speaks as the author.

### From Nicola Chiaromonte's Letter to Mary McCarthy, June 25, 1971

When I turned the last page of *Birds of America* and closed the book, I was charmed. There is no other word. You tell the story of Peter with a tenderness, an irony, and a firmness, that make one think of the most endearing and most intelligent of mothers.

### From Nicola Chiaromonte's Letter to Dwight Macdonald, January 5, 1972

Her last book I found "nice", kind of motherly. But also kind of "adolescent". I don't know how to put it That Peter Levy is a character for an American "bibliothèque rose"[. . . .] Don't tell her.

### From Janet Flanner's Letter to Natalia Danesi Murray, May 15, 1971

Mary McCarthy sent me her new novel which looks painfully harmless, called *Birds of America*, and she dedicated it to me handwritten, "To Janet, an eagle." Very sweet indeed. Her head is beautifully shaped, isn't it? A beauty of a photo of her on the dustcover of the new book.

"Adolescent" was hardly the most damning adjective brought to bear on her latest book. But thanks to a sizable advertising budget and the author's willingness to go out and do battle for it, her "painfully harmless" novel hopped briefly onto the best-seller list. The Literary Guild managed to sell 120,000 copies, but by November Jovanovich was estimating total Harcourt sales at about 35,000. Back when she had been struggling to finish the novel, she had written Edmund Wilson, "It has reached the stage of being an incubus, and I think if I ever get rid of it, I shall never be so foolish as to start another." From the look of it she had not changed her mind. She was beginning to talk seriously about doing a book on the Gothic, not unlike *The Stones of Florence*. First, though, she had asked to cover the Medina trial for *The New Yorker*.

In June 1972, she was working hard on expanding her *New Yorker* report into a short book when, only weeks before George McGovern was slated to lock up the Democratic nomination, five intruders were apprehended trying to plant listening devices in the Washington offices of the Democratic National Committee. Like most of America, she had little time for a bungled late-night break-in at an elaborate riverside complex hitherto known only as the home of Martha Mitchell, the loose-lipped wife of Nixon's irascible attorney general. For one thing, she was trying to make sense of the implications of the shooting of George Wallace, whose promise to get America out of Vietnam had posed a serious threat to Nixon. For another, she was privy to, if not exactly taking part in, the elaborate preparations Jim West was making for a lavish party at a Paris restaurant to celebrate her sixtieth birthday.

That July, while she and most of America were watching George McGovern begin to self-destruct, *The Washington Post* reported that the money used to buy the silence of the five Watergate intruders could be traced back to the Nixon White House and its Committee to Re-elect the President. In August Nixon felt it necessary to announce on television that John Dean, the White House counsel, had looked into the allegations and determined that they were groundless. In November, surprising no one, Nixon was reelected by an overwhelming margin. Everywhere news of Watergate was hard to come by. But in Paris such news as there was came filtered through the French press.

**MARGO VISCUSI** There was all this stuff going on in the United States and we Americans in France felt cut off. The French were totally mystified by it. They wondered how a country could turn against its president. In France the president was a grand figure. There was the *International Herald Tribune*, of course, but it couldn't replace the U.S. papers and TV. There was no CNN back then. We all read the Sunday papers from London and she would have been in touch with Bob Silvers, but still . . .

The French might see no cause to make a fuss, but as winter turned to spring an ever increasing number of Americans found it difficult to laugh off the Watergate break-in. In April 1973, when she was making a flying visit to America—to collect a handful of academic awards and visit old friends—she found the country in an uproar. Judge John Sirica was holding hearings in the U.S. District Court in Washington; and there had been testimony implicating such administration stalwarts as Jeb Magruder, Charles Colson, John Mitchell, John Ehrlichman, and H. R. Haldeman. The FBI was under siege and Richard Kleindienst, who had replaced John Mitchell as attorney general, had been forced to step down in favor of Elliot Richardson.

In May, Archibald Cox was appointed special Watergate prosecutor. Furthermore, a special Senate committee had been convened, headed by Sam Ervin, the senior senator from North Carolina. Not since the days of Joe McCarthy had Washington seen anything like it. Once the Senate hearings began to be broadcast live on television, the whole country was riveted. Word had it that John Dean, who had been implicated by testimony in a massive Watergate cover-up, had agreed to talk in exchange for immunity.

Five years before, Mary McCarthy had watched the events of May from her Paris desk. Feeling that she was out of her depth, she had resolutely kept the 1968 revolt out of *Birds of America*. But that did not mean that she did not take an interest.

**SALLY HIGGINSON BEGLEY**  I remember one night we were all at Sarah Plimpton's—my husband was there, Mary McCarthy and her husband, and a small group of Americans and there was much discussion of why the students were rebelling. Someone said it was out of sympathy with the workers. Someone else said it had to do with the overcrowded classes at the universities. Everyone had some theory or other. Finally, Mary said, "Has it occurred to you that they don't *know* why they are rebelling?"

**THOMAS MALLON**  I remember Mary talking one time about the '68 rebellion and saying, "I guess you could say I *like* emergencies."

Watergate, as she saw it, was a national emergency and she was not content to watch from the sidelines. In June 1973, instead of heading for the coast of Maine, she set off for Washington, to cover the Ervin hearings for *The Observer of London*.

**MARGO VISCUSI**  I believe *The Observer* came to her. Mary knew she was in an odd position, seen as someone connected to American politics and at the same time a writer who lived outside her own country. She used to talk about how not seeing people's faces and hearing them on TV you lost something. I think she felt she could do best as the eyes and ears of someone visiting Washington from England. She couldn't hope to keep up with a reporter who had been there from the beginning.

*The Observer* put her up in a suite at the new hotel that served the now infamous Watergate complex. For her birthday on June 21, Hannah Arendt wired her African daisies and a telegram saying "CONGRATULATIONS BIRTHDAY AND OBSERVER," from Switzerland, where she was spending *her* summer. Although the *Observer*'s correspondent was part of the working press, she was also, by virtue of her celebrity, soon part of the story.

FROM "DEAN'S FIRST DAY," IN "TALK OF THE TOWN,"
*THE NEW YORKER*, JULY 9, 1973
Taped to the press tables are pieces of yellow copy paper with the names of the news organizations for which the seats are reserved; nearly every prominent newspaper, magazine, wire service, and broadcasting company in the United States, Great Britain, and Canada is represented, as are such European journals as *Der Spiegel* and the Stockholm *Dagens Nyheter*. (Places are reserved for at least seven London papers alone; the *Observer*'s correspondent is the writer Mary McCarthy, who takes notes continuously in a small, dense hand.)

FROM "PEOPLE," *TIME*, JULY 9, 1973
"He's extremely intelligent. He has so much common sense. He's become a sort of folk hero." Could it be that the lady praising Sam Ervin was Novelist Mary McCarthy, whose tongue is generally sharp enough to crack ice at 30 paces? Indeed it was. In Washington to cover the Watergate hearings for the London *Observer*, Mary became such a fan of Ervin's that she asked for a little talk with him. How had the Senator got his legal talent? she inquired. "He told me that he comes from a long line of lawyers from North Carolina—and one who practiced away." Where was that? "South Carolina," the Senator answered.

Day after day she could count on seeing Norman Mailer and Richard Goodwin. One day, Dick Cavett, who had once interviewed her on television, asked her to join him and his wife, Carrie Nye, for lunch. With all the invitations pouring in, she had no need to dine alone. The trouble was, she was working on an extremely tight deadline. With her two Vietnam books she'd had several weeks to write up her notes. With *Medina* she'd had a good six months. *The Observer*, which came out once a week, was asking her to file copy every Friday. Working under the gun was exciting, but left little time for an active social life. More important, it left little time to polish and revise.

**MARGO VISCUSI**  It was a brutal schedule. She had to finish what she was writing and go down to where *The Observer* was receiving copy and file her report by midnight every Friday night. But she loved learning the language of any profession. She loved all this business of filing and a deadline.

There was no money in *The Observer*'s budget for an assistant to help with the research and legwork. For one week, however, she had the company of her Paris secretary, who made use of a free round-trip air ticket.

**MARGO VISCUSI**  I was there the week John Ehrlichman testified. Monday morning I got on a long line at eight thirty, along with the other hoi polloi. The hearings started at ten or eleven. At some point Mary swept into the hallway and picked me out of the crowd. I couldn't sit next to her but I got to sit where you could come and go with no restriction. She said, "Norman

Mailer has gotten some floozy of his in as his research assistant, so the least I can do is get you in."

During the weeks she covered the hearings, she heard testimony from Maurice Stans, Jeb Magruder, John Mitchell, John Dean, John Ehrlichman, and H. R. Haldeman. She also heard Alexander Butterfield inadvertently reveal the existence of a potentially damaging archive of White House tapes. What she wrote may have lacked the perspective that comes with distance, but it provided her British audience with a gallery's worth of memorable portraits—some as memorable as any they were likely to find in Orwell, or even Dickens. These portraits she would refine and embellish some months later, when she brought them together in a small book called *The Mask of State*, published simultaneously in hard- and softcover. "She played by the rules and based them only on what she knew at the time," Margo Viscusi would later say.

### FROM *THE MASK OF STATE*

[T]here was something turnipy about Mitchell, the off-white (or tattletale gray) face with occasional mottlings of purplish pink, the watery, squelchy voice, the smooth bald pate. He was educated at Fordham University and Fordham Law School, by the Jesuits, though he is a Protestant, and vocally and visually he has that root-cellar quality of the Jesuitic world, at least as I knew it in my Catholic childhood—the small lifeless eyes, like those of a wintering potato, the voice sprouting insinuations[. . . .]

[Ehrlichman] looks like somebody of a deeply criminal nature, out of a medieval fresco: the upward sneering curl of the left-hand side of the mouth matched, on the bias, by the upward lift of the right eyebrow, above which there is a barely discernible scar; the aggressive tilted nose that cameramen say has been growing all week, the sinister (literally) thrust of the jaw[. . . .]

Haldeman, all agreed, was made of stone. Instead, there appeared a modest figure in a rather badly cut suit, slighter and smaller than his co-worker, bony, with a spine that made an awkward bump in the back of his jacket[. . . .] The fearsome crew cut was moulting into baldness, and he had rather appealing ears.

Writing about Watergate, she felt free to quote a French friend who had observed that "the Americans are using Watergate to cleanse themselves of guilt for Vietnam" and to go him one step further by adding that without Vietnam the break-in might have been just another "tempest in a teapot." She also felt free to discuss the wider implications of what she saw and heard.

There can be no greater boredom, I think, than that engendered by a steady dosage of lies. As Mitchell testified, the occasional laughter of the first day that met his toneless disavowals, the hisses that susurrated once through the room were replaced by an almost total vacuum, which in some dulled helpless way matched the calculated void of his contribution.

The Senate hearings, punctuated by a series of unanticipated revelations, dragged on until mid-August. Finally, faced with the possibility that the hearings might devour most of her vacation with Jim West, she chose to leave for Castine three days before the committee was scheduled to adjourn for the summer. As she saw it, she had no choice. Jim West, who was being forced to retire from the State Department, was eager to head for Maine. The least she could do was keep him company. At Castine she would be able to watch the hearings with friends who did not share her aversion to owning a television. Moreover, she would be able to learn how the hearings played to the local citizenry.

### FROM MARY MCCARTHY'S LETTER TO HANNAH ARENDT, AUGUST 10, 1973

The Ervin show became a tremendous success. Here the plumber's wife had it on all the day long in the shop and she tells me that now she misses it. Her remark, that it has been an education, is often heard, I understand. Also it has been entertainment; I don't know how to judge that, and it's probably too soon to try to do so. She wrote me a note— about housewives: their soap operas, she said, had trained them to tell the good characters from the bad characters. . . .

At Castine she finally heard again from Hannah Arendt, who had found Watergate and "the Ervin show" no less alarming than she had once found the political and social upheaval of Lyndon Johnson's last years in office.

### FROM HANNAH ARENDT'S LETTER TO MARY MCCARTHY, AUGUST 17, 1973

God knows why I did not write earlier, thinking of you all the time and reading the *Observer*, especially the Haldeman-Article, with the greatest admiration[. . . .] I did not write because I was kind of depressed about the whole affair. I had the impression that Nixon would actually emerge as victor in the guise of savior of the nation from Watergate, to be blamed not on him or the White House but on Congress. But I just read excerpts of his speech and a few comments on the reaction and I am reassured. He seems to have been again on the defensive[. . . .] The main fact remains that only 31% (?) support him but that no one wants him impeached. In other words, no one really minds about the massive invasion of crime into the political process. Or, more likely, people are mortally frightened of what might happen if anything is actually done about it. And this I can understand.

Since Nixon actually behaved like a tyrant his downfall would be a kind
of revolution.

Although it was Mary McCarthy's intention to return to Washington in
September for the next round of hearings, she never did. For one thing,
Jim West—who had been cut loose by the United States government but
permitted to stay on at his old job by the OECD, which was now paying
his entire salary—was still very much in need of her company. For
another, she was putting together an introduction to her collected Vietnam writing.

She was in Paris for the resignation of Vice President Spiro Agnew and
for the Justice Department bloodbath immediately dubbed the Saturday
Night Massacre. She was also in Paris when Nixon bowed to the inevitable
and released the much disputed tapes. From the rue de Rennes she was
able to savor the revelation that a crucial $18\frac{1}{2}$ minutes had been erased
by a preternaturally maladroit Rose Mary Woods. Even without those
missing minutes, she felt free to pass judgment: "To my mind, there can
be no doubt that Nixon himself ordered Watergate and was kept informed
of the cover-up, which of course he did not need to order—as the testimony repeatedly brought out, the necessity of a cover-up was taken for
granted as soon as news of the arrests reached the Nixon organization."

As far as she was concerned, the case against Richard Nixon was airtight. As far as the French were concerned, it didn't matter one way or
the other. For them the break-in and the dirty tricks were the stuff of
everyday politics. But once she returned to Castine for the summer of
1974 she could count on finding people who took Watergate as seriously
as she did. On August 8, watching her own small black-and-white television, she was rewarded with the spectacle of seeing Richard Nixon forced
from office.

**KEVIN BUCKLEY**    For several days Frankie [FitzGerald] and I had been separated from newspapers and television, but on the way over to Mary and
Jim's we picked up the paper. It looked like Nixon was going to step down
that night, but with Nixon there was no way of knowing. Frankie and I
parked the car and were walking toward the house when I heard the sound
of a champagne cork popping. I whispered, "The republic is safe." We
watched Nixon's resignation speech with Jim and Mary and we talked about
it. Everybody was happy that he had resigned. And that he had been driven
from office without the use of tanks.

If she felt cheated of the revelations that might have attended a full-
scale impeachment, there was still much to be grateful for. But she was
barely back in Paris when she received the news that Gerald Ford had
granted Nixon a full pardon. "I cannot prolong the bad dreams that con-

tinue to reopen a chapter that is closed," Ford offered as justification. "[T]he cover-up continues," she wrote Hannah Arendt.

To foresee the worst is one thing. To deal with it quite another. In the postscript of her book she could make sense of the pardon only by taking Ford's words to mean that Nixon had suffered a nervous breakdown and the pardon was "a move to shut him up, strait-jacket him, for his own sake, as well as that of the public, which in Ford's conventional view could not stand the shock of so much mud flying."

She had believed that America was prepared to submit to any cleansing necessary to atone for its sins in Vietnam. Now it was clear that there were limits to what the country was prepared to endure. Apparently Hannah Arendt was right. Nevertheless, she continued to hold fast to a long cherished belief in the saving power of truth. Now, when it looked as if the truth was going to take its own good time, she refused to believe it was for the best.

By the end of the summer of 1974, she had real cause for distress. Not only had she watched Nixon walk away from Watergate a free man but she had seen her collected Watergate reporting neglected, discounted, and dismissed out of hand. Here she could not lay the blame on Gerald Ford. Her troubles were of her own making. By choosing to bring out *The Mask of State* within months of *The Seventeenth Degree*, she had encouraged reviewers to lump the two books together. Whenever they did this, they went on, more often than not, to bludgeon *The Mask of State* with the same stick they were using on her Vietnam book.

### FROM JAMES FALLOWS'S REVIEW IN *THE WASHINGTON MONTHLY,* MAY 1974

Pure Sensitivity, untainted by fact or research, can go only so far, and then it runs into things that are actually different than they seem. *The Seventeenth Degree* and *Mask of State* are full of these deceptions, cases in which Mary McCarthy, for one reason or another, is not able to draw valid conclusions from what she sees—and, far from reserving her opinion, goes on to interpret the situation boldly and incorrectly[. . . .] [Her Watergate conclusions] are neither more profound nor more provably true than those reached at dinner-table conversations in half the households of America each night.

### FROM GLORIA EMERSON'S REVIEW IN *WASHINGTON POST BOOK WORLD,* JUNE 2, 1974

I am aware that McCarthy does not see herself running on the same track with Seymour Hersh or Bob Woodward and Carl Bernstein, but what lessons they could teach her and how it would help! Dipping in and out, anxious not to miss a dentist appointment or a dinner party in Paris perhaps, she does not pay the price and it shows. She does not understand that there is a required drudgery, that telephone calls must be made, the mean questions have to [be] asked, and that it is not enough, ever, just to be there.

Sales for *The Mask of State* were consistently lackluster. Some of this had to do with the negative reviews. Some had to do with a new preference on the part of readers for the "inside dope." Not only were readers intent on hearing what Woodward and Bernstein had to say but they were eager to hear from the indicted White House felons themselves. For the majority of readers it didn't matter that a best-selling novelist had brought a fresh eye and an exacting ear to the Senate Caucus Room. And for that best-selling novelist it was small consolation that the Sunday *New York Times* reviewer, defending her against the charge that she was no journalist, ranked her Watergate reporting with the very best American nonfiction. He was not alone in this. Nor was he alone in believing that she had a special affinity for her subject.

### FROM RICHARD GOODWIN'S REVIEW IN *THE NEW YORK TIMES* ### BOOK REVIEW, JUNE 30, 1974

[T]he Washington journalist becomes so immersed in the world of professional politics that he swiftly absorbs the fascination with tactical details and the reluctance to give public expression to harsh private judgments that pollute the air of that company town[. . . .] This is why some of our best political reporting comes from outside Washington, and from writers whose profession is not politics. The line runs from Tocqueville, Bryce and Henry Adams (who did live in Washington) to Norman Mailer, Hunter Thompson and Mary McCarthy[. . . .] It is no deprecation of Mary McCarthy's other talents to say that she is one of America's finest journalists. It is good for all of us that she has turned her powers to the inner tribulations of this country, which, despite a long exile, she appears to care for very much.

**GORE VIDAL**    I thought her Watergate book was very good. She had a subject. She was not very good at subtlety, at subtle points, which is probably why she wasn't much of a novelist. She had to work in rather broad brush strokes. Ehrlichman or somebody like that was a natural for her. There he is. Finer brushwork and the thing would have fallen apart or you would have been in Dostoyevsky-land.

In his review in *The New York Review of Books,* Harold Rosenberg went further than Richard Goodwin in making light of Fallows's objections. After granting that "McCarthy's political writing does indeed belong to the genre of people talking to one another," he went on to assert that what made this political writing special was "not any secret access to the truth but its high analytical quality and metaphorical reference—as talk, it ranks with the best we have." The trouble was, Rosenberg's review did not come until the very end of October. During most of September 1974,

Mary, who prided herself on having no use for self-pity, was suddenly feeling very sorry for herself. To Hannah Arendt, who had stayed a week with her in Castine, she let slip how bad she felt. But in fact it was Hannah who had helped bring her to such a pass.

### FROM MARY MCCARTHY'S LETTER TO HANNAH ARENDT, SEPTEMBER 9, 1974

Thank you for coming up. It was sad to watch you go through the gate at the airport without turning back. Something is happening or has happened to our friendship, and I cannot think that in noticing this I am being over-sensitive or imagining things. The least I can conjecture is that I have got on your nerves.

**WILLIAM JOVANOVICH** On one occasion I defended Hannah Arendt to Mary McCarthy, who telephoned me, almost in tears, to say Hannah had left her and Jim at Bangor Airport without even looking back. I reminded Mary that Hannah, like a lot of Europeans, simply left or said good-bye, sometimes abruptly, at the end of a time spent together, whereas we Americans like to linger.

Bill Jovanovich's words offered some consolation, and Hannah Arendt herself had been quick to reassure her, but in her next letter to Hannah she made no effort to disguise her anger and disappointment over the rough treatment her two books had received.

### FROM MARY MCCARTHY'S LETTER TO HANNAH ARENDT, SEPTEMBER 30, 1974

I can't help feeling, though I shouldn't, that if one of my friends had been in *my* place, *I* would [have] raised my voice. This leads to the conclusion that I am peculiar, in some way that I cannot make out; *indefensible*, at least for my friends. They are fond of me but with reservations. In any case, none of this involves you, because you were in the hospital and then recovering when it happened, because you weren't in the U.S. and didn't see those unpleasant pieces and because, finally, even if you had been on Riverside Drive and in the peak of condition, you *couldn't* have helped since people would have said that you were repaying the Eichmann debt.

Fortunately, just as she was not given to self-pity she was not inclined to stay depressed for long. In the birthdays and holidays that many people secretly find wearisome she had always taken an almost unseemly pleasure. Now, instead of going off to Scotland or Amsterdam or Rome, she chose to celebrate an old-fashioned Christmas in Castine. By early December she was making preparations. Eleanor Perényi and her mother, Grace Zaring Stone, Kevin McCarthy and his daughter Lillah, Alison West, the writer Penelope Gilliatt, *and* Hannah Arendt were all invited to Castine for the holidays.

**ELEANOR PERÉNYI**  We arrived Christmas eve, in a snowstorm, and found the house, and the local inn too, filled with their families and friends. There was a huge dinner that night, and another the next day. In the front hall was a long table laden with presents. You helped yourself. Then copies of a medieval miracle play were passed around, with parts for each of us, which were read aloud. All this had been planned and provided for in Paris and transported to Maine, God knows how. One incident I particularly treasured was the sight of Mary and Hannah Arendt washing up glasses. Or rather, Hannah washed and Mary dried, and she wasn't at all satisfied with Hannah's performance, and kept handing the glasses back. "No, Hannah, that's *not* clean." And Hannah meekly redipped the glass.

For her first Christmas in Castine she brought together her friends from the literary world and her friends from Maine and, against all odds, they passed the holiday without getting entangled in any serious arguments. If she missed Robert Lowell, she had learned to live without his company. If she had been badly upset by Hannah's inexplicable coolness, all that had been smoothed over. Indeed, she had gone so far as to relent on her vow to never again start another novel. With the Vietnam War winding down and Nixon forced from office, she was free to devote all her time to writing anything she wished.

Although there had been personal losses over the past years and disappointments with reviewers, there would be new friends to turn to and new chances to confound her critics. Even on her worst days, when the arthritis in her back wouldn't let her ignore the fact that she was sixty-two years old, she possessed the energy of writers half her age.

Sadly, there would never again be a new novel bearing "a beauty of a photo." The dust jacket of *The Mask of State* showed a handsome Maine dowager with her short gray hair clipped to one side. The avenging dark angel of American letters was nowhere to be found. But as she stood beside Hannah and scrupulously wiped each long stem of each fragile wineglass, she could take comfort in the settled life she had worked so hard to establish and look forward with some confidence to the prospect of many more Christmases with those she loved.

# Chapter Twenty-four

# DEATH OF OLD FRIENDS

"Something is happening or has happened to our friendship," Mary McCarthy had written Hannah Arendt that dark September of 1974. On receiving this anguished letter, Hannah did not pick up the telephone and make a special transatlantic call. Instead, she sat down to compose a written response. "For heaven's sake, Mary, stop it, *please*," she wrote. "I say that of course for my own sake and because I love you, but I think I also may say it for your sake." If she had not looked back at the airport, she suggested, it was merely an oversight. That was all.

Having done her best to treat with due seriousness a cry that defied all reason, Arendt held onto the letter a full day before mailing it. When she picked it up again, all she could add was the sort of excuse that might be offered up by any beleaguered lover. "I am not sensitive and rather obtuse in psychological matters. But this you must have known for a long time."

Mary McCarthy chose to believe her. From the time twenty-five years earlier when Arendt had walked up to her at the Astor Place station and suggested they bury the hatchet, Arendt had been both friend and teacher, serving as moral authority and intellectual arbiter. Throughout those years the friendship had flourished. That it was a joy for both parties was never a secret.

"In examining my life-history you probably don't give enough importance to *friends*," McCarthy had written Doris Grumbach in 1966. Just in case Grumbach missed the point she had added, "I would date my own life more by friendships than by love affairs on the whole. Friends and teachers; for me it has often been the same thing." As self-assessments go, it was reasonably accurate. But while friends had often served as teachers, her closest friends had served at times as something akin to an extended family.

The fact that she was an orphan may have had something to do with this. Certainly it left her more vulnerable to loss. As it happened, most of her best friends were older than she was. Not a few were heavy smokers; several were inclined to drink more than was good for them. Of course no one had really known about the long-term effects of cigarettes and alcohol back when they were young and sowing their fair share of wild oats. By the time word was out, the damage had been done.

In 1970, Mannie Rousuck, who in his effort to live up to the standard of a fine Edwardian gentleman had eaten and imbibed more than was good for him, died while being shaved by a manservant in his Park Avenue apartment. The model for Mr. Sheer in "Rogue's Gallery," Emmanuel J. Rousuck had long ago put his seamy past behind him, replacing the "Mannie" with "Jay" and ending his career as a friend and advisor to Mellons and Whitneys and second in command at the Wildenstein Gallery.

As a child Reuel had observed that Mannie was "a good getter." Edmund Wilson had attributed McCarthy's fondness for him to her "outlaw side." But this fondness seemed to derive from something more than a wayward streak or pure self-interest. At his death, when a fund was set up in his name at the Morgan Library, she sent a check for five hundred dollars—an amount far more generous than most of his millionaire friends had seen fit to contribute. "If more is needed, I can probably help again when I'm feeling slightly richer," she wrote. To this letter she added a brief postscript: "I liked him as Jay, but I loved him as Mannie." Looking back seventeen years later, she would write, "[H]is death in 1970 was the first in a series that brought down the pillars of my life."

Although this first death came with no warning, she had received ample notice that more than one pillar was crumbling. In 1961 Nicola Chiaromonte had been felled by his first heart attack. The same year, Heinrich Blücher had suffered a serious stroke. Placed on strict regimens, both men had chosen to follow their doctors' instructions only when it suited them. Both had gone on to survive subsequent setbacks and both had come to be treated by their wives as semi-invalids. Then, late in October 1970, within months of Mannie Rousuck's death, Heinrich Blücher died suddenly of a massive cerebral hemorrhage. As lovers he and Arendt had gone their separate ways, but they had remained fond companions. For Arendt, who believed she had learned to live with the constant threat of losing him, his death was at once a loss and a shock.

"HEINRICH DIED SATURDAY OF A HEART ATTACK," Blücher's widow cabled from New York. There was no need to say more. As soon as Mary received word of what had happened, she purchased a plane ticket. Not only did she make a special trip to New York for Heinrich's funeral but she made a series of special arrangements to distract Heinrich's widow—

first insisting that Hannah join her and Jim West for a nine-day Easter holiday in Sicily and then that she join them for the month of July in Castine. More important, she made sure the widow did not accept W. H. Auden's proposal of marriage—a proposal encouraged by Stephen Spender. ("It's typical of a homosexual—I mean Spender—to have been married for twenty years and know so little about marriage that he could venture such a thought," she wrote Arendt.)

She might be able to prevent an empty and potentially disastrous marriage, but there were limits to her powers. As in a fairy tale, the spell had been broken. Suddenly everyone was at risk. Thirteen months after Heinrich Blücher's funeral, Hannah wrote to say her doctor had diagnosed some recent chest pains as angina. Upon receiving this unwelcome news, Mary replied at once: "Your angina report naturally perturbs me, though I do persist in thinking that it *may* have something to do with mourning. . . . In any case, do as the doctor tells you and keep to a healthy regime and don't overdo. And keep me informed."

Her words fell on ears that for all practical purposes might have been deaf. Hannah Arendt had a book she was determined to finish. Envisioned as a sequel to *The Human Condition*, where she had investigated man's life in the world, this new book was going to investigate man's life with himself—a life that comprised the activities of thinking, willing, and judging. Writing *The Life of the Mind*, Arendt had her work cut out for her. Always when she worked she smoked. Only so long as it did not interfere with her writing was she prepared to give up her cigarettes.

In life it is rarely the things you dread which deliver the blow that knocks you flat. A month later, Arendt was still at her typewriter, an ashtray within easy reach, and Nicola Chiaromonte was dead, having suffered a massive heart attack in an elevator of the Italian Radio Building, where he had just finished a broadcast. Five months later, in June 1972, Edmund Wilson, plagued by everything from high blood pressure to the aftereffects of a bad fall, died at his home in Talcottville.

Responding to news of Wilson's death, McCarthy felt it sufficient to say to *Time*, "He was an immense landmark. He was active, full of industry and now he's not there anymore. I don't see any replacement for Edmund Wilson." In the end, she had parted with the Minotaur on terms that could be said to be cordial, having enlisted James Baldwin and Stephen Spender in a campaign to secure him a literary prize worth some five thousand dollars. But if there was no replacement for Edmund Wilson, his death was by no means an irreparable loss.

Nicola Chiaromonte's death was of a different order. From the first she had loved and admired him and with time her love had been reciprocated. "You won me over, Mary, yours was the magic touch that broke my sullenness and my shyness," he had written when she was about to leave for Hanoi. In 1971, intent on finishing her Medina report and counting on visiting him in Rome once it was finished, she had put off a planned Christmas visit. Now it was too late.

At his death Nicola Chiaromonte was sixty-seven years old—nine years younger than Edmund Wilson and only eight years older than she was. Although there had been warnings sufficient to prepare her, she found it difficult, if not impossible, to take in the fact of his dying. Faced with his loss, she turned to the one friend she believed capable of comprehending the magnitude of her distress.

### FROM MARY MCCARTHY'S LETTER TO HANNAH ARENDT, JANUARY 19, 1972

[He was] dead in a minute—no pain, or so one thinks. That morning he'd been well and in high spirits. I talked to Miriam, who was in an extraordinary state of control and, yes, sweetness. Of course she had been preparing herself for a long time[. . . .] That he's dead, though, is still unbelievable to me. I have not yet started missing him because he is still *there*. I suppose one had got used to his *not* dying for so long that one took him for eternal. I loved him so much[. . . .] As Jim said, it is *hateful*[. . . .] This grief makes me think doubly of you, triply perhaps. You will understand.

### FROM ARENDT'S LETTER TO MCCARTHY, JANUARY 25, 1972

Mary, look, I think I know how sad you are and how serious this loss is. (I sometimes find myself now going through New York and looking at all the houses which Death has emptied during the last years. And God knows I have some experience in the presence of absence, and can't bear the notion of ever leaving this apartment precisely because here this absence is there and alive in every corner and at every moment.) Still—if you just say "hateful" you will have to say hateful to many more things if you want to be consistent. One could look upon one's whole life as a being-given *and* being-taken away; that starts already with life itself, given at birth, taken away with death; and the whole time in-between could easily be looked at as standing under the same law.

By the time she received Hannah's letter, she had said good-bye to Nicola Chiaromonte in a fashion that was at once singular and in keeping with her character. The day after his death, she and Jim had arrived in Rome.

**JAMES WEST** When Nicola died, it was very strange. On our last visit to Rome he'd invited us into his study, which was tiny, with a little desk and all his notes, and he seemed fine. Then we went back after his death and he was in the coffin in that little study. As there sometimes are, there were little wads of cotton in various places. And there was Mary, forcing herself I suppose to get down as close as she could, studying his face and studying the whole experience of her dead friend. That was very hard on Mary. But it was an experience.

Faced with Chiaromonte's death, she was not going to shrink from the terrible fact of it. But she was also going to do everything in her power to keep his memory alive—first by lobbying his Italian publisher to bring all his essays back into print and urging William Jovanovich to bring his work to the attention of American readers; then by agreeing to write appreciations and introductions; and finally by using every means at her disposal to get the Agnelli Foundation to cover the cost of bringing together all his uncollected essays and letters. Although she was intent on doing Chiaromonte justice, she was also thinking of the widow he had left behind. Immediately she turned to a friend who knew Gianni Agnelli well, asking her to intercede on Miriam's behalf.

**GAIA SERVADIO** When Nicola Chiaromonte died, she wanted Miriam to edit all his books. Of course there was no money to support her and Mary thought of the Agnelli Foundation. I did it only for Mary. I never saw the great intellect in Nicola. Never. Mary always reproached me silently for not seeing it. She always protected him.

**ROBERT SILVERS** Chiaromonte was a central figure for her because she admired his great integrity and his judgment, but above all, I think, she admired him for what she saw as his purity. She was particularly drawn to people—Nicola, Carmen, Hannah—she thought of as uncompromised, not spoiled by worldly or low ambition.

The next pillar of her life to crumble had never been known for his purity or his lack of ambition. The mere suggestion that *he* might possess such attributes would have been enough to provoke from Philip Rahv a snort of disgust. Still, in his own way he was thoroughly uncompromising. If she had gone so far as to mock him in print for his political cynicism and intellectual arrogance, she had also come to take these aspects of his character in stride.

**ROBERT SILVERS** They spoke about each other with what seemed to me real affection and he liked to amuse her. He would say she was a "naughty girl." And she thought he was rather sly.

In 1969, Philip Rahv had broken with *Partisan Review*. Teaching at Brandeis and living in Boston, he had begun making plans for a new magazine called *Modern Occasions*. For his first issue he had gotten her to agree to a written interview. With a new bride, Betty, in tow and full of plans for the future, he had then visited her in Castine just before *Birds of America* came out—a visit that prompted a lengthy report.

### FROM MARY MCCARTHY'S LETTER TO ELIZABETH HARDWICK, SEPTEMBER 14, 1970

I need more strength than I have to tell about the Rahv visit. I don't think she'll succeed in running him; he's still a force of pretty massive resistance. But who knows? I didn't dislike this "Betty," but she stunned me. He looked tired, but possibly that's the honeymoon[. . . .] Just to keep my stock down, he made the following marvelous remark, shortly after arrival: "I read your chapter in the *Atlantic*. People tell me the one in *Playboy* is better." Total comment. He had the appropriate bane for everyone[. . . .] "The Puritans? Religious fanatics. Kicked out of England. Couldn't make it in Holland. Religious nuts, and after them came *bums*!" That alone was worth the visit, as the Michelins say[. . . .] And yet I'm fond of him[. . . .] But I'm worried for him about his magazine.

Hardwick, as another former lover of Rahv, was likely to share her fears for the magazine, just as she was likely to savor this report of Rahv's antics. Sadly, by the time Rahv died three years later, *Modern Occasions* had folded and his marriage to Betty had hit the rocks. Found dead in his Boston apartment by friends just before Christmas, he was not released for burial until an autopsy had been performed. There was talk of a fatal combination of pills and alcohol. Hardwick, who had kept in touch with him and attended the small funeral, treated all the talk as proven fact. Unwilling to believe the end had been so sordid, McCarthy chose to listen to a second, more heartening, version of Rahv's final hours.

### FROM MARY MCCARTHY'S LETTER TO HANNAH ARENDT, MARCH 1, 1974

I had a nice letter from Frankie FitzGerald, who, with her boy friend, was with him, by coincidence, the night he died, and she says they had a marvelous evening. From her description of the things they talked about, it sounds as if he was very much the old Philip in his benign and confidential aspect. This leads me to doubt Lizzie's picture of his utter *"isolation,"* heavy drinking, sleeping drugs, total disintegration. I had suspected her account anyway, so hysterical and insistent—a good deal of projection, I think, of her own assessment of her position onto him[. . . .]

It's strange, but his death has hit me harder than anybody's, even Nicola's, though I was much closer to Nicola and saw him all the time[. . . .] Maybe love, even such a long-ago one, gets at your vital center more than friendship and admiration. I realize that I *must* have loved him when we lived together and continued to do so, though unaware of it. Anyway, his death hurts. Jim says maybe it's because I feel he had an incomplete, tentative sort of life. But does anybody have a complete life?

For Rahv, there was no fund to which she could contribute. No unpublished essays and letters for her to edit. Friends who had remained close to him would see to that. From her nothing was expected, and nothing was asked. There was no way she could make up for the sadness of his last year or for the times she had failed him. Never one to walk away from a challenge, she set out to give Rahv what she believed to be his due with a tribute read by Frances FitzGerald at his funeral and then published in *The New York Times Book Review*.

"So he's gone, that dear phenomenon," her tribute began. "If no two people are alike, he was less like anybody than anybody else. A powerful intellect, a massive, overpowering personality and yet shy, curious, susceptible, confiding." The Rahv she described had "remained an outsider" always. She traced the outsider back to the boy who had come on his own from Russia to join his older brother in Rhode Island, where "already quite a big boy, he went to grade school still dressed as an old-fashioned European schoolboy, in long black trousers and black stockings, looking like a somber little man among the American kids." By invoking Tolstoy, she tried to suggest what Rahv was like at his best.

## FROM "PHILIP RAHV, 1908–1973," *THE NEW YORK TIMES BOOK REVIEW*, FEBRUARY 17, 1974

I said, just now, that he was unlike anybody but now I remember that I have seen someone like him—on the screen. Like the younger Rahv anyway: Serge Bondarchuk, the director of *War and Peace*, playing the part of Pierre[. . . .] Saying good-bye to my old friend, I am moved by that and remember his tenderness for Tolstoy [. . .] and Tolstoy's sense of Pierre as the onlooker, the eternal civilian, as out of place at the Battle of Borodino in his white hat and green swallow-tail coat as the dark "little man" in his long dark East European clothes eyeing the teacher from his grammar-school desk in Providence.

When the tribute ran on the front page of the *Book Review* there was every assurance that, for a few hours at least, attention would be paid. For William Barrett, who as a young editor at *PR* had been left bruised and battered by more than one brush with McCarthy's gentle "Pierre," her portrait was enough to prompt him to write a memoir, looking back on his own experience with Rahv. For William Phillips, Rahv's partner in what Dwight Macdonald had once called a bad marriage held together by a magazine, the portrait was very much in keeping with what he saw as the romantic side of the portraitist's nature. For Hannah Arendt, who had, on occasion, had her own brushes with Rahv, the *Times* eulogy was all that such a piece should be, even if the accompanying photograph was not.

### FROM HANNAH ARENDT'S LETTER TO MARY MCCARTHY, FEBRUARY 25, 1974

I saw Lizzi [*sic*] yesterday and it occurred to me that I did not write you about the Rahv essay—so beautiful, so tender, so absolutely convincing in every memorable detail—i.e. every detail that deserves to be remembered. And nice that the *NY Times* put it on the frontpage. The photo is abominable. Either he had changed beyond recognition since I last saw him—many years past—or just one of those snapshots which are always wrong.

### FROM *INTELLECTUAL MEMOIRS*

[W]hen Philip died and I wrote a little obituary on him, Hannah, on reading it, was astonished. "So, my dear, you loved him. I never knew." Maybe, till she said it, I had not known it myself.

One thing was certain: she had cared for Rahv more than she had realized. Four months later, she was still trying to come to terms with that fact when Hannah Arendt suffered a serious heart attack. The attack came without warning on the eve of Arendt's second series of Gifford Lectures at the University of Aberdeen.

The year before, Mary McCarthy had made the journey to Scotland for the start and finish of the first series of lectures. This time, owing to commitments in France and America, she was planning to be at Aberdeen only at the tail end—a plan that made practical sense since she was scheduled to give a talk at the University of Aberdeen during the first week in May. As luck would have it, William Jovanovich was at the hotel with Hannah Arendt when the attack took place. A heart patient himself, Jovanovich had immediately recognized what was happening and responded accordingly. In no time Arendt was in an oxygen tent at the nearest hospital, and in almost no time Mary was there at Hannah's bedside. Later, when she had to return to Paris, Hannah's friend Lotte Kohler came from New York to take her place.

The doctors had declared the attack to be serious. The smoking must be cut back from her two packs a day, and the workload must be eased, at least for the time being. The patient was not well enough to work or travel, but she was sufficiently recovered to listen to the talk Mary planned to deliver at Aberdeen. By listening she was performing a service—one which gave everyone a chance to feel, at least for the moment, that nothing was in any way different.

**LOTTE KOHLER**    Their gifts were complementary, but fortunately they were in different fields. That was very important. They were not competing. Whenever I saw them together, I felt that Hannah loved Mary more than

Mary loved Hannah. But I think Mary loved being loved by Hannah. I think that Mary may have taken Hannah's love for granted, which may explain why later in that letter she asks, What happened, why do you seem so cold.

The talk, which had been given in a slightly different form the previous month in Pittsburgh, was titled "Art Values and the Value of Art" and was inspired by the recent theft of a priceless Vermeer from its home at Kenwood House, in Hampstead, England. The terrorists who had spirited away the Vermeer had threatened to destroy it unless a large sum of money was paid out for a massive food drop and unless two imprisoned IRA car bombers were immediately transferred to a jail in Ireland. In the end their demands had gone unmet and the Vermeer had been returned virtually unharmed.

The Kenwood Vermeer was hardly the first work of art to be threatened or vandalized. Nonetheless the case had stayed in McCarthy's mind. For her the Vermeer was irreplaceable. The jailed car bombers were not. In an effort to come to terms with this attitude, she went on to consider not only why works of art were suddenly attracting vandals and terrorists but why "[q]uite poisonous people, on the whole, are attracted by the visual arts." She did not stop there, however. She ended by questioning whether beautiful objects were really good for anything at all. The trouble was, once she had concluded that beauty was either "a mysterious something we today cannot put our finger on" or "good for nothing," she could not bring herself to accept such a dispiriting conclusion.

### FROM "LIVING WITH BEAUTIFUL THINGS," THE PUBLISHED VERSION OF "ART VALUES AND THE VALUE OF ART"

> If beauty is a god, and I still think he is, he requires some private service and domestic rituals. The objects we own—I am speaking of people like myself—are generally commemorative. Of an occasion—the day we bought them—or of the friend who brought them back to us[. . . .] They are objects of piety, and the little bit of beauty that is in them is valued both for itself and as a souvenir, for the memories that attach[. . . .] When we die, the collection they constitute will fall apart; they will go their separate ways, be dispersed, like our bodies.

Although the talk at Aberdeen was by no means closely reasoned, not a few of its assertions were guaranteed to provoke a heated response. If nothing else, it was rich in paradox. Not surprisingly, mortality was very much on her mind. Hannah Arendt was sufficiently engaged by what she heard to tell her she should draw on the talk for a novel. Ever after Arendt would receive full credit for that suggestion. For the moment, however, the prospective author showed little inclination to heed her advice. Not until six months had passed and she had been buffeted by the reviews for her Watergate and Vietnam books would she have second thoughts. By then she had come up with a plot, which promised to tax her powers of invention but also promised to get around what she believed to be a grave handicap—the fact that she was "utterly out of touch," as she would later tell an interviewer, and thus not fit to "write a novel that is set in America now."

Her plot was anything but simple. In early 1975, eight prominent liberals fly to Iran to investigate reports of torture under the Shah. Their group includes Gus Hurlbut, an aged Episcopal bishop; Frank Barber, the rector of a fashionable New York parish; Aileen Simmons, a fifty-year-old college president in search of a husband; Sophie Weil, a young smartly dressed "new journalist"; Victor Lenz, an American academic who drinks more than is good for him; and Jim Carey, a skeptical and widowed silver-haired senator. In Paris they are joined by a pleasant enough Scottish don and Henk van Vliet de Jonge, a dashing and happily married Dutch deputy. Their plane, which turns out to have a group of wealthy art collectors traveling in first class, is hijacked between Paris and Teheran. Among the collectors is a socialite who owns a world-famous Vermeer. The hijackers are a mixed lot—Germans and Arabs, a former KLM stewardess and a Dutch giant by the name of Jeroen. Their plan is to hold the liberals for ransom. When their leader, Jeroen, learns of the collectors on board, that plan is scrapped and Jeroen decides to barter the lives of the collectors for their most valuable works of art.

The idea for this new novel, which was eventually called *Cannibals and Missionaries*, had not been her own. And the prospect of her devoting years to it was not going to please William Jovanovich, who had been pushing her to write an intellectual memoir—a book he envisioned as picking up where *Memories of a Catholic Girlhood* left off. Such a memoir, he believed, would play to her strengths. For the moment, though, she believed she had one more novel in her. Furthermore, as she confided to Elizabeth Hardwick, there were too many people still alive who might be offended by what she wrote.

### FROM MARY MCCARTHY'S LETTER TO ELIZABETH HARDWICK, OCTOBER 12, 1973

> For me, in a memoir the problem isn't myself; it's other people. Perhaps I delude myself but I don't find it so hard to be honest about myself. Just to be honest about others or one's feeling toward them is too cruel. That wasn't a problem in *Catholic Girlhood*, because the people I might have been hurting were far away in the past and the only ones I cared about really—my grandparents, Preston—were dead. Yet even there I had some twinges of pain for them, for instance when I wrote about my grandmother's face-lift operation: she wouldn't have liked that[. . . .] Fiction is different, at least for me.

The distinction she drew between putting other people in a novel and putting them in a memoir may have struck some old friends as questionable, but there was no question that this novel was something she wanted to write. "[B]eing a perverse creature, I've been seduced by the temptation of difficulty," she wrote Arendt.

The new novel would be unlike anything she had ever written. In addition, it would offer her a chance to show reviewers she could write a work of fiction whose preoccupations could not be dismissed as the stuff of women's magazines. But while the ideas bandied about in this novel might be the stuff of academic seminars, in essence she was writing a thriller. As such, it would be held to certain standards by both reviewers and readers. Unfortunately, all work on the book had to be put aside for the big 1974 Christmas gathering at Castine, but by mid-February she had completed a first chapter, with the Episcopal rector as protagonist, and was far enough along to come up against her own limitations as a writer of fiction.

### FROM MARY MCCARTHY'S LETTER TO HANNAH ARENDT, FEBRUARY 17, 1975

I find I am steering down a channel with some very familiar landscape on either side. On the one hand he keeps sounding like the girls in *The Group* and on the other like Peter Levi. Scylla and Charybdis. It is sad to realize that one's fictions, i.e., one's "creative" side, cannot learn anything[. . . .] Those confining boundaries, I suppose are set by my life-experience, which lies in vaguely upper-middle-class territory lying between those girls and Peter. My mental experience is broader, but that doesn't seem to count for the imagination[. . . .] It all leads to the awful recognition that one *is* one's life; God is not mocked.

Whatever the first chapter's limitations, she was sufficiently satisfied with it to celebrate with a car trip with Jim West and their Stonington friend Eleanor Perényi, who had treated herself to three months in Paris with her typewriter and her cat. Although their tour of the restaurants and churches of central France was hardly an unqualified success, it would be the first of several they would make over the years.

**ELEANOR PERÉNYI** The same planning that went into Christmas in Castine went into our motor trips around France. Itineraries worked out in advance, which always included something *I* particularly wanted to see: the vegetable garden at Villandry, the Lascaux cave, for which you had to have special permission, and so on. Guidebooks, piled between them, including all the restaurant guides. I sat in the backseat of their very grand car and it was like travel with my parents when I was a child. They dressed very formally, Jim in a three-piece suit, and Mary, who loved couture clothes, in those French tweed suits, with a large jewel in her lapel. We made an impression when we arrived at hotels and restaurants, and I couldn't quite suppress naughty thoughts of Henry James and Edith Wharton processing across Europe in her Rolls, it was all so old-fashioned and ever so slightly absurd. We were quite often lost, too, in spite of all the maps and guides, which I believe used to happen to Henry and Edith.

#### FROM MARY MCCARTHY'S LETTER TO HANNAH ARENDT, FEBRUARY 17, 1975

We had Eleanor Perényi (you remember) and her cat along—she a trying passenger but the cat as good as gold. She suffers from acute anxieties of every description, no sooner is one allayed than another erupts[. . . .] Last night I arrived at the formulation that her problem was that she is a soured hedonist. She assumes I am a hedonist, too, likening Jim and me to Scott Fitzgerald's friends the Murphys (*Tender Is the Night*) with their "gift for living." I decided that any attempt at correction here would be invidious and let it go.

During her first year at work on the book, she was touring with a zest that would knock most tourists flat and plunging into the research with a rigor that would daunt most fellow practitioners. Early on she had determined that her hijackers would retreat with their captives to a farmhouse situated in Flevoland, a remote district of sparsely inhabited farmland that the Dutch had recently reclaimed from the sea. If a hideaway smack in the middle of Europe would be highly unlikely, that seemed not to bother her. If the research necessitated a series of trips to Holland that was all the better.

**CEES NOOTEBOOM**    Mary liked the Dutch people for their moral virtue, for their standing up against their enemies, for their stance in international affairs, and for their reclaiming the land, which has to do with creativity. This is why she always referred to Holland as an imaginary country. She could never understand why I had difficulties with the Dutch. On her first trip in 1962 we went to the fabulous planetarium of Eyse Eysinga in Friesland, in the north of the Netherlands. For me it is somehow symbolic. This was a working-class man of the eighteenth-century who built his own house and in his house he built a complete planetarium. I remember her intense happiness seeing the attic, which has the wooden machinery that makes the planetarium work downstairs. I remember especially that she liked this big wheel that has to be wound once in twenty-nine years for the planet Mars. There was everything in that attic. It was neat. It was small. It was ingenious. It proved the possibilities of the human will and mind. It functioned and endured.

In Holland she wore a good suit with a jewel in the lapel but there was a sense of freedom—not only in the company of Cees Nooteboom and his companion, the singer Liesbeth List, but with Hans van Mierlo, leader of a liberal faction in the Dutch parliament, who had helped the prime minister form his cabinet.

**HANS VAN MIERLO**   When Mary was in Holland, she had something special with the group here. She gave the impression that Amsterdam was something out of her normal life. She was a bit naughty. And childish. Very cheerful. A bit boyish. She wanted to drink and to go to the clubs. Jim was almost always with her. But sometimes she would go alone to Amsterdam for two or three days. A lot of drinks and literature and museums and friends. She never stayed with Cees in the house, I think—she would stay in a hotel. But Cees was really the key to Holland for Mary.

She might find Amsterdam congenial, but her Dutch friends did not always find her easy.

**HANS VAN MIERLO**   We instantaneously liked each other, but sometimes I was a little afraid of her. She was nice but at the same time very sharp. She was a difficult woman. She was difficult for herself and difficult for others—she was for Cees.

**CEES NOOTEBOOM**   Five or six years after Mary and I met, my first novel was finally translated into French. Mary read it and immediately said, "This is very bad translation. I cannot hear you in it." She was severe. But the friendship remained.

Believing as she did that the great novelists invariably got all the details right, it behooved her to find out how a jumbo jet was laid out, how it felt to be confronted by real terrorists, and exactly how the Dutch government would react in the event of a real hijacking. Jim West was able to secure a seating plan from Air France. Her friend Thomas Quinn Curtiss was able to tell her what it had been like when his plane had been hijacked in Egypt. Hans van Mierlo was able to provide her with access to the Dutch prime minister, who agreed to join her and a party of friends for dinner at a restaurant of their choosing.

**HANS VAN MIERLO**   Joop den Uyl was a very sober man. His lifestyle was simple. At six or seven we sat down to dinner. Cees said, "Okay, I want to have oysters." And Mary said, "I want oysters, too." Everybody was eating oysters and expensive food and Joop, as was his custom, ordered something very simple. After two hours he had to go. By then he had answered all the questions Mary wanted to ask. We said to him, "Now we know how to organize a hijacking. What you do is you say to the prime minister that you want to write a book on it and then you find out exactly what he is doing and what the police are doing and then you know how to do it."

One year into the novel she was caught up in the adventure of writing and researching a book whose setting owed much to her fondness for one particular Dutchman. From the way it sounded, she was enjoying every minute of it. And hard as she might be working, she still felt free to take time off to see friends she cared about. Early that spring she had met Hannah Arendt in Copenhagen and in June she had joined Hannah for a stay at Marburg. Although there had been no visit to Castine by Hannah that summer, she had seen her in New York before returning to Paris. If anyone's health was on her mind it was her own.

### FROM MARY MCCARTHY'S LETTER TO HANNAH ARENDT, NOVEMBER 12, 1975

> Just to tell you that I now have the results of the tests, which show nothing wrong except a surplus of white blood corpuscles, indicating an infection. That I had an infection I already knew. However, the doctor has prescribed some antibiotics to try to get rid of it—the bronchial cough, I mean. Meanwhile I've perhaps stumbled on the source of the trouble. My dentist the other day found a quite large cyst or abscess in the bone above a dead tooth, has curetted it, and taken six or seven stitches in the gum.

If Hannah's health was a source of concern, the concern had ceased to be pressing. If Hannah looked drawn or tired, that was to be expected. Every other Sunday the two of them spoke on the telephone, and every other Sunday Mary urged her friend to take better care of herself. After his first heart attack, Nicola Chiaromonte had lived for more than a decade. Heinrich Blücher, too, had dragged on for years. So she was not at all prepared for the news that on Thursday, December 4, Hannah Arendt had suffered a second, and fatal, heart attack while taking her ease in an armchair in the living room of her Riverside Drive apartment, in the company of two friends who had joined her for dinner.

Once again Mary had to rush to New York for a funeral. And once again Jim West was not free to accompany her. This time, however, there was no close friend she could unburden herself to. What she saw and heard when she arrived at the funeral chapel only made matters worse.

**JEROME KOHN** [*Arendt's research assistant at the New School*]  My first memory of Mary is at the funeral home: We were going into the room where the body was, the night before the funeral, and Mary looked at the door and she said, "The name is spelled wrong. It has to be changed." They had spelled Hannah without the final "h." She really made a fuss. Then she went over to where Hannah was lying and she peered into the coffin for a long, long time. She knew she would never see her again. It was as if she couldn't get enough of her.

Later she would say that the only spot that seemed familiar were the "roughened furrows of her neck."

**LOTTE KOHLER**   Although Hannah's husband was not Jewish, his funeral had been at the Riverside Chapel. But nothing Jewish was done. Friends spoke and he was cremated. When Hannah suddenly died, Jovanovich sent one of his right-hand people to help me and I said I wanted the funeral done exactly the same way. But when Hannah's relatives from Israel arrived for the funeral, they wanted something Jewish. Mary said, "No, it was out of the question. Hannah wasn't religious." It became very unpleasant. I stood there and cried and cried. To see this. Finally I was asked to decide. I said to Mary, "Look, they are the relatives and if they think a psalm should be read in Hebrew it's going to be read in Hebrew." Which was done.

In the end the family prevailed. And in the end the argument over the service made for bad feeling. None of this might have mattered if she had not been named executor responsible for the Hannah Arendt Literary Trust. As such she would have to answer to the family for the royalties she collected and the permissions she granted, just as she would have to work with her co-executor, Lotte Kohler, who was handling the business side of the estate. For the moment, though, her primary concern was to get her part of the service right.

Four people were slated to speak at the funeral: Mary McCarthy, William Jovanovich, Jerry Kohn, and Hans Jonas. William Jovanovich stunned the packed chapel when he announced, "I loved her fiercely." Her love was no less fierce and her words caused no less of a stir. Having first touched on her dear friend's plans for her final book, she went on to "try to bring her back as a person."

### FROM "SAYING GOOD-BYE TO HANNAH"

Hannah is the only person I have ever watched *think*. She lay motionless on a sofa or a day bed, arms folded behind her head, eyes shut but occasionally opening to stare upward. This lasted—I don't know—from ten minutes to half an hour. Everyone tiptoed past if we had to come into the room in which she lay oblivious[. . . .]

She was a beautiful woman, alluring, seductive, feminine[. . . .] She had small, fine hands, charming ankles, elegant feet. She liked shoes; in all the years I knew her, I think she only once had a corn[. . . .]

The summer after Heinrich's death she came to stay with us in Maine, where we gave her a separate apartment, over the garage, and I put some thought into buying supplies for her kitchen—she liked to breakfast alone. The things, I thought, that she would have at home, down to instant coffee (which I don't normally stock)[. . . .] I was rather pleased to have been able to find anchovy paste in the village store. On the afternoon of her arrival, as I showed her where everything was in the larder, she frowned over the little tube of anchovy paste, as though it were an inexplicable foreign object. "What is that?" I told her. "Oh." She put it down and looked thoughtful and as though displeased, somehow. No more was said. But I knew I had done something wrong in my efforts to please. She did not wish to be *known,* in that curiously finite and, as it were, reductive way. And I had done it to show her I knew her—a sign of love, though not always—thereby proving that in the last analysis I did not know her at all.

For some listeners her words were no less moving than Jovanovich's impassioned declaration. But for others there was something unseemly about it. Indeed you did not have to be devoted to Arendt to find fault.

**RENATA ADLER**   Mary had observed that, in her own apartment, Hannah liked anchovy paste at breakfast. (So did my parents.) When Hannah came to visit, Mary had bought anchovy paste and put it on the breakfast table. Hannah didn't take any, didn't seem to like finding it there—maybe didn't like having her habits observed quite so closely. In her eulogy, Mary spoke of that. There was something very fine and complicated about the anecdote, also delicate. The thoughtfulness of putting it there, and also of recognizing the intrusion.

**IRVING HOWE**   Mary spoke beautifully. I felt that she was really speaking from the heart.

**WILLIAM PHILLIPS**   I remember when she said Hannah had beautiful ankles. Hannah had good legs, but I wouldn't put that in a memorial. That was Mary.

**JEROME KOHN**   Some people took umbrage at what she said. I had lunch with someone this year who didn't know either Mary or Hannah well and he said, "That's the most offensive thing I've read in my life."

At the funeral, it wasn't only her farewell to Hannah that caused consternation.

**HELEN WOLFF**   Bill Jovanovich came to the service with his wife, Martha, and sat down with her. He has a charming wife, but Mary always somehow managed to totally ignore that fact. At the service Mary simply came over and pulled him from his pew and made him sit next to her, as if the wife did not exist. I've never seen such brazen behavior. Her brother was there with her. But she wanted to have a handsome man at her side who was not her brother. I can remember it so well because fortunately Martha has a sense of humor. After the service, when it came time to leave, Mary arranged for Bill Jovanovich to walk down the aisle with her. I was sitting next to Martha Jovanovich, who whispered into my ear, "All she needs is for the organ to play Mendelssohn's wedding march."

Mary had done her best to say good-bye to her dear friend in a way that would do her justice, but she was not quite prepared to part with her yet. At the time of her death Hannah Arendt had finished the first two sections of *The Life of the Mind* and had started the third. In her typewriter was a sheet of paper on which she had typed two epigraphs for the final section, which would deal with the act of judging. Although between them Lotte Kohler and Jerome Kohn could conceivably have put the book together, she felt she owed it to Hannah to do it herself—not only to track down every quote and attribution and "English" the sentences, the way she had helped "English" them for years, but to piece together an abbreviated final section, "Judging," from lectures and class notes from the New School.

**LOTTE KOHLER**   The manuscript was there, but it still needed a lot of work for Hannah and also for an editor. I was very pleased that Mary took the time to work on it.

**WILLIAM JOVANOVICH**   Some of Hannah's students asked me if Mary McCarthy was competent to edit what remained. I said yes. . . . Of course, Mary learned to read German late and not perfectly. *That* would have occasioned some question.

Helping her with the manuscript she had Jerome Kohn, who *did* read German perfectly and had been working with Arendt since 1968.

**JEROME KOHN**   Mary McCarthy had a reputation of being tough and Hannah had the reputation of being formidable. My experience with them was virtually the opposite. Everyone told me when I had to go to work with Mary, "Oh, you're in for it." But I have never dealt with anyone who was as straightforward as she was. She was very direct. In that she and Hannah were alike. But Hannah was a nervous person, with little patience. Neither of them suffered fools easily. But Hannah not at all.

When Mary embarked on the project, she had already completed five chapters of her novel and was planning to work on both books simultaneously. Early on it became apparent that for *The Life of the Mind* she would need all the energy and concentration she could muster. It was her hope that the knowledge she had gained of German from three years of lessons with a private tutor would make it easier to smooth out or untangle the most vexed passages. But she soon discovered that the actual writing in the manuscript was the least of the challenges she faced. Fortunately, she had Jerome Kohn to help her and Margo Viscusi to type her edited manuscript.

**JEROME KOHN**   Mary did the Englishing. In the end I did the footnotes. We had a very interesting correspondence, because she would write, "What do you think this means? What do you think that means?" Apparently there were pages missing from the Xeroxing or they'd never been in the version that Mary got. To be honest, I think there are still some missing pages. Then, there was the matter of all the quotations. In the end I did the footnotes.

Hannah hated dealing with references, and they were often far from clear or not there at all in the manuscript. For the footnotes Mary wanted to know if this or that translation of Kant, for instance, was being cited. It usually turned out to be a combination of different translations, but with a lot of Hannah's own words as well. Probably the most accurate thing to say is that with languages she knew Hannah consulted standard translations but composed the translation herself. As for the Englishing, Mary had done this kind of work for Hannah before. But then Hannah had always been there to ask about matters of interpretation. Without her, I think Mary found it much harder. She had a tremendous sense of responsibility.

**CEES NOOTEBOOM**   Of course there will be somebody saying that it was an escape from the novel. I don't think so. I don't think Mary did. And she was candid enough to have given it a thought.

**MARGO VISCUSI**   I have never seen anyone work harder in my life—I don't care what kind of work we're talking about, whether it's construction work or what.

Not only was the work difficult but early on it was impeded by illness. In the spring of 1976, only months after Arendt's death, it was determined that she was suffering from a malignant tumor of the breast.

**MARGO VISCUSI**   She was in New York staying with Lizzie and got something prosaic like the flu and Lizzie sent her to her doctor, Annie Baumann, who was also Elizabeth Bishop's doctor. Annie Baumann, who was nothing if not thorough, checked Mary's breasts and discovered a lump. When Mary got back to Paris and consulted with a doctor there, he said it was a miracle that someone had spotted the lump so early.

Although she had always had energy to spare, she had never enjoyed consistently good health. At best her illnesses had provided an occasion for a much needed rest; at worst they had been a nuisance; but rarely had they been life threatening. This time, she was going to have to take immediate action. Sadly, she had no Hannah to turn to for advice. Rather than merely make light of this tumor, she chose to keep it a secret.

**MARGO VISCUSI**   She didn't want to tell people. It was not long after Susan Sontag had breast cancer and wrote about it. Mary never said there was anything wrong about that, but she didn't feel comfortable making her cancer public. She told Lotte and Cees Nooteboom, but she told hardly anybody else. It was then I began to realize how close she was to Cees.

The treatment Mary chose for the tumor was a simple lumpectomy, preceded and followed by weeks of cobalt radiation. She was scheduled to give the commencement talk at Vassar on May 16 and to receive an honorary degree from Bard a few days later. By altering her plans slightly she would be able to make the commencement at Vassar, but the Bard visit would have to be scrapped.

## FROM MARY MCCARTHY'S LETTER TO LOTTE KOHLER, MAY 3, 1976

The bore is that I must start the cobalt again not more than a week after the operation and continue regularly for at least three weeks. That knocks out Bard, but the doctor was very emphatic: "If you don't promise to be back here by Monday the 17th, I won't operate."[. . .] I've had to invent a cover story for the change of plans. So [Bard President] Botstein and Lizzie have been told that I'm in the midst of a dental crisis, involving surgery and follow-up visits. The impression, I hope, has been left that I'll be a toothless or semi-toothless horror between May 17 or 18 and the end of the month—unfit to be seen in public. (I find I enjoy making up an elaborate lie; it's "creative.")

Her lie was a source of some amusement. It was neat and economical and it had "plausibility," since she was actually undergoing dental surgery, although not to the extent that it would be "disfiguring." (Indeed her visits to the oral surgeon could be said to be public knowledge, thanks to Robert Lowell, who had lifted a passage from a 1969 letter in which she had written "[T]he real motive for the trip [to New York] is dentistry. A descending scale. I used long ago to come to New York to see a lover, then a psychoanalyst, then an editor or publisher, then a lawyer, and finally the dentist." Without so much as a by your leave, Lowell had altered the passage slightly, and then used it in a poem called "For Mary McCarthy 3.") In the spring of 1976, when she had so little to amuse her, she made the best of such diversion as came her way.

**HANS VAN MIERLO**   I visited her in Paris that spring, when she was ill, and I sat on the side of her bed. She disliked it very much that she couldn't get up. She had much pain, but she went on with her work. She was busy with the enormous work of Hannah Arendt's last book. The whole bed was filled with papers of Hannah Arendt.

In the end, the project took more than two years. If the book was not the book Arendt might have written, it was as good as her literary executor could make it. To the manuscript she appended a "postface" explaining what the author had intended to accomplish, then telling of her previous experiences working with the author and the personal difficulties she had faced in working on this particular text without the author to turn to for advice and—above all—for company. "When she was alive, the editing was fun," she wrote, "because it was a collaboration and an exchange."

Not only did she do her best for the text but she saw to it that Harcourt gave it the best presentation possible—insisting on large type and wide margins and simultaneous publication in two slender volumes, just the way Hannah had wanted. Then she asked William Shawn if he would be willing to look at it, and Shawn surprised her by taking almost the entire section "Thinking." Later, he would say he had done so even though it was the most difficult of all the Arendt pieces he had considered for publication and he "wasn't sure that more than a handful of people would read it." But gratifying as Shawn's decision was, it entailed a good deal of extra work. Not only was she on the phone for hours with the magazine's proofreaders and checkers but just before publication she also had to spend a week at *The New Yorker*'s offices going over proofs.

If she was hoping to create anything like the stir generated by *Eichmann in Jerusalem*, she was destined for disappointment. When the book came out three months later, it received respectful attention but nothing more. The fact was, it was not an easy book to like, much less understand. Almost invariably journalists and reviewers found her efforts on Arendt's behalf worthy of mention, using words like "exquisite care" and "devotion" to describe what she had done. But as far as her British publisher was concerned the exquisite care she had taken had been a waste of valuable time. As far as some of Hannah's New York friends were concerned, she could have saved herself the trouble. And as far as Arendt's relatives were concerned she was lucky to have the job.

**GEORGE WEIDENFELD**  It is my personal opinion that the world would have been greatly enriched if she had resisted indulging her two great passions—the Vietnam War and Hannah Arendt. They took over her life and literally stifled her creative ability. In my view these were the best years of her life as a writer and she was spending too much time doing things she wasn't particularly good at.

**HELEN WOLFF**  When you have a friendship with an outstanding person, you should be a little discreet about it. In the postscript of *The Life of the Mind*, for instance, look how personal Mary gets. She doesn't write about Hannah but her relationship to Hannah. I was stunned when I read it because it was absolutely not of the level of Hannah's own work.

**LOTTE KOHLER**  There was animus by the relatives to begin with. Then Mary, who at that time wasn't making much money because she was working on *Life of the Mind*, decided that she should get 25 percent of the advance and royalties, with the rest to go to the Hannah Arendt Literary Trust. She was in charge of the literary trust and had the power to make the decision, even if it was in her favor. Of course what Mary could have done was write to the relatives and say, I hope you realize that this is a lot of work and it has to be done by somebody who has a head on his shoulders, and I need to be paid. She didn't do that. The relatives felt that Mary should be gratified and proud simply to be able to edit the manuscript. Of course the relatives had an overblown idea of Hannah.

For all her work on the book Mary McCarthy had received $10,000 from Harcourt, but as the relatives saw it, this was far too much. When the literary trust was set up in 1978, they soon had more than the royalty she paid herself to fret about. Lotte Kohler had offered to assist her with the trust. But she was intent on doing it herself, just as she did her own income taxes—collecting the money that came in from Hannah's publishers and distributing it to the heirs.

**LOTTE KOHLER**   Mary was the last person to deal with anything like bookkeeping. For example, Mary sent a check for $7000 to the main heir and the check bounced. An unpleasant experience. So Mary wrote a long letter saying, "I didn't realize there was nothing in the account because I had opened another account where I thought I would get more interest and I forgot to transfer that. Anyway, I thought the bank was supposed to do that." Mary had her own bank account at the bank where the trust was. She got royalties on her own books and instead of depositing the money in her account, she deposited it into the trust account. Then, realizing what she had done, she transferred it to her own account. All of this looked very strange to the relatives. Mary prided herself on being the most honest and straightforward person in the world. But it is important to be meticulous about money matters. She was meticulous about spelling and grammar, but this was beyond her.

If the bookkeeping occasionally got confused, she had reason to be distracted. By the time the trust was established, she was back at work on her novel. Although she was able to pick up where she had left off, a certain momentum had been lost. Whether this was owing to difficulties inherent in the narrative or to the two-year hiatus, she was soon having troubles with her publisher. Early in 1978 William Jovanovich made comments about chapter six that made her wonder whether he had actually read the text. Later he would say that he was "convinced" that the novel was hurt by her taking all that time off: "She lost some aspects she had in mind, and when in conversation I mentioned this to her, she seemed perplexed."

Certainly, with this novel she had her work cut out for her. Having chosen to cram twenty-eight fictional characters into one modest Flevoland farmhouse, it was up to her first to keep her characters straight and then to breathe something approximating life into a passable number of them, while coping with the myriad practical details of a major hijacking. Compared to this, her efforts on behalf of the eight girls in *The Group* had been child's play. But compared to the existence she was now leading, her days back then had been wonderfully uncomplicated. Not only did she have the Hannah Arendt Literary Trust to administer, she also had to contend with a full social calendar and the management of two separate households. For all she might wish to deny it, now that she was in her sixties she had difficulty coping with the volume of work she had once been known to tear into with gusto.

At a certain point another writer might have put her social life on hold. But Mary McCarthy was not another writer. In June 1978, when at last she was rushing toward the finish, she and Jim celebrated her sixty-sixth birthday with yet another big party. Jim had always had an eye for attractive women and his flirtations did not go unnoticed, but he was a proud and attentive husband who shared his wife's love of festive occasions. Alison came to Paris from Munich, and Cees made the trip, as he did almost every year. Always Cees was a favored guest. As the years passed, the special attention accorded him by his hostess did not go unremarked.

**MARGO VISCUSI**    After Nicola Chiaromonte died, Cees became the person she could talk to about her life and work as a fellow artist-intellectual. Jim sometimes showed annoyance with Cees, who God knows could be provocative and whose shop talk with Mary sometimes left him with nothing to do but pour the wine. I suppose some people thought the relationship was sexual, but I'm quite convinced it wasn't. I witnessed them together a fair amount, especially one time when Cees and I were both houseguests in Castine. I also heard them speak of each other a lot. I was particularly struck by Mary's tenderness toward Cees's women companions. I think it was just one of those unfathomable friendships that defy differences in background, gender, and age.

That summer she had Margo Viscusi and her husband come stay for a week at a nearby Castine inn and *then* had Gaia Servadio and William Mostyn-Owen and their three children come stay for two weeks in the apartment over the garage. It was her fond hope that she could make up for these interruptions when she began her stint as a resident in writing at the American Academy at Rome. There for two to four months she would have a suite overlooking the city and almost no social obligations, save for those she wished to honor.

This time, her hopes proved to be well founded. By February 1979, she had a finished manuscript. Her way of dealing with the unwieldy cast of characters was to treat them the way she would in a novel of manners— focusing on social behavior and class conflicts, on petty venalities and small kindnesses, and on dreary details of life with no change of clothing, no food worth mentioning, and no adequate bathroom facilities. Like any good writer, she tried to stick with what she knew, or could extrapolate from her own experience.

Her way of dealing with the death and destruction which are the nuts and bolts of any self-respecting thriller was to pass over that business as quickly as possible. Where another writer might have drawn out the tension once the hijacking reached its crisis, she rushed headlong toward a climax which made up in sheer body count for any violence that had hitherto been lacking. At the end only two characters were permitted to walk away intact.

## FROM THE "ENVOI" TO *CANNIBALS AND MISSIONARIES*

Aileen and Frank were taking the plane—KLM—to New York. They had been the only ones to survive without serious injury when Jeroen blew himself and the house up. Most had been killed instantly: Jeroen and Greet, Archie and the Senator, the Germans, Carlos, Denise. Two of the Arabs had died from burns before they could be evacuated; the cookstove, run on propane, had caught fire. Ahmed had died two days later in the hospital; his lung had been punctured by a falling joist, and transfusions could not save him. Sophie was in a *kliniek*, having lost an arm. Henk was at home now, still in bed; he had had a concussion and gone into a deep coma. For a time it had been feared that his brain, if he lived, would be affected.

This time, William Jovanovich had no difficulty figuring out what had happened. He wrote quickly to say it was the best novel he'd read in five years. Her characters were "not verbalizing stick figures" and her ending managed to ask "the question of what's really worthwhile without sounding like a tract." What he had difficulty with was the way this bloodbath had been relegated to a paragraph.

## FROM WILLIAM JOVANOVICH'S LETTER TO MARY MCCARTHY, FEBRUARY 23, 1979

It's too abrupt, this totting up of who lived, who died. I felt cheated, as one does in some mystery or adventure story in which the reader follows people along for 300 pages, gets involved in their lives, and then is summarily told in a few paragraphs what happened to them.

He wanted her to work more on the "Envoi" and he wanted her to let him push her publication off from the fall of 1979 until the following January, when, as he put it, "ads and promotion are freer of competition." He soon learned she was not about to make significant changes in her "Envoi." (She, after all, had killed off the heroine of *A Charmed Life* with a haste which was seen by many as cavalier or deliberately perverse and which prompted James Merrill to remark, "She wouldn't ever, even as a novelist I guess, begin to envision what dying might be like.") Furthermore, she was not about to let him push her publication date off until after Christmas. For one thing, with the Shah of Iran in exile and hijacking on the wane, her plot was rapidly becoming dated. For another, she needed the money and attention.

**FROM MARY MCCARTHY'S LETTER TO WILLIAM JOVANOVICH, MARCH 1, 1979**

> It all means in effect that the book could not begin producing income till 1980 or after, and I've no other expectations of revenue for the time being. But it's not the feeling of being "frozen" financially—i.e., of the book as a frozen asset—that troubles me, really. It's the simple desire to be read again after such a long silence. I haven't published even an essay or a book review since I began this damned book.

What she was insisting on was a big fall publication, much like the one she'd had for *The Group*. In return, she was prepared to do her part to help publicize the "damned book." In the end, Jovanovich was forced to relent, and she agreed to fly to San Diego in May for the Harcourt sales conference and then to submit to interviews with *The Observer*, *The New York Times*, and *People*. She also agreed to do a television interview. But while she was able to carry the day with her publisher, she could not bring like pressure to bear on readers and reviewers.

**JAMES MERRILL**   The book that really lost me was *Cannibals and Missionaries*. She interrupted it to do Hannah Arendt's volumes. You can't do that to your own work. In the last years was there much energy left for the writing? Had her domestic life taken over? And all her various projects? I don't know.

**JOHN GROSS**   A falling off in the later fiction happens, you know. One of my favorite English novels is *Vanity Fair*. That was virtually Thackeray's first real novel, and then he wrote one or two others which are not nearly as good, and then he went on. I remember Bernard Shaw said that Thackeray imposed his later novels on the public like sentences of penal servitude. You may say that it's an exception, the novelist who follows his or her genius all the way through. A few novelists have gone on burning brightly until the end, but many many—perhaps the majority—have not. Does anyone really think *Resurrection* is as good as *Anna Karenina*?

From the start there were friends who liked the novel because they had helped with it or saw aspects of themselves in it. But for most of them the novel marked a falling off. Friends tend to hold their tongues when they don't like something, but the same cannot be said for reviewers. "[B]y the time this particular terrorist caper arrives at its dead end, one has long since lost interest in it," wrote Christopher Lehmann-Haupt in the daily *New York Times*. "Somewhere between Arthur Hailey's *Airport* and Thomas Mann's *Magic Mountain*, *Cannibals and Missionaires* gets fog-bound in the author's good intentions," wrote *Time*'s book critic. Fortunately, the review that could be said to be the most favorable appeared where publishers tend to believe it will count the most: in the Sunday *Times Book Review*, where it was featured on the front page.

**FROM MARY GORDON'S REVIEW IN *THE NEW YORK TIMES* BOOK REVIEW, SEPTEMBER 30, 1979**

> In response to the truly frightful prospect of anarchic terrorism, Mary McCarthy has written one of the most shapely novels to come out in recent years: a well-made book. It is delightful to observe her balancing, winnowing, fitting in the pieces of her plot. The tone of *Cannibals and Missionaries* is a lively pessimism. Its difficult conclusion is that to be a human being at this time is a sad fate: even the revolutionaries have no hope for the future, and virtue is in the hands of the unremarkable, who alone remain unscathed.

A former student of Elizabeth Hardwick's, Mary Gordon had received a blurb from the author of *Cannibals and Missionaries* for her first novel, *Final Payments*. Even without that blurb, this reviewer would have been disposed to like any novel Mary McCarthy had written. She, after all, had once dreamed of marrying Mary McCarthy's son so she could have her for a mother-in-law. Such a union was not in the cards; however, thanks to that review, Mary Gordon was invited to introduce the author of *Cannibals and Missionaries* at the 92nd Street Y, where she had occasion to tell a packed audience how much this writer had meant to her. Although the introduction hit exactly the right note, the same could not be said of the meeting backstage.

**FROM MARY GORDON'S INTRODUCTION OF MARY MCCARTHY AT THE 92ND STREET Y, NEW YORK CITY, OCTOBER 5, 1979**

> For me the writing of Mary McCarthy has been a species of inspirational literature. Two sentences will, I hope, explain this. The first is from *Memories of a Catholic Girlhood*: "Though I often stood first in my studies, a coveted pink ribbon for good conduct never came my way." The second, from the story "The Man in the Brooks Brothers Shirt," occurs when the heroine, having spent the night with the impossible man who picked her up in the train, awakes to groan, "Oh, sweet Jesus, when I open my eyes he won't be there." Both these sentences have been of immense comfort to me throughout my life.

**MARY GORDON**   I was very nervous but I managed to ask if she had been thinking of Simone Weil when she gave Sophie Weil her name. She said, "Of course not. There are many people named Weil. It's very common." What shocked me was how provincial she looked—like a banker's wife. I found her eyes wonderful and her smile wonderful, but her hair and dress were not good. As a matter of fact, I recall her wearing a little velvet bow instead of a barrette. She had little bows on her shoes, too. I notice shoes a lot and I was quite shocked by that. Physically she was nothing like what I'd expected.

The Mary McCarthy of "The Man in the Brooks Brothers Shirt" had vanished forever. Mary Gordon was not the only young woman to come up against this startling fact. Kate Crane, a law student who was not about to marry Mary McCarthy's son but was soon to marry her brother, ran into it headlong when Kevin brought her up for a first visit to Castine.

**KATE MCCARTHY**   The first time I met Mary was Labor Day weekend of 1978. Kevin and I had been going together for about a year and a half. I had read about four of Mary's books and from her writing I expected her to be open, the way Kevin was. I had this really beaten-up Volvo, which had no air-conditioning, and it was one of those awfully hot summer days and the drive took forever—ten hours. I was twenty-seven years old and I had on these lit-tle short shorts and this little French T-shirt and my hair was down to my waist. I remember laughing with Kevin when we got to the Bucksport Bridge and the two of us saying I should put my hair up in pigtails and go in to Mary's blowing bubbles. Well, I didn't do that. It was bad enough the way I did go in. Mary looked me up and down and turned to ice. And I knew I had made a grave, grave mistake.

Kate Crane may have been the unhappy beneficiary of her not incon-siderable fears on behalf of Kevin and may have suffered from the fact that she bore an uncanny resemblance to the young Mary McCarthy, but you did not have to be a beautiful young woman to run up against a sense of decorum befitting a Maine dowager. Or to recognize that she was prepared to bend the rules when it suited her.

**J. D. MCCLATCHY**   When I first met Mary, in the late seventies, something happened that I found exemplary. Jimmy Merrill, David Jackson, and Eleanor Perényi were staying with Mary for a weekend, and I came over to fetch them and take them to a place I had rented in Brooklin. I arrived after lunch, but we were taken back to the garden for coffee and she was showing me around. Feeling a bit of an intruder, I was making the kind of bland remarks you make when you first meet someone—in this case, I was gush-ing about Maine, how beautiful it was. "Oh, really," she said. "Well, what *exactly* do you find beautiful about it?" I said how lovely the wildflowers were by the road. "*Which* wildflowers do you like?" Of course, at questions like that the mind goes blank. I couldn't have told a black-eyed daisy from a rag-weed at that point. The decorum of the social occasion was not being observed. Though she was herself so punctilious about meals and domestic details, when it came to personal relationships she could easily take a little Fabergé hammer to the conventional egg and then—boom—everything would fall apart. At the same time, of course, she had cut right through to the ignorance I was trying to hide. So I was both annoyed and ashamed. And my feeling of being annoyed was overwhelmed by the sense that I had failed the quiz, and I was somehow going to have to study harder.

If McCarthy was not always quick to embrace a new friend, she was noticeably reluctant to part with an old one. By the time *Cannibals and Missionaries* came out she had lost Robert Lowell, Harold Rosenberg,

Fred Dupee, and James Farrell. One after another, some more valued than others, these pillars had toppled. For Fred Dupee and James Farrell she wrote tributes that were eventually published in *The New York Review of Books.* "A person of courage and irony," she wrote of Fred Dupee and then went on to make much of the fact that although "there was something permanently subversive about him," Dupee was "never a bohemian; he was too much attracted to style for that." To be fair, she added that it wasn't only a love of style: "In his own way, he was an upholder of order and legitimacy, or, let's say, a wry sympathizer with their efforts to stay in place."

Of James Farrell she wrote, "There was a drollery about him that rarely showed in his writing." While she gave due attention to the writing, it was Farrell himself who concerned her most. "To be a friend of Farrell's was a reassurance; it told you that there must be more good in you than you had sometimes suspected," she wrote. With both men there had been a long estrangement during her marriage to Bowden. But she had grown closer to both after her marriage to Jim West.

For Robert Lowell, who had moved back with Elizabeth Hardwick in Castine for the summer of 1977, just before his sudden death from a heart attack, she had no words to contribute. Indeed most of her attention was directed toward helping her friend Elizabeth. After the divorce, she had continued to see Lowell, even when she disapproved of what he was doing. One time, when he was determined to use Hardwick's letters in a new series of poems he was about to publish, she had tried, with mixed success, to intercede on Hardwick's behalf. He had been impossible at times and he had been terrifying in his madness. Still, she could not help but grieve at his death.

**Isaiah Berlin** I remember at Lowell's memorial service in London she cried nonstop. She was in continual tears, sitting in front of me in a church in Grosvenor Square. She was very emotional. I used to meet her with him in New York. She adored Lowell and he liked her. Mary had profound feelings and deep loves and hatreds.

For Harold Rosenberg, who had offered to defend her against Rahv's lawsuit over *The Oasis* and who had gone on to defend her Vietnam and Watergate books, there were no mixed feelings. At the memorial service, held at the New York Public Library almost a year after his death, she delivered a long tribute. While most listeners were moved by her words, one chose to take umbrage.

**From the Tribute Delivered on April 25, 1979**
For me, Harold's death was the conclusion of a series, which began with Heinrich Blücher, went on with Philip Rahv, Nicola Chiaromonte,

Edmund Wilson, Hannah Arendt, and finishes with him. He was the last tall pine in the forest to go down. There is no tree left standing in that noble array to look up to or mourn for; the axe has fallen on a generation, mine, of intellectuals and bold thinkers; *consummatum est*. And reviewing the scene through the present flat perspective, I cannot help feeling that in those days there were giants in the earth.

**SAUL STEINBERG**   She gave a beautiful speech, a worthwhile one. I remember Renata Adler was jittery about her speech and I told her, "Look, you are too old to be timid." And Mary said then, "One is never too old to be timid."

**SAUL BELLOW**   Everyone spoke and made nice speeches about Harold and then Mary got up. Now, the room was full of old friends. Old lovers, too. And she said, "All the tall pines have gone. Chiaromonte's gone. And Philip Rahv"—whose life she made miserable—"And now Harold the last of them." And there was Dwight Macdonald sitting there, still a buddy of hers. And Meyer Schapiro, whom everybody revered in that circle. So what the hell was she talking about? It was just too much for her. It was an occasion to louse everybody up.

**IRVING HOWE**   Mary was very generous with people after they died. She was a great obituary writer. Rahv. Jim Farrell, whose work she didn't especially like.

While this inclination to be gracious toward old friends at their deaths was so marked as to elicit some comment, she was suddenly no less inclined to extend herself for old friends still alive. In the fall of 1979 a big party for *Cannibals and Missionaries* was held at Elizabeth Hardwick's New York apartment. At the party you could find Arthur Schlesinger, Bob Silvers, Eugene McCarthy, Cleo Paturis, Nancy Macdonald, and Andy Dupee. You could find Vida Deming, who had taught with her at Bard and Sarah Lawrence; Evelyn Hofer, who had taken the photographs of Florence; Elisabeth Niebuhr Sifton, who had conducted the *Paris Review* interview; Renata Adler, who had briefly been engaged to Reuel; and Frani Blough Muser, who had been her best friend at Vassar and who was putting her up at her apartment for the week. There were friends who had never made it into her novels and friends she had used in this new one with barely any disguise. In some respects the party could be said to be the apotheosis of conciliatory dinners and lunches she had been giving for years.

**FROM ELIZABETH HARDWICK'S REMARKS AT MARY MCCARTHY'S MEMORIAL SERVICE, NOVEMBER 8, 1989**
I know a number of people who might be said to have sat for their portraits in her work, unwillingly of course, and who perhaps did not want the sketch hanging on the wall, but I also noted that they always made up. She always made up with them and these sitters, if you can call them that—some obscure and some known people—would become,

after the book was out, the object of Mary's intense friendship. I would think, Oh, we're going to have to see them for dinner for the rest of our lives [. . .] and that turned out to be true.

In *Cannibals and Missionaries* the silver-haired senator was "an improvisation on the theme 'Gene McCarthy' "; the "new journalist" owed a lot to Renata Adler; the Dutch deputy was mostly Cees Nooteboom with a touch of Hans van Mierlo; the rector was a dead ringer for her Castine friend Ed Miller, who had once served as rector at St. George's in New York; the good bishop was a perfect likeness of another Castine neighbor, the late Will Scarlett, a former bishop of St. Louis, to whom the book was dedicated; and, finally, Aileen Simmons (who owed something to Sarah Gibson Blanding, Vassar's president back at the time of the *Holiday* article) bore more than a passing resemblance to Elizabeth Hardwick.

If the party's hostess spotted any of her own attributes in the flirtatious and unfailingly pragmatic president of Lucy Skinner College, she gave no sign of it. For Hardwick, who was herself enjoying a great critical success with her novel *Sleepless Nights* (dedicated to her daughter, Harriet, and her good friend Mary McCarthy), the party afforded an opportunity to be generous. For others it was a chance to revise a prior assessment or simply catch up.

**ELISABETH NIEBUHR SIFTON**   Physically she seemed very different from when I first knew her, and she wasn't as I'd imagined she'd be when she grew older. She was slowed down, more muted. I mean, take Hannah Arendt: there was a woman who blazed into old age with undiminished libidinous intellectual vitality, who even in late-middle age radiated a kind of energy. I expected Mary would be like that, but she wasn't.

**ARTHUR SCHLESINGER**   At a certain stage in life, friends begin to disappear and die. You cling all the more to the people who remain. I had this sense with Mary in those last years. We'd known each other for a long time and had been very fond of each other, but hadn't seen all that much of each other. Suddenly in the last half dozen years or so, I felt a greater mutual dependence and warmth. The circle narrows all the time when you're in your seventies and you value what's left.

But for every dear friend from the past who was present at the party there seemed to be at least one missing. Even though, she might half laughingly confide to William Jovanovich that she now believed in "universal reconciliation," there were times when a final reconciliation defied her best efforts. For Elizabeth Bishop, whom she had admired and respected and offended without ever intending to, there would be no memorial tribute and no making amends while she was still alive.

Upon returning home from Frani Muser's, she had done her very best to set things right. In a letter to Elizabeth Bishop dated October 28 she had sworn that she had not been thinking of Bishop, or her Brazilian friend Lota when writing about Lakey in *The Group*. This letter, which was returned unopened, arrived the day Bishop died of a cerebral hemorrhage. Sadly, Bishop's death was not the only Vassar death to haunt her that November. Helen Sandison, her beloved teacher of Shakespeare, already blind and rapidly going deaf, had taken sleeping pills and drowned herself in her bathtub.

### FROM MARY MCCARTHY'S LETTER TO FRANI BLOUGH MUSER, NOVEMBER 11, 1979

> [S]ince coming back, I've not been able to get Miss Sandison out of my mind; I think of her in the bathtub, of course—I mean while I'm taking my bath. There's something terrible and also touching about her determination, which may have been a little mad. Since she took the overdose of sleeping-pills anyway, why was she bent on drowning herself too? Did she trust that she would submerge on becoming unconscious and thus make doubly sure? But how could she have counted on that? I keep thinking of it and of her and her awful isolation within an active brain.

As the decade drew to a close and she saw her brother Kevin start a new family (Kate had given birth to a baby girl, whom they were naming Tess, so that there would again be a Tess in the McCarthy family), Mary was experiencing more than an occasional intimation of mortality. To Miriam Gross, who had interviewed her for *The Observer*, she had announced, "I absolutely hate being old." Part of it had to do with physical deterioration: "[S]ome days I wake up very irritable and I realise that what I thought was me was just my constitution." And part of it had to do with the losses she had sustained: "[I]n a sense there's almost no one to talk to any more."

Of course there were friends from the past she could turn to for company. And young friends like Margo Viscusi and Cees Nooteboom. But at this juncture in her life she sorely missed Hannah Arendt. Not simply for the pleasure of a running conversation with someone whose mind was as fine as any she'd had the privilege to encounter, but for some matter-of-fact advice.

At the end of the year Jim West was going to have to retire as information officer for the OECD. It was a posting he had never especially cared for and yet it had provided both of them with privileges and perquisites that made their life in Paris comfortable. No less important, it had provided him with the satisfaction and sense of accomplishment that comes with a job well done. Friends had warned her that retired husbands can become irritable. Now, not only would Jim West be at loose ends but the two of them would soon be living on his two pensions instead of a generous government salary. For some time he had been talking of spending five months a year in Maine. Castine was fine for the summer, but it was hardly New York or Paris—or even Rome. Nonetheless, as "Mary West," the devoted wife she had always prided herself on being, she would be expected to follow him.

The trouble was, she was not ready to retire. If anything she was busier than ever. After Christmas she was slated to deliver the North-cliffe Lectures in London at University College. She had always felt appreciated in London. And she could count on still finding many old friends alive there. Karl Miller, an old friend who headed the English department at the college, had invited her to choose her topic. She had decided to give four lectures on the subject of "Ideas and the Novel," undeterred by the fact that she had concluded that her own novel-writing days were over.

To Miriam Gross she had confided, "Something I've observed is that one loses one's social perceptions, they get blunted and dimmer as one gets older—it's partly a matter of eyesight. You can continue writing poetry and essays and so on, but to be a novelist you have to have this alert social thing." Before long she would confide to an audience numbering in the hundreds that she knew her novel-writing days were over when she realized that she could visit a friend's apartment without checking out the contents of the medicine cabinet.

She would no longer be writing fiction, but once the four lectures were delivered, she would not be lacking for a project. After demurring for almost a decade, she had decided to give William Jovanovich the book he wanted. Already she had started work on the first chapter. The contract had been signed and a sizable advance had been paid for her intellectual memoirs. This new memoir, which would inevitably cover old ground, did not promise to be taxing. Furthermore, the main reservation she had voiced to Elizabeth Hardwick was fast becoming irrelevant. The way things were going, with one pillar in her life toppling close upon another, there would soon be no one left to offend.

# Chapter Twenty-five

# THE HELLMAN SUIT

Although Mary McCarthy had long since parted company with the reckless young woman who woke up in a strange Pullman berth, only to groan, "Oh sweet Jesus," that "coveted pink ribbon for good conduct" seemed somehow to elude her. To help publicize *Cannibals and Missionaries* she had agreed to do a limited number of interviews. She balked, however, at a full-scale profile—even one commissioned by the *New York Times Magazine*. She had been burned at least four times. There had been the 1962 Brock Brower profile for *Esquire* and the *Newsweek* profile that ran when *The Group* came out; there had been Doris Grumbach's *The Company She Kept*; finally, in 1978, there had been a profile in a short-lived English-language biweekly paper called *Paris Metro*.

Joan Dupont, the reporter for *Paris Metro*, had set the tone for the profile by invoking the chain-smoking, typewriter-smashing Lillian Hellman played by Jane Fonda in *Julia*, the recently released film adaptation of a section from Hellman's memoir *Pentimento*. "Now, that's the kind of spirit the public likes to see women writers display: mannish, manic," wrote Dupont, before describing her first sighting of a very different kind of writer: "I saw Mary McCarthy standing on the Place de la Concorde at high noon, a Sulka shopping bag clutched to her side, her face powdered pale, dressed in pearl-grey like a widow, hair and handsome chin set. She stepped cautiously, feet splayed in sober pumps, as if she might fall unless she took it very easy."

The profile was titled "Portrait of a Lady," and nothing in the twelve columns of newsprint that followed did anything to soften this portrait of an aging writer with an unfortunate tendency to make pronouncements like a "garden club" matron. Indeed the one time Dupont got what she regarded as a satisfactory response was when she brought up Lillian Hellman. "I can't stand her" said the lady with the sober pumps, and went on to explain why.

Much of her antipathy, it seemed, stemmed from their meeting in 1948 when she was teaching at Sarah Lawrence and Hellman was visiting Harold Taylor. As she told it, she had arrived at the president's house to find Hellman telling a group of wide-eyed students that John Dos Passos had deserted the Loyalist side during the Spanish Civil War not because the Loyalists were being taken over by the Communists but because "he didn't like the food in Madrid!" Her first response had been to keep silent. "I didn't introduce myself and I think [Hellman] thought I was another student. Anyway, she paid no attention to me. She was just brain-washing those girls—it was really vicious. So finally I spoke up and said, I'll tell you why he broke with the Loyalists, you'll find it in his novel, *The Adventures of a Young Man*, and it wasn't a clean break. [Hellman] started to tremble. She had rather aging wrinkled arms, bare, and on them were a lot of gold and silver bracelets—and all the bracelets started to jangle. It was a very dramatic moment of somebody being caught absolutely red-handed. And so, somebody like that writes a book like *Scoundrel Time*, and I think that it's still scoundrel time, as far as she's concerned."

"This has been not, her longest speech, for she has been monologuing, but the most impassioned," noted Dupont, with something like approval and something less than perfect syntax. "The past is very present suddenly. She is still angry. Anything about the Stalinists gets her going."

Carlos Freire, the mutual friend who had brought Dupont and McCarthy together and accompanied Dupont to the rue de Rennes apartment, would later say, "I knew at once it was a mistake." Certainly McCarthy had no intention of making that particular mistake again. Ruling out the *Times Magazine*, she decided to trust to her friend Miriam Gross at *The Observer* in London; her brother Kevin, who had been asked to do a piece for *People*; and to a staff reporter for the daily *Times*. For her one big television interview she chose Dick Cavett, who had taken pleasure in her company during earlier broadcasts and had taken her to lunch when he ran into her at the Watergate hearings. Unlike William Buckley, Cavett was not about to take her to task for her politics. If anything, he enjoyed a reputation for being all too ready to delight in the dearly held convictions of his more celebrated guests.

Her interview with Dick Cavett was taped for WNET, the Public Broadcasting System's outlet in New York, on October 17, 1979. "When she was on camera she was never exactly relaxed," Cavett would later recall. "She often looked like she wished she had a cup of coffee or a cigarette. But I don't think she would have done it if she didn't enjoy it, and I looked forward to having her on."

This time Cavett was sufficiently enthralled with her company to permit the interview to spill over into a second session. Unfortunately, the two sessions, which were taped to coincide with the publication of *Cannibals and Missionaries*, did not air until the following January—too late to be of much help to the novel. By then, thousands of copies were languishing in bookstores or on their way back to the warehouse. And by then, she was delivering the first two of her four Northcliffe lectures at the University of London.

Several times before she had touched on her topic, "Ideas and the Novel," but that did not mean she had tired of it. Indeed, she was more than delighted to tell her London audience how the novel had taken a turn for the worse when Henry James and Virginia Woolf came along and began to act as if sensibility was everything and a heady blend of gossip, hard facts, and ideas was somehow in bad taste. As she saw it, James and Woolf, between them, had drained the blood from the novel, leaving a wan husk for their successors—so that what you had now were old-fashioned novels written by hacks for a mass audience and a very small number of modern, or "art," novels, written by gifted writers for a handful of readers.

Her lack of sympathy for James and Woolf was by now common knowledge. Just as her admiration for Austen, Dickens, and Tolstoy was no secret. But to these lectures she brought a special intensity, perhaps because she had so recently grappled with writing a novel herself. Certainly *Cannibals and Missionaries* seemed to be very much on her mind when she spoke of how gifted writers might make use of an old-fashioned, or popular, form to get an idea across.

To London friends like the Mostyn-Owens, who attended the lectures, her arguments seemed nothing short of "brilliant." To Karl Miller, who had invited her to speak, her arguments seemed perhaps "a vindication of her own practice." But that was only natural, he would add. "Human beings are given to that. They start theories up which are designed to explain why they have done what they've done."

Because she was in London on January 24 and 25, she did not see her interview with Cavett when it aired in the United States. She did not even know that it was being broadcast. If she had known, she probably would not have thought twice about it; for the most part, she had only been repeating things she had said before. Some of those things, of course, had been said in passing, at some cocktail party or dinner. But, so far as she or Cavett could tell, the worst she had done was to attack the Kennedy family by saying that the Kennedys might be Catholics but they were not Christians.

"Now, this is a provocative statement," Cavett had noted. "Do you think it is libelous?" she had asked. On reflection, he had concluded that in all likelihood it was not. Having settled this question to their mutual satisfaction, if not the satisfaction of WNET's lawyers, they moved on to her attack on John Hersey's *Hiroshima*; her reputation for being "contrary"; her desire to write a letter to Solzhenitsyn, who believed America had been wrong to pull out of Vietnam; and, above all, her desire to write Vietnamese Prime Minister Pham Van Dong to find out exactly what was going on in those re-education camps in the South.

Here Cavett pressed her harder than was his custom, asking why she did not write Pham Van Dong that letter or simply ring him up on the telephone. He even went so far as to ask if she could have been "just wrong about him in the first place." And here she faltered for a moment, acknowledging that Pham Van Dong was undeniably old and perhaps powerless "so that the letter could still be written but the real . . . the result might be nil, might be nil, anyway."

She might have gone on in this vein indefinitely if Cavett, mindful of his audience, had not pushed her on to a topic suggested to him by the production assistant who had interviewed her prior to the broadcast. When Cavett asked if there were any writers she considered overrated, she hedged a bit, saying twenty years earlier she might have named Pearl Buck and John Steinbeck but there were no overpraised writers anymore. However, when prodded, she did allow as how there might be one such writer. After that she saw no reason to mince words.

### FROM THE TRANSCRIPT OF *THE DICK CAVETT SHOW,* OCTOBER 18, 1979, TAPING

> McCARTHY: The only one I can think of is a holdover like Lillian Hellman, who I think is tremendously overrated, a bad writer, and dishonest writer, but she really belongs to the past, to the Steinbeck past, not that she is a writer like Steinbeck
>
> CAVETT: What is dishonest about her?
>
> McCARTHY: Everything. But I said once in some interview that every word she writes is a lie, including "and" and "the."
>
> CAVETT: I'm sure she would write you and correct that, but you won't believe it if she did, would you? Have you ever run into Miss Hellman lately?
>
> McCARTHY: I haven't seen her for about . . . and I never really knew her. I think I met her once. I tell you, it was 1948. That is how long ago it is.

She had in fact met Hellman twice and the interview in which she had said all this before had been the recent one for the *Paris Metro*, where, prodded by Joan Dupont, she had declared "every word she writes is *false,* including 'and' and '*but*' [italics added]." Cavett, unlike Dupont, did not make much of her anger. But Cavett, unlike Dupont, enjoyed a sizable audience. Among those watching at eleven o'clock on the night of January 25 were Ben O'Sullivan, her longtime lawyer; Jane Kramer, a young friend who had recently taken over *The New Yorker*'s "Letter from Paris"; Diana Trilling and Irving Howe, two acquaintances who had never considered themselves friends; and Lillian Hellman herself, who, like just about everyone else, was watching from bed.

**BEN O'SULLIVAN**   I remember I was reading, but the TV was on—my wife, Sonya, was sleeping—and I heard Mary say these things. I literally fell out of bed. I said, "Sonya, you should have heard what Mary just said." She, who was half asleep, said something like "It sounds pretty good to me."

**JANE KRAMER**   I like watching old movies in bed, and I had turned on the television and there was Mary with Dick Cavett. I heard Mary being asked this question. With that smile of hers, she said, "Everything is a lie." And he was saying "You're sure you want to say that?" "Yes," she said. My husband, Vincent, was reading in his study, and I yelled, "Vincent, come in here, listen to Mary."

**IRVING HOWE**   Mary was so reckless. She was great. I jumped out of my chair. "She's crazy," I said to my wife. Mary was absolutely right. About the whole thing.

**DIANA TRILLING**   Mary thought Lillian was a liar, so she said it. It was a theatrical performance and she said it in a dramatic and witty way. I saw that program and I was smiling about it the next day.

Although she was legally blind, Lillian Hellman saw enough to ensure that she was not smiling the next morning. Instead, she was on the phone first with her lawyer, Ephraim London, and then with Dick Cavett.

**DICK CAVETT**   The next day the phone rang and the familiar voice rasped out, "Why the hell didn't you defend me?!" Startled, I remember stammering out something like "Gee, Lillian, I don't ever think of you as someone who needs defending by me." And adding that I thought Mary's remark, greeted by audience laughter and punctuated by that legendary smile, was largely a joke that passed quickly. She felt otherwise—that her basic being had been attacked, and attacked violently. I failed to convince her that there might be some sections of the world where it was not being discussed.

Within three weeks Lillian Hellman had sued Mary McCarthy, Dick Cavett and his production company, and WNET, for $2.25 million—$1.75 million for the pain and suffering inflicted by the defamation of her character and $500,000 for punitive damages. Although the actual words "libel" and "slander" were never used, Hellman's lawyer characterized McCarthy's statement about his client as "false, made with ill will, with malice, with knowledge of its falsity, with careless disregard of the truth, and with intent to injure the plaintiff personally and in her profession."

**JANE KRAMER**  I knew that there was no way Mary would not get in trouble with what she said. It was of course entirely accurate.

**DIANA TRILLING**  Lillian reared up because Lillian was a monster. She could not accept any criticism. She had her publisher, Little Brown, refuse to publish a book of mine for which they were contracted because it had literally four sentences of criticism of *Scoundrel Time*. Very mild criticism—factual corrections. She lied, lied, lied. No word of truth to it. Mary was perfectly right. No word of truth came out of her mouth.

The first word the defendant received of the suit was when Herbert Mitgang of the *Times* tracked her down in London, where she was about to deliver the last two of her Northcliffe Lectures.

### MARY MCCARTHY AT CITY ARTS & LECTURES,
### SAN FRANCISCO, MAY 10, 1985

Herbert Mitgang got me on the phone and he said he wanted to tell me that Lillian Hellman was suing me for libel, and I laughed. He said, "You won't laugh when I tell you it's for two and a quarter million dollars." I think I did laugh again.

Whether or not she actually laughed a second time, she sounded noticeably unrepentant, while Hellman came across as puzzled and aggrieved.

### FROM "MISS HELLMAN SUING A CRITIC FOR 2.25 MILLION,"
### BY HERBERT MITGANG, *THE NEW YORK TIMES*, FEBRUARY 16, 1980

Reached in California, Miss Hellman said that she found it difficult to understand why Miss McCarthy had offered the remarks about her. "I haven't seen her in 10 years, and I never wrote anything about her. We have several mutual friends, but that would not serve as a cause for her remarks. I think she has always disliked me. It could go back to the Spanish Civil War days, in November or December of 1937, after I had returned from Spain"[. . . .]

Reached in London, Miss McCarthy recalled the remarks she had made about Miss Hellman and made no effort to modify what she had said about Miss Hellman during the broadcast. "I barely knew her," Miss McCarthy said. "My views are based on her books, especially *Scoundrel Time*, which I refused to buy, but borrowed. I did not like the role she had given herself in that book, which seemed to be hypocritical."

Seeing things the way she did, she saw no reason to retract what she had said. And no reason to cancel her plans to go on with Jim West to a party being given in their honor by David and Ellie DuVivier, old friends from Paris who had taken a fine house on Lord North Street.

**JOHN GROSS**  My most dramatic memory of Mary is at the DuViviers'. The news had come in that very day that Lillian Hellman was going to sue. Mary wasn't exactly lighthearted—she wouldn't be that—but was fairly jokey about the thing. And Jim's body language made it clear that we ought to be taking this thing rather more seriously.

While she persisted in regarding the suit as a joke, her host, who was a senior partner in a prominent international law firm and a former head of the Legal Aid Society, saw it rather differently.

**DAVID DuVIVIER**   I'm sure that everything Mary thought about Lillian Hellman was based on fact, but she made a gross and arrogant error and she was conned into this by Cavett. He wanted the excitement, but he did her a great disservice. He got her in the mood—first, he talked about the Kennedys and how they were great Catholics—and then he led into this thing. She was feeling good because she'd scored another laugh. Not that she would seek laughter, but in this case, on television, it was different. It's my understanding that some years earlier, she'd had a bet with Kenneth Tynan that he would use the word "fuck" on British television. So she was vulnerable to this kind of thing. She did get carried away.

If she got carried away, she'd had ample provocation. As she saw it, in *Scoundrel Time* Hellman had been more than hypocritical. She had been fundamentally dishonest—making no mention of the fact that well into the 1950s she had remained a fellow traveler and, by some accounts, a full Party member. In addition, she had been self-aggrandizing—making much of her offer to testify to the House Committee on Un-American Activities as long as her testimony did not implicate others and glancing over the fact that she, like virtually every witness hauled before the committee, ended up taking the Fifth.

With *Scoundrel Time* and the two memoirs that had preceded it, Lillian Hellman had turned herself into a popular heroine. Having enjoyed a good run as a Broadway playwright with such successes as *The Little Foxes* and *Toys in the Attic*, she was now enjoying an even greater success as a memoirist. Not only was she widely believed to be the beloved partner of Dashiell Hammett but she was widely acclaimed as a woman who had suffered for her politics and had courageously told the House committee that she would not "cut [her] conscience to fit this year's fashions."

**JASON EPSTEIN**   Lillian was a Stalinist, but she would never admit it. Mary really took that stuff very seriously. She was of a generation that would. That was what the attack on Lillian was all about. It was a political argument. It was a delayed reaction. Diana Trilling is of the same generation as Mary. They had all either joined the Party or come very close to joining, so they all felt compromised by it. They felt betrayed by it. The damned thing took advantage of your best impulses and then betrayed you. It was like a terrible marriage. You never got over it.

**EILEEN FINLETTER** I didn't know Lillian well, but in the early fifties my first husband and I were in London, staying with Donald Ogden Stewart and his wife, Ella, as was Lillian. I can tell you this: She was an absolute thousand percent Stalinist. Ella was a Stalinist and she and Lillian were in absolute accord on everything—the trials, executions, etc. If anything, she went further than our hostess. Instead, she paints herself as a nice liberal. Lillian was rewriting history. Mary was so scrupulously honest, she never would have been able to stand that.

**FRANCES FITZGERALD** About Lillian Hellman I don't think Mary cared all that much. I don't think she did at all. Except that again you have her passion for the truth. And she wouldn't spare anything. And, of course, she thought that to say Lillian had never said a word of truth, not even an "and" or a "the," was a joke. It *was* a joke. But she really felt that way about Lillian. And Lillian's work. It wasn't personal. It was about her work.

**ELIZABETH HARDWICK** There wasn't anything to it, you know, except Lillian was an appalling liar. And a very bad person. Mary hated her—not personally. She didn't really know her. It wasn't an old enmity. I knew Lillian much better. There was a time I wrote something in *The New York Review* against *The Little Foxes* and Lillian started such a campaign. I thought, Oh, I must have done that so I wouldn't have to see her ever again.

In the late seventies, everywhere you turned you were likely to run into Lillian Hellman. You could find her played by Jane Fonda in the movie *Julia*, looking pert and pretty and risking her life to carry fifty thousand dollars to a friend active in the anti-Nazi resistance. Or you could find her in the pages of almost every major magazine, sporting a Blackglama mink coat and looking like nothing so much as a bewigged W. H. Auden, identified not by name but by the question "What becomes a Legend most?"

**JASON EPSTEIN** I knew Lillian very well. Did I like her? Yes and no. But she was fascinating. Here she was far from good-looking and with a very small talent, but she turned herself through sheer will into if not a great beauty then a very desirable woman to whom the world ascribed enormous talent. It was a great theatrical performance. Pure theater. She did it all with mirrors. It worked with fewer and fewer people as time went by, but it worked. For instance, Lillian convinced herself and Hammett and then other people that she and Hammett had a real love affair, which I don't think they ever did—they had something, but Hammett was probably too drunk to have a love affair and had contracted a serious sexual disease when they were together. He was fascinated by her, though. She could do that. She could mesmerize you. But she never told the truth. And Mary was right about everything but the "ands" and "buts." Those were probably true.

**DIANA TRILLING** Lillian was the most charming person you could hope to meet. Mary did not have that kind of charm. You could go see Lillian when she was ill, for instance, and you'd sit at the side of her bed and before you knew it you were having the best time. She could turn anything into a good time. Just by the nature of her mind and her character. In addition, she had such wonderful parties. I've never known anything like it. She was vicious. She was monstrous. But until you couldn't stand her, you were absolutely beguiled by her.

**MAX PALEVSKY**   Life is an endless set of difficulties and Lillian was there to talk to. We became friends in 1977. I was admiring because she was of a fabled generation, and she was interested in me because I was rich. With Lillian, wanting money was a steady complaint. I knew that it was not true. It was part of a game. I would send her a check every month. The money that I gave her and the money that was potentially there from me—that was money so she didn't have to feel so wildly at risk. Peter Feibleman tells a story of saying to Lilly, "Why do you need money from Max?" "The rent." "But, Lilly, you own this apartment." "For the rent I'd have to pay if I didn't." Lilly liked to be taken care of.

**SUSAN SONTAG**   At one point Lillian called a lot and she invited me a lot and I went along because I was curious, because I was flattered, because why not. She called you all the time and then you sort of felt, God, it's Lillian Hellman, I should call her sometimes. And so you started calling her and saying, "Hi, Lillian, it's Susan. How are you?" And she seemed so pleased. Of course the next step was you didn't call her for a week or so, and then you did call and she said, "Why didn't you call?" The other person who was taken up around the same time was Renata Adler. And we once compared notes about how possessive Lillian was. And how once you got her attention she really wanted you to be in attendance. She was clinging. People liked it. They liked the warmth of it. I don't think Lillian was any less of a monster than Mary—in fact she may very well have been more of a monster—but she was a warm monster. She was a touchy-feely kind of monster. I responded to that.

Like any self-respecting monster, Lillian Hellman could be endearing. But she could also be terrifying when enraged. And she had a knack for self-preservation. (For instance, when Elizabeth Hardwick had taken a jaundiced look at *The Little Foxes* back in 1967, she had mustered everyone from her friend Richard Poirier to Edmund Wilson to speak out on her behalf in the letters page of *The New York Review of Books*.) Why, then, did she bring a lawsuit guaranteed to bring her attention which might be unflattering and even potentially damaging?

**FRANCES FITZGERALD**   Had Mary known Lillian better, she would have known Lillian's only fun at the end of her life was to sue people. I knew Lillian very well—since I was a child—and I could have predicted it.

**RENATA ADLER**   At one point, years before this particular trouble, I remember Lillian's saying, "I'm rich enough now to sue anybody, even if I'm going to lose." By then it had become clear to me from reading Lillian that she was, by temperament and in fact, not a victim of persecutions and denunciations, but a natural informer, an initiator of persecutions and denunciations. She could be amusing company; she was also a much feared bully.

**ROGER STRAUS**  Lillian made it clear to me she was out to hurt Mary. When I said to her, "Oh, come on, Lillian, why don't you let the matter rest?" she said, "No, I'm gonna teach her a thing or two."

**JOHN GROSS**  Why else would she have done it except to bankrupt Mary? Even if she did it in a blind brainstorm the first time round, within days she'd have realized what she'd launched herself into. It was a form of persecution—even if Lillian was to lose the case, the threat was there.

Almost immediately after receiving news of Hellman's lawsuit, McCarthy was felled by a bad bout of bronchitis, forcing her to reschedule her fourth Northcliffe Lecture. So long as she was in London, she continued to make light of the threat. However, once she returned to Paris and the quiet of her apartment it was difficult to be quite so cavalier about it. Just before the broadcast she had signed a release in which she agreed to hold Cavett's production company and WNET "harmless from and against any and all liability, judgments, claims, losses and expenses, including reasonable attorney's fees, resulting from any statement, act, pose or routine made or performed by me during my 'appearance.' " She might laugh about how it was a release designed for a belly dancer, but it meant she was going to be held financially responsible for what she had said. Moreover, David DuVivier had warned her that her New York bank accounts could be frozen and her future earnings confiscated. Quickly she transferred her funds to a bank in Maine, where they would be safe from the New York courts. But while she had managed to protect her assets, there was no way she could avoid the suit itself.

**BEN O'SULLIVAN**  At first Mary didn't call me at all and I was wondering what she was doing about the suit. And then about two weeks later she sent me a set of the papers she'd received in Paris. She hadn't done anything. And she needed help.

### MARY MCCARTHY AT CITY ARTS & LECTURES, SAN FRANCISCO, MAY 10, 1985

I said, "I hope you'll represent me in court, Ben," though he is not a trial lawyer. He said, "I certainly will not." And I said, "What? Why?" And he said, "If it comes to court I will have committed suicide."

Having made and lost several fortunes, Lillian Hellman was a millionaire several times over. In addition she had Ephraim London, who received a generous stipend as counsel and co-chairman for her Committee for Public Justice. Some people, including Ben O'Sullivan, believed that London was charging Hellman nothing for his labors. Others believed that the suit was being underwritten by Max Palevsky, who had sold his company, Scientific Data Systems, to Xerox, for a nice profit. One thing is certain: Palevsky gave Hellman about $100,000 over a period of time. "What she did with it was up to her," he would later say.

The Wests, on the other hand, had no wealthy benefactor and no lawyer on retainer. Although they had both earned good money, they had also spent it—they lived well and they were famously generous. Indeed virtually all that remained from the large sums that had poured in from *The Group* was Jim West's beautiful white Mercedes convertible, which now resided in Castine, where it was increasingly plagued by breakdowns.

### MARY McCARTHY AT CITY ARTS & LECTURES, SAN FRANCISCO, MAY 10, 1985

All the lawyers on my side were determined to do everything to keep it out of court, because that's when the costs go so high—not the court costs but the costs of the papers and the preparation of the papers, the lawyers' costs, and bringing witnesses, and so on[. . . .] Our side had made an appeal—or a motion, rather—for a summary judgment. That means dismissing a case on sheerly legal grounds—nothing to do with the facts, right or wrong—on First Amendment grounds. One of our points, the point usually made in such cases, was that Hellman was a public figure. If you're a public figure, like any appointed or elected official, you're expected to take more criticism than if you're a housewife. And so we maintained that she was a public figure and that I was exercising my right of free speech as a literary critic.

**BEN O'SULLIVAN**   You might say there were three parts to our position: *Number one* was that what Mary said was opinion expressed in exaggerated form, which everybody should understand. Hyperbole is accepted as not being libelous and is accepted as something not to be taken literally in a libel suit. The *second* was that Lillian was a public figure. And I guess the *third*— which was sort of subterranean—was to suggest that if we ever had to try the case we might have won it on grounds of truth.

In New York, Ben O'Sullivan's firm set about putting together all the paperwork necessary to file a motion for summary judgment. And in Paris, the defendant wrote her publisher asking him to bring out her Northcliffe Lectures in book form so as to buttress her assertion that she was only exercising her right as a critic. Having gotten William Jovanovich to agree, she tried her best to work on her new memoir, while giving due attention to a veritable banquet of damning Hellman tales being served up for her benefit.

Hellman, it seemed, had received an appointment from the romance languages department at Hunter College and done nothing to earn the $45,000 stipend that came with it. More delicious yet, Hellman, in her role as Dorothy Parker's executor, had tried to break Parker's will, so that literary rights left to the NAACP would be hers for life. More to the point, in *Pentimento* Hellman had written of Hammett's putting down Ernest Hemingway at the New York's Stork Club at a time when Hemingway was in Cuba, trying to finish *For Whom the Bell Tolls*. Finally, in *Pentimento* Hellman had taken the life of a real anti-Nazi heroine, Muriel Buttinger, and confected the legend of a beautiful and doomed childhood friend she called "Julia"—presenting *herself* as a heroine who, at the behest of Julia, smuggled money into prewar Berlin in the lining of a fur hat, making it possible for Julia to buy the lives of German Jews. And that was only the beginning.

**ROSALIND MICHEHELLES** *[Paris secretary from 1977 to 1981]* People came out of the woodwork to corroborate Mary's experience by giving her examples of their own. Mary was just alight with excitement. She was hot on the trail of something. She loved every minute of it. I don't think she ever lost a moment's sleep over the fact that this could cost a lot of money. Jim, I think, felt differently. Mary was bursting for battle.

Given her early passion for detective novels, it was not surprising that Mary delighted in tracking down all these leads. If nothing else it made her feel she was accomplishing something. At the same time, it made her friends feel as if they, too, could pitch in and help. Catching Lillian Hellman in the act was a bit like an old-fashioned barn raising. Everyone— from Lizzie Hardwick to Sam Taylor to Stephen and Natasha Spender—was coming forward with some useful insight or information.

### FROM MARY MCCARTHY'S LETTER TO BEN O'SULLIVAN, AUGUST 17, 1980

Lizzie has had a very sharp, indeed brilliant, thought about "Julia." As she said, if the story was *true*, what made Hellman change the names? Nobody could have been hurt by giving "Julia"'s right name. It could only have redounded to the dead friend's credit to have the story told and her name honored. In fact it was H.'s *duty* to proclaim "Julia"'s heroism. Once thought of, this is unanswerable.

**SAMUEL TAYLOR** I was able to help her quite a bit because I knew things about Hellman she and her lawyer didn't know. For example, I pointed out to her that Lillian had used Julia once before, under a different name, in her play *Watch on the Rhine*.

The Spenders caused some consternation when they let her know that they remembered her scene with Hellman as taking place in *their* house at Sarah Lawrence rather than on Harold Taylor's sunporch. Eventually it would be determined that there had been two separate incidents. But while they briefly introduced an unsettling element of confusion on this one point, they were also of enormous help.

**STEPHEN SPENDER**   I had been a friend since I was in my early twenties with Muriel Gardiner Buttinger and I may have been the one to tell Mary that Muriel was the Julia in Hellman's story. At one time Muriel and Lillian had the same lawyer, Wolf Schwabacher, who lived on Muriel's estate. I think Schwabacher was the short circuit whereby Lillian Hellman got to know about the heroism of Muriel, and used it to invent the "Julia" business.

**NATASHA SPENDER**   Muriel had already told us that when *Pentimento* first came out, people would stop her on the street or ring her up and say, "You have to be Julia. There's nobody else who fits that description." Anyway, Muriel then wrote to Lillian Hellman, saying, "This is happening to me everywhere and can you please phone me." But Lillian never answered that letter. Later, the director of the Austrian Archives of the Resistance went into it very carefully, and there wasn't any other person who studied at the Freud Institute and was a rich American who went on to be a hero of the resistance. It clearly was Muriel and she saved countless lives.

**STEPHEN SPENDER**   It seemed such an amazing piece of meanness to write about this great heroine and then when the real-life heroine is named to deny that she has anything to do with it. Then at some point after this thing with Mary got started, Lillian rang Muriel and asked whether she could come visit her. Lillian said she'd be bringing a charming young man with her who happened to be her lawyer. And Muriel realized that Lillian was up to something—that she was trying to get some statement out of her—so Muriel said she'd be absolutely delighted to see her and she was also going to invite a charming young man who was *her* lawyer. Lillian never turned up for the appointment.

In the end, Muriel Gardiner Buttinger never met Lillian Hellman, but she did meet Mary McCarthy in Paris in November 1980. After that meeting, she tried her best to assist her, first contacting the director of the Austrian Archives of the Resistance and then adding an introduction to the wartime memoir she was writing, pointing out her undeniable resemblance to Hellman's "Julia."

Lawsuits, like politics, can make for strange bedfellows. Through the Spenders, McCarthy met Muriel Buttinger and through her old Saigon friend Jonathan Randal she started a correspondence with the journalist Martha Gellhorn, who had been Ernest Hemingway's third wife and who was writing a piece for *Paris Review* asserting that both Lillian Hellman and Stephen Spender were liars, or "apocryphers"—guilty of telling stories about Hemingway she knew to be untrue.

The following year, when the piece was about to come out, Gellhorn sent her galleys, along with a four-page letter offering what she called "tips on how you should do research," and pointing out logical inconsistencies or sheer absurdities in Hellman's memoirs. Many of them could be found in "Julia." For one thing, she noted, it was ludicrous to propose that one fur hat could be made to accommodate fifty thousand dollars worth of one-hundred-dollar bills. For another, there were no undertakers on the London street where Hellman said she picked up Julia's body. Finally, records showed that the ship used to transport the body to America did not sail from a British port.

Although she had little use for Gellhorn's writing ("For some reason Mary thought that Martha was a minor person beneath the salt," Jonathan Randal would later say), McCarthy found Gellhorn's letter sufficiently enlightening to pass it on to Ben O'Sullivan, just as she forwarded other tips she received. At least these offerings provided some diversion. Whether they were of any value was something else again.

**RENATA ADLER**  To have us all searching around for all the layers and instances of lying, which I must say was on an amazing scale, turned out to be almost absolutely futile. If you tried to prove that what Mary said was literally true—that is, that "every word" Lillian ever wrote was literally false—you were in the soup. Suppose just 70 percent was false, where were you? You could lose. The point was: you don't want a trial; you want it thrown out.

On both sides of the Atlantic, lines were drawn and sides were taken, frequently—but not always—owing as much to personal preference as to any overriding principle.

**JOHN GROSS**  I'd never liked Lillian Hellman. I'm going more on her public reputation, but such meetings as we had confirmed that impression. I'd rather have been wrong with Mary than right with Lillian Hellman.

**JAMES MERRILL**  I just didn't like Hellman's writing. So from that point of view I was entirely on Mary's side. Though it seemed to me a great deal of fuss about nothing. It was stupid of Lillian to claim truth, whereas anybody would know that you rearrange. Your memory does it for you, whether you think you're telling the truth or not.

**SUSAN SONTAG**  In the quarrel between Lillian and Mary I was 100 percent on Mary's side. That goes without saying. It's outrageous that Mary should have been sued for so blatantly hyperbolic a remark. I mean, the very fact that she put it that way—almost as if she'd been coached by a lawyer and told that you can't be sued for that if you say "even the 'ands' and 'thes.' " And then by God she was.

In March, the Mitgang article was followed by a much longer article by Michiko Kakutani, in which Hellman and McCarthy were described as "grandes dames of literature, alike in their wit, alike in their tough-mindedness," who differed in several important respects, not least among them being the fact that Hellman was "an elderly woman suffering from emphysema."

In this six-column article you could find virtually every self-respecting New York intellectual over fifty—save for Lionel Abel and Alfred

Kazin, who had no use for either woman, and Norman Mailer, who "elected to keep his own counsel"—eager to volunteer an opinion. There was Hellman's friend Richard Poirier dismissing McCarthy's "attack" as "dizzy rather than funny" and saying, "McCarthy brought some old toys from the New York intellectual attic and some of the old gang will want to play just like the 40's and 50's." There was Hellman's dear friend John Hersey saying, "One has to ask what the critics of Hellman are doing about social questions today," while pointing out that Hellman, as a founder of the Committee for Public Justice "remained alive to a challenging world." And there was McCarthy's old nemesis Malcolm Cowley, saying, "Lillian Hellman is not a bad writer and I thought Mary's attack on her was gratuitous."

To cap it off, Ephraim London, Hellman's lawyer, shifted the terms of the debate from anti-Stalinism to pure female jealousy, saying, "*Missionaries and Cannibals* [sic] is an absolute disaster. It must be a bitter pill to swallow to see someone who you think is a less good writer than you are to be so much more successful."

Arguing in McCarthy's behalf were Dwight Macdonald, who called *Scoundrel Time* "a disgraceful book," and Meyer Schapiro, who pointed out that Hellman "had great success, yes, but she hasn't made it with the people who prefer Mary's work." Also on her side were Irving Howe; Norman Podhoretz, who had tangled with her over *Eichmann in Jerusalem*; and Diana Trilling, who had been so critical of her Vietnam writing.

### FROM "HELLMAN-MCCARTHY LIBEL SUIT STIRS OLD ANTAGONISMS," BY MICHIKO KAKUTANI, *THE NEW YORK TIMES*, MARCH 19, 1980

"It's not just two old ladies engaged in a cat fight," said Irving Howe, the co-editor of *Dissent*. "The question involved—of one's attitude toward communism—is probably the central political-cultural-intellectual problem of the 20th century[. . . .] I might have at least granted Lillian Hellman the 'the's' and 'and's,' " he added. "But aside from that, I'm sure Mary's right."[. . .]

"People on the Left can't bear the fact that they're not victims," [Norman Podhoretz] said[. . . .] "It's a part of their image as heroic dissenters who are always subject to persecution. But given that Lillian herself has been a great protester for civil liberties, I think there is something outlandish in her libel action."[. . .]

"What is important is that people think of [Lillian Hellman] as a heroine of culture," said Mrs. Trilling. "It's as if she's the only person who faced down the House Un-American Activities Committee, when she actually took the Fifth like everyone else who didn't want to go to jail. There's a younger generation that of course doesn't know these things." Asked if she thought Miss Hellman's work dishonest, Mrs. Trilling replied demurely, "Let's say she's a gifted writer of fictions."

## FROM MARY MCCARTHY'S LETTER TO BEN O'SULLIVAN, MARCH 21, 1980

Thinking over the list of my champions (Podhoretz & Co.), I feel rather disturbed. What has happened, obviously, is that the whole business as seen by the press has been a lining-up of political sides. This is really *her* doing. In fact my remark on the Cavett Show wasn't political overtly or covertly. To me the woman is false through and through. It's not just the fresh varnish she puts on her seamy old Stalinism. In one of the "autobiographical" volumes she tells some story about "Dash" and a pond on her property full of turtles; I no more believe that than I do her account of her House un-American performance[. . . .] P.S. Can we make anything of the fact that she can't even get her *Who's Who* entry right?

While it was distressing to be defended by old enemies and to see her attack on Hellman misrepresented, it was laughable to find Norman Mailer not only stepping forth in the *Times Book Review* as a self-appointed arbitrator but proclaiming the whole business to be nothing more than a painful "quarrel between the nearest and best of one's relatives."

## FROM "AN APPEAL TO LILLIAN HELLMAN AND MARY MCCARTHY," BY NORMAN MAILER, *THE NEW YORK TIMES BOOK REVIEW*, MAY 11, 1980

Mary McCarthy has an absolute right to detest Lillian's work, but not to issue the one accusation against which no writer can defend himself or herself[. . . .] Of course, Lillian Hellman is dishonest. So is Mary McCarthy, Norman Mailer, Saul Bellow, John Updike, John Cheever, Cynthia Ozick [. . .] we are all dishonest, we exaggerate, we distort, we use our tricks to invent[. . . .] Given my respect for Mary McCarthy, I must say then that it was a stupid remark to utter on television and best left unsaid. To Lillian Hellman I would plead: Forswear your suit, drop it.

Although McCarthy was careful to make no public comment, others were not so tolerant. Richard Poirier took Mailer to task in the letters column of the *Book Review*, saying, among other things, "This is not an opportunity for Mr. Mailer to patch a family quarrel or to " 'make nice.' " Diana Trilling sent no letter to the *Book Review* but took Mailer to task in Peter Manso's *Mailer: His Life and Times*, where she said, "What a patronizing letter of Norman's that was! Its tone of condescension was really intolerable." A decade later Diana Trilling felt no different. Mailer, on the other hand, was prepared to look back at his efforts with something like amusement.

**DIANA TRILLING** When Norman jumped into that dispute, I thought he had no right to do that in the world. I thought that was a terrible lot of nerve.

**NORMAN MAILER** I thought Mary was wrong to say what she said—it was needlessly cruel perhaps. So what if Lillian was a liar? But Lillian had done something more grievous. I believe that in later years Mary decided on balance that my letter was all right. Lillian never forgave me. We were old friends. She half forgave me. We didn't speak for a year and then we did. My good motive for entering the dispute was that I thought it was terrible for writers to sue each other. My bad motive was I thought it would be wonderful if for once I was a peacemaker.

In the end, Mailer's peacemaking efforts came to nothing. In October the defendant was deposed in New York by Ephraim London.

**ESTHER BROOKS** I had recently given a deposition and I remember saying to Mary, who was going down to New York to be deposed, "I don't envy you, it's the worst possible thing you can go through." Mary said, "That's perfect nonsense, I'm looking forward to it." And I realized, Yes, I guess she is.

In her deposition Mary was characteristically direct and straightforward. When asked "What books and what plays written by Plaintiff or attributed to the Plaintiff have you read?," she tried to answer as precisely as possible, whether or not it served her well. She stated that of the plays she had seen *The Children's Hour* in 1934, *Candide* in 1956, and read *The Little Foxes* circa 1969. Of the memoirs she had read parts of *An Unfinished Woman*, including all of chapter 14, in 1970; she had read "Turtle," "Julia," and some other "bits" of *Pentimento* in 1973; all of *Scoundrel Time* in 1976; and all of *Maybe* in 1980. She had read "the remainder" of *An Unfinished Woman* and *Pentimento* in 1980.

She took care to deny that her statements about Hellman were "statements of fact" and to make clear that they were merely "expressions of my opinion." It was her opinion, she went on to say, that Hellman's three memoirs "distort events which are part of the history of plaintiff's time, distort and aggrandize her relationship to those events and are harshly unfair to many individuals, a few of whom are still living (or were at the time of publication), but most of whom are dead and unable to defend themselves."

She made no mention of Hellman's being a public figure—she left that to her lawyer. In any event, she hardly had the time or the space. Asked to "set forth the substance of each published or written and unpublished statement made or written by Plaintiff that you know to be untrue," she objected that this information would be "unduly burdensome to assemble" and then went on to describe in great detail and with evident relish the weaknesses and discrepancies and sheer absurdities to be found in Hellman's *Scoundrel Time* and "Julia."

This time she declared that she had met the plaintiff twice: once in 1937, at the home of Robert Jay Misch (the model for Pflaumen in her story "The Genial Host"), and once in 1948 at the home of Harold Taylor, in Bronxville, New York. She said that no words had been exchanged at the home of Robert Jay Misch, but that an account of the exchange at Harold Taylor's could be found in the *Paris Metro* interview.

When asked if she had made any published statements about Hellman prior to the airing of the Cavett interview, she scrupulously listed "Dry Ice," a review of Eugene O'Neill's *The Iceman Cometh*, where she spoke of "audiences accustomed to the oily virtuosity of George Kaufman, George Abbott, Lillian Hellman, Odets, Saroyan"; a negative review of the musical *Candide* in *The New Republic* where she did not mention Hellman by name; a negative review of the World War II film *North Star* in *Town and Country*, where again she did not mention Hellman, who wrote the screenplay, by name; and her interview with Kevin in *People*, in which he asked, "What do you have against Lillian Hellman?," and she answered, "Well, I've never liked what she writes," going on to give an account of the Sarah Lawrence incident.

Both she and Ben O'Sullivan were satisfied with her answers. Whether or not her performance at the deposition had anything to do with it, before the month was out Ephraim London had called up Ben O'Sullivan and suggested the two of them have lunch. If there was a turning point in the suit, that lunch probably marked it. After that, there was no going back.

**BEN O'SULLIVAN**   I went to lunch with London and in effect he said if my client consented to say something in the form of a retraction—to say that she did not mean to call Hellman a liar—his client would drop the case. Hellman was asking for a statement that would be circulated saying something of the order of "I didn't mean to suggest that Lillian Hellman was a liar." I don't think he took the case seriously. I don't think he expected it would ever be tried. I told Mary what London's offer was. I said would she consider trying to deflate this thing. And she got mad. She really didn't like Hellman. She really meant every word she had said. She wanted to stand on it. She would have been happy to face Hellman in court. She said, "Well, if I said that I didn't mean Lillian Hellman's a liar, I would not be telling the truth." She was obstinate and firm and, I guess, brave.

**JAMES WEST**   I'm not sure if it was specified whether it would be a public apology or a private one. But I think it went as far as public. Lillian wanted blood. They both did, you know. She wanted Mary to say, "I'm sorry I said that." And Mary said she wouldn't. It wasn't courageous or brave of Mary. It was in character.

**EILEEN FINLETTER**   Mary said to me that if she had been living in America and had seen Lillian Hellman, she would have been more careful. She said, "You can't believe that I would attack a blind, dying old lady." But Mary had been living abroad and she didn't think of her as an old, old lady. She had no image of her. She couldn't write a letter of apology. Mary was stub-

born, and once she had said it and it was on record, she could not take it
back. It became a matter of principle. She didn't believe in a retraction. And
if she'd said, "If only I'd known she was a blind old lady," she'd have gotten
in deeper.

In November 1980 Mary McCarthy's Northcliffe Lectures were published under the title *Ideas and the Novel* to favorable reviews. In the daily
*New York Times* John Leonard wrote, "Miss McCarthy has been over this
ground before in *On the Contrary* and *The Writing on the Wall*, but never
more deftly, with such charm, her quick mind bouncing off the wall of a
thesis at odd angles with a backspin." If nothing else, the publication of
*Ideas and the Novel* brought her name back to the attention of concerned
bystanders. That month, she received word from William Jovanovich,
who was also Diana Trilling's publisher, that Trilling was trying to put
together a committee for her defense.

**DIANA TRILLING**   John Gross, who is an old friend of both of ours, was
here in America and we were talking about the suit, and he said that we
ought to do something to help Mary. He said we could form a committee of
defense for Mary. He said, "I'll take care of the English end and you can take
care of the American end."

Little as she cared for Diana Trilling, she was considering accepting her
help until Jovanovich sent her a copy of a letter from Trilling, in which
she explained that the committee would not attempt to "raise money"
but would try to "mobilize sentiment on Mary's behalf and extrude Lillian from the community of the fair-minded."

**DIANA TRILLING**   Word was passed on, I don't think by me, I don't remember by whom. And word came back from Mary that she didn't want any help
from us. It was really from *such as us*. By this she meant politically such as us.

### FROM MARY MCCARTHY'S LETTER TO BEN O'SULLIVAN, NOVEMBER 29, 1980

This is the first I've heard of a defense committee, and I find the idea
appalling. Even if it comes from other sponsors rather than from that
Cold-War Bellona, I'd resist it[. . . .] I did mention a *defense fund* to [Bill
Jovanovich]. And I still think that [it] might be all right, since it speaks
for itself of the bottomless hole I'm in. But, as you see, she waves that
aside; what interests her isn't helping me pay some of the costs but
extruding Lillian from the community—I love that word[. . . .] By rights
I ought to be cross with Bill, too, and I am, but he has the excuse of
being moved by friendship, concern, affection—something human at
any rate.

Although there was to be no defense fund, her lawyer Ben O'Sullivan
had announced that he was charging her only half his customary fee.

Even so, her legal costs for 1980 came to $15,711.29. After first insisting that O'Sullivan be sure to send her a bill, she took care to pay it before the new year. In 1980 most of her time had been directed toward proving Lillian Hellman a liar. She had done almost no work on her memoir and earned very little money.

On the plus side, both she and Ben O'Sullivan were satisfied with her responses to the interrogatories. It looked as if all her detective work had paid off. If all went as expected, she would soon be free to return full-time to her writing. Once the plaintiff and her codefendants completed their respective depositions to the court's satisfaction, Ben O'Sullivan could file his motion for summary judgment. Unfortunately, owing to delays on both sides, that motion would not be filed for another $2^1/2$ years.

Not until May 14, 1983, would Lillian Hellman complete her "Affirmation in Opposition to Motion for Summary Judgment." In it she would swear that Mary McCarthy "has been attempting to discredit me for many years" and go on to say that the account of the exchange in Harold Taylor's sun parlor was "in every respect untrue." She would also swear that "[m]y opinion of Ms. McCarthy has not been expressed publicly, and I have not responded to any of her increasingly virulent attacks before the latest." Somehow it would escape her memory that her opinion of Ms. McCarthy had been expressed firmly and unequivocally in a 1965 *Paris Review* interview, where—after being told by the interviewer that Mary McCarthy had accused her of "being too facile, relying on contrivance"—she had said, "I don't like to defend myself against Miss McCarthy's opinions, or anybody else's. I think Miss McCarthy is often brilliant and sometimes even sound. But, in fiction, she is a lady writer, a lady magazine writer. Of course that doesn't mean that she isn't right about me. But if I thought she was, I'd quit."

As Hellman would tell it, her sole motive for bringing this lawsuit was to protect herself against future unprovoked attacks. "[I]f I did not take action I would suffer more vicious slanders," she would argue. But, above all, Hellman would contend she was not a public figure—at least in the context of the term's "special meanings in libel law"—since she was not "a person who 'assumes roles of special prominence in the affairs of society' or who occupies a position of 'persuasive power and influence.' "

The motion for summary judgment was filed on June 6, 1983. By then Martha Gellhorn's *Paris Review* piece had received a lot of attention, Muriel Buttinger's *Code Name Mary* had been widely reviewed and Renata Adler had published *Pitch Dark*, a novel in which both Hellman and her lawsuit made a brief appearance—the lawsuit as *Teagarden v. Denneny* and Hellman as Viola Teagarden, a woman who "spoke with a kind of awe of what she called 'my anger,' as though it were a living, prized possession, a thoroughbred bull, for instance, to be used at stud."

Once the motion for summary judgment was filed, a defendant could usually look forward to receiving a decision in anywhere from two weeks to six months. Certainly, for this case a decision was long overdue. As it turned out, Mary would have to wait another eleven months. All told, it would take four years to get a judge to rule on her petition. Although there would never again be a legal bill quite so substantial as that first bill from Ben O'Sullivan, the suit would exact a financial toll.

Making her legal costs doubly punishing was the fact that they were coming on the heels of Jim West's retirement. In 1981 she signed a contract for her intellectual memoirs, guaranteeing her an advance of $100,000, a quarter of which was payable on demand. But even with Harcourt's generous advance, there was simply less money in the family coffers. Still, she and Jim West continued to live pretty much the way they always had. Indeed she managed to carry off their straitened circumstances with style and even humor.

**GAVIN YOUNG**  I heard these stories about how much it was costing from Jim. But Mary wasn't distraught about it. She wasn't saying, "Sorry, we're having scrambled eggs and toast tonight." Maybe they cut back on some things, but I didn't notice it.

**JAMES MERRILL**  Indeed there were financial problems. My little foundation gave her an award one year because I understood that she had already spent nearly a hundred thousand dollars on lawyers. One of the last times I saw her—which would have been the fall before she took ill—Mary looked perfectly beautiful but she was inching along. She could hardly move. And she was wearing a kind of Lillian Hellman Blackglama mink coat and I think she said to me, "This is your generous foundation grant."

Not only did Mary suffer financially but she was plagued by a succession of physical ailments. Always subject to bronchial infections, she was soon struggling with illnesses of a very different order. Possibly they had nothing to do with the lawsuit—after all, she was sixty-eight years old. But in the spring of 1980, when she was served with the actual papers, she was stricken with a very painful case of shingles, exacerbated by a gallbladder attack. Although a latent chicken pox virus may be responsible for shingles, there seems to be a psychological component as well. If she was alarmed by Hellman's lawsuit, however, she tried not to show it. And if she was worried by those angry blisters girdling her torso, she refused to let them slow her down.

**ELEANOR PERÉNYI**  The summer she got shingles, I told her I wouldn't come to Castine unless she absolutely promised not to lay on anything special. The night I arrived, there was a dinner for twelve, and the next day there was a plan to drive to Bar Harbor and to visit the Rockefeller garden. Well, the beautiful white Mercedes broke down—not for the first time, I must say. Anyway, it meant we had to walk an enormous distance. Fortunately, Renata Adler was with us and she managed to flag down a passing station wagon. But in the meantime I could see that Mary was exhausted. She kept stopping to sit on rocks and lean against trees. I was appalled. I had never seen her in such a weakened condition.

The shingles bothered her all that summer, but by November the scars from the blisters were fading and by the following June she was telling Monique Wittig, "In fact the Hellman suit, to be fair, was a kind of antidote since it distracted my mind from the pain of the shingles—something literary composition could never have done." Sadly, her health troubles were far from over. It wasn't long before she was beset by a condition less painful but far more debilitating and so mysterious as to confound all her doctors.

Walking had always been a great source of pleasure—particularly in Paris, where she made it a point to search out the finest produce and freshest flowers. Walking had also served as her chief form of exercise. Having been known to stride resolutely across the Boulevard St. Germain, holding up one arm to stop traffic, she was now hesitating on quiet street corners, uncertain of her balance. Not only were her legs failing her but she was suffering from terrible headaches. To friends she tried to make light of what was happening, but by the fall of 1982 she was consulting neurologists in Boston and New York. From the doctors who examined her there was talk of Parkinson's disease, of ataxia, of water on the brain. But no doctor was prepared to come up with a definitive diagnosis or a program of treatment.

## FROM MARY McCARTHY'S LETTER TO CARMEN ANGLETON, AUGUST 27, 1982

I've finally had the results of all those tests at the Eastern Maine hospital at Bangor. For a time they thought there was an indication of hydrocephalus, i.e., water on the brain. If that had been established, it would have been operable[. . . .] Unfortunately, it turns out that I don't have water on the brain, and all the other tests came out negative except for the spinal tap, which indicated a slight excess of protein in the spinal fluid, but not enough, the neurologist decided, to be significant. So I am back where I was with the uncertainty of gait and the concomitant fatigue, coming, I think, from the will power exercised to make myself walk straight. The etiology is still traced to "youthful alcoholism" though the young doctor, ignorant of the drinking habits of our youth, is getting a little shaky in sustaining that theory. But the alternative, I gather, would be tertiary syphilis (locomotor ataxia), and I don't have that, the tests say. There is nothing much to be done but hope that further deterioration will not occur. He reduced my vitamin prescription by one half and upped the permissible alcohol intake to one glass of wine per day with dinner.

She might be down to two cigarettes and one glass of wine per day and she might be spending much needed cash on lawyers, but she was not about to let the lawsuit poison her life or to let her failing health keep her from enjoying it. If she did not have the energy she had hitherto taken for granted, she had a formidable and enduring curiosity. In the first months of the suit, when someone else might have been inclined to pull back, she went out of her way to draw three younger women into her life. The first was a novelist and critic from San Francisco who, upon arriving in Paris in the fall of 1979 with an introduction from Barbara Epstein at *The New York Review of Books*, had received an invitation to lunch.

**DIANE JOHNSON**    That day at lunch, Mary seemed to me rather didactic and elegant and grand. She was interested that I was writing a book about Dashiell Hammett. Later, when the lawsuit began, she was very forgiving about my whole association with Lillian. She even read the manuscript for *Hammett*. She was extremely nice about it and then she said, "After all, you are too young to remember just how it was to be a Trotskyite." She accurately saw that I didn't really understand the passions of those thirties Communists. Mary didn't lavish you with praise or anything, but she was the one who put me up for an award that I ultimately got from the American Academy of Arts and Letters. I think she liked the idea of my being a novelist *and* a critic. And she loved my husband, John. I think maybe if she'd had to choose between us, she'd have taken John.

The second was a writer and academic from New Orleans, who arrived at Castine with no introduction other than a recently completed biography of Henry Ford, a postcard announcing her arrival, and a very strong desire to write a biography of *her*.

**CAROL GELDERMAN**    She invited me for tea and I was there for several hours. Finally, I said I wanted to write a book about her and she said she thought it was a very poor idea to do a living person. The thing that gave her pause was I said, "I want to do it now because the people who are important in your life are dying." But I don't think that's what finally convinced her. I had gone to school with the Mesdames of the Sacred Heart and Kevin thinks it was the Sacred Heart connection. I think he may be right, though we didn't talk about the Sacred Heart at all.

The third was a much younger woman she had met briefly when she was trying to get a visa for Hanoi, who shared not only her Catholic girlhood but her Vassar education, and who would go on to become her good friend as well as her third biographer—although there was no talk of biography in the beginning.

**CAROL BRIGHTMAN**   I wrote Mary asking to do an interview with her in the fall of 1979. We ended up doing it the following September. When I was with her I found it easy to talk to her. I realize now she was kind of using me to jog her memory for the intellectual autobiography that she was writing. She was having a rough time then. She had shingles and she was just beginning to deal with the libel suit, which I think frightened her and bothered her because she couldn't speak about it publicly. I later thought that her vehemence on the subject of Simone de Beauvoir during the interview might have been some of the energy she was not allowed to express about her troubles with Lillian Hellman. We had that first long interview—maybe it was two afternoons—and then we had no contact for four or five years. I transcribed the interview—all forty-three pages of it—and sent it around, but nobody was interested.

Given what had happened with Lillian Hellman, she was astonishingly open and trusting. One might argue that she welcomed the attention and the distraction. Of course there are forms of distraction and attention decidedly less perilous. But she had every reason to want to prove that she was able to carry on as she always had—not merely to perform beautifully in her role as Mary West but to fill to perfection her role as Mary McCarthy.

Perhaps because she was now spending almost half the year in Castine, she seemed to find her more public role as Mary McCarthy particularly gratifying. In February 1982, when the shingles were behind her but the balance problems were beginning to seriously trouble her, she returned to Vassar, at the invitation of Virginia Smith, as the first "President's Distinguished Visitor." Once Vassar's enterprising president had persuaded her chosen candidate to return for a week with the faculty and students, she set about making arrangements for this visit with the help of Dixie Sheridan, her assistant, and Thomas Mallon, a young member of the Department of English, who as a senior at Brown had written his honors thesis on Mary McCarthy and then, with the innocence of the very young, sent it to her to read. Between the three of them, they managed to put together a schedule of activities.

**THOMAS MALLON**   I got asked to help because Virginia Smith knew I had corresponded with Mary McCarthy on and off over the years. In the first letter Mary wrote me after reading my thesis, she ended by saying that she wished me luck in the future and asked what I wanted to become—a poet, a critic, a novelist? I now see her addressing a very young person. The tip-off in that sentence is "poet." There was no reason she could possibly think I could become one. But that sentence meant to me that Mary McCarthy thought that I *could* possibly become a writer. It gave me a license to try. We kept in touch, and in 1979, when *Cannibals and Missionaries* came out, I wrote

her, "You'll laugh when you hear where I ended up as a college professor." I
finally had my first encounter when she arrived for the first reception. I came
up to her and said, "Oh, Miss McCarthy, I'm Tom Mallon." And she said, "I
*guessed.*" I added up and she had won a point. Not an argumentative point
but a point in a board game.

**VIRGINIA SMITH**   She entered into the program fully. I remember in the
Villard Room she participated in a panel with several faculty members on a
variety of topics—primarily on politics and international relations but ranging quite broadly. Mary was at her best with questions and answers. The
give-and-take of discussions engaged and excited her. Nor did she avoid controversy. Before a press conference during the program, we warned her that
there would be questions from the press about the Hellman matter and we
told her that if she didn't want to talk about it, she should just say that she
didn't care to comment. But she talked about it anyway; talking about it
seemed a kind of necessity for her.

**DIXIE SHERIDAN**   Students don't find many people who are that opinionated, that smart, and that outspoken. I don't think I ever saw her being
abrupt or dismissive. She never held back.

**VIRGINIA SMITH**   Mary tended to be straightforward and I am, too. We
both came from Seattle, and we were both westerners. Westerners tend to be
more direct. I don't think Mary cared much for institutions. But when she
came back as the President's Distinguished Visitor, Mary found people she
liked and she felt comfortable with them. These people came to represent
Vassar for her.


In the course of that week she saw enough of Virginia Smith to know
she liked her and enough of Thomas Mallon to know she wanted to see
more of him. The morning after a big dinner given in her honor at the
president's house, just as a photographer started to snap her picture, she
reached for Mallon and her son, Reuel, seeing to it that in the photograph
she would be flanked by both of these younger men.

That summer, when Thomas Mallon was in Maine, he and a friend
spent two days with the Wests in the apartment over the garage. The visit
was a success and in December, when Mallon was on sabbatical in England, he visited them in Paris. There he was more aware of her balance
problems and of her struggle to negotiate the smallest distances. And
there he got to see how the suit had made her more cautious. He also
noticed how so long as it didn't affect the suit, she was prepared to be
anything but circumspect.

**THOMAS MALLON**   Edmund Wilson's *The Forties* was due out, full of what
Mary said were libels against her. They weren't even part of the diaries but
just some document Wilson cooked up after the breakup, she said. She and
Wilson had remained friendly for years, she said, and all the while there had
been this loaded gun waiting to go off. She didn't want to sue because that

would undermine her position in the Hellman case. It would look as if she were against free expression. By a lucky accident her lawyers had obtained a memo by one of the Farrar Straus lawyers saying that the passages were indeed libelous and shouldn't be printed. So it looked as if everything might be all right after all. When I told her I was using Edmund Wilson's diaries in my "Confessions" chapter of my book on diaries, she said, "That's where they belong." Later that month Mary was scheduled to debate George Steiner on the new Channel Four in London. Steiner's thesis was that the best writers of our day are the oppressed ones and that it was impossible for a Western writer living in freedom to match someone like Solzhenitsyn. She was appalled by this line of thinking. She and Jim and I tried to come up with things she could use to refute his theory. Did Nazi Germany, for instance, produce any flowering of oppressed writers?

When the debate took place in London on December 21, 1982, Thomas Mallon and Jim West were not there to cheer Mary on, but there were others more than happy to do so, including the moderator of the panel, Al Alvarez. Having been put off by what he believed to be the self-righteous tone of her writing against the Vietnam War, Alvarez had come to believe there was nothing worse than a reformed sinner. But that night his reformed sinner was sounding like her old self again.

**AL ALVAREZ**  The program was on very late at night, when most of the world was asleep. I was supposed to be the chairman, but as often as not I got caught up in the arguments. One of the best shows we did was on political repression and the arts, with Mary and Joseph Brodsky taking on George Steiner. Steiner was pronouncing, in his usual high-flown way, about the artistic advantages of persecution. He was saying that all the best writing was coming out of Eastern Europe because the Eastern Europeans were made to suffer for their art; they were censored, harassed by the police, sent into internal exile, etc. All this was stuff Brodsky, of course, knew about firsthand and he was outraged by the way Steiner seemed to be laying claim to it. There was a moment when Steiner started sounding off about what he called "all this noise"—about how the cultural scene in the West is full of this noise, which distracts serious minds from true thinking. Mary looked at him icily and said, "George, haven't you considered that the kind of thing you're doing and saying is just adding to the noise?"

Unfortunately, there were also times when, for one reason or another, she did not have it in her to rise to an occasion. One such occasion was a formal dinner at Vassar in June 1983, to celebrate her class's fiftieth reunion. Although twenty years had passed since the publication of *The Group*, not everyone in her class was prepared to forgive her. Indeed, when Frani Blough Muser first proposed she be invited to give a speech at the big dinner, more than one member of the planning committee had strenuously objected. After some discussion, a compromise was reached

whereby there would be *two* speeches, from the two writers in the class—
Mary McCarthy and Lucille Fletcher Wallop, author of *Sorry, Wrong Number*. Like most compromises it pleased no one.

**HELEN DAWES WATERMULDER**     Mary came to our fiftieth reunion—really
against most people's wishes—but she was invited and her subject was supposed to be in praise of professors of our year. Unfortunately, she strayed
from the subject and gave us more about herself. It was not a good speech.
There was all this malice toward Miss Lockwood and no real justice done to
Miss Kitchel. Some of the speech turned up later in *How I Grew*. When Mary
finished, there was no applause.

**MARY GAZLEY**     In the end Lucille's speech was so much better. We were
all practically in tears. In fact they put some of it in the *Quarterly*. Mary's
speech dropped the ball. In the first place she didn't get there until late. Her
Mercedes supposedly broke down. And her speech was very disorganized.
We decided she'd written it on the way.

**LUCILLE FLETCHER WALLOP**     In all fairness, Mary wasn't well and she had
a terrible time getting there. She looked as if she'd gone through hell. She
wasn't groomed up for the occasion. She had on an old sweater and a short
silk dress and everybody was in evening clothes. She just had a few pieces
of paper in her hand and she looked distraught. Their car had broken down
and they were very late. And she hadn't had any dinner.

It was one thing to face an admiring audience of faculty members and
undergraduates who regarded her as a distinguished lady of letters. And
quite another to face not just a class that had been prepared to publicly
disown her, but also some of the original models for *The Group*.

**KAY MCLEAN**     I went up to Mary after she gave her speech and she really
didn't recognize me. It was an awful shock. Mary had changed very little—
at least I had seen her on TV and I was prepared for changes. But she was-
n't expecting me to be there. I said hello and she said for a minute she didn't
realize who it was. Her husband offered to get me a drink. She'd gone back
into the main living room, where she was sort of sitting in a chair where people would go up to her as they went in. She made no effort to get up out of
her chair. I didn't know until later that she was not only very tired from her
trip there, but was seriously ill.

Frani Blough Muser was not the only friend who had been working
hard to see that Mary McCarthy received her due. Other efforts met with
a less qualified success. In the spring of 1984 it was announced that
McCarthy would receive both the MacDowell Medal and the National
Medal for Literature, which came with a cash prize of $15,000. If these hon-
ors owed something to the efforts of friends, what matter? She *had* done
good work over the years. And wasn't that the way awards were bestowed

anyway? (Inspired by the announcement of the National Medal for Literature, Carol Brightman took out her long interview from the fall of 1980, cut it, and sold it to *The Nation*.)

On May 3, 1984, Mary McCarthy was given the National Medal for Literature at a ceremony at the New York Public Library. Invitations were mailed to old friends like Frani Muser, Dwight Macdonald, the DuViviers, Arthur Schlesinger, Stephen Spender, Margo Viscusi, and Deborah Pease, and new friends like Virginia Smith and Thomas Mallon. Since she would be arriving straight from Paris, she made it a point to ask NYPL president Vartan Gregorian to have a car pick her up at the airport. Because she made no mention of how much trouble she was having walking, he assumed she was merely throwing her weight around.

The National Medal for Literature was not the Nobel Prize or even the National Book Award, but it was very nice to have—particularly when she was still waiting to receive some decision on her motion for summary judgment. Four years into the lawsuit, she seemed to be making no progress. When Ephraim London had initiated it, Ronald Reagan had been about to run for president against Jimmy Carter. Now Reagan was preparing to defend his presidency against Carter's vice president, Walter Mondale, a politician from Minnesota she was happy to claim as her own. She had grown to detest the sight of Reagan and she found the prospect of Mondale's candidacy positively heartening. So much so that she did not hesitate to make mention of it when receiving her bronze medal from Brooke Astor before an audience of literary luminaries and invited guests.

**THOMAS MALLON**   I remember Brooke Astor commending Mary for her explorations of the moral consequences of our "*au*-ctions." And I remember Mary saying "Thank you, Mrs. Astor" in her most patrician voice. She was very pleased by the fact that she was finally getting an award after what she thought was neglect and even hostility. I don't know that she said this directly, but it was clearly meant to be inferred by the audience. There was a sense that the award was a sort of upset and that we all might be in for another upset. She said she was more optimistic about the presidential election than most people. That she thought Walter Mondale might in fact "knock Ronnie off his Exercycle."

Although her hair was tightly curled and she was wearing a striped silk dress with a little bow at the neck, she was not likely to be mistaken for a garden club matron. But while she was delighted to give vent to her feelings about Reagan, she took care not to share a sense of foreboding she had about her lawsuit. Precisely one week later, just as she and Jim West were settling in for their six months in Castine, she learned from Ben O'Sullivan that her "premonition" had been all too accurate.

On May 10, 1984, Lillian Hellman won the first round of the lawsuit. She won in large part thanks to Judge Harold Baer of the New York State Supreme Court, who took the plaintiff at her word and ruled that the plaintiff was *not* a public figure. At the same time, Judge Baer ruled that the defendant had not proven to his satisfaction that she had merely been expressing an opinion that was unmistakably hyperbolic. To his ears it sounded too much like a statement of fact. Adding insult to injury, he penalized the defendant for her honesty on the interrogatories, saying that they showed that she had only "limited exposure" to Hellman's works. He also dropped Dick Cavett from the suit, ruling that he had not been responsible for the editing of the broadcast. It looked to be an unqualified victory for Hellman. But in the Hellman camp the time for celebration was long past.

**MAX PALEVSKY**   Lilly was pleased she won the first round, but she was not dumb and I think Lilly understood very well that she was doing something she shouldn't do—in the sense that this was a quarrel between two literary people and to take it to court was an exaggerated response. I never discussed the suit with her seriously because she became quite provoked by it. The whole thing became painful for her. She had mixed feelings and that's why I think she ended up expending so much emotion on it. She would get into a fury. And everyone would say, "Oh, Lilly, come on." She was a very sick old woman.

While it looked to be a defeat for McCarthy, not everyone was so quick to concede that the game was over. The night the decision was handed down, Bob Silvers of *The New York Review of Books* telephoned. The following day she wrote Ben O'Sullivan not to bemoan what had happened to her but to let him know that she had an "idea for future strategy"—the idea being to contest the judge's ruling that Hellman was *not* a public figure, by providing ample evidence that she *was*. If she was sounding remarkably upbeat it may have had something to do with a plan Bob Silvers had proposed.

**FROM MARY MCCARTHY'S LETTER TO BEN O'SULLIVAN, MAY 11, 1984**
As he told me last night, he would like to organize a fund to take care of my legal costs in appealing. As he described it, I would have nothing to do with the money-raising and would only be the beneficiary, and it sounded as if he thought the *magazine* could launch the fund and handle it. I said I didn't know, that I had a reluctance to posing as a Scottsboro Boy, but that I would talk to you about it.

Unfortunately, by the time she received a call from Deborah Pease a couple of days later, she was not sounding so cheerful.

**DEBORAH PEASE**   Maine in early May can be cold and grim. I thought of Mary up there with this awful news, and I called and got Jim on the phone. When I asked how she was, he said "Poorly." I was surprised to hear that she was in bed. Jim said, "We've got to start all over again." I said, "Isn't it going to be awfully costly?" He said, "Well, Bob Silvers said something about maybe starting a defense fund, but I don't know." I said, "I'll give him a prod."

What Deborah Pease did first was to call Elizabeth Hardwick. Deborah Pease had inherited some money a couple of years earlier and wanted very much to help start the defense fund. It seemed to her that if Bob Silvers could announce that he had a certain sum in hand, then soon more money would come in—the way it does with a matching grant. Before going any further with this idea, Hardwick suggested that they check it out with Mary.

Deborah Pease was not a close friend. Years had passed since she had spent time with Mary in Paris. But, then, many of Mary's closest friends had failed to see how low she was. Deborah Pease's offer of $25,000 was accepted, with a grateful phone call, the very next day.

Once this seed money was in place, a dinner was arranged by Bob Silvers and Renata Adler to introduce Mary to Floyd Abrams, a First Amendment lawyer best known for *"The New York Times" v. Sullivan,* where he had successfully defended the right of newspapers to criticize public figures.

**FLOYD ABRAMS**   I had followed the suit all along in the papers. And I remember trying to make a realistic and restrained depiction to her of the case and what her chances were and what the trial would be like and when the trial would occur, if it did. She said with a half smile, "You really want to do this, don't you?" I didn't think she *knew.* I'd been a fan of hers for a long time. The thing that was disturbing about the suit was that it was so disturbing to Mary. She was very concerned about the cost and about the time it took and the preoccupation of it. She did not treat it as a light matter. It was not two old literary heavyweights just having a final go against each other for the crowd. It seemed to me a suit which was truly brought for the purpose of "chilling" speech. Of hurting her and punishing her and preventing her from saying critical things in the future. Meeting her, I was struck by her. Here at a time when she was so obviously concerned and was having such severe balance problems, she could still smile.

As Floyd Abrams saw it, his first task was to make sure that the case did *not* come to trial.

**FLOYD ABRAMS**   Our strictly legal argument was that you simply cannot, under the First Amendment, treat hyperbolic language as if it is intended to be taken literally. You can't seriously understand that line to mean that every time Hellman used the words "the" and "and" she was lying. No one could mean that. And I think that Judge Baer incorrectly concluded that she *did* mean that. Conceptually, that was what was wrong with the opinion. And that's why I think we would likely have won on appeal. Hellman's being a public figure was secondary. But it seemed to me particularly offensive that this lawsuit should have been allowed to continue when it was brought by a public figure against a public figure about language which could not rationally be read to be a purported statement of literal truth.

As it turned out, there was no appeal and no trial. On June 30, 1984, before any appeal could be mounted, Lillian Hellman died of cardiac arrest at her home in Martha's Vineyard. Her front-page obituary in the *Times* took note of her feud with Diana Trilling and her suit against Mary McCarthy and of her famous "anger," but, for the most part, it left the legend intact and took her at her own value. Among McCarthy's friends there was great elation, although there was some fear that Hellman's estate might pursue the lawsuit. Any fears they had in that quarter were soon allayed. "You sure play hardball," an old friend told Floyd Abrams, but for Abrams there was a sense of disappointment. For the defendant there was disappointment as well as relief.

**FLOYD ABRAMS**   I had spent a good deal of time thinking about how to cross-examine an aged legend. I was reading articles on truth telling. Articles about "Julia." Articles about a wide range of statements made by Mary. It would have been a great trial. It would have been a great cultural and political event, because it would have revisited all those open wounds left from the late thirties and early forties. All those people played politics for keeps.

**JAMES WEST**   After the suit's going on all that time, there's a bit of a letdown when the suit gets dropped. Particularly when you know you've got a man who is a master of the First Amendment and you see a light coming up. Mary wanted to see the sun all the way. There was a part of Mary that would have liked to have gone on. She believed she would have won the case eventually.

With any official decision still in abeyance, there was no way she could publicly express either disappointment or elation. But she had more than enough to occupy her. Although her doctors had not been able to come up with a definitive diagnosis, she had decided to trust to Dr. Plum, her neurosurgeon at New York Hospital, who believed that walking might be much improved by an operation to relieve the pressure of water on her brain.

### FROM MARY MCCARTHY'S LETTER TO CARMEN ANGLETON, JULY 7, 1984

I guess I didn't tell you that I'm going to New York Hospital to have the operation called the *shunt* on Monday the sixteenth. This is on the assumption that what's been troubling me is partly "water on the brain." They drill a hole in your head and insert a tiny tube to drain off the fluid. If the operation is successful and if that is what's the matter with you, the former use of your legs is immediately restored. The doctor told us (Jim and me) that there's a fifty-fifty chance of this and that, if it doesn't work, I'll be no worse off than I am now. So we've decided to do it, and I'm trying not to hope too much.

If she was frightened at the prospect of brain surgery she did not let on. She spoke, instead, of missing her garden during the week she would be in the hospital. Knowing that she would be temporarily disfigured, she didn't hesitate an instant. Knowing that there was no guarantee that the ninety-minute operation would make her better, she was nonetheless eager to proceed.

**SUSAN ANDERSON**   She wasn't upset about having her head shaved for surgery. She was not a narcissistic person at all. She never complained about any kind of inconvenience. She just accepted suffering as part of life.

In a matter of weeks she was able to return to her house in Maine. By mid-August she was well enough to make plans for the trip to New Hampshire to receive the MacDowell Medal. To Carmen Angleton she wrote of her new medal for "literary good behavior" and of how her "incapacitating headaches" were now "greatly diminished." But first and foremost she wrote of the latest turn in her terrible legal battle.

### FROM MARY MCCARTHY'S LETTER TO CARMEN ANGLETON, AUGUST 15, 1984

This is to tell you that the Hellman case is over. Mr. Abrams, my appeals lawyer, called Friday to tell me that this had been confirmed to him by Hellman's lawyer. He is going to send me a check for the part of the retainer I paid him (with Deborah's money), and I shall use it and a bit more, I guess, of Deborah's bounty to pay Ben O'Sullivan for the 1983 bill that he'd not yet had the heart to send me.

For Floyd Abrams the time had come to return all but $1500 of his $10,000 retainer, and for Mary McCarthy the time had come to give up any lingering hope that she might one day get her own back in court. If there was any consolation, it was that at last she was free to speak out in public. Indeed, she was free to say pretty much anything she pleased.

Tucked away in Castine, she had little opportunity to avail herself of this new freedom. But that soon changed when she stepped forth to accept her medal at the MacDowell Colony on August 26. Knowing a perfect opportunity when she saw one, she ended her acceptance speech by making one last pitch for Mondale. But before settling that bit of business to a gratifying round of applause, she let Samuel G. Freedman of *The New York Times* know how she felt about her recent legal travails. "I'm absolutely unregenerate," she told him. "I suppose that if I had thought about it, I might have. . . . No. If someone had told me, 'Don't say anything about Lillian Hellman because she'll sue you,' it wouldn't have stopped me. It might have spurred me on." She then went on to say, "I didn't want her to die. I wanted her to lose in court. I wanted her around for that."

That November, Walter Mondale did not go on to knock Ronald Reagan off his exercise bicycle. But in time Mary McCarthy got to see Lillian Hellman's reputation grow so tarnished that even Hellman's own biographers would concede that her memoirs owed as much to artistry as they did to truth. Indeed, in 1997, an older and wiser Max Palevsky would tell an interviewer, " 'Julia' was a total fabrication. Lilly made it up out of whole cloth."

She did not live long enough to hear these words from Palevsky or to see Harold Baer step down from New York State Supreme Court because, as he argued in a *Times* Op-Ed piece, inadequate facilities and huge caseloads made it "impossible" for "a judge who strives to be conscientious to provide the public with the quality of justice that is their right." Nor did she live to see Harold Baer face impeachment three years later, when as a newly appointed judge in the United States Federal Court he threw out the evidence in a Washington Heights drug bust, ruling that the police had no right to stop and search three black men because they cut and ran. For her, Baer was simply bad luck.

But if character is destiny, then Mary McCarthy was destined to clash with Lillian Hellman and remain locked in that struggle until the case was finally decided one way or the other. Even though it cost her dearly, she simply could not retract those words once she had uttered them. In the end, while she didn't have the satisfaction of winning in court, she did survive long enough to have the *last* word. And that last word she brought forth time and again at the slightest provocation. She wanted Hellman alive so she could beat her. And she didn't care who knew it. "There is no satisfaction in having an enemy die," she liked to say.

From the vehemence of her words one would think she had passed the years of the lawsuit in unrelieved agitation and torment, but that of course was far from the truth. Through it all she had managed to see and entertain old friends and go out of her way to embrace new ones. She had managed to serve beautifully prepared meals and tend her garden, to teach and deliver speeches, to collect awards and honors, and even to acquire a new biographer.

Despite everything, she had somehow even managed to complete more than half of her new memoir and to write more than a half dozen long book reviews and essays—the most memorable being a glowing review of *Green Thoughts: A Writer in the Garden*, by Eleanor Perényi; an acute introduction to a new edition of *The King of the Cats*, by F. W. Dupee; a talk delivered at Vassar on the three types of prose narratives, "Novel, Tale, Romance"; a somewhat tentative review of Joan Didion's *Democracy*; and a long, unsparing essay on "The Very Unforgettable Miss Brayton," her old Newport neighbor.

She had somehow managed not only to produce a more than respectable body of work but to retain her capacity to be diverted and delighted by what happened to come her way. In the process, however, she had drawn on reserves of energy that were rapidly dwindling. She might believe that it was no fun to have an enemy die and she might see in her enemy's dying intimations of her own mortality. But with Hellman dead, she would have more time to devote to the things she cared about. She would be free, if all went well, to give her undivided attention to the seductive but altogether serious business of enjoying her life.

# Chapter Twenty-six

# A FULL LIFE

"It is not true, by the way, that as you get old recent events slip away but early memories flood in. Almost the opposite in my case," Mary McCarthy had written to Frani Blough Muser in the summer of 1979, when she was about to embark on her intellectual memoirs and soon to run afoul of Lillian Hellman. Why she remembered "recent things better" she could not say. All she knew was that her grasp on the past was "getting shaky suddenly." When she tried to recapture details from what she chose to call her intellectual awakening, they had all but evaporated. So far all she had been able to recall were scenes she had described in *Memories of a Catholic Girlhood*.

As she saw it, the reason for this failure was simple enough: "[O]nce you have written about something, all you can recall is what you wrote." No doubt she was right. Still, it could be argued that the memory she so prided herself on was being affected by whatever was starting to make it difficult to keep her balance. In addition, it could be argued that her life was now so crammed with event there was little room for those early memories to flood in.

Certainly she had her hands full. Not only was she beginning to work on her new memoir but she was also planning four lectures on the novel and conducting a vigorous, not to say arduous, social life. Her work on the memoir was further impeded that winter when Lillian Hellman sued her. Caught up in her efforts to prove Hellman a liar and racked by severe health problems, she ended up putting the manuscript aside for a year. But even after she managed to complete a couple of chapters to her satisfaction and sign a contract with William Jovanovich, names and faces continued to elude her.

In truth, it was not her habit to dwell upon the past. The original stories for *Memories of a Catholic Girlhood* had been written over the course of many years. Writing them, she had felt free to invent whenever memory failed her. Later, trying to separate fact from fiction, she'd had her brother Kevin to help her. At times she had made it a family project, drawing on her brother Preston and even her uncles Louis and Harry, who had taken it on themselves to correct any part they believed to be unfair to the McCarthy family.

For much of her life she had lived in the moment—not only blessedly free of anxiety about the future but rarely troubled by second thoughts. Unfortunately, writing an autobiography forces you to tote up your mistakes and setbacks as well as your accomplishments and triumphs. It forces you to take stock. "I remember laughing one day at hearing B.B. up in Vallombrosa announcing that he was a failure and being joined by [Kenneth] Clark and Johnnie Walker of the National Gallery," she wrote William Jovanovich in the summer of 1979. "[W]hat would a *real* failure have thought listening to them? And yet now I see they weren't necessarily insincere."

By the time Mary McCarthy spoke at MacDowell, she'd had a good four years to look at the hopes and ambitions she'd set out with and had been forced to conclude that she'd accomplished far less than she'd hoped to. Particularly when it came to the Vietnam War. Finally, though, any sense of failure was offset by a refusal to accept defeat. She had not lost her taste for doomed causes or her appetite for battle. Just as she had once attacked novelty and fashion in the realm of ideas, she now cried out against credit cards, word processors, and Cuisinarts.

At MacDowell, she used her bully pulpit to take a stand against what she saw as a dismaying falling off and others saw as progress. She had reached an age, however, where she was likely to be more admired for what she represented than for any burning desire to set things right. She was one of the youngest members of her generation, and therefore one of a handful of survivors; as such, she had acquired a special value. At the same time she was receiving awards for what she chose to call "good behavior," she was receiving requests from eager young historians and biographers, all of them hungry for any anecdote or insight she cared to serve up.

She was being encouraged to dwell upon the past and being paid handsomely to do so. At this point in her life, money was a very real consideration. Left to her own devices, she might have started working full-time on the book she had long been planning on Gothic art and architecture. But it was a memoir that William Jovanovich wanted from her. And it was a memoir he was willing to pay her $100,000 for.

As it happened, it wasn't only this new intellectual memoir that had acquired considerable value. Already as an adolescent she'd had sufficient sense of her own importance to hold onto the poems and stories she wrote for Miss Dorothy Atkinson. Only once—when she failed to keep up payments for a trunk she had stored after the breakup of her first marriage—had she let a significant bundle of letters slip from her grasp. In recent years, with the help of various secretaries, she had put together an elaborate filing system. If she had not been in need of money, these letters and manuscripts might have remained in her possession forever. But shortly after her stint as the first President's Distinguished Visitor, Virginia Smith made her a proposition she could not resist.

By July 1983, the last shipment of boxes brimming with everything from manuscripts and letters to photographs and department store receipts had been packed up and shipped to Vassar, to be examined and cataloged before the college made a final offer. Had she sold her papers to the University of Texas, she might have gotten more for them. And had she played Vassar off against another institution she might have been in a better bargaining position. But she had never been one to haggle long over money when personal relations were at stake.

The fact was, during her week's stay at Vassar she had been welcomed by a faculty and student body that gave every evidence of enjoying her company as much as she enjoyed theirs. While it was flattering to hear that her papers would be joining Elizabeth Bishop's in the library's Special Collections, it was especially gratifying to know that they would reside at a place that had taken on a face she not only recognized but liked.

Whether it was owing to the Hellman suit or simply to her time of life, she had reached a point where she welcomed such reconciliations. By the time she received her medal at MacDowell, she had made her peace with Vassar and she had made her peace with Reuel, who back in 1978 had cut short a Castine visit, claiming that she had scheduled so many dinners and activities that he had no time alone with her.

In 1978 Reuel's first marriage had been breaking up and he had been in need of sympathy and advice. When he returned in the summer of 1983 he was happily remarried to Natsuko Murase, a Japanese pianist, and had a new baby daughter, Sophie. This time, he took care to maintain a certain distance. Instead of staying in the apartment over the garage, he took a room at a local inn. When he came back the following summer, bringing his new wife and young daughter, he stayed at the inn again. Both times his mother was pleased to report to Carmen Angleton on their new improved relations. Reuel "is in marvelous form, almost like what he was as a boy at Harvard," she wrote in July 1984, just as he was about to leave for his home in Canada and she was about to go into the hospital in New York.

Although her health problems were increasingly debilitating, she had tried to ignore them. Nonetheless, by the summer of Reuel's second visit, she could barely walk. When she chose to go ahead and risk an operation to relieve the pressure of water on the brain, she had every hope that her life would soon be back to normal. Already by mid-September she was once again writing her autobiography and in mid-October she was strong enough to make a trip to New York, to give a talk at Lincoln Center. But by the end of that visit, it was evident that the shunt was not working the way Dr. Plum had hoped that it would. Indeed, it was not working well at all.

### FROM MARY MCCARTHY'S LETTER TO CAROL GELDERMAN, JANUARY 27, 1985

Let me bring you up to date in the meantime on what's been happening. I had not only a second operation—revision of shunt—but a third. The second was October 23, and the third was November 30 or 31 [sic]. What had happened was the brain's surface—the "subdurals" got flooded because the shunt, probably, was running too fast; hematoma formed. They had to drill holes in the skull to drain the subdurals—what the shunt had been draining was the *inside*, the ventricles—change the valve, shut it off temporarily. When it became apparent, after a month, that that was only half-effective, they devised a new kind of shunt, in the form of a Y, to drain both the inside and the outside. At the time of our departure—we got back [to Paris] December 16—this was not yet working perfectly either, but it was better—the hematoma still left on one side had shrunk—and the neurologist, Dr. Plum, thought that humanity dictated that we leave.

**JAMES WEST** For the third operation she was just in overnight. But for someone who liked ideas and had the highest respect for what goes on in the brain, there was reason to be afraid of what might happen, and I suppose she was, but she didn't cry on about it, ever.

**SUSAN ANDERSON** Later on, I asked her how she was able to cope with all that and she said, "I throw myself into my work." Many people bring books to the hospital, but very few can read after surgery. She was always reading. After the second operation, when she was back in the room, she asked, "Susan, where's my manuscript?" I said, "What are you talking about?" She said that on the way to the operating room somebody had given her a set of galleys. So I went and talked to the operating room nurses. They looked at me as if now they'd finally heard everything. The manuscript must have gone down the laundry chute.

Despite the difficulty of laying her hands on some of her *own* manuscripts and articles, she managed to put together a third collection of essays.

### FROM MARY MCCARTHY'S LETTER TO CAROL GELDERMAN, JANUARY 27, 1985

In the midst of this trying business, Pat (my [Castine] secretary) and I managed somehow to put together a book—a collection of utterances from 1968 on. It's called *Occasional Prose*. A somewhat heroic performance, above all, on her part, since we didn't have any of the original pieces on hand, all of my papers being in the Vassar library and labeled in some instances unrecognizably[. . . .] But it was done, and Jim delivered the ms.—only one copy could be made—to the HBJ office on the day before Thanksgiving. Jovanovich had risen very handsomely to the felt need, and will have the book out by the end of April—incredible speed.

Back in Paris for Christmas she ended up at the American Hospital, with a "severe feverish bronchitis" and what her doctor took to be "an acute gall-bladder attack." There was no pre-Christmas party, no tree, and no decorations, but for once that suited her fine. "I felt too tired," she wrote Carol Gelderman. The fact was, she was still suffering from "mysterious pains and weakness." Her blood pressure was "acting up," she was almost certain that the shunt was still not working correctly, and she very much missed Dr. Plum, her surgeon at New York Hospital. "[I]t spoils one, I must say, to fall upon a good doctor; most of them haven't changed since Moliere's time, not a hair," she confided.

Fortunately, by April not only was the shunt still working but her hair had grown back and the tight page boy—which made some friends think of George Washington and others of Samuel Johnson—had given way to soft white curls. *Occasional Prose*, whose publication date had been put off until May, was due any moment in the stores. Best of all, she was walking again.

**JAMES WEST**   In Paris I had begun to pace myself with Mary when we went for a walk. I slowed my pace way down without thinking about it and of course she finally noticed what I was doing. Then all of a sudden I began to practically run to catch up with her. She sped right ahead.

Not only had Mary picked up her pace but she was making arrangements for a trip to Los Angeles, where she planned to stay the weekend with her brother Kevin and his family, before going on to San Francisco, to give a talk to help publicize *Occasional Prose*. Afterward, she hoped to do a bit of research for her autobiography: to compare notes with an old school friend now living in Mendocino; to drive up the coast with her uncle Frank Preston, now in his nineties; and to once again visit the Annie Wright Seminary, now simply called the Annie Wright School. The plan was for Jim West to join her at some point between San Francisco and Seattle. But her first stop, at Kevin's new house in Sherman Oaks, she was to make on her own.

**KATE McCARTHY**   It was her first visit and there was such trepidation. We practically repainted the entire house. We called in so many cleaners. We even went out and rented furniture.

While relations with Kevin's new young wife were better, they had never fully recovered from their first unhappy Castine encounter.

**KATE McCARTHY**   I was in law school back when we first met, but Mary had a way of utterly discounting that. Later on, when I began writing fiction, we were all at Sam Taylor's and I was talking about how I'd just gotten a computer and Mary said, "Well, no serious writer uses a computer." I remember feeling devastated, although I guess Mary might have said the same thing to a chef who was using a Cuisinart.

During that weekend visit there was no talk of word processors or Cuisinarts.

**KATE McCARTHY**   Mary stayed in our daughter Tess's room. She was jet-lagged and she was getting up at four or five in the morning. She did a lot of reading then. She was reading *Bright Lights, Big City*, mostly because she'd heard gossip about it from friends in New York. We had a couple of dinners and a cocktail party outside and she helped me a lot in the kitchen. She liked doing that. It was probably the most relaxed time I ever had with her, and I think some of it had to do with the fact that it was my territory. I remember her saying that she was impressed with how happy Kevin and I were in our domesticity. I think she was happy to see Kevin happy. Then, at the end of the visit we received word that Frank Preston had died. He was her last link to all the Prestons and she had been looking forward to seeing him. It was the only time I'd seen her cry. I remember Kevin took the plane to Seattle, to represent the family at the funeral.

Back in 1979, Mary and Jim West had joined Frank Preston and his second wife, Myrtle, for a trip to Ireland. In 1980 the Wests had visited them in Seattle. Now, while Kevin made the journey to Seattle, she went on to San Francisco. At this point hundreds of tickets had been sold for her appearance at the Herbst Auditorium. Moreover, Diane Johnson had been planning a big party for her.

Once she arrived in San Francisco, she had little time to cry over the loss of her uncle. As the celebrated writer Mary McCarthy, she was expected to hold center stage in an enormous auditorium and to respond to her interlocutor's questions with answers that ranged from merely quotable to highly controversial. In short, she was expected to give good value. But it wasn't only her audience who counted on her for that.

**SYDNEY GOLDSTEIN**   *[founder and director of the City Arts & Lectures reading program]* Mary McCarthy was a heroic figure to a lot of us. When I first met her in 1980 or '81, she more than lived up to all my notions about her. After that I did everything I could to bring her out here as often as possible. Some people are wonderful at writing warm and generous letters and then when you meet them they have difficulty being the same person. But she was the same person as she was in her letters. She was totally herself. And she felt comfortable being affectionate and friendly. She didn't feel a need to protect herself, I think. Now, I have a practice of never photographing anyone I have out here. If I'm asked to photograph them, I will, but I really feel that it is an invasion of their privacy, that I am the person protecting them. Somehow I made an exception with her, which she didn't seem to mind at all.

She *did* mind being pestered with questions she saw as trivial or somehow beside the point. Seated on the stage of the Herbst Auditorium and interviewed by Sedge Thomson, a local public radio personality, she spoke about everything from her various lawsuits to the recipe for something she described in *Memories of a Catholic Girlhood* as "chauffeur fried potatoes." Even when she found her interviewer's questions irritating, she did her best to treat them with due seriousness. She balked at one of the first questions he took from the audience, but did eventually get around to answering it.

### MARY MCCARTHY AT CITY ARTS & LECTURES, SAN FRANCISCO, MAY 10, 1985

As for feminism, I am not a feminist. I don't see how anyone could fail to be a sympathizer of feminism on economic grounds—that is, on the grounds of equal pay for equal work. But I don't see it in the domestic sphere—that is, I don't see the absolute equal sharing of tasks[. . . .] I never felt oppressed. I felt oppressed by individual men, starting with that terrible uncle, who was really no relation to me, but I never felt oppressed by men[. . . .] I wouldn't be a man for anything in the world. I do not envy them, including the responsibilities that they have, including the clothes they have to wear[. . . .] Exceptional women in my generation certainly profited I suppose—without thinking of it that way—from the fact that women in general were rather looked down upon. So if [men] found one they didn't look down upon, they raised her up a bit higher than she might have deserved. I'm enough of a feminist not to like the kind of praise that says, "She has the mind of a man." I always hated that[. . . .] [But] I cannot give my heart to emotions that are filled with envy and self-pity. They are very, very alien to anything I feel or anything I believe in.

With the Equal Rights Amendment passed by Congress and some reason to believe that two thirds of the states would ratify it, there was no avoiding the subject of feminism. That September, it came up during an interview for CBS News. And it came up again in the fall of 1986, during a second appearance in San Francisco, when a member of the audience raised her hand and asked what she had against feminism. Once again she responded with irritation. But she unbent so far as to admit that her views owed something to the company she kept and to announce there were some feminists whose company she found congenial.

### MARY MCCARTHY AT CITY ARTS & LECTURES, SAN FRANCISCO, OCTOBER 17, 1986

Well, you know, most women who write or produce things, or even the political activists I've known—none of them have been feminists. Hannah Arendt was very much against it. More than I am. I think she slightly influenced me. She would come up with little aphorisms like "What do we lose if we win?[. . .] There are so many kinds of feminists. I'm sort of sympathetic with the wrong kind. That is, with Betty Friedan and so on. I happen to like her.

It so happened that she had recently gotten to know Betty Friedan at a dinner in Paris after Friedan had asked some friends to ring her up and say she'd "love" to meet her.

**BETTY FRIEDAN**   I liked her writing and I liked her guts. I think she may have said I was her favorite feminist because I have never thought being a feminist meant that you were against marriage, men, love, children, or any of the rest of that. All I know is that the two of us hit it off.

As her token feminist she had chosen someone who believed in home and hearth and who had shown every evidence of liking her. In so doing she had shown some of the perversity which had once inclined her to champion "Miss Gowrie." But on this second San Francisco visit she had offended her brother Kevin's young wife, who, having no way of knowing how tired she was of being asked what she had against feminism, had raised her hand and asked yet again.

**KATE MCCARTHY**   Later on, she said that she hadn't realized that it was me. Maybe that's true. At the time I felt rather insulted and hurt. Then, afterward we were all at a reception and she came up to me and said, "Kate I didn't realize you were such a feminist." And Sydney Goldstein said, "You know, Mary, most of us are."

Whether it was her age or living in France, a gulf was widening between Mary and young women who were disposed to admire her. Some might say she had lost touch. Others might say she was simply refusing to embrace a passing ideological fashion. Certainly she was not the only woman writer of her generation to feel as she did about this subject.

**BETTY FRIEDAN**   The first wave of feminism stopped not long after the winning of the vote in 1920 and the second wave began in the sixties. Mary McCarthy was in the generation in between. Listen, when I was at Smith I hardly ever heard the word "feminism" and I was a lot younger than she was. The few women who made it sort of made it as exceptions and they didn't identify with other women—at all. For them, it was men, other women, and myself.

**MAUREEN HOWARD** Mary McCarthy backed away from the feminist movement as did Doris Lessing and Lillian Hellman. Partially, in the early sixties, having performed so well on their own, they did not want to be associated with the disenfranchised. I remember thinking, Yes, they're right. I just want to be a writer. A short-lived opinion that passed quickly from my mind.

She refused to apologize for being an exceptional woman, just as she refused to apologize for being an elitist in her writing. She might go so far as to humor her publisher by writing a memoir, but she was not about to pander to him or to her readers. She was just putting together writing that pleased her. In the end, the selections she made in *Occasional Prose* pleased virtually all of her reviewers, who treated her as a grand lady writer of considerable allure.

### FROM MARY GORDON'S REVIEW IN *ESQUIRE*, NOVEMBER 1985

She is, of course, the *femme de lettres*, and in her case both sides of the phrase have weight. The voice is above all assured, and the assurance is twofold: an intellectual assurance that allows her to range freely around the culture of the West, not literature only, but philosophy, history, politics, music, gardening, art. But the assurance has a second source: it is the assurance of a woman certain always of her power to attract.

### FROM JULIAN MOYNAHAN'S REVIEW IN *THE NEW YORK TIMES BOOK REVIEW*, MAY 5, 1985

Everywhere in *Occasional Prose* appear bracing opinions tartly expressed—Americans are slow, tedious talkers; big-time art collectors are not very nice people; the word "drugget" must never be used for stair carpeting; everybody misuses prepositions because nobody studies Latin in school anymore[. . . .] May she continue to call us all to attention ("No slumping in the back seats!"), showing us the world of her imagination, thought and rich experience.

Perhaps it was her age or the battering she had taken from Lillian Hellman, but Mary McCarthy had never received better reviews. But even as the reviewers made much of her strength and vitality and continued viability, the reviews seemed to partake of an elegiac flavor. In that respect, they could be said to look forward to the atmosphere at a ceremony held at Vassar that September to mark the acquisition of her papers—an occasion where there were moments she might have been sitting in on her own memorial service.

If such a thought crossed her mind as she sat on the platform set up for the occasion on the lawn in front of Thompson Library, she gave no indication of it, just as she gave no indication that she was anything but pleased with the deal she had struck. Such reservations as she harbored had been reserved for intimates. "[Y]ou will scold me for the price, but they didn't get all of them, only what I gave them when they came," she had written Elizabeth Hardwick that spring.

The price, which was never officially announced, was something around $110,000—a respectable-sounding sum until you heard what writers were being offered by better endowed institutions. Lisa Browar, who had been hired especially to take charge of the papers, believed that owing in large part to the character of the seller, the buyer of McCarthy's papers made out very well indeed.

**LISA BROWAR** The papers were in wonderful order and she was remarkably open with us, telling stories and identifying photographs. Mary also left us alone to do our work of sorting and packing. In similar situations, owners of papers or their heirs have remained with us as we packed collections. Mary could be a real zealot in going after people she thought were intellectually pretentious or dishonest—she held herself and the world to a very high standard—but I think she saw people as basically good and true and honest. She was a fundamentally trusting person who believed others shared her values and adhered to her standards, and she was often disappointed when the reality proved otherwise. Except for the files she needed for the book she was working on, Mary let us take everything.

The weather the morning of the September 14 ceremony was warm enough for her to get by with wearing a crisp pin-striped dress with a softening ruffle at the neck. Seated with the various speakers on the wooden platform, Mary McCarthy looked better than she had in years— a bit like the Queen of England, only prettier. Unlike the Queen, she was at liberty to cross her legs at the knee, but whenever the wind kicked up, she would reach down and adjust the folds of her skirt. The sun was so strong that almost everyone present was wearing dark glasses. She was not. Whenever she smiled, her eyes crinkled almost shut, and as she watched one speaker after another stand up and do her honor, she found occasion to smile a lot.

Virginia Smith, who was the first to step up to the podium, spoke of how important it was—particularly in an age of "word processing, with its instantaneous deletion of material"—to have a collection of papers where students could "trace the creation of a work of literature through its various stages." She did not speak of how she was stepping down at the end of the year as Vassar's president, but, with her customary directness, she touched on McCarthy's special relationship with the college.

## FROM VIRGINIA SMITH'S REMARKS AT VASSAR COLLEGE, SEPTEMBER 14, 1985

Over the years Mary has shared her intelligence with us during informal visits to the campus as well as on formal occasions[. . . .] As a social observer, at times she has directed her intelligence *at* us as well. Our relationship has been a family one.

William Jovanovich called her a "rare person" and a "rare writer" and then tried to define what made her writing unique.

### FROM WILLIAM JOVANOVICH'S REMARKS AT VASSAR COLLEGE, SEPTEMBER 14, 1985

It seems to me that she combines a tremendous sense of tradition—in fact, she's one of the few people I know who takes her values largely from literature—with always being in her own time and in her own place. You always know in a McCarthy piece—whether it's a critical piece or a novel—where she is, who's there, what the sky looks like, what someone's wearing, how things are said.

Frances FitzGerald began by saying how "lucky" Vassar was to get this collection. She pointed out that Mary McCarthy's works were "so large and various" that the only places you might not expect to find them in a bookstore were under headings like the "the Occult, Baby and Child Care, Self-Help, and Science Fiction," and went on to say that McCarthy's correspondence was no less large and various, since "probably she knew most of the writers and intellectuals of note and of staying power in the middle of the twentieth century, including a few people she wasn't married to." Finally, she spoke of McCarthy's politics.

### FROM FRANCES FITZGERALD'S REMARKS AT VASSAR COLLEGE, SEPTEMBER 14, 1985

Politics is for her something quite down to earth. It's not so much theory as it is just life[. . . .] She wants to know not just what our leaders say but how they say it. And what kind of smile was playing over the lips of Richard Nixon when he said, "I am not a crook." This is the novelist in her; it's also the soundest kind of politics. That way you can't lose touch with reality.

As a newly tenured professor at Vassar, Thomas Mallon had actually had a chance to examine the papers. He spoke of finding a 1956 engagement calendar, old royalty statements from Harcourt Brace, checks made out to the Madison Curtain Cleaners, and a letter to Dwight Macdonald, dated February 8, 1966, in which she asked, "What are you doing about Vietnam?" He spoke of the chastening experience of coming upon his own correspondence in one folder and of what having the collection so close at hand was going to mean to him.

### FROM THOMAS MALLON'S REMARKS AT VASSAR COLLEGE, SEPTEMBER 14, 1985

I am conscious at this moment of failing Mary McCarthy, of falling

back, as always, on the personal, of streaking myself with the sentimental. I am conscious of failing to rise to the lessons she taught me:
lessons of rigor, clarity, joy in the truth. But it is the awareness of such
failure that will send me back to her books, and to this extraordinary
gathering of documents, for decades to come. In all the years that I'm
at Vassar [. . .] I will know that a few hundred yards from my desk in
Avery Hall, these papers are staying—quiet, alive, folded, assertive—
staying here and being to me what her work always was: a translucent
explanation and a stinging rebuke.

Elizabeth Hardwick, who had not laid eyes on the collection, was no less
aware of the part she played in it. "I believe that herein are institutionalized many follies of my own," she noted. Once again she paid homage
to the remarkable "self-confidence" manifest in Mary McCarthy's earliest published work, this time going so far as to say, "I for one have of
course no doubt that she was born from the head of Zeus." And once
again she spoke of the "cheerful skepticism" and "liberal humane conviction" that left Mary McCarthy "little to apologize for in the way of
moral positions taken."

### FROM ELIZABETH HARDWICK'S REMARKS AT VASSAR COLLEGE, SEPTEMBER 14, 1985

Character, fully formed and always there amidst changing events, is
the key somehow. Character leaves its marks on the writing—the novels, the essays, the voice. The firmness to some extent, especially in
the fiction, is that of a steady eye for folly. For the folly of overreach-
ing, for the trap of ideas or something less than ideas perhaps, for
reigning trends—the trap that leads the innocent and the foolish
astray.

Mary McCarthy had not lost her eye for folly, but that day she was on
her best behavior. After listening to these attempts to characterize her,
she did not try to set right any wayward perceptions. And she did not
give a speech of her own. Instead, she chose to honor both the past and
present by putting on her glasses and reading part of the Vassar chapter
from her memoir in progress. Afterward she took care to see that Mary
Gordon, who had not been invited to speak, was seated beside her at
lunch. But if her public behavior that day had been a model of tact and
diplomacy, her behavior the previous day had been anything but.

Seated on a bench on that same patch of lawn and interviewed by
Faith Daniels of CBS News, she had burst forth with a stream of opinions
guaranteed to give pause to the average television viewer. There was no
old enemy she wasn't prepared to demolish. The interview, which took
almost an entire morning, was edited down to six minutes. In the course
of it she took out after Ronald Reagan who, despite all her efforts on

behalf of his opponent, was still residing in the White House. "I can't stand to look at his face," she said. "His fleshiness around the neck and jowls and that self-satisfied idiot smile." But it wasn't only Reagan's looks that bothered her. "I'm getting less and less able to confront pictures of myself," she said. "I was really quite good-looking and maybe it would have been better not to be really good-looking and then you wouldn't have lost much." She spoke candidly of why she disliked growing older and no less candidly of why she was very much for legal abortions. "I've had several abortions," she said, "I've forgotten how many I've had, but I've had several. I've even had a legal one[. . . .] You are taking away life and so you have to pay for it with a little twinge of conscience. But that's not the same as having the majority tell you, or a vocal minority tell you, what you can or cannot do, must or must not do." She spoke candidly of many things that day, but first and foremost she spoke of why she had made peace with the institution that was honoring her.

### FROM MARY MCCARTHY'S INTERVIEW WITH FAITH DANIELS, SEPTEMBER 13, 1985

I'm very fond of Vassar, even when I've been on the outs with Vassar. I'm very fond of the place, and let's say I'm fond of, and amused by, the idea of the Vassar girl of all ages, because all are recognizable to me. Their desire to be superior—superior to others, superior to their community. There is a certain daringness, sometimes simply a wish to be daring and sometimes the reality, because they're not all that way. And, on the positive side, I think they are very well educated on the whole. I mean, you can't educate everybody. I'm exposed to some Smith women and it makes one appreciate a Vassar education, as the things and people that a Smith graduate has never heard of are shocking to a Vassar girl.

Mary McCarthy prided herself on speaking the truth, even when it meant offending some Smith women, but, no less important, she prided herself on confounding those who believed they knew her best. Call it a desire to shock; call it pure contrariness. Certainly she was not about to be pinned down by anyone. Not even by the school that she had just credited in her memoir with doing so much to form her.

Vassar had paid good money for her papers and, in return, she had given them good value. But that had not kept her from flirting with another suitor. That August, even as she had been preparing for the great event at Vassar, she had been entertaining Fritz and Margaret Shafer, friends from the old days at Bard who had come to Castine full of news of Bard's newly created Charles Stevenson Chair in Literature.

**MARGARET SHAFER**   I told her there was an opening because somebody was endowing a chair in literature. There was a short list of candidates and she was very high on the list. I also asked if she had any names to suggest. Frankly, I thought she had dropped Bard. But when she heard about this new professorship, she said, "I'd like it."

The Charles Stevenson Chair came with a handsome stipend and required that its occupant teach only two courses each year. When she sent word to Bard President Leon Botstein that she *herself* might be interested, he was delighted. It was what he had been hoping for all along. Botstein, who had come to Bard in 1975, had been a student of Hannah Arendt's. He'd first met McCarthy at Arendt's funeral. A year later he'd come up with the idea of awarding her an honorary degree. She sent Eve Stwertka in her place. Knowing that she had just delivered the commencement address at Vassar, and not knowing that she'd had to return to Paris immediately for radiation therapy, he'd sensed in her "a whiff of condescension toward Bard." This was a condescension that he believed to be unwarranted, since "Bard had many fine traditions" and "Vassar was not Bologna." But in 1980, when he spoke at an NYU symposium on Hannah Arendt, relations between them improved markedly.

**LEON BOTSTEIN**   Mary, who was in the audience, liked what I had to say. I then became part of a game which Mary played vis-à-vis Bard and Vassar. She had a mischievous side to her. And this mischievousness was not unintentional. In February of 1982 she was invited to be some kind of super Vassar lecturer and Virginia Smith asked her whom she wanted to invite to come for dinner at the President's House. So she gave Virginia Smith a list mostly of Bard people. Now, I'd never been to the President's House at Vassar under any circumstances. It was one of the most amusing events, because Mary then seated me at her table. Virginia Smith was not at her table. It was the oddest thing. Mary surrounded herself with Bard people.

In the winter of 1982, she had apparently taken a certain pleasure in playing Bard off against her alma mater. In the summer of 1985 she was given a chance to partake of that pleasure again. By September, there was an understanding but no written agreement. That November, on her way back to Paris, she stopped by to see Leon Botstein and it was agreed that if she came to Bard, she'd have to teach only during the fall semester.

At Bard she would be only minutes away from the cemetery where Hannah Arendt and Heinrich Blücher were buried. She would be back where she had been young and beautiful and, at least in retrospect, very happy. She would have the company of friends she had shared that happy year with—not only the Shafers but Irma Brandeis and Andy Dupee, who had come back after the death of her husband, Fred. She would also be cutting short the half year she was now spending in Maine, where a retired Jim West seemed content to stay forever but where she found three summer months sufficient. And she would be earning a sizable amount of money.

**JAMES WEST**   We never had a great sum of money at hand, that's for sure. Never. In fact, toward the end of our days together, we were talking about money for some reason and I said, "I'd like to do that, too, but you know I don't have much money." And she said, "What about the stocks your father left you?" And I said, "Oh, it only amounts to a couple of hundred thousand dollars." "Oh, Jim." "Mary, do you want me to convert that to money?" "Yes." "Well, why?" "So you can spend it."

**BARBARA DUPEE**   I got the impression that she desperately needed the money—to buy all those breakfronts and chairs she and Jim were always buying and all those clothes. She couldn't stand to leave Paris because Jim wanted to be in Maine and she would have died in Maine. One time I asked her, "Why not New York?" And she said, "We can't sell the apartment in Paris for enough to buy something in New York."

It made her decision easier knowing Virginia Smith was about to leave Vassar. An announcement was put off until the spring of 1986 when Virginia Smith's successor had been installed. By then she had worked out the final details of her arrangement with Bard. This time, she'd driven a hard bargain. It had been agreed that she would teach a seminar in Russian literature, open only to literature majors, and a regular class called "The Place of Ideas in Fiction," open to everyone. It was also agreed that in addition to a generous stipend, she would be provided with a pretty house furnished to her taste, practically next door to Andy Dupee, which would remain available to her the entire year. Bard would also find her a secretary.

**SARA POWERS**   I was a senior and a writing student and William Wilson, who was one of my professors suggested me because he thought that with my sharp eyes and her sharp eyes we would get along. Mary had a nice Dutch-style cottage. She used those words to describe it in a letter. Apparently she gave quite explicit instructions to Leon Botstein's assistant about certain things she wanted in the house. I remember she had certain Egyptian rugs that were bought in Blue Hill, Maine, that the college paid for. And I believe she also requested a certain type of linen and a certain type of china. That same semester the British philosopher A. J. Ayer came to teach and of course A. J. Ayer didn't think to request anything. The college gave him an apartment at the end of a dormitory building furnished with tacky dormitory furniture.

She demanded the very best from Bard, but she also demanded the very best from herself. During August 1986, she was busy putting together two elaborate reading lists for her classes, choosing appropriate texts, and getting as much of her own reading done as possible. Fortunately, she had already turned in the first volume of her intellectual memoirs, which she was now calling *How I Grew*.

**ELIZABETH HARDWICK** Mary had a contract at Bard and she wanted to fulfill it. She took it so much more seriously than most writers do. She was very, very serious about it. She'd taught at Bard just before she married Bowden, and she had friends up there, so she was sentimental about it.

If preparation alone made for a good teacher, then she promised to be a very good one indeed. As far as Leon Botstein was concerned, she more than lived up to her side of the bargain. As far as Elizabeth Frank, a poet and teacher in the literature division, was concerned, she was a definite addition. But not everyone in the division was totally enchanted.

**LEON BOTSTEIN** She was a much better teacher than I would have expected—and I didn't expect her to be bad. She had none of the sort of common academic viciousness. And she was able to be very tough without being hurtful. I loved it because she didn't mince words. She didn't play games. She was direct. Very direct. In a nice way.

**ELIZABETH FRANK** *[faculty member]* She would come to class dressed in beautiful suits. And Jim West would be dressed in even more beautiful suits and would come at the end of class to pick her up. I would run into them sometimes at Olin, this brand-new building, where the division's classes were held, and I'd see these two beautifully dressed older people. It would make me feel good just to see them.

**BENJAMIN LAFARGE** *[literature division chairman at the time]* She was wholeheartedly committed to her teaching. Once she told me she put her own writing aside during the fall semester. But her notion was that everyone ought to be literate in a way that she and her generation had been. She was merciless to any kid who didn't live up to this impossible standard. At Bard we have a sort of rite-of-passage exam the students take at the end of sophomore year, called "Moderation." The students submit papers but they also have to go before a three-member panel. At one such exam a student of mine was insisting on being a double major in dance and literature, and I remember Mary saying to him, "You're not a literary person. You don't know how to write." I'm not suggesting Mary was invariably wrong in her judgments, just that she was harsh and unrealistic. She did not attract many of the best students, but this wasn't only because of her old-fashioned "literary" standards. Word got out that she was not an *interesting* teacher. I heard again and again that she talked around the subject. She talked personally about the authors, if she knew them or even if they were long dead. She gossiped.

Benjamin LaFarge had come away from his first meeting with her sensing that she didn't much like him. Whether or not this was the case, there was definitely no sense of connection. Elizabeth Frank came away from *her* first meeting with a very different impression. Like Benjamin LaFarge, she did not sit in on any of Mary McCarthy's classes.

**ELIZABETH FRANK**   I was on panels with her for Moderation and also for Senior Projects. She had this absolute killer smile and she'd fire this smile at a student and you'd expect her to say something about the kid's deepest thoughts and she'd be talking about the commas. I think the students were taken aback. I never saw cruelty from her. Some kids found her boring as a lecturer. But some kids find everyone boring. Some signed up for a course with a great literary star and wondered why she wasn't more interested in what *they* had to say. What she had to say and the experiences she had lived through would have been valued by the right kind of student. There simply aren't that many of those students in the United States today. Most of the students weren't prepared for her.

One student's boring gossip is another's meat and potatoes and among her students at Bard there were at least two who benefited from her teaching. Both took "The Place of Ideas in Fiction" in the fall of 1987. One, the son of the philosopher A. J. Ayer, had been educated in England and had taken her seminar in the Russian novel the previous fall. The other was a political science major who would go on to take a doctorate at Columbia, where he would write his dissertation on the Nuremberg trials.

**NICHOLAS AYER**   They were very selective about the people who were allowed to take her seminar in the Russian novel. There must have been ten of us. She made us work hard—we read a book a week—but people tried to keep up. The class had a good spirit. She allowed me to make a fool of myself and then gave me that wonderful smile that told me I'd made a complete fool of myself. All my life I'd been around people like her. I knew the writers she was talking about—or at least knew *of* them. She talked about Ford Madox Ford an awful lot and Nabokov. But these students were there to pick apart books. She was fantastic for the Russian novel, but Ideas in Fiction was a mistake. There you were in a huge cross-section of people. The students were younger and a lot of them didn't like her. But I think that had to do with the fact that if you made a mistake she pointed it out. She wasn't a trained teacher, who has been trained to be kind and all that sort of thing.

**PETER MAGUIRE**   She was quite ill by then, but she was very impressive. Just a real warrior. Very few people in that class had a right to be critical of her because so few people did the work. There would be these pregnant pauses. It was embarrassing. It was my last semester and I was writing my thesis for Senior Project, but I was getting up at five in the morning and doing two or three hours reading so I would know someone in that class had done something.

**NICHOLAS AYER**   She and Jim West gave parties for both those classes. Mary would have her little group of disciples all around her—you could see she was expecting it, though I don't think she much liked it—and then Jim would be feeding everyone else drinks in the kitchen. I was in the kitchen.

**Peter Maguire**  She treated us all like adults and it was very funny because some of these eighteen- and nineteen-year-olds didn't have a clue. I remember one girl came in and Mary McCarthy said, "I'll take your coat," and the girl said something like, "But I'm cold," and Mary had to wrestle the coat off this girl. There would be no coats in *her* dining room. There was a lot of liquor, though. Bottles and bottles of beaujolais. She liked seeing how everybody handled it. She and I got along. I got past her grandmotherly exterior immediately. Underneath she wasn't even marginally grandmotherly. We had a lot of fun.

It wasn't only her students who took pleasure in her company outside the classroom.

**Elizabeth Frank**  She invited me to dinner soon after she came to Bard. She was respectful, kind, generous, and terribly nice to me about my book on Louise Bogan. One time she told me this story of how Louise Bogan and Edmund Wilson had for years been just pals but at some point after Louise's divorce the two of them had ended up naked in bed together, and then Louise had asked Edmund to get her a glass of water. When he came back with the water he stumbled and ended up spilling it all over her and the bed, at which point they both laughed and Louise suggested it might be a good idea if they called the whole thing off.

**Leon Botstein**  People submerge their pasts, it's like an iceberg—the ice that has been accumulated recently you see and what's submerged you don't see. But Mary kept a lot of her past active, so in her present the past was somehow integrated in a way that was not nostalgic. One of the most unusual things about her was that she never aged. In other words, she was never a woman in her seventies. That's very hard to pull off and it was not self-conscious. She was always sexy, even though she was old. The style was that of someone not conceited but conscious of her own attractiveness. And she was playful to the end. And funny to the end. Witty without being silly.

At Bard, she was being given a chance to take a second or third look at books she hadn't read in years. To this part of her classroom preparation she brought the same passionate attention she had brought to her studies at Vassar and Annie Wright. And she seemed to derive the same satisfaction. But with her return to Bard she soon found herself far busier than she had ever been as a student—or than she'd been as a single parent teaching for the first time.

**Sara Powers**  That fall she had a number of engagements to speak. Then, she was rushing toward the publication of *How I Grew*. She was busy collecting photographs and then at the middle of that semester the galleys came and she was proofreading them. She was also managing all the Hannah Arendt stuff. And she was trying to keep up what seemed to me to be an extraordinary number of social obligations. She made a number of trips down to New York.

**LOTTE KOHLER**   There was so much to do: the estate, keeping track of Hannah Arendt's mail and permissions, all of which seemed to overwhelm Mary. She spent winters in Paris in their elegant apartment and summers in that wonderful house in Castine. Mary liked to live in grand style. It was too tempting to continue this arrangement. But she wasn't well. I liked her very much and, of course, couldn't and wouldn't suggest any change.

It would seem that she shared a desire to "have it all" with those feminists whose self-pity she had no use for. Thanks to her job at Bard, she could afford to maintain substantial residences on two continents. There was no need to sacrifice one for the other. And no need to come into direct conflict with her husband, who had become more irritable since his retirement. In Paris she persisted in arranging her days much as she always had, and with Maria there to help, it was fairly easy to do so. She continued to write every morning, to meet with her German teacher regularly, and to meet with her secretary at least two afternoons a week. In 1981, Patsy Leo, the wife of the minister at the American Cathedral in Paris, had replaced Rosalind Michehelles as her secretary. Soon Patsy Leo and her husband could be found at dinners and parties. And she could be found repaying their visits on the occasional Sunday, sitting in the back of the cathedral church and taking part in the Episcopal service.

**PATSY LEO**   Mary and my husband, Jim, would talk about religion and she would come to church periodically. We asked her to come once in a while. And sometimes she would. It was always very nice when she did. She knew the prayer book backward and forward. She knew a lot about the hymnal. And in a lot of her books she uses a religious vocabulary. Nicky King and Mary always had great discussions about religious things.

**NICHOLAS KING**   While she knew a few Catholics, it was as if with the Episcopal church she came into another spiritual realm where she could have her opinions and her mind had some play. The clergy were fairly educated people and they talked her language. She was attracted to them. She found the Roman church a brick wall. And then of course the whole business about her spiritual situation is always debated. She declares herself an atheist, but I don't know.

Although she had not gone so far as to become a believer, she was experiencing something which she had first experienced at Annie Wright and which she now wrote about in her new memoir.

FROM *HOW I GREW*

I remember singing a new (to me) Christmas hymn, "A Virgin Unspotted," as we marched in procession into chapel, and the strange emotion that came over me as I caroled the words out, my heart singing for joy in Mary Virgin, though Mary I was and virgin I was not. In the Episcopal hymns and liturgy, I was experiencing what psychiatrists call "ideas of reference." With the Advent hymns now posted in chapel I recognized my Jewish relations and raised my voice for their safety: "Rejoice, rejoice! Em-ma-a-anuel will ransom captive I-i-srael." Without ever recovering a trace of the faith I had lost in the convent, I was falling in love with the Episcopal church. I did not believe in God's existence, but, more and more, as Christmas approached, I liked the idea of Him, and chapel, morning and evening, became my favorite part of the day.

Winters in Paris, she continued to juggle a busy social schedule with her writing; to entertain visitors, even when she wasn't feeling quite up to it; and to make welcome fellow Americans.

**ROBERT SILVERS**  At her parties and at her lunches and dinners, she took great pains over every detail. It meant a lot to her, even when she was ill.

**DIANE JOHNSON**  Mary had a set of after-dinner cups—Meissen. Every time that you had coffee, Mary would say that these were real Meissen cups and the way you knew was that the saucers had no ridges. She prized those cups, but she used them. She didn't save them.

**TERENCE KILMARTIN**  I remember once I was in Paris by myself, and Mary was ill, and instead of putting me off, she had me come over. Mary was in bed with a temperature, and Jim said, "It doesn't matter. You and I are going to have supper here and Mary is going to have her supper in bed." Jim and I were in the dining room and Mary was in the bedroom, which was some distance away, but she insisted on having the door open. She wasn't going to miss a thing. Jim and I started by having a little conversation *à deux*, but Mary was interrupting in no time.

**JANE KRAMER**  She had, I think, a sense of responsibility to the American community—which most people I know avoid like the plague, or selectively dip into. She really had it. She was very much the doyenne of that community and she wanted to be.

At her parties one could find old hands like Ivan Nabokov and his wife, Claude, Kot Jelenski, Anjo Levi, Jonathan Randal, and Tom Curtiss. Over time they had been joined by Jim and Patsy Leo; the Brazilian photographer Carlos Freire and his wife, Heloïsa; Diane Johnson and her husband, Dr. John Murray; Jane Kramer and her husband, Vincent Crapazano; and Edgar and Charlotte de Bresson. Vincent Crapazano and Edgar de Bresson had gone to Harvard with Reuel.

**JANE KRAMER**   Not long after I took over *The New Yorker*'s Paris beat, Mary had a party for Reuel at her apartment, and that was the first time I ever saw them together. He's very smart, Reuel, and I've always wondered what it was like for him to see his friends adore his mother and to have his mother take such good care of his friends. She was terrific to us, and she was terrific to Edgar and Charlotte. Twice when Mary was still alive, Reuel was in Paris doing research. Most of that time Mary was in America and the apartment was empty. Reuel came and used it as a study, but he didn't live there. He had a walk-up with two rooms in the Cité Université, and he and his wife slept in the living room and Sophie slept in the bedroom. Now, Mary loved Sophie. She had drawings by Sophie propped up on the mantlepiece, which always touched me. But I'm not sure that Sophie ever stayed in that apartment.

The rue de Rennes had never been lovely and with time it had become less so. Under Pompidou, Le Tour Montparnasse, a hideous black office tower, had been erected at the top of the thoroughfare, casting a shadow down its entire length. The shops had long since been given over to discount appliances and cheap clothing. By night the gutters were clogged with litter. Terrorists on their way to bomb the tower had ended up tossing their bomb into an Arab-owned clothing shop across the street. Whether they were newcomers or habitués, most of her visitors seemed not to take much notice of this. The apartment, after all, looked out over a courtyard in the back. But just as the neighborhood had grown a little shabbier, her parties had lost some of their glamor, or luster. They continued, however, to exert an appeal.

**JANE KRAMER**   It was a bourgeois salon that happened to have intellectuals. Or an intellectual salon that happened to be bourgeois. Unlike most of the French intellectuals we both knew, Mary was not at all ethnocentric. Her apartment was one of the few places in Paris where you met people from all over Europe. She had old friends who were Polish émigrés. She was a friend of the Calvinos. As a hostess, she was a combination of worldliness and innocence. Innocence can carry off anything. I believe she knew she was an innocent, and traded on it. At her place, all sorts of people were thrown together. Sometimes her dinners were deadly, but at most of them the boring people would just be thrown in with the others and reduced.

**PHILIP ROTH**   At dinner, one of the things I noticed was that her response to anything that was said was she would laugh. I know that response. There was always something amusing to be found. I had been seduced by her early stories. I read the diaphragm story when it came out. She acted like a woman for whom it was still possible to be found attractive. I liked her a lot. She liked me, I think, and that helps. She had this clean, crisp American thing and when you saw it in Paris it struck you. You were in a room with Yanks.

If her parties were sometimes more staid than they had once been, that may have had something to do with age and also with Jim West, who continued to exert a strong influence.

**JANE KRAMER** When I first came to Paris I would go and talk to Mary and Jim about my work, really about the ethics of reporting, and Jim was often quite profound talking about it. He was smarter than many people gave him credit for. He had to have been for Mary to be interested in him. He was immensely well read. One time I remember him warning Mary and me against sentimentalizing our relationships with the people we were writing about, or agonizing about "betrayal." I remember him saying, "You girls, you're lying to yourselves if you think you can find a rhetoric to excuse or to cover up what you're doing. You've got to accept that in some sense you're the hunters and they're the prey and that's what you do when you write." They were an interesting team because Mary had a frame of reference as wide as anybody I've ever known. She never forgot anything and her reading was staggering. She didn't flaunt it, but it was always there. And Jim was full of practical wisdom, which had to do with his comment about "you girls." At the time, I thought they complemented each other.

**IVAN NABOKOV** The last time I saw Mary, she came to dinner and Jim was going to come, too. But he was coming directly from the airport. He'd been in Warsaw. It was very touching. She made it up the stairs. She was shuffling. Jim's plane was due in at nine. At ten the doorbell rang. Mary got up and greeted him. "Oh, Jim." They kissed. She was so moved that he'd come back to her. It was a great love match.

Always the bond between them remained strong. She would have liked for Jim to use his talents in some pursuit of his own, but it never happened. With Jim's retirement and her refusal to let illness hold her back, there were moments of strain.

**ESTHER BROOKS** Jim told me once that his day consisted of getting up in the morning and not being able to have coffee because he had to go down and get Mary's coffee, and then just as he would be ready to have his own coffee Mary would ask him to wash her back for her. He would have to get her into the tub and get her out, so he really didn't get his breakfast until around eleven o'clock.

**SARA POWERS** Her life was so much bigger than his. I remember he drove the galleys of *How I Grew* down to New York City to hand-deliver them. And he drove around all over Rhinebeck and that area looking for a certain type of rose water that she insisted on having. And occasionally he would drive up to Maine to bring things down and to get the car overhauled. But most of the time he was there in the house. I remember seeing him sitting in the living room reading the paper. I don't know what there was for him to do except to see to her needs.

**ANGÉLIQUE LEVI** Jim is charming, but he can be hard on occasion. It is possible that he is a misanthrope. He would get angry over little things. Mary had to please him. Once in a while she did not succeed. Retirement was difficult for Jim. In Paris, he was often at home. When we were working, he was in the other room. In Castine he was happy. There he was always working in the garden. He was a different man. But for Mary I think it was hard in Castine sometimes. There were too many people around.

In Castine, Jim was busier and happier, but with all her summer guests and her entertaining, she rarely had many hours to herself. Starting in 1987, when Maria ceased to accompany them to America, she had less free time than ever. Even so, she refused to make the sort of compromises anyone else might make. Year after year, with little in the way of help in the house and the kitchen, she continued to welcome summer visitors, to partake of her favorite warm weather activities, and to acquire still another bit of information about this quiet corner of New England where she was spending more time than she might have liked.

**NICHOLAS KING**   We would go to Hatch's Pond almost ritually. We'd drive down there and we'd picnic. I used to make the mayonnaise with her. The last years, we'd sit making the mayonnaise and talking. She was very concerned about why the elms never came back after the blight. The elm was the great tree of towns and villages in the northeast. The trees now are much lower, and you don't have this vaulting, arching beautiful canopy that the elm provided. In certain domains I knew more than she did. She liked that, too. I'd point out a great blue heron or a black-bellied plover. She enjoyed knowing the names of things. It was a kind of anchor. Learning a fact pleases you and it strengthens you and makes you less dissatisfied with yourself— for a moment anyway.

Most summers she could count on the company of Elizabeth Hardwick. And, if she was lucky, she would sometimes have Hardwick there for a few days in the fall.

**JON JEWETT**   Lizzie liked to go out first thing every morning in her little rental car, to comb the streets and see what was up. At some point she'd almost always stop by at Mary's for a visit, to pass on to Mary some little story she'd heard or whatever. Every day they'd talk. I will always remember coming in the kitchen door rather early one unforgettable Thanksgiving morning—it was snowing and my assignment had been to shovel the walk out and get some firewood—and finding Lizzie and Mary with aprons in the kitchen, standing at that big marble chopping table, chopping oysters for the turkey dressing and discussing Sonia Orwell's spleen.

She was in Castine in the summer of 1985, when Charles McGrath, her new editor at *The New Yorker*, called for some last-minute work on two chapters from her memoirs, which the magazine had purchased several years earlier.

**CHARLES MCGRATH**   We took the chapters and it was my job to make a piece of them. I went about this with some nervousness, partly because, to be honest, the writing was not in every instance all that one would have hoped. There were flashes of brilliance but a funny kind of mellowness had seeped in. There were passages that could almost have been the memoirs of a club lady. It was odd. Anyway, my first hint of what might lie ahead came when I sent her a set of galleys and they came back with a number of places where she had marked this or that typo and one place where she just wrote: "This has been sadly dis-improved in the editing." We held on to the thing forever, and then suddenly it had to go in two weeks. I was finally able to reach her in Castine. She had just arrived and she was running around frantically trying to get settled, and here I was on the phone all the time. I'd never met her. I think I was partly afraid to. I began with some trepidation, but she was very quick and very bright. It was one of those times when you find the editor and the writer just seem to be on the same wavelength. The steely formidable side, which I'd been expecting, was there, but there was also this other, very friendly, almost maternal, side. In the background I could sense that they were throwing a party. Something was going on in the house. There was this very elaborate busy social life going on and, meanwhile, she was running upstairs, trying to close the piece. She was juggling everything, and yet when she sat down with the galleys she was extremely professional.

*How I Grew* finally came out in the spring of 1987. By then chapters had appeared not only in *The New Yorker* but *Vanity Fair* and *Paris Review*; there had been an interview in *The New York Times Magazine* that had not displeased her; and her publisher had reason to believe he might sell out his first printing. With hard work she had eventually managed to pin down many of the details that she had once believed were lost to her forever—the books she had read and the girls she had gone to school with. She had gone on to flesh out details with healthy chunks of social history, placing not only the Annie Wright Seminary and Miss Preston but Vassar and Harold Johnsrud firmly in their time and place. Finally, however, in her excavations of the past, she had taken off in a direction William Jovanovich had never anticipated—striving for something like confession and coming up with something closer to full disclosure—or, at any rate, the fullest disclosure she was capable of.

With scarcely a blush she wrote of losing her virginity at the age of fourteen to a semiliterate twenty-six-year-old Seattle rake in a Marmon roadster, of her subsequent brush with a Seattle lesbian notorious for her sexual preference and her artistic salon, of her dismaying adolescent penchant for lying, of her sexual misadventures with an older Seattle painter who made her do things she could hardly bear to think about, and of losing her virginity for the third time to Harold Johnsrud, whom she went on to marry even after he had killed her love for him. She wrote of the lack of character that led her to disguise her true fondness for Vassar in letters to "Ted" Rosenberg and of the far from courageous part she played when faced with her classmates' anti-Semitism; and she wrote of the mixed motives and pure self-interest that had resulted in her sharing rooms her senior year with the girls she later portrayed in *The Group*.

Taking care to separate fact from fiction, she used this memoir to confess to almost every sin she could possibly be held accountable for. In the process, it could be argued, she also gave William Jovanovich some of what he was looking for. The Marmon roadster, after all, was part of her education. No less a part than finding herself suddenly an orphan at the age of six or living with that horrible aunt and uncle in Minneapolis. As she saw it, all of these experiences had helped shape her both as a writer and as a person.

## FROM *HOW I GREW*

[O]ver the years I have found a means—laughter—of turning pain into pleasure. Uncle Myers and Aunt Margaret, my grandmother, too, in her own style, amuse me by their capacity for being awful[. . . .] Laughter is the great antidote for self-pity, maybe a specific for the malady. Yet probably it does tend to dry one's feelings out a little, as if by exposing them to a vigorous wind. So that something must be subtracted from the compensations I seem to have received for injuries sustained. There is no dampness in my emotions, and some moisture, I think, is needed to produce the deeper, the tragic, notes.

Reasoning things through had always given her enormous pleasure, even when she reached conclusions that might have driven another writer to take refuge in silence. Here, delighted with all she had learned from her excavations of the past, she did not think twice about providing reviewers with ammunition they could draw on when pointing out the failings of her book.

## FROM CHRISTOPHER LEHMANN-HAUPT'S REVIEW IN *THE NEW YORK TIMES*, APRIL 13, 1987

The trouble is, when the feelings dry, we are left mostly with facts. True, the facts are often beguiling[. . . .] Indeed, the thought kept occurring to this reader that if *How I Grew* had been written by someone unknown instead of the person Norman Mailer once called "our First Lady of Letters," it would probably have been celebrated as a historical "find"[. . . .] But as a work by someone as familiar as Mary McCarthy, one can't help noting the absence of those feelings that, according to her own ripe metaphor, get dried out when exposed to the "vigorous wind" of laughter[. . . .] It is hard not to believe that something emotionally a little more damp wasn't flowing beneath the surface of these events, something like the victim's quest for self-punishment. But lacking a psychoanalytical bent, Ms. McCarthy prefers merely to rub her nose in the facts.

With *Occasional Prose* reviewers had treated her with kid gloves. With *How I Grew* the gloves frequently came off. They found the writing uneven, the tone unappetizing, the lists of books and schoolmates endless. Time and again, they compared the new autobiography with *Memories of a Catholic Girlhood*. In *The New York Times Book Review*, Wilfrid Sheed went so far as to say that by reading the two books together you would discover "where all the moisture went" and also end up with "a genuine artwork as original as any of her fiction." But most reviewers were not that kind. Nor were they the only ones to find the book wanting.

### FROM JAMES WOLCOTT'S REVIEW IN *THE NEW REPUBLIC*, MAY 11, 1987

[I]f McCarthy prizes friendship so highly, why does *How I Grew* read like a series of small punctures, petty beyond belief? Friendship isn't nearly so potent or present in this book as McCarthy's brisk air of exclusivity. She masks her hauteur with a smile set in cool marble, as she plays hostess, passing around amusing anecdotes on the snack tray. But the mask, alas, keeps slipping. Where *Memories of a Catholic Girlhood* was *written*, its sentences engraved on the soft recesses of the past with a silver stylus, *How I Grew* has the mild fuss of an ongoing monologue. "But I am digressing in the middle of a digression, piling Ossa on Pelion, we Latinists would say."

**SAMUEL TAYLOR**   I kept urging her, I kept saying, "Mary, I want to know more about you and what you thought about your life." And I don't think she wanted to do that. Why, I don't know. I didn't say this to Mary, but I did say to somebody, that too often *How I Grew* was like a laundry list. She would not be judgmental about her life, but she was a woman who always judged. I didn't understand that, and I never talked to her about it.

**MARGO VISCUSI**   I found it a very sad book—a book full of regrets. And I wish I'd been able to talk to her more about it. There's a strong undercurrent of sadness. There's a feeling that she was not happy with herself, morally or spiritually. In looking back at the younger Mary, she is very self-critical. She doesn't quite approve of a number of her actions, her attitudes toward people. Part of it is simply relating anecdotes but part of it is "Look what an unfeeling thing I did."

If there were those who found *How I Grew* disappointing or disturbing, there were others who felt they understood why it had turned out the way it had.

**FRANCES FITZGERALD**   I don't see Mary disapproving of her young self so much as casting a cold eye and facing up to it. I mean, she was not the same person that she was when she was younger and I think she probably had some sympathy for this kid but not much.

**CEES NOOTEBOOM**   There was something about the book which nobody touched upon. It was like an incantation—all those names of all those girls. It was like a sort of good-bye song also. By the incantation she was trying to get the whole thing going. To almost sing herself into a mood.

By the time the memoir came out she had started its sequel, a second volume that William Jovanovich believed would be more like the book he had originally envisioned. Once again she was struggling to find a fresh way into old material. Instead of opening with the wedding she had given Kay in *The Group*, she chose to portray her marriage to Harold John-srud from the perspective of its dissolution. Skipping three years, she began with an exuberant young Beekman Place matron marching in a May Day parade with John Porter, her handsome young lover.

If she bore little physical resemblance to that young woman march-ing into a future in which a brief flirtation with communism would lead to a longtime battle with Joseph Stalin, that young woman was nonethe-less very much on her mind—first because she herself was writing about it, then because she had been working since 1985 with Carol Brightman, who—having published their interview with great success in *The Nation*—was hoping to use further interviews to write a biography that would con-centrate on her generation's political and intellectual legacy.

Just as she continued to maintain relations with two very different colleges, she now had two very different biographers in her life. Carol Gelderman's research had unearthed unexpected details about her child-hood, and Carol Brightman's interviews were helping her to see her political past with fresh eyes.

But it wasn't only her political past that she was taking a second look at. In June 1987 she celebrated her seventy-fifth birthday. For her sev-entieth birthday there had been an elaborate masque incorporating the title of her books and a great influx of friends from all over the world. This time, there was a brother she hadn't seen in years. To Carmen Angleton she wrote of how it had been "at Carol Brightman's suggestion, which proved to be inspired."

**ELIZABETH HARDWICK**   Preston had been around all these years—worked in a bank or something in Maryland—but I never saw him until then. He and his wife, Ethel, came up for Mary's seventy-fifth birthday and Mary had them to dinner, and then they were down here for drinks. They stayed two or three days at the inn. He was the mildest person on earth. But there must have been some break.

**KEVIN McCARTHY**   Mary didn't see much of Preston, but I didn't see much of Preston myself—once a year or once every two years. He was a banker, living a different kind of life. Then one time Preston got up to Castine and the three of us said, "Why *didn't* we see more of one another?" Preston's a good guy. Quite articulate. He's got fairly strong opinions about things. But you think of him as having something to do with the world of business and commerce.

**ETHEL MCCARTHY**  The first time, when we drove up, she came to the door and gave me a big hug. You hear these wild tales about her, but I never saw any of that. I thought Mary was a wonderful person. I felt cheated not knowing her more. That first night there was a cocktail party at Elizabeth Hardwick's. Mary didn't say much. She sat and smiled and took everything in. She didn't have to make a fuss to be the center of everything.

**PRESTON MCCARTHY**  That night, Kevin arrived with a video camera. He just doesn't walk in. He bursts in. He's so outgoing. Mary wasn't. And I'm not. Mary could be quiet and still and be the focus. Mary could be on the couch and say, "Preston, come sit by me." I wish I could have talked more with Mary—to see if we could piece together our memories from childhood. But everybody would be talking to her and there'd be no time for a long talk—to say I did not think of Shriver and Aunt Margaret as abusive people. He simply believed in the old theory "spare the rod and spoil the child."

There was no time to really get to know this brother she had rediscovered. Or to hear him out. There was time, however, to finish the first chapter of her new intellectual memoir and to do a bit of preparing for her classes in the fall. But once she began again at Bard, the memoir had to be put aside.

**MARGO VISCUSI**  It's only my personal take on this, but I felt Mary's teaching at Bard took time from her writing. It's been presented to me as a very enriching experience for her. And the company of young people probably was good. But in the last years she must have been overwhelmed. I know she would come down and stay with us and she'd be correcting papers or writing evaluations. She'd take all of that extremely seriously. Always I'd ask her, "Are you getting any of your own work done?" She'd sort of sigh. Sometimes she'd say, "I've finished a chapter." But more often toward the end it was, "Well, I haven't been able to get to it." So when I saw her correcting undergraduate papers, I personally had a sort of resentment.

By her second fall of teaching, walking had become painful. That November, she came down with a bad case of bronchitis, which turned rapidly into pneumonia in both lungs.

**NICHOLAS AYER**  She seemed very frail that term. Jim West was obviously very worried about her. He came up to me one day and said, "Please try and get her to stop putting so much into this class." So I went up to her and said, "Look, why bother going in?" She got all the way up in the elevator that day and just turned around and went back down. She was that ill.

### FROM MARY MCCARTHY'S LETTER TO LOTTE KOHLER, NOVEMBER 18, 1987

Yesterday, today, and tomorrow, I got up and had my classes at home, chairs being furnished by Buildings and Grounds. Tomorrow afternoon I have another examination and possibly another x-ray but hope that the germs will have departed. We still count on going to Castine for Thanksgiving.

The X ray her doctors took that fall showed her lungs to be clear but a biopsy in Maine that Thanksgiving turned up another malignant lump in her breast—a lump that was removed on the spot. That January, in Paris, she began radiation. Having dealt with breast cancer once before, she was optimistic about her prospects.

### FROM MARY MCCARTHY'S LETTER TO ELIZABETH HARDWICK, JANUARY 7, 1988

Now my own news, which is good. I saw Dr. Bataini Monday night, to learn that those radium implants were not to be thought of in my case—the reasons are too complicated to explain—and that he will simply do radiation for six weeks. He feels this will take care of the little tumor, which is only half a centimeter big (I'd understood it was a centimeter). I must go three days a week—or is it five days a week?— for six weeks. His remarks, incidentally, tally perfectly with Dr. Palmer's findings. Now I must get to work to tell at least a dozen people that I'm not having radium implants and I must say I feel rather foolish doing so.

Five times a week she had to go out to a clinic in Neuilly. And it was in character for her to feel an obligation to set the record straight just as it was in character for her to speak of a "little tumor."

**SUSAN ANDERSON**   What was funny about Mary was that she had this very high level of sophistication about art and literature but when it came to medicine she had almost her own vocabulary. She would refer to cancer cells or a tumor and she'd say "cancer germs." And she'd always put everything into the diminutive. She'd say she had had "a small heart attack," "a little breast cancer." Or she'd say, "Now I take a little pill for my heart attack." I guess it was a way of reassuring herself and those around her.

She would later tell William Jovanovich that the trip to Neuilly provided a chance to see "a camellia bush bloom outside the clinic toward the end of the treatments." But the treatments resulted in one devastating side effect.

### FROM MARY MCCARTHY'S LETTER TO WILLIAM JOVANOVICH, APRIL 14, 1988

While I was having the radio-therapy I got a bad bronchial flu, with the result, apparently, that the rays affected a lung. I felt absolutely terrible for some time and suffered, above all, from shortness of breath, which made for great difficulty in walking and even in sleeping. It has finally been discovered, by my regular doctor, not the radiologist, that I have a severe insufficiency of oxygen in my blood, and so now I am being treated with a cortisone derivative, which appears to be working, though I'm not wholly recovered. What a bore.

She did not mention that she'd had to spend a week at the American Hospital. Or that she had been subjected to a battery of tests, which led her doctors to conclude that tissues in her lung had been "*sclérosés*" by the double assault of X rays and bronchial flu. Nor did she mention that after one of those tests—a bronchoscopy—there had been an episode that her doctors suspected had been a heart attack. All in all, her stay at the hospital had not been a happy one, although she had carried it off with her customary élan.

**DIANE JOHNSON** I remember visiting her when there was some problem with her lungs arising from radiation. She had flowers in the room and she looked beautiful. As a French friend of mine said, she had this way of being *toujours souriante*. She was always smiling, as though she were about to be photographed at any moment. Her expression was as though addressed to some larger circumstance. Her eyes were sparkling. And she was having her German lesson. Some aspect of her ongoing life was going on. She was fun to visit in the hospital. But my visit was interrupted by palpitations, and nurses rushing in, tearing off her clothes and "lie down next to this EKG machine," at which point I tiptoed out.

Confined to her hospital bed, she managed not only to have a German lesson but to give dictation to her secretary. And her very first night home, she put on a good dress and went out to a dinner party at Jane Kramer's. When it came time to leave for Castine, she had to use a wheelchair at the airport. By midsummer she had been put on cortisone for two weeks and was using two inhalators, eight times a day. Because the cortisone had dangerous side effects, her doctors could not leave her on it for very long. Somehow, through it all, she managed to work on her second intellectual memoir. And she managed to get herself back to Bard in the fall of 1988, but by then she was not the only one whose health was suffering.

**BARBARA DUPEE** It began to seem like every time they came to Bard, Jim got sick or Mary got sick. Someone had to drive them to the hospital or tell them what doctor to go to. Someone had to take them shopping.

**LEON BOTSTEIN** People take illness and debility in various ways. And what it showed in Mary's case was a capacity for intimacy, an enormous capacity for caring, a very affectionate and, finally, a very good person. Sharpness of tongue notwithstanding, a person of great character.

**JULIAN MULLER**   She was having trouble with her breathing. She had given up cigarettes and was intent on losing weight to ease the burden on her lungs. She was marvelous. She really stuck to it. She lost a lot of weight. After lunch one day, we talked as we strolled along. We'd stop and Mary would turn to talk to me. Then, after a little while, we'd stroll on. Once again we'd stop. And I suddenly realized that she needed these pauses to catch her breath, that this really was a serious problem for her. I don't think she liked that one damn bit. I don't think Mary liked the idea of being dependent upon anything, including her body.

It wasn't only her breathing that made walking so difficult. She was suffering from a blocked artery in her leg and from arthritis of the spine. For the moment, spinal surgery was out of the question, but a claudication, to remove the plaque from that troublesome artery, was a real possibility. That December, she and Jim West did not return to Paris for Christmas. Instead, they stayed on in their little Dutch house so that first thing in January she could have her operation at New York Hospital. Reuel was invited down to join them. There would be a big party the day after Christmas, which also happened to be the day after his birthday.

**MARGARET SHAFER**   Mary and I were talking and you know how Mary loved tradition. She said she was thinking of having a party on December 26, and I said, "St. Stephen's Day." "Oh, *St. Stephen's Day*," she said. Then she put that on the invitation. I think they were made up at Tiffany's. She had any number printed. They listed what was to be eaten: ham, eggnog, fruitcake. Some people laughed at her listing what was going to be served. Other people laughing annoyed Andy. She said Mary wanted people to know that it wouldn't be supper and it wouldn't be just eggnog and they could plan accordingly. The invitations didn't have any day of the week or anything like that so they could be used forever.

**BENJAMIN LAFARGE**   That was the first time I met Reuel and I liked him immensely. It couldn't have been easy to be the son of Edmund Wilson and Mary McCarthy, but I had the feeling that he'd dealt with it well enough. As best he could: by leaving the country, by being a professor of Slavic languages. I found Reuel to be a nice man, and that raised my estimation of Mary as a person. Of course that may be completely unrealistic, but I figured she couldn't have been a bad mother if her only child turned out to be a decent human being.

The claudication went as uneventfully as one might hope and she was well enough by the end of February to go on her own to London, to help celebrate Stephen Spender's eightieth birthday. Rather than stay at a hotel, she stayed with the Mostyn-Owens, who did not feel she was at all well. But then they themselves were in the throes of a divorce.

**KARL MILLER**   I saw Mary last in rather sad circumstances really. It was the conclusion of a marriage of two people that she had been friendly with for many years. Gaia Mostyn-Owen gave a dinner party for a large number of people. When I was talking to Mary, up came some Mediterranean man of about fifty or sixty who said he was a writer in Italy and then said, "I very much admire your *Stone of Florence*." She said, "*Stones*." I remember her saying it in that very sharp attractive way she had of speaking emphatically. She had this rheumatism in her hands, and she did seem frail. But her spirit was strong.

She was strong enough to correct a bit of misinformation and to seek a reconciliation with an old friend whose poor opinion of Hannah Arendt had caused her pain. And she was strong enough to make one last Easter visit to Italy.

**ISAIAH BERLIN**   We had a tremendous *froideur*, a great row—not a row, but a period of coolness—in later life. It lasted for three or four years. It was entirely about one thing, and one thing only: Hannah Arendt. Mary had profound feelings and deep loves and hatreds. I last met her at Stephen Spender's eightieth birthday and she was extremely affectionate to me. I was rather surprised. But I was delighted. And I responded. After our difficulties I didn't expect it.

**GORE VIDAL**   Barbara Epstein, Mary, and Jim were in Rome and we all had dinner out at a restaurant. Between us we ate about eight lobsters. We were all very fat and very very happy. "Should I have another?" Mary asked. It was my dinner. "Have three," I said. "We will soon be dead and the lobsters are dying, too." She ordered three more.

Back in Paris in April she took time to write a memorial for James Baldwin, whose writing she had always admired and who had joined with her and Stephen Spender to secure a prize for an ailing Edmund Wilson. Then, with death clearly on her mind, she wrote a piece for *Boston College Magazine*, in which she went as far as she would ever go in delineating the limits of her religious faith—a piece they never published, claiming that it arrived too late.

### FROM "A BELIEVING ATHEIST," PUBLISHED POSTHUMOUSLY IN *VASSAR VIEWS*, NOVEMBER 1992

Insofar as I, a believing atheist, have a foot in any religion, I am a Protestant. When I go to church on Easter Sunday, I go to a Protestant church, and when I die I hope that some kindly Protestant pastor will say last rites over me even though I am outside his Church. At least I am baptized, which will help[. . . .] I do not believe in God or an afterlife or in the divinity of Christ. But I am aware that Jesus did. He thought he was God's messenger to mankind. I feel that was a tragic mistake, but tragedy is no joke. He found virtue in suffering and taught the *Via Crucis*. I agree with that, though I certainly do not aim to illustrate it by imitation. He had an amusing mind, much given to paradox, as in the case of Magdalen, whom none of my relatives would have had in the house. I wish I believed in redemption, but I can't. Nonetheless it moves me, almost shakes me—depending on the music—to hear the *Qui tollis peccata mundi* of the *Agnus Dei*.

That spring Jim West was mugged in the hallway of their apartment building. Soon afterward, he had an operation on his leg. Although her own health wasn't up to it, she had already accepted several invitations. The first week in May, she was to be inducted into the American Academy of Arts and Letters. She was also slated to receive honorary degrees from Tulane University and Colby College and to deliver a talk at Yale. Because of his operation Jim West would not be able to accompany her to Tulane. He would have to join her later. Having accepted these invitations, she could not bring herself to cancel a single one of them, even though her husband was very much against her going on ahead without him. That April, before leaving for America, she threw one last big party, to which she invited Werner Stemans, her German teacher.

**WERNER STEMANS**  At the last party Mary had to sit down. Some people asked, "What are you going to do next?" And she said, "I want to do three books of my intellectual memoirs and then I want to do a book on Gothic cathedrals." I was flabbergasted. At that moment I knew there was something wrong. She wanted life. She wanted to live. So she was saying, I shall go on and on and on and I have to go very far and I see some sort of end but it's not mine and there, at that end I shall have finished all those books and after that we shall see.

She was no longer meeting with Werner Stemans twice a week. Once a week was almost more than she could manage; sometimes she would doze off before their session had ended. And she was no longer entertaining as much as she once had. But before she left for America she gave a final dinner party, to which she invited Diane Johnson, Cees Nooteboom, and Nathalie Sarraute.

**NATHALIE SARRAUTE**  There was a time when Mary and I didn't see much of each other. And then we saw each other again. I began to see her again because with time you forget things and I liked her very much. I loved her in a way. I was so sorry when I heard how ill she was. The last time I saw her, when I went to her house for dinner, she really looked tired. Mary seemed to know that life was unbearable, but she had parties anyway. She was more than brave. She was gallant.

**CEES NOOTEBOOM** Every time one went away in the last years, one thought, This will be the last time I see her. It was surprising how long it went on. After dinner, I walked Nathalie Sarraute home.

At her last session with her German teacher they actually finished the novel they were reading, *Marionett en Theater*, by Heinrich von Kleist. In all the years they had been together, it was the first time they came to the end of a book just as she was about to leave for Castine. The day she was to leave, Maria came to help her pack.

**MARIA FOURRIER** Ordinarily she never asked me to help her, but that time she could not fit all her things into her valise. That was the last time I saw Madame West and it was a sad moment because normally she was so happy. She embraced me but it wasn't the same as always. I sensed that other things were on her mind.

Jim West had warned that her spring itinerary would be too much for her, and he was right. But she felt she owed it to the people who had invited her. Once the two of them were back in Castine, it looked as though she would be able to take it easy. But without Maria she was doing almost all of the cooking. The young Polish girl Jim West had brought with him from Paris was of little help in the kitchen and then only with careful supervision. Furthermore she spoke only Polish and Russian.

**ALISON WEST** My stepmother was a very good cook, but that last time in Maine there was a bizarre lack of accompaniments. Too little spinach or too few vegetables. All of a sudden the planning started to fall off. And there just was never enough.

Alison came to stay. And Rosalind Michehelles, her old secretary, dropped by for a brief weekend visit in early August. Carol Brightman, who was now working on a volume of her correspondence with Hannah Arendt as well as a biography, came for lunch and stayed the night. Then, almost immediately, Kevin and Kate arrived with their children. And as soon as they left, Preston arrived with his wife Ethel.

**CAROL BRIGHTMAN** She was complaining about her respiratory weakness and she was coughing, but I didn't see her as being physically weaker. I saw her concentration was not what it had been. I was interviewing her for the Hannah Arendt book and she was jumping into the interviewing with enthusiasm but there was a more rambling quality to the discussions. There was a sort of make-work quality to our sessions, which there never had been before. I remember we talked about D. H. Lawrence. She was reading *Sons* *and Lovers* because she was going to be teaching a course on Hardy and Lawrence in the fall.

**PRESTON MCCARTHY**  The second year we came up, she was going to have a little cocktail party for Ethel and me. It turned out to be the whole town of Castine. People would call and ask if they could come, and she'd say of course. She was failing, but she insisted on having it, and on letting them all come. The week before she'd given one for Kevin.

**MARGARET BOOTH**  When it came time to leave, they were determined that they would drive from Castine to Bard in one day, and nothing anybody could say would deter them. That's the way they'd always done it and that's the way they were going to do it. There were going to be no concessions made by Mary.

The trip to Bard was made in one day, and they arrived in time to celebrate Labor Day with Rosalind Michehelles at a pig roast at Barrytown, where she had spent Christmas her senior year at Vassar with Maddie Aldrich and her family. But it was soon apparent that something was very wrong.

**BARBARA DUPEE**  Looking back on it, obviously from the very first moment she came, she was not feeling well. Jim had been noticing all summer that she was breathing strangely. Finally, she agreed to let Jim take her to this doctor in Red Hook. I called up when they got back, and Mary said, "Well, the doctor said that the cancer in the breast has leaked into around the lung." I said, "Oh, for God's sake, Mary, that can't be true." Then there were all these awful days and it was really doom. She wouldn't go to the hospital. And she wouldn't call the doctors in New York. For a couple of days Mary was sort of up and eating at the table. But she was getting sicker by the minute.

**MARGARET SHAFER**  The last time Fritz and I saw her, she had that beautiful look that dying people have, when their skin is so taut, the flesh is so taut. The eyes were very large and brilliant. It was an effort for her to talk, but she was terribly interested in what she was talking about. She was giving me the history of somebody's love affairs. She described this person's sexual history and life history, all the while finding it very hard to breathe. It wasn't malicious. It was just this is how people behave, this is what they're up to now.

**JAMES WEST**  I had begged her to go to the hospital. We finally had a little fight—not really, but I couldn't take it anymore. Her pain went through me. I loved her so much. And do. I said, "Mary, I have to tell you something. This is the seventh time this morning that you have told me how almost unbearable the pain is. I have urged you for a week to consider a doctor and a hospital and you must do that. You're not a doctor and I'm not, and we've got to help you." "Jim, what is the matter with you," she said. "I'm worn out, Mary, that's all, because you will not take the necessary steps to get on with this."

I knew at the same time I said it that she didn't want to go to the hospital because she was afraid it would be the last time. And she did want to live.

For a time at New York Hospital things seemed to be better. As always when she was in the hospital, her room was full of flowers and visitors. And as always, she was the perfect hostess as well as the perfect patient. Never complaining about the food. Never demanding of the nurses. Never asking for sympathy or pity.

**THOMAS MALLON**   When I went to see her in the hospital, she told me exactly how many cc's of fluid had been drained from her lungs. Now, you would say to another person, "Don't trouble yourself by telling me all that. Let's talk about something more pleasant." But you didn't think of doing that with her because you knew that she wanted to master her own illness—at least intellectually—the way she would master anything else. She was making deductions about it, trying to figure it out. To talk about such details provided her with an opportunity to *think* about the illness. That was the last thing you would deny her, because you would be denying her her chief pleasure in life.

She was not getting any stronger and it began to look as if she would not be teaching *Sons and Lovers* that term, or ever.

**MARGO VISCUSI**   Even at the end she was worrying about her students. I arrived at the hospital at noon to find she had put in a call to Bard and was expecting a call back. Susan Anderson was there and Mary could hardly speak—she had practically no breath—but she had dictated to Susan a list of questions for a class assignment. When someone from the school called, I read the list over the phone. I remember one of the questions had to do with Byron's *Don Juan* and the lady was all confused, so I spelled it out for her. That evening Mary went into intensive care. She was put on a respirator and we never heard her speak again.

**SUSAN ANDERSON**   I was supposed to be there just as a guest visiting but very quickly I realized how sick she was and I said, "Mary, why don't you let me stay around here for a while?" It was providential that I did. In the afternoon I accompanied her to a bone scan to see if the cancer had metastasized to the bone and all of a sudden she said, "I can't breathe." I told the technician to get a doctor right away. I was afraid she would have a cardiac arrest. They got her back to her hospital room, but her blood gases were terrible and they put her on the respirator. When I left her that night, she had been transferred to intensive care. She couldn't speak, but she pounded on my chest to try to tell me, "You knew I was sick." Then with her finger she drew a big question mark in the air, as if asking whether she was going to survive. I couldn't reassure her that she would, since her condition had become critical. I just told her I loved her very much and would be rooting for her. It was ten thirty at night by then and I asked, "Mary, do you want Jim and Margo to go home now?" She nodded yes.

From September 25 to October 25 she remained in intensive care, in a room with four beds, unable to speak, breathing on a respirator, with her hands tied down so that there would be no risk of her pulling out the tubes that were keeping her alive. During a good part of that time she appeared to be fully aware of what was going on around her and during a good part of that time she continued to have visitors.

**JAMES WEST**   I went three times a day to the hospital and as soon as I got there I would give her a little list of the people that had called. She was very pleased to know that Stephen Spender called from England or Anjo Levi called from France. A bunch of people. I went in one day and I listed five people and then Madame Hardy, who had sent her highest respects to Mary. Mary of course couldn't talk, but she smiled a little bit and then she burst into smiles and happiness because Madame Hardy was one of our white roses, which she loved and which had tiny little green dots on it.

**KATE MCCARTHY**   Jim and Alison took me in to see her and for a long time I held Mary's hand. I can't call it a reconciliation. There had been no falling out, just as there had never been a coming together. But I felt as though I could forgive her for whatever I might have been angry at her about. I felt that something was communicated to me. And I felt that hard as it had all been, she meant a great deal to me.

**DEBORAH PEASE**   She was not physically demonstrative, but she liked it when it was forthcoming from other people. I learned this with time.

**MIRIAM CHIAROMONTE**   I remember her at the hospital, when she was attached to all sorts of machines and couldn't speak, and she was really beautiful. I wouldn't have believed it. She was always beautiful.

**GAVIN YOUNG**   She was in this tiny little room with three other people bleeding and dying. You could hardly walk between the beds. I could see from her eyes that she did know that I was there. I held her hand and said things like "Mary, come on, get up, we'll go back to France and drink some champagne." I went back to see her four or five times. But I was going to California. I had to work.

**MARGO VISCUSI**   Reuel Wilson flew in from Paris, where he was spending a sabbatical year with his wife and young daughter. Outwardly he seemed calm, but I knew him enough to see that he was terribly distraught. He couldn't stay on forever, and leaving his mother in intensive care, on life support, must have torn him apart.

Diane Johnson's husband, John Murray, a pulmonary specialist, flew from Paris to New York to see if there was anything that could be done to treat the cancer, or, failing that, if there was any way they could get her off the respirator.

**CAROL BRIGHTMAN**   You did want to think that she could rise out of that bed, but gradually the information that I was getting from the doctors and nurses made it clear that that was not going to happen. There was one awful moment—we were all out in the hall, and Kevin was there and Reuel and Jim, and John Murray was describing the situation and fastening on this last hope, which was to try to make the pleural lining stick to her chest wall, to get the breathing tube out so that she could speak. I had been the last one in her cubicle or I had gone back in and she was in real distress. There was no nurse in there. She was tossing her head from side to side and I remember trying to hold my peace, but saying finally to John Murray, "There's no one in there with her and she seems to be in trouble." He went back in and that was the last time I saw her.

**MARY GORDON**   I waited too long to visit her. She couldn't speak at all, but she was in terrible pain, you could tell. It was only about three or four days before she died. I just held her hand because I knew she wouldn't know who I was. I just wanted to be there. Jim came in, and it was just terrible because this woman who had been so articulate had lost speech and could only groan in anguish. Jim came over to her and held her hand and he said, "You know who I am? I'm the guy who's been in love with you for twenty-eight years." That calmed her down.

**SUSAN ANDERSON**   There was something in Mary that made you want to take care of her and protect her. That made her friends want to do anything they could to help. Elizabeth Hardwick was very devoted to Mary and so was Margo Viscusi. Elizabeth can appear frail but she's very strong. She would take the crosstown bus, and she was there faithfully, day after day. I said to Mary, "I never really got to know Elizabeth before, but I see now why she's such a great friend." Mary smiled. She loved life and she'd fight to the finish, but I think the last week she'd given up—with good cause. That last week, when I'd get ready to leave, she'd start to cry. She'd never cried before. I asked her if she was afraid. And she shook her head no. I asked if she was depressed and she indicated no. I asked, "But are you in agony?" And she nodded yes. I came in one day and said, "You've really had it, haven't you?" And she indicated that yes, she'd had enough. She died in midafternoon. About two thirty. Jim was there with her. I'd expected it. I'd seen her the afternoon before. Elizabeth and Margo had been there that night.

She died on October 25, 1989, five weeks after she checked into the hospital, and by the time she died no one who cared for her wanted to keep her alive another minute. But that did not keep them from wishing it had not turned out the way it had.

**JAMES WEST**   I asked her in Paris one day, when I felt that I could, "Mary, what do you think of death?" We never had conversations like that. Period. Tears came in her eyes. "Jim, I cannot bear the idea that my life—all the music I've heard, the paintings I've seen, the books I've read, the things I've written—all the experience I've had will *stop* like that and then it's nothing." I can't think of Mary with equanimity.

**MARGO VISCUSI**   The thing that I miss the most—and it's curious because it has nothing to do with her literary genius or even her intelligence, though her intelligence is wrapped up in it—is this outpouring of affection. When you came into the room, her face would light up with pleasure. It was extraordinary. I've never gotten it from anyone else. Never.

**ELIZABETH HARDWICK**   When you entered the room and you were talking to her, something was always happening. She was so intelligent. And, you know, very eccentric in many ways. As I guess every person is when you really get to know them. Her mind was always full of something fresh and new. It was a great pleasure to be around her. I miss her terribly—every day.

**JANE KRAMER**   I feel very sentimental about her and I don't know why. I was never really sure what Mary really thought about me. Usually I like people who like me, and it's very clear-cut. If I don't know people's feelings about me, I'm very wary of them. With Mary I sometimes wondered, but it ultimately didn't matter. Mary was the one person I loved unequivocally.

**FRANCES FITZGERALD**   She was the bravest woman I ever met. In every respect. She would try anything. She was absolutely afraid of no one. And nothing. It wasn't that she was arrogant, either. It wasn't that at all. Watching her die, you realized how brave she was.

# Epilogue

The funeral was held at the Universalist Church in Castine. For her funeral she did not get the church where she had found a warm welcome, but she did get one large enough to accommodate the more than seventy people who came to pay their respects. Furthermore, she got a service she would have found admirable, conducted by Ed Miller—the retired Episcopal minister who had contributed so much to *Cannibals and Missionaries*—and planned with the help of Nicholas King, who shared her views on such matters.

The three musicians who played at the service had been secured by Sam Taylor. The 130th Psalm, which begins, "Out of the depths have I cried unto thee, O Lord," was read by Alison West. Elizabeth Hardwick and William Jovanovich delivered the eulogies. The hymn "O God Our Help in Ages Past" was chosen not merely because it would be familiar to most of the mourners but because it had been written by a dissenter, Isaac Watts.

She was buried on Halloween. The weather was so warm it was almost balmy, perfect for putting to rest a garden or for doing work in the yard. Unfortunately, the warm weather was not nearly so perfect for flying. Her brother Kevin's plane had been delayed by fog at Boston. But the rest of his family had made it in good time. His daughters Lillah and Mary were at the church, along with his wife, Kate. Preston had come with his two sons. Daniel West had flown in from Los Angeles. Reuel had remained in Paris.

Friends as well as family had made the long journey to Castine. At the service were the Viscusis, Eileen Finletter, Ben O'Sullivan, Rosalind Michehelles, the Stwertkas, David DuVivier, Andy Dupee, and the Shafers. Also in attendance were Elmer Wardwell and Woody Bateman, who worked on the property, Philip and Margaret Booth, the Tolmans, the Hatches, Jon Jewett, and Jim's aunt, Hope West. Alison had put a notice on the blackboard at the variety store down by the harbor, saying that everyone was welcome to come to the service.

From the church people went by car and by foot to the cemetery, which was a little less than a mile away, up on a hill overlooking Penobscot Bay. At the graveside Ed Miller read the 121st Psalm, which begins "I will lift up mine eyes unto the hills, from whence cometh my help" and then read "I am the Resurrection and the Life," from the Episcopal service. The day had remained soft and gray, with patches of sun breaking through the haze. As the casket was being lowered and Ed Miller was about to pronounce "ashes to ashes, dust to dust" for the final commital, Kevin came running up the hill. For a moment all was silent, while the crowd around Ed Miller parted and Kevin was pushed forward so he could stand by his sister's grave.

Afterward, Alison invited all the mourners to join the family back at the house for lunch. From a restaurant in Blue Hill, Alison had ordered filet de boeuf, warm potato salad, smoked salmon, petits fours, and extra glasses. It was agreed that the food was up to the deceased's high standard and that the occasion partook of that special excitement guests had come to expect at her parties. In the pantry were baskets filled with fruit and vegetables and eggs, arranged the way she always arranged them. Everywhere one turned, the rooms looked just as they always had when she was there.

The afternoon was warm enough for Nicholas King to make a careful survey of the garden and discover one great pale pink rose, Dr. Van Vleet, in full bloom. As the day wore on, guests began to start the long journey home. Some spoke of meeting again the following week at a memorial at the Morgan Library in New York. Both Alison and Daniel West stayed behind in the house with their father. That night, after the children in the village had returned from their trick or treating, Jim West lay down on the freshly turned earth at the cemetery for a quiet visit with his wife.

In theory the Morgan Library was ideally suited for a memorial service. The trouble was, the library's paneled auditorium could hold only two hundred people, and so on the afternoon of Wednesday, November 8, a fair number of friends and acquaintances found themselves locked out. Fortunately, this time Kevin was able to join Elizabeth Hardwick and William Jovanovich in paying tribute to his sister. Three of her friends also spoke. Reuel was unable to attend.

At the memorial service, Kevin read from *Memories of a Catholic Girlhood* and Elizabeth Hardwick made mention of his sister's unremitting hospitality to those who might see themselves as victims of her satire. James Merrill read "One Art," a poem by her fellow Vassar graduate Elizabeth Bishop, and William Jovanovich noted that, like all people of genius, she was "a contradiction to herself." Arthur Schlesinger recalled being dazzled by her beauty the first time he met her in the company of a husband seventeen years her senior and Nicholas King spoke of meeting her not many years later, when she was a beautiful young Portsmouth housewife. He did not speak, however, of his good friend Bowden Broadwater, her partner in this Portsmouth domesticity—whom she continued always to ask after and whom he secretly regarded as the major reason she had kept him part of her life.

Peter Maguire had not made it into the Morgan auditorium: "This door opened," he would later say, "and all of a sudden I'm getting elbowed aside by all these old men and old ladies and the next thing I know I'm standing outside in my Sunday best." Undaunted, he had gone off with Sara Powers to a nearby coffee shop, where they held their own memorial. By the time they were finished with their coffee and memories, the official ceremony had ended. Checking out the library one last time, they found Jim West among the stragglers on the sidewalk, standing off to one side, looking as if he did not know what to do next. In the end, they were able to tell him how sorry they were for his loss.

She had been Jim West's great love and in the last years she had taken up most of his waking hours. No matter how bad things had stood with her, there had been some comfort in knowing that he was necessary to her. Now, there was nothing more that she asked of him. For the moment, all he could do was return to a house everywhere marked by her tastes and prejudices, where he could take consolation in the tributes and obituaries that continued to drift in, while putting aside for safekeeping the letters of condolence he could not summon the energy to answer.

The morning after her death there had been a front-page obituary in *The New York Times*, by Michiko Kakutani, in which his late wife had been identified as "one of America's pre-eminent women of letters." The obituary, like a magazine profile by Kakutani that had preceded it, was at once rigorous and admiring. After touching on the tragedy of her childhood, her marriages and friendships, her courage and independence, and her legal troubles with Lillian Hellman, Kakutani had ended up recalling how in a recent interview she had said, "I couldn't live without feeling I know more than I did yesterday." The following day there was a brief editorial in the *Times*, celebrating her long career as a "contrarian" and speaking of her death as "a death in the family."

The Paris papers, too, had made much of her dying. But for them she was "*un personnage combattant*," an "*intellectuelle de toutes les batailles*," or "*une des pionnières du feminisme*," a literary Rosa Luxemburg or an American Simone de Beauvoir. The first might have amused her, the second not at all. But she might have been amused by Jane Kramer's memorial in the *International Herald Tribune*, particularly when Kramer, making much of the improbability of her dying, wrote, "[S]he had such a cajoling will, and such authoritative and relentless charm that I think most of us expected her to stand at death's door, looking beautiful in her lace stockings and her good pearls and one of her plaid pleated skirts, and flash her famous Mary McCarthy smile and say in that implacably gracious Vassar voice, 'I'm sorry, I have other plans.' "

Not surprisingly, the most acute and most moving tributes came from women who had known her. In the London *Observer*, Alison Lurie wrote, "Before Mary McCarthy, if an educated girl did not simply renounce ambition and agree to dwindle into a housewife, there seemed to be only two possible roles: the Wise Virgin and the Romantic Victim. You could give up love and devote yourself to intellectual pursuits, or you could abandon yourself to your emotions and feed the creative flame with bits of a broken heart. Mary McCarthy's achievement was to invent herself as a totally new sort of woman who combined sense and sensibility, who was both coolly intellectual and boldly passionate."

In *Time* magazine, Martha Duffy wrote, "Her most autumnal public moment came in a speech at the MacDowell Colony five years ago. 'We all live our lives more or less in vain,' she said. 'The fact of having a small *name* should not make us hope to be exceptions, to count for something or other.' For once, this piercing observer and tough social critic was wrong. She was emphatically an exception, and she counted."

During the five weeks she had been at New York Hospital, friends like Elizabeth Hardwick, Mary Gordon, and even Leon Botstein had filled in for her at Bard, but after her death her class was taken over by a teacher brought in from Fordham University. The Dutch cottage was packed up and the pretty Polish girl sent to live with Andy Dupee, who eventually found her a position with a family in the area.

For company his first winter alone in Castine, Jim West had a small portable television, set up on the counter in the kitchen, and two kittens found for him by Danny and Alison—one of whom he christened "B.B." after Bernard Berenson. During the winter half the roses in the garden were killed by frost, among them two beautiful climbers she had especially liked. It was the first time the garden had sustained such a loss.

That spring the apartment in Paris was put on the market and early that summer Jim West returned to France long enough to arrange for all the furnishings to be packed up and shipped to Maine. In late autumn the apartment in Paris was sold. In December, Jim West married Barbara Byrne, a widow from Bangor, whom he had first met as a student at Bowdoin and whom he met again that November when she spotted him while filing through his home on a local house tour. (The two of them would still be living there when he died in September 1999.)

According to French law, half the proceeds from the sale of the rue de Rennes apartment had to go to the offspring of the apartment's legal owner. Thanks to French law, Reuel received several hundred thousand dollars. There had been no such bequest in his mother's will. She had taken great care to arrange that Margo Viscusi and Eve Stwertka would serve as her literary executors, but she had made few other provisions for her death. Her last will had been written in 1982 and by its terms virtually all of her property had gone to Jim West.

Back when she was about to set off for Vietnam, she had viewed the writing of a will rather differently. Indeed, she had taken a positive pleasure in working out the details of a posthumous distribution of her favorite pieces of jewelry. But as death ceased to partake of the aura of a great romantic adventure and began to figure as a very real possibility, she had apparently lost her appetite for such pleasures.

At her death, she left no new will but she did leave a new, or final, chapter for the second volume of her autobiography—a chapter which she had sent off to *The New Yorker* just before her last trip to Bard and which had languished in the magazine's offices for months before it was returned to her executors, who then placed it with the *Paris Review*. This chapter told of how she came to marry Edmund Wilson—a tale owing much to a tantalizing blend of bemusement and rue and sheer unadulterated anger.

If there had been anything like a reconciliation with Wilson, there was no hint of that here. No hint that there had been a bittersweet reunion in the sixties when—as the two of them sat over drinks in Paris—she had admitted, "I was too young," and Wilson, caught up in the spirit of the moment, had countered by saying that, no, on the contrary, he had been "too old." The farthest she would go was to acknowledge that upon rereading the letters of their courtship she had discovered far more affection for him than she remembered ever having.

What she gave readers in this new chapter was the Minotaur at the height of his power, luring an innocent maiden into his lair and then tearing her from the arms of the younger man who truly loved her—a younger man whom she now realized she had loved very much.

The story as she told it read like a novel; indeed, the outline of this story already existed in *A Charmed Life*. In filling in this outline she painted Edmund Wilson as an overbearing villain and Philip Rahv as a great romantic hero. This change of heart may have owed something to the time bomb Wilson had left for her in his journals from the forties, where, years after the marriage had ended, he had inserted a long description of the lunatic behavior that had compelled him to commit her to Payne Whitney. And it may have owed something to the fact that if you are going to write about one great love, it is easier if you don't have to face him every morning over breakfast or rely on him to soap your back because you can no longer manage by yourself.

*Intellectual Memoirs* came out in the spring of 1992 and, thanks in large part to that third chapter, reviewers credited it with possessing the sort of moisture they had found lacking in its predecessor. The reviews were in fact mixed, but once again her opinions were a subject for debate and for the first time in years a book by her quickly sold out its first printing. Close to death, she had managed to startle those who believed they knew her. Even Elizabeth Hardwick, who had written the book's introduction, found cause to marvel at her candor.

In 1989, one could find college students who had never heard of Mary McCarthy. Ten years later she was better known—not for *The Group* or for any book she herself had written, but simply for the life she had led. *Intellectual Memoirs* played a part in this, as did Carol Brightman's biography and her annotated edition of the correspondence with Hannah Arendt. Also important was a change in intellectual fashion: as the second wave of feminism began to seem altogether too lacking in humor and altogether too ready to embrace the role of victim, Mary McCarthy was winning admirers among the more outspoken members of the next wave.

While she would have been amused to see Katie Roiphe and Camille Paglia rushing to embrace her, she would have been no less amused to see that every writer who saw himself blessed with a terrible childhood was writing a confessional memoir. Above all, she would have been amused to see that she had become the real-life model for characters in novels by two friends of hers.

In Diane Johnson's *Le Divorce*, she shows up as Olivia Pace, an American writer who serves coffee in Meissen cups on saucers without ridges and who has cast her spell upon the novel's narrator and heroine, teaching her that "it is not abnormal to have bitter or illiberal reactions to things, but it is wrong to act on them." In Thomas Mallon's *Aurora 7*, she appears as Elizabeth Wheatley, a fifty-year-old novelist who has just left her husband of eleven years at the altar (Bellini's altarpiece at the Frari in Venice) and who believes "*Someone* has to point out the world's general falling off in beauty, grammar and good sense." Elizabeth Wheatley goes on to save the life of the novel's eleven-year-old hero.

Not long after Mary McCarthy's death, Irving Howe would tell an interviewer, "I don't think *most* of her stuff will last. She wasn't a natural fiction writer. She was a satirist essentially, and satire, unless it's very remarkable, is always of the moment." Jason Epstein would do him one better, saying, "Her stuff was interesting—it was really first-rate—but she was very much of the moment and very much a personality and I don't think *anything* is going to last. But that doesn't mean much because most of what was written by her contemporaries isn't going to last. A lot of it was journalism—or journalism disguised as fiction."

Alison Lurie, whose early work she had championed, would beg to differ with the second estimate, noting, "What Mary McCarthy has done is pass into the common imagination. A lot of what was once new and surprising is no longer new and surprising." William Maxwell, who had first encouraged her to submit stories to *The New Yorker* and later served as her editor, would see things much as Alison Lurie did. He would in fact take Lurie's argument one step farther, saying, "The whole concept of lasting is based on a belief that posterity will be smarter than we are. And they won't be. There will just be other people like us living in a different time. I don't think *Memories of a Catholic Girlhood* will suffer in the slightest. That and the early stories. They are the most solid. And timeless. Even though they are about a particular period. The anguish underneath the highly polished surface is so real. Nobody could fail to respond to that. If people still have hearts, a hundred years from now they'll respond to it."

She herself might not have put it quite that way. But, all things considered, it sounds about right.

# Cast of Characters

*By Andrea Chapin*
*with Sally Arteseros and Trent Duffy*

**DANIEL AARON** (1912– ) is a writer and editor who was a longtime friend of Edmund Wilson and wrote the introduction to Wilson's *Letters on Literature and Politics*. He taught at Harvard for many years. His own books include *Writers on the Left: Episodes of Literary Communism*. His son, **JONATHAN AARON,** studied at the Sorbonne in 1962 and was a model for the character of Peter Levi in McCarthy's novel *Birds of America*.

**LIONEL ABEL** (1910– ) is a playwright, drama critic, professor, and translator. Among his books are *Metatheater* and *The Intellectual Follies*.

**WILLIAM ABRAHAMS** (1919–1998), a writer and editor, worked with such authors as Joyce Carol Oates, Pauline Kael, Lillian Hellman, Thomas Flanagan, Francis Steegmuller, and Jessica Mitford. He was also the editor of *Prize Stories: The O. Henry Awards* for more than three decades.

**FLOYD ABRAMS** (1936– ), a renowned First Amendment lawyer, successfully defended the right of newspapers to criticize public figures in *"The New York Times" v. Sullivan*.

**RENATA ADLER** (1938– ), a novelist, journalist, and film critic, was on staff at *The New Yorker* for twenty years. Her books include the novels *Speedboat* and *Pitch Dark* and a study of libel and the media, *Reckless Disregard*.

**A(LFRED). ALVAREZ** (1929– ) is a literary critic and author of books of fiction, nonfiction, and poetry. Among his works are *The Savage God: A Study of Suicide*, *The Biggest Game in Town*, and *Night*.

**SUSAN ANDERSON** was working as a registered private duty nurse when she met Mary McCarthy in 1984. She tended McCarthy during several of her illnesses.

**ROGER ANGELL** (1920– ) is well known for his baseball writing, published in *The New Yorker* and collected in such books as *The Summer Game, Five Seasons, Late Innings*, and *Once Around the Park*. He is a fiction editor at *The New Yorker*.

**CARMEN ANGLETON,** a longtime friend of Mary McCarthy, is the sister of James Angleton who was chief of counterintelligence for the CIA from 1954 to 1974.

**HANNAH ARENDT** (1906–1975), a close friend of Mary McCarthy, was a philosopher and writer. A student of Martin Heidegger and Karl Jasper in Germany before she immigrated to the United States, Arendt published over twenty books, including *The Origins of Totalitarianism, The Human Condition*, and the controversial *Eichmann in Jerusalem*.

**ARTINE ARTINIAN** (1907– ), a French literary scholar born in Bulgaria and educated in America, was chairman of the humanities division when Mary McCarthy taught at Bard College in 1945–46.

**EVE AUCHINCLOSS,** a writer and editor, has worked at *Mademoiselle* and *Connoisseur*, among other places.

**LOUIS AUCHINCLOSS** (1917– ), a lawyer and writer from an old New York family, has published over forty novels and short story collections, including *The Rector of Justin* and *The Partners*, and twenty books of nonfiction.

**SALLY AUSTIN** knew Mary McCarthy from Castine, where her family had a house since 1901. Her father, Chick Austin, was the director of the Wadsworth Atheneum in Hartford.

**NICHOLAS AYER**, the son of British philosopher A. J. Ayer, was a student of Mary McCarthy's at Bard College in the 1980s.

**JAMES BALDWIN** (1924–1987) is best known for his novels and essays. Several essays from his first collection, *Notes of a Native Son*, originally appeared in *Partisan Review*. His novels include *Go Tell It on the Mountain* and *Giovanni's Room*.

**WILLIAM BARRETT** (1913–1992) became an editor at *Partisan Review* in 1945 and began teaching philosophy at New York University in 1950. He published *The Truants: Adventures Among the Intellectuals*, a memoir of his *Partisan Review* years, in 1982.

**BERNICE BAUMGARTEN** (1903–1978) was Mary McCarthy's literary agent at Brandt & Brandt until her retirement. She was married to the writer James Gould Cozzens.

**SYBILLE BEDFORD** (1911– ) was born in Germany and lives in London. She is the author of seven books, including the novels *A Favourite of the Gods*, *A Legacy*, and *A Compass Error*.

**SALLY HIGGINSON BEGLEY** knew Mary McCarthy in New York and later in Paris. She has been a journalist and book reviewer.

**SAUL BELLOW** (1915– ), whose books include *The Adventures of Augie March*, *Herzog*, *Mr. Sammler's Planet*, and *Humboldt's Gift*, won the Nobel Prize for Literature in 1976.

**BERNARD BERENSON** (1865–1959) was an art historian and critic who lived outside Florence. He advised the art collectors Isabella Stewart Gardner and Henry Clay Frick; his many books include *Italian Painters of the Renaissance*.

**ISAIAH BERLIN** (1909–1997), a professor of philosophy at Oxford University for many years, was a legendary historian of ideas and a proponent of liberalism. His famous essays include "The Hedgehog and the Fox" and "Two Concepts of Liberty."

**GEORGES BERNIER** was the publisher of the French art magazine *L'Oeil* when he and his then wife, Rosamond, commissioned Mary McCarthy to do a book on Venice; the result, *Venice Observed*, was published in 1956.

**ROSAMOND BERNIER** is the author of *Matisse, Picasso, Miro As I Knew Them*. She is known for her lectures on art at New York's Metropolitan Museum of Art.

**JOHN BERRYMAN** (1914–1972) won the Pulitzer Prize in Poetry in 1965 for *77 Dream Songs* and the National Book Award in 1969 for *His Toy, His Rest*.

**ELIZABETH BISHOP** (1911–1979), a class behind Mary McCarthy at Vassar, was a poet, prose writer, and translator. In 1956, she won the Pulitzer Prize in Poetry for *Poems: North and South*.

**WALTER BLAIR** was a professor of English at the University of Chicago. In the summer of 1939, he leased his apartment to Edmund Wilson and his family.

**LOUISE BOGAN** (1897–1970), a poet, translator, and the poetry critic for *The New Yorker* for thirty-eight years, was a close friend of Edmund Wilson.

**PHILIP BOOTH** (1925– ) is a poet whose books include *Margins, Available Light*, and *Before Sleep*. He and his wife, **MARGARET,** were Mary McCarthy's neighbors in Castine, Maine. Their daughter, **MARGOT,** is a psychiatric social worker in private practice in Austin, Texas.

**NINA BOURNE** (1916– ) was Richard Simon's secretary at Simon and Schuster when Mary McCarthy's *The Company She Keeps* was published in 1942. She is now Vice President, Advertising, at Alfred A. Knopf. Her poems have appeared in *The New Yorker*.

**LEON BOTSTEIN** (1946– ), a historian, conductor, and music critic, is the president and chancellor of Bard College.

**MARY BRADY** was the wife of a Foreign Service officer at the American embassy in Moscow when Mary McCarthy met Jim West. Later, when her husband was stationed in Paris, she was McCarthy's secretary from 1967 to 1969.

**ALICE BRAYTON** entertained Mary McCarthy and Bowden Broadwater at Green Animals, her Portsmouth, Rhode Island, estate. Its topiary garden is now open to the public.

**CAROL BRIGHTMAN** (1939– ), a member of the Vassar class of '61, is a writer, editor, and teacher. Her biography, *Writing Dangerously: Mary McCarthy and Her World*, won a National Book Critics Circle Award. She edited *Between Friends: The Correspondence of Hannah Arendt and Mary McCarthy, 1949–1975*.

**BOWDEN BROADWATER** and Mary McCarthy were married in December 1946. The marriage lasted fifteen years. Now retired and living in New York City, Broadwater has worked as a writer, editor, and teacher.

**CLEANTH BROOKS** (1906–1994), co-editor of *The Southern Review* with Robert Penn Warren from 1935 to 1941, is the author of *The Well Wrought Urn: Studies in the Structure of Poetry*.

**ESTHER AND PETER BROOKS** met Mary McCarthy through Elizabeth Hardwick and Robert Lowell. The Brooks house in Dublin, New Hampshire, is where Mary McCarthy stayed after she was awarded the MacDowell Medal in 1984.

**LISA BROWAR** was a librarian at the Special Collections of Vassar College in the mid-1980s. She is now the Lilly Librarian at Indiana University.

**KEVIN BUCKLEY** (1940– ) was a Vietnam war correspondent for *Newsweek* and is now features editor at *Playboy*. He is the author of *Panama: The Whole Story*.

**TOM BUCKLEY** (1930– ) was a *New York Times* war correspondent when he met Mary McCarthy in Saigon in 1967. He is the author of *Violent Neighbors: El Salvador, Central America, and the United States*.

**WILLIAM S. BURROUGHS** (1914–1997) was a friend of Jack Kerouac and Allen Ginsberg. He is the author of the novel *Naked Lunch*. Among his other books are *Junkie* and *Cities of the Red Night*.

**MARGARET CARSON** was the publicist at the MacDowell Colony when Mary McCarthy received its medal for excellence in 1984.

**DICK CAVETT** (1936– ) was the host of a talk show on PBS when Mary McCarthy's 1980 interview resulted in a lawsuit by Lillian Hellman.

**JOHN CHAMBERLAIN** (1904–1995), a book critic and author, wrote for such publications as *The New York Times, The Wall Street Journal, Fortune,* and *Life.*

**ELEANOR "NELLIE" GRAY CHENEY** was Mary McCarthy's classmate at Vassar.

**NICOLA CHIAROMONTE** (1905–1972), a refugee from Mussolini's Italy, fought against Franco in the Spanish Civil War. In 1941, he came to the United States, where he went on to publish articles in *The Nation, The New Republic, Partisan Review,* and *politics.* Later, in Rome, he was cofounder and co-editor of *Tempo Presente,* a publication of the Congress for Cultural Freedom. He and his wife, **MIRIAM,** were Mary McCarthy's close friends.

**ELEANOR CLARK** (1913–1996), a class behind Mary McCarthy at Vassar, wrote for *Partisan Review* and was the author of such books as *Rome and a Villa* and *The Oysters of Locmariaquer.* She married Robert Penn Warren in 1952.

**CYRIL CONNOLLY** (1903–1974), a British critic and novelist, edited the British literary quarterly *Horizon,* which published Mary McCarthy's *The Oasis* in 1949. His collections of essays include *Enemies of Promise* and *The Unquiet Grave.*

**JANE COOPER,** the author of several poetry collections including *The Weather of Six Mornings* and *Scaffolding, New and Selected Poems,* taught poetry at the MFA program at Sarah Lawrence for more than twenty years.

**PAT COVICI** was owner of the publishing firm Covici-Friede, where Mary McCarthy worked as an assistant after her 1936 divorce. He was later an editor at Viking.

**MALCOLM COWLEY** (1898–1989), a critic, historian, editor, translator, and poet, was the literary editor of *The New Republic* from 1929 to 1940. His books include *Exile's Return: A Literary Odyssey of the 1920s.* His son, **ROB COWLEY,** has been both a book and magazine editor.

**THOMAS QUINN CURTISS** wrote theater reviews for the *International Herald Tribune.* His books include *The Smart Set: George Jean Nathan and H. L. Mencken.*

**AUGUSTA DABNEY,** Kevin McCarthy's first wife, is an actress who has appeared on Broadway in such plays as *Abe Lincoln in Illinois* and Edward Albee's *Everything in the Garden.*

**JOHN DAVENPORT** (1906–1966), for many years the literary critic for *The Observer,* was co-author with Dylan Thomas of *The Death of the King's Canary.* He had an affair with Mary McCarthy, which began in Rome in 1956.

**SIMONE DE BEAUVOIR** (1908–1986), French existentialist, novelist, autobiographer, essayist and editor, is the author of such books as *The Second Sex* and *The Mandarins,* which won the Prix Goncourt in 1954.

**PAUL DE MAN** (1919–1983), a Belgian-born writer and critic, first met Mary McCarthy when he worked at a bookstore in Grand Central Station. She recommended him for a teaching position at Bard. He went on to teach at Harvard, Cornell, Johns Hopkins and Yale, where he became one of the originators of deconstructionism. After his death, his reputation became clouded by the discovery that as a young man he had made extensive contributions to a pro-Nazi newspaper.

**VIDA GINSBERG DEMING** was an instructor at Bard College in drama and English literature when Mary McCarthy taught there in 1945–46. They later taught at Sarah Lawrence together and continued to see each other over the years.

**MADDIE ALDRICH DE MOTT** was Mary McCarthy's classmate at Vassar. Her first marriage was to the *New Yorker* writer Christopher Rand. She was the director of the Nairobi-based "Flying Doctors" for several years.

**JOHN DOS PASSOS** (1896–1970), author of such novels as *Manhattan Transfer*, *The 42nd Parallel*, and the *U.S.A.* trilogy, built his reputation as a left-wing writer. His views later shifted to the right. Dos Passos and his wife were friends of Edmund Wilson and lived on Cape Cod.

**F. W. "FRED" DUPEE** (1904–1979), a noted critic, was the literary editor of *New Masses* before he became an editor of *Partisan Review*. He later taught in the English department at Bard College. A collection of criticism, *The King of the Cats* (1965), was reissued in 1983 with an introduction by Mary McCarthy. While at Bard he married his former student, **BARBARA "ANDY" ANDERSON.**

**DAVID DUVIVIER,** a lawyer, and his wife, **ELEANOR,** were Mary McCarthy's friends in Paris. When he and his wife later moved to London, Mary McCarthy and Jim West often stayed with them.

**JEAN EAGLESON** was a classmate of Mary McCarthy at the Annie Wright Seminary in Tacoma, Washington.

**LEON EDEL** (1907–1997) received both the Pulitzer Prize and the National Book Award in 1963 for the second and third volumes of his five-volume biography of Henry James.

**HELEN KELLOGG EDEY,** Mary McCarthy's classmate at Vassar, went to medical school after having four children and became a psychiatrist.

**JASON EPSTEIN** (1928– ), an editor at Random House for more than forty years, helped start *The New York Review of Books* in 1963 with Barbara Epstein, his then wife; Elizabeth Hardwick; and Robert Silvers.

**JAMES FALLOWS**, former editor of *U.S. News & World Report,* is the author of *Breaking the News: How the Media Undermines American Democracy.*

**JAMES T. FARRELL** (1904–1979), a prolific writer of short stories and novels including the *Studs Lonigan* trilogy, published over seventy books.

**EILEEN FINLETTER**, a friend of Mary McCarthy from Paris, continued to see her after moving back to the United States.

**ELLEN BRADY FINN** was a young girl when Mary McCarthy moved down the road from her family in Portsmouth, Rhode Island, in 1949.

**FRANCES FITZGERALD** (1940– ) met Mary McCarthy in 1962, when she went to Paris after graduating from Radcliffe. The winner of the Pulitzer Prize and the National Book Award for her book on Vietnam, *The Fire in the Lake*, FitzGerald is also the author of *America Revised* and *Cities on a Hill.*

**JANET FLANNER** (1892–1978) wrote the "Letter from Paris" for *The New Yorker* for over fifty years. In 1966, her book *Paris Journal* won the National Book Award.

**MARIA FOURRIER** was the nurse to Jim West's children in Poland and accompanied them to France. Later, she served as Mary McCarthy's housekeeper in Paris and Castine.

**ELIZABETH FRANK** (1945– ), author of *Jackson Pollock*, won the Pulitzer Prize in 1986 for her biography of Louise Bogan. She started teaching at Bard College in 1982.

**SAMUEL G. FREEDMAN** was a reporter at *The New York Times* when he interviewed Mary McCarthy in 1984. He is the author of *Upon This Rock: The Miracles* *of a Black Church* and *The Inheritance: How Three Families and America Moved from Roosevelt to Reagan and Beyond.*

**BETTY FRIEDAN** (1921– ), noted writer and lecturer, is the author of the ground-breaking *The Feminine Mystique.*

**CHRISTIAN GAUSS** (1878–1951) was a professor of Romance languages and literature and later a dean at Princeton. Among his students were F. Scott Fitzgerald, Edmund Wilson, and John Peale Bishop.

**MARY GAZLEY** was a classmate of Mary McCarthy at Vassar College.

**CAROL GELDERMAN** (1935– ) is the author of *Mary McCarthy: A Life.* She has also published biographies of Henry Ford and Louis Auchincloss and the book *All the Presidents' Words.*

**MARTHA GELLHORN** (1909–1998), one of the first female war correspondents, also published novels, novellas, and a travel book. Her journalism was collected in *The Face of War* and The *View from the Ground.*

**BRENDAN GILL** (1914–1998), a longtime staff writer for *The New Yorker,* published novels, short stories, essays, film and dance reviews, architecture and literary criticism, and biographies of Tallulah Bankhead, Charles Lindbergh, Cole Porter, and Frank Lloyd Wright. He was a member of the MacDowell Colony's Board of Directors.

**JOSEPH GIOVANNINI** arrived in Paris in 1967 to pursue a master's degree in French. He is a practicing architect and has published architectural criticism in *The New York Times, Art in America,* and *Vanity Fair.*

**ROBERT GIROUX** (1914– ) was editor in chief at Harcourt Brace from 1948 to 1955. He became a partner at Farrar, Straus and Giroux in 1955. As a writer, he is known for *The Education of an Editor* and *The Book Known as Q: A Consideration of Shakespeare's Sonnets.*

**SYDNEY GOLDSTEIN** is founder and executive director of City Arts & Lectures, Inc., a reading and lecture program in San Francisco.

**MARY GORDON** (1949– ) received an enthusiastic quote from Mary McCarthy for her first novel, *Final Payments.* Gordon's subsequent books include the novels *Of Men and Angels, The Company of Women,* and *Spending* and a memoir of her father, *The Shadow Man.*

**HAROLD GRAY** was president of Bard College when Mary McCarthy taught there in 1945–46.

**CLEMENT GREENBERG** (1909–1994) was an art critic and an editor at *Partisan Review* and *Commentary.* His first essay on art and culture, "Avant-Garde and Kitsch," was published in *Partisan Review.* He is credited with promoting Jackson Pollock's career and helping to establish Abstract Expressionism as a major art movement.

**DAVID GRENE**, a classics scholar from Ireland, audited Edmund Wilson's lectures at the University of Chicago during the summer of 1939. For many years he has been a member of the Committee on Social Thought.

**BETH GRIFFITH** was a classmate of Mary McCarthy at Annie Wright Seminary in Tacoma, Washington.

**JOHN GROSS** (1935– ), a writer and editor, is theater critic of the *London Sunday Telegraph.* He was editor of the *Times Literary Supplement* and served on the staff of *The New York Times.* His books include *Shylock: A Legend and Its Legacy.*

**MIRIAM GROSS** (1939– ) has been literary editor of the *London Sunday Telegraph* since 1991 and was deputy literary editor at *The Observer.* Her publications include *The World of George Orwell* (editor) and *The World of Raymond Chandler* (editor).

**DORIS GRUMBACH** (1918– ) is a biographer, literary critic, and novelist. Her book about Mary McCarthy, *The Company She Kept,* was published in 1967. She is the former literary editor of *The New Republic.* Recent books include *Extra Innings: A Memoir* and the novel *Life in a Day.*

**PEGGY GUGGENHEIM** (1898–1979) was one of the twentieth century's major collectors of contemporary art. In 1946 she settled in a *palazzo* in Venice, where she stayed for the rest of her life. Mary McCarthy portrayed her as Polly Herkimer Grabbe in the short story "The Cicerone."

**ELINOR COLEMAN GUGGENHEIMER,** Mary McCarthy's classmate at Vassar, became commissioner for consumer affairs for New York City and served on its Parks Commission.

**DAVID HALBERSTAM** (1934– ) began his career as a war correspondent for *The New York Times* and political reporter. His books include *The Best and the Brightest, The Powers That Be,* and *The Reckoning.*

**JANET HALVERSON** was a designer and an art director at Harcourt Brace when she was assigned to work on Mary McCarthy's *The Stones of Florence.*

**ANNA MATSON HAMBURGER** became friends with Mary McCarthy when the Wilsons moved to Cape Cod in the fall of 1939. Her husband, Norman Matson, and Edmund Wilson had known each other for years. She later married Philip Hamburger.

**PHILIP HAMBURGER** (1914– ) became a staff writer for *The New Yorker* in 1939. His book *Friends Talking in the Night: Sixty Years of Writing for The New Yorker* was published in 1999.

**ELIZABETH HARDWICK** (1916– ), a noted critic and fiction writer, was one of Mary McCarthy's closest friends. A founding editor of *The New York Review of Books,* she is the author of four collections of essays, including *Seduction and Betrayal: Women and Literature* and *Sight Reading.* Her novel *Sleepless Nights* won the National Book Award. She married Robert Lowell in 1949; they were divorced in 1972.

**FRANCIS HASKELL** (1928– ), a noted British art historian, met Mary McCarthy in Venice in 1955. His books include *Patrons and Painters, Rediscovered in Art,* and *History and Its Images.*

**ROSILLA HORNBLOWER HAWES,** Mary McCarthy's classmate at Vassar, joined the National Consumer's League soon after graduation.

**DAPHNE HELLMAN,** married for many years to Harry Bull, editor of *Town and Country,* was a New York debutante who worked as a model and later became a professional jazz harpist.

**LILLIAN HELLMAN** (1905–1984) was the author of many successful plays, including *The Children's Hour* and *The Little Foxes.* Her three volumes of memoirs—*An Unfinished Woman, Pentimento,* and *Scoundrel Time*—brought her even greater success. She sued Mary McCarthy for slander in 1980 for $2.25 million.

**EVELYN HOFER,** a German-born photographer, is known for her fine photographs of buildings, cities, and landscapes. She was the photographer for Mary

McCarthy's book *The Stones of Florence* and collaborated with the writer V. S. Pritchett on *London Perceived* and *New York Proclaimed.*

**SIDNEY HOOK** (1902–1989), a philosopher, political theorist, writer, and educator, was one of the first important members of the American Communist Party to turn against Stalin. In the late 1940s he was a member of *Partisan Review*'s editorial board. His books include *Marx and the Marxists: The Ambiguous Legacy.*

**MAUREEN HOWARD** (1930– ), author of such novels as *Grace Abandoning* and *Expensive Habits*, has also edited several collections of essays.

**IRVING HOWE** (1920–1993) was a literary critic and the founding editor of *Dissent* magazine. Among his books are *Politics and the Novel, Decline of the New*, and *World of Our Fathers,* which won the National Book Award in 1976. For many years he was a professor of English at the City University of New York.

**RANDALL JARRELL** (1914–1965), a poet, critic, and novelist, won the National Book Award in Poetry for *At the Washington Zoo.* Gertrude, one of the main characters of his novel, *Pictures from an Institution*, bears a striking resemblance to Mary McCarthy.

**GARDNER JENCKS** was a concert pianist and composer. He, his wife, **RUTH,** and their children were friends of Mary McCarthy on Cape Cod. His daughter, **PENELOPE,** is a sculptor; his son, **CHARLES,** is an architectural historian.

**EUNICE CLARK JESSUP,** Mary McCarthy's classmate at Vassar, wrote for *Fortune* and *Common Sense* and published a translation of fables by La Fontaine. Her first husband was Selden Rodman and her second was Jack Jessup, editor of *Fortune.* In 1946 she gave the wedding reception for Mary McCarthy and Bowden Broadwater.

**JON JEWETT** lives in Castine, Maine, and is a licensed real estate agent.

**DIANE JOHNSON** (1934– ), the author of fiction, biography, essays, and memoir, divides her time between Paris and San Francisco. Her novels include *The Shadow Knows* and *Le Divorce.*

**HAROLD JOHNSRUD** (1903–1939), an actor, playwright and director, was the first of Mary McCarthy's four husbands. They were married in June 1933 and divorced in 1936. Johnsrud, who acted in such classics as Maxwell Anderson's *Winterset* and Archibald MacLeish's *Panic*, was in the cast of *Key Largo* when he died in a fire at the Hotel Brevoort.

**JAMES JONES** (1921–1977) won the National Book Award in 1951 for *From Here to Eternity.* Subsequent novels include *The Pistol* and *The Thin Red Line.* Mary McCarthy became friends with Jones and his wife, **GLORIA,** when they lived in Paris.

**WILLIAM JOVANOVICH** (1920– ) became Mary McCarthy's publisher at Harcourt Brace in 1955. His books include *New Barabbas*, a collection of essays.

**WARD JUST** (1935– ) was a highly regarded correspondent in Vietnam for *The Washington Post.* He went on to write many novels, including *Jack Gance* and *A Dangerous Friend.*

**PAULINE KAEL** (1919– ) wrote about movies for *The New Yorker* for more than twenty years. Her film criticism is collected in thirteen volumes, including *I Lost It at the Movies* and *Deeper into Movies*, for which she won the National Book Award.

**ALFRED KAZIN** (1915–1998), writer, literary critic, and teacher, is the author of such books as *On Native Grounds, A Walker in the City*, and *An American Procession.*

**GEORGE KENDALL** (1902–1998) was the director of the MacDowell Colony from 1951 to 1970.

**BARBARA KERR,** an old friend of Adlai Stevenson who worked in his 1952 campaign for the presidency, has been managing editor of *Mademoiselle*, executive editor at *Essence*, an editor at *Harper's Bazaar*, and an editorial writer for the *Boston Traveler*.

**TERENCE KILMARTIN** (1922–1991), literary editor at *The Observer* from 1952 to 1986, is best known for his translations of Proust, including *Remembrance of Things Past* (revision of the C. K. Scott Moncrieff translation). He was editor and translator of *Marcel Proust: Selected Letters*.

**NICHOLAS KING** (1924–1992) met Mary McCarthy when she was living in Portsmouth, Rhode Island, with Bowden Broadwater. King worked for the Associated Press in Paris and then at the American embassy. At the time of his death he was head of the Foreign Press Association in New York City.

**ANNA KITCHEL** (1882–1959), Mary McCarthy's advisor at Vassar, was the author of *George Lewes and George Eliot* and *Quarry for Middlemarch*.

**ARTHUR KOESTLER** (1905–1983), the Hungarian-born British novelist, was an anti-fascist and anti-Communist. His books include *Darkness at Noon*.

**LOTTE KOHLER,** who immigrated to the United States in 1955, taught German at City College in New York City for many years. The co-executor, with Mary McCarthy, of Hannah Arendt's estate, she has edited *The Correspondence of Hannah Arendt and Karl Jaspers* and a forthcoming volume of letters between Arendt and her husband, Heinrich Blücher.

**JEROME KOHN** worked as Hannah Arendt's research assistant at the New School for Social Research from 1969 to 1975. He has been on the faculty there since 1976 and also teaches philosophy at Cooper Union. He is the editor of Hannah Arendt's *Essays in Understanding: 1930–1954*.

**JANE KRAMER,** whose books include *The Last Cowboy*, *Unsettling Europe* and *The Politics of Memory*, became *The New Yorker*'s Paris correspondent in 1978.

**BENJAMIN LAFARGE** was the chair of the literature division of Bard College when Mary McCarthy taught there in the 1980s. He is a distant cousin of Maddie Aldrich De Mott.

**BARBARA DOLE LAWRENCE** was a classmate of Mary McCarthy at the Annie Wright Seminary.

**ROBERTA LEIGHTON** was a copy editor for Harcourt Brace for many years. She worked on all of McCarthy's books from *The Stones of Florence* through *How I Grew*.

**MARIA LEIPER** was a talented young editor at Simon and Schuster when she acquired Mary McCarthy's *The Company She Keeps*. She died in an automobile accident in 1998.

**PATSY LEO** became Mary McCarthy's secretary in 1981 while her husband was the minister at the American Cathedral in Paris.

**ANGÉLIQUE "ANJO" LEVI,** a Paris friend of Mary McCarthy, translated *The Company She Keeps* and many of McCarthy's other books into French. She and her husband, **MARIO,** became close to McCarthy during summers in Bocca di Magra, Italy.

**HARRY LEVIN** (1912–1994) was a professor of comparative literature at Harvard and a contributor to *Partisan Review*. Among his books are *Symbolism and Fiction*,

*Grounds for Comparison,* and *Memories of the Moderns.* He and his wife, **ELENA,** were friends of Edmund Wilson for many years.

**HELEN DOWNES LIGHT** was Mary McCarthy's classmate at Vassar.

**ROBERT LINSCOTT** was Mary McCarthy's editor at Houghton Mifflin and brought her with him when he moved to Random House.

**ROBERT "CAL" LOWELL** (1917–1977) was a poet, writer, and translator. His many collections of verse include *Lord Weary's Castle, Life Studies,* and *The Dolphin,* which won the Pulitzer Prize in Poetry in 1974. He was married to the writers Jean Stafford, Elizabeth Hardwick, and Caroline Blackwood.

**ALISON LURIE** (1926– ) has written children's books and nonfiction, but is perhaps best known for her novel *The War Between the Tates.* She won the Pulitzer Prize in Fiction for *Foreign Affairs.*

**J(AMES). H(ENRY). MCCARTHY,** Mary McCarthy's paternal grandfather, managed the family's grain elevator holdings in Minneapolis. His wife was **ELIZABETH "LIZZIE" SHERIDAN MCCARTHY.** They had three sons, **HARRY, ROY** (Mary's father), and **LOUIS.**

**KEVIN MCCARTHY** (1914– ), Mary McCarthy's brother, has had a successful career as a stage, movie, and television actor. He played leading roles in many Broadway productions, was in the movie version of *Death of a Salesman,* and starred in the original *Invasion of the Body Snatchers.* **KATE CRANE MCCARTHY,** his second wife, is a lawyer and writer.

**PRESTON MCCARTHY** (1915– ), Mary McCarthy's brother, is a retired bank executive in Wilmington, Delaware. **ETHEL MCCARTHY** is his wife.

**J. D. MCCLATCHY'S** books of poetry include *Scenes from Another Life, Stars Principal,* and *The Rest of the Way.* He is the editor of the *Yale Review.*

**DWIGHT MACDONALD** (1906–1982) was an editor at *Fortune* magazine and a writer for *The Nation* before he joined the editorial board of *Partisan Review.* In 1944 he created and edited the magazine *politics.* Until his death he was a staff writer for *The New Yorker.* His first wife, **NANCY RODMAN MACDONALD,** a schoolmate of Mary McCarthy at Vassar, was the business manager at *Partisan Review,* managing editor at *Politics,* and founder of Spanish Refugee Aid. One of their sons, **MIKE MACDONALD,** was a childhood friend of Reuel Wilson. **GLORIA MACDONALD** was Dwight Macdonald's second wife.

**KAY MCLEAN** was Mary McCarthy's classmate at Vassar.

**MARTHA MCGAHAN,** Mary McCarthy's classmate at Vassar, managed the San Francisco office of Time-Life for many years.

**CHARLES MCGRATH,** McCarthy's last editor at *The New Yorker,* is the editor of *The New York Times Book Review.*

**PETER MAGUIRE** was a student of Mary McCarthy at Bard College in the 1980s.

**NORMAN MAILER** (1923– ) is the author of novels, short stories, screenplays, nonfiction, and essays. His novels include *The Naked and the Dead* and *Ancient Evenings.* Among his works of nonfiction is the Pulitzer Prize–winning *The Armies of the Night.*

**THOMAS MALLON,** a novelist and essayist, is the author of three books of nonfiction: *A Book of One's Own, Stolen Words,* and *Rockets and Rodeos and Other American Spectacles.* His novels include *Aurora 7, Henry and Clara,* and *Dewey Defeats Truman.* Mallon met Mary McCarthy when he was teaching English at Vassar in 1982.

**ELISABETTA "NICKY" MARIANO** was Bernard Berenson's companion for many years. In 1965, she published *Berenson Archive: An Inventory of Correspondence Compiled on the Centenary of the Birth of Bernard Berenson.*

**MARGARET MARSHALL** (1901–1974) was co-author, with Mary McCarthy, of a five-part series for *The Nation* titled "Our Critics, Right or Wrong." Marshall was the literary editor of *The Nation* for twenty-five years.

**WILLIAM MAXWELL** (1908– ), an editor at *The New Yorker* for forty years, worked with Mary McCarthy on her fiction. He is best known for the novels *The Folded Leaf* and *So Long, See You Tomorrow*. Among his other books are *All the Days and Nights: The Collected Stories*; *Ancestors: A Family History*; and *The Inmost Dream,* a collection of essays and reviews.

**MARY MEIGS,** the author of *Lily Briscoe: A Self-Portrait*, was a young painter in Newport, Rhode Island, when she first met Mary McCarthy and Bowden Broadwater. Later Meigs bought a house next to theirs on Cape Cod.

**JAMES MERRILL** (1926–1995) was the author of over twenty books of poetry, including *Divine Comedies* and *The Changing Light at Sandover*. Awarded the National Book Award in Poetry twice and the Pulitzer Prize in Poetry, he was also a novelist, playwright, and essayist.

**ROSALIND MICHEHELLES,** the niece of Mary McCarthy's Vassar classmate Maddie Aldrich De Mott, served as McCarthy's secretary in Paris from 1977 to 1981.

**KARL MILLER,** head of the English department at London University and founder of *The London Review of Books*, met Mary McCarthy in the 1950s when he was at Harvard University on a graduate fellowship. His books include *Doubles: Studies in Literary History, Authors*, and *Rebecca's Vest: A Memoir.*

**MARGARET MILLER**, who was a year behind Mary McCarthy at Vassar, remained her friend until her third marriage.

Czesław Miłosz (1911– ), a poet, critic, essayist, novelist, and translator, emigrated from Poland to the United States in 1960. His books include *Collected Poems 1931–1987* and *Facing the River: New Poems*. He was awarded the Nobel Prize for Literature in 1980.

**INGE MORATH** (1923– ) was the photographer for Mary McCarthy's book *Venice Observed* (1956). Among her books are *Portraits* and *Chinese Encounters,* a collaboration with her husband, the playwright Arthur Miller.

**GEORGE L. K. MORRIS** was the primary backer of the new *Partisan Review,* contributing about $3000 annually in operating costs. An abstract painter from an old New York family, Morris was considered a political innocent by his *PR* colleagues.

**WILLIAM MOSTYN-OWEN** (1929– ) was a young British art researcher who worked for Bernard Berenson at I Tatti from 1953 to 1959. In 1956 he prepared a new edition of Berenson's *Lorenzo Lotto*. He later worked at Christie's. More than once, the Wests spent Christmas with Mostyn-Owen and his then wife, Gaia Servadio, in Scotland.

**JULIAN MULLER** was editor in chief at Harcourt Brace for years, shepherding many of Mary McCarthy's books to publication.

**NATALIA DANESI MURRAY**, a longtime friend of Janet Flanner, was the head of the New York office of the Italian publishing house Mondadori and later the director of the New York office of Rizzoli.

**FRANI BLOUGH MUSER** was a close friend of Elizabeth Bishop at boarding school. At Vassar, she became Mary McCarthy's best friend. For many years she was active and published in the field of musicology.

**NICHOLAS NABOKOV,** a Russian-born composer and an ardent anti-Stalinist, was Vladimir Nabokov's cousin. His son, **IVAN NABOKOV,** returned from the United States to live in Paris in 1963, where he is now an editor at Editions Plon.

**VLADIMIR NABOKOV** (1899–1977), a Russian émigré, was a celebrated novelist, literary critic, translator, and essayist. His books include the novels *Lolita* and *Pale Fire* and the memoir *Speak Memory.*

**LUISA VERTOVA NICOLSON** is an art historian. She worked as Bernard Berenson's assistant from 1945 until his death in 1959, and also translated his books into Italian.

**CEES NOOTEBOOM** (1933– ), a Dutch poet, travel writer, playwright, and novelist, became Mary McCarthy's close friend after meeting her in Edinburgh at the International Writers' Conference in 1962. His novel *Rituals* won the 1982 Pegasus Prize for Literature.

**ELLEN ADLER OPPENHEIM** was Mary McCarthy's student at Bard College. She is the chair of the Stella Adler Conservatory of Acting.

**GEORGE ORWELL** (1903–1950) is known for his short novels *Animal Farm* and *Nineteen Eighty-four*, as well as for *Homage to Catalonia* and *Shooting an Elephant and Other Essays.*

**SONIA BROWNELL ORWELL** was a young editor at the literary quarterly *Horizon* when she married Orwell four months before he died of tuberculosis. She later worked as an editor at Weidenfeld and Nicolson. Her friendship with Mary McCarthy was close and on occasion vexed.

**BENJAMIN O'SULLIVAN** was Mary McCarthy's longtime lawyer.

**MAX PALEVSKY,** who sold his company, Scientific Data Systems, to Xerox for a substantial sum of money, was a good friend of Lillian Hellman in the years before her death.

**DEBORAH PEASE,** a poet and former publisher of *Paris Review*, was taking her college year abroad in Paris when she met Mary McCarthy in 1964. Her books include the novel *Real Life* and *Another Ghost in the Doorway.*

**ELEANOR PERÉNYI** (1918– ) is the author of a biography of Franz Liszt published in 1974 and *Green Thoughts: A Writer in the Garden.*

**WILLIAM PHILLIPS** (1907– ) was one of the two founding editors of *Partisan Review*. His books include *A Sense of the Present* and *A Partisan View: Five Decades of Literary Life.*

**GEORGE PLIMPTON** (1927– ), cofounder and editor of *Paris Review*, has written many books on sports, including *Paper Lion* and *Shadow Box*, and has published oral biographies of Edie Sedgwick (with Jean Stein) and Truman Capote.

**DAWN POWELL** (1897–1965), the author of fifteen novels, was a close friend of Edmund Wilson. Her novels include *Come Back to Sorrento* and *Angels on Toast.*

**SARA POWERS** was Mary McCarthy's secretary at Bard College in the fall of 1986.

**HAROLD PRESTON** (1858–1938), Mary McCarthy's maternal grandfather, was a

Seattle lawyer who served as president of the Washington State Bar Association in 1898 and of the Seattle Bar Association in 1909–10. His wife was **AUGUSTA MORGENSTERN PRESTON.** Their children were **FRANK, TESS** (Mary's mother), and **HAROLD JR.**

**PHILIP RAHV** (1908–1973), a Russian-born intellectual and political theorist, was one of the founding editors of *Partisan Review.* His *Essays on Literature and Politics, 1932–1972,* published in 1978, included a memoir by Mary McCarthy. Rahv and McCarthy lived together from the late spring of 1937 until just before her marriage to Edmund Wilson in 1938.

**JONATHAN RANDAL** (1933– ), a *New York Times* correspondent in Vietnam, met Mary McCarthy in Saigon in 1967. He has worked at *The Washington Post* since 1969 as a roving correspondent and has been based in Paris for many years.

**JOHN RICHARDSON** (1924– ) is an art critic, editor, and biographer whose books include *Manet.* To date, two volumes of his *Life of Picasso* have been published: *The Early Years, 1881–1906,* and *The Painter of Modern Life, 1907–1917.*

**YALE RICHMOND** was in the Foreign Service in Warsaw with James West when he met Mary McCarthy in December 1959.

**ROBINSON RISNER** was a prisoner of war in North Vietnam for seven years. He is the author of *The Passing of the Night* (1974).

**SELDEN RODMAN** (1909– ), a poet, critic, free-lance travel writer, and well-known collector of Haitian art, was one of the founding members of the left-wing intellectual journal *Common Sense.*

**HAROLD ROSENBERG** (1906–1978) was a writer, lecturer, and art critic for *The New Yorker* from 1966 to 1978. He is credited with coining the term "action painting" to define the work of a group of New York artists in the 1950s, which included Jackson Pollock, Willem de Kooning, and Arshile Gorky.

**EMMANUEL "MANNIE" J. ROUSUCK,** Mr. Sheer in Mary McCarthy's story "Rogue's Gallery," was her sorely beset boss at the Carleton Galleries. Later he became the head of Wildenstein Gallery's department of European painting and a friend and advisor to Paul Mellon.

**COUNTESS CRISTINA RUCELLAI,** a Florentine aristocrat, met Mary McCarthy in the spring of 1957.

**JULIA DENISON RUMSEY** was Mary McCarthy's classmate at Vassar.

**ANTHONY SAMPSON** (1926– ) was a member of the editorial staff of *The Observer* for twelve years. His many books include *Anatomy of Britain* and *Company Man: The Rise and Fall of Corporate Life.*

**FATHER PATRICK SAMWAY,** a Jesuit priest with a doctorate in philosophy, has written *Walker Percy: A Life* as well as several books on Faulkner.

**CYNTHIA MCCARTHY SANDBERG,** a first cousin of Mary McCarthy, is the daughter of Louis McCarthy, Roy McCarthy's younger brother.

**HELEN SANDISON** (1884–1978) was the chairman of the English department at Vassar College and an Elizabethan scholar. Her lifetime work was an edition of the works of Sir Arthur Gorges.

**NATHALIE SARRAUTE** (1900–1999) a pioneer of the *nouveau roman,* was born in Russia and educated in Paris. She practiced law in Paris before publishing her first book, *Tropisms.* She was the author of novels, essays, plays, and the memoir *Childhood.*

**JEAN-PAUL SARTRE** (1905–1980), French existentialist and author of novels, plays, screenplays, biographies, literary and political criticism, refused the Nobel Prize in Literature in 1964. He wrote more than eighty books, including *Nausea* and the play *No Exit*.

**NORA SAYRE** is known for her articles, essays, and book reviews. She is the author of *Previous Convictions: A Journey Through the 1950s*.

**ARTHUR M. SCHLESINGER JR.** (1917– ) has written over fifteen books on American political history, including *The Age of Jackson, The Age of Roosevelt*, and *A Thousand Days: John F. Kennedy in the White House*. He has received the Pulitzer Prize for History and for Biography, and two National Book Awards. His first wife, **MARIAN SCHLESINGER,** published the memoir *Snatched from Oblivion*. Their daughter, **CHRISTINA SCHLESINGER,** is an artist.

**DELMORE SCHWARTZ** (1913–1966) was a poet and short story writer whose "In Dreams Begin Responsibilities" was the lead piece of fiction in the first issue of the new *Partisan Review*. It was also the title story of a collection published in 1938, which was followed by *The World Is a Wedding* in 1948. Saul Bellow's *Humboldt's Gift* presents a fictionalized version of his tragic decline.

**GAIA SERVADIO,** an Italian journalist and novelist, was married for many years to William Mostyn-Owen. Several of her books have appeared in English; McCarthy's favorite was *Melinda*.

**FRITZ SHAFER** was the college chaplain and a lecturer in philosophy when Mary McCarthy taught at Bard in 1945–46. He and his wife, **MARGARET,** became friends of McCarthy.

**WILLIAM SHAWN** (1907–1992) was the editor of *The New Yorker* from 1952 to 1987. He worked with McCarthy on her Venice and Florence pieces for the magazine as well as on Hannah Arendt's *The Life of the Mind*.

**DIXIE SHERIDAN** was the assistant to Vassar President Virginia Smith in 1982, when Mary McCarthy was a "distinguished visitor" to the campus.

**ELISABETH NIEBUHR SIFTON** was in Paris studying on a Fulbright Fellowship when she met Mary McCarthy in the early 1960s. An editor and writer, she is currently senior vice president of Farrar, Straus and Giroux.

**ROBERT B. SILVERS** (1929– ), editor and translator, is cofounder and co-editor of *The New York Review of Books*.

**EILEEN SIMPSON** is the author of *Poets in Their Youth*, which portrays the early promise of her first husband, John Berryman, and his friends. She saw Mary McCarthy often in Paris in the 1960s.

**VIRGINIA SMITH** was president of Vassar from 1977 to 1986.

**SUSAN SONTAG** (1933– ) has written novels, short stories, plays, screenplays, criticism, and essays. Her books of nonfiction include *Against Interpretation and Other Essays* and *Illness as Metaphor*. Her novel *The Volcano Lover: A Romance* was published in 1992.

**STEPHEN SPENDER** (1909–1995), a British poet, playwright, essayist, translator, novelist, short story writer, memoirist, and editor, published more than seventy books. He and his wife, **NATASHA,** were longtime friends of Mary McCarthy.

**JEAN STAFFORD** (1915–1979), author of the novel *Boston Adventure*, won the Pulitzer Prize in 1970 for *The Collected Stories of Jean Stafford*. She was married to Robert Lowell from 1940 to 1948.

**SAUL STEINBERG** (1914–1999), the well-known *New Yorker* artist, was a good friend of Nicola Chiaromonte and a member of the Europe-America Groups.

**GRACE ZARING STONE** (1891–1991) was the author of *The Bitter Tea of General Yen*. Her daughter is Eleanor Perényi.

**ROGER W. STRAUS JR.** (1917– ), founder of Farrar, Straus and Co. in 1945, published Mary McCarthy's collection of theater columns in 1956 and *On the Contrary*, her landmark essay collection, in 1961.

**EVE GASSLER STWERTKA** studied with Mary McCarthy at Bard College in the 1940s and worked at *Partisan Review*. She earned a doctorate in English literature, taught English at State University of New York–Purchase, and has written books for young adults. She is one of the trustees of the Mary McCarthy Literary Trust.

**NATHALIE SWAN,** a classmate of Mary McCarthy's at Vassar, became an architect and later married Philip Rahv. Swan's mother was cofounder of the Junior League.

**MARTIN SWENSEN** (1913–1998) attended the University of Minnesota with Kevin and Preston McCarthy and moved to New York City with them in 1938.

**HAROLD TAYLOR** was the president of Sarah Lawrence when Mary McCarthy taught there in 1948. The author of such books as *The World as Teacher* and *Students Without Teachers*, he contributed salient characteristics to the college president named Maynard Hoar in McCarthy's novel *The Groves of Academe*.

**SAMUEL TAYLOR** (1912– ) was living in Blue Hill, Maine, when he met Mary McCarthy in Castine. A successful playwright, he is best known for *Sabrina Fair* (later made into the movie *Sabrina*).

**PAUL TILLICH** (1886–1965), a minister and Protestant theologian, published over forty books on theology.

**DIANA TRILLING** (1905–1996) and her husband, **LIONEL** (1905–1975), were at the center of the New York intellectual world in the 1940s and 1950s. Lionel was a distinguished critic and professor at Columbia University whose many books include *The Liberal Imagination*. After he died, Diana edited a twelve-volume edition of her husband's work and wrote several books, including *The Beginning of the Journey*.

**NICCOLÒ TUCCI** (1908–1999), a frequent contributor of fiction to *The New Yorker*, gave the dinner party at which Mary McCarthy met her third husband, Bowden Broadwater. His books include *Before My Time*, *Unfinished Funeral*, and *The Son and the Moon*.

**WILLIAM TUOHY** (1926– ), who went to Vietnam as a reporter for *Newsweek* in 1964, was the Saigon bureau chief for *The Los Angeles Times* when he met Mary McCarthy there in 1967. He won the 1969 Pulitzer Prize in International Reporting.

**KENNETH TYNAN** (1927–1980) became the chief drama critic of *The Observer* when he was twenty-seven. He was the literary manager of Laurence Olivier's National Theatre, co-creator of the musical *Oh! Calcutta!* and author of many books on the theater. **KATHLEEN TYNAN** (1937–1995), author of *The Life of Kenneth Tynan* and several novels, was his second wife.

**JOHN UPDIKE** (1932– ) has published over seventy books, including short stories, poetry, and essays. Among his many novels are the Pulitzer Prize–winning *Rabbit Is Rich* and *Rabbit at Rest*, as well as *Couples*, *The Witches of Eastwick*, and *Toward the End of Time*.

**CANDACE VAN ALEN,** a Vassar classmate, met McCarthy again in Newport.

**HANS VAN MIERLO,** a leader of the Dutch progressive party, helped Prime Minister Johannes den Uyl form his center-left government after the 1973 election.

**GORE VIDAL** (1925– ), essayist, novelist, short story writer, and screenwriter, is the author of more than fifty books, including *Myra Breckinridge, Burr,* and *Screening History.*

**MARGO VISCUSI** was Mary McCarthy's secretary in Paris from 1969 to 1977 and became one of the two executors of the Mary McCarthy Literary Trust. She worked for many years as a writer and editor for the United Nations and is now president of Poets House, a library and literary center in New York. She is on the boards of Yaddo and Glimmerglass Opera.

**CHARLES AND ADELAIDE WALKER** ran the Theatre Union, a left-wing theater group that performed in the Old Civic Repertory Theatre in New York City. Charles Walker translated plays by Sophocles and Aeschylus and earned his living as a labor arbitrator.

**LUCILLE FLETCHER WALLOP,** Mary McCarthy's Vassar classmate, wrote the radio play *Sorry, Wrong Number,* as well as the script of its 1948 film version.

**ROBERT PENN WARREN** (1905–1989) was cofounder and editor of *The Southern Review,* which published Mary McCarthy's first story. A poet, novelist, and playwright, he won the Pulitzer Prize in Fiction in 1947 for *All the King's Men.* He married the writer Eleanor Clark in 1952.

**HELEN DAWES WATERMULDER** was Mary McCarthy's classmate at Vassar.

**GEORGE WEIDENFELD** was the head of the British publishing house Weidenfeld and Nicolson.

**LAEL WERTENBAKER** (1909–1997) wrote fiction, nonfiction, and children's books. Her memoir, *Death of a Man,* was adapted for the theater as *A Gift of Time* by Garson Kanin and produced on Broadway in 1962.

**JAMES WEST** (1914–1999), Mary McCarthy's fourth husband, retired in 1979 from his post as public relations officer for the Paris-based Organization for Economic Cooperation and Development. His children by his former wife Margaret are **DANIEL, JONATHAN,** and **ALISON WEST;** the latter is an art historian and author of *From Pigalle to Preault: Neoclassicism and the Sublime in French Sculpture, 1760–1840.*

**DAME REBECCA WEST** (1892–1983), born Cicily Isabel Fairfield, was a British journalist, novelist, biographer, and critic. Her 1941 book on Yugoslavia, *Black Lamb and Grey Falcon,* is considered a classic. Among her many works of fiction are the novella *The Return of the Soldier* and *The Thinking Reed.*

**KATHARINE S. WHITE** (1892–1977) was on the staff at *The New Yorker* for thirty-six years and edited most of Mary McCarthy's stories for the magazine. The wife of E. B. White and the mother of Roger Angell, she also wrote on gardening. *Onward and Upward in the Garden,* a collection of her pieces for *The New Yorker,* was recently reissued.

**GALEN WILLIAMS,** a friend of the young Reuel Wilson on Cape Cod, was the founder of Poets and Writers. She is a landscape architect in East Hampton, New York.

**EDMUND WILSON** (1895–1972), Mary McCarthy's second husband, was a noted literary and social critic. Among his most celebrated works of nonfiction are *Axel's Castle, The Wound and the Bow, To the Finland Station,* and *Patriotic Gore.* He was also the author of the novel *Memoirs of Hecate County* and five volumes of diaries and notebooks from the 1920s through the 1960s. Wilson married **ELENA MUMM THORNTON** after his divorce from Mary McCarthy in 1945. **ROSALIND WILSON** is Wilson's daughter by his first wife, Mary Blair.

**REUEL WILSON** (1938– ), the son of Mary McCarthy and Edmund Wilson, is a professor of Russian and comparative literature in the Modern Languages Department at the University of Western Ontario. He received his doctorate in comparative literature from the University of Chicago.

**MONIQUE WITTIG** (1935– ) is a French radical feminist writer who began teaching in the United States in 1976. Mary McCarthy met Wittig in Paris and championed her first novel, *The Opoponax*.

**HELEN WOLFF** (1906–1994) founded Pantheon Books in 1942 with her husband Kurt and went on to establish the Helen and Kurt Wolff imprint at Harcourt Brace Jovanovich in 1961. The Wolffs were responsible for introducing many important foreign authors to American audiences, including Günter Grass, Umberto Eco, and Italo Calvino.

**MEG WOLITZER** (1959– ) a fiction writer, is the author of *Hidden Pictures*, *This Is Your Life*, and *Friends for Life*.

**SIR PEREGRINE WORSTHORNE** (1923– ), a writer and editor, served on the editorial staff of *The Times*, the *Daily Telegraph*, and the *London Sunday Telegraph*. Among his books are *Peregrinations: Selected Pieces* and *Tricks of Memory*, his autobiography.

**GAVIN YOUNG** (1928– ), who met Mary McCarthy in Vietnam, was a foreign correspondent for *The Observer* for over three decades. He is also a travel writer whose books include *Halfway Around the World*, *Slow Boat Time*, and *In Search of Conrad*.

# Notes

Full citations for all books cited can be found in the bibliography. These short-ened forms are used throughout for manuscript collections in the notes:

Bryn Mawr  Katharine White Papers, Bryn Mawr College Library, Bryn Mawr, Pennsylvania
Columbia  F. W. Dupee Papers, Butler Library, Columbia University, New York City
Harvard-H  Robert Lowell Papers, Manuscript Department, Houghton Library, Harvard University, Cambridge, Massachusetts
Harvard-IT  Bernard Berenson Papers, Harvard University Center for Italian Renaissance Studies, I Tatti, Florence
HRUT  Elizabeth Hardwick Papers, Harry Ransom Humanities Research Center, University of Texas at Austin
JFK  Arthur M. Schlesinger Papers, John F. Kennedy Library, Boston
NYPL  Farrar Straus Giroux Records, New York Public Library, New York City
Vassar  Mary McCarthy Papers, Special Collections, Vassar College Library, Poughkeepsie, New York
Vassar/EB  Elizabeth Bishop Papers, Special Collections, Vassar College Library
Yale-B  Beinecke Rare Book and Manuscript Library, Yale University Library, New Haven (All papers from the Beinecke Library are from the Edmund Wilson Collection, unless otherwise specified in the note.)
Yale-S  Dwight Macdonald Papers, Sterling Manuscript and Archives, Yale University Library, New Haven

Other abbreviations used in the notes are:

HA  Hannah Arendt
BB  Bowden Broadwater
NC  Nicola Chiaromonte
EH  Elizabeth Hardwick
MM  Mary McCarthy
DM  Dwight Macdonald
EW  Edmund Wilson

BF        *Between Friends: The Correspondence of Hannah Arendt and Mary McCarthy, 1949–1975*

CWMM   *Conversations with Mary McCarthy*

HIG       *How I Grew*

IM        *Intellectual Memoirs*

MCG      *Memories of a Catholic Girlhood*

OC        *On the Contrary: Articles of Belief, 1946–1961*


**PREFACE**

12 "Balance is *not* . . .": MM to Carol Gelderman, Dec. 30, 1987, Vassar.

**1. MacDowell**

15 "I went swimming . . .": MM to Carmen Angleton, Aug. 15, 1984, Vassar.

15 "It looks as if . . .": Ibid.

15 "Every word she . . .": Transcript of *The Dick Cavett Show*, p. 50, in *Lillian Hellman v. Mary McCarthy, Dick Cavett, and Educational Broadcasting Corporation*, Supreme Court of the State of New York.

18 "The operation worked . . .": MM to Frani Blough Muser, Aug. 15, 1984; letter courtesy of Ms. Muser.

22 All excerpts from EH's address are from *Colony Newsletter* 14, no. 1 (Summer 1984), published by the MacDowell Colony, Inc.

23 For all excerpts from McCarthy's speech, see ibid.

25 Lovestoneite: Followers of Jay Lovestone, onetime head of the American Communist Party, who broke with Stalin in the 1930s.

26 "Mary McCarthy, literary lioness . . .": Samuel G. Freedman, "McCarthy Is Recipient of MacDowell Medal," *The New York Times*, Aug. 27, 1984, p. C14.

27 The Auchincloss memo is at Vassar.

28 "cheering effect": MM to Louis Auchincloss, Sept. 5, 1984, Vassar.

**2. Minneapolis**

33 "My own son . . .": MM, *MCG*, p. 5.

33 "It is our parents . . .": Ibid.

34 "Everybody's childhood . . .": MM, *The Writing on the Wall*, p. 107.

34 "your lovely mother . . .": Harry McCarthy to MM, Mar. 8, 1952, Vassar. I have also retained all of Harry McCarthy's original spelling in this and other excerpts from the same letter.

34 "My father, I used to maintain . . .": MM, *MCG*, p. 11.

35 "Our father had put . . .": Ibid., pp. 29–30.

35 "father advanced . . .": Harry McCarthy to MM, Mar. 8, 1952.

36 "Myers was the perfect type . . .": MM, *MCG*, p. 60.

37 "I am not sorry . . .": Ibid., p. 24.

38 "Looking back, I see . . .": Ibid., pp. 18, 21, 23.

38 "[W]hen I was ten . . .": Ibid., pp. 63, 64.

39 "i readily admit . . .": Harry McCarthy to MM, Mar. 8, 1952.

39 "A distinction must be made . . .": MM, *MCG*, pp. 65, 66.

40 "[W]e were put . . .": Ibid., pp. 67–68.

40 "Independently of each other . . .": Ibid., pp. 40–41.

42 "I sometimes wonder . . .": Ibid., p. 16.

43 "Compensating . . .": Quoted in *CWMM*, p. 180.

**3. Seattle**

46 For the floor button to summon the maid, see MM, *MCG*, pp. 199–200.

46 "The other thing . . .": Ibid., p. 200.

47 "Meanwhile my brothers . . .": Ibid., pp. 139–40.

47 "from 1927 to 1938 . . .": Harry McCarthy to MM, Mar. 8, 1952, Vassar.

47 "This body of hers . . .": MM, *MCG*, p. 225.

48 "the first time I saw . . .": Harry McCarthy to MM, Mar. 8, 1952.

48 "'Your grandmother's tragedy' . . .": MM, *MCG*, pp. 240–41.

49 "At this point I had not given . . .": MM, *HIG*, pp. 46–47.

49 "you definitely . . .": Harry McCarthy to MM, Mar. 8, 1952.

50 "curtsies dipped in the hall": MM, *MCG*, p. 102.

50 "[O]ur days were . . .": Ibid., p. 92.

50 "sufficient knowledge": Ibid., p. 91.

50 "You're just like . . .": Ibid., p. 96.

51 "People are always asking . . .": Ibid., pp. 111–12, 115.

52 "your mother told me . . .": Harry McCarthy to MM, Mar. 8, 1952.

52 "Contrary to what the McCarthys . . .": MM, *MCG*, p. 125.

52 "In fact, had it not been . . .": MM, "A Believing Atheist," *Vassar Views*, Nov. 1992.

55 "just, laconic, severe . . .": MM, *MCG*, p. 166.

56 "In my first year . . .": MM, *HIG*, pp. 64–65, 74.

57 "We never took her too seriously . . .": Quoted in Carol Brightman, *Writing Dangerously*, p. 55.

58 "Mary was pretty shocking . . .": Quoted in Carol Gelderman, *Mary McCarthy*, p. 40.

58 "Then, at exactly the psychological moment . . .": Pp. 5–6 of an untitled story, Vassar.

58 "I was attracted . . .": MM, *HIG*, p. 153.

58 "She made no advances . . .": Ibid., pp. 154, 155.

58 "On the whole, . . .": Ibid., pp. 155–56.

59 "Mary McCarthy is a student . . .": Ibid., pp. 169–70.

59 "In her worst nightmare . . .": Ibid., p. 170.

59 "the child Mary": Ibid., p. 179.

59 For the stopovers in Minneapolis and New York, see ibid., pp. 186–92.

## 4. VASSAR

61 "Like Athena . . .": MM, *OC*, p. 193.

61 "not a gentleman . . .": Ibid., pp. 194–95.

61 "the very best college in America": Ibid., p. 198.

62 "blue-eyed Republican girls": Ibid., p. 199.

62 "Bucolically set . . .": Ibid., p. 197

62 "I myself was an ardent . . .": Ibid., p. 196.

63 "bareheaded Yale boys": Ibid., p. 197.

63 "aesthete": Ibid., p. 199.

63 "royalist": MM, *HIG*, p. 206.

64 "To the returning alumna . . .": MM, *OC*, pp. 209–10.

64 "'To the Class of Thirty-three' . . .": MM, *The Group*, p. 25.

65 "Having seen me installed . . .": MM, *HIG*, pp. 194, 198.

65 "My group lived in 'Main' . . .": Lucille Fletcher Wallop, unpublished memoir; manuscript courtesy of Ms. Wallop.

66 "Those were the years . . .": Eunice Clark Jessup, "Memoirs of Literatae and Socialists, 1929–33," *Vassar Quarterly*, undated clipping [c. 1979], p. 16, Vassar.

66 "Miss Mary McCarthy . . .": MM to Ted Rosenberg, Nov. 1, 1929, Vassar.

67 "Delightfully eager . . .": Anna Kitchel's comment card is courtesy of Vassar College.

68 "She was the secret Catholic girl in Mary": Interview with Charles Michener.

69 "A young person . . .": MM, *HIG*, pp. 205, 206.

69 "All my friends . . .": MM to Ted Rosenberg, n.d. [c. May 4, 1930], Vassar. MM's letters are often undated, giving only the day of the week, but the exact date can be discerned from the postmark or inferred from their content.

69 "[S]he was lined up . . .": Fletcher Wallop, memoir.

70 "witty": MM, *HIG*, p. 201.

70 "I lost my virginity . . .": Ibid., p. 202.

71 "John and I were engaged . . .": Ibid.

71 "[A]s soon as I read . . .": Fletcher Wallop, memoir.

71 "We considered Mary McCarthy . . .": Clark Jessup, "Literatae," p. 17.

72 "At Vassar, my Davison friends . . .": MM, *HIG*, pp. 214–15.

73 "[A]s Elly's house guest . . .": Ibid., p. 216.

74 "Ladies and gents . . .": Elizabeth Bishop quoted, ibid., p. 227.

75 "At Cushing we belonged . . .": Ibid., p. 226.

75 "[M]ost nights at the dinner-hour . . .": Ibid., pp. 229–31.

75 "I am writing . . .": MM to Frani Blough, Dec. 25, 1931; letter courtesy of Frani Blough Muser.

76 "You see me installed . . .": MM to Frani Blough, July 22, 1932; letter courtesy of Frani Blough Muser.

76 "Mr. Sheer was a dealer . . .": MM, *The Company She Keeps*, pp. 25, 27, 35.

77 "We had a month . . .": MM, *HIG*, pp. 249, 252.

78 "'You people were aesthetes . . .'": MM, *The Group*, pp. 125–26.

79 "By senior year . . .": MM, *HIG*, p. 136.

79 "I think they were practicing . . .": MM to Miss Rosenbaum, Feb. 6, 1964, draft version (unmailed), Vassar.

80 "who just loved . . .": Interview with Frani Blough Muser.

80 "The official literary magazine . . .": Clark Jessup, "Literatae," p. 17.

81 "When the Huxley book . . .": [MM], "Two Crystal-Gazing Novelists," *Con Spirito* 1, no. 1 (Feb. 1933), pp. 1–2, Vassar.

81 "the modern water closet": "Touchstone Ambitions," Vassar.

82 "[Rebecca West] had a great influence . . .": "Mary McCarthy in Conversation with Sedge Thomson," May 10, 1985, City Arts & Lectures, San Francisco; transcript courtesy of City Arts & Lectures.

82 "[T]he course senior year . . .": MM, *HIG*, p. 262.

83 "tramping . . .": MM to Mrs. Earl Blough, Apr. 11, 1933; letter courtesy of Frani Blough Muser.

83 "It was not clear . . .": MM, *HIG*, pp. 255–57.

84 "It was mid-June . . .": Ibid., p. 266.

84 "[T]here was not one of them . . .": MM, *The Group*, pp. 10–11.

85 "two-plus children . . .": MM, *OC*, p. 149.

85 "[T]he statistical fate . . .": Ibid., p. 202.

## 5. MRS. HAROLD JOHNSRUD

90 "Odets, where is thy sting?": Quoted in MM, *IM*, p. 5.

91 "Pokey made use . . .": MM, *The Group*, p. 7.

91 "[I]t was exactly one week . . .": MM, *HIG*, pp. 266–67.

92 "Kay's first wedding present . . .": MM, *The Group*, pp. 12–13.

92 "six silver Old-Fashioned spoons . . .": MM, *IM*, p. 14.

92 "[I]n New York . . .": MM, *OC*, pp. 78–79.

92 "What, perhaps, might be asked nowadays . . .": EH, foreword to *IM* by MM, p. xx.

93 "I was . . . intensely sorry . . .": MM to Frani Blough, July 21, 1933; letter courtesy of Frani Blough Muser.

93 a colored print called *Geometry*: MM, *IM*, p. 13.

95 "I find that I am . . .": MM to Frani Blough, Dec. 7, 1933; letter courtesy of Ms. Muser.

96 "We on this paper . . .": Quoted in MM, *IM*, p. 11.

96 "For the most part . . .": MM, "Minority Report," *The Nation* 142, Mar. 11, 1936, p. 327.

96 "Mr. Graves . . .": MM, "Vivified History," *The Nation* 138, Apr. 13, 1934, pp. 679–80.

96 "She was a prodigy . . .": EH, in *IM*, p. xvi.

97 "[O]ne by one we mounted . . .": MM, *IM*, pp. 6–7, 8–9.

97 "Mexican critics . . .": MM, "Coalpit College," *The New Republic* 78, May 2, 1934, p. 343.

97 "Cowley had second thoughts . . .": MM, *IM*, pp. 9, 10.

98 "This book is of worth . . .": "O.C.F.," afterword to MM, "Coalpit College," p. 343.

98 "[T]hrough our professional . . .": MM, *OC*, pp. 82–83.

99 "At Dwight Macdonald's . . .": MM, *IM*, pp. 18–19.

100 "Johnsrud and I joined . . .": Ibid., pp. 16–17.

100 "There was something . . .": MM, *OC*, pp. 81–82.

101 "Today, after four sidecars . . .": MM to Frani Blough, n.d. [c. Apr. 25, 1934]; letter courtesy of Ms. Muser.

101 "Did you hear about Merlin? . . .": MM to Frani Blough, Sept. 23, 1934; letter courtesy of Ms. Muser.

102 "any extended effort . . .": Margaret Marshall and MM, "Our Critics, Right or Wrong. V: Literary Salesmen," *The Nation* 141, Dec. 18, 1935, p. 719.

102 "Unequipped to deal . . .": Margaret Marshall and MM, "Our Critics, Right or Wrong. II: The Anti-Intellectuals," *The Nation* 141, Nov. 6, 1935, pp. 542–43.

102 "The Marxist critic . . .": Margaret Marshall and MM, "Our Critics, Right or Wrong. IV: The Proletarians," *The Nation* 141, Dec. 4, 1935, p. 653.

102 "The main topic of conversation . . .": John Chamberlain, "Books of the Times," *The New York Times*, Dec. 12, 1935.

103 "All we had in common . . .": MM, *IM*, p. 22.

103 "'FelLOW WORKers, join our RANKS!' . . .": Ibid., p. 1.

104 "So we meet her here . . .": EH, foreword in ibid., p. xxi.

104 "John Porter was tall . . .": MM, ibid., pp. 36–37.

104 "I had 'told' John . . .": Ibid., pp. 35–36.

104 "the Sphinx of the smoking-room": MM, *HIG*, p. 226.

105 "She could not bear . . .": MM, *The Company She Keeps*, pp. 3, 11.

105 "He took it hard . . .": MM, *IM*, p. 38.

106 "*She liked him*. Why, . . .": MM, *The Company She Keeps*, pp. 95, 105–6.

106 "a country gentlewoman . . ": MM, "Paris, 1848," *The Nation* 143, Aug. 15, 1936, p. 191.

106 "Jewish *diseuse* . . .": Ibid., p. 192.

107 "The first Moscow trial . . .": MM, *OC*, pp. 92–93. Writing "My Confession" fifteen years after the book review, McCarthy confused the Paris Commune of 1871 with the Revolution of 1848; the latter is the focus of *Summer Will Show*.

107 "[Sophia] works, singing . . .": MM, "Paris, 1848," p. 192.

107 "I am ashamed to say . . .": MM, *IM*, p. 42.

108 "If it had not been for me . . .": Ibid., p. 43.

109 "No psychoanalyst . . .": Ibid., p. 38.

## 6. PARTISAN REVIEW

111 "Learn to live without love . . .": Quoted in MM, *IM*, p. 52.

111 "This thought greatly . . .": Ibid.

111 "dimple-faced, shaggy-head, earnest": MM, *OC*, p. 95.

111 "This was in September . . .": Ibid., pp. 93–94.

111 "The one-room apartment . . .": MM, *IM*, pp. 47–48.

111 "'great' decisions": MM, *OC*, p. 76.

111 "whims of chance" and with "inadvertence": Ibid., pp. 105, 77.

111 "Trotsky himself . . .": Ibid., p. 105.

113 "A matter of memory . . .": James T. Farrell to MM, Sept. 15, 1967, Vassar.

113 "I knew you were complimenting . . .": MM to James T. Farrell, Oct. 25, 1967, Vassar.

113 "I remember a downtown meeting . . .": MM, *IM*, pp. 73–74.

114 "Suddenly you knew . . .": MM, *The Company She Keeps*, pp. 154–55. The murdered Andrés Nin was a leader of POUM, an anarchist group fighting in Spain with the Loyalists.

115 "If I may give an opinion . . .": MM, *IM*, pp. 60–61.

115 "short, stocky, dark, well-fed body": Ibid., p. 60.

115 "Once I got started . . .": Ibid., p. 62.

116 "Maybe nobody *does* feel . . .": Jean Strouse, "Making the Facts Obey," *The New York Times Book Review*, May 24, 1992, pp. 16–17.

116 "It would be a mistake . . .": Richard Eder, "A Posthumous Catalogue of Carousing," *Los Angeles Times*, May 12, 1992.

116 "I was able to compare . . .": MM, *IM*, pp. 62–63.

117 "Zeal-of-the-Land-Busys": Ibid., p. 56. This is the name of a Puritanical character in Ben Jonson's *Bartholomew Fair*.

118 "long-nosed . . .": Ibid., pp. 64, 65.

118 MM's comments on Cornell and Fontanne are from "Our Actors and the Critics," *The Nation* 144, May 8, 1937, p. 538.

118 "The time was the winter . . .": Transcript courtesy of the 92nd Street Y, New York City.

119 "Most of us . . .": MM, *OC*, pp. 101–2.

120 St. Valentine's Day: MM, *IM*, p. 59.

121 "Manic-impressive": James Atlas, *Delmore Schwartz*, p. 98.

121 "Philip was tall, powerfully built . . .": Lionel Abel, *The Intellectual Follies*, p. 50.

121 "For some reason . . .": Quoted in Diana Trilling, "An Interview with Dwight Macdonald," *Partisan Review* 51, no. 4 (Fall 1984–Winter 1985), pp. 807–8.

122 "I remember when I first knew . . .": MM, *Occasional Prose*, p. 4.

122 Rahv gave Fitzgerald credit: Philip Rahv, *Essays in Literature and Politics, 1932–1972*, p. 23.

123 "the happy center of things": MM, *The Company She Keeps*, p. 170.

124 "Though we felt some . . .": William Phillips, *A Partisan View*, pp. 62–63.

124 "Your letter made us all . . .": Philip Rahv to DM, Aug. 4, 1937, Yale-S.

125 "When Helene met . . .": Delmore Schwartz, "The Complete Adventuress," Yale-B (Schwartz Papers). A handwritten note at the beginning of this two-page fragment says, "Mary & Philip (1937)."

125 "Rahv sat on the sofa . . .": William Barrett, *The Truants*, pp. 6–7.

126 "The 'boys' were still committed . . .": MM, *Mary McCarthy's Theatre Chronicles*, p. ix.

127 "To my youthful eyes . . .": Barrett, *Truants*, p. 7.

128 "If I made mistakes . . .": MM, *Theatre Chronicles*, p. x.

129 "*Partisan Review* is . . .": "Editorial Statement," *Partisan Review* 4, no. 1 (Dec. 1937), p. 3.

129 "The *New Yorker* is . . .": DM, "Laugh and Lie Down," ibid., pp. 48, 50.

131 "Though Mr. Anderson . . .": MM, *Theatre Chronicles*, pp. 7–8.

## 7. EDMUND WILSON

136 "any extended effort . . .": Margaret Marshall and MM, "Our Critics, Right or Wrong. V: Literary Salesmen," *The Nation* 141, Dec. 18, 1935, p. 719.

137 "more suited to a wedding reception": MM, *IM*, p. 88.

137 "angry": Ibid., p. 95.

138 "though derived . . .": Ibid., pp. 98–99.

138 "She did not understand . . .": MM, *A Charmed Life*, p. 103.

139 "One day . . .": MM, *IM*, p. 98.

139 "The only thing that shamed . . .": MM, *A Charmed Life*, pp. 205–6.

139 "With Mary at the Little Hotel . . .": EW, unpublished journal entry of Jan. 1, 1943, Yale-B.

140 "He bustled into our office . . .": MM, *IM*, p. 89.

141 "Let people who have never . . .": EW, "The Old Stone House," in *The Portable Edmund Wilson*, p. 17.

141 "From the time I first . . .": Alfred Kazin, "Midtown and the Village," *Harper's* 248, Jan. 1971, p. 88.

141 "A man of immense . . .": William Phillips, *A Partisan View*, p. 63.

142 "Well, good-bye . . .": MM to EW, Nov. 29, 1937, Yale-B.

142 "I don't know . . .": Ibid.

143 "You left your book . . .": EW to MM, Nov. 29, 1937, Vassar.

143 "Sunday was a bad day . . .": MM to EW, Nov. 30, 1937, Yale-B.

143 For MM's comments on Byron, see ibid.

143 "Byron was always . . .": EW to MM, Dec. 2, 1937, Vassar.

143 For comments on Delmore Schwartz, see MM to EW, Dec. 3, 1937, Yale-B.

143 "bummed a cigarette . . .": MM to EW, Dec. 6, 1937, Yale-B.

144 "You remember my telling you . . .": MM to EW, n.d. [c. Dec. 14, 1937], Yale-B.

144 "I think you're wonderful . . .": MM to EW, n.d. [c. Dec. 20, 1937], Yale-B.

144 "You know the delight . . .": Ibid.

144 "writing a lot of inconsequential . . .": EW to MM, Jan. 18, 1938, Vassar.

144 "You are wrong . . .": MM to EW, Jan. 19, 1938, Yale-B.

145 "the intimacy and friendliness . . .": MM, *IM*, p. 99.

145 "What do you want . . .": Ibid., p. 107.

146 "It was a crushing blow . . .": Diana Trilling, "An Interview with Dwight Macdonald," *Partisan Review* 51, no. 4 (Fall 1984–Winter 1985), p. 807.

147 "So finally I agreed . . .": MM, *IM*, p. 101.

147 "do something" . . . "imaginative writing": Ibid., p. 103.

147 "self-interest" . . . "Marxist explanation": Ibid., p. 104.

147 "That was all . . .": Ibid., p. 105.

147 "The account of the moral struggle . . .": EH, foreword to ibid., p. xiii.

148 "Again and again . . .": Jean Strouse, "Making the Facts Obey," *The New York Times Book Review*, May 24, 1992, p. 17.

148 "If it had been left . . .": MM, *IM*, pp. 103–4.

149 "During that bad night . . .": Ibid., p. 114.

149 "to be hung . . .": EW to W. W. Norton, May 26, 1938, in EW, *Letters on Literature and Politics*, p. 304.

150 "[W]ith the extramarital . . .": MM, *The Company She Keeps*, p. 4.

151 "Late in the evening . . .": Affidavit of Mar. 12, 1945, *Mary McCarthy Wil-*

*son v. Edmund Wilson,* Supreme Court of the State of New York, p. 2, in Vassar.

152 For the first hours at Payne Whitney, see ibid., p. 3.

152 "rough-weave yellow . . .": MM, *The Group,* pp. 314–15.

152 "I laughed . . .": Ibid., p. 315.

152 "'Harald committed me?' . . .": Ibid., pp. 316–17.

152 "yellow roughly woven curtains": Quoted in Carol Brightman, *Writing Dangerously,* p. 175.

153 "I discovered . . .": EW's affidavit of Feb. 23, 1945, *McCarthy v. Wilson.*

153 "I made fewer entries . . .": EW, manuscript, Yale-B.

154 "In June 1938 . . .": Lewis Dabney, note to EW, *The Sixties,* p. 225.

155 "I had an extremely . . .": MM to EW, June 9, 1938, Yale-B. With *"your* insane asylum," MM is alluding to EW's 1932 hospitalization for a nervous breakdown.

156 "It was just the same . . .": Ibid.

156 "I can't come . . .": EW to MM, June 17, 1938, Vassar.

156 "without psychosis; anxiety reaction": A slip of paper in the EW Collection, Yale-B, gives this diagnosis as well as the dates of her stay and the referring physician.

157 For visit by Scott Fitzgerald, see EW to Christian Gauss, Oct. 27, 1938, in EW, *Letters,* pp. 313–14.

158 "I thought the first . . .": EW, "Riposte," *Partisan Review* 4, no. 2 (Jan. 1938), p. 63.

159 "I told him I had joined . . .": William Barrett, *The Truants,* p. 63.

159 "She had to walk up . . .": Interview with Rosilla Hornblower Hawes.

161 *"Picnic with Gerry Allard . . .":* EW, *The Thirties,* p. 718.

161 "We've been having . . .": EW to John Dos Passos, July 16, 1939, in EW, *Letters,* p. 320.

162 "There were some happy . . .": Rosalind Baker Wilson, *Near the Magician,* pp. 99–100.

162 "I keep thinking . . .": EW to MM, July 31, 1939, Vassar.

162 "As I told you . . .": EW to MM, Aug. 14, 1939, Vassar.

163 "I can't buy you . . .": EW to MM, Aug. 19, 1939, Vassar.

163 "absolutely mad about him": MM to EW, n.d. [Aug. 1939], Yale-B.

164 "My grandmother understood . . .": MM, *MCG,* pp. 242–43.

164 "Before we were married . . .": Affidavit of Feb. 23, 1945, p. 1, *McCarthy v. Wilson.*

164 "After I became pregnant . . .": Ibid., pp. 1–2.

## 8. THE MINOTAUR

166 "monster" . . ."the minotaur": MM, *IM,* p. 100.

166 "I may have felt . . .": Ibid.

166 "he was even related . . .": Ibid.

168 "If the weather was good enough . . .": EW, *The Thirties,* p. 716.

168 "Martha had forgotten . . .": MM, *A Charmed Life,* p. 16.

169 The poem appeared in *Partisan Review* 6, no. 5 (Fall 1939), p. 102.

169 "You people are getting . . .": EW to F. W. Dupee, May 16, 1940, Columbia.

170 "Full moon . . .": EW, *The Thirties,* pp. 724–25 (entry dated Mar. 23, 1940).

170 The reports on the death of Johnsrud, which appeared in *The New York Times* on Dec. 23 and 24, 1939, are reprinted in MM, *HIG,* pp. 273–74.

170 "I guess I hadn't adjusted . . .": Interview with Maddie Aldrich De Mott.

171 "[T]he essence . . .": MM, *A Charmed Life,* p. 12.

172 "Today we cleared . . .": EW, *The Forties,* p. 27 (entry dated May 21, 1942).

172 "Many years later . . .": Alfred Kazin, "Midtown and the Village," *Harper's* 248, Jan. 1971, p. 89.

173 "Old stuffed shirts . . .": EW, *The Thirties*, p. 726. Nina Chavchavadze was EW's Russian teacher.

173 Details on EW's studio are from Rosalind Baker Wilson, *Near the Magician*, p. 106.

173 "She had, I thought . . .": Alfred Kazin, *Starting Out in the Thirties*, p. 155.

174 "Yeats . . .": EW to John Peale Bishop, Jan. 14, 1941, in EW, *Letters on Literature and Politics*, p. 329.

176 "When I inherited . . .": The Carol Brightman interview, "Mary, Still Contrary," is reprinted in *CWMM*, pp. 234–49; quotation on p. 244.

176 "Let me suggest . . .": MM, *The Company She Keeps*, p. 296.

177 "mind" and "beauty": Ibid., p. 300.

177 "On the street . . .": Ibid., pp. 301–2, 304.

178 "It was a strange . . .": Kazin, "Midtown," pp. 88, 89.

178 "I'm not sure . . .": EW to Christian Gauss, Sept. 8, 1941, in EW, *Letters*, p. 344.

179 "Your letter pleases . . .": MM to F. W. Dupee, n.d. [1941], Columbia.

179 "And if she had felt . . .": MM, *The Company She Keeps*, p. 112.

180 "Softly, she climbed . . .": Ibid., p. 107.

180 "The scene was . . .": Eileen Simpson, "Ode to a Woman Well at Ease," *Lear's*, April 1990, p. 136.

182 "Anglo-American . . .": Philip Rahv, "10 Propositions and 8 Errors," *Partisan Review* 8, no. 6 (Nov.–Dec. 1941), p. 499.

182 "In a sense this war . . .": Ibid., p. 506.

182 "In what sense . . .": Reply by Greenberg and DM, ibid., p. 508.

182 "At the beginning . . .": The Elisabeth Niebuhr interview, "The Art of Fiction XXVII: Mary McCarthy—An Interview," is reprinted in *CWMM*, pp. 3–29; quotation on p. 14.

183 "[I]f we look . . .": Reprinted from *Partisan Review* in *The Selected Essays of Delmore Schwartz*, p. 372.

185 "'When did you have it last?' . . .": MM, *The Company She Keeps*, p. ix.

185 "Several years ago . . .": John Chamberlain, "Books of the Times," *The New York Times*, May 16, 1942.

186 "Mary McCarthy . . .": William Abrahams's *Boston Globe* review of May 13, 1942, is excerpted in *Book Review Digest 1942*, p. 492.

186 "*The Company She Keeps* is not . . .": Malcolm Cowley's *New Republic* review of May 25, 1942, ibid.

186 "Miss McCarthy is no novelist . . .": Clifton Fadiman's *New Yorker* review of May 16, 1942, ibid.

186 "*The Company She Keeps* is a shrewd . . .": Robert Penn Warren, "Button, Button," *Partisan Review* 9, no. 6 (Nov.–Dec. 1942), pp. 537, 540, 539.

187 "Why was it that she . . .": MM, *The Company She Keeps*, pp. 245–46.

187 "What I really do . . .": Quoted in *CWMM*, p. 8.

187 "its satire . . .": Chamberlain, "Books of the Times."

188 "Two of the characters . . .": Ibid.

188 "Now about Mary's book . . .": Vladimir Nabokov to EW, May 6, 1942, in *The Nabokov-Wilson Letters*, p. 61.

188 "My wife and I . . .": Randall Jarrell to EW, Aug. 5, 1941, in Jarrell, *Letters*, p. 49.

190 "I found those pictures . . .": EW to MM, Sept. 22, 1942, Vassar. EW was in Wellfleet while MM was in New York City.

191 "She was Anna Karenina . . .": R. Wilson, *Near the Magician*, p. 111.

191 "Dos and Katy thought . . .": Ibid.

192 "I came down . . .": EW to MM, Aug. 10, 1942 (written on stationery of Princeton Club, New York), Vassar.

193 "But what does Harry . . .": MM to Bernice Baumgarten, May 29, 1943, Vassar.

193 "Your letter arrived practically . . .": MM to Bernice Baumgarten, June 23, 1943, Vassar.

194 "I've decided to take it . . .": EW to Helen Muchnic, Oct. 10, 1943, in EW, *Letters*, p. 401.

195 "I'd go to a movie . . .": Quoted in *CWMM*, p. 14.

195 "Here is a check . . .": MM to Bernice Baumgarten, May 27, 1944, Vassar.

196 "Martha's story . . .": MM, *A Charmed Life*, p. 18.

196 "On July 5, 1944 . . .": Affidavit of Feb. 23, 1945, *Mary McCarthy Wilson v. Edmund Wilson*, Supreme Court of the State of New York, p. 2, in Vassar.

196 "Their penultimate quarrel . . .": MM, *A Charmed Life*, p. 105

207 "on a purely, friendly basis": All quotations from EW to MM, July 13, 1944, Vassar.

208 "I remember I wrote . . .": Quoted in *Contemporary Authors: New Revision Series* 16, pp. 253–54.

209 "This is the note . . .": MM to EW, n.d. [c. Dec. 1944], Vassar.

209 "kick me, bite me . . .": EW's affidavit of Feb. 23, 1945, *McCarthy v. Wilson.*

210 "Mary was the underdog": Interview with Adelaide Walker.

## 9. THE SUMMER OF '45

212 "I should interpret . . .": EW, *The Wound and the Bow*, p. 240.

213 "[D]on't take too seriously . . .": EW to Helen Muchnic, Feb. 14, 1945; letter courtesy of Ms. Muchnic.

213 "analytic exuberance": William Barrett, *The Truants*, p. 42.

214 "There was no other man . . .": Quoted in *CWMM*, p. 180.

215 "I got Greenberg . . .": Diana Trilling, "An Interview with Dwight Macdonald," *Partisan Review* 51, no. 4 (Fall 1984–Winter 1985), pp. 806–7.

216 "The office aesthete": Interview with Roger Angell.

218 "If you have . . .": MM to Bernice Baumgarten, June 20, 1945, Vassar.

218 "Surely you must come . . .": MM to BB, June 23, 1945, Vassar.

219 "Did I write you . . .": MM to BB, n.d. [July 1945], Vassar.

219 "Reuel has infected toe . . .": MM to BB, Aug. 3, 1945, Vassar.

220 "The Robert Nathans . . .": MM to BB, June 23, 1945.

220 "Clem was perfectly odious . . .": MM to BB, n.d. [July 1945].

220 "Nottingham was . . .": MM, "The Lost Week," p. 22, Vassar.

221 "By adroit manipulation . . .": Ibid., p. 5.

221 "[H]e never entered . . .": Ibid., p. 55.

221 "[S]he practiced self-criticism . . .": Ibid., p. 43.

221 "Reuel is well . . .": MM to EW, July 18, 1945, Yale-B.

222 "At a cocktail party . . .": Eileen Simpson, "Ode to a Woman Well at Ease," *Lear's*, Apr. 1990, p. 136.

225 "We talked about Tolstoy . . .": The Carol Brightman interview, "Mary, Still Contrary," is reprinted in *CWMM*, pp. 234–49; quotation on p. 241.

225 "I heard a characteristic . . .": MM, preface to NC, *The Worm of Consciousness and Other Essays*, p. xiv.

225 blue ruffled apron: Carol Gelderman, *Mary McCarthy*, p. 120.

226 "Hatred and grief . . .": MM, introduction to Niccolò Tucci, *The Rain Came Last and Other Stories*, p. ix.

228 For salutations and closings, see MM's letters of June 23 and July 1945 and BB's letters of early July, July 23, and Aug. 10, 1945, all in Vassar.

228 "[Clement Greenberg] told me . . .": MM to BB, n.d. [July 1945].

228 "In Wellfleet met . . .": MM to BB, Aug. 3, 1945.

228 "Gardner Jencks . . .": MM to BB, n.d. [c. Aug. 8, 1945], Vassar.

229 "Slight discussion . . .": MM to BB, Aug. 3, 1945.

229 "Long visit from . . .": Ibid.

230 "I think the whole thing . . .": *CWMM*, p. 180.

230 "I never ever feel that": MM quoted by Eve Gassler Stwertka in our interview.

230 "[V]iolence obliterates . . .": Simone Weil, "The Iliad or, The Poem of Force," translated by MM, *politics* 2, no. 11 (Nov. 1945), p. 326.

231 "May I add . . .": MM, *OC*, p. 3.

231 "I remember reading . . .": Ibid., p. 267.

231 "Really in frightful state . . .": MM to BB, Aug. 21, 1945, Vassar.

232 "a coarse leer": MM to BB, n.d. [c. Aug. 22, 1945], Vassar.

232 "feel utterly rejected": MM to BB, n.d. [c. Aug. 24, 1945], Vassar.

232 "Everything looks . . .": Ibid.

232 "large and vaguely unpleasant": Ibid.

233 "observance . . . slave of convention": MM, "The Lost Week," pp. 46, 47.

233 "Herbert Harper could not . . .": Ibid., p. 6.

234 "acting out a novel . . .": EW to Muchnic, Feb. 14, 1945.

## 10. BARD

235 "esthetic" . . . "social prophet": EW, *The Wound and the Bow*, p. 160.

235 "It is sometimes true . . .": Ibid., p. 169.

236 "You can take Reuel . . .": EW to MM, Sept. 11, 1945, Vassar.

237 "an Episcopal men's college . . .": *Bard College Bulletin* 129, no. 5 (Sept. 1990), p. 1.

238 "it was quite a bit like Bard": Quoted in *CWMM*, p. 9.

238 "Dear Fred . . .": MM to F. W. Dupee, n.d. [c. Sept. 1945], Columbia.

240 "I liked teaching . . .": *CWMM* p. 10.

240 "were quick to discover . . .": MM, *The Groves of Academe*, p. 81.

240 "Well, you had to call . . .": *CWMM*, p. 10.

241 "It was all quite mad . . .": Ibid., pp. 9, 10.

243 "Bowden makes Mummy laugh": Interview with Barbara Dupee.

243 "Is Bowden only a jester?": MM to BB, Sept. 19, 1945, Vassar.

244 no one had informed St. Bernard's: EW to MM, Sept. 26, 1945, Vassar.

244 Reuel's setback: MM to EW, Nov. 4, 1945, Yale-B. EW's response, in which he continues to blame her, is Nov. 13, 1945, Vassar.

245 "Hate it here . . .": MM to BB, Sept. 19, 1945.

245 "I can't write . . .": MM to BB, Nov. 13, 1945, Vassar.

246 "Cat's been going . . .": Reuel Wilson to BB, Nov. 3, 1945, Vassar. The letter is written in MM's hand.

246 furnace tender: MM to BB, n.d. [c. late Sept. 1945], Vassar.

247 "First a wild lunge . . .": MM to BB, Oct. 1, 1945, Vassar.

247 "According to that . . .": NC to MM, Nov. 25, 1945, Vassar.

249 "By the way, I forgot . . .": MM to BB, Dec. 18, 1945, Vassar.

251 "Must tell you my discovery . . .": MM to BB, Feb. 13, 1946, Vassar.

251 "The last disaster . . .": MM to Charles Henri Ford, n.d. [c. Fall 1945], Yale-B (Ford Papers).

251 "There is no time . . .": MM to Bernice Baumgarten, Nov. 27, 1945, Vassar.

252 "I can't get through . . .": MM to EW, n.d. [c. Feb. 1946], Yale-B. The list of monthly expenses is in this letter.

252 He let her know: BB to MM, Feb. 21, 1946, Vassar.

253 "You will remember . . .": EW to MM, Mar. 21, 1946, Vassar.

253 "lying around . . .": MM to Bernice Baumgarten, Feb. 19, 1946, Vassar.

254 "military funeral": MM to BB, Mar. 20, 1946, Vassar.

255 "You're just like . . .": MM, *MCG*, p. 94.

255 "The only news . . .": MM to BB, May 9, 1946, Vassar.

256 "for fear of getting . . .": MM to Reuel Wilson, n.d. [c. June 1946], Yale-B.

256 "Warnings of . . .": MM, "Lausanne," *Town and Country*, Nov. 1946, p. 130.

257 "a hatbox from a Royal hatter" . . . "Hell Express": Ibid., pp. 262, 267.

257 "Wedged into the train . . .": Ibid.

258 "[A] sinister Swiss doctor . . .": Ibid., p. 267.

258 "Poor Keats lies dead . . .": Ibid., p. 262.

258 "Can you stuff . . .": MM to Bernice Baumgarten, Aug. 28, 1946 (written in Venice), Vassar.

259 "part of the baggage . . .": MM, "Lausanne," p. 262.

259 "an explorer": MM, *Cast a Cold Eye*, p. 110.

259 "On the troopship . . .": Virgil Thomson, *Virgil Thomson*, p. 382.

## 11. Mrs. Bowden Broadwater

262 EW's evaluation of the apartment is in EW to MM, Oct. 25, 1946, Vassar.

262 MM discusses Reuel's health and the rental market in her letter to EW of Dec. 17, 1946, Yale-B.

263 "Actually, as I remember . . .": "The Art of Fiction XXVII: Mary McCarthy— An Interview," conducted by Elisabeth Niebuhr of *Paris Review,* is reprinted in *CWMM*, pp. 3–29; quotation on pp. 15–16.

264 "tall and small-boned . . .": MM, *A Charmed Life*, p. 5.

264 "He had stern faith in Martha . . .": Ibid., p. 8.

264 "The morning of February 18 . . .": BB, "Ciao," *Paris Review* 7, Winter–Spring 1961, pp. 41–42, 49.

265 "it wasn't a mansion . . .": Interview with Reuel Wilson.

265 "I don't remember . . .": Ibid.

267 "very nice": Ann Hulbert, *The Interior Castle*, p. 137.

267 "[T]he greatest snobs . . .": Ibid., p. 172.

267 "They were torturing affairs . . .": Diana Trilling, *The Beginning of the Journey*, pp. 330–31.

267 "An evening at the Rahvs . . .": EH, foreword to MM, *IM*, pp. xvii–xviii.

268 "One writer whom the circle . . .": William Barrett, *The Truants*, p. 48.

268 For de Beauvoir on MM, see her *Letters to Sartre*, p. 428.

270 "People were fond of wondering . . .": Randall Jarrell, *Pictures from an Institution*, pp. 74–75.

271 "skull's grin": Ibid., p. 65.

271 "Torn animals . . .": Ibid.

273 "My mother was not . . .": Interview with Reuel Wilson.

273 "positive and negative elements": Interview with Kevin McCarthy.

273 "visiting Existentialist": MM, *OC*, p. 6.

274 "cold and beautiful . . .": Simone de Beauvoir, *America Day by Day*, p. 286.

274 "In January, 1947 . . .": MM, *OC*, p. 24.

274 "I think she's odious . . .": *CWMM*, p. 20.

274 "Did I say that? . . .": "Mary McCarthy in Conversation with Sedge Thomson," May 10, 1985, City Arts & Lectures, San Francisco; transcript courtesy of City Arts & Lectures.

274 "She's not utterly stupid . . .": The Carol Brightman interview, "Mary, Still Contrary," is reprinted in *CWMM*, pp. 234–49; quotation on p. 246.

274 "I always felt . . .": "MM in Conversation."

275 "A Letter to the Editor of *politics*" and the essays "Tyranny of the Orgasm" and "Gandhi" are all reprinted in MM, *OC*; quotation about Kinsey's findings is on p. 167.

275 George Orwell: I am grateful to Phillip Lopate for this observation.

276 "We both glanced . . .": MM, *OC*, pp. 73–74.

277 "To audiences accustomed . . .": MM, *Mary McCarthy's Theatre Chronicles*, pp. 81, 85, 88.

277 "You are an ordinary . . .": Ibid., pp. 131, 134.

277 "'Attention must be paid' . . .": MM, *Sights and Spectacles*, p. xvi.

279 "As a detector . . .": Kenneth Tynan, "Above the Crowd," *The Observer* [London], May 10, 1959, p. 2-b.

279 "Whenever we children . . .": MM, *MCG*, p. 29.

280 "White hair, glasses . . .": Ibid., p. 33.

281 "in a less categorical form": MM to Harry McCarthy, Apr. 4, 1952, Vassar.

281 "Sexual intercourse . . .": MM, *Cast a Cold Eye*, p. 113.

282 "I read to her . . .": Jacqueline Bograd Weld, *Peggy: The Wayward Guggenheim*, pp. 353–54.

282 "He had a sharp tongue . . .": William Phillips, *A Partisan View*, p. 143.

282 "I think it was . . .": Quoted in Carol Brightman, *Writing Dangerously*, p. 310.

283 "gadfly of the philosophical journals": MM, *The Groves of Academe*, p. 8.

283 "photogenic, curly-haired . . .": Ibid., p. 11.

284 "[Hellman] was telling a group . . .": MM to Ben O'Sullivan, Feb. 26, 1980, Vassar. O'Sullivan was MM's longtime lawyer (see chapter 25).

## 12. *THE OASIS*

286 "Byron was always . . .": EW to MM, Dec. 2, 1937, Vassar.

287 "the weak link": Interview with Irving Howe.

287 "what ought to be": DM, *Memoirs of a Revolutionist*, p. 29.

289 "small libertarian movements": Elisabeth Niebuhr, "The Art of Fiction XXVII: Mary McCarthy—An Interview," in *CWMM*, p. 16.

289 "to change the world . . .": Ibid.

289 Chiaromonte to take money: Transcript of Michael Wreszin's interview with MM (courtesy of Mr. Wreszin); Carol Brightman, *Writing Dangerously*, p. 308.

290 "There was too much . . .": Quoted in Brightman, *Writing Dangerously*, p. 306.

290 "totalitarianism": Wreszin transcript.

290 "We worked through . . .": Ibid.

291 "We came together . . .": The full text of the statement was provided by Miriam Chiaromonte.

292 "the main political-intellectual figure": Interview with Irving Howe.

292 "Hook, they felt . . .": William Barrett, *The Truants*, pp. 84–85.

292 "People do what . . .": Delmore Schwartz, *Portrait of Delmore*, p. 104.

292 "I have never seen . . .": William Phillips, *A Partisan View*, pp. 134–35.

293 For Koestler at his hotel room, EH, and MM's rationale, see Brightman, *Writing Dangerously*, p. 301.

293 "complete adventuress": James Atlas, *Delmore Schwartz*, p. 99.

293 "[W]e were tipped off . . .": Wreszin transcript.

294 "The PR boys . . .": DM to NC, July 9, 1948, Yale-S.

294 letter from Chiaromonte: Dated July 9, 1948, this letter to MM is at Yale-S.

294 For MM on Camus, see Wreszin transcript.

294 "He told me frankly . . .": NC to MM, July 9, 1948.

295 "[M]y preliminary impression . . .": MM to DM, n.d. [late July 1948], Yale-S.

295 On derivation of the title, see Brightman, *Writing Dangerously*, p. 300.

295 "old and famous": The announcement of *Horizon*'s 1948 summer competition is in Vassar.

296 "Why hasn't Mary . . .": NC to DM, Sept. 3, 1948, Yale-S.

296 "Yesterday had a reply . . .": DM to NC, Sept. 14, 1948, Yale-S.

296 For the revised statement's covering letter, see DM to NC, Dec. 10, 1948, Yale-S.

296 "We (Mary and I . . .": Ibid.

296 "better than the first . . .": NC to DM, Dec. 15, 1948, Yale-S.

296 "unexceptional . . .": DM to NC, Dec. 10, 1948.

297 "EAG has always . . .": Ibid.

298 "sparkless and lethargic": Ibid.

298 "the carefully selected jury . . .": Cyril Connolly to MM, n.d. [late 1948], Vassar.

298 " . . . bowling down the hill to Hollywood": Ibid.

299 "Tall, red-bearded . . .": MM, *The Oasis*, p. 8.

299 "the reign of justice and happiness": Ibid., p. 15.

299 "a notion of themselves . . .": Ibid., p. 22.

299 "the widest latitude . . .": Ibid.

299 "confidences . . ." Ibid., p. 36.

299 "dark features": Ibid., p. 16.

299 "peculiar short harsh laugh": Ibid., p. 17.

299 "A kind of helplessness . . .": Ibid., pp. 38–39.

300 I am not quite happy . . .": Connolly to MM, n.d. [late 1948].

300 "she perhaps lacks . . .": Cyril Connolly, "Introduction," *Horizon* 19, no. 110 (Feb. 1949), p. 74.

301 "English readers . . .": Ibid.

301 flicking ashes: Diana Trilling, *The Beginning of the Journey*, p. 348.

301 "tinkled in her mouth . . .": MM, *The Oasis*, p. 11.

301 "The targets of his satire . . .": Ibid., p. 103.

301 "Have you read . . .": DM to NC, Apr. 7, 1949, Yale-S.

301 "Mary's story . . .": NC to DM, Apr. 11, 1949, Yale-S.

302 Joe Loucheim: For the Random House edition, the character's name was changed to Joe Lockman.

302 "[H]e had a legitimate cause . . .": "MM in Conversation with Sedge Thomson," May 10, 1985, City Arts & Lectures, San Francisco; transcript courtesy of City Arts & Lectures.

302 "I just ran into Mary . . .": This is the story that Bellow told me in our interview; a slightly different version appeared in the *San Francisco Chronicle*, Jan. 11, 1991.

302 "The best satire . . .": MM to Doris Grumbach, Feb. 22, 1966, Vassar.

303 "The circle gathered . . .": Barrett, *Truants*, pp. 67–68.

303 "relevant passage": Philip Rahv to DM, Mar. 24, 1949, Yale-S.

303 "[W]e believe this thing . . .": H. J. Kaplan to Philip Rahv, Mar. 19, 1946, quoted in ibid.

304 "I just read . . .": HA to MM, Mar. 20, 1949, in *BF*, p. 1.

304 "welcomed in America": Interview with Lionel Abel.

305 "There had been a number . . .": "MM in Conversation."

305 "She was being so deliberately naughty . . .": Reprint in *CWMM*, p. 42.

305 "There'd be other people . . .": "MM in Conversation."

306 "Elizabeth, nice . . .": MM to DM, n.d. [late July 1948].

307 "[W]e got the tickets . . .": Wreszin transcript.

308 "They said that this . . .": Diana Trilling, "An Interview with Dwight Macdonald," *Partisan Review* 51, no. 4 (Fall 1984–Winter 1985), p. 810.

308 "Hook simply turned . . .": Wreszin transcript.

309 "The Conference had little . . .": DM, "The Waldorf Conference," *politics*, Winter 1949, p. 32A.

309 "[W]e took the precaution . . .": Wreszin transcript.

309 "We did have our . . .": Ibid.

309 For DM's, MM's, and Lowell's questions, see DM, "Waldorf Conference," pp. 32B–C.

310 "it takes considerable skill . . .": Irving Howe, "The Culture Conference," *Partisan Review* 16, no. 5 (May 1949), p. 510.

310 "the most moving . . .": DM, "Waldorf Conference," p. 32D.

310 "But of course the sensation . . .": Trilling, "Interview with DM," p. 810.

310 "They gave him the floor . . .": Wreszin transcript.

311 "The conference, on the whole . . .": Howe, "Culture Conference," p. 511.

311 "Tidings from the Whore": Barrett, *Truants*, p. 67.

311 "had forced himself on her": Brightman, *Writing Dangerously*, p. 340.

311 "[Delmore] went around . . .": Ibid.

312 "P[hilip] R[ahv] observed . . .": Schwartz, *Portrait of Delmore*, p. 335.

312 "the mothball odor . . .": Dawn Powell, "Reader Left Parched in McCarthy Oasis," *New York Post*, undated clipping, Vassar.

312 "caricatures": Margaret Marshall, "Notes by the Way," *The Nation* 169, Sept. 17, 1949, p. 281.

312 "The author's failure . . .": Donald Barr's *New York Times* review of Aug. 14, 1949, is excerpted in *Book Review Digest* 1949, p. 581.

313 "She was wit and gusto . . .": Marshall, "Notes by the Way," p. 281.

313 "Did you see Dawn . . .": MM to Bernice Baumgarten, Aug. 22, 1949, Vassar.

313 "Did you see Margaret . . .": MM to EH, Sept. 23, 1949, Harvard-H.

## 13. NEWPORT

315 Details on moving in are from MM to EH, June 24, 1949, Harvard-H.

315 "four-square" and "frugal": MM to Katharine White, July 20, 1949, quoted in Carol Gelderman, *Mary McCarthy*, p. 156.

315 For the kitchen and the invitation to visit, see MM to EH, June 24, 1949.

316 "As you see . . .": Ibid.

317 All quotations from Jean Stafford's "American Town" are from *The New Yorker*, Aug. 28, 1948, pp. 26–34.

318 "This neighborhood . . .": MM to EH, Aug. 22, 1949, Harvard-H.

319 "We have been working . . .": MM to Reuel Wilson, n.d. [c. July 1949], Yale-B.

320 she wrote to apologize: MM to DM, June 29, 1949, Yale-S.

321 "Wm. Phillips says Chambers . . .": MM to EH, July 7, 1949, Harvard-H.

321 "a mental defective": MM to EH, July 20, 1949, Harvard-H.

322 "I must say . . .": MM to Robert Linscott, Oct. 6, 1949, Vassar.

323 "instantly decided . . .": MM to BB, Oct. 18, 1949, Vassar.

323 "Then P. read me . . .": Ibid.

323 "I've begun to feel . . .": Ibid.

324 "[The] older Vassar career woman . . .": MM, *OC*, pp. 203–4.

324 "[T]he story was circulated . . .": MM to Bernice Baumgarten, Feb. 8, 1951, Vassar.

325 "The whole thing . . .": Ibid.

325 "This letter is a premonition . . .": MM to DM and Nancy Macdonald, Nov. 20, 1949, Yale-S.

326 "Saw Mary once this fall . . .": DM to NC, Dec. 21, 1950, Yale-S.

326 "Dwight was here . . .": MM to EH, Nov. 28, 1950, HRUT.

326 "the Lesbian . . .": MM to Arthur Schlesinger, Feb. 20, 1950, JFK.

327 "A blue-eyed . . .": Draft of "Greenwich Village at Night" in Vassar.
327 "everybody rushed to buy the *Post*": Interview with Nicholas King.
327 "Cast a cold eye . . .": MM, *Cast a Cold Eye*, p. 147.
327 "It seems to me . . .": MM to Bernice Baumgarten, Oct. 19, 1948, Vassar.
328 "They'd gone down . . .": Interview with Nicholas King.
328 "Miss McCarthy's eye . . .": Dudley Fitts, "Portraits Cut in Acid," *The New York Times Book Review*, Sept. 24, 1950, p. 9.
328 "Whoever thought . . .": Robert Halsband, "Jaundiced Eye," *Saturday Review of Literature* 33, Oct. 7, 1950, p. 23.
328 "The title, borrowed . . .": Louise Bogan, "Ecstasy and Order," *The New Republic* 123, Nov. 27, 1950, pp. 18–19.
329 "like some queer topiary animal herself": MM to EH, July 20, 1949.
329 "Despite the late start . . .": MM, *Occasional Prose*, pp. 338–39.
329 "fabulist": Ibid., p. 329.
331 "A terrible thing . . .": MM to EH, Jan. 25, 1951, Harvard-H.
331 talking exclusively: Interview with Elena Levin.
331 "always sort of on the sidelines": Interview with Marian Schlesinger.
331 "something of a reputation": Interview with Diana Trilling.
331 "How can . . .": Ibid.
332 "I've read your book . . .": MM to HA, Apr. 26, 1951, in *BF*, pp. 1–2.
333 For the description of Furness, see MM, *The Groves of Academe*, pp. 93–94.
333 "In lieu of an inscription . . .": MM to F. W. Dupee, Feb. 5, 1952, Columbia.
334 "Furness, now that we mention it . . .": MM to F. W. Dupee, May 19, 1952, Columbia.
334 "Miss McCarthy's satiric . . .": Alice Morris's *New York Times* review of Feb. 24, 1952, is excerpted in *Book Review Digest* 1952, p. 577.
334 "We see from the first . . .": Brendan Gill, "Books: Too High, Too Low," *The New Yorker*, Feb. 23, 1956, pp. 106–7.
334 "Miss McCarthy, as a friend . . .": Delmore Schwartz, "Fiction Chronicle: The Wrongs of Innocence and Experience," *Partisan Review*, May–June 1952, p. 355.
335 "taste for colonial . . .": MM, *The Groves of Academe*, p. 86.
335 "even-handed justice": MM to Dupee, May 19, 1952.
336 "Mary's new novel . . .": DM to NC, Feb. 14, 1952, Yale-S.
336 "Miriam has read . . .": NC to DM, Apr. 24, 1952, Yale-S.
337 "I can't believe . . .": MM to HA, Mar. 14, 1952, in *BF*, p. 5.
337 Committee for Cultural Freedom: This was a successor group to the Americans for Intellectual Freedom mentioned in chapter 12.
338 "The ideas circulate . . .": MM, *OC*, pp. 35, 42.
338 "the deepest impression intellectually": DM, "Notes on the Conference, 'In Defense of Free Culture,' Called by the American Committee for Cultural Freedom, at the Waldorf-Astoria Hotel, March 19, 1952," Yale-S.
338 "The real threat . . .": Eastman's remarks are in ibid.
338 "half-truths . . .": DM, "Notes of Meeting of Committee for Cultural Freedom at the Columbia Club, April 23, 1952," Yale-S.
338 "with the air . . .": Ibid.
339 "The initiated anti-Communists . . .": MM, *OC*, pp. 50–51, 54.
339 For the idea of going to law school, see Brent Brower, "Mary McCarthyism," reprinted in *CWMM*, p. 41, and HA to MM, Sept. 22, 1952, in *BF*, p. 7.
340 "I so envy your going . . .": MM to HA, Mar. 14, 1952, in *BF*, p. 6.
340 For BB's Newport stories, see MM to EH, Dec. 13, 1949, Harvard-H, and MM to EH, Oct. 17, 1951, Harvard-H.
341 "Crushed between . . .": MM to DM, Oct. 14, 1952, Yale-S.

341 "I liked living . . .": Interview with Reuel Wilson.

## 14. NEW YORK

342 "[I]t's extraordinarily beautiful . . .": MM to HA, Oct. 7, 1952, in *BF*, p.9

342 "the only political. . .": MM to HA, Sept. 22, 1952, ibid., p. 8.

343 MM called Ascoli "cowardly" in her interview with Carol Brightman, "Mary, Still Contrary," *The Nation*, May 19, 1984, reprinted in *CWMM*, p. 234.

343 For reviving *politics*, see DM to NC, Dec. 21, 1950, Yale-S.

343 not doing justice: MM to DM, n.d. [1951], Yale-S.

343 ". . . absolutely false and evil . . .": MM to DM, Nov. 14, 1952, Yale-S.

343 "The election results . . .": MM to HA, Dec. 2, 1952, in *BF*, pp. 10–11.

343 "concentrate fire": Ibid.

343 "definitely second-best": Ibid.

344 "with no ideal . . .": MM to Richard Rovere, Dec. 4, 1952, JFK. MM added a handwritten note to a carbon of this letter when she forwarded it to Schlesinger.

344 "the only person I see . . .": MM to EH, Apr. 10, 1952, HRUT.

344 "Too many irons . . .": MM to HA, Dec. 2, 1952, in *BF*, p. 12.

345 a detailed plan: "CRITIC: A Prospectus for a New Magazine," Vassar.

345 "I've always had . . .": *CWMM*, p. 234.

345 The contributors and potential articles are from the prospectus.

345 "Here is the prospectus . . .": MM to Katharine White, Feb. 18, 1953, Bryn Mawr.

346 "I went to see . . .": MM to Arthur Schlesinger, Mar. 6, 1953, JFK.

347 "Jack Kaplan . . .": MM to Arthur Schlesinger, Apr. 17, 1953, JFK.

347 "Arthur, it isn't you . . .": MM to Arthur Schlesinger, Apr. 21, 1953, JFK.

347 "getting a new head of steam on": MM to Arthur Schlesinger, June 3, 1953, JFK. This is also the source for the fund-raiser's advice.

348 "[E]verything is in . . .": MM to Arthur Schlesinger, June 9, 1953, JFK.

348 "[T]he writer must be . . .": MM, *OC*, p. 241.

349 "The weather is so enchanting . . .": MM to HA, Oct. 4, 1953, in *BF*, pp. 14–15.

349 "In theory . . .": MM to EH, Oct. 27, 1953, HRUT.

350 "like a warrior's ritual purification": MM to HA, Oct. 4, 1953, in *BF*, p. 14.

350 "Mary and I have been . . .": Transcript courtesy of the 92nd Street Y, New York City.

350 Kazin was snubbing: MM to HA, Aug. 10, 1954, in *BF*, p. 20.

350 "I thought we were going . . .": *CWMM*, p. 235.

351 "On the one hand . . .": Brent Bower, "Mary McCarthyism," ibid., p. 42.

351 "Hannah convinced me . . .": Ibid.

352 MM's 1985 account of the apology to Rahv is in Carol Brightman, *Writing Dangerously*, pp. 371–72.

353 "Rahv's Marxist assurance . . .": MM to HA, Aug. 10, 1954, in *BF*, pp. 19–20.

353 "He was the only one . . .": Quoted in Brightman, *Writing Dangerously*, p. 372.

353 "wise counselor": Ibid., p. 371.

356 "Dottie did not mind . . .": MM, *The Group*, pp. 67–68.

357 "'You've done this before?' . . .": Philip Roth, *Goodbye Columbus*, p. 82.

358 For Bellow cutting MM, see MM to HA, Aug. 10, 1954, in *BF*, p. 20.

358 "I think we are each . . .": Robert Lowell to Elizabeth Bishop, Apr. 19, 1959, Vassar/EB.

358 "I also had a little . . .": MM to Bernice Baumgarten, Mar. 5, 1952, Vassar.

360 "I tried hard to get . . .": Randall Jarrell to EW, Nov. 1942, in Jarrell, *Letters*, p. 68.

360  For the Jarrell visit to Wellfleet, see William H. Pritchard, *Randall Jarrell*, p. 3.

360  "I find Mary a bit . . .": Robert Lowell to Elizabeth Bishop, July 30, 1968, Vassar/EB.

361  "I'm getting off a blurb . . .": Elizabeth Bishop to Pearl Kazin, Feb. 22, 1954, in Bishop, *One Art*, p. 289.

361  "Gertrude is so large . . .": Randall Jarrell to Philip Rahv, Aug. 1953, in Jarrell, *Letters*, p. 383.

362  "I'd like to be able . . .": MM to Roger Straus, Nov. 12, 1954, NYPL.

363  "The model, I think . . .": MM to Roger Straus, Oct. 22, 1954, NYPL.

364  "experience of practical life": MM to White, Feb. 18, 1953.

364  "People still keep asking . . .": MM to Straus, Oct. 22, 1954.

## 15. THE CAPE

365  "I've long felt . . .": MM to DM, Oct. 14, 1952, Yale-S.

366  "A painter might run . . .": MM, "The Lost Week," unpublished manuscript, p. 27, Vassar.

366  "asylum for derelicts . . .": Ibid., p. 22.

366  "walking case-histories . . .": Ibid., p. 26.

366  *The Little Blue Light* is found in EW, *Five Plays*, pp. 421 ff.

367  "in some ways . . .": EW to Vladimir Nabokov, Feb. 25, 1952, in *The Nabokov-Wilson Letters*, p. 273.

367  "Newport, or rather . . .": MM to DM, Oct. 14, 1952.

367  For the noisy, "indiscreet" plumbing, see Mary Meigs, *Lily Briscoe*, p. 149.

367  "Mary and Bowden . . .": Ibid., p. 147.

369  "Later she read . . .": Arthur Schlesinger, remarks at MM Memorial Service, Nov. 8, 1989, Morgan Library, New York City; copy of speech courtesy of Mr. Schlesinger.

370  "Mary goes into . . .": "Talk with Pearl Kazin about Mary McCarthy," Nov. 14, 1955, Time-Life Morgue.

370  "Reuel's lessons . . .": EW to MM, Aug. 25, 1948, Vassar.

370  "Mary very patiently . . .": Interview with Margaret Shafer.

371  "Alfred [Kazin] was here . . .": MM to HA, Aug. 20, 1954, in *BF*, p. 20.

372  MM reports on Gloria Macdonald and on the Newport house in her letter to HA of Sept. 16, 1954, ibid., pp. 28, 27.

372  "The summer has been vile . . .": MM to Bernice Baumgarten, Sept. 16, 1954, Vassar.

373  "[John and Martha] liked . . .": MM, *A Charmed Life*, pp. 18, 3.

373  "By the way . . .": MM to Bernice Baumgarten, Sept. 16, 1954.

374  "curiously flattened out . . .": MM, *A Charmed Life*, p. 109.

374  "It's your own shit . . .": Ibid., p. 126.

374  "An hour and a half . . .": Ibid., pp. 197, 200–201.

375  "Around a blind curve . . .": Ibid., pp. 312–13

376  "Is it very unsatisfactory . . .": MM to Bernice Baumgarten, May 1, 1955, Vassar.

376  "One thing I'm anxious . . .": MM to HA, Aug. 10, 1954, in *BF*, pp. 18–19.

377  "a real joy": HA to MM, Aug. 20, 1954, ibid., p. 22.

377  "The chief fallacy . . .": Ibid., p. 24.

377  "My novel is going ahead . . .": MM to HA, Dec. 8, 1954, in *BF*, pp. 30–31.

378  "She made a face . . .": MM, *A Charmed Life*, p. 206.

379  "I got within . . .": MM to Roger Straus, Nov. 12, 1954, NYPL. MM was reading the manuscript of *Lolita* in New York, while visiting Edmund Wilson; she could not finish it before she had to leave.

379 "As to Nabokov's book . . .": Roger Straus to MM, Nov. 15, 1954, NYPL.
379 "Nasty subjects . . .": EW to Vladimir Nabokov, Nov. 30, 1954, in *The Nabokov-Wilson Letters*, p. 288.
380 "About Vladimir's book . . .": MM to EW, n.d. [Nov. 1954], ibid., pp. 288–89.
380 "The stuff that . . .": Charles Poore, "Books of the Times," *The New York Times*, Nov. 3, 1955.
380 "Does Martha still . . .": Virgilia Peterson's *New York Herald Tribune* review of Nov. 13, *1955*, is excerpted in *Book Review Digest 1955*, p. 582.
381 "Miss McCarthy once . . .": John Chamberlain, "Books in Review: Heavy Artillery," *National Review*, Dec. 21, 1955, pp. 27–28.
381 "[I]t's a pity . . .": Louise Bogan to May Sarton, Dec. 1, 1955, in Bogan, *What the Woman Lived*, p. 302.
382 "He's not really meant . . .": MM to Arthur Schlesinger, Nov. 13, 1955, JFK.
382 "We have finished . . .": Ruth Jencks to BB, n.d. [ca. late 1955], Vassar.
383 "It was as though . . .": Meigs, *Lily Briscoe*, p. 153.
383 *"style indirect libre"*: Interview with Mary Meigs.
383 "Of all my friends . . .": Mary Meigs to MM, Feb. 9, 1982, Vassar.
383 "[B]y the invention . . .": MM to Mary Meigs, Jan. 20, 1982; letter courtesy of Ms. Meigs.
384 "He was like a pelican . . .": Meigs, *Lily Briscoe*, pp. 148–49.
384 Philip Rahv: Notes in Time-Life Morgue.
386 "A writer's witchcraft is at work": Meigs, *Lily Briscoe*, p. 150.
386 "literally crawled . . .": MM to HA, June 4, 1955, in *BF*, p. 34.

## 16. VENICE

388 The *Time* profile, in the Books section and entitled "Cye," is in the issue of Nov. 14, 1955, pp. 126–30.
389 "lacking in depth and soundness": See definition of "clever" in *Merriam-Webster's Collegiate Dictionary*, 10th edition.
389 "freak hurricane": MM to Bernice Baumgarten, Aug. 19, 1955, Vassar.
390 "open in her manners": MM to BB, Aug. 18, 1955, Vassar.
390 "an 'interesting' profile": Ibid.
391 three-page typed letter: Ibid.
391 "Between ourselves . . .": MM to Bernice Baumgarten, Aug. 19, 1955.
391 For discussions on the book and her misgivings, see MM to BB, Aug. 29, 1955, Vassar.
392 "'You will want, perhaps' . . .": Ibid.
392 "glorious gold Florentine . . .": Ibid.
393 For conclusions on the Berniers, see ibid.
393 "retained a hold . . .": MM to BB, Aug. 31, 1955, Vassar.
393 "It has a romantic . . .": Ibid.
393 For Peggy Guggenheim, see MM to BB, Aug. 19, 1955.
394 "coincide precisely with Ruskin's judgment": MM to Carmen Angleton, Sept. 2, 1955, Vassar.
394 "This is *no place* . . .": MM to BB, Sept. 2, 1955, Vassar.
394 "The fact is . . .": MM to Angleton, Sept. 2, 1955.
395 "[O]ut of the blue": Ibid.
395 "I feel as if . . .": Ibid.
395 *"le peuple"*: MM to BB, Sept. 13, 1955, Vassar.
395 "festering with loneliness": MM to BB, Sept. 2, 1955.
395 "Hannah seems tired . . .": MM to BB, Sept. 9, 1955, Vassar.
396 "almost good-natured contempt": MM to BB, Sept. 23, 1955, Vassar.

396 congress magazines: Congress of Cultural Freedom publications included *Preuves* in France and *Tempo Presente* in Italy.
396 "naive, crude . . .": MM to BB, Sept. 23, 1955.
397 "His first remark . . .": Ibid.
399 "[I met] Bernard . . .": MM to HA, Sept. 29, 1955, in *BF*, p. 37.
399 "B.B., who met me . . .": MM to BB, Oct. 7, 1955, Vassar.
400 "perhaps didn't like . . .": Ibid.
400 "B.B., appalling to say . . .": MM to BB, Oct. 8, 1955, Vassar.
400 "Did I ever say . . .": MM to BB, Oct. 10, 1955, Vassar.
401 "That you don't like me . . .": MM to BB, Oct. 8, 1955.
403 Objects were borrowed: MM to BB, Nov. 14, 1955, Vassar.
405 "'I envy you' . . .": MM, *Venice Observed*, pp. 12–13.
405 "My shrewd, clowning signora . . .": Ibid., p. 153.
406 "blanched creatures": Ibid., p. 24.
406 "[I] take them. . .": Ibid., p. 25
406 "Earth is . . .": Ibid., pp. 110–11.
407 For MM's appraisal of Tintoretto, see ibid., p. 140.
407 "When I go . . .": Ibid., pp. 157–58.
409 "Our Italian trip . . .": MM to Bernice Baumgarten, June 22, 1956, Vassar.
409 "I've done no writing . . .": MM to HA, Aug. 1956, in *BF*, pp. 39–40.
409 "the revel . . .": MM quotes Byron on p. 125 of *Venice Observed*.
410 "Here is one . . .": Dawn Powell, "The Sack of Venice," *The Nation* 183, Dec. 22, 1956, p. 543.
410 "You are wrong . . .": MM to Bernard Berenson, Feb. 25, 1957, Harvard-IT.
421 "More than a century . . .": "The Floating City," *Time*, Nov. 26, 1956, p. 110.
421 "This is a first . . .": Sacheverell Sitwell's *New York Times* review of Nov. 18, 1956, is excerpted in *Book Review Digest 1956*, p. 589.

## 17. B.B. AND J.D.

424 "Well, here I am . . .": MM to BB, May 16, 1956, Vassar.
424 For MM's other impressions of her first day and night at I Tatti, see ibid.
425 For the transatlantic crossing and Tillich, see MM to BB, May 7, 1956, Vassar.
425 "been having quite . . .": MM to BB, May 23, 1956, Vassar.
426 For impressions of Florence and visits to the Sitwell and Acton villas, see ibid.
427 "[T]he entry to the subject . . .": MM to BB, May 7, 1956.
427 For the Rome conference, see MM to BB, June 9, 1956, Vassar.
428 "My excuse . . .": John Davenport to MM, June 3, 1956, Vassar.
428 MM's comments on Davenport are from her letter to BB of June 9, 1956.
429 "I miss you in Rome": MM to John Davenport, June 6, 1956, Vassar.
429 "The most alarming . . .": MM to John Davenport, July 3, 1956, Vassar.
429 Bowden let her know: Carol Brightman, *Writing Dangerously*, p. 366,
430 " . . . Now you're interested . . .": MM to John Davenport, July 21, 1956, Vassar.
430 "might as well be in New York": MM to HA, Aug. 9, 1956, in *BF*, p. 42.
430 "giving a lot . . .": MM to Bernard Berenson, Aug. 28, 1956, Harvard-IT.
430 "Why is she . . .": Ibid.
431 "Nothing special here . . .": MM to John Davenport, Aug. 18, 1956, Vassar.
431 "She discerned . . .": MM to BB, Sept. 28, 1956, Vassar.
432 "Dear Hannah, it's been wonderful . . .": MM to HA, n.d. [c. early Oct. 1956], in *BF*, pp. 43–44.
432 "The part of your letter . . .": John Davenport to MM, Nov. 15, 1956, Vassar.
432 "common little creatures": Interview with Nora Sayre.
432 "Whom the gods wish to . . .": Cyril Connolly, *Enemies of Promises*, p. 109.

434 "[I]t needs some new turn . . .": MM to BB, Sept. 22, 1956, Vassar.

434 "At that moment . . .": MM, *MCG*, p. 245.

434 "These memories of mine . . .": Ibid., pp. 3–4.

435 "Miss McCarthy, who writes . . .": W. T. Scott's *New York Herald Tribune* review of May 26, 1957, is excerpted in *Book Review Digest 1957*, p. 577.

436 "Miss McCarthy's new book . . .": Victor Lange, "The Women and the Orphan Child," *The New Republic* 136, June 24, 1957, p. 18.

436 "No virtue is . . .": Phyllis McGinley, "Mary Was an Orphan," *Saturday Review* 40, June 8, 1957, p. 31.

436 "Mary McCarthy's *Memories* . . .": N. W. Logal, review in *Catholic World* 186, Nov. 1957, p. 157.

437 "Mr. Hughes is not . . .": MM to BB, May 9, 1957, Vassar.

437 "The only true part . . .": Ibid.

438 "You are entitled . . .": Ibid.

438 "a physical reaction . . .": MM to BB, May 12, 1957, Vassar.

438 For Hughes's views of Davenport, see ibid.

438 "morbidly sad": Ibid.

439 "[A]las, they sound tense . . .": MM to BB, May 20, 1957, Vassar.

439 "[I] had given up . . .": MM to HA, May 21, 1957, in *BF*, p. 46.

439 "delicate broths . . .": MM to BB, May 20, 1957.

439 "Of all your books . . .": HA to MM, June 7, 1957, in *BF*, p. 48.

439 gratifying bit of information: Ibid.

440 "Mary, dear, I am afraid . . .": Ibid., pp. 48–49.

441 "He entered, wearing . . .": MM to BB, May 25, 1957, Vassar.

442 "Countess Rucellai strikes me . . .": MM to Bernard Berenson, June 7, 1957, Harvard-IT.

442 "The aspiring Countess. . .": Bernard Berenson to MM, June 11, 1957, Vassar.

443 "that fabulous odalisque . . .": Bernard Berenson to MM, April 27, 1957, Vassar.

443 "I am still . . .": Berenson to MM, June 11, 1957.

444 "Forgive me for blaming . . .": MM to BB, Sept. 14, 1957, Vassar.

445 "godawful" and "pure treacle": MM to BB, Sept. 18, 1957, Vassar.

445 "he would make . . .": MM to BB, Sept. 23, 1957, Vassar.

445 "not in a mind . . .": MM to BB, Sept. 25, 1957, Vassar.

445 essence of Florence: MM to BB, Oct. 3, 1957, Vassar.

446 "There was also . . .": Ibid.

446 "Beaton book": MM to Bernard Berenson, Jan. 20, 1958, Harvard-IT.

446 "tooled-leather" portrait of "a dear . . .": MM, *The Stones of Florence*, pp. 14, 16.

447 "I ought to have . . .": MM to HA, June 145, 1958, in *BF*, p. 51.

448 "almost total solitude": MM to Nicky Mariano, Aug. 21, 1959, Harvard-IT.

448 "superb": HA to MM, Aug. 28, 1959, in *BF*, p. 61.

449 "a brilliant, wonderful . . .": EH to BB, Sept. 6, 1959, Vassar.

449 "The Florentines . . .": MM, *The Stones of Florence*, p. 121.

449 "'How can you stand it?' . . .": Ibid., p. 1.

449 adjectives she favored: Ibid., p. 45.

449 "The statuary of Florence . . .": Ibid., p. 34.

450 "No one has ever . . .": Charles Poore, "Books of the Times," *The New York Times*, Oct. 22, 1959.

450 "[A]greement or . . .": Lincoln Kirstein's *Nation* review of Dec. 12, 1959, is excerpted in *Book Review Digest 1960*, p. 852.

450 "[B]y temperament Miss McCarthy . . .": "Feeling One's Way in Florence," *The Times Literary Supplement*, Nov. 13, 1959.

451 "Roberto looks older . . .": MM to BB, Dec. 12, 1959, Vassar.

451 "far too much insider . . .": DM to NC, Oct. 19, 1959, Yale-S.

452 "[m]any questionable . . .": NC to DM, Nov. 15, 1959, Yale-S.
452 "Of course, it is dry . . .": Ibid.
452 "I am wild . . .": Bernard Berenson to MM, Mar. 29, 1958, Harvard-IT.
452 "in a very bad state": MM to BB, n.d. [May 1958], Vassar.
452 "He's so shrunken . . .": MM to BB, May 30, 1958, Vassar.
452 "Mary scarcely . . .": Bernard Berenson, *Sunset and Twilight*, p. 435.
452 "The only way . . .": MM to BB, May 30, 1958.
453 "Poor old Berenson . . .": MM to HA, June 23, 1958, in *BF*, p. 54.
453 "We've thought . . .": MM to Nicky Mariano, Aug. 21, 1959, Harvard-IT.
453 "[B]y now friends . . .": John Davenport to MM, Nov. 28, 1957, Vassar.
453 "It would not . . .": John Davenport to MM, Mar. 10, 1958, Vassar.
454 "I should like to see *you*": MM to John Davenport, Aug. 18, 1958, Vassar.
454 "Of course I must see you": John Davenport to MM, Aug. 25, 1958, Vassar.
454 ". . . Isak Dinesen . . .": MM to John Davenport, Sept. 26, 1958, Vassar.

## 18. JIM WEST

455 work on the Vassar novel: MM to HA, June 28, 1959, in *BF*, p. 56.
455 "So far, no . . .": Ibid.
456 For the Jerusalem profile, see MM to HA, Aug. 17, 1959, ibid., p. 60.
457 "No one has . . .": MM to HA, Nov. 11, 1959, ibid., p. 63.
458 "I feel rather . . .": MM to BB, Oct. 27, 1959, Vassar.
459 "bright, energetic . . .": Interview with Yale Redmond.
461 "Saul Bellow and I . . .": MM to Nicky Mariano, Apr. 21, 1960, Harvard-IT.
461 "Saul and I parted . . .": MM to BB, Feb. 4, 1960, Vassar.
465 "What he has been doing . . .": MM to HA, Apr. 21, 1960, in *BF*, pp. 67–68.
466 "If I do this . . .": Ibid., p. 68.
466 "He's the most wholly . . .": Ibid., pp. 68–69 (the last part of this excerpt, beginning with "it's as though" and elided from *BF*, is taken from the original at Vassar).
466 "You know that I am frightened . . .": HA to MM, May 3, 1960, ibid., p. 70
466 "To add to the shock . . .": HA to MM, May 18, 1960, ibid., p. 75.
466 "We're living meanwhile . . .": MM to Mariano, Apr. 21, 1960.
467 "Dear Bowden, what shall . . .": MM to BB, Apr. 25, 1960, Vassar.
467 "I grow fonder . . .": MM to HA, May 15, 1960, in *BF*, p. 73.
468 For MM on BB and the marriage, see ibid., p. 74.
468 "He was never so nice . . .": HA to MM, May 18, 1960, ibid., p. 75.
468 "[Bowden] has written . . .": MM to HA, May 15, 1960, ibid. p. 73.
469 "I *got* hurt . . .": MM to HA, May 9, 1960, ibid., pp. 71–72.
469 "I felt it was better . . .": Ibid., p. 72.
469 "getting hurt": HA to MM, May 18, 1960, ibid., pp. 74–75.
470 "[P]lease don't fool yourself . . .": Ibid., p. 75.
470 "My presence here . . .": MM to HA, June 29, 1960, ibid., pp. 82, 84.
471 "Yesterday we drove out . . .": Ibid., p. 84.
471 "I can't see . . .": Ibid., p. 85.
471 forty-seven days: MM to HA, Aug. 30, 1960, ibid., p. 89.
472 written Bowden one last time: MM to BB, June 9, 1960, Vassar.
472 "[Carmen] reports . . .": MM to HA, Aug. 30, 1960, in *BF*, pp. 90–91.
473 "He is under . . .": HA to MM, Sept. 16, 1960, ibid., p. 92.
473 "This is not a game": MM to BB, Oct. 9, 1960, Vassar.
474 "It strikes me . . .": MM to HA, Oct. 7, 1960, in *BF*, p. 97.
474 explain at some length: MM to HA, Oct. 26, 1960, ibid., p. 102.
475 "As I see it . . .": HA to MM, Nov. 11, 1960, ibid., pp. 103–4
475 "a marvelous comedy of modern life": MM to HA, Oct. 26, 1960, ibid., p. 101.

475 "I've had to pick . . .": Ibid., pp. 100–101.

476 "Reuel seems to be . . .": MM to HA, Nov. 23, 1960, ibid., p. 107.

476 "[T]he business with Margaret . . .": Ibid., p. 105.

477 "I give you . . .": MM to EW, Mar. 30, 1961, Yale-B.

477 "[H]e's a very nice . . .": Ibid.

477 "Mary McCarthy was here . . .": Robert Lowell to Elizabeth Bishop, Feb. 15, 1961, Vassar/EB.

477 "I think, as I told . . .": DM to NC, Apr. 6, 1961, Yale-S.

478 "Mary's wedding . . .": DM to NC, Apr. 23, 1961, Yale-S.

478 "I had no doubt . . .": NC to DM, May 9, 1961, Yale-S.

479 "Jim's goose . . .": MM to Carmen Angleton, May 1, 1961, Vassar.

480 "My arm and hand . . .": MM to HA, May 24, 1961, in *BF*, p. 118.

## 19. LADY OF LETTERS

482 "I've been half sick . . .": MM to HA, May 4, 1962, in *BF*, p. 128.

483 rue de Rennes apartment: Ibid., pp. 128–29.

483 "[D]o you have . . .": HA to MM, May 20, 1962, ibid., p. 131.

484 "He's an intensely . . .": MM to HA, Jan. 11, 1962, ibid., p. 123.

485 "ugly mood": MM to HA, Mar. 28, 1962, ibid., p. 125.

485 "For my part . . .": MM to HA, June 1, 1962, ibid., p. 134.

485 "a flood of publications . . .": MM to HA, Mar. 28, 1962, ibid., p. 125.

488 "too many official parties": MM to HA, June 1, 1962, ibid., p. 134.

489 "I wonder what B.B. . . .": MM to Nicky Mariano, Apr. 21, 1960, Harvard-IT.

490 "The only other . . .": MM to HA, Aug. 30, 1960, in *BF*, p. 88.

490 "To do any sustained . . .": MM to Katharine White, n.d. [c. Dec. 1960], Bryn Mawr.

491 "There has probably never . . .": Virgilia Peterson's *New York Herald Tribune Books* review of Sept. 24, 1961, is excerpted in *Book Review Digest 1961*, p. 891.

491 "Mary McCarthy will be . . .": Robert Lowell to Elizabeth Bishop, Aug. 31, 1961, Vassar/EB.

491 "I have been greatly . . .": Janet Flanner to Natalia Murray, Mar. 9, 1962, in Flanner, *Darlinghissima*, p. 313.

491 "I just *must* tell . . .": NC to MM, Sept. 16, 1961, Vassar.

492 "Rational discourse is not . . .": MM, *Mary McCarthy's Theatre Chronicles*, pp. 231–32.

492 "the queen of the patrician *bas bleus*": Kenneth Tynan, "Above the Crowd," *The Observer* [London], May 10, 1959.

493 "Who is to inherit . . .": MM, *The Writing on the Wall*, p. 35.

493 "Mary Darling . . .": Janet Flanner to MM, n.d. [c. 1962], Vassar.

493 "no pleasure . . .": MM to HA, June 1, 1962, in *BF*, p. 133.

493 "I did hear . . .": MM to William Maxwell, June 16, 1962; letter courtesy of Mr. Maxwell.

494 "a commonplace man . . .": MM, *The Writing on the Wall*, p. 3.

494 "*Pale Fire* is . . .": Ibid., pp. 15, 33–34.

494 "I really fell in love . . .": MM to HA, June 1, 1962, in *BF*, p. 133.

495 "About *Pale Fire* . . .": EW to MM, July 7, 1962, Vassar.

496 "She is of medium height . . .": The interview, "The Art of Fiction XXVII: Mary McCarthy—An Interview," is reprinted in *CWMM*, pp. 3–29; quotation from pp. 3–4.

496 "What I really do . . .": Ibid., pp. 8, 16–17, 19–20, 25, 29.

497 "Mary McCarthy has . . .": *CWMM*, pp. 30, 35.

497 "In case you saw . . .": MM to EW, July 27, 1962, Yale-B.

498 "I read the *Esquire* . . .": William Jovanovich to MM, July 24, 1962, Vassar.

498 "there is a secret . . .": *CWMM,* p. 45.

498 "[O]ne startling aspect . . .": Ibid. pp. 43–44.

499 "action painting": MM to William Phillips, Sept. 3, 1969; letter courtesy of Mr. Phillips.

499 "Life this year . . .": MM to Carmen Angleton, Aug. 29, 1961, Vassar.

500 "taken on the look . . .": Ibid.

500 For impressions of Bocca di Magra in 1962, see MM to Carmen Angleton, Aug. 8, 1962, Vassar.

500 "populated by fishermen . . .": MM, "The Hounds of Summer," *The New Yorker,* Sept. 14, 1963, p. 47.

502 MM described her shipboard meeting with Rebecca West in a letter to HA, Mar. 28, 1962, in *BF,* p. 125.

502 "People jumping up . . .": MM to HA, Sept. 28, 1962, ibid., p. 139.

502 nation-state was dying: Ted Morgan, *Literary Outlaw,* p. 333.

503 "The *Naked Lunch* . . .": MM quoted, ibid.

503 "Mary McCarthy was the queen . . .": Janet Flanner to Natalia Murray, Aug. 8, 1962, in Flanner, *Darlinghissima,* p. 319.

504 "Of course everyone's . . .": Paul Bowles to Allen Ginsberg, Oct. 30, 1962, in Bowles, *In Touch,* p. 341.

505 "no real intellectuals . . .": MM, "Hounds," p. 60.

506 "That is one . . .": HA to MM, Sept. 16, 1963, in *BF,* p. 145.

506 "[I] hope you have . . .": Katharine White to MM, Sept. 23, 1963, Vassar.

506 "I don't want you . . .": MM to William Maxwell, Oct. 9, 1962; letter courtesy of Mr. Maxwell.

507 "[P]hysical conditions . . .":MM to Carmen Angleton, Dec. 14, 1962, Vassar.

507 "I've been fearfully . . .": Ibid.

508 "[I]n the new apartment . . .": Ibid.

## 20. *THE GROUP*

509 "I'm not a collector . . .": MM to Roger Straus, Nov. 12, 1954, NYPL.

510 "I'm working on my novel . . .": MM to William Maxwell, Aug. 17, 1959; letter courtesy of Mr. Maxwell.

510 "It's rather like . . .": MM to BB, Sept. 28, 1960, Vassar.

511 "about the idea of progress . . .": The interview, "The Art of Fiction XXVII: Mary McCarthy—An Interview," is reprinted in *CWMM,* pp. 3–29; quotation on p. 5

511 "These girls are essentially . . .": Ibid., p. 24.

511 "too depressed": Ibid., p.37.

511 "[A] *very* strong . . .": William Jovanovich to MM, Aug. 7, 1962, Vassar.

511 "Is there any way . . .": William Jovanovich to MM, Aug. 23, 1962, Vassar.

511 "get a jump . . .": William Jovanovich to MM, Feb. 20, 1963, Vassar.

512 "I rather like the idea . . .": MM to William Maxwell, Feb. 28, 1963; letter courtesy of Mr. Maxwell.

512 holiday in Rome: Carol Brightman, *Writing Dangerously,* p. 497.

513 "I hear Mary's book . . .": NC to DM, June 15, 1963, Yale-S.

513 "A lovely apartment . . .": Robert Lowell to Elizabeth Bishop, Aug. 12, 1963, Vassar/EB.

513 "an awful fatuous superficial book": Robert Lowell to Elizabeth Bishop, July 5, 1963, Vassar/EB.

513 "I've now read it through . . .": Lowell to Bishop, Aug. 12, 1963.

514 "Paying the driver . . .": MM, *The Group,* p. 3.

514 "like a country lass . . .": Ibid., p. 7.

514 "for her decorum . . .": Ibid., p. 23.

515 "You people were . . .": Ibid., p. 125.

515 "a neuter . . .": Ibid., p. 108

515 "the droll member . . .": Ibid., p. 100.

515 "a fat . . .": Ibid., p. 6

515 "a high-bred tempestuous creature": Ibid., p. 16.

515 "one of those . . .": Ibid., p. 205.

515 "rather colorless": Ibid., p. 224.

515 "dyed-in-the-wool liberal": Ibid., p. 26.

515 "the taciturn brunette . . .": Ibid., p. 7.

516 "At college the group . . .": Ibid., pp. 356–57.

517 "THE GROUP NUMBER ONE . . .": William Jovanovich to MM, n.d. [c. Oct. 1963], Vassar.

518 "In her persistently . . .": Arthur Mizener, "Out of Vassar and on the Town," *The New York Times Book Review*, Aug. 25, 1963, p. 14.

518 "*The Group* is in many . . .": Granville Hicks, "What to Be After Poughkeepsie," *Saturday Review*, Aug. 31, 1963, is excerpted in *Book Review Digest 1963*, p. 642.

519 "Mary McCarthy's *The Group* . . .": Louise Bogan to Ruth Limmer, Sept. 8, 1963, in Bogan, *What the Woman Lived*, p. 353.

519 "only real woman of letters": Contrary Mary—Vassar '33," *Newsweek*, Sept. 2, 1963, in *CWMM*, p. 51.

519 "mustache of middle age": Ibid., p. 49.

519 "[T]he reader who approaches . . .": Ibid., p. 48

520 "A somewhat cynical critic . . .": Norman Podhoretz, "Mary McCarthy and the Leopard's Spots," *Show*, October 1963, p. 52.

520 "Maisie had always . . .": Xavier Prynne [EH], "The Gang," *The New York Review of Books*, Sept. 26, 1963, p. 22.

521 All quotations from Norman Mailer's review, "The Mary McCarthy Case," *The New York Review of Books*, Oct. 17, 1963, pp. 1–3.

521 "I suppose you saw . . .": MM to HA, Oct. 24, 1963, in *BF*, pp.154–55.

521 "I read Mailer's review . . .": HA to MM, n.d. [Fall 1963], ibid., p. 156.

522 "had the brilliant idea": Ibid.

522 "Talking to the interviewer . . .": John Gross, "Class of '33," *The New Statesman* 96, Nov. 15, 1963, p. 703.

523 "[T]he big dailies . . .": DM to NC, Oct. 9, 1963, Yale-S.

523 her best novel so far: NC to DM, Oct. 5, 1963, Yale-S.

523 little use for the novel: NC to MM, Sept. 16, 1961, Vassar.

523 "This review of your book . . .": William Phillips to MM, Dec. 12, 1963, Vassar.

523 "Miss McCarthy's mastery . . .": William Abrahams, "After the Daisy Chain," *Partisan Review* 31, no. 1 (Winter 1964), p. 110.

524 "I have a dozen impressions . . .": EH to MM, Aug. 3, 1963, Vassar.

524 "I've always been honest . . .": Katharine White to MM, Sept. 23, 1963, Bryn Mawr.

524 "This isn't a letter . . .": MM to Katharine White, Oct. 26, 1963, Bryn Mawr.

526 "I am very much distressed . . .": EH to MM, Nov. 30, 1963, Vassar.

526 "Dear Cal, I was afraid . . .": MM to Robert Lowell, Jan. 9, 1964, Harvard-H.

526 "nary a chill . . .": Sheila Tobias, "Miss McCarthy's Subjects Return the Compliments," *New York Herald Tribune*, Jan. 7, 1964.

526 had made her girls "dull": Lowell to Bishop, Aug. 12, 1963.

527 "Now I've just read . . .": Elizabeth Bishop to May Swenson, Oct. 3, 1963, in Bishop, *One Art*, p. 419.

530 MM explains the origins of Polly Andrews in her letter to Irvin Stock, Mar. 19, 1969, Vassar.

531 "'She had that harsh . . .'": Tobias, "Miss McCarthy's Subjects."
532 "getting a collection of . . .": MM to Miss Rosenbaum, Feb. 6, 1964, Vassar. All these quotations are from the final version of the letter, which was mailed (see below).
532 "Libby is a blend . . .": Ibid.
532 "still wincing . . .": MM to Miss Rosenbaum, Feb. 6, 1964, draft version (unmailed), Vassar.
533 "[T]he group and my position . . .": Ibid.
533 "Reading this over . . .": Ibid.
534 "Lying isn't one . . .": MM to Elizabeth Bishop, Oct. 28, 1979, Vassar/EB.
534 "While I couldn't . . .": Julia Denison Rumsey to MM, Mar. 8, 1964, Vassar.
534 "laughed out loud": Frani Blough Muser to MM, Mar. 13, 1964, Vassar.
534 "I was relieved . . .": MM to Frani Blough Muser, Mar. 26, 1964; letter courtesy of Ms. Muser.
535 "During this time of excitement . . .": Eileen Simpson, "Ode to a Woman Well at Ease," *Lear's*, April 1990, p. 134.
537 "I find New York . . .": Philip Rahv to MM, Apr. 9, 1965, Vassar.
539 "notion" . . ."culture heroine": Pauline Kael, *Kiss Kiss Bang Bang*, p. 77.
539 "Mary McCarthy has always . . .": Ibid., pp. 96–97.
539 "This is not a question . . .": MM to Pauline Kael, Mar. 24, 1970, Vassar.
540 "perverted outlook on life": Letter of Oct. 2, 1964, from a reader, Vassar.
540 "God-given talents" writing "such filth": Letter of Apr. 10, 1969, from a reader, Vassar.
540 "oily virtuosity": MM, *Mary McCarthy's Theatre Chronicles*, p. 81.
540 "I think Miss McCarthy . . .": Quoted in George Plimpton, ed., *Women Writers at Work*, p. 131.

## 21. FAME

542 "Yes, fame is . . .": HA to MM, n.d. [Fall 1963], in *BF*, p. 156.
542 "to find it . . .": MM to William Maxwell, Mar. 11, 1963; letter courtesy of Mr. Maxwell.
543 "To a Jew . . .": HA, *Eichmann in Jerusalem*, p. 104.
543 "The whole truth . . .": Ibid., p. 111.
543 "[T]he only one . . .": Marie Syrkin, "Hannah Arendt: The Clothes of the Empress," *Dissent* 10, no. 4 (Autumn 1963), p. 347.
543 "The disparity between . . .": Michael Musmanno's May 19, 1963, review was reprinted in a special anniversary issue of *The New York Times Book Review*, October 6, 1996, p. 86.
543 "If a man . . .": Lionel Abel, "The Aesthetics of Evil," *Partisan Review* 30, Summer 1963, p. 219.
543 Arendt had refused to defend: HA to MM, Oct. 3, 1963, in *BF*, p. 151.
544 "As things are going . . .": MM to Philip Rahv and William Phillips, Sept. 25, 1963, Vassar.
544 "It occurs to me . . .": MM to HA, Oct. 24, 1963, in *BF*, p. 155.
544 "I am afraid that . . .": HA to MM, n.d. [Fall 1963], ibid., p. 156.
545 "bad, full of errors . . .": William Phillips to MM, n.d. [Fall 1963], Vassar.
545 "When I read . . .": MM, *The Writing on the Wall*, pp. 54–55, 56–57.
546 "I took the book . . .": Ibid., pp. 67–68, 66.
546 "not in the best taste": William Phillips to MM, Dec. 30, 1963, Vassar.
546 "Polemics ought to be gay . . .": MM to Robert Lowell, Jan. 9, 1964, Harvard-H.
546 "Your piece, I think . . .": HA to MM, Feb. 2, 1964, in *BF*, p. 160.
547 "I have just received . . .": NC to MM, Feb. 29, 1964, Vassar.

547 "You have not answered . . .": Philip Rahv to MM, Apr. 14, 1964, Vassar.

547 scoring "debaters' points": William Phillips, in "Arguments: More on Eichmann," *Partisan Review* 31, Spring 1964, p. 278.

547 "Till Miss McCarthy's sally . . .": Marie Syrkin, ibid., pp. 253, 254–55.

548 "If anyone is willing . . .": MM, ibid., p. 277.

548 "Hannah, let me tell you . . .": MM to HA, June 9, 1964, in *BF*, p. 166.

548 "Just one word . . .": HA to MM, June 23, 1964, ibid., p. 168.

549 "And yet when . . .": MM to HA, June 9, 1964, ibid., p. 163.

549 For NC on MM, see his letter to DM, Mar. 10, 1964, Yale-S.

550 "an evasion . . .": MM to HA, June 9, 1964, in *BF*, p. 163.

550 "The book won't be a satire . . .": Ibid., p. 165.

551 "I couldn't do . . .": *CWMM*, p. 121.

552 "I am gasping . . .": MM to HA, June 22, 1965, in *BF*, p. 184.

553 "I had met . . .": James Jones, *The Merry Month of May*, p. 163.

554 "We had a party . . .": MM to HA, Jan.18, 1965, in *BF*, p. 174.

555 "All considered . . .": NC to DM, Mar. 9, 1965, Yale-S.

556 "Models [for Peter Levi] . . .": MM to HA, June 9, 1964, in *BF*, pp. 164–65.

558 "The only other visit . . .": MM to HA, Sept. 12, 1967, ibid., p. 203.

559 "floods in the cellar . . .": MM quoted in Carol Gelderman, *Mary McCarthy*,
p. 268.

560 "Simone de Beauvoir . . .": MM, *The Writing on the Wall*, pp. 97–98.

561 She concluded the piece: Ibid., p. 101

561 "This has started . . .": MM to HA, Dec. 22, 1964, in *BF*, pp. 169–70

562 "go to bed . . .": Interview with Cees Nooteboom.

566 "My policy has been . . .": Doris Grumbach to MM, Oct. 23, 1965, Vassar.

566 "Thank you for writing . . .": MM to Doris Grumbach, Dec., 16, 1965, Vassar.

567 "clarifications" and "verbatim": Doris Grumbach to MM, Feb. 7, 1966, Vassar.

567 "I must tell you . . .": MM to Doris Grumbach, Feb. 22, 1966, Vassar.

567 "lost virginity . . .": Ibid.

567 "I have *no* intention . . .": Doris Grumbach to MM, Mar. 2, 1966, Vassar.

567 "I'm rather good . . .": MM to Doris Grumbach, July 4, 1966, Vassar.

568 "In regard to . . .": EW to John J. Geoghegan, Sept. 24, 1966, copy (with EW's
handwritten note to MM) in Vassar.

568 "Straight off . . .": MM to Doris Grumbach, Sept. 26, 1966, Vassar.

569 she added a typed postscript: this was on Sept. 29, 1966, per the original at
Vassar. In fact, it was MM who was mistaken about the spelling of her grandmother's maiden name; EW was correct.

569 "I've not had a syllable . . .": MM to HA, Oct. 11, 1966, in *BF*, pp. 196–97. Portions of this letter, elided from *BF*, are from the original at Vassar.

570 "It all started . . .": Doris Grumbach, "The Subject Objected," *The New York
Times Book Review*, June 11, 1967, pp. 6–7, 36–37.

570 "the reformer who . . .": Doris Grumbach, *The Company She Kept*, p. 216.

570 "The urge to scribble . . .": Ellen Moers, "Fictions and Facts," *The New York
Times Book Review*, June 11, 1967, pp. 6–7.

571 "In discussing Mary McCarthy's . . .": Mary Ellmann, "Mary, Mary," *Washington Post Book World*, May 28, 1967, p. 3.

571 "This novel is dragging . . .": MM to William Maxwell, Nov. 22, 1967; letter
courtesy of Mr. Maxwell.

571 "I am glad to see you . . .": HA to MM, Sept. 16, 1963, in *BF*, p. 146.

## 22. VIETNAM

573 "What are you . . .": MM to DM, Feb. 8, 1966, Yale-S.

573 "I read with slight relief . . .": MM to HA, Apr. 2, 1965, in *BF*, p. 178.

573 "I've been reading about . . .": HA to MM, May 18, 1965, ibid., p. 183.

574 For Grumbach's appraisal of MM's politics, see *The Company She Kept*, p. 62.

574 "I am not sure . . .": MM to DM, Mar. 15, 1965, Yale-S.

575 "The moment is past . . .": Edwin Newman's interview was conducted in Paris, Dec. 4, 1966. A transcript is reprinted in *CWMM*, pp. 68–87; quotation on p. 86.

576 "[Jim] now feels . . .": MM to Carmen Angleton, Jan. 7, 1967, Vassar.

577 "I had fun . . .": MM, *The Seventeenth Degree*, p. 18.

577 "[F]or an hour . . .": Ibid., pp. 14–15.

578 "To hear from a novelist . . .": Ibid., p. 27.

580 "witty and sardonic": Ibid., p. 138.

580 "I confess that when . . .": Ibid., p. 63

581 "To an American . . .": Ibid., pp. 65, 77–78, 82.

581 "The worst thing . . .": Ibid., p. 93.

581 "We draw a long face . . .": Ibid., pp. 93, 145–46.

582 "May I say that . . .": NC to MM, Mar. 31, 1967, Vassar.

582 "a good person": DM to MM, Mar. 27, 1967, Yale-S

582 "Thank you for telling . . .": MM to DM, Apr. 4, 1967, Yale-S.

582 "One of the best . . .": DM to MM, May 17, 1967, Yale-S.

583 "[R]ecently I've run . . .": DM to NC, July 5, 1967, Yale-S.

583 "most likely the 'revelations' . . .": NC to DM, July 18, 1967, Yale-S.

583 "What Mary's articles . . .": Ibid.

584 "In June, when I . . .": MM, *The Seventeenth Degree*, pp. 17–18.

584 "It's true, I suppose . . .": MM to William Jovanovich, May 11, 1967, Vassar.

584 "As for another . . .": William Jovanovich to MM, May 18, 1967, Vassar.

585 "solution" . . . "a booby trap": MM, *The Seventeenth Degree*, pp. 149, 150.

585 "willingness to face . . .": EH to MM, Dec. 27, 1967, Vassar.

585 "I too oppose . . .": Diana Trilling's letter, which originally appeared in *The New York Review of Books*, Jan. 18, 1968 (with MM's response, as "On Withdrawing from Vietnam: An Exchange," pp. 5–10), is reprinted in MM, *The Seventeenth Degree*, pp. 171-74; quotation on pp. 173–74.

586 "Mrs. Trilling . . .": MM, *The Seventeenth Degree*, pp. 174–75, 187.

586 "Jim is disgusted . . .": MM to HA, Jan. 26, 1968, in *BF*, p. 210.

587 "I read your answer . . .": HA to MM, Feb. 9, 1968, in ibid., p. 213.

587 "The students all mentioned . . .": Ibid., pp. 211–12.

588 "All was clinking glasses . . .": "People," *Time*, Mar. 29, 1968, p. 39.

589 "I don't know . . .": Janet Flanner to Natalia Murray, Mar. 14, 1968, in Flanner, *Darlinghissima*, p. 410.

589 "What I saw was . . .": MM, *The Seventeenth Degree*, pp. 35–36.

590 "'the American aggressors' . . .": Ibid., p. 268.

590 "Under the cover . . .": Ibid., pp. 224–25.

591 "The Vietnamese, one hears . . .": Ibid., pp. 299–300.

591 eight suitcases: Interview with Carol Brightman.

591 "Everybody knows . . .": MM, *The Seventeenth Degree*, pp. 313–14.

592 "*Vous avez . . .*": Ibid., p. 317.

592 "I wanted to write . . .": HA to MM, June 13, 1968, in *BF*, p. 218.

593 "In the winter . . .": Ward Just, "Fabulous North Vietnam," *Washington Post*, undated clipping [c. 1968], Vassar.

594 "[*Vietnam* was] a sharp . . .": Tom Buckley, "On the Subject of Hanoi, a Muted Voice," *Washington Post Book World*, Dec. 1, 1968, p. 24.

595 "On the one hand . . .": Frances FitzGerald, "A Nice Place to Visit," *The New York Review of Books*, Mar. 13, 1969.

596 "I too have been . . .": MM to Robert Lowell, Feb. 7, 1969, Harvard-H.
598 "It all seems . . .": MM, *The Seventeenth Degree*, p. 325.
598 "yawned, stretched . . .": Ibid., p. 327.
598 "a letter from a credit company": Ibid., p. 399.
598 "If there were American . . .": Ibid. p. 389.
598 the men of Company C: Ibid., pp. 401–2.
599 "counter-culture": Ibid., p. 404.
599 "bitterness [lead] her . . .": Keith R. Johnson, "Verdict on My Lai," *Time*, July 31, 1972, p. 60.
599 "struggling to maintain his composure": *Times* reporter Homer Bigart is quoted in Gloria Emerson's review, "The Famous Little Sting," *The New York Times Book Review*, Aug. 13, 1972, p. 21.
599 "Miss McCarthy is quite . . .": Ibid., pp. 21–22.
601 "I attrribute my . . .": MM, *The Seventeenth Degree*, p. 413.
602 "I sat at the end . . .": Robinson Risner, *The Passing of the Night*, pp. 174–75.
602 "This was Robinson . . .": MM, *The Seventeenth Degree*, p. 299.
603 "Although I am . . .": MM, "On Colonel Risner," *The New York Review of Books*, Mar. 7, 1974, p. 11
603 comment on the immorality: Robert Silvers to MM, Feb. 6, 1974, Vassar.
603 "Looking back, I can see . . .": MM, "On Colonel Risner," pp. 11–12.
604 "review by insinuation . . .": Doris Grumbach, "Fine Print: The Art of Reviewing by Innuendo," *The New Republic* 170, no. 11 (Mar. 16, 1974), p. 33.
605 "Mary McCarthy's hatchet . . .": James Fallows, "Mary McCarthy—The Blinders She Wears," *The Washington Monthly*, May 1974, pp. 6–7
605 "She obviously enjoys . . .": Ibid., p. 11.
606 "a punishing chunk of lard": Gloria Emerson, "Mary, Mary, Quite Contrary," *Washington Post Book World*, June 2, 1974, p. 5.
606 "I shall be glad . . .": MM, *The Seventeenth Degree*, p. 6.
606 "better reporting . . .": Emerson, "Mary, Mary, Quite Contrary," p. 6.
607 "As for my current . . .": The Miriam Gross interview, "A World Out of Joint," is reprinted in *CWMM*, pp. 170–78; quotation on p. 174.
608 "It is not that . . .": MM to HA, Sept. 30, 1974, in *BF*, p. 368.
608 gave her full credit: Harold Rosenberg, "Up Against the News," *The New York Review of Books*, Oct. 31, 1974, p. 17.
608 "I never dream . . .": MM, *The Seventeenth Degree*, p. 30.
609 "Probably this is . . .": Ibid.


## 23. CASTINE

610 "disfiguring itself": MM, *The Seventeenth Degree*, p. 317.
610 "I have the impression . . .": HA to MM, Feb. 9, 1968, in *BF*, pp. 211–12.
610 "For the first time . . .": Ibid., p. 212.
610 "I feel very strongly . . .": MM to HA, Mar. 7, 1968, in ibid., p. 215.
610 "a moment not . . .": Ibid.
611 "[T]here's not a cake rack . . .": MM to Carmen Angleton, Aug. 2, 1964, Vassar.
611 For Hardwick on the house and the village, see EH to MM, Mar. 15, 1967, Vassar.
612 a British interviewer: This interview, "Mary McCarthy Talks to James Mossman About the Vietnam War," originally appeared in *The Listener*, January 18, 1968. It is reprinted in *CWMM*, pp. 88–94; quotations on p. 94.
613 "Painters are here . . .": MM to Frani Blough Muser, July 20, 1967; letter courtesy of Ms. Muser.
613 "Can you come up . . .": MM to DM, Aug. 6, 1967, Yale-S.

614 "But I must say . . .": Ibid.

617 "He is taking some . . .": MM to HA, Sept. 12, 1967, in *BF*, p. 204.

618 "I have the sense . . .": MM to HA, June 6, 1968, ibid., p. 219.

619 "Oh my goodness me . . .": Sonia Orwell to MM and James West, Aug. 26, 1968, Vassar.

619 "Your eight-inch softwood . . .": Robert Lowell, "For Mary McCarthy 1," *History*, p. 157.

620 "Both hands talking . . .": Philip Booth, "Mary's, After Dinner," *Relations*, p. 192.

620 "I find Mary . . .": Robert Lowell to Elizabeth Bishop, July 30, 1968, Vassar/EB.

620 "ascending the social ladder . . .": Lowell to Bishop, Mar. 18, 1962, Vassar/EB.

621 "What he really had . . .": MM, *The Writing on the Wall*, p. 163.

621 "married in his last illness": Ibid., p. 153.

621 "enough human weaknesses . . .": Ibid., p. 165.

621 "Surely he would have . . .": Ibid., pp. 168–69.

622 "If he had lived . . .": Ibid., pp. 169, 159.

623 Walker Percy: Arnold W. Ehrlich, "Mary McCarthy," in *CWMM*, p. 125.

623 Anthony Burgess's review appeared in *The New York Times Book Review*, Mar. 8, 1970, p. 4.

623 "Peggy and Truman . . .": Courtesy of John Richardson.

624 "I'd just as soon . . .": William Jovanovich to MM, June 25, 1969, Vassar.

626 "[N]o creature . . .": Helen Vendler, review of *Birds of America*, *The New York Times Book Review*, May 16, 1971, p. 18.

627 "Forsaking the group . . .": Anatole Broyard, "An Unfriendly Ornithologist," *The New York Times*, May 19, 1971.

627 "When the action lapses . . .": John W. Aldridge, "Egalitarian Snobs," *Saturday Review*, May 8, 1971, p. 22.

627 "bitchiness": *CWMM*, p. 123.

628 "I am late . . .": HA to MM, May 28, 1971, in *BF*, p. 292.

628 "When I turned . . .": NC to MM, June 25, 1971, Vassar.

628 "Her last book . . .": NC to DM, Jan. 5, 1972, Yale-S.

628 "Mary McCarthy sent me . . .": Janet Flanner to Natalia Murray, May 15, 1971, in Flanner, *Darlinghissima*, p. 458.

628 "It has reached . . .": MM to EW, Sept. 15, 1970, Yale-B.

628 "CONGRATULATIONS BIRTHDAY AND OBSERVER": HA to MM, June 21, 1973, in *BF*, p. 338.

631 "Taped to the press tables . . .": "Dean's First Day," in "The Talk of the Town," *The New Yorker* 49, July 9, 1973, p. 42.

631 "'He's extremely intelligent' . . .": "People," *Time*, July 9, 1973, p. 29.

632 "She played by the rules . . .": Interview with Margo Viscusi.

632 "[T]here was something turnipy . . .": MM, *The Mask of State*, pp. 55, 94–95, 108.

632 "the Americans are using . . .": Ibid., p. 24.

632 "There can be no . . .": Ibid., p. 54.

633 "The Ervin show . . .": MM to HA, Aug. 10, 1973, in *BF*, p. 339.

633 "God knows why . . .": HA to MM, Aug. 17, 1973, ibid., p. 341.

634 "To my mind . . .": MM, *The Mask of State*, p. 134.

634 "I cannot prolong . . .": Ibid., p. 178.

635 "[T]he cover-up continues": MM to HA, Sept. 9, 1974, in *BF*, p. 364

635 "a move to shut . . .": MM, *The Mask of State*, p. 182.

635 "Pure Sensitivity . . .": James Fallows, "Mary McCarthy—The Blinders She Wears," *Washington Monthly*, May 1974, pp. 9, 11.

635 "I am aware . . .": Gloria Emerson, "Mary, Mary, Quite Contrary," *Washington Post Book World*, June 2, 1974, p. 6

636 "[T]he Washington journalist . . .": Richard Goodwin, review of *The Mask of State*, *The New York Times Book Review*, June 30, 1974, pp. 5–6.

636 "McCarthy's political writing . . .": Harold Rosenberg, "Up Against the News," *The New York Review of Books*, Oct. 31, 1974, p. 18.

637 "Thank you for coming . . .": MM to HA, Sept. 9, 1974, in *BF*, p. 364.

637 "I can't help feeling . . .": MM to HA, Sept. 30, 1974, ibid., p. 368.

## 24. DEATH OF OLD FRIENDS

639 "Something is happening . . .": MM to HA, Sept. 9, 1974, in *BF*, p. 364.

639 "For heaven's sake, Mary . . .": HA to MM, Sept. 12, 1974, ibid., p. 365

639 "In examining my life-history . . .": MM to Doris Grumbach, Sept. 26, 1966, Vassar.

640 "a good getter": Quoted in MM to Mannie Rousuck, Nov. 4, 1965, Vassar.

640 "outlaw side": Quoted in MM, *HIG*, p. 248.

640 "If more is needed . . .": MM's letter is quoted in Brendan Gill, *A New York Life*, p. 107.

640 "[H]is death in 1970 . . .": MM, *HIG*, p. 249.

640 "HEINRICH DIED SATURDAY . . .": HA to MM, n.d. [Nov. 1 or 2, 1970], in *BF*, p. 265.

641 "It's typical of a homosexual . . .": MM to HA, Dec. 1, 1970, ibid., p. 272.

641 her doctor had diagnosed: HA to MM, Dec. 8, 1971, ibid., p. 302.

641 "Your angina report . . .": MM to HA, Dec. 23, 1971, ibid., p. 304.

641 "He was an immense landmark . . .": "Edmund Wilson: 1895–1972," *Time*, June 26, 1972, p. 90.

641 "You won me over . . .": NC to MM, Mar. 9, 1968, Vassar.

642 "[He was] dead . . .": MM to HA, Jan. 19, 1972, in *BF*, pp. 305–6.

642 "Mary, look . . .": HA to MM, Jan. 25, 1972, ibid., p. 307.

644 "I need more strength . . .": MM to EH, Sept. 14, 1970, HRUT.

644 "I had a nice letter . . .": MM to HA, Mar. 1, 1974, in *BF*, pp. 354–55.

645 "So he's gone . . .": MM, *Occasional Prose*, p. 3.

645 "remained an outsider": Ibid., p. 6.

645 "already quite a big . . .": Ibid., p. 5.

645 "I said, just now . . .": Ibid., p. 7.

646 "I saw Lizzi . . .": HA to MM, Feb. 25, 1974, in *BF*, p. 353.

646 "[W]hen Philip died . . .": MM, *IM*, p. 96.

647 "[q]uite poisonous people . . .": MM, *Occasional Prose*, pp. 120, 123.

647 "If beauty is a god . . .": Ibid., pp. 124–25.

648 grave handicap: Nan Robertson, "Mary McCarthy Mellows as an Expatriate in Paris," *The New York Times*, July 31, 1979, p. C5.

648 "For me, in a memoir . . .": MM to EH, Oct. 12, 1973, HRUT.

649 "Being a perverse creature . . .": MM to HA, Nov. 20, 1974, in *BF*, p. 371.

649 "I find I am steering . . .": MM to HA, Feb. 17, 1975, ibid., p. 373.

650 "We had Eleanor . . .": Ibid., p. 372.

652 "Just to tell you . . .": MM to HA, Nov. 12, 1975, ibid., p. 388.

652 "roughened furrows of her neck": MM, *Occasional Prose*, p. 42.

653 "I loved her fiercely": Quoted in *BF*, p. 391.

653 "try to bring her back . . .": MM, *Occasional Prose*, p. 38.

653 "Hannah is the . . .": Ibid., pp. 41, 39, 41–42.

657 "The bore is that . . .": MM to Lotte Kohler, May 3, 1976; letter courtesy of Ms. Kohler.

656 "plausibility": Ibid.

657 "disfiguring": MM to EH, Apr. 28, 1976, HRUT.

657 "[T]he real motive . . .": MM to Robert Lowell and EH, Oct. 20, 1969, Harvard-H.

657 "When she was alive . . .": MM, editor's postface to HA, *The Life of the Mind*, vol. 1, *Thinking*, p. 220.

658 "wasn't sure . . .": Interview with William Shawn.

659 "She lost some aspects . . .": Interview with William Jovanovich.

661 "Aileen and Frank . . .": MM, *Cannibals and Missionaries*, p. 353.

661 "not verbalizing . . .": William Jovanovich to MM, Feb. 23, 1979, Vassar.

661 "She wouldn't ever . . .": Interview with James Merrill.

662 "It all means . . .": MM to William Jovanovich, Mar. 1, 1979, Vassar.

662 "[B]y the time . . .": Christopher Lehmann-Haupt, "Books of the Times," *The New York Times*, Oct. 4. 1979.

662 "Somewhere between . . .": R. Z. Sheppard, "When Worlds Collide," *Time*, Oct. 1, 1979, p. 89.

663 "In response to the truly . . .": Mary Gordon, "A Novel of Terrorism," *The New York Times Book Review*, Sept. 30, 1979, p. 35

663 "For me the writing . . .": Transcript courtesy of the 92nd Street Y, New York City.

665 "A person of courage . . .": MM, *Occasional Prose*, pp. 43–44.

665 "There was a drollery . . .": MM, "For Jim Farrell's Funeral," *The New York Review of Books*, Nov. 8, 1979, p. 52.

665 "For me, Harold's death . . .": The remarks were reprinted as MM, "Ideas Were the Generative Force of His Life," *The New York Times*, May 6, 1979, sect. 2, p. 12.

666 "I know a number . . .": EH, remarks at MM Memorial Service, Nov. 8, 1989, Morgan Library, New York City; transcript courtesy of Kevin McCarthy.

667 "an improvisation . . .": MM quoted in Kevin McCarthy's 1979 *People* interview, in *CWMM*, p. 183.

667 "universal reconciliation": William Jovanovich, remarks at MM Memorial Service, Nov. 8, 1989.

668 "[S]ince coming back . . .": MM to Frani Blough Muser, Nov. 11, 1979; letter courtesy of Ms. Muser.

669 "I absolutely hate . . .": *CWMM*, pp. 177–78.

669 "Something I've observed . . .": Ibid., p. 178.

669 medicine cabinet: Interview with Thomas Mallon.

## 25. THE HELLMAN SUIT

670 full-scale profile: MM to James Atlas, Aug. 12, 1979; letter courtesy of Mr. Atlas.

670 "Now, that's . . .": The Joan Dupont interview, "Mary McCarthy: Portrait of a Lady," appeared in *Paris Metro*, Feb. 15, 1978, and is reprinted in *CWMM*, pp. 157–69; quotation on p. 157.

670 "garden club": Ibid.

670 "I can't stand her": Ibid., p. 164.

671 "he didn't like the food . . .": Ibid.

671 "This has been, not . . .": Ibid.

671 "I knew at once . . .": Interview with Carlos Freire.

671 "When she was on camera . . .": Interview with Dick Cavett.

672 "brilliant": Interview with Gaia Servadio.

672 "a vindication . . .": Interview with Karl Miller.

672 For the Kennedys and the exchange on libel, see the transcript of *The Dick*

*Cavett Show*, p. 35, in *Lillian Hellman v. Mary McCarthy, Dick Cavett and Educational Broadcasting Corporation*, Supreme Court of the State of New York.

673 "just wrong about him . . .": Ibid., p. 48.

673 "The only one I can . . .": Ibid., p. 50.

673 "every word she writes . . .": Quoted in *CWMM*, p. 164.

674 "false, made with ill will . . .": Quoted in Herbert Mitgang, "Miss Hellman Suing a Critic for 2.25 Million," *The New York Times*, February 16, 1980, p. 12.

675 "Herbert Mitgang . . .": "MM in Conversation with Sedge Thomson," May 10, 1985, City Arts & Lectures, San Francisco; transcript courtesy of City Arts & Lectures.

675 "Reached in California . . .": Mitgang, "Miss Hellman Suing," p. 12.

676 "cut [her] conscience . . .": Ibid.

678 Peter Feibleman: A writer and friend of Hellman who was the principal beneficiary of her last will.

679 "harmless from . . .": This release, dated Oct. 18, 1979, is part of the *Hellman v. McCarthy et al.* file.

679 belly dancer: MM to William Jovanovich, Feb. 26, 1980. Vassar.

679 "I said, 'I hope . . .'": "MM in Conversation."

680 "What she did with it . . .": Interview with Max Palevsky.

680 "All the lawyers . . .": "MM in Conversation."

680 For Hellman at Hunter College, see MM to Ben O'Sullivan, Feb. 26, 1980, Vassar.

681 For Hammett and Hemingway, see Lillian Hellman, *An Unfinished Woman*, pp. 70–72; MM to Ben O'Sullivan, Oct. 27, 1980, and Martha Gellhorn to MM, May 29, 1981, both in Vassar.

681 Muriel Buttinger: Interview with Natasha and Stephen Spender.

681 "Lizzie has had . . .": MM to Ben O'Sullivan, Aug. 17, 1980, Vassar.

682 For Muriel Buttinger's assistance, see, for instance, MM to Ben O'Sullivan, May 29, 1982, Vassar.

682 "tips on how . . .": Gellhorn to MM, May 29, 1981.

683 "For some reason Mary . . .": Interview with Jonathan Randal.

683 "grandes dames of literature . . .": Michiko Kakutani, "Hellman-McCarthy Libel Suit Stirs Old Antagonisms," *The New York Times*, March 19, 1980, p. C21.

684 "It's not just . . .'": Ibid.

685 "Thinking over the list . . .": MM to Ben O'Sullivan, Mar. 21, 1980, Vassar.

685 "quarrel between . . .": Norman Mailer, "An Appeal to Lillian Hellman and Mary McCarthy," *The New York Times Book Review*, May 11, 1980, p. 33.

685 "Mary McCarthy has . . .": Ibid., pp. 3, 33.

685 "This is not an opportunity . . .": Richard Poirier, letter in *The New York Times Book Review*, June 15, 1980, p. 33.

685 "What a patronizing . . .": Quoted in Peter Manso, *Mailer: His Life and Times*, p. 611.

686 "What books and what plays . . .": "Defendant Mary McCarthy's Answers to Plaintiff's First Interrogatories," p. 2, in *Hellman v. McCarthy et al.*

686 She took care to deny: Ibid., p. 7.

686 "set forth the substance . . .": Ibid., pp. 8–9.

686 For the meetings of Hellman and MM, see ibid., p. 23.

687 For earlier published statements, see ibid., p. 24.

687 "audiences accustomed . . .": MM, *Mary McCarthy's Theatre Chronicles*, p. 81.

687 "What do you have against . . .": *CWMM*, p. 184.

688 "Miss McCarthy has been . . .": John Leonard, "Books of the Times," *The New York Times*, Nov. 18, 1980, p. C12.

688 "mobilize sentiment . . .": Diana Trilling to William Jovanovich, Nov. 16, 1980, Vassar.

688 "This is the first . . .": MM to Ben O'Sullivan, Nov. 29, 1980, Vassar.

689 "has been attempting . . .": "Affirmation in Opposition to Motion for Summary Judgment," p. 1, in *Hellman v. McCarthy et al.*

689 "in every respect untrue": Ibid., p. 2.

689 "[M]y opinion . . .": Ibid., p. 3.

689 1965 *Paris Review* interview: George Plimpton, ed., *Women Writers at Work*, p. 131.

689 "[I]f I did not . . .": "Affirmation in Opposition," p. 3.

689 she was not a public figure: Ibid., p. 5.

689 "spoke with a kind of awe . . .": Renata Adler, *Pitch Dark*, p. 4.

691 "In fact the Hellman suit . . .": MM to Monique Wittig, June 8, 1981, Vassar.

691 "I've finally had . . .": MM to Carmen Angleton, Aug. 27, 1982, Vassar.

698 "idea for future strategy": MM to Ben O'Sullivan, May 11, 1984, Vassar.

698 "As he told me . . .": Ibid.

700 "You sure play hardball": Interview with Renata Adler.

700 "I guess I didn't . . .": MM to Carmen Angleton, July 7, 1984, Vassar.

701 she wrote of her new medal: MM to Carmen Angleton, Aug. 15, 1984, Vassar.

701 Amount of Abrams retainer is from "MM in Conversation."

702 "I'm absolutely unregenerate . . .": Quoted in Samuel G. Freedman, "McCarthy Is Recipient of MacDowell Medal," *The New York Times*, Aug. 27, 1984, p. C14.

703 "'Julia' was a total fabrication . . .": Interview with Max Palevsky.

703 "impossible" for "a judge . . .": Harold Baer Jr., "Why I Quit the New York Bench," *The New York Times*, Oct. 1. 1992.

703 "There is no satisfaction . . .": MM to Faith Daniels, Sept. 13, 1985; videotape at Vassar.

## 26. A FULL LIFE

704 "It is not true . . .": MM to Frani Blough Muser, Aug. 16, 1979; letter courtesy of Ms. Muser.

705 "I remember laughing . . .": MM to William Jovanovich, Aug. 16, 1979, Vassar.

705 MacDowell speech: "Mary McCarthy's Acceptance," *Colony Newsletter* 14, no. 1 (Summer 1984), published by the MacDowell Colony, Inc.

705 "good behavior": MM to Carmen Angleton, Aug. 15, 1984, Vassar.

706 "is in marvelous form . . .": MM to Carmen Angleton, July 7, 1984, Vassar.

707 "Let me bring you . . .": MM to Carol Gelderman, Jan. 27, 1985, Vassar.

707 "In the midst . . .": Ibid.

708 The Christmas 1984 medical news is from ibid.

710 "As for feminism . . .": "MM in Conversation with Sedge Thomson," May 10, 1985, City Arts & Lectures, San Francisco; transcript courtesy of City Arts & Lectures.

711 "Most women who write . . .": The transcript of MM's talk in San Francisco on Oct. 17, 1986, was also provided by City Arts & Lectures.

712 "She is, of course . . .": Mary Gordon, *Good Boys and Dead Girls*, p. 57.

712 "Everywhere in *Occasional* . . .": Julian Moynahan, "You Pay Attention, You Learn Something," *The New York Times Book Review*, May 5, 1985, p. 15.

713 "[Y]ou will scold me . . .": MM to EH, Apr. 9, 1985, HRUT.

713 "word processing . . .": All excerpts from Virginia Smith's remarks are from a tape of the ceremony of Sept. 14, 1985, provided by Vassar.

714 "rare person": William Jovanovich remarks are from ibid.

714 how "lucky" Vassar was: Frances FitzGerald remarks are from ibid.

714 1956 engagement calendar: Thomas Mallon's remarks are from a typescript of his speech that he provided.

715 "I believe that herein . . .": EH's remarks are from the tape of the event, provided by Vassar.

716 "I can't stand to look . . .": MM to Faith Daniels, Sept. 13, 1985; videotape at Vassar.

717 "a whiff of condescension . . .": Interview with Leon Botstein.

723 "I remember singing . . .": MM, *HIG*, p. 80.

728 "[O]ver the years . . .": Ibid., pp. 16–17.

728 "The trouble is . . .": Christopher Lehmann-Haupt, "Books of the Times," The New York Times, Apr. 13, 1987.

729 "where all the moisture . . .": Wilfrid Sheed, "Her Youth Observed," *The New York Times Book Review*, Apr. 19, 1987, p. 6.

729 "[I]f McCarthy prizes . . .": James Wolcott, "Nose Jobs," *The New Republic*, May 11, 1987, p. 35.

730 "at Carol Brightman's . . .": MM to Carmen Angleton, June 30, 1987, Vassar.

732 "Yesterday, today, . . .": MM to Lotte Kohler, Nov. 18, 1987; letter courtesy of Ms. Kohler.

732 "Now my own news . . .": MM to EH, Jan. 7, 1988, HRUT.

732 "a camellia bush . . .": MM to William Jovanovich, Apr. 14, 1988, Vassar.

733 *"sclérosés"*: MM to Lotte Kohler, Mar. 21, 1988, Vassar.

733 For heart attack after bronchoscopy, see MM to Carmen Angleton, June 10, 1988, Vassar.

735 "Insofar as I . . .": MM, "A Believing Atheist," *Vassar Views*, Nov. 1992.

### EPILOGUE

743 For most of the details of the Castine funeral, I am indebted to Nicholas King's written account of Nov. 5, 1989.

744 Jim West lay down: Interview with James West.

745 "a contradiction to herself": William Jovanovich, remarks at MM Memorial Service, Nov. 8, 1989, Morgan Library, New York City; transcript courtesy of Kevin McCarthy.

745 "The door opened . . .": Interview with Peter Maguire.

745 "one of America's . . .": Michiko Kakutani, "Mary McCarthy, 77, Is Dead; Novelist, Memoirist and Critic," *The New York Times*, Oct. 26, 1989, p. A1.

745 "I couldn't live . . .": Ibid., p. B10. The interview was Kakutani's *New York Times Magazine* 1987 profile

745 "contrarian": "Topics of the Times: The Contrarian," *The New York Times*, Oct. 27, 1989.

745 *"un personnage combattant"*: Jean-Pierre Léonardini, "Un Personnage Combattant," *L'Humanité*, Oct. 27, 1989.

745 *"intellectuelle . . ."*: Nicole Zand, "La Mort de Mary McCarthy," *Le Monde*, Oct. 27, 1989, p. 1.

745 *"une des pionnières . . ."*: Bertrand de Saint-Vincent, "Adieu à Mary McCarthy," *Le Quotidien de Paris*, Oct. 27, 1989.

746 "[S]he had such . . .": Jane Kramer, "The Private Mary McCarthy: Unfinished with Life," *International Herald Tribune*, Oct. 31, 1989.

746 "Before Mary McCarthy . . .": Alison Lurie, "Battling to the Bitter End," *The Observer* [London], Oct. 29, 1989, p. 47.

746 "Her most autumnal . . .": Martha Duffy, "She Knew What She Wanted," *Time*, Nov. 6, 1989, p. 87.

747 "I was too young . . .": EW, *The Sixties*, p. 322.

748 "it is not abnormal . . .": Diane Johnson, *Le Divorce*, p. 63.
748 "*Someone* has to point . . .": Thomas Mallon, *Aurora 7*, p. 34.
748 "I don't think . . .": Interview with Irving Howe.
748 "Her stuff was interesting . . .": Interview with Jason Epstein.
749 "What Mary McCarthy . . .": Interview with Alison Lurie.
749 "The whole concept . . .": Interview with William Maxwell.

# Bibliography

## BOOKS BY MARY MCCARTHY

Where a reprint edition of one of McCarthy's works was used, the year of original publication is given in brackets.

*Birds of America*. New York: Harcourt Brace Jovanovich, 1971.
*Cannibals and Missionaries*. New York: Harcourt, Brace, 1979.
*Cast a Cold Eye*. New York: Harcourt, Brace, 1950.
*A Charmed Life*. New York: Harcourt, Brace, 1955.
*The Company She Keeps*. New York: Simon and Schuster, 1942.
*The Group*. New York: Harcourt Brace, 1963.
*The Groves of Academe*. New York: Plume/NAL, 1974 [1952].
*How I Grew*. San Diego: Harcourt Brace Jovanovich, 1987.
*Intellectual Memoirs: New York 1936–1938*. San Diego: Harvest/Harcourt Brace, 1993.
*Mary McCarthy's Theatre Chronicles: 1937–1962*. New York: Farrar, Straus, 1963.
*The Mask of State: Watergate Portraits*. New York: Harvest/Harcourt, Brace, 1975 [1974].
*Memories of a Catholic Girlhood*. San Diego: Harvest/Harcourt Brace Jovanovich, 1986 [1957].
*The Oasis*. New York: Random House, 1949.
*Occasional Prose*. San Diego: Harcourt Brace Jovanovich, 1985.
*On the Contrary: Articles of Belief, 1946–1961*. New York: Farrar, Straus and Cudahy, 1961.
*The Seventeenth Degree: How It Went; Vietnam; Hanoi; Medina; Sons of the Morning*. New York: Harvest/Harcourt Brace, 1974.
*Sights and Spectacles: 1937–1956*. New York: Farrar, Straus and Cudahy, 1956.
*The Stones of Florence*. New York: Harvest/Harcourt Brace, 1963 [1959].
*Venice Observed*. San Diego: Harvest/Harcourt Brace, 1963 [1956].
*The Writing on the Wall: And Other Literary Essays*. San Diego: Harvest/Harcourt Brace, 1970.

## OTHER BOOKS

Abel, Lionel. *The Intellectual Follies: A Memoir of the Literary Venture in New York and Paris*. New York: Norton, 1984.
Adler, Renata. *Pitch Dark*. New York: Knopf, 1983.
Arendt, Hannah. *Eichmann in Jerusalem*. New York: Viking, 1963.

——. *The Life of the Mind*. 2 vols. New York: Harcourt Brace Jovanovich, 1978.

Arendt, Hannah, and Mary McCarthy. *Between Friends: The Correspondence of Hannah Arendt and Mary McCarthy, 1949–1975*. Carol Brightman, ed. New York: Harcourt Brace, 1995.

Atlas, James. *Delmore Schwartz: The Life of an American Poet*. San Diego: Harvest/Harcourt Brace Jovanovich, 1982.

Barrett, William. *The Truants: Adventures Among the Intellectuals*. Garden City, N.Y.: Anchor/Doubleday, 1982.

Beauvoir, Simone de. *America Day by Day*. New York: Grove Press, 1953.

——. *Letters to Sartre*. Quintan Hoare, trans. New York: Arcade, 1992.

Berenson, Bernard. *Sunset and Twilight: From the Diaries of 1947–1958*. Nicky Mariano, ed. New York: Harcourt Brace, 1963.

Bishop, Elizabeth. *One Art: Letters*. Robert Giroux, ed. New York: Farrar, Straus and Giroux, 1994.

Bogan, Louise. *What the Woman Lived: Selected Letters of Louise Bogan, 1920-1970*. Ruth Limmer, ed. New York: Harcourt Brace Jovanovich, 1973.

Booth, Philip. *Relations: Selected Poems, 1950–1985*. New York: Penguin, 1986.

Bowles, Paul. *In Touch: The Letters of Paul Bowles*. Jeffrey Miller, ed. New York: Farrar Straus Giroux, 1994.

Brightman, Carol. *Writing Dangerously: Mary McCarthy and Her World*. New York: Clarkson Potter, 1992.

Chiaromonte, Nicola. *The Worm of Consciousness and Other Essays*. Miriam Chiaromonte, ed. New York: Harcourt Brace Jovanovich, 1976.

Connolly, Cyril. *Enemies of Promises*. New York: Persea, 1983.

*Contemporary Authors*. New Revision Series, vol. 16. Detroit: Gale Research Company, 1986.

Flanner, Janet. *Darlinghissima: Letters to a Friend*. Natalia Danesi Murray, ed. San Diego: Harvest/Harcourt Brace Jovanovich, 1986.

Gelderman, Carol. *Mary McCarthy: A Life*. New York: St. Martin's, 1988.

——, ed. *Conversations with Mary McCarthy*. Jackson, Miss.: University Press of Mississippi, 1991.

Gill, Brendan. *A New York Life: Of Friends and Others*. New York: Poseidon Press, 1990.

Gordon, Mary. *Good Boys and Dead Girls: And Other Essays*. New York: Viking, 1991.

Grumbach, Doris. *The Company She Kept*. New York: Coward-McCann, 1967.

Hellman, Lillian. *An Unfinished Woman*. Boston: Little Brown, 1970.

Hulbert, Ann. *The Interior Castle: The Art and Life of Jean Stafford*. New York: Knopf, 1992.

Jarrell, Randall. *Pictures from an Institution*. Chicago: University of Chicago Press, 1986.

——. *Randall Jarrell's Letters*. Mary Jarrell, ed. Boston: Houghton Mifflin, 1985.

Johnson, Diane. *Le Divorce*. New York: William Abrahams/Dutton, 1997.

Jones, James. *The Merry Month of May*. New York: Delacorte, 1971.

Kael, Pauline. *Kiss Kiss Bang Bang*. Boston: Atlantic/Little Brown, 1968.

Kazin, Alfred. *Starting Out in the Thirties*. Boston: Atlantic/Little Brown, 1965.

Lehman, David. *Signs of the Times: Deconstruction and the Fall of Paul de Man*. New York: Poseidon, 1992.

Lowell, Robert. *History*. New York: Farrar Straus Giroux, 1973.

Macdonald, Dwight. *Memoirs of a Revolutionist*. New York: Farrar, Straus and Cudahy, 1957.

Mallon, Thomas. *Aurora 7*. New York: Ticknor & Fields, 1991.

Manso, Peter. *Mailer: His Life and Times*. New York: Simon and Schuster, 1985.

Meigs, Mary. *Lily Briscoe: A Self-Portrait*. Vancouver: Talonbooks, 1981.

Mellen, Joan. *Hellman and Hammett: The Legendary Passion of Lillian Hellman and Dashiell Hammett*. New York: HarperCollins, 1996.

Morgan, Ted. *Literary Outlaw: The Life and Times of William S. Burroughs*. New York: Henry Holt, 1988.

Nabokov, Vladimir, and Edmund Wilson. *The Nabokov-Wilson Letters: Correspondence Between Vladimir Nabokov and Edmund Wilson, 1940–1971*. Simon Karlinsky, ed. New York: Harper & Row, 1979.

Phillips, William. *A Partisan View*. Briarcliff Manor, N.Y.: Stein & Day, 1983.

Plimpton, George, ed. *Women Writers at Work: The Paris Review Interviews*. New York: Viking Penguin, 1989.

Pritchard, William H. *Randall Jarrell: A Literary Life*. New York: Farrar, Straus and Giroux, 1990.

Rahv, Philip. *Essays in Literature and Politics, 1932–1972*. Arabel J. Porter and Andrew J. Dvosin, eds. Boston: Houghton Mifflin, 1978.

Risner, Robinson. *The Passing of the Night: My Seven Years as a Prisoner of the North Vietnamese*. New York: Random House, 1973.

Roth, Philip. *Goodbye Columbus: And Five Short Stories*. New York: Modern Library/Random House, 1966.

Schwartz, Delmore. *The Selected Essays of Delmore Schwartz*. Donald A. Dike and David H. Zucker, eds. Chicago: University of Chicago Press, 1970.

——. *Portrait of Delmore Schwartz: Journals and Notes of Delmore Schwartz, 1939–1959*. Elizabeth Pollett, ed. New York: Farrar, Straus and Giroux, 1986.

Thomson, Virgil. *Virgil Thomson*. New York: Obelisk/Dutton, 1985.

Trilling, Diana. *The Beginning of the Journey: The Marriage of Diana and Lionel Trilling*. New York: Harcourt Brace, 1993.

Tucci, Niccolò. *The Rain Came Last and Other Stories*. New York: New Directions, 1990.

Weld, Jacqueline Bograd. *Peggy: The Wayward Guggenheim*. New York: Dutton, 1986.

Wilson, Edmund. *Five Plays*. New York: Farrar, Straus and Young, 1954.

——. *The Forties: From Notebooks and Diaries of the Period*. Leon Edel, ed. New York: Farrar, Straus and Giroux, 1983.

——. *Letters on Literature and Politics: 1912–1972*. Elena Wilson, ed. New York: Farrar, Straus and Giroux, 1977.

——. *The Portable Edmund Wilson*. Lewis M. Dabney, ed. New York: Viking, 1983.

——. *The Sixties: The Last Journal, 1960–1972*. Lewis M. Dabney, ed. New York: Farrar, Straus and Giroux, 1993.

——. *The Thirties: From Notebooks and Diaries of the Period*. Leon Edel, ed. New York: Farrar, Straus and Giroux, 1980.

——. *The Triple Thinkers and The Wound and the Bow: A Combined Volume*. Boston: Northeastern University Press, 1984.

Wilson, Rosalind Baker. *Near the Magician: A Memoir of My Father, Edmund Wilson*. New York: Grove Wiedenfeld, 1989.

# Acknowledgments

$M$any people helped me during the long, nine-year process of trying to see Mary McCarthy with clarity, in all her many aspects—to see her plain.

This book would not have been possible if I had not had the assistance of Thomas Mallon. A friend and keen observer of Mary McCarthy, he encouraged me at the outset, steered me past many pitfalls, read early versions of the manuscript, and put me in touch with important sources.

I am enormously grateful to Margo Viscusi and Eve Stwertka, McCarthy's literary trustees, for their assistance, their patience, and their faithful support.

I would like to thank Nancy MacKechnie, who presides over the Vassar Library's Special Collections, where Mary McCarthy's papers are housed. I would also like to thank Patricia Willis at the Beinecke Library at Yale, who assisted me with the Edmund Wilson Papers, and Judith Ann Schiff at the Sterling Library, who helped with the Dwight Macdonald letters. In addition, I would like to thank Lisa Browar, who during her time as Assistant Director for Rare Books and Manuscripts at the New York Public Library helped me find my way to *The New Yorker* papers and the archives of Farrar Straus Giroux.

Toward the end of her life, Mary McCarthy asked if all her efforts had been in vain. I wish I could tell her, no, that her work and her example live on through her friends, family members, neighbors, colleagues, and students, many of whom talked to me about her and are quoted in this book. Almost two hundred people shared their thoughts and stories about Mary McCarthy from her childhood through her years at Vassar, in New York, on the Cape, at Newport; her time in Italy, in Paris, in Vietnam, in Maine, and at Bard. Their names appear in the text and they also form a part of the Cast of Characters, so I will not list them all here again.

In particular, I would like to thank James West, Elizabeth Hardwick, Alison West, Lotte Kohler, and Nicholas King.

I would also like to thank those people who helped with this book whose names do not appear in the book. First of all, I would like to thank Steven Barclay and Robert Pounder, who assisted me in more ways than I can count. In addition, I would like to thank: James Atlas, Lu Ann Walther, Maria Campbell, Cleo Paturis, Vickie Karp, Linda Healy, Idanna Pucci, Vincent Giroud, Susan Gillespie, Corlies Smith, Pat Strachan, Vance Muse, Lori Masuri, Barbara Epstein, Glenn Horowitz, M. G. Lord, Alice Gordon, Charles Michener, Linda Davis, Marcelle Clements, Patricia Towers, Carlos Freire, Heloisa Freire, Mark Rudkin, Nancy Crampton, Vincent Crapanzano, "Little Mary" McCarthy, Robert Jones, David Rieff, Emily Maxwell, Kate Risse, Edith Kurzweil, Sophie Consagra, Patricia Weaver, Virginia Foote, Matt Wolf, Nicholas Macdonald, Liz Calder, Irene Skolnick, Daphne Merkin, Dee Wells, Edgar and Charlotte de Bresson, Caroline Blackwood, Andrew Solomon, Cynthia Macdonald, Chris Barnes, William Banks, George Nicholson, John Murray, Linda Asher, Tom Putnam, Betty Ann Solinger, Helen Wilson, and John Heilpern.

I especially want to thank Frani Blough Muser and the other women who knew Mary McCarthy at Vassar and were willing to share their memories.

My agent, Virginia Barber, first encouraged me to write this book and has been encouraging throughout. Two previous biographers, Carol Gelderman and Carol Brightman, have been unfailingly generous. Michael Wreszin, the biographer of Dwight Macdonald, provided me with precious tapes.

At Norton, my original editor, Gerald Howard, helped me shape the manuscript; this book bears his stamp and I thank him. Starling Lawrence and Patricia Chui were wise and resourceful in guiding me through the final stages.

Along with Thomas Mallon, I would like to thank Sally Arteseros, Andrea Chapin, and Bobbie Bristol for their astute early reading of the manuscript; George Nicholson for his help at the end; Trent Duffy for expert copy editing; and Charlotte Staub for the design of the book. Phillip Lopate and Wendy Weil were helpful to me from the beginning.

Finally I would like to thank my dear friend Alice Adams, my family, and especially my husband, Howard, for unwavering support.

# Sources

Every effort has been made to contact the copyright holder of each of the selections. Rights holders of any selections not credited should contact W. W. Norton & Company, Inc., 500 Fifth Avenue, New York, NY 10110, in order for a correction to be made in the next printing of our work.

*Intellectual Follies: A Memoir of the Literary Venture in New York and Paris* by Lionel Abel, copyright © 1984 by Lionel Abel, reprinted with permission of the author and W. W. Norton & Company, Inc. The review "The Aesthetics of Evil" (*Partisan Review,* Summer 1963) reprinted with permission of Lionel Abel.

Louis Auchincloss's 1984 memo to Mary McCarthy reprinted with permission of Louis Auchincloss.

Excerpts from *The Truants: Adventures Among the Intellectuals* by William Barrett (New York: Anchor/Doubleday, 1982) reprinted with permission of Susan E. Barrett.

Excerpts from letters in the Elizabeth Bishop Papers reprinted with permission of Special Collections, Vassar College Libraries, Poughkeepsie, New York.

Excerpt from "Mary's, After Dinner" by Philip Booth reprinted with permission of Philip Booth.

Excerpt from "Ciao" by Bowden Broadwater (*The Paris Review,* Winter 1961) reprinted by permission of *The Paris Review.*

Excerpts from Brock Brower's "Mary-McCarthyism" (*Esquire,* July 1962) and *Other Loyalties: A Politics of Personality* (New York: Atheneum, 1968) reprinted with permission of Brock Brower.

Excerpts from Nicola Chiaromonte's correspondence with Mary McCarthy reprinted with permission of Miriam Chiaromonte.

Excerpts from James Fallows's "Mary McCarthy—The Blinders She Wears" (*Washington Monthly,* May 1974) reprinted with permission of James Fallows.

Excerpts from the reviews "A Novel of Terrorism" (*New York Times Book Review,* September 30, 1979) and "When Beauty Is Truth, Truth Beauty" (*Esquire,* November 1985) by Mary Gordon reprinted with permission of Mary Gordon. Quotations from Mary Gordon's October 5, 1979, introduction to Mary McCarthy's reading from *Cannibals and Missionaries* at the 92nd Street Y reprinted courtesy of the 92nd Street Y Unterberg Poetry Center.

Excerpt from Mariam Gross's "A World Out of Joint" (*Observer,* October 14, 1979) reprinted with permission of Mariam Gross.

Excerpt from Doris Grumbach's October 23, 1965, letter to Mary McCarthy reprinted with permission of Doris Grumbach.

Excerpts from Elizabeth Hardwick's correspondence with Mary McCarthy reprinted with permission of Elizabeth Hardwick and Harry Ransom Humanities Research Center, The University of Texas at Austin. Quotations from November 8, 1989, Morgan Library memorial reprinted with permission of Elizabeth Hardwick.

Anne Hollander and John Phillips's interview with Lillian Hellman (*The Paris Review,* 1965) reprinted with permission of *The Paris Review.*

Excerpt from *The Merry Month of May* by James Jones (New York: Delacorte, 1971) reprinted with permission of Gloria Jones.

Excerpts from William Jovanovich's July 24, 1962, and February 23, 1979, letters to Mary McCarthy and from his 1985 talk at Vassar reprinted with permission of William Jovanovich.

Excerpt from Ward Just's review "Fabulous North Vietnam" (*Washington Post,* May 1974) reprinted with permission of Ward Just.

Excerpt from "The Making of *The Group*" in *Kiss Kiss Bang Bang* by Pauline Kael (Boston: Atlantic/Little Brown, 1968) reprinted with permission of Pauline Kael.

Excerpts from Robert Lowell's letters to Elizabeth Bishop and from "For Mary McCarthy 1" reprinted by permission of the Estate of Robert Lowell.

Excerpt from Alison Lurie's tribute to Mary McCarthy in the London *Observer* reprinted with permission of Alison Lurie.

Excerpts from Mary McCarthy's correspondence with Bernard Berenson reprinted with permission of Villa I Tatti, Harvard University Center for Italian Renaissance Studies.

Excerpts from Mary McCarthy's correspondence with Frani Blough Muser reprinted courtesy of Frani Blough Muser.

Quotations from Mary McCarthy's May 10, 1985, and October 17, 1986, City Arts & Lectures programs reprinted with permission of Sydney Goldstein, Executive Director, City Arts & Lectures, Inc.

Excerpts from Mary McCarthy's letters from the F. W. Dupee collection at Columbia University reprinted with permission of Barbara Dupee.

Reprinted by permission of Harcourt, Inc.: Excerpts from *Between Friends: The Correspondence of Hannah Arendt and Mary McCarthy 1949–1975,* copyright © 1995 by the Literary Trust of Hannah Arendt Blucher, Lotte Kohler, Trustee; copyright © 1995 by the Literary Trust of Mary McCarthy West, Margo Viscusi and Eve Stwertka, Trustees. Excerpt from the dust jacket of *Birds of America,* copyright © 1971 by Mary McCarthy. Excerpt from *Cannibals and Missionaries,* copyright © 1979 by Mary McCarthy. Excerpt from *Cast a Cold Eye,* copyright © 1947 and renewed 1975 by Mary McCarthy. Excerpts from *A Charmed Life,* copyright © 1947 and renewed 1975 by Mary McCarthy. Excerpts from *The Group,* copyright © 1963 by Mary McCarthy and renewed 1991 by James Raymond West. Excerpts from *How I Grew,* copyright © 1987 by Mary McCarthy. Excerpts from "How It Went" in *The Seventeenth Degree,* copyright © 1974 by Mary McCarthy. Excerpts from *Intellectual Memoirs: New York 1936–1938,* copyright © 1992 by The Mary McCarthy Literary Trust. Excerpts from *The Mask of State: Watergate Portraits,* copyright © 1973, 1974 by Mary McCarthy. Excerpts from *Memories of a Catholic Girlhood,* copyright © 1957 and renewed 1985 by Mary McCarthy. Excerpts from *Occasional Prose,* copyright © 1985 by Mary McCarthy. Excerpts from *Venice Observed* by Mary McCarthy. Excerpts from *The Writing on the Wall and Other Literary Essays,* copyright © 1964 by Mary McCarthy and renewed 1992 by James R. West.

Note: Page numbers in *italics* refer to illustrations.